1969

A STUDY OF
HISTORY

The Royal Institute of International Affairs is an unofficial and non-political body, founded in 1920 to encourage and facilitate the scientific study of international questions.

The Institute, as such, is precluded by its rules from expressing an opinion on any aspects of international affairs; opinions expressed in this book are, therefore, purely individual.

A STUDY OF HISTORY

BY

ARNOLD J. TOYNBEE

Director of Studies in the Royal Institute of International Affairs
Research Professor of International History in the University of London
(both on the Sir Daniel Stevenson Foundation)

But at my back I always hear
Time's wingèd chariot hurrying near.
ANDREW MARVELL

ποιεῖν τι δεῖ ἇς γόνυ χλωρόν.
THEOCRITUS: Κυνίσκας Ἔρως, l. 70

γηράσκω δ' αἰεὶ πολλὰ διδασκόμενος.
SOLON

My times are in Thy hand.
Ps. xxxi. 15, in the A.V.

But Thou art the same, and Thy
years shall have no end.
Ps. cii. 27, in the A.V.

VOLUME VII

Issued under the auspices of the Royal Institute of International Affairs

OXFORD UNIVERSITY PRESS
LONDON NEW YORK TORONTO
1954

Oxford University Press, Amen House, London E.C.4
GLASGOW NEW YORK TORONTO MELBOURNE WELLINGTON
BOMBAY CALCUTTA MADRAS KARACHI CAPE TOWN IBADAN
Geoffrey Cumberlege, Publisher to the University

PRINTED IN GREAT BRITAIN

THE PLAN OF THE BOOK

PREFACE

THESE four volumes contain Parts VI–XIII of the thirteen parts which are set out in the plan of the book on p. v above, and their publication brings the book to a close.

I was not able to begin writing these concluding eight parts till I had been released from work as a temporary civil servant during the Second World War. By the summer of A.D. 1946, when I found myself free to return to my normal occupations, more than seven years had passed since the publication of volumes iv–vi in the summer of A.D. 1939, forty-one days before Great Britain had gone to war with Germany, and more than seventeen years had now passed since the latest of the notes for the book, which had all been written between June 1927 and June 1929, had been put on paper.

If these notes had not still been in existence—as they were, thanks to their safe-keeping during the war in the hands of the Council on Foreign Relations in New York—I might have found it beyond my power to take up my work again after a seven years' interruption during which there had been a break in my personal life as well as in the life of the society into which I had been born. On the other hand, I should assuredly have failed at this stage to carry the work to completion if, after having set my thoughts moving again by reacquainting myself with my notes in their original form, I had not thrown them into the melting-pot and recast them.

The world around me and within me had, indeed, met with a number of challenging and transforming experiences in the course of the nineteen years and more that, by the summer of A.D. 1946, had already passed since the first of the original notes for the book had been written. The focus and perspective in which the earlier millennia of the Age of the Civilizations presented themselves to the eyes of our generation had been appreciably modified in the meantime by further discoveries in the field of Archaeology. The prospects of a contemporary Western Civilization, and of an *Oikoumenê* which this civilization had enveloped in its world-encompassing net, had become clearer and graver since the National Socialist movement in Germany had given to Western Man—and to his non-Western contemporaries likewise—a horrifying practical demonstration of the moral depths to which the heirs of a Christian civilization were capable of dragging themselves down. A new dimension of the Spiritual Universe had been brought to light by the psychologists, and a new dimension of the Material Universe by the atomic physicists. An Einstein and a Rutherford, a Freud and a Jung, and a Marshall and a Woolley, as well as a Gandhi, a Stalin, a Hitler, a Churchill, and a Roosevelt, had been changing the face of the Macrocosm; and at the same time my inner world had been undergoing changes which, on the miniature scale of an individual life, were, for me, of proportionate magnitude. The cumulative effect of these divers changes in my universe had been so far-reaching that, when in A.D. 1946 I was once more free to think of resuming and finishing my work,

I found that the reawakening of my original thoughts was only the beginning of my next task. In order to carry out my purpose, I should have to think again in the light of the revolutionary experience which the nineteen intervening years had been thrusting upon me and my contemporaries.

The effort required for performing this act of mental rejuvenation might have been beyond my capacity if I had been left to attempt it in solitude; but at this point I was effectively helped on my way by the timely receipt of a series of invitations to give public lectures on the topics that were the agenda for the still unexecuted parts of the plan of the book. In a set of Edward Cadbury Lectures delivered at the University of Birmingham, England, in the autumn of 1946 I dealt with the subjects of Parts VI–VIII; in a set of Mary Flexner Lectures delivered at Bryn Mawr College, Pennsylvania, in the spring of 1947 I dealt with the subject of Part IX; in a set of Bampton Lectures delivered at Columbia University, New York, in April 1948 I dealt with the subject of Part XII, and, later in the same month, with the subject of Part XIII in a set of Rushton Lectures delivered at Southern College, Birmingham, Alabama. The subject of Part XI was my theme in a set of Chichele Lectures delivered in the autumn of 1948 in the University of Oxford on an invitation from All Souls College. The subject of Part X was broached in a couple of lectures delivered in April 1949 in the University of Chicago on an invitation from the Committee on Social Thought.

I was fortunate in being given these opportunities of feeling my way back into a study of History for the immediate practical purpose of sharing my thoughts and feelings with responsive audiences. The congenial necessity of writing notes for these lectures gave me the stimulus that I needed in order to recast my original notes for the book in a new form answering to the new experiences, public and personal, that I had encountered since the summer of 1927. In the outcome, the original plan of the book still stood and the execution of Parts VI, VIII, X, and XIII was carried out more or less on the lines of the original notes. The subjects of Parts VII, IX, XI, and XII, on the other hand, came, in the event, to be treated very differently from the original design—and the subject of Part XI, in particular, so differently that the title of this Part had to be changed from 'Rhythms in the Histories of Civilizations' to 'Law and Freedom in History'.

When these invitations to lecture had thus given me the impetus required for finishing the book in the light of my experience since 1927, I should have found myself overwhelmed by the accumulation of seven years' arrears of work on the Chatham House *Survey of International Affairs*—work which was the first call on my time and energy—but for the imagination, considerateness, and generosity of the Royal Institute of International Affairs, the Rockefeller Foundation of New York, and the Institute for Advanced Study at Princeton, N.J., in co-operating with one another to release the major part of my time, for a period of five years beginning on the 1st July, 1947, for writing the rest of *A Study of History*, partly in England and partly in America, under ideal conditions. My debt to the Rockefeller Foundation, and to the authorities at Bryn Mawr College who were the Foundation's consultants when it was considering this project, is a greater one than I can put into words.

My acknowledgements and thanks for the help of many kinds, from many quarters, which I have received in the writing of the book as a whole are set out at the end (in volume x, on pp. 213–42), since they run to too great a length to allow of their being included in a preface; but I cannot bring myself to postpone my expression of gratitude for certain essential pieces of help in the production of this last batch of four volumes.

The index to the volumes now published, like the two indexes to the preceding six volumes, has been made by my wife and colleague and co-author of the *Survey of International Affairs*. If the reader ever loses the thread of my thought, he will find it again here—as I know from having often found it, myself, in the indexes to the two previous batches of volumes. My gratitude is not lessened by the happy knowledge that this skilful and exacting task has been a labour of love.

Miss Bridget Reddin has completed the enormous tasks—begun in the winter of 1930–1—of typing from a manuscript that has always been complicated, and of deciphering a handwriting that has not improved in the course of putting on paper some millions of words. Both the printer and I would have been at a loss if Miss Reddin had not returned to give us this help after having served during the Second World War, with my wife and me, in the same department of the Government of the United Kingdom.

The book that I am finishing in the act of writing this preface has had a long history on the Time-scale of an individual human life. Now that I have finished it, I can see in retrospect that, without knowing it, I was already at work on it in rather early days. For instance, the Annex to Part VI C (ii) (*c*) 3 first found its way on to paper, in the form of a child's coloured illustrations to the text of Herodotus, Book VII, chaps. 61–99, in a drawing-book, dated August 1903, which is on my table at my elbow at this moment. Upon it lies the manuscript—running to sixty-four pages of sermon paper and ending with a quotation from the Book of the Prophet Ezekiel xxxvii. 1–10—of an essay on 'the Philosophy of History' read at Oxford to an undergraduate society at some date in the academic year 1910–11. In the summer of 1920, after the philosophic contemporaneity of the Western and Hellenic civilizations had been borne in on me by the experience of the First World War, I for the first time consciously tried—and, at this first attempt, signally failed—to write the present work in the form (dictated by a Late Medieval Italian education in the Greek and Latin Classics) of a commentary on the second chorus (ll. 332–75) of Sophocles' *Antigone*. I did not succeed in finding my way into my subject till more than a year later.

On Saturday, 17 September, 1921, I was travelling with my schoolfellow and life-long friend Theodore Wade-Gery in the Orient Express *en route* from Constantinople to England. Before dawn we had been awakened by the rumbling of our train as it crossed the bridge over the

Maritsa, below Adrianople, and, for the rest of that day, we were travelling on westward up the valley of a river that had once been famous as the Hebrus. As I stood, hour after hour, at the corridor window, watching the stream glide by, with an endless fringe of willows and poplars marking out, as they slid past, the curves of the gently flowing waters' course, my mind began to dream of historical and legendary events of which an Hellenic Thrace and an Ottoman Rumili had been the theatre: the legendary violent death of the Prophet Orpheus; the historic violent deaths of the Emperors Valens and Nicephorus; the entrenchment of the Ottoman Power on the European side of the Straits in the reign of Sultan Murād I. When a group of inquisitive Bulgarian peasants clustered round the door of our coach as the train lingered in a wayside station, my eye was caught by the fox-skin cap that one of these Thracian contemporaries of mine was wearing; for this was the headgear in which Herodotus (in Book VII, chap. 75) had paraded the Asiatic Thracian contingent of Xerxes' expeditionary force, and a picture of a Thracian fighting-man in just such a cap, which I had copied into my drawing-book eighteen years ago, had left its imprint on my memory. These stimulating sights and reminiscences must have released some psychic well-spring at a subconscious level. That evening I was still standing at the window, overwhelmed by the beauty of the Bela Palanka Gorge in the light of a full moon, as our train bore down upon Nish. If I had been cross-examined on my activities during that day, I should have sworn that my attention had been wholly absorbed by the entrancing scenes that were passing continually before my outward eye. Yet, before I went to sleep that night, I found that I had put down on half a sheet of notepaper a list of topics which, in its contents and in their order, was substantially identical with the plan of this book as it now stands printed in volumes i, iv, and vii. The path that had thus unexpectedly—and, as it might seem, casually—opened at last before my feet was to carry me farther than I then foresaw on a journey that was to take nearly thirty years to complete; but, once open, the path went on unfolding itself before me till today I find myself at this long journey's end.

ARNOLD J. TOYNBEE

LONDON
16 *August* 1951

SINCE writing this preface, I have begun to be able to see ahead to the next stage of this Study beyond the moment when I shall have delivered the last proofs of volumes vii–x to the printer.

While these four volumes have been in the press, I have been co-operating with my friend Professor E. D. Myers, of Washington and Lee University, Lexington, Virginia, and with my former colleague Mrs. Gomme, who was the head of the cartographical section of the Foreign Office Research Department during the Second World War, in producing the maps, and compiling the gazetteer of place-names that are either shown on these maps or are mentioned in the text of volumes i–x, which are to be published together in a forthcoming volume xi. This eleventh volume, which is mostly Professor Myers' and Mrs. Gomme's work, will, I believe, be welcomed by readers of volumes i–x.

On the 26th February, 1953, the Rockefeller Foundation once again came to my aid in a most imaginative and effective way by giving my wife and me a grant to cover the costs of travel with a view eventually to revising this book. Our first use of this kind grant was to pay a visit to Mexico, from the 14th April to the 16th May, 1953, for the threefold purpose of seeing at first hand some of the monuments of the Middle American Civilization and of the Spanish Empire of the Indies in the former Viceroyalty of New Spain and some of the aspects, in the Mexican field, of the current encounter between the World and the Modern West. Thanks to the hospitality and help of the Federal Ministry of Public Instruction and the Autonomous National University of Mexico, we were able to use our precious time in Mexico to good advantage. We look forward to following up this reconnaissance in Middle America by visiting Japan and Peru in 1956 on a journey to and from Australia which is to take us round the World. When, after that, we settle down to the task of revision, our plan is, first, to produce a volume of 'reconsiderations' (*retractationes* in Saint Augustine's usage of the Latin word). Since the first publication of the first batch of volumes in 1934, there have been additions to our historical knowledge, particularly through the wonderful work of the archaeologists, which have changed the appearance of some tracts of the historical landscape. There have also been comments and criticisms, both general and particular, on the ideas presented in the book and on some of the citations of facts by which these ideas have been illustrated and supported. While I have already profited greatly by many of these criticisms in writing the later volumes, I shall not have drawn the full benefit from them till I have taken a synoptic view of them; and this will be the second topic in the volume of *retractationes* that my wife and I are planning to produce.

We also have other books on the stocks, and we should be happy if there could be said of us what Clarendon has said of himself in his autobiography:

> 'In all this retirement he was very seldom vacant . . . from reading excellent books or writing some animadversions and exercitations of his own. . . . He left so many papers of several kinds, and cut out so many pieces of work, that a man may conclude that he never intended to be idle.'[1]

ARNOLD J. TOYNBEE

LONDON

18 *February* 1954

[1] *The Life of Edward Earl of Clarendon*, written by himself, *ad fin.* (Oxford 1817, Clarendon Press), vol. ii, p. 567, quoted in the present Study, III. iii. 321.

SCRIPTORIS VITA NOVA

O silvae, silvae, raptae mihi, non revidendae,
O mea, Silvani filia, musa dryas,
non dolet: hoc Paeto dictum immortale profata
Arria procudit mi quoque robur et aes—
mi quoque; non solus tamen exsulo: nonne priores
clara creaverunt tristi opera exsilio?
Exsul—et immeritus—divom, Florentia, carmen
edidit, alma intra moenia tale tua
nil orsus, vates. Non iuste expulsus Athenis,
Pangaei clivis advena Threïciis,
scripsit postnatis in perpetuom relegendam
vir, bello infelix dux prius, historiam.
His ego par fato: par sim virtute. Fovetur
acrius aerumnis magnanimum ingenium.
Me patriae excidium stimulat nova quaerere regna.
Troia, vale! Latium per maria atra peto.
Silvae, musa dryas, praesens Silvane, penates,
'non' mihi clamanti 'non' reboate 'dolet'.

Quae sibi nil quaerens quaerenti tanta ministrat,
quae nil accipiens omnia suppeditat,
quae constanter amat non tali robore amata,
quae dare—et hoc totis viribus—ardet opem,
nonne haec digna suo Beronice nomine sancto?
Quod patet ante oculos, improbe, nonne vides?

Cui tam cara comes, non exsulat exsul: ubique
patria qua praesens coniugis adsit amor.

Caece diu, tandem vidisti clarius. Audi:
Perdita mortali gaudia flere nefas:
non datur humanis in perpetuom esse beatos:
mox marcent vitae praemia: segnities
Elysii pretiumst: hebetat dulcedo: doloris
sopitam recreant volnera viva animam.
Haec non quaesitae tibi ianua aperta salutis:
tu fato felix: te nova vita vocat.

Gavisus iuvenis vitae describere metas,
  ausus eram fatum prospicere ipse meum.
Prospexi triplicem—fauste ducentis Amoris,
  Musarum comitum, coniugis—harmoniam,
amens, qui, vasti peragrans vagus aequora ponti,
  non cavi fulmen, saeva procella, tuom.
Non iterum de me dictabo oracula: nosti,
  qui me servasti, Tu mea fata, Deus.

CONTENTS OF VOLUMES VII–X

VOLUME VII

VI. UNIVERSAL STATES

VII. UNIVERSAL CHURCHES

ANNEXES

TABLES

VOLUME VIII

VIII. HEROIC AGES

IX. CONTACTS BETWEEN CIVILIZATIONS IN SPACE (ENCOUNTERS BETWEEN CONTEMPORARIES)

ANNEXES

TABLE

VOLUME IX

X. CONTACTS BETWEEN CIVILIZATIONS IN TIME (RENAISSANCES)

XI. LAW AND FREEDOM IN HISTORY

ANNEXES

TABLES

VOLUME X

XIII. THE INSPIRATIONS OF HISTORIANS

ANNEX

A NOTE ON CHRONOLOGY

ACKNOWLEDGEMENTS AND THANKS

INDEX TO VOLUMES VII–X, by V. M. TOYNBEE

A KEY TO THE CROSS-REFERENCES

IN THE FOOTNOTES TO VOLS. VII–X

THE final text of this book, like the original notes for it, has been written (except for some of the annexes) in the order in which the chapters appear in the Table of Contents. At each step in both making the notes and writing the text, the writer has always tried to see the particular passage on which he has been working at the moment in its relation to the plan of the whole book; and he has printed in his footnotes to the text the resulting network of cross-references because he believes that a method of continually taking his bearings, which has been an indispensable guide and discipline for the course of his own thought, is likely also to be of some help to his readers.

Since, in the nature of the case, the quantity of these notes of cross-references has increased as one Part of the book after another has been written out in full, the writer has sought, in the printing of this concluding batch of four volumes, to spare the reader's eye—and, in the act, to lighten the printer's labours—by reducing the bulk of his cross-references to a minimum. Accordingly, each reference has been cut down to three entries: a large Roman numeral indicating the Part, a small Roman numeral indicating the volume, and an Arabic numeral giving the page, with an n. to stand for 'footnote' when the reference is to one of these. For example, a reference which in volumes i–vi would have appeared in a footnote in the form 'See IV. C (iii) (*c*) 2 (γ), Annex, vol. iv, p. 637, above', would appear in the four present volumes as 'See IV. iv. 637'. Neither the printer nor the reader, the writer believes, is likely to regret this compression.

VI
UNIVERSAL STATES

A. ENDS OR MEANS?

THE starting-point of this book was a search for fields of historical study which would be intelligible in themselves within their own limits in Space and Time, without reference to extraneous historical events. An empirical pursuit of this inquiry led us to find the self-contained units for which we were seeking in societies of the species called civilizations,[1] and so far we have been working on the assumption that a comparative study of the geneses, growths, breakdowns, and disintegrations of the twenty-one civilizations that we have succeeded in identifying would comprehend everything of any significance in the history of Mankind since the time when the first civilizations emerged among the primitive societies which had previously been the only existing form of human social organization. Up to the present stage of our investigation this assumption has perhaps on the whole been justified by results; yet from time to time we have stumbled upon indications that our first master-key might not serve to unlock all the doors through which we have to pass in order to reach our mental journey's end.

Near the outset, in the act of identifying as many representatives as possible of the species of society that we had set ourselves to study, we found that certain civilizations were related to one another by a tie that was closer than the mere common characteristic of being representatives of the same species. We described this more intimate relation as one of 'apparentation-and-affiliation';[2] and we found, on analysis,[3] that the evidences of apparentation-and-affiliation were certain characteristic social products of a Dominant Minority, an Internal Proletariat, and an External Proletariat into which the 'apparented' society split up in the course of its disintegration. It appeared that dominant minorities produced philosophies which sometimes gave inspirations to universal states, that internal proletariats produced higher religions which sought to embody themselves in universal churches, and that external proletariats produced heroic ages which were the tragedies of barbarian war-bands.

In the aggregate, these experiences and institutions manifestly constitute a link between an 'apparented' and an 'affiliated' civilization that cannot be ignored. And this link in the Time-dimension between two non-contemporary civilizations is not the only kind of relation between civilizations that a comparative study of universal states, universal churches, and heroic ages brings to light. Though civilizations may be intelligible fields of historical study and self-contained units of social life on the whole—at any rate by comparison with the relatively parochial and ephemeral political communities into which they are apt to articulate themselves in their growth stage—the fractions, in the shape

[1] See I. i. 17–50. [2] See I. i. 44. [3] See I. i. 52–62.

of social classes, into which they disintegrate after breaking down acquire a liberty to enter into social and cultural combinations with alien elements derived from other contemporary civilizations.[1] This receptivity of theirs is revealed in the institutions that are their products. Some universal states have been the handiwork of alien empire-builders; some higher religions have been animated by alien inspirations;[2] and some barbarian war-bands have imbibed a tincture of alien culture.[3]

Universal states, universal churches, and heroic ages thus link together contemporary, as well as non-contemporary, civilizations in relations that are closer and more individual than an affinity consisting in the bare fact of their being representatives of the same species of society; and this observation raises the question whether we have been justified in treating these historical phenomena as mere by-products, in each case, of the disintegration of some single civilization and in assuming that the civilizations themselves are the sole objects of historical study which we need to take into account. Now that we have found that universal states, universal churches, and heroic ages cannot, for their part, be studied intelligibly within the framework that the history of a single civilization provides, ought we not to study them on their own respective merits, with a view to testing the validity, or at any rate the sufficiency, of the assumption on which we have been proceeding hitherto? Until we have examined the respective claims of institutions of each of these three kinds to be intelligible fields of study in themselves, and have also considered the alternative possibility that they might be parts of some larger whole embracing them and the civilizations alike, we cannot be sure that we have brought within our purview the whole of human history, above the primitive level, in all its aspects.

This further inquiry was the task that we set ourselves at the end of Part V of this Study.[4] We shall now try to acquit ourselves of it in Parts VI, VII, and VIII; and happily in this case we are in a position to proceed straight from the formulation of our question to an attempt to answer it, without having to go through the laborious process of seeking, sifting, assembling, and comparing those historical facts that are indispensable raw materials for the empirical method of investigation that we are following in this Study. An incidental survey of philosophies and universal states, higher religions and universal churches, heroic ages and war-bands has already been taken in our review of the dominant minorities and the internal and external proletariats of civilizations in disintegration,[5] and the results have been summarized in four tables printed in volume vi[6] and reprinted here.[7]

Accordingly, without further preliminaries, we can now investigate the claims of universal states, and may begin by asking whether they are ends in themselves or means towards something beyond them.

Our best approach to this question may be to remind ourselves of certain salient features of universal states that we have already ascertained.

[1] See V. v. 338–40.
[2] See I. i. 40–41 and 57; II. ii. 213–16; and V. v. 360–1.
[3] See V. v. 351–9.
[4] See V. vi. 325–6.
[5] See V. v. 35–337.
[6] vi. 327–31.
[7] Tables I–III, pp. 769–71 of the present volume, below, and Table I, in vol. viii, pp. 734–5.

In the first place, universal states arise after, and not before, the breakdowns of the civilizations to whose bodies social they bring political unity. They are not summers but 'Indian Summers', masking autumn and presaging winter.[1] In the second place, they are the products of dominant minorities: that is, of once creative minorities that have lost their creative power.[2] The negativeness which is the hall-mark of their authorship and also the essential condition of their establishment and maintenance is brought out in the following passages from the works of a nineteenth-century French philosopher and a twentieth-century English satirist.

'The result of the Roman conquest was the destruction of all the city-states in the greater part of the then known world, just as the result of all the partial conquests that merged in the Roman conquest had been already to reduce their numbers. Thereafter one city-state alone, the arch-aggressor, remained standing; but on the very morrow of the establishment of the Empire we see Rome herself promptly divesting herself of her original character, gradually losing her power of aggression and withdrawing into herself. Her dominant aim at this stage is no longer conquest but conservation; the Roman city-state, in short, disappears in order to make way for the Roman Empire.

'But what order, what state of society, did this empire stand for? Was the aim of conservation, which we have just attributed to the Roman Empire, expressed in a new dogma, in a corresponding social hierarchy, as the Roman conquest had been expressed and organised by the religious dogmas and the social institutions of the Roman city-state? Unquestionably, no: in casting our eyes over this immense empire, we do not find anywhere, in all its vast extent, any sentiments, ideas or habits that do not go back to the preceding institution—that of the city-state. And these sentiments, ideas and habits are deprived of energy, are no longer able to receive any [practical] social application, and therefore no longer provide positive links between individuals. In short, the Roman Empire in no sense constitutes a society; for, in its capacity as an empire, it has no religion, no goal, and no general practical aim whatsoever; it represents merely a vast aggregation of human beings, a shapeless congeries of the débris of societies. The imperial administration—in spite of being so far-flung, so complicated, so meticulous, and of giving so great an appearance of symmetry at first glance—does not constitute a political order or a social hierarchy at all; this administration is in strict truth nothing but a vast office for administering Rome's conquests. . . .

'These are the characteristics and the causes of the demoralisation of Rome that has made so lively an impression on the mind of Posterity. This demoralisation had almost reached full measure before the Empire had completed the first century of its existence. Thereafter, this huge body appears to maintain itself merely by a kind of mechanical equilibrium; and, if it does not actually dissolve, that is not so much because there is any positive reason for it to maintain itself as because there is no positive reason, either, for it to undergo any change.'[3]

The point thus illustrated by Bazard from 'real life' in the instance of

[1] See IV. iv. 56–119, especially 59–60.
[2] See V. v. 35–58.
[3] Bazard, A: 'Exposition de la Doctrine Saint-Simonienne', in *Œuvres Complètes de Saint-Simon et d'Enfantin*, vol. xlii (Paris 1877, Leroux), pp. 181–5.

the Roman Empire is brought out more wittily by Huxley in his imaginary Anti-Utopia:

' "The Nine Years' War, the great Economic Collapse. There was a choice between World Control and destruction. Between stability and. . . .

' "It's curious . . . to read what people in the time of Our Ford used to write about scientific progress. They seem to have imagined that it could be allowed to go on indefinitely, regardless of everything else. Knowledge was the highest good, truth the supreme value; all the rest was secondary and subordinate. True, ideas were beginning to change even then. Our Ford himself did a great deal to shift the emphasis from truth and beauty to comfort and happiness. Mass production demanded the shift. Universal happiness keeps the wheels steadily turning; truth and beauty can't. And of course, whenever the masses seized political power, then it was happiness rather than truth and beauty that mattered. Still, in spite of everything, unrestricted scientific research was still permitted. People still went on talking about truth and beauty as though they were the sovereign goods. Right up to the time of the Nine Years' War. *That* made them change their tune all right. What's the point of truth or beauty or knowledge when the anthrax bombs are popping all around you? That was when science first began to be controlled—after the Nine Years' War. People were ready to have even their appetites controlled then. Anything for a quiet life. We've gone on controlling ever since. It hasn't been very good for truth, of course. But it's been very good for happiness. One can't have something for nothing. Happiness has got to be paid for. . . ."

' "Art, science—you seem to have paid a fairly high price for your happiness," said the Savage. . . . "Anything else?"

' "Well, religion, of course," replied the Controller: "There used to be something called God—before the Nine Years' War. . . ." '[1]

This, however, is not the whole picture; for, besides being accompaniments of social breakdown and products of dominant minorities, universal states display a third salient feature: they are expressions of a rally—and a particularly notable one—in a process of disintegration that works itself out in successive pulsations of lapse-and-rally followed by relapse;[2] and it is this last feature that strikes the imagination and evokes the gratitude of the generation that lives to see the successful establishment of a universal state set a term at last to a Time of Troubles that had previously been gathering momentum from successive failures of repeated attempts to stem it.[3]

Taken together, these features present a picture of universal states that, at first sight, looks ambiguous. Universal states are symptoms of social disintegration, yet at the same time they are attempts to check this disintegration and to defy it.

The tenacity with which universal states do cling to life, when once established, is revealed by a survey of their endings. The divers types into which these endings can be analysed form an illuminating series when arranged in an ascending order of the obstinacy with which a universal state rebels against being condemned to death. To comprehend,

[1] Huxley, Aldous: *Brave New World* (London 1932, Chatto & Windus), pp. 56 and 269–70 and 271.

[2] This rhythm has been analysed and illustrated in V. vi. 278–321.

[3] See V. vi. 181–2 and 191.

and compare with one another, these divers typical endings of universal states, we must view each of them in the setting of its own particular version of the common plot of the tragedy of decline and fall; and an attempt at a survey on these lines will be found in an annex to the present chapter at a later point in this volume.[1] The analysis of the divers types of endings of universal states, which this survey of their histories yields, may be summarized here as follows:

When the establishment of a universal state by indigenous empire-builders has been forestalled by the intrusion of an alien society, the impulse, in the body social of the disintegrating society, to pass through the universal state phase before going into dissolution is powerful enough sometimes to be able to constrain the triumphant alien aggressor to provide his victims with the institution which his very triumph has made it impossible for indigenous hands to set up. The Central American, Chibcha Andean, main Orthodox Christian, and Hindu civilizations all succeeded in exacting this social service from alien intruders; the Hindu Civilization actually succeeded in exacting it from two intruders in succession: first from Mughal representatives of the Iranic Muslim Civilization and then from British representatives of the Western Civilization.

When an indigenous universal state has been overthrown by the intrusion of an alien civilization before the exhaustion of the social rally which the foundation of the universal state has inaugurated, the impulse in the body social of the invaded disintegrating society to complete the universal state phase before going into dissolution is powerful enough sometimes to be able to constrain the triumphant aggressor to provide an alien substitute for the indigenous institution which he himself has destroyed, and sometimes to enable the invaded society to bide its time —for many centuries if need be—until at last it finds its opportunity to expel the intruder, re-establish the long ago overthrown indigenous universal state, and, this time, carry it through to the completion of its natural course. The Andean and the Babylonic Society succeeded in exacting from their alien conquerors the social service that they required—the Andean Society from Spanish representatives of the Western Civilization, the Babylonic actually from two intruders in succession: first from Achaemenid representatives of the Syriac Civilization and then from Seleucid representatives of the Hellenic. The Syriac and the Indic Society succeeded in biding their time and eventually re-establishing their overthrown indigenous universal states.

When an indigenous universal state has collapsed after the exhaustion of the social rally which its foundation has inaugurated, the impulse in the body social of the disintegrating society to complete the universal state phase, before going into dissolution, is powerful enough to be able to achieve the restoration of the prostrate indigenous universal state, sometimes—as the Hellenic, Sinic, and Sumeric civilizations achieved this—by self-help alone, and sometimes—as the Orthodox Christian Civilization in Russia achieved it—by self-help reinforced by the reception of an alien civilization.

[1] On pp. 569–76, below.

After an indigenous universal state has reached the term of its natural expectation of life and has duly given place to the social interregnum in which the dissolution of a moribund civilization is normally consummated, the impulse in the body social of the moribund society to retrieve its life from the jaws of death may be powerful enough—as is witnessed by the Egyptiac Civilization's achievement of this *tour de force*—to be able to restore the defunct universal state and thereafter to maintain it in existence by one means or another until the moribund society, preserved within this institutional mummy-case in an uncanny state of life-in-death, has succeeded, like King Menkaure in the folk-tale,[1] in doubling the span of life allotted to it by the Gods.

Indeed, after a universal state has reached the term of its natural expectation of life, the determination of the body social of the moribund society not to taste of death may be obstinate enough—as is witnessed by the history of the Far Eastern Civilization in China—to be able to maintain the senile universal state in existence, without a break, for an additional term by inducing a vigorous and victorious barbarian invader to shoulder the burden of preserving an institution which he might have been expected to destroy.

These divers endings of universal states bear concordant witness to the craving for life by which these institutions are animated. So strong is this craving of theirs that they refuse to forgo their claims to be brought into existence and to be allowed to live out their normal terms, and sometimes even refuse to pass out of existence after having duly realized their natural expectation of life. In other words, universal states show a strong tendency to behave as though they were ends in themselves, whereas in truth they represent a phase in a process of social disintegration and, if they have any significance beyond that, can only have it in virtue of being a means to some end that is outside and beyond them.

The judgement of History on their idolization of themselves is pronounced in one of the masterpieces of a Modern Western poet:

It is not growing like a tree
In bulk, doth make Man better be,
Or standing long an oak, three hundred year,
To fall a log at last, dry, bald and sere:
A lily of a day
Is fairer far in May,
Although it fall and die that night—
It was the plant and flower of light.
In small proportions we just beauties see,
And in short measures Life may perfect be.[2]

[1] See IV. iv. 409 and V. v. 2.

[2] Ben Jonson.

B. UNIVERSAL STATES AS ENDS

(I) THE MIRAGE OF IMMORTALITY

A Paradoxical Misapprehension

AS we have seen in the last chapter, the endings of universal states indicate that these institutions are possessed by an almost demonic craving for life; and, if we now look at them, no longer through the eyes of alien observers, but through those of their own citizens, we shall find that these are apt not only to desire with their whole hearts that this earthly commonwealth of theirs may live for ever,[1] but actually to believe that the immortality of this human institution is assured—and this sometimes in the teeth of contemporary events which, to an observer posted at a different standpoint in Time or Space, declare beyond question that this particular universal state is at this very moment in its last agonies. To observers who happen to have been born into the history of their own societies at a time when these have not been passing through the universal state phase, it is manifest that universal states, as a class of polity, are by-products of a process of social disintegration and are stamped by their certificates of origin as being uncreative and ephemeral.[2] Why is it, such observers may well ask, that, in defiance of apparently plain facts, the citizens of a universal state are prone to regard it, not as a night's shelter in the wilderness, but as the Promised Land, the goal of human endeavours? How is it possible for them to mistake this mundane institution for the *Civitas Dei* itself?

This misapprehension is so extreme in its degree that its very occurrence might perhaps be called in question, were this not attested by the incontrovertible evidence of a cloud of witnesses who convict themselves, out of their own mouths, of being victims of this strange hallucination.

The Aftermaths of the Roman Empire[3] and the Arab Caliphate[4]

In the history of the Roman Empire, which was the universal state

1 This desire appears to be the characteristic sentiment of citizens of universal states that have been established and maintained by indigenous empire-builders, in contrast to the aversion commonly felt for universal states of alien origin (see V. v. 341–51). An indigenous origin is, of course, the rule, and an alien origin the exception. The love and hatred inspired by these two different kinds of universal state both show a tendency to grow stronger with the passage of time.

2 An imperfection that is transparent in universal states is, of course, characteristic of all states of all kinds in all circumstances, as is pointed out by a Modern Western Christian philosopher in the following passage:

'What men call peace is never anything but a space between two wars: a precarious equilibrium that lasts as long as mutual fear prevents dissension from declaring itself. This parody of true peace, this armed fear, which there is no need to denounce to our contemporaries, may very well support a kind of order, but never can it bring Mankind tranquillity. Not until the social order becomes the spontaneous expression of an interior peace in men's hearts shall we have tranquillity; were all men's minds in accord with themselves, all wills interiorly unified by love of the supreme good, then they would know the absence of internal dissension, unity, order from within, a peace, finally, made of the tranquillity born of this order: *pax est tranquillitas ordinis*. But, if each will were in accord with itself, all wills would be in mutual accord, each would find peace in willing what the others will. Then also we should have a true society, based on union in love of one and the same end' (Gilson, E.: *The Spirit of Mediaeval Philosophy*, English translation (London 1936, Sheed & Ward), p. 399).

3 See xi, map 29.

4 See xi, map 37.

of the Hellenic World, we find the generation that had witnessed the establishment of the *Pax Augusta* asserting, in evidently sincere good faith, that the Empire and the City that has built it have been endowed with a common immortality.[1]

Tibullus (*vivebat circa* 54–18 B.C.) sings of the 'aeternae urbis moenia',[2] while Virgil (*vivebat* 70–19 B.C.) makes his Iuppiter, speaking of the future Roman scions of Aeneas' race, proclaim: 'His ego nec metas rerum nec tempora pono:/imperium sine fine dedi.'[3] A soldier-historian may show somewhat greater caution than a philosopher-poet by expressing the same expectation in the form, not of a divine communiqué, but of a human hope. In recording the adoption of Tiberius by Augustus, Velleius (*vivebat circa* 19 B.C.–A.D. 31) speaks of a 'spem conceptam perpetuae securitatis aeternitatisque Romani imperii'.[4] An historian-propagandist can perhaps afford to be less circumspect, and Livy (*vivebat* 59 B.C.–A.D. 17) writes with the assurance of Tibullus: 'in aeternum urbe conditâ';[5] 'urbem . . . diis auctoribus in aeternum conditam'.[6] But Horace, who was both a poet and a sceptic, was doubly audacious in claiming immortality for his own verse and in taking, as his concrete measure of eternity, the repetition, *in saecula saeculorum*, of the annual round of the religious ritual of the Roman city-state:

Exegi monumentum aere perennius
regalique situ Pyramidum altius,
quod non imber edax, non Aquilo impotens
possit diruere aut innumerabilis
annorum series et fuga temporum.
non omnis moriar . . .: usque ego posterâ
crescam laude recens dum Capitolium
scandet cum tacitâ virgine pontifex.[7]

These lines ring ironically in the ears of a Modern Western student of history as he reflects on the unsuccessful rearguard action that was fought by an outgoing Roman Paganism, only four centuries after Horace's day, to induce a Christian Roman Government to reinstate in the Senate House the statue and altar of Victory that had been placed there by 'Caesar the God' in Horace's lifetime.[8] If some good-natured deity had forewarned Horace, in time, of this not far distant demise of Rome's native religious institutions, we may guess that the poet would have heartily thanked his informant and hastily changed his measure of duration. Whether Horace's poetry was, as its author believed it to be, immortal, Time, in A.D. 1952, had still to show; but this etherial creation of an individual genius had already lasted, *volitans viva per ora virum*, four or five times longer than the rites that are the second term of the poet's unlucky comparison. As a sceptic, the Roman poet Horace finds

[1] 'The little rivulet of disbelief which runs counter to the main stream of popular faith, and which takes the form of a belief in an "allotted span" for the Roman state', is traced from the last century B.C. to the fifth century of the Christian Era by D. A. Malcolm in 'Urbs Aeterna', in *The University of Birmingham Historical Journal*, vol. iii, No. 1 (1951), pp. 1–15.

[2] *Carmina*, Book II, Elegy 5, ll. 24–25.

[3] *Aeneid*, Book I, ll. 278–9.

[4] Velleius Paterculus, C.: *Historia Romana*, Book II, chap. 103.

[5] Book IV, chap. 4, § 4.

[6] Book XXVIII, chap. 28, § 11.

[7] *Carmina*, Book III, Ode xxx, ll. 1–9.

[8] See V. vi. 89, with n. 3.

his match in the English historian Gibbon; yet Gibbon, who was inspired on the 15th October, A.D. 1764, to record 'the triumph of Barbarism and Religion' over the Roman Empire by hearing friars singing Vespers in the Temple of Iuppiter as he sat musing among the ruins of the Capitol[1] nearly 1,772 years after the date of Horace's death on the 17th November, 8 B.C., no doubt believed in the immortality of Horace's verse as confidently as the justifiably conceited poet had believed in it himself.

The same ludicrously inadequate ritual 'yard-stick' that had been taken by Horace as a measure for the duration of his personal literary work was taken by Livy as a measure for the duration of his historical theme the Roman Empire: 'Vestae aedem petitam et aeternos ignes et conditum in penetrali fatale pignus imperii Romani.'[2] The 'guarantee' (*pignus*) of the Roman Empire's survival is the Palladium.[3] In thus reading his modern political symbolism into an archaic religious rite, Livy was perhaps taking a cue from his Imperial patron, and Augustus a cue from his Imperial predecessors on the throne of an earlier universal state which had failed after all to discover the elixir of life. According to an eminent authority,[4] the interpretation of Vesta's undying flame as a symbol of the eternity of an oecumenical ruler was a Roman adaptation of an Achaemenian idea[5] that was adopted by Augustus when, in 12 B.C., he became Pontifex Maximus and consecrated a new temple of Vesta in his house on the Palatine. Augustus's successors, from the Antonines onwards, gave publicity to this idea by making it their practice to have Vesta's fire carried in procession in front of them.[6]

During the century and a quarter that elapsed between the death of Augustus in A.D. 14 and the accession of Pius in A.D. 138, the concept of the eternity of Rome and the Roman Empire had been cherished by two bad emperors who both had met their deserts by coming to untimely personal ends. Nero had instituted games 'quos pro aeternitate imperii susceptos appellari [ludos] maximos voluit'.[7] The *Acta Fratrum Arvalium* record 'aeterni[tati imperi vaccam]' among the proceedings of A.D. 66,[8] and 'vota si custodieris aeternitatem imperii quod [susci]piendo ampliavit (Domitianus)'[9] under the years A.D. 86, 87, and 90.

In the Age of the Antonines we find a Greek man of letters expressing the Augustan belief in the more delicate form of a prayer, without a suspicion that he was living in an 'Indian Summer' and was praying that

1 See IV. iv. 59–60 and XIII. x. 103 and 104.

2 Book XXVI, chap. 27, § 14. Cp. Book V, chap. 42, § 7.

3 See Cicero: *Pro Scauro*, chap. xxiii, § 48: 'Palladium illud quod quasi pignus nostrae salutis atque imperi custodiis Vestae continetur'; *Philippicae*, Speech xi, ch. x, § 24: 'signum . . . de caelo delapsum . . . quo salvo salvi sumus futuri', quoted by Malcolm, D. A.: 'Urbs Aeterna', in *The University of Birmingham Historical Journal*, vol. iii, No. 1 (1951), p. 4.

4 Cumont, Fr.: 'L'Éternité des Empereurs Romains', in *Revue d'Histoire et de Littérature Religieuses*, vol. i (Paris 1896; printed at Macon), pp. 436 and 441–2.

5 In the Achaemenian *Weltanschauung* the symbolization of eternity by fire was connected with a belief in the divinity and eternity of the heavenly bodies (Cumont, op. cit., pp. 443–4).

6 See Cumont, op. cit., pp. 437 and 442.

7 Suetonius Tranquillus, C.: *The Lives of the Caesars*, 'Nero', chap. 11, § 2.

8 *Acta Fratrum Arvalium Quae Supersunt*, ed. by G. Henzen (Berlin 1874, Reimer), p. lxxxi.

9 Ibid. pp. cxv, cxix, cxxvi.

a fugitive October might be miraculously transformed into a perpetual June.

'Let us invoke all the gods and all the children of the gods, and let us pray them to grant this empire and this city life and prosperity world without end. May they endure until ingots learn to float on the sea and until trees forget to blossom in the spring. And long live the supreme magistrate and his children likewise. Long may they be with us to carry on their work of dispensing happiness to all their subjects'.[1]

Thereafter, when the touch of winter begins to make itself felt, its victims defy a change of season, which they have not foreseen and cannot face, by insisting more and more emphatically that they have been privileged to enjoy an everlasting midsummer's day.[2] In the Severan Age and its bleaker sequel, the contrast between the official eternity of the emperors[3] and the ephemeralness that was their actual lot makes a painfully strange impression.[4] It is still more strange to hear the watchwords of the Augustan poets being no less confidently repeated, in the same Latin, and this by men of letters whose mother-tongue was Greek,[5] on the eve of the final collapse of all but the easternmost extremity of the Latin-speaking portion of the Empire.[6] And, even after the truth has been proclaimed, in a deed more eloquent than any words, by Alaric's capture and sack of Rome herself, we can hear, above the reverberations of this resounding blow, the high voice of a Gallic poet reasserting the immortality of Rome as he travels back from the no longer inviolate Imperial City to his own war-ravaged native province.

Erige crinales lauros seniumque sacrati
  verticis in virides, Roma, refinge comas. . . .
astrorum flammae renovant occasibus ortus;
  lunam finiri cernis, ut incipiat.

1 Aristeides, P. Aelius: *In Romam*, edited by Keil, B., *Aelii Aristidis Quae Supersunt Omnia*, vol. ii (Berlin 1898, Weidmann), p. 124 (Or. XXVI, § 109).

2 See V. vi. 370–5.

3 In this age of the Roman Empire's decline 'Your Eternity' gradually comes to be used, like 'Your Majesty' in Modern Western Europe, as the stock style and title for a crowned head (Cumont, op. cit., p. 435).

4 The inscription 'Aeternitas Augusti' first appears on the Senatorial copper coinage of the Roman Empire in the reign of Vespasian (*imperabat* A.D. 69–79), gradually wins its way on to coins of other series, and holds its own till the close of the fourth century of the Christian Era (Cumont, op. cit., p. 438). Severus (*imperabat* A.D. 193–211), whose accession, like Vespasian's, had cost the Empire a disastrous civil war, perhaps had as much—or little—warrant for inscribing on his coinage the motto 'Aeternitas Imperii' and for evoking a dedication 'pro aeternitate imperii et salute Imperatoris Caesaris L. Septimi Severi' (C.I.L., vol. ii (Berlin 1869, Reimer), p. 31, No. 259). But the same motto becomes a bad joke on coins issued in the names of Caracalla and Geta as well as their father; and it makes a farcical effect on coins bearing the name of a Philip or a Carus. (See Cumont, op. cit., p. 437.)

5 In the *Res Gestae* of the Antiochene historian Ammianus Marcellinus the Tibullan phrase 'urbs aeterna' is used as a stock periphrasis for 'Rome': e.g. in Book XIV. vi. 1: in Book XV. vii. 1 and vii. 10; in Book XVI. x. 14; and in eight other passages, according to Charlesworth, M. P.: 'Providentia and Aeternitas', in the *Harvard Theological Review*, vol. xxix, No. 22 (April 1936). The same conviction is expressed in the circumlocutions 'victura dum erunt homines Roma' (Book XIV, vi. 3) and 'victura cum saeculis Roma' (Book XXVI. i. 14). The Alexandrian poet Claudian, in his *De Consulatu Stilichonis*, Book III, ll. 159–60, declares: 'Nec terminus unquam/Romanae ditionis erit', and spends a dozen further lines on variations on this Virgilian theme.

6 For the *tracée* of the geographical line of division between the Latin-speaking and Greek-speaking portions of the Roman Empire, see IV. iv. 326, n. 2.

victoris Brenni non distulit Allia poenam;
  Samnis servitio foedera saeva luit.
post multas Pyrrhum clades superata fugasti;
  flevit successus Hannibal ipse suos.
quae mergi nequeunt nisu maiore resurgunt,
  exsiliuntque imis altius acta vadis.
utque novas vires fax inclinata resumit,
  clarior ex humili sorte superna petis.
porrige victuras Romana in saecula leges,
  solaque fatales non vereare colos. . . .
quae restant, nullis obnoxia tempora metis:
  dum stabunt terrae, dum polus astra feret.
illud te reparat quod cetera regna resolvit:
  ordo renascendi est, crescere posse malis.
ergo age, sacrilegae tandem cadat hostia gentis:
  submittant trepidi perfida colla Getae.
ditia pacatae dent vectigalia terrae;
  impleat augustos barbara praeda sinus.
aeternum tibi Rhenus aret, tibi Nilus inundet,
  altricemque suam fertilis orbis alat.[1]

Perhaps the strangest testimony of all is Saint Jerome's description of the shock that he suffered when the news of the fall of Rome reached him in his remote and still secure retreat at Jerusalem. The saint was devoted to the service of a Church that avowedly placed its hopes in the Commonwealth of God, and not in any earthly polity; yet this news, mundane though it might be, affected Jerome so profoundly that for the moment he found himself incapable of proceeding with his literary labours of theological controversy and scriptural exegesis;[2] and the language in which he describes his admiration for what Rome has once been and his grief for the fate that has now overtaken her anticipates the language of Rutilius in verbal correspondences that can hardly be accidental.[3] Their common stupefaction, perhaps even more than their common sorrow, at the break-up of the universal state that was their common social universe was an emotion strong enough to bridge the moral gulf between the would-be exclusively Christian saint and the aggressively pagan *Praefectus Urbi emeritus*.

The shock administered by the fall of Rome in A.D. 410 to the citizens of a transient universal state which they had mistaken for an everlasting habitation[4] has its counterpart in the shock suffered by the subjects of the Arab Caliphate when Baghdad fell to the Mongols in A.D. 1258.[5] In

[1] Rutilius Namatianus, C.: *De Reditu Suo*, Book I, ll. 115–16, 123–34, 137–46. The poet's exhortation to his heroine in ll. 141–2 was duly acted upon by her when, a century and more after Rutilius's day, Justinian annihilated the Visigoths' Ostrogothic cousins in a fight to the finish on Italian soil, and even struck some shrewd blows at the Visigoths themselves in the distant retreat that they had found for themselves in Spain after having sacked Rome *en route*. The sequel, however, was just the opposite of what Rutilius so confidently looks forward to in ll. 143–6. So far from restoring the Empire's revenues, Justinian's reconquest of some of the Empire's lost Latin provinces was achieved at such a cost, in blood and treasure, to the hitherto still sound Greek and Oriental core of the Hellenic universal state that his extravagant régime was quickly followed by a collapse which proved to be irretrievable (see IV. iv. 326–8 and 397–8, and V. vi. 224–5).

[2] See Saint Jerome, Ep. cxxvii, cap. 12, quoted in V. v, 223, n. 2.

[3] See V. v. 345, n. 4.

[4] Luke xvi. 9.

[5] A touch of the emotion caused by this catastrophe can be felt in the last words of the passage quoted from Falak-ad-Dīn Muhammad b. Aydīmir in IV. iv. 446.

the Roman World the shock was felt from Palestine to Gaul; in the Arab World, from Farghānah to Andalusia.

'It is difficult to estimate the bewilderment that Muslims felt when there was no longer a Caliph on whom the blessing of God could be invoked in the *khutbah*; such an event was without precedent throughout the previous history of Islam. Their suffering finds expression in the prayer offered in the great mosque of Baghdad on the Friday following the death of the Caliph: "Praise be to God who has caused exalted personages to perish and has given over to destruction the inhabitants of this city. . . . O God, help us in our misery, the like of which Islam and its children have never witnessed; we are God's, and unto God do we return".'[1]

The intensity of the psychological effect is even more remarkable in this than in the Roman case, for, by the time when Hūlāgū gave the 'Abbasid Caliphate its *coup de grâce*, its sovereignty had been ineffective, for three or four centuries past, over the greater part of the vast domain that was nominally subject to it.[2] It is perhaps comprehensible that, even for that length of time, a shadow should continue to be mistaken, half deliberately, for the substance by a dominant minority for whom the moribund universal state represented their own latest achievement and last hope; a more astonishing testimony to the hold that a universal state can acquire over the hearts and minds of contemporaries is the fascination which it also exerts upon members of the now victoriously insurgent internal and external proletariats, who do not so much refuse to admit as, apparently, fail altogether to realize that they are in the act of pulling down with their own hands an institution which, in their eyes, is so venerable that it would be inconceivably impious even to imagine its disappearance.

On the strength of this widespread and long-lasting hallucination, which is itself a psychological and political fact to be reckoned with by the roughest-handed and hardest-headed carvers-out of indigenous or barbarian successor-states, the holders, in lawful succession, of the sovereign authority in a universal state may retain—for generations or even centuries after their loss of all genuine power over their nominal dominions—a by no means negligible status as the sole dispensers of legitimacy. Indeed, this monopoly of an imponderable political commodity usually counts for so much that it is rare to find a barbarian conqueror of an imperial province allowing himself the satisfaction of openly boasting that he has seized his prize by force and is holding it by right of conquest.[3] The heretic Arian Vandal conquerors of Roman

[1] Arnold, Sir T. W.: *The Caliphate* (Oxford 1924, Clarendon Press), pp. 81–82.

[2] For the stages in the progressive decline of the 'Abbasid Caliphate from the ninth century of the Christian Era onwards, see Arnold, op. cit., pp. 57–69.

[3] 'The minister who manages to establish an ascendancy over the ruler . . . appropriates the power without giving an inkling of his desire to usurp the throne; he contents himself with the [substantial] advantages of royalty: that is to say, the power of enjoining and prohibiting, of binding and loosing, of deciding and annulling. By this policy he leads the notables of the empire to believe that he is acting under instructions transmitted to him by the sovereign from his cabinet, and that he is merely executing the prince's orders. Although he has appropriated the whole of the authority, he takes care not to usurp the marks, emblems and titles of sovereignty, in order to avoid exciting any suspicions of his ambitions. The curtain which, since the foundation of the empire, has made the sultan and his ancestors invisible to the public, likewise serves to conceal the encroachments of the minister and to make the public believe that this officer is just the

Africa, and the heretic Shīʿī Katāma Berber conquerors of ʿAbbasid Ifrīqīyah and Egypt, did permit themselves this indulgence; indeed the Katāma's self-declared but unauthenticated 'Fātimid' leaders were not content with repudiating the authority of the legitimate Sunnī ʿAbbasid Caliphs at Baghdad, but pretended to the title of Caliphs themselves. For such presumption these two avowedly usurping war-bands both paid the penalty of being liquidated—the Vandals by Belisarius's Roman expeditionary force, and the Fātimids by the Sanhāja Berbers in Ifrīqīyah and by Saladin in Egypt.[1] These, however, are exceptions that prove a rule. The Amalung leaders of the Arian Ostrogoths and Buwayhid leaders of the Shīʿī Daylamīs[2] were wiser in their generation in seeking title for their conquests by ruling them, in official theory, as vicegerents of the Emperor at Constantinople[3] and the Caliph at Baghdad[4] respectively; and, though this tactful handling of a senile universal state did not avail, in their case, to avert the doom to which both of these war-bands condemned themselves by clinging to their distinctive heresy instead of commending themselves to their subjects by adopting the orthodox faiths of Catholic Christianity and of Sunnī Islam,[5] the same political manœuvre was brilliantly successful when executed by fellow barbarians who had the sagacity or good fortune to be at the same time impeccable in their profession of religious faith. Clovis, for instance, who was the most successful of all founders of barbarian successor-states of the Roman Empire, found it worth while to follow up his conversion from paganism to Catholicism in A.D. 496 by obtaining in A.D. 510 from Anastasius, the reigning Emperor at Constantinople, the title of proconsul with the consular insignia.[6] In the history of the decline of the ʿAbbasid Caliphate there are notable examples of a corresponding practice.

'Throughout the whole period of the decline of the Caliphate up to the date of the death of Mustaʿsim (A.D. 1258), the Caliph was to all orthodox Sunnīs[7] the Commander of the Faithful, and as Successor of the Prophet

prince's lieutenant and nothing more.'—Ibn Khaldūn: *Muqaddamāt*, French translation by de Slane, Baron McG. (Paris 1863–8, Imprimerie Impériale, 3 vols.), vol. i, p. 379.

[1] See V. v. 252 and 358. In the former passage, the Sanhāja have been correctly described as Sunnīs but incorrectly as Murābits. In the latter passage, the deposition of the Fātimids in Egypt has been erroneously ascribed to Saladin's uncle and companion in arms Shīrkūh, who died before the process of extinguishing the Fātimids was completed by Saladin in A.D. 1171.

[2] For the Buwayhids, see I. i. 356 and V. v. 358.

[3] In this device for saving Roman 'face', Theodoric had been anticipated by his predecessor and victim Odovacer.

[4] See Arnold, op. cit., pp. 60–68, especially the account, on pp. 65–68, of the particularly piquant farce that was played in A.D. 980, at the Caliphial Court of Baghdad, by the Buwayhid 'mayor of the palace' ʿAdūd-ad-Dawlah, who chose the occasion of his presentation of an ambassador from his fellow heretic the Fātimid anti-Caliph at Cairo as his moment for obtaining from the ʿAbbasid Caliph Tāʾiʿ a formal commission to exercise those plenary powers of government in the Caliph's dominions which he had long since usurped *de facto*.

[5] For the contrast between the respective fortunes of barbarian conquerors who retain an heretical form of religion or a tinge of alien culture and those who adopt the culture and faith of the subject population which they have taken over from a derelict universal state, see V. v. 351–8.

[6] See J. B. Bury's footnote in his *editio minor* of Edward Gibbon's *The History of the Decline and Fall of the Roman Empire*, vol. iv (London 1901, Methuen), p. 119.

[7] For the mass-conversion to Islam that accompanied the decline of the ʿAbbasid Caliphate and anticipated the dissolution of the Syriac Society, see pp. 397–400, below.—A.J.T.

he was held to be the source of all authority and the fountain of honour. The Caliph by his very name led men's thoughts back to the founder of their faith, the promulgator of their system of sacred law, and represented to them the principle of established law and authority. Whatever shape the course of external events might take, the faith of the Sunnī theologians and legists in the doctrines expounded in their textbooks remained unshaken, and, even though the Caliph could not give an order outside his own palace, they still went on teaching the faithful that he was the supreme head of the whole body of Muslims. Accordingly, a diploma of investiture sent by the Caliph, or a title of honour conferred by him, would satisfy the demands of the religious law and tranquillise the tender consciences of the subjects of an independent prince, though the ruler himself might remain entirely autonomous and be under no obligation of obedience to the puppet Caliph. . . . Even the Buwayhids, though their occupation of Baghdad was the culmination of the rapid growth of their extensive dominions, and though the Caliph was their pensioner and practically a prisoner in their hands, found it politic to disguise their complete independence under a pretence of subserviency and to give a show of legitimacy to their rule by accepting titles from him.'[1]

The precedent set by the heretical Buwayhids was followed by their Sunnī rivals, supplanters, and successors in the scramble for fragments of the ʿAbbasid heritage.[2] Mahmūd of Ghaznah (*dominabatur* A.D. 998–1030)[3] obtained a title from the ʿAbbasid Caliph Qādir bi'llāh (*imperabat* A.D. 991–1031) to legitimize the dominion which he had won for himself *de facto* by successful rebellion against a Sāmānid master whose Transoxanian principality was itself the fruit of previous successful usurpation at the ʿAbbasid Caliphate's expense.[4] The Saljūq Turkish Nomad supplanters of the Sāmānids and the Buwayhids took over the Buwayhids' ascendancy at Baghdad in A.D. 1055 under the pretext of delivering the ʿAbbasids from it. At the opposite extremity of Dār-al-Islām, *circa* A. D. 1086, Yūsuf b. Tāshfīn, the founder of a Murābit Berber principality embracing derelict provinces of both the ʿAbbasid Caliphate of Baghdad in North-West Africa and the Umayyad Caliphate of Cordova in the Iberian Peninsula, obtained a title and insignia from the ʿAbbasid Caliph Muqtadī (*imperabat* A.D. 1075–94), who, by his complacency in granting his uncouth petitioner a style barely distinguishable from his own,[5] rather easily won the empty distinction of being the first of his House whose Commandership was recognized—though not, of course, obeyed—by the Faithful in Andalusia. In A.D. 1175 Saladin, having appropriated, in the preceding year, the heritage of his own dead master Nūr-ad-Dīn's lawful heir, sought and obtained from the reigning Caliph Mustadī (*imperabat* A.D. 1170–80) a retrospective legitimization of the dominion which he had already acquired *de facto* by his act of usurpation. How could the Caliph refuse this request from an orthodox Sunnī champion who had restored the recitation of the Caliph's name in the bidding prayer (*khutbah*) in the mosques of Egypt after an interval of

[1] Arnold, op. cit., pp. 77 and 78. [2] See ibid., pp. 78–88.

[3] For Mahmūd of Ghaznah see I. i. 360, n. 1, and V. v. 303.

[4] For the role of the Sāmānids as wardens of the North-Eastern Marches of the Syriac World, see II. ii. 142.

[5] Yūsuf was now entitled to style himself the Amīr-al-Muslimīn, in the Maghrib, of the Amīr-al-Mu'minīn at Baghdad.

more than two hundred years during which it had been recited there in the names of heretical pseudo-Fātimids?[1] How could he disappoint a hero who had broken an aggressive Frankish Power that, by its lodgement in Syria, had almost severed the geographical link between the Asiatic and the African portion of Dār-al-Islām? And how could he say 'No' to a war-lord whose territories lay next door to the Caliph's own, and who could march, if provoked, on Baghdad as easily as on Cairo, Jerusalem, or Damascus?

In the thirteenth century of the Christian Era a special need for the Caliph's good offices was felt by the 'Slave Kings' of Delhi,[2] who were masters of a vast new domain that had been added to Dār-al-Islām by the conquest of Hindustan between the years 1191 and 1204 of the Christian Era. The rule over this new dominion was transmitted, not by hereditary succession from father to son, but by acquisition by slave from slave, and each 'Slave King' who mounted the throne, in his turn, by this contentious avenue required a personal ablution from the 'Abbasid fount of honour to make his tenure secure. The practice was initiated by the first ruler of the series, Iltutmysh, who made himself master of Delhi in A.D. 1211 and obtained a retrospective diploma of investiture from the Caliph Mustansir (*imperabat* A.D. 1221–42) in A.D. 1229.

'The document was solemnly read out in a vast assembly held in Delhi, and Iltutmysh from that date put the name of the Caliph on his coins. His successors followed this pious example. The name of the last 'Abbasid Khalīfah of Baghdad, Musta'sim (*imperabat* A.D. 1242–58) first appears on the coins of 'Alā-ad-Dīn Mas'ūd Shāh (*dominabatur* A.D. 1241–6); and, though Musta'sim was put to death by the Mongols in A.D. 1258, his name still appears on the coins of successive Kings of Delhi, e.g. Mahmūd Shāh Nāsir-ad-Dīn (*dominabatur* A.D. 1246–65), Ghiyāth-ad-Dīn Balban (*dominabatur* A.D. 1265–87), and Mu'izz-ad-Dīn Kayqubād (*dominabatur* A.D. 1287–90), the last monarch of the so-called 'Slave' dynasty; and the first of these continued to have the name of Musta'sim mentioned in the *khutbah*.

'A new dynasty arose, that of the Khaljī [or Khiljī]; the same need for legitimization was apparently still felt, and the coins of Jalāl-ad-Dīn Fīrūz Shāh II (*dominabatur* A.D. 1290–5) continued to bear the name of Musta'sim, though this Caliph had been trampled to death by the Mongols more than thirty years before.[3]

1 Saladin employed the manœuvre of acting in the name of an august puppet twice over. He had established himself in Egypt as the Sunnī Wazīr of the Shī'i Fātimid Caliph whom he deposed (the inverse of the situation at Baghdad two centuries earlier, when Sunnī 'Abbasid Caliphs had been in the power of Shī'i Buwayhid 'mayors of the palace' (see p. 13, n. 4, above)). Saladin now secured legitimization for his acquisitions by holding them, in turn, as the vicegerent of the 'Abbasid Caliph Mustadī.

2 See II. ii. 131; III. iii. 30 and 31, n. 1; IV. iv. 99, with n. 1.

3 Though Hūlāgū Khan was a pagan under the influence of a Nestorian Christian wife (see II. ii. 238 and 451), he did not take the 'Abbasid Caliph's life without some searchings of heart:

'The awe with which the institution of the Caliphate was regarded, even in these days of its weakness, may be realised by the fact that, cruel and bloodthirsty savage though Hūlāgū was, even he hesitated to put to death the Successor of the Prophet, for the Muhammadans who accompanied him in his army in the expedition against Baghdad had warned him that, if the blood of the Khalīfah was shed upon the ground, the World would be overspread with darkness and the army of the Mongols be swallowed up by an earthquake' (Arnold, op. cit., p. 81).

'What was an unfortunate Muslim monarch to do, who felt that his title was insecure? He knew that it was only his sword that had set him on the throne, that his own dynasty might at any time be displaced, as he had himself displaced the dynasty that had preceded him, while his legal advisers and religious guides told him that the only legitimate source of authority was the Khalīfah, the Imām; and he realised that all his devout Muslim subjects shared their opinion. So he went on putting the name of the dead Musta'sim on his coins, because he could find no other, and the Muslim theory of the State had not succeeded in adjusting itself to the fact that there was no Khalīfah or Imām in existence. His [Jālāl-ad-Dīn's] successor, 'Alā-ad-Dīn Muhammad Shah I (*dominabatur* A.D. 1295–1315), got out of the difficulty by ceasing to insert Musta'sim's name and by describing himself merely as Yamīn-al-Khilāfat Nāsir Amīri'l-Mu'minīn, "the Right Hand of the Caliphate, the Helper of the Commander of the Faithful", and this was sufficient for the satisfaction of tender consciences, though in reality he was giving no help at all to any Caliph, any more than either of his predecessors had done, who had seen the unhappy Musta'sim trampled to death without moving a finger, though they had gone on making use of his name for their own selfish purposes.'[1]

The Aftermaths of the Manchu,[2] Ottoman,[3] and Mughal[4] Empires

The belief in the immortality of universal states which is attested by their ability to maintain their status as dispensers of legitimacy long after they have lost the realities of power—or even after they have actually ceased altogether to exist—can be illustrated from other histories besides those of the 'Abbasid Caliphate at Baghdad and the Roman Empire at Constantinople.

The Government of the Manchu incarnation of the Far Eastern universal state in China—surrounded, as the Middle Kingdom was accustomed to find itself, by tributary states, such as Korea, Annam, and the Mongol principalities, whose rulers did receive investiture from the Son of Heaven at Peking—affected to believe that all sovereigns, in any part of the World, with whom the Celestial Empire might be drawn into diplomatic relations, derived their title from the same unique source of legitimacy.[5]

In the decline of the Ottoman Empire, during the critical period between the disastrous end of the great Turco-Russian War of A.D. 1768–74 and the ignominious end of Sultan Mahmūd II's final trial of strength with Mehmed 'Alī Pasha in the hostilities of A.D. 1839–40, the ambitious war-lords who were carving out successor-states for themselves *de facto*—a Mehmed 'Alī in Egypt and Syria, an 'Alī of Yannina in Albania and Greece, a Pasvānoghlu of Viddin in the north-western corner of Rumelia—were sedulous in doing in the Pādishāh's name all that they were doing to his detriment in their own private interests; and, even when the greatest and most successful of them all, Mehmed 'Alī, had to submit to seeing the verdict of ordeal by battle between himself and his lawful master reversed by the irresistible decision of the Concert

[1] Arnold, op. cit., pp. 86–88.
[2] See xi, map 54.
[3] See xi, map 51.
[4] See xi, map 52.
[5] See, for example, the letter, addressed in A.D. 1793 by the Emperor Ch'ien Lung to King George III of the United Kingdom of Great Britain and Ireland, that has been quoted in I. i. 161.

of Powers of an infidel Western World, his mortification at being awarded the loss of Syria as the fruit of his victory was tempered by his satisfaction at securing from the Powers, as his *quid pro quo*, a diploma, drawn in the Pādishāh's chancery, which conferred the Pashalyq of Egypt on Mehmed 'Alī and his heirs in perpetuity.

Even when an Ottoman Emperor who had been wont to style himself 'Sultan of the Two Continents, Khāqān of the Two Seas',[1] had thus declined into being the 'Sick Man' of Europe,[2] dependent for his very existence on the infidel Powers finding it convenient still to keep the life in his body for fear of falling out awkwardly among themselves over the disposal of his estate, it became one of the regular practices of Western diplomacy, for the best part of a century, to mitigate, by maintaining the fiction of legitimacy, the shock that was being administered to Muslims, inside and outside the Ottoman Empire, by its progressive break-up. On the model of the Danubian Principalities of Wallachia and Moldavia and the Khanate of the Crimea, the embryos of the Ottoman Empire's Orthodox Christian 'successor-states' were required to serve terms in the transitional status of 'autonomous' principalities or provinces under the 'suzerainty' of a Pādishāh[3] who had emphasized this aspect of his office by changing his style, as was done by Sultan Mahmūd II (*imperabat* A.D. 1808–39), to 'Sultan of the Sultans of the Age'.[4] Serbia served this apprenticeship from A.D. 1830 to A.D. 1878; Samos from A.D. 1832 to A.D. 1913; Bulgaria and Eastern Rumelia from A.D. 1878 to A.D. 1908; Crete from A.D. 1898 to A.D. 1913. The juridical independence of Rumania and Serbia dated only from 1878 and that of Bulgaria only from 1908. The Powers themselves conformed to the formality which they imposed upon their Ottoman Christian creatures and protégés. It was in the name of the Sultan at Constantinople that the Hapsburg Monarchy administered Bosnia-Herzegovina from A.D. 1878 to A.D. 1908 and Great Britain administered Cyprus from A.D. 1878 and Egypt from A.D. 1882 until she found herself at war with Turkey in A.D. 1914.

The Ottoman and Manchu Empires' success in still retaining, in their decline, a monopoly of the prerogative of serving as a fount of legitimacy was not, however, so remarkable as the Mughal Empire's performance of the same diplomatico-psychological *tour de force*; for the Timurid Mughal Dynasty continued to assert this prerogative in its dealings with alien Powers who held the shadow of a *ci-devant* Mughal Empire at their mercy after it had sunk to a degree of impotence to which neither the Ottoman nor the Manchu Empire ever sank until its dying day.

Within half a century of the Emperor Awrangzīb's death in A.D. 1707, an empire which had once exercised an effective sovereignty over by far the greater part of the Indian sub-continent had been whittled down to a

[1] See Arnold, op. cit., p. 147.

[2] The phrase seems to have been struck out by the Tsar Nicholas I of Russia in conversation with Lord Aberdeen in A.D. 1844, but the celebrated occasion of its use by its coiner was in A.D. 1853, on the eve of the Crimean War.

[3] 'Pādishāh' was the Persian for 'Foot Shah', meaning a potentate who had his foot on the necks of other potentates. It was thus the equivalent of 'Shāhinshāh' or 'King of Kings'.

[4] See Arnold, op. cit., pp. 147–8.

torso that was no more than some 250 miles long by some 100 miles broad,[1] and within a hundred years of A.D. 1707 this truncated dominion had been reduced to the circuit of the walls of the Red Fort at Delhi; yet, 150 years after A.D. 1707—the date which had marked the palpable beginning of a decline that had been germinating long before that—a descendant of Akbar and Awrangzīb was still squatting on their throne in their imperial palace, and he might have been left undisturbed there for an indefinite time to come, even by British rulers of India who had retorted to 'the Great Mogul's' claim still to be their suzerain by insisting that he had now become their pensioner, if, in A.D. 1857, his apparently fantastic pretension to be still seised *de jure* of his mighty ancestors' imperial authority had not been unexpectedly vindicated by a flagrant act which the Mughal Emperor could not avert and which his British masters could not overlook.

In 1857, to the Emperor's own dismay and to his British masters' indignation, the British East India Company's mutinous sepoy army insisted upon exploiting a puppet Emperor's not yet exhausted prestige by inaugurating in his name[2] the government of a revolutionary counter-rāj which they were seeking to substitute by force of arms for the unconsecrated dominion of their British employers.

'There is much evidence . . . of the King's distrust of and distaste for the Army. . . . But there is also no doubt that he clothed their acts with the mantle of his authority';[3]

and, in insisting upon acting in a now impotent 'Great Mogul's' name, the Mutineers in A.D. 1857 were taking practical account of a persisting state of Indian public opinion with which their predecessors had likewise found it necessary to reckon. This was the consideration that had moved the British East India Company, in acquiescing in the terms of the imperial farmans of A.D. 1764 and 1765, to acknowledge the Emperor's suzerainty as the *quid pro quo* for his formal conferment upon them of the right to conduct the administration and collect the revenue in the imperial provinces of Bihar and Bengal; and the same consideration had moved successive Marāthā war-lords of the House of Sindia, from A.D. 1755 to A.D. 1803, to exercise their offensively asserted *de facto* domination over the remnant of the Mughal Empire in the doubly modest official role of deputies for an absentee regent (in the person of the Marāthā Peshwa at Poona) over a puppet Mughal Emperor's shrunken dominions.[4]

The most striking demonstration that this imponderable remnant of Mughal imperial power did in fact possess a genuine specific gravity that could not be ignored with impunity was afforded by British experience. Though, as early as A.D. 1773, the British had revoked[5] the recognition, accorded by them in A.D. 1765, of the Mughal Emperor's continuing suzerainty over Bihar and Bengal, they were confronted as late as A.D. 1811 with a reassertion of the Emperor's title to a formal sovereignty in

[1] See Spear, T. G. P.: *Twilight of the Mughuls* (Cambridge 1951, University Press), p. 5.

[2] See ibid., pp. 205–7.

[3] Ibid., p. 224.

[4] See ibid., pp. 24, 26, 34, 225.

[5] See ibid., pp. 32 and 34.

these long-since ceded provinces which they did not find it altogether easy to quash;[1] and in the Emperor's last stronghold at Delhi within the walls of the Red Fort the controversy over the question whether he was the suzerain or a pensionary of the British East India Company[2] remained unsettled throughout the fifty-five-years' interval between the British military occupation of Delhi in A.D. 1803 and the suppression of the Mutiny in A.D. 1858. The British East India Company's explicit public declaration in A.D. 1811 that it was 'unnecessary to derive from the King of Delhi any additional title to the allegiance of our Indian subjects'[3] was a form of words that, to Indian minds, was less significant than the British Resident's continued performance of a subject's customary visible acts of homage when he attended the Emperor's durbar;[4] and the British thesis was overtly challenged in A.D. 1829, when a new incumbent of the office of Nizām of Hyderabad applied to the Mughal Emperor for investiture,[5] as his predecessor had applied in A.D. 1803.[6]

'Those who took the imperial claims at their face value and those who regarded the Imperial Court as a mere puppet show, alike erred. . . . The British were prone to the latter mistake. But that it was a mistake was shown by the eagerness with which so realistic a man as Madho Rao Sindia sought the cloak of imperial authority for his acts, or a prince like the Nizām solemnly sought confirmation of his accession from Delhi as late as 1803 [and as 1829]. The truth was as nearly expressed as possible by Major Browne when he wrote: "I take the Shah's name to be of as much importance as an Act of Parliament in England if supported by as strong a force." '[7]

The justice of this comparison was to be demonstrated, half a century later, when the British East India Company's own mutinous Indian soldiery followed Sindia's example by cloaking their force under the name of the last occupant of Akbar's imperial throne.

Ghosts of Defunct Universal States

A still more remarkable testimony to the tenacity of the belief in the immortality of universal states is the paradoxical practice of evoking their ghosts after they have proved themselves mortal by expiring. The 'Abbasid Caliphate of Baghdad was thus resuscitated in the shape of the 'Abbasid Caliphate of Cairo,[8] the Roman Empire in the two rival shapes of the Holy Roman Empire of the West[9] and the East Roman Empire of Orthodox Christendom;[10] the Empire of the Ts'in and Han Dynasties in the shape of the Sui and T'ang Empire of the Far Eastern

1 See ibid., pp. 42–43.
2 See ibid., pp. 37 and 41–45.
3 Dispatch from the Court of Directors, quoted ibid., p. 44.
4 See ibid., pp. 38 and 50. When Francis Hawkins, who had succeeded to the Residency in A.D. 1831, sought to break this practice by the flagrant act of riding right into the innermost court of the Mughal imperial palace, he was so far from carrying his principals with him that he 'found himself relieved first of his charge of the palace and then of the Residency altogether' (see ibid., pp. 77–78).
5 See ibid., p. 49.
6 See ibid., p. 9.
7 Ibid., pp. 8–9.
8 See Arnold, op. cit., chaps vii, viii, and xii, and the present work, I. i, 67, n. 2, 70, 360, and 396; II. ii. 75–76; and X. ix. 15.
9 See I. i. 343; III. iii. 276; IV. iv. 378–9; V. v. 477, n. 1; and X. ix. 9.
10 See I. i. 64, n. 3, 65, 66, and 70; IV. iv. 320; and X. ix, 15.

Society in China.[1] Such ghosts of universal states are conspicuous products of the historical phenomenon of 'renaissance' or contact in the Time-dimension between a civilization of the 'affiliated' class and the extinct civilization that is related to it by 'apparentation',[2] and, in that aspect, they are dealt with in a later part of this Study.[3]

The four representatives of this spectral species of polity that are here in question display wide differences from one another both in the timing of their evocation and in their subsequent fortunes. Whereas the Sui and T'ang Empire in the Far East and the Holy Roman Empire in the West were not evoked till after an interval of more than four hundred years since the *de facto* break-up of the universal state of which each of them was respectively a revival,[4] and the East Roman Empire not till after an interval of some hundred and fifty years,[5] the 'Abbasid Caliphate was resuscitated at Cairo less than three and a half years after its extinction at Baghdad.[6] From the date of their prompt installation in A.D. 1261 by the strong hand of the Mamlūk Sultan Baybars to the date of their almost unnoticed cessation as a result of the conquest and annexation of Egypt by Sultan Selīm I 'Osmanli in A.D. 1517, the Cairene 'Abbasid Caliphs were never anything more than the puppets that they were intended to be.[7] The Holy Roman Empire, after starting as a mighty power in virtue of being imposed upon the Austrasian Frankish state at the culminating moment of its history, shared in the collapse which Charlemagne brought upon his ambitious political structure by recklessly overstraining its resources, and was never more than partially rehabilitated by the successive efforts and sacrifices of Saxon, Franconian, and Swabian heirs of this fatal incubus; yet it survived, at least as a name—the ghost of a ghost—for nearly a thousand years after Charlemagne's death.[8] On the other hand the East Roman Empire in the main body of Orthodox Christendom and the Sui and T'ang Empire in the Chinese portion of the Far Eastern World fulfilled the intentions of their respective founders by becoming and remaining solid political realities—the East Roman Empire for more than 250 years[9] and the Sui and T'ang Empire for not

[1] See II. ii. 376; III. iii. 449; and X. ix. 16.

[2] For this relation of Apparentation-and-Affiliation between civilizations of different generations, see I. i. 44, 45–6, 51–2.

[3] In X. ix. 7–21.

[4] The Empire of the Posterior Han became impotent *de facto circa* A.D. 175; the Far Eastern Society in China was united politically under the Sui Dynasty in A.D. 581. The Roman Empire in the West became impotent *de facto* after the *Clades Gothica* of A.D. 378 or, at latest, after the death of the Emperor Theodosius I in A.D. 395; Charlemagne was crowned Emperor in St. Peter's at Rome on Christmas Day, A.D. 800.

[5] The Roman Empire in the East ran out between the death of Justinian in A.D. 565 and the overthrow of Maurice in A.D. 602; the East Roman Empire was constructed by Leo Syrus (*imperabat* A.D. 717–40).

[6] See Arnold, op. cit., p. 82, following Suyūtī: *Husn-al-Muhādarah*, vol. ii, pp. 53 seqq. and 57. The Caliph Musta'sim was put to death at Baghdad in February 1258; his uncle was installed at Cairo as the Caliph Mustansir in June 1261.

[7] When the first of them, Mustansir, showed signs of taking his office seriously, his Mamlūk patron Baybars packed him off to his death, on the forlorn hope of reconquering Baghdad from the Mongols, and installed another member of the 'Abbasid House in his stead. This lesson was not forgotten by Caliph Hākim and his successors (see Arnold, op. cit., pp. 94–95).

[8] Charlemagne died in A.D. 814; the Emperor Francis II Hapsburg renounced the title of Roman Emperor in A.D. 1806 (see I. i. 343 and X. ix. 11).

[9] From the raising of the second Arab siege of Constantinople in A.D. 717 to the outbreak of the Great Romano-Bulgarian War in A.D. 977.

much less than 300[1]—but this at the cost, on which their founders certainly never reckoned, of exhausting the strength of the still immature societies on whose life-blood these two lusty vampire-states waxed fat for a season.[2] The common feature, conspicuous above these differences, that concerns us here is the status which these ghosts, like their originals, acquired and retained as founts of legitimacy.

The Haunting of Cairo and Istanbul by the Ghost of the Caliphate

The Mamlūks had been quick to install a refugee ʿAbbasid at Cairo because, being themselves usurpers of their Ayyubid masters' heritage, and being faced with the problem of handing it down thereafter from slave to slave, they had the same urgent and recurring need of legitimization as their contemporaries and counterparts the Slave Kings of Delhi. The Mamlūk Sultans and their subjects appear to have treated their ʿAbbasid puppets with contempt from first to last,[3] and at Mecca their names were never recited in the *khutbah*.[4] Distance, however, lent them an appearance of dignity, and contemporary Muslim rulers in Hindustan made the same use of the Cairene ʿAbbasid Caliphs as their predecessors had made of the last Baghdadī ʿAbbasid Caliph Mustaʿsim. A diploma of investiture was sought and obtained from the Cairene ʿAbbasid Caliph of the day not only by the parricide and tyrant Muhammad b. Taghlaq (*dominabatur* A.D. 1324–51) but by his estimable successor Fīrūz Shāh (*dominabatur* A.D. 1351–88), who had not his predecessor's incentive for seeking external sanction for his régime.[5] Even Timur Lenk's grandson Pīr Muhammad seems to have thought of taking the same step as a manœuvre in the contest for Timur's heritage, and the Ottoman Pādishāh Bāyezīd I (*imperabat* A.D. 1389–1402) seems actually to have applied in A.D. 1394 to the reigning Cairene ʿAbbasid for a grant of the title of Sultan.[6]

Bāyezīd's descendant Selīm I felt himself in no need of legitimization, and did not covet a title borne by a puppet of his defeated and executed opponent the last Mamlūk Sultan Tūmān Bey.[7] A new generation of *de facto* rulers of a nascent Iranic Muslim World esteemed the blood of the Eurasian Nomad war-lord Chinghis Khan to be a nobler liquid than that of any Meccan Holy Family, and they were also well aware that the strength of their own right arm was their only valid title in the last resort. In these revolutionary circumstances the maintenance of ʿAbbasid Shadow-Caliphs at Cairo, and the occasional utilization of these *fainéants*' services as rubber-stamps by other Muslim potentates besides

[1] From the foundation of the Sui Empire in A.D. 581 to A.D. 878, when the T'ang régime became impotent *de facto* (see IV. iv. 87–88 and V. vi. 311, n. 3).

[2] For this fatal effect of the success of the East Roman Empire on the fortunes of the main body of the Orthodox Christian Society, see II. ii. 368 and IV. iv. 320–408.

[3] See Arnold, op. cit., pp. 99–102.

[4] See ibid., p. 101.

[5] See ibid., pp. 103–5.

[6] See ibid., pp. 105–6.

[7] See ibid., chap. xii. 'The fiction that the last ʿAbbasid Caliph of Egypt handed over his dignity, by a formal act of transfer, to Sultan Selīm, was first enunciated in A.D. 1787 by' the Levantine Christian scholar 'Constantine Mouradgea d'Ohsson in his monumental work *Tableau Général de l'Empire Othoman*' (ibid., p. 146), thirteen years after the negotiation of the Russo-Turkish peace treaty of Küchük Qaynārja, which seems to have been the first occasion on which the Ottoman Pādishāh made any attempt to turn his title of Caliph to any practical account (see p. 23, below).

their own Mamlūk slave-masters, had not deterred ex-barbarian *novi homines* from confidently assuming for themselves, and politely applying to one another, the style of 'Caliph' as a synonym for the effective sovereign of a state that was not oecumenical but was merely a Great Power.[1] This inflationary style had already been accepted by Bāyezīd I 'Osmanli's father and predecessor Murād I (*imperabat* A.D. 1360–89) from the pens of the rulers of neighbouring Turkish principalities in Anatolia.[2] In these circumstances the history of the Khilāfat might have been expected to come to an end with the death, in obscurity, of the last Cairene Caliph in A.D. 1543; yet this was not, after all, the last chapter in this long-protracted story. After having thought nothing of the Caliphate for more than four hundred years after the unwarrantable ascription of the office to Sultan Murād I, the 'Osmanlis discovered belatedly, in the days of their decline, that this long despised and neglected ornament was worth bringing out of their lumber-room and polishing up.

'During the century which began with the negotiation of the Russo-Turkish peace treaty of Küchük Qaynārja in A.D. 1774 and ended with the accession of 'Abd-al-Hamīd II to the Ottoman throne in 1876 the Ottoman Caliphate ceased to be merely titular and became for the first time an active factor in international affairs. This change was the consequence of three new developments: first, the continual transfer of ex-Ottoman provinces, containing Muslim populations, to the rule of Western Governments; second, the successive extinction of all sovereign independent Sunnī Powers of any importance, with the single precarious exception of the fast diminishing Ottoman Empire, and their replacement by the colonial empires of Western Powers (the most conspicuous example of this second development being India, where a large Muslim population passed from the Mughal Rāj to the British Rāj after a short interval of anarchy); and, third, the gradual emergence in Islamic society of a new sense of solidarity and a new desire to express this feeling in some practical form—a development which was a natural and, indeed, almost inevitable reaction to the other two. As a result of these three related developments, interest in the Caliphate revived, and at the same time a confusion of thought arose regarding the character of an office which had been obsolete, in all but name, for many centuries.

'This confusion was due to the misinterpretation of both the history and the theory of the Caliphate by insufficiently instructed Western observers, who drew a false analogy between an Islamic institution which they failed to understand and a Western institution with which they were familiar. They equated the Caliphate with the Papacy; explained it as a "spiritual" office in the Western sense (an abstraction

[1] See Arnold, op. cit., chaps. ix and xi. This rapid depreciation of a title connoting a unique oecumenical sovereignty into one applied by courtesy to any sovereign of any consequence in a comity of parochial states has its parallel in the fate of the title of 'Emperor' in the Western World. The usurpation of this title by Napoleon Buonaparte on the 18th May, 1804, was followed—when the last legitimate Holy Roman Emperor Francis II Hapsburg had opened the flood-gates in proclaiming himself 'Hereditary Emperor of Austria' on the 10th August, 1804, and renouncing his own legitimate title of 'Roman Emperor' on the 6th August, 1806—by the crowning of Dom Pedro I as 'Constitutional Emperor of Brazil' on the 12th October, 1822 (see X. ix. 11).

[2] See Arnold, op. cit., pp. 130–1.

which was quite foreign to Islamic thought); assumed that the double title of Sultan-Caliph implied a personal union of the "spiritual" and "temporal" powers in the Ottoman Pādishāh; and inferred that these powers could alternatively be divided between different persons. Their error obtained a wide currency in the West[1] (except among a few scholars without influence in international affairs) and even among Muslims who had received a Modern Western in place of a Classical Islamic education. It was consciously and skilfully exploited by ʿAbd-al-Hamīd in his dealings with Western Governments, with Muslim peoples under Western rule, and with his own Muslim subjects.'[2]

In at least three peace treaties signed between the years A.D. 1774 and A.D. 1913[3] the Ottoman negotiators slily took advantage of this Western Christian misconception of the Caliphate as a 'spiritual' office in order to secure, in territories that the Sultan was being compelled to cede as Pādishāh, a recognition of his continuing authority there as Caliph—a concession which, if maintained and fully implemented, would have restored to him under one title the political authority that he was surrendering under another. As it turned out, the Christian parties to two of these treaties quickly detected the ruse and insisted—in the one case within seven years and in the other within eleven years of the date of signature of the original instrument—on the cancellation of the insidious provisions.[4]

Although, however, the Caliphate, thus refurbished and passed off as a 'spiritual' office, did not, after all, prove an effective instrument for staving off, or even attenuating, the loss of Ottoman political control over ex-Ottoman territories that the Sultan-Caliph had been compelled to surrender owing to the turning of the tables in the military and political relations between the Ottoman Empire and its Western or Westernizing neighbours since the close of the seventeenth century of the

[1] It seems to have been popularized by M. C. M. d'Ohsson in the first volume of his *Tableau Général de l'Empire Othoman* (Paris 1787), in which 'he speaks of the "sacerdotal authority" of the Sultan and styles him the "Pontiff of the Musulmans" ' (Arnold, op. cit., p. 170).

[2] Toynbee, A. J.: *Survey of International Affairs, 1925*, vol. i (Oxford 1927, University Press): 'The Islamic World since the Peace Settlement', pp. 32–33.

[3] The Russo-Turkish peace treaty signed at Küchük Qaynārja on the 21st July, 1774, Art. 3; the Italo-Ottoman preliminaries of peace signed at Ouchy on the 15th October, 1912; the Turco-Bulgarian peace treaty signed at Constantinople on the 29th September, 1913 (see Toynbee, op. cit., pp. 34–36).

[4] See Toynbee, op. cit., p. 36. The extent to which the minds of the ruling element in Russia had been Westernized by A.D. 1774 is revealed by the success of Ottoman diplomacy in playing this trick upon the representatives of a still officially Orthodox Christian Power; for in Orthodox Christendom the Christian distinction between Church and State had been confounded in the constitution of Leo III's East Roman Empire (see IV. iv. 352–3 and 592–623); and this East Roman 'Caesaro-papism', transmitted to Russia, had been carried a step farther by Peter the Great when, in A.D. 1700, he had allowed the Patriarchate of Moscow to lapse and then, in A.D. 1721, had made the Orthodox Church in his dominions into a department of state in form as well as in fact by placing it under the administration of a 'Holy Synod' (see p. 38 below). Thus, in the post-Petrine Russian Empire of A.D. 1774, Church and State were so nearly fused together into an indistinguishable unity that it ought not to have been difficult for Russian statesmen of that age to appreciate, by analogy, the non-existence, in Islam, of any differentiation of a 'spiritual' from a 'temporal' sphere of social life. The less obvious implications of the status of the Oecumenical Patriarch of Constantinople as a servant of the East Roman Emperor had been realized immediately by the less sophisticated Bulgars upon their conversion to Orthodox Christianity in A.D. 865 (see IV. iv. 377–81).

Christian Era, it did produce psychological effects which were imponderable yet appreciable factors in international politics. It gave pause to aggressive-minded Western or Westernizing Powers which had taken the measure of the Ottoman Empire's present political weakness but still remained in awe of the explosive religious force of Islam. Conversely, it made the Ottoman Empire—shrunken though it was—a moral rallying-point for a Muslim diasporá, not only in ex-Ottoman provinces which had passed under the rule of Orthodox Christian 'successor-states', but in distant regions, on other fringes of Dār-al-Islām, which had never been under the rule of an Ottoman or any other Caliph. By the date of the abolition of the Ottoman Caliphate in A.D. 1924 the Muslim minorities in the British Indian Empire, the Soviet Union, and the Chinese Republic alone numbered considerably more than a hundred million in the aggregate, and these outlying millions—unlike the Arab peoples and others in the solid core of the Islamic World, including the Ottoman Turks themselves—had little prospect of ever being able to attain the current political ideal of a Westernizing World by exchanging the alien rule under which they were living at the time for national states of their own.[1] Their situation was not unlike that of their predecessors in the tenth, eleventh, and twelfth centuries of the Christian Era, when Dār-al-Islām was being overrun by barbarians and partitioned among military adventurers, and in these circumstances the Ottoman Caliphate gave them something of the same cohesion and encouragement that the 'Abbasid Caliphate of Baghdad had given to Muslims of that earlier age.[2]

These psychological effects of the Ottoman Caliphate, as turned to account by Sultan 'Abd-al-Hamīd II (*imperabat* A.D. 1876–1909), were such manifestly valuable assets for the Ottoman body politic that the 'New 'Osmanli' liberal opponents of a tyrannous Hamidian autocracy sought, not to abolish the Ottoman Caliphate, but to preserve it for manipulation as an instrument of their own Turkish national policy. The sovereign was styled Caliph, as well as Sultan and Pādishāh, in the Ottoman Constitution of A.D. 1876, and the Caliphate survived 'Abd-al-Hamīd's successful *coup d'état* of 1877 and unsuccessful attempt to repeat it in 1909 after the re-establishment of the Constitution in 1908.[3] It even survived the abolition of the Sultanate and the vesting of the sovereign power in Turkey in the Great National Assembly at Ankara by a law voted by that body on the 1st November, 1922.[4] This drastic piece of legislation was a retort to the hostile action of the last Sultan-Caliph Mehmed VI Vahīd-ad-Dīn (*imperabat* A.D. 1918–22), who, seeing

[1] On this point see Toynbee, op. cit., p. 39. By the time when the present passage was being written, the abolition of the Ottoman Caliphate was already more than a quarter of a century old, and the Indian Muslims had succeeded in establishing a separate national state of their own in the shape of Pakistan; but it would have been premature to assume that this was necessarily the end of the story.

[2] For the alertness of Sultan 'Abd-al-Hamīd II in making use of railways, newspapers, and other Modern Western means of communication and propaganda for keeping in touch with a Muslim clientèle all over the World, see Toynbee, op. cit., pp. 39–40.

[3] See Toynbee, op. cit., pp. 42–43, and the present Study, IX. viii. 261–3.

[4] The text of this law of the 1st November, 1922, is printed in Toynbee, op. cit., pp. 50–51.

the monarch's opportunity in the country's adversity, had thrown in his lot with the Empire's ex-victorious adversaries in the late wars of 1914-22 in the hope of putting back the constitutional clock to the point at which it had been marking time before the Revolution of A.D. 1908. In the same law the Caliphate was declared to reside in the House of 'Osmān, and the right of election to the office to lie with the Turkish Great National Assembly. On the strength of a legal opinion (*fetvā*), rendered by the Commissary for the Islamic Law (*Sherī'ah*) in the Government ruling the country in the Assembly's name, to the effect that the office of Caliph had been forfeited by Vahīd-ad-Dīn Efendi, the Assembly voted, on the 18th November, 1922, that the office was now vacant, and on the same day they elected another member of the House of 'Osmān, 'Abd-al-Mejīd Efendi, as Caliph without any other title.[1]

In attempting to draw this distinction between two traditional titles which historically and juridically were, both alike, emblems of political authority, the followers of Ghāzi Mustafā Kemāl Atatürk were unintentionally playing on themselves the trick which their ancestors had deliberately played on the Russians in A.D. 1774,[2] and, once again, the equivocal situation created by a false interpretation of the nature of the Caliph's office proved untenable—notwithstanding the suitably inoffensive character of the Assembly's unlucky nominee. When the law of the 1st November, 1922, was followed by another of the 29th October, 1923, proclaiming Turkey a republic and declaring the President of the Republic to be Chief of the State, the incompatibility between the legal position thus created in Turkey and the prerogatives of the Caliphate according to the *Sherī'ah* became so glaring that it was bound to be used as ammunition by Turkish opponents of the régime and to cause overt anxiety among Indian Muslims. The premature publication, in opposition newspapers at Constantinople, of a letter from two eminent Indian Muslims, the Agha Khan and Mr. Ameer Ali, to the Prime Minister of Turkey, intimating, in studiously tactful language, the distress that the Turkish Great National Assembly's actions had been producing among Muslims abroad,[3] precipitated the passage by the Turkish Great National Assembly, on the 3rd March, 1924, of a law abolishing the Caliphate and banishing the members of the Ottoman Imperial family from the territories of the Republic of Turkey.[4] When the news reached Delhi—where, as we have seen, the Caliphate had been revered for seven hundred years with a *naïveté* seldom corrected by first-hand acquaintance—the shock declared itself in a dramatic incident at a Red Crescent tea-party which offers a burlesque counterpart to the

[1] See Toynbee, op. cit., p. 51.

[2] The innocent misapprehension under which the Assembly acted in November 1922 was attested in a speech delivered by Mustafā Kemāl Pasha himself on the 30th October, 1922, in the debate preceding the passage of the Law of the 1st November. To the question 'What becomes of the Caliphate when the temporal power is taken away from it?' the Ghāzi gave the Levantine d'Ohsson's erroneous answer: in the days of the 'Abbasid Caliphs at Baghdad and of their successors at Cairo, 'the spiritual and temporal power existed separately side by side'. The relevant passage of the speech is printed in Toynbee, op. cit., pp. 54–55.

[3] The text is printed in Toynbee, op. cit., pp. 571–2.

[4] Ibid., p. 575.

tragic scene in Saint Jerome's cell at Bethlehem when the Christian scholar received the news of the fall of Rome.[1]

'A mission from the Turkish Red Crescent Society, which was collecting funds in India at the moment when the news of the abolition of the Ottoman Caliphate arrived, found it advisable to cut short its activities and return home. (*The Times*, 5th March, 1924; *Oriente Moderno*, IV, 3, p. 181). The news was actually received during a tea-party at Delhi, where the members of the Turkish mission were being entertained by their Indian co-religionists. Upon the recital of the telegram containing the text of the Turkish Law of the 3rd March, [1924,] all but two of the Indians present immediately left the room.'[2]

At the time when the present chapter was being written, it looked as if this had really been the end of the Caliphate, for an immediate attempt on the part of the Hāshimī King Husayn of the Hijāz to assume the office (on the eve, as it turned out, of his own ejection from his ancestral patrimony by Ibn Sa'ūd) was—in spite of the Sharīf's unimpeachable Qurayshī lineage and his sovereignty, at the moment, over the two Holy Cities of Mecca and Medina—as dismal a failure as most of his other enterprises.[3] Nor did any practical action result from a Caliphate Congress held at Cairo on the 13th–19th May, 1926.[4]

Yet, even if this forecast were to prove correct—though, in the light of previous history, it would not be safe to sign a death certificate for so resilient an institution as the Caliphate until it had been in abeyance for at least a quarter of a millennium[5]—the marvel would be, not that the Caliphate should have petered out at last, but that, on the strength of having been an effective sovereignty over a span of less than two hundred years,[6] it should have been able within that time to acquire a prestige sufficient to keep it alive, and twice revive it,[7] for another eleven hundred

[1] See the passage quoted in V. v. 223, n. 2.

[2] Toynbee, op. cit., p. 63, n. 7. Indian Muslims might have inoculated themselves against this shock by previously exposing themselves to another. 'The present writer once heard, from a British resident in Constantinople, of one instance in which this ignorance [of realities in Turkey] was cruelly dispelled. His informant had been in commercial relations with an Indian Muslim merchant who was a capable man of business and a loyal subject of the British Indian Government, but who cherished a keen sentimental regret for the lost dominion of Islam in India and consoled himself with the belief that in the Ottoman Caliphate there survived one Islamic Power which was as splendid as the Mughal Empire and as efficient as the British Rāj. After sustaining his self-respect as a Muslim upon this illusion for many years, this Indian merchant saved enough money to make a pilgrimage to the seat of the Caliphate at Constantinople—which meant more to him than the Holy Land of the Hijāz—and there became the guest of his British correspondent. The contrast between his long-cherished dream of the Caliphate and the sordid reality of the Ottoman Empire caused him a distress which it was painful to witness. He was appalled by the vast difference of standard between Muslim government in *Dār-al-Islām* and British government in India; and he went home with his spirit broken' (Toynbee, op. cit., p. 39, n. 1).

[3] See Toynbee, op. cit., pp. 63–66.

[4] See ibid., pp. 81–90.

[5] Its latest interregnum had lasted from the death of the last Cairene 'Abbasid Caliph Mutawakkil in A.D. 1543 to the drafting of the Russo-Turkish Treaty of Küchük Qaynārja in A.D. 1774.

[6] From the death of the Prophet Muhammad in A.D. 632 to the death of the 'Abbasid Caliph Amīn (*imperabat* A.D. 809–13), in a civil war with his brother and supplanter Ma'mūn (*imperabat* A.D. 813–33) over the heritage of their father Hārūn-ar-Rashīd (*imperabat* A.D. 786–809).

[7] i.e. at Cairo in A.D. 1261 and at Constantinople in A.D. 1774.

years[1] during which it never emerged from the state of political impotence into which it had begun to decline in the reign of Hārūn-ar-Rashīd's son Ma'mūn (*imperabat* A.D. 813–33).

'The Holy Roman Empire'[2]

This life-curve of the Caliphate, with its successive evocations at Cairo and Istanbul, has its counterpart in the aftermath of the Roman Empire in the West, with its abortive revival there in the shape of the Holy Roman Empire.[3] The Roman Power which Pope Leo III and Charlemagne tried to raise from the dead on Christmas Day, A.D. 800, had been effective in the West for rather more than four hundred years.[4] The Austrasian Power, which thus rashly shouldered the formidable burden of the Roman mantle, was effective for not more than 127 years at the longest reckoning.[5] Yet, on the strength of these two spasmodic 'jet-propulsions', the Holy Roman Empire not only materialized in the heyday of Austrasia's fortunes, but survived thereafter for all but a thousand years more[6] in a state of paralysis into which it fell at the death of Charlemagne, the first holder of the title (*regnabat* A.D. 768–814; *imperabat* A.D. 800–14), and from which it never afterwards more than partially recovered.[7] The shadowy aftermath of the Roman Empire in the West thus attained a span of more than fourteen hundred years in all.[8] A millennium and a half is no doubt an infinitesimally short span of time on the Time-scale of the age, up to date, of the Human Race or of Life or of the Earth or of the Stellar Cosmos,[9] but it is a period of almost Egyptiac longevity on the scale of the six-thousand-years-old history of the species of human societies called civilizations.

[1] Reckoning from the death of the Baghdādī 'Abbasid Caliph Amīn in A.D. 813 to the deposition of the Constantinopolitan 'Osmanli Caliph 'Abd-al-Mejid in A.D. 1924.

[2] See xi, map 37.

[3] In conformity with our procedure in reckoning back the history of the Caliphate to its inauguration at Mecca in A.D. 632, and not merely to the evocation of its ghost at Cairo in A.D. 1261, we have to reckon back the history of the institution liquidated at Vienna in A.D. 1806 to the foundation of the Roman Empire itself by 'the crafty nephew of Julius' in the year 31 B.C.—as Lord Bryce makes his reckoning in the famous exordium of *The Holy Roman Empire* (quoted in I. i. 343).

[4] Reckoning from the Battle of Actium in 31 B.C. to the Battle of Adrianople in A.D. 378, or at latest to the death of the Emperor Theodosius I in A.D. 395 (see p. 20, n. 4, above, and p. 40, n. 2, below).

[5] Reckoning to the death of Charlemagne in A.D. 814 from the Battle of Textri in A.D. 687 in which Charlemagne's great-grandfather Pepin of Heristal had ended the anarchy let loose by the decay of the Merovingian Power and had brought Neustria as well as Austrasia under the effective rule of the House of Arnulf. The period would be still shorter if its initial date were to be reckoned from Charles Martel's victory over the Arabs at Tours in A.D. 732 or from the crowning of Pepin III in A.D. 754 as King of the Franks (see IV. iv. 488, n. 1), or from the crowning of Charlemagne himself as Emperor on Christmas Day, A.D. 800.

[6] Reckoning from the death of Charlemagne in A.D. 814 to the renunciation of the title by Francis II in A.D. 1806.

[7] In Charlemagne's time, and likewise at each of the successive revivals of the Holy Roman Empire after its first rapid lapse into impotence in the hands of Charlemagne's Carolingian successors, this Western ghost of the Roman Empire was an effective political power only in so far as it played the part of a continental march for Western Christendom. Under Charlemagne and the Saxon Emperors the Holy Roman Empire served as a march against the Continental European barbarians (see II. ii. 166–70); under the Hapsburgs it served as a march againt the 'Osmanlis (see II. ii. 177–90).

[8] Reckoning from the death of Theodosius I in A.D. 395 to A.D. 1806.

[9] For time-scales, see Zeuner, F. E.: *Dating the Past* (London 1946, 2nd ed. 1950, Methuen), and the present Study, I. i. 173.

It is noteworthy that, like the 'Abbasid Caliphate, the Holy Roman Empire retained, even at the vanishing-point of its effective power, a certain market value as a unique fount of honour.

'To [the] strange political fiction [that the 'Abbasid Caliphs of Baghdad were still ruling after they had ceased to govern] there is a parallel in the history of the Holy Roman Empire during the fifteenth century [of the Christian Era]. While the unfortunate Emperor Frederick III, having been driven out of Vienna, was wandering about from monastery to monastery as a beggar, making what money he could out of the fees paid by those on whom he conferred titles, a contemporary jurist, Aeneas Piccolomini (afterwards famous as Pope Pius II), could write that the power of the Emperor was eternal and incapable of diminution or injury, and that anyone who denied that the Emperor was lord and monarch of the whole Earth was a heretic, since his authority was ordained by Holy Writ and by the decree of the Church.'[1]

In A.D. 1952, when nearly a century and a half had elapsed since the self-liquidation of the Holy Roman Empire in A.D. 1806 by a voluntary act of the then reigning Emperor, the title of 'Count of the Holy Roman Empire' was still being conferred by the Sovereign Pontiff of the temple-state of the Vatican—who would perhaps have pleaded a victor's right to dispose of the sole remaining spoils of a rival institution which his own predecessors had brought to the ground in the tremendous struggle between Papacy and Empire during the so-called 'Middle Ages' of Western history.[2]

The Haunting of the 'Osmanlis and the Mongols by 'Ghosts of Ghosts'

While the Holy Roman Empire was compensated for the briefness of its effective reign, and the Cairene Caliphate for being cheated of any effective reign at all, by the inordinate length of a dim epilogue, the East Roman Empire in Orthodox Christendom and the Sui and T'ang Empire in the Far East had to pay for a longer spell of full-blooded life by suffering a more swift and drastic liquidation. No milder remedy than this could have saved from an immediate and premature death the societies on whose life-blood these two vampires had been feasting. The collapse, when it came, was in both societies so extreme that the exhausted civilization was fain to receive its respite and rest-cure in the shape of a universal state from the hands of alien empire-builders—the 'Osmanlis performing this unwelcome and indispensable service for the main body of Orthodox Christendom, and the Mongols for China.[3]

These aliens began by filling the social void which they found in their field of reconstruction work with characteristic institutions of their own,[4] and they also eked out their own talents by enlisting ability wherever else they could lay hands on it, rather than from among the demoralized and discredited *ci-devant* dominant minority of the prostrate society for whose government the high-handed conquerors had now made themselves responsible. The Mongols organized their government of China

[1] Arnold, op. cit., pp. 77–78. [2] See IV. iv. 512–84.
[3] See V. v. 348–51, and pp. 570 and 576, below.
[4] For the institutions that the 'Osmanlis brought with them into Orthodox Christendom from the Eurasian Steppe, see III. iii. 22–50.

with the help of Muslims from the western fringes of their spreading dominion, or of Western Christians from beyond its verge, of whom the most famous was Marco Polo. The 'Osmanlis drew on Western Christian renegades as well as on children of their own Orthodox Christian *ra'īyeh* whom they had first 'denatured' by a Platonic system of education. In the governments of both these alien universal states it is the more remarkable to observe, on closer inspection, the presence of a number of institutional survivals of the liquidated vampire polities, and to find the evicted native dominant minority stealthily winning their way back into power as the mandarins who inducted Mongol and Manchu war-lords into the arts of Chinese administration, and as the Phanariots who made themselves indispensable to their Ottoman masters as soon as these were driven to enter into serious diplomatic relations with the Powers of the Western World owing to the loss of their own former military ascendancy.[1] Though the institutional survivals, as they catch our eye, present themselves largely in the forms of outward ceremonial and official insignia and costume, we may infer with confidence, from these outward visible signs, an inward psychological legacy from the East Roman Empire to an Ottoman 'Qaysar-i-Rum' and from the Sui and T'ang Empire to a Mongol 'Son of Heaven'.

'The Great Idea' of the Modern Greeks

The legacy that descended on the victorious 'Osmanlis did not cease to weigh upon the discomfited Greeks. Though the East Roman Empire came to grief in A.D. 1071[2] through the nemesis of the suicidal policy of military aggression on all fronts[3] which had preceded, precipitated, and followed the great Romano-Bulgarian war of A.D. 977–1019, and though the rally led by the Emperor Alexius Comnenus (*imperabat* A.D. 1081–1118)[4] brought no more than a passing relief, the Byzantine political incubus that was crushing the life out of the Greek people not only made a profound impression on their imaginations but also secured an enduring hold on their affections. When the Western military adventurers whose enterprise was nicknamed 'the Fourth Crusade' gave the stricken East Roman Empire its *coup de grâce* by storming and sacking Constantinople in A.D. 1204, they found the prestige of the battered Imperial Throne at Constantinople still standing so high among the conquered Greek population that they decided to enthrone one of their own number as a usurping 'Latin Emperor', in the hope—a vain one, yet the only hope that they had—that the double magic of the Imperial City and Name might commend their hated rule to their recalcitrant subjects.

These lures did indeed exercise an irresistible attraction upon the East Roman Empire's refugee Greek 'successor-state' at Nicaea in North-Western Anatolia, which had first successfully defied the invaders and had afterwards anticipated the career of the 'Osmanlis by bestriding the Dardanelles and gathering in fragments of ex-Imperial territory in the Balkan Peninsula.[5] The able princes of Nicaea were

1 For the Phanariots see II. ii. 222–8 and IX. viii. 187–9.
2 See IV. iv. 392, n. 2.
3 See IV. iv. 391–404.
4 See V. vi. 298.
5 See III. iii. 27.

obsessed from first to last by the ambition of reoccupying Constantinople and there assuming the Imperial style and title; and in A.D. 1261 Michael Palaiológhos duly achieved these Epimethean ambitions at the cost of losing to Turkish interlopers the best part of that precious Anatolian ground from which his principality had drawn its strength. This loss condemned the outwardly restored Empire to impotence from the start. Yet even the two-centuries-long agony of this shadow of a shadow of the Roman Empire, from the reoccupation of Constantinople in A.D. 1261 to its capture by the 'Osmanlis in A.D. 1453, did not cure the Greeks of their infatuation with a polity that had proved their ruin. Year by year, till these years had mounted up to little less than half a millennium,[1] the Greeks of Constantinople continued, under Ottoman rule, to expect the restoration of the East Roman Empire by a miraculous intervention of God.[2] And, in spite of invariable disappointment, 'the Great Idea'[3] had power to entice Ypsilandi into making his fatuous raid across the Pruth in A.D. 1821[4] and Venizelos into embarking in A.D. 1919 on an Anatolian adventure that was to meet with such a tragic ending in 1922. Nothing less than the eviction of a Greek diasporà of some

[1] A.D. 1453–1923.

[2] This expectation was sufficiently intense and persistent to find its way into Modern Greek folk-lore, where it expressed itself in the two parallel motifs of the miraculously interrupted service in the Cathedral Church of Ayía Sophía in Constantinople and the miraculously interrupted frying of the fishes.

A folk-song about the miraculous interruption of the service on the eve of the capture of the Imperial City by Sultan Mehmed II Fātih in A.D. 1453 is printed in Politis, N.G.: *'Εκλογαὶ ἀπὸ τὰ Τραγούδια τοῦ 'Ελληνικοῦ Λαοῦ* (Athens 1914, Estia), pp. 4–5, and a folk-song about the miraculous interruption of the fish-frying in Passow, A.: *Carmina Popularia Graeciae Recentioris* (Leipzig 1860, Teubner), p. 147, No. cxcvii. A folk-tale about the fish-frying is published by Politis in two versions in his *Μελέται περὶ τοῦ Βίου καὶ τῆς Γλώσσης τοῦ 'Ελληνικοῦ Λαοῦ: Παραδόσεις* (Athens 1904, Sakellarios, 2 parts), part i, p. 21 (texts), and part ii, pp. 656–7 (commentary). The writer has been able to run these sources of the legend to earth thanks to the learning and the kindness of Professor R. J. H. Jenkins.

In one of these three pieces of popular Romaic Greek literature—the folk-song about the fishes—the episode of the miracle heralding the fall of Constantinople stands by itself—*τὰ ψάρια πεταχτήκανε, τὰ ψάρια ζωντανέψαν, / κι' ὁ ἀμηρᾶς εἰσέβηκεν ἀτός του καβαλάρης* —without the promise of an equally miraculous future retrieval of Greek fortunes which is the sequel in both the other two places. The first of the two prose versions of the legend about the fish, as given by Politis, runs as follows:

'At the time when the Turks were besieging the City, a monk was frying seven fishes in a frying-pan. He had already fried them on one side and was just turning them over on to the other when someone comes and tells him that the Turks have taken the City. "Never will the Turks set foot in the City," says the monk. "I will wait to believe that till I see these fried fishes come to life again." The words were not out of his mouth before the fishes leapt out of the frying-pan alive and dropped into a piece of water close by; and, down to this day, those fishes that came alive are in Balyqly [*Anglicè* 'Fishwych' —A.J.T.] and will continue to be found there, still half-fried yet alive again, until the hour comes for us to take the City. Then, they say, another monk will come and finish frying them.'

'The fishes are pointed out in the holy well of the Zoodhókhos, outside the walls [of Constantinople], not far from the Gate of Silymbria (*alias* Piyí)', according to Politis, *Μελέται*, part ii, p. 656. According to a Turkish version of the tale (ibid., n. 1), there were originally seven fishes, but only five are now left.

The writer of this Study visited Balyqly in A.D. 1921, but did not see even a residue of five half-fried fishes swimming there, though, in a year when Eastern Thrace was under Greek military occupation again for the first time since A.D. 1360, the possibility that the Greeks might reoccupy Constantinople too seemed less remote than at any other date, either earlier or later, since A.D. 1453.

[3] *'Η Μεγάλη 'Ιδέα*, meaning a conception of Modern Greece as being the heir of the East Roman Empire.

[4] See II. ii. 226–7 for Ypsilandi (in Greek spelling 'Hypsêlantês') and his adventure.

1,280,000 souls from Anatolia and Eastern Thrace[1] availed to banish from Greek minds the persistent dream of restoring the East Roman Empire; and the previous potency of the ghost that was thus at last exorcised is demonstrated by the sequel. Though the Graeco-Turkish war of A.D. 1919–22 had inflicted greater devastation and suffering on both sides than any of its predecessors, it was followed within eight years by a Graeco-Turkish *entente*;[2] and this apparent paradox admits of only one explanation. The loading of the atmosphere with a new charge of hate was far outbalanced by the lightening of it through the dissipation of an old illusion.

'At Ankara, a silent witness of the historic event of October 1930 was one of the most famous monuments of Classical Antiquity: the longest extant Latin inscription in the World, in which the first of the Roman Emperors had recorded his achievements. The Roman Empire had bequeathed its name to its former dominions in the Near East (Rum, Rum-ili, Romania) and to the peoples which had inherited them. The 'Osmānlīs had been known as Romans (Rūmīs) among their Muslim neighbours in Iran and Hindustan, while the modern Greeks had called themselves Romans (Romaioi) until a romantic nationalism, acquired in the West, had taught them to think of themselves as Hellenes. The hold of Rome upon the Near Eastern imagination had only relaxed with the break-up of the Ottoman Empire, which was the Roman Empire's last and strangest reincarnation. The Greeks really repudiated their Imperial Roman heritage when they rose in insurrection in A.D. 1821, the Turks when they signed their National Pact in A.D. 1920. Therewith, the ghost of the Roman Empire, which had so long haunted the Near East, was finally exorcised. The Imperial City of Constantine—the New Rome on the Bosphorus—had ceased to be the capital of an empire or even of a "successor-state". Indeed it was no longer a bone of contention between the states into which the defunct empire had been partitioned. The Oecumenical Patriarch, who had once laid claim, in his very title, to be the head of the Orthodox Church through all the World, had seen his flock diminish until now it was merely represented by that Orthodox Christian minority—less than 100,000 strong—which was recognised as "established" in Constantinople by the terms of the convention of the 10th June, 1930. . . . A meeting, at Constantinople, between the ecclesiastical head of the ancient Greek Church and the political head of the modern Greek State had ceased to be an event of political significance. If there were any statesmen living in 1930 who could claim to have "made history", they were Mustafā Kemāl and Elefterios Venizelos.'[3]

'*Moscow the Third Rome*'[4]

While 'the Great Idea' of the Greeks had been a minor tragedy and major curiosity of history, the sowing of the same seed in Russia had been big with consequences of historic importance which, at a date midway through the twentieth century of the Christian Era, had perhaps not yet come to full harvest.

[1] See the figures given by V. M. Boulter in *Survey of International Affairs, 1925*, vol. ii (London 1928, Milford), p. 276.

[2] For this beneficent revolution in Graeco-Turkish relations, see Toynbee, A. J., and Boulter, V. M.: *Survey of International Affairs, 1930* (Oxford 1931, University Press), pp. 157–68.

[3] Toynbee and Boulter, op. cit., p. 168.

[4] See xi, map 49.

When the lingering shadow of a restored East Roman Empire—the ghost of the ghost of an Hellenic universal state—was finally effaced by the Ottoman conquest of Constantinople in A.D. 1453, the Russian offshoot of Orthodox Christendom[1] was about to enter into a universal state of its own. The establishment of this Russian universal state may be dated from the annexation of the Republic of Novgorod[2] between

[1] For the relation of Russian Orthodox Christendom to the original home of the Orthodox Christian Civilization in Anatolia and the Balkan Peninsula, see I. i. 132–3.

[2] See IV. iv. 88; V. v. 312; V. vi. 191 and 309; and IX. viii. 126. Prince Dmitrī Obolensky comments:

'Is there not some danger of over-estimating the importance of this union? I would say that the annexation of Novgorod and its dependencies by Ivan III, though of course it vastly increased the territories and economic resources of Muscovy, was in itself only a stage in the lengthy process by which the Muscovite sovereigns succeeded in annexing the greater part of their Kievan predecessors' "patrimony" (except, of course, the south-western regions). This process began *circa* A.D. 1300 and may be said to have ended in A.D. 1533, with the death of Basil III; and the annexations of Tver, the Chernigov and Seversk lands, Pskov, Smolensk and Ryazan, which took place in the latter part of Ivan III's reign and in the reign of Basil III, were perhaps in the long run as important landmarks in this process of "gathering" as the conquest of the Novgorodian lands.

'It seems to me, moreover, that the term "universal state" is more applicable to the multi-national Empire that arose out of Ivan IV's Eastern conquests than to the still essentially Russian states of Ivan III and Basil III. For the annexation of Smolensk (A.D. 1514) and the incorporation of the Ryazan principality (*circa* A.D. 1520) into Muscovy mark the final political unification of the Great Russian lands under Muscovite dominion, while the conquest of Qāzān, Astrakhan and Western Siberia in the reign of Ivan IV, which brought into the Muscovite realm large areas of non-Russian population and culture, may perhaps be regarded with greater justification as the opening chapters in the history of the Russian "universal state".'

On consideration of the first of the two points here made by Prince Obolensky, the writer of this Study does not find himself persuaded that the union of Novgorod with Muscovy was not, after all, the crucial event in the process of the political unification of the territorial patrimony of a Russian Orthodox Christendom under Muscovite rule. Among the parochial states that had sprung from the ruins of the ascendancy of the principality of Kiev, Novgorod was surely unique in being a commercial community with a vast economic hinterland extending north-eastwards to the shores of the White Sea and the Arctic Ocean as far as the estuary of the River Obi on the farther side of the Urals, and in maintaining an active intercourse with the Hanseatic states members of a contemporary Western city-state cosmos on the cultural as well as on the economic plane. In exchange for the furs produced by her north-eastern hinterland, Novgorod had imported from her Western customers the political institution of self-government on the city-state scale. In virtue of this combination of commercial wealth with political liberties, Novgorod was surely the one other Russian parochial state in this age that might perhaps have competed seriously with Moscow for the role of becoming the nucleus of a Russian universal state which, had it crystallized round Novgorod instead of crystallizing round Moscow, would have had a different êthos, as well as a different geographical centre, from the Muscovy that actually performed this historic service for a Russian Orthodox Christendom. On this account the writer remains convinced that, in the building of the Russian universal state, the subjugation of Novgorod by Moscow was the decisive event that may be taken as marking the Russian universal state's establishment (though, of course, the precise dating of the consummation of any historical process is inevitably arbitrary and conventional and consequently open to dispute).

Prince Obolensky's second point turns, as will be seen, on the choice of a different criterion for the epiphany of a universal state from the criterion chosen in the present Study. The term 'universal state' is used here to denote an empire that is 'oecumenical' in the sense of embracing the whole geographical domain of the 'world' constituted by some single civilization, while Prince Obolensky is inclined to appropriate the same term for the different (though, no doubt, equally legitimate) purpose of denoting a state that is universal in the sense of embracing at least parts of the domains of more civilizations than one. In a later chapter (pp. 61–67, below) we shall observe that most of the universal states that had been 'oecumenical' in the sense of embracing the whole domain of some single civilization had also been 'cosmopolitan' in the sense of including parts of the domains of alien civilizations as well; but this feature in the composition of a universal state, though usual, will prove to be neither essential nor indeed invariably present. The essential and never-absent mark of a universal state, in the sense in which the term is used in this Study, is the political unification, within its frontiers, of the whole domain of some single civilization.

A.D. 1471 and A.D. 1479 by the Grand Duke of Moscow, Ivan III (*imperabat* A.D. 1462–1505). This swift sequence of momentous events in the main body of Orthodox Christendom and in its Russian off-shoot, and the dramatic contrast between the final downfall of Orthodox Constantinople and the definitive triumph of Orthodox Moscow, made a profound effect upon the Russian imagination.

'The expansion of every nation, the growth of every empire, is usually the outward sign of an inward conviction of the people that they have a special mission to perform. The striking transformation of the small Moscow principality into one of the largest states of the World was the result of the deep-rooted belief of her people that they were called upon to defend Eastern Orthodoxy.'[1]

Other Orthodox Slav princes before the Muscovite Ivan III had coveted the dazzling insignia of the East Roman Empire and had audaciously stretched out greedy hands to snatch them from the person of a legitimate Emperor reigning at Constantinople; but, unnerved by their own impiety, they had faltered and failed, with disastrous ulterior consequences for their own principalities. After missing, in A.D. 913, a chance of mounting the Imperial Throne at Constantinople, Khan Symeon of Bulgaria had proclaimed himself 'Emperor of the Romans and Bulgars' in A.D. 925, and the Archbishop of Preslav 'Patriarch' of his hybrid empire in the year after;[2] but within less than a century the Bulgarian state had been erased from the political map of Orthodox Christendom: a war to the death had ended in the outright annexation of all Bulgaria by an East Roman Empire which Khan Symeon had aspired to supplant.[3] The Bulgar Khan had rashly challenged the East Roman Empire at its zenith; at its nadir, when the possession of the beggarly remnant of its domain was being contested between a legitimate Palaiológhos and the pretender John Kandakouzinós, the Serb war-lord Stephen Dushan had had himself crowned by the Patriarch of Bulgaria and by his own Serbian Archbishop of Peć on Easter Day, A.D. 1346, as 'King of Serbia . . . Albania and the sea-board, prince of the Empire of Bulgaria, and lord of almost all the Empire of Romania'.[4] The misgivings revealed in this cautiously accurate enumeration had afterwards been veiled in the bolder style and title of 'Emperor and Autocrat of Serbia and Romania';[5] yet the waning shadow of the East Roman Empire had eluded Dushan's grasp, and, within less than half a century, the Serb war-bands had been scattered like chaff by their 'Osmanli competitors for the prize of becoming the founders of a universal state for the main body of Orthodox Christendom. The Muscovites, who afterwards trod with impunity the perilous path down which a Bulgarian Symeon and a Serbian Stephen had carried their ephemeral empires to destruction, were not even inspired directly by either of these two magnificent failures; they drew their inspiration from a Second

1 Zernov, N.: *The Russians and their Church* (London 1945, S.P.C.K.), p. 49.
2 See IV. iv. 384 and 386. 3 See IV. iv. 390–2.
4 'Serviae . . . Albaniae, maritimae regionis rex, Bulgariae imperii princeps et fere totius imperii Romaniae dominus' (Gibbons, H. A.: *The Foundation of the Ottoman Empire* (Oxford 1916, Clarendon Press), p. 88).
5 Gibbons, loc. cit.

Bulgarian Empire which had dragged out its undistinguished existence during the two centuries (A.D. 1186–1393) between the collapse of the East Roman Empire in South-Eastern Europe and the political unification of the main body of Orthodox Christendom by the 'Osmanlis.

'The Second Bulgarian Empire with its centre at Trnovo had for a time controlled the Balkans; its rulers had styled themselves Tsar and Autokrátôr, and at their court there had been a literary revival when Greek works were translated into Bulgarian. Among these translated works was the verse chronicle of Manasses. In this chronicle the decline of the Roman Power in Western Europe was described: the Old Rome of the West had failed, but Constantinople had taken its place and still stood young and vigorous. In the Bulgarian version Constantinople disappears, and in its stead the chronicler's praise is transferred to "our new Tsarigrad" and the Bulgarian Tsar. Trnovo claimed for itself the imperial glory of the city of Constantine. In A.D. 1393 the Bulgarian Empire fell before the attack of the Turks, and many exiles fled from Bulgaria to Moscow. A Bulgarian, Kiprian, at this time became Metropolitan of Moscow. It looks as if these *émigrés* had carried with them the imperial theory which on Bulgarian soil had been shattered by the Turkish victory. It was Kiprian who, when a dispute had arisen between Moscow and the [East Roman] Empire, wrote to the Patriarch of Constantinople: "We have a church but no Emperor, and we do not recognise him." Byzantium replied by a re-assertion of its sole claim to imperial sovereignty. In A.D. 1438–9 came the Council of Florence and the union of the Eastern and Western churches. Orthodoxy had been betrayed by the Greeks: The Metropolitan Isidor [of Moscow], who had played the traitor's part at the Council, was cursed as a renegade.[1] In A.D. 1453 Constantinople itself fell into the hands of the Turks. The lesson thus taught by history was obvious: here was the hand of God.'[2]

The Muscovites took full advantage of the opportunity that now lay open to them. In A.D. 1472 the Grand Duke Ivan III married Zoë (*Russicè* Sophia) Palaiológhos, a niece of the last Constantinopolitan Orthodox Emperor Constantine,[3] and adopted as his own coat-of-arms the two-headed East Roman eagle.[4] In A.D. 1480 he repudiated the

[1] Isidore was not only discredited; he was ejected and replaced by a successor of Russian, instead of Greek, nationality; and at the same time the Oecumenical Patriarch's ecclesiastical suzerainty over the Metropolitan See of Moscow was repudiated. See IX. viii. 398.—A.J.T.

[2] Baynes, N. H., and Moss, H. St. L. B.: *Byzantium* (Oxford 1948, Clarendon Press), pp. 383–4. Cp. Zernov, N.: *Moscow the Third Rome*, reprint of 2nd ed. (London 1944, S.P.C.K.), p. 34: 'This catastrophe, comparable only to the destruction of Jerusalem or the sack of Rome, required an explanation, and this was found in the apostasy of the Emperor and the Oecumenical Patriarch.'

[3] The Thirteenth, counting from Constantine the Great, on one reckoning, the Eleventh on another.

[4] These two events are, however, given a different complexion by Prince Obolensky in 'Russia's Byzantine Heritage', *Oxford Slavonic Papers*, vol. i (Oxford 1950, Clarendon Press), p. 46:

'Of course there can be no doubt that Russian Tsarism welcomed the theory that the seat of Imperial sovereignty had migrated to Moscow after the fall of Constantinople; the Tsar's adoption of Byzantine titles, heraldry and ceremonial can be regarded as a visible symbol of this claim. But . . . the Christian universalism of East Rome was transformed and distorted within the more narrow framework of Muscovite nationalism. The really significant fact is that the beginning of Russia's turning away from her Byzantine heritage in the late fifteenth century coincided with the growth of her connexions with the West; Ivan III's marriage with Zoë was a harbinger of these connexions; for the

suzerainty of the Tatars of Bātū Khan's Appanage and proclaimed his own independence under the title of Autocrat. His second successor Ivan IV the Terrible (*imperabat* A.D. 1533–84) had himself crowned Emperor in 1547. In A.D. 1551 a Council of the Russian Church asserted the superiority of the Russian version of Orthodoxy over all others.[1] In the reign of Tsar Theodore (*imperabat* A.D. 1584–98), in A.D. 1589, the Metropolitan of Moscow was elevated by the Oecumenical Patriarch of the day to the status of Patriarch of All Russia.[2] In taking these successive steps the Russians were on stronger ground than their Bulgar and Serb precursors whose ventures had ended so ignominiously. They were not usurpers challenging living legitimate bearers of the Imperial title, but residuary legatees taking over a vacant heritage; and, so far from being conscious of sin, they were confidently self-righteous.

'The feeling that the Greeks had betrayed their Orthodoxy, and were therefore punished by God, was particularly strong in the remote Church of Russia, where anti-Latin tendencies were very pronounced. . . . To the Russians it seemed that, if the Greeks were rejected by God for the betrayal of Orthodoxy, they themselves were restored to political independence because of their devotion to the Church. The Russian nation was the last stronghold of the Orthodox Faith, and would thus inherit all the privileges and duties of the Christian Roman Empire.'[3]

This Russian belief in Russia's high destiny was fortified by Biblical and Patristic authority. The four successive universal states that were a prominent motif in the Book of Daniel[4] had been identified by the Christian Father Hippolytus (*florebat circa* A.D. 230)[5] as the Empires of Babylon,[6] the Achaemenidae, Alexander the Great, and Rome.

'During the ascendancy of the Fourth Realm the greatest events in human history were expected to take place, including the Second as well

niece of the last Byzantine Emperor came to Russia from Italy accompanied by a papal legate, and the marriage had been arranged in Rome.'

1 See Zernov, op. cit., p. 58.

2 See Zernov, ibid., pp. 69–73. In spite of his assumption of this style and title, the Patriarch of Moscow did not succeed immediately in extending his ecclesiastical domain beyond the previous limits of the Muscovite Metropolitan See. Russian Orthodox Christians who were political subjects of the United Kingdom of Poland-Lithuania and who did not become Uniate ecclesiastical subjects of the Roman Church continued to be ecclesiastical subjects of the Oecumenical Patriarchate of Constantinople until after Kiev had fallen under the political sovereignty of Muscovy—as it fell provisionally in A.D. 1667 and definitively in A.D. 1686. After the death of the reigning Metropolitan of Kiev in A.D. 1671, the Muscovite Government deliberately kept the See vacant; and, when in A.D. 1684 they gave their consent at last to the holding of a new election, they stipulated that the new incumbent should be the ecclesiastical subject of the Patriarch of Moscow, and no longer of the Oecumenical Patriarch of Constantinople. The Metropolitan of Kiev who was elected on the 29th June, 1685, accordingly obtained investiture from the Patriarch of Moscow; and, when the Oecumenical Patriarch refused to recognize the alienation of the See of Kiev from his own ecclesiastical jurisdiction, he was compelled to give way by the Sultan acting at the instance of the Tsar, whom the Porte was eager to appease, in the vain hope of deterring Moscow from joining the Western Christian coalition against the Ottoman Empire (see Doroshenko, D.: *History of the Ukraine*, English translation (Edmonton, Alberta, 1939, The Institute Press), pp. 324–8).

3 Zernov, op. cit., pp. 34–36.

4 Daniel ii. 27–49; vii. 1–28; ix. 24–27.

5 Though Hippolytus lived and worked in Rome, he wrote in Greek—which was the language of the proletariat, and therefore of the Church, in the Imperial City till after his day—and his works were therefore current in Eastern Orthodox Christendom.

6 i.e. the Neo-Babylonian Empire of Nebuchadnezzar, not the original Babylonian Empire of Hammurabi.

as the First Coming of the Messiah. The collapse of the western part of the Roman Empire in the fifth century did not affect this conviction, for the Eastern Christians believed that Constantinople was the New or Second Rome. They ascribed to her the same promises of indestructibility which were originally made in regard to Rome herself. When Moscow became the only capital among the Eastern Christians free from the control of the Infidels, it was natural that she should be elevated to the position of the Third and Last Rome.'[1]

This belief was given its classical formulation by an elder of a monastery in Pskov, Philotheus, in an epistle addressed to the Grand Duke Basil III (*imperabat* A.D. 1505–33).

'The Church of Old Rome fell [because of] its heresy; the gates of the Second Rome, Constantinople, were hewn down by the axes of the infidel Turks; but the Church of Moscow, the Church of the New Rome, shines brighter than the Sun in the whole Universe. Thou art the one universal sovereign of all Christian folk; thou shouldst hold the reins in awe of God. Fear Him who hath committed them to thee. Two Romes are fallen, but the Third stands fast; a fourth there cannot be. Thy Christian kingdom shall not be given to another.'[2]

Two generations later, a paraphrase of this famous passage was written into the installation charter of the first Patriarch of Moscow[3] over the signature of his creator the Oecumenical Patriarch Jeremiah:

'Because the Old Rome has collapsed on account of the heresy of Apollinarius, and because the Second Rome, which is Constantinople, is now in [the] possession of the godless Turks, thy great kingdom, O pious Tsar, is the Third Rome. It surpasses in devotion every other, and all Christian kingdoms are now merged in thy realm. Thou art the only Christian sovereign in the World, the master of all faithful Christians.'[4]

The Russians' bold application to their own universal state of the belief in the immortality of an oecumenical Roman Empire seems to have moved a Muscovite Government—in so far as this 'great idea' had any practical influence on Muscovite policy—to concentrate its attention and effort more steadily than ever upon working for the Russian aims of saving a still inviolate 'Third Rome' from suffering 'the Second Rome's' and 'the First Rome's' fates and of liberating from Western political and ecclesiastical domination the Russian Orthodox Christian lands and peoples that had fallen under the rule of Poland and Lithuania since the fourteenth century,[5] without allowing itself to be diverted by Western diplomacy into fancying itself in the romantic role of a divinely appointed liberator of non-Russian Orthodox Christians who had fallen under Otto-

[1] Zernov, N.: *The Russians and their Church*, p. 50.

[2] Philotheus of Pskov, op. cit., as cited in Zernov, *The Russians and their Church*, p. 51. In this passage, Philotheus has taken his cue from earlier Russian expressions of the same idea. For instance, 'the chronographer of A.D. 1512 writes: "Constantine's city is fallen, but our Russian land through the help of the Mother of God and the Saints grows and is young and exalted. So may it be, O Christ, until the end of Time!" The words which the Bulgarian translator of Manasses had applied to Trnovo are here claimed for Moscow' (Baynes, N. H., and Moss, H. St. L. B.: *Byzantium* (Oxford 1948, Clarendon Press), p. 384).

[3] For the establishment of the Patriarchate of Moscow in A.D. 1589, see p. 35, above.

[4] Text as cited in Zernov, op. cit., p. 71.

[5] See IX. viii. 126–8.

man Muslim rule as a penalty for 'the Second Rome's' apostasy.[1] The political mission of 'the Third Rome' would be neither to rescue nor to reform 'the Second Rome', but to supplant her, as it had been the Christian Church's mission to supplant the Jewish Church. The effect, in Russian souls, of the concept of 'Moscow the Third Rome' seems to have been to precipitate, focus, and express a Russian sense of the uniqueness of Russia's own destiny as the sole surviving repository and citadel of an impeccably orthodox Christianity; and this sense of destiny subsequently demonstrated its strength by surviving some very formidable opposition.

While 'it is an open question whether Jeremiah himself fully understood the Russian text [of his charter] and shared the interpretation given by the Russians to the act committed by him',[2] it is certain that, when the four Greek Patriarchs of Constantinople, Alexandria, Antioch, and Jerusalem jointly accorded recognition to the Patriarchate of Moscow in A.D. 1593, they assigned to the new Patriarch the fifth and not the first place in their order of precedence.[3] Thereafter, in the seventeenth and eighteenth centuries, the ideal of 'Moscow the Third Rome' was signally defeated first by Greek Orthodoxy and then by the secular civilization of the West.

In consequence of a schism within the bosom of the Russian Church, arising from the championship of Greek as against Russian ritual practice[4] by no less a person than the reigning Patriarch of Moscow, Nikon,[5] the four Greek Patriarchs—Ottoman *ra'īyeh* though they were—became for a moment the arbiters of Russia's ecclesiastical destiny. At a Council held at Moscow in A.D. 1666–7, over which the Patriarchs of Alexandria and Antioch presided, the opponents of Nikon's Graecizing reforms were excommunicated, and the Russian hierarchy were compelled to sign a statement renouncing the pretension, put on record by the Council of A.D. 1551, that Muscovite Orthodoxy was an ensample for the rest of the Orthodox Church. At the same time Nikon himself was deposed and unfrocked.[6]

[1] See Prince Dmitri Obolensky in *Oxford Slavonic Papers*, vol. i (Oxford 1950, Clarendon Press), pp. 46 and 62, together with the further observations from him and from B. H. Sumner that are quoted, in an annex, on pp. 577–9, below.

[2] Zernov, op. cit., p. 71.

[3] See Zernov, op. cit., loc. cit.

[4] 'The cause of these differences in ritual, discovered by the Russians in the seventeenth century, was their long separation, under the Tatar yoke, from the rest of Eastern Christendom. For, whilst the Church of Byzantium had gradually altered liturgical customs, the Russians had preserved intact the ritual received by them at the time of their conversion in the tenth century' (Zernov, op. cit., p. 100). It will be seen that the circumstances in which this issue between the Russian and Greek versions of Eastern Orthodoxy arose in the seventeenth century were remarkably similar to those in which the issue between the Irish and Roman versions of Western Catholicism had arisen in the seventh century (see the present Study, I. i. 29 and II. ii. 333–6). There is a singular resemblance between the masterful characters, and parallelism between the chequered careers, of Nikon and Wilfrid. The two prelates won a conspicuous and enduring victory for the causes of Constantinople and Rome respectively, and both of them eventually brought personal discomfiture and downfall on themselves through the intolerable hybris bred in their imperious souls by the brilliance of their previous successes.

[5] Nikon *patriarchico munere fungebatur* A.D. 1652–66.

[6] Zernov, op. cit., pp. 103–4. This Greek ecclesiastical ascendancy in Muscovy proved ephemeral. 'In general, the religious and cultural links between the [Russians and the Greeks], which had been steadily increasing during the first three-quarters of the

In the next generation, Peter the Great applied his extraordinary genius to a revolutionary attempt to transform Muscovy from a Russian Orthodox Christian universal state, believing itself to be charged with a unique oecumenical mission, into an efficient parochial state member of the contemporary Western comity. Peter transferred the capital of his dominions from Russian Orthodox Moscow to a new city, founded by him in the maritime Western March of the Russian World and named after its founder; and, on the culturally as well as physically virgin soil of St. Petersburg, a Westernizing Russia was to have a seat of government that would be Western from the start, uncontaminated by any antecedent deposit of Orthodox tradition.[1] Peter also instilled a tincture of Westernism into the Muscovite Church by filling the key posts in the Russian Orthodox hierarchy, hitherto held by Muscovites, with Ukrainian clerics from Kiev and the Ukrainian territories lying east of the River Dniepr that had been acquired by Muscovy from Poland-Lithuania in A.D. 1667;[2] for, under a Roman Catholic ascendancy, the Ukrainian Orthodox clergy, whether they opposed Romanization or yielded to it, had been constrained to study Roman theology and in the process had been mentally re-oriented to a partially Western outlook.[3] Finally, after having left the Patriarchal Throne of Moscow lying vacant for twenty years, Peter replaced the Patriarchate in A.D. 1721 by a 'Holy Synod' composed of ecclesiastics appointed by the Emperor himself and explicitly acknowledging his supremacy; and, to make sure that his control should be effective, he placed the Synod under the supervision of a lay Procurator.[4]

This rain of blows might have been expected to be crushing, yet the ideal once conveyed in the concept of 'Moscow the Third Rome' clung to life in its traditional religious expression and eventually found for itself new expressions in terms of the ideologies of a Westernizing World whose atmosphere the Russians were now constrained to breathe. The

seventeenth-century, had declined in the last quarter, when Kiev [ceded to Muscovy by Poland-Lithuania in A.D. 1667], not Constantinople, proved itself the leading Orthodox cultural influence on Russia. When in A.D. 1685–6 the Metropolitanate of Kiev was placed under the jurisdiction of the Moscow Patriarchate, this was effected without previous agreement with Constantinople, and the [Oecumenical] Patriarch could do nothing but register unavailing protests. Ukrainians, not Greeks, became the leading representatives, in Russia, of new trends in Orthodox thought and education. Constantinople no longer, as in the days of Nikon, represented for Russia the fountainhead of learning and of Orthodox tradition' (Sumner, B. H.: *Peter the Great and the Ottoman Empire* (Oxford 1949, Blackwell), p. 64). Both Peter the Great and his ambassador at Constantinople, P. A. Tolstoi, seem to have disliked and despised the Phanariot Greek Orthodox Christian prelates (see ibid., pp. 63–65).

[1] A corresponding consideration had been in the mind of Constantine the Great when he had transferred the capital of the Roman Empire from Old Rome to his own foundation of New Rome or Constantinople. The seat of Government of a converted Roman Empire was to be Christian from the outset, unaffected by the archaistic paganism that was dying so hard in its Senatorial fastness on the banks of the Tiber (see V. vi. 89). In making the transfer, both Constantine and Peter were, of course, moved by political and strategic motives in addition to the cultural motive here in question (see II. ii. 157–8 and pp. 221–3, below).

[2] The Zaporozhian Cossacks, who controlled the southern fringe of the Ukraine, below Kiev (see II. ii. 154–7 and V. v. 283), had transferred their allegiance from Poland-Lithuania to Muscovy already between the years 1648 and 1667.

[3] See Zernov, N.: *Moscow the Third Rome*, pp. 89–91.

[4] See Zernov, op. cit., pp. 81–82; eundem, *The Russians and their Church*, pp. 122–4; and the present chapter of the present Study, p. 23, n. 4, above.

excommunicated opponents of Nikon succeeded in establishing and maintaining, under the Petrine régime, the dissident church of the Old Believers,[1] and in a Western Age of Romanticism the Russian faith in Russia's unique destiny and oecumenical mission acclimatized itself to the spiritual temperature of a secular Western culture under the guise of the Slavophil Movement.[2] When the Petrine political régime collapsed in A.D. 1917, the Patriarchate of Moscow was re-established[3] and the political capital was retransferred to Moscow from Petrograd.

It might have been expected, again, that, after this flicker of life, the ideal of 'Moscow the Third Rome' would have received its *coup de grâce* from the Bolshevik régime; for did not Lenin and his companions out-Peter Peter? Was it not the aim of the Communists to complete the Westernization of Russia on a radical futurist pattern? Were they not setting themselves to uproot, not merely Orthodoxy, but the very belief in the existence of God? Did they not deliberately eliminate the name of Russia from the official style of their 'Union of Soviet Socialist Republics'? The answers to these rhetorical questions are necessarily affirmative, yet they leave unsolved the enigma of the ambiguity in the nature of Bolshevism which has been touched on at an earlier point in this Study[4] and which still remained obscure at a time when the Soviet Government had been in existence for a third of a century.

The would-be disciples of Marx might prove to be involuntary disciples of Philotheus. It was they, after all, who had repaired Peter's breach with Muscovite geographical tradition by bringing back to Moscow from Leningrad the capital of the Empire which the Soviet régime had inherited from Peter, and Peter from Ivan III; and, though this deliberate act of theirs had no doubt been prompted by other motives,[5] it was improbable that, once ensconced in the Kremlin, they would be impervious to an atmosphere from which their clear-sighted precursor had taken

[1] See V. vi. 120–1 and IX. viii. 131–2.

[2] See Kohn, Hans: 'Dostoevsky's Nationalism', in the *Journal of the History of Ideas*, October 1945, vol. vi, No. 4 (New York 1945, College of the City of New York), pp. 385–414, and the present Study, IX. viii. 131–2.

[3] Tikhon, the Metropolitan of Moscow, was elected Patriarch on the 5th November, 1917 (i.e. after the Bolsheviks had come into power), by a Church Council, including lay as well as ecclesiastical members, which had been convened on the 15th August (Zernov, *The Russians and their Church*, p. 154).

[4] In III. iii. 200–2. See further IX. viii. 133–6 and 607–8.

[5] These motives are discussed, in an annex, on pp. 690–1, below. One motive of the Bolsheviks in retransferring the capital from Leningrad to Moscow on the 12th March, 1918, had been to entrench themselves in a strategic position covering the eastern exit of an overland avenue of attack from Western Europe along which the Germans had marched, in Polish and French footsteps, in two world wars. Another of their motives had been to establish their hold over, and spread their doctrine among, the mass of the people whom they had set out to rule, by planting themselves at a point which, besides covering the most dangerously exposed of all Russia's twentieth-century frontiers, had the second advantage of lying much nearer than Leningrad lay to the heart of the country. This was the motive that likewise led the British Government of India to retransfer the capital of the Indian Empire from Calcutta to Delhi in A.D. 1912, the Kemalist Government of Turkey to remove the capital of Turkey from Constantinople to Ankara in April 1920, and the Kuomintang Government of China to retransfer the capital of China from Peking to Nanking in A.D. 1928. Such moves are likely to have two-way cultural effects. While they may fulfil the migrating Governments' purpose of strengthening their own influence over the interior of their dominions, these Governments will also be exposing themselves, by their migration, to the influence of the traditional culture of the interior. (For transfers of capitals and some of their causes and effects, see II. ii. 112–208 and pp. 193–228, below.)

such pains to extricate the new ruling element in his own anti-traditional régime. The spirit of Moscow was a faith in Russia's destiny;[1] and, at the time of writing, the Russians' consciousness of a unique destiny was sharing with the Americans' possession of a unique weapon the invidious distinction of being one of two titanic facts that, between them, were darkening the horizon of a world which had condemned itself to political unification by its two feats of disintegrating the Atom and 'annihilating distance'. This was an impressive testimony to the strength of the belief in the immortality of a Roman Empire which in reality had ceased to exist not less than thirteen hundred years ago.[2]

The Riddle of the Prestige of the Imperial Office in Japan

A similar testimony to the endurance of the prestige of the Ts'in and Han Empire is perhaps afforded by the history of the Imperial House of Japan.[3]

At an earlier point in this Study[4] an explanation has been offered for the ebbing away of power from the Imperial Government in Yamato to the feudal nobility in the Kwanto. We have still to explain why an Imperial House which exercised effective authority for less than three hundred years after the reorganization of the Imperial Government on a Chinese model in A.D. 645 should have survived for another thousand years in impotence as the sole fount of honour and dispenser of legitimacy. All the *de facto* rulers of Japan, since the time in the tenth century of the Christian Era when the Imperial Government had lost control, had felt it necessary to do their ruling in the Emperor's name. At the time of writing, an utterly victorious occupying Power was finding it convenient to administer the country through a native Japanese Government acting in the name of the Emperor of the day.

This extraordinary vitality of the prestige of the Japanese Imperial House had been attributed by the Japanese themselves to their own official belief that the Imperial Family were descendants, in unbroken line, from the Sun Goddess Amaterasu. But, though, no doubt, this myth went back to the dawn of Japanese history, the deliberate exploitation of it for a political purpose seemed to be no older than the Meiji Period, when the new masters of Japan, who had wrested the *de facto* power from the last of the Tokugawa shoguns in A.D. 1868 and had appropriated to themselves the manipulation of the indispensable Imperial puppet under pretence of 'restoring' him to the status enjoyed by his forefathers, were concerned to enhance the prestige of the institution in whose name they had to rule. Moreover, the Emperor Hirohito did not seem to have forfeited his hold on the allegiance of the Japanese people by his public declaration to them, on New Year's Day 1946, that he was not a god but a man.[5] It therefore looked as if there were some

[1] For the persistence of this faith and the fundamental identity of the Slavophil and the Communist manifestation of it, see Kohn, op. cit., p. 414.

[2] Reckoning that even the relatively tough Greek and Oriental core of the Roman Empire went to pieces within the hundred years following the death of Justinian in A.D. 565. In the West the Empire went to pieces some two hundred years earlier (see p. 20, n. 4, and p. 27, n. 4, above).

[3] For the relation of the offshoot of the Far Eastern Civilization in Japan to the main stem in China, see I. i. 132–3.

[4] In II. ii. 158–9.

[5] In his rescript of that date, the Emperor Hirohito declared: 'The ties between us and

firm foundation, other than the Sun Goddess myth, for the immense esteem which the Imperial House had continued to enjoy through all vicissitudes of their fortunes and Japan's, and this foundation might perhaps be discovered in the historic 'reception', in A.D. 645, of the Chinese Imperial Constitution of that age. This bureaucratic system of administration was far too elaborate and refined to be practicable under the rude conditions of contemporary Japanese society. Yet its exotic character, which doomed it to a speedy failure in the field of practical politics, may have been the very feature that ensured its age-long preservation as a palladium of the Japanese polity; for the Japanese Imperial Constitution of A.D. 645 was modelled on that of the then reigning Chinese dynasty of the T'ang, and the T'ang Empire had been a resuscitation of the Han Empire, which had been the Sinic Society's universal state. On this showing, the Japanese Imperial Office in the twentieth century of the Christian Era was living on political capital that had been accumulated by Han Liu Pang in the second century B.C.

The Grounds of the Illusion

We have perhaps now sufficiently established the fact that the belief in the immortality of universal states survives for centuries and millennia after it has been decisively confuted by plain hard facts. What are the causes of a phenomenon that looks strange at first sight?

One manifest cause is the potency of the personal impression made by the founders of universal states and by their successors who enter into the fruits of their labours[1]—an impression that their contemporaries, who receive it at first hand as the direct beneficiaries of these great men's achievements, hand on to a receptive Posterity with an emphasis which, by the cumulative effect of transmission, exaggerates an imposing truth into an overwhelming legend. From among the many famous testimonies to the impression made by the Emperor Augustus, we have singled out already, in another context, the almost lyrical tribute paid by Philo,[2]

our people have always stood upon mutual trust and affection. They do not depend upon mere legends and myths. They are not predicated on the false conception that the Emperor is divine and that the Japanese people are superior to other races and fated to rule the World' (English text published in *The New York Times*, 1st January, 1946).

[1] A survey of representatives of these two generations of 'saviours with the sword' has been given in V. vi. 189–97. See further V. vi. 370–5.

[2] See V. vi. 181, n. 3. The Alexandrian Jewish man of letters' private and personal tribute to Augustus has an official counterpart in a decree passed—probably in the year 9 B.C.—by the *Κοινόν* of the Province of Asia, providing that in this province in future Augustus's birthday shall be kept as New Year's Day and that the first month of the new calendar year shall be called 'Caesar'. This inscription (No. 458 in W. Dittenberger: *Orientis Graeci Inscriptiones Selectae*, vol. ii (Leipzig 1905, Hirzel), pp. 48–60) expresses the same sentiments as Philo in outright religious language:

'[The Most Divine Caesar] has re-established a Universe that had everywhere been in disintegration and had degenerated into a lamentable state. He has put a new face on the whole Cosmos—a Cosmos that would have been only too happy to pass out of existence if, at the critical moment, Caesar had not been born to be the Universe's universal blessing. . . . The Providence that has organised every detail of Human Life has exerted and surpassed Itself in order to bring Life to perfection in producing Augustus—whom It has filled with virtue to be the benefactor of Mankind, sending him to us and to Posterity as a saviour whose mission has been to put an end to War and to set the Universe in order.'

This official eulogy is capped by one from Halicarnassus (No. 94 in *The Collection of Ancient Greek Inscriptions in the British Museum*, Part IV, section i (Oxford 1893,

who, as a Jew, a Hellenist, an Alexandrian, and a philosopher, can hardly be suspected of having gone to exceptional lengths in his enthusiasm for the Roman founder of an Hellenic universal state. The prestige to which such tributes gave a flying start can be seen gathering momentum during the next two centuries.

'A very important "virtue", which emerges and takes shape slowly, ... is the *Providentia* (in Greek *πρόνοια*) of the ruler. This ... "foresight" or "forethought" ... as we meet it in Cicero ... appears to be a virtue at once of the wise magistrate, who foresees and so forestalls dangers, and of the loving father, who makes provision for the welfare and future of the family of which he is the head. Both these senses tend to blend and come together, as they naturally might in a ruler who was at once a magistrate ... of the Roman People and a father for the whole Empire.

'Through a hundred years it develops till it reaches its first climax under Trajan, "the most provident prince".... This aspect of the rule of Trajan and Hadrian and the Antonine Emperors, stressed as it was on coins, on buildings, by speakers and publicists, was bound to have its effect. Slowly the common people learnt to look for help and aid to the *Providentia* of their all-powerful ruler—he knows, he cares, he can act: he is like some Hercules, who visits all corners of the World putting down injustice and ending misery. Remembering this, we can form for ourselves some faint idea of how tremendous the effect of Hadrian's great journeys must have been on the provincials: here was an Emperor who did not stay in Rome (or, if he left it, leave merely for campaigns), but who visited every part of his realm to put things in order and to restore. ... As years pass, this *Providentia* of the one ruler becomes more comprehensive. ... When men are in distress and trouble they turn to the one person of whose help they can be sure: oppressed tenant-farmers on an Imperial estate in Africa appeal for aid to the *Divina Providentia* at Rome, and the harassed colonists of Scaptopara in Thrace beg the Emperor to pity them and help them by his *θεία πρόνοια*.[1]

'There is something very touching in this faith, this belief in the *providentissimus princeps*: however far away he may be in Rome, he cares for them, he pities them, he cannot be deceived, and he exerts always, to quote the fine phrase of one of Hadrian's officers, "a care that is never tired, with which he watches unrestingly on behalf of the good of Mankind (*infatigabilis cura, per quam adsidue pro humanis utilitatibus excubat*)". ... Justice, clemency, duty, warlike prowess—these are fine things; but even more important is it that the subject peoples and provincials over this vast area should have believed in a ruler who was not merely a soldier but who cared for them and provided for their needs.'[2]

Clarendon Press), pp. 63–65), which must have been drafted not earlier than the year 2 B.C., since it cites Augustus's title 'Pater Patriae':

'Considering that the eternal and immortal Nature of the Universe has lavished upon Mankind the greatest blessing, redounding to superlative benefactions, in bringing forth Caesar Augustus, who in the blissful life of our generation is the father of his own fatherland the goddess Rome, and is the ancestral Zeus and saviour of the whole Human Race, whose providence has not only fulfilled but has surpassed the prayers of all Mankind—for there is peace on land and sea, the commonwealths flourish in law-abidingness, concord and prosperity, and there is a peak and a fecundity of every blessing: of good hopes for the future and of good cheer in the present, in a world whose inhabitants have been given full measure of matches and monuments and celebrations. ...'

[1] 'La notion de l'éternité des Césars est ... étroitement unie à celle de leur divinité' (Cumont, Fr.: 'L'Éternité des Empereurs Romains', in *Revue d'Histoire et de Littérature Religieuses*, vol. i (Paris 1896; printed at Macon), pp. 439–40).

[2] Charlesworth, M. P.: *The Virtues of a Roman Emperor: Propaganda and the Creation*

This epiphany of the ruler of a universal state as the one shepherd whose oecumenical monarchy makes one fold for all Mankind[1] appeals to one of the Human Soul's deepest longings, as, in Dostoyevski's fable, the Grand Inquisitor reminds a subversive Christ.

'Thou mightest have taken . . . the sword of Caesar. Why didst Thou reject that last gift? Hadst Thou accepted that last counsel of the mighty spirit, Thou wouldst have accomplished all that Man seeks on Earth—that is, someone to worship, someone to keep his conscience, and some means of uniting all in one unanimous and harmonious ant-heap; for the craving for universal unity is the third and last anguish of men. Mankind as a whole has always striven to organise a universal state. There have been many great nations with great histories, but the more highly they were developed the more unhappy they were, for they felt more acutely than other people the craving for world-wide union. The great conquerors—Timurs and Chingis Khans—whirled like hurricanes over the face of the Earth, striving to subdue its people, and they too were but the unconscious expression of the same craving for universal unity. Hadst Thou taken the World and Caesar's purple, Thou wouldst have founded the universal state and have given universal peace. For who can rule men if not he who holds their conscience and their bread in his hands?'[2]

Another cause of the persistence of the belief in the immortality of universal states is the impressiveness of the institution itself, as distinct from the prestige of the succession of rulers who are its living incarnations. A universal state captivates hearts and minds because it is the embodiment of a rally from the long-unhalted rout of a Time of Troubles, and it was this aspect of the Roman Empire that eventually won the admiration and love of originally hostile Greek men of letters.

'There is no salvation in the exercise of a dominion divorced from power. To find oneself under the dominion of one's superiors is a "second best" alternative; but this "second best" proved to be the best of all in our present experience of a Roman Empire. This happy experience has moved the whole World to cleave to Rome with might and main. The World would no more think of seceding from Rome than a ship's crew would think of parting company with the pilot. You must have seen bats in a cave clinging tight to one another and to the rocks; and this is an apt image of the whole World's dependence on Rome. In every heart to-day the focus of anxiety is the fear of becoming detached from the cluster. The thought of being abandoned by Rome is so appalling that it precludes any thought of wantonly abandoning her.

'There is an end of those disputes over sovereignty and prestige which were the causes of the outbreak of all the wars of the past; and, while some of the nations, like noiselessly flowing water, are delightfully quiet—rejoicing in their release from toil and trouble, and aware at last that all their old struggles were to no purpose—there are other nations which do not even know or remember whether they once sat in the seat of power.

of Belief (London 1937, Milford), pp. 15, 16, 17, and 19–20. Cf. eundem: 'Providentia and Aeternitas', in the *Harvard Theological Review*, vol. xxix, No. 2, April 1936. See also Cumont, Fr.: 'L'Éternité des Empereurs Romains', in *Revue d'Histoire et de Littérature Religieuses*, vol. i (1896), pp. 435 seqq., cited by Charlesworth.

[1] John x. 16.

[2] Dostoyevski, F.: *The Brothers Karamazov*, Part II, Book V, chap. 5: 'The Grand Inquisitor'.

In fact we are witnessing a new version of the Pamphylian's myth (or is it Plato's own?). At a moment when the states of the World were already laid out on the funeral pyre as the victims of their own fratricidal strife and turmoil, they were all at once presented with the [Roman] dominion and straightway came to life again. How they arrived at this condition, they are unable to say. They know nothing about it, and can only marvel at their present well-being. They are like sleepers awakened who have come to themselves and now dismiss from their thoughts the dreams that obsessed them only a moment ago. They no longer find it credible that there were ever such things as wars; and, when the word "war" is mentioned to-day, it has a mythical sound in most peoples' ears. . . .

'The entire Inhabited World now keeps perpetual holiday. It has laid aside the steel which it used to wear of old and has turned, care-free, to festivities and enjoyment of all kinds. All other rivalries have died out, and one form of competition alone now pre-occupies all the cities—a competition in making the finest show of beauty and amenity. The whole World is now full of gymnasiums, fountains, gateways, temples, workshops, academies; and it is now possible to say with scientific certainty that a World which was in its death-agonies has made a recovery and gained a new lease of life. . . . The whole Earth has been laid out like a pleasure park. The smoke of burning villages and the watch fires (lit by friend or foeman) have vanished beyond the horizon, as though some mighty wind had winnowed them away, and their place has been taken by an innumerable multitude and variety of enchanting shows and sports. . . . So that the only people who still need pity for the good things that they are missing are those outside your empire—if there are any such people left. . . .'[1]

If there are, they are hardly worth speaking of in the estimation of those inside, and this is another reason why the belief in their immortality that universal states inspire is so blindly persistent. Universal states are the supreme expressions, on the political plane, of a sense of unity which is one of the psychological products of the process of social disintegration.[2] During the Times of Troubles through which disintegrating civilizations make their rough passage, the vision of unity grows ever clearer and the yearning for it ever more poignant as the reality of it continues to elude the storm-tossed wayfarers; and, when, at the lowest ebb of hope, the long-pursued goal is at last unexpectedly attained, and this in a monumental form, the psychological effect is overwhelming.

'Ahuramazda, the creator of Heaven and Earth, has made the King of the Persians "ruler, far and wide, over this great Earth"—made "him, the one [lord], to be ruler over many"; made him "king over many lands and tongues", "over the mountains and plains this side of the Sea and beyond it" [Babylonian Inscription *H*]. He can style himself "the lord of all men from sunrise to sunset" [Aeschines, iii. 132]. All the peoples whose representatives are portrayed on the seat of his throne render him obedience, bring him tribute and serve in his armed forces.'[3]

This sense of unity and universality is not a peculiarity of the

[1] Aristeides, P. Aelius: *In Romam*, edited by Keil, B., in *Aelii Aristidis Quae Supersunt Omnia*, vol. ii (Berlin 1898, Weidmann), pp. 110–11 (Or. XXVI, §§ 68–70) and p. 120 (Or. XXVI, §§ 97–99).

[2] See V. vi. 1–49.

[3] Meyer, E.: *Geschichte des Altertums*, vol. iii (Stuttgart 1901, Cotta), pp. 24–25.

Achaemenian Empire;[1] it is the hall-mark of universal states, which stamps those that bear it as authentic representatives of this class of polity. In his eulogy of Rome, the Greek man of letters, quoted above, makes a point of the universality of her rule as well as of the new lease of life that she has brought to a lacerated Hellenic Society.

'Of this city of Rome you could not say either that it was left unfortified with a Lacedaemonian bravado or that it was enclosed in fortifications of a Babylonian magnificence. . . . You have not, however, you Romans, neglected to build walls; only you have run them round your empire and not round your city. You have placed them in the uttermost parts of the Earth; yet they are magnificent walls which are worthy of you and are a sight for the eyes of all who live within their shelter—though it would take an intending sight-seer months or even years to reach them if Rome itself were the starting-point of his journey; for you have pushed your way beyond the outermost circuit of the Inhabited World and there, in no-man's-land, you have drawn a second circuit with a more convenient *tracée* which is easier to defend—for all the world as though you were simply fortifying a city. . . . This circuit is utterly impregnable and indestructible at every point; it outshines all others; and no system of fortifications that was ever constructed before bears any resemblance to it.'[2]

In this passage, a literary contemporary of Marcus Aurelius, in whose anxious reign Rome's magnificent world-wall was beginning to crack, was re-expounding the theme of a writer of the preceding generation, in whose day the World's defences did indeed look impregnably secure. During the last two centuries, says Appian of Alexandria (*vivebat circa* A.D. 90–160) in the preface to his *Studies in Roman History*,

'The [Roman] State has reached its highest point of organisation and the public revenue its highest figure, while a long and stable peace has raised the whole World to a level of secure prosperity. A few more subject nations have been added by the Emperors to those already under the

[1] In the sentence immediately preceding the passage quoted above, Eduard Meyer suggests that 'the Empire of the Achaemenidae is the first state known to history to have put forward the claim to universality'. This is surely incorrect. The Sumeric universal state founded by Ur-Engur, *alias* Ur-Nammu (*imperabat circa* 2143–2126 or 2079–2062 B.C.), and re-established by Hammurabi (*imperabat circa* 1792–1750 or 1728–1686 B.C.), advertised a claim to universality by entitling itself 'The Realm of the Four Quarters'; and, though Hammurabi was a contemporary of the epigoni of the Egyptiac Twelfth Dynasty, we may guess that, from the standpoint of 'the Middle Empire', which was the Egyptiac universal state, even the Sumeric 'Realm of the Four Quarters' was an exception, hardly worth speaking of, to Pharaoh's universal rule even at a date when this had in truth fallen into decadence. 'The New Empire's' claim to universality is better attested than 'the Middle Empire's', and also better founded, since, in 'the New Empire's' day, 'the Realm of the Four Quarters' was extinct and its former dominions in Syria and Mesopotamia had become provinces or dependencies of the Emperors who were reigning at Thebes. The Emperor Ikhnaton, who broke so sharply with his predecessors' traditions on so many points, both cherished and accentuated their oecumenicalism. Universality was the leading note of his revolutionary cult of the Aton; and the impartial benevolence with which the Aton showed the light of His countenance to all peoples was symbolized in the foundation of an 'Aton city' in Nubia, and perhaps another in Syria, as counterparts of the original 'Aton city' which Ikhnaton had laid out in Middle Egypt on the site subsequently known as Tall-al-ʿAmarnah (see Breasted, J. H.: *The Development of Religion and Thought in Ancient Egypt* (London 1912, Hodder & Stoughton), pp. 322–3).

[2] Aristeides, P. Aelius: *In Romam*, edited by Keil, B., in *Aelii Aristidis Quae Supersunt Omnia*, vol. ii (Berlin 1898, Weidmann), pp. 114–15 (Or. XXVI, §§ 79–84).

Roman dominion, and others which have revolted have been reduced to obedience; but, since the Romans already possess the choicest portions of the land and water surface of the globe, they are wise enough to aim at retaining what they hold rather than at extending their empire to infinity over the poverty-stricken and unremunerative territories of uncivilized nations. I myself have seen representatives of such nations attending at Rome on diplomatic missions and offering to become her subjects, and the Emperor refusing to accept the allegiance of peoples who would be of no value to his government. There are other nations innumerable whose kings the Romans appoint themselves, since they feel no necessity to incorporate them into their Empire. There are also certain subject nations to whom they make grants from their treasury, because they are too proud to repudiate them in spite of their being a financial burden. They have garrisoned the frontiers of their Empire with a ring of powerful armies, and keep guard over this vast extent of land and sea as easily as if it were a modest farm.'[1]

In the view of an Appian and an Aelius Aristeides, the Roman Empire was eternal[2]

> sicut summarum summa est aeterna, neque extra
> qui locus est quo dissiliant neque corpora sunt quae
> possint incidere et validâ dissolvere plagâ.[3]

In the lines of the Latin poet, Democritus's argument looks as impregnable as the Roman *limes* itself.

> Nec rerum summam commutare ulla potest vis;
> nam neque quo possit genus ullum materiai
> effugere ex omni, quicquam est [extra], neque in omne
> unde coorta queat nova vis irrumpere et omnem
> naturam rerum mutare et vertere motus.[4]

A universal state has indeed as little to fear from outer barbarians as the Universe has from stray star clusters that are *ex hypothesi* non-existent; yet the argument is a fallacy nevertheless, for, as we have seen in an earlier context, 'things rot through evils native to their selves'.[5] In Physical Nature there are elements whose atoms disintegrate by spontaneous radiation, without requiring any bombardment from extraneous bodies; and, in human social life, universal states 'are betrayed by what is false within'[6] into revealing, for those who have eyes to see through their specious appearance of impregnability, that, so far from being immortal, these are spontaneously fissile polities.

[1] Appian of Alexandria: *Studies in Roman History*, Preface.

[2] A modern Western student of the religions that were contemporaries of Christianity traces to Syria the association, in Roman minds, of the idea of the Roman Empire's eternity with the idea of its universality:

'L'origine de cette association des deux idées doit sans doute être cherchée en Syrie, où un seul et même mot *'olmo* signifie *aevum* et *mundus*, de telle sorte que le même titre, qu'on trouve porté par un dieu, peut se traduire aussi bien par "maître du monde" que par "maître de l'éternité"' (Cumont, Fr.: 'L'Éternité des Empereurs Romains', in *Revue d'Histoire et de Littérature Religieuses*, vol. i (Paris 1896; printed at Macon), p. 450, n. 2).

[3] Lucretius: *De Rerum Natura*, Book V, ll. 361–3.

[4] Lucretius, op. cit., Book II, ll. 303–7.

[5] Menander, fragment 540, quoted in IV. iv, 120, n. 3.

[6] Meredith, George: *Modern Love*, stanza 43, last line, quoted in IV. iv. 120.

(II) THE DOOM OF TITHONUS

If it were the truth—as the course of history had so far invariably indicated it to be—that a universal state is not the goal of human endeavours, the watchword for citizens of universal states should be 'here have we no continuing city'.[1] Yet the impulse to idolize any institution is so strong,[2] and the particular institution with which we are here concerned wears so radiant a halo in the deceptive light cast by the mirage of immortality, that it is not surprising to find its citizens persistently mistaking this Gilead for the Promised Land, and translating their error into action by attempting to settle down there in comfort instead of proceeding manfully on their pilgrimage. Transjordan is indeed a better-watered and more smiling land than Palestine, and its woods and pastures appear to offer to the weary fugitive from the desert of a Time of Troubles a home which he can make his own without having to face the final ordeal of crossing Jordan's stream. The penalty of this intellectual and moral aberration is the doom of Tithonus.

An obscure divinity of the Nubian marches of the Egyptiac universal state[3] was transfigured by the genius of Hellenic mythology into a mortal king of the Ethiopians who had the misfortune to be loved by Eôs, the immortal Goddess of the Dawn. The goddess besought her fellow Olympians to confer on her human lover the immortality which she and her peers enjoyed; and, jealous though they were of their divine privileges, she teased them into yielding at last to her feminine importunity. Yet even this grudging gift was marred by a fatal flaw; for the eager goddess had forgotten that the Olympians' immortality was mated with an everlasting youth, and the other immortals had spitefully taken care to grant her no more than her bare request. The consequence was both ironic and tragic. After a honeymoon that flashed past in the twinkling of an Olympian eye, Eôs and her now immortal but still inexorably aging human mate found themselves condemned for eternity to grieve together over Tithonus's hapless plight. A senility to which the merciful hand of Death could never set a term was an affliction that no mortal man could ever be made to suffer, and an eternal grief was an obsession that left no room for any other thought or feeling.

The tragic irony of the Hellenic myth has been transposed into the realism of a Flemish picture by the sardonic imagination of Jonathan Swift in the character of Gulliver's cicerone on the air-borne island of Laputa.

'He gave me a particular account of the Struldbrugs among them. He said they commonly acted like mortals till about thirty years old, after which by degrees they grew melancholy and dejected, increasing in both till they came to fourscore. . . . When they came to fourscore years, which is reckoned the extremity of living in this country, they had not only all the follies and infirmities of other old men, but many more which arose from the dreadful prospects of never dying. They were not only opinionative,

1 Heb. xiii. 14.

2 For the idolization of institutions, see IV. iv. 303–423.

3 For the authentic god Tetwen, see Meyer, E.: *Geschichte des Altertums*, vol. i, Part II, 3rd ed. (Stuttgart and Berlin 1913, Cotta), p. 210.

peevish, covetous, morose, vain, talkative, but uncapable of friendship and dead to all natural affection. . . . Envy and impotent desires are their prevailing passions. But those objects against which their envy seems principally directed are the vices of the younger sort and the deaths of the old. By reflecting on the former, they find themselves cut off from all possibility of pleasure; and whenever they see a funeral they lament and repine that others are gone to an harbour of rest to which they themselves never can hope to arrive. They have no remembrance of anything but what they learned and observed in their youth and middle age, and even that is very imperfect. And, for the truth or particulars of any fact, it is safer to depend on common traditions than upon their best recollections. . .

'The language of this country being always upon the flux, the Struldbrugs of one age do not understand those of another, neither are they able after two hundred years to hold any conversation (farther than by a few general words) with their neighbours the mortals; and thus they lie under the disadvantage of living like foreigners in their own country. . . .

'They were the most mortifying sight I ever beheld. . . . Besides the usual deformities in extreme old age, they acquired an additional ghastliness, in proportion to their number of years, which is not to be described; and among half a dozen I soon distinguished which was the eldest, although there was not above a century or two between them.'[1]

For any human soul or human institution, an immortality in This World would prove a martyrdom, even if it were unaccompanied by either physical decrepitude or mental senility.

Eadem sunt omnia semper.
si tibi non annis corpus iam marcet et artus
confecti languent, eadem tamen omnia restant,
omnia si pergas vivendo vincere saecla,
atque etiam potius, si nunquam sis moriturus.[2]

'In this sense it would be true to say that any man of forty who is endowed with moderate intelligence has seen—in the light of the uniformity of Nature—the entire Past and Future';[3] and, if this estimate of the capacity of human souls for experience strikes the reader as an inordinately low one, he may find the reason in the character of the age in which the philosopher-emperor happened to live; for an 'Indian Summer' is an age of boredom. The price of the Roman Peace was the forfeiture of Hellenic liberty;[4] and, though that liberty might always have been the privilege of a minority, and this privileged minority might latterly have turned irresponsible and oppressive,[5] it was manifest in retrospect that the turbulent wickedness of the Ciceronian climax of an Hellenic 'Time of Troubles' had provided a wealth of exciting and inspiring themes for Roman public speakers which their epigoni in a smugly ordered Trajanic epoch might conventionally condemn as

[1] Swift, Jonathan: *Travels into Several Remote Nations of the World by Lemuel Gulliver*, Part III: 'A Voyage to Laputa, &c.', chap. x.

[2] Lucretius: *De Rerum Natura*, Book III, ll. 945–9.

[3] Aurelius Antoninus, Marcus: *Meditations*, Book XI, ch. 1, quoted in VI. vi. 137.

[4] 'Caesar Augustus . . . dedit . . . iura quis pace et principe uteremur' (Tacitus: *Annals*, Book III, chap. 28).

[5] 'Corruptissimâ re publicâ plurimae leges . . . continua discordia, non mos, non ius; deterrima quaeque impune ac multa honesta exitio fuere' (Tacitus, loc. cit.).

horrors not *nostri saeculi*[1] but must secretly envy as they found themselves perpetually failing in their laborious efforts to substitute far-fetched artifice for the stimulus of importunate life.[2]

The doom of Tithonus may overtake a whole society as well as an individual soul.

> 'Un peuple marche, vit, fonctionne, souvent même grandit après que le mobile générateur de sa vie et de sa gloire a cessé d'être.'[3]

On the morrow of the breakdown of the Hellenic Society, Plato, seeking anxiously to safeguard the Hellenic Civilization against a further fall by pegging it in a securely rigid posture,[4] had idealized the comparative stability of the Egyptiac culture;[5] and a thousand years later, when this Egyptiac culture was still in being while the Hellenic Civilization had arrived at its last agonies, the last of the Neoplatonists pushed their reputed master's sentimentality to an almost frenzied pitch of uncritical adoration.[6]

Thanks to the obstinacy of the Egyptiac universal state in again and again insisting on returning to life after its body, like Êr's, had been duly laid upon the salutary funeral pyre,[7] the Egyptiac Society lived to see its contemporaries—the Minoan and Sumeric civilizations and the Indus Culture—all pass away and give place to successors of a younger generation, some of which passed away in their turn while the Egyptiac Society still kept alive. Egyptiac students of history could have observed—if they had had the curiosity to observe—the birth and death of the First Syriac,[8] Hittite, and Babylonic offspring of the Sumeric Civilization, and the rise and decline of the Syriac and Hellenic offspring of the Minoan. Yet, even if they had made the most of this intellectual opportunity, would it have been worth the spiritual price? The fabulously long-drawn-out epilogue to the broken-down Egyptiac Society's natural term of life[9] was an alternation between dull stretches of boredom, in which the victim lay prone, an ἄχθος ἀρούρης,[10] in a cataleptic trance, and hectic bouts of demonic energy into which this somnolent society was galvanized by the impacts of alien bodies social.

The Egyptiac reactions to these impacts of foreign bodies may be likened to the successive explosions that keep a jet-plane in the air. The first recurrence of the Egyptiac universal state in the form of 'the New Empire' was a consequence of Amosis' 'Zealot' reaction against the tincture of Sumeric culture in the Hyksos barbarians who had swooped

[1] Traianus, Marcus Ulpius, in *Correspondence between C. Plinius Secundus and M. Ulpius Traianus*, Letter xcvii [xcviii].

[2] This point is made by Tacitus in his *Dialogus de Oratoribus*, chap. 36, § 1, chap. 38, § 2, and chap. 41, § 5, quoted in V. vi. 80, n. 5.

[3] De Gobineau, J. A.: *Essai sur l'Inégalité des Races Humaines* (Paris 1853–5, Firmin-Didot, 4 vols.), vol. i, p. 52.

[4] For this practical purpose of the construction of utopias, see III. iii. 88–106.

[5] See, for example, *Timaeus*, 21A–25D, especially the passages quoted in IV. iv. 24–25.

[6] For the êthos of these cranky but not ignoble fighters of Hellenism's last rearguard action, see V. v. 565–7 and 680–3.

[7] For the myth of Êr the Armenian, see Plato: *Respublica*, Book X, 614B–621D, to which Aelius Aristeides alludes in the passage cited on p. 44, above.

[8] For this abortive First Syriac Civilization, see II. ii. 388–91.

[9] See I. i. 136–46 and IV. iv. 84–86.

[10] *Iliad*, Book XVIII, l. 104, *et alibi*.

down to batten on the carcass of 'the Middle Empire' after this original Egyptiac universal state had gone into dissolution in due course.[1] The subsequent re-establishment of the Egyptiac universal state in the northern half of the Egyptiac World under the Saïte régime was a consequence of the 'Zealot' reaction of Psammetichus I (*imperabat* 663–609 B.C.)[2] against the Babylonic culture of Assyrian invaders.[3] Psammetichus and his Saïte successors liberated Egypt from the Assyrians, and kept her free from the Assyrians' Neo-Babylonian successors, by employing the prowess of Ionian and Carian mercenaries. The infiltration of Hellenic culture that seeped into Egypt in the wake of these 'brazen men from the sea'[4] produced, within a hundred years, a 'Zealot' reaction against Hellenism in which Amasis (*dominabatur* 566–526 B.C.) usurped the throne of the too complacently xenophile Saïtes with a popular mandate to put the intrusive Hellenes in their place. The Achaemenian conquest of Egypt *circa* 525 B.C.—which the conqueror, Cambyses, rendered doubly odious by persecuting the Egyptiac religion and culture with an un-Achaemenian intolerance[5]—evoked a spate of insurrections, the first in 485–484 B.C., the second lasting from 465 to 449, and the third from 404 to 343, that gave Egypt successive interludes of freedom from alien rule. The Achaemenian reconquest of Egypt in 343 B.C. was final only because it was followed within the next few years by a Macedonian conquest of the whole Achaemenian Empire. Yet the Egyptiac capacity for provocation by alien impacts was not exhausted. The Macedonian conquest of Egypt in 332 B.C. was followed, before the close of the third century B.C., by a fresh spate of insurrections,[6] through which the native Egyptiac community wrung notable concessions from their Hellenic masters. It was not till after the Ptolemaic had given place to a Roman régime that these explosions of xenophobia which had been following one another in the Egyptiac World since the sixteenth century B.C. gave way at last to a counter-movement towards assimilation that culminated in the conversion of the provincial capitals (*metropoleis*) of the 'nomes' into simulacra of Hellenic city-states;[7] and it was not till the fifth century of the Christian Era that this long-delayed liquidation of the petrified Egyptiac culture was completed by a mass-conversion to Christianity.[8]

1 See I. i. 138–9; II. ii. 112; V. v. 351–3; and V. vi. 190.

2 See II. ii. 116 and IV. iv. 476.

3 The Psammetichan reaction seems to have surpassed the Amosan in vehemence, if this can be measured in terms of Archaism. The Archaists of the Eighteenth Dynasty, under the mild stimulus of the Sumeric tincture in the Hyksos, sought to leap no farther back up the stream of Egyptiac history than the age of 'the Middle Empire'; the Archaists of the Twenty-Sixth Dynasty, more violently stimulated by the full-blooded Babylonic Civilization of the Assyrians, sought to carry their flying leap right back to the age of 'the Old Kingdom'.

4 Herodotus, Book II, chap. 152.

5 See V. v. 704–5.

6 The first of these native Egyptiac revolts against the Ptolemaic régime broke out *circa* 213/212 B.C. according to *The Cambridge Ancient History*, vol. vii (Cambridge 1928, University Press), pp. 151–2; in 216 B.C. according to Tarn, W. W.: *The Hellenistic Age* (London 1927, Arnold), pp. 161–4. The next insurrection followed *circa* 189–184 B.C.

7 See IX. viii. 408 and 586.

8 Even this final apostasy from their ancestral civilization did not cure the Egyptians of a xenophobia which, by that time, had been their breath of life for two thousand years. The Christianity to which they and their Hellenic contemporaries were simultaneously converted did not bridge the gulf between the Egyptians and their alien masters. Before the fifth century was over, the Egyptians had transferred their religious allegiance from the Catholic—or, as they termed it, 'Imperial' (Melchite)—Church (see II. ii. 236, n. 1,

The same rhythm of trance-like somnolence alternating with outbursts of fanatical xenophobia can be discerned in the epilogue to the history of the Far Eastern Civilization in China.[1] The tincture of Far Eastern Christian culture in the Mongols who had forced upon China an alien universal state evoked a reaction in which the Mongols were evicted and their dominion over China was replaced by the indigenous universal state of the Ming. Even the Manchu barbarians, who stepped into a political vacuum created by the Ming's collapse and whose taint of Far Eastern Christian culture was less noticeable than their receptivity in adopting the Chinese way of life, aroused a popular opposition which, in Southern China at any rate, never ceased to maintain itself underground and broke out into the open again at last in the T'aip'ing insurrection of A.D. 1852–64.[2] The infiltration of the Early Modern Western Civilization, in its Catholic Christian form, in the sixteenth and seventeenth centuries of the Christian Era provoked the proscription of Catholicism in the first quarter of the eighteenth century. The blasting open of the sea-gates of China for Western trade by military force between A.D. 1839 and A.D. 1861 provoked the retort in kind of the anti-Western 'Boxer' Rising of A.D. 1900; and the Manchu Dynasty was overthrown in A.D. 1911 in retribution for the double crime of being ineradicably alien itself and at the same time showing itself incompetent to keep the now far more formidable alien force of Western penetration at bay.[3]

In the trance-like phases of this ghastly alternating rhythm, the Egyptiac and the Chinese Society recall the figure of Lot's wife transformed into a pillar of salt as the retribution for her forbidden backward glance at the perishing Cities of the Plain. In the furious bouts in

and IV. iv. 86) to a Monophysitism that could serve them as an expression of their anti-Hellenic feelings. This 'cultural isolationism' survived down to the twentieth century of the Christian Era, some seven centuries after the mass-conversion of all but a small minority of the Egyptian people from Monophysitism to Islam and after the complete replacement of Coptic by Arabic as the living language of Christian and Muslim Egyptians alike. In the twentieth century of the Christian Era, when a Westernizing Egyptian intelligentsia was aspiring to make Egypt the cultural and perhaps even the political metropolis of the Arabic World of the day, the Egyptian fallāhīn—Arabic-speaking Muslims though they now were—felt no more at home with their Asiatic Arab co-religionists than their progenitors had felt with the Hyksos, Assyrians, Persians, and Hellenes. The home-sickness of the Egyptian labour corps that had been sent to Palestine and ʿIrāq during the war of A.D. 1914–18 was one of the causes of the Egyptian insurrection of A.D. 1919 against a British régime.

1 See IV. iv. 86–88; V. v. 3–4, 54, and 348–51.

2 For the T'aip'ing insurrection, see V. v. 107 and 112. Since the T'aip'ing movement was to some extent stimulated by Western Protestantism, its suppression by the Imperial Government was also in some sense an anti-alien movement, like the contemporary suppression of the Muslim insurrections in Kansu and Yunnan. But the Imperial Government did not get the upper hand over the Western-stimulated T'aip'ing until it had itself enlisted Western military leadership and organization by placing its own forces under the command of General Gordon (see V. vi. 208).

3 The 'Boxer' Rising was anti-Manchu mainly for the reason that the decrepit Manchu régime of the day was only ineffectively anti-Western. From the T'aip'ing insurrection onwards, all Chinese revolts that were directly anti-Manchu were also indirectly anti-Western. We are reminded of the anti-Western impetus of the Wahhābī reaction against the Ottoman Empire of Sultan Selīm III and the Mahdist reaction against the Egypt of Khedive Ismāʿīl (see IV. iv. 76–78; V. v. 294–6, 329, and 333–4; and IX. viii. 601–2). The two subsequent counter-movements towards assimilation—to Western culture through the Kuomintang and to Russian culture through Communism—were counterparts of the successive conversions of an Egyptiac Society to Hellenism and to Christianity under the Roman Empire.

which these same societies are galvanized into action by the stimulus of an alien energy that they abhor, they call up the more horrifying image of Life-in-Death as she displayed herself to the Ancient Mariner.

The western wave was all aflame,
The day was wellnigh done!
Almost upon the western wave
Rested the broad, bright Sun;
When that strange shape drove suddenly
Betwixt us and the Sun. . . .

Are those her ribs through which the Sun
Did peer, as through a grate?
And is that woman all her crew?
Is that a Death? and are there two?
Is Death that woman's mate?

Her lips were red, her looks were free,
Her locks were yellow as gold:
Her skin was as white as leprosy,
The Nightmare Life-in-Death was she
Who thicks man's blood with cold.[1]

Happily in this instance life is kinder than legend, for the sentence of immortality that mythology has passed on Tithonus and the Struldbrugs is commuted in real life to a not interminable longevity. Marcus's disillusioned man of forty must die at last though he may outlive his zest for life by fifty or sixty years; and a universal state that kicks again and again against the pricks of death will weather away, in the course of ages, like the pillar of salt that was fabled to be the petrified substance of a once living woman. The struggle for the dreadful prize of immortality is actually foredoomed to failure.

Nec prorsum vitam ducendo demimus hilum
tempore de mortis nec delibare valemus
quo minus esse diu possimus forte perempti.
proinde licet quot vis vivendo condere saecla:
mors aeterna tamen nilo minus illa manebit,
nec minus ille diu iam non erit, ex hodierno
lumine qui finem vitai fecit, et ille
mensibus atque annis qui multis occidit ante.[2]

[1] Coleridge, S. T.: *The Rime of the Ancient Mariner*. In XII. ix. 412–13 this image is applied to the Western Civilization's situation in the twentieth century of the Christian Era.

[2] Lucretius: *De Rerum Natura*, Book III, ll. 1087–94.

C. UNIVERSAL STATES AS MEANS

(I) THE PRICE OF EUTHANASIA

THE attempt to secure immortality in This World is a vain effort, whether blind or deliberate, to thwart the economy of Nature.

> Cedit enim rerum novitate extrusa vetustas
> semper, et ex aliis aliud reparare necessest . .
> materies opus est ut crescant postera saecla;
> quae tamen omnia te vitâ perfuncta sequentur;
> nec minus ergo ante haec quam tu cecidere, cadentque.
> sic alid ex alio nunquam desistet oriri,
> vitaque mancipio nulli datur, omnibus usu.[1]

The fate of Tithonus testifies that 'whosoever will save his life shall lose it'; but is it likewise true that 'whosoever will lose his life for My sake, the same shall save it?'[2] In an earlier version of this saying, it is driven home still more pointedly that the sacrifice has to be altruistic in order to be efficacious. 'Whosoever shall lose his life for My sake and the Gospel's, the same shall save it.'[3] On this showing, a universal state that eschews the vain quest for immortality and aspires to euthanasia must emulate the Phoenix. It must not only sacrifice its own life; it must make this sacrifice for the sake of something beyond itself. Such voluntary altruism is unheard-of in any universal state and indeed in any institution, since the besetting sin of all institutions is to become idolized ends in themselves.[4] There had indeed been universal states which, through a fortunate failure to bring upon themselves Tithonus's fate, had won the Phoenix's reward without having risen to the Phoenix's virtue. The Phoenix's reward for the agony of being burnt alive is to conjure up his own double out of his ashes; and there had been universal states which, by dying betimes, had won this reward for the moribund civilizations of which they had been the last political embodiments. For example, the Western and Orthodox Christian civilizations had sprung from the ashes of the Roman Empire,[5] which had been the Hellenic universal state; the Iranic and Arabic civilizations from the ashes of the 'Abbasid Caliphate,[6] which had been the Syriac universal state; the Hellenic and Syriac civilizations themselves from the ashes of Cnossos, the seat of 'the thalassocracy of Minos';[7] the Babylonic and Hittite civilizations, and perhaps the Indic Civilization too, from the ashes of the Empire of the Four Quarters,[8] which had been the Sumeric universal state; the Hindu Civilization from the ashes of the Guptan Empire,[9] which had been the Indic universal state; the Far Eastern Civilization from the ashes of the Han Empire,[10] which had been the Sinic universal state; the Mexic and Yucatec civilizations from the ashes of the 'First Empire' of the Mayas,[11] which had been the Mayan universal state and

1 Lucretius: op. cit., Book III, ll. 964–5 and 967–71, quoted in I. i. 48.
2 Luke ix. 24; cf. Matt. xvi. 25 and x. 39.
3 Mark viii. 35.
4 See IV. iv. 303–423.
5 See xi, maps 33 and 34.
6 See xi, map 50.
7 See xi, maps 15 and 16.
8 See xi, map 11.
9 See xi, map 30.
10 See xi, maps 27A and 28.
11 See xi, maps 70 and 71.

which, on one interpretation of the fragmentary and cryptic evidence as to the circumstances of its demise, would have been the only universal state so far known to history that had gone into voluntary liquidation.[1] It is indeed something of a miracle that an institution that is a by-product of social disintegration should play any part at all in a fresh act of creation. Yet, before we attempt to assess what the Phoenix's reward amounts to, we must ask ourselves whether the mere reproduction of its own kind is after all the highest purpose that a broken-down civilization can hope to serve. We will not beg that question, but will reserve it for discussion later.[2] What concerns us in our present inquiry is the possibility that a universal state may find euthanasia in spite of itself; and we can see at once that this unsought and unmerited good fortune can only be obtained through the tender mercy of God in the guise of stern compulsion.

> 'Lead me, O Zeus, and thou too, Fate, to that goal, whatsoe'er it be, to which ye have posted me. I will follow without flinching—though, if I turn coward and hang back, I shall follow just the same.'[3]

The hard but saving truth thus baldly stated by a Stoic philosopher has been expressed by a Christian seer in more movingly mysterious words.

> 'When thou wast young, thou girdedst thyself and walkedst whither thou wouldest; but, when thou shalt be old, thou shalt stretch forth thy hands and another shall gird thee and carry thee whither thou wouldest not.'[4]

The grace of God can lead even the reluctant soul or society into sharing in God's creative work. In the simile of the sowing of the seed[5] the issue between freedom and compulsion is left dormant.

The destinies of universal states thus prove to be paradoxical. These imposing polities are, as we have seen,[6] the last works of dominant minorities in the disintegrating bodies social of moribund civilizations, and these dominant minorities are far indeed from consciously accepting the role of self-abnegation that is evidently the only condition on which their latest handiwork can bear fruit. Their conscious purpose, in every case, is to preserve themselves by conserving the wasting energies of the society with whose fortunes their own are bound up, and their intention in establishing a universal state is to use it as a means to this self-regarding end. This intention, however, is never fulfilled. A universal state, however long its life may be drawn out, always proves to have been the last phase of a society before its extinction, and the pursuit of the mirage of immortality, into which a dominant minority is misled through mistaking its ephemeral universal state for the goal of human endeavours, leads the deluded pursuer towards the unsuspected and uninviting goal of petrifaction, from which the only means of release is the ignominious

[1] For alternative possible explanations of the abandonment of the cities of the First Empire of the Mayas, see Morley, S. G.: *The Ancient Maya* (Palo Alto, Cal. 1946, Stanford University Press), pp. 67–72, and the present Study, I. i. 125–6 and II. ii. 413–20.

[2] On pp. 422–3, below.

[3] Cleanthes: *Hymn to Zeus*. The original Greek text has been quoted from von Arnim, J.: *Stoicorum Veterum Fragmenta*, vol. i (Berlin and Leipzig 1905, Teubner), p. 118, in III. iii. 47, n. 1, and in V. v. 421.

[4] John xxi. 18.

[5] See III. iii. 256–9 and V. vi. 99.

[6] In V. v. 35–57.

fate of eventually being swallowed up and assimilated by an alien civilization.[1] If a dominant minority takes the contrary path that leads through self-abnegation to a fresh opportunity for sharing in a creative act, it always does so in spite of itself. A dominant minority is incapable either of the resignation with which Moses accepted the sentence that he should see the Promised Land, but should not go over thither, or of the selflessness with which he carried out his instructions to charge, encourage, and strengthen his designated successor Joshua for the enviable mission of reaping the fruits of Moses' own thankless labours.[2] A dominant minority will never show the generosity of David in assembling the materials for a Temple which not he but Solomon is to build,[3] or the humility of John the Baptist in confessing 'I am not the Christ';[4] 'he that cometh after me is preferred before me';[5] 'he must increase, but I must decrease'.[6] The actor who has thus been forced into playing the forerunner's part after having failed in an attempt to pose as the heir of the Kingdom[7] is not a sublime or sympathetic figure; yet even a grudging performance may fulfil the playwright's purpose by carrying out his plot to its designed denouement.

The makers and masters of a universal state have perhaps one excuse for thus kicking against the pricks. However low their handiwork may rank in the general scale of creative achievements, it is at any rate indisputably the highest representative of its kind. Whereas parochial states prey on one another, and for this pernicious purpose cause human beings to shed one another's blood and to regard an anti-social practice as a public virtue, universal states come into existence in order to put a stop to wars and to substitute co-operation for bloodshed. If even universal states prove to be, not permanent ends in themselves, but merely ephemeral creatures whose happiest destiny is to find euthanasia by spending themselves in the service of others, this suggests that, in the hierarchy of human institutions, the place of states in general must be a relatively low one.

If a universal state finds its significance as a means for the performance of services, who are its beneficiaries? They must be one or other of three possible candidates for the part—the internal proletariat or external proletariat of the moribund society itself, or some alien civilization which is its contemporary—and in serving the internal proletariat a universal state will be ministering to one of the higher religions that make their epiphany in the internal proletariat's bosom. In the traditional language of an outgoing Early Modern Age of Western Christian history,

'Tous les grands empires que nous avons vus sur la terre ont concouru par divers moyens au bien de la Religion et à la gloire de Dieu, comme Dieu même l'a déclaré par ses prophètes.'[8]

1 For this fate, which is one of the alternative possible ends of a disintegrating civilization, see IV. iv. 76–114.

2 Deut. xxxiv. 1–6; cf. Deut. iii. 23–28 and Num. xxvii. 12–14.

3 1 Chron. xxii.

4 John i. 20 and iii. 28.

5 John i. 15.

6 John iii. 30.

7 For the relation between heirs of the Kingdom and their forerunners in the series of saviours with the sword, see V. vi. 185–95.

8 Bossuet, J.-B.: *Discours sur l'Histoire Universelle*, 3rd ed. (Paris 1700), Troisième Partie, chap. i.

(II) SERVICES AND BENEFICIARIES

(a) THE CONDUCTIVITY OF UNIVERSAL STATES

Our next task is to make an empirical survey of the services involuntarily offered by universal states and of the uses made of these facilities by internal proletariats, external proletariats, and alien civilizations; but we have first to find the answer to a preliminary question: How can any services at all be rendered to anyone by an institution that is passive, conservative, archaistic, and in fact negative in every respect?

'The world empire of Rome was a negative phenomenon: the result, not of any surplus of power on the one side (the Romans ceased to enjoy that after [their victory at] Zama), but of an absence of resistance on the other side. It would be quite untrue to say that the Romans conquered the World. They merely took possession of something that was lying about for anyone to pick up. The Roman Empire was brought into existence, not by an extreme exertion of Rome's total military and financial energies, as these had once been exerted against Carthage, but through a renunciation, by the contemporary Oriental World, of the externals of self-determination. . . . The petrified remains of Imperialism are to be seen in empires like the Egyptian, the Chinese and the Roman and in societies like the Indian World and the World of Islam, which remain in existence for hundreds and thousands of years and may pass from one conqueror's hand to another's: dead bodies, shapeless masses of humanity from which the soul has departed, the used-up material of a great historical past.[1] The imperialism that leaves such débris is the typical symptom of social dissolution.'[2]

How—in terms of the expressive Sinic notation for the rhythm of the Universe[3]—can so unpromising a Yin-state give rise to a new burst of Yang-activity? It is easy, of course, to see that, if once a spark of creative energy has been kindled in the shelter of a universal state, it will have a chance of swelling into a steady flame which it might never have had if it had been exposed to the buffeting blast of a Time of Troubles. The establishment of a universal state marks the beginning of the second rally in the succession of bouts of the rhythm of Rout-and-Rally through which the life of a civilization runs out from breakdown to dissolution,[4] and this second rally is usually the most vigorous in the series. But this service, though valuable, is negative. What feature in the social situation arising under a universal state is the positive source of that new capacity to create, which is the supreme benefit that a universal state confers on its beneficiaries, though it is apparently unable to profit by it for its own account? Perhaps one clue is to be found in the tendency shown by

[1] This aspect of the psychological condition of the subject populations of universal states has been discussed in the present Study in V. v. 60–95.—A.J.T.

[2] Spengler, Oswald: *Der Untergang des Abendlandes*, vol. i, 11th–14th edition (Munich 1920, Beck), p. 51. Cp. vol. ii, 1st–15th edition (Munich 1922, Beck), p. 529, quoted in V. v. 620, n. 1. The pith of the point that Spengler is making in these two passages is concentrated in Francis Bacon's dictum, quoted on p. 110, below, that 'it was not the Romans that spread upon the World, but it was the World that spread upon the Romans'.

[3] For the Sinic conception of Yin and Yang, see II. i. 201–3.

[4] This rhythm of disintegration has been analysed in V. vi. 278–87.

Archaism to defeat itself by being inveigled into construction in its efforts to justify itself by 'making things work'.[1]

A universal state is pushed into constructive action primarily, no doubt, by the impulse, which is strong in every state, to work for its own self-preservation and do whatever may prove necessary for this purpose. But, though this impulse may be the primary one, it is not the predominant one in this case; for a universal state is not subject to the pressure from other representatives of its kind which is so potent an influence in the life of parochial states—especially at the climax of a Time of Troubles, when the struggle for existence between the warring parochial states of a disintegrating society is apt to attain its highest degree of intensity. The establishment of a universal state brings with it an abrupt transition from internecine warfare to profound peace; and the victims of a change that is a blessing for Society as a whole might appraise the victorious empire-builders' achievement by applying to it the ironic judgement: 'Ubi solitudinem faciunt, pacem appellant.'[2] A universal state is established through a knock-out blow by which some single parochial state wipes all competitors off the map and so emerges from the struggle as the sole survivor. A universal state is *ex hypothesi* unique within its own world; and the prestige of this uniqueness works together with the *vis inertiae* of an exhausted society to keep a universal state in being when once it has come into existence. A universal state on the morrow of its foundation thus has little cause to be concerned over its own security. Instances can, no doubt, be found in which this has been the motive of a universal state's policy. For example, the first founder of the Sinic universal state, Ts'in She Hwang-ti, deliberately obliterated the old inter-state frontiers and remapped his now unified Sinic World into a new pattern of artificial provinces which cut across the old pattern of historic principalities; and the second founder, Han Liu Pang, who began by discarding Ts'in She Hwang-ti's new political map as an unnecessarily revolutionary innovation, was led by his own experience virtually to reimpose it.[3] The Napoleonic Empire,[4] which was the abortive universal state of the medieval Western city-state cosmos,[5] employed the same device in its efforts to wipe out the traces of the states that it had supplanted.[6] Again, the Inca makers and masters of an Andean universal state modified and systematized the institutions of the conquered peoples, though this without destroying them;[7] and the Imperial Roman Government displayed what might seem to be an excessive nervousness in suppressing all manner of private associations, and showing some suspicion even of such humble and apparently harmless varieties of the species as friendly societies and funeral clubs. Such symptoms are, however, rare on the whole, and this is an indication

[1] This self-defeat of Archaism has been examined in V. vi. 94–97.

[2] Tacitus: *Agricola*, chap. 30, § 7.

[3] See pp. 169–74, below.

[4] See xi, map 60.

[5] See V. v. 619–42.

[6] This remapping of the medieval Western city-state cosmos by Napoleon and of the Sinic World by Ts'in She Hwang-ti and Han Liu Pang is an instance of the breach in institutions that is one of the manifestations of Futurism (see V. vi. 107–11).

[7] See Markham, Sir C.: *The Incas of Peru* (London 1910, Smith Elder), p. 161. See also the other authorities quoted in the present Study, V. v. 90, n. 2.

that, in the policy of universal states, the motive of self-preservation does not play an important part.

A different motive for action, which is strong in proportion to the weakness of the universal state's concern for self-preservation, is supplied by the need for conserving, not a state that is universal in virtue of having no surviving competitors, but the society itself that has been unified politically in the universal state—or, rather, what remains of this society and its institutions by the time when the tardy and violent imposition of peace by a single surviving Power has put an end at last to the long-drawn-out and ever-mounting agony of a Time of Troubles. In the course of that terrible experience, most of the institutions inherited from the age of growth have either been destroyed outright or else been so badly hurt that, even after the process of attrition has been arrested by the establishment of the universal state, they crumble and collapse, one after another, through the delayed but inescapable effects of fatal injuries previously received. The inclusion of the surviving fabric of the shattered society within the universal state's political framework does not avail either to restore what has already perished or to prevent the progressive collapse of the remainder; and the menace of this immense and constantly extending social vacuum compels the Government of the universal state to act against its own inclinations by constructing stop-gap institutions to fill the void, as the only means open to it of conserving Society itself—the fundamental task that is the universal state's *raison d'être*.

A classic illustration of this necessity of stepping ever farther into an ever-widening breach is afforded by the administrative history of the Roman Empire during the two centuries following its establishment in 31 B.C. as a result of the Battle of Actium. The Roman *arcanum imperii* was the principle of indirect rule. The Hellenic universal state was conceived of by its Roman founders as an association of self-governing city-states[1] with a fringe of autonomous principalities in regions where the Hellenic culture had not yet struck political root. The burden of administration—which, even at the end of an Hellenic Time of Troubles, was still, in the public estimation, an honourable and covetable load—was to be left resting on the shoulders of these responsible self-governing local authorities; the Imperial Government was to confine itself to the twofold task of keeping the local communities in harmony with one another and protecting them against attack on the part of the outer barbarians; and, for these limited Imperial activities, a slender military framework and light political superstructure were all that was required. This fundamental policy was never deliberately revised; yet, if we resurvey the Roman Empire as it emerged from a spell of two centuries of Roman Peace, we shall find that its administrative structure had in fact been transformed as a result of innovations that were reluctant and piecemeal but were far-reaching in their cumulative effect because they were all in the same direction.

By the end of the reign of Marcus Aurelius (*imperabat* A.D. 161–80) the last of the client principalities had been *gleichgeschaltet* with the

[1] See IV. iv. 310.

provinces,[1] and, more significant still, the provinces themselves had become organs of direct administration instead of remaining mere frameworks for local groups of self-administering city-states. The cause of these far-going moves towards a centralization of world-government was not any desire on the part of the Imperial authorities to take over the responsibility for details; it was a progressive loss of efficiency on the part of the local authorities that forced the Imperial Government to step in. In the generation of Augustus the government provided by client princes of the stamp of Herod the Great had in general been as effective as it had been ruthless. Among other things, it had been observed that these were more active than the Roman governors of adjoining provinces in defending their territories against the raids of pirates from beyond the pale.[2] The city-states, again, whatever their juridical status, had been mostly successful in still finding sufficient numbers of citizens of sufficient public spirit, integrity, ability, and affluence to administer their affairs without remuneration and to consider themselves richly rewarded by the honour and prestige which local office still carried with it. In the course of the next two centuries the human resources for the conduct of local government gradually ran dry, and the Central Government, faced with this increasing dearth of the local administrative talent on which it had been accustomed to rely, found itself constrained not only to replace client princes by Imperial governors but to put the administration of the city-states in the hands of 'city managers' who were appointed by the Imperial authorities instead of being elected (as the city-state magistrates were) by the local notables, and who were responsible, through the provincial governor, to the Emperor himself.

In the second century of the Empire's existence, at the very opening of a delusive 'Indian Summer',[3] we can follow the progress of this disquieting administrative development in the famous correspondence between the Emperor Trajan (*imperabat* A.D. 98–117) and his friend and subordinate Pliny the Younger during the latter's term of service as governor of the province of Bithynia. Before the end of the story, the whole administration of the Roman Empire, from top to bottom, had passed into the hands of a hierarchically organized bureaucracy, while the self-complacent local magistrates and town councillors of the once self-governing city-states had been degraded into becoming the unwilling

[1] See further p. 166, below. The religious consequences of this process of *Gleichschaltung*—which is not a peculiarity of the Roman Empire but is characteristic of universal states as a species—have been touched upon in V. vi. 36.

[2] Strabo, writing on the morrow of the establishment of the Augustan Peace, makes the following observation at the end of his description of the piratical raids into the domain of the Hellenic universal state which were at that time the main source of livelihood for the barbarians (Achaei, Zygi, Heniochi) inhabiting the strip of inhospitable country between the crest of the North-Western Caucasus Range and the north-eastern coast of the Black Sea:

'In places under [the] autocratic rule [of princes of client states of the Roman Empire] the victims [of these piratical raids] are afforded some protection by their rulers; for the princes make frequent counter-attacks and bring the war-canoes down, crews and all. The territory under direct Roman administration receives less effective protection owing to the indifference shown by the non-permanent lieutenant-governors sent out from Rome' (Strabo: *Geographica*, Book XI, chap. ii, § 12 (C 496)).

[3] For these 'Indian Summers' in the lives of universal states, see IV. iv. 58–70.

instruments of the central exchequer for extracting ruinously heavy taxes from the local notables.[1]

The central authorities themselves had been no more eager to impose these changes than the local authorities had been to suffer them. Both alike had been the victims of *force majeure*; and, in yielding to such necessity, the government of a universal state is indeed defeating its own ends, since the new institutions which it reluctantly constructs with a conservative intention inevitably have an innovating effect. The consequences are revolutionary because these new institutions are highly 'conductive'. In a previous context[2] we have seen that two leading motifs in the *Zeitgeist* of an age of social disintegration are a sense of promiscuity and a sense of unity; and, though these two psychological tendencies may be antithetical from the subjective standpoint, they conspire to produce an identical objective result. Receptivity is a distinguishing mark of the empire-builders themselves,[3] notwithstanding their conservative intentions, and this undesired and unvalued characteristic of theirs may have been one of the causes of their victory in their life-and-death struggle, during a Time of Troubles, with their competitors in command of the other parochial states of their world for the prize of surviving to become the founders of the ultimate universal state. This dominant spirit of the age endows the new stop-gap institutions thrown up by a universal state with a 'conductivity' comparable to that which the Ocean and the Steppe derive, not from a human psychological atmosphere, but from their own physical nature.[4]

> 'As the surface of the Earth bears all Mankind, so Rome receives all the peoples of the Earth into her bosom, as the rivers are received by the sea.'[5]

And the spectacle of the same universal state had suggested the same simile to the writer of this Study, before he had become acquainted with the passage, just quoted, from the pen of a Greek man of letters who knew the Roman Empire at first hand during the last days of its 'Indian Summer'.

"The writer can best express his personal feeling about the Empire in a parable. It was like the sea round whose shores its network of city-states was strung. The Mediterranean seems at first sight a poor substitute for the rivers that have given their waters to make it. Those were living waters, whether they ran muddy or clear; the sea seems just salt and still and dead. But, as soon as we study the sea, we find movement and life there also. There are silent currents circulating perpetually from one part to another, and the surface water that seems to be lost by evaporation is not really lost, but will descend in distant places and seasons, with its bitterness all distilled away, as life-giving rain. And, as these surface-waters are drawn off into the clouds, their place is taken by lower layers continually rising from the depths. The sea itself is in constant and creative motion, but the influence of this great body of water extends far beyond its shores.

[1] See III. iii. 99–100.

[2] In V. v. 439–568 and V. vi. 1–49.

[3] See V. v. 439–45.

[4] The conductivity of Nomadism has been noticed in III. iii. 391–4.

[5] Aristeides, P. Aelius: *In Romam*, § 62 in B. Keil's edition (*Aelii Aristidis Quae Supersunt Omnia*, vol. ii (Berlin 1898, Weidmann), p. 108), quoted in V. v. 344.

One finds it softening the extremes of temperature, quickening the vegetation, and prospering the life of animals and men, in the distant heart of continents and among peoples that have never heard its name.'[1]

The social movements that make their way through the conductive medium of a universal state are in fact both horizontal and vertical. Examples of horizontal motion are the circulation of medicinal herbs in the Roman Empire and the spread of the use of paper from the eastern to the western extremity of the Arab Caliphate.

'Different herbs', says Pliny the Elder, 'are brought from different quarters to and fro all over the World for the welfare of the Human Race. The immense majesty of the Roman Peace reveals to one another not merely human beings, in all their diversity of countries and nationalities, but also the mountains and the ranges that tower up into the clouds, with their fauna and flora. God grant that this divine benefaction may be eternal. The gift bestowed by the Romans on Mankind can only be described as a new form of light.'[2]

As for the transit of the Far Eastern invention of paper across the conductive expanse of the Arab Caliphate, this was impressively rapid. Reaching Samarqand from China in A.D. 751, the use of paper had spread to Baghdad by A.D. 793, to Cairo by A.D. 900, to Fez (Fas), almost within sight of the Atlantic, by about A.D. 1100, and to Jativa in the Iberian Peninsula by A.D. 1150.[3]

The vertical movements are sometimes more elusive but often more important in their social effects—as is illustrated by the history of the Tokugawa Shogunate,[4] which was the universal state of the Far Eastern Society in Japan. The Tokugawa régime set itself to insulate Japan from the rest of the World, and was successful for nearly two and a half centuries in maintaining this political *tour de force*; but it found itself powerless to arrest the course of social change within an insulated Japanese Empire, in spite of its efforts to petrify a feudal system, inherited from the preceding 'Time of Troubles', into a permanent dispensation.

'The penetration of money economy in Japan . . . caused a slow but irresistible revolution, culminating in the breakdown of feudal government and the resumption of intercourse with foreign countries after more than two hundred years of seclusion. What opened the doors was not a summons from without but an explosion from within. . . . One of [the] first effects [of the new economic forces] was an increase in the wealth of the townspeople, gained at the expense of the samurai and also of the peasants. . . . The *daimyō* and their retainers spent their money on luxuries produced by the artisans and sold by the tradesmen, so that by about the year [A.D.] 1700, it is said, nearly all their gold and silver had passed into the hands of the townspeople. They then began to buy goods on credit. Before long they were deeply indebted to the merchant class, and were obliged to pledge, or to make forced sales of, their tax-rice. . . . Abuses and disaster followed thick and fast. The merchants took to rice-broking,

[1] Toynbee, A. J., in *The Legacy of Greece* (Oxford 1922, Clarendon Press), p. 320.
[2] Plinius Secundus, C.: *Historia Naturalis*, Book XXVII, chap. i (i), § 3.
[3] See Carter, T. F.: *The Invention of Printing in China and its Spread Westward*, revised ed. (New York 1931, Columbia University Press), pp. 97–100; Lévi-Provençal, E.: *L'Espagne Musulmane au Xème Siècle* (Paris 1932, Larose), p. 185.
[4] See xi, map 55c.

and then to speculating. . . . It was the members of one class only, and not all of them, who profited by these conditions. These were the merchants, in particular the brokers and money-lenders, despised *chōnin* or townsmen, who in theory might be killed with impunity by any samurai for mere disrespectful language. Their social status still remained low, but they held the purse and they were in the ascendant. By the year 1700 they were already one of the strongest and most enterprising elements in the state, and the military caste was slowly losing its influence.'[1]

If we regard the year 1590 of the Christian Era, in which Hideyoshi overcame the last resistance to his dictatorship, as the date of the foundation of the Japanese universal state, we perceive that it took little more than a century for the rising of the lower layers of water from the depths to the surface to produce a bloodless social revolution in a society which Hideyoshi's successor Tokugawa Ieyasu and his heirs had sought to freeze into an almost Platonically utopian immobility. This social upheaval was a result of the operation of internal forces within a closed system, without any impulsion from outside the frontiers of the Japanese universal state.

The extent of the resultant change is impressive—and the more so, considering that, for a universal state, the Tokugawa Shogunate was culturally homogeneous to an unusually high degree. Apart from a little pariah community of Dutch business men who were strictly segregated on the islet of Deshima,[2] the only heterogeneous element in the otherwise culturally uniform Japanese life of that age was a barbarian Ainu strain that was socially impotent in so far as it was not already culturally assimilated.[3] In most universal states, such partially assimilated barbarians have been one only—and this the least alien one—of several alien cultural elements. Owing to the tendency of the parochial states of a broken-down civilization in its Time of Troubles to sharpen their weapons in fratricidal conflicts with one another and to take advantage of this dearly bought increase in their military proficiency to conquer neighbouring societies with their left hands while continuing to fight one another with their right hands,[4] most universal states have embraced not only a fringe of conquered barbarians but substantial slices of the domain of one or more alien civilizations as well. Some universal states, again, have been founded by alien empire-builders, and some have been the product of societies within whose bosoms there has already been some degree of cultural variety—even on a reckoning which does not differentiate between march-men and the denizens of the interior of the same social world.[5] Such cultural diversity, which is the rule rather than the exception in the structure of universal states, is apt to heighten the effects of the social 'conductivity' that is characteristic of them all.

1 Sansom, G. B.: *Japan: A Short Cultural History* (London 1931, Cresset Press), pp. 460–2. See further eundem: *The Western World and Japan* (London 1950, Cresset Press), chaps. ix–xi (pp. 177–289).

2 See II. ii. 232–3.

3 For the barbarian frontier of the Far Eastern World in Japan, and for the effect of this frontier on Japanese history, see II. ii. 158–9.

4 See III. iii. 139–53.

5 For the distinction between marches and interiors, and its historical importance, see II. ii. 112–207.

No other universal state known to History appears to have been as homogeneous in culture as Japan under the Tokugawa régime. In 'the Middle Empire' of Egypt,[1] in which a fringe of barbarians on the Nubian glacis of its Theban march was one element of variation from the cultural norm of the Egyptiac Society of the age,[2] there was another and more positive feature of cultural diversity in the Empire's culturally Sumeric provinces and client states in Palestine and Coele Syria. As for 'the New Empire',[3] which was a deliberate revival of the original Egyptiac universal state, it accentuated the pattern of its prototype by completing the assimilation of the barbarians of Nubia[4] and by embracing the domain of an abortive First Syriac Civilization in Syria and North-Western Mesopotamia;[5] and this culturally tripartite structure—in which the cultural domain of the civilization through whose disintegration the universal state has been brought into existence is flanked by culturally alien territories annexed at the expense of both barbarians and neighbouring civilizations—appears to be the standard type.

For example, in the Mauryan Empire,[6] which was the original Indic universal state, an Indic cultural core was flanked by an alien province in the Panjab, which had been at least partially Syriacized during a previous period of Achaemenian rule[7] after having been partially barbarized by an antecedent Völkerwanderung of Eurasian Nomads,[8] while in other quarters the Mauryan Empire's Indic core was flanked by ex-barbarian provinces in Southern India and possibly farther afield in both Ceylon and Khotan as well. The Guptan Empire,[9] in which the Mauryan was eventually reintegrated, possessed an ex-barbarian fringe, with an alien Hellenic tincture, in the satrapy that had been founded by Saka war-bands in Gujerat and the North-Western Deccan,[10] and a Hellenized fringe, with a Kushan barbarian dilution, in the territories under its suzerainty in the Panjab. In a Han Empire[11] which was the Sinic universal state, the Sinic World proper was flanked by barbarian annexes in what was eventually to become Southern China, as well as on the Eurasian Steppe, and by an alien province in the Tarim Basin, where the Indic, Syriac, and Hellenic cultures had already met and mingled before this cultural corridor and crucible was annexed to the Han Empire for the first time in the second century B.C. and for the second time in the first century of the Christian Era.[12] In the Roman Empire,[13] which was the Hellenic universal state, a culturally Hellenic core in Western Anatolia, Continental European Greece, Sicily, and Italy, with outlying enclaves in Cilicia, in Syria, at Alexandria, and at Marseilles, was combined with the domain of the submerged Hittite Civilization in Eastern Anatolia, with the homelands of the Syriac and Egyptiac civilizations in Syria and in the Lower Nile Valley, with the colonial domain of the Syriac Civilization in North-West Africa, and with ex-barbarian hinterlands in North-

[1] See xi, map 13.
[2] See II. ii. 115.
[3] See xi, map 14.
[4] See II. ii. 115.
[5] For this abortive First Syriac Civilization, see II. ii. 388–91.
[6] See xi, map 23.
[7] One cultural legacy of the Achaemenian régime here was the Kharoshthī script (see V. v. 500).
[8] See pp. 651–2, below.
[9] See xi, map 30.
[10] See V. v. 603–4.
[11] See xi, maps 27A and 28.
[12] See V. v. 144–6.
[13] See xi, map 29.

West Africa and in Western and Central Europe as far as the left bank of the Rhine and the right bank of the Danube.[1]

There are other cases in which this standard cultural pattern has been enriched by some additional element.

In the Muscovite Tsardom[2] a Russian Orthodox Christian core was flanked by a vast ex-barbarian annex extending northwards to the Arctic Ocean and eastwards eventually to the Pacific, and by an Iranic Muslim annex consisting of the sedentary Muslim peoples of the Volga Basin, the Urals, and Western Siberia. This pattern was afterwards complicated by Peter the Great's deliberate substitution of a Westernized for a traditional Orthodox Christian cultural framework for the Russian Orthodox Christian universal state, and by the subsequent annexation of additional alien territories—at the expense of the Islamic World on the Eurasian Steppe and in the Crimea, the Caucasus, and the Oxus–Jaxartes Basin, and at the expense of Western Christendom in the Baltic Provinces, Lithuania, Poland, and Finland.

In the Achaemenian Empire,[3] which was the original Syriac universal state, there was an antecedent cultural diversity, within the Syriac core itself, between the Syrian creators of the Syriac Civilization and their Iranian converts,[4] and a geographical gap between Syria and Iran that was still occupied by the dwindling domain of the gradually disappearing Babylonic culture.[5] The Achaemenian Empire also embraced the domain of the submerged Hittite culture in Eastern Anatolia, the best part of the domain of the Egyptiac Civilization,[6] fringes torn from the Hellenic and Indic worlds, and pockets of partially reclaimed barbarian highlanders and Eurasian Nomads. Moreover, after its life had been prematurely cut short by Alexander the Great, its work was carried on by his political successors, and especially by the Seleucidae, whom it would be more illuminating to describe as alien Hellenic successors of Cyrus and Darius. In the Arab Caliphate,[7] in which the Achaemenian Empire was eventually reintegrated,[8] the Syriac core—in which the earlier diversity between Syrian creators and Iranian converts had been replaced by a cleavage, along approximately the same geographical line, between ex-subjects of the Roman and ex-subjects of the Sasanian Empire—was united politically, by Arab barbarian empire-builders, with barbarian annexes—in North-West Africa, in the fastnesses of Daylam and Tabaristan between the Elburz Mountains and the Caspian Sea,[9] and on the fringes of the Eurasian Steppe adjoining the Oxus–Jaxartes Basin—and with fragments of alien civilizations: a slice of the new-born Hindu World in Sind;[10] the potential domain of an abortive Far Eastern Christian Civilization in the Oxus–Jaxartes Basin;[11] an

[1] Leaving out of account the late-acquired and early-lost Transdanubian bridgehead in Dacia.

[2] See xi, map 49.

[3] See xi, maps 20 and 21.

[4] See I. i. 79–82.

[5] For the gradual assimilation of the Babylonic Society by the Syriac, see I. i. 79 and 119; II. ii. 138; IV. iv. 100–3 and 471; V. v. 122–3 and 370.

[6] For the permanent political partition of the Egyptiac World from the middle of the seventh century B.C. onwards, see II. ii. 116.

[7] See xi, map 37.

[8] See I. i. 76–77.

[9] See II. ii. 377–8.

[10] See I. i. 105–6 and II. ii. 130.

[11] See II. ii. 369–85 and 446–52.

Orthodox Christian diasporà in Syria and Egypt; and a fossil of the by then elsewhere extinct Babylonic Society at Harran.[1]

In the Mongol Empire,[2] which was a universal state imposed by alien empire-builders on the main body of the Far Eastern Society in China, the annexes to a Chinese core were unusually extensive—including, as they did, the whole of the Eurasian Nomad World, the whole of Russian Orthodox Christendom, and the ex-Sasanian portion of a Syriac World which by that time was *in extremis*. The Mongols themselves were barbarians with a tincture of Far Eastern Christian culture.[3] In the Manchu empire-builders,[4] who subsequently repeated the Mongols' performance on a less gigantic yet still imposing scale, there was the same tincture in a more diluted form;[5] and the Chinese universal state in its Manchu avatar once again embraced, in addition to its Chinese core, a number of alien annexes: a 'reservoir' of barbarians in the still unfelled backwoods and still virgin steppes of Manchuria, the whole of the Tantric Mahayanian Buddhist World in Tibet, Mongolia, and Zungaria,[6] and the easternmost continental outposts of the Islamic World in the Tarim Basin, the north-western Chinese provinces of Kansu and Shansi, and the south-western Chinese province of Yunnan.[7]

In the Ottoman Empire,[8] which provided, or saddled, the main body of Orthodox Christendom with its universal state, the alien ʿOsmanli empire-builders united an Orthodox Christian core with a fringe of Western Christian territory in Hungary, with the whole of the Arabic Muslim World except Morocco, the Sudan, and South-Eastern Arabia, and with pockets of barbarians and semi-barbarians in Serbia, Bosnia, Albania, the Mani, the Caucasus, the Crimea, and on the Arabian Steppe. In the Mughal Empire,[9] which was the Ottoman Empire's counterpart in the Hindu World, the pattern was simpler, since, apart from the Iranic Muslim empire-builders and their co-religionists who had been deposited in the Hindu social environment by earlier waves of invasion from the Middle East and Central Asia,[10] the Mughals' only non-Hindu subjects were the Pathan barbarian highlanders on the north-western fringe of their dominions. When, however, the Mughal Rāj was replaced by a British Rāj,[11] the pattern of the Hindu universal state became more complex; for the advent of a new band of alien empire-builders, which substituted a Western element for an Islamic at the political apex of the Hindu universal state, did not expel the Indian Muslims from the stage of Hindu history, but merely depressed their status to that of a numerically still formidable alien element in the Hindu internal proletariat, so that the Hindu universal state in its second phase combined elements drawn from two alien civilizations with a Pathan barbarian fringe and a Hindu core.

There had been other universal states in which, as in the Mughal

1 See IV. iv. 101, n. 1; V. v. 125, n. 1; and IX. viii. 408, n. 5.
2 See xi, map 47.
3 See V. v. 348–51.
4 See xi, map 54.
5 See loc. cit.
6 See I. i. 35 and 90–2; II. ii. 405, n. 1; IV. iv. 497; and V. v. 309–10.
7 See V. v. 116.
8 See xi, map 51.
9 See xi, map 52.
10 See II. ii. 78; II. ii. 130–1 and 149; IV. iv. 96–99.
11 See xi, map 53.

Empire, the cultural pattern had been less complex than the standard type yet not so simple as that of the Tokugawa Shogunate.

The Empire of Sumer and Akkad,[1] which was the Sumeric universal state, included no representatives of an alien civilization—unless Byblus and other Syrian coast-towns are to be counted as such in virtue of their tincture of Egyptiac culture. On the other hand, the Sumeric Civilization itself was represented in two varieties at least—a Sumero-Akkadian and an Elamite[2]—and in no less than three if the domain of the Indus Culture should prove also to have been included in 'the Empire of the Four Quarters of the World'.[3] Moreover, the Babylonian Amorites, who eventually restored a polity that had been first constructed by the Sumerian Ur-Engur (*alias* Ur-Nammu) of Ur,[4] were not merely marchmen but marchmen with a barbarian tinge. So, on a broader and a longer view, the cultural pattern of the Sumeric universal state proves to have been less homogeneous than might appear at first sight. 'The thalassocracy of Minos',[5] again, which was the Minoan universal state, probably included representatives of the continental Mycenaean variety of the Minoan culture as well as the creators of that culture in its Cretan homeland, even if it did not embrace any representatives of an alien civilization.

In the Central American World[6] two once distinct sister societies—the Yucatec Civilization and the Mexic—had not yet lost their distinctive characteristics, though they had already been brought together by force of Toltec arms, when the task, and prize, of establishing a Central American universal state was snatched, at the eleventh hour, out of the hands of barbarian Aztec empire-builders by Spanish representatives of an utterly alien Western Christendom.[7] In the Andean World the Empire of the Incas,[8] which was the Andean universal state, already included representatives of the Kara variety of the Andean culture as well as the creators of that culture in the Peruvian coastlands and its propagators on the Peruvian, Bolivian, and Argentinian sections of the Andean Plateau,[9] before the indigenous Incan empire-builders were suddenly and violently replaced by Spanish *conquistadores* from Western Christendom who turned the Andean World upside-down, with a vigour reminiscent of Alexander the Great's, by proceeding to convert the indigenous population to Christianity and to variegate the social map by studding it with immigrant Spanish landlords[10] and self-governing municipalities.[11]

The Danubian Hapsburg Monarchy,[12] which served as a carapace for Western Christendom against the assaults of the 'Osmanlis, and which,

1 See xi, maps 10 and 11.

2 For the distinction between them, see I. i. 117, n. 4.

3 This possibility has been suggested in I. i. 108.

4 See I. i. 106 and V. vi. 297–8.

5 See xi, maps 15 and 16.

6 See xi, map 71.

7 See I. i. 123–4.

8 See xi, map 68.

9 If we compare the Andean and Sumeric societies in their respective universal state phases, we may see in the coastal communities of Chimu and Nazca the cultural counterparts of Sumer; in the highland communities, south of Ecuador, the counterparts of Akkad; in the Karas of Ecuador the counterparts of Elam; and in the Chibchas of Colombia the counterparts of the makers of 'the Indus Culture'.

10 See p. 144, below.

11 See pp. 135 and 145, below.

12 See xi, map 51.

seen from the south-east, wore the deceptive appearance of being a full-blown Western universal state,[1] set itself, like the Tokugawa Shogunate, to achieve domestic cultural uniformity, but lacked both the ruthlessness and the insularity which, between them, enabled the Japanese isolationists for a time to put their policy into effect. In pursuing its aim of being totally Catholic, the Hapsburg Power did succeed, more or less, in extirpating Protestantism within its frontiers; but the very success of its stand, and eventual counter-attack, against the Ottoman embodiment of an Orthodox Christian universal state broke up the Danubian Monarchy's hardly attained Catholic homogeneity by transferring to Hapsburg from Ottoman rule a stiff-necked minority of Hungarian Protestants and a host of Orthodox Christians of divers nationalities, most of whom proved unwilling to accept the ecclesiastical supremacy of Rome, even when the yoke was proffered in the easy form of Uniatism, while, among those who did accept this relatively light burden, the rank and file remained nearer in heart and mind to their dissident Orthodox ex-co-religionists than they ever came to be to their fellow Catholics who were of the Latin Rite.

The Neo-Babylonian Empire,[2] which was the Babylonic universal state, similarly forfeited its cultural purity—and thereby worked unwittingly for the eventual extinction of the Babylonic Civilization itself—when Nebuchadnezzar conquered and annexed the homeland of the Syriac Civilization west of the Euphrates; and the impress of the indigenous Babylonic culture became progressively fainter as the domain which Nebuchadnezzar had bequeathed to a short line of native successors was incorporated first into the barbaro-Syriac Empire of the Achaemenids and then into the Hellenic Empire of the Seleucids.

Our survey has shown that, in the cultural composition of universal states, a high degree of diversity is the rule; and, in the light of this fact, it is evident that one effect of the 'conductivity' of universal states is to carry farther, by less violent and less brutal means, that process of cultural pammixia that is started, in the antecedent Times of Troubles, by the atrocities that these bring in their train. The refugees, exiles, deportees, transported slaves, and other *déracinés* of the more cruel preceding age are followed up, under the milder régime of a universal state, by merchants, by professional soldiers, and by philosophic and religious missionaries and pilgrims who make their transit with less tribulation in a more genial social climate.

The cumulative cultural effect of these voluntary and involuntary migrations within the ambit of a disintegrating society has been examined at earlier points in this Study[3] and need not be resurveyed here. The Israelites who were deported by the Assyrians to the cities of the Medes and the exiles from Jerusalem whose memories made them weep by the waters of Babylon may serve as typical representatives of the *déracinés* of a Time of Troubles. In the Papal emissary Friar William of Rubruck's poignant account of how he spent Palm Sunday, A.D. 1254, in the Mongol capital, Qāraqorum, in the company of fellow Catholic deportees from

[1] See II. ii. 177–88 and V. v. 325–7.
[2] See xi, map 19.
[3] Especially in V. v. 58–194 and 439–80.

far-away Western Christendom,[1] we can catch the anarchy of a Time of Troubles in the act of turning into the orderly peace of a universal state. In the secret and silent circulation of the waters of that seemingly motionless sea, the Orontes discharges into the Tiber and the sands of the Shāmīyah are deposited on the banks of the Tyne. The missionary of Christianity, Saint Paul, travels from Antioch to Rome, and, 'as an inscription from South Shields informs us, a Romano-Oriental from Palmyra could marry a Romano-British wife and settle down for the rest of his days in the neighbourhood of Hadrian's Wall'.[2]

Judgements passed on the effects of this pammixia diverge, poles apart, according to the divers social, political, and historical standpoints of the observers who make them. A grandchild of those European Greeks whose heroic resistance against enormous odds had barely saved them from being incorporated, at the blossoming-season of their own civilization's growth, into the world-empire of the Achaemenidae, can write of 'the appalling present condition of the populations under the Persian yoke, which have been quite disintegrated by being interlarded and kneaded up together'.[3] Another Greek, born more than five hundred years later into the 'Indian Summer' of an Hellenic universal state which he could readily appreciate because it was so long overdue, could say to Rome, as the highest praise that he could give her: 'You have made one single household of the entire Inhabited World';[4] and a Gallic poet, writing more than two hundred years later again, at a moment when the Roman Empire in the West had already received its death-blow, could give the Greek stylist's phrase a Latin echo in the famous epigrammatic line: 'Urbem fecisti quod prius Orbis erat.'[5] On this controversial question of the value of the result, points of view may differ completely; but there is no disputing the facts themselves, however depreciatory or laudatory may be the literary framework in which they are presented.

'I am not unaware', writes a Roman encyclopaedist towards the end of the first century of the Roman Peace, 'that it may justly be regarded as the lapse of an insensitive and lazy mind to have given so brief and cursory a description of a country that is the nurse of all countries—their nurse and their parent and the chosen vessel of divine grace for the mission of making the skies themselves clearer, gathering the scattered realms into one flock, softening harsh traditional practices, bringing together into mutual converse, through a common medium of linguistic exchange, the discordant and barbarous tongues of innumerable peoples, conferring humanity on Man, and, in a word, becoming the single fatherland of all nations throughout the World.'[6]

What Pliny writes of Roman Italy and of the world-empire that she had built up around herself is true, in some degree, of every universal state.

[1] See the passage quoted from Friar William's narrative in V. v. 113–14.

[2] Toynbee, J. C. M.: 'Catholicism and the Roman Imperial Cult', in *The Month*, vol. clviii, November 1931, citing *Ephemeris Epigraphica*, vol. iv (Berlin 1881, Reimer), p. 212, No. 718 *a*: 'D. M. Regina, liberta et coniuge, Barates Palmyrenus, natione Catuallauna, an. xxx.'

[3] Plato: *Leges*, 693A, quoted already in V. v. 124, n. 2.

[4] Aristeides, P. Aelius: *In Romam*, § 102 in B. Keil's edition (*Aelii Aristidis Quae Supersunt Omnia*, vol. ii (Berlin 1898, Weidmann), p. 121), quoted already in V. v. 343.

[5] Rutilius Namatianus, C.: *De Reditu Suo*, Book I, l. 66, quoted already in V. v. 345.

[6] Plinius Secundus, C.: *Historia Naturalis*, Book III, chap. v. (vi), § 39.

(*b*) THE PSYCHOLOGY OF PEACE

A universal state is imposed by its founders, and accepted by its subjects, as a panacea for the ills of a Time of Troubles. In psychological terms it is an institution for establishing and maintaining concord;[1] and this is the true remedy for a correctly diagnosed disease. The malady from which a broken-down civilization is suffering as the penalty for its breakdown is that of being a house divided against itself, and this schism in Society is a double one. There is a horizontal schism between contending social classes as well as a vertical schism between warring states, and a universal state is born of a paroxysm which exacerbates this twofold strife to an unprecedented and intolerable degree of intensity and, in the same act, puts a sudden stop to it for the time being. The immediate and paramount aim of the empire-builders, in making a universal state out of the Power that emerges as the sole survivor from a war of annihilation between the parochial states of the preceding age, is to establish concord among themselves and with their fellow members of the dominant minority of their society who are survivors of the former ruling element in those parochial states that have succumbed in the fratricidal struggle. Non-violence, however, is a state of mind and principle of behaviour that cannot be confined to one compartment of social life; it must apply in some degree to all social relations if it is to apply to any; and therefore the concord which a dominant minority, in urgent need of being at peace within itself, is moved to seek and ensue[2] in its own domestic life has to be extended to the dominant minority's relations with the internal and external proletariats and with any alien civilizations with which the disintegrating civilization is in contact. In these relations, if there cannot be perfect and permanent peace, there must at least be an armistice and a *modus vivendi*.

This universal concord, which is the prevailing psychological climate under the dispensation of a universal state, profits its divers beneficiaries in different degrees. While it enables the dominant minority to recuperate to some extent—and indeed is the condition *sine qua non*, if it is to recuperate at all—it brings a greater relative access of strength to the proletariat. Concord is, in itself, a negative boon. 'A bruised reed shall he not break, and the smoking flax shall he not quench.'[3] The practical effect of such forbearance varies with the quality of the flax and the reed; and, in the case in point, the life has already gone out of the dominant minority and cannot be revived by a belated relief from attrition, whereas the same relief enables the proletariat, which has been stimulated and not crushed by its foregoing tribulations, to 'shoot up and thrive'.[4] Accordingly, during the armistice inaugurated by the establishment of a universal state, the proletariat must increase but the dominant minority must decrease.[5] Under the common régime of concord the dominant minority's conservation of energy freezes into

[1] See V. vi. 2–13.
[2] 1 Pet. iii. 11.
[3] Isa. xlii. 3, quoted in Matt. xii. 20.
[4] The phrase used by Herodotus (Book I, chap. 66) to describe the progress of Sparta under the impetus that she received from the institution of the Lycurgean *agôgê*.
[5] John iii. 30.

Archaism,[1] and this Archaism rankles into Esotericism—a regressive Esotericism distinguishable from the progressive form of the same social aberration which is one of the perilous stepping-stones of a civilization in its growth-phase. On the other hand the toleration practised by the founders of a universal state for the sake of getting rid of fratricidal strife among themselves incidentally gives the internal proletariat a chance to found a universal church, while the atrophy of the martial spirit among the subjects of a universal state, resulting from the monopoly of the military profession by the Imperial Power, gives the external proletariat or a neighbouring alien civilization a chance of breaking in and seizing for itself the dominion over an internal proletariat that has been conditioned by the peculiar climate of a universal state to be passive on the political plane, however active on the religious.

The relative incapacity of the dominant minority to profit by conditions which it itself has called into existence through the act of establishing a universal state is strikingly illustrated by its almost invariable failure to propagate a philosophy or a 'fancy religion' of its own from above downwards.[2] In this matter the political pressure which the sovereign or the ruling element in a universal state is able to bring to bear upon the mass of the population seems to be a positive obstacle to the attainment of the ruler's desire, and his will here defeats itself in attempting to gain its ends by means that generally prove effective in other spheres. The working of this psycho-social 'law' has been examined in this Study already in an earlier passage[3] which need not be recapitulated.

It is all the more remarkable to observe how effective a use the representatives of the internal proletariat are apt to make of the opportunity offered by the pacific atmosphere of a universal state for propagating, from below upwards, a higher religion and eventually establishing a universal church. We may recall the more striking examples from a fuller survey that we have made in a previous chapter of this Study.[4]

'The Middle Empire' of Egypt, for instance, which was the original Egyptiac universal state, was used to this effect by the Osirian Church.[5] The Neo-Babylonian Empire, which was the Babylonic universal state, and its successive alien successor-states, the Achaemenian Empire and the Seleucid Monarchy, were similarly used by Judaism and by its sister-religion Zoroastrianism[6]—a creation of the Iranian wing of the proletariat of the Babylonic World which made converts of the Achaemenid empire-builders but escaped the blight that might have been the penalty for its having become the religion of the powers that be, thanks to the studied religious tolerance of all the Achaemenidae except, perhaps, Cambyses and to the personal religious laxity of the later rulers of the dynasty from

[1] See V. vi. 49–97.

[2] The most striking apparent exception is the successful establishment of Confucianism as the official philosophy of the Sinic universal state by the Emperor Han Wuti. The success of this imposition of a philosophy of the dominant minority upon the internal proletariat of the Sinic World is at least partly explicable by the fact that the 'Confucianism' which thus became a going concern was an amalgam in which an element of authentic philosophy was heavily alloyed with popular superstitions (see V. v. 418–19, 555–7, 654–5, and 708).

[3] See V. v. 646–712.

[4] In V. v. 58–194.

[5] See V. v. 149–52.

[6] See V. v. 120–4.

Artaxerxes II onwards.[1] The opportunities offered by the Roman Peace were seized by a number of competing proletarian religions—by the worships of Cybele and Isis and by Mithraism and Christianity,[2] as well as by the Babylonic philosophy of astral determinism.[3] The corresponding opportunities offered by a *Pax Hanica* in the Sinic World were competed for by an Indic proletarian religion, the Mahāyāna, which had arisen out of a philosophy of the Indic dominant minority in the crucible of the Kushan Empire,[4] and by the indigenous Sinic proletarian religion of Taoism, which likewise created itself out of a philosophy in emulation of the equally astonishing genesis of its Indic rival.[5] The Arab Caliphate provided a comparable opportunity for Islam—thanks to the êthos of the Umayyad Caliphs, who, with the exception of ʿUmar II, were as tolerant and as lax as the Achaemenidae[6]—and the Gupta Rāj in the Indic World for Hinduism.[7] The Mongol Empire, which for a moment extended an effective *Pax Nomadica* over the Continent from the west coast of the Pacific Ocean to the east coast of the Baltic Sea and from the southern fringes of the Siberian tundra to the northern fringes of the Arabian desert and the Burmese jungle, struck the imagination of the missionaries of a host of rival religions by the portentous scale of the opportunity which this almost literally universal state appeared to offer; and, considering how brief this passing moment actually was, it is remarkable to observe how successfully it was turned to account by the Nestorian and the Western Catholic Christian churches and by Islam, as well as by the Lamaist Tantric sect of Mahayanian Buddhism.[8] The successive Ming and Manchu avatars of the universal state which the Mongol Empire had provided for the main body of the Far Eastern World gave Western Catholic Christianity a second opportunity of attempting the conquest of a new world,[9] and the same church made a simultaneous attempt to take advantage of the foundation of a Japanese universal state in the shape of the Tokugawa Shogunate.[10] The Ottoman Empire gave an opening for Bedreddinism, Imāmī Shīʿīsm, and Bektāshism,[11] and the Mughal Rāj in the Hindu World for Kabirism and Sikhism.[12]

The exponents of the higher religions that had thus so frequently profited by the favourable social and psychological climate of a universal state had in some cases been conscious of the boon and had ascribed its bestowal upon them in an auspicious hour to the providence of the One True God in whose name they had been going forth converting and to convert their fellow men. In the eyes of the authors of the Books of 'Deutero-Isaiah', Ezra, and Nehemiah,[13] the Achaemenian Empire was the chosen instrument of Yahweh for the propagation of Judaism,[14] and

1 See V. v. 704–5.
2 See II. ii. 215–16 and V. v. 80–82.
3 See V. v. 56–57.
4 See V. v. 139–40.
5 See V. v. 146–7.
6 See V. v. 675–7 and 704–5.
7 See V. v. 137–8.
8 See V. v. 112–17.
9 See V. v. 365–7.
10 See V. v. 365.
11 See V. v. 111.
12 See V. v. 106.
13 According to van Hoonacker, A.: *Une Communauté judéo-araméenne à Elephantine aux vie et ve siècles avant J.C.* (London 1915, Milford), pp. 22–23, Nehemiah (whose first mission this scholar dates in 445 B.C.) really preceded Ezra (whose mission he dates in 398 B.C.).
14 See V. vi. 17, 122, n. 3, and 130, n. 3. In inverse form and in non-supernatural terms the same conception of the relations between Judaism and the Achaemenian

this conception of the final cause of a universal state was applied to the Roman Empire by a Father of the Christian Church in a passage so felicitous that it gave birth to a patristic commonplace.

'The incarnation of the Word of God united divine nature with human nature so [completely] that God's nature was able to stoop to the depths and ours to be raised up to the heights. In order that the effects of this ineffable act of grace might be spread throughout the World, God's providence previously brought into existence the Roman Empire. Its territorial acquisitions were carried to the lengths required for enabling all nations everywhere to become neighbours in the intimate contact that is established in a universal state. It was thoroughly consonant with the divine plan of action that many kingdoms should thus be confederated in a single empire and that the evangelization of all Mankind should find itself able to make an unimpeded and rapid progress through the ranks of peoples held together under the rule of a single polity.'[1]

The inspiration, direct or indirect, of this passage in a fifth-century Christian sermon can be discerned in an ode from the pen of a seventeenth-century Christian poet, when he imagines Nature put out of countenance by her Maker's overwhelming act of becoming incarnate.

But He, her fears to cease,
Sent down the meek-eyed Peace;
She, crown'd with olive green, came softly sliding
Down through the turning sphere,
His ready harbinger,
With turtle wing the amorous clouds dividing;
And, waving wide her myrtle wand,
She strikes a universal peace through sea and land.

No war or battle's sound
Was heard the world around:
The idle spear and shield were high uphung;
The hookèd chariot stood

Empire is presented by Eduard Meyer: 'Once again [i.e. in the light of the newly discovered Elephantinê papyri] it is made unquestionably manifest that Judaism is a creation of the Persian Empire: the Babylonian Jews actually set in motion [for their own purposes] the engine of the Imperial Government and made use of its authority to impose on the Jews in Palestine and the Disporà the Law which Ezra had composed' (Meyer, E.: 'Zu den aramäischen Papyri von Elephantinê' in the *Mittheilungen* of the Königliche Preussische Akademie der Wissenschaften, Gesammtsitzung vom 23 November, 1911). According to Van Hoonacker, op. cit., p. 20, Meyer exaggerates the extent of the new departure in the development of Judaism in the fifth century B.C.

[1] '[Verbum] caro factum ita divinam naturam naturae univit humanae ut illius ad infima inclinatio, nostra fieret ad summa provectio. Ut autem huius inenarrabilis gratiae per totum mundum diffunderetur effectus, Romanum regnum divina providentia praeparavit; cuius ad eos limites incrementa perducta sunt quibus cunctarum undique gentium vicina et contigua esset universitas. Disposito namque divinitus operi maxime congruebat ut multa regna uno confoedarentur imperio et cito pervios haberet populos praedicatio generalis quos unius teneret regimen civitatis' (Leo the Great, Pope: Sermo lxxxii, chap. 2, in Migne, J.-P.: *Patrologia Latina*, vol. liv, col. 423). Leo the Great has been cited as an exponent of the gentle response of Christianity to the challenge of social disintegration in V. v. 77. Another passage in the same sermon, on Rome's debt to the Christian Church, is quoted on p. 697, below. The present passage is anticipated in an address to an Antonine emperor by Bishop Melito of Sardis, which is quoted by Eusebius: *Historia Ecclesiastica*, Book IV, chap. xxvi, §§ 7–8.

Unstain'd with hostile blood;
The trumpet spake not to the armèd throng;
And kings sat still with awful eye,[1]
As if they surely knew their sovran Lord was by.[2]

An opportunity so marvellous as to seem truly heaven-sent is indeed presented to a higher religion by the establishment of an imperial peace; yet, in the relation between a successful missionary church and the universal state within whose framework it is carrying out its purpose of converting Mankind, the climate of toleration, which gives the work of conversion so favourable a start, does not always persist till the end of the story and is sometimes actually transformed into its own opposite by the very success of the tolerated religion in taking advantage of it during the first chapter.

There have, no doubt, been cases in which there has been no such sinister termination of the armistice between an internal proletariat and a dominant minority that is inaugurated by the establishment of a universal state.

For example, in the history of the Osirian Church in the Egyptiac World, the apprehensive hostility which the rising proletarian religion evoked in the hearts of the ruling element in the Egyptiac Society at as early a date as the eve of the Time of Troubles[3] does not appear to have led on to any overt trial of strength between this would-be universal church and 'the Middle Empire' that was the Egyptiac universal state; and in the ensuing interregnum the rival religions of the Egyptiac internal proletariat and dominant minority actually made common cause against the religion of an external proletariat with an alien cultural tinge, and entered into an alliance which proved to be the prelude to amalgamation.[4] Peace likewise seems to have been preserved in the Sinic World between the Mahāyāna and the Taoist Church on the one side and the Han Empire on the other until the Sinic universal state went into dissolution towards the end of the second century of the Christian Era.

When we come to Judaism and Zoroastrianism, we cannot tell what their ultimate relations might have been with either the Neo-Babylonian or the Achaemenian Empire, since each of these universal states in turn had its life cut short by an alien conqueror at an early stage of its history. We only know that, when the Achaemenian régime was abruptly replaced by the Seleucid and eventually, west of the Euphrates, by the Roman, the impact of an alien Hellenic culture, of which the Seleucid and the Roman Powers were the successive political instruments,

[1] This image is perhaps a reminiscence of a passage of Latin poetry (Lucretius: *De Rerum Natura*, Book V, ll. 1222–5) depicting the psychological effect produced by the descent from heaven, not of Peace, but of a thunderbolt:

Non populi gentesque tremunt, regesque superbi
corripiunt divom percussi membra timore
nequid ob admissum foede dictumve superbe
pœnarum grave sit solvendi tempus adultum?

[2] Milton, John: *Ode on the Morning of Christ's Nativity*.

[3] See I. i. 140–3. This presentation of Osirism, which had been adopted by the writer of this Study from J. H. Breasted: *The Development of Religion and Thought in Ancient Egypt* (London 1912, Hodder & Stoughton), pp. 29 and 140, is contested by Breasted's successor, J. A. Wilson, in his *The Burden of Egypt* (Chicago 1951, University Press), p. 32, n. 12.

[4] See I. i. 143–4.

deflected both Judaism and Zoroastrianism from their original mission of preaching a gospel of salvation to all Mankind, and transformed them into weapons of cultural warfare in the Syriac Society's retort to the Hellenic Society's aggression.[1] If the Achaemenian Empire, like its post-Hellenic avatar, the Arab Caliphate, had run out its full course, we may conjecture that, under the auspices of a tolerant or indifferent Achaemenian Imperial Government, either Zoroastrianism or Judaism or some syncretism of these two higher religions would have anticipated the achievement of Islam, which—profiting by the indifference of the Umayyads and the conscientious observance, by the ʿAbbasids, of the tolerance, prescribed by the *Sharīʿah*, towards non-Muslims who were 'People of the Book'[2]—made gradual headway, uncompromised by the frustrating assistance of the civil arm, until the collapse of the ʿAbbasid régime brought a landslide of voluntary mass-conversions among ex-subjects of the Caliphate seeking shelter, in the courtyard of the Mosque, from the storm of an approaching political interregnum.[3] Similarly, under a Guptan Empire which was a reintegration of the original Mauryan Hindu universal state, the ousting of the philosophy of Buddhism by the post-Buddhaic higher religion of Hinduism was not only unopposed by a dynasty who were, themselves, adherents of the rising Hindu faith, but was also unimpeded by any left-handed stimulation of the outgoing philosophy through acts of official persecution that would have been alien to the intrinsically tolerant and syncretistic religious êthos of the Indic Civilization.[4]

In contrast to these cases in which a higher religion, profiting by the peace of a universal state, had been tolerated by the Imperial Government from first to last, there were other cases in which its peaceful progress had been interrupted by official persecutions that had either nipped it in the bud or had denatured it by goading it into going into politics and eventually taking up arms or, at the lightest, had compelled it to pay a heavy toll of suffering as the price of spoiling the Egyptians.

Western Catholic Christianity, for example, was almost completely extirpated in Japan by the Tokugawa régime in the seventeenth century of the Christian Era,[5] and was effectively checked in China in the eighteenth century by the less drastic measures then taken against it by the Manchu Power.[6] Shiʿism was crushed in the Ottoman Empire in A.D. 1514 by Sultan Selīm the Grim.[7] Islam was persecuted by the pagan Mongol khāqāns—partly because of the Muslims' steadfastness in refusing to abandon Islamic ritual observances that were offensive to Mongol tribal custom, and partly owing to the influence, in Mongol counsels, of Islam's Nestorian Christian enemies[8]—and, though this persecution was more than counter-balanced in the long run by a temporary political union, under Mongol rule, of China and Dār-al-

[1] See I. i. 90–91; II. ii. 203, 234–6, 285–6, and 374; V. v. 125–6 and 657–61.

[2] See V. v. 674–5 and 678. [3] See V. v. 678. [4] See V. v. 706.

[5] The faithful remnant was driven underground, like the Jews and Muslims in Catholic Spain and Portugal (see II. ii. 232–3 and 244–8 and IX. viii. 569).

[6] See V. v. 365–7. [7] See I. i. 365 and 382–3 and V. v. 365.

[8] For the adverse consequences of this influence for Islam, see II. ii. 122, n. 2, 237–8, and 449–52; V. v. 3, n. 3, and 250; in the present volume, pp. 256–7 below; IX. viii. 355; and X. ix. 36.

Islām which led to the permanent introduction of Islam into China,[1] Islam in China under the Mongols, like Western Catholic Christianity in China under the Ming and the Manchus, missed its possible destiny of becoming the universal church of the main body of the Far Eastern Society. Islam gained no substantial foothold in China outside the two far north-western provinces of Kansu and Shensi and the new south-western province of Yunnan which was added to China's patrimony by force of Mongol arms; and, even in these two lodgements, the Islamic community in China never became anything more than an alien minority which was goaded, by the precariousness of its position, into recurrent outbreaks of militancy.

This denaturing effect of official persecution, which thus left its mark in China on Islam, is more signally exemplified in the perversion of Sikhism in India in reaction to the sustained and violent persecution to which this possible embryo of a Hindu universal church was subjected by the Mughal Rāj.[2] In allowing itself to be provoked into militancy, Sikhism renounced its spiritual birthright and opted for the limited and uncreative role of becoming a local political community in a single province of the Hindu World, where, down to the time of writing, the height of its political success had been the dubious achievement of having once carved out one of the ephemeral successor-states of the Mughal Empire.

In contrast to the cases just cited, the untoward after-effects on Christianity of the trial of strength that was the prelude to its triumph over the Roman imperial régime were comparatively slight.[3] During the three centuries ending in the conversion of Constantine, while Christianity was benefiting by the facilities unintentionally offered to it by the Roman Peace, it was never out of danger of falling foul of Roman policy; for, besides the suspicion of private associations of all kinds that haunted the Roman State in the Imperial Age,[4] there was an older and more deeply graven Roman tradition of special hostility to private associations for the practice and propagation of foreign religions; and, though the Roman Government had relaxed this hardset policy in two notable instances—in its official reception of the worship of Cybele at the psychological crisis of the Hannibalic War[5] and in its persistent toleration of Judaism as a religion, even when the Jewish Zealots forced Rome's hand and ultimately compelled her to obliterate the last vestiges of a Jewish state[6]—the suppression of the Bacchanals in the second century B.C. was an augury of what the Christians were to suffer in the third century of their era.[7] Unlike the Sikh community under the Mughal

[1] See Broomhall, M.: *Islam in China* (London 1910, Morgan & Scott); de Thiersant, D.: *Le Mahométisme en Chine et dans le Turkestan Oriental* (Paris 1878, Leroux, 2 vols.); Devéria, G.: *Musulmans et Manichéens Chinois* (Paris 1898, Imprimerie Nationale); and the present Study, IV. iv. 496 and V. v. 116. This was an incidental consequence of the Mongols' general policy of intermixing the peoples and cultures of their empire (for an instance of this see V. v. 350–1).

[2] See V. v. 187 and 665–8.

[3] These untoward after-effects are considered again, in a different connexion, on p. 439, below.

[4] See p. 57, above.

[5] See II. ii. 216 and V. v. 685–8.

[6] See IV. iv. 224–5; V. v. 68 and 657–9; and V. vi. 120–3.

[7] See II. ii. 216.

Rāj, the Christian Church under the Roman régime resisted the temptation to retort to official persecution by perverting itself from a religious into a politico-military association; and it was duly rewarded for remaining substantially true to its own nature by becoming a universal church and an heir of the future. Yet the Christian Church did not come through this ordeal unscathed. Instead of reading and taking to heart the manifest lesson of the triumph of Christian gentleness over Roman force, she presented her discomfited persecutors with a gratuitous vindication and a posthumous moral revenge by taking to her bosom the sin which had consummated their failure. The habit of resorting to persecution as a would-be short cut to overcoming opposition to her practice and beliefs was adopted by the Christian Church before the close of the fourth century of the Christian Era[1] and clung to her thereafter. Even the desperate remedy of clutching at tolerance at the cost of losing hold of faith—an expedient in which Western Christendom had been experimenting since the latter part of the seventeenth century[2]—had not proved a lasting cure for this wantonly contracted spiritual disease.

Such sinister legacies, bequeathed to higher religions by universal states, are not, however, of the same order of significance as the benefits which are offered to a higher religion by the facilities that a universal state provides. It was within, and with the aid of, this political and social framework that Christianity, Islam, Hinduism, and the Mahāyāna won their way to becoming universal churches.

While the internal proletariat, as the creator of the higher religions, is thus the principal beneficiary on the spiritual plane from the dominant minority's impermanent yet momentous achievement of establishing a universal state, the benefits on the political plane are harvested by other hands; and this distribution of advantages arises from the very nature of the situation. The enforced peace of a universal state gives the internal proletariat its opportunity for spiritual prowess in so far as it debars it from the privilege of exercising political power and relieves it of the necessity of bearing arms; and even the empire-builders, bled white by the supreme effort of imposing peace through a knock-out blow that has been the climax of a crescendo of fratricidal warfare, lose the zest that has carried their forefathers to victory in their struggle for existence in the foregoing Time of Troubles. The military service once readily accepted as an honour and as an opportunity for ambition now comes to be shunned as an unwelcome burden; and, in looking about for stalwart and willing shoulders to which this load might be transferred, the imperial authorities are apt to draw an ever larger quota of their military recruits from the ranks of an untamed external proletariat.[3] The psychology of peace under the auspices of a universal state thus unfits the rulers themselves for the task of retaining their own political heritage; and accordingly the political beneficiaries of this process of psychological disarmament that is induced by the moral climate of a universal state are neither the rulers nor the ruled; they are intruders from beyond the

[1] See IV. iv. 226–7. [2] See IV. iv. 227–8 and V. v. 669–71.

[3] See VIII. viii. 43–44. The consequent barbarization of the dominant minority has been discussed in V. v. 459–80.

imperial frontiers who may be either members of the disintegrating society's external proletariat or representatives of some alien civilization.

At an earlier point in this Study[1] we have, in fact, observed that the event which registers the extinction of a civilization—as distinct from the event which precipitates its antecedent breakdown and disintegration—is usually the occupation of the domain of the defunct society's universal state either by barbarian war-lords from beyond the pale or by conquerors coming from another society with a different culture, or in some cases by both kinds of invader, one following at the heels of the other. Barbarians overran the Empire of Sumer and Akkad, the Guptan Empire, the Empire of Ts'in and Han, the Roman Empire, the Arab Caliphate, 'the thalassocracy of Minos', and both 'the Middle Empire' and 'the New Empire' of Egypt.[2] The Neo-Babylonian Empire, which was the Babylonic universal state, was cut short by Iranian barbarians who were in the act of becoming converts to the Syriac Civilization and architects of the original Syriac universal state; and this Achaemenian Empire, in its turn, was cut short by Macedonian barbarians who had already become disciples and missionaries of Hellenism before the whirlwind campaign in which Alexander the Great overthrew the Achaemenian Power. The Mauryan Empire, which was the Indic universal state, suffered the Achaemenian Empire's fate, 150 years later, at the hands of an Hellenic successor of the Achaemenian Empire in Bactria; and the Empire of the Incas, which was the Andean universal state, was similarly cut short by militant apostles of Western Christendom whose leader emulated the demonic energy, but not the chivalrous generosity, of the Macedonian Alexander. At the break-up of the Ottoman Empire, which had provided an alien universal state for the main body of Orthodox Christendom, incipient barbarian invasions were overtaken, and were then either brought to a halt or changed in character, by the mightier march of Westernization: partly in the form of conquests by Western or Westernizing Powers, and partly through the cultural conversion of the subject peoples of the Empire and of the invading barbarians themselves.[3] At the break-up of the Mughal Empire, which had provided an alien universal state for the Hindu World, incipient barbarian invasions were stopped dead by the restoration of the universal state in the form of a British Rāj.[4]

The benefits secured by barbarian or alien aggressors who have succeeded in taking advantage, for their predatory purposes, of the psychological climate induced by a universal state are palpable and, on a short view, imposing. Yet we have observed already,[5] and shall be verifying in a later part of this Study, that the barbarian invaders of the

[1] In IV. iv. 56–119.

[2] The Hyksos barbarians who came in at the death of 'the Middle Empire' of Egypt had acquired *en route*, as we have seen, a tincture of the alien Sumeric culture, and this is one possible explanation of the fanatical fury with which the Egyptiac Society rose against them, drove them out, and restored a universal state that had already run its full course before the Hyksos had appeared on the scene (see VI A, Annex, pp. 574–6, below, and the references there given to previous passages in this Study that bear upon this point).

[3] See IV. iv. 68–70 and 76–78.

[4] See V. v. 304 and 305, n. 2.

[5] In I. i. 58–62 and V. v. 194–337, *passim*.

derelect domain of a crumbling universal state are heroes without a future;[1] and Posterity would assuredly have recognized them as being the disreputable adventurers that they are, but for the retrospective glamour of romance and tragedy that is cast over their sordid escapades by their redeeming intuition of their fate and their marvellous capacity for writing their own epitaphs on their own terms in the language of high poetry.[2] As for the achievements of the militant missionaries of an alien civilization, these too, though seldom so short-lived as the triumphs of the barbarians, are, like them, delusive and disappointing by comparison with the historic achievement of an internal proletariat that has taken advantage of a *pax oecumenica* by founding, under its aegis, a universal church.

In two instances in which we know the whole story, we have seen that a civilization whose universal state has been prematurely cut short by alien conquerors is capable of going to earth, hibernating for centuries, biding its time, and eventually finding its opportunity to expel the intrusive civilization and resume the universal state phase of its history at the point where this has been interrupted. The Indic Civilization achieved this *tour de force* after nearly six hundred years, and the Syriac after nearly a thousand years, of submergence beneath an Hellenic flood; the monuments of their achievement were the Guptan Empire and the Arab Caliphate, in which they respectively resumed the universal states originally embodied in the Mauryan Empire and in the Achaemenian Empire.[3] On the other hand the Babylonic and Egyptiac societies were eventually absorbed into the body social of the Syriac, though the Babylonic Society succeeded in preserving its cultural identity for about six hundred years after the overthrow of the Neo-Babylonian Empire of Nabopolassar and Nebuchadnezzar by Cyrus the Achaemenid, while the Egyptiac Society[4] maintained itself for no less than two thousand years after the termination of its natural expectation of life had been signalled by the collapse of 'the Middle Kingdom' in which we have seen its original universal state.[5]

On the evidence of past history there are thus two alternative denouements to attempts on the part of one civilization to devour and digest another civilization by force. The evidence shows, however, that, even when such an attempt is ultimately successful, there may be a period of probation, lasting for centuries or even millennia, before the result is assured; and the Time-scale here revealed might incline twentieth-century historians to be chary about forecasting the outcome of the Western Civilization's latter-day attempts to swallow its contemporaries, considering how relatively short the time had been since even the oldest of these attempts had been inaugurated, and how little had yet been seen of the gradually unfolding story.

In the case of the Spanish conquest of the Central American World, for example, in which the alien conquerors had actually anticipated the

[1] See VIII. viii. 45–72. [2] See VIII. viii. 73–81.

[3] See I. i. 75–77 and 85–86 and pp. 569–76, below.

[4] See p. 575, below, with the references there given to previous passages in this Study.

[5] See pp. 49–50, above, and pp. 569–76, below.

establishment of a universal state by indigenous empire-builders, it might well have been supposed that, when the alien substitute, in the shape of the Spanish Viceroyalty of New Spain,[1] had in due course been supplanted by a Republic of Mexico which had sought, and gained, admission into the comity of Western states, the assimilation of the Central American Society into the body social of the Western Society had become an irreversibly accomplished fact. Yet the Mexican Revolution of A.D. 1821, which might thus have appeared to have completed the incorporation of the Central American into the Western World, had been followed by the Revolution of A.D. 1910, in which the buried but hibernating indigenous society had suddenly bestirred itself, raised its head, and broken through the crust of culture deposited by officious Castilian hands on the grave into which the *conquistadores* had thrust a body that they believed themselves to have slain. This portent from Central America raised the question whether the apparent cultural conquests of Western Christendom in the Andean World and elsewhere might not likewise prove, sooner or later, to have been no more than superficial and temporary.

The Far Eastern Civilization in China, Korea, and Japan, which had succumbed to the influence of the West within the last century before the time of writing, was manifestly far more potent than the Central American Civilization had ever been; and, if the indigenous culture of Mexico was reasserting itself after a four hundred years' eclipse, it would be rash to reckon that the Far Eastern Society was destined to be assimilated by the West or by Russia. As for the Hindu World, the inauguration of two 'successor-states' of the British Rāj in A.D. 1947 might be interpreted as a peacefully accomplished counterpart to the establishment of a Republic of Mexico by revolution in A.D. 1821, and at the time of writing it seemed possible that in this case, as in that, an act of political emancipation which had superficially set the seal upon the process of Westernization by bringing the emancipated state into the comity of Western nations, might prove in retrospect to have been the first step towards the cultural emancipation of a civilization that had been temporarily submerged by a Western tide.

The Arab countries, again, which had recently been gaining admission to the Western comity of nations as sovereign independent states,[2] had been able to achieve this ambition in virtue of their success in shaking off an Ottoman political ascendancy and an Iranic cultural veneer by which they had been overlaid for four centuries.[3] Was there any reason to expect that the latent survival power of the Arabic culture, which had enabled the Arabs to resist assimilation to the kindred culture of a sister society, would not assert itself, sooner or later, against the influence of the far more alien culture of the West? And, if the permanent Westernization of the Arabic World was not assured, there was also no assurance that the Ottoman Turkish converts from the Iranic culture, or even the Greek, Serb, Ruman, Bulgar, Georgian, and Russian converts from the Western Society's sister civilization, Orthodox Christendom, would abide in their new cultural allegiance. We can merely speculate on the

[1] See xi, map 72. [2] See IV. iv. 82 and 107. [3] See IV. iv. 113–14.

possibility that cultural conversions which, like those of the Aztecs, the Incas, and the Hindus, have been initiated by force of alien arms may prove less stable than conversions which have been entered into on the converts' own initiative, like those of the Irish,[1] the Scandinavians,[2] the Orthodox Christians,[3] the Japanese,[4] and the Jews[5] to the culture of the West, or the assimilation of the Manchus to the Far Eastern Civilization in China.[6]

The general effect of this survey of the ultimate consequences of 'cultural conversions' is to confirm our conclusion that the sole sure beneficiary from the services afforded by a universal state is the internal proletariat. The benefits obtained by the external proletariat are always illusory, while those obtained by an alien civilization are apt to be impermanent.

(c) THE SERVICEABILITY OF IMPERIAL INSTALLATIONS

1. *Communications*

An Analysis of Imperial Institutions

Having now examined the effects of two general characteristics of universal states—their conductivity and their peace—we may go on to survey the services afforded to their beneficiaries by particular concrete institutions which they themselves deliberately create and maintain, but which are apt to find their historic mission in roles for which they had never been cast by their makers. These imperial institutions may be grouped under the three heads of installations, currencies, and corporations, and each of these heads may be subdivided. The principal installations set up by a universal state are its communications, its garrisons and colonies, its provinces, and its capital city. Its most important currencies are its official language and script, its legal system, and its money, weights and measures, and calendar. Its major corporations are its army, its civil service, and its citizen body. If we consider each of these institutions in turn, we shall find it serving some unintended beneficiary in some measure.

The Spider's Web

Communications head the list, because they are the master-institution on which a universal state depends for its very existence. They are the instrument not only of its military command over its dominions but

1 The first act in the assimilation of the Irish was their voluntary decision, at the time of the Reformation, when their English rulers turned Protestant, to maintain their allegiance to a Catholicism which had been thrust upon them in the Early Medieval Age of Western history (see II. ii. 421–3). The second act was the captivation of the Irish, in the nineteenth century of the Christian Era, by the contemporary Western movement of Nationalism. (For recent Irish Linguistic Archaism as a symptom of Nationalism, see V. vi. 65–67 and 71).

2 See II. ii. 347–60 and V. vi. 64–65 and 71.

3 For the Westernization of the Modern Greeks, see II. ii. 226–7; V. vi. 68–70 and 71; and IX. viii. 161–84. For the deliberate attempt to transform the Russian Orthodox Christian universal state into a member of the comity of Western states, see IV. iv. 88–91.

4 See IV. iv. 88–91.

5 See II. ii. 252–4; V. vi. 70–71; and IX. viii. 286–8.

6 See V. v. 348–9 and 352.

also of its political control through overt imperial inspectors and unavowed secret service agents. For this imperial life-line does not consist merely of the physical media of travel. The highways offered ready-made by Physical Nature, in the shape of rivers,[1] seas,[2] and steppes,[3] do not provide practicable means of communication except in so far as they are effectively policed;[4] and the same political condition governs, *a fortiori*, the use of artificial or regulated inland waterways and man-made roads. Nor is the maintenance of public security enough in itself to make the potentialities of communication practically operative. In a geographical area so large as is the domain of even the least extensive universal state if measured by the standard of an individual human being's mobility even in a technologically efficient society, the traveller may be hard put to it to reach his destination unless he is given the privilege of using public means of transportation. In most of the universal states so far known to History, these means had taken the form of an imperial postal service; and the imperial postmaster-general at the seat of the central government, with his host of subordinates strung out along the roads radiating from the capital to the frontiers, had been apt to acquire the additional function of a chief of secret police whose most important duty, in the eyes of his masters, had been to turn his opportunities of intelligence to the central government's account by reporting on the conduct and ambitions of provincial governors and frontier commanders, and on the public opinion and temper of imperial troops and subject populations.

A public postal service seems to have been part of the machinery of government of the Empire of Sumer and Akkad. In its metropolitan territory of Shinar, the embankments of the irrigation canals appear to have served as highways for land-traffic.[5] 'The New Empire' of Egypt, which established its authority over the derelict Syrian and Mesopotamian provinces of the Empire of Sumer and Akkad after an interlude of barbarian Hyksos rule, used the roads which it inherited here from its predecessors for keeping control over the native princelings by a service of diplomatic couriers and travelling inspectors. In the Achaemenian Empire we find the same installations apparently raised to a higher level of organization and efficiency—though this apparent superiority in

[1] In the geographical structure of an Egyptical universal state the natural waterway provided by the River Nile served as a spinal cord, and a corresponding service was performed by the rivers Euphrates and Tigris for the Empire of Sumer and Akkad.

[2] 'The [Mediterranean] Sea stretches in a belt across the middle of the Inhabited World and across the middle of your [Roman] empire; and round the sea the continents extend "grand and grandly" (μεγάλαι μεγαλωστὶ κέκλινται)—continually supplying your needs with consignments of their products' (Aristeides, P. Aelius: *In Romam*, §§ 10–11 in B. Keil's edition (*Aelii Aristidis Quae Supersunt Omnia*, vol. ii (Berlin 1898, Weidmann), p. 94)). For the role of the Mediterranean Sea in the life of the Roman Empire, see further pp. 216–20, below.

[3] For the conductivity of the Steppe, see III. iii. 391–4. The centrally situated medium of communication which was provided for the Roman Empire by the Mediterranean Sea—as depicted by Aelius Aristeides in the passage quoted in the preceding footnote—was provided by the Great Western Bay of the Eurasian Steppe (see III. iii. 401) for the Nomad empires of the Royal Scythians, the Khazars, and the Golden Horde (see V. v. 281–9), and by the entire Eurasian Steppe for the short-lived Nomad Empire of the Mongol khāqāns who ruled from Qāraqorum (see p. 198, below).

[4] See the passage quoted from Epictetus in V. vi. 3 and 142, and on p. 92, below.

[5] See Woolley, L.: *Abraham* (London 1936, Faber), p. 122.

standard may be an illusion reflecting a mere difference in the amount of our information.

'The farther the bounds of the Empire were extended, the more powerful became the position of the provincial governors; and this made it the more necessary to create institutions for preserving the Empire's unity and for ensuring a prompt and unhesitating execution of Imperial commands. Instruments for holding the Empire together were the great roads converging on Susa and traversing the Empire in all directions in the track of the previously existing trade-routes. . . . These roads were measured in parasangs and were permanently maintained in good condition. The Imperial Highway[1] was provided, at intervals of about four parasangs on the average, with "imperial post-stations and excellent inns".[2] The provincial boundaries and the river crossings were guarded by strongly garrisoned fortresses (πύλαι)[3] (the desert frontier of Babylonia, among others, was provided with defences of the same kind).[4] At these points the traffic was subjected to searching supervision. All post-stations were manned by mounted couriers whose duty it was to convey imperial commands and official dispatches post-haste, travelling day and night without a break—"swifter than cranes", as the Greeks put it.[5] There is also said to have been a system of telegraphic communications by beacon-signals. To keep the satraps under control, the Emperor would take every opportunity of sending out into the provinces high officials, like the Emperor's "eye" or his brother or son, with troops at their back. These would arrive, without warning, to inspect the administration and report abuses. Further safeguards against misconduct on the satraps' part were provided by the presence of the imperial secretary who was attached to the provincial governor,[6] and of the commandants of fortresses and other military officers in his province, who all served as instruments of supervision. These checks were supplemented by a highly developed espionage system. The Emperor had a ready ear for denunciations.'[7]

This Achaemenian policy of utilizing the imperial communications system as an instrument for maintaining the central government's control over the provinces reappears in the administration of the Roman Empire, which eventually fell heir to the former Achaemenian dominions west of the Euphrates, and of the Arab Caliphate—a reincarnation of the Achaemenian Empire in which the Syriac universal state found its

1 i.e. the Great North-West Road connecting Susa with Sardis and Ephesus (see xi, map 20). The central section of this Achaemenian Imperial Highway, between Assyria and Cappadocia, had originally been opened up, as early as the third millennium B.C., by Assyrian pioneer traders whose settlements in Cappadocia had subsequently been embraced in the Empire of Sumer and Akkad (see I. i. 110–11).—A.J.T.

2 Σταθμοί τε πανταχῇ εἰσι βασιλήϊοι καὶ καταλύσιες κάλλισται (Herodotus, Book V, chap. 52).

3 The corresponding installations were called κλείσουραι (i.e. 'clausurae') in the East Roman Empire and 'derbends' in the Ottoman Empire.—A.J.T.

4 See Xenophon: *Expeditio Cyri*, Book I, chap. 5, § 5.—A.J.T.

5 Reminiscences of Herodotus's account of the Achaemenian system of communications, blending with the tenth verse of the seventh chapter of the Book of Daniel (quoted in the present Study, V. vi. 34), may have inspired Milton to write:

His state
Is kingly. Thousands at His bidding speed
And post o'er land and ocean without rest.
They also serve who only stand and wait.

The poet's application of this Achaemenian imagery is, of course, all his own.—A.J.T.

6 See Herodotus, Book III, chap. 128.—A.J.T.

7 Meyer, E.: *Geschichte des Altertums*, vol. iii (Stuttgart 1901, Cotta), pp. 66–68.

second avatar after the long interruption caused by the intrusion of the Hellenic Civilization upon the Syriac World between the Macedonian conqueror Alexander's crossing of the Hellespont in 334 B.C. and the Roman Emperor Heraclius's withdrawal behind the Amanus in A.D. 636.[1] In the case of the Caliphate a twentieth-century historian had at his disposal a wealth of information; for a full and accurate account of the ʿAbbasid road network and postal system had been extracted from the official records and preserved for Posterity in a corpus of treatises which was a notable monument of the classical Arabic literature,[2] while a picture of the Roman road network and postal system had been pieced together from archaeological and epigraphical evidence by Modern Western classical scholars.[3]

The Roman Imperial Cursus Publicus was instituted by Augustus himself—perhaps consciously on the Achaemenian pattern[4]—and the burden of providing the service, which was originally imposed on the local public authorities, appears to have been progressively taken over by the Imperial Treasury in the reigns of Hadrian and Septimius Severus, though this without ever ceasing to bear heavily on the populations of the territories through which the imperial highways ran.[5] Official dispatches were carried overland by corps of *tabellarii* and *cursores*, and oversea by *naves tabellariae*.[6] The Achaemenian inspiration of this Roman institution is betrayed in a characteristic use of couriers as spies. The emissaries of the Roman Imperial Government who went under the euphemistic names of *frumentarii* ('foragers') in the Age of the Principate and of *agentes in rebus* in the post-Diocletianic Age were counterparts, in Roman dress, of an Achaemenian emperor's 'eye'. Their administrative duty of superintending the conduct of the imperial postal service was coupled with the political duty of espionage.[7]

In the Caliphate under the ʿAbbasid régime the administration of the public postal service was turned to account for purposes of intelligence and police.

'At the capital of each of the large provinces into which the mighty empire was articulated there was a postmaster (*Sāhib al-Barīd*)[8] whose

1 See I. i. 75–77.

2 The Arabic texts of this corpus had been published by de Goeje, M. J., in his *Bibliotheca Geographorum Arabicorum* (Leyden 1870–94, Brill, 8 vols.). A masterly summary and appreciation of the facts was to be found in Le Strange, Guy: *The Lands of the Eastern Caliphate* (Cambridge 1905, University Press).

3 See Hirschfeld, O.: *Die kaiserlichen Verwaltungsbeamten bis auf Diocletian* (Berlin 1905, Weidmann), pp. 190–204, 'Die Reichspost', and pp. 205–11, 'Die Italischen Strassen'.

4 See ibid., p. 190.

5 See ibid., pp. 192–3.

6 See ibid., pp. 200–4.

7 See Grosse, R.: *Römische Militärgeschichte von Gallienus bis zum Beginn der byzantinischen Themenverfassung* (Berlin 1920, Weidmann), pp. 105–6. The postal service itself must, all the same, have been efficient—at any rate during the halcyon days of an Antonine Indian Summer. Otherwise Aelius Aristeides would hardly have ventured to write:

'An administrator sitting [in Rome] can govern the whole Inhabited World with the greatest facility by correspondence. The despatches are no sooner written than they are delivered, just as if they had travelled by air' (*In Romam*, edited by Keil, B., in *Aelii Aristidis Quae Supersunt Omnia*, vol. ii (Berlin 1898, Weidmann), p. 101 (Or. XXVI, § 33)).

8 This word *barīd*, which is used in Arabic to mean 'postal system', is derived from the Latin *verēda* meaning 'mail-cart'.—A.J.T.

duty it was to keep the Caliph continually informed of all affairs of any importance. The postmaster had even to keep an eye on the conduct of the governor and was thus a confidential agent of the Central Government's, appointed direct by them. The report of a Chief Postmaster of Baghdad, addressed to the Caliph Mutawakkil, has come down to us. . . . We even know the form of appointment of a postmaster. The Caliph commissions him therein to report from time to time on the conduct of the financial officials and of the administrators of the crownlands, on the state of agriculture, on the situation of the peasants, on the behaviour of the officials, and on statistics of the minting of gold and silver coin. He was also to be present when the troops were being reviewed and paid. It is clear that the postal service, as we understand it, was quite a secondary consideration.'[1]

The primary consideration was what it had been under the Achaemenian Government.

'The postmasters . . . were the sensitive octopus-arms which the Court of Baghdad extended into the provinces. . . . The postal system was made to serve the purposes of espionage: in this far-flung empire the intelligence service was most efficiently organized. In the later parts of his work, Tabarī gives the dates, not merely of the events themselves, but of the arrival at Court of the news of them.'[2]

The same institutions reappear in two empires built by representatives of an Iranic Muslim Civilization that was affiliated to the Syriac and had retained a memory of the parent society's achievements. Seventeenth-century Western observers of the Ottoman Empire avowed their admiration for the imperial highways—the like of which were not to be found in the Western Europe of that day—and for the courier service, staffed with mounted Tatars, who emulated the hard riding of Darius's Persian equerries. The contemporary empire of the Timurid Mughals in India never attained the Ottoman standard either in the material quality of its roads or in the effectiveness of its public police, but these shortcomings did not prevent it from operating an espionage and intelligence system in the Achaemenian and ʿAbbasid tradition. Confidential news bulletins were systematically sent in from each province by an official reporter (*wāqiʿah nawī*) and were submitted to the Emperor by his *mīr bakhshī*.[3] When the Mughal Power went to pieces in the eighteenth century of the Christian Era, this intelligence organization continued to function longer than most other parts of the dilapidated imperial administrative machine.

Napoleon, who was an active and ubiquitous builder of roads during the short life of the transitory universal state[4] which he provided for an abortive Medieval Western city-state cosmos,[5] was in this, as in so much of the rest of his work, making a conscious attempt to evoke a ghost of the Roman Empire; and the Petrine Russian Empire had deliberately set itself to acquire the Western technique which it used in its latter days for establishing and consolidating its hold over Transcaucasia, Trans-

[1] von Kremer, A. *Culturgeschichte des Orients unter den Chalifen* (Vienna 1875–7, Braumüller, 2 vols.), vol. i, pp. 193 and 195; English translation by S. Khuda Bukhsh: *The Orient under the Caliphs* (Calcutta 1920, University Press), pp. 230 and 232.

[2] Wellhausen, J.: *Das Arabische Reich und sein Sturz* (Berlin 1902, Reimer), p. 350.

[3] See Ibn Hasan: *The Central Structure of the Mughal Empire* (Oxford 1936, University Press), pp. 220–1.

[4] See xi, map 60.

[5] This aspect of the Napoleonic Empire has been examined in V. v. 619–42.

caspia, the Oxus–Jaxartes Basin, and a Maritime Province on the Pacific coast of the Continent by railway-building on a scale that outstripped all contemporary achievements in the United States and Canada. But similar circumstances and requirements likewise called similar administrative machinery into existence in other universal states which could not have drawn their inspiration, even at second or third hand, from the practice and experience of imperial chanceries at Ur or Susa or Rome or Baghdad.

Ts'in She Hwang-ti, the revolutionary founder of a Sinic universal state, was a builder of roads radiating from his capital, which he used for making political inspections and carrying out statistical surveys.[1] The inspectorate was elaborately organized. An Inspector-General, with two deputies, in the capital was served by a numerous staff of subordinates both in the capital and in the provinces, and there were special inspectorates, besides, for 'subject barbarians' and 'subject states'.[2] The Incas, likewise, were builders of roads and fortresses.[3] Like the Roman conquerors of Italy, the Incas, in their systematic northward conquests, used these instruments to consolidate each gain of ground, in preparation for the next advance.[4] The completed system consisted of two main roads running parallel, south and north, one along the Andean Plateau and the other along the Pacific Coast, with transverse connecting roads at intervals. These roads were carried across the rivers by bridges of stone and wood, by suspension bridges of rope, or by cable and basket.[5] There were store-houses strung along the route, and relays of post-runners[6] were stationed at intervals of one and a half leagues. A message could travel from Cuzco to Quito—a distance of more than a thousand miles as the crow flies and perhaps half as much again by road—in as short a time as ten days.[7] The organization of this service was attributed to the eighth Inca, Pachacutec (*imperabat circa* A.D. 1400–48).[8] The travelling facilities were used by the Inca himself and by itinerant imperial inspectors, intendants, and judges.[9]

'The surveillance [of the Central Government over the provinces] was provided for by inspectors, drawn from the ranks of the *orejones*,[10] who

[1] See Hackmann, H.: *Chinesische Philosophie* (Munich 1927, Reinhardt), p. 168; Fitzgerald, C. P.: *China, A Short Cultural History* (London 1935, Cresset Press), p. 138; Franke, O.: *Geschichte des Chinesischen Reiches*, vol. i (Berlin and Leipzig 1930, de Gruyter), p. 233. Ts'in She Hwang-ti imposed a standard measure for the axle-length of carts, in order that any cart might be able to travel over any of the deeply rutted roads in the loess country in the North and North-West. In the foregoing period of the Contending States, when each locality had had a customary axle-length of its own, through-traffic had been hampered by the necessity, at frequent intervals, of either changing the axles of the cart or else trans-shipping the freight to another cart of the right axle-gauge for the next stage of the journey (Fitzgerald, op. cit., p. 138; Franke, op. cit., vol. cit., p. 233).

[2] See Franke, op. cit., vol. cit., pp. 230 and 231.

[3] See Joyce, T. A.: *South American Archaeology* (London 1912, Lee Warner), p. 56.

[4] See ibid., p. 94.

[5] See ibid., pp. 106–7; Baudin, L.: *L'Empire Socialiste des Inka* (Paris 1928, Institut d'Ethnologie), pp. 189–96.

[6] See ibid., pp. 196–8.

[7] See ibid., p. 197.

[8] See Joyce, op. cit., p. 108.

[9] See ibid., p. 109; Markham, Sir Clements: *The Incas of Peru* (London 1910, Smith Elder), pp. 162–3; Baudin, op. cit., pp. 198–9.

[10] The nickname given to the ruling minority in the Inca Empire by their Spanish conquerors (see V. v. 50–51).—A.J.T.

made general tours of the Empire every three years, and by secret agents of the Inca . . . who paid visits, incognito, to all districts. These agents' instructions were to observe, to listen to complaints, and to report, but it was not within their competence to take measures for the suppression of abuses. Under this system, several brothers of the Inca Tupac Yupanqui were successively appointed inspectors. . . . The duties of inspector-in-chief were performed by the Inca himself; he travelled over the Empire in his golden litter, and during the whole period of his visits—which were very long, considering that he sometimes remained absent [from the capital] for as much as three or four years—he would be hearing petitions and dispensing justice.'[1]

While the means of communication with which the Inca Empire equipped itself were thus assiduously used by the public authorities, including the Emperor in person, they were not at the disposal of private travellers—in contrast to contemporary practice in Central America, where travelling companies of merchants, organized in a guild, were continually extending the field of their private economic enterprise[2] in advance of the expansion of the Aztec Empire,[3] like the Roman *negotiatores* who, in their irrepressible eagerness for profits, used to push their way in advance of the legions into perilous no-man's-lands,[4] and linger there after the legions had retreated.[5] This active international trade in private hands seems to have been part of the heritage of the Mexic Civilization from its Mayan predecessor.[6] On the other hand no evidence had survived to show that the Aztec Empire had been prompted by memories of 'the First Empire' of the Mayas when it had turned its commercial travellers to account as sources of military and political intelligence[7] or when it had constructed the installations with which it had confirmed its hold on its conquests in the manner of the contem-

[1] Baudin, op. cit., pp. 120–1. This particular duty afterwards devolved upon the Inca's alien successor the Spanish viceroy. 'The welfare of the Indians was presumed to be his special care, and he was expected to devote a part of two or three days each week to the consideration of Indian petitions' (Haring, C. H.: *The Spanish Empire in America* (New York 1947, Oxford University Press), p. 119).

[2] On this point see Joyce, T. A.: *Mexican Archaeology* (London 1914, Lee Warner), pp. 126–7; Gann, T.: *Mexico from the Earliest Times to the Conquest* (London 1936, Lovat Dickson), pp. 172–4; Vaillant, G. C.: *The Aztecs of Mexico* (London 1950, Penguin), pp. 122–3 and 208.

[3] See xi, map 71.

[4] As, for example, those who were massacred in Anatolia in 88 B.C. by Mithradates Eupator—to the number, it was said, of eighty thousand (see V. v. 69).

[5] As, for example, those whom, in A.D. 448, the Constantinopolitan envoy Priscus found doing their business in Attila's ordu in the former Roman province of Pannonia (for Priscus's mission see V. v. 473–4).

[6] See Gann, T., and Thompson, J. E.: *The History of the Maya* (London 1931, Scribner), pp. 200–1.

[7] 'In the Aztec period the travelling merchants became a special class, and their security of body and property, preserved at first for the advantages which each town could derive from their wares, was guaranteed by the force of Aztec arms. . . . Having to move step by step, and to intimidate or win over town after town, [the Aztecs] needed patience and knowledge of geographical and political conditions. One reason for the honour in which merchants were held was the information of this character which they could furnish from their travels. . . . In time they performed an important political function, spying out towns to conquer and reporting on the tribute which could be exacted. There is a very modern touch about the economic and political functions of these merchants who so often brought military conquest in their train' (Vaillant, op. cit., pp. 122–3, 208, and 213).

It will be seen that these merchants played in the acquisition of the Aztec Empire the role that in the maintenance of the Achaemenian Empire was played by 'the King's Eye', and in the maintenance of the 'Abbasid Empire by the postmasters.

porary Inca Power. The Aztec Imperial Government built and maintained highroads, threw bridges of stone, wood, or rafts across the rivers, and operated on these thoroughfares an imperial postal service manned by relays of couriers at intervals of five or six miles.[1]

In Japan the Great North-East Road,[2] running up the south-eastern side of the Main Island from the civil capital at Kyoto in the interior to the successive military capitals at Kamakura and Yedo, served first to secure the conquests made by the Far Eastern Civilization in Japan at the expense of the Ainu barbarians and afterwards to bring and keep Yamato under the domination of the Kwanto—as the new northern marches came to be called, after the name of the road by which they had been opened up.[3] Under the Tokugawa régime, which provided the Far Eastern Society in Japan with its universal state, this trunk road and its branches ministered to the policy of the Shogun's government at Yedo as an instrument not only for keeping an eye on the impotent Imperial Court at Kyoto, but also for the more formidable task of keeping to heel the feudal lords all over the Empire—especially those 'Outside Lords' (*Tozama*) whose houses had once been rivals of the Tokugawa in the grim struggle for power at the climax of a Japanese Time of Troubles. These *daimyō* were required by the Shogun to reside in Yedo, with their principal retainers, for so many months in the year, and to leave their wives and families there as hostages when they themselves were in residence in their fiefs, with the triple object of keeping them under supervision, loosening their personal hold on the fiefs from which they drew their political and military strength, and weakening them financially by putting them under social pressure to live, while in the capital, in a style beyond their means.[4] The migration, twice a year, of these feudal lords, with their retinues, between their fiefs in the provinces and their residences in the capital was one of the distinctive features of Japanese life in the Tokugawa Age; and the grand trunk road and its ramifications were the media of communication for their perpetual coming and going. While the Government were interested in seeing the means of communication kept up sufficiently well to serve this police purpose, they were equally interested in seeing to it that they should not be kept up well enough to tempt disaffected feudal forces into planning a convergent march on the capital; and they 'deliberately refrained from building bridges and otherwise facilitating communications on the main lines of approach to Yedo'.[5]

The Grand Canal

In the main body of the Far Eastern World in China the long-distance transportation of foodstuffs in bulk came to be one of the besetting

[1] See Gann, op. cit., p. 174.

[2] See xi, map 55A.

[3] See II. ii. 158–9.

[4] See Sansom, G. B.: *Japan, a Short Cultural History* (London 1932, Cresset Press), p. 436; Sadler, A. L.: *A Short History of Japan* (Sydney 1946, Angus & Robertson), p. 217.

[5] Sansom, op. cit., p. 437. Perhaps their scholars had reminded them of the unintended and untoward service that the roads built by Ts'in She Hwang-ti had once rendered to the rebels who had overthrown his régime a few years after his death (see pp. 99–100, below).

problems of public administration, owing to a tendency towards political unification under an oecumenical government seated in the North which persisted after the economic centre of gravity had shifted conclusively from the North to the Yangtse Valley.

'Commercial growth in China never reached a level which would enable it to overcome the localism and narrow exclusiveness of an agricultural economy. [The] regional groupings were highly self-sustaining and independent of each other; and—in the absence of machine industry, modern facilities of transport and communication and an advanced economic organisation—state centralisation in the modern sense was impossible. In the circumstances, the unity or centralisation of state power in China could only mean the control of an economic area where agricultural productivity and facilities of transport would make possible the supply of a grain tribute so predominantly superior to that of other areas that any group which controlled this area had the key to the conquest and unity of all China. It is areas of this kind which must be designated as the Key Economic Areas. . . .[1]

'The Yangtse Valley grew in importance as a productive centre during the Eastern Tsin (A.D. 317–420) and the other Southern dynasties (A.D. 420–589), definitely assuming the position of the Key Economic Area from the time of the T'ang Dynasty (A.D. 618–907).[2] Politically, the centre of gravity still lay in the North. . . . This anomalous situation rendered the development and maintenance of a transport system linking the productive South with the political North a vital necessity. The link was provided by the Grand Canal,[3] which engaged the attention of the best minds of China for more than ten centuries and demanded countless millions of lives and a large portion of the wealth of the country for its improvement and maintenance. . . .[4]

'Although traditionally the canal is ascribed to the genius and extravagance of Yang Ti [*imperabat* A.D. 605–18] of the Sui, it was not built in one period or by one emperor. Like the Great Wall, it was constructed in disconnected sections at different periods.[5] Yang Ti of the Sui completed

[1] Chi, Ch'ao-ting: *Key Economic Areas in Chinese History as Revealed in the Development of Public Works for Water-Control* (London 1936, Allen & Unwin), pp. 4–5. The quotations from this book have been made with the permission of the publishers.

[2] In the time of Han Yü, a writer on the subject of water control who lived from A.D. 768 to A.D. 824, 'Kiangnan' (i.e. the combined areas of the latter-day provinces of Kiangsu, Chekiang, Kiangsi, and Nganhwei) yielded nine-tenths of the total land-tax of the T'ang Empire (Chi, Ch'ao-ting, op. cit., p. 125).

[3] See xi, maps 46, 47, 54.—A.J.T.

[4] Chi, Ch'ao-ting, op. cit., p. 113.

[5] Waterways for the transportation of troops, tribute, grain, and merchandise were already being constructed in the Sinic World before the close of the period of Chan Kuo, 'the Contending States', which was the second and climacteric bout of the Sinic Time of Troubles (see ibid., p. 65).

Han Kou, the earliest canal linking the Yangtse River with the Hwai River, was dug in the second decade of the fifth century B.C. by King Fu Ch'ai of Wu (see ibid., pp. 65 and 117). This Yangtse–Hwai canal was straightened out, after the collapse of 'the United Tsin régime', by the Emperor Mo Ti of the refugee Tsin Dynasty in the South (*imperabat* A.D. 345–61) (see ibid., pp. 112 and 117); and it was restored in A.D. 587, to facilitate the transportation of tax-grain, by Sui Yang Kien (Wên Ti), who, in the ninth decade of the sixth century of the Christian Era, united the North and South of the main body of the Far Eastern World in a single oecumenical empire (see ibid., p. 117). This section was improved by Sui Yang Ti in A.D. 605 (see ibid., p. 117).

The Pien Canal, linking the Hwai River with the Yellow River, is likewise recorded to have been in existence already during the Chan Kuo period of Sinic history (see ibid., pp. 114–15); it appears to have been completed in A.D. 204 (see ibid., pp. 100–1); and under the refugee Tsin it was used by Wang Chün for the conquest of Wu (see ibid., p. 115). The Sui alinement of the Pien Canal was more direct than the preceding

it by linking the various waterways running in a north and south direction into a connected system[1] and adding long sectors both in the North and South.'[2]

While the completion of the Grand Canal, in its original alinement from Hangchow via Loyang to Si-Ngan, was thus the work of Sui Yang Ti, the solution of the problem of provisioning Si-Ngan from Kiangnan was worked out, after the fall of Yang Ti and his house, by the public servants of the succeeding T'ang régime. Granaries were built *en route*—particularly at either end of the Yellow River gorge ('the San Men Gates'), where storage facilities were required in order to allow of a six-mile portage overland.[3] This T'ang system of inland water communications was perfected between A.D. 764 and 780 by a public servant named Liu Yen, who, among other improvements, built five different types of boats for use on different sections;[4] but seven-tenths of the works accomplished under the T'ang Dynasty had been carried out before the outbreak of the devastating rebellion of An Lu-shan (*saeviebat* A.D. 755–66).[5]

This disaster was a premonition of a Time of Troubles that overtook the main body of the Far Eastern Society when the T'ang Dynasty finally went to pieces at the turn of the ninth and tenth centuries of the Christian Era.[6] After this Time of Troubles had entered on its second and more violent bout in the reign of the Sung Emperor Huitsung (*imperabat* A.D. 1101–25),[7] China relapsed into political disunity and,

one; it took off from the Yellow River at a point in the neighbourhood of Loyang, instead of at Kaifêng, and from this point it ran direct to the Hwai (see ibid., p. 115); but in this Hwai–Yellow River section of the Grand Canal, as in the Hwai–Yangtse section, Sui Yang Ti still had the advantage of having had predecessors.

The Yangtse–Hangchow section was dug by Yang Ti in A.D. 610, and thereby a continuous waterway was established between Yangchow and Loyang, the former capital of the Eastern Chóu and the Posterior Han (see pp. 212–13, below), which was erected by Yang Ti into a subsidiary imperial capital. The main capital of the Sui Empire was Si-Ngan, on the site of the Prior Han Dynasty's capital Ch'ang Ngan (see pp. 212 and 213, below); and Yang Ti carried his through-waterway to Si-Ngan from the new 'key economic area' in the South by restoring a canal, cut by Han Wuti in the seventh decade of the second century B.C., which had connected Ch'ang Ngan directly with the Yellow River—by-passing the Wei River, which was difficult to navigate in the gorge through which it made its way out of 'the Country within the Passes' into the Lower Yellow River Plain (see Chi, Ch'ao-ting, op. cit., pp. 81–82 and 119–20).

1 These vast public works were carried out by correspondingly onerous corvées. One hundred thousand men and women are said to have been conscripted by Sui Yang Ti to dig his Yangtse–Hwai canal; one million to dig his Yellow River–Hwai canal (see Chi, Ch'ao-ting, op. cit., pp. 117 and 116); and another million—again including women, to make good a shortage of men—to dig a branch taking off from the Yellow River in the Great Eastern Plain and linking up the main line of the Grand Canal with the Hai Ho Basin (see ibid., p. 120). The terrible harshness and brutality with which the workers on the Yellow River–Hwai (Pien) canal were treated are described in an anonymous contemporary monograph (see ibid., pp. 123–4). The means of communication created at this cost in human suffering served, when in existence, as instruments for enabling a ruling minority to intensify its exploitation of the masses. Hence the unpopularity of Han Wuti and Sui Yang Ti (see ibid., p. 122). The first of the revolts that ended in the overthrow of the Sui Dynasty was provoked by Yang Ti's enterprise of digging his Yellow River–Hai Ho branch of the Grand Canal to bring supplies to Sui armies engaged in a war with the Sui Empire's neighbour the North-West Korean state of Koguryŏ (see Bingham, W.: *The Founding of the T'ang Dynasty: The Fall of Sui and the Rise of T'ang: A Preliminary Survey* (Baltimore 1941, Waverley Press), pp. 37–46).

2 Chi, Ch'ao-ting, op. cit., pp. 113–14.

3 See ibid., pp. 125–7.

4 See ibid., p. 127.

5 See ibid., p. 128.

6 See IV. iv. 86 and 87–88 and V. vi. 306.

7 See V. vi. 307.

therewith, the problem of long-distance grain transport automatically fell into abeyance; but, when unity was restored, and the Time of Troubles brought to an end, by Mongol empire-builders who established a Far Eastern universal state with its capital at Peking, this problem of grain transport presented itself again, and this time in geographical circumstances that made it more difficult to solve than it had been in the days of an oecumenical government seated 'beyond the passes' at Si-Ngan—which the T'ang, like the Sui, had chosen for their capital—and still more difficult than in the days, between A.D. 960 and the disastrous year A.D. 1124, when the Sung had ruled virtually the whole of China from Kaifêng[1]—the most convenient of all possible sites in the Yellow River Basin for water communications with the South, lying, as it did, in the very middle of the Great Eastern Plain.

The Mongols had followed the lead of their forerunners the Kin in choosing Peking for their capital because this site lay just inside the northernmost limits of the cultivated land of China, within convenient proximity to the steppes on which the Nomad conquerors of China were at home. Unlike the Kin, however, who had never succeeded in pushing southward beyond the basin of the Yellow River into the basin of the Yangtse, the Mongols had proceeded to conquer the whole of China right down to Canton inclusive; and this achievement raised for them the questions how they were to administer this vast, populous, and wealthy domain from a capital located on its extreme northern verge and how they were to keep this capital supplied from a southern 'key economic area' which was more remote from Peking than it was from Kaifêng, Loyang, or even Si-Ngan. This problem was inherited from the Mongols by their indigenous Chinese supplanters the Ming, who soon found by experience that the military and political considerations telling in favour of Peking outweighed those considerations of cultural sentiment and economic convenience that had led the founder of the new dynasty to try the experiment of transferring the capital to the historic site of Nanking.[2] But a reunited China could not be governed from Peking without some effective medium of communication for maintaining the Imperial Government's political control over the distant Yangtse Basin and still more distant southern seaboard, and for bringing rice northward in bulk for the two purposes of paying in kind the taxes due to the Imperial Government from the rice-growing provinces and at the same time feeding the vast and increasing population of an economically eccentric capital. This problem was solved by a re-alinement of the Grand Canal which made Peking instead of Kaifêng its northern terminus.

From Peking southwards as far as the River Hwai, the Yüan (Mongol) Grand Canal was an entirely new enterprise, for Sui Yang Ti's branch, linking the Hai Ho with the Yellow River, had not been alined with the direct route between the Hai Ho Basin and the southern sections of the main line, and in any case the whole of the northern part of the Sui canal system had been wrecked by the retreating Sung in A.D. 1128, when they had breached the embankments of the Yellow River in order

[1] See p. 213, below. [2] See II. ii. 121–2.

to check the advance of the pursuing Kin invaders.[1] The cutting of the new northern section was started, from Peking southwards, in A.D. 1292, and the completed Yüan Grand Canal continued to be used, after the expulsion of the Mongols, by their successors the Ming and the Manchus,[2] as the Sui Grand Canal had continued to be used by the Sui's successors the T'ang and the Sung. The Grand Canal served, in fact, as the spinal cord of the Chinese body politic and body economic[3] until the dissolution of the traditional structure of Chinese social life in the course of the nineteenth century of the Christian Era under the economic impact of the West.[4]

In all chapters of its history the Grand Canal was, of course, mainly a medium for the slow transport of commodities in bulk, and it could not take the place of roads as media for a postal service. Accordingly, when the main body of the Far Eastern World was politically united, an oecumenical network of roads, to carry an imperial postal service, had to be maintained side by side with an oecumenical system of inland water transport. The Manchus revived a postal system, once maintained by the Ming,[5] which was perhaps ultimately derived from the system with which a Sinic universal state had been endowed by Ts'in She Hwang-ti.[6]

'*All Roads Lead to Rome*'

It will be seen that, in constructing and maintaining their impressive systems of communications, the makers and masters of universal states usually had a clear and precise idea of the purposes for which they were burdening their subjects with these costly public works. Yet the sequel shows that the most sagaciously organized system of imperial communications may be utilized by other parties than the Imperial Government—and this for purposes to which the official owners and operators of the system would have been either indifferent or hostile if they could have foreseen this unintended use to which their carefully designed installations were to be put.

This variation on the motif of the victory of the dark horse[7] is piquantly illustrated in the history of the magnificent communications system of the Roman Empire.

The splendour of this achievement on the social and political plane is ungrudgingly admitted in a passage already quoted[8] from the pen of a Greek Stoic philosopher, living and teaching near the beginning of the second century of the Roman Peace, who is at the same time sharply

[1] See Chi, Ch'ao-ting, op. cit., p. 140. [2] See ibid., p. 140.

[3] In the last days of the Yüan régime, when the Mongols were losing their grip on the 'key economic area' in the Yangtse Basin which they had linked with Peking by their new alinement of the Grand Canal, they attempted, from A.D. 1352 onwards, to develop a subsidiary source of supply in the immediate neighbourhood of Peking in the Hai Ho Basin; but this policy never had much success (ibid., pp. 144–6).

[4] Chi, Ch'ao-ting, op. cit., p. 149. An interesting account of an excursion on the Yüan Grand Canal that was made in A.D. 1853 by an acute Western student of the Far Eastern Civilization in China will be found in Meadowes, T. T.: *The Chinese and Their Rebellions* (London 1856, Smith Elder), pp. 213–50.

[5] See Michael, F.: *The Origin of Manchu Rule in China* (Baltimore 1942, Johns Hopkins Press), p. 118, n. 16. [6] See p. 85, above.

[7] For other variations on the same elemental theme see IV. iv. 245–584, *passim*.

[8] Epictetus: *Dissertations*, Book III, chap. xiii, §§ 9–13, quoted in V. vi. 3 and 142 (in the latter place, including the moral).

aware of the psychological and spiritual limitations of Caesar's power and, indeed, cites his potency in policing the Hellenic World only in order to bring out this contrast.

'You see that Caesar appears to provide us with a great peace, because there are no longer any wars or battles or any serious crimes of brigandage or piracy, so that one can travel at any season and can sail from the Levant to the Ponent.'

Towards the close of the same century the eulogy was repeated, without the philosopher's reservation, by a Greek man of letters of a school which had recognized the Roman Empire as the Hellenic universal state.

'The common saying that Earth is the all-mother and the universal home has been demonstrated by you Romans to perfection; for to-day Greek or barbarian, travelling heavy or travelling light, is at liberty to go where he pleases, at his ease; and, wherever he goes, he will never be leaving home behind him. The Cilician Gates and the narrow sandy passage through the Arab country to Egypt[1] have both alike lost their terrors. The mountains are no longer trackless, the rivers no longer impassable, the tribesmen no longer ferocious; it is a sufficient passport to be a Roman citizen or indeed a Roman subject; and Homer's saying that "the Earth is common to all men" has been translated into fact by you, who have surveyed the whole Inhabited World and have thrown all manner of bridges over the rivers and have hewn cuttings through the mountains until you have made the Earth *carrossable*—with your post-houses planted in the wilderness and your system and order spreading civilisation far and wide.'[2]

If the makers and the panegyrists of the Roman imperial system of communications could have foreseen the future, they would have found it intolerable no doubt, but not unintelligible in a world in which 'all roads' led 'to Rome', that the thoroughfares which in their time were bringing prisoners, petitioners, and sightseers to the Imperial City should one day bring barbarian war-bands or the armies of rival empires. They might even have taken a rueful pride in the thought that, in their impartial service to foes and friends alike, the Roman roads would still be bearing witness to the Empire's former greatness in those latter days of her adversity. These imperial highways certainly enabled, and possibly inspired, the barbarians to make straight for the heart of the Hellenic World.[3]

The Vandals, for instance, entered Spain within three years, and appeared before the walls of Carthage within twenty-four years, of their passage of the Rhine on the 31st December, A.D. 406. The Arabs arrived in Egypt within six years, at Carthage within sixty-four years, and all but in sight of the River Loire within ninety-nine years of their first raid across the Syrian *limes* of the Roman Empire in A.D. 633. And the Romans' Persian rivals for world dominion reached Calchedon, the

[1] See Herodotus, Book III, chaps. 4–7 and 88.—A.J.T.

[2] Aristeides, P. Aelius: *In Romam*, §§ 100–1 in B. Keil's edition (*Aelii Aristidis Quae Supersunt Omnia*, vol. ii (Berlin 1898, Weidmann), pp. 120–1).

[3] This strategy of the barbarian invaders of the Roman Empire is pointed out by Nilsson, M. P.: *The Minoan-Mycenaean Religion and its Survival in Greek Religion* (London 1927, Milford), p. 33.

Asiatic suburb of Constantinople, within twelve years, and Alexandria within sixteen years, of their crossing of the Mesopotamian frontier of the Roman Empire in A.D. 603.

The inland sea which the Romans had confidently styled *mare nostrum*[1] proved even more serviceable to barbarian raiders than the Empire's overland media of communication. Goths who had won a frontage on the north coast of the Black Sea by descending from the interior of the Continent and seizing the Roman Empire's local client state, the Bosporan principality, took to the water in A.D. 254 and, forcing their way out through the Straits into the Aegean, sacked Athens in A.D. 268. A band of Franks, who had been planted by the Emperor Probus (*imperabat* A.D. 276–82) on the sea-coast of Pontus, to hold for the Empire against the Alans a frontier at the opposite extremity to the sector that was threatened by the Franks themselves from their native lair, seized ships and succeeded in exploring their way 'from the mouth of the Phasis to that of the Rhine'.[2] This Frankish exploit was subsequently surpassed by the Vandals, who, after establishing themselves in Carthage, likewise took to the sea and put Epictetus's limited homage to Caesar out of date by turning a Mediterranean that had been 'a Roman lake' since the morrow of the Battle of Actium into the naval arena that it had been at the climax of the foregoing Time of Troubles, when Sextus Pompeius was defying Augustus, or when the Cilician pirates were challenging the might of a Roman Republic that had overthrown all its peers, or when Carthage was contending with Rome for the dominion of the Hellenic World. Indeed the Vandals achieved what the Pompeians and Cilicians and Carthaginians had hardly dreamed of accomplishing. In A.D. 455 they captured Rome from the sea. Such a sensational reversal of maritime fortunes had not been witnessed in Mediterranean waters since, more than eighteen hundred years before, 'the thalassocracy of Minos' had been overthrown by Vandal-like Mycenaean and Goth-like Achaean sea-rovers.

If Romans of the generation of Domitian or of the seemingly halcyon Age of the Antonines could have foreknown these coming events, they might have been overcome by horror and indignation, yet they would hardly have been bewildered as they certainly would have been if they had been told that, by their time, the superb imperial system of communications had already fulfilled its historic mission by facilitating the journeys of a private Roman citizen of whom they had never heard. When Augustus imposed the Roman Peace on a Pisidia that had not been effectively subdued by either the Achaemenids on the Seleucids, he was unconsciously paving the way for Saint Paul, on his first missionary journey from Antioch-on-Orontes, to land in Pamphylia and travel inland, unmolested, to Antioch-in-Pisidia, Iconium, Lystra, and Derbe. And Pompey had swept the Cilician pirates off the seas in order that Paul might make his momentous last voyage from a Palestinian Caesarea

[1] See p. 81 with n. 2, above, and pp. 216–17, below.

[2] Gibbon, Edward: *The History of the Decline and Fall of the Roman Empire*, chap. xii, following Panegyrici Veteres (the passage will be found on p. 145 of Bährens' edition) and Zosimus, *Historiae*, Book I, chap. lxxi, §§ 3–5. The audacious adventurers sacked Syracuse *en route*.

to an Italian Puteoli without having to brave man-made perils in addition to the ordeals of tempest and shipwreck.

If we think of Antioch-on-Orontes as the base of operations from which Saint Paul achieved his spiritual conquests, we shall realize how successful and enduring Paul's achievements were by comparison with the military and political enterprises of the House of Seleucus, which had operated from the same headquarters from the day when Seleucus Nîcâtôr had ousted his rival war-lord Antigonus Monophthalmus from this key position and had removed the rising city of Antigoneia to a more commanding adjacent site to which he had given the new name of Antioch.[1] The appeal 'Come over into Macedonia and help us',[2] which moved Saint Paul to deliver his triumphantly audacious assault upon the European shore of the Hellenic World's Aegean heart, had been heard, and responded to, by Seleucus Nîcâtôr at the height of his fortunes, in an hour when the overthrow of Lysimachus in succession to the overthrow of Antigonus had made him master of the lion's share of the Achaemenian heritage in Asia; and it had sounded again in the ears of Nîcâtôr's descendant Antiochus the Great, when, after emulating his ancestor's exploits by driving to the wall Lysimachus's Pergamene heirs, he was hovering, like Paul in a later age, in the Asiatic hinterland of the Hellespont. Yet the enterprise which Paul was to carry to so brilliant a conclusion on the spiritual plane had ended in both political and personal disaster for Seleucus I and Antiochus III.

Seleucus—impelled by homesickness to revisit at last the native land which he had not seen since he had crossed the Hellespont with Alexander fifty-three years before—had hardly recrossed the Straits and set foot again in Europe when he was treacherously assassinated by an unscrupulous adventurer; Antiochus, ambitiously aspiring to snatch the championship of the Macedonian cause against Rome out of the hands of Antigonus's descendant King Philip V of Macedon and to avenge, in his rival's stead, the honourable defeat which Macedonian arms had suffered at Cynoscephalae, only brought upon himself his ignominious military fiascos at Thermopylae and Magnesia, and had to pay the political penalty of surrendering all Seleucid possessions in Europe and Asia north-west of Taurus. Following in these inauspicious footsteps, Saint Paul, in his spiritual campaigns, succeeded where the Seleucidae had failed. In the Hellespontine city of Alexandria Troas, which had closed its gates against Antiochus,[3] Paul succeeded in founding a Christian congregation.[4] And the fatuous boast of Antiochus's swashbuckler Aetolian allies that they would pitch their camp on the banks of the Tiber[5] sets a standard by which we may measure Paul's successful fulfilment of his prediction that he was to see Rome as well as

[1] For the relation between Antioch and its forerunner Antigoneia, see Tscherikower, V.: *Die Hellenistischen Städtegründungen von Alexander dem Grossen bis auf die Römerzeit* (Leipzig 1927, Dieterich), p. 61; Bouché-Leclercq, A.: *Histoire des Séleucides* (Paris 1913–14, Leroux, 2 vols.), vol. i, pp. 32–33, and vol. ii, p. 522; Bevan, E. R.: *The House of Seleucus* (London 1902, Edward Arnold, 2 vols.), vol. i, pp. 211–12. See also the present Study, pp. 201–3, below.

[2] Acts xvi. 9.

[3] See Livy, Book XXXV, chap. 42.

[4] See Acts xx. 6–12.

[5] See Livy, Book XXXV, chap. 33.

her Oriental and Greek dominions.[1] He reached Rome as a political prisoner, but, whatever the length of his sojourn there and in whatever way he may have met his end in This Life, it is certain that his presence and action in the Imperial City ensured the survival there of an infant Christian congregation that was to have a greater destiny than any other in the Hellenic World.[2]

The Roman Roads' Service to the Christian Church

If this contrast between Paul's success and the Seleucids' failure is mainly to be explained by the difference of the planes on which the Apostles of Jesus and the Successors of Alexander were operating, the no less striking contrast between Paul's success and the Mauryan Emperor Açoka's failure in a philosophic missionary enterprise in the same Mediterranean area may be ascribed in a large measure[3] to the establishment of the Roman Peace in the Hellenic World between the Buddhist philosopher-king's and the Christian Apostle's day. Açoka has left us a notice of the philosophic missions which he sent to the realms of five of Alexander's successors in the second generation,[4] but no record of his emissaries' activities has come to us from their mission field, and, whatever their fortunes may have been, they made no discernible effect upon the history of Mankind. In seeking to propagate the philosophy of Siddhārtha Gautama beyond the western limits of his own Mauryan Peace, Açoka was unlucky in his generation, for the Achaemenian Peace, which had proved so conductive a medium for Judaism and Zoroastrianism,[5] and had perhaps conveyed to the Hellenic World the Zoroastrian and Indic elements that are to be found in Orphism,[6] had been broken up by force of Macedonian arms two generations before Açoka's time, and the anarchy that racked the Syriac and Hellenic worlds, with little intermission, from this break-up of the Achaemenian Peace to the establishment of the Roman Peace was particularly unpropitious for missionary work.

On the other hand the Roman Peace proved as propitious a social environment for Paul's successors as it had been for Paul himself. In the latter part of the second century of the Roman Empire's existence, Saint

[1] See Acts xix. 21.

[2] Though Rome had been the queen of Christian cities in the history of Christianity so far, it would have been unwarrantable in A.D. 1952 to assume that she was destined to retain her historic primacy in perpetuity. The advent of Christianity was then still a recent event, even on that time-scale of the histories of civilizations which was so infinitesimally short by comparison with the age of the Human Race or with the aeons of geological and astronomical reckonings (on this point see I. i. 173, n. 2). At the time when these lines were being written, Christianity had hardly yet begun to retrieve the loss of its former Nestorian and Monophysite provinces by winning converts beyond the bounds of the two societies—those of Western and Orthodox Christendom—which were the daughter civilizations of the Hellenic Society. By the same date, however, the Western Civilization had already thrown the tentacles of its communications system and its technology round the whole habitable and traversable surface of the planet. If Christianity were to make as good a use of this opportunity as it had once made of the similar opportunity presented by the Roman Empire, there was no knowing where in the World its eventual centre of gravity would be found.

[3] In large measure, yet only in part, for Açoka was handicapped in his spiritual enterprise by his political power. The ineffectiveness of political power as an instrument for propagating philosophies or religions from above downwards has been discussed in V. v. 646–712.

[4] See V. v. 131–2. [5] See V. v. 124–5. [6] See V. v. 85–87.

Irenaeus of Lyon—a Christian Father who was an approximate contemporary of the pagan Greek man of letters Publius Aelius Aristeides—was paying an implicit tribute to the Empire in extolling the unity of the Catholic Church throughout the Hellenic World.

'Having received this gospel and this faith, . . . the Church, in spite of her dispersal throughout the World, preserves these treasures as meticulously as if she were living under one single roof. She believes in these truths as unanimously as if she had only one soul and a single heart, and she preaches them and expounds them and hands them down as concordantly as if she had only one mouth. While the languages current in the World are diverse, the force of the [Church's] tradition is one and the same everywhere. There is no variety in the faith or in the tradition of the churches that have established themselves in the Germanies or in the Spains or among the Celts or in the East or in Egypt or in North-West Africa, or, again, of the churches that have established themselves at the World's centre. Just as God's creature the Sun is one and the same throughout the World, so likewise the Gospel of the Truth shows its light everywhere.'[1]

This successor of Paul's failed to recognize—or at any rate forbore to acknowledge—how much the Christian Church was indebted for her marvellous unanimity-in-ubiquity to the communications system of the Roman Empire. But the connexion was disagreeably evident two hundred years later, in an age when the Church had become the official partner of the Roman State, to a pagan historian bred in the city that had been the spiritual headquarters of Saint Paul and the political headquarters of the Seleucidae.

'[The Emperor] Constantius [II]',[2] writes Ammianus Marcellinus of Antioch, 'found the Christian religion uninvolved and straightforward and proceeded to muddle it up with old wives' superstitions. As his delight in complicated theological hair-splitting was greater than his sense of responsibility for maintaining harmony, he provoked innumerable dissensions, and he added fuel to the galloping flames by organizing acrimonious debates. One consequence was that crowds of prelates made use of the public post-horses (*iumentis publicis*) for rushing to and fro on the business of these "synods", as they call them. The prelates' object was to wrench the whole practice of their religion into conformity with their own caprice; Constantius's achievement was to ham-string the postal service (*rei vehiculariae succideret nervos*).'[3]

The sentiments of Ammianus, a Roman soldier of Greek birth writing history in the Latin tongue, would have been applauded by the Roman administrators who had called the imperial system of communications into existence and by the Greek men of letters who had eulogized it as its apogee. Though the waters of the Mediterranean Sea and the pavement of the chaussées leading inland from its shores were free for all comers to traverse at their own risk, exertion, and expense, the imperial postal service was not a facility provided by the Government for the

[1] Irenaeus: *Contra Haereses*, Book II, chap. x, § 2 (Migne, J.-P.: *Patrologia Graeca*, vol. vii, cols. 552–3), quoted already in V. v. 407, n. 4.

[2] Constantius II *imperabat* A.D. 337–61.—A.J.T.

[3] Ammianus Marcellinus: *Res Gestae*, Book XXI, chap. xvi, § 18.

convenience of the public, but a burden imposed on the public by the Government for strictly official purposes;[1] and, before the bishops took the mail-carts by storm, the passes (*diplomata*) entitling private persons to travel by public post were issued very sparingly, and this only on warrants from the very highest authorities.[2] Itinerant second-century Greek lecturers who would have been happy to receive passes for themselves would have grudged them to itinerant fourth-century prelates if they could have foreseen the appearance of such strange personages above the historical horizon of their conventional-minded age. But the Roman system of imperial communications is not the only one that illustrates the irony of history.

The Beneficiaries of Means of Communication created by Other Universal States

The Empire of Sumer and Akkad was as hard hit by its own efficiency in this department of imperial administration as the Roman Empire was in the last chapter of the story. Its north-eastern highways[3] eventually conveyed both the flood of Mitanni Nomad invasion which swept across Mesopotamia and over Syria into the Nile Delta[4] and the contemporary infiltration of Kassite mountaineers into Shinar—a sluggish flow whose waters, eventually submerging Babylon, turned the latter-day capital of a Sumeric universal state into a cultural morass that it was to take the best part of a thousand years to reclaim.[5] The corresponding north-western highway[6] conveyed Hittite marauders from the Anatolian Plateau on the lightning raid in which they sacked Babylon *circa* 1595 or 1531 B.C.[7] The success with which the barbarians thus used the imperial thoroughfares of the Empire of Sumer and Akkad to break the Empire's power and to plunder its wealth was sensational, yet at the same time it was a performance which was to have little lasting effect on the fortunes of Mankind, as was evident in the perspective of some three and a half millennia of subsequent history. There was, however, another unintended beneficiary from these roads whose influence, under many masks, was still at work in the World in A.D. 1952; for it was the forerunners of this Sumeric

1 See Hirschfeld, op. cit., pp. 190–1 and 204.
2 See ibid., pp. 198–200.
3 See xi, map 11.
4 See I. i. 104–7.
5 The Babylonic Civilization which eventually arose on the derelict site of the Sumeric World must have been in full cultural health in the eighth century B.C., when it began to make major discoveries in the field of astronomy (see IV. iv. 23–24).

'Astronomy was not a science at a fabulously early time; its beginnings as a science date back only to the late Assyrian period, its best-known devotees lived under the Achaemenid Persians, its greatest triumphs were under Seleucid or even Parthian rule. . . . The first advance is attributed to the Babylonian King Nabu-nasir, whose era, beginning 747 and remembered to late classical times, introduced a nineteen-year cycle of intercalation which was later modified but never abandoned in principle. Significant is the fact that the first eclipses quoted by Ptolemy date from exactly this time. Evidently there was a new emphasis on observation. . . . Scientific astronomy was primarily developed from practical considerations, and, in particular, from the need of adjusting the calendar' (Olmstead, A. T.: 'Babylonian Astronomy—Historical Sketch', in the *American Journal of Semitic Languages and Literatures,* vol. lv, April 1938, No. 2, pp. 114 and 117).

6 See xi, map 11.

7 The historical context, as well as the dating, suggested for the Hittite sack of Babylon in I. i. 111 and V. v. 263–4, had to be reconsidered in the light of archaeological discoveries made since the writing of the first six volumes of this Study (see the Note on Chronology in vol. x, on pp. 167–212, below).

imperial communications system that had conveyed the worship of Ishtar and Tammuz, the Mother and her Son, on the first stages of that long journey which—in diverging directions and through continual metamorphoses—was to carry this rudiment of a Sumeric higher religion over Syria to the shrine at Abydos on the banks of the Nile, and over Asia Minor to the Island of Heligoland among the waters of the North Sea.[1]

When the Achaemenidae, establishing a wider empire on the site of Ur-Nammu's and Šulgi's, reconditioned the same north-western highway and extended it to the shores of the Aegean and the Hellespont, they, in their turn, were leading a lightning conductor into the heart of their dominions. Their magnificent installations opened the way for the Pretender Cyrus the Younger to march his invincible ten thousand Greek mercenaries from Sardis to Cunaxa,[2] and for Alexander to follow, from the Granicus to Arbela, the trail which the Ten Thousand had blazed for an Hellenic conquest of South-Western Asia. The lightning speed of Alexander's marches in the western and central provinces of the Empire bears witness to the excellence of the Achaemenian roads as well as to the endurance of the Macedonian troops and to their leader's own demonic energy.[3] The political achievements of Alexander and his successors were, however, as negative and ephemeral as they were astonishing. While it took them no more than five years to break the Achaemenian Empire up, they never succeeded in putting the fragments together again. The true beneficiaries of the Achaemenian empire-builders' constructive work were two higher religions, Judaism and Zoroastrianism, and the tragically efficient destructive ability of the Macedonian *conquistadores* cleared the field, not for a Macedonian reproduction of the Achaemenian Empire, but for an influx of Hellenic culture.

When, after an interval of nearly a thousand years of Hellenic intrusion, the Syriac universal state, originally embodied in the Achaemenian Empire, was reconstituted at last in the shape of the Arab Caliphate,[4] it was the turn of the north-eastern highway—now pushed forward again by Arab empire-builders up to the Transoxanian shore of the Eurasian Steppe[5]—to serve as the suicidally directed lightning conductor for a *Blitzkrieg* in the Nomadic style of warfare. The *coup de grâce* which the Empire of Sumer and Akkad had received from the Hittites, and the Achaemenian Empire from the Macedonians, pouring down the north-west highway from a barbarian reservoir in Europe, was administered to the Caliphate by Turks and Mongols breaking in from the Eurasian Steppe in the track of the Mitanni.[6] Contemporaneously, other barbarian

[1] See V. v. 148–52 and IX. viii. 453.

[2] The efficiency of the Achaemenian system of communications is attested, not only by the ease and rapidity of Cyrus the Younger's south-eastward march, but by the necessity in which the Ten Thousand found themselves, on their subsequent retreat, of abandoning the Imperial Highway, and taking to the trackless mountains of Kurdistan, in order to shake off their pursuers (see Xenophon: *Expeditio Cyri*, Book III, chap. v, §§ 7–18).

[3] North-east of the Caspian Gates, Alexander had a very much rougher and slower passage. An explanation of this contrast has been offered in II. ii. 139–40.

[4] See I. i. 73–77.

[5] See II. ii. 141–2 and 378–84.

[6] On this point see I. i. 104–6.

invaders of the Caliphate were sped on their way by other imperial thoroughfares. The North African coast-road from Alexandria to the Straits of Gibraltar,[1] which the Primitive Muslim empire-builders had opened up, and the road from the Straits of Gibraltar to the Rhône,[2] which they had taken over from the Roman Empire's Visigothic successor-state, served to carry the barbarian Arab Banu Hilāl and Sulaym from east to west, the Western Christian invaders of the Peninsular domain of Dār-al-Islām from north to south, and Berber war-bands—unsuccessfully disguised by the high-sounding names of 'Fātimids', Murābits, and Muwahhids—both eastward to the Nile and northward to the Ebro. Here too, however, the lasting beneficiary from the imperial system of communications was not any barbarian invader. The historic mission of the wonderful organization described in the Corpus of Arab Geographers[3] was to facilitate the propagation of Islam.

A few more illustrations of our theme may be cited to complete the tale. The thoroughfares traversing the Eurasian Steppe in all directions —from the Carpathians, Pamirs, and Kwenlung to Qāraqorum and Peking—that were opened up for the short span of about ninety years[4] by the Mongol Empire, were to serve, not the Mongol empire-builders, but alien religious missionaries. These Mongol-made thoroughfares gave Western Catholic Christianity its first opportunity to attempt the conversion of China;[5] they gave Islam two footholds within China's western borders;[6] and they prepared the way for the eventual conversion of the Mongols themselves and their Calmuck kinsmen to the Tibetan Tantric form of Mahayanian Buddhism.[7] The Grand Trunk Canal which was the *chef d'œuvre* among the public works of the Far Eastern universal state in China served to convey a second wave of Western Catholic Christian missionaries from the southern ports to Peking. The communications system of the Timurid Mughal Empire in India, which was too ramshackle to hold the Empire together, sufficed to carry contemporary Catholic missionaries on successive expeditions from Goa to Agra and made it possible for the Emperor Akbar to assemble at his court a mixed company of exponents of rival faiths whose seances in his presence inspired him to promulgate his own abortive *Din Ilāhī*.[8] The roads efficiently provided by the Aztecs and the Incas enabled Cortés and Pizarro to overrun two new worlds with the lightning speed of a Macedonian Alexander, and thereby opened the way for Catholicism to make lasting spiritual conquests in these evanescent military *conquistadores'* wake. In the Sinic World, Ts'in She Hwang-ti's work was overtaken by the same nemesis.

'The construction of roads was a benefit to the Empire, but it proved a danger to the Ts'in Dynasty. When the great revolt occurred, the armies of the rebels found that the new roads served their purposes as well [as], or better than, those of the soldiers of Ts'in. For all the roads centred on the capital. The rebel armies were thus able to move swiftly and easily into the western hill country, hitherto so difficult of access, while the Ts'in

[1] See xi, maps 33 and 37. [2] See ibid.
[3] See p. 83, above. [4] *Circa* A.D. 1241–1328 (see V. v. 112 and XIII. x. 76, n. 3).
[5] See V. v. 113–15. [6] See pp. 74–75, above, and p. 160, below.
[7] See III. iii. 451; IV. iv. 497; and V. v. 309–10. [8] See V. v. 699–704.

generals, endeavouring to cope with rebellion in all parts of China, were hampered by the lack of lateral communications.'[1]

During a Napoleonic occupation of Dalmatia that lasted less than ten years, the French empire-builders did their road-building so well for the benefit of a Hapsburg Monarchy which was to enter into the fruits of their labours that the subsequent spectacle of these fine public works which the French had left behind them startled the astonished Emperor Francis into exclaiming that it was a pity that the French had not stayed in Dalmatia a bit longer.[2]

An Islamic Pilgrims' Way[3]

There was one famous road, 'the King's Highway',[4] which had played an historic part in the life of one empire after another. This thoroughfare ran north and south, along the border between Syria and the Syrian Desert, from the crossings of the Euphrates, at the point where the river bends nearest to the Mediterranean, through Damascus and Transjordan to the head of the Gulf of ʿAqabah, where the road branched westwards across the Desert of Sinai towards Egypt and south-eastwards into Arabia. This King's Highway had served successively the Empire of Sumer and Akkad, 'the New Empire' of Egypt, the Neo-Babylonian Empire, and the Achaemenian Empire. After the shattering of the Achaemenian Peace by Alexander, the Ptolemies and the Seleucids, holding opposite ends of the thoroughfare, had contended with one another for possession of the whole of it, and the Seleucids had won the contest only to give place to Rome—till the King's Highway had changed hands again from the Roman Empire to the Arab Caliphate and thereafter, in its southern sector, from the ʿAbbasids' Fātimid successor-state to the Crusader Kingdom of Jerusalem.

In the course of its long and chequered history the King's Highway has been used, not only by its official masters of the moment, but by rebels, raiders, and rival Powers. The Elamite and Babylonian war-lords who had twice taken this road in the eighteenth century B.C. in order to reimpose the long dormant authority of an Empire of Sumer and Akkad on the princelings of Syria had been pursued along their own highway on their return march, and been relieved of their booty, by an untamed band of Hebrew Nomads.[5] In the eighteenth or seventeenth

[1] Fitzgerald, C. P.: *China, A Short Cultural History* (London 1935, Cresset Press), p. 138. This mistake of Ts'in She Hwang-ti's was avoided by the Tokugawa (see p. 87, above).

[2] See V. v. 636, n. 3.

[3] See xi, maps 11, 14, 20, and 21A.

[4] Num. xx. 17 and xxi. 22. See Wright, V. E., and Filson, F. V.: *The Westminster Historical Atlas of the Bible* (London 1946, Student Christian Movement Press), p. 40, fig. 25, for an aerial photograph of a section of this road in Transjordan.

[5] See Gen. xiv. The historical events which here loom through a mist of tradition may perhaps be dated some time between the annexation of the Sumerian Empire of Isin by the Elamite State of Larsa *circa* 1799–1793 or 1735–1729 B.C. and the annexation of Larsa by the Amorite State of Babylon in 1762 or 1698 B.C. (see V. vi. 297). The account in Gen. xiv. 13–24 of Abraham's audacious but successful surprise attack on the plunder-laden army of the retreating imperialists is reminiscent of the attack by the Brygi on an Achaemenian army marching along the coast road from the Hellespont to European Greece *circa* 492 B.C. (Herodotus, Book VI, chap. 45) and of the similar attack by Thracians on a Roman army following the same route in 188 B.C. (Livy, Book XXXVIII, chap. 40).

century B.C. the King's Highway had carried a Palestinian barbarian Hyksos war-band to the north-eastern corner of Egypt, and perhaps also an advance guard of the Eurasian Nomad Mitanni to the north-western corner of Arabia, on the last stage of their long trek from the south-western shore of the great Eurasian Steppe.[1] In the fourteenth or thirteenth century B.C. the Children of Israel had been refused a passage along the southernmost section of the King's Highway by the Edomite successor-state of 'the New Empire' of Egypt,[2] and had forced a passage along another section in the teeth of opposition from an Amorite successor-state in the Peraea,[3] on their way to carve out a domain for themselves on the western side of Jordan. In the ninth, eighth, and seventh centuries B.C. the independent principalities of Syria that had emerged from a dark age following the collapse of 'the New Empire' of Egypt and the overthrow of 'the thalassocracy of Minos' had fallen victims to Assyrian aggressors following on Chedorlaomer's track; and when the downfall of Assyria had seemed to promise them relief they had been cheated of it by the immediate substitution of Babylonian for Assyrian rule. On the eve of the overthrow of the Neo-Babylonian Empire by Cyrus the Achaemenid, the King's Highway had once again come to the fore in the play of international politics, and a would-be leader of an anti-Babylonian movement among the remnant of Judah had exhorted his countrymen to recondition this historic route in order to expedite the passage of Cyrus's liberating armies.

'The voice of him that crieth in the wilderness: Prepare ye the way of the Lord; make straight in the desert a highway for our God. Every valley shall be exalted, and every mountain and hill shall be made low; and the crooked shall be made straight, and the rough places plain.'[4]

'The road was to follow much the same route that Nabonidus', the last emperor of the short-lived Neo-Babylonian Empire,[5] 'had taken east of Jordan and through Ammonitis, Northern and Eastern Edom.'[6]

At the break-up of the Achaemenian Empire's Seleucid successor-state, Nabataean intruders from Arabia, treading in the footsteps of the Children of Israel, had followed the King's Highway, without turning off it to pass over Jordan, till they had reached and occupied Damascus; and at the break-up of the Roman Empire the Primitive Muslim Arabs —taking the same war-path, and avenging, in a decisive victory at the passage of the Yarmuk, their discomfiture at Mu'tah in their first encounter with the Roman veterans of the last and greatest Romano-Persian War—had not only captured Damascus but had established

1 See the Note on Chronology in vol. x, and p. 201, n. 3, below.

2 Num. xx. 14–22 and xxi. 4.

3 Num. xxi. 21–32.

4 Isa. xl. 3–4. The technique of making military thoroughfares seems to have been borrowed by successive empire-builders from their predecessors, to judge by the remarkable correspondence between the Pentateuch Greek version of this passage of Deutero-Isaiah, quoted in the Gospels, and a passage in Plutarch's *Lives of the Gracchi* (chap. 28). These two passages have been compared in V. vi. 418–19, and it has there been pointed out that the correspondence cannot be due to any literary influence of either passage on the other.

5 Nabonidus *imperabat* 556–539 B.C.—A.J.T.

6 Smith, Sidney: *Isaiah, Chapters XL–LV: Literary Criticism and History* (London 1944, Milford), pp. 65–66.

there the capital of an empire whose boundaries they had pushed out, within the next hundred years, to Farghānah on the one side and to the Atlantic coasts of Morocco and the Iberian Peninsula on the other. At the break-up of the Arab Caliphate the Crusaders, bursting into Syria through the Cilician Gates and by sea, had forced the passage of the Jordan in the reverse direction to that of the Israelites' trek, and had pushed their way southwards, down the southernmost stretch of the King's Highway, till they had reached the head of the Gulf of ʿAqabah and had thereby momentarily cut the land communications between the African and Asiatic domains of Dār-al-Islām.[1]

This history of the King's Highway over a period of some three thousand years might look like a monotonous repetition of contests between successive universal states claiming legitimate sovereignty over the thoroughfare and outsiders disputing their title by force of arms. Yet the historic importance of the King's Highway lay in none of these episodes. This long-fought-over thoroughfare was to find its destiny at last as an Islamic Pilgrims' Way on which, year by year, a peaceful multitude of Muslims—converging from the far-flung outposts of Dār-al-Islām in Fez and Sarayevo and Vilna and Qāzān and Kāshghar—would make the Hajj, at first on foot or camel-back and latterly by train,[2] to the Holy Cities of the Hijāz.

The Mahāyāna's Transcontinental Royal Road

This pacific exploit of Islam was surpassed by the Mahāyāna, which laid one empire after another under contribution to prepare the way for its astonishing journey from the Ganges to the Yellow River round three sides of the Tibetan Plateau.[3] When Cyrus II had opened a road from Oxus to Indus over the Hindu Kush in order to annex the Panjab to the Achaemenian Empire; when Chandragupta had carried Cyrus's highland highway on south-eastwards, across the whole expanse of the plains of Hindustan, from Taxila to Magadha, in order to clinch his hold on

[1] This curiosity of historical geography had an effective precedent in the Völkerwanderung that followed the collapse of 'the Middle Empire' of Egypt and an Empire of Sumer and Akkad that had been momentarily re-established by Hammurabi, and it also had an abortive parallel in the Völkerwanderung that had followed the collapse of 'the New Empire' of Egypt and 'the thalassocracy of Minos'. In the eighteenth or seventeenth century B.C. an advance guard of the Hurrian highlanders, who had been set on the move by the impact of the Eurasian Nomad Mitanni, had established themselves in the highlands overhanging the Wādi ʿArābah (see Gen. xiv. 6). In the twelfth century B.C., when the main body of the Philistine refugees from the Aegean Basin and invaders of the Egyptiac World had ensconced themselves in the coastal cities of the Shephelah, one war-band of Cherethite intruders from overseas had penetrated into the arid Negeb, south-east of Gaza, and had established themselves there at Ziklag (see 1 Sam. xxvii. 6 and xxx. 14). Possibly they had been attempting the feat, which the Crusader Kingdom of Jerusalem was momentarily to achieve in its day, of gaining possession of a land-bridge between the Mediterranean and the Red Sea. If that had been their objective, they had been foiled by the successful establishment of an Edomite successor-state of 'the New Empire' of Egypt in the Wādi ʿArābah and on the plateau to the east of it, whose Hurrite occupants the Edomite invaders had exterminated (see Deut. ii. 4–5, 12, and 22). See further IX. viii. 358, n. 1.

[2] The building of the Hijāz railway southwards from Damascus along the route of the King's Highway was begun in A.D. 1900 and was completed as far as Medina in A.D. 1908. Put out of action in the war of 1914–18, the Hijāz Railway remained derelict thereafter from Maʿān southwards.

[3] For this adventurous route see II. ii. 405, n. 1.

an Indic universal state which he had founded by expelling Alexander's feeble garrisons from Cyrus's and Darius's derelict Indian provinces; when the Greek princes of Bactria and their Kushan successors had taken an unintended advantage of Cyrus's and Darius's and Chandragupta's work in order to 'abolish the Hindu Kush' by establishing their rule from Farghānah to Bihar;[1] when the Prior Han, feeling their way westward beyond the north-western extremity of Ts'in She Hwang-ti's Wall and crossing the sand-sea in the Tarim Basin from oasis to oasis, had 'abolished the Tien Shan' by descending on Farghānah;[2] when the Posterior Han had contended for the possession of this coveted route with the Kushan Emperor Kanishka:[3] not one of these empire-builders can have suspected that the mighty public works which each had believed himself to be carrying out for his own carefully calculated purposes were mere fragments of a grand design in which he and his rivals and adversaries, and his and their predecessors and successors, were each unconsciously performing their allotted task in the *corvée*. He would have been still more astonished to learn that this gigantic network of communications was being constructed by a press-gang of empire-builders for the benefit, not of some superlative secular empire of Pan-Asian dimensions, but of an Indic philosophy which was being transfigured into a religion[4] as it travelled—along the road that captains and kings had prepared for it—towards its mighty mission field among the peoples of the Far East.[5] This truth was, nevertheless, to be revealed by the course of history; and, where the Mahāyāna had shown the way, a procession of other religions—Manichaeism, Nestorianism, Islam, and Western Christianity[6]—was to follow as soon as facilities were unintentionally provided for them by other empire-builders: the T'ang whose political necromancy succeeded in evoking a ghost of the Sinic universal state to haunt a nascent Far Eastern World,[7] and the Mongols who, after China had been crushed by the incubus of the T'ang's success, imposed on her an alien universal state[8] which momentarily embraced, besides, all the other shores of the vast Eurasian Steppe.

The Challenge to Christianity in a Western Technology's 'Annihilation of Distance'

Our survey has brought to light so many cases in which a brilliantly planned and magnificently executed system of public communications has ultimately been turned to account by unexpected and unintended beneficiaries that we may tentatively regard this tendency as illustrating an historical 'law', and in A.D. 1952 this conclusion raised a momentous question about the future of the Westernizing World in which the writer of this Study and his contemporaries were living.

By the year A.D. 1952 the initiative and skill of Western Man had been engaged for some four and a half centuries in knitting together the whole habitable and traversable surface of the planet by a system of

1 See II. ii. 141, n. 2, and 370–3.
2 See V. v. 143.
3 See II. ii. 373 and V. v. 144–5.
4 See V. v. 136 and 362.
5 See V. v. 139–40, 144–6, and 356.
6 See V. v. 112–17.
7 See pp. 20–21, above, and X. ix. 16 and 20.
8 See V. v. 105 and 116.

communications that was unprecedented in the two features of being literally world-wide and being operated by a technique which was constantly surpassing itself at a perpetually accelerating pace. The wooden caravels and galleons, rigged for sailing in the eye of the wind, which had sufficed to enable the pioneer mariners of Modern Western Europe to make themselves masters of all the oceans, had given way to mechanically propelled iron-built ships of relatively gigantic size;[1] 'dirt-tracks' travelled by six-horse coaches had been replaced by macadamized and concrete-floored roads travelled by automobiles; railways had been invented to compete with roads, and aircraft to compete with all land-borne or water-borne conveyances. Concurrently, means of communication which did not require the physical transportation of human bodies had been conjured up, and put into operation on a world-wide scale, in the shape of telegraphs, telephones, and wireless transmission—visual as well as auditory—by radio. The movement of sea-borne and air-borne traffic had been made detectable at long range by radar. There had been no period in the history of any other civilization in which so large an area had been made so highly conductive for every form of human intercourse.

In the light of the histories of all other known civilizations, the development of this system of communications foreshadowed the eventual political unification of the society in which these technological portents had appeared. At the time of writing, however, the political prospects of the Western World were still obscure;[2] for, even though an observer might feel certain, in his own mind, that political unity would come about in some form sooner or later, neither the date nor the manner of this apparently inevitable unification was yet possible to divine. In a world which was still partitioned politically among sixty or seventy self-assertively sovereign parochial states, but which had already discovered the technique of flying and the 'know-how' of manufacturing the atom bomb, it was manifest that political unity might be imposed by the familiar method of the 'knock-out blow'; and it was also probable that, if peace was thus to be imposed in this case, as it had been in so many others, by the arbitrary fiat of a single surviving Great Power, the price of unification by force, in terms of moral, psychological, social, and political, as well as material, devastation, would be relatively still higher than it had been in other performances of this tragedy. At the same time it was possible that—even if political unification were inevitable and indeed indispensable—it might be achieved by the novel alternative method of voluntary co-operation, without coercion or catastrophe, which had been tried after the war of 1914–18 in the League of Nations and was being tried again after the war of 1939–45 in the United Nations Organization. The prospects of this great political experiment, as they appeared at a date rather more than half-way through the twentieth century of the Christian Era, are discussed in a later part of this Study.[3] But, whether the political future of the Westernizing World of the day was to be rough or smooth, and whatever form of political

[1] See XI. ix. 364–74.

[2] See XII, *passim*, ix. 406–644.

[3] In XII, *passim*, ix. 406–644.

unity was to be attained in this world by whatever road, it could be predicted with some confidence that the world-wide network of unprecedentedly efficient communications which the Western Civilization had already installed for its own purposes would find its historic mission in the familiar ironic role of being turned to account by unintended beneficiaries.

Who would draw the largest benefits in this case? In another context we have seen reason for expecting that, in this Western World that had come to embrace the whole surface of the planet, the barbarians of the external proletariat would play an even less significant part than they had played in the histories of other civilizations.[1] On the other hand the extant higher religions, whose domains had been linked up with one another, and with the dwindling tenements of pagan Primitive Man, by the West European technologist's ever closer-meshed spider's web, had already begun to take advantage of the fresh opportunities thus opened to them, without waiting for the establishment of a universal peace. Saint Paul, who had once travelled from the Orontes to the Tiber under the aegis of a *Pax Romana*, had been eagerly venturing forth on other seas still broader and stormier than the Mediterranean. On board a Portuguese caravel he had travelled on from Rome round the Cape of Good Hope on his second journey to India,[2] and farther afield again, through the Straits of Malacca, on his third journey to China.[3] Trans-shipping to a Spanish galleon, the indefatigable Apostle had crossed the Atlantic from Cadiz to Vera Cruz, and the Pacific from Acapulco to the Philippines. Nor had Western Christianity been the only living religion to take this advantage of Western technique. While Western Catholic Christianity was reaching the Pacific coasts of China and Japan by sea, Eastern Orthodox Christianity, in the train of Cossack pioneers equipped with Western fire-arms, had been making the long trek from the River Kama to the Sea of Okhotsk;[4] and these sixteenth-century and seventeenth-century missionary enterprises of Christianity in Asia had been emulated in Tropical Africa in the nineteenth century by Christianity and Islam in competition. It was not inconceivable that the Mahāyāna might one day recollect its marvellous journey over a succession of royal roads from Magadha to Loyang, and, in the strength of this buoyant memory, might turn such Western inventions as the aeroplane and the radio to as good account for its own work of preaching salvation as it had once turned the Chinese invention of the printing-press.[5]

The issues raised by this stimulation of missionary activities on a world-wide range were not just those of ecclesiastical 'geo-politics'. The

[1] See V. v. 332–4.

[2] Reckoning the Nestorian lodgement in Travancore as the first attempt of Christianity to convert India, and the Jesuit mission to the court of Akbar as the second.

[3] Reckoning the seventh-century Nestorian lodgement at Si-Ngan as the first attempt of Christianity to convert China, the thirteenth-century and fourteenth-century Western Christian missions overland as the second, and the sixteenth-century and seventeenth-century Western Christian missions by sea as the third.

[4] See II. ii. 157 and IV. iv. 497.

[5] For the use of printing in China, from the ninth century of the Christian Era onwards, in the propagation of the Mahāyāna among the masses, see Carter, T. F.: *The Invention of Printing in China and its Spread Westward*, revised edition (New York 1931, Columbia University Press), pp. 17–19 and 39–46.

entry of established higher religions into new missionary fields brought up the question whether the eternal essence of a religion could be distinguished from its ephemeral accidents; the encounters of the religions with one another brought up the question whether they could live and let live side by side or whether one of them would supersede the rest.

The ideal of religious eclecticism had appealed to certain rulers of universal states—an Alexander Severus[1] and an Akbar[2]—who had happened to combine a sophisticated mind with a tender heart; and Akbar's decorous séances had been crudely and clownishly anticipated at the Court of the Mongol Khāqān Mangū.[3] But in each of these instances the attempt to attain religious unity by the political device of confederation had been abortive, and a different ideal had inspired the pioneer Jesuit missionaries—a Francis Xavier and a Matteo Ricci—who were the earliest Apostles of any religion to grasp the opportunities opened for missionary enterprise by the Modern Western technician's titanic conquest of the oceans. These audacious spiritual pathfinders aspired to captivate for Christianity, in their own day, the Hindu and Far Eastern worlds, as Saint Paul and his successors had captivated the Hellenic World in theirs; but—endowed, as they were, with an intellectual genius that matched their heroic faith—they did not fail to recognize that their audacious enterprise could not succeed without fulfilling one exacting condition, and they did not shrink from accepting the consequences in their own missionary strategy and tactics.[4] They perceived that a missionary, if he was to give himself a chance of success, must convey his message in terms—intellectual, aesthetic, and emotional—that would appeal to his prospective converts. The more revolutionary the message in its essence, the more important it would be to clothe it in a familiar and congenial presentation. But this would require that the message should be stripped of the incompatible clothing in which the missionaries themselves happened to have inherited it from their own cultural tradition; and that, in turn, would demand of the missionaries that they should assume the responsibility, and take the risk, of attempting to determine what the essence of their religion might be.

The crux of this policy was that, in removing a stumbling-block from

[1] See V. v. 549. [2] See V. v. 700–1.

[3] See V. v. 115. Mangū was not the only Eurasian Nomad ruler to anticipate Akbar in taking a comparative survey of living higher religions by listening to disputations in his presence between their rival spokesmen. The Khan of the Khazars, who ruled over a parochial steppe empire in the Eurasian Steppe's Great Western Bay (see III. iii. 428–30) is said (see Dvornik, F.: *The Making of Central and Eastern Europe* (London 1949, Polish Research Centre), p. 169, n. 92) to have listened to a disputation of the kind before opting for Judaism in the eighth century of the Christian Era (see II. ii. 410 and V. v. 285); and in the following century a successor of this royal Khazar convert's is said to have given the East Roman Orthodox Christian missionary Constantine-Cyril an opportunity of disputing in his presence with representatives of Judaism, Islam, and paganism. The familiarity of this practice is attested by the two celebrated stories of the disputation between Khazar advocates of Judaism, White Bulgarian advocates of Islam, and East Roman advocates of Orthodox Christianity at the court of the Russian war-lord Vladímir before he opted for the East Roman faith, and of the disputation between Wilfrid and Colman in King Oswiu's presence at Whitby in A.D. 664 (see II. ii. 335).

[4] The policy of the Jesuits in China has been touched upon, by anticipation, in V. v. 366–7.

the path of the non-Christian societies which he was setting out to convert, a missionary would be placing another stumbling-block before the feet of his own co-religionists. On this rock the Early Modern Jesuit missions in India and China suffered an undeserved and tragic shipwreck. They were the victims of an unscrupulous jealousy on the part of rival missionaries of other orders and of a timid conservatism in high places in the Vatican. Yet the frustration of their noble and imaginative enterprise at the dawn of the unification of the Inhabited World (*Oikoumenê*) by Modern Western technique seemed unlikely to be the end of the story; for the underlying issue which they had raised was a crucial one for the destinies of all the higher religions.

If the local swaddling clothes in which Christianity had been wrapped when it came into the World in Palestine had not been masterfully removed by Paul of Tarsus, the Christian artists of the Catacombs at Rome and the Christian philosophers of the divinity school at Alexandria[1] would never have had their chance of presenting the essence of Christianity in terms of Greek vision and thought and thereby paving the way for the conversion of the Hellenic World. And, if, in the twentieth century of the Christian Era, Origen's and Augustine's Christianity could not divest itself of trappings acquired in those successive Syriac, Hellenic, and Western posting-stations at which it had once paused to rest on its historic journey, it would not be able to take advantage of the world-wide opportunity that had now been opened up for every living higher religion by the technical achievements of a Modern Western secular civilization. A higher religion that allows itself to become 'dyed in the wool' with the imprint of a temporary cultural environment is condemning itself to become stationary and earth-bound—to be the slave, and not the master, of the secular civilizations and their works. On the other hand any living higher religion that might save itself from this fate by taking Ricci's lesson to heart and putting his policy into practice would be opening for itself thereby a boundless field for new spiritual action. And, if Christianity itself were, after all, to embrace this manifest destiny, it might repeat in a latter-day *Oikoumenê* what it had once achieved in the Roman Empire.

In the spiritual commerce that had been served by Roman means of communication, Christianity had drawn out of, and inherited from, the other higher religions and philosophies, which it had thus encountered, the heart of what had been best in them. In a world materially linked together by the many inventions of Western technique, Hinduism and the Mahāyāna might make no less fruitful contributions than Isis-worship and Neoplatonism had once made to Christian insight and practice. And if, in a Western World too, Caesar's empire were to rise and fall—as his empire always had collapsed or decayed after a run of a few hundred years—an historian peering into the future in A.D. 1952 could imagine Christianity then being left as the heir of all the philosophies from Ikhnaton's to Hegel's and of all the higher religions as far back as the ever latent worship of a Mother and her Son who had started on

[1] For the significance of the interpretative work of Clement of Alexandria and Origen, see V. v. 366–7.

their travels along the King's Highway under the names of Ishtar and Tammuz.

2. *Garrisons and Colonies*

The Mixture of Motives in the Minds of Imperial Authorities

Whereas Imperial systems of communications are installed by their makers with the single-minded self-regarding aim of maintaining the imperial government's authority, imperial garrisons and colonies have a dual function. Like the public highways along which they are strung, they are, of course, designed primarily to preserve the universal state by whose rulers they have been planted; but in some cases they are also intended to serve the distinct purpose of preserving the civilization whose domain has been embraced within the universal state's frontiers.

Plantations of loyal supporters of the imperial régime—who may be soldiers on active service, militiamen, discharged veterans, or civilians—are an integral part of any imperial system of communications linking the capital of a universal state with its frontiers across intervening tracts of subject territory. The presence, prowess, and vigilance of these human watch-dogs provide the indispensable security without which the most efficient physical installations—roads, bridges, posting-stations, and the rest—would be of no practical use to the imperial authorities (as in fact they eventually fall out of use when the imperial system of security and defence breaks down). This imperial network of practicable communications in the shape of garrisoned roads does not consist merely of the thoroughfares radiating from the capital to the frontiers; the frontiers themselves are part and parcel of the same system; for even the most elaborately fortified frontier lines—such systems as the Military Frontiers of the Hapsburg Empire over against the Ottoman Empire during the century beginning in A.D. 1777[1] or the Roman *limites* in Germany and Britain or 'the Great Wall of China' itself—prove, on analysis, to be lateral highways, skirting the outermost verge of an empire's domain, along which the fortresses have been strung so close together that they have coalesced into a continuous chain.[2]

Some of these frontier garrisons—or lines of garrisons dressed in close order to hold a *limes* or a wall—are new installations, established by the universal state *in partibus barbarorum* where it has had no predecessors. Others, on the other hand, are replacements of garrisons formerly posted along the same line, for defence against the same barbarian or alien adversary, by parochial Powers that have perished in the fratricidal struggle that has ended in the imposition of a universal peace by a single survivor among the competitors. Thus Rome, in the acts of imposing her hegemony on the city-states of Etruria and extinguishing the Carthaginian and Macedonian Powers, was taking upon her own shoulders a

[1] See V. v. 463.

[2] 'The Great Wall' of China and 'the Roman Wall' in Britain between Tyne and Solway were each originally laid out as a chain of garrisoned fortresses strung along a road and connected by an embankment of earthwork which served as a demarcation line rather than as a military barrier. In both cases the construction of an actual wall of masonry, along the line of the embankment, was the last phase. (For the structural evolution of the Chinese Wall, see Franke, O.: *Geschichte des Chinesischen Reiches*, vol. i (Berlin and Leipzig 1930, de Gruyter), pp. 240–2.)

responsibility for holding the former Etruscan frontiers against the barbarians of Northern Italy, the former Carthaginian frontiers against the barbarians of the Iberian Peninsula and North-West Africa, and the former Macedonian frontiers against the barbarians of South-Eastern Europe.[1] In the Sinic World the march state of Ts'in, which won the last round in the long strife of the Contending States, had to pay for its victory by taking over the frontiers previously held by the other two march states, Chao and Yen, against the Nomads of the Eurasian Steppe. The overthrow of these two frontier Powers left a gap in the defences of the Sinic World between the eastern terminus of the sectional anti-barbarian frontier of Ts'in and the Pacific coast of the Sinic World; and, in filling this gap, Ts'in She Hwang-ti, the founder of the Sinic universal state, had at least to double the length of the frontier against the Eurasian barbarians that had been held by his own predecessors.[2] In the Hindu World, likewise, the British Rāj had to take over the north-west frontier of the Sikh principalities against the highlander barbarians of North-Eastern Iran;[3] and in the Egyptiac World, when the alien empire of the Achaemenidae had conquered the Saïte Kingdom, the conquerors found themselves saddled with the defence of their Saïte victims' southern frontier at Elephantinê[4] against the still independent Napatan Power in the southern portion of the Egyptiac Society's domain.

In taking over the defence of derelict frontiers from extinguished parochial Powers, a universal state is, of course, acting in self-preservation as well as in the interests of the society over whose domain it has established its rule. But, besides planting garrisons along frontiers of which it finds itself the residuary legatee, a universal state may be moved to plant colonies in the interior, not for purposes of defence or police, but in order to repair ravages inflicted by the devastating struggle for power during a Time of Troubles before the imposition of the imperial peace.

It was this that was in Caesar's mind when he planted self-governing colonies of Roman citizens on the desolate sites of Capua, Carthage, and Corinth. In the course of the foregoing struggle for survival between the parochial states of the Hellenic World, the Roman Government of the day had deliberately made an example of Capua for her treacherous secession to Hannibal at a moment when Rome had been at the nadir of her fortunes,[5] and of Carthage for the crime of having almost got the better of Rome in the struggle between them for world power, while Corinth had been arbitrarily singled out for the same treatment among the states members of an Achaean League whose declaration of war on Rome had endangered the existence of no state except the puny commonwealth that had so frivolously put itself in the wrong by assuming the role of the aggressor. Under the pre-Caesarean republican régime at

[1] See II. ii. 161–4 and V. v. 212–22.

[2] See Franke, op. cit., vol. cit., loc. cit. ;Fitzgerald, C. P.: *China, A Short Cultural History* (London 1935, Cresset Press), p. 137; and the present Study, II. ii. 119 and V. v. 270.

[3] See V. v. 304–8.

[4] For the crystallization of this frontier *circa* 661–655 B.C., see II. ii. 116.

[5] See II. ii. 19.

Rome, the conservative party had been stubbornly and bitterly opposed to the restoration of these three famous cities. They had succeeded in frustrating or undoing or arresting three attempts to recolonize Capua,[1] and one attempt to recolonize Carthage,[2] before Caesar succeeded in forcing through what amounted to a re-establishment of Capua in his agrarian law of 59 B.C., and thereafter re-established Carthage and Corinth in 45 B.C. over the dead body of the Roman Senatorial régime.

By the time that Capua had lain desolate for 153 years (211–58 B.C.) and Carthage and Corinth for a hundred, while Rome had been confirming her already unchallengeable supremacy, the ground of the opposition to rescinding the three penal sentences had, of course, long ceased to be the original motive of fear. The long-drawn-out controversy in Roman domestic politics over the treatment of the three cities had by that time become the symbol of a wider issue. Was the *raison d'être* of the Roman Empire the selfish interest of the particular Power that had succeeded in establishing it by conquest? Or did the Empire exist to serve the common weal of the Hellenic World of which it was a political embodiment? Caesar's defeat of the Senate was a victory for the more liberal, humane, and imaginative of these two views; and the praise which an English philosopher-statesman has given to the Romans *sans phrase* should be reserved—as it was by Greek men of letters in the Antonine Age—for the Roman Imperial régime which Caesar inaugurated.

'Never any state was . . . so open to receive strangers into their body as were the Romans; therefore it sorted with them accordingly, for they grew to the greatest monarchy. Their manner was to grant naturalisation (which they called "ius civitatis"), and to grant it in the highest degree—that is, not only "ius commercii, ius connubii, ius hereditatis", but also "ius suffragii" and "ius honorum"; and this not to singular persons alone, but likewise to whole families—yea, to cities, and sometimes to nations. Add to this their custom of plantation of colonies, whereby the Roman plant was removed into the soil of other nations, and, putting both constitutions together, you will say that it was not the Romans that spread upon the World, but it was the World that spread upon the Romans.'[3]

This striking difference in moral character between the régime which Caesar inaugurated and the régime which he superseded was not a peculiar feature of Roman and Hellenic history. A similar change of attitude towards the use and abuse of power had accompanied the transition from a Time of Troubles to a universal state in the histories of other civilizations and other empire-builders, and in a general way it would appear that the devastation of cities, destruction of communities, and uprooting of populations are characteristic crimes of the rulers of

[1] Gaius Gracchus's abortive colony projected in 123 B.C. and cancelled after his tragic death in 121 B.C.; Marcus Iunius Brutus's colony planted in 83 B.C. and uprooted in 82 B.C. by Sulla; and the abortive project embodied in an agrarian law introduced by Publius Servilius Rullus in 64 B.C. and withdrawn by its author next year (see Cicero's speech *In Rullum*, which helped to kill the bill).

[2] Gaius Gracchus's colony planted in 123 B.C.

[3] Bacon, Francis: *The Essays, or Counsels Civil and Moral*, xxix: 'Of the True Greatness of Kingdoms and Estates'. Compare the dicta of Oswald Spengler's that have been quoted in the present Study, V. v. 620, n. 1, and p. 56, above.

contending parochial states, while it is a characteristic virtue of the governments of universal states that they attempt to repair the moral and material ravages perpetrated by their predecessors. But, though this historical 'law' may be discernible, it is far from being absolute or exact.

On the one hand we find Times of Troubles generating not only uprooted and embittered proletariats[1] but constructive and successful colonization enterprises on the grand scale—as exemplified by the host of Greek city-states that were planted far and wide over the former domain of the conquered Achaemenian Empire by Alexander the Great and his successors, and by the contemporary colonies of Latins and Roman citizens that were founded by Republican Rome to secure her conquests in Italy.[2] This constructive work of the Hellenic Time of Troubles was the foundation on which Caesar and his successors built in the subsequent Imperial Age—just as Caesar's liberality in conferring Roman citizenship, which was a revolutionary departure from the narrow-hearted policy of the Roman republican régime of the Post-Hannibalic Age, was a reversion to the more generous-hearted policy of the Republic in the age before that,[3] at a time when the Roman governing class of the day had been inspired with confidence by its success in conquering Italy, and had not yet had its heart seared by having to face the formidable issue of world-power or downfall with which Rome was to be confronted in the next chapter of her history by her encounter with Carthage.

Conversely the change of heart on the part of a dominant minority, which is the moral and psychological counterpart of the institutional reform accomplished in the establishment of a universal state,[4] is seldom so thorough or so steadfast that it does not occasionally relapse into the brutal practice of a foregoing Time of Troubles. The Neo-Babylonian Empire, which stood on the whole for a moral revolt of the interior of the Babylonic World against the brutality of its Assyrian marchmen,[5] lapsed into uprooting Judah as Assyria had uprooted Israel, Damascus, and Babylon itself. The Achaemenidae, who permitted and assisted the Jews to return home to Judea from their Babylonish captivity, and who were welcomed as liberators by the Phoenicians,[6]

[1] See V. v. 58–194, *passim.*

[2] A conspectus of the Macedonian and Roman plantations of colonies will be found in Tscherikower, V.: *Die Hellenistischen Städtegrundungen von Alexander dem Grossen bis auf die Römerzeit* (Leipzig 1927, Dieterich); Jones, A. H. M.: *The Cities of the Eastern Roman Provinces* (Oxford 1937, Clarendon Press); eodem: *The Greek City from Alexander to Justinian* (Oxford 1940, Clarendon Press); Beloch, K. J.: *Der Italische Bund unter Roms Hegemonie* (Leipzig 1880, Teubner); eodem: *Römische Geschichte bis zum Beginn der Punischen Kriege* (Berlin and Leipzig 1926, de Gruyter).

[3] Salient examples of this policy are to be seen in the treatment of the Sabines and the Picentes. The Sabines were granted passive Roman citizenship immediately after their conquest by Rome in 290 B.C.; this was converted into active citizenship as early as 268 B.C., and a new Roman tribal constituency was created in 241 B.C. for Sabine voters. The Picentes, who were conquered after 290 B.C., were given passive Roman citizenship in 268 B.C., and this had been converted into active citizenship by 241 B.C., when a new Roman tribal constituency was created for Picentine voters (see Beloch, *Der Italische Bund*, pp. 32, 54–55, and 76).

[4] For this change of heart, which gives the public servant and the philosopher a chance of repairing the ravages of the conqueror, the wastrel, and the hangman, see V. v, especially pp. 38–40 and 47–52.

[5] See II. ii. 135–6 and IV. iv. 468–84.

[6] See V. v. 123, n. 2.

uprooted the Greek city-states Samos, Barca, Miletus, and Eretria,[1] and colonized the inhospitable islands of the Persian Gulf with *déracinés* who appear to have been themselves of Iranian origin.[2] The Jews whom the Persians had repatriated encountered a new Nebuchadnezzar in the Seleucid King Antiochus Epiphanes, whose house was as well liked by the Babylonians as the Achaemenidae had been by the Jews,[3] and they were uprooted for the second time—and this far more drastically than in their first experience at Nebuchadnezzar's hands—by a Roman Imperial Government which had manifested its intention of breaking with the inhuman policy of its republican predecessors when it had re-peopled the desolate sites of Capua, Carthage, and Corinth.

It is true that Nebuchadnezzar's prisoner of state, the ex-King of Judah, Jehoiachin, was released from prison (after he had languished there for thirty-seven years) by Nebuchadnezzar's successor Amel-Marduk;[4] that the Achaemenidae showed concern for the welfare of the Greek communities which they had carried away captive;[5] and that the Romans, in their dealings with the Jews, exercised almost superhuman self-restraint before the Zealots forced their hand in A.D. 66 and finally in A.D. 132[6]. It must be noted, however, on the other side of the account, that the constructive colonization that is characteristic of a universal state is not easy to distinguish sharply from the destructive tearing up of social roots that is characteristic of a Time of Troubles; for, if the hallmark of a Time of Troubles is violence and coercion, it is also true that redistributions of population under the auspices of a universal state are not always, or altogether, voluntary. The selected colonists may be reluctant to make a change of domicile which may be judged by their rulers to be desirable in the public interest without being, on that account, acceptable to the men, women, and children who are required to undergo this ordeal. It is known that the Incas—in spite of the immensity of their prestige and the general benignity and efficiency of their administration—met with resistance, now and again, among loyal populations whom they were proposing to transplant.[7] The Greek veterans whom Alexander the Great had planted in the recalcitrant Eurasian marches of the Achaemenian Empire, north-east of the Caspian Gates, four or five months' journey up country from the Greeks' beloved Mediterranean Sea, left their posts and drifted westwards again *en masse* as soon as they heard the news of Alexander's death; and we may guess that, if we knew the full story of the colonies planted by Rome, we should come across similar cases here.[8] Moreover, a willing or even

[1] See V. v. 124, n. 2. [2] See V. v. 124, n. 2, and p. 602, below.
[3] See V. v. 94, 123, and 347, and V. vi. 442.
[4] See Jer. lii. 31–34; 2 Kings xxv. 27–30.
[5] See Herodotus, Book IV, chap. 204; Book VI, chaps. 20 and 119.
[6] See V. v. 68.
[7] See Baudin, L.: *L'Empire Socialiste des Inka* (Paris 1928, Institut d'Ethnologie), pp. 134–5. In general, the Spaniards found the transplanted elements in the population of the Inca Empire more ready than the un-uprooted elements to leave their domiciles in the service of their new masters (op. cit., p. 135).
[8] Though the Roman peasantry in the Ager Romanus in Italy south of the Appennines had been ruined and uprooted by the Hannibalic War and, after Carthage had

eager candidate for resettlement may have been the victim of social or political upheavals that have uprooted him from a home which he would never have left except under *force majeure*.[1] And in the third place a demand for new homes on the part of one element in the population of a universal state may require for its satisfaction the forcible uprooting of another element. Augustus found farms in Italy for his demobilized veteran soldiers by evicting a civilian peasantry;[2] and in resorting to this ruthless expedient he was following a precedent set by the reactionary war-lord Sulla in an age that had not yet been graced by a Caesarean clemency or an Augustan Peace.

capitulated, by a continuing drain of manpower to maintain the Roman armies of occupation in the former Carthaginian dominions in the Iberian Peninsula, the Roman settlers in the new Latin colony Bononia (Bologna)—founded in 189 B.C., twelve years after the conclusion of peace between Rome and Carthage—had to be bribed with allotments of land of 50 acres each for infantrymen (i.e. more than seven times the pre-war standard allotment of 7 acres) and 70 each for cavalry troopers (see Livy, Book XXXVII, chap. 57). Alarmed at having thus set a precedent that would rapidly use up even the vast tracts of public land available for colonization north of the Appennines, the Roman Government next tried the experiment of converting the bribe to colonists from an economic into a political currency. In founding the colonies Parma and Mutina (Modena) in 183 B.C., they reduced the size of the standard allotments to 8 acres and 5 acres respectively, but, in compensation, they allowed the colonists not only to retain their Roman citizenship but to incorporate themselves in local city-states with substantially the same powers of self-government as they would have enjoyed if they had been constituted as Latin communities instead of being allowed, as they were, to remain within the Roman body politic (see Livy, Book XXXIX, chap. 55). The new political precedent thus set at Parma and Mutina appears, however, to have alarmed the Roman authorities as much as the new economic precedent set at Bononia, and, in founding Aquileia in 181 B.C., they reverted to customary constitutional practice and gave the new colony the Latin status. They found, however, that, in order to induce even ruined Roman peasants to settle in the extreme north-eastern corner of the Po Basin and to pay for this drastic transplantation by forfeiting their Roman citizenship, they must again allot 50 acres to the private infantry soldier and, this time, 70 to the centurion and no less than 140—a veritable estate—to the cavalry trooper (see Livy, Book XL, chap. 34).

1 For example, the colonists from Italy south of the Appennines who were planted in the Po Basin by the Roman Government between 190 and 173 B.C. had been uprooted by the Hannibalic War and its aftermath. The host of landless agricultural labourers whom the Gracchi planted on public land, of which the state had resumed possession for the purpose, was a product of the continuing consequences of the same great social catastrophe—and so were the veterans of the semi-private armies raised by Marius, Sulla, Caesar, the Second Triumvirate, and finally Augustus after the elimination of his two colleagues. An economic interpretation of History would account for the Roman civil wars of the century preceding the establishment of the Augustan Peace as being a desperate device for endowing by force a landless rural proletariat which had failed to obtain satisfaction for their needs by the peaceful methods of Tiberius Gracchus. In effect the armies that fought the civil wars were trade unions of unemployed agricultural workers, and the war-lord politician who raised an army to back him was a labour boss. The understanding between the war-lord and his soldiers was that, if they were to succeed in bringing him into political power by winning a civil war for him, he on his part would use his power to reward their services by planting them on the land in Italy—no matter by what methods or at whose expense. This incentive explains the relative ease with which armies were raised by a succession of Roman war-lords from Marius to Augustus inclusive, in contrast to the difficulty of recruitment during the hundred years between the end of the Hannibalic War and the beginning of Marius's career. (This point has been touched upon, by anticipation, in V. v. 62–3.)

2 The individual exemption of the poet Virgil from this grievous injustice that was being inflicted on his neighbours is the celebrated theme of his First Eclogue. If we can shake off the spell that the poetry casts over us and see the picture through Meliboeus's instead of Tityrus's eyes, we shall be less impressed with the young Octavian's capricious act of generosity towards one man of genius than with the harsh rule that was broken by this facile exception. Meliboeus's fellow sufferers were legion; Tityrus's companions in good fortune were an insignificant minority. The *beau rôle* conferred on Augustus by Virgil's magic words was cheaply bought and ill deserved.

Incaic Examples of Divers Types of Resettlement

Notwithstanding these overlaps and inconsistencies, it is still broadly true that a relatively constructive and humane colonization policy is one of the distinguishing marks of a universal state.

The most extensive, scientific, and beneficent application of such a policy among the instances on record is the system worked out by the Incas.[1] During the relatively short period of little more than a century which intervened between the foundation of the Andean universal state and its overthrow by the Spaniards, if we date its foundation from the accession of the Inca Pachacutec (*imperabat circa* A.D. 1400–48),[2] the Incas redistributed the population of their dominions on so large a scale that, according to the testimony of subsequent Spanish observers, there remained hardly a valley or a village in all Peru where there was not a settlement of *mitimaes*, as these deportees were called. This high-handedly systematic manipulation of human communities as though they were pawns on a chessboard is said to have been initiated by Pachacutec himself.[3]

The resettlements fell into four classes,[4] of which only one was penal, while one was for military and two were for economic purposes.

Rebellious populations were compulsorily exchanged with loyal populations,[5] who received as their reward what was meted out to the rebels as their punishment.[6] But these penal and precautionary deportations in the Assyrian style seem to have been much less characteristic of the Inca régime than those falling within the other three categories. Military colonies, recruited from populations that were both loyal and martial, were settled along the frontiers,[7] where they were employed in agriculture and on public works as well as on their military duties. The honourableness of their status was advertised by the gift of wives, garments, and valuables which they received from the Inca. These military colonies in the marches had their counterpart, in the interior, in civilian settlements of small groups of families which corporately performed the function of permanently domiciled inspectors or spies.[8]

Of the two types of resettlement for economic purposes, one began with transfers of surplus population from overpopulated to underpopulated districts, and developed—through a practice of requiring the settlers to contribute to the food-supply of their original homes—into a systematic linking together of economically complementary districts (e.g. a highland district with a lowland one) with a view to an interchange of products.[9] Settlers of this class were treated by the Govern-

[1] This has been touched upon by anticipation in V. v. 90, n. 2.

[2] See IV. iv. 103.

[3] See Baudin, op. cit., p. 135, n. 2.

[4] Described in Baudin, op. cit., pp. 132–4.

[5] After the conquest of the warlike and recalcitrant Karas of Ecuador, loyal elements were drafted into their country to hold them in check (Baudin, op. cit., p. 135).

[6] 'As has been well said, what the Magyars received as punishment was bestowed upon the non-Magyars as reward' [after the *émeute* of A.D. 1848–9 in the Danubian Hapsburg Monarchy] (Seton-Watson, R. W.: *The Southern Slav Question* (London 1911, Constable), p. 35, quoted in V. v. 293, n. 2).

[7] For example, a military march was organized in Chile over against the unconquered Araucanians (Joyce, T. A.: *South American Archaeology* (London 1912, Lee Warner), p. 224).

[8] See Baudin, op. cit., p. 135.

[9] This type of resettlement and interchange seems to have been an officially organized

ment with studied consideration. They were granted long terms of exemption from all taxation. They were also exempted from the jurisdiction of the local authorities in the districts in which they were planted, and were allowed to form autonomous communities administered by headmen of their own. In addition it was arranged that their kinsmen who had been left at home should come periodically to help them in their agricultural labours at the busy seasons of the year.[1] The second type of resettlement for economic purposes was designed to raise, not the quantity of production, but its quality, and in this case the resettlement was not by whole communities but by single families. Selected families of specially skilful cultivators were settled in districts where the standard of agricultural technique was low, and, conversely, skilled families of artisans were drafted away from centres where there was a surplus of skilled workmanship.

'To sum up, the Inca regulated all displacements of population; he installed good husbandmen where there was a dearth of them, he provided instructors for populations that lacked them, he planted restless and stiff-necked communities in the neighbourhood of submissive ones; he distributed his subjects over the different regions under his rule with a sovereign hand, as though they had been pawns on a chessboard, and brewed together the peoples under his rule in order to unify his empire.'[2]

These different types of resettlement for divers purposes, which were combined and co-ordinated in the Empire of the Incas, have partial counterparts in the institutions of other universal states.

Penal Deportations

A classical case of penal deportation is the treatment of Judah by Nebuchadnezzar (*imperabat* 605–562 B.C.) when this little but never negligible highland principality overlooking the southernmost sector of the coast road between Damascus and Pelusium[3] persistently refused to acknowledge that, in forcing the Saïte Power to withdraw from Asia once for all in 605 B.C.,[4] the Neo-Babylonian Empire had become the legitimate heir to all its Assyrian predecessor's rights and titles in the

and systematically applied version of practices that had grown up piecemeal and haphazard before the establishment of the Inca Empire. For example, Aymará settlers from the highlands had already migrated to the coastal lowlands, not under governmental auspices, but under the spur of economic need, and in their new settlements they had maintained commercial relations with their former fellow countrymen. Conversely, the Chincha and Chimu lowlanders had already acquired landed property in the highlands, which they used for pasturing llamas in order to obtain a wool-supply for their clothing industry (Baudin, op. cit., p. 133). There was also an interchange of products between the highlands and the tropical forest-clad lowlands to the east of them, on the western fringe of the Amazon Basin (see Markham, Sir C.: *The Incas of Peru* (London 1910, Smith Elder), p. 199).

[1] This practice of mutual aid survived the overthrow of the Inca imperial régime by which it had been fostered. An instance in which it operated for the benefit of a community that had been the victim of Spanish atrocities is recorded by the Spanish historian Cieza de Leon (see Markham, op. cit., p. 166).

[2] Baudin, op. cit., pp. 135–6.

[3] This road—which followed the present track of the Hijāz Railway from Damascus to Haifa, running down the gorge of the Yarmuk and along the Vale of Esdraelon to Megiddo, where it found its way between Mount Carmel and the Hill Country of Ephraim and so descended into the Shephelah—was a variant of the southernmost section of 'the King's Highway' (see pp. 100–2, above), from which it branched off in the Hawrān.

[4] See 2 Kings xxiv. 7.

former Assyrian dominions and dependencies between the Middle Euphrates and the Desert of Sinai. King Jehoiachin's recalcitrance was punished in 597 B.C. by the deportation to Babylon of the contumacious king himself, the royal family, the members of the court and administrative service, 7,000 fighting-men, and 1,000 metal workers and other artisans, the total number of deportees amounting to about 10,000 souls in all.[1] The subsequent rebellion of Zedekiah, whom Nebuchadnezzar had set on the throne of Judah, in Jehoiachin's stead, to play the part of a quisling, was punished in 586 B.C. by the execution of Zedekiah's sons before their father's eyes, the blinding and relegation to Babylon of the rebel king himself, the burning of Jerusalem—including private houses as well as public buildings—and a second deportation which was perhaps larger and less discriminating than that of 597 B.C.[2]

Ts'in She Hwang-ti's penal deportations seem to have been more sweeping than Nebuchadnezzar's—even allowing for the difference in scale between the Sinic World of the third century B.C. and the Babylonic of the sixth. The founder of the Sinic universal state deported no fewer than 120,000 families of feudal notables from the conquered and extinguished parochial states that had once been rivals and adversaries of Ts'in, and planted them in the citadel of Ts'in, 'the Country within the Passes' (the latter-day Province of Shensi).[3] This tide of compulsory migration from the East and South to the North-West was crossed by another flowing in the opposite direction, if we are to credit the statement that Ts'in She Hwang-ti clinched his hold on the ex-barbarian territories that he was annexing in the South-East and South by colonizing them with deported criminals.[4] There are parallels in the Achae-

[1] See 2 Kings xxiv. 14–16.

[2] Eduard Meyer estimates the numbers deported in 586 B.C. at something between 30,000 and 50,000 (*Geschichte des Altertums*, vol. iii (Stuttgart 1901, Cotta), p. 175). This estimate appears to be based on the record, preserved in the Book of Nehemiah, chap. vii, of the numbers that returned from Babylonia to Judaea in 538 B.C. after Nebuchadnezzar's sentence of deportation had been rescinded by Cyrus. The total given in this document amounts to no less than 42,360 free persons and 7,337 slaves, and the figures are convincing, since they are the sum total of thirty-nine precise items, while there is also a note of one group that was of doubtful legitimacy and of another that was definitely rejected. All the same, Eduard Meyer's estimate for the deportation of 586 B.C. seems hazardously high in the light of the information (fragmentary and ambiguous though it is) in the second Book of Kings and in the Book of the Prophet Jeremiah. Even in 586 B.C. Nebuzar-adan, Nebuchadnezzar's captain of the guard, 'left of the poor of the people, which had nothing, in the land of Judah, and gave them vineyards and fields at the same time' (Jer. xxxix. 10; cf. 2 Kings xxv. 12); and this statement means, on the face of it, that the agricultural population of Judah was not only left undisturbed, even in 586 B.C., but was given possession of the former property of the executed or deported notables. Even the deportation of 586 B.C. may have been confined to the inhabitants of Jerusalem, and we cannot be certain that the urban population was deported *en masse* even on this second occasion. 'Now the rest of the people that were left in the city, and the fugitives that fell away to the King of Babylon, with the remnant of the multitude, did Nebuzar-adan . . . carry away' (2 Kings xxv. 11; cf. Jer. xxxix. 9) has to be taken with a grain of salt considering that the same authority declares that Nebuchadnezzar had 'carried away all Jerusalem' in 597 B.C. (2 Kings xxiv. 14). Moreover, a quite incompatible set of figures, on a far smaller scale, is given from some different source in Jer. lii. 28–30: 3,023 persons deported by Nebuchadnezzar in 597 B.C.; 832 deported by Nebuchadnezzar in 586 B.C.; 745 deported by Nebuzar-adan in 581 B.C.; making only 4,600 souls in all.

[3] See Fitzgerald, C. P.: China, *A Short Cultural History* (London 1935, Cresset Press), p. 139.

[4] See Franke, O.: *Geschichte des chinesischen Reiches*, vol. i (Berlin and Leipzig 1930, de Gruyter), pp. 244–6, cited in the present Study, V. v. 141.

menian Government's policy of marooning *déracinés* on the islands of the Persian Gulf[1] and in the Muscovite Government's policy of granting toleration to religious dissenters from the Orthodox Faith when these consented to serve the interests of the Muscovite empire-builders by going out as pioneers into the wilderness to prepare the way for future advances of the Muscovite Empire's frontiers.[2]

Garrisons along the Frontiers

A classical example of a chain of military garrisons strung along a frontier is afforded by the Roman Empire, which held by this means its two cross-country *limites* in Germany and Britain, its three river lines along the Rhine, the Danube, and the Euphrates, and its two desert frontiers over against the Syrian Desert and the Sahara. This Roman institution was reproduced, whether consciously or not, with remarkable similarity in the Military Frontier over against the Ottoman Empire[3] that was the *raison d'être* of the Danubian Hapsburg Monarchy.[4]

The Hapsburg frontiersman[5] was liable to military service from the age of eighteen onwards,[6] but, like the Roman legionary cantoned on the military frontiers organized by Augustus, he was also a cultivator of the soil on regimental lands corresponding to the Roman *prata legionum*. During the static last phase of the Hapsburg-Ottoman frontier, after the ʿOsmanlis had been expelled from their conquests in Hungary and Croatia-Slavonia, but before they had ceased to be a formidable military power, a continuous strip of Hapsburg territory, extending from the Adriatic coast of Croatia, between Fiume and Dalmatia, to the south-western extremity of the Carpathian Mountains, where these overhang the north bank of the Danube at the Iron Gates,[7] was kept administratively separate from the Crownlands through which it ran, and was articulated into a number of local regimental districts under the direct control of the military authorities at Vienna.[8] The Hapsburg Military Frontier was organized along this line in A.D. 1777[9] and was reabsorbed into Croatia-Slavonia between the years 1871 and 1881,[10] when both the military and the political situation had been transformed by the cumulative effect of the departure of the Turkish military garrisons from Belgrade and the other Ottoman fortresses in Serbia in A.D. 1867, the

[1] See V. v. 124, n. 2, and p. 602, below. [2] See II. ii. 222.

[3] *Vojna Krajina* in the Serbo-Croat language that was the mother tongue of a majority of the troops composing the garrisons in the last phase of this Hapsburg military installation.

[4] The Danubian Hapsburg Monarchy took shape after the overthrow of the Kingdom of Hungary at the Battle of Mohacz in A.D. 1526 in order to provide Western Christendom with a new and more effective anti-Ottoman carapace (see II. ii. 177–90 and V. v. 325–8). [5] In Serbo-Croat, *granichar* (see V. v. 462–3).

[6] See Seton-Watson, R. W.: *The Southern Slav Question* (London 1911, Constable), pp. 22–23.

[7] The Hapsburg-Ottoman frontier came to rest along this line in the peace settlement concluded at Belgrade in A.D. 1739.

[8] A list of eleven such districts will be found in Seton-Watson, op. cit., p. 373. The territories of the six most easterly Grenzregimenten, and the Czaikistenbataillon cantoned in the angle between the Danube and the Tisza, are shown in the map inset in the bottom right-hand corner of Plate 75 of Spruner, K. von, and Menke, T.: *Hand-Atlas für die Geschichte des Mittelalters und der Neueren Zeit*, 3rd edit. (Gotha 1880, Perthes). The name 'Czaikisten' ('boatmen') is derived from the Turkish word *qayÿq*. [9] See Seton-Watson, op. cit., p. 44. [10] See ibid., p. 93.

Austro-Hungarian *Ausgleich* of 1867 and Hungaro-Croatian *Ausgleich* of A.D. 1868, and the evaporation of the last vestiges of Ottoman power from the regions adjoining the Hapsburg frontier as a result of the Russo-Turkish War of 1877–8 and the consequent grant, at the Berlin Conference of 1878, of independence to Serbia and Rumania, autonomy to Bulgaria and Eastern Rumelia, and a mandate to Austria-Hungary to occupy Bosnia-Herzegovina.[1] It is one of the more interesting curiosities of history that, for some 350 years from first to last—reckoning to the morrow of the Berlin Conference from the morrow of the Battle of Mohacz—so close a replica of the Roman system of frontier defence should have been installed by Hapsburg Emperors who laid claim to *Caesarea Majestas* over against Ottoman Pādishāhs styling themselves *Qaysar-i-Rūm*.

By comparison with either the Danubian Hapsburg Monarchy's or the Roman Empire's problems of frontier defence,[2] 'the New Empire' of Egypt had a simple task when once it had tacitly abandoned the attempt to retain an effective hold over its Asiatic dominions.[3] Thereafter, it was in a position to seal its frontiers against attack from any quarter by maintaining one fortress at the north-eastern corner of the Delta barring the coast road from Asia, a second fortress at the north-west corner of the Delta barring the coast road from North-West Africa, and a third at some point on the Upper Nile to block invasions from farther upstream. In a different context[4] we have noticed that the north-eastern frontier fortress, Ramses, actually became the capital of the Empire in the thirteenth century B.C., when this frontier was being subjected to cumulative pressure from the Nomads of the North Arabian Steppe, the Hittite Power from beyond the Taurus, and 'the Sea Peoples' pouring out of the Aegean Basin in a Völkerwanderung precipitated by the collapse of 'the thalassocracy of Minos'.

After the Libyan barbarians had succeeded in gaining by 'peaceful penetration' the entry into Egypt which had been denied them when they had sought to break in by force of arms,[5] and had subsequently demonstrated their incapacity to serve the Egyptiac Society as a military caste by their utter ineffectiveness when, at the turn of the eighth and seventh centuries B.C., the Assyrians and the Ethiopians had borne down, from opposite quarters, upon the heart of the Egyptiac World,[6] the founder of the Saïte Power, Psammetichus I (*regnabat* 663–609 B.C.), who eventually succeeded in getting rid of both invaders, perceived that he must find more mettlesome troops than the official defenders of

[1] See p. 17, above.

[2] The Roman Empire's problem was aggravated by the Empire's failure to carry its European land-frontier forward to the short line across the waist of Eastern Europe, between the north-west corner of the Black Sea and the south-east corner of the Baltic, and its further failure to maintain its Asiatic land-frontier along the short line across the waist of South-Western Asia, between the head of the Persian Gulf and the south-west corner of the Caspian Sea (for the European frontier see V. v. 591–5; for the Asiatic frontier see I. i. 390).

[3] Egyptian rule in Syria seems to have ceased to be more than nominal by the time of the infiltration of the Israelites, which appears to have taken place in the thirteenth century B.C. The existence of the Egyptian régime is ignored in the Hebrew tradition (see V. v. 611, n. 3).

[4] In II. ii. 113.

[5] See IV. iv. 422, n. 3; V. v. 269–70 and 353.

[6] See II. ii. 116.

the country to garrison the frontiers, if Egypt was to be preserved from the fate of again becoming a battlefield for neighbouring Powers. At the cost of alienating the established Libyan military caste, and perhaps even provoking some of their number to emigrate from the Saïte dominions to new cantonments offered them by the rival Ethiopian Power on its own southern frontier between the White and Blue Niles,[1] Psammetichus recruited Greek and Jewish mercenaries[2] to man his three frontier-fortress Daphnê-by-Pelusium, Marea barring the approaches from the Western Desert, and Elephantinê at the First Cataract,[3] where the frontier between the Saïte and Napatan Powers, between whom the Egyptiac World was now partitioned, settled down about 655 B.C.[4]

When the Saïte Power was extinguished by Cambyses, the Achaemenian Government continued to maintain the two fortresses of Daphnê and Elephantinê.[5] Persian garrisons were posted at both places,[6] but at Elephantinê an economy was made in the employment of Persian manpower by taking over and retaining the Jewish military colony which the Saïtes had planted there.[7]

1 For the expansion of Ethiopia up-river, see II. ii. 117. For the story of 'the Deserters', see Herodotus, Book II, chap. 30.

2 The Ionian Greeks' exploits in the Saïte Government's service in the seventh and sixth centuries B.C. have been touched upon, in another context, in IV. iv. 21. The Greek inscriptions carved upon the two southern colossi of the Great Temple at Abu Simbel prove that Greek troops in Saïte service were at least once employed in an expedition against Ethiopia in the reign of Psammetichus II (*regnabat* 593–588 B.C.), but there seems to be no evidence of their having shared with the Jewish military colony at Elephantinê the duty of permanently garrisoning the southern frontier of the Saïte dominions. The reception of Jewish settlers on Egyptiac ground had precedents of very long standing in Egyptiac history. Whatever may be the truth about the Israelite tradition of a sojourn of Israel in the north-eastern marches of 'the New Empire' of Egypt, there is documentary evidence that under 'the Middle Empire', in the sixth year of the reign of the Emperor Senwosret II (i.e. in the year 1892 B.C.), a 'barbarian chief' called Ebsha, with thirty-seven 'Amu followers from the desert, made application to the Imperial Warden of the Eastern Desert for permission to settle on Egyptiac territory (Meyer, E.: *Geschichte des Altertums*, vol. i, Part II, 3rd ed. (Stuttgart and Berlin 1913, Cotta), pp. 283–4).

3 See Herodotus, Book II, chap. 30.

4 See II. ii. 116.

5 See Herodotus, Book II, chap. 30.

6 See Herodotus, loc. cit.

7 Modern Western archaeological enterprise had unearthed a cache of documents, written on papyrus in Aramaic, which threw a flood of light on the life and fortunes of this community under the Achaemenian régime during the fifth century B.C. This information had been sifted and interpreted by Eduard Meyer in *Der Papyrusfund von Elephantinê* (2nd ed.: Leipzig 1912, Hinrichs) and by A. van Hoonacker in *Une Communauté Judéo-Araméenne à Eléphantine en Égypte aux vi^e et ve siècles avant J.-C.* (London 1915, Milford). This Jewish community was treated by the Achaemenian Government with studied consideration. For instance, Cambyses spared their temple at Elephantinê when he destroyed the temples of the Egyptians (Meyer, p. 36; van Hoonacker, p. 42). In 410 B.C. the Egyptian priests of the local temple of Khnum took advantage of the absence of the Governor-General of Egypt, Arsham, on a visit to Susa to induce the local Persian commandant Widarnag (*Graecè* Hydarnes) to destroy the Jewish temple. The Jewish community's protest at this outrage appears to have moved the Achaemenian Government to put Widarnag and his son to death (Meyer, op. cit., pp. 78–79; van Hoonacker, op. cit., pp. 40–42 and 45–46). The Achaemenian Government had as good reasons for retaining and conciliating the Jewish military colony at Elephantinê as it had for mistrusting and disbanding the Greek garrison at Daphnê. The Greeks were the Persians' rivals for the immense prize of domination over the Egyptiac, Syriac, and Babylonic worlds, which had been left exhausted, and incapable of defending themselves against any vigorous aggressor, by the appalling after-effects of the last and most ferocious bout of Assyrian militarism (see IV. iv. 475–6). The Jews were the Achaemenids' protégés, whom they had liberated from the yoke of the Neo-Babylonian Empire and allowed to return home from their Babylonish

A Persian frontier garrison of which the Achaemenidae were justly proud was the isolated outpost at Doriscus, on the Thracian coastal road from the Hellespont to Continental European Greece, which, after the disastrous outcome of Xerxes' attempt in 480–479 B.C. to unite the Hellenic World under Achaemenian rule by force of arms, was the sole surviving fragment of the pre-war Achaemenian province between the Hellespont and the Strymon styled 'Those beyond the Sea' in the official lists.[1] This vestige of a lost dominion was preserved for the Empire, in the teeth of Athenian sea-power and in defiance of repeated assaults, for perhaps not less than half a century after the disasters of 480–479 B.C., by the valour of its commandant Mascames and his descendants.[2]

While we are thus informed about the Achaemenian garrisons at Doriscus and Elephantinê, we have no record of any corresponding installations for the defence of the north-east frontier of the Empire over against the Eurasian Steppe, though this frontier, on which Cyrus himself had met his death, must always have been the most critical and most important of all in the estimation of the Government at Susa.[3] This silence may be due to an accidental gap in our knowledge; but it is also possible that the north-eastern frontier was not in fact guarded by imperial frontier garrisons of the kind familiar on the west because its defence was provided for otherwise. On its Sogdian sector this frontier was screened by a military alliance with a Nomad horde in Farghānah described in the official lists as 'the Hauma-(?)drinking Saka' (Saka Haumavarga, *Graecè* Amyrgioi);[4] and, behind this screen of barbarian *foederati*, a defence in depth that would undoubtedly be more effective than any fixed garrisons could be for foiling Nomad raids was afforded by the presence of a warlike feudal nobility throughout the broad territories, running back from the north-east frontier to the Caspian Gates, that constituted the imperial marches in this quarter. This mobile feudal cavalry based on almost impregnable castles was master, like its counterpart in a Medieval Western Christendom,[5] of the local military situation.

captivity to Judaea. Moreover, in Egypt the Jews, though they had originally been planted at Elephantinê by a native Egyptian régime, were as odious as the Persian conquerors themselves in the sight of the native Egyptian population in the fanatical temper that was invariably aroused in Egyptian hearts by alien domination (see V. v. 351–3; pp. 5–6 and 49–50, above; and Meyer, op. cit., p. 75). The Jewish colony at Elephantinê fell a victim to this temper in the end, if there is truth in the conjecture that it was finally wiped out by massacre during the Egyptian nationalist revolt against Achaemenian rule that was led by Amyrtaeus II in 404 B.C. (see van Hoonacker, op. cit., pp. 51–52). This Jewish garrison at Elephantinê under the Achaemenian régime has a counterpart in the cluster of Bosniak garrisons, planted in A.D. 1520 by the 'Osmanli conqueror of Egypt, Selīm I, who held for the Ottoman Empire the Nubian march, between the First and the Third Cataract, which it had taken over from the extinguished Mamlūk régime (see Budge, E. A. Wallis: *The Egyptian Sudan, Its History and Monuments* (London 1907, Kegan Paul, 2 vols.), vol. ii, pp. 207–8; Toynbee, A. J.: *Survey of International Affairs, 1925*, vol. i (London 1927, Milford), p. 236).

[1] See pp. 682–4, below.

[2] See Herodotus, Book VII, chaps. 105–6. It is to Xerxes' credit that he singled Mascames out for appointment to this post in place of the previous commandant installed by Darius.

[3] On this point see II. ii. 138–9.

[4] See pp. 644–5, below.

[5] The trouble which this feudal nobility in the north-eastern marches of the Achaemenian Empire gave to Alexander the Great has been noticed above in II. ii. 139–40.

When the Arab Caliphate re-established the Syriac universal state of which the Achaemenian Empire had been the first embodiment, and took over from its own immediate predecessors, the Sasanidae, the responsibility for defending the north-eastern borders of the Syriac World, the Arab empire-builders garrisoned Khurāsān—which had been the frontier province since the submergence of the Oxus–Jaxartes Basin under a flood of Eurasian Nomad invasion in the second century B.C.[1]—with Arab tribal cantonments of the kind that they had already established in the interior of their dominions;[2] and, when, in the eighth century of the Christian Era, the north-eastern frontier of the Caliphate was carried forward from Khurāsān to Farghānah, the political reunion of the Oxus–Jaxartes Basin with the rest of the Syriac World was confirmed by the establishment of similar Arab cantonments in the newly conquered territories.[3] The north-western frontier of the Caliphate was not stabilized until the Umayyads' ambition to complete their conquest of the Roman Empire had been quenched by the disastrous ending, in A.D. 718, of their second attempt to capture Constantinople and by the overthrow of the Umayyad Dynasty itself twenty-two years later. After the ʿAbbasids had transferred the capital of the Caliphate from Damascus, within short range of the East Roman frontier, to the more distant site of Baghdad, the north-western marches were stabilized and organized by Hārūn-ar-Rashīd (*imperabat* A.D. 786–809). The forward zone, in which the two principal military centres were Tarsus[4] and Malatīyah,[5] became known as the Thughūr ('the barrier fortresses'),[6] the rearward zone as the ʿAwāsim ('the [places] that give protection').[7]

The Ottoman Empire practised on the grand scale the policy, followed by the Achaemenian Empire at Elephantinê, of drawing on loyal peoples who were not themselves members of the ruling nationality for the purpose of frontier defence, and thereby kept down to a minimum the proportion of their own admirable professional army[8] that had to be locked up in garrisons and so withdrawn from active service in the field. On their critical eastern frontier over against the Safawī Power, the ʿOsmanlis induced the local Kurdish tribal chiefs to serve as wardens of the Ottoman marches by investing them with the insignia of Ottoman feudatories without requiring them to give up their own ancestral

Our records do not tell us whether these barons were the native aristocracy of the North-East Iranian peoples, or whether they were incomers of Persian origin who had been endowed with fiefs in these territories at the time when the Achaemenian Power had salvaged them from Nomad occupation (see II. ii. 138).

1 The consequent segregation of the Oxus–Jaxartes Basin from the main body of the Syriac World between the Saka conquest in the second century B.C. and the Arab conquest in the eighth century of the Christian Era has been noticed in II. ii. 141, with n. 2.

2 For the cantonments in Khurāsān, see Wellhausen, J.: *Das Arabische Reich und sein Sturz* (Berlin 1902, Reimer), pp. 256–9, and the present Study, II. ii. 141, n. 3. The cantonments in the interior are dealt with on pp. 130–1, below.

3 See Wellhausen, op. cit., pp. 272–3.

4 See II. ii. 368, n. 1.

5 See V. v. 254.

6 See Ahmad al-Balādhurī: *Kitāb Futūh-al-Buldān*, English translation by Khitti, P. Kh., vol. i (New York 1916, Columbia University Press), pp. 253–65.

7 See op. cit., pp. 202–3; and the present Study, II. ii. 368, with n. 1, and p. 150, n. 3, below.

8 For the recruitment, training, and êthos of the Ottoman professional army, see III. iii. 22–50.

hereditary tenures.[1] And, with the same audacious disregard for Human Nature's sensitiveness to climate which the Incas showed in interchanging the populations of the Andean Plateau and the Pacific coastal plain, the ʿOsmanlis planted Bosniaks in Nubia in the sixteenth century of the Christian Era to hold a new frontier there,[2] and Circassians in Transjordan in the nineteenth century to guard an old Ottoman frontier against the Arab Nomads of the Hamād.

The policy by which the ʿOsmanlis enlisted the services of the Kurds for the defence of their frontier against the Safawīs has an almost exact counterpart in the Manchus' policy towards the Mongols. The Manchus roped these elusive Nomads into their system of frontier defence against the Zungar Calmucks and the Russians by giving the Mongol tribes the nominal status of 'banners' (i.e. units of the Manchu Government's regular standing army), without attempting in practice to interfere with the traditional Mongol tribal organization.[3] In this light-handed treatment of the Mongol tribesmen the Manchu Imperial Government was applying to them a policy which its predecessor the Ming Imperial Government had previously applied to the Imperial Manchus' own tribal ancestors; for the original nucleus of the Manchu state had been a Manchu war-band which the Ming had organized into a feudatory statelet in order to use it as a frontier garrison of barbarian *foederati*.[4]

Garrisons in the Interior

In turning our attention from garrisons on the frontiers to garrisons in the interior of a universal state, we shall find, as might be expected, that, the more efficient the defence of the frontiers and the more successful the pacification of the subject peoples inside them, the smaller, in general, are the forces that an imperial government finds it necessary to maintain for the preservation of internal law and order.

In the Roman Empire Augustus was so successful in dealing with pockets of recalcitrant barbarism within the vast area embraced by his new frontiers along the Rhine, the Danube, and the Euphrates that by the end of his reign three legions sufficed to keep in order the highlanders of North-Western Spain,[5] and nine colonies of time-expired soldiers to overawe Pisidian highlanders who had defied successive attempts of Achaemenids, Seleucids, Attalids, and Galatians to subdue them.[6] The newly subjected Alpine peoples seem to have required no

[1] See I. i. 389–90. In the Mughal Empire the Rājput chiefs were given a similar status *de facto*.

[2] See p. 119, n. 7, above.

[3] See Lattimore, O.: *The Mongols of Manchuria* (London 1935, Allen & Unwin), pp. 145–6 and 148–51, quoted in the present Study, V. v. 315, n. 3.

[4] See Michael, F.: *The Origin of Manchu Rule in China* (Baltimore 1942, Johns Hopkins University Press), p. 39.

[5] See Sutherland, C. H. V.: *The Romans in Spain, 217 B.C.–A.D. 117* (London 1939, Methuen), p. 150. One of these three legions was withdrawn with impunity by Claudius soon after A.D. 43 (op. cit., p. 177), and another by Vespasian in A.D. 71 (op. cit., pp. 190 and 191–2). The single remaining legion sufficed to keep the Roman peace in Spain thenceforward.

[6] Augustus's Roman military colonies in and round Pisidia were Pisidian Antioch (an originally Seleucid foundation which was reinforced with a Roman military colony in or before 27 B.C.); Olbasa, Comama, Cremna, Parlais, Lystra, Germe, and Ninica, all founded in 6 B.C.; and Isaura of uncertain date (see Hahn, L.: *Rom und Romanismus im Griechisch-Römischen Osten* (Leipzig 1900, Dieterich), pp. 93–94). Claudius found it necessary to add Claudiopolis, Seleucia Sidera, and Iconium (Hahn, op. cit., p. 148).

garrisons at all. In the heyday of the Roman Peace the only garrison on the road between Rome and the Upper Rhine via the Riviera and the Rhône Valley was a battalion, perhaps 1,200 men strong, at Lyon; and this was merely one of the *Cohortes Urbanae* ('Metropolitan Battalions')—an armed police force that could hardly be counted as part of the Roman combatant army.[1] A sister-battalion at Carthage was the only garrison, in the opposite direction, between Rome and the frontier of the Empire in the desert hinterland of North-West Africa. In the latter days of an Antonine 'Indian Summer', it could be declared that

'The cities are free from garrisons, and mere battalions (μόραι) and squadrons (ἴλαι) are sufficient to provide for the security of whole nations. Even these units are not posted in large numbers in every city in each national territory. They are scattered so thinly over the countryside in such small numbers that there are many nations that do not know where their garrison is posted. . . .

'Yet [, in spite of your devotion to the arts of peace,] you have not made the mistake of depreciating the god of War. . . . Nowadays, however, Arês dances his unceasing dance on the banks of the frontier rivers, and he keeps his arms unsullied by the stain of blood.'[2]

Less secure or less well-ordered régimes have to devote a higher proportion of their military resources to the preservation of internal peace. When Hammurabi (*imperabat circa* 1792–1750 or 1728–1686 B.C.) had succeeded in restoring the Empire of Sumer and Akkad after a 260-years-long eclipse,[3] he sought to safeguard the results of his efforts by building fortresses[4] and by endowing his army with fiefs of land in order to keep it in being.[5] Similar measures were taken for the same purpose by the Achaemenidae.

In addition to the detachments of troops which they posted at river-crossings, mountain-passes, and other strategic points on the roads connecting the capital with the frontiers,[6] the Achaemenian Government maintained standing garrisons in fortresses in the interior.[7] All these units were under the command of the Central Government and not of the Governor of the province within whose boundaries their posts happened to lie.[8] The Achaemenian Crown was also generous in rewarding distinguished services by the grant of appanages in conquered territories,[9] and, whether as a fortuitous or as a designed result of this policy, an Iranian feudal nobility like that in the north-eastern marches[10] struck root in other parts of the Empire where the mass of the population

[1] See Arnold, W. T.: *Studies of Roman Imperialism* (Manchester 1906, University Press), p. 110.

[2] Aristeides, P. Aelius: *In Romam*, in *Aelii Aristidis Quae Supersunt Omnia*, edited by Keil, B., vol. ii (Berlin 1898, Weidmann), p. 110 (Or. XXVI, § 67) and pp. 122–3 (Or. XXVI, § 105).

[3] This eclipse had lasted from the overthrow of Ibbi-Sin of Ur by Elamite insurgents *circa* 2025 or 1961 B.C. to the overthrow of the Elamite war-lord Rimsin of Larsa by Hammurabi in 1762 or 1698 B.C. (V. vi. 297).

[4] See Meyer, Eduard: *Geschichte des Altertums*, vol. i, 3rd ed. (Stuttgart and Berlin 1913, Cotta), Part II, Book 2, p. 630.

[5] See Meyer, op. cit., vol. cit., p. 627.

[6] See the passage quoted from Eduard Meyer on p. 82, above.

[7] See Meyer, E.: op. cit., vol. iii (Stuttgart 1901, Cotta), p. 68.

[8] See ibid., p. 70.

[9] See ibid., pp. 36 and 60–61.

[10] See p. 120, above.

was non-Iranian.[1] Cappadocia, from the north-western slopes of Taurus to the coast of the Black Sea, became in this way a New Iran on a small scale;[2] and the top dressing of Iranian population and culture that was deposited under the Achaemenian régime continued to make its presence felt after the Achaemenian Empire's downfall. The Iranian barons in Cappadocia managed to avoid being conquered by either Alexander or any of his Macedonian successors; and two of the leading local Iranian feudal houses succeeded, with the support of their peers, in founding here, on this distant Hittite ground, two of the three earliest of the Achaemenian Empire's Iranian successor-states.[3] The greatest statesman whom these dynasties produced, Mithradates Eupator, King of Pontic Cappadocia (*regnabat* 115–63 B.C.), almost succeeded in undoing all that Alexander the Great had done[4] and achieving all that Xerxes had failed to achieve. And, though both the Iranian dynasties of Cappadocia sought and obtained admission, at an early date, into the comity of Hellenic states, the Cappadocian kingdoms were slower than Transjordan or Bactria in accepting anything more than a tincture of Hellenic culture. It was not till the fourth century of the Christian Era that Cappadocians, educated at Athens, won a tardy distinction as Greek men of letters who found their field of action in the Christian Church.

The policy of planting the interior of a universal state with feudal barons of the ruling nationality was applied, with a thoroughness unknown to the Achaemenidae, by the architects of the Ottoman Empire.[5]

The Ottoman network of military fiefs extended over all the European provinces of the Empire, the provinces in Asia Minor in which the predominant element in the population was Muslim and Turkish-speaking, and some of the provinces beyond the Taurus in which the population was Muslim and Arabic-speaking.[6] It was in fact almost ubiquitous except for Ottoman Kurdistan, where the native hereditary chiefs were incorporated into the Ottoman feudal system only nominally,[7] and Egypt, where the Ottoman conquerors tolerantly—but, as it turned out, unwisely—allowed the Mamlūks to perpetuate themselves under

1 See Meyer, op. cit., vol. cit., p. 37.

2 The success with which an Iranian feudal nobility struck root here may perhaps be accounted for partly by the presence in Cappadocia of an earlier stratum of Iranian population—the sediment left by the invasion of the Cimmerian Nomads (see III. iii. 404 and 431, n. 1, and the present volume, pp. 606–10, below)—and partly by the physical similarity between the Anatolian and the Iranian Plateau, which would make a settler from Media or Persis feel at home in Cappadocia.

3 The third was the principality of Media Atropatênê (Azerbaijan).

4 See V. v. 69.

5 Convenient summaries of our information about the Ottoman feudal system will be found in Bélin, F. A.: 'Du Régime des Fiefs Militaires dans l'Islamisme et particulièrement en Turquie' (*Journal Asiatique*, vi^e série, tome xv, Paris 1870) and in Tischendorf, P. A.: *Das Lehnswesen in den Moslemischen Staaten, insbesondere im Osmanischen Reiche* (Leipzig 1872, Giesecke & Devrient). The principal Ottoman sources on which these Western scholars draw are the treatise of 'Aynī 'Alī (written *circa* A.D. 1606, when an attempt was being made to retrieve the Ottoman feudal system from the decay into which it had fallen by that date) in Ahmed Vefīk Efendī's edition, and a *Mémoire sur les Causes de Décadence de l'Empire* written in A.D. 1630 by Khoja Beg (*alias* Kuchi Bey) and translated by Behrnauer in the *Zeitschrift der Deutschen Morgenländischen Gesellschaft* for 1861, pp. 272–332 (see Bélin, op. cit., pp. 237–8).

6 While effective in Syria and the Jazīrah, the Ottoman feudal system was very imperfectly established in the province of Baghdad (see Bélin, op. cit., pp. 259–89).

7 See p. 121, above.

Ottoman rule.[1] The military obligation incumbent on a fief-holder was to reside on his fief,[2] to serve personally in the field, and to bring with him a retinue of men-at-arms (*jebeli-ler*), whose number was determined by the officially registered annual value of his fief in terms of money,[3] whenever the feudal force of his province was called up for active service by the Central Government. In all provinces the fiefs were on two standard scales;[4] but any fief-holder who distinguished himself might be rewarded by the grant of an additional 'portion', the tenure of which was personal to the recipient and automatically terminated at his death.[5] Though in both Rumili and Anadolu there were fiefs that were hereditary freeholds,[6] this was exceptional. In general the indispensable condition for legal investiture with even the smallest fief was the receipt, from the Pādishāh himself, first of a waiting-ticket of candidature[7] and then of a warrant of appointment—and this whether the fief in question was officially registered in the 'ticket' or the 'non-ticket' category (*teskereli* or *teskeresiz*).[8]

When the Ottoman feudal system was in its heyday, the fief-holders were recruited from two sources only: from the sons of deceased fief-holders and from the issue of members of the Pādishāh's slave-household, who were invested with fiefs as a consolation prize to compensate them for the personal hardship inflicted on them by the rigid rule debarring the grandsons of administrative officials and of troopers in the household cavalry ('Sipāhīs of the Porte'),[9] and the sons of all public slaves of lower categories, from being admitted into the slave-household themselves.[10] No allowances were paid to the sons of a fief-holder in their father's lifetime, but the father might retire in favour of one of his sons, and, if the father died in battle, a 'portion' might be given to his son as a retaining fee while he was a candidate for a vacant fief.[11] The rules governing the assignment of 'portions' and the award of fiefs to sons of fief-holders were worked out by Sultan Suleymān the Magnificent[12] (*imperabat* A.D. 1520–66). He ruled that more than one son of a deceased fief-holder might be enfeofed.[13] Sons of fief-holders offering themselves as candidates were, however, required to substantiate their claim to be their fathers' sons.[14] Suleymān rather grudgingly admitted, under strict

1 See III. iii. 30–31.
2 See Tischendorf, op. cit., p. 95.
3 See ibid., p. 87. In the province of Anadolu the fief-holders themselves were exempt from personal service and were required merely to send men-at-arms (see Bélin, op. cit., p. 254).
4 The holders of the larger fiefs (*timars*) were known as *timarjy-lar*, those of the smaller fiefs (*zi'āmets*) as *zā'im-ler*.
5 See Bélin, op. cit., p. 240; Tischendorf, op. cit., pp. 37–38. Conversely, any excess of the actual income of a fief over its registered value had to be surrendered by the fief-holder to the Treasury, which applied it to the creation of a separately bestowable 'portion' (see Tischendorf, op. cit., p. 87).
6 See Bélin, op. cit., pp. 253–4; Tischendorf, op. cit., pp. 98–99.
7 See Tischendorf, op. cit., p. 95. During the period of probation the candidate had to serve in the field as a volunteer who had 'staked his head' (*serden gechdi*) on a forlorn hope (see Bélin, op. cit., pp. 232–3).
8 See Bélin, op. cit., p. 251.
9 These privileged members of the Pādishāh's slave-household must not be confused with the provincial feudal cavalry, who were also known as sipāhīs.
10 On this point see the present Study, III. iii. 34, n. 2.
11 See Tischendorf, op. cit., pp. 37–38 and 95; Bélin, op. cit., p. 250.
12 See Tischendorf, op. cit., p. 44.
13 See ibid., p. 47.
14 See ibid., p. 40.

control and limitations, a father's right to bequeath to his son a fief of the *yurd* or *ojāq* category of tenure.[1] He did not show the same hesitation about giving protection to the peasantry (*ra'īyeh*) by whom the fiefs were cultivated and the rents paid. He affirmed their right to bequeath their holdings to their children, and he made it illegal for fief-holders to bestow vacant peasant holdings upon their own relatives.[2] The peasant was thus deliberately given a security of tenure which was no less deliberately withheld from the holder of the fief on which the peasant lived and worked.[3] All these regulations were enforced by a strict system of official control. The records of the fiefs were kept in provincial registers, and these were called in and examined at the Porte by Suleymān when he made his general review of the Ottoman feudal system.[4]

As a basis of Ottoman military and political power, this feudal system was second in importance only to the Pādishāh's slave-household itself; and, though, after the death of Suleymān, the feudal system was affected by the general decay of the Ottoman body politic which then set in, determined efforts were made, some seventy years later, to bring the system back to its former level of efficiency. During the years A.D. 1632–7, in the reign of Sultan Murād IV (*imperabat* A.D. 1623–40),[5] musters of fief-holders were held, and fiefs found vacant were given to members of the Pādishāh's slave-household in lieu of pay.[6] The two fundamental institutions of the Ottoman Empire were finally abolished by the same reforming hand. After destroying the Janissaries in A.D. 1826,[7] Sultan Mahmūd II (*imperabat* A.D. 1808–39) liquidated the feudal system as well. The fiefs were reabsorbed into the public domain, and the living fief-holders were pensioned off, under the terms of the *Khatt-i-Sherīf-i-Gülkhāneh* of A.D. 1839.[8]

While the Ottoman feudal system was more highly organized than the Achaemenian, both institutions alike were of secondary importance—both for the defence of the imperial frontiers and for the maintenance of the Imperial Government's authority in the interior of the Empire—by comparison with the garrisons and mobile formations of professional troops in the Imperial Government's service. By contrast, the Mughal Imperial Government, which made similar efforts to maintain a professional force drawing its pay from the Imperial Treasury and therefore directly subject to the Emperor's control, found itself unable to prevent this Imperial Army from disintegrating into a host of feudal contingents, each virtually at the disposal of its own commander in consequence of their coming to be paid out of provincial land-revenue assigned to their commanders for collection by them without this revenue any longer passing into and out of the Imperial Treasury on the way.

While even the later Mughal emperors did succeed in keeping up a

[1] See Tischendorf, op. cit., p. 47. [2] See ibid., p. 49.

[3] Ottoman fief-holders had no political authority over their peasants, and a peasant had the right to prosecute his feudal lord in the qādi's court (see Bélin, op. cit., p. 189).

[4] On this occasion Suleymān confirmed in their holdings any *ra'īyeh* whom he found in actual occupation of fiefs.

[5] For Murād IV's herculean efforts to put the Ottoman Empire on its feet again, see V. vi. 207.

[6] See Tischendorf, op. cit., p. 105. [7] See III. iii. 49–50 and IX. viii. 239.

[8] See Bélin, op. cit., p. 294; Tischendorf, op. cit., p. 110.

small body of artillerymen, matchlockmen, and cavalry organized and commanded, as well as paid, by the imperial authorities themselves,[1] the Imperial Government, as early as Akbar's day, depended for the recruitment and maintenance of the greater part of its cavalry on *bloc* grants of divers grades of salary to office-holders (*mansabdārs*) who, in return, were required to produce proportionate numbers of troops. Even when these *mansabdārs* were paid their salaries—as Akbar made a point of paying them—out of the Imperial Treasury, the Imperial Government seems to have failed to secure from them the upkeep of their full stipulated quotas of men-at-arms; and, after Akbar's death, his successors lapsed into the slovenly and perilous practice—traditional among pre-Mughal Central Asian Muslim *conquistadores* in India—of compounding for the payment of the *mansabdārs*' salaries by assigning to them the right to collect particular local allotments (*jāgīrs*) of provincial revenue up to an equivalent value. In thus signing away its own right to collect the local revenue, the Imperial Government was in effect relinquishing its hold on the local administration as well; and the effect of a widespread grant of *jāgīrs* was thus no less pernicious for the political integrity of the Mughal Empire than it was for the military efficiency of the Mughal Imperial Army.[2]

The deadliness of Feudalism in the history of the Mughal Empire in India throws into relief, against a foil of Mughal inefficiency, the masterliness of the Tokugawa Shogunate in Japan. A traditional institution that was the death of the Mughal Empire was deliberately adopted by the Tokugawa as the basis for the establishment of an oecumenical peace after a Time of Troubles; yet the Tokugawa régime's experience in Japan was just the opposite of the Mughal régime's in India. In Japan, down to the moment when the internal play of forces was suddenly upset by the impact of the Western Civilization in the nineteenth century of the Christian Era, the local feudal lords, so far from progressively shaking off the Central Government's control, found themselves caught more and more tightly in its toils as time went on.

Immediately after the inauguration of their rule the Tokugawa were so successful in insulating the Japanese Archipelago from contact with the outside world that, for some two and a half centuries ending at the appearance of Commodore Perry's squadron in Yedo Bay in A.D. 1853, they were not called upon to provide for frontier defence. But their very success in relieving Japan from foreign pressure must have reduced almost to vanishing-point, in Japanese minds, one powerful motive for loyalty to the Tokugawa régime, and this must have added to the intrinsic difficulty of the Tokugawas' crucial political problem of maintaining their domination over the great feudal lords who had submitted to their suzerainty only under *force majeure*, and then only at the

[1] See p. 319, below.

[2] See H. Blochmann's note on the Mughal *mansabdārs* on pp. 236–47 of vol. i of his translation of the *'Ayn-i-Akbarī* (Calcutta 1873, Baptist Mission Press); Irvine, W.: *The Army of the Indian Moghuls* (London 1903, Luzac), chaps. 1, 2, and 6; Smith, V. A.: *Akbar the Great Mogul, 1542–1605*, 2nd ed., revised (Oxford 1919, Clarendon Press), pp. 360–7; Moreland, W. H.: *India at the Death of Akbar* (London 1920, Macmillan), pp. 65–68.

eleventh hour. Some of these lords had been more powerful than the Tokugawa themselves had been until the eve of the establishment of their ascendancy; many of them could boast of a much more illustrious past; and even under Tokugawa overlordship they still retained much of their former wealth and prestige.[1] To hold them in check and gradually reduce their power was a delicate and difficult task. In another context[2] we have noticed the device of requiring the periodic residence of the *daimyō* and their families at the Shogun's capital at Yedo. Another method of 'belling the cat' was to make Feudalism itself serve as an instrument for keeping Feudalism in order.

'The Shogunate . . . depended for its supremacy on the balance of power of its possible opponents. The *daimyōs* were by this time divided into three classes: first, the Related Houses (*Shimban* or *Kamon*), sons of Ieyasu [the first Tokugawa Shogun] and their descendants; second the Vassal Clans (*Fudai*), hereditary vassals of his house and their descendants; the third, Outside Feudatories (*Tozama*), or lords who did not come under this head. The *Bakufu* [i.e. the Shogunal Government] arranged that all the strategic positions should be held by the first two classes,[3] and that the "Outside Lords" should be so placed that they were separated by these, and adjacent to unfriendly neighbours. Thus these "Outside Lords" mutually checked each other and were in turn restrained by the hereditary vassals. The Related Houses also might in an emergency be controlled by the hereditary vassals, and both these classes were finally overawed by the Shogun's personal bodyguard, the *Hatamoto*, whose interests were entirely bound up with those of the *Bakufu*. How successful was this system that Ieyasu put together with such shrewdness can be seen from the fact that from this day till the latest period of the Shogunate in 1850 there was not a single rebellion of any of these feudatories.'[4]

While the Achaemenian institution of a feudal system thus found its classic application in Japan under the Tokugawa Shogunate, the Achaemenian institution of imperial garrisons posted at key-points in the interior of the Empire was likewise unconsciously reproduced, in a more thoroughgoing form, in a Far Eastern universal state in China under the Ming régime and its Manchu successor. The Ming planted garrisons of hereditary professional troops throughout their empire—not only along the frontiers over against the Eurasian Steppe and the Manchurian forests, but also along the coasts (which were harried by Japanese pirates) and along the vital inland waterway of the Grand Canal.[5] In the interior of the Empire the military districts occupied by such garrisons were thinly scattered enclaves in the territory under ordinary civil administration;[6] but the south-western corner of Manchuria, outside the Great

[1] See Sansom, G.: *Japan, A Short Cultural History* (London 1932, Cresset Press), p. 436. [2] See p. 87, above.

[3] 'The hereditary vassals, though not so rich in estates as the great *Tozama*, were assigned lands at points of strategic importance, commanding the main highways and towns, or so situated with relation to the domains of possible enemies of the Shogun as to threaten their flank or rear should they ever venture to march upon Yedo' (Sansom: op. cit., p. 436).

[4] Sadler, A. L.: *A Short History of Japan* (Sydney 1946, Angus & Robertson), pp. 209–10.

[5] See Michael, F.: *The Origin of Manchu Rule in China* (Baltimore 1942, Johns Hopkins University Press), pp. 29–30. [6] See ibid., loc. cit.

Wall but inside the Willow Palisade, which had been a Chinese-inhabited country since the Age of the Contending States, was mapped out into military districts exclusively.[1] The original nucleus of the Manchu state that was to be the Ming's successor had, as we have observed,[2] been a local Manchu tribe whom the Ming had fitted into their military system; and this system was the model followed by the architect of the Manchu Power, Nurhachi.[3]

The organization of the Manchu military establishment in 'banners' on the Ming pattern preceded the beginning of the Manchu conquest of the Chinese-inhabited country between the Willow Palisade and the Great Wall.[4] A social and administrative, as well as a military, revolution was carried out in A.D. 1601 when the Central Government of the nascent Manchu Power registered its subjects, organized them in 'banners' for civil as well as military purposes, and decreed that this new order was to override all traditional feudal claims and ties.[5] After the subsequent Manchu conquest of China, these 'banners' were the units out of which a Manchu Imperial Government reigning in the former Ming Imperial Government's stead constituted the garrisons that it stationed in Peking, the imperial capital, and in the Chinese provinces inside the Great Wall, as well as outside the Great Wall in both the Chinese-inhabited and the Manchu-inhabited zone of the Dynasty's previous domain. In the standard 'banner' of the Manchu Imperial Government's professional army after the Conquest, one battalion of Manchu troops was brigaded with one of Chinese and one of Mongols;[6] but there were some 'banners' in which the Manchu component had no Chinese or Mongol complement. The standard garrison consisted of detachments[7]—corresponding to the *vexillationes* of the Roman Imperial military organization—drawn from four 'banners' in each case originally and afterwards from eight; but there continued to be some garrisons of less than eight units, while some were raised to a still higher number, though the maximum was always less than sixteen.[8]

Sedentary barbarians, like the Manchus,[9] find less difficulty than Nomads, like the Mongols, in assuming the role of an imperial people. The antecedent attempt of the Mongols to impose an alien peace on China on their own account had been markedly less successful than the Manchus' repetition of the enterprise, in which the Mongols had to be content to serve as the Manchus' junior partners. It is true that the Mongols were handicapped not only by their Nomad background but

1 See ibid., pp. 30–31.

2 On p. 122, above.

3 See Michael, op. cit., pp. 33, 62, and 75.

4 See ibid., p. 63.

5 See ibid., p. 64.

6 These Mongol battalions of hereditary professional soldiers, individually recruited, in the 'banners' of the Manchu imperial army must be distinguished from the so-called Mongol 'banners', which were the war-bands of the Mongol tribes under Manchu suzerainty (see p. 122, above).

7 See Michael, op. cit., pp. 65–66.

8 See Lattimore, O.: *The Mongols of Manchuria* (London 1935, Allen & Unwin), pp. 146–8, and eundem: *Manchuria Cradle of Conflict* (New York 1932, Macmillan), p. 32. The military organization of the Manchus has been touched upon, by anticipation, in V. v. 315, n. 3, and 447.

9 For the social and economic background of the Manchu restorers of a Far Eastern universal state in China, see II. ii. 122, n. 2; III. iii. 16, 19, and 423, n. 1; and V. v. 315.

by a taint of Far Eastern Christian culture which provoked the demonic uprising of the Chinese against them,[1] and we have seen that the Libyan Nomads, who were undefiled—or unredeemed—by any such alien cultural tincture, were suffered by a hyper-sensitively anti-alien Egyptiac Society not only to drift into the Egyptiac World but to remain there without bringing down upon their heads any counter-stroke from the hands of the population on whose labours they had settled down to live as parasites.[2] The Libyans, however, made the fatal mistake of severing their connexion with an ancestral Nomadic way of life in which their martial qualities had been bred. They spread themselves over the Egyptian countryside[3] and, in so doing, forfeited their strength, like Sampson when he allowed Delilah to shear his locks.[4] This Libyan mistake was not repeated by the Primitive Muslim Arab Nomad warriors when they burst into the Roman and Sasanian empires, broke down the seven-centuries-old political partition between them,[5] and thereby re-established a Syriac universal state that had been originally embodied in the empire of the Achaemenidae.[6]

The Arab empire-builders realized that, if they were to retain a lasting hold over the vast dominions which they had so swiftly won, they must preserve the martial qualities of their badawī soldiery and must also keep their garrisons *in partibus agricolarum* in close and constant touch with the reservoir of badawī man-power on the Arabian steppes. Their device for meeting both these requirements was to plant permanent cantonments (*junds*) of badawī professional troops (*muqātilah*)[7] along the borderline between the Desert and the Sown, as the sea-faring empire-builders of a thalassocracy control their overseas dominions from the sea-ports linking them with the metropolitan territory across the water.[8]

The first four Arab Muslim cantonments of this type were planted, along the borderline between the Syrian Steppe and Syria, in Transjordan, at Damascus, at Homs (*alias* Hims, *alias* Emesa), and at Qinnasrīn.[9] These four garrisons were located in existing centres of

[1] See V. v. 348–51.

[2] See IV. iv. 422, n. 3; V. v. 269–70 and 352–3.

[3] The only districts in which the Libyan intruders did not plant themselves were those reserved for the temple-states which were established by their confederates the Egyptiac priesthood.

[4] An elaborately dressed side-lock was part of the insignia of a Libyan warrior.

[5] See I. i. 75–76.

[6] See I. i. 76–77.

[7] Also called 'migrants' (*muhājirah*), because they had left their ancestral tribes or oases in order to become members of one of these newly constituted military communities (see Wellhausen, J.: *Das Arabische Reich und sein Sturz* (Berlin 1902, Reimer), p. 16).

[8] The typical structure of a thalassocracy is illustrated on the Aegean scale by 'the thalassocracy of Minos' and by the Athenian Empire that grew out of the Delian League, and on the Oceanic scale by the British Empire. The British conquered India from three maritime bases: the river-port of Calcutta, the sea-port of Madras, and the inshore island of Bombay. The transfer of the political capital of the British Indian Empire from Calcutta to New Delhi in A.D. 1912 was a step towards the renunciation of British rule over India (on this point see pp. 194–5, below).

[9] See Ahmad Al-Balādhurī: *Kitāb Futūh-al-Buldān*, English translation by Hitti, P. Kh., vol. i (New York 1916, Columbia University Press), p. 202. Quinnasrīn was constituted into a separate *jund* by the Caliph Yazīd (*imperabat* A.D. 680–3). It had previously been included in the Jund of Homs. Balādhurī, in this passage, leaves it uncertain whether there was or was not also a Jund of Filastīn (i.e. Cis-Jordanian Palestine).

population, but their counterparts on other coasts of the desert were all laid out on previously unoccupied sites.[1] 'Irāq was overawed from cantonments at Basrah (*conditum* A.D. 635) and Kūfah (*conditum* A.D. 636) on the right bank of the Euphrates, where the Arab garrisons were not insulated by any water-barrier from their Arabian source of reinforcement.[2] A corresponding site on the right bank of the Nile, just above the head of the Delta, was chosen for Fustāt (*conditum* A.D. 641), 'the camp' from which the Arabs dominated Egypt. North-West Africa was dominated from Qayrawān (*conditum* A.D. 670) on a site, at the meeting-point between the low-lying arid south-eastern zone and the mountain-ribbed fertile north-western zone of Ifrīqīyah, which corresponded topographically to the sites of the cantonments dominating Syria.

Owing to the acquisition of the Caliphate and foundation of a dynasty by an Arab war-lord—the Umayyad Mu'āwīyah—who had started his career, and made his fortune, as governor of Syria, the Arab cantonments, not only on the desert coasts of Syria, but on those of 'Irāq, Egypt, and North-West Africa as well, were garrisoned by Syrian Arab troops.[3] The basis of military organization was tribal. Ziyād, whom Mu'āwīyah appointed as his governor, first of Basrah and then of Kūfah as well, tried to reorganize the military colony at Kūfah on non-tribal lines, but he seems to have achieved no permanent success in this, and in his parallel reorganization at Basrah he did not even make the attempt.[4] Tribal loyalties and rivalries were the governing factors in the life of the Arab cantonments throughout the Umayyad Age; and the resulting disunity and disorder, which was chronic and irrepressible, was no doubt one of the causes of the downfall of the Umayyad dynasty and of the eventual decay and disappearance of the cantonments themselves.

[1] See Wellhausen, op. cit., p. 17.

[2] Wāsit ('the centre') was planted by Al-Hajjāj on the far side of the Euphrates, on an island between two arms of the Shatt-al-Hayy; but this aptly named military centre for the Syrian garrison of 'Irāq was not laid out till A.D. 702, and by that time Arab rule over 'Irāq had long since been securely established.

[3] See Wellhausen, op. cit., pp. 155–6. These troops were 'Syrian' for the most part in the sense of being drawn from those badawī Arab armies, recruited in Arabia, that happened to have been directed to the Syrian theatre of the Primitive Muslim Arab wars of conquest and to have remained in Syria, after its subjugation, under the command of Mu'āwīyah. There were also, however, Syrian Arab troops whose connexion with Syria was less casual. Before the Muslim Arabs had invaded Syria, there had been two Arab infiltrations—one in the last century B.C. and the second since the latter part of the fourth century of the Christian Era—and, since the sixth century, the wardenship of the Arabian marches of Syria had been entrusted by the Roman Government to the Christian Arab dynasty of the Banu Ghassān (see I. i. 73, n. 1, and VIII. viii. 50–51). Alone among the peoples conquered by the Primitive Muslim Arabs, the Christian Arabs already established in the conquered territories were compelled (except for the Banu Taghlib in 'Irāq) to embrace Islam (see Wellhausen, op. cit., pp. 14–15) and were thereby compulsorily included in the ruling element in the Arab Empire. The Umayyad Caliphate might be described as an aggrandisement of the Ghassānid principality, and we may guess that the Syrian garrisons of the Umayyad cantonments were, to quite a large extent, of Ghassānid origin (see Wellhausen, op. cit., p. 83). Analogously the abortive Caliphate of 'Alī b. Abī Tālib, who established his seat of government at the Arab cantonment of Kūfah, on the desert border of 'Irāq, might be described as an aggrandisement of the rival pre-Muslim Arab principality of the Lakhmids who had served as wardens of the Arabian marches of the Sasanian Empire, considering that Kūfah had been planted in the immediate vicinity of Hīrah, the Lakhmids' former capital (see VIII. viii. 51, n. 1).

[4] See Wellhausen, op. cit., p. 79.

Civilian Settlements

The installation of standing military garrisons along the frontiers and in the interior of a universal state by the empire-builders can hardly fail to bring civilian settlement in its train. The Arab military *muhājirah* were allowed to bring their wives and children with them to the cantonments in which they settled.[1] The Roman legionaries, though debarred from contracting legal marriages during their term of active service, were permitted in practice by the military authorities to enter into permanent marital relations with concubines and to bring up families; and, after their discharge, they were able, by an easy process of law, to convert a concubinate into a legal marriage and to obtain retrospective legitimization for their children born out of wedlock. Moreover, the auxiliaries, who, unlike the legionaries, were recruited from among the Roman Empire's subjects, and not from among its citizens, seem to have been given the franchise upon their discharge at the end of the full statutory term of service, and sometimes earlier.[2] Thus the Roman *canabae*[3] and Arab cantonments became nuclei of civilian settlements which, in turn, became sources of recruitment for the garrisons round which they had gathered. The growth of the civilian element in the Arab cantonments was given a further impetus when the Caliph ʿUmar II (*imperabat* A.D. 717–20) granted to members of the non-Arab subject population who became converts to Islam the option of migrating to an Arab cantonment from their home town or village.[4] On these analogies we may infer that the Turkish Muslim civilian population, which amounted, at the beginning of the nineteenth century, to a considerable proportion of the total population of the Ottoman provinces in Europe, and this not only in the towns but also on the land, was a by-product of the Ottoman military fiefs which, by that date, had been in existence in these provinces for about four hundred years on the average. And we may guess that a Persian civilian population had been generated in Cappadocia by the Persian feudal baronies there before the Achaemenian régime was brought to its premature close.

Besides arising as undesigned by-products of military establishments, civilian colonies are also planted by empire-builders as an end in themselves. For example, the North-East Anatolian districts in which the Achaemenidae had granted appanages to Persian barons were colonized by the ʿOsmanlis with Albanian converts to Islam, on whose loyalty they

1 See Wellhausen, op. cit., p. 16.

2 See Last, H., in *The Cambridge Ancient History*, vol. xi (Cambridge 1936, University Press), p. 443, and pp. 140 and 155, below.

3 See Rostovtzeff, M.: *The Social and Economic History of the Roman Empire* (Oxford 1926, Clarendon Press), p. 51.

4 In this ruling, ʿUmar was deliberately rescinding the practice of the celebrated governor of ʿIrāq, Hajjāj (*proconsulari munere fungebatur* A.D. 691–713), who had forbidden converts to migrate and had even forcibly repatriated those who had done so. Under ʿUmar's ruling, migration presumably became the rule, as the theoretical alternative of remaining on the land and continuing to pay, under the less offensive name of 'rent', the tribute (*kharāj*) due from non-Muslims was hardly likely to be attractive to many converts (see Wellhausen, op. cit., p. 175). The fiscal considerations that inclined the earlier Umayyad Caliphs, first and foremost Muʿāwīyah I, to refrain from encouraging the conversion of the Arab Empire's non-Muslim subjects are discussed by Lammens, S.J., le Père H.: *Études sur le Règne du Calife Omaiyade Moʿâwia Ier* (Paris 1908, Geuthner), pp. 424–6.

could count for helping them to hold these anti-Safawī marches.[1] In the commercial centres in the heart of their dominions—Constantinople, Smyrna, Salonica, Sarayevo—the ʿOsmanlis settled civilian communities of refugee Sephardī Jews from Spain and Portugal.[2] In the Roman Empire, not only military cantonments but civilian settlements—of which Caesar's colonies of Roman citizens at Capua, Carthage, and Corinth may be regarded as the exemplars[3]—were planted by Caesar, Augustus, and their successors.

Caesar himself may have been the founder of the Roman colonies in three ports of entry—Dyrrhachium (Durazzo), Buthrotum (Butrinto), and Dyme—from Italy to Continental European Greece; in two other Greek cities—Dium and Philippi—which commanded respectively the southern and the eastern exit from the province of Macedonia;[4] and in four Anatolian ports—Lampsacus, the Bithynian Apamea, Heraclea Pontica, and Sinope—on the coastal shipping route through the Hellespont to the mouth of the Phasis.[5] Augustus reinforced these three groups of Roman civilian colonies by adding Byllis and Patrae to the first, Pella and Cassandrea to the second, and Alexandria Troas and Parium to the third. He did something to repair the ravages of his civil war with Sextus Pompeius[6] by founding other Roman civilian colonies in Sicily, and he made a momentous new departure in policy when in 15 B.C. he planted two Roman civilian colonies in Syria:[7] one at Berytus (Bayrūt)[8] and the other at Heliopolis (Baʿlbak). Claudius added a Roman colony at Ptolemais in Palestine to Augustus's Syrian foundations, and broke new ground in two regions—Cappadocia and Thrace—which had both hitherto shown an exceptional imperviousness to Hellenism. After suppressing the native client kingdom in Thrace which had been ruled for Rome by the princes of the Odrysae, Claudius founded a colony of Roman citizens at Apri, where the Great East Road running from Dyrrhachium and Apollonia through Thessalonica and Philippi forked

1 One of these Albanian settlements in North-Eastern Anatolia, Vezīr Köprü, gave birth to the Köprülü family whose eventual flowering, in a crop of distinguished statesmen, was one of the causes of the rally of the Ottoman Empire in the latter part of the seventeenth century of the Christian Era (see V. vi. 208, with n. 3, and 299).

2 For the motives of this deed of humanity and stroke of statesmanship, see II. ii. 244–6.

3 For the long-drawn-out conflict between opposing policies and political ideals which was the historical background of these three foundations, see pp. 109–10, above.

4 For the plantation of Macedonia with Roman colonies and municipia under the early Principate, see *The Cambridge Ancient History*, vol. xi (Cambridge 1936, University Press), pp. 567–8.

5 See Hahn, L.: *Rom und Romanismus im Griechisch-Römischen Osten* (Leipzig 1906, Dieterich), pp. 60–61.

6 See V. v. 71 and V. vi. 239.

7 See Hahn, op. cit., pp. 92–94. Another civilian settlement of Roman citizens planted by Augustus on Asiatic ground was his Roman colony at Tralles, founded in 26 B.C. (ibid.).

8 This Syrian outpost of the Latin-speaking world was so successful in preserving its Latin character that it became a centre for the study of Roman Law. Justinian treated the academy of law at Berytus as the peer of those at Constantinople and Rome (see Cumont, F., in *The Cambridge Ancient History*, vol. xi, pp. 626–7, and Collinet, P.: *Études Historiques sur le Droit de Justinien*, vol. ii: 'Histoire de l'École de Droit de Beyrouth' (Paris 1925, Recueil Sirey)). According to Collinet, op. cit., vol. cit., pp. 20–22, the law school at Berytus owed its rise to the Imperial Government's practice—established at some date before A.D. 196—of using Berytus, in virtue of its being the easternmost Latin-speaking community in the Empire, as its depot for the distribution, in the Oriental provinces, of the texts of new laws.

on its divergent ways to the Hellespont and the Bosphorus. In Cappadocia, which Tiberius had brought under direct Roman administration, Claudius founded a Roman colony at Archelais, just within the western borders of the province. Vespasian followed up Claudius's initiative in Thrace by founding a Roman colony at Deultum under the name of Flaviopolis, and Claudius's initiative in Palestine—where Vespasian blasted away the Jewish obstruction to Hellenization which Antiochus Epiphanes had failed to overcome—by reinforcing Ptolemais on the coast with two new Roman colonies in the interior: one at Emmaus and the other at Samaria, which Vespasian renamed Flavia Neapolis.[1]

The Roman Imperial Government did not, however, confine its programme of civilian colonization to the establishment of colonies of the ruling Latin nationality. While it did set itself systematically to Latinize—and thereby indirectly Hellenize in Latin dress—the barbarians on whom it had imposed its peace in the Danubian territories beyond the former northern frontiers of Macedonia[2] and in the West European and North-West African territories whose political destinies had been decided by Rome's victory in her struggle with Carthage,[3] the foundation of Roman colonies on Greek or Oriental ground was in this quarter only a side-line of Roman Imperial policy. In European Greece and in all parts of the Empire lying to the east of it the predominant aim of Roman Imperial statesmanship was to preserve and complete the Hellenizing work of Alexander the Great and his successors; and this aim was pursued with a steadiness and effectiveness which were tardily recognized and rewarded when, in the second century of the Imperial Peace, the Empire was at last acclaimed by Greek men of letters as an embodiment, on an oecumenical scale, of the Platonic ideal of the rule of the philosopher-king.[4]

The exemplar of this Hellenizing aspect of the Roman Imperial Government's policy of internal colonization was the synoecism by Augustus, *more Alexandrino*, of a new Greek city on the grand scale under the name of Nicopolis to adorn the scene of his crowning victory at Actium and to keep its memory alive by periodical celebrations in honour of the event. Trajan's foundation of a Greek city of the same name in the Trans-Haeman fringes of the province of Thrace[5] was evidence of the sincerity of the Roman Government's intention to make Thrace a replica of Greek-speaking Macedonia and not of Latin-speaking Moesia.[6] This Hellenization of Thrace in Greek dress at Roman

[1] See Hahn, op. cit., pp. 148–9. [2] See II. ii. 163–4. [3] See I. i. 40.

[4] See V. v. 343–4, and pp. 41–44, above. Aelius Aristeides goes so far as to suggest that Alexander's enduring achievement lay in his having served as Rome's forerunner:

'The only achievement and memorial, worthy of his genius, that Alexander left behind him was the city on the coast of Egypt that bears his name; and it is his merit that he founded Alexandria for you Romans, in order that she might be yours, and that you might be masters of the city which is the greatest in the World, next to your own'—(Aristeides, P. Aelius: *In Romam*, edited by Keil, B., in *Aelii Aristidis Quae Supersunt Omnia*, vol. ii (Berlin 1898, Weidmann), p. 99 (Or. XXVI, § 26). Cp. p. 119 (§ 95)).

[5] The grounds for believing that Nicopolis-ad-Istrum was originally included in the province of Thrace, and not in that of Lower Moesia, are given by Mommsen, Th.: *The Provinces of the Roman Empire*, English translation, vol. i (London 1886, Bentley), p. 307, n. 2.

[6] For the spread of the Latin language all the way down the right bank of the Danube, see IV. iv. 326, n. 2.

hands was consummated by Hadrian when he gave his own name to the Greek city that he founded on a site which, under a Nomad-minded Odrysian régime, had been crying out, unheeded, for synoecism ever since the time, five hundred years back, when the sister-city of Philippopolis had been duly founded by the father of Alexander the Great. Planted, as it was, at the junction of the River Hebrus with its principal tributary, on the military road to the Bosphorus from Aquileia and Sirmium, Adrianople provided Thrace with the convenient urban centre that it had lacked hitherto.[1]

This practice of diffusing Hellenism in the Roman Empire by means of the foundation of city-states was reproduced in the Spanish Empire of the Indies; and the Medieval Spanish institution which was thus propagated in the Americas in an Early Modern Age of Western history was in truth a renaissance of the Hellenic institution that had originally been propagated in Spain by Roman *conquistadores* from Italy.[2] Like the Hellenic cities planted in the post-Alexandrine Age by Macedonian empire-builders in South-West Asia and Egypt and by Roman empire-builders round all the shores of the Mediterranean, these Spanish cities in the Americas had individual founders;[3] they were laid out on the rectangular plan that, in the history of Hellenic town-planning, had been inaugurated in the fifth century B.C.[4] by Hippodamus's layout of the Peiraeus; and each *civitas* had a rural *territorium* 'attributed to' it, to use the Roman technical term.[5] In the more settled regions of the Spanish Empire these municipal *territoria* were conterminous; and, in the undeveloped regions on the fringes, some of them were of vast extent.[6] By A.D. 1574 about a hundred Spanish city-states had already been founded within the area of the Incaic Empire's former domain.[7] 'The Spanish American provinces, therefore, were in many instances a collection of municipalities, the latter . . . being the bricks of which the whole political structure was compacted.'[8]

If these Spanish colonial city-states thus resembled the post-Alexandrine Hellenic colonial city-states in serving as the cells of an intrusive alien régime's administrative and judicial organization, they likewise resembled them in enjoying little more than a simulacrum of local self-government; for they had no sooner been founded than the Crown took into its own hands the appointment of the municipal officers.[9] Above all, they resembled their Hellenic prototypes in being parasitic.

'In the Anglo-American colonies the towns grew up to meet the needs

[1] Though Adrianople was thus marked out by its geographical position for playing the part of a capital city, it had not so far achieved its manifest destiny except during the century ending in A.D. 1453, when it had been the seat of government of the Ottoman Empire. There had, on the other hand, been two periods in which Adrianople had had the misfortune to find itself serving as a frontier fortress: first during the three centuries ending in the annexation of Eastern Bulgaria by the East Roman Empire in A.D. 972 (see IV. iv. 389) and again since the carving of the autonomous principalities of Eastern Rumelia and Bulgaria out of the body of the Ottoman Empire in A.D. 1878 (see p. 17, above).

[2] See Haring, C. H.: *The Spanish Empire in America* (New York 1947, Oxford University Press), p. 159.

[3] See ibid., p. 160.

[4] See ibid., p. 161.

[5] See the present Study, III. iii. 98, with n. 2.

[6] See Haring, op. cit., pp. 161–2.

[7] See ibid., p. 160, n. 4.

[8] Ibid., p. 162.

[9] See ibid., pp. 164–5.

of the inhabitants of the country: in the Spanish colonies the population of the country grew to meet the needs of the towns. The primary object of the English colonist was generally to live on the land and derive his support from its cultivation; the primary plan of the Spaniard was to live in town and derive his support from the Indians or Negroes at work on plantations or in the mines. . . . Owing to the presence of aboriginal labour to exploit in fields and mines, the rural population remained almost entirely Indian.'[1]

The Spanish empire-builders' Inca predecessors' practice of linking together districts that were geographically far apart and at the same time economically complementary[2] has counterparts in the economy of both the Roman Empire and the Arab Caliphate.

The vacant public land which the Roman Government acquired in the Po Basin through the conquest of the country between the years 197 and 173 B.C. and the concomitant eviction of the more recalcitrant of its native Gallic and Ligurian inhabitants[3] was not all transferred to individual ownership through the foundation of Latin and Roman colonial communities of freeholders and the grant of freeholds to other settlers individually (*viritim*). Tracts were also granted to corporations domiciled in Italy south of the Appennines—both ecclesiastical corporations, such as the sorority of the Vestal Virgins and other colleges of priests belonging to the established public service of the Roman State,[4] and political corporations in the shape of self-governing city-states that were incorporated in, or externally associated with, the Roman body politic.[5]

1 Haring, op cit., pp. 160 and 159. 2 See pp. 114–15, above. 3 See V. v. 569–74.

4 See Hyginus: *De Condicionibus Agrorum* (in *Die Schriften der Römischen Feldmesser*, ed. by Blume, F., Lachmann, K., and Rudorff, A., vol. i (Berlin 1848, Reimer), p. 117) and Siculus Flaccus: *De Condicionibus Agrorum* (in op. cit., pp. 162–3).

5 The self-governing communities incorporated in the Roman body politic were colonies and municipia of Roman citizens; those externally associated with it were Latin city-states, whose relations with the Roman State were governed by custom, and *civitates foederatae* which were bound to Rome by written treaties, the terms of which varied in accordance with the particular circumstances in which each community had entered into permanent political association with Rome. Cis-Appennine city-states of both classes received corporate grants of land in the Po Basin from the Roman Government—presumably as a recompense for services rendered by the military contingents from these states in the Roman armies by which the Po Basin had been conquered from its native inhabitants. The aggregate extent of their holdings must have been considerable, to judge by the part that they played in the opposition of the various vested interests to the Gracchan policy of reasserting the Roman State's right of eminent domain over all Roman public land that had not been assigned in freehold to individual proprietors (see Appian of Alexandria: *Studies in Roman History*, 'The Civil Wars', Book I, chap. x, § 6, and chap. xix, § 1, where πόλεις ἰσοπολίτιδες signifies *municipia civium Romanorum*, πόλεις ἄποικοι the *coloniae Latinae*, and Ἰταλιῶται the citizens of *civitates foederatae*).

Both the ecclesiastical and the municipal corporations that possessed these endowments of land in the Po Basin appear to have turned them to account by letting them to tenants. The ecclesiastical tenancies ran for either one-year or five-year periods (Hyginus: *De Condicionibus Agrorum*, in *Die Schriften der Römischen Feldmesser*, ed. cit., vol. i, p. 117). We have two glimpses of the management of the municipal estates in the collected correspondence of Cicero. In a letter written in 46 B.C. (*Ad Familiares*, Book XIII, Letter 11), Cicero introduces to his correspondent, Decimus Iunius Brutus, governor of Cisalpine Gaul, the three commissioners whom the municipal authorities of Arpinum (Cicero's own home town) are sending out with instructions 'to inspect the properties let out on lease (*vectigalia*) which they possess in the Province of Gaul, to collect the rents due from the tenants (*colonis*), and generally to examine and deal with the situation there'. In a letter written in 45 B.C. (*Ad Familiares*, Book XIII, Letter 7), Cicero asks his correspondent Cluvius to intercede with Caesar on behalf of the municipality of Atella in the matter of that community's agricultural property let out on lease (*de agro vectigali municipii*), which was threatened with confiscation. According to Cicero these rents were

In the Arab Caliphate under the Umayyad régime we find a parallel to the Inca practice which is almost exact from the geographer's standpoint though perhaps not so close from the sociologist's. Just as the Incas established economic partnerships between lowland districts and highland districts, so the Umayyads endowed the two cantonments of Basrah and Kūfah not only with arable land on the adjoining plains of ʿIrāq (the fabulously productive 'Black Earth': *As-Sawād*), but also with meadow-land, pasture, and forest in 'the Highlands' (*Al-Jibāl*) through which the Great North-East Road wound its way up towards the frontier of the Syriac World over against the Eurasian Steppe.[1] The difference between the Umayyad and the Inca application of the same device lies in the motive, which in the Umayyads' case seems to have been primarily military and only incidentally economic. The frontier garrisons which the Arab empire-builders pushed forward up the Great North-East Road,[2] first into Khurāsān and eventually into Transoxania,[3] were originally recruited, and subsequently reinforced, by drafts from the cantonments at Basrah and Kūfah;[4] and the grant to these

an important item in the budgets of the municipalities to which they were payable. In the first of the two letters here cited, he writes that the people of Arpinum depend on this source of income for 'all their ways and means of providing for public worship and keeping public buildings, both religious and secular, in a sound state of repair'. In the second letter he goes so far as to write that 'the municipal finances of Atella are entirely dependent on this source of income'.

Evidence of a grant of forest and pasture land in the Po Basin to the *civitas foederata* Aquinum, situated in the distant basin of the Liris (Garigliano), is preserved in the name 'Saltus Galliani qui cognominantur Aquinates' (meaning 'Estates, situate in Cisalpine Gaul, of the city-state of Aquinum') which was borne by one of the self-governing municipalities of Roman citizens in the eighth of the eleven regions into which Augustus grouped the city-states of Italy (see the list in Plinius Secundus, C.: *Historia Naturalis*, Book III, chap. xv (xx), § 116). At some date between the end of the first quarter of the second century B.C. and Augustus's day, the tenants and squatters on this estate must have been incorporated as an autonomous community.

[1] For example, the revenues of the city and district of Dīnawar were payable to the cantonment of Kūfah, and those of Nihāwand to the cantonment of Basrah (Le Strange, Guy: *The Lands of the Eastern Caliphate* (Cambridge 1905, University Press), pp. 189 and 197).

[2] See xi, map 37.

[3] See p. 121, above.

[4] In the Arab military occupation of Khurāsān, it was Basrah, not Kūfah, that played the predominant part, and this fact was unhappily reflected in the transplantation to Khurāsān not only of the Basran soldiery but of the inter-tribal feuds that were Basrah's heritage from a pre-Islamic Arabia (see Wellhausen, J.: *Das Arabische Reich und sein Sturz* (Berlin 1902, Reimer), pp. 247, 256, and 131). The Basran Arab garrisons in Khurāsān were not deterred from pursuing these inter-tribal feuds either by the numerical preponderance of the native Iranian population or by the proximity of the Eurasian Nomad adversary on the farther side of the frontier. Ziyād—whom the Caliph Muʿāwīyah appointed governor not only of Basrah and Kūfah but of all Arab dominions beyond them, as far as Khurāsān inclusive, which were dominated from the cantonments on the Euphrates by way of the Great North-East Road—sent large numbers of Basran and Kufan Arab families to Khurāsān (see ibid., p. 79). Further drafts of 25,000 men each from the two cantonments were sent to Khurāsān by Ziyād's son Rabīʿ, on whom his father's governor-generalship was conferred by Muʿāwīyah after Ziyād's death. By the end of the seventh century of the Christian Era there was in Khurāsān an Arab population of about 200,000, including about 40,000 fighting-men (see ibid., p. 266). The military and political dependence of the greater part of the Iranian Plateau on a Power installed on the plains of ʿIrāq, which was a salient feature in the administrative organization of the Umayyad Empire, has its counterpart in the similar situation after the overthrow of the Achaemenian Empire, when the successors of Alexander were contending for the fragments of the carcass. In that struggle, Seleucus Nicator emerged as one of the victors largely owing to his ability to dominate, from his base at Babylon, all the former Achaemenian dominions lying to the north-east and east of Babylonia, save for an easternmost fringe which he was constrained to cede to Chandragupta in exchange for a park of war-elephants.

two Arab military corporations in ʿIrāq of estates on the Iranian Plateau—whose productive resources were thus laid under contribution for the benefit of Basrah's and Kūfah's war-chests—was an economic reflection of the military fact that the outlying garrisons protecting the Iranian provinces of the Caliphate were detachments from the two great nurseries of soldiers cantoned on the distant borderland between the Euphrates and the Arabian Steppe.

The Inca practice of transporting individually selected skilled workers and their families, in order to improve the quality of production in economically backward districts, has counterparts—economically comparable, though incomparably brutal and indiscriminate from the human standpoint—in both Hellenic and Syriac history. The scientific agricultural exploitation, with imported slave labour, of the coastlands of the Western Mediterranean from the fifth century B.C. onwards and of the seaboard of Lower ʿIrāq in the ninth century of the Christian Era has already been noticed in this Study in another context.[1] There are indications that the Incas may have brought artificers from the culturally maturer lowland region of Chimu to raise the standard of workmanship in their own highland capital at Cuzco.[2] This was certainly the purpose of the Mongols in carrying Chinese, Russian, and Western Christian craftsmen away captive from the extremities of the Old World to its heartland when they were trying to transform Qāraqorum from an encampment of Nomads into a city fit to be the capital of a world empire.[3] Ts'in She Hwang-ti may have had the same end in view in bringing selected settlers from other parts of his empire to recruit the population of Hien-yang,[4] when he was making an imperial capital out of a city that had hitherto only had to serve as a capital for the parochial state of Ts'in.[5] On the other hand Nebuchadnezzar, in deporting to Babylon from Jerusalem 'all the craftsmen and smiths',[6] was probably more concerned to deprive Judah of her armaments industry—and thereby render it impossible for her to make any further attempt at armed insurrection against the Neo-Babylonian régime[7]—than he was to improve the age-old craftsmanship of Babylon, whose practitioners would have felt that they had little to learn from a handful of artisans picked up from a rustic highland principality in a remote corner of the empire.

A type of internal colonization which is apt to become prominent in the last phase of the history of a universal state is the plantation of barbarian husbandmen on lands that have come to be depopulated either as a result of raids perpetrated by these barbarians themselves (or by neighbours of theirs in their former homes in the no-man's-land beyond the *limes*) or as a result of some social sickness, native to the

[1] In V. v. 66 and 129.

[2] Baudin, L.: *L'Empire Socialiste des Inka* (Paris 1928, Institut d'Ethnologie), p. 134.

[3] See the passage quoted from Friar William of Rubruck's narrative in V. v. 113–14, and Olschki, L.: *Guillaume Boucher, A French Artist at the Court of the Khans* (Baltimore 1946, Johns Hopkins University Press).

[4] See V. v. 141.

[5] The successive changes in the location of the capital of the Sinic universal state are dealt with below on pp. 210–13.

[6] 2 Kings xxiv. 14 and 16, cited already on p. 116, above.

[7] This had unquestionably been the motive of the Philistines when, in the eleventh century B.C., they had placed a ban upon the practice of the metallurgical industry in the subjugated territory of Israel (see I Sam. xiii. 19–22).

depopulated empire itself, which has laid it open to barbarian attack by sapping its powers of resistence.

A classic example is presented in the picture of a post-Diocletianic Roman Empire in the *Notitia Dignitatum*, which records the presence of a number of German and Sarmatian barbarian corporate settlements on Roman soil in Gaul, Italy, and the Danubian provinces. The technical term *laeti*, by which these barbarian settlers were known, is derived from a West German word[1] denoting semi-servile resident aliens; and we may infer that the Romans' *laeti* were the descendants of defeated barbarian adversaries of the Roman Imperial Government who had been punished or rewarded for past acts of aggression by being coerced or coaxed into migrating permanently to become peaceful cultivators of the Promised Land on the inner side of the *limes* which they had formerly devastated as raiders. From the Roman Government's standpoint this arrangement would serve the dual purpose of employing the barbarians to repair the damage that they themselves had inflicted and of giving them at the same time an interest in keeping the peace for the future instead of continuing to break it. The *laeti* were cautiously planted in the interior of the Empire, not in the immediate neighbourhood of the *limites*,[2] and in Gaul, at any rate, each settlement of *laeti* was attached to a particular Gallic canton and was required to pay its land-tax to the municipal authorities, not to the Imperial Treasury.[3] In its gazetteer of the western portion of the Empire the *Notitia Dignitatum* mentions twelve *praefecturae* of German *laeti* attached to divers Gallic cantons[4] and twenty-two *praefecturae* of Sarmatian *laeti* in Gaul and Italy,[5] as well as a settlement of Sarmatae and Taifali Gentiles in the Gallic canton Pictavi[6] and a Gens Marcomannorum, administered by a tribune, in the Middle Danube province of Pannonia Prima.[7]

'*The Melting-pot*'

Our survey of garrisons and colonies installed by builders of universal states has perhaps borne out our contention that these systematic transfers of population—which are characteristic of the universal state phase in the decline of a civilization—are on the whole much more humane, in execution as well as in design, than the capricious and vindictive uprooting of individuals and communities which is characteristic of the antecedent Time of Troubles. At the same time our survey has brought to light the truth that these two morally diverse processes produce similar social results. And the cumulative effect of the empire-builders' statesmanship, following upon the war-lords' atrocities,[8] is to

1 *Leto, litu, let, laet, lat* (see Grosse, R.: *Römische Militärgeschichte von Gallienus bis zum Beginn der Byzantinischen Themenverfassung* (Berlin 1920, Weidmann), p. 208).

2 See ibid., p. 209.

3 See ibid.

4 *In Partibus Occidentis*, chap. xlii, §§ 33–44.

5 Ibid., §§ 46–63 and 66–70; cp. Codex Theodosianus VII. 20, 12, of A.D. 400: 'Laetus (MS. luctus) Alamannus, Sarmata'.

6 *In Partibus Occidentis*, chap. xlii, § 65.

7 Ibid., chap. xxxiv, § 24.

8 The successive types of 'saviours with the sword' whose sequence punctuates the stages of the decline and fall of a civilization have been reviewed in V. vi. 178–213.

intensify and accelerate a process of pammixia and proletarianization[1] that is characteristic of Times of Troubles and universal states alike.

Permanent military garrisons installed on the frontiers of universal states become 'melting-pots' in which the dominant minority of a disintegrating society fuses itself with both the external and the internal proletariat. In an earlier part of this Study[2] we have observed that, on the organized military frontier of a civilization over against outer barbarians, the wardens of the marches and the opposing barbarian war-bands tend, with the passage of time, to become assimilated to one another first in military technique and equipment and eventually also in culture and êthos. But, long before the dominant minority of a disintegrating society has been barbarized by hostile contact, across the frontier, with the external proletariat, it will have been vulgarized by fraternization, within the frontier, with the internal proletariat.[3] For empire-builders who have gained their position by emerging as sole survivors from a struggle for existence between the parochial states of their world do not often preserve either sufficient manpower or sufficient zest for the profession of arms to be able to contemplate holding and defending their hardly won empire unaided.

In this quandary their first recourse is to reinforce their own military strength by enlisting, not barbarians from beyond the pale, but subjects of the empire who have not lost their martial virtues. While they seldom push this policy to the extreme to which the Achaemenidae went when they took over into their own service the Jewish military colony that had been installed in the Egyptian frontier fortress of Elephantinê by their Saïte predecessors,[4] they frequently raise new military formations from among their subjects and brigade these with the troops of their own ruling nationality. Thus Augustus and his successors manned the immensely long frontiers of the Roman Empire, which Augustus had staked out, by brigading with the Roman legions *auxilia* recruited from Roman subjects who were not Roman citizens.[5] The detachments of Arab professional soldiery from Basrah and Kūfah, which were posted in Khurāsān to hold the north-east frontier of the Umayyad Empire, enlisted the help of the warlike native Iranian inhabitants of the province and fraternized with their new comrades-in-arms, in contrast to the aloofness of the parent cantonments on the Euphrates from the subject civilian population of 'Irāq.[6] Khurāsānī Arab officers adopted the Iranian custom of surrounding themselves with a *comitatus* of picked Iranian fighting-men, and they also raised separate Iranian military formations under Iranian officers.[7] The local Iranians, on their side, had good reasons for responding favourably to these bids for their co-operation that were made to them by their Arab conquerors.

'As a result of the conquest, their position, on the whole, changed only slightly, and this hardly for the worse. The defence of Khurāsān against enemies from outside—that is, against the Turks—was conducted by the

[1] For this process, see V. v. 439–80, *passim*.
[2] In V. v. 459–80.
[3] See V. v. 439–59.
[4] See pp. 118–19, above.
[5] See V. v. 446, and p. 132, above.
[6] See V. v. 447, and Wellhausen, op. cit., p. 307, quoted in the present Study in V. v. 450.
[7] See Wellhausen, op. cit., p. 309.

Arabs more successfully than it had been managed under the Sasanian régime. . . . The *Mawāli* (as non-Arabs who had become converts to Islam and become adopted members of the Arab tribes were called in Khurāsān, as elsewhere) fought shoulder to shoulder with the Arabs against their traditional national enemy, the Turks. They also fought for Islam against their own Sogdian kinsmen, in so far as the latter were Islam's enemies and the Turks' confederates. . . . The domestic life of Khurāsān was not interfered with by the Arabs very much. They left the administration to the *marzbans* and *dihqans* and did not impinge upon the subject population except through these native intermediaries. Even in the garrison towns and in the seats of administration the native authorities continued to play their part side by side with their Arab colleagues. For one thing, they had to collect the taxes, for the due payment of which, on the agreed scale, they were responsible to their conquerors. However, the burden of taxation had doubtless weighed as heavily on the *misera contribuens plebs* under the Sasanian régime.[1] The Iranians were also left undisturbed in the practice of their religion; in the agreements providing for payment of tribute it is always assumed that they are going to retain their ancestral faith. . . . They appear, all the same, to have had no very serious attachment to Zoroastrianism. . . . The attraction of Islam for the Iranians was in the first instance not so much on account of its intrinsic merits as for the sake of the material advantages which it had to offer. They used it as a means of diminishing the gulf between themselves and the ruling class and of obtaining a share in their privileges by "going Arab". They adopted Arabic names and secured admission into an Arab tribe.'[2]

Even the Manchus—who, as mere restorers of their Mongol predecessors' empire-building work in China, had not to pass through the ordeal that is the usual price of founding a universal state—did not attempt to hold, with their own unaided strength, the vast and populous domain of which they had made so easy a conquest. In the 'banners' of which their garrisons were composed, their general practice was, as we have seen,[3] to brigade a Chinese and a Mongol with each Manchu battalion.

Our records, fragmentary though they are, give us vivid glimpses, here and there, of 'the melting-pot' at work. A piece of first-hand evidence for the mutual assimilation of the Chinese 'bannermen' in Manchu service and their Manchu fellow soldiers has been quoted in this Study at an earlier point.[4] At Elephantinê under the Achaemenian régime—which was particularly liberal[5] in giving openings to non-Persians—the Jewish military unit constituting the garrison had on its strength not only some soldiers of Babylonian origin but also at least one

[1] According to Wellhausen, op. cit., p. 310, Khurāsān was not exempt from the general rule that land-tax continued to be payable, both by native converts to Islam and by Muslim Arabs who had become local landowners, on land originally belonging to the native non-Muslim population. On the other hand, according to the same authority, op. cit., p. 19, non-Muslim subjects of the Caliphate who performed military service for frontier defence were exempted from taxation.—A.J.T.

[2] Wellhausen, op. cit., pp. 308–9.

[3] See pp. 128–9, above, with the references there given.

[4] In V. v. 457–8; cp. p. 449.

[5] On this point see Meyer, E.: *Der Papyrusfund von Elephantinê*, 2nd ed. (Leipzig 1912, Hinrichs), p. 26.

Chorasmian.[1] It is remarkable that this soldier should have found his way to the First Cataract of the Nile from his native land in the delta of the Oxus, at the opposite extremity of the Achaemenian Empire. It is still more remarkable that this representative of the high-spirited Iranian peoples of the north-eastern marches, who were to offer such a stubborn resistance to Alexander the Great,[2] should not have felt it beneath his dignity to serve shoulder to shoulder with Syrians in a regiment of mercenaries.

In the civil life of this Jewish military colony, Babylonic influence was strong, though the colony had originally been founded by the Neo-Babylonian Empire's Saïte rivals and adversaries, and though it is probable that the Saïtes had recruited at least the first nucleus of the force from among those 'die-hards' in Judah who had preferred to be refugees in Egypt rather than deportees in Babylonia.[3] The marriage contracts, for example, that had survived from the community's archives were Babylonian rather than Israelite in form, and this Babylonicizing tendency in Elephantinian Jewish personal law had been strong enough to raise the general status of women above the customary Jewish level of that age.[4] One medium through which this Babylonic influence had seeped in was the Aramaic language and alphabet of the Jewish community at Elephantinê, which were identical with those in use in contemporary Babylonia and Assyria.[5] The tincture of Babylonic polytheism in the Yahweh-worship of the Elephantinê community[6] suggests that there may have been Babylonian elements in the community itself; and this, in turn, suggests that the original nucleus may have been a mixed band including refugees from Samaria as well as from Judah,[7] since the Samaritans were a hybrid community in which a remnant of Israel was mingled with deportees from Babylonia whom the Assyrian war-lord Sargon had planted in place of the Israelites whom he had deported to 'the cities of the Medes'.[8] These facts and probabilities indicate that Achaemenian Elephantinê was a 'melting-pot' indeed; and, on this analogy, we may picture the corresponding role of the Arab military cantonments in the Umayyad Empire.

'[The non-Arabs] went over to Islam in large numbers, and such conversions were particularly numerous among the masses of Iranian prisoners-of-war in Kūfah and Basrah.'[9]

This non-Arab element in the cantonments was continually reinforced by the effect of 'Umar II's ruling that non-Arab converts in the provinces

[1] See Meyer, op. cit., p. 28, and van Hoonacker, A.: *Une Communauté Judéo-Araméenne à Elephantinè en Égypte aux vi^e et ve siècles avant J.-C.* (London 1915, Milford), p. 5.

[2] See II. ii. 140.

[3] See 2 Kings xxv. 26 and Jer. xl-xliii.

[4] See van Hoonacker, op. cit., pp. 25–29.

[5] See ibid., pp. 29–30. For the process of peaceful penetration by which the Aramaic language and alphabet replaced the Akkadian language and cuneiform characters in the homelands of the Babylonic Civilization, see I. i. 79–80, and V. v. 486–91 and 499–501.

[6] See V. v. 125, n. 1.

[7] This is van Hoonacker's conjecture, in op cit., pp. 84–85.

[8] See 2 Kings xvii.

[9] Wellhausen, op. cit., p. 45. For instances, see Ahmad Al-Balādhurī: *Kitāb Futūh al-Buldān*, English translation by Hitti and Murgotten, Part (ii) (New York 1924, Columbia University Press), pp. 105–11.

must migrate to a cantonment if they wanted to avoid the alternative of continuing, after their conversion, to pay the tax imposed on non-Muslim subjects of the Empire.[1] All non-Arab converts had to obtain affiliation to some Arab tribe or clan,[2] and this institution of clientship

[1] For this ruling, see p. 132, above.

[2] See Wellhausen, op. cit., p. 45. For example, the soldiers of a Persian cavalry force in Ahwāz which deserted to the Arabs and turned Muslim *en masse* appear to have settled first in Basrah as clients of the Banu Tamīm and afterwards to have transferred their allegiance to the Banu S'ad. Besides these Persian Asāwirah, there were Sindi deserters from the Persian army known as Zutt (i.e. Jāts), and others known as Sayābijah and Andaghār. Under the Sasanian régime these Zutt had had their pastures on the borders (*tufūf*) of 'Irāq over against the North Arabian Steppe, while the Sayābijah had been settled on the coast of the Persian Gulf, and the Andaghār in the desert borderland between Kirmān and Seistan. These three peoples were all now settled at Basrah as clients of the Banu Tamīm, and they afterwards transferred their allegiance to the Banu Hanthalah (see Balādhurī, op. cit., Part (ii), pp. 105–107, 109, and 111). We also hear of a Persian family from Umān migrating to Basrah via Yamāmah (see ibid., p. 100), and of the inhabitants of the Persian city of Qazwīn surrendering to the Arabs on terms, accepting Islam, and settling in Kūfah, under the name of Hamrā' ad-Daylam, as clients of Zuhrah b. Hawīyah (see ibid., p. 10). Prisoner-converts from Bukhārā were settled by 'Ubaydallah b. Ziyād at Basrah (see ibid., p. 111).

Some of the Zutt and Sayābijah deserters from the Persian army were transplanted in A.D. 669 or 670 by the Caliph Mu'āwīyah I from Basrah to Antioch (see ibid., pp. 110–11, and vol. i (New York 1916, Columbia University Press), p. 250). When the Arabs conquered Sind, another batch of Zutt, whom the conquerors had uprooted from their native pastures, seem to have been sent to Syria by Hajjāj (*proconsulari munere fungebatur* A.D. 691–713) and eventually to have been sent on by the Caliph Walīd I (*imperabat* A.D. 705–15) to join the previous batch of Zutt deportees at Antioch (see Balādhurī, op. cit., Part (ii), p. 111, and vol. i, p. 250)—whence some, again, were sent on by the Caliph Yazīd II (*imperabat* A.D. 720–4) to Massīsah (Mopsuestia) in Cilicia (see Balādhurī, op. cit., vol. i, p. 259). But the bulk of Hajjāj's deportees from Sind—who included representatives of other Sindī tribes besides the Zutt, and who were 'accompanied by their wives, their children and their buffaloes' (Balādhurī, op. cit., Part (ii), p. 109)—seem to have been settled by Hajjāj in 'Irāq, in the Kaskar district. Here their numbers were subsequently recruited, according to Balādhurī (ibid., p. 109), by runaway black slaves and by contumacious clients of an Arab tribe and an Arab grandee; and in the reign of the 'Abbasid Caliph Ma'mūn (*imperabat* A.D. 813–33) they broke out into a rebellion which it took him and his successor Mu'tasim (*imperabat* A.D. 833–42) the best part of twenty years to quell. According to Mas'ūdī (in his *Tanbih*, Baron Carra de Vaux's translation, p. 455) these ninth-century Zutt insurgents in the marches of South-Western 'Irāq were the descendants of immigrants from Sind who had migrated to 'Irāq in large numbers across Kirmān, Fars, and Khūzistān. Whether there had or had not been a voluntary immigration as well as a compulsory deportation of Zutt to 'Irāq from Sind, we may take it that, in the course of the first two centuries of Arab rule, man-power from Western India had, in one way or another, been flowing into a South-Western Asia that, on the eve of the Arab conquest, had been depopulated by the two last and most devastating of the Romano-Persian wars.

After the capitulation of the 'Irāqī Zutt insurgents in A.D. 834, Mu'tasim deported some of them to Jalūlah and Khāniqīn, astride the Great North-East Road, and the rest to 'Ayn Zarbah (*Graecè* Anazarbus) in Cilicia, in the valley of the River Jayhān (*Graecè* Pyramus) to the north-east of Massīsah (see Balādhuri, op. cit., Part (ii), p. 110, and vol. i, p. 264, and the other authorities cited by M. J. de Goeje in *Mémoires d'Histoire et de Géographie Orientales*, No. 3: 'Mémoire sur les Migrations des Tsiganes à travers l'Asie' (Leyden 1903, Brill), pp. 30–31). These were not the first Zutt to be settled at 'Ayn Zarbah; for Zutt from 'Ayn Zarbah had already been drafted by Hārūn-ar-Rashīd (*imperabat* A.D. 786–809) to reinforce the garrison of the neighbouring Cilician fortress Kanīsat as-Sawdā' (see Balādhurī, op. cit., vol. i, p. 264). Thereafter, in A.D. 855, the East Romans descended on 'Ayn Zarbah and carried off into East Roman territory, to the north-west of the Taurus Range, the Zutt deportees there, together with their women and children and buffaloes (Tabarī III, 1426, cited by de Goeje in op. cit., p. 31). This thrice deported detachment of the Zutt were the advance guard of the Gypsies of Orthodox and Western Christendom. We may guess that they were reinforced by their kinsmen at Massīsah and Antioch after the reconquest of Cilicia and Northern Syria by the East Roman Empire in the tenth century of the Christian Era.

It will be seen that the Arab Caliphate played a part in the dissemination of the Gypsies that corresponded to the part played by the East Roman Empire in the dissemination of the Paulicians (see IV. iv. 624–34).

made the relation between non-Arab and Arab Muslims intimate, even though it did not place the two categories of Muslims on a footing of equality with each other. The resulting social fusion went far. Even at Basrah and Kūfah, at least as much Persian as Arabic was spoken in the markets,[1] and in Khurāsān the process naturally went farther still. In the Khurāsānī army which, under Abu Muslim's leadership, overthrew the Umayyad régime in the great insurrection of A.D. 747–50, even the Arabs were predominantly Persian-speaking.[2] The Khurāsānī Arab officer who caught and killed the fugitive Umayyad Caliph Marwān in Upper Egypt in the summer of A.D. 750 gave the word of command in Persian when he ordered his troops to attack.[3]

In the Roman Empire, likewise, the military cantonments and civilian colonies acted as social 'melting-pots'.[4] The ferment must have been particularly active in the Roman colony planted in 45 B.C. by Caesar at Corinth,[5] since the Roman citizens whom Caesar settled here were freedmen;[6] and these 'stepsons of Italy'[7]—as Publius Scipio Aemilianus had once called the free populace of the city of Rome to their face, in contemptuous allusion to the servile source to which so many of them owed their origin, even as early as Aemilianus's day—were drawn from all quarters of the Hellenic World and its hinterlands. In their settlement at Corinth, Caesar's freedman-colonists were merely consummating a process of pammixia of which they themselves were earlier products.

Who are the Beneficiaries?

In promoting this process of pammixia and proletarianization in the body social of a universal state, for whose benefit do civilian colonies and military garrisons chiefly operate?

There have been cases in which the beneficiary has been an alien civilization. For example, the transfers of population on the grand scale, to which the Incas' subjects had been broken in by their rulers' benevolently high-handed policy, prepared the ground for the more revolutionary acts of the Incas' Spanish supplanters and successors. The Spanish authorities were adopting Incaic practice in attempting to regroup the subject 'Indian' population into new local communities[8] and in retaining and protecting the village headmen[9] whom the foregoing Incaic régime had installed.[10] The Spanish Viceroy of Peru, Francisco de Toledo (*proconsulari munere fungebatur* A.D. 1569–81) was said also to have been consciously and deliberately following Incaic precedent when he organized a system of universal compulsory conscription for

[1] See Wellhausen, op. cit., p. 307.
[2] According to Tabarī, cited by Wellhausen in op. cit., p. 308.
[3] See ibid., p. 342.
[4] The Roman Army's role in propagating the Latin version of the Hellenic culture in the Greek-speaking and Oriental provinces of the Roman Empire and at the same time introducing Greek and Oriental influences into the Latin western provinces is described in Hahn, L.: *Rom und Romanismus* (Leipzig 1906, Dieterich), pp. 160–6.
[5] See pp. 109–10, above.
[6] See IV. iv. 270, with n. 4.
[7] 'Quorum noverca est Italia' (Velleius Paterculus, C.: *Historia Romana*, Book II, chap. iv, § 4).
[8] See Haring, C. H.: *The Spanish Empire in America* (New York 1947, Oxford University Press), pp. 70–71, 142, and 174–5.
[9] See ibid., p. 63, n. 44, and p. 215.
[10] See p. 115, above.

civilian labour, under which 'the Indians' were called up in rotation for periods of three or four months' service at a time in numbers that kept one-seventh of the total labour force perpetually mobilized;[1] and the long-suffering native peasantry that was thus periodically rounded up[2] like Ottoman *ra'īyeh* to meet the Spanish colonists' seasonal demands for labour were also placed, when at home, at the disposal of Spanish *encomienderos*.[3] These Spanish counterparts, in the Andean countryside, of the Persian barons whom the Achaemenidae planted in Cappadocia were not the only agents of a Western Christian cultural penetration of the Andean Society under the newly imposed alien régime. The Spanish self-governing municipalities founded at key-points in the Andean World had as potent an effect as the Greek self-governing city-states that were founded in Egypt and South-Western Asia by Alexander and his successors;[4] and these municipalities, like the *encomienderos*, were beneficiaries of an antecedent Incaic Imperial régime which had schooled an uprooted and regimented Andean population to become docile 'Indians' for *conquistadores* from the Old World.

In the European interior of the Western World a quarter of a millennium later, the main body of the Western Society was the beneficiary of the short-lived universal state which was provided for the mouldering remains of a Medieval Western city-state cosmos by the Napoleonic Empire. The stagnation into which the life of Flanders, Western Germany, and Northern Italy had sunk since the Medieval Western city-state cosmos's decay[5] was stirred into fresh and vigorous movement by the intrusion of semi-alien French garrisons; and, brief though this disturbing French visitation was, it had the decisive and historic effect of drawing back into the main stream of Western life the waters of a branch that had become a backwater.[6] The impact of the Napoleonic soldiery, and of their more polished forerunners under the *ancien régime*, on the mustily vegetating society of eighteenth-century Frankfurt and Düsseldorf has been vividly depicted in two masterpieces of German literature.[7]

Such cases, however, as these are as rare as they are interesting, and it is evident that an alien civilization is not the normal beneficiary from the colonies and garrisons that have been installed by a universal state. On the other hand, the barbarians beyond the pale of a civilization derive conspicuous benefits from cantonments screening a universal state's

[1] See Haring, op. cit., p. 64. [2] See p. 112, n. 7, above.

[3] An exact account of the *encomienda* will be found in Haring, op. cit., pp. 44–45 and 62. The strictness with which, at least in juridical theory, the rights of the Crown on the one hand and of the peasants on the other hand were safeguarded in the terms on which an *encomienda* was granted to a Spanish *conquistador* is reminiscent of the limitations on the rights of Ottoman fief-holders (see pp. 124–6, above).

[4] See p. 135, above.

[5] See III. iii. 344–50. [6] See V. v. 619–42.

[7] In Goethe's *Dichtung und Wahrheit*, Book III, there is an account of the impression made on Goethe in his childhood by the French 'town major', Count Thorane of Grasse, who was billeted in Goethe's father's house after the occupation of Frankfurt by the French Army on the 2nd January, 1759. In Heine's *Reisebilder*, in 'Das Buch Le Grand', there is an analogous picture of the impression made on Heine in his childhood by the French drummer who was billeted in Heine's father's house in Düsseldorf. The Jewish child was captivated by the French plebeian, as the Frankfurter patrician child had been by the French aristocrat.

outer frontiers; for the education which the barbarians gradually acquire from these military outposts of a civilization—first as adversaries and later as mercenaries of the imperial power—makes them capable, at the moment when the empire collapses, of swooping across the fallen barrier and carving barbarian successor-states out of derelict imperial provinces. This adventure and its sequel have been discussed in previous parts of this Study[1] and are dealt with further below.[2] At this point it is only necessary to remind ourselves that the barbarians' triumphs are as short-lived as they are sensational.[3] The transfers and mixtures of population in a universal state produce deeper effects, with more important historical consequences, on the relations between the dominant minority and the internal proletariat.

In both the Roman Empire and the Arab Caliphate, for example, the relative positions of these two social factions had undergone a revolutionary change to the dominant minority's disadvantage—though this without any commensurate gain for the internal proletariat—long before the barbarians succeeded in founding their ephemeral successor-states. In the Arab Caliphate this internal social revolution expressed itself politically in the substitution of the 'Abbasid for the Umayyad régime after the short and sharp civil war of A.D. 747–50. In the Roman Empire the political expression of the corresponding social revolution was the replacement of an Augustan 'principate' by a Diocletianic despotism after a long-protracted bout of disorder which, in its most acute phase, rankled into outright anarchy.[4] In both cases the revolution was provoked by the disillusionment of the internal proletariat with a formal enfranchisement which had not made them genuine equals of the dominant minority; in both cases the insurgent internal proletariat succeeded in depriving the dominant minority of the power and privileges which they had retained till then *de facto*; and in both cases, again, the ruin of the dominant minority did not achieve the revolutionists' aim of setting the victorious internal proletariat in their former masters' seat. Equality, indeed, was attained, but on the level of a common servitude to a new master in the shape of a totalitarian régime.

This ironical turn of events through which History cheated the proletarian insurgents of the fruits of their victory was a consequence of the violence with which the revolution had been carried out. This recurrence of disorders characteristic of a Time of Troubles put to rout the social rally that had been achieved through the foundation of a universal state. Therewith, the temporarily arrested disintegration of a declining civilization was set in motion again, and the social effort thenceforth fruitlessly expended on the forlorn hope of saving the life of a civilization that was by that time *in extremis* took such a tremendous toll from the society's fast-dwindling energies that no margin remained for allocation to individual liberties—not even on the restricted scale of inordinate privileges for a small minority. The totalitarian régime, which was a last

[1] In V. v. 194–337 and 459–480. [2] In VIII. viii, *passim*.

[3] On this point, see I. i. 58–62 and VIII. viii. 45–87.

[4] The period of disorder lasted from the death of the Emperor Marcus Aurelius in A.D. 180 to the accession of Diocletian in A.D. 284. The chapter of anarchy ran from the murder of Alexander Severus in A.D. 235 to the official triumph of Aurelian in A.D. 274.

desperate and swiftly bankrupt expedient for staving off social dissolution, demanded, and exacted to the uttermost farthing, the surrender of the individual's residual treasure of personal freedom.

The Triumph of Equality and Despotism in the Arab Caliphate

The dissatisfaction of the non-Arab converts to Islam[1] with their treatment under the Umayyad régime had substantial grounds. For example, non-Arab prisoners-of-war

'secured by conversion their personal freedom,[2] but not the full status of citizens and members of the army, and therefore not the privileges which this status carried with it: they became *Mawāli*, i.e. clients of an Arab clan. It was only on these terms, as subordinate hangers-on of Arab clans, that converts obtained admission to the ranks of the theocracy; for Islam by itself did not suffice to produce this result. The theocracy was in reality a specifically Arab state, an imperium exercised by the Arabs over the conquered peoples.'[3]

Even the Khurāsānī Iranians whom the local Arab military colonists had accepted as their comrades-in-arms[4]

'were not looked upon by the Arabs as being fully their peers. If they served in the army they had to fight on foot and not on horseback, and if they distinguished themselves they were regarded with mistrust. They did receive pay and a share in prize-of-war, but no regular salary. Their names did not appear on the military salary-roll (*dīwān*). Though they were adopted into the Arab tribes, they were still distinguished, as "peasants", from the "tribesmen". And, though they were Muslims, they were not exempted from the tax payable by subjects.'[5]

In their natural dissatisfaction with an Umayyad régime under which they were kept in this ambiguous, uncomfortable, and irritating position, the Iranian converts to Islam found allies in members of the Arab ruling race who were hostile to the Umayyads on religious grounds; and a series of attempts on the part of these two different dissident elements to make common cause, against a régime that was obnoxious to both, resulted eventually in the Umayyads' overthrow.

The first attempt—an unsuccessful one—was made under the auspices of Sabaism, an extreme form of the Shīʿah which glorified the Caliph ʿAlī at the cost of tampering with a fundamental tenet of Islam.[6] This sect struck root in some of the Arab clans in the cantonment of Kūfah, which ʿAlī had made the seat of his government; it gained adherents among the numerous Persian freedmen there; and in the anarchy let loose by the civil war between the adherents of ʿAlī and those of Muʿāwīyah the Sabaïtes momentarily succeeded in overthrowing the ruling Arab aristocracy of Kūfah and substituting a Sabaïte régime

[1] See V. v. 449–50 and 501, n. 2.

[2] 'It was, however, only customary, and not obligatory, to grant their freedom to prisoners-of-war if they accepted Islam.'

[3] Wellhausen, op cit., p. 45.

[4] See the passage quoted from Wellhausen, op. cit., on pp. 140–1, above.

[5] Wellhausen, op. cit., pp. 309–10.

[6] See ibid., pp. 42 and 312–13. The Sabaïtes perverted the Islamic belief in the singleness and transcendence of God by introducing the doctrine that the prophets were successive vehicles of the spirit of God, and that ʿAlī was the next of these avatars in succession to Muhammad.

under which the invidious distinction of status between Arab Muslims and non-Arab converts was abolished.[1] After the collapse of a movement that was too heretical to succeed, the Iranian converts found more effective allies in less extreme representatives of the Shīʿah and in the hyper-orthodox and militantly anti-Umayyad Kharijites (*Khawārij*), who condemned ʿAlī himself for his half-heartedness in the cause of God.[2] Seeds of both Kharijism and Shiʿism were carried from Kūfah to Khurāsān by the drafts of Kufan fighting men that were sent to reinforce the garrisons on the North-East Frontier;[3] and, after the Umayyads and their Syrian Arab war-bands had enjoyed nearly a century of ascendancy over all other elements in the Empire, they were overthrown at last by Khurāsānī Iranian converts to Islam with Arab co-operation and largely under Arab leadership.[4]

The anti-Umayyad movement in Khurāsān which came to a head in A.D. 747 in the armed insurrection of Abu Muslim at Merv, and which ended in the replacement of the Umayyads by the ʿAbbasids, had been set on foot, about A.D. 720, by agitators from Kūfah who had been Iranian converts by descent and shopkeepers and artisans by profession.[5] Abu Muslim himself appears to have been of the same origin,[6] while the nucleus of his rebel army was mainly recruited from peasant Iranian converts in the Merv oasis.[7] But, though the targets of the insurgents' attack were the Arab representatives of the Umayyad régime, Khurāsānī Arabs were in a majority among Abu Muslim's lieutenants and the insurgents were not consciously working for the cause of Iranian nationalism; the insurrection was an *union sacrée* of Iranian and Arab Khurāsānī Muslims in the cause of Islam;[8] yet its very success inevitably transformed it into an Iranian *revanche* for the Arab conquest of the Sasanian Empire a hundred years back.

The Khurāsānī conquerors took full advantage of the admirable network of roads which the Umayyads had inherited from the Sasanidae and from the Romans and from those Powers' Achaemenian predecessors. While it had taken the Primitive Muslim Arabs nineteen years (A.D. 634–51/2) to conquer the Sasanian dominions from the Euphrates to Merv, and the Macedonians five years (334–330 B.C.) to conquer the Achaemenian dominions from the Hellespont to the scene of Darius's death beyond the Caspian Gates,[9] it took the Khurāsānīs

[1] See Wellhausen, op. cit., p. 43.

[2] For the *Khawārij* see Wellhausen, op. cit., pp. 40–41. In the Primitive Islamic community this faction—whose name means 'the Withdrawers'—took the same line towards the political-minded supporters of both ʿAlī and Muʿāwiyah as the synonymous 'Pharisees' took towards the Maccabees in the second century B.C. They differed, however in their consequent tactics, for the *Khawārij* took to militancy while the Pharisees persevered in non-violence (see V. v. 73).

[3] See pp. 137–8, above.

[4] See Wellhausen, op. cit., p. 310.

[5] See ibid., pp. 315 and 320.

[6] See ibid., p. 323.

[7] See ibid., p. 331.

[8] See ibid., pp. 320 and 333–4. In the recently conquered province of Tukhāristān, adjoining Khurāsān on the north-east, Arab conquerors and native Iranians likewise made common cause in this crisis, and likewise accepted a non-Arab as their leader because the Arab aspirants to leadership could not agree among themselves. But this *union sacrée* in Tukhāristān was directed not against the Umayyads but against the Khurāsānī rebels (see ibid., p. 334). This loyalty of the recently conquered Iranians of Tukhāristān to the Umayyad régime is reminiscent of the loyalty of the recently conquered Sikhs in the Panjab to the British Rāj in the crisis of the Indian Mutiny.

[9] See II. ii. 140.

less than three years to sweep over the Umayyad dominions from Merv to the point in Upper Egypt where they caught and killed their quarry the Umayyad Caliph Marwān. The capitulation, in the summer of A.D. 749, of the Syrian Arab garrison of Nihāwand—the fortress commanding the Great North-East Road at an easily defensible point on the western brow of the Iranian Plateau—retrieved the disgrace of the catastrophic defeat of the Persians by the Arabs on the same spot in A.D. 641 or 642. The crushing defeat of Marwān himself by a mere detachment of the Khurāsānī forces in a ten days' battle (*commissum* 16th–25th January, A.D. 750) on the banks of the Greater Zāb wiped out the older score of the equally crushing defeat that had been inflicted in this neighbourhood in 331 B.C. on the last Darius's last army by Alexander's expeditionary force. In bursting out of Asia into Egypt, and obtaining the allegiance of all the former Umayyad dominions in Africa up to the Atlantic coast of Morocco, the Khurāsānī adherents of the ʿAbbasids surpassed the feat of the Sasanian army which had occupied Alexandria in A.D. 619, but had exhausted its impetus some distance short of Carthage,[1] in the course of the last and worst of the Romano-Persian wars. Indeed, they achieved the ambition of the Achaemenid conqueror Cambyses, whose intention of following up his conquest of Egypt by a naval expedition against Carthage had been frustrated by the refusal of the indispensable Phoenician contingent in his fleet to carry out an order to subjugate their colonial kinsmen.[2]

The brilliant victory of the Khurāsānīs in the civil war that swept across the dominions of the Caliphate in A.D. 747–50 was decisive in its negative results. The Umayyad régime and the hegemony of the Syrian Arab military cantonments, of which the régime had been an expression, were overthrown once for all,[3] and the Khurāsānīs ostensibly reigned in their stead under the banner of the ʿAbbasids.

'The Khurāsānīs had won for the ʿAbbasids their victory and they took their own share of the spoils. In a certain sense they became the heirs of the Syrians, though their relation to the Government was not the same.

1 See p. 93, above.

2 'Cambyses gave orders to his fleet to sail against Carthage, but the Phoenicians refused to obey. They submitted that they were bound by solemn engagements and that they would be guilty of a crime if they made war on a daughter-community. This unwillingness of the Phoenicians [to lend themselves to Cambyses' designs against Carthage killed the project, since] the remainder of the fleet was inadequate for the task. So, thanks to their Phoenician kinsmen, the Carthaginians escaped subjugation at Persian hands; for Cambyses felt it impolitic to try to coerce the Phoenicians, considering that they had come under Persian sovereignty voluntarily and that the naval power of the Persian Empire depended entirely on them' (Herodotus, Book III, chap. 19). For the relations of the Phoenician city-states to the Achaemenian Imperial Government, see V. v. 123, n. 2.

3 See Wellhausen, op. cit., p. 347. As this authority here points out, the success of the subjects of the Caliphate in throwing off the yoke of the Arab cantonments on the borders of the Desert and the Sown had the effect of breaking those links between the subject territories of the Caliphate and the reservoir of badawī Arab military man-power on the Arabian Steppe which had been forged with such care and skill by the original Arab empire-builders. 'The ancient home of the Arabs now "went native" (*verwilderte*) again so completely that it actually became a dangerous business to make the pilgrimage.' Cp. Caetani, L.: *Studi di Storia Orientale*, vol. iii (Milan 1914, Hoepli), p. 50. In the post-Syriac interregnum *circa* A.D. 975–1275, in which the ʿAbbasid Caliphate foundered, the Nomads of Arabia played the role, not of upholders of the tottering empire, but of invading barbarians on all fours with the Berbers and the Turks (see III. iii. 445–6).

They were called the *Shī'ah* ('the Party'), the *Ansār* ('the Helpers')[1] or the *Abnā'-ad-Dawlah* ('the Sons of the New Era').[2] They held in their hands the external power; they had a military organization. . . . They constituted the Caliph's standing army, and the Caliph lived in the midst of these guards of his. Baghdad was in fact laid out, not as an oecumenical capital, but as a cantonment for the Khurāsānīs in which the Caliph could reside at a safe distance from Kūfah. In this cantonment they still maintained their links with their home,[3] and the predominance which they had won in the service of the 'Abbasids, both as a party and as a military force, became a predominance of their nation and their country—Eastern Iran—over the rest of the Empire.'[4]

This ostensible hegemony was retained by the Khurāsānī garrison of Baghdad for rather more than a century before the military control over the central government of the 'Abbasid Caliphate passed into the hands of a Turkish slave-bodyguard recruited from the Eurasian Steppe beyond the pale of both Khurāsān and Transoxania; and, in terms of the nationality of the founders of successor-states, the general Iranian political ascendancy in the 'Abbasid dominions may be reckoned to have lasted for more than three centuries, if we place to its credit the Transoxanian Iranian successor-state established by the Sāmānids,[5] and if we take as the terminal date the overthrow of the Daylamī Iranian Buwayhids by the Turkish Saljūqs in A.D. 1055–6.[6] Compared with the ephemeral subsequent triumphs of the barbarian war-bands that came in at the death of the Caliphate—an ill-assorted mob of Turks and Mongols, Arabs and Berbers, Normans and Franks—the Iranian ascendancy in

[1] The original *Ansār* had, of course, been the people of Medina who had invited the Prophet Muhammad to come and rule over them. Under this name they had been distinguished from the *Muhājirīn* who were the Prophet's Meccan fellow refugees. Now that the name *Muhājirīn* had come to signify the Arab military settlers in the cantonments, the adoption of the name *Ansār* by the Khurāsānīs had an obvious political connotation.—A.J.T.

[2] Wellhausen notes (op. cit., p. 347) that the original meaning of *dawlah* was 'new era' and that it was the choice of this term by the 'Abbasids to describe their régime that led to its acquiring the general meaning of 'government' or 'dynasty'. Wellhausen also draws attention to the affinity between the title 'Sons of the Kingdom' and the language of Matt. xvii. 25; 'Of whom do the kings of the Earth take custom or tribute? Of their own children, or of strangers?'—A.J.T.

[3] The geographical situation of Baghdad in relation to the Iranian Plateau corresponded exactly to that of Basrah and Kūfah in relation to the Arabian Steppe. Baghdad was laid out on a site as near to the heart of 'Iraq as a Khurāsānī garrison could post itself without placing a river barrier between itself and its sources of reinforcement in North-Eastern Iran. The 'geopolitical' significance of the sites of Basrah and Kūfah has been noticed on p. 131, above. When Hārūn-ar-Rashīd (*imperabat* A.D. 786–809) organized the North-Western March of the Caliphate over against the East Roman Empire (see p. 121, above), he planted Khurāsānī garrisons at Adana, Tarsus, and 'Ayn Zarbah, *alias* Anazarbus (Ahmad Al-Balādhurī: *Kitab Futūh-al Buldān*, English translation by Khitti, P. K., vol. i (New York 1916, Columbia University Press), pp. 260, 262, and 264).

[4] Wellhausen, op. cit., p. 348.

[5] See II. ii. 142, above. Iranian successor-states of the 'Abbasid Caliphate arose to the west as well as to the east of the 'Abbasid metropolitan province of 'Irāq. The Zanātā Berber Kharijite principality which held the hinterland of Ifrīqiyah from A.D. 761 to A.D. 908 was founded by a Persian adventurer named Rustem, and the ancestor of the so-called 'Fātimids' was said to have come from Ahwāz in the Iranian province of Khūzistān (see I. i. 355). The Ikhshīd, who in A.D. 935 founded for himself and his heirs a successor-state in Egypt and Syria by carrying out the 'Abbasid Government's mandate to suppress the previous local successor-state ruled by the Tulunids, was a Transoxanian Iranian princeling. His ancestral principality was Farghānah (see Lane-Poole, S.: *A History of Egypt in the Middle Ages*, 2nd ed. (London 1914, Methuen), pp. 81–82).

[6] See I. i. 356.

the more palmy days of the ʿAbbasid Era was long-lived and historically important. On the other hand it was unsubstantial by comparison with the antecedent Arab hegemony which had been brought to an end by the Khurāsānī insurrection of A.D. 747–50. The effective immediate heir of the Syrian Arab cantonments in Syria and ʿIrāq was not the Khurāsānī cantonment at Baghdad but the ʿAbbasid totalitarian régime—which did indeed inaugurate a 'new era' when it supplanted its comparatively easy-going Umayyad predecessor.

'The change of dynasty brought with it a transformation of the inward nature of the régime. . . . The Arabs had imposed themselves, by right of conquest, as a ruling nobility over against the populations which they had subjugated. . . . Under the Umayyads this primitive system persisted in essentials. . . . Under the ʿAbbasids it vanished—along with the distinction of classes which was its pre-supposition. The ʿAbbasids did not, like the Umayyads, stand on the shoulders of a strong aristocracy of which they themselves were members; the Khurāsānīs, on whom their power was based, were not their kinsmen; they were merely their tools. The whole Muslim community stood in a uniform relation to the ʿAbbasids, without any gradations of a natural order in the political standing of different elements; the dynasty alone possessed the divine right to rule as heirs of the Prophet. There were no impediments to prevent them from shaping the régime in accordance with technical considerations, as might seem best for efficiency and also for the interests of the dynasty itself. They succeeded in bringing greater order into the administration, especially in the departments of taxation and justice; they were zealous in giving a hearing to, and taking action on, the complaints of subjects who appealed to them as a court of supreme instance.[1] But they suppressed the general living interest in politics—which had formerly been part and parcel of religion—far more thoroughly than had proved practicable for the Umayyads. . . . The State shrank to the dimensions of the Court. . . . And the Court comprised a

[1] This ʿAbbasid and likewise Caesarean *arcanum imperii* was also taken to heart by the ʿAbbasids' Sāmānid successors in the North-East. It was remembered of the Sāmānid prince Ismāʿīl b. Ahmad, surnamed 'Al-ʿĀdil' ('the Just') (*dominabatur* A.D. 892–907) that, even in the depth of winter, when the ground was under snow, he would sit motionless on horse-back, armed cap-à-pie, in open court, in order to render himself continually accessible to petitioners.

'I have read, in the works of our forefathers, that it was the usual practice for the Kings of Persia to have a lofty scaffold erected and to station themselves there on horse-back, to enable them to distinguish, among the multitude assembled on the plain, all petitioners complaining of oppression, and so to give themselves the opportunity of doing justice. The reason for this custom was that, when a prince remains inside a palace with doors, barriers, vestibules, corridors and curtains, perverse and ill-intentioned persons can obstruct the entry of petitioners and prevent them from reaching the royal presence. . . .

'Ismāʿīl b. Ahmad had a practice, when the cold was most severe and when the snow was falling most heavily, of repairing, unattended, to the Great Square [at Bukhārā] and remaining there on horseback till the moment of the dawn prayer. It might happen, he used to say, that some victim of injustice might come to my Court to inform us of his needs, and he might have neither money to cover his expenses nor a roof to shelter him. Because of the rain and the snow, they would not allow him to reach my presence; but, when he knew that I was here, he would come to find me, would obtain satisfaction, and would return home re-assured and rejoicing in complete security.'

This Sāmānid royal practice, thus described by Hasan Abu ʿAlī Nizām-al-Mulk in his *Siyāsat-Nāma*, chap. 3, *ad initium* and *ad finem* (on pp. 12 and 26 of the French translation by Schefer, Ch.: *Siasset Namèh* (Paris 1893, Leroux)), was still being followed, some nine hundred years later than Ismāʿīl b. Ahmad's day, in the Transcaucasian Kingdom of Georgia on the eve of its annexation by Russia, according to a self-complacently contemptuous allusion in the work of a Modern Western publicist (see de Maistre, J.: *Lettres et Opuscules Inédits*, vol. i (Paris 1851, Vaton), p. 215).—A.J.T.

throng of civil servants who were no longer identical with the officers [of the military establishment].[1] Most of these civil servants were creatures and favourites of the sovereign. Freedmen were preponderant among them. Under the previous régime freedmen may have enjoyed the ruler's confidence and exercised a corresponding influence; they now attained to the highest positions in the public service.[2] They were raised from the dust, to be hurled down into the dust again. . . . It was not birth, but the Caliph, that made people's fortunes. . . . The aristocracy was replaced by a Court hierarchy of officials, distributed between recognized grades and kept under one another's surveillance. At the top stood the Wazīr, who was the head of the Caliphial Chancery and eventually became the visible *alter ego* of a Caliph who no longer appeared in public.'[3]

The Triumph of Equality and Despotism in the Roman Empire

This masterly portrayal of the features of the 'Abbasid régime in which it presented so striking a contrast to its Umayyad background could be adapted with little change to portray the corresponding revolution in the Roman Empire which substituted the Diocletianic despotism for the Augustan 'Principate'. The Augustan régime, like the Umayyad Caliphate, had respected in large measure the liberties of an 'ascendancy'[4] as against the Imperial Government at the price of tolerating the maintenance of this 'ascendancy's' privileged position as against the subject population of the Empire. In the Roman Empire under the Principate, as in the Arab Caliphate in the Umayyad Age, these privileges were partly positive and partly negative.

An inner circle of Roman families whose members enjoyed a customary right of entry into the Senate actually shared with the Emperor—who tactfully described himself as 'Leader of the House' (*Princeps Senatus*) in the administration of the Roman dominions. A number of pacific provinces in the interior had been handed back to the Senate by Augustus; and, in the provinces which the Emperor continued to keep in his own hands, with the important and significant exception of Egypt, the governorships were reserved in practice for senators, who were reconciled by the splendour of these posts to the indignity of having to hold them as the Emperor's servants. The senatorial class also staffed the senior posts in the Imperial Army. And, though the administration of Egypt was not the only sphere in which the Emperor delegated the realities of power to non-senatorial agents, the authority still left to the senatorial class was considerable in reality and even more imposing in its carefully-kept-up appearances.

A wider circle of Roman citizens who were not of the senatorial class but who were domiciled in Italy enjoyed a monopoly of the right to serve in the Imperial Guard—the nine 'praetorian' ('headquarters') battalions

1 Compare the segregation of the civil and military services under the Diocletianic régime in the Roman Empire.—A.J.T.

2 Compare the corresponding transformation of the freedmen-stewards of Caesar's private household into virtual ministers of state (see V. v. 452–3). In the Roman Empire this political consequence of social *Gleichschaltung* occurred at an early stage of 'the Principate'.—A.J.T.

3 Wellhausen, op. cit., pp. 348–50.

4 In the sense in which the term came to be used of the Protestant dominant minority in Ireland under the British Crown from the Tudor Era down to the establishment of the Irish Free State.

that were permanently quartered in the City of Rome itself—and further possessed the valuable negative privilege of being exempt from direct taxation. Under the Principate this 'ascendancy' of an inner circle within the Roman citizen body occupied a position not unlike that of the Syrian Arab soldiery on the salary-rolls of the Arab cantonments in the Caliphate under the Umayyad régime. Like the Syrian Arabs, these specially privileged Roman citizens were a small minority of the total population of the Empire; and, just as, in the Caliphate, there came, as time passed, to be an ever larger body of converts to Islam whose conversion proved not, after all, to have made them the peers of their Arab masters, so likewise in the Roman Empire there was an ever larger body of legally naturalized citizens who found themselves still outside the privileged circle.

In the Roman Empire, as in the Caliphate, and indeed for the same reasons, the formal status of membership in the ruling community was easier for members of the subject population to obtain than were the substantial advantages that had originally been associated with that status automatically. The ring of senatorial families was reluctant to see the value of their privileges depreciated by a widening of their circle. Caesar's revolutionary act of making Roman senators out of the uncouth notables of recently conquered Gallic cantons raised so fierce a storm that Augustus beat a retreat in the interests of his policy of reconciling the Senate to the Principate, and it was not till A.D. 48 that it became practical politics for the Emperor Claudius to enrol senators from among the notables of the Aedui, a Gallic canton that had already been Rome's ally before Caesar's conquest.[1] The Roman Imperial Treasury, for its part, was as reluctant to see its sources of revenue diminished as a result of progressive extensions of the Roman franchise to non-citizen subjects of the Empire as the Umayyad Treasury was to suffer a similar loss through the progressive conversion of non-Muslim subjects of the Caliphate to Islam.[2]

The immunity from direct taxation which was enjoyed under the Principate by Roman citizens domiciled in Italy dated from the morrow of the Third Romano-Macedonian War (*gerebatur* 171–168 B.C.);[3] and at that date the entire Roman citizen body had occupied a territory embracing less than half of Italy south of the Appennines.[4] When the

[1] See *The Cambridge Ancient History*, vol. x (Cambridge 1934, University Press), p. 377.

[2] All treasuries are apt to think alike, but the Umayyad Treasury was actually the historical heir to the Roman Treasury's tradition. At the time of the conquest the Primitive Arab Muslim Government had taken on the existing inland revenue organization as a going concern—including the official personnel as well as the records and the practice—in both their ex-Roman and their ex-Sasanian dominions. Ruling, as they did, from Damascus, the Umayyads were influenced by the Roman fiscal tradition predominantly.

[3] Having destroyed in that war the last surviving Great Power in the Hellenic World apart from the Roman Commonwealth itself, the Romans felt that the consequent decrease in their own military and political liabilities, and increase in the external sources of their public revenue, made a combination of new circumstances that justified them in ceasing to impose direct taxation on themselves. They did not, however, abolish the tax of 5 per cent. on the manumission of slaves, which had been introduced as early as 357 B.C. and which had a social as well as a fiscal purpose. This tax remained in force under the Empire (see Hirschfeld, O.: *Die Kaiserlichen Verwaltungsbeamten bis auf Diocletian*, 2nd ed. (Berlin 1905, Weidmann), pp. 106–9).

[4] A map displaying the areas in Italy that were included in the territory of the Roman

Roman citizenship had been subsequently conferred, first on all previously alien Italian communities south of the River Po,[1] and then on all communities between the Po and the Alps,[2] the exemption from direct taxation had accompanied the conferment of the franchise as a matter of course. When, however, under the Principate, the still expanding body of Roman citizens burst even the generous bounds that had been assigned to Italy by Augustus and came to constitute an appreciable and increasing element in the population of the provinces as well, the Imperial Treasury took alarm, and laid down the new doctrine that the immunity from direct taxation which had been one of the attributes of Roman citizenship since 167 B.C. was applicable only to citizens domiciled in Italy; all persons domiciled in provincial Roman territory were now deemed to be liable to direct taxation even if they happened to be Roman citizens;[3] the only exception to this ruling was in favour of Roman citizens domiciled in the territory of a Roman municipality, outside Italy, on which 'Italian status' (*ius Italicum*)[4] had been expressly conferred; and the Imperial Government was very sparing in its grant of this boon: it was obtained by few non-Italian communities of Roman citizens beyond those which were at least partially of Italian origin.[5]

The Roman Treasury could, and did, thus create a class of non-privileged provincial Roman citizens, but it could not prevent this class either from harbouring resentment or from steadily growing in numbers until it found itself strong enough to sweep away by main force the privileges which a favoured minority of the citizen body had so long retained for itself.

The non-privileged element in the Roman citizen body in the Age of the Principate was recruited from various sources. The military policy, inaugurated by Augustus, of insisting that the Roman legionary infantry of the line should continue to be composed exclusively of Roman citizens but should be stationed henceforward mainly on the frontiers and wholly outside Italy[6] ensured, when combined with legal facilities for legitimizing

State between the end of the Hannibalic War and the secession, in 90 B.C., of a confederacy of Italian states hitherto externally associated with the Roman Commonwealth will be found in Beloch, J.: *Der Italische Bund unter Roms Hegemonie* (Leipzig 1880, Teubner), *ad finem*.

[1] By the *Lex Plautia Papiria* of 89 B.C. [2] By Caesar in 49 B.C.

[3] It will be seen that this Roman Treasury ruling was identical with the Umayyad Caliph 'Umar II's ruling, noticed on p. 132, above, that a non-Arab convert to Islam must migrate to one of the Arab military cantonments in order to qualify for obtaining the comparatively favourable fiscal treatment that Arab Muslims enjoyed.

[4] See *The Cambridge Ancient History*, vol. xi (Cambridge 1936, University Press), pp. 455–6. This *ius Italicum* had a juridical as well as a fiscal aspect. Roman citizens not domiciled in territory possessing this status were thereby debarred, not only from the right of exemption from direct taxation, but also from the right of owning land in freehold as *ager privatus ex iure Quiritium*.

[5] 'Italian status' was, for example, possessed by the Roman 'colony' of Vienna Allobrogum (Vienne) in the province of Gallia Narbonensis, in spite of the fact that the Roman citizens inhabiting this titular Roman colony were Latinized natives and not settlers from Italy. Yet Vienna was the only municipality in the province that did possess this *ius Italicum*, though, at an early stage in the history of the Principate, Narbonensis as a whole had become almost as thoroughly Latinized in language and culture as the Transpadane fringe of Italy itself. The less exceptional phenomenon of the possession of the *ius Italicum* by a Roman community situated outside Italy but composed of settlers of Italian origin is illustrated by the case of Lugdunum (see Arnold, W. T.: *Studies of Roman Imperialism* (Manchester 1906, University Press), pp. 99 and 107–8).

[6] See II. ii. 20 and p. 117, above.

the legionaries' children retrospectively,[1] that a warlike population of Roman citizens, who could have the last word in Imperial politics if ever they awoke to a realization of their power, should establish itself on the Empire's fringes. Where militarily suitable citizen recruits for the legions were not forthcoming in sufficient numbers (as, for example, in the Anatolian areas of recruitment for the eastern legions), it is probable that militarily suitable non-citizens were naturalized *ad hoc* in order to make them eligible for enrolment,[2] and it is also probable that soldiers enrolled in the non-citizen formations called *auxilia* could obtain naturalization as Roman citizens upon their discharge from the service, if not before.[3]

Moreover, as the civilian population of one ex-barbarian province after another became Latinized in language and culture, naturalization was granted wholesale by a regular series of stages. The first stage was to confer on a subject community the political status of a city-state externally associated with the Roman Commonwealth on the customary terms traditionally called the *ius Latinum*. A citizen of a Latin community who was elected by his fellow citizens to a local magistracy thereby acquired Roman citizenship automatically, and this door of entry into the Roman citizen body came to be known as the *Latium Minus* after the institution (perhaps in Hadrian's reign)[4] of a *Latium Maius* which automatically conferred the Roman citizenship on a citizen of a Latin community who was elected to his local town council.[5] There were even non-Latin communities—for example, the Gallic canton of the Aedui—whose elected local magistrates became Roman citizens *ipso facto*.[6] Through all these avenues the body of non-privileged Roman citizens was steadily recruited under the Principate for nearly a quarter of a millennium[7] till,

1 See p. 132, above.

2 See Parker, H. M. D.: *The Roman Legions* (Oxford 1928, Clarendon Press), p. 170. Aelius Aristeides seems, in a passage in his *In Romam* (Keil's edition, vol. ii. pp. 112–13 (§§ 75–78)), to imply that, in his day, *all* recruits for the Imperial Army were non-citizens who were enfranchised when they were enrolled.

3 See *The Cambridge Ancient History*, vol. xi (Cambridge 1936, University Press), p. 443, cited on p. 132, above.

4 'Between A.D. 100 and the death of Pius' (*The Cambridge Ancient History*, vol. xi (Cambridge 1936, University Press), pp. 452–3).

5 See Arnold, op. cit., p. 99, n. 2.

6 See ibid., p. 111.

7 It will be seen that the ascendancy of a privileged minority lasted nearly twice as long in the Roman Empire under the Principate as in the Arab Caliphate under the Umayyad régime. This notably greater longevity is perhaps to be explained by the fact that in the Roman case the ascendancy was exercised less crudely and was monopolized less exclusively. The Augustan settlement was a compromise between the monstrously harsh and predatory tyranny which the masters of the Roman State had exercised over the Hellenic World during the last century and a half of the Roman Republican régime and the drastic dictatorship on behalf of the 'under-dog' that had been the ideal, and the death, of Caesar; and the Caesarean element in the genius of the Principate tended to gain ground at the expense of the oligarchic element. For example, the area of recruitment for the Praetorian Guard, which appears to have been confined to Central Italy when Augustus founded the corps (see Tacitus: *Annals*, Book IV, chap. 5), was progressively extended, first up to the limits of Italy within Augustus's boundaries, and later to communities of Roman citizens in adjacent provinces (e.g. Macedonia and Noricum) and in Baetica. There was a corresponding tendency to extend the area of recruitment for the Senate; and, though Senators of non-Italian origin were required by the Emperor Trajan to re-invest one-third of their property in Italian real estate, the proportion was reduced to one-fourth by Marcus Aurelius (see *The Cambridge Ancient History*, vol. xi (Cambridge 1936, University Press), pp. 212, 370, and 419). This policy of gradually widening the privileged circle was eventually applied to the Principate itself. Of the five emperors, from Nerva to Marcus inclusive, whose successive reigns covered the 'Indian Summer'

in the year A.D. 212, the Emperor Caracalla took the logical concluding step of conferring Roman citizenship on all—or, at any rate, all but an insignificant residue—of the still unenfranchised subjects of the Empire by his celebrated *Constitutio Antoniniana*.[1]

This superficially liberal measure might perhaps have been expected to exorcise the danger of a social revolution; for, after all, the inferior form of Roman citizenship that did not carry the *ius Italicum* with it was nevertheless something well worth having. Whatever its fiscal and juridical shortcomings may have been, it was undoubtedly a palladium of civil liberties—as was found by Saint Paul when he put its efficacy to the test on three critical occasions in his missionary career.[2] Yet the *Constitutio Antoniniana* did not avert the upheaval of A.D. 235–74, and may actually have played some part in bringing it to pass. For on the one hand it did not diminish, and possibly increased, the financial burdens of its beneficiaries;[3] and on the other hand it made the inequity of privileges still enjoyed by a minority *de facto* more glaring now that all inhabitants of the Empire had become Roman citizens *de jure*.

The first stroke in the battle against privilege had indeed been struck already by Caracalla's father and predecessor Septimius Severus. This professional soldier of colonial Phoenician origin[4] had been able to seize a vacant imperial throne thanks to finding himself in command of the frontier defence force nearest to Rome at a moment when the Praetorian Guards had unpardonably abused their trust by assassinating an excellent emperor and proceeding to sell the purple by auction to a worthless bidder. When Severus marched on Rome at the head of his Pannonian legions, the Praetorians proved to be as unwarlike as they were murderous and corrupt. They submitted tamely to a sentence of disbandment and banishment, and the provincial war-lord who had thus given these privileged Italian guardsmen their deserts not only cashiered the men but made a complete break in the basis of recruitment of the corps. It was recruited thenceforth from the *élite* of the legions (in practice, from soldiers of the Danubian legions and of one eastern legion, the Sixth

of Hellenic history, two (Trajan and Hadrian) came from Baetica, one (Antoninus Pius) from Narbonensis, while the family of a fourth (Marcus) was of Baetican origin. The only Italian among the five was Nerva, the first—and the least estimable—in the series. No doubt this progressive widening of the privileged inner circle of the Roman citizen body delayed the revolt of the ever-growing mass of Roman citizens of inferior status. Conversely, in the Sinic universal state the ascendency of the victorious empire-building principality of Ts'in was overthrown only twelve years after the establishment of the *Pax Sinica* because it had immediately been made intolerable by the inhumanly revolutionary policy of Ts'in She Hwang-ti.

[1] See V. vi. 7, with n. 4.

[2] In dealing with the magistrates of the Roman colony of Philippi (see Acts xvi. 37–39); in dealing with Claudius Lysias, the Roman military tribune in command of the castle at Jerusalem (see Acts xxii. 23—xxiii. 31); and in dealing with two successive Roman procurators of Judaea: Antonius Felix and Porcius Festus (see Acts xxiii. 31—xxvi. 32).

[3] It is possible that one of the motives and effects of the *Constitutio Antoniniana* was to extend to all inhabitants of the Empire the special taxes—death duties (at the merciful rate of a mere 5 per cent.), a general sales tax (at the rate of 1 per cent.), a special tax on sales of slaves (at the rate of 4 per cent.)—which Augustus had imposed on Roman citizens domiciled in Italy as a device for diminishing the inequality in the distribution of the burden of taxation between this minority and the rest of the inhabitants of the Empire (for details see Hirschfeld, O.: *Die Kaiserlichen Verwaltungsbeamten bis auf Diocletian*, 2nd ed. (Berlin 1905, Weidmann), pp. 93–105).

[4] Severus's home town was the Punic city of Leptis in Tripolitania.

Ferrata). Severus also stationed at Albano, within one short march of Rome, the second of his three new *Legiones Parthicae*. The commanders of these new legions were not of senatorial rank, and the soldiers were probably for the most part Roman citizens from Illyricum and Thrace.[1]

After this decisive demonstration of the military impotence of a still privileged minority, the sequel was almost a foregone conclusion. The upheaval of A.D. 235–74 was a revolt of the provinces against Italy, of the non-senatorial classes against the Senate, and of the uncultivated masses against the heirs of the Hellenic culture; and on all three battlefields the former 'ascendancy' was decisively defeated.[2] The 'ascendancy' did not, indeed, allow itself to be deposed without a struggle. The successful organization of armed resistance to the intolerable Thracian soldier Maximinus was a last triumph of the *concordia ordinum* and *consensus Italiae* that had been the political ideals of Cicero. But the discomfiture of the Senate was made manifest by the exclusion of senators from all military command, direct or indirect, by act of the Emperor Gallienus (*imperabat* A.D. 253–68);[3] and it was sealed when Florianus, the brother of the last senatorial occupant of the imperial throne,[4] was rejected by the Senate itself as a candidate for the succession in favour of the capable Illyrian soldier Probus. This liquidation of the long-respected partnership of the Senate in the government of the Empire was accompanied by a violation of the equally long-respected immunity of Italy from direct taxation. After the devaluation of the currency during the anarchy, the primitive practice of raising a levy in kind (*annona*) for the support of the army and the civil service was applied to Northern Italy as well as to the provinces. After this progressive *Gleichschaltung* of Italy with the provinces and of the Senate with the rest of the inhabitants of the Empire, the inauguration of a totalitarian régime by the Illyrian soldier-statesman Diocletian was inevitable and indispensable.[5] This was the political price that had to be paid for long overdue

[1] See Parker, H. M. D.: *A History of the Roman World from A.D. 138 to 337* (London 1935, Methuen), pp. 60 and 80–84. There is, of course, an almost exact analogy between this measure of Severus's and the substitution, by the 'Abbasids, of a Khurāsānī garrison at Baghdad for the Syrian Arab garrisons at Basrah, Kūfah, and the four cantonments on the desert border of Syria itself.

[2] The social and cultural aspects of this great revolution in the Roman Empire have been imaginatively apprehended and brilliantly portrayed by M. Rostovtzeff in *The Social and Economic History of the Roman Empire* (Oxford 1926, Clarendon Press). The scholarly author of this magnificent piece of historical work has incurred some criticism on the ground that he has read into the history of the Roman Empire in the third century of the Christian Era his own experience of the Russian revolution of A.D. 1917. It is possible, perhaps, that here and there Rostovtzeff may have been carried by this analogy beyond the limits of the evidence; but it is certain that his illuminating and instructive interpretation of a momentous passage of history would not have enriched our whole understanding of History, as it has done, if Rostovtzeff had not lived through that experience as a human being and had not possessed the imaginative power to turn it to account as an historian.

[3] This was a portent, considering that the Emperor who pronounced these aristocrats no longer fit for military command was himself a man of culture. Yet the process of pushing the Senate out of public life, which was thus carried a long step farther by Gallienus, had been covertly set in train by his far more cultivated predecessor Augustus (for Gallienus's measures, see Parker, op. cit., pp. 178–80).

[4] For the significance of the reign of Florianus's brother and predecessor Tacitus (*imperabat* A.D. 275–6), see V. vi. 55.

[5] The complete exclusion of senators from the civil service as well as from military command, and the extension of liability to imperial taxation to Cis-Appennine as well as

acts of social justice by which, in reaction against an invidious former discrimination between classes, every Roman citizen in a Roman World in which virtually the whole population had now been enfranchised was made eligible henceforward for appointment to any post, up to the highest, in the Roman Imperial Army[1] and Civil Service.

The Utilization of Imperial Garrisons and Colonies by Higher Religions

In the sequel to this genuine social but illusory political triumph of an internal proletariat over an 'ascendancy', we have still to discover who were the beneficiaries in the long run; for we have already ascertained that the immediately resulting totalitarian régime was transitory and that the subsequent 'heroic age' of the barbarians was ephemeral. The truth would appear to be that while the internal proletariat was not appreciably more successful than any of the other competitors for the spoils of a disintegrating civilization in so far as it was competing with them in their own currency of material power—economic, political, and military—it did achieve an enduring and momentous success in so far as it placed its treasure in the spiritual enterprise of propagating a higher religion. The ultimate beneficiaries from the organized redistribution and intermixture of population that precipitated a social revolution in both the Roman and the Arab Empire were Christianity in the one case and Islam in the other.

The military cantonments and frontier garrisons of the Umayyad Caliphate manifestly served Islam as invaluable *points d'appui* in that extraordinary deployment of latent spiritual forces by which Islam transfigured itself, and thereby transformed its mission, in the course of six centuries. In the seventh century of the Christian Era, Islam had burst out of Arabia as the distinctive sectarian creed of one of the barbarian war-bands that were carving out successor-states for themselves in provinces of the Roman Empire; by the thirteenth century of the Christian Era, Islam had become a universal church providing shelter for sheep left without their familiar shepherds through the collapse of the ʿAbbasid Caliphate at the dissolution of the Syriac Civilization.[2]

Time and again it looked, on the surface, as if Islam had been cheated of this spiritual destiny by being successfully exploited for political and social ends.

'The original driving-force behind the insurrection of the Khurāsānīs was Islam and not [Iranian] nationalism . . . [but] the nationality of the victors asserted its preponderance over [the cause of] Islam. . . . The international [fraternity of] Islam was a mask for the triumph of the Iranian cause over the Arabs. . . . This was inherent in the situation, though not in the original design.'[3]

Trans-Appennine Italy, do not appear to have taken place before the Diocletianic re-organization. This was the logical fulfilment of the piecemeal reforms of Septimius Severus and Gallienus.

[1] In the post-Diocletianic Roman Army there were no distinctions of class (see Grosse, R.: *Römische Militärgeschichte von Gallienus bis zum Beginn der Byzantinischen Themenverfassung* (Berlin 1920, Weidmann), p. 196). The classless military hierarchy established by Diocletian and Constantine at the turn of the third and fourth centuries of the Christian era lasted, substantially unchanged, until the seventh century (see ibid., p. 107).

[2] This transfiguration of Islam has been touched upon already in V. v. 127–8, 230, and 673–8.

[3] Wellhausen, op. cit., pp. 334 and 348.

In the next chapter of the story it looked, again on the surface, as if the ʿAbbasids had been still more adroit than the Khurāsānīs in making Islam serve their purpose.

'The ʿAbbasids took credit for having brought Islam—which they accused the Umayyads of having repressed—into its due position of dominance. They professed a desire to bring to life again the extinct tradition of the Prophet. They gathered round themselves in Baghdad the doctors of the Islamic Law from Medina, which had been their headquarters hitherto, and they constantly took legal opinions from them; for the ʿAbbasids made a point of handling political questions in juristic form and of seeing that decisions were taken on the basis of the Qur'ān and the Sunnah. In reality, though, they made Islam subservient solely to their own ends. They domesticated the doctors of the Law at their court and secured the stamp of their approval for even the most discreditable of their own measures. [In fact,] they made the pious opposition innocuous by the very act of leading it to victory.'[1]

Yet this ʿAbbasid statecraft, in spite of all its cunning, was no more successful in the long run than Iranian nationalism in harnessing Islam to the service of a political purpose. The ʿAbbasid Caliphate itself was merely the last phase of a universal state, and, as such, it was *ex officio* condemned to death before it was born, notwithstanding the mirage of immortality with which it managed to delude its audacious assailants as well as its loyal supporters.[2] When the Mongol war-lord Hūlāgū took and sacked Baghdad in A.D. 1258, 'the Caliphate that had created Baghdad, and for five hundred years had made it a magnificent centre of art, science and letters, was forever extinguished; but Islam did not die'.[3] It not only retained the allegiance of the ex-subjects of the defunct ʿAbbasid Empire; it also took their savage conquerors captive. In spite of the tincture of Nestorian Christianity with which Hūlāgū, like other Chingisids of his generation, was imbued,[4] his descendants who governed, after him, the appanage of the Mongol Empire which Hūlāgū had established in the derelict domain of the Caliphate, from Merv to the east bank of the Euphrates, did not remain pagans or become outright Nestorians or succumb to the Lamaistic form of the Tantric Mahāyāna which proved so attractive to the main line of the House of Chingis in China and which eventually won the allegiance of those Mongols and Calmucks who had stayed at home on their native steppes;[5] the Mongol Il-Khans of Hūlāgū's line became converts to Islam, and they did not even follow the frequent practice of barbarian converts by adopting the religion of a conquered population in a distinctively heretical version.[6] After playing with the Shīʿah as they had previously played with Nestorianism, the Il-Khans finally embraced Islam in its Orthodox Sunnī form, though this was the form in which it was followed by the Il-Khans' arch-enemies the Mamlūks and by the Mamlūks' puppet ʿAbbasid Caliphs at Cairo.[7]

1 Ibid., p. 350.
2 See pp. 7–16, above.
3 Gilman, A.: *The Saracens* (London 1887, Fisher Unwin, in 'The Story of the Nations' series), p. 441.
4 Hūlāgū himself had a Nestorian Christian wife (see II. ii. 238 and 451).
5 See IV. iv. 497; V. v. 137 and 309–10.
6 For this practice see V. v. 229–30 and 235.
7 See I. i. 363–4.

Within little more than a hundred years of the sack of Baghdad by Hūlāgū the example thus set by his house had been followed by the eastern as well as the western branch of the House of Chaghatāy, which dominated the sedentary Muslim population of the Upper Oxus-Jaxartes Basin from the Central Asian Steppe between the Zungarian Gap and the Sea of Aral.[1] The House of Jūjī ('the Golden Horde'),[2] which dominated the sedentary Muslim populations on the Lower Oxus and the Middle Volga from the Great Western Bay of the Eurasian Steppe between the Sea of Aral and the Carpathians, was finally converted within the same period under the influence of its allies the Mamlūks.[3] Even the dissident 'qāzāq' Nomads who hovered out of range of the Golden Horde's long whip-lash on the steppes of Western Siberia[4] followed the Golden Horde's lead in embracing Islam; and the Mongol Khāqāns in the Far East, who had no penchant towards Islam themselves,[5] helped Islam to win new outposts on the north-western and south-western fringes of China.[6] Meanwhile, Islam continued to make spiritual conquests of comparable magnitude in other quarters: in India, in Indonesia, in Tropical Africa.[7] And thus, so far from dying at the death of the Baghdādī 'Abbasid Caliphate, Islam lived on to become, by the fourteenth century of its own era, one of the four principal higher religions of a World that in that age was being unified on a literally oecumenical scale by the world-wide expansion of the Western Civilization.

What was the secret of Islam's power to survive the death of its founder, the downfall of the Primitive Arab empire-builders, the decline of the Arabs' Iranian supplanters, the overthrow of the 'Abbasid Caliphate, and the collapse of the barbarian successor-states that established themselves, for their brief day, on the Caliphate's ruins? The explanation was to be found in the spiritual experience of the converts to Islam among the non-Arab subjects of the Caliphate in the Umayyad Age. 'Islam, which they had originally adopted mainly for external reasons [of social self-interest], struck root in their hearts as well, and was taken by them more seriously than by the Arabs themselves.'[8] A religion which thus succeeded in winning loyalty in virtue of its intrinsic religious merits was not doomed to stand or fall with the political régimes which had successively sought to exploit it for non-religious purposes; and this spiritual triumph of Islam was the more remarkable considering that such exploitation for political ends had proved fatal to other higher religions and that Islam had thus been placed in jeopardy not only by its founder's successors but by Muhammad himself, when he had migrated

[1] For the successive conversions of the Western and the Eastern Chaghatāy to the Sunni form of Islam, see II. ii. 145.

[2] See III. iii. 429.

[3] The bond of this friendship was a commercial one. The most lucrative export from the domain of the Golden Horde was the supply of slaves, drawn from the martial races inside and beyond the Golden Horde's borders, through which the Mamlūks of Egypt recruited their own ranks. The Golden Horde was finally converted to Islam in the reign of Uzbeg Khan (*regnabat* A.D. 1312–40). The individual conversion of Uzbeg's predecessor Baraqa Khan (*regnabat* A.D. 1256–66), like that of the Il-Khan Ghazan in 1295, had been a premature flash in the pan.

[4] See V. v. 282.

[5] See pp. 256–7, below.

[6] See pp. 74–75 and 99, above.

[7] See Arnold, T. W.: *The Preaching of Islam*, 2nd ed. (London 1913, Constable), especially chaps. 8–12.

[8] Wellhausen, op. cit., p. 309.

from Mecca to Medina and had become a brilliantly successful statesman instead of remaining a conspicuously unsuccessful prophet.[1] In this *tour de force* of surviving its betrayal by its own founder, Islam had borne witness, through the ages, to the spiritual value of the religious message which Muhammad had brought to Mankind, and to the disinterestedness and sincerity of the messenger himself during the heart-breaking and hazardous thirteen years of his thankless mission to his own countrymen at Mecca.

Thus, in the history of the Caliphate, the carefully considered policy of the empire-builders in planting garrisons and colonies and regulating the transfer and intermingling of populations had the unintended and unexpected effect of expediting the career of a higher religion: and corresponding effects were produced by the same causes in the history of the Roman Empire.[2]

In the Age of the Principate the most conspicuously active conductors of religious influences were the military garrisons along the frontiers, and the religions that were propagated the most rapidly along these channels were the Hellenized Hittite worship of the 'Iuppiter' of Dolichê and the Hellenized Syriac worship of the originally Iranian divinity Mithras. We can follow the transmission of these two religions from the Roman garrisons on the Euphrates to those on the Danube, on the German *limes*, on the Rhine, and on the Wall in Britain, and the spectacle recalls the contemporary journey which the Mahāyāna, in the last stage of its long trek from Hindustan round the western flank of the Tibetan Plateau,[3] was making from the Tarim Basin to the shores of the Pacific along the chain of garrisons guarding the frontier of a Sinic universal state over against the Nomads of the Eurasian Steppe. In the next chapter of the story the Mahāyāna succeeded in penetrating from the north-western marches of the Sinic World into the interior and thereby becoming the universal church of the Sinic internal proletariat[4] and eventually one of the four principal higher religions of a latter-day Westernizing World. The destinies of Mithraism and of the worship of Iuppiter Dolichênus were more modest. Bound up, as they had come to be, with the fortunes of the Roman Imperial Army, these two military religions never recovered from the blow dealt to them by the Army's temporary collapse during the turbulent transition from the Augustan Principate to the Diocletianic Autocracy; and, as far as they had any permanent historical significance, it was as forerunners of Christianity and tributaries to the ever-growing stream of religious tradition fed by the confluence of many waters in the bed which Christianity dug for itself as it poured over the Roman Empire along a different channel.

While Iuppiter Dolichênus and Mithras used the frontier garrisons of the Roman Empire as their stepping-stones in a north-westward march which brought them in the end from the banks of the Euphrates to the Empire's opposite extremity on Tyneside, Saint Paul made a corresponding use of colonies planted by Caesar and Augustus in the

[1] See III. iii. 466–72.

[2] See xi, map 29.

[3] See II. ii. 373 and 405, n. 1; III. iii. 131; and V. v. 140.

[4] See V. v. 145.

interior of the Empire as stations on the successive missionary journeys which culminated in his last voyage to Rome itself. On this first journey he sowed seeds of Christianity in the Roman colonies Antioch-in-Pisidia and Lystra;[1] and on his second in the Roman colonies Troas, Philippi, and Corinth as well, while on his third journey he revisited these and other scenes of his previous labours. Paul was, of course, far from confining his activities to places in which Roman colonies had been planted. In the course of his third missionary journey, for instance, he established his headquarters for two years at Ephesus and from that centre systematically evangelized the province of Asia.[2] Nor did all the Christian congregations founded by him in Roman colonies distinguish themselves particularly in the subsequent history of Christianity. Corinth, however, where Paul stayed for eighteen months[3] when he revisited it on his second journey, continued to play an important part in the life of the Church in the post-Apostolic Age, and we may conjecture that the prominence of the Christian community here was due, not only to the unique geographical situation of Corinth at the cross-roads of overland and maritime lines of communication, but also to the cosmopolitan character of the settlement of Roman freedmen that had been planted here by Caesar.[4] While the social origin of the population among which Paul had made his Corinthian converts goes far to explain the moral laxity with which the Apostle had to contend, we may also conjecture that the business ability and the world-wide connexions of this brood of twice-uprooted *déracinés* had something to do with the energy which the Church of Corinth displayed in the next chapter of its history.

The most signal example, however, of a Roman colony being turned to Christian account is not Corinth but Lyons, for the advance of Christianity from colony to colony did not come to a stop when it had reached the metropolis and did not cease with the death of Saint Paul. 'Never was the rise of a great city less accidental and less arbitrary than in the case of Roman Lyons.'[5] Planted in 43 B.C. on a carefully chosen site, in the angle formed by the confluence of Rhône and Saône—a node of land and water communications that rivalled the situation of Corinth itself—Lugdunum was a Roman colony not only in name but in fact; and this settlement of Roman citizens of genuinely Italian origin on the threshold of the vast tracts of Gallic territory that had been added to the Roman Empire by Caesar's conquests had been designed to radiate Roman culture through this Gallia Comata as it had already been radiated through a Gallia Togata by the older Roman colony of Narbonne. Lugdunum, as we have seen, possessed the coveted *ius Italicum*[6] and was the seat of the only Roman garrison between Rome itself and the Rhine.[7] Moreover, it was not only the administrative centre of one of the

[1] It is uncertain whether the Roman colony planted at Iconium by the Emperor Claudius (*imperabat* A.D. 41–54) was in existence at the time of Paul's first or second passage through the place, but it must have been established by the date of his third missionary journey.

[2] See Acts xix. 10.

[3] See Acts xviii. 11.

[4] See IV. iv. 270, with n. 4, and pp. 109–10 and 133, above.

[5] Arnold, W. T.: *Studies of Roman Imperialism* (Manchester 1906, University Press), p. 108.

[6] See p. 154, with n. 4, above.

[7] See p. 123, above.

three gigantic provinces into which Gallia Comata had been divided; it was also the official meeting place of 'the Council of the Three Gauls', where the representatives of the sixty or more cantons comprised in these three provinces assembled periodically round an Altar of Augustus erected here by Drusus in 12 B.C.[1] In fact, Lugdunum had been deliberately called into existence to serve particularly important Roman imperial purposes. Yet by A.D. 177 this Roman colony had come to harbour a Christian community of sufficient vitality to provoke a massacre; and here, as elsewhere, the blood of the martyrs was the seed of the Church;[2] for it was as bishop of Lugdunum during the immediately following quarter of a century that Irenaeus—a Greek man of letters of possibly Syrian origin—worked out the earliest systematic presentation of Catholic Christian theology.

Thus, when the Principate, and the 'ascendancy' of which it was the instrument, collapsed in the third century of the Christian Era, the ultimate beneficiary of this political and social revolution was neither the insurgent mass of previously unprivileged Roman citizens nor the Diocletianic autocracy nor Iuppiter Dolichênus nor Mithras but the Christian Church.

Christianity in the Roman Empire, Islam in the Caliphate, and the Mahāyāna in the Sinic universal state each took advantage of the garrisons and colonies installed by secular empire-builders for their own purposes; yet these unintended religious consequences of orderly redistributions of population were not so signal as those of Nebuchadnezzar's relapse into Assyrian methods of barbarism; for, in carrying Judah away captive, the Neo-Babylonian war-lord did not merely foster the progress of an existing higher religion but virtually called a new one into existence.

Ἄνδρες ἀνάσπαστοι, φῦλον τάλαν, αἰνὰ παθόντες,
οὓς πάρος ἐκ ῥιζῶν Μῆδος ὑπερφίαλος
Ἀσσύριός τ᾽ ἀγέρωχος ἀνέσπασε νηλέϊ θυμῷ,
χαίρετ᾽· ἐγὼ δ᾽ ὑμῖν ὀψιγενὴς ἕταρος.
κἀμὲ κατέπληξεν τοῖος μόρος· ἀλλὰ χαρῶμεν,
ἡμεῖς γὰρ Μεγαλοῦ φίλτατα τέκνα Θεοῦ.
ἡμεῖς τοῖο προφῆται· ἀπήμονας οὐκ ἐμύησεν·
μάρτυρας ἀνθρώποις εἵλετο τούς τάλανας.

3. *Provinces*

The Mixture of Motives in the Minds of Imperial Authorities

Like the garrisons and colonies which the builders of universal states distribute over their dominions, the provinces into which they carve these dominions up have two distinct functions: the preservation of the universal state itself and the preservation of the society for whose body social a universal state provides the political framework. But, whereas in the installation of garrisons and colonies the function of maintaining

[1] See Arnold, op. cit., p. 86.

[2] The passage in which this famous phrase of Tertullian's occurs has been quoted in V. vi. 202, n. 3.

the political supremacy of the empire-builders is, as we have seen, the predominant one, we shall find that, in the organization of provinces, the two functions play less unequal parts—though of course their relative weight will vary, *ad hoc*, according to the particular train of historical events through which a universal state has been brought into existence.

The alternative possible functions of an imperial province can be aptly illustrated from the histories of the Roman Empire and the British Rāj in India.

For example, the Roman provinces of Africa, Macedonia, and Bithynia-et-Pontus owed their origin wholly to the Roman State's concern for its own self-preservation. The Romans installed their own administration there not at all for the benefit of their new subjects, but in order to prevent the resurrection of three rival Powers—the Carthaginian Empire and the Kingdoms of Macedon and Pontic Cappadocia—which had proved such formidable and persistent antagonists of Rome that she did not feel her hard-won victory secure till she had erased them once and for all from the political map. On a similar reckoning, the ex-Carthaginian dominions in the Iberian Peninsula were organized into the two Roman provinces of Nearer and Farther Spain,[1] and the ephemeral conquests of King Tigranes of Armenia at the expense of the last of the Seleucidae into the Roman province of Syria, in order to make sure that these strategically important but politically derelict territories should not again fall into hostile hands. On the other hand, when the Romans accepted invitations to undertake the direct administration of the dominions of the client kingdom of Pergamum, and afterwards to take over Cyrenaica and Cyprus, which had been dependencies of the client kingdom of Egypt, they were tempted, no doubt, by the bait of immediate windfalls for the Roman Treasury and of future profits for Roman tax-farmers, investors, and traders; but, though their motives may have been self-seeking, they were in fact undertaking here a public service from which the previous local rulers were seeking relief because they no longer felt equal to continuing to discharge it themselves.

An element of public spirit in a larger cause than the direct political self-interest of Rome herself is less ambiguously apparent in the creation of the Roman province of Cilicia, which in its original extension embraced the fastnesses of all the wild highlanders of South-Eastern Anatolia. When the Romans had taken over the heritage which the last of the Attalids had bequeathed to them some thirty years before,[2] they had deliberately excluded these unremunerative and burdensome territories from their new province of Asia, and they had thereby created in the expanding no-man's-land between the south-eastern boundary of Roman Asia and the north-western boundary of the fast dwindling dominions of the expiring Seleucidae a breeding-ground for pirates who

[1] 'Why did the Roman Government, whose policy at that time evidently did not contemplate the acquisition of countries beyond the sea, not rid itself of so troublesome a possession? . . . They could not abandon Spain without putting it into the power of any adventurer to revive the Spanish empire of the Barcides' (Mommsen, Th.: *The History of Rome*, English translation, vol. ii (London 1888, Bentley), p. 213).

[2] King Attalus III of Pergamum had died in 133 B.C.; the original Roman province of Cilicia was created in 102–101 B.C.

rapidly extended their activities all over the Mediterranean. The Roman Government's assumption of administrative responsibility for this uninviting no-man's-land that had become a pirates' lair was followed up by the Roman People's successive commissions to Publius Servilius, to Marcus Antonius, and to Pompey to sweep the pirates off the seas,[1] and this series of measures signified Rome's recognition and acceptance of imperial responsibilities. The same motive inspired the restoration of order in Cilicia and the subsidiary operations by which the Romans deprived the pirates of their insular stronghold in Crete and brigaded the island with Cyrene to form a single Roman province.[2] In the mind of Augustus a broad concern for the welfare of the Hellenic World as a whole was evidently combined with the narrower motive of providing for the military security of the Roman State when he extended the area of the province of Hispania Tarraconensis by subduing the wild highlanders of North-Western Spain, and when he carried the frontiers of the Empire up to the line of the Danube at the cost of saddling Rome with the responsibility for administering the vast ex-barbarian territories included in his new provinces of Rhaetia, Noricum, Pannonia, and Moesia.

Similar illustrations of the diversity of the functions that the provincial organization of a universal state may perform are afforded by the history of the British Rāj in India. While the annexations of territory at the expense of the Muslim war-lord Tippu Sahib of Mysore, the Marāthā states in the Deccan and Central India, and the Sikh principalities in the Panjab were mainly dictated by considerations of military and political security for the British Rāj itself, the annexations in the Ganges Basin, from Bengal to Delhi inclusive, were to some extent forced upon the British East India Company by the decay of the Mughal Empire; and, though no doubt the momentous British decision to take over the administration of Bengal was prompted, like the Roman acceptance of the bequest of the last Attalus, by the prospect of lucrative profits for British empire-builders, one of the effects of this self-seeking British act was to meet the Hindu World's need to be delivered from the anarchy that had arisen through the creation of a political vacuum in the place that the Mughal Empire had formerly occupied. Augustus's annexations of barbarian territory in the joint interests of the Roman Empire and the Hellenic World likewise find their counterpart in British annexations of tribal territory on the North-West frontier of India; and the risk of military disaster to which empire-builders expose themselves in their search for 'natural frontiers' is exemplified in the outcome of the First Anglo-Afghan War as well as in the results of Crassus's attempt to subdue the

1 A Roman 'province' in the original meaning of a frontier command had been created in the western and northern fringes of this no-man's-land *circa* 102–101 B.C. (see Mommsen, Th.: *The History of Rome*, English translation, vol. iii (London 1888, Bentley), p. 140, n. *; *The Cambridge Ancient History*, vol. ix (Cambridge 1932, University Press), p. 442; Jones, A. H. M.: *The Cities of the Eastern Roman Provinces* (Oxford 1937, Clarendon Press), p. 202) and was called 'Cilicia' though it appears to have included neither Cilicia Tracheia nor Cilicia Pedias. Servilius received his commission in 79 B.C., Antonius his in 74 B.C., and Pompey his in 67 B.C.

2 Cyrenaica was bequeathed to Rome by Ptolemy Apion in 96 B.C. and was definitively organized as a Roman province in 74 B.C. Crete was annexed in 67 B.C.

Parthians and Augustus's attempt to move the North-West European frontier of the Roman Empire forward from the Rhine to the Elbe.

While the histories of the Roman Empire and of the British Rāj in India thus indicate that the two main alternative functions of the provincial organization of a universal state are to maintain the supremacy of the empire-building Power and to fill a political vacuum arising in the body social of the disintegrating society through the destruction or collapse of its former parochial states, the relative importance and the reciprocal relations of the two functions vary widely from case to case.

There is, no doubt, a general tendency for the function of filling a vacuum to become increasingly important with the passage of time, as the memory—and the loyalty evoked by the memory—of the extinguished parochial states grows fainter, while those that have been allowed to survive as clients of the victorious empire-building Power are progressively rotted by the general process of social disintegration that is still creeping on under the veneer of an oecumenical peace. In the Roman Empire, for example, this tendency had resulted,[1] within a century of the establishment of the Augustan Peace at the Battle of Actium, in the conversion into provinces of all client states except three on the eastern frontier,[2] though it was a seldom broken tradition of Roman statesmanship[3] to shrink from the burden of administering alien subject territories and to confine even unavoidable annexations to a minimum area.[4] *Pari passu*, and this likewise against the grain of traditional Roman policy, the Roman Government found itself constrained, in the administration of its provinces, to leave less and less of the responsibility in the hands of local organs of self-government, and to take more and more of it upon the shoulders of the imperial civil service.[5]

This latter process likewise occurred in the administrative history of the British Rāj in India; on the other hand, the process of annexation did not take the same course here as in the history of the Roman Empire. While they were in the act of empire-building, the British conquerors of India showed less hesitation than the Roman conquerors of the Hellenic World in making sweeping annexations of territory and undertaking wide responsibilities for direct administration. The British-administered

[1] This point has been touched upon already on p. 58, above.

[2] The Nabataean Principality, Commagênê, and Armenia Minor.

[3] The most flagrant breaches—in the shape of unprovoked annexations—were made by the radical imperialists who annexed Gallia Narbonensis in 120 B.C., by Caesar when he invaded and conquered the rest of Gaul, and by Trajan when he extinguished the Nabataean Principality, not, apparently, on account of any incompetence in the native administration, but because he wished to bring this territory under his own direct control as an overture to his ambitiously aggressive attack on the Parthian Empire. On the other hand, Trajan's creation of the new province of Dacia out of the conquered dominions of a dangerous enemy of Rome was in the same category as Pompey's creation of the province of Bithynia-et-Pontus.

[4] For instance, the Roman province of Africa, within its original boundaries, did not include the whole of the former dominions of Carthage in North-West Africa; the western districts were given to Rome's client state Numidia. Similarly, when the Romans created their province of Asia out of the former dominions of the Attalids, they gave some districts to their surviving client states in Anatolia and left others derelict (see p. 164, above). Again, Pompey's new province of Bithynia-et-Pontus embraced only the semi-Hellenized western parts of the former dominions of Mithradates Eupator.

[5] See pp. 58–60, above.

territories in India were expanded in three successive waves. The first wave (A.D. 1757–66) brought under British rule Bengal, Bihar, and the Northern Circars along the north-west shore of the Bay of Bengal; the second (A.D. 1790–1818) brought the Carnatic, the Upper Ganges Basin, and the Western Deccan; the third (A.D. 1843–9) brought the Indus Basin. In the course of this expansion, all other parts of India were lassoed in an encircling belt of British-administered territories and were reduced to the status of client states; and, under Lord Dalhousie's régime, the annexations of the client states of Satára in A.D. 1848, Jhansi in 1853, Nagpur in 1854, and Oudh in 1856 seemed to portend a rapid extension of direct British rule over the whole of the rest of the peninsula. On the other hand, after the mutiny of the Indian units in the British East India Company's Army in A.D. 1857–8, it became the general policy of the British Government of India to keep the surviving client states intact; and, though this new rule was not invariably observed, nevertheless the annexation of the Kingdom of Oudh, which had been reminiscent of the Roman Emperor Tiberius's annexation of the Kingdom of Cappadocia, was, after all, not followed up by the progressive extinction, *more Romano*, of the remaining Indian client states.

The extent to which the founders of a universal state are tempted to resort to the devices of annexation and direct administration as measures of insurance against the danger of a resurgence of the victorious empire-builders' defeated rivals depends, no doubt, on the degree of the loyalty and regret that the abolished parochial states continue to evoke in the minds of their own former masters and subjects after their overthrow by the empire-building Power; and this, in turn, depends on the pace of the conquest and on the antecedent history of the society in whose domain the universal state has established itself. Victorious empire-builders have most reason to fear a violent undoing of their work when they have established their rule at one stroke and when they have imposed it on a world of parochial states long accustomed to enjoy and abuse a status of sovereign independence.

In the Sinic World, for example, effective political unity was imposed for the first time (at any rate, in recorded history) by the empire-building state of Ts'in within a period of no more than ten years (230–221 B.C.). Within that brief span of time, King Chêng of Ts'in overthrew the six other till then surviving parochial states Han, Chao, Wei, Ch'u, Yen, and Ts'i,[1] and thereby became the founder of a Sinic universal state under the title of Ts'in She Hwang-ti. But, in bringing to this sudden end the long-drawn-out struggle for existence in which the contending states of the Sinic World had been engaged since the beginning of the Sinic Time of Troubles, Ts'in She Hwang-ti could not extinguish with equal rapidity the political selfconsciousness and *esprit de corps* of the former ruling elements in the six states that had survived, side by side with Ts'in, until this last swift round in the contest. The political re-unification of the Egyptiac World by Mentuhotep, the ruler of the

[1] See Fitzgerald, C. P.: *China, A Short Cultural History* (London 1935, Cresset Press), p. 70, and Franke, O.: *Geschichte des Chinesischen Reiches*, vol. i (Berlin and Leipzig 1930, de Gruyter), pp. 198–9.

march-state of Thebes who became the founder of 'the Middle Empire',[1] seems likewise to have been achieved by a sudden stroke;[2] and, here too, the victorious empire-builder and his successors had still to reckon with disaffection on the part of nomarchs who had been resubjected by force to an oecumenical authority without having ceased to regret the parochial independence which they had enjoyed in the anarchic sequel to, and reaction against, the inordinately centralized régime of 'the Old Kingdom'.[3]

The political unification, under the Napoleonic Empire, of the relics of an abortive Medieval Western city-state cosmos in Northern Italy, Western Germany, and the Low Countries[4] was also rapidly accomplished, if we reckon that it was begun by the French Revolutionary armies that invaded the Southern Netherlands and the Rhineland in the autumn of A.D. 1792 and was completed on a raft in the River Niemen on the 25th June, 1807, at the personal encounter between Napoleon and the Russian Emperor Alexander I in which the two emperors partitioned between them the European end of the Old World; and, though the French empire-builders had little recalcitrance to contend with among the subjects of the statelets which they had suddenly and unceremoniously swept out of existence, since the once exuberant political vitality of the city-states of Western Christendom had long since sunk into a coma, Napoleon felt his hold on these easily subjugated territories insecure so long as he had not finally disposed of the surrounding Great Powers that had been the peers and competitors of France in the pre-Napoleonic Balance of Power.

The Persian empire-builders who founded the Achaemenian Empire had to cope, like Ts'in She Hwang-ti, with persisting prior parochial loyalties, which flared up into energetic and widespread rebellion upon the assassination of Gaumata in 522 B.C.,[5] when it might have been expected that an established oecumenical peace would have been accepted passively, if not actively welcomed, by populations who, for three hundred years, had had their parochial patriotism pounded out of them by unflagging blows from an Assyrian flail.

This identical problem of having to guard against a resurgence of parochial political feeling was handled by the empire-builders on similar lines in all four cases. They sought to break these traditional parochial loyalties by erasing the traditional parochial frontiers from the political map and replacing the overthrown parochial states by artificially created imperial provinces with new boundaries and a new administrative régime which would ensure the due subordination of the provincial governors to the central government of the parvenu universal state.[6]

[1] See I. i. 137 and 140, n. 2; II. ii. 112; IV. iv. 85; V. v. 267 and 530; and V. vi. 190.

[2] Possible evidences of the rapidity of Mentuhotep's rise to fortune are the indications (if these are the correct interpretations of the archaeological data) that, in the course of his reign, he changed his style and title and remodelled his mortuary temple on more sumptuous lines than those of the original plan (see Meyer, E.: *Geschichte des Altertums*, vol. i, Part II, 3rd ed. (Stuttgart and Berlin 1913, Cotta), pp. 257–8; see further Winlock, H. E.: *The Rise and Fall of the Middle Kingdom in Thebes* (New York 1947, Macmillan), pp. 28–32).

[3] See Meyer, op. cit., vol. cit., pp. 226–30 and 262–4.

[4] See II. ii. 104; III. iii. 344–7; and V. v. 619–42.

[5] See pp. 599–604, below.

[6] These deliberately revolutionary redrawings of the political map are instances of

Administrative Policy in the Sinic Universal State

The issue was sharply formulated in the entourage of the Emperor Ts'in She Hwang-ti, and the radical solution was advisedly adopted by a personal decision of the Emperor, as the result of a clash between opposing schools of policy that has been dramatized by the historian Sse-ma Ts'ien in the form of a tournament of set speeches in the Imperial Council.[1] By whatever processes the issue may have been fought out, it is certain that the radical policy prevailed and that in 221 B.C. Ts'in She Hwang-ti ratified the redistribution of the whole territory of his newly established universal state, including not only the dominions of Ts'in's six former rivals and recent victims but also those of the victorious empire-building state as well, into thirty-six military commands (*chün*), which were each sub-divided into a number of prefectures (*hsien*).[2] Each military command had a civilian administrator as well as a military governor, and the prefectures were administered by civilian prefects.[3]

In applying this non-feudal provincial system to the whole of his empire, Ts'in She Hwang-ti was extending to the territories of the six states which he had just subjugated a régime that had been in force in his own ancestral state of Ts'in for more than a hundred years past. As far back as the year 350 B.C. the entire territory of Ts'in, within its frontiers at that date, had been redistributed into thirty-one *hsien* by the radical reformer Shang Yang.[4] This recasting of the internal administrative map had been one of a number of interrelated political and social innovations which had transformed Ts'in from a feudal state of the same type as its contemporaries and rivals in the Sinic World into a centralized bureaucratic and almost 'totalitarian' state of a new pattern; and it had been this political reformation that had enabled Ts'in, from that time onwards, to gain the upper hand over its antagonists in the Sinic arena in a progressive series of successes which had culminated in Ts'in She Hwang-ti's own sensational and conclusive achievement of overthrowing

the psychological phenomenon of Futurism, which has been illustrated already in the political field in V. vi. 107–11.

[1] Renderings of this debate, as presented by Sse-ma Ts'ien, will be found in Fitzgerald, C. P.: *China, A Short Cultural History* (London 1935, Cresset Press), pp. 139–40; Franke, O: *Geschichte des Chinesischen Reiches*, vol. i (Berlin and Leipzig 1930, de Gruyter), pp. 229–30; Bodde, D.: *China's First Unifier: A Study of the Ch'in Dynasty as seen in the Life of Li Ssŭ* (Leiden 1938, Brill), pp. 78–79.

[2] These two units of non-feudal local administration under the direct authority and control of a central government were not new inventions of Ts'in She Hwang-ti's radical-minded minister Li Sse. They had been made use of in the administration of the former parochial states of the Sinic World from an early stage in the Sinic Time of Troubles. *Hsien* are first heard of in the State of Ts'in itself in 688 B.C., *chün* in the State of Wei (the successor-state of Tsin) *circa* 400 B.C. *Hsien* may have originated as a form of administration for territories conquered by one of the Contending States from another, *chün* as military marches of Sinic states against their Eurasian Nomad neighbours. The radical innovation that was confirmed in 221 B.C. was not the invention of these two units of non-feudal administration but the sudden application to the whole of the Sinic World of a system of non-feudal administration, which had previously been exceptional, in place of a feudal system which had been the general rule (for these points see Bodde, op. cit., pp. 134–43 and 238–46).

[3] See Bodde, op. cit., p. 135; Franke, op. cit., vol. cit., p. 230.

[4] See Bodde, op. cit., p. 143. For this important statesman's life and work, see Duyvendak, J. J. L.: *The Book of Lord Shang* (London 1928, Probsthain).

six rival states in ten years and thereby unifying the Sinic World politically.

In assuming, however, that he could impose abruptly on the rest of the Sinic World a régime that was commended by its proven success in his ancestral state of Ts'in, Ts'in She Hwang-ti was leaving out of his reckoning certain significant differences between Ts'in and her defunct competitors. The statesmen who had carried out these sweeping local reforms in Ts'in with such successful results had been working on an exceptionally malleable human material. In the first place Ts'in was a march-state of the Sinic World,[1] and in the hard school of their perpetual struggle for existence against the outer barbarians the people of Ts'in had been broken in to adapting themselves to any social or technical innovations that might be necessary for securing their own survival. In the second place Ts'in, in virtue of being 'the Country within the Passes', was secluded by physiographical barriers from the rest of the Sinic World, and was culturally backward by comparison with the heart of the Sinic Society on the plains of the lower basin of the Yellow River.[2] Her relation to her western neighbours was like that of Macedon in the fifth and fourth centuries B.C. to the Hellenic city-states beyond the passes of Tempe and Volustana, or like that of Piedmont,[3] in the medieval and early modern ages of Western history, to Lombardy, Venetia, the Romagna, and Tuscany. Like Macedon, Ts'in was culturally plastic, and she thus escaped the cultural ossification which overtook her more cultivated neighbours.

The peoples at the cultural centre of the Sinic World were naturally predisposed to idolize a culture of which they themselves were the principal originators and exponents, and they had latterly been encouraged in this foible by the philosophers of the Confucian school, whose founder had diagnosed the social sickness from which the Sinic Society was suffering in its Time of Troubles as being due to a neglect of traditional rites and practices, and had prescribed as the sovereign remedy a return to the supposed social and moral order of the early Sinic Feudal Age as idealized in retrospect by Confucius himself.[4] This sentimental Confucian canonization of a half-imaginary past had made little impression on the people of Ts'in. The only one of the Sinic philosophical schools of the Confucian and post-Confucian Age that had made its influence felt effectively 'within the passes' was the irreverent ruthless school of the Legists, and it was this radical spirit that had inspired the work of the series of great statesmen from other parts of the Sinic World who had found their field for action in Ts'in, beginning with Shang Yang from Wei[5] (*decessit* 338 B.C.), who had laid the foundations of Ts'in's greatness,[6] and ending with Li Sse of Ch'u (*vivebat*

[1] See II. ii. 118.

[2] For this heart and cradle of the Sinic World, see I. i. 318–21.

[3] See IV. iv. 285–9.

[4] See Fitzgerald, op. cit., pp. 140–1.

[5] i.e. the Wei which was one of the three successor-states of the former state of Tsin, though Shang Yang traced his ancestry back to the princely house of the older state of Wei, still nearer to the heart of the Sinic World (see Fitzgerald, op. cit., p. 99).

[6] See Franke, O.: *Geschichte des Chinesischen Reiches*, vol. i (Berlin and Leipzig 1930, de Gruyter), pp. 183–4.

280–208 B.C.), Ts'in She Hwang-ti's minister, who had raised Ts'in to the pinnacle of power.

The sudden imposition of the institutions of this uncultivated and unfamiliar march-state of Ts'in upon Sinic communities who had been conquered by her through force of arms, without ceasing to regard her as a semi-barbarian stepdaughter of the Sinic family of cultivated peoples, was bound to arouse violent resentment among the *ci-devant* feudal aristocracy of the extinguished states. After having lost the power and status that had been theirs under the régime of parochial independence, they were now deprived of all hope of retaining some vestige of their former position through being taken into the service of the newly established Sinic universal state. In these days of their adversity and impotence, these *chün tze* rallied under the standard of the Confucian school of philosophy whose founder's theories and counsels had been ignored during his lifetime by their predecessors; but Ts'in She Hwang-ti's only retort to this *union sacrée* between the aristocratic and the philosophical devotees of conservatism was to take the offensive against philosophy as well as against feudalism. A petition from the conservatives for the re-establishment of feudal principalities under princes of the House of Ts'in seems to have given the occasion for the famous measure of cultural *Gleichschaltung* known as 'the Burning of the Books'.[1]

In thus recklessly closing every safety-valve, Ts'in She Hwang-ti was inviting an explosion, and the first Ts'in emperor's death in 210 B.C. was followed in 209 B.C. by the outbreak of a general revolt, and in 207 B.C. by the capture of the capital of the Ts'in empire[2] and extinction of the Ts'in dynasty itself by one of the rebel leaders, Liu Pang.[3] Ts'in She Hwang-ti's radicalism had thus defeated its own ends; yet this victory of the violent reaction against the revolutionary work of the founder of the Sinic universal state did not, after all, result in a restoration of the *ancien régime*. It was significant that both Ch'êng Shê, the bold initiator of the revolt, and Liu Pang, the rebel who gave the Ts'in Power its *coup de grâce* by capturing its capital, were peasants from outlying southern provinces,[4] not feudal aristocrats from the centre of the Sinic World; and, in the subsequent struggle among the victorious rebels for possession of the spoils of their joint victory, the peasant Liu Pang again emerged as the victor over his cultivated aristocratic opponent Hsiang Yü, whose ancestors had held an hereditary office in the military hierarchy of the former parochial state of Ch'u.

Liu Pang, unlike either Hsiang Yü or Ts'in She Hwang-ti, succeeded

[1] The connexion is pointed out by Fitzgerald, op. cit., p. 141. 'The Burning of the Books' has been cited already in this Study, as an illustration of Futurism, in V. vi. 111.

[2] The seat of government had remained at Hsien Yang, the city 'within the passes' that had been the parochial capital of Ts'in before her conquest of the rest of the Sinic World in 230–221 B.C.

[3] In this context English students of history will recall that the restoration of the monarchy in England in A.D. 1660 followed within two years of Oliver Cromwell's death and within five years of his remapping of the Kingdom, in A.D. 1655, into ten military commands under major-generals in place of the traditional feudal organs and institutions of English local self-government.

[4] Ch'êng Shê (*alias* Ch'êng Shêng) was a native of the former state of Ch'u in the Middle Yangtse Basin; Liu Pang came from a coastal district, north of the mouth of the Yangtse, in the northern part of the latter-day province of Kiangsu.

in founding a stable and enduring régime because he did not attempt to re-establish either the anachronistic feudal order or Ts'in She Hwang-ti's revolutionary substitute for it. Liu Pang's policy was to feel his way gradually towards Ts'in She Hwang-ti's Caesarean goal through an Augustan semblance of compromise.

In the short interval between the collapse of the Ts'in Power in 207 B.C. and the general recognition of Liu Pang as sole master of the Sinic World in 202 B.C. the experiment of attempting to restore the *ancien régime* had been tried and proved unworkable.[1]

Under Hsiang Yü's auspices, a legitimate scion of the House of the former parochial state of Ch'u had been invested with the oecumenical style and title and ceremonial prerogatives of the ancient Imperial House of Chóu, which Ts'in She Hwang-ti's grandfather had suppressed in 256–249 B.C.; and the other extinguished states, with the exception of Ts'in, had likewise nominally been restored. In order to make sure that Ts'in should not again establish its domination over the rest of the Sinic World, it had been broken up, as a measure of security, into four fragments.[2] Three of these, covering between them the ancient domain of the state, had been granted to high officers of the Ts'in army who had deserted to Hsiang Yü in good time. The fourth, consisting of recently annexed ex-barbarian territories on the north-western fringes of the Yangtse Basin (in the latter-day provinces of Southern Shensi and Ssechuan) had been assigned by Hsiang Yü to Liu Pang as a scurvy reward for his embarrassingly valuable services.[3] Naturally the other rebel leaders had also had to be rewarded with grants of territory, and these new lordships had had to be carved out of the historic dominions of the nominally restored states of the previous era. The parvenu war-lords, as well as the restored representatives of the old houses, had taken the title of king (*wang*), and the king-maker, Hsiang Yü, had styled himself 'suzerain king' (*pa wang*), with the intention of managing this travesty of the pre-Ts'in dispensation in the name of the nominal emperor of the parochial House of Ch'u.

This makeshift arrangement had been neither a genuine restoration of the old régime nor an alternative instrument for furnishing the Sinic World with the sorely needed oecumenical peace that Ts'in She Hwang-ti had effectively provided at an exorbitant price. On the surface the cause of the immediate breakdown of Hsiang Yü's attempt at a settlement had appeared to be the personal antagonism between Hsiang

[1] For the details see Franke, op. cit., vol. cit., pp. 257 and 259–61; Fitzgerald, op. cit., pp. 149–50.

[2] Compare the Romans' experiment of breaking up the Kingdom of Macedon into four autonomous republics in 167 B.C., after the Third Romano-Macedonian War (see Livy, Book XLV, chaps. 29–30). It was not till after the Macedonian insurrection of 149–148 B.C. that the Romans resigned themselves to the necessity of converting Macedon into a province under direct Roman administration.

[3] As this new 'Kingdom of Han' (so called after the Han River which flows into the Yangtse at Hankow) lay 'within the passes', Hsiang Yü was nominally honouring the preliminary agreement that had been made between the restored King of Ch'u and the rebel leaders that whichever of the latter should be the first to penetrate the passes and overthrow the Ts'in Power on its home ground should become King of 'the Country within the Passes'. Liu Pang had qualified for winning this prize by his capture of Hsien Yang, and by rights he should have received the entire territory of the state of Ts'in within its frontiers of 230 B.C., and not merely an outlying semi-barbarian march.

Yü and Liu Pang. A deeper cause had been the bankruptcy of the old feudal aristocracy who had been the mainstay of the historic parochial states. They had not only been decimated in the particularly murderous last round of fratricidal wars that had ended in the victory of Ts'in over all her competitors; their spirit had been further broken by Ts'in She Hwang-ti's subsequent massacres and deportations;[1] and, above all, they had been discredited in the eyes of the vast peasant majority of the population of the Sinic World by the plight to which the anarchy of the Contending States had brought the Sinic Society in the last phase of its Time of Troubles.

With both Ts'in She Hwang-ti's and Hsiang Yü's failures in mind, Han Liu Pang and the succeeding emperors of his dynasty followed a Fabian policy of hastening slowly.[2] In the first act Liu Pang duly conferred fiefs on his most deserving lieutenants, and even left undisturbed the existing fief-holders of Hsiang Yü's régime who had managed to come to terms with the victor. But, one by one, the enfeofed generals were degraded and put to death, while other fief-holders were frequently transferred from one fief to another and readily deposed, without ever being given a chance of establishing any dangerously close personal relation with their temporary subjects. In 144 B.C. Liu Pang's successor Hsiao Ching changed the law of succession for fief-holders by abolishing primogeniture and decreeing that their fiefs should be divided among their sons, and the consequent rapid subdivision of their domains reduced them to final impotence.

Meanwhile Liu Pang had taken effective measures for maintaining and progessively increasing the preponderance of the Imperial Power. The parochial kingships, though they were now no more than shadows of their former selves, were strictly reserved, nevertheless, for members of the Imperial House; the entire 'Country within the Passes' was kept by the Emperor under his own direct administration; and, in the rest of the Han Empire, he retained enough of Ts'in She Hwang-ti's provincial organization to reduce the autonomous kingdoms and fiefs to the position of dwindling enclaves within a steadily expanding network of imperial provinces. Thus, in effect, Ts'in She Hwang-ti's ideal of a universal state controlled from the centre through a hierarchy of artificially mapped out units of local administration was once more translated into fact within a hundred years of Ts'in She Hwang-ti's death; and this time the achievement was definitive, because the Fabian statesmanship of Han Liu Pang and his successors had given the Imperial Government time to create the human instrument for lack of which the first Ts'in emperor's grandiose design for an oecumenical provincial organization had come to grief.

A centralized government cannot be operated without a professional civil service, and, in contrast again to Ts'in She Hwang-ti,[3] the Han Dynasty succeeded in building up a civil service that was acceptable,

[1] See pp. 116–17, above.

[2] For the details see Franke, op. cit., vol. cit., pp. 270–2 and 276; Fitzgerald, op. cit., pp. 152–3.

[3] See pp. 351–3, below.

and therefore effective,[1] by entering into an alliance with the Confucian school of philosophy, which had originally associated itself with the feudal régime and had been driven still farther in that direction by Ts'in She Hwang-ti's intransigence.[2] The failure of Ts'in She Hwang-ti's régime had discredited the Legist school of philosophy, in whose spirit it had been conceived, without rehabilitating the prestige of the Confucian advocates of the old feudal order, and Han Liu Pang, who shared the anti-Confucian feelings of Ts'in She Hwang-ti, inclined, during the *laisser faire* overture to his long-term policy, towards the passive philosophy of Taoism.[3] Yet, before the close of his reign, Liu Pang (*imperabat* 202–195 B.C.) had thought better of his earlier hostility towards Confucianism and had himself initiated[4] that *rapprochement* between the Han Dynasty and the Confucian School which was consummated when his successor Wuti (*imperabat* 140–87 B.C.) made the somewhat debased Confucianism of the day into the official philosophy of the Sinic universal state.[5]

Han Liu Pang and his successors weaned the Confucian philosophers from their former alliance with the old narrow military aristocracy of birth by opening the public service to a new and broader-based aristocracy of cultural merit as measured by proficiency in the Confucian lore. This historic innovation was introduced in a decree promulgated by Liu Pang in 196 B.C.[6] The result was the creation of a new class of public servants—the Confucian litterati—with as strong a vested interest in the preservation of the Empire of the Han as the hereditary feudal nobility had had in the maintenance of the former parochial states. The transition was made so gradually and was managed so skilfully that the new aristocracy inherited the old aristocracy's historic appellation—*chün tze*—without any overt recognition that a momentous social and political revolution was taking place.

Administrative Policy in 'the Middle Empire' and in 'the New Empire' of Egypt

Our relatively abundant information about the vicissitudes of the political struggle which ended in the definitive victory of bureaucracy over feudalism in the Sinic World may help us to piece together the fragmentary surviving record of the similar struggle, in the Egyptiac World, between the nomarchs and the central government of 'the Middle Empire'.

There is, to begin with, a remarkable parallel between the external careers of the respective founders of the Sinic and the Egyptiac universal state, Ts'in She Hwang-ti and one of the Mentuhoteps. Either achieved a dramatic personal success—starting as the ruler of a parochial principality and ending as an oecumenical emperor. Both of them enjoyed long reigns: Ts'in She Hwang-ti was on the throne for thirty-six

[1] For the details see Franke, op. cit., vol. cit., pp. 272–6; Fitzgerald, op. cit., p. 153. See also the present Study, pp. 355–7, below.
[2] See p. 171, above.
[3] See the passage from a paper by Dr. Hu Shih quoted in V. v. 418.
[4] See the anecdote quoted from Hu Shih, op. cit., in V. v. 654.
[5] See V. v. 655.
[6] German translation in Franke, op. cit., vol. cit., pp. 274–5.

years (246–210 B.C.) all told, and this Mentuhotep for fifty-one (*circa* 2061–2010 B.C.).[1] Yet their deaths were followed, after brief intervening reigns of one or two nonentities, by the extinction of their houses and the foundation of new dynasties;[2] and thus, in spite of achievements that might have been expected to make the fortune of the empire-builder's race for many generations to come, either monarch was virtually the last of his line. This apparent paradox is explained in Ts'in She Hwang-ti's case by the known facts that have been considered above; and, on this analogy, we might hazard the guess that a Mentuhotep brought the same catastrophe upon his house by making the same mistake of trying to force the pace too fast in asserting the authority of his newly established oecumenical government over the defeated yet still formidable representatives of a previous parochial régime. At any rate, we find the founder of the succeeding Twelfth Dynasty Amenemhat I (*imperabat circa* 1991–1962 B.C.) and his successors apparently avoiding a frontal attack on the status of the parochial nomarchs, yet at the same time working steadily to reduce their power by stages.

The deposition of particular nomarchs who found themselves on the losing side in the civil war through which Amenemhat I appears to have won the Imperial Crown[3] may have set a precedent for his subsequent practice of overriding the customary right of hereditary succession and transferring the government of nomes from the old princely houses to his own nominees.[4] Historic families that retained their principalities were tactfully allowed to save their face by keeping up their state, and the most magnificent of their tombs are the last in the series.[5] But Modern Western archaeologists had not discovered any such tombs that were of later date than the reigns of Senwosret II (*imperabat circa* 1897–1879 B.C.) and Senwosret III (*imperabat circa* 1878–1843 B.C.), and the inference was that the power of the nomarchs had been finally broken, at the latest, by the reign of Amenemhat III (*imperabat circa* 1842–1797 B.C.). The administrative vacuum created by this progressive reduction in the power of the nomarchs was perhaps[6] filled by the organization of 'the Middle Empire' into three provinces: 'the North' embracing the Delta, 'the South' embracing the Nile Valley from the head of the Delta to the northern boundary of the Theban march, and 'the Head of the South' embracing the Theban march itself within the boundaries of the principality which Mentuhotep had inherited from

1 See Winlock, H. E.: *The Rise and Fall of the Middle Kingdom in Thebes* (New York 1947, Macmillan), p. 22. This Mentuhotep's conquest of Heracleopolis—which had the effect of uniting the Egyptiac World, as the Sinic World was united by Ts'in She Hwang-ti's conquest of Ts'i in 221 B.C.—is dated 1252 B.C. by Winlock in op. cit., p. 28. Winlock's reconstruction of this passage of Egyptiac history is commended by J. A. Wilson in *The Burden of Egypt* (Chicago 1951, University of Chicago Press), p. 127. On the other hand, E. Drioton and J. Vandier, in *L'Égypte* (Paris 1946, Presses Universitaires de France), pp. 234 and 271–2, contest the identification of a Nebhapetre Mentuhotep who united the Egyptiac World with a Nepkherure Mentuhotep who enjoyed a long reign over an Egyptiac universal state.

2 Compare the similar sequels to the deaths of Alexander the Great and Oliver Cromwell.

3 See Meyer, E.: *Geschichte des Altertums*, 3rd ed., vol. i, Part II (Stuttgart and Berlin 1913, Cotta), p. 265. 4 See ibid., p. 269. 5 See ibid., p. 276.

6 Eduard Meyer's reconstruction, followed here, had been challenged by some later scholars.

his forebears before he had brought the rest of the Egyptiac World under his rule.[1]

When this Mentuhotep's empire-building work was repeated some five hundred years after his day by the founder of 'the New Empire', Amosis, the seat of power, which the Twelfth Dynasty had quickly transferred from Thebes to the neighbourhood of Memphis, remained this time at Thebes for two hundred years,[2] and this different location of the political centre of gravity seems to have been reflected in a difference in the grouping of provinces. Under 'the New Empire' two out of the three former provinces of 'the Middle Empire', the Delta and the Nile Valley to the north of the Theban march, which had been united under the rule of the Hyksos, were perhaps brigaded by their Theban 'liberators' in a single province governed by 'the Intendant of the North' or 'of Memphis', while the Theban march was placed under an officer of equal rank, styled 'the Intendant of the Southern Capital', and was divided, perhaps for symmetry's sake, into two sub-provinces, one to the north of the imperial city and the other to the south of it.[3]

Administrative Policy in the Napoleonic Empire

The Napoleonic Empire was overthrown by external forces at so early a stage of its existence that there was little time for the consequences of Napoleon's internal administrative policy to begin to work themselves out. This policy was identical with Ts'in She Hwang-ti's. Starting his career by becoming the ruler of an empire-building parochial state, and finding the home territory of this state newly remapped into artificial administrative divisions in place of the historic territorial units of a past feudal age, Napoleon proceeded to remap the Belgian, Dutch, German, Italian, and 'Illyrian' territories that had been annexed to France outright, or been externally associated with her like the Napoleonic Kingdom of Italy, into departments on the pattern of those of Revolutionary France herself. Before the reaction to this drastic policy had time to declare itself, the Napoleonic Empire came to a premature end because Napoleon was not content with the immense achievement of having won for France that hegemony over the derelict domain of an abortive Medieval Western cosmos of city-states[4] for which she had been contending inconclusively with the other Great Powers of an Early Modern Western World for some three hundred years past.[5]

Napoleon insisted on setting France the further and more formidable task of establishing her supremacy over the whole of an expanding Western World that had come to include the overseas economic dependencies of Great Britain in one direction and the continental hinterland of the Russian Empire in the other; and this task proved too heavy for

[1] For these three provinces, see Meyer, op. cit., vol. cit., pp. 274–5. The march-state of Thebes in the Egyptiac World, like the march state of Ts'in in the Sinic World, had played no part in the history of the civilization during its growth stage and had emerged from its original obscurity only in the course of a Time of Troubles which it had eventually brought to an end by imposing its own rule upon all its rivals.

[2] See pp. 215–16, below.

[3] See Meyer, E.: *Geschichte des Altertums*, vol. ii, Part I, 2nd ed. (Stuttgart and Berlin 1928, Cotta), pp. 59–60. This reconstruction, too, had subsequently been challenged.

[4] See III. iii. 344–7.

[5] See III. iii. 311 and IV. iv. 283.

France's strength.[1] We are left to conjecture whether, in the Napoleonic Empire, the same revolutionary administrative policy would have provoked the same explosive reaction as in the empire of Ts'in She Hwang-ti if Napoleon had not brought his empire to grief by invading Russia in A.D. 1812; and, in the nature of the case, such facts as we have to go upon are insufficient to yield us a conclusive answer; yet, such as they are, they do strongly suggest—for a reason that has been considered at earlier points in this Study[2]—that, even if the Napoleonic Empire had avoided bringing destruction on itself at the hands of foreign Powers, it would have failed sooner or later to secure the acquiescence of its non-French subjects in a thoroughgoing administrative assimilation of the annexed or dependent territories to the French core of the Napoleonic body politic.

The governing fact in the situation was that France herself was not one of those dead-alive successors of the city-states of Medieval Western Christendom which she had just succeeded in gathering together under her rule; the vigour and enterprise which France had displayed in this notable piece of empire-building work were characteristic of the lively Modern Western World in which these mouldering débris of an unsuccessful medieval experiment were embedded. Napoleonic France was a member of this wider and more energetic society, and her membership in it not only led her on into over-ambitious military adventures that resulted in the loss of her newly established dominion over a smaller and tamer world; it also made France the carrier of Modern Western political ideas and ideals that ran clean counter to the spirit and objective of her empire-building enterprise.

The political service that France was performing for the wreckage of an abortive new order in Medieval Western Christendom, which had missed its destiny and broken down as far back as the fourteenth century, was to build the fragments of that shattered world into a universal state; and this service was not unacceptable to Germans, Flemings, and Italians of the generation and outlook of Goethe, who felt themselves stifled by the atmosphere of a Frankfurt, Bruges, or Venice in decay and were eager to escape from it by becoming citizens of the World, without shedding a tear over the extinction of decrepit statelets whose parochial independence had long since lost all meaning and value for their subjects. On the other hand, the political gospel to which France had given her own allegiance, and which she was preaching to her non-French subjects by example, was not Oecumenicalism but Nationalism, and this was the political lesson that the younger generation of Germans, Italians, and Belgians learnt—through both attraction and repulsion—from their intercourse with the very Frenchmen who were the agents of French imperialism. The portent of the German national uprising against French imperial rule in A.D. 1813 makes it evident that, even if the Napoleonic Empire had escaped or survived Napoleon's Russian adventure, the uniform departmental organization of the Napoleonic French administration would have provoked—in the name of the very principles of the French Revolution—the same disruptive national

[1] See V. v. 626–33.

[2] In IV. iv. 283–4 and V. v. 633–42.

movements that were to break a post-Napoleonic Hapsburg hegemony over Italy and Germany within little more than half a century after the Battle of Leipzig. Indeed, the nationalist reaction against a continuance of the drastic process of absorption into the French body politic might have been more vehement than the actual reaction in the 'liberated territories' against a rickety post-Napoleonic restoration of a sluggish *ancien régime*.

Administrative Policy in the Achaemenian Empire

In the administrative history of the Achaemenian Empire the sequence of policies was the inverse of the course of events in the Sinic universal state under the successive régimes of Ts'in and Han. The policy of the first founder, Cyrus II, was not unlike that of Han Liu Pang. He styled his empire 'the Realm of the Lands', and he made it his endeavour to reconcile the conquered peoples to Achaemenian rule by governing each of them as far as possible, at least in outward form, through its own peculiar political institutions.[1] Even the demonic Cambyses, who rode rough-shod over the Egyptians' religious susceptibilities, showed extreme consideration towards the Phoenicians.[2] This policy of deliberate administrative *laisser faire* was proved inadequate by the widespread and obstinate insurrections that broke out in 522 B.C. at the news of the assassination of Cambyses' successor on the imperial throne, who had professed himself to be Cambyses' brother Smerdis; for Smerdis had been the last male representative of the Cyran branch of the Achaemenidae; and, when the assassin Darius, representing the Ariaramnan branch of the house, had succeeded in restoring order and re-establishing the Empire at the cost of almost superhuman exertions, he sought to insure himself and his successors against a repetition of a catastrophe in which the Empire had all but perished by organizing his dominions, behind the façade of the Cyran dispensation, into twenty artificial taxation districts[3] under central control.

The easy-going genius of the Achaemenidae refrained from pushing this new Darian dispensation to the degree of uniformity and centralization that was aimed at in the departmental organization of the Napoleonic Empire or in the network of *chün* and *hsien* into which the Sinic World was remapped by Ts'in She Hwang-ti. Though Darius's successor Xerxes put an end to the constitutional existence of the Babylonian monarchy in form as well as in fact by refusing to repeat, on New Year's Day 484 B.C., the annual ceremony of 'taking the hands of Bel' that was the traditional warrant and sanction of legitimate sovereignty over Marduk-Bel's city,[4] Darius and his successors were as careful as the

[1] See p. 582, below.
[2] As is illustrated by the anecdote quoted on p. 149, n. 2, above.
[3] This was the original number according to the list in Herodotus, Book III, chaps. 89–94. See further pp. 582–4, below.
[4] See Meyer, E.: *Geschichte des Altertums*, vol. iii (Stuttgart 1901, Cotta), pp. 129–30, cited in the present Study, V. v. 123, n. 2. Darius himself had long-sufferingly observed the traditional procedure, in spite of Babylon's having revolted twice during the period of anarchy after Cambyses' death. Xerxes' deliberate discontinuance of the traditional rite was followed immediately by the third and last revolt of Babylon against Achaemenian rule.

Ptolemies and the Caesars were, after them, to rule Egypt in the style of a legitimate Pharaoh;[1] and, though, in the interior of the empire as reorganized by Darius, Cilicia[2] was the only surviving client state that was allowed to retain a juridical status of sovereign independence,[3] there were many smaller principalities, temple-states, and city-states that retained their autonomy as enclaves within the territories under direct administration. Indeed, within the taxation district labelled 'Athurā' ('Syria'), the Phoenician city-states were invested with minor empires of their own.[4]

It was likewise characteristic of the spirit of the Achaemenian régime that the viceroys (satraps) retained extensive powers even under the stricter Darian dispensation.[5] An imperial secretary who presumably reported direct to the Central Government was, however, attached to each of them[6] and appears to have been a member, *ex officio*, of the provincial council, mainly consisting of local Persian notables, whose concurrence the governor had to obtain in the more important of his acts of state. Moreover, in some of the more inveterately nationalist-minded viceroyalties—e.g. in Media, Armenia, Babylon-cum-Beyond the River, and West Anatolia—the likelihood of either a traitorous viceroy or an insurgent pretender being able to carry the whole country with him must have been decidedly diminished by the dissection of these four viceroyalties into four, three, two, and two taxation districts respectively.[7]

Administrative Policy in the Arab Caliphate

In contrast to the four instances, examined above, in which a provincial organization was introduced in a universal state as a means of combating persistent parochial opposition to the establishment of an oecumenical régime, a classical example of the opposite situation, in which a provincial organization was required for the filling of an administrative vacuum, is afforded by the Arab Caliphate. The Arab conquests were comparable, in point of speed, to Ts'in She Hwang-ti's, Mentuhotep's, Napoleon's, and Cyrus's; for it took the Arabs only nineteen years (A.D. 633–51)[8] to conquer the whole of the Sasanian Empire up to Merv, inclusive, on the north-east, as well as not much less than half of the surviving dominions of the Roman Empire up to

[1] It must be added that the tactfully treated Egyptians remained as irreconcilable to Achaemenian rule as the unceremoniously treated Babylonians.

[2] Erroneously reckoned in the Herodotean list as the fourth taxation district. The effects of this error on Herodotus's presentation of the administrative geography of the Achaemenian Empire are discussed on pp. 594–7, below.

[3] Beyond the frontiers of the territory under direct imperial administration there were friendly peoples in treaty relations with the Imperial Government who were allowed to retain a juridical status of equality with their imperial ally in consideration of their service to the Empire in screening it from the assaults of outer barbarians. Two such allied peoples were 'the Hauma-(?)drinking Saka' in Farghānah and the Arabs astride the road up the Euphrates from Babylonia to Syria and along the shore of the Mediterranean Sea from Syria to Egypt (see pp. 644–5 and 658–9, below).

[4] See V. v. 123, n. 2.

[5] For their powers and functions see Meyer, op. cit., vol. cit., pp. 52–54.

[6] See p. 82, above.

[7] See pp. 582–3, below.

[8] The Arab conquests are here reckoned to have begun with the campaigns of A.D. 633, and not with the reconnaissance of A.D. 629 which ended so disastrously for the Muslims at Mu'tah.

the Amanus Range on the north and up to the approaches to Carthage on the west.[1] Yet, in spite of the abruptness of the imposition of their rule, the Arab empire-builders were not confronted with any widespread vigorous movements to restore pre-existing régimes.[2]

The Arabs' administrative task was easy in this respect because the vast populations which they had so swiftly subjugated had by that time been broken in by more than eleven centuries' experience of being ruled by successive foreign empire-builders,[3] till they had grown accustomed to submitting passively to any new masters who might assert their title to rule by overthrowing their predecessors. Moreover, throughout this long period of time in most parts of this wide area, the dominant tendency had been for local self-government and parochial autonomy to give place to direct imperial rule, and this imperial administration itself had tended to become more and more centralized. This tendency had been only partially and temporarily counteracted by the break-up of the Achaemenian Empire and the planting of autonomous city-states on provincial territory by the successors of Alexander and by the Romans in their wake. The Sasanian Persian and Diocletianic Roman régimes which were the Arab Caliphate's immediate predecessors had been more highly centralized, not only than their own respective immediate predecessors the Arsacid hegemony and the Roman Principate, but than any of the other imperial régimes that had followed one another in South-West Asia and Egypt since the days of the Achaemenidae. Thus the mapping out of the Arab Caliphate into provinces was called for, not to meet the challenge of any rival political order, but to carry on an oecumenical system of government which, in virtue of its long monopoly, was the only practical possibility in the field. It is not surprising that the provincial organization of this resuscitated Syriac universal state should have borne, in its best days under the early ʿAbbasid Caliphs, a striking resemblance to the provincial organization with which the original Syriac universal state had been endowed by Darius the Great.[4]

[1] Carthage itself was momentarily occupied by the Arabs for the first time in A.D. 697 and was not definitely conquered by them till perhaps as late as A.D. 703, though they had established themselves in Tripolitania as early as A.D. 647 (see Becker, C. H.: *Islamstudien*, vol. i (Leipzig 1924, Quelle & Meyer), p. 118).

[2] Successful resistance to the imposition of Arab rule was put up only in a few natural fastnesses: in the ex-Sasanian territories between the Elburz Range and the south coast of the Caspian Sea; in the coastal highlands of Syria; and, after the later Arab conquest of the Visigothic successor-state of the Roman Empire in the Iberian Peninsula, in a strip of territory between the Asturian Mountains and the south coast of the Bay of Biscay which was a miniature counterpart of Daylam and Tabaristan (the physiographical similarity of these two regions has been noticed already in II. ii. 446–7). The most sensational of these resistance movements was that of the Mardaïtes in Syria, who managed to hold their own within short range of the four or five Arab cantonments there and within a stone's throw of the Umayyads' capital city, Damascus, itself. The Mardaïtes, however, seem to have drawn their strength and their *moral* largely from the support which they received from the Roman imperial authorities. Their movement was one of infiltration from a base in unconquered Roman territory, and they were sufficiently under the Roman Government's control for it to be able to undertake to withdraw them as part of the *modus vivendi* into which it entered with the Caliph ʿAbd-al-Malik in A.D. 688.

[3] Reckoning from the date of Darius's administrative reorganization of the Achaemenian Empire in the last quarter of the sixth century B.C.—but Syria and Egypt had had a still longer training in the hard lesson of political submissiveness (see V. v. 118 and IX. viii. 90–97).

[4] A statistical comparison of the areas and assessments of the provinces of the ʿAbbasid

Financial Functions of Provinces

A synoptic view of the provincial systems of the divers universal states that have come under consideration in the present chapter brings to light three main functions—a financial, a judicial, and a military—for which a province may serve as the local agency of an oecumenical government. The relative importance of these different functions will be found to vary widely from case to case, in accordance with historic differences in the policies of the respective empire-builders, in the degree of their ability to carry their policies into effect, and in the temper and traditions of their subjects; and there are cases in which one or more of these normal functions has been altogether in abeyance.

The essential and never dormant function is the financial one. Even the Primitive Muslim Arab conquerors of Roman and Sasanian territory, barbarians though they were, appreciated from the outset the importance, in their own interests, of maintaining as a going concern the existing financial administrative machinery—built up gradually through a continuous practice extending over many generations—of surveys, censuses, assessments, collections, and, above all, trained personnel for carrying all these administrative procedures out. Accordingly the Arabs left undisturbed at their posts the host of inland revenue officials whom they found in operation on either side of the former Romano-Persian frontier; and they wisely allowed them to continue to keep their books in Greek and Pehlevi till the reign of the Caliph ʿAbd-al-Malik (*imperabat* A.D. 685–705),[1] by when the lapse of half a century had made the conquerors' language and alphabet sufficiently familiar to their subjects to make it possible to transpose the official book-keeping into Arabic without throwing the financial service into confusion and bringing the collection of revenue to a standstill.[2]

Yet, although the provincial organization of a universal state seems always to be used for some financial purpose, the respective roles of the provincial administration and the central government in the control of finance vary within very wide limits. In both the Arab Caliphate and its prototype the Achaemenian Empire each province was financially autonomous. The provincial government not only carried out the collection of all revenue within its own boundaries; it retained, for provincial use, all receipts beyond a fixed tribute payable to the imperial treasury. On the other hand the financial administration of the British Indian Empire and the Roman Empire was highly centralized, and the imperial treasury here kept in the hands of its own revenue service both the collection of revenue in the provinces and the payment of charges for provincial administration—thus using the provinces as mere organs of the central government for financial purposes.

Caliphate, as recorded by the classical Arab geographers, with those of the taxation-districts of the Achaemenian Empire, as recorded by Herodotus, might yield interesting results.

1 See V. v. 501, with n. 3, and p. 242, below, where an error in vol. v, p. 501, n. 3, is corrected.

2 See Ahmad al-Balādhurī: *Kitab Futūh-Al-Buldān*, English translation by Hitti, P. Kh., vol. i (New York 1916, Columbia University Press), pp. 301 and 465–6.

Judicial Functions of Provinces

The judicial function of provincial governors had likewise varied in importance. This was a prominent feature of a provincial governor's duties in both the Achaemenian and the Roman Empire. Indeed, in the acts of Christian martyrs, in which this aspect of a Roman provincial governor's duties is in the foreground in the nature of the case, the governor is frequently referred to simply as *iudex*. In the government of British India the criminal law was administered, above the level of the petty cases dealt with by village headmen or *panchayats*, by salaried magistrates who, *more Romano*, were usually revenue and administrative officers as well as judges; but civil law at the same level, and criminal as well as civil law at all levels higher than that, was here administered, in accordance with a principle already established in the government of the United Kingdom, by a judiciary separate from, and independent of, the administrative service.[1] Even in the loosely organized Achaemenian Empire there appears to have been a bench of imperial judges whose importance in the scheme of imperial government is indicated by the facts that they were recruited from the leading Persian noble houses and that, if they were discovered to have taken bribes, they were arraigned before the Emperor himself and were punished by him with the utmost severity.[2] In the Roman Empire, again, the judicial discretion of a provincial governor in cases to which Roman citizens were parties was limited by the citizens' right of appeal to Caesar; and this procedure had the curious result that the Praetorian Prefect, who had originally been simply the Commander of the Emperor's bodyguard, in course of time became the president of a central court of final appeal through which the Emperor's prerogative was exercised.[3] Under the Diocletianic constitution this court of appeal was decentralized like the imperial office itself, and the Empire was divided into four praetorian prefectures, each presided over by a prefect of its own who had the last word in all judicial business within his area.

Military Functions of Provinces

The military function of provincial governors had varied in scope and character even more widely than the judicial and the financial.

In the Achaemenian Empire the standing army maintained and controlled by the central government was very small by comparison with the size of the total population and area of the Achaemenian dominions. It consisted merely of a bodyguard attached to the emperor's person and of garrisons stationed at key points along the imperial lines

[1] See the *Report of the Indian Statutory Commission*, vol. i (London 1930, H.M. Stationery Office = Cmd. 3568), pp. 292–7.

[2] See Herodotus, Book V, chap. 25, and Book VII, chap. 194.

[3] Compare the analogous evolution in the Achaemenian Empire by which the Hazarapatiš (*Graecè* Chiliarch), who had originally been the commander of the Emperor's bodyguard of a thousand men, became something like the president of a council of ministers (see Meyer, E.: *Geschichte des Altertums*, vol. iii (Stuttgart 1901, Cotta), p. 43, and Junge, P. J.: 'Hazarapatiš: Zur Stellung des Chiliarchen der Königlichen Leibgarde im Achämenidenstaat', in *Klio*, vol. xxxiii (Neue Folge, vol. xv) (Leipzig 1940, Dietrich), pp. 13–38).

of communication.[1] The title 'hazarapatiš' (commander of one thousand troops'), borne by the imperial officer who eventually came to perform the functions of a head of the civil administration,[2] indicates that the imperial bodyguard had originally been only 1,000 men strong; and, even if the *corps d'élite* known as 'the Immortals', who served in Xerxes' expeditionary force in 480–479 B.C., were a standing professional force and not merely the cream of a Persian national militia, their number was in any case fixed at no more than 10,000.[3] Allowing for the partial recruitment of the imperial garrisons from non-Persian sources[4] and further for the possibility that the original 1,000 Persian picked troops were included in the eventual 10,000 and that these were not all Persians,[5] it will still seem improbable that any considerable number of additional Persian troops can ever have been raised from the thinly populated home territory of the ruling nation in the highlands of Pārsa (*Graecè* Persis, the latter-day Fars) after more than one half of its area, and perhaps not much less than one half of its population, had been detached from Pārsa by Darius I through his act of degrading the dissident Asagartiyā in Kirmān and dissident Yautiyā and Maciyā in Lāristān to the status of subject peoples.[6] Accordingly, when the Achaemenian Imperial Government was called upon to make a serious war effort, it had to draw very largely on provincial militias, and these again were recruited not merely from the local Persian settlers but from the native populations as well.

The training, inspection,[7] and command of these provincial militias were responsibilities of the provincial governors, and the military power which these prerogatives placed in their hands was not effectively kept in check by the presence, within their domains, of a few imperial garrisons under the central government's control—as was demonstrated by the ever-increasing frequency and formidableness of the rebellions on which provincial governors ventured. The Mughal Empire paid the same penalty for lapsing into the slovenly practice—against which Akbar had set his face in vain—of providing for the payment of the imperial officers (*mansabdārs*), charged with the maintenance of contingents of troops, by assigning to them provincial land revenue which they were empowered to collect for themselves, instead of collecting the revenue on its own account and paying the *mansabdārs* out of the Imperial Treasury.[8] In the Ottoman, unlike either the Mughal or the Achaemenian, Empire the central government had at its disposal a

[1] For these garrisons see p. 123, above.

[2] See p. 182, n. 3, above, and p. 344, below.

[3] See Herodotus, Book VII, chap. 83.

[4] See p. 119, with n. 7, above.

[5] On the evidence of the friezes at Susa, A. T. Olmstead holds (see *A History of the Persian Empire* (Chicago 1948, University of Chicago Press), p. 238) that the Ten Thousand were recruited from among the Medes and the Elamites as well as the Persians.

[6] See pp. 583, 622–3, and 637, below.

[7] There would appear to have been periodic musters—presumably for inspection and perhaps also for manœuvres—to judge by the formula 'commander of all the forces whose appointed place of assemblage is the Plain of Castolus', which was part of the terms of appointment issued by Darius II to his son Cyrus in 408 B.C. according to Xenophon: *Expeditio Cyri*, Book I, chap. ix, § 7 (cp. op. cit., Book I, chap. i, § 2, and eundem: *Historia Graeca*, Book I, chap. iv, § 3). See further this Study in the present volume, p. 674, with n. 3, and IX. viii. 548, n. 1.

[8] See p. 127, above.

professional army which, in its best days, was admirably disciplined, mobile, and efficient;[1] yet in wartime the Ottoman Empire, too, had to draw heavily upon provincial forces, and, though, as we have seen,[2] the central government exerted itself to keep under its own control the assignment of the fiefs by which the provincial feudal cavalry was maintained, the feudal contingent of each province was commanded in wartime by the provincial governor.

In the Roman Empire during the Principate, all units of the professional army except the Emperor's Praetorian Guard and the so-called *Cohortes Urbanae* ('Metropolitan Battalions')[3] were under the command of provincial governors; but, in the Augustan constitution, this arrangement did not carry with it that decentralization of military power which was a dangerous weakness of the Achaemenian, Mughal, and Ottoman Empires. At this stage of its history the Roman Empire enjoyed such a decided ascendancy over both the enemy beyond the frontiers[4] and recalcitrant tribesmen in patches of the interior that it was able to keep its troops concentrated in a small fraction of the imperial territory, and this mainly along the borders. In his division of the control over the provinces between himself and the Senate, Augustus was careful to retain in his own hands all provinces in which troops had to be stationed, and the governors of these provinces were the Emperor's own appointees and military subordinates. Constitutionally, therefore, the whole Imperial Army, wherever stationed, remained under the Emperor's own undivided command, and normally this control was effective—though the civil wars of A.D. 69 and A.D. 193–7, in which governors of different imperial provinces who were *ex officio* deputy chiefs of rival army-groups fought one another for the prize of the vacant imperial office, were portents of the greater bout of anarchy, arising from this inherent weakness in the constitution of the Principate, in which the Empire itself was to come within an ace of destruction in the third century of the Christian Era.

By the time when Diocletian (*imperabat* A.D. 284–305) undertook the reorganization of the Roman Empire, the terrible experience of the two preceding generations had demonstrated the danger of combining the civil government of a province with the local military command, even when local commands were constitutionally subordinate to an imperial commander-in-chief and when this dangerous combination of powers was confined to one of two categories of provinces. In Diocletian's day it was no longer practically possible to maintain the distinction between military and civilian provinces which had been of the essence of Augustus's system, for by this time the frontier defences of the Empire had broken down and, in the new military situation, if the Empire could be defended at all, it could be defended only in depth by mobile forces which might need to operate in any part of the imperial territory. These two considerations led Diocletian and his successors to take a radical new departure. They set up a small number of high military commands each embracing a wide area and covering, between them, the whole of

[1] See III. iii. 32–44.
[2] See pp. 125–6, above.
[3] For these see p. 123, above, and pp. 321–2, below.
[4] See p. 320, below.

the Empire,[1] but they confined the powers of this professional military hierarchy to military affairs and placed the civil administration—from governorships of provinces[2] up to praetorian prefectures inclusive—in the hands of a professional civil service. This division of powers continued till the break-up of the Empire in the fifth century of the Christian Era in the west and in the seventh century in the east and centre.[3]

In the Sinic World the experience of the last and most appalling round of the warfare between the Contending States led Ts'in She Hwang-ti, in founding a Sinic universal state, into the path that was to be followed in another society by Diocletian when he refounded the Roman Empire. Though Ts'in She Hwang-ti chose an historic institution of military government—the *chün*—as the major unit of provincial administration for his dominions,[4] he separated the civil administration of his *chün* from the military command and placed the two offices in different hands, while the *hsien*—which in Ts'in She Hwang-ti's system became a subdivision of the *chün*—seems to have been under exclusively civilian control.[5] This division of civil and military powers was, of course, the antithesis of the traditional Sinic feudal régime, yet, like other radical and provocative innovations introduced by the first Ts'in emperor, it ultimately prevailed. The permanent victory of this new principle of Sinic administration was assured when, in consequence of the eventual alliance between the Han Dynasty and the Confucian school of philosophy, the Confucian scholar, selected individually for intellectual merit, replaced the feudal warrior, inducted by right of birth, as the typical representative of the Sinic governing class. And a principle thus established in the Sinic Society in the last chapter of its history was resuscitated—after the social interregnum in which the Han Empire foundered—in the affiliated Far Eastern Society in China.

The Utilization of Provincial Organizations by Alien Civilizations

Who had been the principal ultimate beneficiaries from the systems of provincial administration which universal states had set up?

Conspicuous benefits had been secured by intruders of alien culture. The provincial organization of the Achaemenian Empire, for instance, was taken over and turned to good account by the Hellenic successor-states into which the Achaemenian dominions were partitioned at the turn of the fourth and third centuries B.C. after the overthrow of the Empire by Alexander the Great; and when, in the second decade of

[1] See pp. 322–3, below.

[2] Under the Diocletianic régime the provinces were reduced in size and were increased in number, by comparison with the administrative map of the Roman Empire under the Principate, owing to a progressive transfer of business that had once been handled by local organs of municipal self-government to the shoulders of imperial officials.

[3] When a ghost of the Roman Empire was conjured up in the Orthodox Christian World by Leo Syrus in the eighth century of the Christian Era, this division of civil and military powers was not one of the imperial institutions that were revived. It had proved too complicated an arrangement to weather the storms of a political interregnum, and, even before the crash had come in the centre and the east, the first steps towards a reversal of the Diocletianic policy had been taken here and there by Justinian (*imperabat* A.D. 527–65). See Bury, J. B.: *A History of the Later Roman Empire* (London 1889, Macmillan, 2 vols.), vol. ii, chap. 13.

[4] See p. 169, above.

[5] See Bodde, D.: *China's First Unifier* (Leiden 1938, Brill), p. 135.

the second century B.C., an Hellenic ruler of the ex-Achaemenian province of Bactria emulated Alexander's feat by overrunning the Indic universal state that had been established by Chandragupta Maurya, the provincial organization that had been worked out during the preceding 137 years (322–185 B.C.) by Chandragupta himself and his Mauryan heirs[1] was no doubt similarly serviceable to the Hellenic princes who ruled North-Western India for the next hundred years.[2]

The British Rāj in India was indebted in the same way to the foregoing Mughal Rāj, particularly in the financial sphere;[3] for, though so many Mughal institutions, good and bad alike, had perished during the century of anarchy that had followed Awrangzīb's death in A.D. 1707, the military adventurers—Indian, Afghan, and West European—who had since been contending for the spoils of a derelict Mughal heritage had all been careful—like the barbarian Arab conquerors of the Sasanian and Roman Empires—to preserve an imperial administrative machine for the collection of revenue that was the irreplaceable source of pay for their troops. Accordingly the British empire-builders, when they came on the scene, were not faced with the task of rebuilding from the foundations in the revenue department. Thanks to the legacy which they here inherited from their Mughal forerunners, the organization, information, experience, and, above all, the habits which are indispensable conditions for success in the administration of finance were to a large extent at British disposal as going concerns; and one of the most effective of the devices by which the British made themselves masters of India was the employment of a financial leverage for bringing into British hands the command of the troops and the administration of the territories of successor-states of the Mughal Empire that became the Honourable East India Company's allies.

'Our participation in Indian wars began when the English lent a military contingent to assist some native potentate. The next stage came when we took the field on our own account, assisted usually by the levies of some prince who made common cause with us, and whose soldiery were undisciplined, untrustworthy, and very clumsily handled. . . . What was needed was a body of men that could be relied upon for some kind of tactical precision and steadiness under fire; but for this purpose it was of little use even to place sepoys under European officers unless they could be regularly paid and taught to obey one master. So the system soon reached the stage when the native ally was required to supply not men but money,[4] and the English undertook to raise, train, and pay a fixed number of troops on receiving a subsidy equivalent to their cost. . . . Large sums had been

1 The fragmentary information about this aspect of the Mauryan Empire is presented in Smith, V. A.: *The Early History of India*, 3rd ed. (Oxford 1914, Clarendon Press), pp. 163–4.

2 The scanty information about the provincial organization of the Greek successor-states of the Mauryan Empire is sorted out, with a masterly hand, by Tarn, W. W.: *The Greeks in Bactria and India* (Cambridge 1938, University Press), pp. 230–43 and 259.

3 The administrative and financial organization set up by the Mughal Darius, Akbar (*imperabat* A.D. 1556–1605), is set out in Moreland, W. H.: *India at the Death of Akbar* (London 1920, Macmillan), p. 33.

4 In the Hellenic World of the fifth century B.C. the requirement of money instead of ships was the process by which the Athenians converted a Delian League under Athens' leadership into an Athenian Empire under Athens' thumb.—A.J.T.

hitherto spent by the native princes in maintaining ill-managed and insubordinate bodies of troops, and in constant wars against each other; they might economise their revenues, be rid of a mutinous soldiery, and sit much more quietly at home, by entering into contracts with a skilful and solvent administration that would undertake all serious military business for a fixed subsidy. But, as punctuality in money matters has never been a princely quality, this subsidy was apt to be paid very irregularly; so the next stage was to revive the long-standing practice of Asiatic governments: the assignment of lands for the payment of troops.'[1]

This method of extending direct British rule in India was applied by Lord Wellesley (*proconsulari munere fungebatur* A.D. 1798–1805) with special vigour to the two important successor-states of the Mughal Empire whose respective rulers were the Wazīr of Oudh and the Nizām of Hyderabad, and the territory thus acquired by the British Rāj from Oudh was of crucial importance.

'The result of Lord Wellesley's somewhat dictatorial negotiations was that the Wazīr ceded all his frontier provinces, including Rohilcund, to the Company, the revenue of the territory thus transferred being taken as an equivalent to the subsidy payable for troops. . . . Oudh was thenceforward enveloped by the English dominion. This most important augmentation of territory transferred to the British Government some of the richest and most populous districts in the heart of India, lying along the Ganges and its tributaries above Benares to the foot of the Himalayan Range. It consolidated our power on a broader foundation, brought a very large increase of revenue, and confronted us with the Marattha chief Sindia along the whole line of his possessions in Upper India.'[2]

While the British in India were entering into the heritage of an empire that had collapsed a hundred years before, and the Hellenic supplanters of the Mauryan and Achaemenid empires overthrew régimes that were already in decay, the Spanish *conquistadores* of the Andean World seized an Incaic Empire that was still intact, and they profited from this piece of good fortune notwithstanding the blind brutality and pride which moved them to destroy so many Inca institutions that were valuable in themselves and would have also served the interests of the new masters of the Andean World. The paternal totalitarian êthos of the Inca régime had been faithfully reflected in its system of provincial administration. A hierarchy of administrative units—based on the natural social unit of the family and the natural geographical unit of the valley—ascended through communes, departments, and provinces to the four viceroyalties, reminiscent of the praetorian prefectures of a Diocletianic Roman Empire, from which this Andean 'Realm of the Four Quarters' took its name.[3] Though this elaborate system was too delicate a tool to fit the alien conqueror's rough hand, the habit of obedience that had been inculcated into the population of the Empire by the minutiae of Incaic administration made these subjects most accommodatingly submissive

1 Lyall, Sir A.: *The Rise and Expansion of the British Dominioni n India* (London 1894, Murray), pp. 244–5.

2 Lyall, op. cit., p. 247.

3 For the administrative map of the Inca Empire, see Baudin, L.: *L'Empire Socialiste des Inka* (Paris 1928, Institut d'Ethnologie), pp. 118–19; and the present Study, xi, map 68.

to the more rudimentary administrative methods of the Inca's Spanish supplanters.

The inability of the Spanish *conquistadores* to derive substantial advantage from the administrative system which they found on their hands is characteristic of barbarian conquerors. The German and Sarmatian invaders of the western provinces of the Roman Empire were similarly unable to take advantage of the Diocletianic organization. The signal exception which proves the rule is the success of the Arab invaders of Roman Syria and Egypt in preserving the Roman financial system as a going concern, and this goes far to explain the Arabs' unparalleled achievement of transforming one of the barbarian successor-states of the Roman Empire into an avatar of the Syriac universal state that had once been embodied in the Empire of the Achaemenidae. The administrative receptivity of the Primitive Muslim Arabs has its counterparts in the less striking achievements of the Arsacid 'Parthian', Saka, and Kushan barbarian supplanters of Hellenic empire-builders on former Achaemenian ground in South-West Asia east of Euphrates and on former Mauryan ground in North-West India.[1] But these were all exceptional cases, and, for the most part, the barbarian invaders of universal states had failed to profit from their victims' work in the field of provincial administration.

The Utilization of Provincial Organizations by Churches

On the other hand, the provincial organization of a universal state had more than once been turned to ecclesiastical account.

When the Egyptiac Emperor Thothmes (Tuthmosis) III (*imperabat circa* 1490–1436 B.C.) organized the priests of the parochial divinities of the nomes into a Pan-Egyptiac ecclesiastical corporation under the presidency of the Chief Priest of Amon-Re at Thebes,[2] we may guess that he was extending to the ecclesiastical field the existing political structure of 'the New Empire' of Egypt; for 'the New Empire' was a resuscitation of 'the Middle Empire' after an interregnum of Hyksos barbarian ascendancy, and, as we have seen,[3] 'the Middle Empire' had succeeded, step by step, in extinguishing the autonomy of the once virtually independent nomarchs and eventually bringing the nomes under the direct administration of the imperial government. One of the moves made by the emperors of the Twelfth Dynasty on their road to this objective had been to enter, over the heads of the nomarchs, into direct relations with the priests of the local shrines and to purchase their alliance by sending officials of the Imperial Office of Works to repair and improve their temple buildings at the charge of the Imperial Treasury.[4] Thothmes' historic act set the coping-stone on the construction of this mutually profitable partnership between the local priesthoods and the Imperial Crown.

The hierarchical organization of the local Egyptiac priesthoods into a

[1] See V. v. 442–3. [2] See I. i. 145, n. 5; IV. iv. 421; and V. v. 530–1.
[3] On pp. 174–6, above.
[4] See Meyer, E.: *Geschichte des Altertums*, vol. i, Part II, 3rd ed. (Stuttgart and Berlin 1913, Cotta), p. 274.

Pan-Egyptiac ecclesiastical corporation under a supreme pontiff, on the initiative and under the patronage of the secular Imperial Power, has a parallel in the position accorded to the Magi in the Sasanian Empire (*stabat* A.D. 224[1]–641 or 642[2]). The fundamental difference in structure between the Sasanian Persian Monarchy and the Arsacid 'Parthian' régime which it supplanted lay in the Sasanids' effective assertion of the central government's authority. Provincial governors, appointed by the Sasanian Emperor, now replaced the hereditary local kinglets[3]—seldom effectively under the control of their Arsacid overlord and often in overt rebellion against him—of whom the founder of the Sasanian Empire, Ardashir I, had himself been one before he carried a successful rebellion to its logical conclusion by slaying his master and seizing his throne. This Sasanian centralization of the civil administration of South-West Asia east of Euphrates was reflected in the corresponding organization of the Zoroastrian Church under Ardashir I's auspices and, according to tradition, on his initiative. Ardashir not only made Zoroastrianism the established church of his empire; he organized the Magian priesthood of the imperial religion into a hierarchy[4] rising from the local Magi (*Mōghān*), through the Chief Magi (*Mōghān Mōghān*) of eminent shrines and their superiors the Archimagi (*Mōbadhān*), to a supreme Archimagus (*Mōbadhān Mōbadh*) who was the ecclesiastical counterpart of the Sasanian Emperor himself.[5] This organization had a territorial basis: the empire was divided and subdivided into the equivalents of Christian archbishoprics, bishoprics, and parishes, each under the jurisdiction of an ecclesiastic of the corresponding rank.

Though Ardashir's and Thothmes' acts of state wear the appearance of creations *ex nihilo*, this is doubtless partly an illusion arising from the scantiness of our information about their antecedents. We do know that the Egyptiac priesthood to which Thothmes gave an oecumenical organization had previously ensured its own survival by coming to terms with the perhaps intrusive Sumeric worship of Osiris in an *union sacrée* against the alien religion of the Hyksos;[6] and the Magi—an ancient ecclesiastical caste which had originated in the pre-Zoroastrian age of Iranian paganism—had shown a similar resourcefulness in capturing the revolutionary higher religion founded by Zarathustra after they had come to the conclusion that they could neither stamp it out nor prevent its spread.[7] The Magi had also succeeded in commending Zoroastrianism (in the hardly recognizable form in which it had emerged from the Magian crucible) to

1 The probable date of the overthrow of the last Arsacid king of kings, Artabanes V, by Ardashir I of the House of Sāsān.

2 The date of the Battle of Nihāwand, after which the Sasanian Government was virtually non-existent, though the last Sasanian Emperor, Yazdagird III, survived as a fugitive in Khurāsān till A.D. 651 or 652.

3 This unbridled local autonomy had been so characteristic a feature of the Arsacid régime that this whole episode of South-West Asian history came to be known, in the Arabic version of the Sasanian tradition, as the age of the *mulūk-at-tawā'if* (the parochial princelings who were mere 'kings of shreds and patches').

4 See Christensen, A.: *L'Iran sous les Sassanides* (Copenhagen 1936, Levin & Munksgaard), pp. 112–13.

5 A second order of ecclesiastics, the *Hērbadhān*, who were specialists in ritual, were similarly brigaded together under a supreme *Hērbadhān Hērbadh* (Christensen, op. cit., p. 114).

6 See I. i. 140–5.

7 See V. v. 542 and 705, n. 1; and V. vi. 43, n. 4.

the Arsacid princes of the Azerbaijānī line (*regnabant* A.D. 10/11–224) who had been the Sasanids' immediate predecessors; and, though these latter-day Arsacids had not gone to the length of making Zoroastrianism the official religion of their state, the captivation of these ex-barbarians by the Magi was a more remarkable achievement than this ecclesiastical corporation's alliance with the Sasanidae. In the act of supplanting the Arsacids, the Sasanidae had virtually committed themselves to Zoroastrianism in advance by claiming to be the legitimate successors of the Achaemenidae, since the personal adherence of the great emperors of the Achaemenian Dynasty to the religion of Zarathustra was one of the few facts of pre-Alexandrine Iranian history of which a lively recollection had been preserved in the folk-memory of the Iranian people during the long ascendancy of an alien Hellenic culture.

Thus both the Magi and the Egyptiac Priesthood had known how to help themselves before their fortunes were made by a stroke of the secular arm, and, in the sequel, both ecclesiastical corporations demonstrated their capacity to survive the state that had called them into existence. The Chief Priest of Amon-Re at Thebes, Hrihor,[1] actually took over the Egyptiac Imperial Crown in the eleventh century B.C. from the last decrepit secular pharoahs of 'the New Empire';[2] and, though nothing came of this attempt to keep 'the New Empire' in being through a personal union of the supreme temporal and ecclesiastical offices, the Pan-Egyptiac ecclesiastical corporation instituted by Thothmes III did continue to maintain itself—and, in doing so, to preserve the distinctive character of the Egyptiac Society—for some fifteen hundred years after the Theban priest-king Hrihor's day, under successive alien ascendancies and native Egyptiac reactions against them, until at last, under Roman rule, its close-grained fabric yielded to the solvent of Christianity. As for the Zoroastrian Church, it failed to emulate the tenacity of the Egyptiac priesthood on its native soil; when the Sasanian Empire was overthrown, the Magian hierarchy fell with it; yet, though Zoroastrianism did not succeed in holding its own at home, it did achieve the even more difficult feat of preserving its identity in diasporá, and the credit for this was largely due to the perennial adaptability of the Magi, who retained their hold over their flock, and thereby kept this flock together, by making the most of their role as executants of a ritual and doctors of a religious law after they had lost their ecclesiastical lordship over a territorial empire.[3]

[1] According to recent findings of Modern Western Egyptologists, Hrihor himself was not a priest by profession but was a military adventurer who had usurped the Chief Priesthood of Amon-Re of Thebes without being properly qualified to hold it (see Edgerton, W. F.: 'The Government and the Governed in the Egyptian Empire', in the *Journal of Near Eastern Studies*, vol. iv, July 1947, No. 3 (Chicago 1947, University Press), pp. 152–60). Edgerton makes this statement on p. 153 on the authority of Kees, H.: 'Hrihor und die Aufrichtung des Thebanischen Gottesstaates', in *Nachrichten von der Gesellschaft der Wissenschaften zu Göttingen*, Phil.-Hist. Klasse, Neue Folge, Fachgruppe 1, 2. Band (1936–8), pp. 1–20). If this is the fact, it is a further testimony to the potency of the office in Hrihor's day. If it had not been the most favourable 'jumping-off ground' within Hrihor's reach for going on to usurp the Pharaonic Crown, the Chief Priesthood of Amon-Re would hardly have excited the cupidity of a soldier of fortune.

[2] See II. ii. 116, n. 1; IV. iv. 421 and 515–17; and p. 692, below.

[3] There was, of course, a remarkable similarity between the Zoroastrian and the Jewish response to the identic challenge of exile and dispersion.

The Christian Church showed still greater initiative and independence in turning to its own account the provincial organization of the universal state within whose framework it arose.[1] In building up its body ecclesiastic it availed itself of the city-states that were the cells of the Hellenic body social and of the Roman body politic. From the days of Saint Paul and his fellow pioneers in the Christian mission field, city-states were the primary units of the Church's territorial structure, and, as the traditions of the Hellenic Civilization gradually died out, a city came to mean a town that was the seat of a Christian bishop, instead of meaning a town possessing institutions of civil self-government and chartered as a municipality of the Roman Commonwealth. A local bishop whose see was the administrative centre of a Diocletianic Roman province came to be recognized by the bishops of the other cities of the same province as their superior; such metropolitans or archbishops, in their turn, acknowledged as their primate the bishop whose see was the administrative centre of one of those groups of provinces which, in the Diocletianic system, were known as *diœceses*;[2] and bishops, metropolitans, and primates alike paid ecclesiastical allegiance to regional patriarchs, who corresponded hierarchically to the Diocletianic praetorian prefects, though there was no correspondence at this level, as there was at the lower levels, between the areas of ecclesiastical and civil jurisdiction. In the Diocletianic Empire the west and centre were partitioned between three praetorian prefectures, while the east, from the Lower Danube to the First Cataract of the Nile, and from Thrace and Cyrenaica to Mesopotamia, was united in a single vast circumscription. In the Christian ecclesiastical organization, on the other hand, the Diocletianic Praefecture of the East was eventually divided between the four patriarchates of Alexandria, Jerusalem, Antioch, and Constantinople, while the circumscriptions of the other three praefectures were united in the single vast ecclesiastical domain of the Patriarchate of Rome.

This territorial organization of the Christian Church was not called into existence by the fiat of any Roman Thothmes or Ardashir; it was built up by the Church itself in the days when, in Roman official eyes, Christianity was a *religio non licita*; and all but the top story—whose architecture was implicit in the structure of the lower tiers—was in existence by the time of the conversion of Constantine. In virtue of this original independence of the secular imperial régime whose territorial organization it had thus adapted to its own purposes, the Roman-inspired territorial structure of the Christian Church was able to survive the Roman Empire's disappearance. In Gaul, for example, where a tottering Roman imperial régime had sought at the eleventh hour to rehabilitate itself on a novel basis of local support by instituting periodic regional congresses of notables, the Church, after the Empire had faded

[1] The preservation of the lineaments of an obsolete Roman political map in those of a surviving Christian ecclesiastical map is examined further on pp. 693–5, below.

[2] Though this technical term of Diocletianic Roman administration had been adopted as the designation of the 'diocese' of a Christian bishop, this usage was historically incorrect, since the standard domain of a bishopric was the territory of a city-state or canton, whereas the *diœceses* of the Roman Empire each contained several hundreds of territorial units of that order of magnitude.

out of existence, took its cue from this secular precedent by convening regional congresses of bishops;[1] and, though in many regions once included in the Roman Empire the Church's structure had eventually weathered away like its secular prototype, the indebtedness of the Church to the Roman Empire in this administrative sphere, as well as its ability to survive its Roman model, was apparent on the face of a latter-day map.

On the medieval ecclesiastical map of France, for example, an historian could discern in the mosaic of bishoprics the boundaries of the city-states of Gallia Togata and the cantons of Gallia Comata, while the archbishoprics preserved the outlines of the Diocletianic subdivisions of the four Augustan provinces Narbonensis, Aquitania, Lugdunensis, and Belgica. Even the five patriarchates, which were the precarious superstructure of the Christian ecclesiastical pyramid, were all still in existence —four in Eastern Orthodox hands and one in Western Catholic hands— at the time when these lines were being written; and, though the areas of their circumscriptions, and the distribution and nationality of their ecclesiastical subjects, had undergone vast changes during the fifteen centuries that had elapsed since the date of the Fourth Oecumenical Council (*sedebat Calchedone*, A.D. 451), their mortifying losses had been partially offset by gains that could never have been foreseen at the time when the patriarchates had first taken shape.

For example, the Patriarchate of Rome had lost its African sees to Islam, its South-East European sees to Eastern Orthodoxy, and its North European sees to Protestantism, but it had won hundreds of new bishoprics and millions of new subjects overseas in the Americas and the Indies. The four Eastern Patriarchates within their own historic bounds had suffered losses—to Monophysitism first and to Islam in the sequel—that were far more severe than the corresponding reverses of the Papacy; yet, in drawing up the balance-sheet of fifteen centuries of chequered history, they could still take heart from two signal achievements. They had preserved, as between themselves, their unity of rite and creed without sacrificing their independence of one another as units of ecclesiastical administration; and they had jointly called into existence a number of new sister churches that in rite and creed were at one with the four patriarchates and with one another, while enjoying in the sphere of ecclesiastical administration the same independence as the patriarchates themselves. Thanks to this liberality, this ecclesiastical commonwealth of Eastern Orthodox churches had never yet provoked a secession such as the ecclesiastical autocracy of the Roman Church had brought upon itself in a Protestant Reformation or the secular British Empire in an American Revolutionary War. The British Empire might indeed take credit for having learnt its lesson and converted itself into a commonwealth of fully self-governing communities of equal status; but this wisdom after the event could merely exorcise the danger of further

[1] See Burns, C. Delisle: *The First Europe* (London 1947, Allen & Unwin), pp. 541–2, for an illuminating comparison between an imperial rescript, issued at Constantinople on the 17th April, 418, in the names of the Emperors Honorius and Theodosius II, and a letter, dated the 23rd August, 546, written by Pope Vigilius.

secessions; it could not induce an independent United States to return to the British fold. The Commonwealth of Eastern Orthodox churches had risen to a higher level of statesmanship in being wise in time and thereby managing to retain within its circle the giant Church of Russia to champion the cause of Eastern Orthodoxy in an age when the onset of Western Nationalism, following the inroads of Islam and Monophysitism, had reduced to shadows of their former selves the once mighty patriarchates of Constantinople, Alexandria, Antioch, and Jerusalem.

4. *Capital Cities*

'*Laws*' *governing the Migration of Capital Cities*

The seats of the central governments of universal states show a decided tendency to change their locations in course of time, and this is one of the clearest indications that, whatever may have been the motives and intentions of the founders of a universal state, the true *raison d'être* of their handiwork is not the kingdom, power, or glory of the empire-builders but the welfare of their subjects.

Empire-builders usually begin by ruling their dominions from a seat of government convenient to themselves: either the established capital of their own fatherland, which they have transformed from a parochial into a universal state by overthrowing its rivals and imposing its peace on an entire society; or else some new site on the fringe of the subjugated territories, at a point where these are particularly accessible from the empire-builders' home country. But, as time goes on, the experience of imperial administration or the pressure of events is apt to lead either the original empire-builders or successors of theirs who take their empires over or rebuild them after a temporary collapse to transfer the imperial capital to a new site which is commended by its convenience, not for the original empire-building Power, but for the empire itself as a whole. This new oecumenical outlook will, of course, suggest different new locations in different circumstances. If the first consideration is administrative convenience, the capital is likely to shift to some point, enjoying good facilities for communication, that is geographically central.[1] On the other hand, if the most urgent demand is for defence against some barbarian or alien aggressor, the new capital may gravitate towards the particular sector of the imperial frontiers on which the hostile pressure is heaviest at the time.[2]

We have seen that the founders of universal states are not always of the same origin. Sometimes they are representatives of a civilization which is foreign to the society for whose political needs they are providing. Sometimes the empire-builders are barbarians who have become morally alienated from the society which they are supplying with a universal state, but have nevertheless continued to gravitate towards it. Frequently the empire-builders are marchmen who have vindicated their claim to be members of the society by defending its borders

[1] This point is made by Ibn Khaldūn: *Muqaddamāt*, translated by de Slane, Baron McG. (Paris 1863–8, Imprimerie Impériale, 3 vols.), vol. ii, pp. 308–9.

[2] This last-mentioned determining factor in changes in the locations of capitals of universal states has been examined already in II. ii. 112–208.

against outer barbarians before turning their arms against the interior of their own world and forcibly endowing it with an oecumenical peace. Such marchmen empire-builders are indeed true heirs of the civilization which they salvage from a Time of Troubles; yet, in the sight of their co-heirs for whom they have performed an invidious social service, they are sometimes hardly distinguishable from those outer barbarians with whom the marchmen have become familiar through the intercourse of border warfare. Lastly there are cases—apparently rather rare—in which the empire-builders have been neither aliens nor barbarians nor marchmen but 'metropolitans' from the interior of the world on which they have conferred the boon of political unity.

In universal states founded by aliens or barbarians the imperial capital is apt to start on the edge of the empire and to travel towards the interior. When the empire-builders are marchmen the same tendency sometimes asserts itself, but in this situation there are sometimes counter-pulls which tend to hold the capital in its original location. A margrave-emperor may find himself still tied to his ancestral base of operations in the back-woods by the continuance of pressure from the barbarians whom it is his first duty to keep at bay; and, if he does now succeed in disposing of this barbarian menace once for all by mobilizing against it the total resources of the society which he has united under his imperial rule, this very success may have the effect of extending his dominions so far afield into former barbarian territory that his seat of imperial government at the headquarters of his former march is consequently relegated to the interior of his expanded empire. In universal states founded by metropolitans the capital is, of course, likely to be located from the beginning at some point in the interior which is convenient for oecumenical administration, but nevertheless it may be drawn away towards a frontier if a threat of aggression from that quarter comes to be the imperial government's paramount concern. It is evident that the changes in the location of the seats of government of universal states are subject to certain 'laws' of political geography, but that the operation of these 'laws' is modified, in practice, by such complicated combinations of historical contingencies that particular cases have to be examined and analysed *ad hoc*.

Migrations of the Capital Cities of Alien Empire-builders

The operation of the 'law' governing the location of capitals of universal states founded by alien empire-builders is illustrated in the history of the British Rāj in India.[1] Reaching India, as they did, from overseas, and coming there to trade with the inhabitants before they ever dreamed of ruling over them, the English established their first footholds on Indian ground in the seaports Calcutta, Madras, and Bombay; and, of these three British maritime commercial settlements, Calcutta became the first political capital of British India because the East India Company happened to acquire the political dominion over the two great provinces Bengal and Bihar, in the hinterland of Calcutta, some forty or fifty years before they began to make any comparable acquisitions of territory in the

[1] See xi, map 53.

hinterlands of Madras and Bombay. Calcutta continued to be the capital of British India for more than a hundred years after the design of bringing all India under British rule had been first conceived by Wellesley (*proconsulari munere fungebatur* A.D. 1798–1805) and for more than sixty years after this ambition had been achieved. But the gravitational pull of a politically unified sub-continent eventually proved strong enough to draw the seat of the British Indian central government away from Calcutta, where it had been located for the convenience of a British thalassocracy, and to attract it to Delhi,[1] which was the natural site for the capital of a continental empire including the basins of both the Ganges and the Indus.

Delhi was, of course, not merely a natural site; it was also an historic one. The Mughal predecessors of the British rulers of India had governed India from Delhi since the days of Shāh Jahān (*imperabat* A.D. 1628–59),[2] and before Shāh Jahān's day they had governed it from the neighbouring city of Agra,[3] which was situated, like Delhi, on the banks of the Upper Jumna. The Mughals, like the British, had been aliens in the Hindu World on which they had imposed a universal state, but, unlike the British, they had never tried to govern India from a site on the threshold across which they had made their entry. It is true that the Mughals had arrived in India as fugitives from their own country; yet, when once they had placed the barrier of the Hindu Kush between themselves and their Uzbeg pursuers, they might have been tempted to establish their seat of government on some site in the highlands of North-Eastern Iran, where the climate, scenery, and fruits would have resembled those of their lost but lovingly remembered Farghānah. It is noteworthy that Bābur and his successors never in fact cast Kābul for the role of an imperial capital. As soon as they found themselves strong enough to descend upon the plains of the Panjab and Hindustan, they not only conquered them; they also immediately planted their seat of government on the sultry banks of the Jumna, in the heart of their newly acquired dominions. On the administrative map of the Mughal Empire, Kābul was merely the local capital of the north-western march and was never the overland equivalent of the maritime capital at Calcutta from which India was ruled by British hands for a century.

The Spanish *conquistadores* who established a universal state in Central America and took possession of a universal state in the Andean World were alien intruders from overseas like the British conquerors of India,

1 The transfer of the capital of the British Indian Empire to Delhi in A.D. 1912 has already been touched upon in II. ii. 132.

2 See II. ii. 131, with n. 3, for the establishment of the capital of the Mughal Empire at Delhi from the reign of Shāh Jahān onwards and for the previous history of Delhi, first as a frontier fortress of the Hindu World against Muslim aggression and afterwards as the capital of successive Muslim rulers of Hindustan from the Muslim conquest of the Ganges Basin at the turn of the twelfth and thirteenth centuries of the Christian Era down to the replacement of a Lōdī Afghan by a Mughal Turkish rāj in the sixteenth century.

3 Akbar's attempt to establish a new capital *ex nihilo* at Fātihpūr Sīkrī was no more successful than his attempt to launch a new higher religion, the Dīn Ilāhī (for these two failures of Akbar's, see II. ii. 131, n. 3, and V. v. 699–704). It is noteworthy that Ikhnaton, who likewise tried and failed to launch a new religion of his own invention, also made a similarly unsuccessful attempt to establish a new capital city at Tall-al-'Amarnah (see p. 215, below).

but, in the location of their seats of government, the Spaniards did not make the move from an original capital on the coast to a subsequent capital in the interior; in this matter they went to opposite extremes in the two new worlds of which they made themselves masters. In the Andean World they laid out a maritime capital at Lima which they never abandoned in favour of the inland capital at Cuzco from which the Andean Realm of the Four Quarters had previously been ruled by the Incas. In Central America, on the other hand, they never attempted to govern their dominions from the seaport which they laid out at Vera Cruz. They immediately located their seat of government in the interior on the site of Tenochtitlan—the highland capital of the Aztecs who were in the act of building a Central American universal state when the Spaniards suddenly came on the scene and usurped the Aztecs' role.

Why did the Spaniards thus adopt opposite policies in two at first sight similar situations? The Mexican Plateau may have attracted them by its resemblance to their native plateau of Castile; yet, if that was the decisive consideration, why did it not lead them to pass over Lima, as they passed over Vera Cruz, and locate their Andean seat of government in the highland city of Cuzco, which was the existing capital from which the Andean universal state was actually being governed by the Incas at the time of the Spaniards' arrival? The explanation of this apparent inconsistency may lie in a difference in the previous historical roles of the respective environs of Vera Cruz and Lima. The lowlands lying between the Mexican Plateau and the shores of the Gulf were no longer playing a great part in the life of the Mexic Civilization. By contrast, the lowlands lying between the Andean Plateau and the shores of the Pacific Ocean had been the cradle of the Andean Civilization and had lost none of their economic or cultural importance since their political incorporation into an Andean universal state established by Inca empire-builders from the highlands.[1] Thus, in consulting their own convenience by abandoning the highland capital of the Incas at Cuzco and establishing their own seat of government in the seaport of Lima, the Spaniards were at the same time selecting a site in the cultural heart of the Andean World.

We may even raise the question whether the Incas themselves might have been impelled to transfer their seat of government from their ancestral capital at Cuzco to some site in the coastal lowlands if their dominion had endured for its natural term instead of having been abruptly brought to an end by the Spanish conquest not more than a hundred years after the establishment of an Andean universal state by the Inca Pachacutec (*imperabat circa* A.D. 1400–48). The decisive act in the elevation of the Inca Empire into an Andean universal state had been Pachacutec's conquest of the lowland states along the seaboard; and, with the passage of time, this epoch-making addition to the Empire's domain might well have affected its administrative structure. In the empire which Pachacutec put together and Pizarro took over, Cuzco was not more centrally situated than Lima; for the Incas had won their way by serving as marchmen, and their ancestral city had become an

[1] See I. i. 121–3 and II. ii. 103, n. 2.

imperial capital without ceasing to be a frontier fortress guarding the eastern brow of the Andean Plateau against the fierce and aggressive barbarians of the Amazonian tropical forest.[1] If the Incas had been given a longer time to harvest the experience of administering an empire in which highlands and lowlands were linked together, it seems not unlikely that they might have followed up their scientific redistribution of population[2] by a transfer of the seat of their central government. Indeed, before the Spaniards arrived, the Incas had already built two imperial palaces on the coast.[3]

The Ottoman dominion over Orthodox Christendom and the Mongol dominion over China were established, like the Mughal Rāj in India, by invasion overland, and not, like the British Rāj in India or the Spanish Empire in the New World, by assault from across the sea; yet, in the location of their capital cities, their histories followed the British and not the Mughal pattern.

The ʿOsmanlis started their empire-building operations from a base just beyond the eastern borders of the Orthodox Christian World within the limits to which Orthodox Christendom had been reduced by the turn of the thirteenth and fourteenth centuries of the Christian Era,[4] and, as the ʿOsmanlis' dominions expanded, their seat of government travelled *pari passu*. First it moved from Eskishehr, 'the old city' just within the north-western rim of the Anatolian Plateau, to Yenishehr, 'the new city' in the lowlands within range of the Sea of Marmara. In A.D. 1326 it moved on to Brusa. In A.D. 1366 it leapt the Dardanelles and entered the Balkan Peninsula, into which the centre of gravity of the Orthodox Christian World had already shifted since the Saljūq Turkish conquest of the interior of Anatolia in the later decades of the eleventh century of the Christian Era.[5] The first location of the Ottoman capital in the Balkan Peninsula was at Adrianople, but this was only a halting-place and not its final destination.[6] The Ottoman Sultan Mehmed the Conqueror (*imperabat* A.D. 1451–81), who completed the political unification of the main body of the Orthodox Christian World under Ottoman rule, was also the statesman who brought the Ottoman seat of government to its final resting-place at Constantinople, the former capital of the East Roman Empire and the cultural metropolis of Orthodox Christendom. Constantinople did not lose the status which Mehmed the Conqueror had conferred upon her till after the Ottoman Empire itself had been snuffed out of existence through the reconstitution of an Anatolian remnant of Mehmed the Conqueror's realm into a Republic of Turkey on the 29th October, 1923. In virtue of Article 2 of the Constitution of the 20th April, 1924, Constantinople forfeited juridically to Ankara the role of being the official seat of government of this Turkish successor-state.[7]

1 See II. ii. 207.
2 For this, see pp. 114–15, above.
3 See Markham, Sir C.: *The Incas of Peru* (London 1910, Smith Elder), p. 238.
4 See II. ii. 151.
5 See II. ii. 79–80 and 152.
6 See p 135, n. 1, above.
7 Since the autumn of 1919 Ankara had, of course, been the *de facto* provisional seat of the revolutionary Kemalist movement out of which the Republic of Turkey had sprung.

The progressive advance of the capital of the Ottoman Empire towards the heart of the Orthodox Christian World has a parallel in the series of stages by which the capital of the Mongol Khāqāns followed the China-ward course of Mongol conquest. The first signal successes in Chingis Khan's career were his conquests of the Karāyits and Naimans,[1] the two Nestorian Turkish Nomad peoples whom the Mongols found in occupation of the choicest portion of the High Steppe[2] in the basin of the River Orkhon. By a long-established tradition the Orkhon Basin was the domain of the paramount Nomad community on the High Steppe,[3] and, when the Mongols acquired this paramountcy in their turn by the customary right of conquest, and then proceeded to extend their rule over a number of sedentary societies round about, their first essay in living up to their newly attained dignity and making use of their newly acquired wealth was to lay out a permanent capital for themselves in the Orkhon Basin at Qāraqorum.[4] For the translation of this dream into reality, skilled artificers were uprooted from their distant homes in China, Russia, and Western Christendom and were carried away captive to beautify the Khāqān's rising city on the Steppe;[5] but before the work was finished it was made of no avail by the triumph of Mongol arms on the Chinese front.

The Mongol Khāqān Qubilāy (*imperabat* A.D. 1259–94) achieved what had proved beyond the strength of the Mongol conquerors' Kin and Khitan forerunners. He conquered not merely Northern China but the whole continental domain of the Far Eastern Society, including the Yangtse Basin and the southern seaboard; and the gravitational pull of this Far Eastern sub-continent, now once more politically united, immediately made itself felt in the location of the Mongol Khāqān's capital. In A.D. 1264 Qubilāy began to recondition Peking—the site in the north-east corner of China, just inside the Great Wall, where the previous Kin conquerors of Northern China had placed their seat of government[6]—and in A.D. 1267 he moved his own capital to Peking from Qāraqorum.[7] Though Qubilāy's head dictated this move, his heart remained homesick for its ancestral pastures, and the semi-Sinified

[1] See V. v. 250 and 309.

[2] The Great Eurasian Steppe consisted of two areas which were geographically distinct, though both had been theatres of one uniform Nomad way of life. There was the High Steppe (the Alexandrian Hellenic geographer Ptolemy's Scythia extra Imaum) on the immense plateau which was bounded on the west by the Altai and Tien Shan Mountains, and there was the Low Steppe (Ptolemy's Scythia intra Imaum) which extended westward from the Tien Shan to the Carpathians. The two areas were in communication with one another through the Zungarian Gap between Tien Shan and Altai.

[3] This position had been occupied in succession by the Hiongnu, the Juan Juan, the Northern Turks, and the eastern Turkish successors of the united Turkish steppe-empire of the sixth and seventh centuries of the Christian Era. The eighth-century Turkish masters of the Orkhon Basin had left there a memorial of themselves in their celebrated inscriptions. It was not an accident that the seat of government of a latter-day Soviet Socialist Republic of Outer Mongolia was located in the same neighbourhood, at Urga.

[4] See III. iii. 397 and V. v. 312–15.

[5] See Olschki, L.: *Guillaume Boucher, A French Artist at the Court of the Khans* (Baltimore 1946, The Johns Hopkins Press).

[6] The Kin themselves had taken the site over from their own predecessors the Khitan, who had laid the foundations of Peking's political fortunes by choosing this hitherto obscure spot for the location, not of their central seat of government, but of their southern residence.

[7] See II. ii. 121, n. 3.

Mongol statesman indulged his unregenerate Nomad feelings by building himself a subsidiary residence at Chung-tu, a point on the south-eastern rim of the Mongolian Plateau where the Steppe approached nearest to the new imperial city.[1] But Qubilāy's 'Xanadu' was a 'pleasure dome' and no more; his serious business of state was transacted at Peking. The requirements of a conquered world had won a pacific victory over the inclinations of its conqueror which was to have a more lasting effect than the Mongols' mere military victory over the Empire of the Sung.

When the Manchus followed in the Mongols' footsteps by conquering the whole of China and reconstituting a Far Eastern universal state in the seventeenth century of the Christian Era after an interlude of some two centuries during which China had managed to keep herself free from barbarian rule, history duly repeated itself in the location of the imperial capital. Before the Manchus set about the conquest of China within the Wall, they had already made a new capital for themselves at Mukden,[2] the South Manchurian meeting-point of the Manchus' native forests, the Mongols' pastures, and the arable land, beyond the shelter of the Wall, which had been won for the plough by Chinese peasant pioneers in the course of ages. The Manchus were more firmly planted at Mukden than the Mongols had been at Qāraqorum. Their leaders, at any rate, were already half Sinified before they crossed the Great Wall, and Mukden had become a seat not merely of Manchu government but of Chinese culture. Yet the Manchu conquerors of China took the same decision as the Mongol Qubilāy. The guardians of the Manchu boy-king Shun Chih (*imperabat* A.D. 1644–61), when they proclaimed him Emperor, transferred the Manchu seat of government to Peking[3] and allowed Mukden—which had been 'the education of' the Manchus—to sink to a subordinate status.[4] The Manchu rulers of China made the same concession to their own home-sickness as their Mongol forerunners. They built for themselves a counterpart of Qubilāy's Chung-tu in the shape of a magnificent holiday resort at Jehol, a highland paradise on the road back from Peking to the dynasty's original home in the hill-country of North-Eastern Manchuria. Yet, in spite of this backward gesture, the requirements of a conquered China had overcome the inclinations of her conquerors once again.[5]

1 See vol. cit., loc. cit.

2 Mukden was founded by the second prince of the Manchu Dynasty, T'ai Tsung (*extra Murum regnabat* A.D. 1625–43).

3 See II. ii. 123.

4 Mukden (*Sinicè* Shêngking) did retain some vestiges of its former status. For instance, the Manchu Emperor Ch'ien Lung (*imperabat* A.D. 1736–96) directed in A.D. 1782 that one of four fair copies of the manuscript of his Ssu-k'u Ch'üan Shu ('The Four Treasuries') which were designed for official use was to be lodged at Mukden in a building specially erected to hold it (see Mayers, W. F.: 'Bibliography of the Chinese Imperial Collections of Literature', in the *China Review*, vol. vi (1877–8), No. 5, p. 295). The writer of this Study had the privilege of being taken to see this building, the Wên So Ko, with Ch'ien Lung's immense *corpus scriptorum Sinarum* still safely housed in it, on the 17th November, 1929. The corresponding buildings for housing the other three official fair copies were located respectively in the precincts of the Imperial Palace at Peking, at Yüan-ming Yüan, and at Jehol (see further X. ix. 56).

5 When the gravitational pull of a united China had drawn the Mongols' capital to Peking from Qāraqorum and the Manchus' capital to Peking from Mukden, why, in both cases, did the change of location go thus far and no farther? Why did the seat of imperial

We may conclude this survey of the histories of the capital cities of alien empire-builders by considering one of those exceptions that sometimes prove a rule.

When the successors of Alexander were contending for the spoils of the Achaemenian Empire, Seleucus Nicator made his fortune by concentrating his efforts on gaining possession of the vast interior. There was less keen competition for this prize than for provinces with seaboards on the Mediterranean that offered their Macedonian holders an easy access to the heart of the Hellenic World round the shores of the Aegean Sea; yet the prize on which Seleucus had set his heart was attractive for an empire-builder with the vision to divine its possibilities. Babylonia, which Seleucus had selected for his base of operations, had been both the granary and the industrial workshop of the Achaemenian Empire,[1] and, apart from its economic value, it was the strategic key to the political control of all the ex-Achaemenian provinces to the north-east of it, up to the southern borders of Nomads' Land in Central Asia and the western borders of Chandragupta's Indic Empire in Eastern Iran.[2] Seleucus saw this prize, won it, and made statesmanlike provision for retaining it by laying out, and stamping with his own name, a new metropolis in Babylonia on the right bank of the Tigris at the point where Tigris and Euphrates approached nearest to one another. Seleucia-on-Tigris was a better site than Babylon both for the administration of Babylonia itself and for the command of the great North-East Road linking the Lower Tigris–Euphrates Basin with the Upper Oxus–Jaxartes Basin over the crown of the Iranian Plateau. Thanks to the skill which Seleucus displayed in its location,[3] Seleucia-on-Tigris remained an important city and a flourishing centre of Hellenic life and culture for more than five centuries after its foundation towards the end of the fourth century B.C.[4] But it missed its political destiny through an error of political judgement committed by the founder himself.

The sagacity of Seleucus's original design for constructing a successor-state of the Achaemenian Empire out of its dominions east of Euphrates was conclusively demonstrated after the Seleucid Dynasty's demise by

government come to rest at Peking, instead of travelling on to Loyang on the Yellow River or to Nanking on the Yangtse? Loyang and Nanking had been historic imperial capitals in the past. Why did History fail to repeat itself to this extent on these two occasions? And why did it eventually repeat itself to this extent in A.D. 1928? An attempt to find the answers to these questions has been made in II. ii. 121–7.

[1] According to Herodotus, Book I, chap. 192, Babylonia supplied the Achaemenian court's and mobile army's requirements in kind for four months out of every twelve (cp. p. 205, n. 4, below).

[2] For the analogy between the Seleucid and the Umayyad control over the Iranian Plateau from a base on the plains of the Land of Shinar (*alias* Babylonia, *alias* 'Irāq 'Arabī), see p. 137, n. 4, above. This portion of the former Achaemenian Empire lying east of Euphrates, which Seleucus marked out for his own share, was the portion which the last Darius had proposed to retain for himself when, during the interval between the battles of Issus and Arbela, he had offered to divide the Empire with Alexander.

[3] Whereas Seleucia was an artificial foundation deliberately located with an eye to its possibilities as an oecumenical capital, Babylon had become an oecumenical capital through the accident that the Amorite marchmen of the Sumeric World, who had established themselves there on the borders between the Desert and the Sown, had eventually played the part of restorers of a Sumeric universal state (see II ii. 133, and pp. 226–8, below).

[4] The exact date of the foundation of Seleucia-on-Tigris is not known (see Bouché-Leclercq, A.: *Histoire des Seleucides* (Paris 1913–14, Leroux, 2 vols.), vol. ii, pp. 524–5.

the histories of the Arsacid and Sasanian Powers, each of which lasted for some four hundred years within these limits, whereas the Sasanian Empire came to grief still more quickly than its Seleucid predecessor when it seriously attempted, under the misguided impulsion of Khusrū Parwīz, to extend its dominions westward to the shores of the Mediterranean and the Bosphorus. Seleucus was enticed to his own death and his dynasty's eventual undoing by the completeness of the triumph of two successive coalitions of Macedonian war-lords in which Seleucus found himself each time on the winning side. In 301 B.C. at the Battle of Ipsus, Seleucus of Babylonia, in alliance with Ptolemy of Egypt and Lysimachus of Thrace, succeeded in overthrowing their common adversary Antigonus, who, from his commanding central position in Syria and Anatolia, had aspired to reassemble all the fragments of the Achaemenian Empire under his own rule at the expense of his fellow successors. Thereafter, in 281 B.C., at the Battle of Corupedium, Lysimachus, in his turn, was overthrown by Seleucus and Ptolemy. The cumulative effect of these two decisive successes was to give Seleucus Nicator, who had originally made his way without access to the western seas, both a Syrian seaboard on the Mediterranean and an Ionian seaboard on the Aegean; and this westward expansion of his empire exposed Nicator and his successors to temptations which they failed to resist.

Nicator himself took over Antigonus's half-built capital city Antigoneia-on-Orontes, within one short day's march from the north-east corner of the Mediterranean, and removed it to a more commanding adjacent site to become the capital of his own monarchy under the name of Antioch,[1] and he met his death on his road to Macedon by way of his newly acquired and precariously far-flung dominions in Western Anatolia and Thrace.[2] In the sequel, Seleucus's successors drained away the resources of Babylonia and the Iranian provinces on the farther side of Babylonia in an inconclusive struggle with a mobile and elusive Ptolemaic sea-power for the command of the coasts of the Levant all the way round from Gaza to the Hellespont;[3] and even the ultimate success of the Seleucidae in this warfare between the elephant and the whale was fraught with disaster. When, in 200–198 B.C., Antiochus the Great conquered Coele Syria from Ptolemy Eurgetes' feeble successor Ptolemy Epiphanes, he was bequeathing to his successors the insoluble problem of dealing with the Jewish temple-state in the hill-country between the two branches of 'the King's Highway';[4]

[1] See p. 94, above.

[2] See p. 94, above.

[3] One object of this misguided Seleucid policy was to keep open an overland pipe-line through which soldiers and settlers from the heart of the Hellenic World round the shores of the Aegean could be pumped into the interior of the Seleucid dominions; but these reinforcements of Greek manpower could assuredly have been obtained even if the Seleucid Monarchy had not spent its resources in trying to maintain a maritime frontage. The dominant consideration was the prestige attaching to suzerainty over historic Greek city-states, however insignificant. We may recall the equally misguided Hapsburg policy of spending the resources of the Danubian Monarchy during the eighteenth century of the Christian Era in efforts to retain possession of Silesia, the Southern Netherlands and the Breisgau, at the cost of letting slip a golden opportunity for wresting from the Ottoman Empire the whole of South-Eastern Europe between Vienna and Constantinople (see II. ii. 180–6 and cp. III. iii. 301–6).

[4] See pp. 100–2, above, and xi, maps 11, 14, 20, and 21A.

and, when he proceeded to reassert the claim of his house to Seleucus Nicator's acquisitions on both sides of the Hellespont, the result was an irretrievably disastrous collision with the overwhelmingly superior power of Rome.

While the Seleucidae were absorbed in gaining or losing some canton, city-state, or islet on the western fringes of their expanded dominions, they were losing one province after another in the neglected, exploited, but indispensable East. By 248–247 B.C., fifty-four years after Seleucus Nicator's ill-omened victory at Ipsus, the Parnian Nomads had established themselves in the Seleucid province of Parthia astride the Great North-East Road at the point where it descended from the Iranian Plateau towards the Oxus, and the consequent insulation of the Oxus–Jaxartes Basin from the main body of the Seleucid Monarchy quickly resulted in the establishment of an independent state by the Greek 'ascendancy' there.[1] When the Arsacid war-lords of the Parni went on to occupy Media, where the Great North-East Road[2] made its way through the western mountain ramparts of the Iranian Plateau, and when they proceeded, through this open gate, to descend upon Babylonia itself in 142 B.C., they were tearing out the Seleucid Monarchy's heart; and, after Demetrius Nicator's and Antiochus Sîdêtês' successive attempts in 140 and 130 B.C. to reconquer Babylonia and Media had ended in repeated disaster, the remnant of the Seleucid Empire in Syria was doomed to extinction at an early date. The Seleucid Monarchy met its ignominious end when Tigranes King of Armenia—a hitherto obscure non-Hellenic successor-state of the shattered empire of Antiochus the Great[3]—unconsciously avenged the overthrow of Antigonus Monophthalmus by occupying Antioch-on-Orontes in 83 B.C.

Such was the nemesis of Seleucus Nicator's momentous decision to establish the seat of his central government on a site adjoining his defeated rival Antigonus's abortive capital at Antigoneia-on-Orontes instead of establishing it in a metropolis of his own creation at Seleucia-on-Tigris.[4] Nicator could not conjure away inexorable geographical facts which had once been apparent to him by disguising a virtual reconstruction of Antigoneia under a family name of his own;[5] for a site command-

[1] See II. ii. 143–4. This Greek Power in Bactria seems to have established its independence gradually between 246 and 228 B.C. (see Tarn, W. W.: *The Greeks in Bactria and India* (Cambridge 1938, University Press), pp. 72–74).

[2] See xi, map 20.

[3] The creation of the Kingdom of Armenia Major by the House of Artaxias—a former lieutenant of Antiochus the Great's who declared his independence after his suzerain's disastrous defeat by the Romans in 190 B.C.—is touched upon on p. 626, below.

[4] It is worth noticing that the corresponding false step was avoided by both the Arsacid and the Sasanian successor-states of the Seleucid Monarchy, each of which lasted nearly twice as long as the Seleucid Monarchy itself. The Arsacidae, and the Sasanidae after them, unhesitatingly established their seat of government at Ctesiphon, a suburb of Seleucia-on-Tigris which was presumably called after the name of the Greek who had originally laid it out, and which was situated on the farther side of the river, on its Iranian bank. The Arsacidae did not attempt to govern Babylonia from Hecatompylos, their previous capital at the north-eastern exit of the Caspian Gates between the central desert of Iran and the Elburz Range; and the Sasanidae did not attempt to govern it from Istakhr, their previous capital in Fars. Istakhr and Hecatompylos both gave way to Ctesiphon, as, in the Far Eastern World, Mukden gave way to Peking after the Manchu conquest of China (see p. 199, above).

[5] Seleucus named his new capital in the neighbourhood of Antigoneia 'Antiocheia' after his own father Antiochus.

ing the landward end of the gorge down which the River Orontes forced its way through a coastal range of mountains to the Mediterranean was as unsuitable for the capital of an empire whose heart lay in Babylonia and whose eastern provinces extended across the Iranian Plateau into the Oxus–Jaxartes Basin as it had been felicitous for the capital of an empire which, like Antigonus's empire in its last phase, had been virtually confined to Anatolia and Syria and had not extended farther into the interior of Asia than the western bank of the Euphrates in the section of the river's course in which it approached nearest to the Mediterranean. When eventually the founder's descendants Demetrius Nicator (*imperabat primum* 145–139 B.C.) and Antiochus Sîdêtês (*imperabat* 139/8–129 B.C.) were made keenly aware of the indispensability of Babylonia by the painful experience of the consequences of its loss, the elder brother forfeited his liberty and the younger his life in vainly seeking to undo the untoward effects of the century and a half that had elapsed between the establishment of the capital at Antioch by their ancestor the first Seleucus in 300 B.C. and their own ill-fated expeditions on the forlorn hope of recovering Seleucia. If the change made by Seleucus I in his focus of geographical interest had been the other way about—from the banks of the Orontes, on the western edge of the Achaemenian dominions, to the banks of the Tigris in their heart—the Seleucid Monarchy might have had a longer and a happier history.

Migrations of the Capital Cities of Barbarian Empire-builders

Having now surveyed the shifts in the seats of administration of universal states founded or captured by aliens, we may turn to a consideration of the cases in which the empire-builders were barbarians or marchmen.[1] We may begin with the Persian barbaro-marchmen who gave the Syriac World its universal state, and the Arab barbarians who reconstituted the Empire of the Achaemenidae after a thousand-years-long interlude of Hellenic intrusion.

'The homeland of the Persians lies out of the way of the theatres of historical life. The great highroad that links the West with the Eastern World[2] runs, from Babylon towards the interior, up the valley of the Gyndes [Diyālah] and out of it into the valley of the Upper Choaspes [Karkhah], past the rock of Behistan [*alias* Bisitun], to Ecbatana [Hamadan], and from here it proceeds along the northern rim of the Iranian Plateau. And so we find that, although the Persians, like the Arabs, have repeatedly launched far-sweeping movements, their country has never been able to become the permanent centre of a great state. As soon as the reaction sets in, Persis [Pārsa, Fars] once more disappears, for centuries on end, from the stage of historic life.'[3]

According to a story with which Herodotus concludes his work,[4] Cyrus the Great deprecated a suggestion that the Persian people, now

[1] The Manchu Empire, whose founders were barbaro-marchmen, has been considered already, by anticipation, in connexion with the Mongol Empire in China, whose founders were barbarians with a tincture of alien culture; and the Inca Empire, whose founders were marchmen, in connexion with the Spanish Empire by which it was supplanted.

[2] See xi, map 20.—A.J.T.

[3] Meyer, E.: *Geschichte des Altertums*, vol. iii, 1st ed. (Stuttgart 1901, Cotta), p. 22.

[4] The passage has been quoted in the present Study in II. ii. 21.

that they had become masters of the World, should evacuate their bleak highland homeland and settle in one of the many more agreeable countries that were now at their disposal. But, whether or not it was the Achaemenian Government's policy to discourage the Persian people as a whole from migrating to more genial tracts of their newly acquired empire, it is an historical fact that, more than a hundred years before the Empire was established through Cyrus II's overthrow of his Median suzerain Cyaxares, the Achaemenian Dynasty had transferred its own seat of government from its ancestral highlands—which stood not in Fars (Pārsa) but in Lūristān (Parsuwaš)—to the first piece of lowland territory of which it had gained possession. King Teispes of Parsuwaš (*regnabat circa* 675–640 B.C.), the son and first successor of Achaemenes the dynasty's founder and eponym, figures in the Assyrian records as 'King of the city of Anšan';[1] and Anšan was believed by twentieth-century Western scholars to have lain somewhere in the neighbourhood of both the Babylonian district of Der and the city of Susa, the capital of Elam—perhaps at some point where a fortress would command the corridor of lowland territory linking the plains of Elam with the plains of Babylonia between the south-eastern extremity of the Kabīr Kuh Range's Pusht-i-Kuh foothills and the northern extremity of the swamps through which, in that age, the rivers Kārūn, Tigris, and Euphrates made their separate exits into the Persian Gulf.[2] The importance attached to this earliest acquisition of the Achaemenids in the lowlands is attested in the retention of the title 'King of Anšan' by Teispes himself and by his first three successors in the elder branch of his house—Cyrus I, Cambyses I, and Cyrus II the Great[3]—even after Teispes had taken the opportunity to make himself master of Pārsa, on the far side of Elam, while Elam and Assyria were engaged in the last and most exhausting of the Assyro-Elamite wars (*gerebatur circa* 663–638 B.C.), and even after the reunion of the two portions of Teispes' dominions in the hands of the elder branch of Teispes' line—which seems to have come to pass, in or shortly before the year 547 B.C., through the deposition of King Arsâmês (Aršāma), the son of Cyrus I's younger brother Ariaramnes (Ariyāramna) and the heir of Ariaramnes' appanage Pārsa, by Cambyses I's son and Cyrus I's grandson Cyrus II the Great.[4]

For more than a hundred years after the Achaemenidae had acquired their footing in the lowlands of Anšan, just to the west of Susa, and for not much less than a hundred years after they had gone on to acquire the highlands of Pārsa, to the south-east of Elam, Susa remained in non-Achaemenian hands. The former capital of Elam was annexed by Assyria after she had erased Elam from the political map[5] and was inherited

[1] See Cameron, G. G.: *A History of Early Iran* (Chicago 1936, Chicago University Press), p. 180; Olmstead, A. T.: *A History of the Persian Empire* (Chicago 1948, Chicago University Press), p. 23. [2] See p. 621, below.

[3] See König, F. W.: *Älteste Geschichte der Meder und Perser* (Leipzig 1934, Hinrichs), p. 10; Cameron, op. cit., pp. 212 and 218.

[4] According to F. H. Weissbach in Pauly–Wissowa: *Realencyclopädie der Classischen Altertumswissenschaft*, Neue Bearbeitung, Supplementband iv, cols. 1141-2, s.v. 'Kyros', followed by Kent, R. G., in his *Old Persian: Grammar, Texts, Lexicon* (New Haven, Conn. 1950, American Oriental Society), p. 159.

[5] See Cameron, op. cit., p. 211.

from Assyria by Assyria's Neo-Babylonian successor-state. There was archaeological evidence that Susa was included in the Neo-Babylonian Empire in Nebuchadnezzar's day (*imperabat* 605–562 B.C.);[1] and it was not till after his death[2] that the Achaemenian Kingdom managed to gain possession of a city which, ever since Teispes' acquisition of Pārsa, had insulated the dynasty's major new dominion from its minor original patrimony as awkwardly as, from A.D. 1466 to A.D. 1772, the two sections of the Hohenzollern dominions were insulated from one another by a city-state of Danzig under Polish suzerainty marching with a corridor of Polish territory extending to the shore of the Baltic Sea and thereby cutting East Prussia off from Prussian Pomerania and Brandenburg.

After Susa had at last fallen into Achaemenian hands, it was as inevitable that the capital of the Achaemenian Empire should be transferred to Susa from Anšan as it was that the capital of the Ottoman Empire should be transferred to Constantinople from Adrianople after Sultan Mehmed II's capture of the Second Rome in A.D. 1453; and this step was duly taken by Darius I before the end of the year 521 B.C.[3] It will be seen that the geographical situation of Susa *vis-à-vis* the highlands of Fars, the highlands of Lūristān, and the great plain of Shinar was comparable to the position of Peking *vis-à-vis* the highlands of Eastern Manchuria, the Orkhon High Steppe and the great plain of Northern China. The site lay between the semi-barbarian empire-builders' two main reservoirs of military man-power in a corner of the lowlands that were the Empire's main granary and workshop; and the site's proximity to the military reservoirs was the reason for its selection and retention notwithstanding the inconvenience of its location for the purpose of administering the Empire as a whole.

In Darius's reorganization of the Achaemenian Empire it proved not impossible to lead into Susa both the Great North-East Road and the Great North-West Road; yet this achievement of the Achaemenian ministry of works remained something of a *tour de force*, and the awkwardness, even of Susa, as a seat of government for an empire extending to the Jaxartes, Indus, Nile, and Danube, is attested by the fact that the Achaemenian Imperial Court did not reside in the official capital of the Achaemenian Empire year in and year out, but moved round in an annual migration between Susa and two other imperial residences.[4] The winter residence was Babylon, which was far better placed than Susa, though not quite so well placed as the future Seleucia-

[1] 'Bricks [identical in make with bricks of Nebuchadnezzar's found at Babylon, and stamped] with his name were used to erect buildings in that city, while an alabaster vase with his inscription and a weight with his legend are further witnesses of his control' (Cameron, op. cit., pp. 219–20).

[2] According to Cameron, op. cit., p. 221, Susa, together with the rest of the lowlands of Elam, was lost by the Neo-Babylonian Empire to the Achaemenidae before Nabonidus's accession in 556 B.C. According to Olmstead, op. cit., p. 43, it was lost when, in 546 B.C., the Neo-Babylonian Government's commandant of the citadel of Susa, Gobryas, turned traitor and joined forces with Cyrus II.

[3] See Olmstead, op. cit., p. 119.

[4] According to Xenophon: *Expeditio Cyri*, Book III, chap. v, § 15, and *Cyropaedia*, Book VIII, chap. vi, § 22, the Achaemenian Court used to spend seven winter months in Babylon, two summer months in Ecbatana, and only three spring months out of every twelve at Susa (cp. p. 200, n. 1, above).

on-Tigris, for serving as the point of junction of the two main imperial highways.[1] The summer residence was Ecbatana (Hamadan), the former capital of the Median Power, which lay at the strategically important point on the Great North-East Road where this highway dropped down to the level of the Iranian Plateau after surmounting the Zagros Range that walled in the plateau on the west.[2]

The significant point here for the purpose of our present investigation is that the Achaemenian Court's fixed annual time-table of circulation from one imperial residence to another does not appear to have allowed for any regular annual residence at any site in the Persian homeland of the imperial people. The Achaemenian emperors showed their reverence for Pārsa by being crowned there and their affection for it by being buried there. Cyrus built for himself a tomb (still standing at the time of writing) in the Persian canton of Clan Pasargadae,[3] near the latter-day village of Murghāb; and, lower down the course of the little River Pulvār, Darius and his successors hewed out their sepulchres in the face of a cliff at the point latterly known as Naqsh-i-Rustam.[4] Cyrus is said also to have built for Clan Pasargadae in the course of the years 559–550 B.C. a city called by the clan name;[5] and between 512 and 494 B.C.[6] Darius I

1 Seleucia-on-Tigris was skilfully sited by its Macedonian founder to serve as the point of junction not only between the Great North-East Road and the Great North-West Road, but also between the two alinements of the latter. The north-eastern alinement of the Great North-West Road, as described by Herodotus (Book V, chaps. 52–3), ran from Susa to Ephesus to the east of the middle course of the Tigris and to the north of the central desert of Anatolia. The south-eastern alinement ran from Susa to Ephesus via Babylon and the east bank of the middle course of the Euphrates through the Cilician Gates. The north-eastern alinement traversed the derelict capitals of both Assyria and the Hittite Power. The south-western alinement was followed by Cyrus the Younger in 401 B.C. and by Alexander in 434–433 B.C., and it became the life-line of Seleucus Nicator's dominions after he had extended them to the shores of the Mediterranean and the Aegean, since the more southerly of the two Iranian successor-states of the Achaemenian Empire in Cappadocia succeeded in maintaining itself astride of the north-eastern branch.

2 The choice of Ecbatana for the summer residence of the Achaemenian Court was doubtless partly due to the coolness of its climate and partly to its historic prestige as the former capital of the Median Power which the Achaemenian Empire had supplanted. Under the Achaemenian régime, even after its reorganization by Darius I on a narrower political basis, the Medes were second only to the Persians in the hierarchy of imperial peoples. At the same time the selection of this site at a key-point on the Great North-East Road is also evidence of the high priority of the North-East Frontier among Achaemenian cares of state.

3 According to Herodotus, Book I, chap. 125, the House of Achaemenes was one of the septs of this Clan Pasargadae. Are we to infer that the Pasargadae had migrated from Lūristān to Fars either at the time of the acquisition of Fars by the Achaemenid king of Parsuwaš-and-Anšan, Teispes, or else at the time of its acquisition by Teispes' great-grandson the Cyran Achaemenid King of Parsuwaš-and-Anšan, Cyrus II?

4 The shock administered to the Persian people by their sudden overthrow from their high estate through the prowess of their Macedonian conquerors was so severe that it broke the continuity of their folk-memory; and, after forgetting that these sepulchres had been hewn and occupied by the greatest potentates of their own race, they expressed their continuing sense of wonder at the mightiness of these ancient monuments by naming the locality after a parvenu hero of an epic cycle which was perhaps of Saka origin (see V. v. 602–4). Even the crushing experience of 334–330 B.C. could hardly have produced so extreme a lapse of memory as this if the association of the Persian people in their homeland with the universal state which Persian hands had built had not been rather tenuous.

5 For a description see Herzfeld, E. E.: *Archaeological History of Iran* (London 1934, Milford), pp. 27–28. 'Such a plan cannot be called exactly a town. It looks more like the first settlement of nomads, and such in fact was the case.'

6 The imperial archives disinterred at Persepolis by twentieth-century Western archaeologists indicated that Persepolis had been built between these dates, and that the

constructed at the point where the gorge of the Pulvār opens out into the plain of Marv-Dasht[1] an imperial centre for the Persian people as a whole which, like the civic centres of the cantons of Gaul under the Roman Empire, came to be known by the name of the nation itself[2] and not of the locality in which it happened to have been laid out. The layout of this artificial capital was dominated by a magnificent audience hall,[3] but the visits paid by Achaemenian emperors to Persepolis and Pasargadae were as rare and brief as those paid by Hapsburg king-emperors to their royal palace at Buda or by sovereigns of the United Kingdom to their royal palace at Holyrood. The unusualness of the spectacle of an Achaemenian emperor giving audience in the stupendous *apadāna* looking out on to the plain of Marv-Dasht is attested by the handsomeness of the rare imperial visitor's customary atonement for his necessary misdemeanour of being a chronic absentee. Whenever an emperor did, for once, set foot on Persian ground, he used to give a gold piece to every woman of Pasargadae[4] or, as some Greek men of letters reported,[5] to every man and woman in the whole of Fars.

The munificence of this largesse could be afforded thanks to its infrequency. Persepolis remained unknown to the Hellenes before Alexander fought his way to the spot through a barrage of brigand tribesmen. Its name is not mentioned in the Babylonian, Jewish, Phoenician, or Egyptian records either;[6] and the only indication that Persepolis may after all have been of some political importance is the fact that Alexander felt it worth while to burn the place down. If the intention of this unworthy act of vandalism was to break the prestige and efface the memory of the imperial dynasty that Alexander was aspiring to supplant, he would have employed his destructive energies to better effect on the more arduous task of defacing the gigantic bas-relief and trilingual inscription, recording the mighty deeds of Darius the Great, which the second founder of the Achaemenian Empire had graven on the face of a precipitous cliff far up above the reach of any ordinary saboteur. But, if the Macedonian usurper had set out to destroy this all but impregnable monument, he would not have found it in Fars, but on a crag overhang-

work of construction had been most actively pressed forward between the years 503 and 497 B.C. (see Olmstead, op. cit., p. 176).

1 Olmstead (in op. cit., p. 172) conjectures that Darius's reason for abandoning Pasargadae was its association with the rival Cyran branch of the Imperial House.

2 'Pārsa-tya', in an inscription of Xerxes'. From this usage the Greeks coined the word 'Persepolis', but, in current Greek parlance, to go to this imperial centre of the Persian people was expressed simply as going ἐς Πέρσας (as a Gallo-Roman would say 'Parisios' instead of 'Lutetiam'). On this point see Meyer, E.: *Geschichte des Altertums*, vol. iii, 1st ed. (Stuttgart 1901, Cotta), pp. 31–32.

3 The Sasanidae followed the policy of the Achaemenidae in adorning their native Fars with magnificent monuments as a compensation for the removal of their seat of imperial government to a more convenient site. Eighteen out of twenty surviving Sasanian rock-sculptures were in Fars (Herzfeld, E.: *Archaeological History of Iran* (London 1935, Milford), p. 79).

4 'Whenever the Emperor of the Persians visits Pasargadae, he distributes a largesse of gold to the Persian women. The value of this donative amounts to twenty Attic drachmae per head' (Ctesias: *Persica*, Books IV–VI, p. 116 in J. Gilmore's edition (London 1888, Macmillan). Cp. Nicolaus of Damascus, fr. 65, in *Historici Graeci Minores*, ed. by Dindorf, L., vol. i (Leipzig 1870, Teubner), p. 63).

5 Xenophon: *Cyropaedia*, Book VIII, chap. v, § 21, and chap. vii, § 1; cp. Plato: *Leges*, Book III, 695 D, and Plutarch: *Life of Alexander*, chap. 69.

6 See Olmstead, op. cit., p. 162.

ing one of the stations on the Great North-East Road in the section where the imperial highway climbed the Zagros Range *en route* from Babylon to Ecbatana. In choosing a site for his own sepulchre, Darius might indulge his personal sentiment for the Persian crownland of his Ariaramnan Achaemenid ancestors, and in deciding where to lay out an imperial palace he might feel it politic to flatter the vanity of the imperial people on whose loyalty to his throne and house the stability of his empire and dynasty depended. But, in the location of a monument that was to serve neither piety nor policy but publicity, Darius showed the shrewdness of his judgement by putting his finger on the rock of Behistan, where his record would force itself on the attention of the maximum number of his subjects as they travelled on their lawful occasions along the busiest thoroughfare in his empire.

When the universal state that had been originally provided for the Syriac World by Persian empire-builders from the south-west corner of the Iranian Plateau was eventually reconstituted by Hijāzī empire-builders from the western rim of the Arabian Plateau, history repeated itself with emphasis. Thanks to the intuition of the discordant oligarchs of an oasis-state in the Hijāz, who had invited the rejected prophet of a rival community to make himself at home with them and try his hand at being their ruler, in the hope that he would bring them the concord which they had failed to attain by themselves, Yathrib became, within thirty years of the Hijrah, the capital of an empire embracing not only the former Roman dominions in Syria and Egypt but the entire domain of the former Sasanian Empire.[1] Yathrib's title to remain the seat of government for this vast realm was indisputable on its juridical merits. This remote oasis-state was the territorial nucleus out of which the Muslim Arab world-empire had burgeoned in its miraculously rapid growth, and it was now also hallowed as *Madīnat-an-Nabī*, the City of the Prophet which had recognized his mission and had furnished him with home, throne, and sepulchre. This title was so impressive that *de jure* Medina remained the capital of the Caliphate—at any rate until the foundation of Baghdad by the 'Abbasid Caliph Mansūr in A.D. 762.[2] Yet *de facto* the swiftly expanding dominions of the Prophet Muhammad and his successors were governed from Medina for no longer than thirty-four years; for the fact was that this oasis hidden away in the interior of the Arabian Plateau—a vaster, wilder, barer, emptier counterpart of the Plateau of Iran—had condemned itself to political nullity by the immensity of its political success.

It would have been still less practicable to rule 'the Fertile Crescent' and the Lower Nile Valley and the Upper Basin of the Oxus and Jaxartes from Medina than to rule them from Istakhr or Persepolis or Pasargadae. The last event in Medina's brief career as an operative

[1] Ibn Khaldūn suggests that the Primitive Muslim Arabs' success in conquering the whole of the Sasanian Empire was a consequence of their conquest of the Sasanian imperial capital Ctesiphon, and that their contemporary failure to conquer more than a portion of the Roman Empire was a consequence of their inability to conquer the Roman imperial capital Constantinople (see the *Muqaddamāt*, translated by de Slane, Baron McG. (Paris 1863–8, Imprimerie Impériale, 3 vols.), vol. i, p. 333).

[2] See pp. 148–50, above.

imperial capital was the assassination there of Muhammad's third Caliph Uthmān in A.D. 656. Thereafter, ʿAlī (*imperabat* A.D. 656–61) tried to rule the Caliphate from Kūfah, one of the cantonments of Arab tribal troops on the borderline between the Arabian Steppe and ʿIrāq, and Muʿāwīyah (*imperabat* A.D. 661–80) succeeded in ruling it from Damascus, on the borderline between the Arabian Steppe and Syria. Under the Umayyad régime Medina was never the *de facto* seat of government; it was the academic fastness of embittered orthodox exponents of the Islamic Law; and the usurping dynasty, in its wary handling of this impeccable hornet's nest, seldom allowed itself to be provoked into committing invidious acts of repression; it was usually able to dispose of the fulminations of the Medinese doctors of theology by the more elegant and baffling riposte of a mock-respectful disregard.

When the Umayyad usurpers were supplanted by the semi-legitimate ʿAbbasids, orthodox Medina's situation did not improve but deteriorated, for the road (if it could be called a road) from this West Arabian oasis to the ʿAbbasids' metropolitan territory in ʿIrāq was longer and more arduous than the road from Medina to Damascus. Moreover, the downfall of the Umayyads had put an end to that Arab hegemony in the Caliphate which, under the Umayyad régime, had been a link between the Desert and the Sown. The change of dynasty in the Caliphate was accompanied by a virtual secession of the badu of the Arabian Steppes;[1] and, though this break-away was less overt than the insurrection which had broken out after the death of the Prophet Muhammad, it was, unlike the *Riddah*, enduring in its effects. Medina was insulated from Baghdad by a Nomad no-man's-land; and, while the ʿAbbasid Caliphs might occasionally advertise their piety by visiting the Haramayn as pilgrims,[2] these imperial pilgrimages to a couple of oases at World's End, where a Commander of the Faithful had no political business to transact, were as infrequent as they were hazardous.

To judge by the experience of later, less august and, by the same token, less opulent Muslim pilgrims to the two principal holy cities of Islam, we may assume that the badu made Hārūn-ar-Rashīd and his ever more degenerate successors pay toll for the right of way across their steppes. Recalcitrant tribesmen are no respecters of persons; and we know for a fact that, when the Achaemenian emperors paid their occasional visits of family piety to Persepolis and Pasargadae from Susa, they had to pay toll to the wild highlanders commanding the mountain passes on their route for the privilege of travelling through to scatter their largesse among their own Persian kinsfolk in Fars. When these impudent Uxii[3] imprudently notified Alexander, on his arrival at their borders in

[1] See p. 149, n. 3, above.

[2] The stations on the two pilgrimage routes of the ʿAbbasid Age from ʿIrāq to the Hijāz—one route taking off into the Arabian steppe from Kūfah and the other from Basrah—are plotted out in Spruner-Menke: *Hand-Atlas für die Geschichte des Mittelalters und der Neueren Zeit*, 3rd. ed. (Gotha 1880, Perthes), Map 81.

[3] This was a Greek version of the name of a people which appears as Ūvjiyā (standing for Hūjiyā) in Old Persian. In the Achaemenian official lists of *dahyāva*, the land name Ūvja or Ūja (standing for Hūja) denotes Elam in the widest sense, including the Susian lowland as well as its highland hinterland. In a later age the same country continued to be known by the same name in the form Hūzistān (or Khūzistān), while its latter-day

331 B.C., that they would not let him pass either unless he paid them their customary fee, the conqueror gave the blackmailers the surprise of their lives;[1] and thereafter, in the winter of 324–323 B.C., he diverted himself by conducting a miniature lightning campaign against the Uxians' north-western neighbours and fellow brigands the Kassites,[2] who had likewise acquired a customary right of levying blackmail—presumably also, like the Uxii, from the Achaemenian Emperor himself, since the Kassites' highland fastness lay astride the direct road from Susa to Ecbatana.[3]

Migrations of the Capital Cities of Marchmen Empire-builders

We may now pass from empires founded by barbarians like the Primitive Muslim Arabs, or by barbaro-marchmen like the Persian henchmen of the Achaemenidae and the Manchu conquerors of China, to empires

capital (the provincial successor of an imperial Susa) was called Ahwāz, the Arabic plural of Hūz, which was the singular of an ethnikon corresponding to the old Persian Hūjiyā.

1 See Arrian: *Expeditio Alexandri*, Book III, chap. xvii. If these uncouth brigands of the Southern Zagros had been as ready-witted as the accomplished Tyrrhenian pirate, they might have taken a verbal revenge for their military discomfiture by pointing out to Alexander that he was engaged in a larger way in the same trade that they were practising on a petty scale (see the story as told by Saint Augustine: *De Civitate Dei*, Book IV, chap. 4, and translated in XI. ix. 223, n. 1).

2 See Arrian: *Expeditio Alexandri*, Book VII, chap. xv, §§ 1–3.

3 The Kassites' customary right to take toll from august travellers seeking passage through their country was flouted in 317 B.C. by Antigonus, as the Uxians' had been by Alexander in 331 B.C., but the sequel was not the same, for this time it was the Macedonian war-lord who was given the surprise of his life by the Iranian mountaineers. Antigonus, confronted with the problem of rapidly extricating his troops from a precarious military situation and a formidably high summer temperature in the lowlands of Elam, had decided to evacuate them to Media—the nearest quarter of the Iranian Plateau—to recuperate and refit. For reaching this destination, he had a choice of two alternative routes: a detour, estimated to involve a forty days' march, for the most part through sultry lowlands, or a short cut, amounting to no more than a nine days' march, through the cool highlands of the Kassite country. The detour would have taken him from Susa along the north-east alinement of the Great North-West Road to a point where this road crossed the Babylon–Ecbatana section of the Great North-East Road, and from there he would have marched to Ecbatana, past the rock of Behistan, along the main highway of the Achaemenian Empire. Diodorus Siculus's source rightly characterizes the detour as being καλὴ καὶ βασιλική. The short cut through the Kassite country was presumably the Ecbatana–Susa diversion of the Great North-East Road of which the proper south-western terminus was not Susa but Babylon. Against advice, Antigonus insisted both on taking the short cut through the Kassites' country and on trying to force his passage without purchasing the tribesmen's acquiescence. The Kassites did not get their money, but they made their redoubtable visitor pay dear in soldiers' lives (Diodorus Siculus: Book XIX, chap. 19). So much for the effect of Alexander's flamboyant chastisement of the Kassites only five and a half years before! It is easier to chastise wild tribesmen than to break their spirit or change their habits, as empire-builders have discovered in many different areas and ages. Tribesmen, like bayonets, are awkward to sit on.

When the Ūvjiyā and the Kassites felt the disconcerting weight of Alexander's arm, they could hearten themselves by recalling that they and their ancestors had survived many previous punitive expeditions of the kind (ignorant though they were of Naramsin's stele portraying him chastising the Gutaeans). The Kassites had, indeed, been sitting, unscotched, in their local fastness in the Zagros since at least as early as the eighteenth century B.C., and a detachment of their braves had made history by descending on a Land of Shinar which Hammurabi had just exhausted in the act of re-establishing the Empire of Sumer and Akkad by main force. This momentarily resuscitated Sumeric universal state had come and gone, but the Kassites had battened on their Babylonian prey for five or six hundred years (see I. i. 111). At the time of writing the social condition of this corner of Iran was much like what it had been in the eighteenth century B.C. and in the fourth. In the twentieth century of the Christian Era the Kassites called themselves 'Lūrs' and the Uxii 'Bakhtīyārīs'.

founded by marchmen who were genuine, though rustic, members of the society which they furnished with a universal state. In such cases likewise the normal tendency, as we have noted by anticipation,[1] is for the seat of imperial government to travel from the site of the former parochial capital of the empire-building march-state to some new site nearer the heart of the civilization whose whole domain has now been united politically. A classical illustration of this tendency is afforded by the course of Sinic history.

The cradle of the Sinic Civilization had been the great plain which lay between 'the Country within the Passes' on the west and the hill-country of Shantung on the east, and which was inundated by the waters of the Yellow River in the lower part of its course;[2] but, at an early date, a secondary centre had arisen in the little plain watered by the lower course of the River Wei,[3] the principal right-bank tributary of the Yellow River, which joins the main stream just at the point where the Yellow River bends, in an acute angle, from a south-by-westerly to an east-by-northerly course and forces its way through the mountain barrier that separates the little western plain 'within the passes' from the Great Eastern Plain which was the heart of the Sinic World.

The empire-building march-state Ts'in had started its career as a western outpost of the Sinic World far up the Wei Valley, but, after centuries of progressive expansion, its capital had come—by the time when Ts'in She Hwang-ti united the Sinic World politically by conquering and annexing Ts'in's six rivals[4]—to be located at Hsien Yang, on the left bank of the Lower Wei near the western end of the little western plain 'within the passes'; and Ts'in She Hwang-ti retained this existing capital of his hereditary kingdom as the seat of government for his newly established universal state.[5] Upon the overthrow of the Ts'in régime after Ts'in She Hwang-ti's death and the capture of Hsien Yang by Liu Pang,[6] the former capital of the Ts'in Power was laid waste in cold blood by the arch-rebel Hsiang-yü.[7] This aristocrat had inherited an implacable hatred of Ts'in and all its works from forebears who had been hereditary dignitaries of the state of Ch'u, Ts'in's principal rival.[8] The peasant-born founder of the Han Dynasty had no such vested interest in the vendettas of a dead feudal past. When he had occupied Hsien Yang in 207 B.C. and thereby brought the Ts'in régime to an end, he had achieved this *coup* by the combination of a politic clemency with military force, and had been content to spare the stones and timbers of the city as well as the life of the last Ts'in emperor, when once the latter had resigned the insignia of the imperial office.[9] When, after his successful issue from his inevitable settlement of accounts with Hsiang-yü, Han Liu Pang found himself sole master of the Sinic World, he followed in the footsteps of his Ts'in forerunners, not only in keeping the whole of 'the Country within the Passes' under his own direct administration,[10]

[1] On p. 194, above.
[2] See I. i. 90 and 318–21, and xi, map 25.
[3] See II. ii. 118–19, and xi, map 26.
[4] See p. 167, above.
[5] See p. 171, n. 2, above.
[6] See p. 171, above.
[7] See Franke, O.: *Geschichte des Chinesischen Reiches*, vol. i (Berlin and Leipzig 1930, de Gruyter), p. 259.
[8] See p. 171, above.
[9] See Franke, op. cit., vol. cit., p. 258.
[10] See p. 173, above.

but in locating his seat of government at the western end of the little plain of the Lower Wei. Ch'ang Ngan, where Han Liu Pang laid out his new capital, lay near the right bank of the Wei just opposite the devastated site of Hsien Yang on the farther side of the river.

This avatar of the capital of Ts'in remained the capital of the Han Empire for the duration of the Prior Han Dynasty (*imperabant* 202 B.C.–A.D. 9). When, however, after the interregnum arising from the usurpation of Wang Mang (*dominabatur* A.D. 9–23),[1] the Empire was reinstated by the Posterior Han Dynasty (*imperabant* A.D. 25–221), the seat of government was transferred by them from Ch'ang Ngan in the Lower Wei Valley, just 'within the passes', to Loyang, just outside the passes, on the western verge of the Great Eastern Plain, in the lower valley of the River Lo, which was the next right-bank tributary of the Yellow River below the Wei.[2]

This site, just within the plain that was the heart of the Sinic World, was already historic ground by the time when the Posterior Han decided to plant their capital there. The transfer of the seat of government of the Han régime that was made in A.D. 25 had been anticipated in 770 B.C.,[3] when the Chóu Dynasty had evacuated their previous capital 'within the passes' at Tsung Chóu (a few miles to the south-west of the subsequent site of Ch'ang Ngan) after it had been sacked in 771 B.C. by barbarian raiders from the west, and had taken refuge at Loyang, which had previously been no more than a secondary seat of theirs.[4] Moreover, before the Chóu had established this at first subsidiary

[1] See V. vi. 295.

[2] See II. ii. 119.

[3] See Hirth, F.: *The Ancient History of China* (New York 1908, Columbia University Press), p. 176.

[4] The political sequels of these two coincident shifts in the location of the seat of government of the Sinic World were not the same. When made in A.D. 25, the transfer of the capital gave the Han régime a new lease of life; when made in 770 B.C., it resulted in the Chóu Dynasty's becoming *rois fainéants* who lingered on, in a miniature imperial domain and with merely ceremonial functions, till they were snuffed out by Ts'in She Hwang-ti's grandfather Kung Chao Hsiang of Ts'in in 256–249 B.C. The histories of the Chóu and Ts'in dynasties had, however, run almost exactly parallel in an earlier chapter, and, even in the last chapter, the two denouements resembled one another in being, both of them, ironic.

Either dynasty had started its career as a western outpost of the Sinic World in the upper reaches of the Wei Basin. Both of them had subsequently moved their seat of government down into the little plain of the Lower Wei (Chóu perhaps in 1150 B.C., Ts'in after 770 B.C.). Both had then broken out of their western march-state 'within the passes' and had conquered the heart of the Sinic World on the Great Eastern Plain: Ts'in She Hwang-ti's overthrow of Ts'in's six eastern rivals in 230–221 B.C. had its precedent in Chóu Wu Wang's overthrow of the Shang (*alias* Yin) Power on the Great Eastern Plain at some date, not precisely determinable, between 1122 B.C. (the traditional dating) and about 1050 B.C. In the next chapter the two histories diverged. The Chóu Dynasty attempted to organize the government of its eastern conquests by devolution on feudal lines, and thereby reduced itself, by stages, to impotence: the first shock was suffered by the Chóu Power in 841 B.C., the second in 771–770 B.C., and the end came in 249 B.C. Warned (we may guess) by the miscarriage of the Chóu Dynasty's policy, Ts'in She Hwang-ti sought to confirm his hold on his eastern conquests by a policy of extreme *Gleichschaltung* and centralization, and thereby defeated his own personal and dynastic ends by provoking a violent reaction which extinguished the Ts'in Power for ever within three years of the First Ts'in Emperor's death. Thanks, however, to the genius of Han Liu Pang and to the hardly less notable statesmanship of the founder of the Posterior Han Dynasty, Kwang Wuti, Ts'in She Hwang-ti's empire and system of government lasted, in a modified and on that account more practically effective form, for nearly four hundred years—from Ts'in She Hwang-ti's death in 210 B.C. to the decay of the Posterior Han Power towards the close of the second century of the Christian Era (see II. ii. 118–19).

western seat of theirs at Loyang, the neighbourhood had already been a focus of political power. A site a few miles farther down the course of the Lo River, not far from its junction with the Yellow River, had been one of the successive capitals of the Shang (*alias* Yin) Dynasty, which had ruled in the Great Eastern Plain before the Chóu had descended from 'the Country within the Passes' and had brought this Shang régime to an end.[1]

In the history of the main body of the Far Eastern Society that was affiliated to the Sinic Civilization, this episode of the transfer of a seat of government from the little western plain in the Wei Basin to the Great Eastern Plain repeated itself after the evocation of a ghost of the Sinic universal state by the Sui Dynasty.[2] The Sui, and the T'ang after them, located the capital of a politically united China at Si Ngan (the latter-day Sian-fu),[3] on a site adjoining that of Ch'ang Ngan; and the capital of this resuscitation of the Ts'in and Han Empire remained at this spot as long as the Sui and T'ang dynasties endured (*imperabant* A.D. 589–907). But, after an interregnum following the decay of the T'ang Power that had set in before the close of the ninth century of the Christian Era, the reunion of all but a fraction of the former dominions of the T'ang[4] by the Sung Dynasty in A.D. 960 was accompanied by an eastward shift in the seat of government[5] along the historic west–east axis. This time, Loyang was not the beneficiary; under the Sung régime she did not re-emerge from the secondary position that she had occupied under the T'ang.[6] The Sung laid out their capital more than a hundred miles farther to the east, at Kaifêng, in the middle of the Great Eastern Plain, and not on its western verge.

The course of empire in the Yellow River Basin had had a parallel in

[1] By the time of writing, archaeological discoveries had confirmed the Sinic literary tradition by producing independent evidence for the existence of the Shang culture (see xi, map 25) on the Great Eastern Plain in the second millennium B.C. (The authenticity of the Hsia Dynasty, which was the traditional precursor of the Shang, still remained to be proved.) The capital of the Shang Power was traditionally recorded to have lain in the Lower Lo Valley from 1386 to 1198 B.C. During the last phase of the Shang régime, traditionally dated 1198–1122 B.C., the seat of government was recorded to have lain farther to the north-east, at Mo (see xi, map 25), on the main northern arm of the Lower Yellow River itself. After the overthrow of the Shang Empire, the dynasty survived as hereditary princes of the parochial state of Sung (see xi, map 25) to the east of Loyang in the upper basin of the Huai River. During the Sinic Time of Troubles that resulted from the decay of the Chóu Power, Sung was one of those little states in the centre of the Sinic World which were the stakes in the contest for hegemony between the great states on the fringes.

[2] For this achievement of the Sui Dynasty, and its prolongation by their successors the T'ang, see II. ii. 120; pp. 19–21, above; and X. ix. 16.

[3] See II. ii. 120.

[4] Though inconsiderable in area compared with the total extent of the main body of the Far Eastern World, this fragment of former T'ang territory which the Sung failed to reincorporate into the reunited empire was strategically and historically important. The sixteen districts of which it consisted (see II. ii. 121) lay just within the Great Wall and included the site of the future imperial city of Peking at the northern extremity of the Great Eastern Plain. The Khitan Nomad barbarians, to whom this fragment of territory had been ceded, *circa* A.D. 927–37, during the post-T'ang interregnum, chose this site for their southern residence and thus prepared the way for it to become the capital of their successors the Kin, after these had shifted the centre of gravity of their dominions southward by conquering the Yellow River Basin from the Sung in A.D. 1124–42 (see V. vi. 307).

[5] See II. ii. loc. cit.

[6] At the time of writing, Loyang was serving, under the name of Honan-fu, as the local centre of administration of the central province of Northern China.

the Nile Valley below the First Cataract.[1] In Egyptiac as in Sinic and Far Eastern history, political unity was conferred—or imposed—on the society no less than three times over by a march-state starting from a base of operations up-river;[2] and in Egyptiac history likewise the aggrandisement of a march into a universal state was followed on each occasion by a shift in the location of the seat of government from the former parochial capital of the empire-building marchmen to a new site nearer to the heart of the domain of the politically unified society.

The foundation, *circa* 3100 B.C., of a united kingdom of Upper and Lower Egypt was achieved by empire-builders from the extreme south of the Egyptiac World of the day, in the neighbourhood of the modern Al-Kāb,[3] between Thebes and the First Cataract. The political union, from this base of operations, of the whole of the Lower Nile Basin between the First Cataract and the Mediterranean was immediately followed by a northward shift of the seat of power. The Hieraconpolite empire-builders established their imperial residence at Thinis, and their necropolis at Abydos on the opposite bank of the Nile, down-stream from their ancestral canton; and the *de facto* centre of imperial administration seems soon to have moved on still farther down-stream to Memphis.[4] Thereafter, this ideally convenient site, at the point of junction between the mouth of the Nile Valley and the head of the Delta, remained the seat of government of 'the Old Kingdom' to the end. The *de facto* capital of its spring-time became the *de jure* capital of its summer, when the Thinites were followed by the pyramid-builders of the Third and Fourth Dynasties;[5] and, when summer passed over into autumn, Memphis was still the place from which the demonic pyramid-builders' pious Heliopolitan successors attempted to exert their gradually diminishing authority.[6]

After the Time of Troubles following 'the Old Kingdom's' collapse, the establishment, *circa* 2052 B.C., of an Egyptiac universal state by a prince of the southern march-state of Thebes was similarly followed, in the reign of the Emperor Amenemhat I (*imperabat circa* 1991–1962 B.C.), by a transfer of the capital of 'the Middle Empire' from Thebes to a site, only a few miles up-stream from Memphis, which its founder named 'the Conqueror of the Two Lands' (*Egyptiacè* 'Iz-Taui').[7] Though Thebes was slightly less remote than Al-Kāb had been

[1] This parallel has been pointed out, in another connexion, in II. ii. 118.

[2] See I. i. 140, n. 2, and II. ii. 112–13.

[3] The nucleus of the 'nome' (canton) which was the original domain of these Horus-worshipping empire-builders consisted of a pair of cities facing one another across the Nile: Necheb (*Graecè* 'Eileithuia') on the site of the modern Al-Kāb on the east bank of the Nile, and Nechen (*Graecè* 'Hieracônpolis', in allusion to the hawk ('hierax') which was both the heraldic emblem of the city and the symbol of its god Horus) on the west bank). (See Hall, H. R.: *The Ancient History of the Near East* (London 1913, Methuen), pp. 93–94; Meyer, E.: *Geschichte des Altertums*, vol. i, Part II, 3rd ed. (Stuttgart and Berlin 1913, Cotta), pp. 80 and 111).

[4] See Hall, op. cit., pp. 108–9; Meyer, op. cit., vol. cit., ed. cit., p. 134.

[5] See Meyer, ibid., p. 169.

[6] It is significant that, whereas the Thinites were buried at Abydos, far up the Nile Valley though not so far as Al-Kāb, the Heliopolitans as well as the pyramid-builders chose the neighbourhood of Memphis for the site of their sepulchres (see ibid. pp. 132 and 202–3).

[7] See ibid., p. 267.

from the heart of the Egyptiac World, the gravitational pull of the body social which Theban prowess had reunited proved once again so strong that Thebes on this occasion, like Al-Kāb before her, had to pay for her political achievement by ceasing to be the seat of government of the oecumenical polity which she had called into existence. When, however, after an abortive interregnum,[1] the Egyptiac universal state was restored *circa* 1570 B.C. by another prince of Thebes, as a result of his triumph in a holy war of liberation against the hated alien Hyksos conquerors of Lower Egypt, the power and prestige of Thebes stood so high that this time she was able to resist successfully, for more than two hundred years,[2] the gravitational pull which made itself felt again now that the Egyptiac World was for the third time politically united.

'[The] structure of "the New Empire" presents a very peculiar picture: the seat of government lies far away from the geographical centre in the southernmost part of the [Egyptiac] Civilization's domain, 700 kilometres above Memphis and only 200 kilometres below the frontier at the First Cataract, as the Nile flows [and not as the crow flies]. This makes the impression of a defiance of the conditions set by Nature. . . . In terms of the Kingdom of Prussia,[3] it is as though the seat of government had lain at Königsberg [instead of at Berlin]. . . . The distortion is not appreciably abated by the fact that Nubia has now once again been incorporated into the permanent domain of the empire. This unnaturalness of "the New Empire's" structure bears striking testimony to the truth that the [Eighteenth] Dynasty's hereditary dominions were, and continued to be, the source of the dynasty's strength.'[4]

In this instance, Nature proved unable to reassert herself till a man of genius came to her aid. Applying his revolutionary philosophy consistently, as he did, to every side of life, the Emperor Ikhnaton (*imperabat circa* 1380–1362 B.C.)[5] not only deposed the god Amon-Re of Thebes from his established primacy in the Egyptiac pantheon in favour of an etherialized sun-disk; he also transferred his capital from Thebes to Tall-al-ʿAmarnah, about half-way, as the Nile flows, from Thebes to Memphis. Ikhnaton, like Ts'in She Hwang-ti and Akbar, defeated his own ends by going to extremes that provoked an overwhelming reaction.[6] What can a solitary philosopher-king achieve against the cumulative momentum of a cultural tradition? Ikhnaton's Tell-el-Amarna suffered the fate of Akbar's Fātihpūr Sīkrī. Yet Ikhnaton's discomfiture did not enable Thebes to recapture her geographically unnatural prerogative of serving as the seat of imperial government for a united Egyptiac World. Under Horemheb (*imperabat de facto circa* 1349–1319 B.C.) a still united Egyptiac World was ruled once again from its geographical centre at

[1] See I. i. 137–9.

[2] See p. 176, above. It is worth noticing that this was about the length of time for which, in a Sinic World politically united under the Han régime, Ch'ang Ngan 'within the passes' succeeded in resisting the gravitational pull on the seat of government which eventually caused the capital to travel to Loyang, on the verge of the Great Eastern Plain.

[3] Presumably the writer is thinking of Prussia within the frontiers of A.D. 1866–1918.—A.J.T.

[4] Meyer, E.: *Geschichte des Altertums*, vol. ii, Part I, 2nd ed. (Stuttgart and Berlin 1928, Cotta), p. 60.

[5] Or, on another reckoning, *circa* 1370–1352 B.C.

[6] See I. i. 145–6 and V. v. 695–6.

Memphis; but this time the victory of the interior over the marches was as short-lived as it had been long-delayed. In the next chapter of Egyptiac history the seat of imperial government was prised out, split, and polarized by pressures of unequal magnitude from beyond the frontiers. Two major pressures from the north-east and the north-west drew the principal capital away into the Delta, while a secondary capital arose at Napata, near the foot of the Fourth Cataract, which, under 'the New Empire', had superseded Thebes and Al-Kāb as the southern bulwark of an Egyptiac World that had now expanded southward to take in Nubia.[1]

In Hellenic history the fortunes of Rome are reminiscent of those of Egyptiac Thebes. Rome had won her spurs by taking over from the Etruscans the wardenship of the Italian marches of the Hellenic World over against the Gauls,[2] as Thebes had won hers by taking over from Al-Kāb the wardenship of the First Cataract of the Nile over against the barbarians of Nubia. Like Thebes, again, Rome had afterwards turned her arms inwards and imposed political unity on the society of which she was a member. At the same time the geographical location of Rome in the empire which she eventually gathered round her was so much more central than that of Thebes in either 'the Middle Empire' or 'the New Empire' that Rome might have been expected to remain the seat of the Roman imperial government as long as the Roman Empire lasted. The Roman Empire was, in geographical terms, a Pan-Mediterranean 'thalassocracy', and Rome's own situation at the mid-point of the west coast of Italy, on the banks of a river which was navigable up to Rome by the sea-going vessels of the day, was not far from being the geographically ideal site for the capital of an empire embracing all the shores of the Mediterranean and holding this ring of continental provinces together by a network of maritime communications.[3] As a Greek man of letters, writing in the age of the Antonines, expressed it in an invocation to Rome and the Romans,

> 'The sea stretches in a belt across the middle of the Inhabited World and across the middle of your empire; and round the sea the continents extend "grand and grandly"—continually supplying your needs with consignments of their products.'[4]

Nevertheless, Rome, like Thebes, did eventually lose her imperial pre-

[1] See II. ii. 113–15.

[2] See II. ii. 161.

[3] In a Pan-Mediterranean 'thalassocracy' the ideal seat of imperial government, corresponding to Memphis in the fluvial Egyptiac World, would be one or other of two sites in Sicily—Messina and Marsala—which command respectively the narrower and the wider of the two straits through which the south-eastern and the north-western basins of the Mediterranean communicate with one another. The despots who imposed an imperfect and precarious political unity on the Greek city-states in Sicily and the toe of Italy in the fifth and fourth centuries B.C. (see III. iii. 357, n. 1) had never possessed a sufficient surplus of power to enable them to unite the whole Hellenic World, not to speak of the whole circumference of the Mediterranean, round a Sicilian political centre. Syracuse was the capital of a Mediterranean thalassocracy for the first and last time during the residence there of the Roman Emperor Constans II in the years A.D. 663/4–8 (see IV. iv. 330–1 and 589–91).

[4] Aristeides, P. Aelius: *In Romam*, §§ 10–11 (*Aelii Aristidis Quae Supersunt Omnia*, edidit B. Keil (Berlin 1898, Weidmann, 2 vols.), vol. ii, p. 94), quoted on p. 81, n. 2, above.

rogative of serving as the seat of government for an empire which she herself had created.

While Rome lay not far from the centre of the Mediterranean Basin, she was by no means so centrally situated from the standpoint of an Hellenic World of which she was ostensibly the mistress but in the last resort the servant. The Hellenic Civilization had grown up round the shores, not of the Mediterranean, but of the Aegean, which was a north-eastern bay of the larger sea that, for the Romans, was *mare nostrum*; and, though, by the time when the Roman Empire was established, Continental European Greece had lost its former military, political, and economic pre-eminence, the Hellenic and Hellenized provinces of the Empire in Anatolia and Syria were gaining steadily in population and wealth, while Italy, which had conquered the Mediterranean Basin largely in virtue of her then abundant man-power, began, under the *Pax Augusta*, to fall into the same decline as Greece.[1] Accordingly, under the Roman Empire, though Greek influence continued to radiate into Italy, and Rome herself became for a time a predominantly Greek-speaking city,[2] the centre of gravity of the Hellenic World travelled away from the Aegean Basin, not north-westward towards Rome, but south-eastward towards Antioch and Alexandria. At the same time the centre of gravity of the Empire—which was a hollow ring of land encircling the Mediterranean—was travelling northwards owing to the doubling of the thickness of this ring on its northern side through the annexation of Britain, Gallia Comata, the Danubian provinces, and Cappadocia between the years 58 B.C. and A.D. 84.

These two gradual but persistent displacements of the Empire's economic and social centre of gravity were already exerting a gravitational pull upon the imperial seat of government when, in the third century of the Christian Era, their effect was suddenly and violently accentuated by pressures from beyond the frontiers: a pressure on the Euphrates from the aggressive Sasanian Power that had replaced the lethargic Arsacidae; a pressure on the Lower Danube from semi-nomadicized North European barbarian intruders on the Great Western Bay of the Eurasian Steppe;[3] and a pressure on the Rhine and on the Rhine–Danube *limes* from local sedentary barbarians who had made themselves more formidable neighbours by learning something of the Roman arts of war and of state-building. Through the play of these divers social forces the seat of government of the Roman Empire, like that of the Egyptiac 'New Empire', was prised up, split, and polarized.

[1] This decay of Italy can be traced back to the social effects of the devastation produced by the Hannibalic War (see I. i. 40), and, in Italy south of the Appennines, these effects had already become alarming by the generation of Tiberius Gracchus (*tribunatum plebis gerebat* 131 B.C.). The depopulation of Peninsular Italy was, however, counterbalanced at that stage by the colonization of the Po Basin, and, largely on this account, the relative decline of Italy as a whole, within the Alpine boundaries conferred on her by Augustus, did not begin to become pronounced until about the second century of the Roman Empire's existence, during 'the Indian Summer' of the Antonine Age.

[2] 'Non possum ferre, Quirites, Graecam urbem' (Juvenal: *Satires*, No. III, ll. 60–61, quoted already in V. v. 67) is merely an exaggeration of a truth which is attested, for example, by the extant works of the Christian Father Hippolytus, who lived in Rome and wrote in Greek in the third century of the Christian Era.

[3] See III. iii. 399 and 426–8.

In this case the principal capital was drawn away eastward from the banks of the Tiber to the shores of the Bosphorus. Diocletian was governing the Empire from Nicomedia, at the point where the road from the Asiatic shore of the Bosphorus leaves the sea behind and plunges into the interior of Anatolia, when he gave the signal, in A.D. 303, for the launching of an oecumenical campaign to extirpate the Christian Church. Constantine laid out his New Rome on the European shore of the Bosphorus, on the site of the Greek city of Byzantium,[1] in A.D. 324. Simultaneously a secondary capital likewise detached itself from Rome and then travelled, not eastward, but north-westward—lingering at Milan and coming to a halt at Trier.[2]

Of all the sites open for consideration by any ruler of the Roman Empire who had once shaken himself free from a traditional inhibition against moving the capital from Rome herself, a site on or near the Bosphorus offered the greatest combination of political advantages in the social and strategic circumstances of Diocletian's and Constantine's day. In a city with a harbour opening on to the narrow seas through which the Black Sea communicated with the Aegean, the imperial government would find itself within easier reach of the original heart of a maritime Hellenic World. At the same time it would find itself posted midway between the two frontiers—the Lower Danube and the Middle Euphrates—which in that age headed the list of its military anxieties, while at its doors, in Thrace and Illyricum, would lie the main reservoir of military man-power from which the Empire was now recruiting its armies. The cumulative weight of these considerations was decisive, and a secondary capital in the basin of the Po or the Moselle was necessary merely for looking after those economically backward ex-barbarian provinces in the far west, from Britain to Morocco inclusive, which could not be directly controlled by way of either the sea-routes or the land-routes that radiated out from Constantinople.

At the turn of the third and fourth centuries of the Christian Era the transfer of the principal capital of the Roman Empire from Rome to Constantinople or to some maritime city in that neighbourhood was, in fact, inevitable. But it is remarkable to find evidence that, more than three hundred years earlier, when Rome was towering at the zenith of her power under the auspices of Julius Caesar and Augustus, the Romans were already anxiously foreboding a shift in the seat of the imperial government, and were expecting that the Roman dictator with whom the decision of Rome's destinies now lay would choose his new site in that very region—on or near the shores of the waterway between the Aegean and the Black Sea—which did in fact eventually attract the choice of Diocletian and Constantine.

One of the causes of the unpopularity that gave Julius Caesar's enemies at Rome their opportunity for compassing his death was said to have been a rumour that he was proposing 'to migrate to Alexandria [Troas] or Ilium and at the same time to transfer thither the empire's

[1] The navigational advantages which had previously made Byzantium a key-point in the Hellenic system of maritime communications have been examined in II. ii. 43–48.

[2] See II. ii. 164.

resources after exhausting Italy by levies of man-power and leaving friends of his own as his agents for administering the city of Rome'.[1] This anecdote might have been discounted as an echo of a malicious propaganda campaign were it not for a revelation of the same anxiety in a celebrated passage in one of Horace's odes.[2] The Augustan poet must have written these lines not many years after the Battle of Actium had disposed of the Egyptian Alexandria's attempt to challenge, with Roman arms, Rome's title to be the imperial capital of a politically unified Hellenic World. At that moment[3] Rome stood in solitary omnipotence without any rival to dispute her primacy; and Augustus, who had at last succeeded in winning the support of a *consensus Italiae* by defeating Mark Antony's attempt to transfer the seat of government of the Mediterranean World to the Levant, could not readily be suspected, without substantial evidence, of planning to make on his own initiative a move which had proved a fatal false step for his rival and a damaging insinuation against his predecessor. One of the fundamental principles of Augustus's policy was to steer clear of his adoptive father's fate by eschewing provocatively revolutionary acts and pursuing Caesarean aims by Fabian tactics. Yet it is plain that Horace, writing when and as he did, believed a transfer of the capital of the Roman Empire from Rome to some site on the Asiatic shore of the Hellespont to be both a serious possibility and a dangerous subject. Horace tactfully misrepresents a cold-blooded 'geopolitical' calculation as a pious tribute to the legendary derivation of Rome from Troy, and, after cautiously expressing his disapproval in the form of a mythological conceit, he precipitately breaks off with an apology for trespassing on high matters of state in a mere poet's *jeu d'esprit*.

In the political geography of the Roman Empire,[4] Troy or Alexandria Troas were the equivalents in Augustus's day of Nicomedia or Byzantium in Diocletian's and Constantine's;[5] and the whimsical prophecy, put

[1] Or 'the cities of Italy' if the correct reading is not 'Urbis' but 'urbium'. This passage occurs in Suetonius Tranquillus, C. : *The Lives of the Caesars*, 'Divus Iulius', chap. 79.

[2] Horace: *Carmina*, Book III, Ode iii, ll. 57–72.

[3] This challenge, and the abiding resentment of the Greek citizens of Alexandria Aegyptiaca at their city's defeat in her audacious trial of strength with her great Italian rival, have been touched upon in V. vi. 37, n. 1, and 217–19.

[4] See xi, maps 28 and 29.

[5] Before the addition to the Roman Empire of the continental northern tier of provinces from Britain to Cappadocia inclusive (see p. 217, above), the main route from the European to the Asiatic territories of the Empire had run from Rome via the Via Appia to Brundisium, had crossed the mouth of the Adriatic by a sea-passage to Dyrrhachium or Apollonia, and had then followed the Via Egnatia, via Thessalonica and Lysimacheia, to the Hellespont. By Diocletian's day the corresponding main route had come to be an unbroken overland highway running from Lyons via Milan and Aquileia (or even north of the Alps, from Trier via Augsburg and Vienna) to Belgrade, and thence south-eastwards, up the valley of the Morava and down the valley of the Maritsa, to the Bosphorus. As late as the year A.D. 360, when the Rhine–Danube *limes* had long since been submerged and when Swabia was in the hands of the independent and aggressive barbarian confederacy of the Alemanni, the Emperor Julian took the route north of the Alps in his march upon Constantinople from Northern Gaul. Yet, although by Constantine's day the Bosphorus had thus supplanted the Hellespont in the role of affording the most convenient passage across the narrow seas between Roman Europe and Roman Asia, Constantine is said to have started to build his new imperial capital on a site commanding the Asiatic shore of the Hellespont, at a point between Alexandria Troas and Ilium, before arriving at his eventual decision in favour of a site commanding the European shore of the Bosphorus (see Zosimus: *Historiae*, Book II, chap. xxx, §§ 2–3).

by Horace into the goddess Juno's mouth, that, if Troy were to be refounded by the Romans, she would infallibly be recaptured by the Greeks, did in fact come true of Byzantium after her refoundation as a New Rome by Constantine. Though the Latin-speaking Dardanian founder of Constantinople and his successors down to his Latin-speaking fellow countryman Justinian were resolved to make and keep their new Rome a Latin-speaking city,[1] the Greek language had captured the New Rome by the close of the sixth century of the Christian Era, as it had captured the Old Rome in Juvenal's time, some four hundred years earlier; and at Constantinople, with its Greek-speaking hinterland, the Latin language had no chance of repeating the victorious counter-attack by which at Rome it eventually overwhelmed what had never been more than a Greek-speaking enclave in an elsewhere Latin-speaking Italy.

Unlike Rome and Thebes, both Moscow and Yedo successfully avoided the fate of seeing the imperial throne removed from their precincts and permanently transferred to another site, and in both cases this difference of fortune was due to the same cause. Though Moscow and Yedo were on a par with Rome and Thebes in starting their careers as capitals of march-states which became the nuclei of universal states, and, though again, in both pairs of cases alike, the former march was afterwards relegated to the interior in consequence of a victorious expansion of the society into what had previously been barbarian territory beyond the pale, the eventual sequel was not the same. After Moscow and Yedo had thus changed their relative positions in their respective worlds from a former situation near the edge to a latter-day situation much nearer the centre, the advantage of this change for the purpose of serving as the seat of an oecumenical government was not counteracted in either case by the pressure of hostile forces from beyond the new frontiers which the expansion of the society had called into existence. Neither the Japanese World in its northward expansion up the Main Island of Japan and over the Tsugaru Straits into Hokkaido nor the Russian World in its eastward expansion across the Ural Mountains into Siberia ran into such formidable military commitments as those which Rome, for example, eventually incurred as a result of having expanded her dominions from the line of the Appennines to the line of the Rhine and the Danube.

For this reason the locus, half-way up the eastern seaboard of the Main Island of Japan, which became a seat of abortive oecumenical government at the site named Kamakura during the Japanese Time of Troubles and a seat of effective oecumenical government at the site named Yedo after the foundation of the Tokugawa Shogunate, succeeded in retaining its prerogative for the duration of the Tokugawa régime; and, thanks to Japan's being an archipelago in which Yedo, like every other important centre of population, lay almost within a stone's throw of the sea, the site which had proved itself a convenient seat of government for an insulated Japanese universal state did not forfeit its prerogative when Commodore Perry's expedition, by demonstrating that Japan no longer had it in her power to go on living in isolation as

[1] See V. vi. 224.

a self-contained social universe, precipitated a revolution which sought to transform Japan into a parochial state member of a world-wide society within a Western framework. Yokohama, the port of Yedo, was as handy for sea communications with North America or Western Europe as Kobe or Nagasaki; and therefore Japan's decision to open her doors to the West did not confront her with a geographical as well as a cultural problem. The cultural volte-face of the Meiji Revolution did not require any change in the existing capital except a ceremonial change of name from Yedo to Tokyo to signify the inauguration of a new era.

On the other hand in a land-locked Russia the desirability of providing the seat of government of a Westernizing régime with easy access to a maritime Western World raised a geographical problem for which it was difficult to find a satisfactory solution; and, unlike Yedo, Moscow was temporarily deprived of her prerogative as a result of her rulers' decision to open their doors to the West. So far from being able to retain her historic status at the cheap price of a change of name, Moscow was compelled, for more than two hundred years, to see her empire governed from a capital which was not only given a new name but was planted on virgin soil on a far-distant site.[1]

When Seleucus Nicator chose for the capital of his newly carved-out successor-state of the Achaemenian Empire an Antioch-on-Orontes within a stone's throw of the Mediterranean in preference to a Seleucia-on-Tigris in the heart of South-Western Asia, he was acting in accordance with the feelings of the Hellenic ruling element in his dominions and was ignoring the feelings of a subject population which in his day was politically impotent. The transfer of the capital of the Russian Empire by Peter the Great from Moscow in the heart of Holy Russia to Saint Petersburg on the banks of the Neva, within a stone's throw of the Baltic, is comparable to Nicator's choice in its cultural and geographical aspects.[2] In this case, as in that, the seat of government of a land-locked empire was planted in a remote corner of the empire's domain in order to provide the capital with easy access by sea to the sources of an alien civilization which the imperial government was eager to introduce into its dominions. In its political aspect, however, Peter's act was much more audacious than Nicator's; for, in seeking to supplant Moscow by Saint Petersburg, Peter was ignoring the feelings of the Orthodox Christian ruling element in Muscovy with a brusqueness reminiscent of the revolutionary acts of Julius Caesar and Ts'in She Hwang-ti. The Russians whose capital Peter uprooted and transplanted were not a defeated people; on the contrary, they were at that time in process of defeating their Swedish Western enemy under Peter's own auspices; and the site of the new capital which Peter laid out to take the place of Moscow and to serve as a window for letting in Western cultural influence lay in territory wrested from a Western Sweden by Russian force of arms. In the light of this political situation it is astonishing that Saint Petersburg should have remained the capital of the Russian

[1] See pp. 690–1, below.

[2] This comparison has been suggested already in II. ii. 157.

Empire for more than two hundred years (A.D. 1712[1]–1918[2]). The length of this interlude in Moscow's reign is a testimony both to the force of Peter's personality and to the potency of the alien Western Civilization of which Peter had constituted himself a missionary.[3]

Yet even this combination of forces in Saint Petersburg's favour could not avail either to maintain the seat of government there permanently or to avert the untoward effects of its remaining there as long as it did. In the Russian Empire under the Petrine régime the location of the capital at the extreme north-western corner accentuated the tendency, inherent in the imperial government's Westernizing policy, for a Westernized official class to become alienated, like the Hellenic and Hellenized ruling element in the Seleucid Monarchy, from the unassimilated mass of the population. This social schism was the price paid by the Russian Empire for a reception of the alien civilization of the West which never went far enough on the technological plane to achieve Peter the Great's ambition of making Russia capable of holding her own in war against the strongest Western antagonist who might enter the field

1 This was the date on which Saint Petersburg officially became the capital of the Russian Empire; but the site of the new city had already been the seat of government *de facto* since May 1703, when Peter the Great had started work on the building of Saint Petersburg; for, though the task of conjuring a great city out of a wilderness of waterway and marsh was naturally a labour of many years, the Tsar had at once planted himself on the spot to direct the work in person; and the Tsar, wherever resident, was the Imperial Government incarnate.

2 The seat of government was moved back from Saint Petersburg to Moscow in A.D. 1728, but was retransferred to St. Petersburg in A.D. 1732 (see Sumner, B. H.: *Peter the Great and the Emergence of Russia* (London 1950, English Universities Press), p. 199).

3 There was also a feature in the past domestic history of Russian Orthodox Christendom which may have helped Saint Petersburg to maintain itself as the capital of the Russian Empire for as long as it did. The Empire had been brought into existence through the imposition of the rule of the Grand Duchy of Muscovy upon the city-state of Novgorod between A.D. 1471 and 1479. At that date Novgorod represented one half of Russian Orthodox Christendom, and this not merely in the extent of her territory but also in the complexion and orientation of her culture. The Russian state which had been converted to Eastern Orthodox Christianity by the cultural influence of the East Roman Empire at the close of the tenth century of the Christian Era had been founded by pagan seafarers who had made their way into Russia at her opposite extremity, from Scandinavia. Their port of entry had been Novgorod, on the River Volkhov, which the sea-going ships of the Vikings were able to ascend via the River Neva and Lake Ladoga. When the Scandinavians in their homelands were converted to Western Catholic Christianity—a conversion which was simultaneous with that of the Russians to Eastern Orthodoxy—Novgorod became a point of contact between Russia and Western Christendom, and it continued to perform this function till its subjugation by Muscovy. The heavy hand of Muscovite autocracy extinguished both Novgorod's overseas trade with the West and the self-governing institutions that were her heritage from the pagan Viking Age and that had been favoured by the cultural effects of Novgorod's subsequent commercial intercourse with the Hansa towns. In crushing Novgorod and what she stood for, the Muscovite empire-builder Ivan III and his successors were depriving Russian Orthodox Christendom of a valuable cultural asset, and conversely Peter the Great, in founding Saint Petersburg, was in a sense merely restoring to Russia this treasure of which his predecessors had robbed her. In purely geographical terms, Saint Petersburg was the eighteenth-century counterpart of a medieval Novgorod, taking into account the increase in the size and draught of sea-going ships that had taken place in the meantime. In cultural terms the effect of the removal of the capital of the Russian Empire to Saint Petersburg from Moscow was to create at that stage the situation which would have been created in the fourteen-eighties if at that date the political unification of Russia had been brought about through the city-state of Novgorod's conquering the Grand Duchy of Moscow instead of through Moscow's conquering Novgorod. In the light of this historical background, Peter the Great's act of transferring his capital from Moscow to Saint Petersburg appears somewhat less perverse than Seleucus Nicator's act of transferring his from a site in Babylonia to Antioch.

against her. Peter's successors thus fell between two stools; and this was one of the causes of the progressive decay of an always unsound Petrine régime after the assassination of the Tsar Alexander II in A.D. 1881.

In the War of A.D. 1914–18 the Russian Empire narrowly escaped the fate of the Seleucid Monarchy in 83 B.C. Indeed, Saint Petersburg had come near to proving as fatal to the Russian Empire as Antioch proved to be to the Seleucid Monarchy before the empire-building work of Tsar Ivan III and Tsar Ivan IV was salvaged at the eleventh hour by the Bolsheviks. The Bolsheviks snatched the Russian Empire out of the jaws of destruction in order to transform it into a Union of Soviet Socialist Republics, and the general tendency of the Russian Communist Revolution was to carry the process of Westernization, initiated by Peter the Great, a long stage farther, albeit, at this stage, along a line which was heretical from the orthodox Western standpoint of the day. But in one vital point the Bolsheviks made a change which was unquestionably a return to the Pre-Petrine Muscovite tradition. They retransferred the seat of government from Saint Petersburg to Moscow;[1] and this was perhaps the most effective single step that they could have taken to ensure that the results of their salvaging work should be lasting.

As for the capitals of the Danubian Hapsburg Monarchy and the Napoleonic Empire, we can do no more than speculate about the changes of location that might have taken place if the Napoleonic Empire had been less short-lived and if the Danubian Monarchy had either made good its academic pretensions or seized its golden opportunity. If in the eighteenth century of the Christian Era the Hapsburg Power had not allowed itself to be diverted, by inconclusive contests with rival Western Powers for the possession of relatively small and unimportant morsels of territory, from achieving its manifest destiny of entering into the heritage of the Ottoman Empire in the whole of South-Eastern Europe from the eastern outworks of Vienna to Adrianople and Yannina,[2] it is conceivable that in such circumstances the seat of government might have travelled down the Danube from Vienna to Budapest, or even as far as Belgrade. On the other hand, if by some miracle the Hapsburg Monarchy had succeeded in becoming in reality the oecumenical power, embracing the whole of Western Christendom in a single polity, which it purported to be in its style and title and which it was pictured as being in the imaginations of its own Catholic subjects and of its Orthodox Christian and Muslim neighbours and adversaries on the south-east[3], it is conceivable that in such circumstances the capital might have travelled in the opposite direction—up the Danube from Vienna to Ratisbon or Ulm, or even farther afield to either Milan or Frankfurt. It is likewise conceivable that one or other of the two last-mentioned cities might have eventually superseded Paris as the capital of the Napoleonic Empire if the French empire-builders had known how to perpetuate their momentary success in achieving their own less impracticable task of

[1] Petrograd, as Saint Petersburg had been rechristened in a fit of Slavophil fervour after the outbreak of war between Russia and Germany in A.D. 1914, was poorly compensated for ceasing to be the seat of government by having its name changed once again—this time from Petrograd to Leningrad.

[2] See II. ii. 179–80 and 182, n. 4.

[3] See V. v. 326–7.

unifying politically the debris of an abortive medieval cosmos of city-states in Northern Italy, Flanders, and Western Germany.

Migrations of the Capital Cities of Metropolitan Empire-builders

If we take, in conclusion, a glance at those universal states that had been founded neither by aliens nor by barbarians nor by marchmen but by some metropolitan power, we shall observe here a general tendency for the seat of government to start in a central position and subsequently to travel towards the frontiers of a politically unified world.

The classical example of this tendency is afforded by the history of the Indic universal state, which was both originally founded and subsequently re-established by dynasties whose ancestral domain was the centrally situated state of Magadha. The Mauryas and the Guptas alike retained their seat of government at Pataliputra (the latter-day Patna), which had previously been Magadha's parochial capital. Standing, as it did, at the junction of the Ganges with the Jumna and with two other tributaries, Pataliputra was the natural administrative centre for the Ganges Basin;[1] yet, in spite of the practical advantageousness of the site, which worked together with the imponderable forces of tradition and prestige to preserve Pataliputra's prerogative, the seat of government eventually travelled north-westward in both these two parallel chapters of Indic history, and in both cases alike it was drawn in that direction by politico-military pressures from beyond the frontier in that quarter.

After the derelict domain of an enfeebled Mauryan Empire had been overrun by the Euthydemid Bactrian Greek prince Demetrius in the second decade of the second century B.C., the conqueror transferred the seat of government from Pataliputra to a new site far along the Great North-West Road[2] connecting the former Mauryan capital with Demetrius's own former capital at Bactra (Balkh) on the Central Asian side of the Hindu Kush.[3] Demetrius's New Taxila[4] lay near the old city of the same name, in the neighbourhood of the latter-day Rawalpindi, which, before the foundation of the Mauryan Empire, had been the capital of a parochial Indian state; and it commanded the approaches, on the Indian side, to the difficult section of the highway in which a traveller had to negotiate the three successive obstacles of the River Indus, the Khyber Pass, and the main chain of the Hindu Kush.

This neighbourhood was the natural location for the capital of a Power which was seeking to 'abolish the Hindu Kush' by uniting the Ganges–Jumna Basin with the Oxus–Jaxartes Basin.[5] The Greek war-lord Demetrius's pioneering essay in this audacious defiance of physical

1 See II. ii. 130.

2 See xi, maps 23 and 24.

3 For this road, which ran into the Great North-East Road of the Achaemenian Empire on the steppe of Türkmenistan, between the left bank of the Oxus and the north-eastern edge of the Iranian Plateau, see Tarn, W. W.: *The Greeks in Bactria and India* (Cambridge 1938, University Press), pp. 61–62.

4 See Tarn, op. cit., p. 179.

5 This 'geopolitical' *tour de force* which was achieved by the Bactrian Greek prince Demetrius and was repeated by his Kushan barbarian successors had its counterpart in Western history in the long-continuing political union of Piedmont with Savoy in defiance of the intervening physical barrier of the Alps (see IV. iv. 285–6). In this miniature Western reproduction of the mountain-bestriding realm of Demetrius and Kanishka, Turin corresponded in location to Taxila (Rawalpindi), Vercelli to Sāgala (Sialkot), Susa to Peshāwar, and Chambéry to Bactra (Balkh).

geography proved ephemeral. The Bactrian Greek Power had no sooner overrun the Mauryan Empire than it was broken up by fratricidal warfare which opened the way for Nomad invasions of its dominions on the Indian as well as the Central Asian side of the Hindu Kush;[1] but, when, after more than two centuries of kaleidoscopic political changes,[2] the momentary achievement of the Greek empire-builder Demetrius was repeated in the first century of the Christian Era by the Kushan empire-builder Kadphises I and was perpetuated by Kadphises' successors, the seat of government of this reconstituted political union of North-Western India with Central Asia came to rest not far from the spot originally selected for it by Demetrius. The capital of the Kushan Empire was planted at Peshāwar, on the Great North-West Road between the Indus and the Khyber Pass.[3]

After the Mauryan Empire had been re-established by the Guptas, history repeated itself. The Guptas, like their predecessors, ruled the Indic World from Pataliputra; but, when the Guptan Empire collapsed in its turn and was momentarily restored by the Emperor Harsha (*imperabat* A.D. 606–47),[4] this last of all the rulers of an Indic universal state placed his seat of government, not at Pataliputra, but at Sthanesvara on the banks of the Upper Jumna, above the site of Delhi, covering the north-western approaches to the Ganges Basin from the quarter from which Hun and Gurjara Nomad invaders had swept down on the Guptan Empire from the Eurasian Steppe in the preceding chapter of Indic history.[5]

Like the Mauryan and Guptan empires, 'the Empire of the Four Quarters', which was the Sumeric universal state, was founded by a power situated in the heart of the world on which it conferred political unity. The founder, Ur-Engur, *alias* Ur-Nammu (*imperabat circa* 2143–2126 or 2079–2062 B.C.), was the ruler of Ur, one of the oldest of the Sumerian city-states in the Tigris–Euphrates Delta; and Ur remained the capital till 'the Empire of the Four Quarters', 118 years after its foundation, was broken up by an Elamite revolt. After an interlude of more than two hundred years, the empire of Ur-Engur was at length partially restored by Hammurabi (*imperabat circa* 1792–1750 or 1728–1686 B.C.);[6] but this Amorite saviour of the Sumeric Society did not

[1] During the brief period about half-way through the second century B.C. when Demetrius's dominions were partitioned between one Greek Power in the Oxus–Jaxartes Basin and another in North-Western India, the Greek ruler in India, Menander, placed his capital at Sāgala (Sialkot) on the Great North-West Road a few stages nearer than New Taxila to Pataliputra (see Tarn, op. cit., pp. 247–8).

[2] For this obscure passage in the history of the contact of the Indic, Hellenic, Syriac, and Nomadic civilizations, see V. v. 133, n. 1, following Tarn, W. W., op. cit.

[3] See Smith, V. A.: *The Early History of India*, 3rd ed. (Oxford 1914, Clarendon Press), pp. 261–2. On the political map of the World in A.D. 1952 the role of Taxila (Rawalpindi) in Demetrius's realm and of Peshāwar in Kanishka's was being played by Kābul as the capital of a Kingdom of Afghanistan which had reproduced the structure of the Bactrian Greek and the Kushan Empire by uniting territories lying on opposite sides of the Hindu Kush. The domain of this twentieth-century kingdom of Afghanistan was, of course, much less extensive than those of either of its forerunners. On the north-west it did not extend beyond the left bank of the Upper Oxus, while on the south-east it did not now touch the right bank of the Indus at any point.

[4] See V. vi. 209, n. 3.

[5] See II. ii. 130.

[6] For this chapter of Sumeric history see V. vi. 297–8. For the chronology see the Note in vol. x, pp. 167–212.

reinstate Ur in her former role of serving as the imperial seat of government. Hammurabi governed the empire which he had partially re-established from his own ancestral capital at Babylon—a city which was 'the gate', not only of the Gods, but also of the Amorite barbarians who, during the anarchy following the collapse of the dominion of Ur, had found in Babylon their port of entry from the North Arabian Steppe into the north-west corner of the Land of Shinar.

Regarded from the standpoint of Sumer—the cradle of the Sumeric Civilization in the south-eastern quarter of the Tigris–Euphrates Delta—or even from the wider standpoint of the combined domains of Sumer and its Semitic neighbour and pupil Akkad, Babylon lay on the north-western fringe of the Sumeric World; but the geographical situation had been transformed to Sumer's own detriment, and to Babylon's ultimate profit, by the very success of the Sumeric empire-builder Ur-Engur. The universal state which Ur-Engur had founded and which Hammurabi had partially re-established was not confined to Sumer and Akkad; in its original avatar, at any rate, it embraced the whole of 'the Fertile Crescent', girdling the northern bay of the North Arabian Steppe from the Land of Shinar through Assyria and Mesopotamia as far as Syria and Palestine, which had been opened up during a preceding Time of Troubles by Assyrian traders and Akkadian war-lords; and, in establishing an empire of this extent, Ur had deprived herself and the other cities of Sumer once for all of the central position which they had originally occupied. The expansion of the Sumeric World up-river, north-westward, by commerce and conquest had been an incomparably quicker process than its expansion down-river, south-eastward, by the gradual silting-up of the head of the Persian Gulf.

Thus Ur's empire-building work made Babylon's fortune; and, though Babylon's first innings as the capital of a universal state did not outlast the final collapse of 'the Empire of the Four Quarters' which followed Hammurabi's death, the parvenu Amorite imperial city lived on to enjoy a second innings and a third. After she had recovered her prestige and renewed her youth by bringing the ancient sedentary population of the Land of Shinar into a fraternal union with the interloping Chaldaean tribesmen in an heroic resistance to Assyrian militarism,[1] Babylon was the inevitable capital of Nabopolassar's and Nebuchadnezzar's Neo-Babylonian Empire, which provided a universal state for the Sumeric Civilization's Babylonic successor. And, after the life of this Neo-Babylonian Empire had been cut short by an Achaemenian conquest, the city of Babylon once again survived a political catastrophe to become, as we have seen,[2] the principal capital, *de facto*, of its alien conquerors.

This virtual retention of an onerous imperial status never reconciled Babylon to Achaemenian rule. No doubt the Babylonians were aware that they owed their dubious good fortune, not to their alien masters' goodwill, but to the felicitousness of their city's geographical position, which constrained the Achaemenidae to use her as a political centre, however much political trouble she might give them. No doubt the Babylonian priesthood were quick to regret their folly in having facilitated

[1] See IV. iv. 477–9. [2] On p. 200, n. 1, and on p. 205, n. 4, above.

Cyrus's task by turning against their own emperor Nabonidus; and indeed it is remarkable that Nabonidus's unpopularity should have been so extreme as to inveigle the opposition in his own household into cutting off its nose to spite its face. One cause of this unpopularity was the archaeologist-emperor's tactlessly pedantic religious policy;[1] another cause may have been a fear that his penchant towards awkward innovations might inspire him to transfer the capital from Babylon to some other site. Nabonidus showed a marked interest in the North-West Mesopotamian city of Harrān, which not only happened to be his own home town (if this inference from the evidence is correct),[2] but was well placed for serving as a northern bulwark for the Neo-Babylonian Empire against the Achaemenian successor-state of an expansive Median highland Power which had been encircling 'the Fertile Crescent' from the Zagros to the Antitaurus.[3] Was Nabonidus planning to move the seat of government of his threatened empire to this distant outpost?[4] Or was he perhaps planning to move it to his yet more distant asylum at Taymā in the Hijāz?[5] Nabonidus's hostile Babylonian contemporaries may have had no better intelligence than twentieth-century Western scholars had about what was really brewing in their cranky emperor's mind; but we may guess that their conjectures and anxieties on this score played some part in the prompting of their suicidal policy.

In the event, Babylon succeeded in preserving her imperial prerogative in despite of Nabonidus's caprice as well as the Achaemenids' hostility, and the blow which was to deprive her not only of her status but of her existence was dealt her by her Macedonian deliverers from Achaemenian domination. Seleucus Nicator put Babylon out of court by planting his new foundations of Seleucia-on-Tigris[6] on a site still more convenient than the site of Babylon itself for the oecumenical purpose that Babylon had been serving since the days of Hammurabi. The location of Seleucia-on-Tigris was indeed so well chosen that, as we have seen,[7] the Seleucids' barbarian Arsacid successors and the Arsacids' militantly anti-Hellenic Sasanid supplanters made Ctesiphon, the east-bank suburb of Seleucia, into the seat of government of their dominions; and, under the ʿAbbasid Caliphs, Ctesiphon had an avatar in the shape of Baghdad.[8] As for Babylon herself, she had dwindled to vanishing-point by the first century of the Christian Era. Yet, after she had forfeited to Seleucia-Ctesiphon the imperial role which Hammurabi had first conferred on her, her site once more demonstrated its felicity by reverting

[1] See V. vi. 30 and 94–95.

[2] See Thompson, R. Campbell, in *The Cambridge Ancient History*, vol. iii (Cambridge 1925, University Press), pp. 218–19; Smith, Sidney: *Isaiah, Chapters XL–LV* (London 1944, Milford), pp. 24–25.

[3] The political fortunes of Harrān during the seventy years between the fall of the Assyrian Empire in 610–609 B.C. and the fall of the Neo-Babylonian Empire in 538 B.C. are discussed further on pp. 655–6, below.

[4] After having served as an outpost of the Babylonic Society, Harran became a fastness in which a fossil of the Babylonic Civilization survived the fall of the Neo-Babylonian Empire for some fourteen hundred years (see IV. iv. 101, n. 1, and IX. viii. 408, n. 5).

[5] For the road to Taymā, see p. 101, above. The Neo-Babylonian Emperor Nabonidus's 'funk-hole' at Taymā had its counterpart in the Roman Emperor Honorius's at Ravenna.

[6] See p. 200, above.

[7] See p. 202, n. 4, above.

[8] See p. 150, with n. 3, above.

to the part which it had played under Hammurabi's own ex-Arabian Amorite ancestors. Both Hīrah, the capital of the Lakhmid Arab principality that stood on guard over the Arabian marches of the Sasanian Empire, and Kūfah, the cantonment of the Primitive Muslim Arab conquerors of ʿIrāq and Iran,[1] were virtually west-bank suburbs of Babylon-on-Euphrates.[2]

As a final example of the tendency for the capital of a universal state to travel from the centre towards the fringes when the empire-building Power has been a metropolitan community, we may observe how in Minoan history the imperial sceptre passed from Cnossos to Mycenae. Cnossos was the natural capital for a 'thalassocracy of Minos' ruling the waves of the Aegean from a Cretan base of operations; but, in extending her dominion to the coasts of Continental Greece, Cnossos paved the way for Mycenae to supersede her.

Who are the Beneficiaries?

Having now cursorily surveyed the histories of the capitals of universal states, we may go on to inquire who were the beneficiaries of the insight and will-power that called these capitals into existence. These seats of imperial governments served the divers purposes of both violent and gentle interlopers. Barbarians swooped down on them in quest of mere plunder. Conquerors bred in an alien culture occupied them as a step towards reigning in the stead of a legitimate régime whose inheritance they aspired to usurp. Restorers of dilapidated empires, and revivers of empires that had completely disintegrated, were aided in their reconstruction work by the lingering prestige of the ancient seat of imperial government. Alien cultures, either forcibly imposed by conquerors or voluntarily imported by native 'Herodians',[3] found the capitals of universal states convenient stations for the radiation of their influence. Higher religions found them equally convenient for their own more audacious missionary enterprise of seeking to convert, not merely a cultural *élite*, but Mankind in the mass. During the Babylonish captivity of Nebuchadnezzar's deportees from Judah the capital city of a secular oecumenical empire actually served an embryonic higher religion as the incubator in which it found its soul by exchanging a parochial for an oecumenical outlook.

The seat of government of a universal state is indeed good ground for

1 See p. 131, above.

2 If the Primitive Muslim Arab cantonment at Kūfah may be regarded as an avatar of an earlier Amorite cantonment at Babylon, Kūfah's sister foundation at Basrah may similarly be regarded as an avatar of Obolla (*Latinè* Apologus). Obolla had been one of the cities of Mesênê, a successor-state of the Seleucid Monarchy in the extreme south-east of Babylonia, skirting the head of the Persian Gulf; and this Mesênê was an avatar of the Sea Land which had been a successor-state of the Empire of Sumer and Akkad. The political secession of the Sea Land from the rest of the Land of Shinar after the death of the Emperor Hammurabi may be interpreted as a political expression of a Sumerian national consciousness which had survived the replacement of the Sumerian by the Akkadian language as the living speech of the population of the former territory of Sumer. The special function of the city of Obolla—if its name is derived from the Sumerian word for 'door'—was to serve the Sea Land, as Babylon, 'the Gate', served Akkad, by providing a port of entry from 'the Desert' into 'the Sown'.

3 The contrast between alternative 'Herodian' and 'Zealot' reactions to the impact of an alien civilization is discussed in IX. viii. 580–623.

spiritual seeds to fall into;[1] for a city that is performing this oecumenical function is the epitome of a wide world in small compass. Its walls enfold, at close quarters, representatives of all nations and classes, speakers of all languages, and adherents of all religious connexions and persuasions, while its gates lead out on to highways running in all directions to the World's end. The same missionary can preach on the same day to the populace in the slums and to the Emperor in his palace; and, if, in the power of the spirit, he does gain the Emperor's ear, he may hope to see the mighty machine of imperial administration set in motion in the cause of the Church. Nehemiah's key-position in the Achaemenian imperial household at Susa gave him his opportunity for enlisting the effective patronage of the Emperor Artaxerxes I for a temple-state at Jerusalem which was still the emotional focus of a world religion in the making; and the Jesuit Fathers who sought and won a footing in the imperial court at Agra and the imperial court at Peking in the sixteenth and seventeenth centuries of the Christian Era dreamed of winning India and China for Catholicism by the Nehemian strategy of converting the Great Mogul and the Son of Heaven. Had not the Mongol Khāqān Qubilāy been half-converted by Tibetan missionaries of the Tantric Mahāyāna?

The Pillage of Capital Cities by Barbarians

The barbarian's appetite for plunder was sated in the looting of Delhi by the Marāthās; of Tenochtitlan and Cuzco by the Spaniards; of Susa, Persepolis, and Ecbatana by the Macedonians; of Ctesiphon by the Primitive Muslim Arabs; of Baghdad by the Mongols; of Loyang by the Hiongnu; of Kaifêng by the Kin; of Thebes by the Assyrians; of Rome by the Visigoths and Vandals; of Babylon by the Hittites; of Cnossos by her Mycenaean marchmen; and of Mycenae, in her turn, by her continental backwoodsmen. An imperial capital in which the tribute of a subject world has silted up for centuries is an irresistibly tempting material prize for invaders who have no subtler or more abiding objective; but the seed sown by covetousness so crude as this bears a vindictive karma. The unsophisticated barbarian squanders his ill-gotten gains as quickly as he snatches them; the more cultivated alien conqueror who, in behaving as a barbarian, is sinning against the light of his own higher moral law, brings a more ironic retribution on the society that has bred him. The ill-gotten gains of the Macedonian and Spanish *conquistadores* slipped through their fingers no less quickly than those of the Vandals and the Mongols; but in these two heinous cases the barren harvest was followed by a calamitous aftermath. The Hellenic Society of the fourth century B.C. and the Western Society of the sixteenth century of the Christian Era were not only put to shame by the barbarism into which their militant apostles had relapsed; they were also devastated by it. For a crime which primitive barbarians can commit with economic impunity does not go unpunished in societies that have risen to a money economy. The rifling of the treasure-houses of the Americas and South-Western Asia put into sudden circulation an

[1] Matt. xiii. 8.

avalanche of bullion which produced a catastrophic inflation, and the sins of Spanish plunderers at Cuzco and Macedonian plunderers at Persepolis were expiated by German peasants in Swabia and by Ionian artisans in the Cyclades.[1]

The Exploitation of the Prestige of Capital Cities by Empire-builders

A less barbarous use has been made of imperial capitals by conquerors or successors who have looked beyond the immediate indulgence of crude appetites towards the more constructive aim of supplanting, reconditioning, or reviving the régimes into whose heritage they have entered. Thanks to the camouflaging mirage of immortality that is apt to glimmer round the grave of even a long since defunct universal state,[2] a *ci-devant* imperial capital may retain its prestige long after it has ceased to perform its function; and this prestige may stand an interloping empire-builder in good stead if he inherits or adopts the hallowed site as his own seat of government.

When a usurper takes over his victim's former capital as a going concern, the effect is to lighten his task of hoisting himself into the saddle and keeping himself there. Though Peking was first promoted to be a seat of imperial government by the intruding barbarian Khitan, and not by any thoroughbred Chinese dynasty whose choice of the site might have stamped it with the hall-mark of legitimacy in Chinese eyes, the subsequent domination of the Chinese people by the Kin in place of the Khitan and by the Mongols in place of the Kin was undoubtedly facilitated by the retention, under each of these successive barbarian régimes, of a capital from which a subject Chinese population had gradually grown accustomed to receiving a barbarian master's word of command. *A fortiori*, in a later passage of Far Eastern history, the retention of Peking as the seat of imperial government must have facilitated the usurpation of the Manchu barbarians when they took the imperial city over, not from barbarian predecessors, but from the thoroughbred Chinese dynasty of the Ming.

A similar advantage was secured by the Spaniards when they established the seat of government of the universal state which they imposed on the Central American World on the site of Tenochtitlan, which had been the capital of the Spaniards' Aztec forerunners. The political value of the accumulated prestige of an existing imperial capital was rated so high by the Japanese statesmen who engineered the Meiji Revolution that they kept the seat of government at Yedo and induced the Imperial House to migrate thither from Kyoto, although Yedo was the seat of a 'forcèd power'[3] which had been in the saddle for not much longer than a quarter of a millennium, while Kyoto had been for more than ten centuries (A.D. 795–1869) the seat of the legitimate dynasty which was now being rehabilitated. The decisive consideration in the sagacious revolutionaries' minds was no doubt the hard fact that the Japanese

[1] For the inflation of prices that was inflicted on the Hellenic World by the Macedonians' looting of the Achaemenian treasuries, see Tarn, W. W.: 'The Social Question in the Third Century', in *The Hellenistic Age* (Cambridge 1923, University Press).
[2] See pp. 7–46, above.
[3] Marvell, Andrew: *An Horatian Ode upon Cromwell's Return from Ireland.*

people had by that time become accustomed to being governed from Yedo *de facto*, whereas Kyoto, for the greater part of its long and venerable history, had been an historical museum and political lumber-room.

The restorer of a universal state likewise finds his task eased if his own initial seat of government happens to be the former capital of the prostrate empire which he is seeking to re-erect. When Amosis successfully repeated the achievement of a Mentuhotep by restoring 'the Middle Empire' of Egypt in the form of 'the New Empire', the founder of the Eighteenth Dynasty was assuredly assisted, and conceivably inspired, by the fact that, like his Eleventh-Dynasty predecessor, he had started his career as prince of Thebes. In the history of the Indic Society a corresponding service was rendered by Pataliputra to the Guptas when they set out from the Mauryas' historic capital to restore the Mauryas' imperial régime.

Dethroned imperial captials have sometimes been deliberately reinstated by empire-builders who have not had the good fortune either to find these seats of imperial government still at their disposal as going concerns or to inherit them as the local capitals of parochial successor-states of ruined universal states which they have set out to restore.

We have seen[1] that, when Han Liu Pang had made himself sole master of the Sinic World, he laid out a new oecumenical capital in the immediate neighbourhood of the Ts'in Power's historic seat of government at Hsien Yang, which had been wantonly destroyed by Hsiang Yü after it had been carefully spared by Liu Pang himself. When, some eight hundred years later, Han Liu Pang's Ch'ang Ngan was reinstated by the Sui Dynasty, under the new name of Si Ngan, as the capital of an empire which was intended by its founders to be an avatar of the Empire of Ts'in and Han, this act of Sui statesmanship bore witness to the vitality of the prestige that clings to a site which has once been a seat of oecumenical dominion; for by that date nearly six hundred years had passed since Ch'ang Ngan had been dethroned. When the Posterior Han Dynasty had re-established the Han Power after its momentary collapse in A.D. 9, they had not reinstated the Prior Han Dynasty's capital. They found Ch'ang Ngan in ruins; for in the anarchy of A.D. 9–25 the city laid out by Liu Pang had suffered the fate of Hsien Yang in the anarchy after the death of Ts'in She Hwang-ti; but in choosing a new site the second founder of the Han Power, Kwang Wuti, did not overlook the value of historic associations. His substitute for Ch'ang Ngan was Loyang, which had been the last seat of the Ts'in Power's predecessors the Chóu. The Chóu, as we have seen,[2] had been extinguished by Ts'in She Hwang-ti's grandfather in 249 B.C.; and, for more than five centuries before that, their authority had been as shadowy as was that of the Japanese Imperial House during the ten centuries preceding the Meiji Restoration. In the tiny enclave round Loyang which was all that then remained of their once extensive patrimony within as well as outside 'the passes', the Chóu had continued to perform certain customary ritual functions without retaining a shred of practical power.

[1] On p. 212, above.

[2] On p. 212, n. 4, above.

It is remarkable that this simulacrum of an imperial past should have invested Loyang with a prestige so abiding as to make its fortune more than 250 years after even a nominal primacy had been taken from it. Yet this Sinic case, though extreme, is not unique.

The prestige of Delhi, for example, survived the decline and fall of the Mughal Empire after the death of Awrangzīb so triumphantly that, more than two hundred years later, she compelled the British to transfer the seat of government of a rāj which had been rebuilt on a basis of British sea-power to the inland site of the capital of their Mughal predecessors from the maritime site of their own original capital at Calcutta. Moscow, too, possessed sufficient prestige to allow her to wait, as Delhi waited, for more than two hundred years for her eventual triumph over a parvenu competitor. Saint Petersburg was Calcutta's twin in her fate, as well as in her location.

As for Babylon, it was inevitable[1] that she should be the capital of a Neo-Babylonian Empire that was a political embodiment of Babylon's genius, but it is remarkable that her situation and prestige should have compelled her Achaemenian conquerors to perpetuate Babylon's imperial prerogative by making her one of the seats of government of their own dominions in preference to a loyal though unpractical Persepolis. It is even more remarkable that the situation and prestige of Peking should have compelled the Ming Dynasty to reverse a deliberate break with an odious past. When the Ming had succeeded in expelling the Mongols from Intramural China, they had transferred the seat of government to Nanking from a city whose only role in Far Eastern history till then had been to serve as the capital of successive barbarian conquerors. Peking was obnoxious to Chinese sentiment for the reason that had rendered her attractive to the Mongol successors of the Kin and to the Kin successors of the Khitan. Yet she was able to compel the Ming to reinstate her at the risk of stultifying themselves in the eyes of their own militantly anti-barbarian Chinese supporters.[2]

In a Medieval Western World the 'Roman Emperors' of the German nation could not acquire a perfect title to legitimate investiture with their purple shirt of Nessus without paying at least one visit to the ruins of Rome in order to be crowned in the midst of them by the Pope and acclaimed by 'a Roman People' who in their day were, not the *faex*, but the *faex faecis Romuli*.[3] For German potentates whose strength was derived from hereditary dominions lying north of the Alps, this Italian expedition was always as costly and perilous as it was frequently barren and humiliating. Yet the prestige of a dead Rome's shadow was still so great that, for the sake of it, these moth-kings sacrificed a living Germany's substance; and, though the medieval German Kingdom eventually came to grief through a persistent pursuit of this Roman will-o'-the-wisp, Napoleon's subsequent experience was to indicate retrospectively the difficulties in which the medieval Western Emperors might have involved themselves if they had refused to pay their personal homage to the ex-imperial city's imponderable power.

[1] The reason has been indicated on p. 226, above.

[2] See II. ii. 121–2.

[3] See Cicero: *Ad Atticum*, II. i, § 8.

When Napoleon set to work to build the débris of a cosmos of medieval Western city-states into an empire founded on the might of the most populous and powerful Western national state of his day, he signalized his intention of providing an effective substitute for 'the Holy Roman Empire' by pointedly breaking with the traditional procedure for investiture with the imperial office. Instead of making a pilgrimage to Rome in the wake of an Austrasian Charlemagne and his Saxon and Franconian successors, Napoleon summoned the Pope from Rome to Paris and required him to assist at his coronation in his own imperial capital. Though 'the Corsican usurper' himself was neither Roman nor French, Napoleonic Paris might well feel that she could look contemporary Rome in the face. Had not Paris been the intellectual centre of the Western World since the twelfth century and its cultural centre as well since the seventeenth? And was not her new imperial master now doing for Paris what Augustus had done for Rome when—finding her a city of brick and leaving her a city of marble[1]—he gave her the physical presence that befitted the capital of the World? For the drily rational intelligence of a Napoleon, such considerations might be conclusive; yet the event was to prove that, in the Year Thirteen of the New Era of the French Revolution, Napoleon had under-estimated the longevity of traditional pieties. By flouting Rome and bullying her sovereign pontiff, he won, not respect for his own political power, but sympathy for the helplessness of his venerable victim.

While the Old Rome in the days of her physical impotence thus compelled a series of Western war-lords to reckon with her during a thousand years running from the date of Charlemagne's coronation to the date of Napoleon's, the New Rome gave proof of a comparable power by hypnotizing first the Palaiológhi and then the 'Osmanlis.

When Michael Palaiológhos took Constantinople from its unhappy Western occupants in A.D. 1261, he was relieving them of an untenable position at the cost of creating one for himself and his heirs. In concentrating his efforts on the capture of the ex-imperial city he had let slip through his fingers the best part of his dominions in Anatolia;[2] and, in thus exchanging a countryside that had been the source of his strength for a city that was a liability, he found himself constrained to seek support against the Turkish enemy whom he had neglected from the Latin enemy whom he had affronted. An Eastern Orthodox Christian principality in these straits could not hope to buy military assistance from Western Catholic Christendom except at the price of ecclesiastical submission to the Papacy; and this payment was repeatedly offered by the Palaiológhi, to be invariably rejected by a fanatically Orthodox Greek clergy and people.[3] This insoluble problem of reconciling incompatible terms of appeasement was the rock on which the Palaeologan ship of state eventually foundered:

> Und das hat mit ihrem Singen
> Die Lorelei getan.

[1] Suetonius Tranquillus, C.: *The Lives of the Caesars*, 'Divus Augustus', chap. xxviii, § 3
[2] See V. vi. 298, n. 7, and p. 30, above.
[3] See IV. iv. 615–19.

The Palaiológhi obtained a posthumous revenge; for, in attracting the ʿOsmanlis into their wake and drawing them out of Asia into Europe,[1] they exposed these conquerors and supplanters of theirs to the lure of the siren-city by whom they themselves had been brought to shipwreck. The ʿOsmanlis could not resist the temptation of seizing a prize that had twice eluded the grasp of their Arab co-religionists and ensamples. They were beckoned forward by the legendary figure of the martyr Seyyid Battāl.[2] Yet, when in A.D. 1453 Mehmed ʿOsmanli the Conqueror repeated Michael Palaiológhos's feat, he too was yielding to the magic of the imperial city against the dictates of a sober *raison d'état*. In impelling Sultan Mehmed to conquer her, Constantinople succeeded at last in retrieving her own long-adverse fortunes. By the time of the Conqueror's descendant Suleymān the Magnificent's death in A.D. 1566, Constantinople found herself the capital of a larger empire than she had been ruling in A.D. 565, at the death of Justinian the Prodigal. Yet, by the same token, the commonwealth of which she was the ornament and incubus was by that time once more on the verge of a calamitous decline; and in Ottoman history this decline was to be consummated by a fall before the revolutionary architects of the Ottoman Empire's Turkish successor-state could summon up the courage to transfer the seat of government from Constantinople to Ankara.

This defiance of Constantinople's magic power was indeed the Turkish nationalists' only alternative to committing national suicide; yet even then they could not bring themselves to throw away the millstone that the Ottoman Conqueror of Constantinople had hung about the Turkish nation's neck.[3] Though Atatürk and his fellow revolutionaries dethroned Constantinople, they insisted on retaining possession of her; and in getting their way on this point they did their worst to defeat the governing purpose of all their policy. This governing purpose was to nurse their new-born national state into a vigorous and healthy maturity. The reformers realized in principle that, if they were to give this delicate infant a fair chance of survival, they must allow it to start life free from the grievous burdens that had broken the back of the old Ottoman Empire; and in two cases in point they did not flinch from putting this principle into practice. They renounced bona fide all ambition to re-impose Turkish rule on either the Arabs or the Balkan Christians. Yet, when they had to take their decision about the most formidable burden of all, they opted for clinging to Constantinople and thereby stultified the rest of their acts; for, in burdening the Turkish Republic with Constantinople, they were condemning her, sooner or later, to fall foul of the Soviet Union for the same ineluctable reasons of strategic and commercial geography that had brought the old Ottoman Empire into collision with the old Russia. At the time of writing, it seemed not impossible that Constantinople might once again play her sinister role of luring to destruction a state which had failed to resist the temptation of possessing her.

[1] See III. iii. 27 and V. vi. 184.
[2] See V. v. 255 and 256.
[3] Matt. xviii. 6.

The Use of Capital Cities as Transmitting-stations for the Radiation of Cultures

Having now examined certain passages of history in which an ex-imperial city has enchanted some empire-builder into purchasing the asset of her prestige at a prohibitive price, we may go on to consider cases in which an imperial capital has served as a transmitting-station for the diffusion of an alien culture. This was the role of Vienna in the Danubian Hapsburg Monarchy,[1] of Saint Petersburg in the Petrine Russian Empire, of Antioch-on-Orontes and Seleucia-on-Tigris in the Seleucid Monarchy, of Calcutta in the British Indian Empire, of Mexico City in the Spanish Viceroyalty of New Spain, and of Lima in the Spanish Viceroyalty of Peru.

It will be seen that in most of these instances the imperial 'radio city' was a new foundation planted on virgin soil; and in the founding of Seleucia and Antioch and Saint Petersburg this geographical breach with the past was certainly deliberate. Peter the Great realized that the most effective installation for radiating Western culture into Russia would be a seat of Russian government that had no pre-Western associations, and he rejected Moscow, as Seleucus Nicator rejected Babylon, because she was a citadel of the culture which he was planning to replace. Yet this cultural missionary's rule of thumb was broken with impunity by the Spanish foundation of Mexico City and by the Seleucid

[1] Vienna served as a station for the transmission of the Western culture to sub-Western and non-Western receivers, though the province of Lower Austria, in which Vienna lay, was, like the city itself, an integral part of the Western World. Vienna was situated just to the west of the cultural boundary between the heart of Western Christendom and its eastern marches—the lands of the Crown of the Hungarian King Saint Stephen and the United Kingdom of Poland-Lithuania—in which the Western Christian culture was diluted with a tincture of the Nomad culture of the Eurasian Steppe. Vienna's cultural function was to radiate an authentic Western culture, native to Vienna itself and to its western hinterland, into the imperfectly Westernized eastern marches of the Western World and, beyond these again, into Eastern Orthodox Christendom and Dār-al-Islām. Vienna's performance of this cultural task was facilitated by her geographical location; for, while she lay just to the west of the cultural frontier along the line of the River Leitha (where 'the East begins' according to an illuminating Viennese *bon mot*), she lay just to the east of the Austrian Alps, which constituted 'the natural frontier' of Western Christendom in this quarter. Standing, as she thus stood, with her back to the eastern foothills of the Alps, and looking down the course of the River Danube from a point where, after having threaded its way through the Alps, it is heading for the Hungarian Alföld, *en route* for the Iron Gates and for the western tip of the Eurasian Steppe's Great Western Bay, Vienna could not fail to find her missionary field in the sub-Western and non-Western worlds to the east and south-east of her.

Though the writer of this Study did not pay his first visit to Vienna till the summer of A.D. 1929, at a date more than ten years after she had been reduced politically from being the imperial capital of a cosmopolitan empire to being the national capital of an Austrian Republic whose narrow bounds embraced none of the sub-Western or non-Western territories of a now defunct Danubian Monarchy, he found the evidences of Vienna's historic cultural mission still impressively prominent. In A.D. 1929 the names of the subscribers to the Vienna telephone service, as recorded in the book, testified that this city was a melting-pot in which Rumans, Serbs, and Bulgars, as well as Poles, Magyars, and Croats, were being reminted into pure Westerners (see IX. viii. 530); and, when the observer travelled on eastwards to the 'Saxon' cities of Transylvania, which had been under Rumanian rule since the dissolution of the Danubian Hapsburg Monarchy in A.D. 1918, he found these outposts of a Western Civilization, which were now marooned and in peril of being submerged under the resurgent flood of an alien culture, desperately clinging to a traditional link with Vienna which was their cultural lifeline—as the marooned outposts of Hellenism in Western Iran still clung to their traditional link with Antioch-on-Orontes after the military occupation of Media and Babylonia by the Arsacid Power in the sixth decade of the second century B.C.

foundation of Seleucia-on-Eulaeus. Mexico City was not prevented from fulfilling her revolutionary cultural task by any lingering ghost of an Aztec Tenochtitlan; nor was the Seleucid avatar of Susa inhibited from being an active and long-lived focus of Greek life and letters by the more formidable legacy of a site which had been the national capital of Elam before rising to its political apogee as the imperial capital of the Achaemenidae.

The success of this subsidiary transmitting station for the diffusion of Hellenism on an historic site, which, under the Seleucid régime, had ceased to be a capital city, brings out another prevalent feature in the policy of alien empire-builders who use their seats of government for the diffusion of their culture. The Seleucidae were not content to provide for the radiation of Hellenism from a single centre only. When Seleucus Nicator rejected Seleucia-on-Tigris in favour of Antioch-on-Orontes in choosing the location for his imperial capital,[1] he did not deprive the abortive Tigrine seat of government of its cultural role. Seleucia-on-Tigris 'made history' as the local transmitting-station for Hellenism in Babylonia for the next five centuries, and it was the glory of the Seleucidae that, not only on the banks of the Orontes and the Tigris, but throughout their dominions, from Seleucia-on-Eulaeus to Laodicea-on-Lycus, they sowed with a generous hand a star-dust of Greek city-states which continued, long after the disappearance of the missionary dynasty that had called them into being, to shine like a Milky Way across the face of South-Western Asia.[2]

The Spaniards likewise were not content to confine themselves to the use of Mexico City in Central America, or of Lima in the Andean World, as stations for the radiation of the culture that they had brought with them across the Atlantic from Western Europe. As we have already noticed,[3] the Spanish Crown planted its vast new dominions overseas with settlements of Spanish colonists, organized in self-governing municipalities, who, like the Greek colonists in the Seleucid dominions, were to propagate their distinctive way of life by the display of a living example; and, in rural tracts which the radiation of these scattered Spanish municipalities could not reach, the conversion of the subject population was catered for by the Achaemenian expedient of conferring feudal appanages on grandees of the ruling race. In the Spanish Empire such *encomiendas*[4] were granted to their recipients on the condition that, in return for the economic privilege of being furnished by the Crown with a supply of native labour, they must provide for the instruction of their serfs in the Catholic version of the Christian Faith. In the British Empire in India, Madras and Bombay played their part, side by side

[1] See p. 201, above.

[2] The cultural idealism of the Seleucidae is thrown into relief by the sharpness of its difference from the narrow-hearted cultural policy of the Seleucids' neighbours and rivals the Ptolemies, whose objective was, not to Hellenize their Egyptiac subjects, but to exploit them. On Egyptiac ground the Ptolemies added only the single Greek community of Ptolemais in Upper Egypt to Alexandria and to the pre-Alexandrine Greek settlement at Naucratis. Yet even the Ptolemies emulated the Hellenizing policy of the Seleucidae in their non-Egyptiac dominions—as is witnessed by the names of the Greek cities in Transjordan and along the Palestinian section of the shores of the Mediterranean.

[3] See pp. 135–6, above.

[4] See p. 145, above.

with Calcutta, in the dissemination of an inflowing alien culture, as the provincial centres in Spanish America and Seleucid Asia played theirs side by side with Lima and Mexico City and Antioch and Seleucia; and Saint Petersburg was singular in serving as the sole centre for the diffusion of Western culture, as well as the sole political capital, in the structure of the Petrine Russian Empire.

The Use of Capital Cities as Seminaries for Higher Religions

We have now made some survey of the divers services that imperial capitals perform for alien cultures, for alien or indigenous empire-builders, and for predatory barbarians; but their historic mission lies in the religious field.

The potent effect on the destinies of Mankind which the Sinic imperial city of Loyang was still exercising at the time when these lines were being written was not a consequence of her former political role as the seat of the Eastern Chóu Dynasty and subsequently of the Posterior Han; she was exercising it in virtue of having been the nursery in which the seeds of the Mahāyāna—wafted by the winds of History from India to China over the Eurasian Steppe—were acclimatized to a Sinic cultural environment and were thus enabled to resow themselves broadcast over the face of the Sinic World. It is true that this historic religious mission would not have fallen to Loyang if the Emperor Kwang Wuti had not previously chosen her for the service of a political purpose; but it was the unforeseen religious consequence of the Posterior Han statesman's political choice that gave Loyang her opportunity to make a lasting mark on history.

The abiding significance of other seats of a transitory political power was likewise due to their religious associations. Si Ngan, for example, was still influencing the life of Mankind in the twentieth century of the Christian Era not because, from A.D. 589 to A.D. 907, she had been the political capital of the Empire of the Sui and T'ang but because, under the T'ang régime, she had become a centre for the diffusion of the Mahāyāna, Manichaeism, and the Nestorian form of Christianity. The desolate site of Qāraqorum was still invisibly alive because, as an undesigned effect of this ephemeral steppe-city's meteoric political career in the thirteenth century of the Christian Era, she had brought missionaries of the Roman Catholic Christianity of the West face to face with Central Asian exponents of Nestorianism and Tibetan exponents of Lamaism. Peking, in her turn, had won immortality when, as the political capital of successive Mongol, Ming, and Manchu régimes, she had fallen heir to Qāraqorum's role as a disseminator of higher religions. In A.D. 1928 the city from which a large portion of the Human Race had been governed in succession by Qubilāy and Yung Lo and Ch'ien Lung was at last deprived for a season by a victorious Kuomintang of the political prerogative which she had so long enjoyed; yet, twenty years later, before she had yet found her opportunity of constraining the Kuomintang's Communist successors to serve her purpose by making her the political capital of China once again, she was still making her mark in the life of the contemporary world as an intellectual centre under the non-committal new name of Peiping;[1] and this cultural role, which had thus survived Peking's fall from her imperial estate, had been conferred on her by a succession of religious missionaries who had preached and practised within her gates: the Tibetan Lamas who had gained the ear of Qubilāy; the emissaries of the Roman Church who, twice over,[2] had won a footing in this distant base of operations; and the Protestant educator-evangelists who had followed in the Jesuits' footsteps and had prepared the way for Peiping to fulfil her latter-day function.

In the year A.D. 1952 it was manifest that Peter and Paul, not Romulus or Augustus, had been the true authors of the immortality of Rome. By that date, more than sixteen centuries had run their course since Rome had forfeited to Constantinople and Trèves the prerogative of serving as the political capital of a united Hellenic World; and the paltry political consolation prize which the former imperial city had tardily received when, in A.D. 1870, she had been turned into the national capital of a Modern Western parochial state had been written down to its true value by the humiliation of the Kingdom of Italy in the world war of A.D. 1939–45. The world-wide influence which Rome was nevertheless still exercising—unaffected by political vicissitudes—was a consequence of the work and death, in Rome, of the two Apostles nineteen hundred years before. It was also a consequence of Christianity's subsequently displayed genius for assimilating and transmuting vital elements of other alien religions which had made themselves at home in Rome before the seeds of Christianity had been sown there. The Great Mother who was to play so distinctive a part in the Roman version of Christianity had been escorted in pomp by the Roman Senate and People from Tiber-side to the Palatine[3] 265 years before Paul, after landing at Puteoli, had slipped unnoticed into Rome in the company of the little party that had gone out along the Appian Way to meet him at the Three Taverns.[4]

As for Constantinople, her religious mission was manifest from the moment of her birth; for this New Rome was founded by Constantine the Great, as Saint Petersburg was founded by Peter the Great, with a spiritual as well as a 'geopolitical' purpose.[5] When the first Christian Emperor laid out his new capital on ground that had been cleared by his pagan predecessor Septimius's vindictive erasure of Byzantium, he was founding a city that was to be Christian from the start; and in A.D. 1952 it was apparent that this religious function was of more lasting significance than the superb geographical location[6] that had prompted Constantine to plant his new Christian capital on that particular site. In the course of the following sixteen hundred years, Constantinople had lost and won and lost again the political prerogative of serving as an imperial capital for the Roman Empire, the East Roman Empire, and the Ottoman Empire in turn; and, at the time of writing, such influence

1 Pei-ping meant merely 'northern city', in contrast to Pei-king, which meant 'northern capital'.

2 In the fourteenth century of the Christian Era and again in the sixteenth.

3 See V. v. 685–7.

4 See Acts xxviii. 15.

5 This comparison had been suggested, by anticipation, in V. vi. 343.

6 See p. 218, above.

as she was still exercising in the World of the day was due to her being the seat of a Patriarch who was still recognized by the ecclesiastical heads of the other Eastern Orthodox churches—including the mighty Church of Russia—as *primus inter pares*.

(*d*) THE SERVICEABILITY OF IMPERIAL CURRENCIES

1. *Official Languages and Scripts*

Alternative Possibilities

It can almost be taken for granted that a universal state will have provided itself with official media of mental communication, and that these will include not only one or more languages transmitted viva voce and received by ear, but also some system of visual records that can be preserved and be consulted by the eye after the passing of the minute span of time during which the ear is sensitive to vibrations set in motion by 'winged words'. In the apparatus of nearly all the universal states whose history was within the ken of twentieth-century students, the official system of visual records had taken the form of a visual notation of the meaning of some oral and auditory official language; and, though the Incas had succeeded in creating and maintaining an almost totalitarian régime without the aid of any notational system beyond the wordless semantics of their *quipus*,[1] this *tour de force* was no more than an exception to a general rule that the written word had been an indispensable instrument of oecumenical government.[2]

There had been cases in which some single language and single script had previously driven all other possible competitors off the field throughout the area which the empire-builders had eventually brought under a single government, and in such cases History had virtually decided in advance what the official language and script of the new universal state were to be. In the Egyptiac 'Middle Empire', for example, they were bound to be the Classical Egyptian language and the hieroglyphic characters; in Japan under the Tokugawa Shogunate they were bound to be the Japanese language and the particular selection and usage of Chinese characters that had been worked out already in Japan for conveying the Japanese language visually; in the Russian Empire they were virtually bound to be the Great Russian language and Great Russian variety of the Slavonic version of the Greek Alphabet.[3] This simple situation had not, however, been the usual one; for, in a society that is a 'civilization', more than one language and more than one script are current as a rule, and we have also observed, in another context,[4] that the dominions of universal states are apt to embrace territories of

1 See V. v. 491.

2 See Myres, J. L.: *The Dawn of History* (London, no date, Williams & Norgate), pp. 68–70.

3 It was, of course, conceivable that the Muscovite Government might have adopted for its own secular use the 'Church Slavonic', fashioned by the Greek Christian missionaries Cyril and Methodius out of the living Macedonian Slavonic dialect of the ninth century of the Christian Era, which had continued to be the ecclesiastical language of the Slavonic-speaking Orthodox Christian peoples. This would not have been so extreme a *tour de force* as the Guptas' adoption of Neo-Sanskrit (see p. 253, below).

4 See pp. 62–67, above.

alien culture in addition to the domain of the civilization on which the empire-builders have imposed political unity. More often, therefore, than not, when it comes to deciding what the official language and script of a universal state are to be, the empire-builders find themselves confronted, not with an accomplished fact to ratify, but with a difficult choice to make between a number of competing candidates.

In these circumstances, most empire-builders had given official currency to their own mother tongue, and, if this ancestral language of theirs had hitherto been unprovided with the visual form of presentation which is a necessity for any language that is to be used as an instrument of oecumenical government, they had borrowed or adapted or invented a script for their purpose. There had, indeed, been cases in which empire-builders had passed over their own mother tongue in favour of another language already current in their dominions as a *lingua franca*[1] or even in favour of a classical language which would have been extinct long since if it had not been artificially kept alive or resuscitated.[2] The most usual practice, however, had been for empire-builders to give official currency to their own national language and script without granting these a monopoly. Indeed, in the administration of universal states a plurality of official languages and scripts appears to be the rule; and a medium that enjoys a legal primacy may not in practice be the medium most in use. There may be secondary languages that reign supreme in particular regions of the empire or in particular imperial services; and these may be *lingue franche* that have won this position for themselves *de facto* without having been given recognition *de jure*. *Lingue franche* that are already going concerns may force their way into official or unofficial use in the service of a universal state that has come into existence after they have already won an established position for themselves; and, conversely, the use of a *lingua franca* in the service of a universal state may be a factor in the making of this language's fortune.

These general propositions may perhaps be usefully illustrated in an empirical survey.

A Monopoly for Some Single Language or Script

In the Sinic World the problem was solved in a characteristically drastic fashion by Ts'in She Hwang-ti.[3] The founder of the Sinic universal state gave exclusive currency to the version of the Chinese characters that had been in official use in his own ancestral state of Ts'in[4] and thereby succeeded in arresting the tendency, which had gone

[1] *Lingue franche* are products of social disintegration. A survey of them has been made in V. v. 483–527.

[2] A survey of instances of such archaism in language and literature has been made in V. vi. 62–83.

[3] It would be interesting to know whether, in A.D. 1928, President Mustafā Kemāl Atatürk was aware of this Sinic precedent for his own equally high-handed act of making the use of the Perso-Arabic Alphabet illegal, and the use of the Latin Alphabet obligatory, for conveying the Ottoman Turkish language within the frontiers of the Turkish Republic.

[4] See Fitzgerald, C. P.: *China, A Short Cultural History* (London 1935, Cresset Press), p. 137; Franke, O.: *Geschichte des Chinesischen Reiches*, vol. i (Berlin and Leipzig 1930, de Gruyter), pp. 233–40. Franke gives German translations of the relevant passages in the work of Sse-ma Ts'ien.

far by the end of the foregoing Time of Troubles, for each of the Contending States to develop a parochial script only partially intelligible to litterati outside those parochial limits. Since the Sinic characters were 'ideograms' conveying meanings, not 'phonemes' representing sounds,[1] the effect of Ts'in She Hwang-ti's act was to endow the Sinic Society with a uniform visual language, which would continue—even if the spoken language were to break up into mutually unintelligible dialects—to serve as a means of oecumenical communication by sleight of hand and skill of eye for the very small minority that could learn to read and write so complex a script—just as, in a Western World in A.D. 1952, the Arabic numerals conveyed identical meanings on paper to peoples who, viva voce, called the numbers by different names and wrote these names out in different alphabets.[2] Yet, as this parallel indicates, Ts'in She Hwang-ti's standardization of the Sinic characters would not, in itself, have availed to save the Sinic Society from the curse of a babel of tongues if in the Sinic World there had not been other forces working in favour of uniformity in speech as well as in script.

To begin with, the Sinic World, at the time when the first Ts'in Emperor united it politically under his own rule, happened still to be homogeneous in language to an unusual degree, though by that time it had expanded far and wide from its original nucleus. A great majority of the population even of this vastly extended area spoke some variety of the Chinese branch of the Chinese-Siamese group of the great Asian family of monosyllabic languages,[3] and the heterophone minority largely consisted of speakers of some language of the kindred Tibeto-Burman group. Yet the unifying influence of this original linguistic homogeneity might have been more than counteracted by the combined effect of the geographical expansion and the political disruption of the Sinic Society during its Time of Troubles if Ts'in She Hwang-ti had not opened a new chapter of Sinic history by imposing political unity, and if his Han successors had not underpinned this edifice of oecumenical government by calling into existence, to administer it, the acceptable and therefore effective oecumenical civil service that Ts'in She Hwang-ti had failed to create.[4] These professional civil servants, recruited from all quarters of the Empire and posted in any province except that of their birth, could not conduct their business with one another and with the public solely by brushwork. In addition to the common visual language, provided by Ts'in She Hwang-ti's fiat, which had become the silent shibboleth for admission into the service of the state, the new imperial governing class required a common means of communication viva voce; and it was a standardized official vocalization of a standardized official script that was to save the Sinic Society, and later on the main body of the succeeding Far Eastern Society, from being afflicted with that multiplicity of languages that was to make the Western World an easy prey for the malady of Nationalism.

Ts'in She Hwang-ti's standardization of the Sinic characters may have been anticipated by the founder of a Minoan universal state whose

[1] See V. v. 492. [2] See V. v. 491. [3] See II. i. 318.
[4] See pp. 169–73, above, and pp. 351 and 352, below.

name had not yet been discovered by Modern Western archaeologists in A.D. 1952. Though none of the scripts in use in the Minoan World at divers times and places had yet been deciphered, their sequence gave evidence of a reform in the art of writing that was still more revolutionary than Ts'in She Hwang-ti's. At the transition from 'Middle Minoan II' to 'Middle Minoan III',[1] two separate hieroglyphic scripts, which had made their appearance simultaneously at the beginning of the former period, were suddenly and completely superseded by a single new linear script which was not just one version of the form of writing previously in use, but which drew on its predecessors for the construction of a new form of a different and superior order.[2] In the history of the Syriac Society, we know[3] that Ts'in She Hwang-ti did have a counterpart in the Umayyad Caliph ʿAbd-al-Malik (*imperabat* A.D. 685–705), who substituted the Arabic language and script for the Greek in the ex-Roman provinces of the Arab Caliphate, and for the Pehlevi in the ex-Sasanian provinces, as the official vehicle for the public records, including the all-important registers of the inland revenue.[4] When this change was put in hand, there was evidently some anxiety in official circles as to its possible effect on the efficiency of the public administration, particularly in the vital matter of the collection of the land-tax, and there was a corresponding relief when the transition was achieved without the awkward consequences that had been foreboded.

In the Spanish Empire in the Americas, Spanish became both the official language and the unofficial *lingua franca* of the Viceroyalty of New Spain, which provided the Central American World with its universal state, and it was given the same official status in the Andean universal state which the *conquistadores* had converted into the Spanish Viceroyalty of Peru. In the Andean World, however, the Spanish Crown demonstrated the sincerity of its profession to be a devoted secular agent for the propagation of the Catholic Christian Faith by allowing and encouraging the Roman Church to utilize and develop for its own purposes the Quichuan *lingua franca* to which the Spaniards' Inca predecessors had given an oecumenical currency[5] by making its acquisition compulsory for all their subjects.[6]

[1] The possibility that the break between 'Middle Minoan II' and 'Middle Minoan III' might be the mark left on the archaeological record by the foundation of a Minoan universal state has been suggested in I. i. 92–93; IV. iv. 64–65; V. v. 236; and V. vi. 312.

[2] See V. v. 491, n. 3.

[3] From the testimony of Ahmad Al-Balādhurī (*Kitāb Futūh al-Buldān*, pp. 300–1 and 465–6 in the English translation by Hitti, P. K., vol. i (New York 1916, Columbia University Press)); Tabarī (2, 1034); and Theophanes (*Chronographia*, ed. by de Boor, C. (Leipzig 1883–5, Teubner, 2 vols.), vol. i, p. 376, *sub Anno Mundi* 6199). Theophanes ascribes the innovation, not to ʿAbd-al-Malik, but to his successor Walīd I (*imperabat* A.D. 705–15). Walīd I appears to have completed ʿAbd-al-Malik's work by substituting the Arabic language and script for the Coptic in Egypt, where the Coptic had formerly been used side by side with the Greek. This local change in Egypt, which was carried out in A.H. 87 according to Makrizi, *Khitāt*, i. 98, cited by Wellhausen, J.: *Das Arabische Reich und sein Sturz* (Berlin 1902, Reimer), p. 137, n. 1, seems to have been confused by Theophanes with the previous displacement of Greek throughout the ex-Roman provinces of the Caliphate. In the present Study, V. v. 501, n. 3, Theophanes' error has been carelessly reproduced, notwithstanding Wellhausen's elucidation.

[4] See V. v. 501, and p. 181, above.

[5] See Markham, Sir C.: *The Incas of Peru* (London 1910, Smith Elder), p. 165.

[6] See V. v. 523–4, and p. 251, below.

A Partnership between Several Different Languages or Scripts

We may now pass on to consider some instances of the more frequent practice of providing a universal state with several official languages and scripts, including the empire-builders' own.

In the British Rāj in India the English mother tongue of the rebuilders of a Mughal Rāj was, for certain purposes, substituted for Persian, the official language that had been bequeathed by the Mughals to their British and other successors. In A.D. 1829, for instance, the British Indian Government made English the medium for its diplomatic correspondence, and in A.D. 1835 the medium for higher education in its dominions. But when in A.D. 1837 the final step was taken in the deposition of Persian from its official status in British India, the British Indian Government did not introduce the use of English for all the other purposes that Persian had previously served. In the conduct of judicial and fiscal proceedings, which were provinces of public administration that personally concerned all Indians of every nationality, caste, and class, the British Indian Government replaced Persian, not by English, but by the local vernaculars;[1] and the Sanskritized Hindī vernacular known as Hindustānī was actually manufactured by British Protestant missionaries to provide the Hindu population of Northern India with a counterpart of the Persianized Hindī vernacular, known as Urdu, which the Indian Muslims had already manufactured for themselves.[2] This humane and politic decision to forbear from misusing political power by giving exclusive official currency to the alien empire-builders' own mother tongue perhaps partially accounts for the remarkable fact that when, 110 years later, their descendants voluntarily handed over their rāj to the descendants of their Indian subjects, it was taken as a matter of course, in both of the British Indian Empire's polyglot Indian successor-states, that the English language would remain at least provisionally in use *de facto* for the purposes which it had served under the British régime.

In the Napoleonic Empire in Western and Central Europe, the local vernaculars—Italian, German, and Dutch—which had previously been in use as official languages in parochial states, were allowed to retain their official status side by side with French. In earlier chapters of Western history the French language had made pacific conquests at the expense of Flemish in the Southern Netherlands and of a local High German dialect in Alsace. In both these countries, French had not only become a *lingua franca* but had been accepted as the medium for literature and administration. The Napoleonic Empire had too short a life to furnish any indication whether, if it had endured, its builders' language would have been likely by the same process of peaceful penetration to win for itself over a wider area the position which it had already attained in Alsace and Flanders. The nationalism which the French Revolution had begotten in France, and of which the Napoleonic Empire was inevitably a 'carrier',[3] would in any case have militated against the prestige which the French language and culture had

[1] See V. v. 516, n. 1. [2] See V. v. 518, n. 2. [3] See V. v. 503–4.

acquired in Central Europe under the *ancien régime*.[1] One thing of which we can be certain is that the French language's prospects, whatever they might otherwise have been, would have been blighted if the Napoleonic régime had attempted, in the manner of the Caliph 'Abd-al-Malik, to impose the use of the empire-builders' own mother tongue on their non-French-speaking subjects.

We can assert this with confidence in the light of the then recent failure of the Emperor-King Joseph II (*res gerebat solus* A.D. 1780–90)[2] to impose the use of German on the non-German-speaking peoples of the Danubian Hapsburg Monarchy. Though economic utility and cultural amenity alike told in favour of this attempted *Diktat* of political authority, Joseph's linguistic policy was a disastrous failure. It not only met with prompt defeat in the territories of the Crown of Saint Stephen, where the vigorous survival of medieval constitutional rights had kept a Magyar and a Croat national consciousness alive, and where the diasporà of German urban and agricultural settlers was very thinly sown; it also evoked the first new stirrings of the long since dormant national consciousness of the Czechs and the Slovenes, who by Joseph's time had been so deeply submerged by a flowing tide of Germanization that, in the judgement of even the sharpest-sighted contemporary observer, their complete assimilation at no distant date might have been taken as a foregone conclusion. The only substantial success which the Josephian policy secured was the retention of German, until the break-up of the Monarchy in A.D. 1918, as the universal language of command in a unitary Imperial-Royal Army. In the Imperial-Royal Navy the language of command had been Italian;[3] and the fact that this Hapsburg fighting service continued during the nineteenth century to employ for this purpose the mother tongue of its principal adversaries in that chapter of its history testifies both to the placidity of the Hapsburg êthos and to the vitality of the Italian language as a maritime *lingua franca* in the Mediterranean.

The Turkish masters of the Ottoman Empire never embarked on the policy which was successfully applied in the Arab Caliphate and unsuccessfully in the Danubian Hapsburg Monarchy. The founders' native Turkish was the official language of imperial administration; but in the heyday of the Ottoman Power in the sixteenth and seventeenth centuries of the Christian Era the *lingua franca* of the Pādishāh's slave-household was Serbo-Croat[4] and the *lingua franca* of the Ottoman Navy Italian[5]—for the same reason that prevailed upon the Hapsburg Navy to employ the same language. Moreover, on the civil side the Ottoman Government, like the British Indian Government, followed a policy of allowing its subjects as far as possible to use languages of their own choice in public affairs that were of personal concern to the individual—though it approached this same statesmanlike objective along a different consti-

[1] See V. v. 503, n. 3.

[2] Joseph was Holy Roman Emperor from A.D. 1765 onwards, and from the same date he was also associated with his mother Maria Theresa in the government of the hereditary dominions of the House of Hapsburg; but it was not till after her death in A.D. 1780 that he had a free hand to pursue a policy of his own.

[3] See V. v. 502.

[4] See V. v. 518–19.

[5] See V. v. 502.

tutional avenue. Whereas the British Government in India boldly set aside the previously established Muslim ecclesiastical courts and succeeded in providing an acceptable alternative for its Muslim subjects by applying the Muslim *Sharī'* Law in British courts and by conducting the judicial proceedings in the local vernaculars, the Ottoman Government delegated this great province of public administration to autonomous communal authorities, officially recognized and supported by the Sublime Porte, which conducted their judicial business in languages traditionally employed by them for public purposes.[1] Since these communal authorities were ecclesiastical, the languages which they used for civil as well as for religious affairs were the sacred languages of their respective religions. The law administered in the communal courts of the Muslim community throughout the Ottoman Empire was written in Arabic,[2] the law of the communal courts of the Orthodox Christian community throughout the Empire in Greek, the law of the Gregorian Monophysite community in Armenian, and so on. It will be seen that the 'Osmanlis in the Orthodox Christian and Arabic worlds showed the same restraint as the British in India in limiting the scope of the official currency which they gave to their own mother tongue.

A similar restraint was shown by the Romans in the imposition of Latin as an official language in provinces of their empire in which Greek was either the mother tongue or the established *lingua franca.* They contented themselves with making Latin the exclusive language of military command for units of the Imperial Army, wherever recruited and wherever stationed,[3] and the principal language of municipal administration for colonies of Italian origin on Greek or Oriental ground. For

1 See IX. viii. 184–6. The non-Muslim autonomous communities were known by the name of *millet*—a word of Arabic origin with a meaning betwixt and between the connotations of the Western words 'nation' and 'church'. Though the dominant Muslim community was not called a *millet*, its constitution and status were in essence the same as those of the Jewish *millet* and of the several Christian *millets* of different denominations. Indeed, the *millet* system, which confounded the traditional Christian distinction between Church and State, was an expression of the Islamic conception of Society which could hardly have taken shape in a predominantly Christian political milieu. In the Ottoman Empire there were two privileged groups within the Muslim community—the kinsfolk of the Prophet Muhammad (*Seyyids*) and the members of the Pādishāh's slave-household (*qullar*)—each of which enjoyed a communal autonomy of its own in the judicial sphere (see Lybyer, A. H.: *The Government of the Ottoman Empire in the Time of Suleiman the Magnificent* (Cambridge, Mass. 1913, Harvard University Press), pp. 116 and 216).

2 In addition to the *Sherī'ah* the Ottoman ecclesiastical courts did, however, also administer the *qānūns* (imperial rescripts of the Ottoman *pādishāhs*) and *'ādet* (local customary law). The *qānūns* were written in Ottoman Turkish, while *'ādet*, if written at all, was not necessarily written in either Turkish or Arabic (see Lybyer, A. H.: op. cit., pp. 152 and 223).

3 The two policies of giving Latin a monopoly in the Army and paying deference to Greek ran counter to one another in Thrace. In another context (pp. 133–4 and 134–5 above) we have noticed that, when the Romans annexed the client kingdom of the Odrysae, they carried their respect for the Greek language to the point of making Greek, and not Latin, the *lingua franca* and official language of this new Roman province. At the same time Thrace became as prolific a source of recruitment for the Roman Army as the adjoining provinces along the right bank of the Danube. In consequence, Thrace, as well as Moesia and Pannonia, came to be Latinized to a large extent, though in Thrace, unlike the Danubian provinces, the Latinization was not deliberate. For the penetration of Thracians into the Praetorian cohorts from the Severan revolution of A.D. 193 onwards until the disbandment of these units in A.D. 312 by Constantine the Great, see Durry, M.: *Les Cohortes Prétoriennes* (Paris 1938, Boccard), pp. 248 and 255.

other purposes they continued to employ the Attic *koinê*[1] wherever they found it already in official use;[2] and they made its official status in their own empire conspicuous by giving it a place, side by side with Latin, in the central administration as well. At Rome under the Principate the Imperial Chancery was organized in duplicate, with a Greek as well as a Latin side, so that correspondents using either of 'the two languages' (as Latin and Greek were styled *sans phrase*) could be sure of being able to transact their business with the imperial authorities in the language of their choice.

This Roman forbearance towards the Greek language was something more than a tribute to the pre-eminence of Greek over Latin as a medium of culture; it represented a signal victory of statesmanship over *hybris* in Roman souls; for in those far-flung territories of the Empire, extending from Moesia to Mauretania and from Bruttium to Britain, in which Greek was not in competition with Latin on the morrow of the Roman conquest, the triumph of Latin was so sensational that it might have turned the heads of any but the most sober-minded empire-builders. So far from having to impose the use of Latin upon their subjects and allies in territories outside the Greek language's range, the Romans were in the happy position of being able to enhance its attractiveness by treating the use of it as a privilege that had to be sued for.[3] Nor did Latin win its peaceful victories solely at the expense of languages that had never been reduced to writing or enshrined in a literature. In Italy it had to contend with sister Italic dialects like Oscan and Umbrian, and with Illyrian dialects like Messapian and Venetian, which had once been on a cultural par with Latin—not to speak of Etruscan, which was freighted with the cultural heritage of its Anatolian homeland. In Africa, again, Latin had to contend with Punic. Yet, in these contests with non-Greek 'culture languages' already in the field, Latin was invariably victorious; and, although in Africa the wave of Punic speech continued under Roman rule to advance from the coast into the interior, and to penetrate from the upper to the lower strata of society, at the expense of Berber, it now lost ground to a Latin wave, following hard in its wake, as fast as it gained it from a Berber sump. This triumphal progress of the Latin language west of Syrtis and north of Haemus is the setting in which we have to regard the Romans' deference towards the Greek language in order to appreciate this attitude at its full worth.

An even more remarkable restraint was shown by the Sumerian

[1] See V. v. 494–5.

[2] In Egypt the Romans continued the Ptolemies' practice of employing, side by side with the Greek language and alphabet, the New Egyptian language and the hieroglyphic and demotic scripts for inscriptions addressed to the native Egyptian population. This practice had been copied by the Ptolemies from the Achaemenidae, who, in Egypt, had employed the Egyptian language and scripts side by side with the Aramaic (see p. 248, below).

[3] For example, in 180 B.C. the municipality of Cumae, whose citizens had possessed the passive rights of Roman citizenship (the Roman *civitas sine suffragio*) since 338 B.C., was allowed, in response to a petition from the municipal authorities themselves, to substitute Latin for the community's native Oscan as its official language ('Cumanis eo anno petentibus permissum ut publice Latine loquerentur et praeconibus Latine vendendi ius esset.'—Livy, Book XL, chap. 42).

founders of 'the Realm of the Four Quarters' when they put the upstart Akkadian language officially on a par with a Sumerian which was not only the empire-builders' mother tongue but was the historic vehicle of the Sumerian culture. This large-minded policy was no doubt inspired by the practical consideration that in Ur-Engur's (Ur-Nammu's) day (*imperabat circa* 2143–2126 or 2079–2062 B.C.) Akkadian was gaining ground[1] while Sumerian was on the ebb; and, in the event, Sumerian had become almost a dead language by the time when a universal state which Sumerian-speaking empire-builders had inaugurated reached the end of its chequered career after the death of Hammurabi (*imperabat circa* 1792–1750 or 1728–1686 B.C.).[2] The Amorite restorer of a Sumerian political edifice did 'not strive officiously to keep alive' the moribund mother tongue of his predecessor Ur-Engur; but it is significant that he also appears to have made no attempt to fill the Sumerian language's now all but vacant place with his own ancestral Canaanite dialect, but to have allowed Akkadian—which in his time stood at its zenith—to enjoy, unchallenged, the virtual monopoly which by then it had won for itself *de facto*.

The Achaemenidae gave as modest a place in the government of their empire to their Persian mother tongue as to their Persian mother country.[3] Darius the Great's account of his own acts on the rock of Behistan, overhanging the Great North-East Road, was inscribed in triplicate in three different adaptations of the cuneiform script conveying the divers languages of the three imperial capitals: Elamite for Susa, Medo-Persian for Ecbatana,[4] and Akkadian for Babylon. The same three languages and scripts were likewise employed in the inscription on Darius's own tomb at Naqsh-i-Rustam in Fars,[5] and in official inscriptions on imperial buildings in all parts of the Empire.[6] It is to the credit of the Achaemenidae that they should thus have placed two other languages officially on a par with their own mother tongue, but this conscientious even-handedness was too pedantic and too clumsy to meet the practical needs of current imperial administration. The Elamite tongue, for example, though it did happen to be the language of Susa, was not a *lingua franca* and was already moribund even in its own parochial domain;[7] and the version of the cuneiform script that had been specially devised for the conveyance of the Medo-Persian language failed—in spite of its technical excellence—to win its way into general use, and consequently failed to perpetuate itself. The increasing inaccuracy of its use in the inscriptions of Artaxerxes II (*imperabat* 404–358 B.C.) and Artaxerxes III (*imperabat* 358–338 B.C.) betrays the truth that its proper usage was

1 See V. v. 496–9.

2 See V. v. 485.

3 For the location of the several cities that divided between them the function of serving as capitals of the Achaemenian Empire, see pp. 203–8, above.

4 For Ecbatana, the former capital of the Median Monarchy and the actual summer residence of the Achaemenian Court, see p. 206, above. This Medo-Persian was, of course, also the language of the Persian imperial people's homeland in Fars, but, at the date when the Behistan Inscription was carved, the building of Persepolis was certainly not finished and may not even yet have begun.

5 See pp. 206–7, above.

6 See V. v. 499, n. 3, following Meyer, E.: *Geschichte des Altertums*, vol. iii, 1st ed. (Stuttgart 1901, Cotta), p. 28.

7 See Meyer, op. cit., vol. cit., p. 29.

being forgotten within perhaps less than two hundred years of its invention.[1]

This infelicity in the Achaemenids' original choice of official scripts and languages was only partially offset by their liberality in the use of unofficial languages and scripts which had a regional currency—for example, the Greek language and alphabet in the neighbourhood of the Aegean, and in Egypt the New Egyptian language conveyed alternatively, for different purposes, in the hieroglyphic and in the demotic form of the Egyptiac characters.[2] It seems, indeed, to have been their regular practice to provide translations, in the local vernaculars, of official documents addressed to their subjects.[3] But the stroke of statesmanship by which they saved a situation which their own pedantry had created was their act of giving official currency to the Aramaic alphabet and language—side by side with the three hyper-official languages and scripts—in all provinces of the Empire to the west of Babylonia.[4]

The sequel showed that commerce and culture may be more potent instruments than politics for making a language's fortune. In the Achaemenian Empire the speakers of Aramaic were politically of no account,[5] whereas the speakers of Medo-Persian were politically dominant; and, apart from this political 'pull', the Medo-Persian language was by no means at a disadvantage in other respects. The area over which it was spoken as a mother tongue was probably not less extensive,[6] though it was of course much less populous, than the area over which Aramaic was current at the time not merely as a *lingua franca* but as the language of daily life. Moreover, the unknown man of genius who had adapted the cuneiform characters for the conveyance of the Medo-Persian language had endowed it with a script that was almost as convenient as the Aramaic Alphabet. Taking his cue, we may suppose, from the Alphabet itself, he had achieved with the cuneiform characters what had never been achieved with them by their Sumerian inventors or their Akkadian, Elamite, and Hittite users: he had contrived to convey visually all the sounds of the Medo-Persian language in an all but alphabetic syllabary

[1] See Meyer, op. cit., vol. cit., p. 48.

[2] See Meyer, E.: *Geschichte des Altertums*, vol. iii, 1st ed. (Stuttgart 1901, Cotta), p. 48; eundem: 'Zu den Aramäischen Papyri von Elephantinê', in *Sitz. Kön. Preuss. Ak. Wiss.*, Gesamtsitzung vom 23 November, 1911, Mitth. vom 26 October, p. 1040.

[3] See Meyer, E.: *Geschichte des Altertums*, vol. iii, 1st ed. (Stuttgart 1901, Cotta), pp. 48–49.

[4] See Meyer, E.: *Geschichte des Altertums*, vol. iii, 1st ed. (Stuttgart 1901, Cotta), p. 48; eundem: *Sitz. Kön. Preuss. Ak. Wiss.*, loc. cit.; *Der Papyrusfund von Elephantinê* (Leipzig 1912, Hinrichs), p. 17 (both cited in this Study already in V. v. 123, n. 2). See further Olmstead, A. T.: *A History of the Persian Empire* (Chicago 1948, Chicago University Press), pp. 116–17, 178, 480–1.

[5] Any prospects of political greatness that the Aramaean peoples might ever have been able to look forward to had been blighted when they had lost their long-drawn-out battle with Assyria in the eleventh and tenth centuries B.C. (see II. ii. 134), and the final blow had been the destruction of the south-westernmost of the Aramaean states, the Kingdom of Damascus, in 732 B.C. (see IV. iv. 476). But, at every stage of their military martyrdom, the Aramaeans had snatched cultural victories out of political reverses (see I. i. 79–80).

[6] We do not know the geographical boundaries of the Medo-Persian dialect of the Iranian language in the Achaemenian Age. The dialect of the Oxus–Jaxartes Basin, known in a later form as 'Sogdian', may already have become differentiated from the dialect or dialects of the Iranian Plateau, and we cannot identify the homeland of the Avestan dialect in which Zoroaster composed his *Gathas*.

of not more than thirty-six characters.[1] Yet in the competition between the Medo-Persian and the Aramaic scripts and languages it was the Aramaic that won.

It was not so surprising that the Aramaic language should have beaten the Medo-Persian in a competition for capturing the domain of a faltering Akkadian tongue, for here Aramaic had been the first in the field,[2] and it enjoyed, in addition, the overwhelming advantage of being a sister Semitic language which an Akkadian-speaker might substitute for his own mother tongue without having to make that conscious and laborious effort to speak an utterly alien language which would be required of him if he were to try to make himself at home with an Indo-European dialect. The really remarkable triumph was achieved by the Aramaic script, which succeeded in replacing the cuneiform as the medium for conveying the Medo-Persian language in its post-Achaemenian phase. This victory must appear the more extraordinary considering that it was accompanied by a lamentably perverse retrogression in the art of writing. Whereas the forgotten inventor of the Achaemenian script for the conveyance of the Medo-Persian language had shown his originality by making an exclusively phonetic use of cuneiform characters that had originated as ideograms, the inventors of the Pehlevi script for the conveyance of the same language in its next phase mishandled a ready-made phonetic Alphabet by coining ideograms out of it. Instead of consistently conveying Persian words by spelling them out in Aramaic letters used phonetically, they lapsed into conveying them by writing Aramaic words that were their equivalents in meaning but were, of course, entirely unrelated to them in sound.[3] This ability of the Aramaic Alphabet to capture the Persian language even in a usage that stultified the Alphabet's own distinctive technical excellence gives some measure of the prestige which it must have acquired, by then, in Persian minds; and one source of this prestige was undoubtedly the official status that had been given to the Aramaic Alphabet and language by Achaemenian Emperors whose mother tongue was not Semitic but Indo-European.

The Manchu restorers of a Far Eastern universal state showed the same liberality, and same touch of pedantry, as the Achaemenidae in placing their own mother tongue and the languages of their Mongol allies and Chinese subjects on a footing of official parity. The Manchus, like the Achaemenidae, inscribed their public records in triplicate: the Chinese text in Sinic characters, the Mongol text in an adaptation of a Uighur version of a Sogdian variant of the Aramaic Alphabet,[4] and the Manchu text in an adaptation of the Mongol Alphabet.[5] In the Manchu, as in the Achaemenian, Empire, two out of the three languages and scripts that had thus been made official on rather formal grounds failed to qualify for this privileged position on the strength of their actual or

[1] The inventor of the Medo-Persian cuneiform Alphabet had been anticipated by the inventor of the Phoenician cuneiform Alphabet used at Ras ash-Shamrah on the coast of Northern Syria about a thousand years earlier. But the Ras ash-Shamrah Alphabet had long since fallen into disuse and oblivion, and the inventor of the Behistan Alphabet must have made the same invention independently.

[2] See I. i. 79–80 and V. v. 499.

[3] See I. i. 80 and V. v. 500.

[4] See V. v. 500, n. 6.

[5] See ibid.

prospective currency. The habitat of the Manchus' Mongol-speaking allies was confined to an outlying and sparsely populated glacis of the Manchu Empire; and the northern and north-eastern parts of Manchuria, where, if anywhere, the Manchus' mother tongue had some prospect of surviving, were almost equally remote from the heart of the imperial people's now far extended dominions. In Southern Manchuria the Manchus had entered into a symbiosis with a local Chinese population, and the ruling element among the Manchus had already become half-Sinified before their entry into Intramural China in A.D. 1644. The complete Sinification of the Manchu civil and military 'Bannermen' inside the Wall[1] was manifestly only a matter of time. In fact, the successful achievement of the Manchus' political ambitions had condemned the Manchus' mother tongue to sink *de facto*, whatever its status *de jure*, to the level of a local patois spoken only by the imperial Manchus' country cousins in a 'reservoir' of man-power in the north-eastern marches.[2]

Fortunately for the Manchu Imperial Government, however, the uselessness, for most practical purposes, of two out of the three official languages and scripts of their choice was fully counterbalanced by the all but universal currency, throughout their dominions, of the Sinic characters and the 'mandarin' *lingua franca* of the Chinese civil service.[3] In Eastern Asia in the Manchu Dynasty's day, these two media of visual and oral communication held the field as ubiquitously as the Akkadian language and Akkadian adaptation of the cuneiform characters in South-West Asia in the days of Ur-Engur (Ur-Nammu) and Hammurabi. As compared with the Manchus, the Achaemenidae were unlucky in their generation; for by their time the Akkadian language had lost its former monopoly of serving as a South-West Asian *lingua franca* and was giving way to Aramaic even as the parochial speech of the single province of Babylonia. From Babylon westwards a babel of tongues confronted the Achaemenidae with an administrative problem from which the Manchu rulers of Eastern Asia were exempted by a lucky accident of local linguistic history; and, thanks to this, the Manchus never found themselves compelled like their Achaemenid counterparts to institute a fourth official language in order to redress the inadequacy of three.

In the Mauryan Empire the philosopher-emperor Açoka (*imperabat* 273–232 B.C.) succeeded in reconciling the demands of impartial justice with those of practical convenience by employing a number of different local living vernaculars conveyed in two different scripts, the Brahmī and the Kharoshthī.[4] This happy catholicity in Açoka's choice of media

[1] For the Manchu 'Banners', see pp. 128–9, above; for the civil service of the Manchu Empire, see pp. 346–8, below.

[2] The function performed by 'reservoirs' of this kind in universal states established by semi-barbarian or barbarian empire-builders is brilliantly expounded by Lattimore, O., in *Manchuria, Cradle of Conflict* (New York 1932, Macmillan), pp. 31–52.

[3] For the spread of this 'mandarin' dialect of Chinese, see V. v. 512–14.

[4] See Smith, V. A.: *The Early History of India*, 3rd ed. (Oxford 1914, Clarendon Press), pp. 166–70 and 172–4, and the present Study, V. v. 498 and 500. 'Two recensions of the Fourteen Rock Edicts, inscribed on rocks at places near the North-West Frontier of India, were executed in . . . Kharoshthī. . . . All the other inscriptions [about thirty-two in number] are incised in one or other variety of the early Brahmī Alphabet' (Smith, op. cit., pp. 166–7).

for communication with his subjects was prompted by the single-minded purpose of acquainting them with the way of salvation revealed to Mankind by Açoka's master Gautama,[1] as the Spanish successors of the Incas were moved by their eagerness for the propagation of the Roman Catholic form of Christianity to allow the Gospel to be preached in the Andean World in a Quichuan *lingua franca*.[2] This Quichuan had gained the wide currency that it enjoyed at the time of the Spanish conquest because the Spaniards' Inca predecessors had made the learning of Quichuan compulsory[3] and had imposed this intellectual corvée on themselves as well as on their subjects—if it is a fact that the Incas had an esoteric language of their own which they did not choose to vulgarize.[4]

Empire-builders who have refrained from giving Official Currency to their own Mother Tongue

This Incan self-denying ordinance might have been dismissed as a peculiar product of the Incas' ultra-totalitarian êthos if there were not other examples of imperial peoples refraining from giving any official status to their own mother tongue.

The Mongols, for instance, did not take advantage of their immense conquests in order to propagate the Mongol language from the Pacific to the Euphrates and the Carpathians. The Mongol Khāqāns employed the Sinic characters and the 'mandarin' dialect for the government of China, and the Mongol Il-Khans the New Persian language and the Perso-Arabic Alphabet for the government of Iran and 'Irāq. Even the Khans of Chaghatāy's and Bātū's appanages, who did not transfer their headquarters from 'the Desert' to 'the Sown', nevertheless abandoned the use of their Mongol mother tongue in favour of a Turkish that was current among a majority of their Nomad subjects.

The Turkī dialect that was adopted by the Mongol Chaghatāy Khan's successors from the local Nomads of whom they had taken command in Zungaria had also become the current language of their sedentary subjects in Transoxania; and, when, under the leadership of Timur Lenk (*imperabat* A.D. 1369–1405), the Transoxanians reversed the Mongol political order by force of arms and asserted their own mastery over the Eurasian Nomads,[5] their Turkī tongue was fashioned into a literary language on a Persian model by the Timurid Sultan Husayn's minister Mīr 'Alī Shīr Nawā'ī (*decessit* A.D. 1501).[6] In the next generation Bābur (*vivebat* A.D. 1483–1530)—a scion of the House of Timur who retrieved his family's fortunes by laying the foundations of a new Timurid Empire on the Indian side of the Hindu Kush—made a brilliant use of the vehicle for literary expression that Nawā'ī had provided for him in his own Turkī mother tongue by writing in Turkī his celebrated memoirs.

In the light of these antecedents, it might have been expected that, when Bābur's pioneer empire-building work in India was followed up and completed by his grandson Akbar (*imperabat* A.D. 1556–1605), the Timurid Mughal Dynasty's now literate mother tongue would have

1 See V. vi. 75–76. 2 See p. 242, above. 3 See ibid.

4 See V. v. 523, n. 2, following Joyce, T. A.: *South American Archaeology* (London 1912, Lee Warner), p. 213.

5 See II. ii. 144–8. 6 See I. i. 351 and II. ii. 149.

become one of the official languages of the universal state which these Turkī-speaking empire-builders from Central Asia had imposed on the Hindu World. The architects of the Mughal Rāj in India did indeed select for the official language of their empire one of the established literary languages of the Iranic Muslim Society of which they themselves were members, but the language of their choice was not Turkī but Persian;[1] and, in the unofficial hybrid *lingua franca* that was begotten of the social intercourse between a Mughal Court and Army and a Hindu subject population, it was Persian again, and not Turkī, that was infused into Hindustānī.[2] Even in their own household the Mughal Dynasty in India eventually took to speaking Persian instead of their mother tongue. This defeat of Turkī by Persian on all fronts was the more remarkable considering that the discomfited language was the ancestral speech not only of the Timurids themselves but of the most martial contingent of their polyglot henchmen, and also considering that the Emperor Bābur's literary gift reappeared among his descendants. Bābur's daughter Gulbadan Bēgum wrote a history of her brother Humāyūn, and Humāyūn's grandson Jahāngīr emulated his great-grandfather's literary achievement by writing memoirs of his own life and reign;[3] but Gulbadan's *Humāyūn Nāma* and Jahāngīr's *Tuzūk* were written, not in Turkī, but in Persian. When Bābur's pen as well as Bābur's sword had been thrown into the Turkī scale, the balance would hardly have inclined on the Persian side, as it did, if the prestige of the victorious language had not been allowed to pull its weight by a deliberate forbearance on the part of the gifted Turkī-speaking princes with whom the last word lay.

A similar forbearance was shown by the Emperor Hammurabi (*imperabat circa* 1792–1750 or 1728–1686 B.C.) when he refrained[4] from attempting to substitute his living Canaanite mother tongue for a moribund Sumerian as one of the official languages of a momentarily restored Empire of Sumer and Akkad, and thereby left the way open for the Aramaic dialect of a later wave of Semitic-speaking interlopers from the Arabian Steppe eventually to supersede Akkadian as the *lingua franca* of South-Western Asia. It was even more remarkable that in the eighth and seventh centuries B.C., in the hour of the Aramaic language's triumph, when the Akkadian language was manifestly on the wane, as the Sumerian had been in Hammurabi's day, the Chaldaean leaders of an anti-Assyrian resistance movement and founders of a Neo-Babylonian Empire should have followed Hammurabi in making the Akkadian language and Akkadian version of the cuneiform script their official media of communication. The Chaldaeans had been carried into the marshlands of South-Western Babylonia in the same Völkerwanderung that had swept the Hebrews[5] into Southern Syria and the Aramaeans into Damascus and Mesopotamia, and we may infer that, at the time when these three Semitic peoples simultaneously broke out of Arabia, they were all speaking some variety of a common ancestral Aramaic.[6] If there

1 See V. v. 515.
2 See V. v. 517–18.
3 See II. ii. 149.
4 See p. 247, above.
5 Including under this term Moab and Ammon and Edom and Judah as well as Israel.
6 On this hypothesis, both the Chaldaeans and the Hebrews were originally Aramaic-speaking peoples who eventually readopted their ancestral speech after an interval during

is substance in this conjecture, it speaks volumes for the prestige of Babylon that the Chaldaeans should have been moved to discard an ancestral Aramaic dialect in favour of the Akkadian speech of their Assyrian oppressors because this Akkadian was also the traditional language of an imperial city and treasure-house of culture which Nabopolassar's Chaldaean followers longed to make their own[1] as eagerly as Mehmed the Conqueror's Turkish followers desired to possess 'the Abode of Felicity' on the shores of the Bosphorus.

The adoption of Akkadian by the Chaldaeans as the official language of the Neo-Babylonian Empire may have prolonged the currency of Akkadian as a living language for perhaps five hundred years. Sanskrit was adopted by the Guptas as the official language of a restored Indic universal state perhaps a thousand years after it had died a natural death.[2] It is one of the curiosities of history that the rebuilders of Açoka's Empire should have chosen for their official medium of communication a language which had been passed over, as obsolete, by Açoka himself some seven hundred years earlier.

Who are the Beneficiaries?

If we now pass from our survey of official languages in universal states to a review of the beneficiaries, we shall find that official languages had been turned to account by restorers of the empires in which these languages had enjoyed official currency; by other latter-day secular agencies, both public and private, political and economic; and by the propagators of higher religions and organizers of universal churches.

Akkadian, for example, as we have seen, was taken over from Ur-Engur's 'Realm of the Four Quarters' by Hammurabi, and again from the Neo-Babylonian Empire by the Achaemenidae. Classical Egyptian was taken over by 'the New Empire' from 'the Middle Empire'; Greek by the Umayyad Caliphate from the Roman Empire; and Persian by the British from the Mughal Rāj in India. It may be observed, however, that in a majority of these cases the inherited official language was not permanently retained. The British Indian Empire discarded Persian in favour of English employed in combination with local Indian vernaculars; the Umayyad Caliphs discarded Greek—and likewise Coptic and Pehlevī—in favour of Arabic; the archaistic-minded 'New Empire' of Egypt acquiesced in Ikhnaton's iconoclasm in the one point of sub-

which—unlike their Aramaean kinsmen and northern neighbours—they had succumbed to the languages of the sedentary peoples among whom they had settled—to Akkadian, that is, in the Chaldaeans' case and to Canaanite (hence miscalled 'Hebrew') in the Hebrews'. In both cases this adoption of the established language of the occupied country was to be expected; for the penetration of the Chaldaeans into Babylonia and of the Hebrews into Palestine was, as we know, a gradual process, and in each case the interlopers were mingling with a sedentary population that was more numerous and more cultivated than they were. On the other hand, it is not surprising that the Aramaean conquerors of the desert-port of Damascus and of the sparsely inhabited Mesopotamian Steppe should have preserved their ancestral language and should have been able, in a key-position at the mid-point of 'the Fertile Crescent', to convert an unextinguished local dialect into an oecumenical *lingua franca*.

1 The relations between the Chaldaean tribesmen and the citizens of Babylon in the eighth and seventh centuries B.C. have been touched upon in IV. iv. 476–80.

2 For the artificial revival of Sanskrit which culminated under the Gupta régime, see V. vi. 75–77.

stituting the living Egyptian speech of the day for the now dead classical language; the Achaemenidae found themselves constrained to supplement a waning Akkadian language and script by giving a supernumerary official status to a waxing Aramaic.

Akkadian, again, continued, after the final collapse of 'the Realm of the Four Quarters', to be used as a medium of diplomatic intercourse, commerce, and culture, not only within the former frontiers of the now defunct Sumeric universal state, but also in regions never ruled by either Hammurabi or Ur-Engur, and never even trodden by the great Akkadian war-lords of an earlier age, a Sargon or a Naramsin. In the fourteenth century B.C. the Akkadian language and script were being employed in the archives and libraries of Hittite Kings at Boghazqal'eh, and, *mirabile dictu*, in the correspondence between the Imperial Government of Egypt and its client princes in its own dominions in Syria, as well as in its transactions with such independent Powers as Khatti and Mitanni. A comparable triumph was achieved by the French language after the meteoric rise and fall of the Napoleonic Empire. In the nineteenth century of the Christian Era, French not only retained the role—which, under the *Ancien Régime*, it had already captured from Latin—of serving as the diplomatic language of the Western World; in the less superficial role of a culture-language it now also found new worlds to conquer in the successor-states of a defunct Spanish Empire of the Indies and in an Ottoman Empire that was rapidly going the Spanish Empire's way.[1]

An even more remarkable resilience was shown by Aramaic when, upon the overthrow of the Achaemenian Empire by Alexander, it was brusquely deposed, in favour of the Attic *koinê*, from the official status that the Achaemenidae had conferred on it in their western dominions. Deprived of the imperial patronage which it had enjoyed for two centuries, the Aramaic language succeeded, by the first century of the Christian Era, in completing the process, which it had begun without imperial patronage in the eighth century B.C., of supplanting Akkadian on the east and Canaanite on the west as the living language of the entire Semitic-speaking population of 'the Fertile Crescent'.[2] And, likewise on the strength of its own unaided merits, the Aramaic Alphabet achieved far wider conquests. In A.D. 1599, within less than two thousand years of the Achaemenian Empire's downfall, it was adopted for the conveyance of the Manchu language on the eve of the Manchu conquest of China.[3]

This diffusion of the Aramaic Alphabet was a technological and intellectual conquest which surpassed in its sweep the military and political conquests of the Mongol and Arab herdsmen-warriors, but the ultimate victors in this field were the higher religions which sped the Aramaic Alphabet on its way by taking it into their service. In its 'Square Hebrew' variant it became the vehicle of the Jewish scriptures and

[1] In the Ottoman Empire the way had been prepared for the entry of French by the previous currency of the philologically germane Tuscan *koinê* known as the Lingua Franca; and no doubt the adoption of French as the culture-language of Hispanic America was similarly facilitated by the kinship between French and the two locally current Romance languages: Spanish and Portuguese.

[2] See V. v. 499.

[3] See V. v. 500, with n. 6.

liturgy; in an Arabic adaptation of its Nabataean variant it became the Alphabet of Islam; in its Syriac variant it served impartially the two antithetic heresies of Nestorianism and Monophysitism into which Christianity polarized itself south-east of Taurus; in an Avestan adaptation of its Pehlevī variant it enshrined the sacred books of the Zoroastrian Church; in a Manichaean adaptation it laboured for a heresiarch whom Christians and Zoroastrians agreed in execrating; in a Kharoshthī variant it provided the Emperor Açoka with an instrument for conveying the teachings of the Buddha to his subjects in the former Achaemenian province in the Panjab.[1] This latter-day ecclesiastical use of the Aramaic Alphabet had given it an abiding place in history which it would never have won from its ephemeral secular canonization as one of the official scripts of the Achaemenian Empire; and, in this point, its fortunes were by no means peculiar.

In like manner the Latin and Attic Greek official languages and alphabets of the Roman Empire had won their place in history as the liturgical, theological, and administrative vehicles of the Roman Church in the West and the Greek Church in Orthodox Christendom,[2] while the Neo-Sanskrit official language of the Gupta Empire had justified its resurrection by providing a literary medium for both Hinduism and the Mahāyāna.[3] Even the Emperor Ts'in She Hwang-ti's mighty deed of standardizing the Sinic characters might live to be remembered, not for the service that it had done to ethics and politics by providing the Confucian School of Philosophy and the imperial civil service with a common instrument of literary expression, but for its service to religion in preserving in translation certain indispensable scriptures of the Mahāyāna that were no longer extant in the original Sanskrit. The Incas' pedagogic imposition of compulsory Quichuan on their long-suffering subjects would perhaps similarly be commemorated by these pagan Andeans' Catholic Christian descendants for its unintended assistance in furthering the propagation of Christianity in the New World. And it could be predicted that the Buddha's devoted exponent, the Emperor Açoka, would continue to win the blessings of Pālī-reading Hīnayānian Buddhists for his deliberate adoption of the living languages of his subjects as the media for his inscriptions.[4]

2. *Law*

The Three Provinces of Law

The field of social action which is the domain of Law divides itself into three great provinces: there is an administrative law that lays down the duties of subjects towards a government, and there are a criminal and a civil law, which are alike concerned with acts in which both parties are private persons, but which nevertheless differ, from a government's point of view, in the degree to which they affect governmental interests.

No government, of course, can be indifferent to administrative law;

[1] See V. v. 500–1, and p. 250, above.

[2] For the enlistment of a Neo-Attic Greek language, reconstructed by pagan Hellenic archaists, in the service of the Greek Church, see V. vi. 77–78.

[3] See ibid.

[4] See V. v. 498 and V. vi. 76, and p. 251, above.

indeed, it is no exaggeration to say that this province of law is bound to have priority over any government's other concerns; for the first concern of a government is to keep itself in existence; it cannot exist if it does not effectively impose its authority on its subjects by preventing or repressing all those acts of insubordination—ranging from high treason to arrears in the payment of taxes—in which a subject may show himself recalcitrant to a government's will; and the enforcement of governmental authority requires the formulation and execution of a body of administrative law. The same considerations lead governments, in so far as they have the strength, to concern themselves with the criminal law as well; for, though the criminal may not be attacking his government's authority intentionally or consciously in his assaults upon the life, limb, or property of his fellow subjects, he is in fact trespassing on the government's preserves by arrogating to himself, without official licence, a use of force which the Government must jealously preserve as its own monopoly if it is to maintain its authority intact. It will be seen that, in concerning itself with the criminal as well as with the administrative law, a government is primarily actuated by the motive of self-preservation, and for this reason there is in these two provinces of law a close approach to uniformity in the practice of all governments of both the parochial and the universal type. On the other hand, as far as they concern themselves with civil law, governments are acting for Society's and the individual's benefit more directly than for their own; and accordingly we shall not be surprised to find an empirical survey here revealing wide differences in the practice of those universal states which are our subject in the present Part of this Study.

Instances of Failure and Success in Attempts to impose a Uniform Imperial Law

In the domain of law, universal states, by reason of their historical role and their social function, are faced by a special problem of their own which does not confront parochial states—or, at any rate, not ordinarily in so extreme a degree. Universal states do not start life with a clean slate, and they have not time to work out the development of their institutions gradually. They usually establish themselves in place of their parochial predecessors abruptly, as an emergency measure for forestalling a now imminent social collapse. But those predecessors do not perish without leaving—in the domain of law, as in other fields of social action—a legacy with which their destroyer and successor has to reckon.

There had been at least one instance in which the empire-builders had been so abysmally inferior in culture to their conquered subjects that they had found themselves unable to impose on these any part of their own ancestral law. When the Mongols gave the Chinese main body of the Far Eastern Society its universal state and also roped into their empire both a nascent Iranic Muslim Society and a Russian offshoot of the main body of Orthodox Christendom, their leader Chingis Khan naïvely imagined that the legislator's pen would be as puissant an instrument in his hand as the conqueror's sabre.

' "The Great Yasa" was . . . made obligatory on all, including the head of the Empire, the Khāqān, himself. . . . He drew this immutable law neither from the institutions of the more civilised nations with which he came in contact . . . nor from the revelations of a supreme spirit . . . but from the ancient traditions, usages and ideas of his clan and of his nation. He was convinced that . . . he had established eternal norms, good for all time. But . . . "the Great Yasa" has ceased to be law, and the modern Mongols have lost all recollection of it.'[1]

A fortiori, this Nomad code failed to supersede the existing laws of the Mongol Khāqān's sedentary subjects, and, even when it came into head-on collision with them, it did not prevail, though it had the Mongol sword to back it. It conflicted, for example, with the Islamic *Sharī'ah*[2] by prohibiting the washing of hands in running water and by laying down an incompatible ritual procedure for the slaughtering of cattle. Chingis himself recklessly attempted to ride roughshod over the *Sharī'ah* by making it a capital offence to slaughter cattle in the Muslim fashion;[3] but, instead of thereby breaking-in for himself submissive subjects, he found himself inspiring defiant martyrs. This deliberately savage and provocative ordinance was revived by Chingis' successor Qubilāy (*imperabat* A.D. 1259–94)[4] and was not only inflicted on the Muslim diasporà in the Khāqān's own personal domain in Eastern Asia, but was also applied in the Transoxanian subject territories of the Appanage of Chaghatāy,[5] and in the dominions of the Il-Khan Arghūn (*regnabat* A.D. 1284–91)[6] in Iran and 'Irāq, where the Muslims constituted an overwhelming majority of the sedentary population. Yet this third Mongol persecution of Islam[7] was no more successful than its predecessors; and this defeat of the *Yāsāq* by the *Sharī'ah* was typical of the *Yāsāq*'s fortunes in all the Mongols' immense possessions.[8]

The 'Osmanlis—who, unlike the Mongols, found a long-enduring solution for the problem of stabilizing a Nomad empire over a sedentary population[9]—not only dealt summarily with high treason and firmly with the collection of taxes, but also took care to keep in the Ottoman Imperial Government's own hands the administration of the criminal law—to whatever *millet* the criminal or his victims might belong—with the sole, though portentous, exception of the members of the Pādishāh's slave-household, who had extorted from Sultan Bāyezīd II (*imperabat* A.D. 1481–1512) the privileges of being exempted from the jurisdiction of the courts of the Muslim community and of being made amenable exclusively to the judgement of their own officers.[10] On the other hand,

[1] Vladimirtsov, B. Y.: *The Life of Chingis-Khan*, English translation (London 1930, Routledge), pp. 74–75.

[2] See p. 74, above; IX. viii. 355; and X. ix. 36.

[3] See Howorth, H. H.: *History of the Mongols*, Part I (London 1876, Longmans Green), pp. 111–12.

[4] See ibid., pp. 273–4.

[5] See Cahun, L.: *Introduction à L'Histoire d'Asie: Turcs et Mongols des Origines à 1405* (Paris 1896, Colin), p. 412.

[6] See Arnold, T. W.: *The Preaching of Islam* (London 1913, Constable), p. 226.

[7] There appears to have been a second persecution in the reign of the Khāqān Kuyūk (*imperabat* A.D. 1246–8). See ibid.

[8] The eventual utilization of the Mongol Empire by Islam has been noticed on p. 160, above.

[9] See III. iii. 22–50.

[10] See Lybyer, A. H.: *The Government of the Ottoman Empire in the Time of Suleiman the Magnificent* (Cambridge, Mass. 1913, Harvard University Press), pp. 97, 116, and 216. See also the present Study, IX. viii. 186, n. 2, and X. ix. 37.

as we have seen,[1] the Ottoman imperial authorities showed an equal concern to avoid being implicated in the administration of the civil law, for which the 'peculiar institution' of the Pādishāh's slave-household could not be made to serve as an instrument.

In this province of law the slave-household's only positive concern was its insistence upon enjoying a communal autonomy of its own. As far as other Ottoman Muslims were concerned—apart from the Seyyids (i.e. reputed descendants of the Prophet Muhammad), who enjoyed the privilege of communal autonomy, like the members of the Pādishāh's slave-household[2]—the ʿOsmanlis not only conformed to the traditional practice of their adopted Islamic Faith by leaving all matters of civil law to be administered in accordance with the *Sharīʿah* by the Islamic ecclesiastical courts under the authority of the Sheykh-el-Islām; they took the logical further step—which had been taken by other Muslim governments before them, but had never, perhaps, before been carried out so systematically—of granting the same autonomy, on the same ecclesiastical basis, to the non-Muslim communities under their rule. Indeed, they showed an injudiciously light-hearted consistency in conferring corresponding powers on the foreign colonies of Frankish business men of divers nations whom they permitted to reside in the chief commercial centres of their empire—and thereby opened a chink in the curtain-wall of the Ottoman imperial fortress which was eventually to be enlarged into a breach by the lusty application of Frankish diplomatic and military levers.[3]

Thus in the province of the civil law the tendency in the Ottoman Empire was for an initial diversity to become increasingly accentuated with the passage of time, but in this point Ottoman history would appear

[1] The Ottoman institution of *millets* has been touched upon on pp. 244–5, above, *à propos* of its linguistic aspect. See further IX. viii. 184–6.

[2] See Lybyer, op. cit., pp. 206, 207, and 216.

[3] Though the name 'capitulations', by which these Ottoman charters to colonies of resident aliens came to be known, meant simply 'articles' and not, of course, 'terms of surrender', they did in fact have the effect of putting the Ottoman Empire at the mercy of the Frankish Powers in the latter days of the Empire's weakness. In origin these instruments were unilateral acts by which the Sublime Porte conferred on Frankish Christian residents the same right to administer their own civil affairs that it granted to its non-Muslim subjects. The 'capitulations' were inspired by the same motive of disinclination towards undertaking the distasteful task of administering the affairs of infidels in a field that did not appear to touch the security either of Islam or of the Ottoman State. Moreover, the 'capitulations', as well as the *millets*, had been a going concern in the parochial states whose place the Ottoman Empire had taken. They had originally been granted by the Western Christian Crusader successor-states of the ʿAbbasid Caliphate to colonies of business men from Venice, Genoa, Pisa, Amalfi, and other medieval Italian city-states, and the practice had spread thence both to the dominions of the Egyptian Mamlūks and to the Orthodox Christian successor-states of the East Roman Empire. It was thus easy to understand how the ʿOsmanlis slipped into their error of conferring 'capitulations' not only on the old-established Venetian and Genoese residents but on the French, Dutch, and English who now came bustling in at the Italians' heels. The error lay in failing to perceive that the analogy between charters granted to 'millets' consisting of Ottoman subjects and 'capitulations' conferred on resident colonies of the subjects of foreign Powers was one of form without being one of substance. The essential difference was that, in the second case, the rights and powers were accorded, not to Ottoman subjects, but to foreign governments who, unlike the *millet-bāshī* of the *Millet-i-Rum*, were not in the Pādishāh's power, but, on the contrary, wielded power of their own which they could use, in the hour of the Sublime Porte's weakness, for forcing upon the Porte their own interpretation of the 'capitulations' to the advantage of their subjects *in partibus Ottomannorum*.

to have been exceptional. In most universal states the tendency seems to have run contrariwise, towards uniformity. Indeed, even in Ottoman history there was an undercurrent in this direction; for from the fourteenth to the seventeenth century of the Christian Era the dominant Muslim community in the Ottoman Empire was continually gaining adherents at the subject non-Muslim communities' expense, and, if this process had not been checked by a decline in the 'Osmanlis' prestige in the eyes of their Orthodox and Monophysite Christian subjects when the tide turned against 'the Ghāzis of Rum'[1] in their warfare with the Christians of the West,[2] it is conceivable that eventually the Empire might have arrived at uniformity in civil law through attaining uniformity in religion.

In the more frequent cases in which the tendency towards uniformity had prevailed over opposing forces, this common result had not always been reached by the same means or at the same pace.

In the Sinic World, Ts'in She Hwang-ti characteristically imposed an oecumenical uniformity of law at one stroke by decreeing that the legislation in force in his own ancestral kingdom of Ts'in should be applied throughout the territories of the six rival states which he had suddenly conquered and annexed.[3] This act was doubly revolutionary, for these abruptly imposed Laws of Ts'in did not represent the traditional customs even of that outlandish march-state. They were one of those sweeping innovations executed in Ts'in, rather more than a hundred years earlier, by the philosopher-statesman Shang Yang (*decessit* 338 B.C.) which had prepared the way for Ts'in's decisive victory over her competitors in Ts'in She Hwang-ti's generation. Shang Yang had been one of the pioneer exponents of the so-called 'Legist' School of philosophy,[4] which had challenged the sanctity of customary rights and duties and had preached to the receptive ears of sovereigns the Machiavellian doctrine that all means were legitimate for attaining the socially expedient end of breaking the power of a feudal aristocracy for the benefit of parvenu monarchies.

Ts'in She Hwang-ti's revolutionary act had at least two Modern Western parallels. Napoleon introduced his newly minted codification of French law not only in France within her pre-Napoleonic limits, but in Italian, Flemish, German, and Polish annexed territories and client states of the Napoleonic Empire. The British Government of India introduced 'the Common Law' of England—partly in its original form and partly in adaptations embodied in local legislation—throughout the Indian territories over which it established its own direct rule.

This act of British statecraft, as far as it went, was more audaciously revolutionary than either of the other two, for the new law which Napoleon and Ts'in She Hwang-ti imposed on their subjects had, after

[1] The title by which the 'Osmanlis are saluted by their Timurid Mughal Turkish kinsman Bābur in his memoirs.

[2] For this change in the relations between the 'Osmanlis and their Orthodox Christian subjects see II. ii. 223–5; III. iii. 47–48; V. vi. 203–4, 299, and 300; and IX. viii. 161–5.

[3] See Franke, O.: *Geschichte des Chinesischen Reiches*, vol. i (Berlin and Leipzig 1930, de Gruyter), p. 233; Fitzgerald, C. P.: *China, A Short Cultural History* (London 1935, Cresset Press), p. 136.

[4] For Shang Yang's doctrine and achievements, see pp. 169 and 170, above.

all, come out of the bosom of the society of which the autocrat and his subjects alike were members, whereas the English 'Common Law' was the outcome of Western religious, political, and economic traditions and influences that were alien to the Muslim as well as to the Hindu subjects of the British Rāj. But, though, in this instance, the wind was not tempered to the shorn Indian lamb, his British shearers tactfully made the operation tolerable for him by shaving him only partwise, like a Parisian poodle.

The civil province of law can be divided into two departments, one concerned with what, in laymen's language, may be described as the 'business relations' between private individuals, and the other with what, in the language of the art, is known as 'personal statute'. 'Business relations' are a broad field in which the pocket is touched without deeply affecting the heart; 'personal statute' is a relatively narrow field, but it touches the quick, for its agenda are the intimacies of social life—marriage, wills, inheritance, wardship, and the like. The 'Osmanlis, as we have seen, consigned both these departments of the civil province of law to be dealt with in the separate communal courts of the Muslim community and of the non-Muslim *millets* of the Ottoman Empire in accordance with their respective communal laws. In the derelict domain of a defunct Mughal Empire in India, the British found a *macédoine* of religions, cultures, and peoples closely resembling the contemporary hotch-potch in the Ottoman dominions, but they worked out a different solution for a similar problem. They gave jurisdiction over the whole field to their own newly instituted British Indian courts, but, in prescribing the law that was to be applied in these courts, they confined the application of the English 'Common Law' and its British Indian derivatives to the department of 'business relations', and laid down that cases concerning 'personal statute' should continue to be governed by the communal law of the parties.[1]

Like the British in India, the Incas in their Andean Empire partitioned the field of law—apparently on somewhat similar lines.

'The customary rules, varying from one clan to another, [under which their subjects had lived,] were subordinated by the Incas to their own law, which was rigorous and uniform. The customary rules survived in great numbers, as was natural, in the domain of private law. The Incaic Law, which was by far the more important of the two, constituted a civil and criminal law of very wide scope.'[2]

The Romans were slower than the Incas or the British or Napoleon or Ts'in She Hwang-ti in achieving uniformity of law in their empire.

[1] This was done, not by drawing up any general definition of the field covered by 'personal statute', but by enumerating in each case the subjects in respect of which the existing communal law of the parties was to be applied in the British Indian courts. The area of the field was different in different cases. The legal institution enabling an owner of property, by making a will which, if valid, is recognized and made enforceable by the law, to determine during his lifetime how his property shall be disposed of after his death, was a feature of Islamic Law, as it was of Western Law, but was unknown to Hindu Law. As a consequence of this historical fact, the testamentary province of personal law came, for Hindus, to fall within the field of the English 'Common Law' or its British Indian derivatives, while for British Indian Muslims it continued to be administered in accordance with the *Sharī'ah*.

[2] Baudin, L.: *L'Empire Socialiste des Inka* (Paris 1928, Institut d'Ethnologie), p. 182.

To live under Roman Law was one of the reputed privileges of Roman citizenship, and the progressive conferment of the citizenship on the Empire's subjects was not carried to its completion till the reign of Caracalla (*imperabat* A.D. 211–17).[1] As and when they received the citizenship, however, the inhabitants of the Roman Empire automatically came under the rule of Roman Law in all its provinces and departments, and thus the universal reign of Roman Law, when it did come, was all-embracing. In the parallel history of the Arab Caliphate the reign of the Islamic Law was progressively extended by conversions of non-Muslim subjects of the Caliphate to the empire-builders' religion, and, though the non-Muslim residue in the Caliphate was never reduced to the same infinitesimal fraction of the population as the non-citizen residue in the Roman Empire in its latter days, the mass-conversion to Islam that took place in the Caliphate and its successor-states from the ninth to the thirteenth century of the Christian Era gained in momentum as the effective power of the Caliphate progressively decayed, and this produced a far more homogeneous result than the corresponding process in the Ottoman Empire, which, as we have seen, was checked, instead of being stimulated, by the political decline of the universal state.[2]

The Attempt to stabilize the Law in Japan under the Tokugawa Régime

In the Roman Empire and other universal states in the days of their decline, attempts were made to arrest the course of deterioration by 'freezing' an existing legal or social situation. The Tokugawa Shogunate in Japan was perhaps unique among universal states in applying this prescription of 'freezing' from first to last and in achieving the *tour de force* of arresting change in the outward forms of social life (though not, of course, in the inward realities) over a span of more than 250 years.

In the domain of law the Tokugawa régime, so far from regarding equality before a uniform law as being a desirable ideal, exerted itself to accentuate and perpetuate a caste division between the feudal aristocracy and their retainers on the one side and the rest of the population on the other which was one of the worst of the wounds that the Japanese Society had inflicted on itself during a foregoing Time of Troubles. The cue was given by Tokugawa Ieyasu's predecessor and patron Hide-yoshi in an edict of A.D. 1587 (popularly known as 'the Taikō's Sword Hunt') ordering all non-samurai to surrender any weapons in their

[1] See V. v. 446–7, and pp. 155–6, above, and p. 375, below.

[2] This at first sight puzzling difference is to be explained by a difference in the character of the external enemies by whom a declining Ottoman Empire and a declining 'Abbasid Caliphate were respectively menaced. The most formidable assailants of the 'Abbasid Caliphate were pagan Turkish and Mongol Eurasian Nomads who were as terrifying to the Caliphate's Zoroastrian and Christian subjects as to the ruling Muslim community. In these circumstances the subjects found salvation in adopting Islam themselves and helping their former masters to convert to their now common religion the barbarian conquerors of both parties alike (as the ex-Roman citizen body in Gaul dealt with their pagan Frankish conquerors by converting them to their own recently adopted Catholic Christianity). By contrast, the most formidable assailants of the Ottoman Empire were Western Christians whose culture became extremely attractive to the Ottoman Christians in the secularized version of it that was placed on the international market towards the close of the seventeenth century of the Christian Era, at the very time when the tide of war was turning against the 'Osmanlis.

possession.[1] The recently and arduously established central government further sweetened the pill for the feudal lords whom it had deprived of their long-abused *de facto* local independence by leaving them a very free hand to maintain and develop as they pleased, in all matters that the central government did not consider pertinent to the preservation of its own authority, the variegated 'house laws' which the ruling family of each fief had gradually hammered out and enforced, within the limits of its own parochial jurisdiction, during the later stages of the foregoing Time of Troubles, particularly during the fifteenth and sixteenth centuries of the Christian Era.[2] The edict entitled 'the Laws of the Military Houses' which Tokugawa Ieyasu promulgated in A.D. 1615, on the morrow of his crushing retort to the last challenge to his absolute authority,

> 'is a document which, like the formularies and "house laws" of earlier times, is not so much a systematic collection of specific injunctions and prohibitions as a group of maxims, in somewhat vague language, supported by learned extracts from the Chinese and Japanese classics.'[3]
>
> 'This "Constitution" . . . was regarded by the Shogunate as fundamentally unchangeable. It was re-affirmed by each shogun on his succession, in a solemn ceremony attended by all his vassals; and, though circumstances sometimes forced them to alter it in detail, they never admitted or even contemplated any deviation from its essential principles, and they punished without mercy any breach of its commands.'[4]

It is noteworthy that under this ultra-conservative régime a tendency towards the standardization of local laws did nevertheless declare itself.

> 'Within their own fiefs the barons enjoyed a very full measure of autonomy. . . . But the Shogunate, without interfering, used to keep a sharp watch on the conduct of the feudatories, and it was one of the chief duties of the censors (*metsuke*) and their travelling inspectors to report upon affairs in the fiefs. For this and similar reasons there was a general tendency among the *daimyō* to assimilate their administrative and judicial methods to those of the central authority, and the legislation in which the Shoguns freely indulged soon began to displace the "house laws" of the fiefs where it did not clash with local sentiment and habit.'[5]

The Expedient of Codification

In universal states in which a progressive standardization of the law had resulted in the attainment of approximate uniformity, there had sometimes been a further stage in which a unified imperial law had been codified by the imperial authorities.

In the history of the Roman Law, the first step towards codification was the 'freezing', in A.D. 131, of the *Edictum Perpetuum* that had hitherto been promulgated afresh by each successive Praetor Urbanus at the beginning of his year of office,[6] and the final steps were the promulgation

[1] Sansom, Sir G.: *Japan, A Short Cultural History* (London 1932, Cresset Press), pp. 422 and 450.

[2] For these local 'house laws', see ibid., pp. 418–20.

[3] Ibid., p. 450. [4] Ibid., p. 438. [5] Ibid., p. 449.

[6] Since *circa* 367–366 B.C.—the traditional date at which the practice of annually electing a governing college of three magistrates had been reinstituted (or perhaps in reality introduced for the first time)—or at any rate since 243 B.C., when the number

of the Justinianean *Code* in A.D. 529[1] and *Institutes* and *Digest* in A.D. 533[2] and the subsequent abrogation of the legal validity of all previous legislation and learned comment except in so far as it was reproduced in one or other of the three components of the new *Corpus Iuris Romani.* In the Spanish Empire in the Americas, after two abortive attempts at codification, a Creole Tribonian was found at last, in the person of Antonio León Pinelo, to codify the existing laws of the Indies in a *corpus iuris*, entitled *Recopilación de Leyes de los Reynos de las Indias*, which was completed in A.D. 1635 and eventually published, in a revised version, in 1681.[3] Thereafter the stream of legislation continued to flow till the *Recopilación* had fallen out of date. But a project, first for revising and then for replacing it, which was launched in A.D. 1765, was never carried through.[4] In the Sumeric 'Realm of the Four Quarters' an earlier code compiled under the Sumerian emperors who had ruled this Sumeric universal state from a seat of government at Ur during the first chapter

of annually elected Roman magistrates of the rank of 'praetor' (the next highest rank to the supreme magistracy represented by the two consuls) had been increased from one to two, one praetor had always been detailed to take charge of the conduct of legal business in the metropolis, and hence had come to be known as the Praetor Urbanus. The transformation of a once socially simple peasant community first into one of the Great Powers, and finally into the imperial mistress, of a complicated and sophisticated Hellenic Society had gradually made it necessary for the Praetor Urbanus to interpret—and, by interpreting, to extend—the existing Roman Law in order to make it applicable to an ever-increasing range and complexity of cases. In order to cope with this problem, it had become customary for each successive Praetor Urbanus, on his accession to office, to draw up, in consultation with the best living legal authorities whose advice he could obtain, a declaration of the lines on which he proposed to administer the law during his own term of office. This practice had been regularized by a *Lex Cornelia* of 67 B.C., which had made it thenceforward obligatory, and no longer merely customary, for the Praetor Urbanus to adhere to the terms of his own edict when once he had posted it up, in order that jurymen, judges, litigants, and the general public might know in advance the terms on which the law was going to be administered during the current year (Strachan-Davidson, J. L.: *Problems of the Roman Criminal Law* (Oxford 1912, Clarendon Press, 2 vols.), vol. i, pp. 72–73). From 67 B.C. to A.D. 131 it had still been theoretically open to each successive Praetor Urbanus to ignore the edicts of his predecessors and to draft an entirely new annual edict which, though it would be binding on the draftsman, would no more bind his successors than he himself had been bound to follow the drafts of his predecessors. But, though the word *perpetuum*, as used in the *Lex Cornelia*, had thus meant no more than 'valid for twelve months', the effect had been to confirm the practice—no doubt by then already well established—of carrying over the major part of the edict from year to year, since a Praetor Urbanus who had actually exercised his theoretical right to recast it *in toto* would merely have thrown the administration of the law into confusion if he had accomplished the *tour de force* of executing this herculean labour. Thus from 67 B.C. to A.D. 131 the *Edictum Perpetuum* had been a supple instrument in which the benefits of a substantial continuity had been combined with opportunity for the law to grow in response to changes in the social life with which the law was concerned. The Emperor Hadrian commissioned the legal expert Salvius Iulianus to edit, rearrange, and systematize the *Edictum Perpetuum* of the day, and Iulianus's edition was given the force of law, and at the same time made definitive, by a *senatus consultum* of A.D. 131. The effect, of course, was, not to bring the development of Roman Law to an end, but to transfer to the Senate and the Princeps the virtual legislative power which, under the terms of the *Lex Cornelia* of 67 B.C., the Praetor Urbanus had previously been sharing with them *de facto*.

1 According to Collinet, P.: 'The General Problems raised by the Codification of Justinian', in *Tijdschrift voor Rechtgeschiedenis* (Haarlem 1923, Tjeenk Willink), p. 6, there were two editions of the *Code*, of which the first was ordered on the 13th February, 528, and was promulgated on the 7th April, 529, while the second was promulgated on the 17th November, 534.

2 According to Collinet, ibid., the *Digest* was ordered on the 15th December, 530, and was promulgated on the 16th December, 533; the *Institutes* were promulgated on the 21st November, 533.

3 See Haring, C. H.: *The Spanish Empire in America* (New York 1947, Oxford University Press), pp. 110–15.

4 See ibid., p. 114.

of its history (*imperabant circa* 2143–2026 or 2079–1962 B.C.) appears[1] to have been the basis of the later code, promulgated by the Amorite restorer of the Empire, Hammurabi of Babylon,[2] which was brought to light in A.D. 1901 by the Modern Western archaeologist J. de Morgan in the course of his excavations at Susa, whither the stele on which Hammurabi's code had been engraved had been carried away from Babylon in the twelfth century B.C. by the Elamite raider Shutruk-Nachchunte.[3] In the main body of the Far Eastern World the victory of the law of the Mongols' sedentary subjects over their Nomad conquerors' *Yāsāq*[4] was celebrated in the codification of Chinese law in and after the reign of Hung Wu (*regnabat* A.D. 1367–98),[5] the Chinese patriot leader who had founded the indigenous Ming Dynasty by expelling the Mongols from China-within-the-Wall.[6] In the Napoleonic Empire a labour which elsewhere was usually 'staggered' over a span of many generations was crowded, for once, into the compass of a single lifetime.

The Historical Background of Codification in the Spanish Empire of the Indies

In all these otherwise diverse instances the work of codification was an urgently needed social service. Hung Wu and Hammurabi were confronted with the problem of conjuring order out of the confusion to which the law, like the rest of the apparatus of oecumenical government, had been reduced by the respective intrusions of alien Mongol and alien Elamite conquerors. In the Andean World, where the Incaic Law had been as strictly administered as it had been sternly conceived,

'Things changed completely when the Spaniards arrived. The swift and inexorable justice of the Inca disappeared, there was a multiplication of

1 See *The Cambridge Ancient History*, vol. I, 1st ed. (Cambridge 1924, University Press), pp. 435 and 461; Rostovtzeff, M.: *Caravan Cities* (Oxford 1932, Clarendon Press), p. 9; Hrozný, B.: *Die Älteste Geschichte Vorderasiens und Indiens* (Prague 1943, Melantrich), p. 113. Hrozný ascribes the first essay in codification to the revolutionary reformer Uru-kagina of Lagash, who lived in the third quarter of the twenty-sixth century B.C., or in the first quarter of the twenty-fifth century (see the Note on Chronology in vol. x.).

2 English translations of Hammurabi's Code are given in Smith, J. M. P.: *The Origin and History of Hebrew Law* (Chicago 1931, University of Chicago Press), pp. 181–222, and in Pritchard, J. B.: *Ancient Near Eastern Texts* (Princeton 1950, University Press), pp. 163–80. A convenient summary of the contents will be found in *The Cambridge Ancient History*, vol. cit., ed. cit., pp. 516–21. Pritchard, in op. cit., pp. 159–63, gives translations of fragments of codes promulgated at Isin and at Eshnunna during the interval between the fall of Ibbi-Sin of Ur and the rise of Hammurabi.

3 See Hrozný, op. cit., p. 113.

4 See pp. 256–7, above.

5 'The first Emperor of the Ming Dynasty, immediately following the capture of Wuchang, ordered a revision of the existing law. In the tenth month of the first year of his reign as King Wu, Li San-Chang was appointed Head of the Law Codification Commission, assisted by Yang Shien, Liu Chi and Dao An. The Code was completed in the twelfth month. In the sixth year of the reign of Hung Wu, Liu Wei-chien was designated to compile the Code of Great Ming, which was submitted by Sung Lien to the Emperor for approval the following year. The Code underwent modifications from time to time after that, and was finally completed and revised by Wu Wei-yung and Wang Kwong Yang. It was promulgated in the thirtieth year of the same reign.' (Note communicated to the writer on the 12th December, 1947, by the kindness of the Chinese Ambassador at the Court of St. James's, Mr. F. I. Cheng, from the record in the official History of the Ming Dynasty.)

6 The retransfer of the capital of China from Nanking to Peking by Hung Wu's son and second successor Yung Lo has been discussed in II. ii. 122–3 and on p. 237, above.

interminable suits, the judges were full of tenderness towards criminals and debauchees, and in the markets of the great cities there were Indians to be found who gained their livelihood by serving as witnesses.'[1]

Moreover,

'Under an absolute and paternalistic [Spanish] monarchy, legislation for the Indies soon became very voluminous, touching every aspect of the duties, rights and responsibilities of the colonists and of the officials set to rule over them. This legislation was intended to carry over into America the spirit and intent of the law of the metropolis, as Philip II explicitly declared in A.D. 1571. It implied the transplanting of society and institutions from an Old World to the New. Yet the legislation of Castile itself had in the colonies the force only of supplementary law. From the very first the Crown had to "adapt the distinct physiognomy acquired by traditional institutions" to circumstances, both geographical and historical, which were radically different from those in the metropolis. The peculiar conditions prevailing in America called for the elaboration of a new legislation with a distinct character of its own. Moreover, in spite of the centralist and unifying tendencies of Hapsburgs and Bourbons, the Crown was forced to take into account, both in legislation and in its application by viceroys and governors, the great differences between one region in America and another. A surprising amount of autonomy was often permitted to colonial authorities. There likewise grew up a substantial amount of customary law in the overseas dominions derived from the jurisprudential practices of the times, which had a recognized legal force if accepted by the Crown and if no written legislation was applicable. Much of this customary jurisprudence developed from the modifications of royal orders by viceroys and captains-general to meet the exigencies of a local situation. Finally, the Crown tried to incorporate into its American legislation some of the juridical customs of the aborigines—especially of those, such as the Incas and the Aztecs, who had evolved a strong political and economic organization—customs which were not in contradiction to the fundamental precepts of Spanish organization and control.'[2]

In the *Recopilación de Leyes de los Reynos de las Indias*, 'León Pinelo reduced the laws of the Indies to over 11,000, extracted from some 400,000 royal *cédulas*.'[3] It is little wonder that this clearance of an Augean stable took even that 'zealous and indefatigable' labourer ten years. But it reflects some discredit on the Spanish imperial administration that the task should not have been placed in Pinelo's competent hands until after A.D. 1624, considering that an abortive preceding essay in codification had been commissioned as far back as A.D. 1582. It is perhaps still more discreditable to the authorities that, though Pinelo's draft was completed in A.D. 1635 and was approved by them within the next seven months, the eventual revised version was not published until A.D. 1681.[4]

The Historical Background of Codification in the Roman Empire

This complexity of the historical background of Pinelo's *Recopilación* is surpassed by that of Tribonian's *Corpus Iuris*. The Law of the Twelve Tables, which, according to the traditional chronology, had been pro-

1 Baudin, L.: *L'Empire Socialiste des Inka* (Paris 1928, Institut d'Ethnologie), p. 186.
2 Haring, op. cit., pp. 109–10.
3 Ibid., p. 113.
4 See ibid.

mulgated in 451–450 B.C. by the Board of Decemvirs appointed to draft it, had equipped the still archaic Roman community of the age with an instrument that, by that time, would already have been out of date in the heart of an Hellenic World on whose outskirts Rome then lay. The subsequent progressive and cumulatively enormous revolution in Rome's social and political position demanded, and duly evoked, a flood of new legislation which flowed for ten centuries in a number of different channels: laws enacted by the Populus Romanus; votes, possessing the force of law, passed by the Plebs; the *Edictum Perpetuum* of the Praetor Urbanus; the resolutions of the Senate; and the acts, decisions, and decrees of Caesar after the Republic had been succeeded by the Principate. When the stream of often capricious and inconsequent acts of Plebs and Populus had ceased to flow, the new stream of imperial legislation became, as time went on, even more inconsequent, capricious, and voluminous till, in the western half of the Empire during the century ending in A.D. 476, a climax was reached in a spate of decrees reiterating the same commands on a rising note of hysteria, with threats of ever more savage penalties for disobedience which merely advertised the truth that the imperial legislators in that part of the Empire had by that stage become impotent to enforce their authority. 'Et septemgemini turbant trepida ostia Nili.'[1] The ancient river of Roman legislation had dispersed its waters into a mazy delta on its way to losing them in an 'unharvested sea'.

Yet this maze of legislation was not so formidable as the jungle of learned comment that had sprung up on its marge. Law is by nature conservative, and its ineradicable resistance to change calls always and everywhere for the services of skilled interpreters to ensure that it shall continue to serve the practical needs of social life in spite of perpetually losing its unequally matched race with changing circumstances. In the administration of the Roman Law during the thousand years following the promulgation of the Twelve Tables, the lag—to be made up by interpretation—between the formal state of the law and the social task required of it was enlarged to an unusual degree of magnitude in consequence of the extraordinary political career through which a rustic city-state had grown into an oecumenical empire. If the Roman jurisconsults were to succeed in bridging this formidable gulf,[2] they stood in need of all the intellectual building-materials on which they could lay hands; and, after the reception of Hellenic philosophy at Rome in the second century B.C., the ethics of the Stoic School gradually came to supply the interpreters of the Roman Law with those comprehensive maxims, logical principles, and imaginative vistas that were required for transforming the peculiar local customs of a primitive-minded peasantry into a system acceptable to the Hellenic World.

Under the early Principate as well as under the late Republic, a still persisting aristocratic tradition kept the study and interpretation of the

[1] Virgil: *Aeneid*, Book VI, l. 800.

[2] The archaic title *pontifices* would have described the functions of these secular Roman jurisconsults more aptly than those of the Christian bishop who eventually took it over from the college of pagan priests who were its original bearers.

law in the hands of a governing class—confined to the senatorial and equestrian orders—whose members were expected to be men of action as well as men of culture and would not have been allowed by their superiors or their peers to rise to high positions of political responsibility exclusively in virtue of eminent legal ability, without having also shown at least some aptitude for military command and public administration. This aristocratic way of public life, with its obvious merits and its equally obvious limitations, was abandoned, in the field of law, in the reign of the Emperor Hadrian (*imperabat* A.D. 117–38),[1] whose personal policy was consciously inspired by a zeal for efficiency but at the same time served the purposes of a *Zeitgeist* that was already up in arms against social privileges and political monopolies.[2] Hadrian converted his predecessors' informal and indefinite entourage of advisers into an imperial council of salaried jurisconsults of senatorial and equestrian rank, and he also created a panel of eminent legal authorities (*iuris prudentes*) whom he invested with powers of replying officially to legal queries (*ius respondendi*) and, in effect, of acting corporately as a legislative body, since he provided that their opinion, when unanimous, should have the force of law. By these measures, Hadrian called into existence a professional class of legal specialists; and the consequent lawyers' 'Golden Age' outlasted the Antonine 'Indian Summer' and survived—though not unscathed—the intermittent frosts of the ensuing Severan overture to winter.[3]

The virtues and abilities of Papinian—whom Posterity regarded as the brightest link in all the golden chain of the Roman legal tradition[4]—found a lawyer's mind to appreciate them and a soldier's arm to protect them combined in the person of Septimius Severus, who had been Papinian's predecessor in the office of Advocatus Fisci before becoming his imperial master and patron. Yet even the grim founder of the Severan Dynasty could not save Papinian from paying the extreme penalty for his probity to the savagery of Septimius's brutal son and successor Caracalla; and Papinian's disciple Ulpian was assassinated in his turn, by the praetorian guards, in the presence of his impotent imperial friend and admirer the gentle Alexander Severus. Paul, and Paul only, was left; and when, seven years after the murder of Ulpian, the last Emperor of the House of Severus himself succumbed to the tragic fate from which he had failed to rescue an esteemed and beloved public servant, this culminating political crime heralded a blizzard of anarchy in which liberal legal studies were blasted and seared. Yet, even so, the golden century of Roman legal studies, from the 'freezing' of the Urban Praetor's Perpetual Edict in A.D. 131 to the 'revolt of Caliban' in A.D. 235, had produced a volume of output so enormous that for Tribonian and his colleagues, three hundred years later, the compression of this matter

[1] See p. 262, with n. 6, above. [2] See pp. 152–8, above.

[3] See *The Cambridge Ancient History*, vol. xi (Cambridge 1936, University Press), pp. 314–15 and 816–26.

[4] A rescript of Galla Placidia's, dated the 7th November, A.D. 426, gave Papinian the casting vote in any conflict of authority between two or more of the five classical jurists (Papinianus, Paullus, Gaius, Ulpianus, Modestinus) in which the authorities, including Papinian, were ranged in equal numbers on either side (*Cod. Theod.* I. iv. 3).

into the *Digest* was the heaviest of their three titanic tasks, though they virtually confined their selection of materials to the contents of treatises produced within this relatively short period in the long history of Roman Law.

'Seventeen lawyers, with Tribonian at their head, were appointed by the Emperor [Justinian] to exercise an absolute jurisdiction over the works of their predecessors. If they had obeyed his commands in ten years, Justinian would have been satisfied with their diligence; and the rapid composition of the Digest or Pandects in three years (15th December, A.D. 530—16th December, A.D. 533) will deserve praise or censure according to the merit of the execution. From the library of Tribonian they chose forty, the most eminent civilians of former times; two thousand treatises were comprised in an abridgement of fifty books; and it has been carefully recorded that three millions of lines or sentences were reduced, in this abstract, to the moderate number of one hundred and fifty thousand.'[1]

By comparison with this second of his labours, Tribonian's first feat of compiling the *Code* was easy. In codifying within a term of fourteen months (13th February, A.D. 528–7th April, A.D. 529) the decrees that had been promulgated by successive emperors in the course of the four centuries that had elapsed between the accession of Hadrian[2] and the current year of Justinian's reign, Tribonian could avail himself of the existing works of three forerunners: the unofficial codes compiled by Gregorius (later than the 19th October, A.D. 294, and probably in A.D. 297) and by Hermogenianus (later than the 21st March, A.D. 295)[3] and the official supplement to them promulgated, on the 15th February, A.D. 438, by the Emperor Theodosius II (*imperabat* A.D. 408–50),[4] which covered the years A.D. 312/13–437 for the Eastern Half of the Empire and the years A.D. 312/13–432 for the Western Half.[5] By comparison, again, with the arduousness of compiling the Code, it was child's-play for Tribonian to round off his threefold enterprise by enucleating the elements of Roman Law in the Institutes.

The Historical Background of Codification in the Napoleonic Empire

The *Corpus Iuris Iustinianeum* had a worthy counterpart in the Napoleonic array of codes in respect of both the speed and the immensity of the labours of which it was a monument.

'The difficulties of this undertaking consisted mainly in the enormous

[1] Gibbon, E.: *The History of the Decline and Fall of the Roman Empire*, chap. xliv.

[2] The series did not begin before Hadrian's reign because Hadrian was the initiator of the practice of promulgating imperial decrees undisguisedly as such. 'From Augustus to Trajan, the modest Caesars were content to promulgate their edicts in the various characters of a Roman magistrate; and, in the decrees of the Senate, the epistles and orations of the Prince were respectfully inserted. Hadrian appears to have been the first who assumed, without disguise, the plenitude of legislative power' (Gibbon, op. cit., loc. cit.). This new departure of Hadrian's was at variance with the spirit of the Principate as inspired by Augustus.

[3] A second edition of Hermogenianus's code was published (probably by Hermogenianus himself) in the reign of Constantine the Great (*imperabat* A.D. 306–37), and a third during the joint reign of Valentinian and Valens (A.D. 364–75).

[4] The Theodosian Code had taken just under nine years to compile, since the commissioners had been appointed on the 26th March, 429.

[5] See Seeck, O.: *Geschichte des Untergangs der Antiken Welt* (Stuttgart: Metzler), vol. vi (1920), pp. 164–83, and vol. vi, Anhang (1921), pp. 428–32.

mass of decrees emanating from the national assemblies, relative to political, civil and criminal affairs.'[1] This amorphous product of more than eleven years of French revolutionary legislation[2] was comparable with the spate of decrees of the Roman Emperors, from Hadrian to Justinian, which Papinian had to confine within the dykes of the Justinianean *Codex*. The resemblance extended beyond the sheer volume to the intrinsic nature of the materials. 'Many of these decrees, the offspring of a momentary enthusiasm, had found a place in the codes of laws which were then compiled; and yet sagacious observers knew that several of them warred against the instincts of the Gallic race.'[3] The French legislators had been attempting, like the Roman jurists, to transfigure a litter of ancient local customary laws by suffusing it with a modern philosophy; but they had sought to achieve at a stroke what their Roman ensamples had been content to accomplish in the course of three or four hundred years, and they had gone to work with an inferior intellectual instrument; for the self-confident iconoclastic humanism of Rousseau or Voltaire was a jejune spiritual elixir by comparison with the ripe and rueful wisdom of a Stoicism that had been refined by many generations of suffering.

The Napoleonic codifiers were therefore well advised in rejecting their revolutionary heralds' academic ideal of making a clean break with the past; yet they could not contemplate reinstating the antediluvian law as it had stood.

'Old French law had been an inextricable labyrinth of laws and customs, provincial privileges, ecclesiastical rights, and the later undergrowth of royal decrees; and no part of the legislation of the revolutionists met with so little resistance as their root-and-branch destruction of this exasperating jungle. Their difficulties only began when they endeavoured to apply the principles of the Rights of Man to political, civil and criminal affairs.'[4]

The revolutionary legislators' axes had cleared away the primeval forest to force a rank second growth in the name of simplicity and reason, and it was left for the Napoleonic codifiers to produce a blend of old and new which could serve the practical needs of the Western Society of the day.

In putting this hard but urgent task in hand, Napoleon did not have to start entirely *de novo* or unaided. Before the expiration of the *Ancien Régime* the industry and sagacity of pre-revolutionary French jurists had already gone far towards distilling a common essence out of the divers provincial varieties of French customary law; and, in following up their work, Napoleon had at his elbow, in the Second Consul Cambacérès, a learned and clear-headed lawyer who had stumbled upon the pitfalls of the revolutionary attitude and method in failing, in A.D. 1793, to obtain the approval of the Convention for a draft of a civil code which he and his fellow committeemen had taken six weeks to prepare instead of the month which the Convention had assigned for the completion of the

1 Rose, J. H.: *The Life of Napoleon I* (London 1904, Bell, 2 vols.), vol. i, pp. 287–8.

2 Reckoning from the opening session of the States-General on the 5th May, 1789, to the appointment, on the 12th August, 1800, of a commission to draft a civil code.

3 Rose, op. cit., vol. cit., p. 288.

4 Ibid., p. 288.

work. The four commissioners appointed on the 12th August, 1800, by Napoleon, to try again where the Convention's committee had failed, succeeded in carrying out their instructions to produce a first draft in four months. It was printed on the 1st January, 1801; and, though it then still had to run the gauntlet of the Court of Cassation, the Courts of Appeal, the Legislative Section, and the General Assembly of the Council of State, and thereafter the Tribunate, a civil code of 2,281 articles, embodying the amendments of these successive critics, was duly promulgated between the 15th March, 1803, and the 30th March, 1804, and was thus completed only three and a half years after the drafting commission had been nominated. Within nine and a half years of the same initial date, the entire gigantic task of producing not only a civil code but also a code of civil procedure, a criminal code, a code of criminal procedure, and a commercial code had been completed by the promulgation of the fourth and last book of the criminal code on the 2nd March, 1810.

The extent of Napoleon's own personal contribution to the shaping of these five Napoleonic codes may continue to be disputed. We may believe contemporary reports that, in some episodes of the thirty-five sittings, out of eighty-seven in all, at which the First Consul was present and in the chair while the draft of the Civil Code was being debated in the General Assembly of the Council of State, Napoleon 'fatigued the attention of his audience by the confused abundance and the unexpected turns of his thought'.[1] We may follow a recent English master of Napoleonic studies in his verdict that 'the Civil Code was a hasty piece of work, and' that 'the First Consul imported a strong gust of passion and of politics into the laboratory of legal science'.[2] But any student of history who, at however low a level, has had dealings with both scholars and men of action, and has also had it laid upon him to induce them to co-operate with one another on a common task, will not be blind to the significance of Napoleon's decisive intervention, on the 1st April, 1802, to shorten, simplify, and improve the procedure for passing the draft of the Civil Code at a moment when the cumbrous wheels of an academic constitution had almost stopped turning. And he will readily be convinced that, 'without [Napoleon's] driving power, [the Civil Code] would certainly not have come into existence so soon, and might not have come into existence at all'.[3]

The Price of Codification

Who had been the principal beneficiaries of the empire-builders' legal heritage and of their successors' codifying labours?

The victims of codification would hardly have reckoned themselves among the beneficiaries if they could have risen from the dead to inspect their successors' handiwork. Among the codifiers whom we have just passed in review, the Napoleonic team alone could have contemplated with equanimity a personal encounter with predecessors who, in this

[1] Fisher, H. A. L., in *The Cambridge Modern History*, vol. ix (Cambridge 1906, University Press), p. 152.
[2] Ibid., p. 162.
[3] Ibid., p. 163.

exceptional case, would have been compelled, on confrontation, to confess that these deft and elegant surgeons had improved, out of all recognition, the uncouth build of a *corpus vile*. By contrast, the ghosts of Papinian and Ulpian might have protested in all sincerity that they would liefer have felt again, in their own flesh, the agonizing edge of their assassins' swords than have voluntarily submitted the exquisite products of their masterly intellectual labours to be butchered by the rough-and-ready workmanship of Tribonian and his colleagues.

'Instead of a statue cast in a simple mould by the hand of an artist, the works of Justinian represent a tesselated pavement of antique and costly, but too often incoherent, fragments.'[1]

And it is possible that a twentieth-century historian might have felt moved to apply Gibbon's dictum to the Code of Hammurabi if the extant fragments of the underlying work of Hammurabi's Sumerian predecessors[2] that had been preserved independently had been sufficient to enable the latter-day student to extract and reconstruct the copious borrowings from the same source that were to be looked for in Hammurabi's redaction.

The Exceptional Service rendered by the 'Code Napoléon' to a Late Modern Western Society

In their high-handed treatment of their predecessors' work, are the codifiers performing a valuable service for their contemporaries and successors? In the judgement of an eminent post-Gibbonian Western student of Roman Law,

'Justinian's intention was to promulgate legislation applicable to the peoples of diverse race who were living under the law of the Empire of the East, using as his materials the texts of the Roman Law as he found it—first and foremost, the texts of the classical jurists. The basis thus given to his work was the best that he could have taken; for, in the decadent state of the science of Law in his day, he could never have succeeded in obtaining a codification comparable in merit to the system with which his name is actually associated if he had instructed his commissioners to do the drafting themselves. Just because, however, he chose the basis that he did choose, the materials that entered into the composition of his codification, and particularly into the Digest, had to be transformed—as stones from an old building that are being used in a new one are re-cut and re-mortared—in order to be brought into harmony with the exigencies of a civilization that was younger by three centuries at the least, and with the needs of an empire—the Empire of the East—whose boundaries were no longer identical with those of the *Orbis Romanus* of the generation of Gaius or Ulpian.[3] This task of adaptation required the constant employ-

[1] Gibbon, E.: *The History of the Decline and Fall of the Roman Empire*, chap. xliv.

[2] Twenty-five laws, in all, of the code compiled in the Sumerian language by the Emperor Ur-Engur and succeeding sovereigns of the Third Dynasty of Ur had been preserved on two clay tablets from Nippur and one from Uruk (*The Cambridge Ancient History*, vol. i, 1st ed. (Cambridge 1924, University Press), p. 461). Whatever might be the respective merits of the draftsmanship, there seemed to be no doubt that, in the penalties prescribed, the Sumerian emperors' code was superior to Hammurabi's in point of humanity.

[3] According to Collinet, P., *Études Historiques sur le Droit de Justinien*, vol. i, 'Le

ment of an adequate instrument, [and this instrument was found in the device of] interpolation.'[1]

The claim made in this passage on behalf of the authors of the *Corpus Iustinianeum* could undoubtedly be substantiated by the authors of the *Code Napoléon*; but this may be one of those exceptions that prove a contrary rule; for the *Code Napoléon* was the work of empire-builders to whom History, as we have seen, had assigned the peculiar task of providing a universal state for a moribund sub-society within a larger body social that had not yet lost its vitality; and these unusual circumstances, which condemned the Napoleonic Empire itself to an early death, ensured a brilliant career for the code that was its offspring. The *ci-devant* city-state cosmos in Italy, the Low Countries, and Germany, whose incorporation into a universal state was the Napoleonic Empire's historical *raison d'être*, did duly dissolve with the downfall of the Napoleonic political edifice that had housed it in its last phase; but in this unique case the sequel was not the catastrophe of a social interregnum but a 'happy ending' in which an abortive sub-society that had failed to make a success of its deliberate departure from the standard pattern of the Western Civilization now at last succeeded in divesting itself of a separate identity which had long since ceased to be anything but a handicap and an embarrassment to it by re-entering the main stream of Western life from which it had once self-consciously sought to part company. It had been the mission of the French empire-builders to draw their non-French subjects back into a flowing current of life which was the imperial people's own native element, and from which their legal tradition and êthos were derived; and for this reason the successful accomplishment of a French political task, which made the Napoleonic Empire superfluous, launched the *Code Napoléon* on a flood-tide leading on to fortune.

Caractère Oriental de l'Œuvre Législative de Justinien' (Paris 1912, Recueil Sirey), the *Corpus Iustinianeum* was intended to serve the current needs of the Greek and Oriental provinces of the Roman Empire (p. 14). The work is a monument of 'the transformation of Oriental elements, that had previously been merely provincial, into imperial elements [during the interval] between [the generations of] Constantine, who is a Roman emperor reigning in a Roman city, and Justinian, who is an Oriental emperor reigning over an Empire of the East' (ibid., p. 16). Justinian's board of commissioners was composed of representatives of four parties: Constantinopolitan officials, Constantinopolitan professors, Berytan professors, and advocates practising in the court of the Praefectus Praetorio per Orientem at Constantinople (ibid., p. 23)—i.e. the law schools of Constantinople and Bayrūt alone were represented, to the exclusion of those of Rome, Alexandria, Caesarea, and Athens (ibid., p. 23). According to Collinet, the Code was wholly, and the Institutes were mainly, the work of the Constantinopolitan commissioners, while the Berytan commissioners were perhaps principally responsible for the Digest (ibid., p. 24). The *Corpus Iustinianeum* is a codification of the living law of the Roman East (ibid., p. 28); and this was a fusion of Hellenic Law with a Roman Law which had been adapted to Oriental requirements by an abandonment of some of its original native Roman elements (ibid., p. 29). In Justinian's day a Roman Law that, by then, had already become static in the West was still evolving in the East on Oriental lines (ibid., pp. 34, 159, and 314); and, in order to bring the *Corpus Iustinianeum* into conformity with the living Roman Law of the East, a number of traditional Roman legal institutions were jettisoned in the compilation of it (ibid., pp. 213–14). The *Corpus Iustinianeum* was distinguished from contemporary Western Roman Law in two ways: it was more *savant*; and, instead of being stagnant, it embodied the results of regional progress (ibid., pp. 314 and 317).—A.J.T.

[1] Collinet, P.: *Études Historiques sur le Droit de Justinien*, vol. i: 'Le Caractère Oriental de l'Œuvre Législative de Justinien' (Paris 1912, Recueil Sirey), pp. xxv–xxvi.

On the day of its promulgation the Napoleonic Civil Code automatically became law, not only for all inhabitants of France within her pre-Revolutionary frontiers, but for Walloons and Flemings in the Southern Netherlands and Germans west of the Rhine, who on the 21st March, 1804, were already fellow citizens of the French in a Republic that, on the 18th May, was to be converted into an Empire. Thereafter, from A.D. 1804 to A.D. 1811, the Code's domain was being constantly enlarged. It gained ground partly through the enlargement of the French Empire itself, which continued to swallow up satellite states and conquered territories till it stretched north-eastwards as far as Lübeck and south-eastwards as far as Terracina,[1] and partly through the 'reception' of the Code in satellite states that survived or that were increased in stature or that were enlisted as new recruits. On the 30th March, 1806, the Code was promulgated in the Napoleonic Kingdom of Italy, which by that time had been enlarged to include almost all the former dominions of Venice;[2] and, before the Napoleonic edifice collapsed, the Code had become law throughout Continental Italy, including the satellite Kingdom of Naples. It seeded itself in several Swiss cantons. It was promulgated in Holland on the 18th October, 1810. And it made a triumphal progress across Napoleonic Germany, where it was received in the Kingdom of Westphalia on the 15th November, 1807; in the Free City of Danzig on the 19th November, 1807; in Arenburg on the 28th January, 1808; in the Grand Duchy of Baden on the 5th July, 1808; in the Grand Duchy of Frankfurt on the 15th September, 1809; in the Grand Duchy of Berg on the 1st January, 1810; in the newly constituted Lippe and Hanseatic Departments of the French Empire on the 29th May and the 10th December, 1810, respectively; in the Duchy of Köthen on the 28th December, 1810; and in the Duchy of Nassau on the 1st and 4th February, 1811.[3]

The most distant and exotic of the Code's pacific conquests was the Grand Duchy of Warsaw, where it was received in A.D. 1808 in the ex-Prussian nucleus, and in A.D. 1810 in the ex-Austrian annex.[4] In A.D. 1928 it was still in force in a fragment of territory, wedged in between the left bank of the River Niemen and the eastern frontier of East Prussia, which had once constituted the north-eastern extremity of the Duchy of Warsaw and its successor the 'Congress Kingdom' of Poland, but which in 1928 formed part of the *Saisonstaat* of inter-war Lithuania.[5]

This widespread 'reception' of the Code was brought about by a

[1] Without reckoning in the Illyrian Provinces, insulated geographically from the main body of the French Empire by the breadth of the satellite Kingdom of Italy, which France acquired from Austria in the Peace Treaty of Schönbrunn (14th October, 1809).

[2] All, indeed, except the Ionian Islands. The Kingdom of Italy obtained these acquisitions through the Franco-Austrian Peace Treaty of Pressburg (26th December, 1805). In the territorial rearrangements following the conclusion of the subsequent Franco-Austrian Peace Treaty of Schönbrunn (14th October, 1809) the Kingdom of Italy lost Dalmatia but acquired the Trentino.

[3] This calendar of the progressive reception of the Code in Germany is taken from Fisher, H. A. L.: *Studies in Napoleonic Statesmanship in Germany* (Oxford 1903, Clarendon Press), p. 380, n. 2.

[4] See ibid.

[5] This curiosity of legal history was imparted to the writer of this Study one day in that year when he was standing in Kovno and gazing across the Niemen towards its once Napoleonic western bank.

variety of means, ranging from a more or less genuine free choice to sheer and undissimulated coercion.

'The transplantation from one country to another of a code of laws, and of a system of judicial organisation, must in all cases be a delicate proceeding, for, though the elementary principles of justice are universally appreciated, nation differs from nation in the principles of their application. . . . The immediate introduction of the French codes into the Grand Duchy of Berg seemed to the conservative mind of Count Beugnot [the French Imperial Commissioner] to savour of indiscretion. "Germany", as he reminded his Government, "had not, like France, been levelled by the legislation of iconoclastic assemblies." It would require time and instruction before she could properly attune herself to the new melodies of the Code. Nor was there any danger in delay. . . . These representations were received and rejected. On the 12th November, 1809, an imperial decree ordered that the *Code Napoléon* was to have the force of law in the Grand Duchy of Berg from the 1st January, 1810, and at the same time the Imperial Commission was requested instantly to furnish a draft scheme for judicial organization. Beugnot had no option but to obey.'[1]

In the Kingdom of Westphalia, likewise, the *Code Napoléon* was made law, as from the 1st January, 1808,[2] by the terms of a constitution, promulgated from Paris on the 15th November, 1807, which 'may be considered either in the light of a treaty or in that of a guarantee'.[3] But here the peremptoriness of the imperial dictate was mitigated by the tender-handedness of its local application. In the crucial matter of feudalism, for example, a declaration of 'the unconditional abolition of serfage passed through the crucible of successive legal refinements';[4] and when

'some proprietors complained of these proceedings as too revolutionary, the Government replied with justice that, according to the liberal principles of the *Code Napoléon* and of the Act constituting the Kingdom of Westphalia, all rights of serfage and feudalism might have been suppressed. . . .; that the suppression had been general in Genoa, Parma, Piacenza and Tuscany; but that the Westphalian Government had preferred an equitable temperament between the rigour of the laws and the respect due to long possession. They had kept everything which they could keep without violating principle.'[5]

In any case, whatever the political circumstances of its local 'reception' might have been, the intrinsic merits of the *Code Napoléon* were such as to secure its survival when the Napoleonic Empire was overthrown through an irresistible reaction of its non-French subjects and victims against an intolerable abuse of French military and political power.

'When the project for the German Civil Code came before the Reichstag in 1900, it was stated that seventeen per cent of the fifty million inhabitants of the German Empire were still ruled by French law. In the Prussian, Hessian and Bavarian Rhine provinces, and in Alsace-Lorraine, the *Code Napoléon* was administered in its original tongue; while a German translation, only slightly differing from its French prototype, was current in

1 Fisher, op. cit., pp. 197–8.
2 See ibid., p. 232.
3 Ibid., p. 231.
4 Ibid., p. 257.
5 Ibid.

Baden. That the Code should have persisted in any portion of Germany, when all the circumstances of the War of Liberation are taken into account, is a remarkable tribute to its merits. We may admit that its preparation was hurried, that the discussions in the Council of State were often unsatisfactory, and that it is based upon an imperfect survey of practical contingencies. There is doubtless great weight in Savigny's contention that Germany was not ripe for a code, and that the legal system of a country should be the natural result of its historical development. But the choice in 1807 and in 1815 did not lie between pure German and pure French law. It lay between the *Code Napoléon* on the one hand, sketchy, no doubt, and over-simplified, but lucid, intelligible and portable,[1] and an "endless waste of contradictory, conjectural and motley ordinances. . . ." We cannot wonder that, in comparison with this hybrid miscellany, the French Code seemed to many Germans to be the utterance of Reason herself.'[2]

Even in territories where, upon the downfall of the Napoleonic Empire, the *Code Napoléon* was abrogated, along with all other Napoleonic innovations, by the 'Zealotism' of a momentarily restored *Ancien Régime* that was too uncertain of its tenure to venture to be discriminating in its policy, the imported French law was not in every case rescinded *in toto*, while in other cases it crept back, unacknowledged yet effectively operative, in a non-French disguise, when the mounting pressure of nineteenth-century Industrialism and Democracy compelled even unrepentant reactionary régimes to overhaul the antiquated law that they had reinstated in the *Code Napoléon's* place. This happened in several of the temporarily re-erected pre-Napoleonic statelets in Italy; and, when, in belated response to Napoleon's trumpet-call,[3] an Italian Risorgimento

[1] The portability of the *Code Napoléon* proclaims its success; its lucidity and intelligibility account for its portability; and this trinity of virtues was heaven-sent; for the substitution of one system of law for another, *in toto* and at one stroke, is, at best, a formidable undertaking. Even when the substitute exists, ready-made, and has merely to be translated and enacted in order to give it the force of law on paper, it cannot become practically operative without the introduction of a corresponding new code of procedure and without the training up of a new generation of judges, barristers, and solicitors who have familiarized themselves with the new law and new procedure by daily practice in the courts. When the writer of this Study visited Lithuania at Eastertide, 1928, he found that, in their enthusiasm for reorganizing their life on a Lithuanian national basis, the Lithuanians had taken two steps which, in their combined effect, were producing serious practical difficulties. On the one hand they had set themselves to draft a unitary national Lithuanian system of law to replace both the *Code Napoléon*, which was in force in the fragment of Lithuanian territory on the left bank of the Niemen, and the Imperial Russian Law, which was in force in the rest of the country. Simultaneously, in their educational system, they had deposed the Russian language from its former position of being the first foreign language to be learnt by Lithuanian children, and had replaced it by a choice between the leading Western languages. This replacement of the Russian language in the Lithuanian schools was, of course, as quick and easy a step as the replacement of the Imperial Russian Law in the Lithuanian Courts was slow and difficult. By A.D. 1928 the Lithuanians had realized, too late, that their self-imposed task of introducing a new national Lithuanian system of law was not going to be fulfilled as a going concern within any foreseeable period of time; but by 1928 a time could already be foreseen when the Imperial Russian Law would have to be administered in Lithuania by a rising generation of Lithuanian judges and lawyers who would have been brought up without having been taught the Russian language. To tide over the awkward interim stage that could thus be seen ahead, could not the Imperial Russian Law be translated into Lithuanian? Alas, no; for this was not a code but a congeries of 'case law', and the use of it demanded a familiarity with decisions of the Imperial Russian Senate running into hundreds of volumes. In such a situation the merits of the *Code Napoléon* were conspicuous. Happy that small minority of Lithuanian judges, lawyers, and litigants whose business was transacted on the River Niemen's Napoleonic bank. —A.J.T.

[2] Fisher, op. cit., p. 379.

[3] See V. v. 642.

had swept this political lumber away, to make room for an Italian national state that aspired to be liberal as well as united, Italian codifiers frankly took the *Code Napoléon* as their model in drafting the Italian Civil Code that was adopted on the 25th June, 1865, and was brought into force on the 1st January, 1866.

The *Code Napoléon*'s most remarkable triumphs, however, were its conquests of alien worlds on which the claws of the Napoleonic eagle had never fastened. During Napoleon's trial of strength with Great Britain, British sea power had foiled his attempt to conquer Egypt and Syria, forced him to sell Louisiana to the United States,[1] and prevented him from following up his military occupation of Spain and invasion of Portugal by pouncing upon these decrepit Powers' great possessions in the Americas. Yet the *Code Napoléon* struck roots both in the Americas and in the Levant. It became an important constituent of the local law of the State of Louisiana within the North American Union;[2] it influenced the development of the established variety of pre-Revolutionary French customary law in the anti-Revolutionary Canadian Province of Quebec;[3] while in the successor-states of the Spanish Empire of the Indies it came as a god-send to fill the legal vacuum left by the failure of the Spanish Bourbon régime to bring up to date the worthy Pinelo's long-since antiquated *Recopilación de Leyes de Los Reynos de las Indias*.[4]

As for Egypt, it would hardly be an exaggeration to say that the *Code Napoléon* found a second home in this stronghold of Islam after the process of Westernization, foreshadowed in the shattering but transitory visitation of Napoleon's expeditionary force, had been put in hand in good earnest by Mehmed ʿAlī. In the whole field of civil law outside the communal preserve of Personal Statute, the *Code Napoléon* was 'received' in Egypt in A.D. 1876 as the law for the new Mixed Courts and in A.D. 1883 (a sensational triumph, this!)[5] as the law for the new system of civil and criminal jurisdiction,[6] applying to Ottoman subjects in Egypt,

[1] French land power had enabled Napoleon, in a secret convention signed at Saint Ildefonso on the 7th October, 1800, to extort from the Spanish Crown the retrocession to France of the originally French possession of Louisiana, which the French Crown had ceded to Spain in the peace settlement of A.D. 1763; but Napoleon missed his opportunity for seizing this Transatlantic prey during his momentary enjoyment of the freedom of the seas after the conclusion of the Anglo-French Peace Treaty of Amiens on the 25th March, 1802; and the naval war was in full swing again by the 20th December, 1803, when the sale of Louisiana by the French Empire to the United States was completed.

[2] The state law of Louisiana was a blend of several different elements: the local French customary law of the *Ancien Régime*, the law of the Spanish Indies, introduced after the cession of Louisiana by France to Spain in A.D. 1763, and the English 'Common Law' introduced after the retrocession of Louisiana by Spain to France in A.D. 1800 and its purchase from France by the United States in A.D. 1803. The Napoleonic codes were grafted on to the existing local French law *pari passu* with the introduction of the 'Common Law' current in the United States.

[3] This influence was manifest in the Quebec Civil Code of A.D. 1867.

[4] See p. 263, above.

[5] Sensational in view of the gulf between the *Code Napoléon* and the communal systems of law which it was replacing. It did, however, share one vital common source with the Islamic *Sharīʿah* as well as with the communal laws of the several Christian *millets*. All these legal systems alike were derived in large measure from varieties or transmutations of Roman Law. The influence of Roman Law on Islamic Law is discussed on pp. 288–91, below.

[6] The traditional *Sharīʿ* courts retained their jurisdiction in matters of 'personal statute'.

that was introduced in that year. This naturalization of French Law in Egypt goes far to account for the strength of the hold which French culture obtained in Egypt notwithstanding the ultimate discomfiture of France in her military and political struggle with Great Britain for ascendancy there. The French military occupation of Egypt had lasted for little more than three years (reckoning from the landing of Napoleon's expeditionary force on the 1st July, 1798, to the ignominious surrender of ʿAbdallah Menou on the 2nd September, 1801); the second and single-handed British occupation[1] had lasted for fifty-four years (reckoning from the landing of a British expeditionary force on the 20th August, 1882, to the ratification of the Anglo-Egyptian Treaty of Alliance signed on the 26th August, 1936), and in A.D. 1952 the vestiges of British occupation which the terms of the Treaty had preserved had not yet been entirely removed. Yet on the morrow of the General War of 1939–45 the by this time penetratingly Westernized governing class of Egypt bore its Western imprint in the French and not in the British variety of the pattern.

One of the most remarkable episodes in the history of the dissemination of the *Code Napoléon* was the role that it was called upon to play in Japan during the Meiji Era. In embarking on a general programme of Westernization the authors of the Meiji Revolution showed their wisdom in the field of law by hastening slowly. Their first step, taken in A.D. 1870, was to have the French Codes translated into Japanese. Law schools for French, English, and German Law were successively established in A.D. 1872, 1874, and 1887. In A.D. 1875 a commission was appointed to compile a civil code, and, after its draft, which followed the Napoleonic Civil Code very closely, had been submitted to the Japanese Government in A.D. 1878 and had been rejected, a member of the commission, the French jurist Boissonade, was asked in 1880 to prepare a new draft. His draft was published on the 27th March, 1890, and a complementary draft by Japanese jurists, covering the province of 'personal statute', on the 16th October of the same year, and the whole code was to come into force on the 1st January, 1893.

This apparent acceptance, in Japan, of a Napoleonic *Code Boissonade* was the high-water mark in the flow of the *Code Napoléon*'s influence over the face of the globe; and a turn in the tide was not slow to follow. Before the arrival of the date fixed for bringing the *Code Boissonade* into operation, the newly created Japanese Imperial Diet voted, on the 16th May, 1892, for postponing the date till the 31st December, 1896. Thereupon, a third draft was commissioned, and this draft, which was published in instalments in 1896 and 1898 and was brought into force in July 1899, was inspired, not by the *Code Napoléon*, but by the second draft of a German Civil Code, which had been published in 1895.[2]

The controversy in Japan which resulted in this victory of German

[1] In response to the challenge of the French occupation, British troops had already set foot on Egyptian soil from the 8th March, 1801, to March 1803; but on this first occasion they had come by invitation of the lawful sovereign of Egypt, the Ottoman Pādishāh, and in the company of a Turkish expeditionary force.

[2] In the German Empire this draft was subsequently adopted on the 16th August, 1896, and was brought into force on the 1st January, 1900.

over French law had not arisen over the respective merits of two variant Western schools of jurisprudence, but had been

'a deep-seated conflict between two fundamental ideas of law. The immediate enforcement party contended for the juristic idea embodied in the theory of the school of Natural Law, namely that Law was based upon Human Nature, that it is of a universal character, and that, inasmuch as the codification of a civilised country like France was a refined expression of Human Nature or of the universal character of Law, it could be adopted by Japan. The postponement party stood for the juristic idea of the historical school, that Law, like Language, was an expression of national character and a product of History, and that the introduction of a foreign code into Japanese Society was absurd and preposterous.'[1]

On the 16th May, 1892, the majority in the Japanese Diet showed their impartial hostility towards exotic law of all varieties by voting for the postponement of the coming into force, not only of a French-inspired civil code, but of a German-inspired commercial code, which they had already condemned to a first period of postponement in a previous vote on the 16th December, 1890. Nevertheless, in the Japanese civil code that was eventually brought into force in 1898, as well as in the commercial code brought into force in 1899, it was a German, not a Japanese, influence that replaced the French; and this eventual adoption, in Japan, of a German instead of a French model might be read as the opening of a new chapter in the history of the dissemination of Western Law. For the German Civil Code was likewise taken as the basis for the Swiss Civil Code adopted on the 10th December, 1907, and brought into force on the 1st January, 1912; and the Turkish Civil Code, adopted on the 17th February, 1926, was, in its turn, virtually a translation of the Swiss.

The German Civil Code was, indeed, a more scientifically executed piece of work than its famous French forerunner; yet, even if the outlook for German cultural influence abroad had not been blighted by the sinister military and political events of A.D. 1914–45, the ghosts of Napoleon's draftsmen might, not unjustly, have booked the German Civil Code's successes to the credit of their French account. The workmanlike instrument that saw the light in Germany in A.D. 1895 could never have emerged out of the 'hybrid miscellany' of German customary law if the *Code Napoléon* had not pegged out a drove-road for ruminant German jurists to follow; and it would have been surprising, after all, if this German cud had not been well digested when it had been chewed for more than ninety years.

The Normal Failure of Codification to arrest Decay

In any case, whatever verdict History might eventually pronounce on the respective merits and achievements of the Revolutionary French Code and its slow-footed German competitor, our glance at the *Code Napoléon's* nineteenth-century history has perhaps made it evident that

[1] Takayanagi, Kenzo: *Reception and Influence of Occidental Legal Ideas in Japan* (Tokyo 1929, The Japanese Council, Institute of Pacific Relations), p. 11.

this ninety-years-long triumphal progress from Paris to New Orleans and Buenos Aires and Cairo and Tokyo was the exceptional result of peculiar historical circumstances. As a rule—and this rule is inherent in the very nature of the declines and falls of civilizations—the demand for codification reaches its climax in the penultimate age before a social catastrophe, long after the peak of achievement in jurisprudence has been passed, and when the legislators of the day are irretrievably on the run in a losing battle with ungovernable forces of destruction. Justinian himself had no sooner turned at bay against Fate, and thrown up in her face the imposing barricade of his *Corpus Iuris*, than he was driven by the Fury's relentless hounds to sprint on again in a paper-chase in which he was constrained to strew the course with the tell-tale sheets of his *Novellae*. Yet in the long run Fate is apt to deal kindly with the codifiers, even when they have not shared Napoleon's fortune in being moved to do their work at an exceptionally auspicious hour; for the mead of admiration which their outraged predecessors would have refused, with indignation, to accord to them has been offered to their *manes*, in full and overflowing measure, by a Posterity that has been too remote, too barbarous, or too sentimental to be capable of arriving at a soberly correct appraisal of the codifiers' work.

Even this uncritically admiring Posterity, however, finds the consecrated codes impossible to apply in real life until they have suffered a sea change; for it is the tragedy of the codifiers that, in reducing the law of a happier and more cultivated past age to the social, moral, and intellectual level of their own melancholy generation, they have still pegged it so high that it is bound to pass forthwith beyond the reach[1] of a herd running violently down a steep place into the sea.[2]

> 'In the parts in which they were borrowing from the classical law—of which they preserved many useful rules—as well as in Justinian's own personal constitutions and in the interpolations, the [Justinianean] commissioners succeeded, notwithstanding the difficulties of their task, in producing a work which, without being free from contradictions and obscurities, was better suited to the needs of the populations of their countries than were the admirable classical masterpieces. One might even say that, in itself, this work was still too strong meat for the juridically uncultivated minds to which it was addressed. In the East it does not appear to have succeeded in dethroning the Syro-Roman Custumal, which was unquestionably less scientific. In the West its only effect on legal practice was by way of glosses which were never more than mediocre before the study of the Justinianean Law received its impulsion from the School of Bologna.'[3]

In the last phase of the Roman Empire in its last strongholds, Justinian's reign was promptly followed by a deluge of Lombard, Slav, and Arab barbarian invasion; in the last phase of the Empire of Sumer and Akkad, Hammurabi's strenuous work of political and social reclamation on the plains of Shinar was no less promptly waterlogged by a Kassite

[1] See V. vi. 224, with n. 3.

[2] Matt. viii. 32; Mark v. 13; Luke viii. 33.

[3] Collinet, P.: *Études Historiques sur le Droit de Justinien*, vol. i: 'Le Caractère Oriental de l'Œuvre Législative de Justinien' (Paris 1912, Recueil Sirey), p. xxix.

inundation from the hills; in the Andean World the rule of the Inca law-givers was brought to a sudden end by the calamity of the Spanish conquest. Even in the Anatolian core of Justinian's empire, when Leo the Restorer and his successors set to work, after a virtual interregnum of 150 years, to replace the wreckage of Justinian's pretentious imperial edifice by something more modest, more practical, and, above all, more firmly based, they found apter materials in the Mosaic Law than in the Justinianean *Corpus Iuris* for meeting the simple needs of a new society that was struggling to be born under their aegis.[1] In Italy, whom Justinian succeeded in 'liberating' momentarily from barbarian rule at the cost of finally wrecking her social structure and her cultural life, the immediate future lay, not with the secular *Corpus Iuris*,[2] but with the monastic rule of Saint Benedict,[3] which was conceived during the agony of the Great Romano-Gothic War (*gerebatur* A.D. 537–53) and was disseminated to Ultima Thule before Monte Cassino was laid desolate by the Lombards. In the former Transalpine provinces of the Roman Empire that Justinian neither inherited from his imperial predecessors nor reconquered from barbarian war-bands, the Justinianean *Corpus Iuris* did not, of course, obtain even the short-lived currency that it enjoyed in Italy and North-West Africa pending the undoing of Justinian's work there by the Lombards and the Arabs.[4]

The Decay of the Roman Law in the Roman Empire's Teutonic Barbarian Successor-states

In these lost and never even temporarily recovered Transalpine dominions of Rome a Roman subject population was permitted, by the indulgence or indifference of its new barbarian masters, to continue to live under Roman civil law in its locally prevalent pre-Justinianean embodiments; and the milder and more statesmanlike of the emperors' barbarian successors went so far as to anticipate Justinian by promulgating local codes of Roman Law—a *Lex Romana Burgundionum* and a Visigothic *Breviarium Alarici*—for the use of their Roman sheep without a jurisprudent shepherd. The *Breviarium* of the Visigoth King Alaric II, which was mainly based on the Theodosian Code, had also actually preserved extracts from the *Sententiae* of the Severan jurist Paulus which would have been lost to latter-day scholars if the sole surviving

1 See III. iii. 276 and X. ix. 21–27.

2 Collinet, in op. cit., vol. cit., points out that Italy had not yet come under Justinian's rule at the time—A.D. 528–34—when Justinian's *Corpus Iuris* was being compiled (p. 11); and that no Italian jurists were included in the board of commissioners by whom the work of codification was carried out (p. 13). Justinian's legislation did not apply to Italy automatically; it was made applicable there by express provisions, and this only *pari passu* with the progress of the reconquest (p. 12). At the same time, Collinet suggests elsewhere that an already formed design of reconquering Italy may have been one of Justinian's motives in compiling his *Corpus Iuris*. While he did not draw upon the local Italian version of the Roman Law, he did wish to provide himself with a *Corpus Iuris* that would be applicable in Italy (Collinet: 'The General Considerations raised by the Codification of Justinian', in *Tijdschrift voor Rechtsgeschiedenis*, vol. iv (Haarlem 1923, Tjeenk Willink), pp. 7–8).

3 See III iii. 265–7 and V. vi. 224, n. 3.

4 This point is brought out by Burns, C. Delisle: *The First Europe* (London 1947, Allen & Unwin), p. 326.

official anthology of the masterpieces of Roman jurisprudence had been Tribonian's *Digest*. In the first phase of the Visigothic régime in Southern Gaul and Spain, King Euric I (*regnabat* A.D. 466–84) enlisted the services of Sidonius Apollinaris' friend and correspondent the Roman jurist Leo of Narbonne.[1] Yet this precarious survival of Roman Law in the West was limited in its range and, even within those limits, was a wasting asset. Roman subjects of Teutonic barbarian successor-states were subjected, it would seem, from the outset, to a regressive barbarian criminal law providing for the payment of a *wergeld* to the injured party or his heirs, in lieu of punishments imposed and exacted by the state;[2] and, though, in the deliberately conciliatory common law for Romans and Burgundians that was embodied in the Burgundian war-lord Gundobad's *Liber Constitutionum*,[3] the invidious differentiation of scales of *wergeld* was based on differences of class and not of community, in the *wergeld* tariff of the ultra-barbarous Frankish *Lex Salica* 'the life of an ordinary Frank' was 'reckoned worth double that of a Roman'.[4] What is still more significant, the Roman Law was now in retreat even in the tolerated departments of business relations and 'personal statute'.

'The Roman Law survived, but it sank to the level of custom.[5] Since

1 See Apollinaris, Sidonius: *Epistulae*, Book VIII, Letter iii, § 3.

2 See Lot, F.: *Les Invasions Germaniques* (Paris 1935, Payot), pp. 166–8.

3 In Southern Gaul at the turn of the fifth and sixth centuries of the Christian Era the subject Romans gained a notable improvement in their legal status from the play of power politics between their barbarian masters of the moment—the Nomadicized East German Burgundians and Visigoths—and the neighbouring Frankish backwoodsmen from the Lower Rhineland, who, under Clovis' leadership, were now showing themselves formidably aggressive. In the preface to the Burgundian *Liber Constitutionum* it is declared to be the king's benevolent intention to secure justice, unalloyed by either corruption or communal inequality, for Burgundians and Romans alike, by providing a common law for cases between a Burgundian and a Roman, and a separate code for cases in which both parties are Romans (see Dill, Sir S.: *Roman Society in Gaul in the Merovingian Age* (London 1926, Macmillan), p. 65). This Burgundian profession of virtue is borne out by the sixth-century Gallic Roman historian Gregory of Tours. '[Gundobadus] Burgundionibus leges mitiores instituit, ne Romanos opprimerent' (*Historia Francorum*, Book II, chap. 9, *ad fin.*); and the evidence is impressive when a Roman and Francophil Catholic ecclesiastic testifies in favour of a barbarian and Arian Burgundian war-lord whose dynasty had been suppressed by Gregory's Frankish patrons by the time when Gregory was writing. Dill (op. cit., p. 63) dates the first edition of Gundobad's *Liber Constitutionum* about A.D. 501; Burns (op. cit., p. 330) about 503 (the dating turns on an article, dated the 28th May, 502, which appears in the final edition). The *Breviarium* of the Burgundian Gundobad's Visigoth contemporary Alaric II (*regnabat* A.D. 484–507) is dated by Dill (op. cit., p. 94) and by Burns (op. cit., p. 330) *circa* A.D. 506, on the eve of the Battle of Vouillé. This battle, which was fought in A.D. 507, resulted in the conquest of all Southern Gaul save Septimania from the Visigoths by the Franks (see II. ii. 166, 380, and 428; V. v. 217, n. 1, and 221, 222, 225–6). The Burgundian principality had suffered its first Frankish invasion in A.D. 500. These coincidences of date bear out the view that at the turn of the century the Visigothic and Burgundian governments were attempting to offset the odium of their heretical Arian faith by granting genuine equality before the law to their Catholic Roman subjects. Though their conciliatory policy did not induce the Catholic Roman clergy in their dominions to cease working for the victory of their own barbarous Frankish convert Clovis, some of the Roman laity felt differently. A grandson of Sidonius Apollinaris fell at Vouillé fighting for the Visigoths; and, though, when the converted Franks conquered Aquitaine and Burgundy, they left in force the liberal *Breviarium Alarici* and *Lex Romana Burgundionum* and *Liber Constitutionum Gundobadi* that had been enacted by their Visigoth and Burgundian victims, the Aquitanians chafed under the Frankish yoke for centuries thereafter. The Catholic clergy, however, were privileged in all contingencies. Under the barbarian law of the Ripuarian Franks it cost four times as much to kill even a sub-deacon, and nine times as much to kill a bishop, as to kill an ordinary Roman layman (Burns, op. cit., p. 336).

4 Dill, op. cit., p. 47; cp. Lot, op. cit., p. 195.

5 Cp. Collinet, op. cit., vol. cit., pp. 312–13.—A.J.T.

the Empire had disappeared, there was no longer any legislation to put fresh life into the old law by adapting it to new necessities.'[1]

'In the sixth century [of the Christian Era] in the West, the destinies of Roman Law were dominated by one key phenomenon: an arrest in the development of the classical law. When we analyse this phenomenon in order to examine it in its diverse aspects, we can see that there are three elements in it: a traditional persistence of the classical institutions;[2] an evolution of these institutions in which there is nothing creative; and, as an inexorable consequence of these first two facts, a general regression in legal standards. . . .

'The full measure of the feebleness of the evolution comes to light when one measures it by this sixth-century Western World's needs. In the troubled period that marks the end of the Ancient World and ushers in the Middle Ages, the new needs were numerous and pressing. In whatever direction one turns one's eyes—towards the political, the economic, the moral or the religious situation—one sees nothing but the overthrow of the ancient traditional order, the Roman order, of things. At this decisive moment in history, did Italy and Gaul, to confine our attention to them, make any attempt to satisfy these needs in so far as they affected private law? When it had become clear that the barbarian conquest had come to stay, the accomplishment of [legal] reforms that would have sufficed to bring the law in force into harmony with the new way of life—a harmony that was imperatively required—called for energetic and intelligent men (such as were the feudal jurists of a later age) who would labour diligently to bring the [necessary] evolution to pass. Evolution does not take place without effort, and is never automatic. The times called for someone with the courage to apply the pick-axe to the dilapidated edifice of law, and with the authority and ability to build up a new edifice [in place of the old one]. But this was something beyond the powers of the men of [sixth-century] Italy and Gaul. Their impotence is attested by the decadence which had brought them under the yoke of their new masters and had opened the way for the profound transformation of economic life. . . .

'The West [in the sixth century] was "a static society in which nothing could die because nothing was coming to birth there any longer". In this static world, stagnation and decadence had incontestably gained the upper hand over progress. This is the spectacle presented by Roman Law in Italy and Gaul at the very moment when the names of Constantinople and Justinian were lighting up the World with their lustre.'[3]

Thus, in the last chapter of the history of Roman Law in the West, the Theodosian Code played a dwindling part and the Justinianean *Corpus* no part at all. In Western and Orthodox Christendom alike, the Justinianean *Corpus* eventually came into its own, not by showing itself proof against death, but by surmounting a *vitai pausa*[4] through a feat of hibernation. Though in Italy as a whole the *Corpus* had an innings of no more than fifteen years (reckoning from the end, in

[1] Lot, op. cit., p. 166.

[2] e.g. *mancipatio*, which was abolished by Justinian, persisted in Italy down to the ninth century of the Christian Era (Collinet, op. cit., vol. cit., p. 216). *Dictio dotis*, which was likewise abolished by Justinian, was retained by Alaric in his *Breviarium* (ibid., p. 220). See further ibid., p. 308.—A.J.T.

[3] Collinet, P.: *Études Historiques sur le Droit de Justinien*, vol. i: 'Le Caractère Oriental de l'Œuvre Législative de Justinien' (Paris 1912, Recueil Sirey), pp. 309–14.

[4] Lucretius: *De Rerum Natura*, Book III, l. 930.

A.D. 553, of the Ostrogoths' last stand to the beginning, in A.D. 568, of a piecemeal Lombard conquest), it came to life again, some four hundred years later, in an eleventh-century juristic renaissance at Bologna, the principal city in the bridgehead which the Constantinopolitan Government's Italian exarchs had maintained till A.D. 751 in the hinterland of Ravenna. From there from that time onwards, Tribonian's work radiated its influence into extremities and extensions of an expanding Western World that had lain beyond the political horizon not only of Justinian but of Trajan; and, thanks to Bologna's capacity, in the Dark Ages, for intellectual cold storage, a version of Roman Law was eventually 'received' in Modern Holland, Scotland, and South Africa. In Orthodox Christendom the Justinianean *Corpus Iuris* survived, with greater ease, the less exacting ordeal of hibernating for three centuries at Constantinople, and re-emerged in the tenth century of the Christian Era in the Imperial Code (*Vasiliká*) by which the Emperors of the Macedonian Dynasty replaced the Mosaistic legislation of their eighth-century Syrian predecessors. These parallel juristic renaissances in Orthodox and in Western Christendom will occupy our attention in a later Part of this Study.[1] In the present place we are inquiring into cases in which the juristic legacy of a defunct universal state has been inherited direct, not rediscovered as a treasure-trove.

The Failure of the Spanish Empire of the Indies to profit by the Law of the Incaic and Aztec Empires

In the broken history of the Andean universal state, we have seen[2] that some vestiges of the oecumenical law of the Incas did find their way into the heterogeneous and ill-digested *corpus iuris* of the Spanish Empire of the Indies, but the greater part of this precious Incaic legal heritage, which had been so carefully adapted by its authors to the social needs of the Andean World, was sacrificed by the destructiveness of the *conquistadores* and the unimaginativeness of their more reputable successors the *licenciados*. It is true that among the legal advisers of the Spanish Crown in the Indies there were individuals who saw that

'the most difficult problems . . . were those arising from the government of an Indian population which could not be reduced to the norms of Spanish law. Juan Matienzo, judge in the Audiencia of Charcas and intimate adviser to [the Viceroy] Toledo (*proconsulari munere fungebatur* A.D. 1569–81), in his celebrated text-book of Peruvian administration, *Gobierno del Perú* (*circa* A.D. 1570), warns the Spanish authorities not "to try and change the customs abruptly and make new laws and ordinances, until they know the conditions and customs of the natives of the country and of the Spaniards who dwell there; for, as the country is large, so customs and tempers differ. One must first accommodate oneself to the customs of those one wishes to govern and proceed agreeably to them until, having won their confidence and good opinion, with the authority thus secured one may undertake to change the customs." '[3]

[1] See X. ix. 27–34.

[2] On p. 265, above.

[3] Haring, C. H.: *The Spanish Empire in America* (New York 1947, Oxford University Press), p. 110.

But the indigenous customs that were incorporated into Spanish colonial law on the strength of such considerations as those set forth by Matienzo 'had to do, naturally enough, with the life of the lower orders of society: the regulation of labour, the succession and the privileges of native chiefs, Indian village organisation, agricultural practices, etc. . . . Basically . . . people in the Indies, especially in the domain of private law, lived according to the same judicial criteria as in Spain.'[1]

The Infusion of a Decadent Roman Law into the Customary Law of the Roman Empire's Teutonic Barbarian Conquerors

In the more usual situation in which the aggressors who have snatched the sceptre out of the hands of the rulers of a universal state are not the representatives of some alien civilization, but are barbarians, we should expect *à priori* to see the governments of the barbarian successor-states take over much more of the juristic heritage of a former oecumenical Power which has eventually succumbed to force of barbarian arms without having lost its cultural prestige in barbarian eyes. We have, indeed, noticed already[2] that in the Teutonic barbarian successor-states of the Roman Empire the new masters were ready to allow their Roman subjects to continue to live under Roman Civil Law. On the other hand the barbarians' impulse to maintain a distinctive communal culture of their own in the alien social environment in which they have placed themselves through their conquests is apt to declare itself in the field of law, as well as in the fields of religion and poetry in which we have studied it in another context.[3]

The extant collections of the laws of divers Teutonic war-bands on ex-Roman ground gave a latter-day student the impression that these barbarians wanted to accommodate themselves to their new social environment with as little change in their own traditional life as local circumstances might allow. The most archaic of these collections was the Frankish *Lex Salica*;[4] but the same imperviousness to Roman influence was displayed in the rather more sophisticated provisions of the other law-books which had been put into their final form at a later date: for instance, the laws of the Ripuarian Franks, the Alamanni, the Bavarians, the Frisians, the Lombard conquerors of Italy, and the English conquerors of Britain. The backbone of these laws consisted of such utterly un-Roman institutions as ordeal by battle and the atonement for crimes of violence by the payment of compensation to the injured party or his heirs.[5] This contrast in character between the sophisticated Roman Law of a moribund Hellenic World and the archaic barbarian law of the Teutonic war-bands who had settled on the Roman Empire's derelict provinces had its counterpart in a corresponding contrast between the Sumerian Law, as mirrored in Hammurabi's Code, and the law of the

[1] Haring, op. cit., loc. cit.

[2] On pp. 280–1, above.

[3] See V. v. 194–337, *passim*.

[4] See the *aperçu* of it in Dill, Sir Samuel: *Roman Society in Gaul in the Merovingian Age* (London 1926, Macmillan), pp. 43–62.

[5] An illuminating survey and analysis of the history of this institution among the Teutonic barbarian invaders of the Roman Empire and their successors is given by Phillpotts, B. S.: *Kindred and Clan* (Cambridge 1913, University Press).

Hittite barbarians who had settled on a moribund Sumeric World's Anatolian fringes. The difference in the spirit of the law was here twofold. From one point of view the Hittite Law gave the impression of being more advanced than the Sumerian; for, whereas in Hammurabi's Code the punishments prescribed were savage and, in particular, the *lex talionis* was worked out to forbiddingly pedantic extremes,[1] the Hittite law substituted fines for Hammurabi's sentences of death or mutilation as the penalty for a number of offences.[2] From another point of view, however, the Hittite Law represented a regression; for, in dealing with crimes against persons, it substituted a tariff of *wergeld* for the punishments, to be imposed and exacted by the state, that had been prescribed for the same crimes by Hammurabi.[3]

What were the prospects of life for these barbarian systems of law on the alien ground of a decadent civilization whose domain the barbarians had overrun? The Hittite Law, in the redaction in which it happened to have been disinterred by twentieth-century Western archaeologists, dated from the later days of the second phase of Hittite history, for which the Carolingian Age of Western history would be the Frankish equivalent both in cultural terms of the contemporary state of society and in chronological terms of the passage of time since the emergence of a nascent new civilization out of a cultural interregnum.[4] Here we have an historical example of a law of barbarian origin successfully providing for the needs of a civilization in the first chapter of its history. Beyond this point, however, Hittite history does not carry us; for, not long after the date at which the Hittite Code was promulgated in the redaction that had been unearthed, the homeland of the Hittite Society in Eastern Anatolia was overwhelmed by a barbarian Völkerwanderung from the Balkan Peninsula and the Aegean which had been set in motion by the catastrophic dissolution of the neighbouring Minoan Society, and thereafter the Hittite Civilization lingered on only in refugee communities, beyond the Taurus in Northern Syria and overseas along the

[1] The articles in which it was applied are set out in Smith, J. M. P.: *The Origin and History of Hebrew Law* (Chicago 1931, University of Chicago Press), p. 24, n. 2.

[2] See Hrozný, B.: *Die Älteste Geschichte Vorderasiens und Indiens* (Prague 1943, Melantrich), pp. 114 and 167; Götze, A.: *Hethiter, Churriter und Assyrer* (Oslo 1936, Aschehoug), pp. 64–65; Delaporte, L.: *Les Hittites* (Paris 1936, La Renaissance du Livre), p. 231.

[3] See Cavaignac, E.: *Le Problème Hittite* (Paris 1936, Leroux), p. 105. The institution of *wergeld* thus turns out to be a common feature of Teutonic and Hittite barbarian law. 'The idea of settling conflicts by a money indemnity is not peculiar to the Germans. It is found among other peoples and is of a high antiquity. We come across it already, fourteen centuries before the beginning of our Era, among the Hittites of Asia Minor' (Lot, F.: *Les Invasions Germaniques* (Paris 1935, Payot), p. 166).

[4] This Hittite law, as latter-day Western students had it, was a code drafted in the language of the Power that had exercised political hegemony over the Hittite World from the sixteenth century B.C. onwards. It was written in the Akkadian cuneiform script on two clay tablets, containing one hundred paragraphs each, which were discovered on the site of the Hittite Empire's capital, Boghazqal'eh, in A.D. 1906–7. This redaction dated from the fifteenth century B.C. according to Hrozný, op. cit., pp. 166–7; from the thirteenth century according to Cavaignac, op. cit., p. 105. According to Delaporte, op. cit., p. 214, there were three successive redactions, of which the second was made in the fifteenth or fourteenth century B.C. English translations of the disinterred text will be found in Smith, J. M. P.: *The Origin and History of Hebrew Law* (Chicago 1931, University of Chicago Press), pp. 247–74, and in Pritchard, J. B.: *Ancient Near Eastern Texts* (Princeton 1950, University Press), pp. 188–97.

west coast of Italy, which were eventually absorbed by the Syriac and the Hellenic Society respectively.[1] It was as if, in the ninth century of the Christian Era, the collapse of the Carolingian Empire had resulted in the destruction of the nascent Western Christian Civilization at the hands of Scandinavian, Eurasian Nomad, and Muslim Arab invaders. If we are to follow the fortunes of barbarian law in a growing civilization farther than this point, we must turn from Hittite to Western history, where we find the law of the English barbarian settlers on ex-Roman ground in Britain succeeding, without any deliberate or systematic 'reception' of Roman law at any stage,[2] in developing sufficiently, out of its own resources, to be able to provide for the needs of a civilization that has arrived at a high degree of social sophistication and economic complexity.

This unique ability of the English Common Law to keep pace with the growth of the Western Civilization could be explained as the effect of three distinct causes. In the first place, at the time of the post-Hellenic Völkerwanderung, the barbarian law of the English invaders of Britain was largely relieved of such hampering archaic institutions as *wergeld* thanks to the exceptionally rapid disintegration of the kin-group organization of society in a migration across the sea.[3] In the second place the ex-Roman population did not, in Britain, survive under barbarian rule as a distinct community, continuing to live under its own Roman law, as it survived in the Continental Teutonic successor-states of the Roman Empire. In Britain the provincials were exterminated, expelled, or assimilated by the English settlers. In the third place, at the opening of the second chapter of Western history towards the close of the eleventh century of the Christian Era the English law was carried forward and, above all, was effectively enforced, thanks to the exceptionally strong and efficient monarchy that was imposed on a politically united England by a Norman conquest. The survival of the English Common Law, however, was an exception that proved a rule; for the ancestral law of the other Teutonic barbarian invaders of the Roman Empire failed to stay the course. In all other cases we find Roman influence seeping in from an early date.

To begin with, the earliest versions of all the Teutonic law-books, with the significant exception of the English, were drafted in Latin; and, when we turn our attention from this point of form to matters of substance, we catch glimpses of Teutonic custom fighting a stubborn rear-guard action against the moral pressure of Roman concepts and Christian standards. The comparatively enlightened King Liutprand of the ultra-barbarian Lombards declares frankly, in a law promulgated in A.D. 731, 163 years after the Lombards' eruption into the comparatively highly cultivated social environment of Italy, that ordeal by battle is a Lombard

[1] See I. i. 114–15; III. iii. 139; IV. iv. 109; V. v. 88; and IX. viii. 438–9.

[2] This is not, of course, to say that 'the Common Law' of England remained impervious to the influence of Roman Law after this influence had become prevalent in Western Christendom as a whole in consequence of the Justinianean juristic renaissance at Bologna in the eleventh century of the Christian Era (see X. ix. 31–34).

[3] On this point, see the passage quoted from Phillpotts, op. cit., pp. 257–65, in the present Study, II. ii. 90–91.

custom which it is beyond his power to ban, though he is 'uncertain of the judgment of God and' has 'heard that many litigants have unjustly lost their case through' this practice.[1] On the other hand the genial Burgundians had mellowed under Roman influence within less than a hundred years of their crossing the Rhine.

'There is hardly a trace of German ideas or institutions in the legislation of Gundobad.[2] He has no resemblance to the old German chief, surrounded by his assembled warriors. His type and model is the political authority wielded by the Emperor or the great Praetorian Prefects. . . . In the Salian Law pecuniary compensation is almost universal: other punishments are almost unheard of. In Burgundy, besides the pecuniary sanction, there are many and various punishments for crime, some of them even harsh and cruel. This, however, it has been observed, does not prove a less civilised social tone, but rather the reverse.[3] The Burgundian legislator, in fact, is striving to abolish the vindictiveness of private conflicts by making the state the avenger of personal wrongs.'[4]

The Burgundian *Liber Constitutionum* marked a radical departure from archaic Teutonic law not only in its character but in its application; for, while the *Lex Salica* and other Teutonic law-books of that type were merely communal prescriptions for the exclusive use of an intrusive barbarian war-band, Gundobad and Sigismund were enacting, as we have observed already, a 'common law' for their barbarian Burgundian followers and their Roman subjects. The *Edictum Theodorici*,[5] which was promulgated in the Ostrogothic dominions at about the same date, either *circa* A.D. 500 or *circa* A.D. 511–15,[6] was a 'common law' in the same sense of applying alike to Theodoric's Ostrogoth followers and to the Roman population under his rule; and in this case the scales already incline heavily in the Romans' favour. The contents of this barbarian war-lord's edict are drawn from Roman sources—the Theodosian Code and the *Sententiae* of Paulus—and the Ostrogoth masters of Italy are referred to as 'barbarians' throughout the document. It is even more remarkable that the Visigothic *Breviarium Alarici*, which was promulgated within a few years of Theodoric's *Edictum* and Gundobad's *Liber Constitutionum* and was compiled, from the same sources as Theodoric's work, avowedly for the benefit of the Visigoths' Roman subjects, declares in its preamble that its prescriptions apply to 'both Romans and barbarians'.[7]

The promulgation of these three codes of 'common law' by Teutonic war-lords on ex-Roman ground at the opening of the sixth century of

[1] *Liutprandi Leges*, cxviii: 'Incerti sumus de iudicio Dei, et multos audivimus per pugnam sine iusticiam [*sic*] causam suam perdere, sed, propter consuetudinem gentis nostrae Langobardorum, legem ipsam mutare non possumus.'

[2] i.e. in his 'common law' for Burgundians and Romans (see p. 281, above). His version of Roman Civil Law for the use of his Roman subjects among themselves is not in question here.—A.J.T.

[3] Compare the corresponding contrast between the salutary severity of Hammurabi's Code and the inexpedient laxity of the Hittite Code, to which attention has been drawn above.—A.J.T.

[4] Dill, op. cit., p. 66.

[5] See Hodgkin, T.: *Italy and Her Invaders*, 2nd ed. (Oxford 1892–9, Clarendon Press, 8 vols), vol. iii, pp. 276–7 and 309–14.

[6] See Collinet, P.: 'The General Problems raised by the Codification of Justinian', in *Tijdschrift voor Rechtsgeschiedenis*, vol. iv (Haarlem 1923, Tjeenk Willink), pp. 6–7.

[7] Burns, C. Delisle: *The First Europe* (London 1947, Allen & Unwin), pp. 329–30.

the Christian Era was only the beginning of the transfusion of Roman law into the body of Teutonic custom. In the unstable social situation produced by the establishment of barbarian rule over Roman populations, legislation could not stand still. The rulers of the Teutonic barbarian successor-states followed the example of their Imperial Roman predecessors, from the Emperor Hadrian onwards, by issuing a spate of decrees; and these decrees, in their turn, were inevitably coloured by the legal traditions of their Roman social setting. The classic example is the corpus of rescripts, issued in Theodoric's name, which were largely drafted, besides being collected and published, by the Ostrogoth war-lord's Roman minister Cassiodorus. The Ostrogothic régime in Italy, however, met with an early violent end at Roman hands, and the Iberian Peninsula under Visigothic rule was the place where the natural course of events had time to work itself out before the Visigothic Power was overthrown, in its turn, by the more competent rival hands of the Visigoths' fellow barbarian invaders the Primitive Muslim Arabs.

The Visigothic King Receswinth (*regnabat* A.D. 649–72) restored to the former Roman territories under his rule the uniformity of law that they had enjoyed from the time of Caracalla until the Visigothic conquest. In A.D. 654 he put out of commission the *Breviarium* of his predecessor Alaric II (*regnabat* A.D. 484–507) and gave sole force of law to a code[1] compiling the decisions of the Visigothic Kings from Euric down to Receswinth himself.

'These decisions are thoroughly imbued with the spirit of Roman Law. . . . Where else [in the field of Teutonic barbarian legislation] can one find anything comparable to Book I [of Receswinth's *Forum*], entitled *De Legislatore, De Lege*, in which an effort is made to formulate general principles of legislation?'[2]

The end of the story was the blending of Roman with Teutonic law in as many different mixtures[3] as there were local customary laws[4] in Medieval Western Christendom.[5]

The Infusion of a Decadent Roman Law into the Islamic Sharīʿah

This infusion of Roman Law into the custom of Teutonic barbarians who had no future was, however, neither so important an event nor so striking a feat as its surreptitious and unavowed yet unmistakable infiltration into the Islamic law of the Arab barbarian conquerors of other ex-Roman territories. The two elements that blended here were even more incongruous, and the result of their blending was the creation, not

1 Known under the alternative names of *Liber Iudicum* and *Forum Iudiciorum*, and eventually translated into Castilian as the *Fuero Juezgo*.

2 Lot, F.: *Les Invasions Germaniques* (Paris 1935, Payot), pp. 182–3.

3 The close resemblance of medieval Spanish customary law to Scandinavian law leads Lot (op. cit., p. 183) to surmise that, in the Visigothic dominions, an unwritten Gothic customary law survived both the *Breviarium Alarici* and Receswinth's *Forum Iudiciorum*.

4 In France, this diversity of local customary laws survived even the effective political unification of the kingdom and was only ironed out by the legislation of the 'iconoclastic assemblies' convened by the Revolution.

5 The main contributions of Roman Law on the one side and Teutonic Law on the other are set out by Lot, op. cit., pp. 245–7.

just of a parochial law for a barbarian successor-state of the Roman Empire, but of an oecumenical law which was to serve the needs of a restored Syriac universal state and, after surviving the break-up of this political framework, was to govern and mould the life of an Islamic Society that, after the fall of the Caliphate, was to continue to expand until, at the time of writing, its domain had come to extend from Indonesia to Lithuania and from South Africa to China.

Unlike their pagan and Arian Teutonic counterparts, the Primitive Muslim Arabs had been roughly shaken out of their archaic traditional way of life before they administered to themselves the additional shock of a sudden change of social environment by bursting out of the deserts and oases of Arabia into the fields and cities of the Roman and Sasanian empires. A long-continuing radiation of Syriac and Hellenic cultural influences into Arabia had produced a cumulative social effect which had declared itself dramatically in the personal career of the Prophet Muhammad;[1] and his achievements had been so astonishing and his personality so potent that his oracles and acts, as recorded in the Qur'ān and the Traditions, were unquestioningly accepted by his followers as the source of law for regulating, not only the life of the Muslim community itself, but the relations between the Muslim conquerors and their at first many times more numerous non-Muslim subjects. The speed and sweep of the Muslim conquests—which brought half of what remained of the Roman Empire and the whole of the Sasanian Empire under the rule of Muhammad's successors within less than twenty years of the Prophet's death—conspired with the irrationality of the accepted basis of the Muslim empire-builders' new-laid law to create a problem which was hardly more awkward for the non-Muslim population of the Caliphate than it was for their Muslim masters; for, even when the Qur'ān was eked out by the Traditions, the task of wringing out of these unpromising materials an oecumenical law for a sophisticated society was as preposterous as the demands for welling water in the wilderness that the Children of Israel were said to have addressed to Moses.[2]

For a jurist in search of legal pabulum for sustaining social life, the Qur'ān was indeed stony ground. The chapters dating from the non-political Meccan period of Muhammad's mission, before the *Hijrah*, offered far less matter for the practical jurist than he would find in the New Testament; for this literary legacy of the politically disinterested first phase of the Prophet's career contained little beyond a patently sincere and monotonously reiterated declaration of the unity of God and denunciation of the moral and intellectual error of polytheism and idolatry. The chapters afterwards delivered at Medina might look, at first sight, more promising; for at the *Hijrah* Muhammad achieved in his own lifetime a position that was not attained by any follower of Jesus till the fourth century of the Christian Era;[3] he became the head of a state, and his utterances during this Medinese period were mainly concerned with public business. Yet it would be at least as difficult to elicit

[1] See III. iii. 276–7.

[2] Exod. xvii. 1–7.

[3] The difference between the respective political environments in which Christianity and Islam came to birth has been noticed in III. iii. 466–72.

a comprehensive system of law for a sophisticated society from the Medinese *surahs*, unsupplemented, as it would be to perform the same juristic conjuring trick with the Epistles of Saint Paul. Like the apostle-missionary, the apostle-podestà found that the flurry of improvising provisional solutions, *ad hoc*, for a ceaseless succession of emergencies, serious or trivial,[1] left him no breathing-space for attempting to sort out these stray sibylline leaves into anything like a comprehensive or systematic code. Yet, even if Muhammad had succeeded, where Paul had failed, in performing this superhuman labour, the result would have been of less practical use to the Arabian prophet's successors than a Pauline code would have been to the Christian Roman Emperors; for the private business of religious congregations in important cities of the Roman Empire in Paul's day actually had more in common with the public business of the Roman Empire in the fourth century of the Christian Era than had the public business of the agricultural, non-commercial, oasis-state of Medina under Muhammad's rule during the years A.D. 622–32 with the public business of the universal state, embracing all but a fraction of the Syriac World, of which Muhammad's thirty-third successor Muʿtamid found himself master upon his accession in A.D. 870.[2]

In these compelling circumstances the men of action who built the Arab Caliphate let theory take its chance and resorted to self-help. In a legal no-man's-land where the oracles of the Qur'ān were dumb and where even the beaten track (*Sunnah*) of concordant Tradition faded out, they found their way through by the aid of common sense, analogy, consensus, and custom.[3]

'In the oldest period of the development of Islam the authorities entrusted with the administration of justice and the conduct of the religious life had in most cases to fall back on the exercise of their own *ra'y* (common-sense personal judgment) owing to the scarcity of legislative material in the Qur'ān and the dearth of ancient precedents. This was regarded as a matter of course by everyone. . . . Corresponding to this recognition of *ra'y* as an approved source of law are the instructions ascribed to the Prophet and the early Caliphs, which they gave to the officials sent to administer justice in the conquered provinces. . . . In the digests which were developed from these simple origins we find deduction from decisions in allied cases expressly mentioned, i.e. the application of analogy (*qiyās*) as a methodical adjustment of equity (*ra'y*). . . .

'We have—there is evidence for it at a very early period—a kind of popular element adopted among the constitutive sources for the deduction

[1] For these characteristics of Muhammad's personal legislation in the Medinese *surahs*, see Margoliouth, D. S.: *The Early Development of Mohammedanism* (London 1914, Williams & Norgate), pp. 5 and 12. 'It has been noticed that the word which we ordinarily render "reveal", and which literally means "send down", is properly applied to royal rescripts; the suppliant "raises" a petition and the sovereign "sends down" the reply. The faithful at Medinah used to await fresh revelations each day somewhat as we in these days are on the look out for the morning paper.'

[2] i.e. three hundred years after the birth of Muhammad in A.D. 570.

[3] 'It is likely that [Muhammad] meant current practice to continue except where his legislation had abrogated it' (Margoliouth, op. cit., p. 66). To begin with, the custom which counted for most was that of the Arabian oasis-dwellers and Nomads whose conquests re-established a Syriac universal state. The custom which eventually prevailed was that of the Arab empire-builders' converted subjects.

of laws: the conception of consensus (*ijmāʿ*), i.e. the general usage of the community which has been established by agreement in the larger circles of believers independent of the written, traditional or inferred law. . . .

'It was quite natural, from the changed conditions after the conquests, that the formation of the law, not only in its special provisions, but particularly in the point of view they adopted in their method of deductive operation as laid down in *fiqh* (Islamic jurisprudence), was greatly influenced by what the authorities on the development of law in Syria and Mesopotamia were able to learn of Roman Law, sometimes of the special laws for the particular provinces. It was obvious that a quite uncultured people, coming from a land in a primitive stage of social development into countries with an ancient civilization where they established themselves as rulers, would adopt from among their new surroundings as much of the customary law of the conquered lands as could be fitted in with the conditions created by the conquest and be compatible with the demands of new religious ideas. . . . The comparative study of one chapter of private law has yielded the most conclusive proofs of the thorough-going adoption of Roman Law by the jurists of Islam.[1] . . . Roman Law, however, does not exhaust the sources drawn upon in the development of Muslim Law. The receptive character that marks the formation and development of Islam also found expression, naturally first of all in matters of ritual, in borrowings from Jewish Law. According to [von] Kremer,[2] even many of the provisions of Roman Law that have been adopted by Islam only found a place in *fiqh* through the intermediary of the Jews.'[3]

The Mosaic Law's Debt to the Codification of the Sumeric Law by Hammurabi

This Jewish Law, which had so long a history behind it already by the time of Muhammad's *hijrah* from Mecca to Medina, had originated, like the Islamic *Sharīʿah*, as the barbarian customary practice of Nomads who had broken out of the steppes of Northern Arabia into the fields and cities of Syria; and, for meeting the same emergency of an abrupt and extreme change of social environment, the primitive Israelites, like the Primitive Muslim Arabs, had recourse to the existing law of a sophisticated society which they found in operation in the Promised Land.

While the Decalogue—at any rate in a pristine form, in which all the Commandments were couched in the lapidary style still preserved in the Sixth, Seventh, and Eighth[4]—would appear, on the face of it, to be a native Hebrew product, the next piece of Israelite legislation, known to scholars as 'the Covenant Code',[5] betrays its debt to the Code of Ham-

[1] Schmidt, F. F.: *Die Occupatio im Islamischen Recht*, reprinted from *Der Islam*, i (Strassburg 1910).

[2] Kremer, A. von: *Culturgeschichte des Orients* (Vienna 1875–7, Braumüller, 2 vols.), vol. i, p. 535; English translation by Khuda Bukhsh, S.: *The Orient under the Caliphs* (Calcutta 1920, University Press), chap. viii, 'The Origin and Development of Muslim Law', Section 6, 'The Sources of Muslim Law'.

The influence of local Medinese Jewish jurisprudence on the early school of Islamic jurisprudence at Medina is emphasized by Margoliouth, op. cit., p. 74: 'There is no evidence that Roman Law penetrated into this primitive city.'

[3] Goldziher, I., in the *Encyclopaedia of Islam*, vol. ii (London 1927, Luzac), s.v. Fiḳh, quoted with the permission of the publishers.

[4] A conjectural reconstruction of the whole Decalogue in this presumably original style will be found in Smith, J. M. P.: *The Origin and History of Hebrew Law* (Chicago 1931, University of Chicago Press), pp. 6–7.

[5] The Covenant Code 'exists in two forms: one very short, viz. Exodus xxxiv, 17–26;

murabi more patently than the *Sharīʿah* reveals its corresponding debt to a Syrian Roman law-book.

'It has been calculated that, out of forty-five, or possibly fifty-five, judgments preserved in this old Hebrew Law, thirty-five have points of contact with the Hammurabi Code, and quite half are parallel.'[1]

This masterful influx of a code of Sumerian Law into legislation enacted at least nine centuries later in one of the local communities of a latter-day Syriac Society testified to the depth and tenacity of the roots which the Sumeric Civilization had struck in Syrian soil during the millennium ending in Hammurabi's generation. A First Syriac Civilization, affiliated to the Sumeric, had miscarried as a result of the insatiable aggressiveness of the Hyksos barbarians, who, not content with carving out for themselves a successor-state in the Syrian provinces of the Empire of Sumer and Akkad, had driven on into the Egyptiac World and had thereby eventually brought down upon Syria an Egyptiac counter-invasion.[2] On the political plane, Syria had been included, for two centuries, in a reinstituted Egyptiac universal state and thereafter been partitioned, for two further centuries, between this Egyptiac Power and a rival Hittite Empire. On the cultural plane the subject Syrian peoples, while continuing, down to the reign of the Egyptiac Emperor Ikhnaton (*imperabat circa* 1380–1362 B.C.), to employ as their medium of literary expression the Akkadian language, conveyed in the cuneiform characters according to the Akkadian usage, had experimented in working out an Alphabet for the conveyance of their native Canaanite speech, and, after testing the adaptability of the cuneiform characters for alphabetic use,[3] had discarded them in favour of the notation—possibly of Minoan origin—which they immortalized by creating the historic Alpha-

the other more extended, viz. Exodus xx, 23—xxiii, 33. This code is incorporated in two of the documents which compose the Hexateuch: Exodus xxxiv, 17–26, in the J document, and Exodus xx, 23—xxiii, 33, in the E document. These two documents arose in the latter part of the ninth century or the early part of the eighth century B.C., J being probably a half-century or so older than E' (Smith, op. cit., p. 15).

1 Johns, C. H. W.: *The Relations between the Laws of Babylonia and the Laws of the Hebrew Peoples* (London 1914, Milford), p. 49. In the third of the three lectures composing this book, the writer takes up the question whether the indubitable and, indeed, striking points of similarity between Hammurabi's Code and the Covenant Code are to be accounted for as products of a uniformity of Human Nature, in virtue of which we find different individuals or communities independently making similar responses to similar challenges, or whether these particular similarities are to be traced to a process of diffusion through which the Covenant Code has borrowed from Hammurabi's Code or both have borrowed from some common source. Johns' conclusion is that most of the matter which the Covenant Code shares with Hammurabi's Code has been borrowed by the Covenant Code from the earlier of the two compilations. He argues from the similarity, down to arbitrary details, of the provisions in the two codes concerning (i) debt slavery (Johns, op. cit., pp. 56–60; cp. pp. 39–46) and (ii) the prescription of the penalty of burning alive for two particular offences (op. cit., pp. 60–61), and from the grouping of the laws, in both codes, in sets of fives and tens (op. cit., pp. 26–27 and 61). Thus, in Johns' view, Sumerian Law, as finally codified by Hammurabi, is the main common element in the two codes. He does, however, allow for a subsidiary common element in the shape of a primitive customary law of the Semite Nomads of Arabia which may have been imported independently by Hammurabi's Amorite ancestors into Shinar and by the Hebrews, in their turn, into Palestine, and have been injected, in both cases, by the Nomad conquerors into the existing law of the conquered sedentary population (op. cit., pp. vi-vii, 28, and 32–33).

2 See II. ii. 388–91.

3 In this experiment, they were anticipating the work of the creator of the Medo-Persian cuneiform Alphabet, which was invented—to all appearance, quite independently—about a thousand years later (see p. 247, above).

bet out of it. Finally, the Syrians had struck out for themselves, in all departments of life, a new civilization of their own which was affiliated to the Minoan, and not to either the Sumeric or the Egyptiac. Yet the Israelite Covenant Code is evidence that, through all these political and cultural revolutions in Syria, the Sumerian Law, as embodied in Hammurabi's Code, had remained in force among the descendants of Hammurabi's Syrian subjects—and this in such vigour as to impress itself imperiously upon the callow legislation of the Canaanites' Hebrew barbarian conquerors.[1]

In thus entering into the law of barbarians who happened, exceptionally, to be incubators of a higher religion, the Sumerian Law, like the Roman Law, made a greater mark on history than when it was influencing barbarians whose destiny was the usual inglorious exit of their kind. At the time of writing, the Sumerian Law was still a living force in virtue solely of its Mosaic offprint. On the other hand, the Islamic *Sharīʿah* was neither the sole nor the liveliest living carrier[2] of the Roman Law at the same date. In the twentieth century of the Christian Era the chief direct heirs of the Roman Law were the canons of the Eastern Orthodox and Western Catholic Christian Churches. In the domain of law, as in other fields of social action, the master institution created by the internal proletariat was the universal state's principal beneficiary.

3. *Calendars; Weights and Measures; Money*

The Concern of Governments with Standard Measures

Generally accepted and effectively operative standard measures of time, distance, length, volume, weight, and value are necessities of social life at any level above the most primitive. They are needed not only by manufacturers, stock-breeders, and agriculturists, but by hunters of the higher type that does not simply wait passively for game to turn up, but pursues a strategy dependent on ability to forecast and anticipate its

1 The Covenant Code was a selection from the Code of Hammurabi. 'There are 282 laws in the Code of Hammurabi, and only 50 in the Covenant Code' (Smith, op. cit., p. 18); and the selection had been made to suit the requirements of a much more backward society than that for which Hammurabi was legislating. 'The provisions in the case of each law in Hammurabi's Code are much more detailed and elaborate and presuppose a much greater experience with the practices of an advanced social and economic order' (ibid., p. 18). 'It would . . . seem that wages for service were higher in Hammurabi's day than when the Covenant Code was drawn up' (ibid., p. 19). The legislation in Hammurabi's Code on the subject of runaway slaves has no counterpart in the Covenant Code as we have it (ibid., p. 29). 'The Code of Hammurabi is much the more severe of the two and uses the penalty of capital punishment to a much greater extent' (ibid., p. 20), but, as we have seen in comparing the Hittite Code with Hammurabi's and the Teutonic barbarian laws with Roman Law, the absence of severe penalties may be evidence, not of humane feeling, but merely of impotence, on the legislator's part. Moreover, the law concerning the working off of debt by the enslavement of the debtor or members of his household to the creditor is less harsh in Hammurabi's Code than in the Covenant Code. Hammurabi's Code frees male and female debt-slaves alike after three years' service; the Covenant Code exacts six years' service from males and enslavement for life (with certain reservations and exceptions) from females (ibid., pp. 18–19). The Israelite laws prescribing the punishments for divers unnatural forms of sexual practice are likewise harsher than the corresponding provisions in the Hittite Code (see the comparative table in Cavaignac, E.: *Le Problème Hittite* (Paris 1936, Leroux), p. 109, n. 1).

2 The continuous carriers of an institution are, of course, to be distinguished from reconverted renegades who have adopted the same institution *de novo* in a 'renaissance'.

victims' movements and behaviour. Social currencies of these kinds are older—perhaps far older—than governments; and they become matters of concern to governments as soon as these come into existence in their turn. The positive *raison d'être* of governments is to provide central political leadership for common social enterprises, and common enterprises cannot be operated without standard measures. Again, the negative *raison d'être* of governments is to ensure at least a modicum of justice in the private relations between their subjects, and, in most private issues of a 'business' kind, standard measures of some sort are involved. While governments thus find themselves implicated *ab initio* in the maintenance and enforcement of standard measures as one of their essential functions which they cannot afford to neglect, they also eventually discover that the administration of these institutions—for example, of the calendar at one end of the scale and of a coinage at the other—can be turned to account by them incidentally for the secondary purpose of moving their public in the direction of their policy.

In these various ways, standard measures concern governments of every species; but they are of particular concern to the governments of universal states for two reasons. In the first place, such governments start life as parvenus who have to take active steps to win the obedience, respect, and loyalty of subjects whom they have taken over, without consulting their wishes, from the former parochial states that they have overthrown and replaced by force. In the second place, universal states, by their very nature, are confronted with the problem of holding together far greater numbers of subjects and far wider areas of territory than any single one of their parochial predecessors; and for this reason, again, they have a special interest in the social unity and uniformity that standard measures promote when effectively enforced.

Calendrical Cycles

Of all the standard measures here in question, a standard system of registering time is the earliest felt and the most persistently imperative need; and the first necessity here is a measurement of the seasons of the year-cycle, which continues, even in technically advanced societies, to be the indispensable basis of Man's unceasing struggle to win a livelihood from Non-Human Nature.[1] But the problem of measuring the seasons soon carries the pioneer chronometrist into calculations of vastly longer aeons of Time than the single year-period within which the seasons revolve. The measurement of the seasons requires a harmonization of the three different natural cycles of the year, the month, and the day; the discovery that the ratios between these three cycles are not

[1] At first sight it might look as if Man's primeval servitude to the seasons had been thrown off in a Modern Western factory in which the temperature and atmosphere were 'conditioned' by artificial regulation and in which the machinery was worked by shifts of operatives for 24 hours in the day and for 365 days in the year. But this appearance of successfully contracting out of the tyranny of Nature was, of course, an illusion. Factories were fed by raw materials, and factory-workers by food, and in a Westernizing Modern World, no less than in the Higher Palaeolithic Society, the ultimate constituents of both food and raw materials had to be wrested from Nature. Moreover, this continuing war with Nature was still being waged, even in this technologically precocious society, by such 'higher hunters' as the trawler and the whaler, as well as by their younger brothers the husbandman and the shepherd.

simple fractions but surds leads a would-be harmonizer into thinking in terms of vaster cycles—the products, not of observation, but of reasoning—in which the elusive correspondences between the beginnings or between the ends of days, months, and years are found, by a mathematical computation, to recur after a formidably long lapse of time; and, when the habit of reckoning with these ampler periods leads the budding astronomer to take into his account the real or apparent cyclic movements of the planets and the 'fixed' stars, besides those of the Sun, Moon, and Earth, the chronological horizon recedes to a distance which is not easy to express and is still less easy to imagine—narrow-verged though it may seem to a latter-day cosmogonist in whose eyes our particular solar system is no more than one speck of star-dust in the Milky Way, and the Milky Way itself no more than one *ci-devant* nebula out of myriads of nebulae on their way from a flaming birth towards a deathly incineration.

Short of this latest stage in the mental exploration of chronological magnitudes, the 'least common measure' of the recurrent coincidences between the apparent movements of the Sun and those of a single one of the 'fixed stars' had generated the Egyptiac 'Sothic Cycle' of 1,460 years,[1] and a recurrent common cycle of the Sun, the Moon, and five planets the Babylonic *Magnus Annus*[2] of 432,000 years,[3] while, in the

1 These 1,460 years were 'Sothic' years: i.e. years reckoned from heliacal rising to heliacal rising of the star Sothis (Sirius), its heliacal rising being the first occasion in the year on which the star is visible above the horizon before dawn. Throughout the life-span of the Egyptiac Civilization the Sothic-year was virtually coincident in length with the Julian year of 365¼ days, whereas the Egyptiac official year was a conventional one of 365 days. Thus a period of 1,460 Sothic years was exactly equal to a period of 1,461 official years, and in the course of a 1,460-years-long Sothic cycle the New Year's Day of the official year would travel right round the Sothic year-clock. The mathematical device of controlling the palpably inaccurate conventional year by relating it to the much more nearly accurate Sothic year must have been inaugurated in—or been based retrospectively on—some year in which the New Year's Day of the official year actually coincided with the heliacal rising of Sirius. In the latitude of Memphis in the fifth and fourth millennia B.C. this astronomical event occurred on the 19th July of the Julian Calendar, which in that age corresponded to the 15th June of the Gregorian Calendar—a date approximate to the Summer Solstice and also to the beginning of the annual rising of the Nile in the Lower Nile Valley and the Delta. It seems a fairly safe guess that, at the time when the official year of 365 days was first put into commission, it was set to begin on a date which was of such paramount importance for the whole life of the Egyptiac World. The Egyptiac official year did actually open on the 19th July of the Julian Calendar in each of the four-year periods A.D. 140/1–143/4, 1321/1320–1318/1317 B.C., 2781/2780–2778/2777 B.C., and 4241/4240–4238/4237 B.C. Since the Egyptiac Calendar, with its Sothic correction, is known to have been in use at both the two first-mentioned of these dates, the inaugural year—or retrospectively calculated starting-point—must fall within one or other of the two last-mentioned four-year periods. Eduard Meyer opts for the earlier of the two alternatives, i.e. 4241/4240—4238/4237 B.C., on the ground that, by the time of the Old Kingdom, the Calendar was already a long since established institution (see Meyer, E.: *Geschichte des Altertums*, vol. i, Part II, 3rd ed. (Stuttgart and Berlin 1913, Cotta), pp. 28–30).

2 See IV. iv. 23–24 and 37, and V. v. 56–57.

'Quarum [stellarum] ex disparibus motionibus magnum annum mathematici nominaverunt, qui tum efficitur cum Solis et Lunae et quinque errantium ad eandem inter se comparationem confectis omnium spatiis est facta conversio. Quae quam longa sit, magna quaestio est; esse vero certam et definitam necesse est' (Cicero: *De Natura Deorum*, Book II, chap. 20).

'Homines . . . populariter annum tantummodo Solis, id est unius astri, reditu metiuntur; cum autem ad idem, unde semel profecta sunt, cuncta astra redierint, eandemque totius anni descriptionem longis intervallis retulerint, tum ille vere vertens annus appellari potest—in quo vix dicere audeo quam multa saecula hominum teneantur' (Cicero: *Somnium Scipionis*, chap. 7 = *De Republica*, Book VI, chap. 22, in Cardinal Angelo Mai's edition (Rome 1823, Mawman)).

3 This appears to have been the estimate that was traditional in the Babylonic school

stupendous Mayan Grand Cycle of 374,440 years, no less than ten distinct constituent cycles were geared together.[1]

Governmental Methods of Keeping Count of Time

Governments, like astronomers, find themselves concerned with computations of terms of years, as well as with the seasonal articulation of the recurrent year-cycle. Their interest in the seasonal calendar is obvious, for it is the key not only to the livelihood of their subjects, for which governments are held responsible in the last resort, but also to their own ability to command the resources without which they cannot perform a government's recognized functions. Even in a technically advanced and highly industrialized state of society the parochial governments of a Westernized World in the year A.D. 1952 were having their policies dictated to them by the results of the last harvest and the prospects of the next one; and in simpler states of society this domination of weather over policy had made itself felt *a fortiori*. Governments had not been able to mobilize and maintain armies without a sufficient surplus of food stocks with which to feed them, and they had been constrained to time their military campaigns to coincide with the slack season of the agricultural year (whichever of the seasons this might happen to be in the particular climate in which their dominions were situate and under the particular system of agricultural production that was practised there).

In a state of society in which a money economy is either unknown or else only partially operative, the government even of a sedentary agricultural community may have to make an annual round of seasonal migrations to draw on food-supplies which, under the technological conditions of the time and place, are less mobile than even august human bodies. We have already taken note of the Achaemenian Court's regular distribution of its time between three different imperial residences.[2] The Merovingian Frankish rulers of the most barbarous of the Continental Teutonic successor-states of the Roman Empire in one of the most backward of the Empire's former territories used to roam from one estate to another of their royal domain in order to browse on the fat of the land. Where the government has been of Nomad origin and has brought with it, out of 'the desert' into 'the sown', a war-band of Nomad empire-builders who persist, *in partibus agricolarum*, in following their ancestral way of life, this migratory dance of attendance on the

of astronomers (see Cumont, F.: *Les Religions Orientales dans le Paganisme Romain*, 4th ed. (Paris 1929, Geuthner), pp. 164 and 289). Macrobius, in his commentary on the *Somnium Scipionis*, II. 11, rushing in where Cicero had feared to tread, ventures on an estimate of his own in which he reckons the span of the Magnus Annus at 15,000 solar years, and Cicero himself had proposed a figure of 12,954 years in his *Hortensius* (inaccessible in A.D. 1952), according to Tacitus in his *Dialogus de Oratoribus*, chap. 16. Cicero's and Macrobius's shots fell much nearer the mark than their Babylonic predecessors' conscientious calculations, if the true figure is 25,817 solar years (see Pickman, E. M.: *The Mind of Latin Christendom* (London 1937, Oxford University Press), p. 119).

[1] See Morley, S. G.: *The Ancient Maya* (Palo Alto, California 1946, Stanford University Press), pp. 262 and 289; Thompson, J. E. S.: *Maya Hieroglyphic Writing: Introduction* (Washington, D.C., 1950, Carnegie Institution of Washington), pp. 141–56. Like the Egyptiac Sothic Cycle, the Mayan Grand Cycle was a device for correcting the inaccuracy of an official year of 365 days.

[2] See pp. 205–6, above.

seasons is, of course, a still more conspicuous feature of public business. Yet even the most primitive and rudimentary government cannot allow its enslavement to a tyrannous annual round to preoccupy its attention to the exclusion of all provision for reckoning in terms exceeding the length of a single year; for the first concern of every government is to keep itself in existence; the most incompetent government may last for a whole lifetime, and perhaps for a term spanning a number of successive generations; and the most naïve administration soon discovers that it cannot remain in business without keeping some permanent record of its acts.

For this purpose the gigantic astronomical cycles evolved by the chronometrists were, however, as useless as the miniature calendar of the annual round, since the spans of time to which the continuous acts of even the longest-lived governments had run had, in human history up to date, been of a lesser order of magnitude than even the relatively modest length of the Sothic period. Consequently, governments had had to work out methods of their own for dating events over a series of years.

One of their methods had been based on the distinctiveness of every individual human being and on the personal names in which this distinctive individuality was expressed. They had taken to dating their acts by the names of magistrates with an annual term of office, such as the Assyrian *limmu*, the Athenian *archôn epônymus*, and the Roman pair of consuls; alternatively they had dated them by the series of regnal years of successive sovereigns ruling (short of accidents) for life. This system of dating does effectively distinguish every year in the count from every other; its weakness is that, when the continuous life of the institution employed as a time-measure happens to be prolonged for 1,050 years, as the life of the Roman consulate was from the reputed date of its institution in 509 B.C. to its abolition by the Emperor Justinian in A.D. 541,[1] a list of eponymous magistrates becomes far too long to be retained in the memory with the ease with which it is possible, for example, to learn by heart the twenty-six letters of the Latin Alphabet in their arbitrary sequence; and in these circumstances the denotation of a date by the citation of the consuls of the year no longer suffices to call the date to mind without a tiresome search through a list of perhaps a thousand pairs of names. The reckoning by reigns is ultimately open to the same objection, even when the names of individual sovereigns are grouped together under the names of dynasties, and when each individual reign is articulated, not only into single regnal years but into tax-assessment periods each extending over a number of years (the fifteen-yearly 'indictions' of the Later Roman Empire). The difficulty is not overcome by inventing an artificial cycle of official years with 'fancy' names, such as the Sinic cycle in which the years are named after animals (real and mythical) and other objects with auspicious associations; for, if the cycle is kept within the manageably short compass of

[1] See V. vi. 111 and 224. The life-span of the consulate would have to be reckoned as having been 990 years if we were to take as the initial date the traditional year, not of the inauguration of the institution itself (509 B.C.), but of its first restoration (449 B.C.).

the Latin Alphabet, it will recur so frequently that confusion will arise between one of its occurrences and another, while, if such confusion is to be avoided, this can only be done by drawing out the series towards the unmanageable length which the Roman consular *fasti* had reached by the year A.D. 541.

The only satisfactory way out is to adopt the different method of choosing some particular year as an initial date and reckoning subsequent years from that date onwards in a numerical sequence which can, if necessary, be continued *ad infinitum* without in any way diminishing the convenience of the system for ready reckoning.[1] The dates chosen as the starting-points for new eras had in some cases been those of events of which the authenticity and the time of occurrence had been established beyond dispute. Classical examples were the eras starting from the Fascist occupation of Rome on the 28th October, 1922; from the establishment of the First French Republic on the 22nd September, 1792; from the Prophet Muhammad's *hijrah* from Mecca to Medina on the 15th July, A.D. 622;[2] from the assumption of a formal claim to oecumenical authority in the Indic World by the Gupta Dynasty on the 26th February, A.D. 320; from the definitive establishment of the Seleucid Empire's Hasmonaean successor-state in Judaea in 142 B.C.; and from the triumphal re-entry of the founder of the Seleucid Monarchy, Seleucus Nicator, into Babylon in 312 B.C. (an event which, for chronometrical convenience, was retrospectively equated with the 1st of the Macedonian month Dius (October) of that year).

There were other cases in which eras had been reckoned from events of which the precise date had been disputable. For example, there was no evidence that Jesus had in fact been born in the first year of a Christian Era that did not become current in divers provinces of Western Christendom till divers dates in and after the sixth century from the birth of Christ according to this computation;[3] there was likewise no evidence that the city of Rome had in fact been founded in the year 753 B.C. from which later generations of Romans had reckoned their era *post urbem conditam*; and the year 776 B.C., which figured as the first year of 'the First Olympiad' quadriennium, was admittedly not the ascertained first year in which the Olympian Festival had been celebrated, but merely the first year in which there was a record of the name of a victor in the games at the chronometrist's disposal for use as an eponym. In the third place there were cases in which eras had been reckoned from an imaginary event in the cosmogonical scheme of some particular school of theology: for example, the supposed instantaneous creation of the World by the fiat of a unique and omnipotent personal God, which had been discrepantly dated the 7th October, 3761 B.C., by the Jews, the 1st September, 5509 B.C., by the Eastern Orthodox Christians,[4] and

1 'New eras' have already been discussed, as symptoms of 'Futurism', in V. vi. 339–45.

2 This is the proper correction for the popular traditional date 16th July, 622. D. S. Margoliouth dates the *Hijrah* the 20th September, 622 (*Mohammed and the Rise of Islam* (3rd ed.: London 1905, Putnam), p. xx).

3 The traditional Christian Era is said to have been instituted in A.D. 525 at Rome, by the Abbot Dionysius Exiguus, at the instance of the Pope. Even within the limits of Western Christendom it did not become generally prevalent till the ninth century.

4 The Eastern Orthodox Christian reckoning by 'Years of the World' appears to have

6.0 p.m. on the evening before the 23rd October, 4004 B.C., Old Style, by the Anglo-Irish chronologist-archbishop Ussher (*vivebat* A.D. 1581–1656).[1]

The Inability of New Eras to establish themselves without Religious Sanctions

In the two preceding paragraphs the eras passed in review have been marshalled in a descending order of the cogency of the evidence for the events chosen by their originators for setting their initial dates; but, if we now resurvey these same eras from the standpoint of their relative success or failure in gaining a wide and lasting currency, we shall observe that the talisman by which their destinies had been decided had not been the touchstone of historical attestation, but the presence or absence of a religious sanction. In A.D. 1952 the historically dubious Western Christian Era was in the ascendant in the World on the unexpended strength of its ancient appeal to the former religious sentiment of its once Christian Western disseminators. The Islamic Era of the Hijrah, which was now on the defensive against the Christian Era, was still holding its own, in so far as it was succeeding in doing so, in virtue of its living appeal to the surviving religious sentiment of a majority of its hereditary adherents, and not at all in virtue of its being, as it was, as impeccable historically as the Christian Era was vulnerable to assaults of the higher criticism. At the same date the Jews were still persistently reckoning by their hallowed version of the date of the Creation. The vitality that was thus being displayed by the religious eras in A.D. 1952 was thrown into sharp relief by its contrast with the mortality rate of these consecrated eras' unhallowed secular counterparts. The Era of the First French Republic had been discarded by Revolutionary France herself in its fourteenth year on the 1st January, 1806; the Era of the Italian Fascist Revolution had shared the downfall of Fascism itself; and even the Seleucid and Gupta eras, after remaining in use for centuries, and being adopted or imitated by successive epigoni and supplanters of their originators, had long since fallen out of use.[2]

It is also significant that other secular events which, in the minds of contemporaries and Posterity, were no less epoch-making than those cited above, were never taken as the starting-points of new eras—not even of new eras that were abortive. Cases in point are the beginning, in May 1703, of the building, at St. Petersburg, of a new capital for Russia that was to be Western from the start;[3] the landfall of the Pilgrim Fathers in New England on the 21st December, 1620; the

arisen at Constantinople in the seventh century of the Christian Era. In Russia, it was abrogated by Peter the Great, in favour of the Western Christian reckoning by 'Years of Our Lord', as from the 1st January, 1700. The celebration of New Year's Day thenceforward on the 1st January, in lieu of the 1st September, was made obligatory (see Brückner, A.: *Peter der Grosse* (Berlin 1879, Grote), p. 227).

1 See XI. ix. 178. Bishop Ussher's chronology found its way into the margin of the Church of England's Authorized Version of the Bible.

2 'The tenacity of the Seleucid calendar was remarkable: Doura used it when under Roman rule and Jews down to the eleventh century, and it is said to have still been in use among Syrian Christians at the beginning of the present century' (Tarn, W. W.: *The Greeks in Bactria and India* (Cambridge 1938, University Press), p. 65).

3 See p. 221, above.

opening of a new chapter in Western history towards the close of the fifteenth century of the Christian Era (an event which could have been dramatically symbolized either in the crossing of the Alps by King Charles VIII of France in A.D. 1494, or in da Gama's landfall at Calicut on the 20th May, 1498, or in Columbus's landfall on one of the Antilles on the 12th October, 1492, or in the publication of the first Western printed book in A.D. 1445–6). We might add to this catalogue the beginning, in the year A.D. 324, of the building, at Constantinople, of a new capital for the Roman Empire that was to be Christian from the start,[1] and the crossing of the Hellespont by Alexander the Great in 334 B.C.

Evidently the recognition of the authenticity and the importance of an event is not enough, in itself, to make such an event eligible for serving as a mark for the measurement of Time. If the historic event is not consecrated by some religious sanction, its intrinsic merits as a starting-point for an era may count in practice for little or nothing. There is indeed a traditional association, which cannot be dissolved with impunity, between the measurement of Time by human intellects and the hold of Religion over human souls, and the ground for this is not difficult to descry. Religion dominates every side of life or aspect of the Universe that is recognized by Man as being out of his control, and in this respect there is a striking contrast between Man's relation to the heavenly bodies whose cyclic movements give him his measures of Time and the divers objects which he subjects to measurements of length, volume, weight, and value. Man has at least an illusion of being master of the flour that he metes out in a man-made vessel after having ground it from grain produced by a harvest that Man himself has sown and reaped; he has a still greater sense of mastery over the piece of metal that he strikes into a coin after having smelted it from ore that he has detected in, and extracted from, the bowels of the Earth; but the stars in their courses overawe him by their inexorable aloofness, though in truth the astronomer's intellectual mastery over them is a more wonderful achievement than any physical feats of miner, miller, husbandman, or metallurgist.

In caeloque deûm sedes et templa locarunt,
per caelum volvi quia nox et luna videtur—
luna, dies et nox et noctis signa severa,
noctivagaeque faces caeli flammaeque volantes . . . .
nam cum suspicimus magni caelestia mundi
templa super stellisque micantibus aethera fixum,
et venit in mentem solis lunaeque viarum,
tunc aliis oppressa malis in pectora cura
illa quoque expergefactum caput erigere infit,
nequae forte deûm nobis immensa potestas
sit, vario motu quae candida sidera verset.[2]

So far from readily falling into the delusion that he can affect the move-

[1] See pp. 218 and 238, above. The dedication date of the completed city was the 11th May, 330.
[2] Lucretius: *De Rerum Natura*, Book V, ll. 1188–91 and 1204–10.

ments of the heavenly bodies, Man has found it difficult to shake off the contrary delusion that these movements influence human destinies.

The persistence of this superstition in the inaccessible subconscious depths of the Psyche, even in societies that had attained a degree of sophistication at which Astrology had been professedly discredited and repudiated, was attested by the rarity of the instances in which a revolutionarily rational reform of the Calendar had succeeded in establishing itself. The French Revolution, whose rationalized codes of law went forth, conquering and to conquer, to the ends of the Earth[1] and whose pedantically new-fangled weights and measures—grammes and kilogrammes and milligrammes, metres and kilometres and millimetres —enjoyed a *succès fou* and ran like wildfire round the globe, was utterly defeated in its attempt to supersede a pagan Roman calendar that had been rejuvenated through being consecrated by the Christian Church, though the substitute which the lucid French Reason offered was the attractive one of a neatly proportioned new series of picturesquely renamed months—a Brumaire, a Ventôse, a Germinal, a Fructidor—each cut to a uniform length of thirty days grouped in three ten-day weeks. The batch of five supernumerary days that made up the tale of the ordinary (non-leap) year 'hardly marred the most sensible calendar ever invented—too sensible for a country which calls the tenth, eleventh and twelfth months of the year October, November and December'.[2] Yet, while the fantastically erroneous lunar year of an archaic Meccan oasis-state had been adopted, as the calendar of Islam, by hundreds of millions of people over a vast area extending almost from end to end of the Old World, the 'sensible' calendar devised by French votaries of Reason did not manage to outlive its fourteenth year, and the shortness of its life testified that, after all, the French revolutionaries had been less wise in their generation than the Roman conservatives.

The Roman misnomers pointed out by a distinguished Modern Western historian in the passage quoted just above were neither casual nor imbecile but deliberate and sagacious. The six months originally denoted in the Roman calendar by numerals, and not by the names of gods, had not, of course, been wrongly numbered when their names had first been bestowed on them. Originally the Roman official year had begun on the 1st March, in the spring of the solar year, and this month had been a convenient starting-point for the annual round of administration and warfare, as well as agriculture, so long as the Roman Government's range of action had extended no farther afield than a few days' march from the Pomoerium; for, under those conditions, an annual magistrate elect who had entered on his term of office on the 15th March could still take up the local command, assigned to him by the Senate, in time to take advantage of the spring campaigning season. When, however, in and after the Hannibalic War, the field of Roman military operations expanded out of Italy overseas into the Balkan Peninsula and the still more distant Iberian Peninsula, a magistrate,

[1] See pp. 271–8, above.

[2] Thompson, J. M.: *The French Revolution* (Oxford 1943, Blackwell), p. ix.

appointed to one of these distant commands, who had to wait till the 15th March before setting out from Rome might find himself unable to get into action before the summer was at its height and the autumn was approaching.

During the half-century immediately following the end of the Hannibalic War, this hampering loss of the best part of each annual campaigning season, with which the Roman state was threatened now that it had come to be fighting its wars in theatres at a distance of as much as several months' journey from the Italian homes of a Roman peasant soldiery, was at first largely offset by a discrepancy between the Roman official calendar and the actual cycle of the seasons resulting from the Pontifical College's cumulative neglect to keep the official year in step with the solar year by inserting intercalary months of the requisite length at the requisite intervals. For example, in the year 190 B.C., in which a Roman army inflicted a decisive defeat upon a Seleucid army on the Asiatic battlefield of Magnesia, the legions found time to arrive on the threshold of Sardis before the current season was over, because in that year the official 15th March fell on a day that was in reality the 16th November of the preceding solar year, while in the year 168 B.C., in which another Roman army inflicted an equally decisive defeat on a Macedonian army at Pydna, the official 15th March fell on a day that was in reality the 31st December of the solar year 169 B.C.[1] In these two militarily critical years the campaigning season was thus salvaged for Roman military operations thanks to a calendrical error; but, whether this error had been dictated by military considerations or by superstition, its efficacy diminished as the Roman calendar was progressively brought back nearer to correspondence with the solar year. The additional time now needed for arriving at a theatre of war before the campaigning season would be too far advanced had therefore to be provided by some alternative means; and, with this eminently practical consideration in mind, the Roman Government secured the passage of a law providing that, as from the year 153 B.C. onwards, the date on which the annually elected magistrates were to enter on their term of office was to be advanced, by two and a half months, from the 15th March to the 1st January,[2] and in consequence January instead of March became the first month of the year.[3]

Finding themselves thus constrained by *raison d'état* to call upon their

[1] In these two cases the magnitude of the Roman calendar's deviation from the current solar year can be calculated because Livy has recorded the dates of eclipses in terms of the day of the official Roman month (see Bouché-Leclercq, A.: *Histoire des Séleucides* (Paris 1913–14, Leroux, 2 vols.), vol. i, p. 205).

[2] The original provision in the United States for a four months' interval between the election of a President's electors and the President Elect's assumption of office was made with the similar practical purpose of ensuring that he should have sufficient time to convey himself to Washington by horse-traction from his home state, even if this happened to be Georgia or New Hampshire. Within half a century of the year in which the Constitution had been adopted, the invention of steam-traction by railroad had stultified the practical purpose which this provision had originally been designed to serve, but it was not till the 6th February, 1933, that the interval was shortened by 36 days through the coming into force of the Twentieth Amendment to the Constitution (see XII. ix. 496).

[3] The definitive replacement of the 1st March by the 1st January as the Roman New Year's Day seems to have taken place on the 1st January 45 B.C. as part of Julius Caesar's reform of the Roman Calendar.

public to put up with one shock to its habits and prejudices, the Roman authorities forbore to aggravate an already somewhat vexatious demand upon the Roman People's capacity for adaptation by simultaneously asking them to alter the traditional names of six of their twelve months merely out of respect for a different kind of reason which would have been, not political, but sheerly pedantic. Satisfied with their success in meeting the bare practical need of the day, the Conscript Fathers let the names of the months alone, and more than a century was allowed to pass before two out of the six resultant misnomers were corrected. At length the architects of the Principate took the bold step of renaming the first two of those six months which a Roman poverty of imagination had hitherto left unanimated and unhallowed by the names of gods. The month that was now the seventh, though still called 'the fifth' (*Quinctilis*), was renamed after Divus Iulius, and the following month (previously *Sextilis*) after Divus Augustus. The audacious innovation caught on, and in A.D. 1952 the calendars of both the Orthodox Christian and the Western World were still bearing the superscription of those two Roman statesmen in the month-names 'July' and 'August'.

Such currency is indeed apotheosis, if not immortalization; yet, in thus achieving a nomenclatory *tour de force* that proved beyond the capacity of French revolutionary enthusiasts, the astute authors of the Julian Calendar were exceptionally successful. In the United Kingdom in the supposedly enlightened eighteenth century of the Christian Era, disturbances were caused by an Act of Parliament, passed in A.D. 1751, for replacing the inexact Julian by the virtually perfect Gregorian calendar. This amended calendar had first been introduced by Pope Gregory XIII as far back as A.D. 1582, and in the meantime it had been adopted in most of the leading states of the Western World. But, in the sacrosanct sphere of the Calendar, religious susceptibilities long inhibited English Protestants from embracing a Papistical innovation, even if it were astronomically correct; and, sure enough, when the Act was published, it became suspect of having a catch in it. By the year 1752, in order to bring the current Julian reckoning into line with the Gregorian reckoning when this was substituted for it, it was necessary to drop eleven days out of the calendar year in which the change was being inaugurated. In their superstitious fear of calendrical magic, the British public were impervious to the simple truth that the eleven days which were to be dropped were only theoretical days on paper; they jumped to the conclusion that they were being cheated of eleven days' pay,[1] or perhaps even being docked of eleven days of life, and vociferous crowds went about demanding to have their stolen eleven days given back to them.

The Conservation of Pagan Calendars by Churches

Who had been the beneficiaries of calendars inherited by universal states from a dim religious past and rationalized by them at their peril?

[1] In fact, of course, everyone who was paid by the year or the month stood to gain, while anyone who was paid by the week or the day did not stand to lose, by the omission of eleven days in the month of September, 1752.

The marvellously exact, though formidably complex, Mayan calendar was bequeathed by 'the Old Empire' of the Mayas to the Yucatec and Mexic societies that were affiliated to the Mayan Civilization. The Sinic calendar was similarly bequeathed by the Empire of Ts'in and Han to the Far Eastern society affiliated to the Sinic Civilization. The Sumerian calendar, after having been bequeathed by 'the Realm of the Four Quarters' to the Babylonic Society affiliated to the Sumeric Civilization, and having survived to serve the Neo-Babylonian and Achaemenian Empires in their turn,[1] acquired at this stage a new lease of life through being adopted by the Jewish Church that was the enduring monument of Judah's fifty-years' exile by the waters of Babylon. The Roman calendar was bequeathed by the Roman Empire to the Christian Church and was transmitted[2] by this original legatee to secondary recipients—in the first place to the Orthodox Christian and Western societies, and thereby eventually to a number of universal states founded by Orthodox Christian and Western empire-builders: e.g. the Muscovite Empire in the Russian offshoot of Orthodox Christendom; the Danubian Hapsburg Monarchy; the Spanish Empire of the Indies; the British Rāj in India. By a still stranger caprice of Fortune the archaic lunar calendar of Mecca, thanks to its adoption by Islam and by the Caliphate, became the calendar of the Iranic and Arabic Muslim societies and hence the calendar of the Ottoman Empire and of the Timurid Mughal Empire on Indian ground.

This brief survey shows that in the histories of calendars the function most frequently performed by a universal state had been to take over a calendar from a primitive pagan past and to transmit it to a higher religion. In the process of transmission the universal state had sometimes stamped the pagan calendar with its own political imprint; yet, when once a calendar had been adopted from a universal state by a 'higher religion', it was apt, notwithstanding the patent evidence of its unhallowed origin, to acquire the sacrosanctity with which the higher religions had been tempted to invest their casually acquired external accessories as well as their inner spiritual essence; and a calendar that had received this consecration had to be taken as it had been found by civilizations and universal states of a later generation who had inherited it from some higher religion that had incubated them. The accoutrements of a church usually cannot be refurbished by any party except the Church's own recognized supreme authority, whatever that authority may be. In Northumbria in the seventh century of the Christian Era the abandonment of a traditional method of reckoning the date of Easter, which had survived in a Far Western Christendom, in favour of a

[1] In the Jewish garrison-community at Elephantinê under the Achaemenian régime, the Babylonian calendar was current officially and the Egyptiac unofficially (Meyer, E.: 'Zu den Aramäischen Papyri von Elephantinê', in *Kön. Preuss. Ak. Wiss.*, Gesammtsitzung vom 23 November, 1911: *Mitt.* vom 26 October, pp. 1040–1).

[2] With the important addition of a reckoning by Jewish weeks as well as by Roman months. The Jewish community's original count of weeks—from the forgotten initial date at which this had been started—was still being kept, in A.D. 1952, in all living communities with a Jewish, Christian, or Muslim background. This was an historically notable common practice of the three religions—though Christianity and Islam had taken care to differentiate their practice from the Jews' and from one another's by choosing a different day of the week for their own equivalent of the Jewish Sabbath.

novel method which was a Roman innovation, implied a recognition of the Roman Church's supremacy over the churches of 'the Celtic Fringe'.[1] In a Western Catholic Christendom in the sixteenth century of the Christian Era the Julian Calendar—work of pagan genius though it was—could not have been reformed by any other authority than the Papacy; and the act of Pope Gregory XIII was as effective as it was uncharacteristic of the normally conservative êthos of an established universal church.

The Defeat of a Duodecimal by a Decimal System of Reckoning

When we pass from calendars and eras to weights and measures and money, we enter a province of the field of social currencies in which the rationalizing intellect holds sway uncensored by those religious scruples that had sometimes welled up forcefully from the subconscious depths of the Psyche when Reason had sought to extend her rule over the reckoning of Time.

The French Revolutionaries, who suffered such a shattering defeat in their attempt to inaugurate a rational new calendar and new era unfortified by an augur's indispensable religious prestige, scored with their new weights and measures an oecumenical success that eclipsed even the triumph of the Napoleonic Codes. And a kindred spirit, Ts'in She Hwang-ti, the revolutionary founder of a Sinic universal state, succeeded in imposing the current weights and measures of his own hereditary parochial state of Ts'in upon the conquered remainder of the Sinic World[2] without, apparently, provoking in this case the stultifying reaction by which, in other fields, his work, like that of his French *confrères*, was so largely undone within a few years of its recklessly sweeping execution.

Though it is evident that weights and measures are a sphere in which the revolutionary intellect can disport itself with an unusual impunity, a comparison of the respective fortunes of the French and the Sumeric new model metric system suggests that the dazzling success of the French reformers' work was due, above all, to their judicious moderation in setting common-sense bounds to their pursuit of their ideal. They were uncompromising in reducing the bewilderingly variegated tables of the *Ancien Régime* to one single system of reckoning; but they showed their practical good sense in irrationally following for this purpose the inconvenient decimal system which had been unanimously adopted by all branches of the Human Race, neither on its merits nor as the result of some laboriously achieved diplomatic compromise between conflicting better plans, but simply because the normal human being was born with ten fingers and ten toes.

It was one of Nature's unkind practical jokes that she had furnished some of the tribes of her vertebrate brute creation with six digits apiece for each of their four limbs without endowing the possessors of this

[1] See II. ii. 326, 332, and 335.

[2] See Fitzgerald, C. P.: *China, A Short Cultural History* (London 1935, Cresset Press), pp. 136–7; Franke, O.: *Geschichte des Chinesischen Reiches*, vol. i (Berlin and Leipzig 1930, de Gruyter), p. 233.

admirable natural abacus with the intellectual capacity for mathematical calculation, while she had dealt out to the *Genus Homo* a niggardly allowance of appendages that added up, not to dozens and double dozens, but only to decades and scores. Given the human anatomy, a decimal notation of Man's mathematical affairs was as inevitable as it was unfortunate. It was unfortunate because, on a decimal count, the basic scale of reckoning is divisible only by the low-powered number Two and the not very useful number Five, while the lowest number divisible alike by all the three key-factors Two, Three, and Four is Twelve. The decimal notation was nevertheless inevitable because, by the time when any wits in any society had come to appreciate the intrinsic superiority of the number Twelve over the number Ten, the decimal notation had become ineradicably entrenched in practical life, in language, and perhaps even already in written records.

The reformers of the French weights and measures forbore to kick against these ten-pronged pricks, but they had Sumerian predecessors who had been less wise in their generation. The Sumerian discovery of the virtues of the number Twelve was a stroke of pure intellectual genius, for there were no obvious sets of twelve articulations on the surface of the human body to guide a pioneer mathematician to the ideal choice for a scale of reckoning. The Sumerians not only saw the advantages of the number Twelve; they took the revolutionary step of recasting their system of weights and measures on a duodecimal basis; but apparently they did not realize that, unless they could also achieve the further, and far more difficult, step of leading their fellow men to substitute a duodecimal for a decimal basis of reckoning for all purposes,[1] the convenience of acquiring, for the simple purpose of weighing and measuring, a basic scale divisible by both the numbers Three and Four would be far more than offset by the inconvenience of having two incommensurable scales in operation side by side. This hopeless irreconcilability of an ideally convenient Twelve with a practically ineradicable Ten foredoomed an intrinsically superior duodecimal system of weights and measures to ultimate defeat, and assured a whole-hogging decimal system of a rapid victory. In the course of the four thousand years preceding the inauguration of the French decimal metric system the Sumeric duodecimal metric system had spread, notwithstanding its inherent handicap, to the ends of the Earth. Yet this long start in Time and Space did not save it from being almost entirely supplanted by its latter-day decimal competitor within 150 years of this rival system's promulgation. By A.D. 1952 the twelve ounces constituting a troy-weight pound and the twelve pence constituting a shilling in the antediluvian

[1] Technically the step would be simple enough in a society employing the originally Hindu 'Arabic' numerals or any other application of the device of making the numerical value of a figure depend on its relative location in a group. All that would be needed would be the invention of two new figures to represent the numbers Ten and Eleven. The notations 10 and 11 would then be released to stand respectively for Twelve and Thirteen. Twelve would be represented by 10, Twenty-four by 20, One Hundred and Forty-four by 100, and so on. The difficulty would lie, of course, not in cyphering, but in thinking, duodecimally; for in the common cultural tradition of the Human Race the decimal count was so immemorially old a piece of mental furniture that it had come to be virtually a fixture.

metronomy of the United Kingdom were almost the last surviving monuments of an unpractical stroke of Sumerian genius; and in an obstinately decimal-minded world it could not be maintained that this piously conservative loyalty to a provedly unsuccessful intellectual experiment was anything but a hindrance to the dispatch of business.

The Invention of Coinage

As soon as it has come to be recognized and accepted that honest dealing in weights and measures is a matter of social concern transcending the personal interests of the parties directly involved, and that therefore any government that aspires to be worthy of the name must make the giving of false weight and measure a prosecutable and punishable offence at law, the invention of money lies just round the corner. Yet this corner can only be turned by the taking of certain precise successive steps, and the requisite combination of moves in fact remained unachieved in the history of any society in process of civilization before the seventh century B.C., though by that time the species of societies called civilizations had already been in existence for perhaps as long as three thousand years.

The first step was the invention of the commercially useful expedient of giving some particular commodity or commodities the special function and status of serving as media of exchange and thereby acquiring a secondary use independent of their intrinsic utility. But this step did not, in itself, lead on to the invention of money when the commodities selected as media of exchange were multifarious and not exclusively metallic. In the Mexic and Andean worlds, for example, by the time of the Spanish conquest, the substances known and coveted in the Old World as 'the precious metals' existed in quantities that seemed fabulous to the Spanish *conquistadores*, and the natives had long since learnt the art of extracting, refining, and working this local gold and silver; but, though they valued it as material for works of art and ornaments, they had not thought of turning it to account as an exclusive medium of exchange,[1] though they, too, had hit upon this secondary use of com-

[1] Chronological facts forbid the otherwise almost irresistible conjecture that some report of this Mexic and Andean practice (so strange to the ears of denizens of the Old World) of estimating gold and silver, like any other commodity, at a valuation based on their mere intrinsic utility inspired a famous passage of More's *Utopia*:

'They keep an inestimable treasure, but yet not as a treasure. . . . Gold and silver . . . they do so use as none of them doth more esteem it than the very nature of the thing deserveth. And then who doth not plainly see how far it is under iron—as without the which, men can no better live than without fire and water, whereas to gold and silver Nature hath given no use that we may not well lack, if that the folly of men had not set it in higher estimation for the rareness' sake. . . . Whereas they eat and drink in earthen and glass vessels, which indeed be curiously and properly made, and yet be of very small value, of gold and silver they make commonly chamber-pots and other vessels that serve for most vile uses. . . . Furthermore, of the same metals they make great chains, fetters and gyves, wherein they tie their bondmen. . . . Thus by all means possible they procure to have gold and silver among them in reproach and infamy' (More, Sir Thomas: *Utopia*, English version, Book II: 'Of their Journeying or Travelling Abroad').

Utopia, however, was published before the end of A.D. 1516, and 'it is important to remember that the Inca Empire of Peru, which in more than one detail had a likeness to Utopia, was not known till some fourteen years later; Cortés had not yet conquered Mexico' (Chambers, R. W.: *Thomas More* (London 1935, Cape), p. 143). Evidently these dates rule out the possibility that the passage in *Utopia*, quoted above, could have been inspired by reports of Central American or Andean institutions. It may, however,

modities independently of the Old World and perhaps also independently of one another.

In the Mexic World the Spaniards found cacao beans, cotton cloths, T-shaped pieces of copper, and quills stuffed with gold dust circulating as media of exchange;[1] in the Andean World they found pimento, dried fish, cotton, maize, chuño, birds' feathers, salt, coca, and copper being used for the same purpose.[2] There was also at least one instance in which they found sea-shells being employed in this way, as the cowrie shell likewise was employed round the shores of the Indian Ocean.[3] It will be seen that the civilizations of the New World came near to employing standard units of metal in the fashion which, in the Old World, had led to the invention of money more than two thousand years earlier, while the employment of shells—a commodity without any intrinsic value of its own—was an anticipation of that use of paper money which in the Old World had already arisen, before the Spaniards' conquest of the Americas, as a sequel to the use of metallic coin.[4] Yet, though the civilizations of the New World thus came within an ace of inventing money, they failed to take the final step, and the verdict of History on their achievements in this sphere is that 'a miss is as good as a mile'.

In the commercially interwoven Egyptiac, Babylonic, Syriac, and Hellenic worlds by the date of the invention of money in the Hellenic World in the seventh century B.C.,

> 'the use of the precious metals in bar form as measures of value had been a regular institution for thousands of years past. They circulated, not in the form of coin minted by a state and guaranteed as legal tender, but as units of weight which passed from hand to hand in established forms such as rings, plaques, ornaments and so on, but which, in the act of payment, had to be verified by being weighed like any other commodity.'[5]

This usage had perhaps become customary in the Sumeric World in the time of its universal state;[6] but a regular metallic medium of exchange was the raw material of money without being the thing itself.

have been inspired by reports of already discovered fringes of the Americas where 'the precious metals' were given the same valuation by the inhabitants as in Mexico and Peru—whether in consequence of the radiation of one or other or both of these indigenous civilizations of the New World, or because even the more backward among the 'native' peoples had arrived independently, by the light of Nature, at the same common-sense valuation of gold and silver as their more progressive neighbours. 'We can only understand *Utopia* if we remember the Europe for which it was written; . . . the travels of Vespucci in every man's hands: Vespucci, who had found folk holding property in common and not esteeming gold, pearls or jewels' (ibid.).

Though the historic institutions of the Incaic Empire did not inspire *Utopia*, the imaginary institutions of More's ideal society did inspire one of the more beneficent and successful attempts, on the part of the Spanish conquerors of the New World, to fill the social vacuum which they themselves had produced by brutally shattering the fabric of Central American and Andean society. The Spanish philanthropist Vasco de Quiroga, who arrived in the Indies in A.D. 1530 as an enthusiastic disciple of More, succeeded in founding Indian *pueblos* on lines that were a deliberate attempt to reproduce *Utopia* in real life (Haring, C.: *The Spanish Empire in America* (New York 1947, Oxford University Press), p. 193). The present writer visited some of these on the 23rd–26th April, 1953.

1 See Gann, T.: *Mexico from the Earliest Times to the Conquest* (London 1936, Lovat Dickson), p. 174; Vaillant, G. C.: *The Aztecs of Mexico* (London 1950, Penguin), p. 132.

2 See Baudin, L.: *L'Empire Socialiste des Inka* (Paris 1928, Institut d'Ethnologie), p. 174.

3 See ibid.

4 See pp. 312–13, below.

5 Meyer, E.: *Geschichte des Altertums*, vol. iii, 1st ed. (Stuttgart 1901, Cotta), p. 79.

6 See Rostovtzeff, M: *Caravan Cities* (Oxford 1932, Clarendon Press), p. 11.

The decisive steps which conjured money into existence were taken in the seventh century B.C. by some Greek city-state, or perhaps by several of the commercially foremost Greek city-states of the day simultaneously, when their governments went beyond the existing practice of putting metallic media of exchange on a par with other commodities and thereby including them under the common ruling that made it an offence at law to give false weight and measure in the transfer of any commodity from hand to hand. These pioneer city-states now took the two revolutionary steps of making the issue of these metallic units of value a government monopoly and of stamping this exclusive governmental currency with a distinctive official image and superscription as a guarantee that the coin was an authentic product of the governmental mint and that its weight and quality were to be accepted as being what they purported to be on the face of them. When a government had assumed this prerogative, the clipping or filing of authentic coins became a political crime against the state and not merely an offence in civil law against some private individual on whom the fraudulently reduced lump of metal had been palmed off, and counterfeit coining by private individuals became a crime of the same order—a crime which would be not a whit less heinous if the unauthorized coiner's politically bad money happened to be as good in weight and quality as the legitimate coinage of the realm.[1]

The Diffusion of the Use of Coinage

Since the management of a coinage is evidently least difficult in a state with a minimum area and population, it was perhaps no accident that city-states should have been the political laboratories in which the invention was made. At the same time it is equally evident that the utility of a coinage increases with every enlargement of the area and population in which it circulates as legal tender. Such Greek city-states as Phocaea, Lampsacus, Miletus, Aegina, and Corinth, which were pioneers in minting coin, were of miniature material dimensions; and the narrow range of currency of these city-state issues was not appreciably extended when, as happened in several notable instances, two or three city-states situated in different quarters of the Hellenic World—one, perhaps, in Ionia or on the Hellespont, a second in Continental European Greece, and a third in Sicily or Magna Graecia—went into commercial partnership and arranged to issue uniform coinages which could all circulate *de facto*, if not *de jure*, throughout the issuing governments' combined domains. In the wide world beyond, where the writ of these petty governments did not run, their minted coinage was not accepted at its face value but was still treated like any unminted standard unit of metal whose value had to be assayed by weighing, every time the piece changed hands.[2]

[1] It will be seen that the invention of coinage is analogous, in the field of commerce, to the epoch-making change that takes place in the field of criminal law when a government takes to treating crimes as political offences against itself instead of regarding them merely as personal injuries to be avenged by the private self-help of the victim or his surviving kinsmen, in regard to which the government's own responsibility, at its widest, is limited to promulgating a tariff of *wergelds*.

[2] In out-of-the-way places with no coinage of their own, this practice of treating

A regional jump in scale was achieved when, in the earlier decades of the sixth century B.C., the Lydian Monarchy conquered all the Greek city-states round the western coasts of Anatolia except Miletus, as well as the interior of the peninsula as far east as the River Halys, and issued a coinage of electron (gold alloyed with silver), based on the local standard of the subjected Greek city-state of Phocaea, which was given a general currency throughout the Lydian dominions. The last and decisive step was taken when the Kingdom of Lydia, with its subject Greek city-states, was incorporated, in its turn, into the Achaemenian Empire. The Achaemenidae had the imagination to perceive the value, for a universal state, of this new invention which they had stumbled upon on the far western fringe of their South-West Asian World. They issued a gold coinage superior to the Lydian both in weight and in purity of metal, with a subsidiary silver coinage to supplement it, and they made the coining of gold an imperial monopoly. At the same time, with characteristic liberality, they permitted autonomous Greek and Phoenician city-states, client principalities, and even the Persian viceroys of imperial provinces, to issue, on their own account, not only small change in copper, but also silver money to circulate side by side with the silver issues of the imperial mints.[1]

In a more jealous vein the Roman Imperial Government in its day monopolized, throughout its dominions, the coining of silver as well as gold, and left nothing but copper cash to be issued by autonomous and allied states members of the Roman Commonwealth.[2] The prerogative, asserted by the Roman Imperial Government, of monopolizing the coining of gold was tacitly respected by the Arsacid Government, in spite of an insistence on their political independence which they vindicated successfully by force of arms on several critical occasions; and, when the easy-going Arsacidae were supplanted by militant Sasanidae who asserted, not merely their independence of Rome, but a political parity with her, these self-conscious successors of the Achaemenids in the Cis-Euphratean portion of the former Achaemenian dominions found themselves debarred by economic inability from emulating their Achaemenian ensamples and flouting their Roman contemporaries by taking to coining in gold as well as in silver.

After the Primitive Muslim Arabs had achieved the unfulfilled ambitions of the Sasanidae by reuniting under a single oecumenical régime, for the first time since the death of Alexander the Great, the bulk of the

foreign coins as if they were pieces of uncoined metal lasted for at least twelve hundred years after the invention of coinage on the shores of the Aegean. For example, 'at Mecca in Muhammad's day Roman gold pieces and Persian dirhems were already in circulation, but in commercial transactions they were valued by their weight' (Kremer, A. von: *Culturgeschichte des Orients* (Vienna 1875–7, Braumüller, 2 vols.), vol. i, p. 169).

[1] See Meyer, E.: *Geschichte des Altertums*, vol. iii, 1st ed. (Stuttgart 1901, Cotta), pp. 80–82. A viceroy who presumed to issue a silver coinage with as low a content of alloy as the alloy content of his Achaemenian imperial master's gold coinage was, however, found guilty of high treason by Darius *ipso facto*, according to Herodotus, Book IV, chap. 166.

[2] A provincial silver coinage was issued at Alexandria, and for a time at Antioch as well, by local branches of the Imperial Mint; on the other hand, in the western provinces even the copper cash in circulation was mostly of Roman and not of local mintage (see Rostovtzeff, M.: *The Social and Economic History of the Roman Empire* (Oxford 1926, Clarendon Press), p. 171).

former Achaemenian dominions, including the latterly Roman provinces in Syria and Egypt as well as the entire domain of the Sasanian Empire,[1] successive attempts were made by the Umayyad Caliphs Muʿāwīyah I (*imperabat* A.D. 661–80) and ʿAbd-al-Malik (*imperabat* A.D. 685–705) to restore the long-lost monetary unity of the Syriac World.[2] There are indications,[3] however, that, in the matter of coinage, weights, and measures, the Caliphate did not in practice succeed in re-establishing a unity which was so triumphantly re-established under its aegis on the social, cultural, and spiritual planes.

The Invention of Paper Money

The oecumenical Achaemenian gold coinage had given the then still recent invention of money an impetus that had sped it—as the Revolutionary French decimal metric system and the Napoleonic Codes were to be sped in a later age—on an irresistible and almost ubiquitous course of conquest. Coined money was launched on its historic career in India by the temporary annexation of the Panjab to the Achaemenian Empire itself.[4] The more distant Sinic World became ripe for adopting the new institution after Ts'in She Hwang-ti's revolutionary empire-building work had been salvaged through being tempered by the tactful hands of Han Liu Pang. In its first fumblings with this puzzling alien device, the Prior Han régime betrayed its failure to apprehend one of the essential principles involved when in 175 B.C. the Emperor Hsiao Wên (*imperabat* 180–157 B.C.) sought to make up a shortage of currency by abandoning the imperial monopoly of issue and giving licences to local governors and princes of the Imperial House to mint copper cash.[5] The consequent inflation was eventually cured in 113 B.C. by the drastic steps of demonetizing all current coins and issuing a new imperial currency minted exclusively at Ch'ang Ngan under the direct control of imperial officials,

1 See I. i. 76–77.

2 See Wellhausen, J.: *Das Arabische Reich und Sein Sturz* (Berlin 1902, Reimer), pp. 135–6. According to Ahmad Al-Balādhurī: *Kitāb Futūh-al-Buldān* (English translation by Hitti, P. K., and Murgotten, F. C. (New York: Columbia University Press), vol. i (1916), pp. 383–4, and part ii (1924), pp. 263–6, ʿAbd-al-Malik started coining gold (in ex-Roman territory) at Damascus in A.H. 74, and his eastern viceroy Al-Hajjāj silver (in ex-Sasanian territory) at Kūfah at the end of A.H. 75. The same authority reports that the occasion was a quarrel between the Umayyad and Roman Governments over a delicate question of images and superscriptions. According to Al-Balādhurī, the Caliphate had been selling to the Roman Empire Egyptian papyrus (which the Romans could not do without) in exchange for Roman gold coin (for circulation in the ex-Roman part of the Umayyad dominions). The water-mark on the papyrus (which was processed in Egypt before export) had been provocatively changed by ʿAbd-al-Malik from the sign of the Cross to the Qur'anic text 'Say: He alone is God'. The Romans had threatened to retaliate by inscribing their—as they believed, indispensable—gold pieces with strictures on the Prophet Muhammad. This threat moved the Caliph ʿAbd-al-Malik to start coining gold for himself. According to the East Roman chronicler Theophanes, *sub* A.M. 6183 (*Theophanis Chronographia*, ed. C. de Boor, vol. i (Leipzig 1883, Teubner), p. 365), the Roman Imperial Government refused to accept these new Damascene gold pieces in payment of the tribute which had been one of the stipulations in the treaty of A.D. 688 prolonging the peace settlement of A.D. 685, and this was the occasion of the recrudescence of war between the Umayyad Power and the Roman Empire in A.D. 692 (see Bury, J. B.: *A History of the Later Roman Empire* (London 1889, Macmillan, 2 vols.), vol. ii, p. 322; von Kremer, op. cit., vol. i, pp. 168–70.

3 See Wellhausen, op. cit., loc. cit.

4 See Meyer, op. cit., vol. cit., p. 80.

5 See Fitzgerald, C. P.: *China, A Short Cultural History* (London 1935, Cresset Press), p. 161.

while at the same time granting an amnesty to the host of convicted coiners[1] who had continued to mint cash without licence in defiance of the Imperial Government's reassumption of its monopoly. But in 119 B.C., in the reign of the Emperor Wuti, in the course of preliminary gropings after some less arduous method of reinstituting a sound currency, the Imperial Government redeemed its compromised reputation for financial acumen by a quaint expedient based on a brilliant intuition of the hitherto undiscovered truth that metal is not the only stuff of which good money can be made.

'In the imperial park at Ch'ang Ngan the Emperor had a white stag, a very rare beast, which had no fellow in the empire. On the advice of a minister the Emperor had this animal killed, and made a kind of treasury note out of its skin, which, he believed, could not be copied. These pieces of skin were a foot square, and were made with a fringed border and decorated with a pattern. Each piece was assigned the arbitrary value of 400,000 copper coins.[2] The princes, when they came to pay their respects to the Throne, were compelled to buy one of these pieces of skin for cash, and present their gifts to the Emperor upon it. This precaution ensured the circulation of "the White Stag Notes". The skin of the white stag was, however, a limited quantity, and the time soon came when this device ceased to supply the Treasury with much needed money.'[3]

Leathern money—in this case apparently made from sable pelts—turns up again in Russia in the thirteenth century of the Christian Era, at a time when she was politically associated with China under a common Mongol domination;[4] but the invention of currency notes did not become effectively applicable till it had become associated with the two subsequent inventions of paper (invented in the penultimate chapter of Sinic history under the Posterior Han Dynasty)[5] and printing (invented in the early summer of the affiliated Far Eastern Society under the T'ang Dynasty).[6]

Negotiable paper ('flying money'), in the form of cheques tallying with stubs retained by the Imperial Treasury at Si Ngan, was issued by the T'ang Government in the years A.D. 807 and A.D. 809;[7] but there is no evidence that the inscriptions on these cheques were printed. Paper money on which there was probably an imprint was issued in the Chinese province of Szechwan—first by a group of private men of business, and later by the local government through the agency of a bank established for the purpose—during the interval (*durabat* A.D. 907–60) of political disunity in China between the extinction of the T'ang Dynasty and the re-establishment of an all but oecumenical régime by the Sung.[8] In A.D. 970 the invention of printed paper money was taken up by the Sung Government, and in China and its dependencies from that date onwards until the reign of the third Ming sovereign Yung Lo

[1] See Fitzgerald, op. cit., p. 165.

[2] Not 400,000 but 40,000, according to Ma Tuan-Lin: *Wên Hsien T'ung K'ao*, quoting from the Dynastic History of the Prior Han, as translated in Carter, T. F.: *The Invention of Printing in China and its Spread Westward*, revised edition (New York 1931, Columbia University Press), pp. 222–3.—A.J.T.

[3] Fitzgerald, op. cit., pp. 164–5.

[4] See Carter, op. cit., pp. 76 and 225.

[5] See ibid., pp. 1–6 and 190–1.

[6] See ibid., pp. 28–32 and 201–4.

[7] See ibid., pp. 70–71 and 223.

[8] See ibid., pp. 71–72 and 223–4.

(*regnabat* A.D. 1403–25) paper money was continuously and ubiquitously current.[1] In the latter part of the twelfth century of the Christian Era the practice was taken over from the Sung by the Kin barbarian invaders who had wrested the Yellow River Basin out of the hands of the Sung in A.D. 1124–42; and from the Kin it was taken over in succession by their more redoubtable supplanters the Mongols.[2]

The Mongols' sweeping conquests round all the shores of the Great Eurasian Steppe carried the western frontiers of an empire based on China up to the Euphrates and the Carpathians and thereby made China momentarily accessible to Iranic Muslim and Western Christian observers; and the paper money current in China at the time is mentioned by Marco Polo[3] and at least seven other pre-Renaissance Western authors, as well as by a number of Muslim authorities.[4] In Hūlāgū Khān's appanage of the Mongol Empire in Iran and 'Irāq, in the reign of his descendant Gaykhātū Khān (*dominabatur* A.D. 1291–5), in the year A.D. 1294, an issue of printed paper notes, with a bilingual inscription in Chinese and Arabic, was uttered in the commercial capital, Tabrīz. The local business community did not take kindly to the innovation, and their protests were so violent that the issue had to be withdrawn after two or three days' trial. It has been conjectured that some of this historic but unprofitable printed paper money may have been unloaded on to the hands of the Venetian and Genoese merchants residing in Tabrīz at the time.[5]

The Utility of a Monetary Currency as a Medium for Governmental Propaganda

Who had been the principal beneficiaries from this institution of money in the divers material media in which it had been issued by innumerable governments—parochial and oecumenical, ephemeral and rather longer-lasting—since its invention in the Hellenic World in the seventh century B.C.? Undoubtedly this device had proved, on balance, a convenience in the private transactions of the issuing governments' subjects—in spite of the socially subversive fluctuations of inflation and deflation, and temptations to borrow and lend at usurious rates, which the invention had brought in its train. But a greater benefit had assuredly accrued to the issuing governments themselves; for the issue of money is an *acte de présence* which brings a government into direct and constant contact with at least an active, intelligent, and influential minority of its subjects, even where the circulation does not extend through the entire population; and this monetary epiphany—which does not cease to be

1 Yung Lo withdrew it from circulation (no doubt in view of the inflation that had occurred in the latter days of the Mongol régime in China, and, before that, in the latter days of the Sung). No further issues of paper money were made in China till A.D. 1851, when the Manchu Dynasty, in its turn, was declining towards its fall (see Carter, op. cit., p. 76).

2 See Carter, op. cit., pp. 72–76 and 224–5.

3 An English translation of the passage, accompanied by valuable notes, will be found in *The Book of Ser Marco Polo*, translated into English and edited by Sir Henry Yule, 3rd ed., revised by Henri Cordier (London 1903, Murray, 2 vols.; 1920, supplementary volume), vol. ii, pp. 423–30.

4 See Carter, op. cit., pp. 76–79 and 225–6.

5 See ibid., pp. 128–9 and 238.

impressive by becoming familiar—not only automatically fosters a government's prestige and authority; it also gives a government a magnificent opportunity for deliberately indoctrinating its subjects with sentiments, beliefs, and views.

The hypnotic effect of a coinage even on the minds of a population under alien rule who resent this political yoke and abominate the Power by whom it has been imposed, is conveyed in a classic passage of the New Testament.

'They send unto Him certain of the Pharisees and of the Herodians, to catch Him in His words. And when they were come, they say unto Him: "Master, we know that thou art true, and carest for no man; for thou regardest not the person of men, but teachest the way of God in truth. Is it lawful to give tribute to Caesar, or not? Shall we give, or shall we not give?"

'But He, knowing their hypocrisy, said unto them: "Why tempt ye me? Bring me a penny, that I may see it." And they brought it, and He saith unto them: "Whose is this image and superscription?" And they said unto him: "Caesar's". And Jesus answering said unto them: "Render to Caesar the things that are Caesar's, and to God the things that are God's".'[1]

'And they could not take hold of His words before the people, and they marvelled at His answer, and held their peace.'[2]

This automatic moral profit which the prerogative of issuing money yielded, even in a formidably adverse political and religious environment, was of incomparably greater value to the Roman Imperial Government than any mere financial gains which the management of the mint might incidentally bring in. The Emperor's likeness on a coin gave the Imperial Government a certain status in the minds of a Jewish population which not only regarded Rome's dominion as illegitimate but treasured, as the second of ten commandments believed to have been received by Moses from Yahweh viva voce, the explicit injunction:

'Thou shalt not make unto thee any graven image or any likeness of anything that is in Heaven above or that is in the Earth beneath or that is in the water under the Earth. Thou shalt not bow down thyself to them nor serve them; for I the Lord thy God am a jealous god.'[3]

When in 167 B.C. the Seleucid sovereign Antiochus IV Epiphanes had placed a statue of Olympian Zeus in the Holy of Holies of Yahweh's temple at Jerusalem, the horror and indignation of the Jews at seeing the 'abomination that maketh desolate'[4] 'standing where it ought not'[5] were so intense that, thenceforward, they could not rest until they had thrown off every vestige of Seleucid rule. Again, when in A.D. 26 the Roman procurator Pontius Pilate smuggled into Jerusalem, draped and under cover of night, Roman military standards bearing the Emperor's image in medallions, the reaction of the Jews was so vehement as to compel Pilate to remove the offensive emblems from the precincts of the Holy City.[6] Yet in their holy land the Jews had schooled themselves

1 Mark xii. 13–17. Cp. Matt. xxii. 15–21; Luke xx. 20–25.
2 Luke xx. 26. Cp. Matt. xxii. 22; Mark xii. 17.
3 Exod. xx. 4–5. Cp. Deut. v. 8–9.
4 Dan. xi. 31 and xii. 11.
5 Mark xiii. 14. Cp. Matt. xxiv. 15.
6 Josephus: *Antiquitates*, Book XVIII, chap. iii, § 1; *Bellum Iudaïcum*, Book II, chap. ix, §§ 2–3.

meekly, not only to seeing, but to handling, using, earning, hoarding, and by all these compromising actions progressively countenancing, the abominable image on Caesar's coinage, and had thereby anticipated in action the observation of their future Roman chastiser Vespasian that sordid money does not smell.[1]

The Roman Government was not slow to perceive the value of an oecumenical coinage as an instrument of policy.

'From the middle of the first century onwards the Imperial Government had appreciated, as few governments have done before or since, not only the function of coinage as a mirror of contemporary life—of the political, social, spiritual and artistic aspirations of the age—but also its immense and unique possibilities as a far-reaching instrument of propaganda. Modern methods of disseminating news and modern vehicles of propaganda, from postage-stamps to broadcasting and the press, have their counterpart in the imperial coinage, where yearly, monthly—we might almost say, daily—novelties and variations in types record the sequence of public events and reflect the aims and ideologies of those who control the state.'[2]

The designers of the Roman imperial coinage could make play with a combination of image and superscription for giving visual form to the issuing government's political directives. The Umayyad successors of the Roman Empire in Syria, Egypt, and North-West Africa, and the innumerable Muslim governments that had succeeded the Umayyads in their turn down to the time of writing, were required to perform the still more skilful feat of conveying their messages to their subjects by superscription alone, since the Jewish tabu on graven images had been adopted by the Prophet Muhammad. In this inverted Psyche's task of spinning straw out of gold, they were fortunate in operating with a version of the Alphabet whose beauty, like that of the Sinic characters, when displayed by a master of calligraphy, could still be appreciated even by an eye whose owner's mind was illiterate. This capacity of a superscription, even when unsupported by an image, to transmit to the users of a coinage the message impressed on it by its makers was attested by the variety and abundance of the issues uttered by Muslim states.

The User's Demand for Conservatism in the Reproduction of Coin Types

There is, however, one golden rule that has to be rigidly observed if a coinage, iconic or aniconic, is to produce its psychological effect. A type that has once caught the imagination of its clientèle will not retain its hold unless it is reproduced in successive issues with blind fidelity.

The abortive first essay in an Umayyad gold and silver coinage—made by the founder of the dynasty, Muʿāwīyah, himself—is recorded

1 'Reprehendenti filio Tito, quod etiam urinae vectigal commentus esset, pecuniam ex primâ pensione admovit ad nares, sciscitans num odore offenderetur; et, illo negante, "Atquin", inquit, "e lotio est"' (Suetonius Tranquillus, C.: *The Lives of the Caesars*, 'Divus Vespasianus', chap. xxiii, § 3).

2 Toynbee, J. M. C.: *Roman Medallions* (New York 1944, The American Numismatic Society), p. 15. See further eandem: *The Hadrianic School: A Chapter in the History of Greek Art* (Cambridge 1934, University Press), pp. 2–5 and 24–159, for the 'province' coin series; p. 5 for the 'exercitus' coins; and Sutherland, C. H. V.: *Coinage in Roman Imperial Policy, 31 B.C.–A.D. 68* (London 1951, Methuen).

to have been boycotted by the public because it did not bear on its face the reassuringly familiar symbol of the Cross which was the hall-mark of the antecedent Christian Roman mintage.[1] Vexatious experiences of this kind no doubt explain the rigid conservatism of the Attic and Achaemenian mints, which continued to strike their primitive Athenian 'owls' and Daric 'archers' in latter days when the artificers' fingers must have itched to replace these stiff archaic types by something in a more lifelike modern style. Such sedulously mummified coin-types may indeed continue not only to pass current but to be uttered for centuries after the disappearance of the government whose image and superscription they bear. Silver *dirhems* (drachmae) bearing the image of Athena's owl were still circulating in the highland fastness of the Yaman[2] down to the date of the Umayyad Caliph ʿAbd-al-Malik's (*imperabat* A.D. 685–705) new oecumenical gold and silver issue, though by that time more than nine centuries had gone by since the native Attic issues of silver 'owls' from an Athenian mint had been discontinued by the Athenians themselves.[3]

After a brief taste of the novel experience of being a province of a universal state, the Yaman promptly took advantage of the weakening of the Caliphate's hold in the latter days of the ʿAbbasid régime in order to revert to her familiar way of life as a 'hermit kingdom'; and in A.D. 1952 the most popular monetary medium of exchange in the dominions of the Imām of Sanʿā, as well as in the adjoining Arabian regions of the Hadramawt and the hinterland of Aden, was the Maria Theresa dollar of an extinct Danubian Hapsburg Monarchy which, in the Hapsburg dominions themselves, had ceased to be legal tender as long ago as A.D. 1858.[4] The writer of this Study, when he was travelling on foot in

[1] See Wellhausen, J.: *Das Arabische Reich and Sein Sturz* (Berlin 1902, Reimer), p. 136.

[2] See ibid., p. 136. During the interval between the annexation of the Yaman to the Medinese nucleus of the Arab Empire, in the last days of the Prophet Muhammad's lifetime, and the Caliph 'Abd-al-Malik's new issues, these Himyarite silver 'owls' were actually in circulation, in small numbers, throughout the Arab dominions, side by side with Sasanian silver and with Roman silver and gold.

[3] This change of Attic coin types appears to have been made soon after the liberation of Athens from Macedonian occupation in 229 B.C. (see Ferguson, W. S.: *Hellenistic Athens* (London 1911, Macmillan), p. 245).

[4] See Hans, J.: *Zwei Jahrhunderte Maria-Theresien-Taler, 1751–1951* (Klagenfurt 1950, Hans), p. 16.

Of the 320 million MTT that had been minted since A.D. 1751, more than 150 million had been minted within the thirty years ending in A.D. 1950 (see ibid., pp. 3 and 10). Between A.D. 1751 and A.D. 1866, 82,727,621 had been minted in divers Hapsburg mints; between 1867 and 1935, 163,202,763 had been minted at Vienna; between 1935 and 1949, 72,326,022 had been minted at Vienna, Rome, London, Paris, Brussels, and Bombay (see ibid., pp. 14–15). The number minted at Vienna and exported to the Levant had been 15 million in 1925 and 15½ million in 1927 (see ibid., pp. 3 and 22); and, during the years 1935–9, 19,445,000 MTT, minted at Rome, had been imported by the Italian authorities into Abyssinia (p. 34).

The type of the MTT which thus made its fortune so far afield from the Queen-Empress' dominions was the issue minted at Günsburg in A.D. 1780, which was the last year of Maria Theresa's reign (p. 7). More than a hundred years later, in the last decade of the nineteenth century of the Christian Era, MTT of this type were circulating in a vast area extending in Africa from Algeria to the Upper Niger and to Madagascar and in South-West Asia as far as Maskat and Trebizond (according to a map, cited by Hans, p. 16, in Peez, C., and Raudnitz, J.: *Geschichte des Maria-Theresien-Thalers* (Vienna 1898)), and they were also circulating in China, side by side with Mexican dollars, *circa* A.D. 1900, according to Kann, E.: *The Currencies of China* (Shanghai 1928), cited ibid. In Abyssinia the MTT was the officially recognized coin of the realm from about the begin-

out-of-the-way districts of the Kingdom of Greece in A.D. 1911–12, found that gold 'Napoleons' of the French Second Empire were the most convenient coins to carry in his stocking; for the image and superscription of a bankrupt French political adventurer then still retained all their prestige in the eyes of Greek peasants and Vlach shepherds, though forty years had passed already since Napoleon III's capture by the Prussians and deposition by his own French subjects. On this showing, it might be anticipated that the English gold 'sovereign', of which Englishmen saw the last in A.D. 1914, might still be circulating in Albania for generations, and in Arabia for centuries, after that portentous date.[1]

ning of the nineteenth century until the Italian occupation in the years A.D. 1936–41 (Hans, p. 24).

For more than a hundred years, dating from the Ottoman Government's unsuccessful attempt in and after A.D. 1837 to replace the MTT by the Mejīdīyeh in its Arabian provinces as well as in the rest of the Empire (p. 21), the MTT triumphantly resisted repeated attempts to drive it out of circulation by the substitution of alternative metallic currencies. It did not begin to lose its hold upon the loyalty of its Abyssinian and Arabian addicts until after the liberation of Abyssinia from Italian occupation in A.D. 1941, and then it succumbed, not to any more attractive metallic currency, but to a belated adoption of the latter-day Western institutions of paper money, cheques, and bonds. In A.D. 1867 a British expeditionary force in Abyssinia had found itself compelled to import large quantities of MTT, specially minted at Vienna for its use, because the Abyssinian public had been unwilling to take payment in gold sovereigns (p. 20); in A.D. 1941 another British expeditionary force in Abyssinia found the public eager to surrender MTT in exchange for British East African paper money (see Hans, op. cit., p. 41, citing Lord Rennell of Rodd: *British Military Administration of Occupied Territory in Africa during the years 1941–1947* (London 1948, H.M. Stationery Office): see pp. 365–7, 370–1, 373–4, 379). Yet there were indications (see Hans, op. cit., pp. 50–51 and 53–54) that in A.D. 1950 the MTT was still being hoarded in large quantities in its old domain. A fine silver coin was, after all, proof against the two dangers, to which a paper note was exposed, of being eaten by termites and being devalued by politicians.

1 During the general war of 1914–18, both the Albanians and the Arabs welcomed the opportunity of being paid by the belligerents for continuing to conduct their own intertribal feuds in the role of their respective foreign paymasters' partisans. So long as they might go on fighting one another, they did not greatly care whether it was the Entente Powers or the Central Powers that were financing their customary activity, but they were unanimous and intransigent in insisting that they must be paid for their services in gold, cash down—not because they foresaw a coming catastrophic depreciation of paper money with a prescience denied to the wily financiers of Lombard Street and Wall Street, but for the simpler reason that, in Albania and Arabia, an invention that had been made in China only a thousand years back (see pp. 312–13, above) had not succeeded in acclimatizing itself yet by the beginning of the twentieth century of the Christian Era. The European belligerent governments—fighting, as they were, for their lives, and therefore clutching at straws—could not resist purchasing the nominal support of rival Albanian and Arab war-bands, and, to buy this dubious asset, they ruefully disgorged some of the gold that they had so ruthlessly withdrawn from circulation at home. An amusing sequel to this war-time tragi-comedy was witnessed by the writer of this Study at the Paris Peace Conference of A.D. 1919–20. The moving spirit of the Hashimite Hijāzī Arab delegation was Colonel T. E. Lawrence, and, when he was on his delegation's official business, he used to make a point of wearing the highly distinctive uniform of an officer of the Hijāzī Army. One day, in a corridor of the Hotel Majestic, the present writer had the good fortune to see this picturesque and animated figure run into a weary-looking official of the British Treasury. In a flash, Lawrence had whipped out from under the folds of his robe a magnificent dagger with a head of chased gold, and was holding it under the Treasury official's nose, saying: 'Do you know what that is made of?' 'No, I don't,' said the Treasury official rather testily. 'A hundred and fifty of your sovereigns,' Colonel Lawrence retorted; and the intended shock was duly registered by his victim. During the antecedent hostilities, while Colonel Lawrence had been having the fun of carrying bags of 'sovereigns' on camel-back and dispensing them to the Hijāzī allies of His Britannic Majesty's Government, the Treasury official had been saddled with the vexatious task of trying in vain to induce these Arab recipients of 'sovereigns' to part with them again in exchange for Indian piece goods, which he had dangled, like carrots, before a knowingly irresponsive donkey's nose. The Arabs had found a better use for British 'sovereigns' than that. So long as the gold remained in the form of minted coin, it might

(*e*) THE SERVICEABILITY OF IMPERIAL CORPORATIONS

1. *Standing Armies*

The Difficulty of Creating and Maintaining a Mobile Standing Army

Our survey of imperial installations and imperial currencies has indicated that these had been features in the life of all the universal states that had come into existence down to the time of writing; and indeed it is difficult to imagine any universal state establishing or maintaining itself without roads and postal arrangements, garrisons and colonies, a provincial organization, a capital city, one or more official languages and scripts, a code of law, a calendar, a set of weights and measures, and the rudiments or equivalents of money. By contrast, imperial corporations—standing armies, civil services, and citizenships—were to be found in the life of different universal states in various degrees of development ranging over the whole gamut between the rudimentary bud and the full-blown flower; and, because of this, they provided criteria for arranging the score of universal states on our panel in a tentative order of comparative maturity.[1]

In the role played in the lives of universal states by organized military force, the extent of the variation had been particularly great.

In the history of 'the Old Empire' of the Mayas there was no certain evidence for the existence of armed forces even in the form of a police cordon to keep out barbarians from beyond the imperial frontiers. The Spanish Empire of the Indies had been almost equally innocent of armaments on land during the two centuries and more that had elapsed between the domestication of the epigoni of the *conquistadores* and the establishment of a common land-frontier between the Spanish and the British dominions in the New World in the territorial settlement after the Seven Years War. During the intervening age the only permanent professional troops in the Indies had been the few hundred halberdiers in the ceremonial bodyguards of the Viceroys of New Spain and Peru. It had not been till A.D. 1762 that the Spanish Empire in the Americas had found it necessary to provide itself with a standing army and a militia.[2]

In the Achaemenian Empire, the Caliphate, and the Mughal Rāj the

(they felt) slip through their fingers; so they had converted it into dagger handles, which were not only more beautiful but more secure, since they could be carried more snugly on the person and were riveted to an automatic caretaker in the shape of a formidable steel blade.

[1] Of our twenty-one civilizations, the Hittite, Iranic, Arabic, Mexic, and Yucatec had apparently failed to produce universal states. On the other hand, the Egyptiac, Syriac, Indic, and Far Eastern societies had produced recurrent universal states, while, in the histories of the Sumeric, Hindu, Andean, and Russian universal states, there had been a break of continuity which not only permitted but constrained a student of History to treat as separate instances the Sumerian régime at Ur and the Amorite régime at Babylon; the Mughal Rāj and the British Rāj; the Incaic Empire of the Andes and the Spanish Empire of the Indies; and the pre-Petrine dispensation and the post-Petrine dispensation in Russia. See the table of contents of the atlas in vol. xi.

[2] Haring, C. H.: *The Spanish Empire in America* (New York, 1947, Oxford University Press), pp. 124, 125, and 145. The Empire of the Indies was not, of course, as defenceless as it might appear to have been, for down to A.D. 1763 it was more or less effectively insulated by the Spanish Navy from direct contact with the dominions of any other Power except France in Louisiana.

standing army included garrisons at strategic points along the frontiers[1] and in the interior[2] as well as the emperor's personal bodyguard at the headquarters of the imperial administration;[3] the 'small but efficient standing army', which even the later Mughal emperors managed to keep up 'consisted of cavalry and matchlockmen, and its kernel was the imperial park of artillery, without which no great fortress could be forcibly reduced';[4] but, when there was a call for mobile armies of any considerable strength, all three empires depended upon levies *ad hoc*. In all three the first ban was furnished by the imperial people itself. The Mughal and Achaemenian empires could call up their feudal cavalry, and the Caliphate its henchmen quartered in the cantonments (Arabs under the Umayyad Caliphs and Khurāsānīs under the ʿAbbasids). When, however, it was a question of a major military enterprise, these empires had to call upon the population at large.[5] When Xerxes invaded European Greece in 480 B.C., he not only mobilized his personal bodyguard and his Persian fief-holders and the rest of the manhood of the Perso-Median imperial people; he also raised levies from the subject population of all the provinces.[6] The regular spring and autumn raids from Cilicia into the East Roman Empire which were one of the institutions of the Caliphate for some two hundred years, until the tide of war turned in the East Roman Empire's favour at last in the second quarter of the tenth century of the Christian Era, were made by Muslim volunteers from all over the Caliph's dominions who assembled and dispersed behind the double screen of fortresses known as the Thughūr and the ʿAwāsīm.[7]

On the other hand, standing armies capable of providing mobile forces for campaigns, besides imperial bodyguards and provincial garrisons, were maintained by the Roman, Han, Manchu, Ottoman, Danubian Hapsburg, and Napoleonic empires, by the British Rāj in India, and by the post-Petrine Russian imperial régime.[8] The histories of these standing armies show that mobility is difficult to maintain. With the lapse of time a mobile professional force tends to degenerate into a sedentary militia.

The Danubian Hapsburg Monarchy and the British Rāj counteracted this tendency by deliberately organizing a local militia, distinct from the mobile army, to man chronically restless *limites*. There were the Croat

[1] See pp. 120–1, above.

[2] See pp. 123–4 and 130–1, above.

[3] See pp. 182–3, above.

[4] Spear, T. G. P.: *Twilight of the Mughuls* (Cambridge 1951, University Press), pp. 7–8. 'The Mughul train of artillery, in maintaining internal security, had something of the potency of the Tudor monopoly of gunpowder. The artillerymen were generously paid, Europeans were freely engaged at high rates, and even supplied with servants so that they should be relieved of all labour save that of aiming the guns' (ibid., p. 8).
A detailed account of the Mughal artillery is given in Irvine, W.: *The Army of the Indian Moghuls* (London 1903, Luzac), chaps. 10–12.

[5] See p. 183, above.

[6] See the army list in Herodotus, Book VII, chaps. 61–99.

[7] See II. ii. 368, with n. 1, and the present volume, p. 121, above.

[8] After the Russian Empire had been equipped with a Western-model professional army by Peter the Great, efforts continued to be made to improve this army's professional standards. In A.D. 1731 an officer's cadet corps was founded, with places for 150 Russian nobles and 50 Livlanders. In A.D. 1732 garrison schools were started (see Mettig, C.: *Die Europäisierung Russlands im Achtzehnten Jahrhundert* (Gotha 1913, Perthes), pp. 82 and 314).

and Serb territorial regiments which, in the eighteenth and nineteenth centuries of the Christian Era, held the line of the Save for the Hapsburg King-Emperor against their Bosniak and Turkish hereditary adversaries;[1] and there were the Pathan militias whom the British Indian military authorities on the North-West Frontier of India recruited during the century beginning in A.D. 1849 from among the wild tribesmen on the principle of setting a thief to catch a thief. These Danubian Hapsburg and British Indian sedentary *limitanei* were of minor importance compared to the mobile armies which they supplemented, whereas in the Ottoman military system the Kurdish *foederati* who, under the command of their own tribal chiefs, held the Ottoman frontier over against Persia,[2] and the Turkish feudal cavalry whose fiefs were sown thick over the Empire except in the more remote of the Arab provinces,[3] together considerably outnumbered the Pādishāh's Slave-Household. Yet the existence of this border militia and provincial feudal array did not preserve the Janissaries, after the death of Suleymān the Magnificent, from losing their mobility and changing, in their turn, into a militia, cantoned in Constantinople and the provincial capitals, which became ever more unwarlike and ever more seditious *pari passu*, till there was nothing to be done with this once magnificently soldierly force except to annihilate it in order to rebuild an Ottoman professional army from the foundations—this time on an alien new model derived from the West.[4] In the Manchu and Roman empires the originally mobile 'banners' and legions likewise struck root through vegetating in fixed stations—the 'banners' in the interior of China and the legions on the frontiers of the Roman World.

The Creation of a Mobile Standing Army in the post-Diocletianic Roman Empire

In the history of the Roman Imperial Army this loss of mobility—of which the danger did not become apparent so long as the prestige of the Empire stood so high that no outsider ventured seriously to attack it[5]—was one of the causes of the catastrophe in which the Empire all but came to grief in the third century of the Christian Era. The improvisation of a new mobile army was the creative act of that desperate age; and, though it was achieved in adverse circumstances at the eleventh hour, it proved so great a success that it prolonged the life of the Empire for one and a half centuries even in the West and for three and a half centuries in the East and the Centre.[6]

[1] See pp. 117–18, above. [2] See I. i. 389–90, and pp. 121–2, above.

[3] See pp. 124–6, above.

[4] For Sultan Selīm III's tragic failure, and Sultan Mahmūd II's grim success, in coping with the task of superseding the Janissaries, see III. iii. 48–50 and IX. viii. 239.

[5] See p. 184, above.

[6] This impressive chronological evidence of the success of the Diocletiano-Constantinian reorganization of the Roman system of imperial defence would seem, to a layman's eyes, to suffice in itself to refute Zosimus's savage critique of it in his *Historiae*, Book II, chap. xxxiv. Zosimus submits that the withdrawal of units from the frontiers to create a mobile reserve in the interior exposed the Empire to uncontested invasion, located the troops in places not requiring defence, brought ruin upon the cities in which they were stationed, and demoralized the troops themselves in the process. Zosimus does not mention the telling truth that, during the century ending in A.D. 284, when the

The truth that a military force can be kept mobile only by relieving it of sedentary tasks had been perceived and translated into action by the genius of Julius Caesar. Out of the thirty-two legions that he had in hand at the close of his civil wars, he posted twenty-six on the frontiers and kept six in reserve.[1] Thereafter, Augustus posted all his twenty-eight legions[2] on the frontiers[3]—whether from lack of his adoptive father's strategic insight or because a further bout of civil wars had left him with that amount less of man-power and sinews of war at his command.[4] Apart from the 4,500 men in the nine praetorian cohorts constituting the Emperor's personal bodyguard[5] and the 1,500 men in the original three urban cohorts,[6] which—as their designation ('Metropolitan Battalions') pointedly proclaimed—were a semi-civic force, Augustus's army possessed no striking force, no field army, no reserves, and the only means of reinforcing the garrison of one sector of the imperial frontier was the drafting of a detachment (*vexillatio*) from the garrison of another sector.[7] Domitian carried the process of immobilizing the legions one stage farther by ruling that each legion was to have a camp of its own.[8] After Hadrian had made a rule of the already prevailing tendency for the legions, like the *auxilia*, to be recruited locally,[9]

Augustan system of frontier defence had still been in operation, the Empire had suffered far more grievously from barbarian invasion than it suffered thereafter, under the new system, during the century ending in A.D. 378. His flagrantly incorrect ascription of the Augustan system to Diocletian, the pagan innovator whose reforms a Christian Constantine had merely carried through to completion, seems to indicate that Zosimus's critique of a policy which he falsely attributes to Constantine's initiative was at least partly prompted by religious animus.

1 See Grosse, R.: *Römische Militärgeschichte von Gallienus bis zum Beginn der Byzantinischen Themenverfassung* (Berlin 1920, Weidmann), p. 55.

2 This appears to have been the establishment of Augustus's standing army in 16 B.C. The number was reduced to 25 by the loss of three legions in Varus's disaster in Germany in A.D. 9. This number was raised to 27 by Gaius or (more probably) by Claudius. By the end of the civil wars of A.D. 69 the number had perhaps risen to 31. It was reduced to 29 by Vespasian, but had been raised again to 30 by A.D. 83; and this seems to have been regarded as the standard establishment for the next 110 years. To maintain this figure, Trajan appears to have replaced one legion lost by Domitian in Sarmatia in A.D. 92, and another lost by himself, and Marcus Aurelius to have replaced two lost (perhaps) by Hadrian in Britain and in Palestine respectively. Thereafter, Septimius Severus raised the standing army to a higher strength than it had ever yet possessed by adding his three *Legiones Parthicae* to Marcus's thirty (see Parker, H. M. D.: *The Roman Legions* (Oxford 1928, Clarendon Press), chaps. 3 and 4, pp. 72–117, and compare the *Cambridge Ancient History*, vol. x (Cambridge 1934, University Press), pp. 123 and 221).

3 See p. 184, above.

4 At the moment when this final bout of civil wars was brought to an end by the overthrow of the last of Augustus's competitors for the mastery of the Roman World, the victor had on his hands perhaps as many as sixty legions. In his *res gestae*, Augustus claims to have replanted 300,000 discharged soldiers in civilian life by either repatriating them in their original communities or settling them in new colonies. Twenty-eight legions was presumably the maximum establishment that, in Augustus's view, an exhausted world could be expected to support.

5 The original strength of both a praetorian and an urban cohort was 500 men. The strength of the praetorian cohorts was raised from 500 to 1,000 momentarily during the crisis of A.D. 69 and then permanently in A.D. 193 by Septimius Severus. Septimius also raised the strength of the urban cohorts from 500 to 1,500 (see Durry, M.: *Les Cohortes Prétoriennes* (Paris 1938, Boccard), pp. 82–87).

6 For these, see pp. 123 and 184, above. By Vespasian's time (*imperabat* A.D. 70–79) the number of urban cohorts appears to have risen to four stationed in Rome and the two posted in the provinces at Lyons and at Carthage respectively (see the *Cambridge Ancient History*, vol. xi (Cambridge 1936, University Press), p. 135).

7 See Grosse, op. cit., p. 55.

8 See Suetonius Tranquillus, C.: *The Lives of the Caesars*, 'Domitianus', chap. 7.

9 See Durry, op. cit., p. 246.

and had carried to completion the Augustan system of fixed frontier defences, 'the whole Roman Army was degraded into being a bevy of gendarmes and customs officials'.[1] In the third century, 'when the whole empire became one single gigantic fortress assaulted simultaneously from all sides, the old method of frontier-defence inevitably proved totally inadequate, and the need for a strong field army that could be brought into action rapidly at any point inevitably declared itself ever more insistently'.[2] Before the third century was over, this need had been met. Gallienus (*imperabat* A.D. 260–8) made a beginning by detaching the cavalry from the legions and grouping them under an independent command,[3] and the work of reorganization was continued by Aurelian (*imperabat* A.D. 270–5)[4] and was completed by Diocletian (*imperabat* A.D. 284–305).

Out of the best of the battered units of the Augustan Army, without any discrimination between legionary *vexillationes*[5] and auxiliary cohorts and *alae*, the third-century reformers built up a mobile army of all arms; and, within this category of troops trained and equipped to accompany the emperors on campaign (*Comitatenses*),[6] there were gradations of mobility, proficiency, and privileged proximity to a throne that dire necessity of state had now transformed into a portable camp-stool which was pitched from day to day wherever the need for the emperor's presence might happen at the moment to be the greatest.[7] Within the *Comitatenses* there came to be an *élite* of *Palatini*,[8] an inner guard composed of the *Scholae*[9] and the *Candidati*, and a personal bodyguard of *Protectores* and *Domestici*[10] who provided the new mobile army with the

[1] Grosse, op. cit., p. 56.
[2] Ibid., p. 56.
[3] See ibid., pp. 15, 18, and 56.
[4] See ibid., pp. 56–57.

[5] By Diocletian's time the Augustan legions seem to have been already broken up into detachments (*vexillationes*) of the strength of the cohorts which had always been the units of the *auxilia* and had also been the principal subdivisions of the legions themselves since the reforms of Marius. At the same time the auxiliary cohorts of infantry and *alae* of cavalry had become detached from the legions with which they had been brigaded under the Principate. After this dissolution of the Augustan legion of 10,000 to 12,000 men (including its complement of *auxilia*), the name legion came to denote a *vexillatio* of perhaps no more than 500 men. The fifth-century *Notitia Dignitatum* catalogues 174 legions, as against the 33 in the army of the Principate after the addition of three to the previous total by Septimius Severus (see Grosse, op. cit., pp. 30–32).

[6] A Latin inscription (*C.I.L.* vi. 2759) witnesses that the *Comitatenses* were in existence at latest by A.D. 301 (see Grosse, op. cit., p. 59).

[7] After the foundation of Constantinople on a site where the new political capital of the Roman Empire could simultaneously serve as a military base for the defence, in depth, of both the Lower Danube and the Upper and Middle Euphrates frontier (see pp. 217–18, above), the Imperial camp-stool was pitched here more often than not; and this gravitation of the Imperial headquarters to the shores of the Bosphorus is reflected in the distribution of the standing cantonments of the Comitatensian infantry legions (excluding the *Palatini*) according to the *Notitia Dignitatum*. No less than twenty of these units were cantoned in Thrace, as compared with nine apiece in Oriens and Gaul, eight apiece in Eastern Illyricum and Africa, and five apiece in Western Illyricum, Italy, and Spain (see Grosse, op. cit., p. 90).

[8] First heard of in A.D. 365 (see ibid., p. 61). The name was, of course, by that time an anachronism; for it was more than a century since the Roman Empire had been governed from the Palatine Hill.

[9] The *Scholae*, once unofficial clubs organized by officers, in the Empire's halcyon days, to provide amenities for their leisure hours, had become part of the working organization of the Army in consequence of their feat of surviving the general dissolution of institutions in the third century.

[10] The Praetorian Cohorts had perished in the last gusts of the hundred-years-long social tornado by which the Roman Empire had been ravaged. Diocletian had depressed

equivalent of a much-needed staff college.[1] The leavings of the Army, when the mobile *Comitatenses* had been formed out of it, were assigned to a frontier force (*Ripenses*, *Riparienses*, *Limitanei*)[2] which was frankly permitted to be the sedentary militia[3] that the Army of the Principate had tended to become *sub rosa*[4] ever since it had been cantoned along the frontiers by Augustus, while the mobile standing army embodied in the *Comitatenses* constituted at last, after a dearly paid-for delay of nearly 350 years, that mobile reserve which had been designed, on a smaller scale, by *Divus Iulius*.[5]

Esprit de corps

The superiority of a mobile standing army over a sedentary militia in professional technique is surpassed both in degree and in importance by its superiority in *esprit de corps*. A militiaman tends to be drawn back into civilian life and êthos by a fixed domicile, by marriage, and by the pressure on him to engage in gainful occupations in order to support a family which cannot live on a soldier's pay. This masterful process of demilitarization overtook the Roman Army of the Principate after the removal, by Septimius Severus, of the ban on marriage while with the colours,[6] and it overtook the Janissary Corps after the relaxation of its discipline upon the death of Suleymān the Magnificent. By contrast, a professional soldier in a mobile standing army is 'conditioned' by an insulating way of life and a differentiating discipline into being first and

their status and reduced their importance by keeping them at the long since evacuated seat of imperial government at Rome (Grosse, op. cit., p. 59, citing Aurelius Victor, 39, 47, and Lactantius, *De Mortibus Persecutorum*, 26). Thereafter, Constantine the Great had abolished them after they had fought on the losing side at the Battle of the Milvian Bridge on the 28th October, A.D. 312 (see Durry, op. cit., pp. 170 and 393; Grosse, op. cit., p. 60).

1 See ibid., pp. 61–63 and 93–96.

2 See ibid., pp. 66 and 68.

3 We are ignorant of the date at which the soldiers of the frontier garrisons became *adscripti glebae* by being given personal and hereditary holdings of land to cultivate, but there is no doubt that, from the fourth to the sixth century of the Christian Era, the frontier troops were in fact 'a militia of sedentary peasants' (ibid., pp. 64–65).

4 In theory the Army of the Principate was always mobile, and the symbol of this theory was the legal inability of the serving soldier to contract a valid marriage so long as he was with the colours. Considering, however, that, upon a soldier's honourable discharge, a permanent illicit union could be converted into a legal marriage and children already born of it be legitimized retrospectively (see p. 132, above); that the soldiers' families were allowed to live in civilian *canabae* adjoining the camps; and that the men were free, while still on active service, to cultivate the *prata legionum*, it is evident that the difference *de facto* between the pre-Severan legionary and the post-Diocletianic *limitaneus* was not by any means as great as the difference in theory. The rights of contracting a legal marriage while on active service and of leasing plots in the *prata legionum* were granted to soldiers by Septimius Severus (see Grosse, op. cit., p. 248; *The Cambridge Ancient History*, vol. xii (Cambridge 1939, University Press), p. 32).

5 Not the least part of this price of a long delay was a formidable increase in the total strength of the Army in an age when the economic resources of the Empire were dwindling. Even after Septimius Severus had increased the number of the legions from 30 to 33, the Army of the Principate had amounted to not much more than 300,000 men. Diocletian raised the figure by perhaps something like two-thirds, from about 300,000 to about 500,000 (see Grosse, op. cit., p. 253). Within this total, the field army may have had a nominal strength of 148,000 infantry and 46,500 cavalry (see ibid., p. 254).

6 See Grosse, op. cit., p. 248. In the post-Diocletianic Army, both the soldier and his wife (if he were married in lawful wedlock) were tax-free after he had completed five years' service (see ibid., p. 202). Nevertheless, private soldiers as well as officers were still apt to get entangled in civilian business concerns in the sixth century of the Christian Era (see ibid., p. 278).

foremost a member of his corps and paying only a secondary and conditional allegiance to the civilian community which bears the cost of keeping him under arms; and, if and when the interests of community and corps diverge, the professional soldier is apt to become, in relation to the community, that portentous creature, the unsocial human being, who, as Aristotle sees him, is 'either a beast or a god'.[1] In this predicament the professional soldier can, indeed, either sink to a depth of inhumanity or rise to a height of heroism that are alike beyond the range of his brethren who have not put themselves outside the pale of civilian life through being initiated into a professional military fraternity.

In sacrificing himself to his professional duty the soldier is, of course, happiest when *esprit de corps* gives the same orders as patriotism.

> Ὦ ξεῖν', ἀγγεῖλον Λακεδαιμονίοις ὅτι τῇδε
> κείμεθα, τοῖς κείνων ῥήμασι πειθόμενοι·

and this famous epitaph by Simonides on the Three Hundred Spartans who fell, to the last man but one,[2] at Thermopylae was to inspire a worthy counterpart in Housman's epitaph on a British army of mercenaries that likewise faced and met certain death in pitting itself against overwhelming odds in order to purchase eventual victory for its cause by checking the first onset of a formidable invader.

> These, on the day when Heaven was falling,
> The hour when Earth's foundations fled,
> Followed their mercenary calling
> And took their wages and are dead.
>
> Their shoulders held the sky suspended;
> They stood, and Earth's foundations stay;
> What God abandoned, these defended,
> And saved the sum of things for pay.

No doubt, in all situations, the professional soldier's First Commandment is

> Theirs not to reason why,
> Theirs but to do and die;

yet there are degrees of heroism which can be measured by the desperateness of the situation in which the soldier obeys the call to give his life. The Spartan soldier who died in 480 B.C. and the British soldier who died in A.D. 1914 in the act of saving a civilization was not confronted with so severe an ordeal as the Assyrian soldier who, in 610–609 B.C.,[3] made the same supreme personal sacrifice in the baneful cause of striving to undo the World's accomplished deed of liberating itself from the scourge of Assyrian militarism; for the *moral* of Assyria's last army, which took the field again and perished in that last campaign, had been proof against the shock of seeing Assyria herself laid desolate and her fortress-capital Nineveh taken by storm and put to the sack two years

1 Aristotle: *Politics*, Book I, chap. i, §§ 9–12 (p. 1253A), quoted in I. i. 173, n. 3.

2 The tragic story of the sole survivor Aristodâmus has been told, with sympathetic insight, by Herodotus, Book VII, chaps. 229–31, and Book IX, chap. 71 (see III. iii. 63, n. 3).

3 See IV. iv. 475 and 480.

earlier.[1] In 610 B.C. Assyria still lived within a defeated but undismayed army's lines at Harrān, as in A.D. 1848 Austria survived in Radetsky's camp within the Quadrilateral of Hapsburg fortresses in Lombardy.

> In deinem Lager ist Österreich,
> Wir Andern sind einzelne Trümmer.[2]

While manfully standing to arms for a new trial of strength with adversaries who had won the preceding round, the Assyrian army in 610 B.C. hoped as sanguinely against hope as Radetsky's army in A.D. 1848 that, this time, they would retrieve their country's fortunes by rescuing her from the very jaws of destruction. While the Assyrians duly failed in their forlorn hope, Radetsky's army played a capital part in winning for the Danubian Hapsburg Monarchy a seventy years' reprieve from her eventually inevitable doom of disruption by the mounting force of Nationalism.[3] Yet, though Radetsky's success might be less romantic than the Assyrians' failure, it was the fruit of a greater *tour de force* in the art of leadership.

The Assyrian army of 610 B.C., like the British Light Brigade of A.D. 1854 and Expeditionary Force of A.D. 1914, was a military formation of a homogeneous national texture fighting in its own national cause without any conflict of mutually incompatible loyalties, whereas the Austria that, in A.D. 1848, was incarnate in Radetsky's camp on the banks of the Po was a miniature reproduction of the house divided against itself in the valley of the Danube. The troops who in that year held together in Lombardy under Radetsky's command had to withstand a twofold psychological assault upon their *esprit de corps*. They were being asked to go on fighting for a state which not only appeared to have dissolved already in their rear, but which, for many of them, was not their own country but was, rather, their country's hereditary oppressor whose yoke had just been broken, not by their Italian opponents in the field, but by their own kinsmen on the home front in a revolutionary upheaval that was threatening to rankle into an outright civil war. Radetsky's army in the Quadrilateral was a mixed multitude in which German

1 This steadfastness of Assyrian military *moral* in 610–609 B.C. will appear the more remarkable when it is recalled that, although by that date the Assyrian state had been in serious adversity for no longer than about sixteen years, since the death of Asshurbanipal in 626 B.C., the Assyrian soldier had been living under a severe personal strain for more than a hundred years past, ever since the opening of the fourth and final bout of Assyrian militarism in 745 B.C. (see IV. iv. 476–7) had first carried him away from home on distant, protracted, and consecutive campaigns. In the fragments of Assyrian law, dating from an earlier chapter of Assyrian history, that Modern Western archaeologists had recovered, a significantly high proportion of the legislation was concerned with situations arising from a soldier's return home from foreign service after so long an absence that his wife had given him up for dead. (Convenient English translations and commentaries will be found in Smith, J. M. P.: *The Origin and History of Hebrew Law* (Chicago 1931, University of Chicago Press), pp. 233–45, and in Pritchard, J. B.: *Ancient Near Eastern Texts* (Princeton 1950, Princeton University Press), pp. 180–8.) An Englishman who had lived through the World War of A.D. 1939–45 would be reminded of the similar marital troubles arising from the absence of British troops from home for years on end in the Middle East and Burma. A student of Roman history would be reminded of the personal strain on the Roman peasant-soldier during the four generations that elapsed between the beginning of the Hannibalic War and the creation of a professional army by Marius.

2 Grillparzer, Franz: *Feldmarschall Radetzky* [written at the beginning of June 1848].

3 See II. ii. 182–6.

Austrians found themselves cheek by jowl with Magyars whose kinsmen at home were repudiating a German ascendancy, and with Slavs whose kinsmen—in the hope of winning Imperial-Royal support in their struggle to throw off the ascendancy of German and Magyar alike—were rallying to a refugee King-Emperor whose flight from Vienna had been as humiliating as Radetsky's ejection from Milan. When full allowance has been made for the momentum of a habit of co-operation that had been inculcated by more than two centuries of professional military discipline, it will still seem little less than a miracle that Radetsky's troops did not turn their arms against one another when their spirits, already depressed by the experience of defeat at the front, were further unsettled by the news of national uprisings in their rear.[1]

Die Gott als Slav' und Magyaren schuf,
Sie streiten um Worte nicht hämisch,
Sie folgen, ob deutsch auch der Feldherrnruf,
Denn: Vorwärts! ist ung'risch und böhmisch.[2]

A greater miracle of the same kind was worked by the *esprit de corps* that, in the Tropical African theatre of the World War of A.D. 1914–18, kept von Lettow-Vorbeck's Bantu askaris in the field for more than four years in a cause that was not their own, with no hope at all of reinforcements, and none of fresh supplies except such as they might succeed in capturing from the enemy. Yet the armistice imposed on them by Ludendorff's failure of nerve in a reverse that had not yet carried the war on to German territory in Europe found these mercenary askaris still fighting gamely for their German masters in Portuguese East Africa after having been driven out of German East Africa by the tardy pressure of a decisively superior enemy force. Equally noteworthy was the loyalty to the British Rāj, during the mutiny of the East India Company's older sepoy-troops in A.D. 1857–8, of the regiments then daringly recruited from a warrior community of Sikhs who, only nine years before, had

[1] The *esprit de corps* of the Austrian Army, which gave such a good account of itself in Radetsky's camp in Lombardy in A.D. 1848, eventually succumbed to the ordeal of the World War of A.D. 1914–18. In that war, Czech regiments deserted *en masse* to their Russian fellow Slavs, and after the armistice of 1918 the Army of the Isonzo, as it drifted back from a defensive campaign which, with German help, it had carried on to enemy territory, dissolved into mutually hostile national elements. This end of an army that had been called into existence, four hundred years back, to defend the eastern flank of Western Christendom against the 'Osmanlis, had been described to the writer of this Study by an Austrian friend of his who, being at that moment a civilian, had been caught in the eastward-ebbing tide of self-demobilizing troops as he was trying to make his own way, across the current, from Graz to Innsbruck. The Imperial-Royal comrades-in-arms of yesterday, as they sorted themselves out into Czechs, Germans, Magyars, Poles, Ukrainians, Rumans, and Yugoslavs, were eyeing one another suspiciously, with forebodings of the fratricidal conflicts into which they were to be drawn on the morrow. Since Radetsky's day the unitary tradition of a once professional Austrian Army had been undermined by the introduction of universal compulsory short-term military service, which, in a general mobilization, inevitably filled the cadres to bursting-point with men who were civilians and nationalists at heart while they were soldiers and servants of the King-Emperor against the grain. Yet, even in this war that was the old Austrian Army's death, the Hungarian, German, and Polish subjects of the Dual Crown, whose national interests happened to coincide with the interests of the Monarchy, still gave a good account of themselves; and the Croats, among whom a military tradition of personal loyalty to the Dynasty was still alive, fought valiantly against their Serb fellow Yugoslavs.

[2] Grillparzer, op. cit.

fought the British for the second time and, this time, had paid for a second defeat the penalty of forfeiting, at one stroke, their ascendancy over the other communities in the Panjab and their own political independence. Yet all these signal triumphs of professional *esprit de corps* were surpassed by the unsung achievement of the sepoy mutineers themselves, in which the honours had to be divided between the British officers who had once inculcated the discipline and the Indian non-commissioned officers and privates who succeeded in maintaining it in spite of the deadly wounds which they had dealt to their own *moral.* The mutineers had committed the militarily and morally unforgivable sin of breaking faith with their employers and murdering their superiors; and by this treachery they had deprived themselves of an alien leadership which had held together a mixed multitude of mutually antipathetic Hindus and Muslims and had welded them into a professional army that had not met its match east of Indus. Yet, disabled though they were by these self-inflicted handicaps, they had the spirit to challenge their British makers, and in the ensuing struggle they came within an ace of repeating the feat of those Mamlūks who, in Egypt six hundred years earlier, had wrested the sceptre irrevocably out of the hands of their Ayyūbid masters.[1]

The Problem of Controlling Alien or Barbarian Troops

This professional military *esprit de corps* is both more necessary and more notable in a universal state than it is in a parochial state; for, in contrast to the standing armies of parochial states, which are usually homogeneous in their personnel, the armies of universal states are usually composed of heterogeneous elements that have to be inspired by artificial influences of discipline and tradition with a community of feeling which the recruit does not bring with him, ready-made, from civilian life. While one of these artificially associated elements, and this the leading one, had generally, though not invariably, been the imperial people itself, the empire-builders, however generous they might have been in taking outsiders into their ranks, had seldom had the numbers or the strength to win and hold their empire unaided. In most of the universal states that had come into existence up to date, the rulers had found it expedient to take into military partnership in their standing armies the military *élite* of their subjects within their frontiers or of the barbarians beyond their pale, or even to enlist representatives of an alien civilization.

The unpopularity of the Napoleonic Empire, which was one cause of its premature fall, was due in large measure to the 'blood-tax' which Napoleon imposed not only on the French but on the non-French populations incorporated into the Empire and on the peoples of the client states. When he invaded Russia in A.D. 1812, he compelled even Prussia and Austria to furnish contingents—if only as hostages to ensure that these two discomfited Great Powers should not rise and attack him in the rear after he had traversed their dominions on his eastward march. In the Grand Army that started to cross the Niemen on the

[1] See III. iii. 30–31.

24th June, 1812, only about 120,000 out of 363,000 men were Frenchmen.

The Mongols swiftly won and momentarily held their far-flung dominion over the sedentary peoples round the periphery of the Great Eurasian Steppe by first taking into partnership all but a small fraction of the rest of the Eurasian Nomads and then drafting troops from one conquered sedentary sub-continent to assist in the conquest of another. In the Mongols' service Chinese military engineers played their part in the capture of Transoxanian cities, while Muslim troops from Transoxania, and Orthodox Christian Alan cavalry from the northern slopes of the Caucasus,[1] were brought into action in China against the recalcitrant Empire of the Sung.

The Mughal conquerors of India reinforced their own scanty numbers with drafts of fellow Muslims from an Iranic World out of which they themselves had issued; and in their dearth of martial man-power they did not hesitate to accept recruits from among the barbarous Uzbegs who had driven Bābur out of Farghānah and the heretical *qyzyl-bāshīs* with whom he had allied himself, against his conscience, in a vain attempt to recover the Transoxanian heritage of his ancestor Timur from the Uzbeg invader.[2] Yet even the most generous-handed sharing of the spoils of India with fellow Iranic Muslims enlisted at the eleventh hour did not give the Mughals the strength to complete the conquest of the peninsula, or even to hold securely what they had already won, against the obstinate resistance of the epigoni of earlier Muslim conquerors; and they found themselves constrained to sin against the spirit and tradition of Islam by enlisting the services of the infidel chivalry of their Rājpūt client states in their fratricidal wars against their True Believing rivals.

The Achaemenian Empire, which on the military plane was perhaps the least efficient of all the universal states in our catalogue, exposed its own incompetence to the World and to itself by embarking on the formidable enterprise of trying to conquer European Greece. The humiliating outcome of the thirty years' war (480–450 B.C.) that Xerxes had wantonly brought upon himself and his successors convinced the Achaemenian Government of their need for a mobile standing army; but, instead of building up one of their own out of the excellent military man-power and abundant economic resources that the Empire could afford, they contented themselves with the unimaginative, slovenly, expensive, and dangerous makeshift of hiring Greek to meet Greek. After the break-down of the Hellenic Civilization had been signalized by the outbreak of the Atheno-Peloponnesian War, the daric could purchase any number of seasoned soldiers from among the uprooted citizens of the faction-ridden city-states of Hellas; but, of course, the latter-day Achaemenids' Greek mercenary army, so far from arresting the Hellenic Society's counter-offensive, invitingly blazed a trail for their fellow Hellenes into the heart of South-Western Asia. After ten thousand Greek mercenary troops in an Achaemenid pretender's

[1] See the passages of Marco Polo quoted in V. v. 350–1.
[2] For this episode in Bābur's history, see I. i. 375–80.

service had demonstrated their ability to march unhindered from Ephesus to Cunaxa and back again from Cunaxa to Trebizond, it was evident that the thirty-six thousand Greeks whom Alexander led across the Hellespont would suffice to overthrow the Achaemenian régime and to conquer the Empire from the Aegean to the Pamirs.

The fate of the Arab Caliphate shows that a standing army of barbarians from beyond the pale may be almost as great a political danger as one recruited from the *déracinés* of an alien civilization. When, on the Khurasanian frontier of the Umayyad Power, the local garrisons of Arab empire-builders had fraternized and blended with comrades-in-arms enlisted from the local Iranian subject population,[1] the ruling element in the Caliphate had been strengthened by this broadening of its basis. But when, after the revolution that had brought the ʿAbbasids into power, the Khurāsānī henchmen of the new régime were supplanted, in their turn, by Turkish mercenaries from beyond the Oxus, the mastery of the Caliphate passed first to these Transoxanian Turkish praetorians and eventually to the Nomad Turkish Saljūqs from the Eurasian Steppe. In 'the New Empire' of Egypt a similar consequence followed from the recruitment of a mercenary army of Minoan *déracinés* and Achaean and Libyan barbarians. Though this hazardous expedient appeared to have vindicated itself when, at the turn of the thirteenth and twelfth centuries B.C., the barbarians in the Egyptian service loyally assisted their native Egyptian comrades-in-arms to repel successive waves of barbarian invasion,[2] the policy stood condemned when, in the event, the discomfited Libyans sauntered back, unopposed, into the Egyptiac World and settled down upon the land as an incubus-militia.[3]

The ʿOsmanlis in their heyday were unique among empire-builders in debarring the imperial people itself from participation in either the defence or the government of their empire, and in relying exclusively on the services of subjects and aliens. In a different context[4] we have seen how they achieved this *tour de force* by detaching their recruits from all previous ties of family, nationality, and religion, and reconditioning them through a strenuous course of broadly conceived and skilfully devised education. The system was so efficient that it produced its transforming effect not only upon tribute-children subjected to it at a tender age but also upon adult prisoners-of-war and renegades; but, when the system broke down owing to the defiance of human nature which was the price at which its efficiency had been purchased, and the free Muslim population of the Empire was grudgingly admitted to a long-overdue participation in public power and responsibility, the Ottoman Empire began to go the way of the ʿAbbasid Caliphate and 'the New Empire' of Egypt.

When the long military retreat that had started under the walls of Vienna in A.D. 1683 was converted into a rout by the disastrous outcome of the Great Russo-Turkish War of A.D. 1768–74, both the Sublime

[1] See V. v. 450, and pp. 140–1, above.
[2] See I. i. 93 and 101; IV. iv. 85 and 422; V. v. 269 and 352; and V. vi. 207.
[3] See IV. iv. 422; V. v. 269–70, 352–3, and 463.
[4] In III. iii. 31–44.

Porte and its increasingly independent lieutenants in the provinces found themselves leaning on a broken reed in their belated reliance on a free Turkish squirearchy and peasantry that were untutored alike in the old Ottoman school of warfare followed by the Pādishāh's now demoralized Slave-Household and in the new Western school that had originally been inspired by an Ottoman ensample. In these straits the distracted rulers of a tottering empire turned, in their desperate search for martial man-power, to the rude but still untarnished valour of barbarian Albanians and Bosniaks.[1] In Continental European Greece they even authorized the enrolment of a militia of Christian Greek highlanders, under native captains, to guard the passes.[2] And, on the analogy of what happened in other universal states in similar situations in which the process was not checked by the intervention of a third force, we may guess that these and other barbarians would have duly entered into the Ottoman heritage if the Ottoman World had not fallen, at that juncture, under the shadow of the West.[3] As a result of this new turn in their fortunes, the 'Osmanlis succeeded in building up a new Western-model Ottoman Army which put the pashas' Albanian house-carls out of business, brought the Kurdish tribes to heel, saved the Turkish core of the Empire from being partitioned by the European Powers, and eventually shepherded their country into the fold of Western political life as an independent Turkish national republic.[4]

The ruling element in the British Rāj in India, like the rulers of the Spanish Empire of the Indies, were peculiar in being a company of pilgrims and sojourners who were neither born nor educated nor superannuated nor buried within the bounds of the universal state that they garrisoned and governed during the prime of their working lives;[5] and in British India, which, unlike the Spanish Indies, found itself unable to dispense with a standing army, this permanent geographical and social segregation of a West European imperial people from an Indian subject population was a military safeguard, though in some ways a political stumbling-block.

The standing army of the British Rāj in India was composed of three elements: West Europeans from the United Kingdom, Indians from British Indian territory and from the Indian client states, and barbarians recruited mainly from the independent Gurkha states of Nepal and Bhutan and from the autonomous Pathan tribes in the zone between the north-western boundary of British-administered Indian territory and the Indo-Afghan political frontier. The British troops, the Gurkhas, the Pathan *limitanei* in the North-West Frontier militias, and the Indian troops maintained by the client states were organized in separate units,

[1] See IV. iv. 76.

[2] See V. v. 297–9.

[3] See IV. iv. 76–78 and V. v. 299–302.

[4] For the Westernization of Turkey and the part played in the process by the new Western-model Ottoman Army, see further IX. viii. 234–9.

[5] In the Spanish Indies there was, of course, a considerable Creole population of Spanish blood, descended from the *conquistadores*, and both there and in British India there was a half-caste population (the *mestizos* and the 'Eurasians', latterly renamed 'Anglo-Indians'). But in both empires power and responsibility remained in the hands of thoroughbred West Europeans born and brought up in the European countries of which these two universal states were political dependencies.

each of which was homogeneous in its personnel;[1] the Hindu and Muslim British Indian troops and the Pathans in the mobile regular army (as distinct from sedentary Pathan militiamen) all served together in the same regiments, though not usually in the same companies or squadrons. From A.D. 1849 onwards, when the British Rāj took over the North-West Frontier of the Panjab from the Sikhs and thereby established direct contact with the Pathans, there was a tendency for the ratio of soldiers of transfrontier barbarian origin in the British Indian Army to increase;[2] but down to A.D. 1947, when the British authorities withdrew the last British troops from India and handed over the former British Indian Army to the governments of the Indian Union and Pakistan, this increase in the relative numerical strength of the barbarian contingent in the armed forces of the Rāj had not seemed to be preparing the way for an eventual barbarian domination over India such as had threatened to overtake the Ottoman Empire and had actually overtaken the ʿAbbasid Caliphate and 'the New Empire' of Egypt.

If in British India this danger had been successfully kept at arm's length, the success may have been due to a combination of causes which were all bound up with the special character of the British Rāj. There were no Gurkha or Pathan units in the British Indian Army that were furnished to the British authorities *en bloc*, under national or tribal commanders of their own, by the Gurkha states or the Pathan tribes themselves. The only units that were permitted that degree of corporate individuality and autonomy were the contingents furnished by the Indian client princes, of whose loyalty the British Indian authorities were sure. The Gurkha and Pathan soldiers enrolled in units of the British Indian Army were recruited, not corporately, but individually, and were commanded, not by leaders drawn from their own community, but by British officers. A further safeguard was that the British troops in India, consisting, as they did, exclusively of soldiers born and bred in the United Kingdom, and being segregated, as they were, from their Indian, Pathan, and Gurkha comrades-in-arms in self-contained units of their own, retained their pristine martial qualities from one generation to another—in contrast to their immediate predecessors the Mughals and other earlier alien empire-builders in India, who, by making India their home and by intermarrying with the native inhabitants, had merged themselves in the mighty mass of the Indian people and, in thus losing their alien identity, had forfeited their ascendancy over their Indian subjects. In A.D. 1952, when these former British counterweights to the menace of a barbarian preponderance in a now divided Indian Army had all been removed, the outlook was still obscure, but it was

[1] After A.D. 1858, when the British Crown took over the administration of British India from the British East India Company, there were no units of British troops in India that were not part of the Royal Army of the United Kingdom. Under the Company's régime the Company had maintained an army of its own which had included British as well as Indian units. The Gurkha and British Indian regular units and the Pathan militias were under British command and had a complement of British officers—though they also had non-British commissioned officers of special grades. The forces maintained by the Indian client states were officered by Indians but were uniform with the British Indian Army in their training and equipment.

[2] See II. ii. 128, n. 1.

evident that the Pathans had a brighter prospect of capturing the army of Pakistan, and the Gurkhas of capturing the army of Hindu India, than either of these two barbarian peoples—martial though both of them were—had ever had of capturing the army of the British Rāj.

The success of the British Rāj in India in employing with political impunity the military services of barbarians beyond its pale, as well as those of its own Indian subjects, was emulated by the Manchu restorers of a Far Eastern universal state in China. As we have noticed in another context,[1] Chinese and Mongol battalions were brigaded with Manchu battalions in varying numbers and ratios in the Manchu Power's army corps known as 'banners'. Even when the Manchu Government's domain was still confined to territories lying outside the Great Wall, the Chinese members of the community outnumbered the Manchus and Mongols;[2] and, after their passage of the Wall in A.D. 1644, it was the South Manchurian Chinese contingent in the banners that gave the invaders the man-power requisite for completing the conquest of Intramural China. While the Manchus thus succeeded in enlisting Chinese to help them win and hold China for a Manchu régime, they were no less successful in dealing with the equally delicate problem presented by the Mongols, martial barbarians with memories of a great imperial past of their own and with a tincture of alien culture[3] that made them no less difficult to assimilate than the intensely cultivated Chinese.

The Manchus attacked their Mongol problem from two directions. On the one hand, in the organization of the Mongol battalions of the banners they anticipated the policy of the British military authorities towards the Gurkhas and Pathans by recruiting their Mongol soldiers individually, and not in tribal *blocs*, and by placing them under the command of Manchu officers. On the other hand, they handled the Mongol tribes on the Steppe as the 'Osmanlis had handled the Kurdish tribes in the Zagros Mountains. Without attempting to destroy their tribal organization, they contented themselves with dividing the tribes up into tribal atoms of a minimum size, and with imposing a strict delimitation of the boundaries between their respective pastoral ranges. The Mongol tribes, thus reduced in size and penned within fixed limits, were allowed to remain autonomous under the rule of their own tribal chiefs, while, to save appearances, these Mongol tribal chieftainships were nominally given the status of 'banners', as the Kurdish tribal chieftainships had been officially classified as Ottoman fiefs in the books of the Pādishāh.[4] The political success of this Manchu military organization is attested by the fact that, when the Manchu régime in China was liquidated in A.D. 1911, the revolution was not the work of the Manchus' comrades-in-arms in the Chinese and Mongol battalions of the banners.

The success of the Manchus in China and the British in India in

[1] See pp. 128–9, above.
[2] See Michael, F.: *The Origin of Manchu Rule in China* (Baltimore 1942, Johns Hopkins University Press), p. 71.
[3] See II. ii. 237–8; III. iii. 451; V. v. 309 and 348.
[4] See Michael, op. cit., pp. 96–97. It will be seen that, in post-Diocletianic Roman terminology, these Mongol and Kurdish tribes were *foederati* of the Manchu and the Ottoman Empire respectively.

employing the professional military services of barbarians with political impunity was eclipsed by the Carthaginian architects of a colonial Syriac universal state in the area opened up by Phoenician maritime enterprise in the western basin of the Mediterranean. Though the citizens of Carthage never exempted themselves entirely from serving personally in the field, they did not hesitate, in the heyday of their wealth and power, to enrol Libyans and Iberians—and these not only from among their own subjects, but also from among the untamed barbarians beyond their pale—on a scale which quite dwarfed the Carthaginians' own citizen force. This, on the face of it, perilous policy did, sure enough, bring the Carthaginian Empire, and Carthage herself, to the verge of destruction when, at an hour in which Carthage's prestige was at a low ebb owing to her defeat in the First Romano-Punic War (*gerebatur* 264–241 B.C.), the Carthaginian Government imprudently, though characteristically, exasperated their mercenaries by proposing to interpret their agreed terms of service on lines so niggardly as, in the mercenaries' view, to create a breach of contract. Yet Carthage did succeed in quelling the Great Mutiny of 240–237 B.C.; and this discreditable incident in her military annals apparently did so little permanent damage to her mercenary army's discipline and *moral* that in the next generation the successors of the discomfited mutineers, when led by a captain of genius who inspired them with a personal devotion to himself, all but succeeded in inflicting on Rome the fate that Carthage herself was eventually to suffer at Roman hands.[1]

The Consequences of the Enlistment of Barbarians in the post-Diocletianic Roman Army

The problem which was solved by the Carthaginians in the Western Mediterranean, by the Manchus in China, and by the British in India, but which defeated the Ramsids and the 'Abbasids, overtook the Roman Empire likewise in its post-Diocletianic age.

Though, in all ages, able-bodied adult Roman citizens were legally liable to be called up compulsorily for military service, the standing army of the Principate had in fact been recruited by voluntary enlistment; for, though service in the Army was confined to Roman citizens for the legions and to free Roman subjects for the *auxilia*, to the exclusion of both slaves and aliens, the strength of the Army in that age was a very low percentage of the total man-power available in the two eligible categories. This easy state of affairs was brought to an end once for all by Diocletian's military reforms, involving, as they did, an increase in the strength of the Army by perhaps as much as two-thirds, from about 300,000 men to about 500,000.[2] From that time onwards there was perpetual difficulty in finding suitable recruits in sufficient numbers.[3]

The civil authorities, whose responsibility it was to produce the men

[1] See V. v. 465–6. [2] See p. 323, n. 5, above.

[3] Vegetius complains (probably with reference to conditions in the western provinces of the Empire in the fifth century of the Christian Era) of the difficulty of filling the cadres—especially in the legions, to which the *auxilia* were preferred by recruits (see Vegetius, Book I, chap. 5, and Book II, chap. 3, quoted by Grosse, op. cit., p. 266).

for their military colleagues,[1] dealt with the Roman citizen-body—which, since the *Constitutio Antoniniana* of A.D. 212, embraced nearly the whole of the native-born free population of the Empire[2]—by sifting it, for military purposes, into different categories which received differential treatment ranging between the two extremes of compulsion to serve and prohibition to enlist.[3] In the conscription of agricultural serfs, which was by far the largest reservoir of citizen man-power at the recruiting authorities' disposal, there were elaborate arrangements—unfortunately frustrated to a large extent by fraud, bribery, and pressure—for distributing the burden equitably between province and province and between estate and estate.[4] Conscripted serfs, however, were naturally apt to be of poor martial quality, even if they had been forthcoming in sufficient numbers to cover Diocletian's formidable increase in the Army's strength, and the recruiting authorities therefore looked for an additional source of supply. The ban on the enlistment of slaves was not lifted, and it was still in force in Justinian's day (*imperabat* A.D. 527–65).[5] From Diocletian's reign (*imperabat* A.D. 284–305) onwards, however, all barriers to the recruitment of aliens were removed,[6] and barbarian alien recruits were now the more highly esteemed the more barbarous they were.[7]

For Roman military purposes an unreclaimed barbarian had the double attraction of bringing with him a native martial tradition and of being a volunteer who had not had the edge taken off his zest for military service through being pressed into it,[8] as were the majority of the post-Diocletianic recruits of Roman origin.[9] Even barbarian prisoners-of-war, if distinguished by rank or prowess in their native social environment, were able to bargain with the Roman recruiting authorities, as a condition of enlistment in the Roman Army, that they should start their career as officers;[10] and the number of high officers of barbarian origin in the post-Diocletianic Roman Army indicates either that this privilege of a flying start was frequently secured by barbarian recruits or else that high promotion was frequently earned by men who

[1] See Grosse, R.: *Römische Militärgeschichte von Gallienus bis zum Beginn der Byzantinischen Themenverfassung* (Berlin 1920, Weidman), p. 158. We may conjecture that this task was assigned to the civil authorities in the post-Diocletianic Roman Empire for the reason that led the Government of the United Kingdom, during the World War of A.D. 1939–45, to assign it to the Ministry of Labour and National Service. Whereas the military authorities were bound to think of their own needs first, the civil authorities might be expected to look at the problem of man-power as a whole, and to do their best to keep the Army up to strength with the least possible detriment to civilian services, such as the production of foodstuffs and the manning of the merchant marine, which, on a comprehensive view, might be seen to be not less essential than military defence itself for the welfare, or even for the survival, of the community.

[2] See V. vi. 7, n. 4, and p. 156, above.

[3] See Grosse, op. cit., pp. 202 and 204–6.

[4] See ibid., pp. 210–15.

[5] See ibid., p. 198.

[6] See ibid., p. 200.

[7] See ibid., pp. 200–1.

[8] See ibid., pp. 201–2.

[9] A majority, but not all; for, as late as the sixth century of the Christian Era, in what remained of the Illyrian provinces of the Empire, there was a native Latin-speaking rural population of Roman citizens in which an historic local martial tradition was still sufficiently alive to inspire two Dardanian peasants—the future Emperor Justin I and his brother—to seek their fortunes by coming to Constantinople to enlist (see Grosse, op. cit., p. 203).

[10] See ibid., p. 203.

started as privates.[1] Conversely, the citizen recruit came to be rated so low that in A.D. 440, at a date when, in the West, the Empire was at its last gasp, Roman citizens were freed from all military obligations save for taking part in the manning of city-walls in an emergency.[2]

The increasingly numerous and important barbarian intake into the post-Diocletianic Roman Army was recruited and organized on two systems, each of which had its own disadvantages and dangers. Besides the barbarian soldiers who enlisted individually in Roman military formations, there were national units, commanded by officers of their own nationality, that were furnished to the Roman Army by autonomous barbarian communities with the status of *foederati*.[3] On the face of it, the system of individual enlistment might seem the less hazardous of the two—the more so, in view of the success of the Manchus in China and the British in India in keeping in order the barbarian soldiers whom they enrolled in this way. If the Romans ran into disaster where the British and the Manchus steered clear of it, the explanation of this difference in the outcome perhaps lies in a difference in the extent to which the dilution of regular units with barbarian personnel was carried; and, if, in this delicate matter, the Roman military authorities trespassed beyond the margin of safety, the culprit is to be found in the Emperor Theodosius I (*imperabat* A.D. 378–95).[4] Theodosius tipped the hazardous balance in the post-Diocletianic Roman Army in the barbarians' favour.[5] He drafted them into the Roman regular formations in a ratio so high as to produce a break in the Roman military tradition and discipline.[6] The disastrous consequences are reflected in Vegetius's picture[7] of the Army going to pieces. The troops can no longer be induced to submit to training,[8] drill,[9] or assaults at arms;[10] they are unwilling to carry burdens;[11] they are slack in the performance of their military duty in general;[12] and they are unwilling to undertake the hard labour of fortifying camps.[13] 'The Roman Army had ceased to exist. It had never succumbed to the Germans; it had simply been supplanted by them.'[14]

The Roman Army, and consequently the Roman Empire itself, was thus confronted, by Theodosius's ill-judged abandonment of all restrictions on the admission of barbarian recruits, with the imminent threat of a barbarian ascendancy. This doom was not accepted by the Roman

1 See ibid., p. 196.

2 See ibid., p. 202.

3 Strictly, *foederati dediticii* (see Grosse, op. cit., p. 206), presumably because, since the *Constitutio Antoniniana*, *dediticii* were the only category of inhabitants of the Roman Empire who did not possess the Roman franchise.

4 See Grosse, op. cit., p. 262, n. 2.

5 See Zosimus: Book IV, chaps. xxx and xxxi, cited by Grosse, op. cit., p. 260.

6 The effect, according to Zosimus, chap. xxxi, §§ 1–2, was a dissolution of military discipline and a breakdown of the system of registering effectives—with the result that the professed 'deserters' from barbarian tribes beyond the Roman imperial *limes* who had been registered as serving soldiers in the Roman regular army took to going home, sending substitutes to fill their places, and falling into the ranks again whenever it took their fancy.

7 Cited as evidence by Grosse, op. cit., p. 261.

8 Vegetius: Book I, chaps. 20 and 28. Compare Book I, chap. 26, Book II, chaps. 18 and 24, and many other passages.

9 Ibid.: Book I, chap. 8.

10 Ibid., chaps. 11, 12, and 18.

11 Ibid., chap. 19.

12 Ibid.: Book III, chap. 8.

13 Ibid.: Book I, chap. 21; Book III, chap. 10.

14 Grosse, op. cit., p. 262.

element in the Army without a struggle; but, while the Roman reaction was ubiquitous, the results were quite different in different sections of the Empire. In the East and Centre the untoward effects of Theodosius's error were reversed in the nick of time, while in the West the vantage surrendered by him to the barbarians was not, in the end, retrieved.

In the East the coming conflict was heralded, before Theodosius's death, by a clash at Philadelphia between Egyptian and barbarian troops which was provoked by the barbarians' intolerable treatment of the civilian population and in which the barbarians suffered more than two hundred casualties;[1] but the crucial trial of strength in the East—in which the utter discomfiture of the barbarians made history by producing a permanent parting of the ways between the fortunes of the eastern and western sections of the Empire[2]—came in A.D. 400. In the East in that year there was a general civil war between the Roman and barbarian soldiery in which 35,000 Gothic troops were wiped out;[3] and the victors confirmed and enhanced the effects of their signal triumph by taking advantage of the breathing-space that they had thereby won for themselves in order to introduce effective measures for precluding, in the East, a recurrence of the barbarian peril. In the East the imperial authorities had the courage thenceforward to dispense with a barbarian instrument whose dangerousness had proved greater than its value. Almost all the surviving names of military officers in the East in the records of the next fifteen years are Graeco-Roman;[4] and, though this resolute purge of barbarian military man-power may have had adverse short-term military effects, its long-term political result was that the Empire managed, in the East, to stave off for two centuries longer the final catastrophe that now swiftly descended upon the West.[5]

Before the close of the fifth century of the Christian Era the East had tapped a native source of martial man-power by making serviceable Roman soldiers out of the wild highlanders of the Taurus;[6] and these Isaurian troops showed themselves a match for the barbarians from beyond the pale in the Great Romano-Gothic War of A.D. 537–53.[7] At the same time the Roman military authorities in the East continued to draw recruits from the general population, even in the least warlike of the eastern provinces. In the documents preserved on Egyptian papyri dating from the sixth and seventh centuries, none of the soldiers there mentioned bear barbarian names,[8] and, according to a Modern Western scholar who was an eminent authority on the subject, the first mention of *foederati* serving in Egypt was to be found in the chronicle of John of Nikiû, who lived to record the Arab conquest.[9] By that time

[1] See Zosimus: Book IV, chap. xxx, §§ 4–8, cited by Grosse, op. cit., p. 263.

[2] The historic importance of this event has been pointed out already in IV. iv. 324.

[3] See Grosse, op. cit., p. 264.

[4] See ibid.

[5] See ibid., pp. 264–5.

[6] See IV. iv. 324–5.

[7] In the Modern Western World the Government of the United Kingdom pursued the same policy with similar success when it enrolled the wild highlanders of Scotland in the British Army after their last outbreak in A.D. 1745.

[8] See Grosse, op. cit., p. 277.

[9] The authority for this statement is Grosse, op. cit., p. 281, but the page (p. 531) of Zotenburg's edition of the chronicle of John of Nikiû which he cites as his reference does not exist in Zotenburg's definitive edition: *Chronique de Jean, Evêque de Nikiou*, texte éthiopien publié et traduit par H. Zotenberg (Paris 1883, Imprimerie Nationale),

the *foederati* in the East had been transformed from national contingents furnished by autonomous barbarian communities under native commanders into units of the Roman regular army which were, indeed, still barbarian in their personnel but were of mixed nationality and were under the command of Roman officers.[1] These sixth-century barbarian regulars to whom the name *foederati* now attached were a mobile cavalry force which was the cream of Justinian's army.[2] In fact, by Justinian's day the Roman Army of the East had learnt the secret of how to employ barbarian troops with military profit[3] without political risk. The only non-Romans whom Justinian enrolled were prisoners-of-war[4] or deserters.[5] His barbarian troops were relatively few in numbers, but it was they who won his victories for him.[6]

This Roman military recovery in the East was not reproduced in the West. The anti-barbarian reaction that had started in Constantinople in A.D. 400 did indeed have repercussions on the farther side of the Adriatic. It made its influence felt in the assassination of the Vandal generalissimo Stilicho in A.D. 408 and in the ineptly brutal accompanying massacre of the families of barbarian soldiers, domiciled in Italy, by Roman troops.[7] Moreover, for the next half-century the perilously dictatorial western military office of generalissimo (*magister peditum in praesenti*)[8] was held by five successive incumbents, from Constantius to

and the reference is presumably to the preliminary edition published in the *Journal Asiatique* in 1879. In the French translation accompanying the definitive edition, it is mentioned (p. 421, chap. cvii) that, when Heraclius in Africa revolted against Phocas, he raised mercenary troops from the barbarians of Tripolitania and Pentapolis and that a strong contingent of these was included in the expeditionary force which marched on Egypt under the command of Nicetas. These barbarian mercenaries are mentioned subsequently on three occasions in the chronicler's account of the ensuing military operations in Egypt (pp. 426–7, chap. cvii; p. 428, chap. cviii; p. 431, chap. cix). Again, in the account of the military operations arising out of the invasion of Egypt by the Arabs, there is a reference to 'toutes les troupes d'Égypte et les troupes auxiliaires' (p. 434, chap. cix). If these are the passages that Grosse has in mind, he is presumably taking it for granted that Nicetas' 'barbarians' and Theodore's 'auxiliaries' were *foederati* in the then current technical meaning of the term.

1 See Grosse, op. cit., pp. 280–1.

2 Ibid., pp. 282–3.

3 One index of the re-establishment of discipline in the Roman Army of the East, after the *dégringolade* following the dilution of the Army with barbarians in the reign of Theodosius I, may be found in the survival, in Justinian's day, of the laborious practice of fortifying camps (as described by the 'Anonymus Köchly', chaps. 26–29 (Köchly, H., and Rüstow, W.: *Griechische Kriegschriftsteller*, Zweiter Theil, Zweite Abtheilung, pp. 136–47) cited by Grosse, op. cit., p. 302). As Grosse points out (op. cit., pp. 305–6), this survival of the tradition of camp-making in the Roman Army of the sixth century of the Christian Era is the more noteworthy considering that camp-making was an infantry technique, whereas by this time the principal arm of the Roman Army had long since come to be the cavalry.

4 e.g. Vandals.

5 See Grosse, op. cit., pp. 277–8.

6 See ibid., pp. 279–80.

7 See Zosimus: Book V, chap. xxxv, §§ 7–8, cited by Grosse, op. cit., p. 265.

8 The *magistri militum* of the post-Diocletianic Empire were the commanders of the mobile army (the *Comitatenses*) that Diocletian had called into being. Since the *Comitatenses* were divided into an infantry and a cavalry arm, there was originally a pair of *magistri*—a *magister peditum* and a *magister equitum*—attached to the Emperor, or one pair to each of the emperors at times when the imperial office was in commission. In this college of commanders-in-chief the *magister peditum* ranked senior to his colleague commanding the cavalry (see Grosse, op. cit., p. 183). When an Empire that had been re-united in the hands of Theodosius I was divided again, upon his death, between his sons Arcadius and Honorius, the *magister peditum* at the imperial headquarters (*in praesenti*) in the West came to overshadow his junior colleague the *magister equitum in praesenti* so completely as to become virtually a permanent military dictator within the western emperor's domain (see ibid., pp. 188–9)—a situation which was recognized in

Aëtius inclusive,[1] who were Roman in nationality. When, however, with the accession of Ricimer to the generalissimate in A.D. 456, an army which in the West was still overwhelmingly barbarian in its personnel[2] found itself once more under the supreme command of an all-powerful barbarian war-lord, the fate of the Empire in the West was sealed,[3] and Ricimer's death in A.D. 472 could not prevent his fellow barbarian Odovacer from taking his place and completing his work by making appearances in the West more nearly conform with realities.[4]

The Roman Army's Legacy to the Christian Church

If we now ask ourselves who had been the beneficiaries of the institution of mobile standing armies in universal states, we can answer at once that these military corporations had been apt to make the fortunes of

the practice that grew up of investing him, almost *ex officio*, with the title of *patricius* (see Grosse, op. cit., p. 182).

'This dominance of the office of imperial generalissimo was one of the principal factors in the fall of the West Roman Empire; the German *magister militum* eventually supplanted the Emperor. Ricimer laid the foundations of the German supremacy in Italy and thereby prepared the way for Odovacer's usurpation. Theodoric, in the next chapter of history, was, from the Roman standpoint, simply the East Roman Emperor's *magister militum utriusque militiae* [i.e. area commander, in Italy, of both arms of the mobile branch of the Roman Imperial Army]'—(ibid., p. 190).

This development, which worked itself out in the West with such fatal consequences for the Empire, was avoided in the East thanks to precautions taken there by Theodosius I to prevent the concentration of military authority in a single pair of hands. In the first place the two *magistri praesentales* at Constantinople were given equal and coordinate rank with one another, and the command of the mobile troops of both arms at the eastern imperial headquarters was divided equally between them. In the second place, under the co-ordinate commandership-in-chief of the two eastern *praesentales*, the army groups of *Comitatenses* stationed in the eastern and central provinces were divided between three different area commands—per Orientem, per Thraciam, per Illyricum—under the regional command of three subordinate *magistri equitum* who were styled *magistri utriusque militiae* because they were in command of the infantry as well as the cavalry units of the mobile army within their respective areas (see ibid., pp. 185–6). Since the area command per Orientem was still dangerously large, Justinian reduced its size by carving out of it a fourth eastern area command per Armeniam (see ibid., p. 190). This institution of subordinate area commands *utriusque militiae* was not confined to the East. In the West there was, for example, an area command per Gallias. In the West, however, this decentralization did not avail to curb the power of the senior *magister militum praesentalis*.

Though Zosimus lived to see the western provinces of the Roman Empire overtaken by a disaster from which the central and eastern provinces were saved by Theodosius's precautions, the pagan historian professes (in Book IV, chap. xxvii, §§ 3–5) to see no more in the Christian Emperor's statesmanlike division of commands than a wantonly extravagant inflation of the imperial budget for military salaries.

[1] For the career and the significance of Aëtius, see V. v. 471–2.

[2] See the rhetorical, yet nevertheless revealing, catalogue, given by Sidonius Apollinaris (*Carmen* V, ll. 474–9), of the barbarian peoples represented in the army with which the unhappy emperor Majorian crossed the Alps from Italy into Gaul in A.D. 458.

[3] There were, of course, other, and perhaps more potent, causes of the dissolution of the Roman Empire in the West at this juncture. One underlying cause, from which all the rest derive in some measure, was the general social and economic backwardness and feebleness of the western provinces by comparison with those of the Centre and the East. One symptom of this was an unhealthy concentration of such wealth as there was in the West in the hands of great rural landowners who in the fifth century of the Christian Era virtually escaped the control of the imperial authorities and, in particular, defied the efforts of the inland revenue authorities to collect from them the taxes which they alone had the means to pay. (On this point see Grosse, op. cit., p. 269.)

[4] The conformity achieved was far from being complete, for, though Odovacer did depose the puppet-emperor Romulus Augustulus in whose name he had been ruling Italy, he did not venture to assume authority in his own name by naked right of his *de facto* power, but sought and obtained investiture as the vicegerent, in Italy, of the Imperial Government at Constantinople.

the aliens or barbarians who had been enrolled in them. The latter-day Achaemenids' recruitment of a mobile professional force of Greek mercenaries led to the conquest of the Achaemenian Empire by Alexander and its partition between a number of Macedonian Greek successor-states. The enrolment of barbarians in the bodyguard of the 'Abbasid Caliphs and in the standing armies of the Roman Empire and 'the New Empire' of Egypt led to the establishment of barbarian rule in the dominions of the Caliphate, in the Egyptiac World, and in the western provinces of the Roman Empire. We can also espy cases in which the beneficiary had been an alien secular culture. The Hellenic culture made its entry into the Hittite, Syriac, Egyptiac, Babylonic, and Indic worlds at the heels of thc Macedonian *conquistadores*. The creation of a new army on a Western model in the Russian Empire by Peter the Great, and in the Ottoman Empire by Selīm III and Mahmūd II, led to the progressive Westernization of other sides of Russian and Ottoman life.[1] The enrolment of Italian, Flemish, and West German troops in the Napoleonic army expedited the re-absorption of the debris of a city-state cosmos in Northern Italy, Western Germany, and Flanders, which had differentiated itself from the rest of Western Christendom in the medieval age of Western history,[2] into a Modern Western body social represented by contemporary French society. It is more surprising to see the mantle of an army descending upon the shoulders of a church—and the more so when the recipient of this military inspiration is a church with an anti-military tradition and êthos.

In their conscientious objection to the shedding of blood, and consequently to the performance of military service, the Primitive Christians were at variance with both the Jewish and the Roman tradition.

'In the last resort, the Jew literally drew the sword and forestalled the Messiah. . . . The Christian, on the other hand, was instructed to await the coming of his victorious Christ.'[3]

In striking contrast to the series of Jewish insurrections against first Seleucid and then Roman rule during the three hundred years running from 166 B.C. to A.D. 135,[4] the Christians never once rose in armed revolt against their Roman persecutors during the approximately equal period of time that elapsed between the beginning of Jesus' mission and the conclusion of peace and alliance between the Roman Imperial Government and the Church in A.D. 313.[5] As for service in the Roman Army, this was a stumbling-block for Christians because it involved not only the shedding of blood on active service but also, among other things, the passing and execution of death sentences, the taking of a military oath of unconditional loyalty to the Emperor, the worship of the Emperor's genius and offer of sacrifice to it, and the veneration of military standards as idols.[6] Service in the Army was, in fact, expressly

[1] The penetration of an alien culture through a military door is examined further in IX. viii. 126–53.

[2] See III. iii. 344–7 and V. v. 619–42.

[3] Harnack, A. von: *Militia Christi: Die christliche Religion und der Soldatenstand in den Ersten Drei Jahrhunderten* (Tübingen 1905, Mohr), p. 9.

[4] See V. v. 68.

[5] See Harnack, op. cit., p. 44.

[6] See ibid., p. 46.

declared to be unlawful for Christians by successive Early Christian Fathers—by Origen,[1] by Tertullian,[2] and even by Lactantius in a work published after the conclusion of the Constantinian peace between the Christian Church and the Roman State.[3] In his downright assertion—'We do not march with the Emperor, not even if he presses us'—Origen retrospectively justified Celsus's complaint (of which the record has been preserved by Origen himself) that the Christians refuse to perform military service.[4]

It is significant that this ostracism of the Roman Army by the Christian Church broke down, and this through developments in the position and outlook of the Christian community at a time when the Army of the Principate was still being recruited by voluntary enlistment—indeed, more than a hundred years before the issue was raised on the Roman Government's side through the reintroduction of compulsory military service as a corollary to the expansion of the Army by Diocletian.

Down to about the year A.D. 170, occasions for conflict over this issue were, it would seem, avoided; for down to that time Christian civilians apparently abstained as a matter of course from enlisting in the Army, while, if a pagan serving soldier became a convert, the Church tacitly acquiesced not only in his serving out his term with the colours but in his continuing to perform all acts that the Army expected of him, including those requirements that deterred Christians from enlisting. Possibly the Church justified to herself this laxity on a question of principle on the same ground on which, in this first chapter of her history, she tolerated other social anomalies or enormities in her bosom, such as the continuance of the institution of slavery even when master and slave alike were members of the Christian community. In the Church's expectation in this age, the time remaining before Christ's Second Coming was so short that the Christian soldier-convert might just as well pass it under arms as the Christian slave-convert in bondage.[5]

> 'The incompatibility [of Christian principles] with the State, the social order, public life and the like, first impinged upon the Christians' conscience in its full force when the Christians began to suspect and to recognise that they were going still to have to do with these affairs for quite a long time to come, and were also going to incur their share of responsibility for them.[6]

In the third century of the Christian Era, when the Christians did begin to make their way in rapidly increasing numbers into the politically responsible classes of Roman society—partly by themselves rising in the world, and partly by winning upper-class converts—they answered in practice the question raised for them by the social impor-

[1] *Contra Celsum*, Book VIII, chap. 73 (see Harnack, op. cit., pp. 31, 72, and 104).

[2] See the passages cited by Harnack, op. cit., pp. 58–68, especially those from the *De Coronâ*.

[3] *Institutes*, Book VI, chap. 20, § 16 (see Harnack, op. cit., p. 72).

[4] See Harnack, op. cit., p. 54.

[5] For this possible application of the eschatological outlook on life to the delicate case of the soldier-convert, see Harnack, op. cit., pp. 49–50.

[6] Harnack, op. cit., pp. 50–51. Compare p. 69.

tance of the Roman Army without ever solving it in theory and without waiting for the conversion of the State of which this army was an organ. In Diocletian's army the Christian contingent was already so large, so conspicuous, and so influential that the persecution launched in A.D. 303 was directed against Christianity in the Army in the first instance.[1] The Army was, in fact, the testing ground of the issue between the Imperial Government and the Church.[2] The strength of the Christians in the Army even in the West, where at the opening of the fourth century the percentage of Christians in the population was very much lower than in the contemporary East, is indicated by Constantine's manifesto in the Church's favour in A.D. 312, on the eve of the critical battle at the Milvian Bridge.[3] The future pioneer of Christian monachism, the Egyptian Pachomius, was converted to Christianity as a soldier in the expeditionary force with which Constantine was then marching against Maxentius.[4] The completeness of the eventual identification of Church and Army in an age when the names 'Christian' and 'Roman' had become virtually synonymous is symbolized in the record that, when, in the fifth century, the flood of barbarian invasion finally engulfed the Upper Danubian *limes*, and the last unit of local *limitanei* dissolved, their commanding officer found alternative service as a bishop.[5]

Still more significant than this breakdown of the Christian Church's original boycott of the Roman Army is the influence of the Army on the Church in the age in which the ban was still in force.

> ' "War" is one of the fundamental forms of Life, and there are inalienable virtues that find their highest, or at any rate their symbolic, expression in the warrior. . . . Accordingly, no higher religion can do without imagery derived from war, or, in consequence, do without "warriors" [of its own].'[6]

In the Jewish tradition, which the Christian Church had retained as a treasured part of its own heritage when it had parted company with Judaism, war was consecrated both in the literal sense as an indispensable means of realizing the messianic hope and in a symbolic sense in the metaphorical language of the authors of the Books of the Prophets and the Psalms;[7] and, though the Church dropped the literal application, she retained the symbol.[8] While, however, the Jewish martial tradition was thus a potent literary influence on the life of the Primitive Christian Church, the Roman martial tradition presented itself to Christians as a living and impressive reality. Baneful and hateful though the Roman Army of the Republic had been to the population of the Hellenic World in the cruel age of the Roman conquests and the still more cruel age of the ensuing Roman civil wars, the Roman Army of the Principate, which lived on its pay instead of lining its pockets by looting,

1 See Harnack, op. cit., p. 80.
2 See ibid., p. 82.
3 This point is made by Harnack, op. cit., pp. 86–87.
4 See Harnack, op. cit., p. 85.
5 Eugippius: *Vita Sancti Severini*, chap. iv, § 2, and chap. xx, § 1, cited by Grosse, op. cit., pp. 269–70.
6 Harnack, op. cit., p. 2.
7 See ibid., pp. 8–9.
8 This abandonment, by the Christian Church, of Jewry's literal militancy was perhaps originally sub-conscious, or at any rate tacit. Origen, however, frankly admitted a change of principle, on this point, as between the New Testament dispensation and the Old (see Harnack, op. cit., pp. 26–27 and 72).

and which was stationed on the frontiers, to defend Civilization against the barbarians, instead of infesting and devastating the civilized interior, came to win the involuntary respect, admiration, and even affection of Rome's subjects, as an oecumenical institution that ministered to their welfare and that was a legitimate object for their pride.

'Let us observe', wrote Clement of Rome, about the year A.D. 95, in his First Epistle to the Corinthians,[1] 'the conduct of the soldiers who serve our rulers. Think of the orderliness, the pliancy, the submissiveness with which they carry out their orders. Not all of them are legates or tribunes or centurions or options or officers of the grades below these. But each serving soldier in his own unit carries out the commands of the Emperor and the Government.'

In thus commending the discipline of the contemporary Roman Army as an exemplar for his Christian correspondents, Clement was seeking to establish a rule of organization for the Church. Obedience, he was saying, is due from Christians, not only to God, but to their ecclesiastical superiors. '*All* Christians are soldiers; but, just for that reason, they have to obey their leaders the presbyters.'[2] This equation of 'soldier of God' with 'member of the Church' would have seemed a matter of course to Mithraists; for, of the seven grades of initiation in the Mithraic Church, the third from the bottom was *miles*, and it is probable that most initiates never rose higher than that level.[3] In the evolution of the Christian Church's military imagery, however, the original equation of 'soldier' had been not with 'convert' but with 'missionary'; and from this equation its author, Saint Paul, had drawn two inferences: the missionary must disencumber himself from the impedimenta of civilian life, and the missionary has the same claim to be supported by his flock as the soldier has to receive his pay out of the contributions of the tax-payer.[4]

'The two military axioms that were adopted by the Christian community in its earliest phase—that the Christian missionary and teacher should receive his maintenance from others, and that on the other hand he should not entangle himself in civilian business life—are in a relation of polarity to one another and just on that account already contain in themselves the germs of a whole hierarchical system.'[5]

Yet, whatever influence the Roman Army may have had on the development of the Church's institutions, the Church owed more in that sphere to the influence of the Roman civil service,[6] and the Army's example produced its principal effect on the life of the Church in the more elusive but more intimate realm of ideas and ideals. The Roman military imagery that was introduced into the Christian Church's terminology by Saint Paul, and that was adopted and developed by Clement of Rome, was extended by Saint Ignatius, whose letters, written early in the second century of the Christian Era in Greek, bristle

[1] Chap. 37.
[2] Harnack, op. cit., pp. 18–19.
[3] See ibid., pp. 37–8.
[4] See ibid., pp. 14–16, citing 1 Tim. i. 18 and 2 Tim. ii. 3.
[5] Harnack, op. cit., p. 17. Compare pp. 17–18.
[6] See pp. 191–3, above, and pp. 369–70, below.

with transliterated Latin military technical terms.[1] Tertullian (*vivebat circa* A.D. 155–222), who was the son of an army officer, worked out the simile of the *militia Christi* consistently and thoroughly,[2] and in this he was followed up by his North-West African compatriot Saint Cyprian.[3]

The Christian initiation-rite of baptism is equated by Cyprian with the military oath (*sacramentum*) required of the recruit upon his enrolment in the Roman Army.[4] Once enrolled, the Christian soldier must wage his warfare 'in accordance with the regulations' (*νομίμως*).[5] He must eschew the unpardonable offence of desertion,[6] and likewise the grave misdemeanour of dereliction of duty.[7] 'The pay of delinquency is death', as Tertullian translates the phrase in Saint Paul's Epistle to the Romans[8] which appears as 'the wages of sin' in the Authorized English Version of the Bible. The ritual and moral obligations of the Christian life are equated by Tertullian with military fatigues. In his terminology a fast is a stint of sentry-go (*statio*),[9] and the Christian duty which is declared in the Gospel according to Saint Matthew to be so well within the compass of human powers is 'the Lord's light pack' (*levem sarcinam Domini*).[10] Moreover, the Christian soldier's faithful performance of his duty is duly recompensed. If 'the pay of sin is death', it must be reckoned on the other side of the account between the spiritual soldier and his heavenly paymaster that 'God's gratuity is life' (*donativum autem Dei vita*).[11] And, short of receiving a gratuity, the soldier can look forward to drawing his rations so long as he gives satisfaction to the master with whom he has taken service.[12] 'Your deposits [of deferred pay] are your works, [and you bank them] in order that you may [eventually] draw your receipts on an appropriate scale.'[13] The Cross is a military standard (*σύσσημον*) which Jesus has raised to inspire his troops.[14] The Christian soldier's general (*imperator*) is Christ,[15] and the soldier must never forget that he is under his general's eye.[16] Thus inspired, led, and disciplined, Christ's army can challenge comparison with Caesar's. If Christians are civilians (*pagani*) from the standpoint of Caesar's army, so are Caesar's

1 See Harnack, op. cit., pp. 19–20.

2 See ibid., pp. 32–33 and 35.

3 See ibid., p. 41.

4 See ibid.

5 2 Tim. ii. 3–5, cited by Harnack, op. cit., p. 17.

6 *Ποῖος δὲ κόσμος δέξεταί τινα τῶν αὐτομολούντων ἀπ' αὐτοῦ;* (1 Clem. ad. Cor., chap. 28). *Μήτις ὑμῶν δεσέρτωρ εὑρεθῇ* (Ignatius ad. Polycarpum, chap. 6). These passages are printed in Harnack, op. cit., pp. 94–95.

7 *Δικαῖον οὖν ἐστὶν μὴ λιποτακτεῖν ἡμᾶς ἀπὸ τοῦ θελήματος αὐτοῦ* (1 Clem. ad. Cor., chap. 21, printed in Harnack, op. cit., p. 94).

8 Rom. vi. 23.

9 See Harnack, op. cit., pp. 35–36.

10 Matt. xi. 30, as translated into Latin by Tertullian: *De Monogamiâ*, chap. 2 (Harnack, op. cit., p. 36).

11 Rom. vi. 23, as translated into Latin by Tertullian.

12 *Ἀρέσκετε ᾧ στρατεύεσθε, ἀφ' οὗ καὶ τὰ ὀψώνια κομίζεσθε* (Ignatius *Ad Polycarpum*, chap. 6, printed in Harnack, op. cit., p. 95).

13 *Τὰ δεπόσιτα ὑμῶν τὰ ἔργα ὑμῶν, ἵνα τὰ ἄκκεπτα ὑμῶν ἄξια κομίσησθε* (Ignatius, op. cit., loc. cit.).

14 Ignatius *Ad Smyrnaeos*, chap. i, cited by Harnack, op. cit., p. 20. (N.B. This phrase occurs in the Septuagint Greek translation of Isaiah v. 26 and xlix. 22, and it therefore seems more likely that Ignatius is here quoting from the Septuagint than that he is employing a Roman military term current in his own day.—A.J.T.)

15 Cyprian (see Harnack, op. cit., p. 41).

16 'Spectat militem suum Christus' (Cyprian, Ep. lviii, ch. 4, cited by Harnack, op. cit., p. 42).

soldiers from the standpoint of Christ's.[1] Justin Martyr (*florebat circa* A.D. 150) goes so far as to claim that the Christians' devotion to their service is greater than the Army's is to theirs.[2]

With a great Modern Western scholar's aid, enough evidence has now been cited to show that the Roman Army's impress on the Christian Church had cut deep. The mark that it had made had been enduring; and, in virtue of it, a mundane military organization which had finally lost its own identity in wars to the death with Persian and Arab adversaries in the seventh century of the Christian Era was still a living force in the World in A.D. 1952.

2. *Civil Services*

The Difficulty of Creating a Professional Civil Service

The variety which our survey of imperial standing armies has brought to light in the degree of development of the institutional organization of the universal states in our catalogue makes itself apparent again when we pass to the consideration of imperial civil services.

These vary, in degree of development, between two extremes illustrated by the Achaemenian Empire at the lower end of the scale and by the Ottoman Empire at the upper end. The Achaemenian professional civil service always remained rudimentary. Its most important representatives were the imperial secretaries who were resident at the headquarters of the provincial governors but were independent of the satraps and reported directly to the Central Government. As a further check, the satraps were also kept under observation by itinerant inspectors, expressively nicknamed 'the Emperor's eyes'.[3] The need for a central authority to gather together, hold, and manipulate these widely ramifying threads of administrative control seems to have been met, in the organization of the Imperial Court, by the evolution of an officer who was known in Old Persian as 'the Hazarapatiš' and in Greek as 'the Chiliarch', because he had begun by being simply the commander of an inner imperial bodyguard of one thousand men, into an Imperial Chancellor or Minister of State performing some, at any rate, of the functions that, in the Roman Empire, through a parallel process of evolution, came to be performed by the commandant of the Emperor's praetorian guards (*praefectus praetorio*).[4] While the Achae-

[1] Tertullian: *De Coronâ, passim,* cited by Harnack, op. cit., pp. 68–9, who points out that *paganus* is likewise used in the sense of 'civilian' in *Digest,* XLIX. xix. 14.

[2] See Harnack, op. cit., p. 21.

[3] The Achaemenian network of imperial communications, which made this system of inspection a practical possibility, has been noticed on p. 82, above.

[4] See p. 182, n. 3, and p. 183, above, and Junge, P. J.: 'Hazarapatiš: Zur Stellung des Chiliarchen der königlichen Leibgarde im Achämenidenstaat', in *Klio,* vol. xxxiii (Neue Folge, vol. xv) (Leipzig 1940, Dietrich), pp. 13–38. The Hazarapatiš could not have performed his duties without being served by a skilful, organized, and numerous administrative and clerical staff. The scale of his Chancery is indicated by the quantity of the imperial archives. By A.D. 1940 no less than 30,000 clay tablets, inscribed in the Elamite language, had been discovered at Persepolis alone by Modern Western archaeologists (see Junge, op. cit., p. 14, n. 2), and the collection at Susa, the principal seat of the Achaemenian imperial administration, must have been far larger (see ibid., p. 30, n. 3). These bulky, heavy, and brittle records on clay, together with the staff whose duty it was to keep them up to date and to consult them for administrative purposes, must have

menian civil service never developed beyond this point,[1] the Ottoman Government provided for its corresponding administrative needs by doing everything that human ingenuity could devise, and human determination accomplish, to produce a civil service that was to be no mere professional fraternity but a secular equivalent of a religious order, so rigorously segregated, austerely disciplined, and potently 'conditioned' as to be transfigured into a super-human, or sub-human, race —as different from the ordinary run of human kind as a thoroughbred and broken-in horse, hound, or hawk is from the wild life that has been the breeder's and trainer's raw material.[2]

At divers points between these two extremes we may place the professional civil services that were taken over by the Umayyad Caliphate from the Roman and Sasanian empires and by the Manchus from the Ming; those that were inherited from the pre-imperial past of the empire-building state by the Ts'in Empire in the Sinic World, the Mongol Empire in the Far Eastern World, and the Spanish Empire of the Indies; those that were modelled in the British Rāj in India, in the Napoleonic Empire, and in the Danubian Hapsburg Monarchy on home-grown institutions of the metropolitan countries that were themselves new creations; those that were worked out more or less *ab initio* in the Han Empire, the Roman Empire, and 'the Middle Empire' of Egypt; and those that, like the professional civil service of the Petrine Russian Empire, were fashioned on a last of an alien mould.

The Taking Over of an Existing Civil Service by a Barbarian Conqueror

The taking over of the existing civil service of a conquered polity is an expedient that almost forces itself upon empire-builders when these are barbarians who have won their empire by a sudden stroke and when the conquered polity itself has been a universal state whose imperial civil service has still been a going concern at the time of the conquest. Yet, though, in this situation, the main lines of action may be dictated by circumstances, there will still be some room for the free play of statesmanship. The barbarian empire-builders may be more or less receptive, and the subjugated civil servants more or less pliant; and it is a question of judgment how far the conquering ex-barbarian imperial

remained, year in and year out, in the administrative centre, whichever one it might be, where they had originally been inscribed and deposited; they cannot have accompanied the Emperor and his Court on their seasonal migration between Susa, Babylon, and Ecbatana, or on their occasional state visits to Persepolis (see pp. 205–7, above). Junge conjectures (ibid., p. 33 and p. 34, n. 4) that, besides being responsible for the Imperial Chancery, the Hazarapatiš was invested with the command over the imperial garrisons in the provinces.

[1] The differentiation from one another of the Imperial Household, the Imperial Treasury, and the Imperial Chancery, which was a feature of the subsequent Sasanian régime, was still unknown to the Achaemenidae (see Junge, op. cit., p. 30, n. 4). The Emperor's Bow-Bearer and Lance-Bearer served, no doubt, as his adjutants (see ibid., p. 22), and perhaps as his private secretaries. The post of Cup-Bearer, which came to be frequently, and in the end perhaps exclusively, held by eunuchs, seems to have carried with it the comptrollership of the Corps of Pages and of the whole personnel of the Household (see ibid., pp. 19–21). The Book of Nehemiah indicates how well placed the Cup-Bearer was for winning the Emperor's ear, and there seems to have been a tendency for him to gain in power at the Hazarapatiš's expense (see Junge, ibid., p. 37).

[2] For the ideal inspiring the creation of the Ottoman Pādishāh's Slave-Household, see the passage quoted from Lybyer in III. iii. 32–34.

people is to resign itself to taking over the conquered ex-imperial civil service lock, stock, and barrel as a permanent solution for its own problem of having to administer an empire, and how far it shall venture to reject or modify the institution that has so providentially fallen into its hands, for the sake of trying to preserve at any rate the more valuable elements in its own native communal tradition and êthos.

The Umayyad princes, on whom the sweeping conquests of the Primitive Muslim Arabs had conferred an unexpected dominion over ex-Roman and ex-Sasanian territories, compelled their Christian and Zoroastrian civil servants in the third generation to substitute Arabic for Greek, Coptic, and Pehlevi as the official language of the public records,[1] without attempting to take over the business of administration themselves; and, though under the ensuing ʿAbbasid régime—especially from the ninth century of the Christian Era onwards, when the ʿAbbasid Caliphate was declining towards its fall—the process of conversion to Islam became a landslide which carried into the Islamic fold a majority of the population of the Caliphate of all classes and occupations, the residual unconverted Christian minority continued to play a part in the civil service, and especially in the revenue administration, that was out of proportion to its eventual numbers.

In the less abrupt course of the establishment of the Manchu Empire over China, the reciprocal relations of Manchu and Chinese administrative institutions came to be adjusted more subtly.

In the Manchu polity a Chinese-inspired bureaucracy had already prevailed over both the original clan system and the subsequently engrafted feudal system, that had been the Manchus' own communal heritage, in the organization of the Manchu 'banners'[2] that had been created in A.D. 1601, forty-three years before the Manchus had embarked on the conquest of Intramural China.[3] To staff a bureaucratic administration of their newly established banners, the Manchu Central Government commandeered Chinese scholar-serfs from the Manchu feudal lords,[4] and, if a new element had not entered into the situation thereafter, the Manchu Power might have followed independently the path that the Ottoman Power took when it provided for the government of its empire by building up the Pādishāh's Slave-Household. In the history of the Manchu Empire, however, this embryonic servile civil service never came to maturity; for the Manchu empire-builders soon came to recognize the expediency, and indeed necessity, of taking Chinese civil servants into the Manchu service as free men enjoying the status that was traditionally theirs under an indigenous Chinese régime.[5]

[1] See p. 242, n. 3, above. [2] See p. 129, above.

[3] See Michael, F.: *The Origin of Manchu Rule in China* (Baltimore 1942, Johns Hopkins University Press), pp. 61 and 64. [4] See Michael, op. cit., pp. 58 and 68.

[5] See ibid., p. 68. While the Manchus took the Chinese into their service on these generous terms at an early date and of their own free choice, the 'Osmanlis did not take the corresponding step of employing Greeks as freemen, unconverted to Islam, until they were constrained by the breakdown of the Pādishāh's Slave-Household and by a turn in the tide of war, in favour of the Western Christian Powers, which for the first time made the Ottoman Government feel the need for diplomacy and consequently appreciate the qualifications of their Greek Christian *raʿīyeh* for negotiating with Western diplomats on their Ottoman masters' behalf (see II. ii. 223–5; III. iii. 47–48; and V. vi. 299).

The epoch-making event that produced this change in the Manchus' attitude and policy towards Chinese litterati was the desertion in A.D. 1618, from the Ming to the Manchu service, of Li Yung-fang, the Chinese commandant of Fushun, a strategic point just inside the Great Wall at its eastern extremity on the coast of the Gulf of Chihli. The possibility of Li's adhesion to their cause promised the Manchus so important an advantage that they offered him admission to their service on terms of equality. He accepted the offer, and this bargain created a precedent by which Li's compatriots benefited from that time onwards.[1] In fact, 'the Chinese forced their standards on the invader'.[2] In A.D. 1631, thirteen years before the Manchus' passage of the Great Wall, a conference of Manchu feudal lords and high officials decided in favour of adopting the traditional Chinese bureaucratic organization for the central government;[3] and the Manchu administrative system was duly Sinified by Prince Dorgon, the son of the founder of the Manchu Power, Nurhachi (*regnabat* A.D. 1618–25), and the younger brother of Nurhachi's successor T'ai Tsung (*regnabat* A.D. 1625–43).[4]

'Feudalism had given the Manchus their first integrating power. The acceptance of bureaucracy in the banner and central administration made them a state. It was the Chinese system, Chinese officials and Chinese ideas that enabled the Manchus to conquer China.'[5]

The tottering Ming régime was given its *coup de grâce*, not by the Sinified Manchu Power beyond the Great Wall which was to succeed, in the event, to the fallen Ming régime's heritage, but by a rebel who had raised his horn in the interior of China. As against the Manchus, Li Tse-chêng, after occupying Peking, had the double advantage of being in possession and being Chinese. In the revolutionary breaks in the history of the Chinese state, native Chinese rebels, no less than barbarian invaders, had found themselves unable to gain possession of the Empire without the use of force,[6] and for this reason the aspirants to supreme power in times of anarchy, whether barbarians or Chinese, had usually been men who had little to lose and who had had to fight to hold even what they had.[7] Li Tse-chêng, the extinguisher of the Ming, conformed to the historic type of successful Chinese rebel in being an illiterate proletarian. On the other hand, the *ci-devant* barbarian Manchus were by this time in the second generation of Sinification and, in the process, had become men of substance with something to lose and therefore with a motive for hesitating to put their fortunes to the touch by playing for the greater but more hazardous prize of oecumenical dominion.[8]

In the circumstances, that prize might have remained in the bandit Li Tse-chêng's hands if the issue had depended on him and the

1 See Michael, op. cit., pp. 69–72.

2 Ibid., p. 75. As has been noticed in III. iii. 31, n. 1, Chinese litterati at the Manchu Court were styled 'officials' (*ch'en*), whereas Manchu officials were styled 'slaves' (*nu*). This distinction of nomenclature lasted down to the fall of the Manchu régime in A.D. 1911 (see ibid.).

3 See ibid., pp. 76–77.

4 See ibid., pp. 78 and 92–93.

5 Ibid., p. 79.

6 See ibid., p. 9.

7 See ibid., p. 41.

8 The Manchu Government had even waited till A.D. 1636 to repudiate the suzerainty of the moribund Ming over their extramural principality (Michael, op. cit., pp. 100 and 103).

Manchus alone. In the history of the antecedent Sinic Civilization, Liu Pang had become the founder of the Han Dynasty through a very similar career. In the crisis of A.D. 1644, however, the issue was decided otherwise by the suffrages of a third party. The Chinese civil service, and the scholar-gentry from whose ranks they were drawn, could not stomach the illiterate usurper, while they felt that there was a future for them under an ex-barbarian Power which had already given practical proof of its esteem for the Confucian culture by Sinifying itself of its own accord.[1] The Manchus crossed the Great Wall with at least the hint of a mandate to make the Empire safe for the Chinese scholar-gentry against the barbarian from within; and, though there proved to be nationalist-minded elements in the South of China which refused to recognize the Manchus' cultural mission and which remained unreconciled to the Manchu domination to the end of the story, the unenthusiastic yet efficacious support of the Chinese cultivated class enabled the Manchus to make themselves masters of China and to hold their prize for more than a quarter of a millennium.

'The Manchu State was growing in the Chinese World at the edge of the Chinese Empire. Its development can only be understood in its relationship to the Chinese Empire, as it was—though a conquering force—still a part of China all the time.'[2]

At the same time the Manchus did not become Chinese altogether without reservations. While they adopted the Confucian philosophy and educated their young men in it, they interpreted Confucian virtue in military terms[3] that would have been more acceptable to the Sinic hereditary feudal nobility of Confucius's day than to Confucius himself or to the latter-day *chün tze* of the Han Age who bore the by then extinct feudal class's historic name, while teaching and practising what they believed to be Confucius's philosophy.[4] T'ai Tsung warned his Manchus against assimilation to the Chinese civilian way of life.[5] 'The banners had at first been the Manchu state. Now'—as a consequence of the Manchu Power's momentous act of taking over the Chinese State as a going concern under the administration of the established Chinese professional civil service—the banners 'became a state within a State'.[6] In this equivocal position they did, however, maintain their existence and retain their identity till the Manchu régime in China fell, in its turn, in A.D. 1911.

Experiments in Recruiting a Civil Service from an Existing Aristocracy

The Manchus and the Primitive Muslim Arabs were exceptional among empire-builders in the scantiness of the indigenous cultural and institutional heritage that they brought with them. Most of their peers had come into the saddle better equipped, and, in addressing themselves to the unfamiliar and formidable task of governing an empire, they had naturally been apt to turn to account as far as possible, for

1 See Michael, op. cit., pp. 113–14.
2 Ibid., p. 99.
3 See ibid., pp. 104–6.
4 See pp. 355–6, below.
5 See Michael, op. cit., p. 107.
6 Ibid., p. 118.

this new purpose, the social heritage of the pre-imperial age of their own national history.

The Manchus themselves, as we have seen, had developed the rudiments of a tribal and feudal aristocracy before they embraced the Confucian culture and virtually put themselves in the hands of the Chinese civil service as the price of their acquisition of the Chinese Empire. Longer-established national aristocracies were in existence, by the time of their accession to oecumenical power, among the Persian henchmen of the Achaemenidae and among their Macedonian supplanters; among the clansmen of the Inca Emperors and among their Spanish supplanters; and in the hereditary dominions of the Hapsburg founders of the Danubian Monarchy. There was an incapable aristocracy in Muscovy at the time when Peter the Great took her Westernization in hand, and a highly capable one in the Roman Republic at the date of the foundation of the Principate.

In each of these cases the aristocracy descending from a previous age was drawn upon by the founder or reorganizer of a universal state as material for the building of an oecumenical administrative structure. The motives prompting an identical policy were, however, widely diverse. While Peter the Great tried to dragoon the old-fashioned Muscovite nobility into becoming the cultivated, efficient, and industrious administrators in the contemporary Western style whom he needed urgently in large numbers, Augustus took the politically experienced Roman Senatorial Order into a cautiously regulated partnership with his own new dictatorial régime, not so much because he needed or desired their collaboration as because he judged this policy of appeasement to be a prudent measure of insurance against suffering his adoptive father's fate at the hands of an old governing class whose thirst for power was still unsatiated, and because he realized that, in spite of their shameful and notorious betrayal of their trust during the last 150 years of their government of the Roman body politic, the Senatorial Order had not yet exhausted the credit of an accumulated prestige.

These antithetical problems that confronted respectively Augustus and Peter the Great are the horns of a dilemma that is apt to catch the architect of a universal state who finds himself with an imperial people's pre-imperial aristocracy on his hands. If the aristocracy is capable and experienced, it will probably be resentful of the change in its fortunes that has left it no opening, except the unpalatable service of a dictator, for still exercising those administrative capacities which it has developed through having been in power on its own account before losing its old political supremacy to its new master. Conversely, if the aristocracy is easy-going, the dictator who seeks to make use of its services will probably find that the innocuousness of his tool is offset by the bluntness of its edge. After Peter the Great's attempt to turn Muscovite nobles into Western-style administrators had been tried for two generations,[1] the Petrine Imperial Government gave it up as a bad

[1] Peter and his successors tried to use the Russian nobility in the provincial, as well as the central, administration by enrolling them in colleges of Landrats modelled on those

job[1] and granted the hereditary nobility a conditional exemption from public service in A.D. 1762.[2] On the other hand, Augustus, who was as anxious to dispense with his *viri senatorii* as Peter was to make use of his *boyars*, had to be content with making them ineligible for the single governorship of Egypt (a province that was a personal conquest of his own, and whose resources were so extensive and so efficiently concentrated in government hands that no Roman emperor could afford to see a Roman senator in control of them). The best part of three centuries was to pass before Augustus's successor Gallienus (*imperabat* A.D. 260–8) could venture, in the equalitarian revolutionary atmosphere of the third century of the Christian Era,[3] to set about excluding the senatorial class systematically from key positions of public responsibility and power; and, even then, nearly half a century elapsed before Gallienus's work was completed by Diocletian (*imperabat* A.D. 284–305).[4]

Among the other national aristocracies, mentioned above, whose fortune it was to be called upon to share in the administration of a universal state, the Macedonian, like the Roman, nobility was competent but recalcitrant. In the generation of anarchy in Macedon preceding the accession of Philip II these spirited and turbulent Macedonian rural barons had enjoyed as great a licence as the Polish nobility in the age preceding the Partition of A.D. 1772, and they fiercely resented being called upon to become the devoted humble servants, *more Persico*, of a once constitutional king of their own blood who had formerly been proud to recognize them as his social peers (ἑταῖροι). They rebelled against this demand even when it was made of them by a legitimate king of the Argead line who had won a position of unique eminence by overthrowing and supplanting the last Achaemenid. Still less willing were the Macedonian nobility to serve a despotic master when their lawful King Alexander was replaced by a batch of noble-born usurpers of the royal title, in whose shoes any other Macedonian noble military adventurer might have found himself standing if the luck of the game, in the scramble for power after Alexander's death, had happened to come his way instead of playing into the hands of his peers the Ptolemies, Antigoni, and Seleuci. In these psychological circumstances it was no wonder that the Seleucids and the Ptolemies had to look for ministers and administrators for their successor-states among the adaptable

that were a going concern in the Baltic Provinces that Peter had conquered from Sweden (see Brückner, A.: *Peter der Grosse* (Berlin 1879, Grote), p. 505).

[1] Peter found himself constrained, by an effective passive resistance, to revoke, after a two years' trial, his edict of A.D. 1714, ordering all landowners and civil servants to send their children, between the ages of ten and fifteen, to his newly founded secular elementary schools. Peter vainly tried to enforce this edict by making a school-leaving certificate a pre-requisite—in the case of all persons subject to the edict—for a licence to marry (see Sumner, B. H.: *Peter the Great and the Emergence of Russia* (London 1950, English Universities Press), p. 153, and the present Study, III. iii. 282, n. 2). A would-be bridegroom had to satisfy the examiners in arithmetic, geometry, and navigation (see Mettig, op. cit., p. 412).

[2] See Mettig, C.: *Die Europäisierung Russlands im Achtzehnten Jahrhundert* (Gotha 1913, Perthes), p. 413; Sumner, op. cit., pp. 197–8.

[3] For this revolutionary movement and its triumph, see pp. 152–8, above.

[4] See Grosse, R.: *Römische Militärgeschichte von Gallienus bis zum Beginn der Byzantinischen Themenverfassung* (Berlin 1920, Weidmann), pp. 4–9. Between Augustus's day and Gallienus's, Septimius Severus (*imperabat* A.D. 193–211) had followed the precedent set by Augustus in Egypt when he enlarged the Roman Empire by adding the new

citizens of the city-states of the Hellenic World rather than among their intractable fellow noblemen from Hellas' Macedonian march.

By contrast, the grandees of Spain were ready enough to serve the Spanish Crown as viceroys and captains-general of the kingdoms of the Indies, even though the crown was worn by foreign Hapsburg and Bourbon heads, while, in the Danubian dominions of the eastern branch of the House of Hapsburg, the nobility of the dynasty's Austrian hereditary dominions was likewise willing to serve an Imperial-Royal-Archiducal master in the task of attempting to knit into a unity the congeries of kingdoms and lands which had been shaken into the lap of the *Caesarea Maiestas* by the shock of the Ottoman victory at Mohacz in A.D. 1526.[1] These Austrian and Spanish aristocrats, however, were as sluggish as they were loyal. In fine, of all the aristocracies to whom Fortune had offered an opportunity for distinguishing themselves by sharing in the administration of a universal state, the Persian *megistânes* and the Inca *orejones* alone had risen to the occasion—and, in rising to it, had redeemed the credit of their caste by acquitting themselves so well that, in the hour of their defeat and humiliation, they extorted a posthumous tribute of praise from the mouths of the very adversaries who had beaten and supplanted them.[2]

Experiments in Recruiting a Civil Service from Novi Homines

Such pre-imperial aristocracies were the principal, but not the only, national administrative material that empire-builders had brought with them for setting about their oecumenical task. The blue-blooded viceroys whom the Spanish Crown sent out to New Spain and Peru would hardly have succeeded in turning the offspring of the unmanageable *conquistadores* into governable Creoles if they had not had the assistance of middle-class lawyers whose natural ability was fortified by a professional training and tradition. As for the Mongols, they would assuredly have failed to retain, even for one lifetime, their hold on China, Russia, Iran, and 'Irāq if they had not had the good sense to enlist the secretarial services of Nestorian Christian Uighurs whom they took over from their Karāyit and Naiman predecessors in the hegemony of the High Steppe.[3] But the most formidably—though, as it turned out, fatally—well equipped of all empire-builders was Ts'in She Hwang-ti.[4]

While the six rival contending states that succumbed to the last king of Ts'in and first emperor of a Sinic universal state were still living under the traditional feudal régime of the Chóu dispensation, the corresponding régime in the State of Ts'in had been liquidated by the revolutionary reforms of the Lord of Shang nearly a hundred years before the future First Emperor's accession to the parochial throne of

province of Mesopotamia and enlarged the Roman Army by adding the three new *Legiones Parthicae*. Members of the Senatorial Order were disqualified from holding either the governorship of Mesopotamia or any of these three new legionary commands (see Grosse, op. cit., p. 4).

[1] The Danubian Hapsburg Monarchy was created and kept in being by Ottoman military pressure, as has been noticed in II. ii. 177–88.

[2] See V. v. 50–52.

[3] See II. ii. 237–8; III. iii. 451; V. v. 309 and 348.

[4] See pp. 169–74, above.

Ts'in in 246 B.C.[1] as King Chêng. In place of the liquidated aristocracy of Ts'in the reformer had installed a professional bureaucracy, and the concentration of power in the royal government's hands as a result of this drastic administrative reorganization was the secret of Ts'in's subsequent advance from strength to strength which culminated in King Chêng's feat of overthrowing all his competitors and thereby making himself master of the entire Sinic World in 230–221 B.C. The cause of Ts'in's dramatic triumph was, however, likewise the cause of the equally dramatic reversal of her fortunes on the morrow of the First Ts'in Emperor's death.

The unimaginatively revolutionary-minded conqueror had committed the fatal blunder of trying to hold his conquests by the use of the same instrument that had won them. Not content with subduing and annexing the six rival states, he deposed their feudal aristocracy as well as their royal houses, and put their administration in the hands of bureaucrats from his own hereditary kingdom of Ts'in, without realizing that he was imposing on his victims a sharper affliction than they could bear. Even in Ts'in a century back, Lord Shang might have failed to carry through his revolution at the local aristocracy's expense if Ts'in had not been a rude and backward march-state where tradition had less strong a hold than in more mellow countries nearer the heart of the Sinic World. The abrupt imposition of the rule of the bureaucracy of Ts'in upon the people of these other countries a hundred years later brought the loss of their independence home to them in a direct personal way. It was a misfortune for the ambitions of Ts'in She Hwang-ti that, owing to Lord Shang's revolutionary service to his royal predecessors, he found himself in possession of the means to carry out the intolerably sweeping administrative revolution which his own successful successor Liu Pang deliberately forbore to emulate on the morrow of the swift undoing of Ts'in She Hwang-ti's revolutionary work.

The builders of two other universal states had drawn, with happier results, upon the practice and personnel of a civil service which the empire-building community had not inherited from the past but had created to meet its own domestic needs at home in the same generation in which the task of imperial administration had descended on its shoulders. This was the means by which the French equipped themselves for administering the Napoleonic Empire in a politically stagnant Central Europe, and the British for reconstructing a derelict Mughal Rāj in India.

The character and achievements of the British Indian civil service can hardly be understood without being looked at against the background of an immediately preceding chapter of administrative history in the United Kingdom.

'The institution of factory inspection by the Act of 1833 was a stage in the development of a new kind of civil service. . . . Bentham's passion for substituting science for custom, his view of administration that it was a

[1] In 246 B.C. according to Fitzgerald, C. P.: *China, A Short Cultural History* (London 1935, Cresset Press), p. 70; in 247 B.C. according to Franke, O.: *Geschichte des Chinesischen Reiches*, vol. i (Berlin and Leipzig 1930, de Gruyter), p. 226.

skilled business, had in this instance results that were wholly satisfactory: under his inspiration England created a staff that brought to its work training and independence; unlike the English Justice of the Peace, the new Civil Servant had knowledge; unlike the French *intendant*, he was not the mere creature of a government. The English people learnt to use educated men on terms that preserved their independence and their self-respect. . . . For the moment, the chief occupation of this educated class was to throw a searchlight on the disorder of the new world. Nobody can study the history of the generation that followed the passing of the first Reform Bill without being struck by the part played by lawyers, doctors, men of science and letters in exposing abuses and devising plans.'[1]

The new fraternity of middle-class professional administrators which took a passage to India, after having thus made its way peacefully to the front in England, had, in France, to force an outlet for itself by an explosive outbreak of its artificially dammed-back energies.

'The French bourgeoisie of '89 belonged to a class proud of its economic independence and of its social standing. Its members had earned or inherited a competence derived from honest toil. They cherished a self-respect that set them no further from the *aristos* above them than from the *sansculottes* below. Yet they resembled the English aristocracy, and differed from that of their own country, in being a class, not a caste. Their ranks were not fixed, but fluid. There was always an element in them surging up from *roturier* to *bourgeois*, and from *bourgeois* to noble. . . . Hitherto they had been kept out of the government of a country which they enlightened and enriched. But nothing had been able to exclude them from the management of its trade, its agriculture, or its administration. Here they had become apprenticed to political power. Here, during half a century of political outlawry, they had been educating themselves for 1789.'[2]

The new field of action that the French *bourgeoisie* now opened up for themselves was a bureaucratic public service, which was called for to fill an institutional vacuum created in France by the Revolution itself before the French conquests abroad, which the Revolution set in motion, enlarged this vacuum to embrace Flanders, Italy, and Western Germany and to give a French bureaucracy *in partibus peregrinis* a different function from that which it had recently been called into existence to perform at home.

'The French had long lost the feeling for local autonomy, and the efforts to decentralise the government of the *Ancien Régime* had not had time to fructify before the Revolution supervened. That catastrophe eliminated the aristocracy, sowed hate and jealousy in every village, and prevented any further development of the constitution on the lines laid down by Turgot and Necker. A centralized bureaucracy was a necessity for France, being, as it were, not only a kind of anaesthetic or healing drug, but also the elementary condition for the preservation of all that was precious in the revolutionary movement. Among the lethargic inhabitants of Westphalia the mission of the bureaucracy was not to calm but to excite, not to preserve but to communicate. . . .[3]

[1] Hammond, J. L. and Barbara: *The Rise of Modern Industry* (London 1925, Methuen), pp. 256–7.

[2] Thompson, J. M.: *The French Revolution* (Oxford 1943, Blackwell), p. 26.

[3] Fisher, H. A. L.: *Studies in Napoleonic Statesmanship in Germany* (Oxford 1903, Clarendon Press), pp. 269–70.

'It was not merely by their laws that the French left a permanent mark upon the Duchy [of Berg]. Their administration was a pattern and a precedent. The Prussians, indeed, had done good bureaucratic work in Mark and in Münster before the French occupation, but it was the French who first adequately expounded the arts of finance and administration to the whole region. To the slovenly government of the Bavarians in Berg, the French methods, combining, as they did, strict control with prompt, orderly and intelligent action, and distinguished always for their clear definition and distribution of functions, were related as the railway train is related to the stage coach.'[1]

Napoleon was seeking to carry out in a subjugated Central Europe the long overdue administrative reformation that Ts'in She Hwang-ti had tried to impose upon the subjugated states of the Sinic World 'outside the passes', and the great demonic French innovator's tragedy was the same as his Sinic counterpart's. In forcing the pace of revolutionary change without mercy on Human Nature, he defeated his reformatory purpose and brought his own work to grief.

'There has been no greater master in the art of using, driving, and inspiring men. He found great disorder and demoralisation; he created a bureaucracy more competent, active, and enlightened than any which Europe had seen. But, as the Consulate passed into the Empire, and as the growing palsy of despotism spread over France, the quality of the work declined. The best men hated the never-ending wars and saw insanity written in large tokens over their master's schemes. . . . All criticism, all independent political thought, expired. Resolutely closing his eyes to unpleasant facts, Napoleon insisted that his servants should be blind also, and, being despotic and irritable, he was able to exact a constant supply of nutriment for his illusions. The men who spoke the truth and thought justly were dismissed or scolded; and, as compliance came to be rated more highly than ability, the most precious qualities were excised from public life.'[2]

The Metamorphosis of an Hereditary Aristocracy into a Professional Civil Service

If Napoleon and Ts'in She Hwang-ti deservedly failed in their attempt abruptly to force an alien bureaucracy on their subjects, Augustus and Han Liu Pang well deserved the success that attended their humane and statesmanlike policy of calling a new civil service into existence to answer to the needs of the devastated, disorganized, and weary world for whose welfare each of them found himself responsible. The administrative systems founded by the Hellenic bourgeois and the Sinic peasant saviour of society were perhaps the two finest secular institutions that, down to the time of writing, had yet been fashioned by the wisdom and benevolence of Man; yet, when they are compared with one another, their merits can be seen to be as unequal as their longevity. The Roman imperial administrative system, which went to pieces in the seventh century after its inauguration by Augustus, was not on a par with the Han system which had been founded 150 years earlier and which lasted, with at least a thread of continuity, down to A.D. 1911.

[1] Fisher, op. cit., p. 222. [2] Ibid., pp. 374–5.

The defect of the Roman imperial civil service was its reflection of the discord between the old republican senatorial aristocracy and the new imperial dictatorship which an Augustan compromise had glozed over but had not healed. In the Roman imperial civil service under the Principate there were two rigidly segregated hierarchies and two mutually exclusive careers in which the senatorial and the equestrian civil servant went their respective ways. This schism in the heart of the service was, as we have seen, eventually brought to an end in the third century of the Christian Era, not by the achievement of that *concordia ordinum* which the public interest had always required, but by a high-handed elimination of the Senatorial Order from all posts of administrative responsibility. Their discomfiture, however, did not leave their equestrian rivals in enjoyment of a monopoly of the imperial service; for by this time the decay of local civic self-government had so swollen the volume of the imperial service's work[1] that Diocletian found himself compelled to make an inordinate increase in the permanent establishment of the civil service as well as the army; and in a post-Diocletianic Age the entry into the service was open to any Roman citizen possessed of the necessary degree of education, without discrimination between classes. The contrast with the history of the Han imperial civil service[2] is instructive. The opening of careers to talent, which was not achieved in the Roman Empire till more than three hundred years after the establishment of the Augustan Peace, was inaugurated in the Han Empire by Han Liu Pang himself, within six years of his restoration of order in 202 B.C., in an ordinance, issued in 196 B.C.,[3] in which he directed the provincial public authorities to select candidates for the public service on a test of merit, and to send them to the capital for appointment or rejection by the officers of the Central Government.

This new Sinic civil service received its definitive form when Han Liu Pang's successor Han Wuti (*imperabat* 140–87 B.C.) decided that the merit required of candidates should be a proficiency in reproducing the style of the classical literature of the Confucian canon and in interpreting the Confucian philosophy to the satisfaction of the Confucian litterati of the day.[4] Under the skilful handling of the Han emperors the transition from the old feudal order of the Chóu Age to the new bureaucratic order of the Han Age was made so smoothly—notwithstanding the violence of the abortively revolutionary Ts'in interlude—that old names acquired new meanings, and old doctrines new interpretations, by insensible degrees.

'The disappearance of feudalism was rendered possible by the policy of the Han emperors towards a very important and hitherto irreconcilably reactionary class, the *chün tze*. The aristocracy had been virtually destroyed by the revolutionary measures of She Hwang-ti, but they transmitted their ideals and their political outlook to a new class, the scholars and officials of the centralised empire. From this time onwards the *chün tze* cease to be an hereditary nobility distinguished by membership of a

[1] See pp. 59–60 and 166, above. [2] See pp. 173–4, above.

[3] Franke, O.: *Geschichte des Chinesischen Reiches*, vol. i (Berlin and Leipzig 1930, de Gruyter), pp. 274–5, gives a German translation of the text as recorded in the official history of the Prior Han Dynasty. [4] See V. v. 418–19, 654–5, and 708.

limited number of clans. The revolution had destroyed the territorial and clan basis of the old aristocracy for ever. The *chün tze*, including many of the old aristocratic families, became a class marked off from the mass of the people by education, and only by education. . . . The very meaning of the old terms became obscure. *Chün tze* had meant the son of a lord, member of a noble clan. Under the new régime it gradually came to mean a gentleman in much the same sense as [that in which] that word is used in modern English—one who had received a polite education.

'The later Han emperors adroitly favoured the new educated class. Themselves of peasant origin, with no trace of divine or noble blood to fortify their claim to the throne, it was of vital importance to the new emperors to discover some principle of legitimacy for their power. Noble blood and divine descent they could not claim; force, upon which the Ts'in had relied, had proved to be a double-edged weapon. The master-stroke of the Han emperors was to enlist in support of the centralised state the very school which had upheld feudalism to the last. . . . Their supreme achievement was to persuade the new scholar class, to whom the Feudal Age was personally unknown, that the doctrines of Confucius could be applied to the new political régime. . . .

'She Hwang-ti tried to destroy the memory of the past; the Han sovereigns, more subtle than he, succeeded in distorting it. The interpretation of the Confucian doctrine which gained currency during the Han Dynasty proved one of the most enduring results of the revolution. The ideal of a centralised state became closely associated with the scholar class and the followers of the Confucian School. Henceforward fissiparous movements are always opposed by the scholars, the very class who had defended ancient feudalism.'[1]

The Confucian School of the second century B.C. which was thus tactfully coaxed into partnership with the Han imperial régime would have astonished Confucius himself by the enormity of its intellectual, as well as its political, departure from the founder's own standpoint. The break in scholarly tradition caused by Ts'in She Hwang-ti's burning of the books, and the syncretism in religion produced by the levelling of the former barriers between contending parochial states and by the inclusion of a host of semi-barbarous peoples within the pale of the Sinic Society through their subjugation by force of Ts'in and Han arms, had made of the epimethean philosophy of Confucius a melting-pot for exotic superstitions.[2] To translate the course of this chapter of Sinic social history into Hellenic terms, we should have to imagine the Emperor Marcus Aurelius making the Stoicism of his day[3] into the official philosophy of the Roman civil service,[4] and this Stoically rigged Roman ship of state being freighted with as heavy a cargo of superstition as Neoplatonism eventually took on board.[5]

To complete this imaginary parallel, however, we must picture the Stoic School in the next chapter of its history, after it has become the

[1] Fitzgerald, C. P.: *China, A Short Cultural History* (London 1935, Cresset Press), pp. 153–5. The quotations from this book have been made with the permission of the publishers.

[2] See V. v. 549 and 555–6.

[3] For the flush of religious feeling that suffused the Stoicism of the second century of the Christian Era, see the passage quoted from Dill in V. v. 550–1.

[4] Marcus's conscientious abstention from misusing his political power for the purpose of propagating his philosophic faith has been noticed in V. v. 705.

[5] See V. v. 565–7 and 680–3.

official philosophy of a universal state, deliberately purging its doctrine and practice of the superstitious accretions of the preceding age, and abandoning to its unofficial rival, Neoplatonism, the mission of supplying a demand for a popular religion under a philosophical veneer. In the Sinic World in the course of the last three centuries of the Han régime, the Confucian School did jettison the superstition that it had picked up in its rough passage through a revolutionary last phase of the Sinic Time of Troubles and first phase of the universal state established by Ts'in She Hwang-ti and refounded by Han Liu Pang. Yet, although 'the rather arid doctrines of the Confucian scholars had little appeal for the mass of the people', and in consequence 'the popular religion, which Confucianism had rejected', fell into the hands of 'the principal heterodox philosophy, Taoism',[1] even the dehydrated official philosophy of the Han imperial civil service was a more effective inspiration for a corporate professional way of life than the merely literary archaistic culture that was the shibboleth of a post-Diocletianic Roman civil service.[2]

A comparable vein of literary archaism was, indeed, carried to perhaps even greater lengths of absurdity by the Confucian School in the Han Age,[3] with the same unfortunate effect of cutting off a civil service that plumed itself on this conceit from the realities of contemporary life outside its own charmed circle; but the pedantic canon of literary taste to which the Han imperial civil service had subjected itself was always the handmaid of a rule of conduct which, however pedantic it, too, might be, still gave its followers a social cohesion among themselves, even when they had lost human touch with the rest of Society. This bond of a common traditional ethic was lacking among the Han civil servants' Roman counterparts; and no doubt this was one of the reasons for the difference in the fortunes of these two official corporations during the interregna following the break-up of the universal states whose respective servants they had been.[4]

1 Fitzgerald, op. cit., p. 261.

2 See V. vi. 71–81.

3 See V. vi. 81–83.

4 This difference is explored further on pp. 370–2, below. While one cause of it was the Roman imperial civil service's lack of a corporate philosophy such as the Han imperial civil service acquired in the shape of a purged Confucianism, another cause was the lack of a spacious fastness, impregnable to barbarian attack, such as the Han imperial civil service found for itself in the South of the Sinic World, where the expansion of the Sinic Civilization during its Time of Troubles had been carried forward, by the united forces of the subsequent universal state, until the conquest of Nan Yüeh (the present Chinese provinces of Kwangsi and Kwangtung, together with Tongking) by Han Wuti in A.D. 111 brought an expanding Sinic World to the 'natural frontier' of the sea coast (see Fitzgerald, op. cit., p. 181). The Yangtse Basin and the Southern Seaboard, unlike the Yellow River Basin, were unpropitious *terrain* for the cavalry of the Eurasian Nomad barbarian invaders of the Sinic World during the post-Han interregnum; and their defeat in A.D. 383 at Fei Shui (see Franke, op. cit., vol. ii, pp. 95–97; the date is given as A.D. 387 by Fitzgerald, op. cit., p. 257) was a decisive battle which may be compared, in respect of the magnitude of its consequences, to the defeats of the Mongols by the Egyptian Mamlūks in A.D. 1260, 1281, 1299–1300, and 1303 (see I. i. 350), since this battle insured the birth of a Far Eastern Civilization, affiliated to the Sinic, as those insured the birth of an Arabic Civilization affiliated to the Syriac. The Roman Empire embraced no fastness of comparable size that was immune against attack by the same Eurasian Nomad barbarian enemy, and in any case the barbarian invaders of the Roman Empire included sedentary peoples—highland Berbers and non-nomadicized West Germans—who were less sensitive to the nature of the *terrain* than their more highly specialized Nomad fellow aggressors. In the politico-strategic geography of the Roman

In the art of converting an aristocracy of birth into a professional civil service, both Augustus and Han Liu Pang were to be surpassed by Peter the Great; for the wisdom of hastening slowly, which Han Liu Pang had learnt from the fate of Ts'in She Hwang-ti's revolutionary handiwork, and Augustus from the fate of Julius Caesar's, was not only learnt by Peter from his own experience but was taken to heart by him in time to retrieve a first false start.

After having discovered, by trial and error, the unwisdom of attempting either to dragoon feudal nobles into becoming professional administrators[1] or to supersede them by a wholesale substitution of *novi homines* and foreigners, Peter set himself in A.D. 1722 gradually to convert the Muscovite nobility into an effective instrument of Russian Imperial administration by instituting an official hierarchy of military and civil ranks, in fourteen grades.

'Through each of these it was necessary to pass, beginning from the bottom, just as it had been Peter's practice to make his guards officers, like himself, start from the ranks. Promotion from grade to grade was to be partly by length of service and partly by exceptional merit. Standing in the state service took precedence of birth, even in the court and social hierarchy. The privileges of the land-owning class—notably those of owning serfs and of being exempt from the poll-tax—were extended hereditarily to all persons, whether Russians or foreigners, who reached the eighth grade, and in the case of the Army and Navy even from the lowest grade.

'Throughout his life Peter picked men for multifarious duties without regard to birth or class, in the interests of recruitment for military or state service. From this time forward the land-owning class began to receive an influx of newcomers, who in the course of the next two generations broadened its composition and changed its complexion. . . . Despite subsequent alterations, the table of ranks had a profound influence on the future. It set the stamp on the hierarchal, bureaucratic ordering of the upper class in military and state service, which during the next two centuries became so prominent a feature of the social structure of Russia. Rank, in the sense of position in the table of ranks, largely displaced birth or wealth in the administrative and social scale.'[2]

Empire the nearest counterpart to the great southern fastness of the Han Empire was Anatolia; but even Anatolia was constantly overrun by invading and occupying Persian and Arab armies in the seventh century of the Christian Era; and the measure of the break in administrative continuity, even here, is given by the contrast between the Diocletianic administrative organization, as it survived in Anatolia in the reign of Justinian, and the system of local government through army corps districts (*themata*), as it had emerged there within a hundred years of Justinian's death. Only the precincts of Constantinople remained inviolate, and this Constantinopolitan fastness was too small, and too alien in experience and outlook from the exposed and harried countryside, to play the part which the New South of the Sinic World was able to play in the affiliation of a new-born civilization to an extinct one. The administrative continuity between the Roman Empire that foundered in the seventh century of the Christian Era and the ghost of it that was evoked in the eighth century by Leo Syrus was one of form without substance, whereas in the Sinic World 'the flight of the scholars after the fall of Loyang [under the impact of Hiongnu Eurasian Nomad invaders in A.D. 311] brought civilisation into the South, and gave these provinces an importance which they had not possessed in the Han Empire, but which was to grow more and more marked in succeeding ages' (Fitzgerald, op. cit., p. 260). Observers of the Sino-Japanese war of A.D. 1931–45 would have been reminded of the similar effect of a similar migration of a Westernized intelligentsia from Peking and the treaty ports into the south-western provinces of contemporary China. See further X. ix. 649–81.

[1] See IX. viii. 554–7.

[2] Sumner, B. H.: *Peter the Great and the Emergence of Russia* (London 1950, English

In the judgement of an acute and sensitive Russian student of Russian history,

'La noblesse, cette nouvelle élite infiniment plus large, plus agile, plus capable d'avenir que l'ancienne, était sans doute, avec la nouvelle capitale, le don le plus précieux du tsar [Pierre] a la Russie future. Malgré Lomonossov et d'autres "parvenus" de génie, tout ce que la Russie a produit jusqu'au milieu du siècle suivant de grands hommes et de valeurs culturelles vient de cette classe ou du moins n'a pu éclore que dans le milieu formé par elle. . . . L'ascension culturelle, politique et sociale de la Russie, de Pierre 1er a Alexandre 1er, est l'œuvre de la noblesse.'[1]

Experiments in Providing an Education for New Recruits

While the Han Empire and the Roman Empire created their magnificent civil services[2] out of their own respective social and cultural heritages, Peter the Great and his successors in Russia, when they were in search of administrative support for their enterprise of Westernizing their empire and had found the hereditary Muscovite nobility a broken reed,[3] forced the pace in the first stage of the manufacture of their new bureaucratic 'nobility of service' by copying Western institutions and even enlisting Western personnel.[4] The Cabinet Secretary instituted by Peter on a contemporary Western model[5] performed for the autocrat of a Westernizing Muscovy the service that an Achaemenian emperor received from his hazarapatiš and a Roman Emperor from his praetorian prefect. The contemporary organization of Western governments likewise suggested the Senate that was established by Peter on the 22nd February, 1711, and was endowed with far-reaching executive powers,[6] and the Administrative Colleges that were set up in A.D. 1717–18. Most of these colleges started life with Russian presidents and foreign vice-presidents to induct the Russians into new-fangled Western methods of administrative work.[7] To provide the staff, Swedish prisoners-of-war were roped in, and Russian apprentices were sent to acquire a Prussian training at Königsberg.[8] In A.D. 1722 the office of Procurator-General was created for the purpose of keeping a 'king's eye'[9] (to use the Achaemenian term) on both the colleges and the Senate.[10] An historian who was a Westerner himself would like to believe—against the presumptive

Universities Press), pp. 155–6. See also Brückner, A.: *Peter der Grosse* (Berlin 1879, Grote), p. 506, and the present Study, III. iii. 282, n. 2. Though the creation of this professional civil service was Peter's personal achievement, he did not have to start entirely from the beginning. For the pre-Petrine rudiments, see Mavor, J.: *An Economic History of Russia*, 2nd ed. (London 1925, Dent, 2 vols.), vol. i. p. 73.

1 Weidlé, W.: *La Russie Absente et Présente* (Paris 1949, Gallimard), p. 68.

2 See V. v. 38–39.

3 See pp. 349–50, above.

4 The first wave of immigrant Western bureaucrats consisted of German aristocrats from the Baltic Provinces after the conquest of these from Sweden by Peter the Great (see Sumner, B. H.: *Peter the Great and the Emergence of Russia* (London 1950, English Universities Press), p. 119). The second wave came from Germany itself during the sixteen years (A.D. 1725–41) immediately following Peter's death (see ibid., p. 192). During Peter's reign, however, there were no non-Russians in the taxation service, the provincial governorships, or the Senate, and very few in the Ministry of Foreign Affairs and in the diplomatic service (see ibid., pp. 204–5).

5 See Brückner, op. cit., p. 497; Sumner, op. cit., pp. 64 and 131.

6 See Brückner, op. cit., pp. 499–500; Sumner, op. cit., pp. 123–5 and 127.

7 See Brückner, op. cit., pp. 501–2; Sumner, op. cit., pp. 125–7.

8 See Brückner, op. cit., pp. 501–2.

9 See p. 82, above.

10 See Sumner, op. cit., pp. 127–8.

evidence of contemporary Venetian practice—that this official organization of espionage on the new Westernizing Russian civil service[1] was not likewise inspired by Western models.

Where, as in the Petrine Russian Empire, an imperial civil service is thus called into existence in conscious imitation of alien institutions, the need for special arrangements for the training of personnel is, of course, particularly evident.[2] At the same time, this need arises in some degree in all the divers situations in which an imperial civil service has to be provided, since it is inherent in the nature of a universal state and in the invariable circumstances of its advent in history.

An oecumenical polity of this type normally takes shape rather suddenly out of a cluster of contending parochial states that have brought a Time of Troubles to its climax and conclusion by an obstinate refusal to adapt themselves to the necessities of a new age. The problems, experience, institutions, and êthos of these anachronistic predecessors are manifestly unlikely to be of much use to the new polity that has at last belatedly superseded them. A fledgling universal state nearly always has, in the main, to supply its own needs for itself; and it cannot afford to imitate its parochial forerunners' comfortable habit, in the spacious days of their long-since vanished youth, of waiting upon experience to give them the necessary instruction; for the universal state has been brought into being as a response to the urgent challenge of its parochial predecessors' protracted failure to meet the World's political requirements; its mission is to grapple at once with the troubles of a society on the verge of dissolution; and, if it cannot draw profitably on its predecessors' experience and cannot wait to learn by experience of its own, it must take a leaf out of the book of Utopia[3] and must improvise the education of a new type of administrator for a new form of government. Most universal states will be found to have worked out arrangements of some kind for educating the administrators that they need.

In the Incaic, Achaemenian, Roman, and Ottoman empires the Emperor's personal household was both the hub of the wheel of imperial government and the training-school for the administrators required for making the machinery of government work, and in a number of cases this educational function of an imperial household had been catered for by the creation, within it, of the special institution of a corps of pages.

At the Inca Emperor's court at Cuzco there was a regular course of education—with tests and ordeals at successive stages of initiation—in which the young men of the Inca's own imperial clan were brigaded

[1] See Brückner, op. cit., p. 504.

[2] Peter the Great sought to meet this need *quam celerrimè* by sending batches of young Russians to be educated abroad from A.D. 1697 onwards. In A.D. 1697–8 he voluntarily performed, himself, a task that he was imposing on his subjects when he went abroad for eighteen months on 'the Great Embassy' in the suite of his Swiss-born ambassador Lefort (see Brückner, A.: *Peter der Grosse* (Berlin 1879, Grote), pp. 174–5; Sumner, B. H.: *Peter the Great and the Emergence of Russia* (London 1950, English Universities Press), pp. 34–41; and the present Study, III. iii. 281 and IX. viii. 556–7).

[3] We have seen that Utopias are products of Times of Troubles. They are attempts to arrest the decline of a disintegrating civilization by 'pegging' it at the highest level still attainable. The price of this bid for survival is a sacrifice of plasticity; but, in a chapter of history in which plasticity represents a danger of disintegration rather than an opportunity for growth, rigidity comes to seem a blessing and not a curse (see III. iii. 88–111).

with the sons of the chiefs and notables of the subject peoples.[1] In the Achaemenian Empire 'all Persian boys of noble birth' were 'educated at the Emperor's court (ἐπὶ ταῖς Βασιλέως θύραις)',[2] 'from the age of five to the age of twenty, in three things and three only: riding, shooting, and telling the truth'.[3] This Achaemenian method of breaking in noblemen for the public service was copied in the Hellenic kingdom of Macedon, which, on the political map of the Achaemenian world order, was a barbarian principality lying just beyond the pale of the universal state; and the borrowed institution proved its efficacy, to its Persian inventors' detriment, first in the service of the historic Macedonian Monarchy by which the Achaemenian Empire was eventually overthrown, and thereafter in the service of upstart Macedonian successor-states whose domains were carved out of a defunct Achaemenian Empire's carcass. The Petrine Russian Empire, whose relation to the Western World was not unlike Macedon's relation to the Achaemenian Empire, was likewise imitating its neighbours when it instituted a corps of pages.[4]

The Ottoman Court made similar provision for the education of pages in its early days at Brusa,[5] and it was still treading a well-worn path when Sultan Murād II (*imperabat* A.D. 1421–51) established a school for princes at Adrianople, which was the capital of the Empire in his time;[6] but his son and successor, Sultan Mehmed II Fātih (*imperabat* A.D. 1451–81), struck out a new line of his own when, after the conquest of Constantinople, he built his father's foundation at Adrianople into a new educational edifice, centred in his own palace in the conquered metropolis of Orthodox Christendom, which was not only laid out on a larger scale but was designed for the different purpose of staffing the Ottoman imperial administrative service, no longer with independent-minded princes of the Imperial House and sons of 'Osmanli Muslim noblemen, but with Christian slaves—including renegades and prisoners-of-war from Western Christendom, as well as 'tribute children' levied from the Pādishāh's Orthodox Christian subjects[7]—whose status of servitude, and still more, perhaps, their segregation from their ancestral environment, would make them peculiarly susceptible to the skilful process of 'conditioning' to which they were to be subjected as cadets in the Pādishāh's Slave-Household. This 'peculiar institution' of the Ottoman Empire[8] has been described in a previous passage of this

[1] See Joyce, T. A.: *South American Archaeology* (London 1912, Lee Warner), pp. 106 and 112–16; Markham, Sir Clements: *The Incas of Peru* (London 1910, Smith Elder), pp. 128–34 and 142.

[2] Xenophon: *Expeditio Cyri*, Book I, chap. ix, § 3.

[3] Herodotus, Book I, chap. 136. See Meyer, E.: *Geschichte des Altertums*, vol. iii, 1st ed. (Stuttgart 1901, Cotta), pp. 35–36.

[4] In A.D. 1759, according to Mettig, C.: *Die Europäisierung Russlands im Achtzehnten Jahrhundert* (Gotha 1913, Perthes), p. 83; in A.D. 1730, according to Sumner, B. H.: *Peter the Great and the Emergence of Russia* (London, 1950, English Universities Press), p. 153.

[5] See Miller, B.: *The Palace School of Muhammad the Conqueror* (Cambridge, Mass. 1941, Harvard University Press), p. 20.

[6] See Miller, op. cit., p. 22.

[7] Though the 'tribute children' accounted for less than half the total intake of imperial slaves, they were in a great majority among the *élite* selected for training and service in the Palace, which was the avenue to subsequent employment in the administrative service instead of employment in the standing army (see Miller, op. cit., p. 75).

[8] The Ottoman Pādishāh's Slave-Household was a characteristic product of the Eurasian Nomad Society out of which the original nucleus of the Ottoman community had

Study[1] which need not be recapitulated here. At its zenith the Ottoman public slave-education system for entry into the administrative service was a graded pyramidal edifice of nine colleges ranged in four tiers, rising to the Hall of the Imperial Bedchamber at the apex.[2]

This establishment for training recruits for the administrative branch of the Slave-Household was built on such solid foundations of *esprit de corps*[3] that, when in the last quarter of the sixteenth century of the Christian Era the free Muslim subjects of the Empire at last succeeded in forcing an entry into the military branch,[4] the colleges composing the Palace School managed for another century and a half to keep their doors closed to boys of free birth and to continue to supply the Ottoman civil service with admirably trained slave-administrators.[5] Even after Sultan Mahmūd II (*imperabat* A.D. 1808–39), in his thoroughgoing replacement of obsolete indigenous Ottoman institutions by substitutes of a Western pattern, had swept away the six colleges inside the palace precincts after his destruction of the Janissaries in A.D. 1826,[6] he spared the Galata Seray, which in Mahmūd's day was the sole survivor of the former three extramural schools;[7] and an abortive attempt, made by Mahmūd himself in A.D. 1828, to put the Galata Seray on a Western basis was eventually carried through successfully in A.D. 1868.[8] As a *lycée* recog-

come, but it was a revolutionary innovation in the life of the Orthodox Christian sedentary society on which the Ottoman conquerors had imposed their rule. The Ottoman Sultans Murād II and Mehmed II were not the first Turkish-speaking empire-builders of Eurasian Nomad origin to found schools of public administration. When the Saljūq Turkish barbarian invaders of the dominions of the 'Abbasid Caliphate took over responsibility for carrying on the government of their august protégé-puppet, their gifted Minister of state, the Nizām-al-Mulk, included a division for training in public administration, as well as one for instruction in Islamic theology, in the celebrated *madrasah* which he founded at Baghdad in A.D. 1065–7 (see Miller, op. cit., p. 12). His Nizāmīyah was a resident college (see ibid., p. 16). Was this Saljūq precedent in the minds of the Ottoman Sultans Murād II and Mehmed II (see ibid., p. 20)?

[1] In III. iii. 35–45. Since the publication of that volume of this Study, the Western World's understanding of the Pādishāh's Slave-Household, and of the educational institutions embedded in it by which it had provided for its own self-perpetuation, had been increased by the publication of two works of Western scholarship in addition to those mentioned in vol. iii, p. 32, n. 1. These subsequent published works were Penzer, N. M.: *The Harēm* (London 1936, Harrap); Miller, B.: *The Palace School of Muhammad the Conqueror* (Cambridge, Mass. 1941, Harvard University Press).

[2] The component institutions of this educational pyramid were, to enumerate them in ascending order: (i) three schools outside the precincts of Mehmed II's Palace at Constantinople, namely Murād II's school at Adrianople; a school in the Galata Seray on the opposite side of the Golden Horn from Istanbul; and Ibrāhīm Pasha's school in Istanbul, near the Hippodrome, which catered for cadets of Bosniak and Albanian origin. These three outside schools were preparatory for (ii) the Great and Small Halls inside the Palace. These, in turn, were preparatory for (iii) three vocational schools inside the Palace: the Hall of the Expeditionary Force (*Seferli Oda*) and the Halls of the Commissariat and the Treasury. The three vocational schools were preparatory for (iv) the Hall of the Imperial Bedchamber (see Miller, op. cit., pp. 43–44 and 126).

[3] The pages of the Palace School displayed a steady loyalty that was in strong contrast with the turbulence of the Janissaries (see Miller, op. cit., p. 8).

[4] See III. iii. 45.

[5] See Miller, op. cit., p. 174.

[6] See ibid., p. 182.

[7] See ibid., p. 80. Compare the present Study, III. iii. 49, n. 4.

[8] See Miller, op. cit., pp. 182–3; Engelhardt E.: *La Turquie et le Tanzimat*, vol. ii (Paris 1884, Pichon), pp. 12–15; Davison, R. H.: *Reform in the Ottoman Empire, 1856–1876* (thesis submitted to Harvard University for degree of D.Phil., 1st April, 1942, typescript copy in the Harvard University Library). The lines on which the Galata Seray was to be reconstructed were laid down in March 1867 in consultations between Fu'ād Pasha and a French mission, and it was decided that it should be transformed into a secondary school on a Western model in which French was to be the language of instruction. This *lycée*

nized by the Ministry of Education in Paris, the Galata Seray came, in the last chapter of the history of the Ottoman Empire, to be once again the *alma mater* of men of mark, not only among the Muslim ruling class of a truncated Turkey, but also among the Orthodox Christian elder statesmen of Turkey's Bulgarian successor-state.

While the Ottoman Pādishāhs deliberately expanded their personal slave-household into an instrument for the government of a rapidly enlarged empire to the exclusion of the free 'Osmanlis who were the Ottoman imperial people, the Roman emperors, when they found themselves driven to make a similar use of Caesar's slave-household in an administrative emergency arising from the bankruptcy of the Roman republican régime, took steps first to limit and then to reduce the role of the imperial freedmen in the task of world government.

We have already noticed that Augustus reserved for members of the Senatorial Order the posts of highest dignity and heaviest responsibility in the service of the Princeps, quite apart from the senatorial monopoly of the administration of those provinces that the founder of the Principate handed back to the Senate under his system of 'dyarchy'.[1] No imperial freedman was ever appointed to the governorship of a major imperial province or to the command of a legion; and, when members of the Senatorial Order were eventually disqualified from holding these high posts,[2] it was the Equestrian Order that entered into their heritage. The freedmen's stronghold in the administration of the Roman Empire in the early days of the Principate was the central government, in which five administrative offices in Caesar's household—*ab epistulis*, *a rationibus*, *a libellis*, *a cognitionibus*, and *a studiis*[3]—had grown into imperial ministries of state;[4] and even in these posts, which were traditionally the freedmen's preserve, the freedmen became politically impossible as soon as they had impoliticly made themselves conspicuous. The scandal caused by the spectacle of Claudius's and Nero's freedmen-ministers exercising inordinate power led, under the Flavian emperors and their successors, to the transfer of one of these key posts after another from the hands of imperial freedmen to those of members of the Equestrian Order,[5] which was the equal of the Emperor's slave-household in

was to be open to members of all Ottoman communities, and students who were successful in passing the leaving examination were thereby to acquire a right of entry into the Ottoman public service. The text of the Imperial Firman in which this project was given effect will be found in G. M. Young: *Corps de Droit Ottoman* (Oxford 1905–6, Clarendon Press, 7 vols.), vol. ii, pp. 377–80. The new-model Galata Seray was opened on the 1st September, 1868. Out of the 341 students enrolled, 147 were Muslims, 48 were Armenian Gregorian Monophysite Christians, 36 were Greek Eastern Orthodox Christians, 34 were Bulgar Eastern Orthodox Christians, 34 were Jews, 23 were Roman Catholics of the Latin rite, 19 were Roman Catholics of the Armenian rite. By December 1869 there were 622 students, including 277 Muslims, 91 Gregorian Armenian Christians, 85 Greeks, 65 Roman Catholics of the Latin rite, 40 Bulgars, 29 Jews, 28 Roman Catholic Uniat Armenian Christians, and 7 Protestant Christians. The Armenians and the Bulgars proved to make the best students.

1 See pp. 349–50, above.

2 See p. 350, above.

3 See *The Cambridge Ancient History*, vol. x (Cambridge 1934, University Press), pp. 687–8.

4 See V. v. 452–3.

5 The first equestrian secretary of state *a rationibus* was appointed by Trajan (*imperabat* A.D. 98–117) according to *The Cambridge Ancient History*, vol. xi (Cambridge 1936, University Press), p. 220.

business ability, and which could be placed in charge of the central administration of the Empire without offence to other free-born Roman citizens.

Thus in the history of the Roman civil service under the Principate the equestrian middle class gained ground at the expense of the slave underworld and the senatorial aristocracy alike. The Equestrian Order's victory over its rivals on either hand was justified by the efficiency and integrity with which the equestrian civil servants performed their official duties, and this redemption of a class which, during the last two centuries of the republican régime, had risen to wealth and power by a predatory exploitation of army contracts, tax-farming, and usury, was perhaps the most remarkable of the Principate's moral triumphs. The British Indian civil servants, whose record during the last four or five generations of the British Rāj, in the service first of the East India Company and afterwards of the Crown, could bear comparison with the record of the Roman equestrian civil servants at their best, were conjured out of much the same unpromising human materials as their Roman counterparts.

The antecedents of these British Indian civil servants likewise were commercial. They had originated as the employees of a private trading organization whose purpose had been pecuniary profit; one of their original incentives for taking employment far from home in an uncongenial climate had been the possibility of making money for themselves by personal trading on the margin of their work for their employers; and, when the break-up of the Mughal Rāj had suddenly transformed the East India Company from a mere commercial concern into the virtual sovereign of the Mughals' largest and most lucrative successor-state, the Company's servants had yielded to the temptation to make illegitimate and inordinate pecuniary profits out of the political power that Fortune had thrust into their hands,[1] with much the same shamelessness and irresponsibility as the Roman equites had shown when they had found a prostrate Hellenic World at their mercy after Rome's victory over Carthage in the Hannibalic War. In the British, as in the Roman, case, this start might have seemed so bad as to be beyond hope of retrieving;[2] yet in the British, as in the Roman, episode of administrative history a predatory band of harpies was converted in a surprisingly short time into a body of public servants whose incentive was not personal pecuniary

[1] See IV. iv. 511–12. The metamorphosis of the East India Company's servants 'from pettifogging traders . . . into imperialistic swashbucklers and large-scale extortionists' was accomplished between A.D. 1750 and A.D. 1785 (see Spear, T. G. P.: *The Nabobs* (London 1932, Milford), p. 23). 'The transformation of factors into soldiers and statesmen . . . meant that soldiers and officials brought commercial minds to their new duties, in which, if they were not always over-careful of the Company's coffers, they never forgot their own' (ibid., p. 28). In Bengal the European adventurers' reign of terror was at its height from A.D. 1761 to A.D. 1771–2, when it was curbed by Warren Hastings' reforms (see ibid., pp. 32–33).

[2] In the early years of the nineteenth century of the Christian Era the highest reasonable hope might well have been thought to be the conversion of a piratical Clive into a chicken-livered Jos. Sedley (see IV. iv. 641). At Calcutta, where the transition from a respectable obscurity to a corrupt ascendancy had taken place between A.D. 1756 and 1765, there was a reversion towards respectability under Cornwallis' régime (*proconsulari munere fungebatur* A.D. 1786–93). The nineteenth-century era of virtuous aloofness was inaugurated by Wellesley (*fungebatur* A.D. 1798–1805). See Spear, op. cit., p. 26.

gain and who had come to make it a point of honour to wield enormous political power without abusing it.[1]

This redemption of the character of the British administration in India was due in part to the East India Company's decision to educate their servants for bearing the new political responsibilities that had fallen upon their shoulders. The Company acquired the financial administration of Bengal, Bihar, Orissa, and the Northern Circars in A.D. 1765; it opened its college in Hertfordshire for probationer-appointees to its administrative service in India in A.D. 1806; and the college played an historic role during the fifty-two years (A.D. 1806–57) for which it performed this function.[2]

The influence of an educational tradition and environment on the professional êthos of a civil service may be no less profound when the aspirants for admission to its ranks are educated in non-official institutions. In the history of the British Indian civil service, this was shown when in A.D. 1853–5, on the eve of the transference of the Government of India from the Company's hands to the Crown's, Parliament's decisions to recruit the service in future by competitive examination and to close the Company's vocational school for cadets opened the door to candidates drawn from the wider field offered by such non-official institutions as the universities of the United Kingdom and the so-called 'public schools' from which the English universities were almost exclusively recruited at that date.

In making this new departure in educational policy for the English contingent in the personnel of a British Indian civil service, Her Britannic Majesty's Government were unconsciously following the precedent set by Han Wuti when he decided to place the education of a Sinic imperial civil service in the hands of the Confucian school of philosophy.[3]

[1] See V. v. 47–48.

[2] The East India Company's College was installed in Hertford Castle at its opening in February 1806, but was moved into new buildings at Haileybury in A.D. 1809. There were about 100 students; the length of the course was two years; and the age of admission ranged between 16 and 19. A student obtained admission through a nomination by one of the Directors of the East India Company which assured him not only of a place in the college but of a post in India thereafter. This method of admission was abolished by an Act of Parliament, passed in A.D. 1853, which provided for the future recruitment of the Indian Civil Service by open competitive examination. The first examination of the kind was held in London in A.D. 1855, and the College was closed, by an Act of A.D. 1855, as from the end of the calendar year 1857.

Besides the contribution that it made to the improvement of British administration in India, the College had the distinction of contributing to the advancement of the science of human affairs through the work of Malthus, who was a professor on its staff from A.D. 1806 until his death in A.D. 1834.

[3] In the histories of the Confucian and the British Indian civil services the experiments in official and unofficial education of aspirants for admission were made in an inverse order. While the British began by setting up a vocational college and then, on second thoughts, decided to rely, instead, on a traditional system of higher education in non-governmental institutions, Han Wuti entrusted the education of civil servants to the Confucian school of philosophy, and the alternative method of training them in a state college was not introduced until the renaissance of the Han Empire, in the shape of the Sui and T'ang régimes, in the history of a Far Eastern Civilization, affiliated to the Sinic, which arose after the social interregnum following the Han Empire's dissolution. When the political unification of the main body of the Far Eastern World by the short-lived Sui Dynasty had been repeated by the second sovereign, but actual founder, of the T'ang Dynasty, T'ai Tsung, one of his measures for placing his political achievement on enduring foundations was to give his unified empire a unitary civil service of Confucian scholars on the Han model. During the interregnum the Confucian scholar-

The indigenous Indian contingent in the personnel of the British Indian civil service—which always vastly outnumbered the handful of Europeans occupying the key posts at the top—was recruited, both under the Company and under the Crown, from the alumni of Western Christian missionary schools and colleges in India, and of Indian universities built up round them or founded side by side with them, whose curricula and standards were largely governed by those of the universities of the United Kingdom, particularly the University of London.[1] On the whole, it would seem that, the less direct the hand that a government finds it necessary to take in the training of candidates for its civil service, the more satisfactory the results are likely to be. The limits to the possibility of compulsory training and enrolment are illustrated by the experience of Peter the Great and his successors in Russia. Peter himself, as we have seen,[2] debarred Russian noblemen from contracting a legal marriage without having passed examinations in arithmetic, geometry, and navigation; and in A.D. 1736 a course of compulsory education from the age of seven to the age of twenty was imposed on noblemens' sons, with a series of three examinations in which a failure entailed the penalty of serving in the Army as a common soldier.[3] Yet, as we have also seen,[4] the disappointing experience of two generations of unprofitable coercion led the Russian Imperial Government in A.D. 1762 to grant an unsuccessfully dragooned hereditary nobility a conditional exemption from compulsory public service.

Our survey of the methods and sources of recruitment of imperial civil services suggests that neither a pre-imperial hereditary nobility nor an imperial slave-household provides the best human materials for the purpose. Neither the attractiveness of the Persian *megistânes* and Inca *orejones* nor the impressiveness of the Ottoman Pādishāh's *qullar* can obscure the manifest truth that the most promising recruiting ground for an imperial civil service is a middle class which has served an apprenticeship in the responsible management of important and intricate non-official business. It was no accident that, in the history of the Roman imperial civil service, the Equestrian Order steadily gained ground at

administrator had survived in a fastness in the South (see p. 357, n. 4, above, and X. ix. 667). But, though the South was united politically with the North under the Sui and T'ang régimes, as it had been under the Han, the remnant of the scholar-administrator class in the South could not be expected suddenly to provide the personnel for staffing the whole of T'ai Tsung's united empire. Like the Ottoman Sultan Mehmed II after his conquest of Constantinople, T'ai Tsung filled an awkward vacuum by enlarging an existing imperial college and using it for the training of professional administrators. The new faculty of Confucian studies was instituted by him in A.D. 628, and in A.D. 630 he took action to provide the Confucian cadets for his resuscitated imperial civil service with the requisite means of instruction and examination by giving orders for the preparation of an official standard edition of the Confucian classics and—what was perhaps of still greater practical convenience—an official digest and elucidation of the existing commentaries (see Fung Yu-lan: *A Short History of Chinese Philosophy* (New York 1948, Macmillan), p. 266). As it emerged from T'ai Tsung's hands, the imperial college at Si Ngan had a student body of 8,000, of whom 3,260 were residents. T'ai Tsung further increased the Imperial Government's control over its intake of recruits into the imperial civil service by instituting a system of public examinations which was afterwards perfected by the Sung and later dynasties (see Fitzgerald, op. cit., pp. 304, 312, and 381–2).

1 The nature, genesis, and unhappiness of an intelligentsia have been touched upon in V. v. 154–9.

2 On p. 350, n. 1, above.

3 See Mettig, op. cit., p. 412.

4 On p. 350, above.

the expense of the Senatorial Order on the one hand and of the imperial freedmen on the other. Nor, perhaps, again, is it an accident that the Roman 'knight' and the English 'gentleman', drawn, as they both were, from an ex-commercial class fumigated with an aristocratic literary culture, should have to yield the palm to a Chinese scholar-administrator educated in an aristocratic philosophy without any skeleton of a commercial past in the cupboard of his family history.

Who are the Beneficiaries?

If we turn now to consider who had been the principal beneficiaries from the imperial civil services that universal states had called into existence for their own purposes, we shall see that the most obvious benefits had been obtained by these empires' non-barbarian successor-states:[1] the Latin American successors of the Spanish Empire of the Indies; the Central and East European successors of the Napoleonic Empire and the Danubian Hapsburg Monarchy; the Soviet Union that had succeeded the Petrine Russian Empire; the two British Dominions —an Indian Union and a Pakistan—that had succeeded the British Indian Rāj; and the indigenous successor-states of the Han Empire in the Yangtse Basin and along the southern seaboard of an expanded Sinic World, where a remnant of the Confucian scholar-administrator class had been able to hibernate until the evocation of a ghost of the Han Empire by the Sui and the T'ang had given this academic Rip van Winkle an opportunity to play his professional part again on the old oecumenical scale in the life of a new Far Eastern Civilization.[2] A fledgling successor-state that is struggling to establish itself is seldom inhibited by political animosity from taking over from its imperial predecessor a vital administrative technique or even an existing professional personnel that knows how to make the wheels of administration keep on revolving. The British Rāj in India, which was perhaps unique among universal states in having voluntarily liquidated itself, had taken pains during the transitional thirty years 1917–47 to prepare the way for its successors by progressively Indianizing the previously European-manned higher ranks of the Indian civil service, and the Napoleonic French administrators in Central Europe had been equally conscious of having an educational mission, though perhaps not equally aware that it was of the essence of their task to educate their non-French flock to a level of administrative efficiency at which these pupils would be able to do without the services of their blandly self-assured masters.

'If, as Napoleon said, experience is everything in administration, faith also goes for something. The French administrators in Westphalia were not only experienced, but they had faith in their own value. It is only necessary to read the letters of Beugnot or the speeches and circulars of Siméon to see how saturated men can become with the belief in the superiority of the language and civilization of their own country. They

[1] Barbarian hands are seldom gentle and deft enough to make effective use of so subtle and delicate an administrative implement as a professional civil service.

[2] See p. 357, n. 4, above, and X. ix. 667.

speak kindly, considerately, condescendingly to the poor Westphalians, explaining everything in the lucid French manner, as a master might expound a beautiful text to a class of stupid and backward boys, now calling attention to a grace of phrase, now to its inner logical coherence, now to its bearing on life. The official letters and documents of this time have all the air of being written by men who regarded themselves as missionaries of Civilisation, and who wish to impart the mysteries of their creed.'[1]

A characteristic exposition of this condescending outlook is given in the following passage from the pen of an eminent representative of the French missionary-administrator fraternity:

'It was then a position in Europe to be a Frenchman, and it was a great position to represent the Emperor anywhere; save that I should not have abused my office with impunity, I was in Germany what the proconsuls were in Rome. . . . We were at that time under the charm of the Peace of Tilsit, the invincibility of the Emperor had not yet received a wound. I came from Paris, where I had passed my life at his Court, that is to say, in the midst of the memorable works and miracles of his reign. In his councils, I had admired this genius who dominated human thought; I believed that he was born to chain up Fortune, and it seemed to me quite natural that people should be prostrate at his feet. . . . I presented myself in the Grand Duchy [of Berg] under the empire of these ideas. . . . I worked from morn to night with a singular ardour, and astonished the natives of the country, who did not know that the Emperor exerted upon his servants, however distant, the miracle of the Real Presence.'[2]

This radiation of the demonic influence of Napoleon's personality was as fruitful at long range in raising administrative standards in the Napoleonic Empire's non-French successor-states as it was fatal at short range to the perpetuation of French rule over non-French populations for whom, at close quarters, the upsetting effect of a genially high-handed re-education in the administrator's art decidedly outweighed the stimulus.

While serving the administrative needs of its imperial creators and their successors, a professional civil service may also be performing the historically more important function of propagating a culture. In the minds of Beugnot and his colleagues, their political and cultural missions were manifestly inseparable; and the Western culture that these Napoleonic French missionary-administrators were dispensing, on their own doorstep, to a still semi-medieval Central Europe, was likewise being propagated farther afield, in various forms and divers degrees of maturity, by Spanish administrators in the Central American and Andean worlds; by Austrian administrators among semi-Western Magyars, Croats, and Poles and among Orthodox Christian Rumans, Serbs, and Ukrainians; by Petrine administrators (many of them of Baltic German or other Western origin) in Russian Orthodox Christendom; and by British Indian civil servants (of Indian as well as European

[1] Fisher, H. A. L.: *Studies in Napoleonic Statesmanship in Germany* (Oxford 1903, Clarendon Press), p. 256.

[2] Beugnot, Count: *Mémoires*, vol. i, pp. 312–13, as translated in Fisher, op. cit., pp. 191–2 (the original French text will be found on pp. 263–4 in the single-volume 3rd ed.: Paris 1889, Dentu).

blood) among the variegated population of a sub-continent. As for the Confucian scholar-administrators who found asylum in the South after the break-up of the Han Empire, they succeeded—during a social interregnum in which the homeland of the moribund Sinic Civilization in the Yellow River Basin was submerged by the influx of barbarian conquerors and of an alien higher religion—in raising a recently incorporated and hitherto backward southern fringe of the Sinic World in its last phase to a cultural level that could compare with that prevailing in the northern focus of the Sinic Civilization under the Han.

The most important beneficiaries from imperial civil services had, however, been neither successor-states nor secular civilizations but churches. In surveying in an earlier chapter the provincial structure of universal states and its after-effects, we have noticed a number of cases in which the hierarchical organization of a church had been based on that of an empire.[1] This basis was provided by 'the New Empire' of Egypt for the Pan-Egyptiac Church that was organized by Thothmes III under the presidency of the Chief Priest of Amon-Re at Thebes; by the Sasanian Empire for the Zoroastrian Church; and by the Roman Empire for the Catholic Christian Church. The ecclesiastical pyramid reproduced the features of its secular model from base to apex. At the summit, the Chief Priest of Amon-Re at Thebes was created in the image of a Theban Pharaoh; the Zoroastrian Chief Mōbadh (Mōbadhān Mōbadh) in the likeness of a Sasanian Shāhinshāh; the Pope in the likeness of a post-Diocletianic Roman Emperor.[2] Secular administrative corporations had, however, performed more intimate services for churches than the mere provision of an organizational last. They had also influenced their outlook and êthos, and in some cases these intellectual and moral influences had been conveyed, not merely by example and mimesis, but by the social translation of a personality, in whom they had been incarnate, from the secular to the ecclesiastical sphere.

Three historic figures, who each gave a decisive turn to the development of the Catholic Church in the West, were recruits from the secular Roman imperial public service. Ambrosius (*vivebat circa* A.D. 340–97) was the son of a civil servant who had reached the peak of his profession by attaining the office of praetorian prefect in the Gauls; and the future Saint Ambrose was following in his father's steps as a young and promising governor of the two North Italian provinces of Liguria and Aemilia when in A.D. 374, to his astonishment and consternation, he was dragged out of the rut of an assured official career and was hustled into the episcopal see of Milan by a popular impetus that did not wait to ask his leave. Flavius Magnus Aurelius Cassiodorus Senator (*vivebat circa* A.D. 490–585) spent his working life on the thankless—and, as his colleague Boethius's fate proved, perilous—task of administering a Roman Italy in the service of a barbarian war-lord. It was only after his retirement from secular public life that Cassiodorus found a creative use for a literary archaism that had been an impediment to his draftsmanship as

[1] See pp. 188–93, above.

[2] See Toynbee, J. C. M.: 'Catholicism and the Roman Imperial Cult', in *The Month*, vol. clviii, November 1931, pp. 390–2.

a Minister of State. In his latter days he turned a rural property of his in the toe of Italy—the Vivarium, in the district of Squillace—into a monastic settlement that was the complement of Saint Benedict's foundation at Monte Cassino. Saint Benedict's school of monks broken-in, by the love of God, to hard physical labour in the fields[1] could not have done all that it did do for a nascent Western Society if it had not been wedded, at the start, to a Cassiodoran school that was inspired by the same motive to perform the mentally laborious task of copying the Classics and the Fathers.[2] As for Gregory the Great (*vivebat circa* A.D. 540–604),[3] he abandoned the secular public service, after serving as *Praefectus Urbi*, in order to follow Cassiodorus's example by making a monastery out of his ancestral palace in Rome, and he was thereby led, against his expectation and desire, into becoming one of the makers of the Papacy.

After citing the names of these three great luminaries, we may single out, among the lesser lights, two country gentlemen, Gaius Sollius Modestus Apollinaris Sidonius of Auvergne (*vivebat* A.D. 430–83) and Synesius of Cyrene (*vivebat* A.D. 370–415), who were both drawn out of a life of innocent but uncreative literary dilettantism when their local countryside was engulfed in the oecumenical catastrophe of their age. Both of them responded nobly to this personal challenge by taking on their shoulders the burdens, anxieties, and perils of local leadership; and each found that he could best perform an arduous duty, that he would not shirk, by allowing himself to be made bishop of his local community.[4]

Diverse as the origins and histories of these five personalities were, they had four things in common. For all of them except, perhaps, Cassiodorus, their ecclesiastical career went against the grain. Ambrose was aghast at being made a bishop, while Synesius and Sidonius half-whimsically acquiesced in a role which evidently struck them as being, to say the least, incongruous. Gregory was as reluctant to be made seventh deacon, apocrisiarius, and pope, and even to become abbot of his own monastery, as he had been eager to enrol himself as an ordinary monk. The second common feature in these five ecclesiastical careers was that all these *ci-devant* lay notables were constrained, willy-nilly, to employ their secular administrative gifts and experience in the Church's service. In the third place, they found a scope for the use of this mundane faculty in the ecclesiastical field which they had not found in secular life.[5] And, finally, they eclipsed their own performance as ecclesiastical administrators by their prowess on the spiritual plane.

Thus, when the break-up of the universal state for whose administrative service they had been educated had deprived these Roman *honestiores* of the possibility of following secular public careers, they responded to this formidable challenge by entering the service of the Christian Church and devoting all their powers to assisting in the creation of a new order of society. An instructive contrast is presented

[1] See III. iii. 266. [2] Ibid., p. 267.

[3] Ibid., p. 267–9.

[4] Synesius was made metropolitan bishop of the Cyrenaic Pentapolis *circa* A.D. 410; Sidonius was made bishop of Auvergne in A.D. 469 or 470.

[5] See IV. iv. 55.

by the very different reaction of their Sinic counterparts. Under the same ordeal the Confucian scholar-administrator did not paradoxically save his life by losing it;[1] he kicked obstinately against the pricks;[2] he put up a stouter fight than the Roman civil servant against overwhelmingly powerful forces of disintegration;[3] he declined to confess that 'we have no armour against Fate'; and, if he can be said to have performed any service at all for any church, it was the negative and unintentional service of leaving to Buddhist scholar-monks and Taoist philosopher-medicine-men the thankless task of carrying on a secular administration for the Eurasian Nomad war-lords of the defunct Han Empire's barbarian successor-states.

'The fall of the Ḥan Empire, and the partitions and barbarian invasions which followed, opened the road to Buddhism and effected a religious revolution which was the most significant development in what the historians of Confucian tradition describe as an "Age of Confusion". . . . The northern Tatar dynasts extended their favour to Buddhist monks in the conquered provinces. The Confucian scholars had for the most part fled south when Loyang fell [in A.D. 311]. Those who remained in the North were not favoured by the invaders, who rightly suspected this class of secret loyalty to the Chinese Emperor and hostility to the new conquerors. The new sovereigns, needing the assistance of a literate class, found in the Buddhists and Taoists, who had been the opponents of the orthodox Confucians, a body of scholarly men who were trustworthy and loyal. . . . In A.D. 405[4] the [Confucian] historians confess that nine out of every ten families in the northern empire had embraced the Buddhist faith. The proportion is significant, for the non-Buddhist tenth fairly represents the educated class of Confucian scholars and Taoist sectaries who alone remained detached from the new religion. . . . A hundred years later, in A.D. 500, it is admitted that the whole of China, North and South alike, was Buddhist. . . . A few Confucian scholars refused for themselves the salvation which their own families, and particularly the women, eagerly embraced.'[5]

For this uncreative obstinacy, the epigoni of the Han imperial civil service had their reward.[6] Though, by the end of the interregnum between the disappearance of the Sinic and the emergence of an affiliated Far Eastern Civilization, 'the Han civil service based on scholarship was almost forgotten',[7] the Confucian scholar never abdicated. The tide was running all against him, for

'these melancholy conditions and the apparently incurable anarchy of the times tended to encourage the progress of Buddhism. . . . The doctrines

1 Matt. x. 39 and xvi. 25; Mark viii. 35; Luke ix. 24; John xii. 25.

2 Acts ix. 5 and xxvi. 14.

3 In the last phase of the dissolution of the Han Empire, in A.D. 166, the Confucian civil servants founded an association for combating the pernicious influence of the eunuchs, and thereby drew down upon themselves a crushing counterstroke in A.D. 168, partly because they were not sufficiently adaptable to succeed in co-operating with the fighting service, even in this supreme common cause (see Fitzgerald, op. cit., pp. 248–9).

4 According to Sir Charles Eliot: *Hinduism and Buddhism* (London 1921, Edward Arnold, 3 vols.), vol. iii, p. 250, this religious landslide in the North of a disintegrating Sinic World had already taken place by the year A.D. 381.—A. J. T.

5 Fitzgerald, C. P.: *China, A Short Cultural History* (London 1935, Cresset Press), pp. 275–6.

6 Matt. vi. 2, 5, and 16.

7 Fitzgerald, op. cit., p. 259.

of the new religion offered comfort to men living in a world of violence and instability. To renounce society, abandon possessions, and seek peace in a monastery among the mountains became the fashion among thoughtful men. Those who could not take the extreme step contributed to the building of temples and pagodas and their enrichment with artistic treasures.'[1]

If, in these psychologically propitious circumstances, Buddhism eventually failed after all to anticipate Christianity's triumphant success in making the future decisively her own, the explanation lies in the Confucian scholar's feat of holding out in a situation in which the Roman civil servant at last despaired of the republic.

The Confucian civil service produced no Buddhist or Taoist equivalent of an Ambrose or a Gregory the Great. So far from giving the Buddhist Church wings to fly with, it sullenly bided its time for clipping the wings that she had.

'Even at the height of Buddhist fervour, the political power remained in the hands of laymen who were Confucian in training, even if Buddhist in sympathy and the practice of daily life.'[2]

The Confucian scholar's monopoly of a literary culture that was indispensable for the practice of a latter-day Sinic administrative technique, in combination with his cult of a family solidarity which was as close-knit as it was narrow-hearted, armed him with two weapons that enabled him not only to retain his power in the South but actually to recover it in the North by eventually establishing his ascendancy over the epigoni of the barbarian conquerors.[3] By the persistent exercise of these prosaic arts at the price of closing his eyes to the vision of an Other World which the disintegration of his own world might have revealed to him, the Confucian scholar lived to achieve in the end his blinkered mundane ambition of reanimating a defunct universal state with which he had come to identify his own existence so completely that he had ceased to be able to imagine the possibility of felicity in any other social setting.

3. *Citizenships*

The Initial Gulf between Subjects and Rulers

Since a universal state usually arises in the first instance[4] from the forcible unification of a number of contending parochial states at the end of a Time of Troubles in the history of a disintegrating civilization, it is apt to start life with a great gulf fixed between rulers and ruled. On the one side of this sharp political dividing line stands an empire-building community representing the survivors of a dominant minority in a protracted struggle for existence between the rulers of the com-

[1] Fitzgerald, op cit., p. 259. [2] Ibid., p. 286.

[3] An illuminating study of the Confucian recovery in the North, in which the evidence latent in the official records of the *ci-devant* barbarian To Pa dynasty is extorted by a brilliant use of 'third-degree' statistical methods, will be found in Eberhard, W.: *Das Toba-Reich Nord Chinas* (Leiden 1949, Brill).

[4] In contrast to the re-establishment of a universal state after a break caused by the intrusion of an alien civilization, as, for example, 'the Middle Empire' of Egypt was re-established in the shape of 'the New Empire,' the Achaemenian Empire in the shape of the Arab Caliphate, and the Maurya Rāj in the shape of the Gupta Rāj.

peting local communities of the preceding age; on the other side lies a conquered population which, in spite of a superiority in numbers that may be very great, finds itself militarily and politically at the mercy of its conquerors. This standard initial political pattern can be detected even in the history of the Ottoman Empire, which afterwards followed the singular course of excluding the free ʿOsmanli imperial people themselves from political power in favour of professional slaves recruited from among their subjects and their neighbours. It is also common form—as can be observed in the subsequent history of the Ottoman Empire as well as in the careers of universal states of the standard type—for the effectively enfranchised element in the body politic[1] of a universal state to become, as time goes on, a relatively larger fraction of the total population as a result of the admission of recruits from the subject majority. It had, however, been unusual, in the universal states that had come into existence up to date, for this process to go to the length of completely obliterating the initial division between rulers and ruled by enfranchising politically the whole of the originally subject element.

The Obliteration of the Gulf by the Statesmanship of Han Liu Pang

The outstanding instance in which a comprehensive political enfranchisement had been achieved—and this within a quarter of a century of the foundation of the universal state—was in the Sinic World. In the Sinic universal state established in 230–221 B.C. through the conquest of six other parochial states by their victorious competitor Ts'in, the supremacy of Ts'in was brought to an end when Hsien Yang, the capital of the Ts'in Power, was occupied by Liu Pang in 207 B.C. and was sacked by Hsiang-yü in 206 B.C.[2] The political enfranchisement of the whole population of a Sinic universal state that had collapsed after Ts'in She Hwang-ti's death and had been restored by Han Liu Pang may be dated from the ordinance of 196 B.C.[3] in which the first Han emperor directed that candidates for posts in the imperial civil service should be selected by merit. Though this political act did not, and could not, change at a stroke the fundamental economic and social structure of the Sinic Society, it was, as we have seen, revolutionary in its effects on the political plane. The Sinic Society continued, it is true, to consist of a mass of tax-paying peasantry supporting a small privileged ruling minority, but henceforward the avenue giving entry into the Sinic political paradise was genuinely open to talent, in the sense that admission was no longer confined either by a national restriction to inhabitants of the former state of Ts'in or by a class restriction to scions of the former Sinic hereditary nobility.

The historical explanation of this exceptionally rapid and thoroughgoing political enfranchisement of the originally subject population of a Sinic universal state is to be found in the previous destruction of a

[1] In the Greek terminology of Hellenic political science the meaning of this clumsy English periphrasis is accurately conveyed by the single word πολίτευμα.

[2] See pp. 211–12, above.

[3] See p. 355, above

former monopoly of political power in the hands of the Sinic hereditary nobility. This was accomplished, as we have seen, in the State of Ts'in through the reforms introduced by Lord Shang in the fourth century B.C.,[1] and in the rest of the Sinic World after 221 B.C. through still more drastic measures on the part of Ts'in She Hwang-ti.[2] The sequel indicates that Ts'in She Hwang-ti did his work less effectively than Lord Shang had done his; for there appears to be no record that Han Liu Pang ever had to reckon with attempts on the part of the people of Ts'in to recapture for their state the political dominion over the rest of the Sinic World which, after striving for it for a hundred years, Ts'in had held from 221 B.C. to 207 B.C.—though, if any sense of disappointed imperialism had been alive in the Ts'in people's hearts, it would assuredly have been inflamed by the experience of coming under the rule of a foreign usurper whose home country lay at the farther extremity of the region 'outside the passes', in the borderland between the former territories of Ts'in's conquered rivals Ts'i and Ch'u. The politically dangerous nostalgia for the past that gave Han Liu Pang anxiety was cherished by the dynasties and aristocracies of the former parochial states 'outside the passes' whose hereditary authority their conqueror Ts'in She Hwang-ti had done his utmost to eradicate. To forestall a second outburst, in these quarters, of the political explosion that had shattered the work of Ts'in She Hwang-ti was the main object of Han Liu Pang's carefully planned face-saving policy.

Han Liu Pang's choice of a territory for his own imperial demesne would hardly have fallen on the former parochial domain of Ts'in solely on the ground of the strategic strength of 'the Country within the Passes' unless he had felt the local population to be amenable to his rule; and for this he could hardly have counted on their gratitude to him for his clemency in 207 B.C.—even though this had been thrown into relief by the atrocities committed in Ts'in by Hsiang-yü in the following year. There must be some further explanation of the amenability which the people of Ts'in manifestly displayed in these apparently provocative circumstances, and we may perhaps find the explanation in the political annihilation of the nobility in Ts'in to the profit of the Crown more than a hundred years earlier. This concentration of power in the Crown's hands had made the people of Ts'in a formidably pliant military instrument for the overthrow of all the other parochial states in a war to the death; but it had given the state this military predominance at the cost of depriving it of the political vitality embodied in an experienced and self-conscious aristocracy; and accordingly, when the legitimate hereditary dynasty, in its turn, was extinguished in 207 B.C., the people of Ts'in were left as sheep without a native shepherd, at the mercy of the first competent stranger to arrive on the scene and round them up. The combined effect of Lord Shang's revolutionary work 'inside the passes' and Ts'in She Hwang-ti's outside them would seem to account for Han Liu Pang's success in obliterating, within the span of a single generation, the dividing line between rulers and ruled in the Sinic universal state.

[1] See p. 351, above.
[2] See p. 352, above.

The Inefficacy of a merely Juridical Enfranchisement

The unifying effect produced by living historical forces, operating over a long period of time, cannot be reproduced by the mere formality of conferring a uniform juridical status. The uniform status of Europeans, Eurasians, and Asiatics under the British Rāj in India, and of Europeans, Creoles, and 'Indians' in the Spanish Empire of the Indies, as subjects, in either case, of one Crown, did not have any appreciable practical effect in diminishing the gulf between rulers and ruled in either of these polities. In the Danubian Hapsburg Monarchy, on the other hand, the common allegiance of the divers religious and national communities to one dynasty, and the opening of careers in the Emperor-King-Archduke's service to talent, wherever this might be forthcoming among the Hapsburg monarch's motley collection of subjects, might in time have had the same effect as the same cause in the Han Empire, if in the Danubian Monarchy the tendency towards political equality had not been overtaken and reversed in the last chapter of its history by a nationalism, derived from Western Europe, which eventually split the Monarchy into pieces.[1] The classical instance in which an initial gulf between rulers and ruled was successfully obliterated by a gradual merger of a once privileged ruling minority in the mass of its former subjects is to be found in the history of the Roman Empire, and here, too, as we have seen,[2] the substance of political equality was not communicated by the mere conferment of the juridical status of Roman citizenship. After the promulgation of the *Constitutio Antoniniana* in A.D. 212 all inhabitants of the Roman Empire were Roman citizens with the possible exception of an inconsiderable residue of *dediticii*; yet, after that, it still required the political and social revolution of the third century of the Christian Era to bring the realities of life into conformity with the law, because the effective governing element (πολίτευμα) under the Principate had not been coextensive with the Roman citizen body, but had been a narrower oligarchy whose privileges had survived the progressive extension of the status of Roman citizenship to former Roman subjects.

Imperial Citizenships and Ecclesiastical Allegiances

The ultimate beneficiary from the political egalitarianism towards which the Roman Empire was moving in the Age of the Principate and at which it arrived in the time of Diocletian was, of course, the Catholic Christian Church, and this in more than one way.

In the first place, the Catholic Church borrowed the Roman State's master institution of dual citizenship—a constitutional device that had solved the technical and psychological problem of how to enjoy the advantages of membership in an oecumenical community without having to repudiate narrower loyalties or to cut local roots.[3] In the Roman Empire under the Principate, which was the political framework within which the Christian Church grew up, all citizens of the world-city of Rome, except a small minority whose ancestral domicile was the

[1] See II. ii. 182–6.
[2] On pp. 152–8, above.
[3] See IV. iv. 307–14.

metropolis itself or its immediate environs, were also citizens of some local municipality that, though within the Roman body politic, was an autonomous city-state with the traditional Hellenic form of city-state self-government and the traditional hold of such a local motherland upon the affections of her children. On this Roman secular model a growing and spreading Christian ecclesiastical community built up an organization and a corporate feeling that was both local and oecumenical. The Church to which a Christian gave his allegiance was both the local Christian community of a particular city-state and the Catholic Christian community in which all these local churches were embraced in virtue of a uniform practice and doctrine and a perpetual intercourse through which they kept in touch and in step with one another.

The Catholic Church became, in another sense, a beneficiary of the Roman Empire in its post-Diocletianic phase when—after the conversion of Constantine to Christianity had been followed by Theodosius's proscription of all non-Christian religions[1] except Judaism—the terms 'Catholic Christian' and 'Roman citizen' became almost interchangeable. The politico-ecclesiastical equation thus established in the Roman Empire towards the close of the fourth century of the Christian Era reappeared in the constitutions of those 'ghosts' of the Roman Empire that were afterwards conjured up in Western and in Orthodox Christendom. In the medieval 'Holy Roman Empire', and even in the modern Danubian Hapsburg Monarchy, at least down to the Austro-Hungarian *Ausgleich* of A.D. 1867, it was hardly possible to be a fully approved and privileged subject of the Imperial Crown without at the same time being a Roman Catholic Christian, while in the East Roman Empire and in the Russian Empire, even in its post-Petrine phase, full membership in the political community could hardly be enjoyed without a profession of Eastern Orthodox Christianity. In A.D. 1952 a philological fossil of this once living state of politico-religious affairs was still preserved in the Modern Greek appellation *Rômyós*, to which an unsophisticated Greek peasant or a hyper-sophisticated cultivator of the vulgar tongue would answer rather than to the artificially revived name *Hellên* with which he would have been indoctrinated at school. Though *Rômyós*, in the philologist's ear, merely rang a slight change on the Ancient Greek word Ῥωμαῖος, it had long since ceased, on the lips of its Modern Greek users, to mean 'Roman' in the historical sense. It had come to mean an Orthodox Christian whose mother tongue was Modern Greek and whose true fatherland was an ideally still existing East Roman Empire with its capital at Constantinople.[2]

In the convergent histories of the Roman Empire and the Catholic Christian Church, the Roman citizen body and the Christian ecclesiastical community had made their *rapprochement* from entirely different origins in extremely diverse social and cultural milieux; and, though, at an early date in the history of Christianity, they had acquired an outstandingly important common member in the person of Saint Paul, they did not coalesce until the Christian Church was nearly four hundred, and the Roman State more than a thousand, years old. In the histories

[1] See IV. iv. 226–7.

[2] See pp. 29–31, above.

of the Arab Caliphate and the Sunnī form of Islam, the higher religion that was eventually to be embraced by all but a remnant of the population of the universal state was associated from the outset with the imperial people; and, so far from converging—as the Catholic Christian Church and the Roman citizen body converged, to the point of eventual coalescence—by extending their membership from opposite quarters to include by degrees almost the whole population of the state, the imperial people and the Islamic community ceased to be coextensive as Islam proceeded to convert the Primitive Muslim Arab empire-builders' non-Arab subjects. The revolution that carried the ʿAbbasids on to the imperial throne of the Caliphate in place of the Umayyads corresponded, as we have seen,[1] to the revolution in the Roman Empire in the third century of the Christian Era in breaking down a previous political barrier between a dominant minority and a subject majority. Since, however, in the pre-ʿAbbasid Caliphate, the ruling element had been distinguished from its subjects, not by a secular citizenship to which non-citizens could be admitted by naturalization, but by the incommunicable physical heritage of Arab descent and by a communicable religious allegiance to Islam that did not give a non-Arab convert Arab status,[2] the effect of the ʿAbbasid revolution was to open the way towards egalitarianism in the Caliphate, not by making Arabs as well as Muslims out of an increasing number of the Caliphate's non-Arab subjects, but by substituting the Muslim for the Arab community as the imperial people.[3] Thus in the Caliphate, in contrast to the Roman Empire, the political distinction between rulers and ruled was eventually effaced by their merger, not in both a common citizenship and a common religion, but in a common religion alone. In the Caliphate an oecumenical faith had to do duty for an oecumenical citizenship as well.

The role of Islam in the Caliphate in the last phase of the history of the Syriac Civilization recurs in the histories of the Mughal Rāj and the Ottoman Empire, in which Muslim empire-builders imposed universal states on the Hindu World and on Orthodox Christendom respectively. In both these cases, Islam once again served as a unifying and a levelling political force.

In the Ottoman Empire after the death of Suleymān the Magnificent the free Muslim community, who for the best part of two centuries past had been paradoxically excluded from a share in the government, were stimulated by a sense of the incongruity between their profession of Islam and their unfavourable political status into wresting out of the hands of the Pādishāh's infidel-born Slave-Household its monopoly of political power. In the Mughal Rāj, which developed only the rudiments of a counterpart of the ʿOsmanlis' 'peculiar institution',[4] no revolution

[1] On pp. 147–52, above.

[2] The most that could be communicated to a non-Arab subject of the pre-ʿAbbasid Caliphate who embraced Islam and sought to associate himself with an Arab patron was a relation of clientship that was an intolerably inferior status compared with that of the Arab imperial people itself.

[3] The deposition of the Arabs from their former political supremacy in the Caliphate as a result of the fall of the Umayyads was comparable to the deposition of the people of Ts'in from their supremacy in the Sinic World as a result of the fall of the Ts'in Dynasty.

[4] See III. iii. 31, n. 1.

was needed in order to merge the Transoxanian Turkī henchmen of the Timurid imperial house with their fellow Muslims who had made their way into India before them or who came in afterwards from Central Asia or Iran to reinforce them.

In the Caliphate, the Ottoman Empire, and the Mughal Empire alike, Islam also brought recruits to the imperial people in the form of converts from the non-Muslim subject population, but failed to drive rival religions entirely off the field, as Christianity virtually succeeded in superseding its rivals in the Roman Empire; and for this difference in the outcome we can see two reasons. One is that Islam had to contend with higher religions—Zoroastrianism and Orthodox, Monophysite and Nestorian Christianity in the Caliphate; Hinduism in the Mughal Rāj; Orthodox Christianity in the Ottoman Empire—which were all already well established before Islam's advent, whereas Christianity in the Roman Empire had better chances. She was running a neck-and-neck race with coeval higher religions which, like her, had still to establish their positions, while the older religions that were already established in the Hellenic World of that age had no chance of holding their own against any higher religion that might enter the lists against them, since they were worships either of a Non-Human Nature who had been deprived of her prestige by Man's establishment of his mastery over her, or of some parochial human community which had lost its prestige in losing its sovereign independence. Islam's second handicap, by comparison with Christianity, was its honourable obligation, under one of its own articles of faith, to grant toleration to other 'Peoples of the Book' so long as they accepted Muslim political supremacy and gave practical proof of their acceptance of it by paying tribute; and, though, on a strict interpretation of the Islamic Law (*sharī'ah*), the Jews and Christians were the only sects that were entitled to claim this status, the same privileges were accorded in practice to both Zoroastrians and Hindus,[1] partly perhaps, owing to an intuitive perception that their faiths, too, were 'higher religions', and partly, no doubt, on account of the sheer political impracticability of proscribing any religion that commanded the allegiance of the solid mass of a numerous subject population —which was the position of Hinduism in the Mughal Rāj in India and of Zoroastrianism in the eastern provinces of the Caliphate down to at least the ninth century of the Christian Era.

While these handicaps were operative in all the three cases under consideration, there was a notable difference in the extent of Islam's success in the conversion of non-Muslim subject populations in the Caliphate on the one hand and in the Mughal and Ottoman empires on the other. In the Caliphate, by the time of the extinction of the last lingering shadow of the 'Abbasid Power by the Mongols in A.D. 1258, the process of conversion had gone so far—particularly during the last two or three centuries, under the spur of successive Eurasian Nomad barbarian invasions—that the non-Muslim residue in the population had been reduced to a numerically insignificant minority.[2] In the Otto-

[1] See IV. iv. 225–6; V. v. 674, n. 2; and V. vi. 204–5.

[2] For the process, see, further, Tritton, A. S.: *The Caliphs and their Non-Muslim*

man Empire and the Mughal Rāj the corresponding missionary activity never made a comparable impression on the non-Muslim mass, and in both states the process was arrested in the course of the seventeenth century of the Christian Era by an increase in the vigour and confidence of the reaction of the Orthodox Christian and the Hindu subject population respectively.

The explanation of this marked difference in results is probably to be found in differences on the non-Muslim side in this competition between Islam and rival faiths. Among Islam's rivals in the Caliphate, Zoroastrianism and Orthodox Christianity had forfeited their popular appeal through their adoption by the Sasanian and Roman Imperial governments as established official religions.[1] The Nestorian Christians in the ex-Sasanian provinces and the Monophysite Christians in the ex-Roman provinces were not disposed to resist a change of masters when their former Zoroastrian and Melchite oppressors were deposed by the Primitive Muslim Arabs, though they were slow to adopt Islam themselves in place of faiths which they had originally embraced of their own accord and not under compulsion. This divided religious opposition to Islam in the Caliphate was evidently less difficult to overcome than the united front that Hinduism opposed to it in the Mughal Rāj and Orthodox Christianity in the Ottoman Empire. In the contest between Islam and Orthodox Christianity for the spiritual allegiance of the Ottoman *raʿīyeh* the scales were eventually weighted against Islam by the impact of Western Christendom after the tide of war between the ʿOsmanlis and the Western Powers had begun to flow in favour of the West. This change in military fortunes lowered the prestige of Islam in the Orthodox Christians' eyes and inspired them with the new ideal of remoulding themselves in the cultural image of their heterodox Western co-religionists.[2] The West had impinged on India likewise before Awrangzīb's abandonment of the Islamic tradition of toleration evoked a militant Hindu counter-attack, but in this case Islam's arrest must be ascribed to an error in Mughal statesmanship and not to any influences emanating from Western onlookers who, in India at this date, had not yet acquired prestige by a display of their military strength.

These considerations on oecumenical citizenships, ecclesiastical and secular, conclude our survey of universal states—an institution whose evil genii had been the Ts'in She Hwang-tis and its good genii the Han Liu Pangs.

Subjects (London 1930, Milford), and Browne, L. E.: *The Eclipse of Christianity in Asia from the Time of Muhammad till the Fourteenth Century* (Cambridge 1933, University Press).

1 For the effect of this on Zoroastrianism, see V. v. 125–6 and 659–61. For the ostracism of the Orthodox Church, as the religion of the Melchites ('Imperialists'), by Syriac and Coptic Christians, see IV. iv. 593, n. 3.

2 See IX. viii. 161–5.

VII

UNIVERSAL CHURCHES

A. ALTERNATIVE CONCEPTIONS OF THE RELATION OF UNIVERSAL CHURCHES TO CIVILIZATIONS

(I) CHURCHES AS CANCERS

IN entering now upon our study of universal churches we may find it convenient to start by examining their relation to the social environment in which they arise.

We have seen that a universal church is apt to come to birth during a Time of Troubles following the breakdown of a civilization, and to unfold itself within the political framework of a universal state which is the institutional manifestation of a temporary arrest in a broken-down civilization's decline and fall. Our study of universal states has brought out two facts about them:[1] first that, in so far as their achievements bear fruit, the harvest is apt to be reaped, not by the sowers themselves, but by alien hands; and, second, that, in so far as they become creative in this indirect, second-hand, vicarious way, through the creative acts of their alien beneficiaries, they are creators unintentionally and indeed against their will. Their own primary aim is, not to be creative, but to survive, and the experience of losing their lives in order to find them again in the lives of their beneficiaries does not reconcile them to their fate; it provokes them to recalcitrance and indignation. Our survey in the preceding Part of this Study has shown that the principal beneficiaries of universal states are universal churches; and it is therefore not surprising that the champions of a universal state, at a stage in its history at which its own fortunes are manifestly on the wane, should dislike the spectacle of a universal church within its bosom profiting by services that the universal state is continuing to render without any longer being able to turn them to its own benefit. The church is therefore likely at first sight to wear the appearance of a social cancer; for in this situation and state of mind the universal state's devotees are apt, not merely to observe and resent the fact that the church is increasing while the state decreases,[2] but to take it for granted that the beneficiary is also a parasite, and that the patent profit which it draws from its host is the cause of the host's malady. This diagnosis is as attractive as it is exacerbating; for it is always easier, both intellectually and morally, to debit one's ills to the account of some outside agency than to ascribe the responsibility to oneself.

In the decline of the Roman Empire an indictment of the Christian Church, which had been mounting up since the firing of the first telling

[1] See Part VI, *passim*, above.

[2] John iii. 30.

shot by Celsus (*scribebat circa* A.D. 178), came to a head in the West when the Empire was in its death agonies there. An explosion of this hostile feeling was evoked in A.D. 416, in the heart of a 'die-hard' pagan Gallic devotee of Imperial Rome,[1] by the sad sight of desert islands colonized—or, as Rutilius would have expressed it, infested—by Christian monks:

Processu pelagi iam se Capraria tollit.
squalet lucifugis insula plena viris.
ipsi se monachos Graio cognomine dicunt,
quod soli nullo vivere teste volunt. . . .
quaenam perversi rabies tam stulta cerebri,
dum mala formides, nec bona posse pati?[2]

Rutilius's impersonal hostility towards the monks of Capraia was, however, a less painful feeling than the pang which, before his voyage was over, he was to suffer at the sadder sight of another island that had captivated a fellow countryman and acquaintance of the poet's own.

Adsurgit ponti medio circumflua Gorgon
inter Pisanum Cyrnaïcumque latus.
aversor scopulos, damni monumenta recentis:
perditus hic vivo funere civis erat.
noster enim nuper iuvenis maioribus amplis,
nec censu inferior coniugiove minor,
impulsus furiis, homines terrasque reliquit,
et turpem latebram credulus exul adit.
infelix putat illuvie caelestia pasci,
seque premit laesis saevior ipse deis.
num, rogo, deterior Circaeis secta venenis?
tunc mutabantur corpora, nunc animi.[3]

Through these lines there breathes the spirit of a still pagan aristocracy in the dissolving western provinces of the Roman Empire who saw the cause of the ruin of the body politic in the abandonment of the traditional worship of the Hellenic pantheon by pagan converts to Christianity and in the suppression of Paganism by the Christian Emperor Theodosius.[4]

This controversy between a sinking Roman Empire and a rising Christian Church raised an issue of such deep and general interest that it had stirred the feelings, not only of contemporaries directly concerned, but of a Posterity contemplating this historical spectacle across a great gulf of time and change. In the statement 'I have described the triumph of Barbarism and Religion',[5] Gibbon not only sums up the seventy-one chapters of his book in nine words but proclaims himself a partisan of

[1] The most striking of Rutilius Namatianus's expressions of this devotion have been quoted in V. v. 345–7.

[2] Rutilius Namatianus, C.: *De Reditu Suo*, Book I, ll. 439–42 and 445–6.

[3] Rutilius, Book I, ll. 515–26.

[4] It was, of course, in answer to this pagan thesis that Saint Augustine wrote his *De Civitate Dei* (see V. v. 225, n. 1 and XIII. x. 88–89).

[5] Gibbon, E.: *The History of the Decline and Fall of the Roman Empire*, chap. lxxi, quoted in the present Study in IV. iv. 58. Cp. Pope: *An Essay on Criticism*, ll. 692–3:

'A second deluge Learning thus o'er-run,
And the Monks finish'd what the Goths begun.'

Celsus and Rutilius; and we can divine that, in his eyes, the cultural peak, as he saw it,[1] of Hellenic history in the Antonine Age stood out clear across an intervening span of sixteen centuries which, for Gibbon, was a cultural trough. Out of the miry clay[2] of this slough, the generation of Gibbon's grandfather in the Western World had tardily gained a footing on the slopes of another mountain, and from this point of vantage the twin peak was once again visible in all its majesty.[3] 'On the morrow of the death of the Emperor Marcus,' we seem to hear Gibbon saying to himself, 'the Roman Empire, as I have described it in its glory,[4] went into its decline. On the standards of value that I, Gibbon, and my kind in my world share with our kindred spirits in the world of Tacitus and Hadrian, a depreciation of values then set in, and this in every province of life. Religion and Barbarism triumphed, and this lamentable state of affairs continued to prevail for hundreds and hundreds of dreary years, until only the other day, no longer ago than the close of the seventeenth century, a rational civilization began to emerge again.'

This view, which is subtly implicit in Gibbon's work, has been put clearly and sharply[5] by a twentieth-century Western anthropologist who is a figure of comparable stature in his own field:

'The religion of the Great Mother, with its curious blend of crude savagery with spiritual aspirations, was only one of a multitude of similar Oriental faiths which in the later days of paganism spread over the Roman Empire, and by saturating the European peoples with alien ideals of life gradually undermined the whole fabric of ancient civilisation.

[1] Gibbon's view on this point has been criticized in the present Study, IV. iv. 59–63.

[2] Psalm xl. 2.

[3] The writer owes the following valuable note to his friend and colleague Mr. Martin Wight, who was so kind as to read the draft of Part VII of this Study in typescript:

'This conception of the Middle Ages is discussed, with interesting illustrations, by W. P. Ker in his *The Dark Ages* (Edinburgh 1904, Blackwood), pp. 1–4. He quotes the most explicit and refined statement of the Gibbonian view that I have come across, in a passage from James Cotter Morison (the Victorian biographer of Gibbon, Macaulay and Saint Bernard):

"The Graeco-Roman world had descended into the great hollow which is roughly called the Middle Ages, extending from the fifth to the fifteenth century, a hollow in which many great, beautiful, and heroic things were done and created, but in which knowledge, as we understand it, and as Aristotle understood it, had no place. The revival of learning and the Renaissance are memorable as the first sturdy breasting by Humanity of the hither slope of the great hollow which lies between us and the Ancient World. The modern man, reformed and regenerated by knowledge, looks across it and recognises on the opposite ridge, in the far-shining cities and stately porticoes, in the art, politics and science of Antiquity, many more ties of kinship and sympathy than in the mighty concave between, wherein dwell his Christian ancestry, in the dim light of scholasticism and theology."—J. C. Morison: *The Service of Man: an Essay towards the Religion of the Future* (London 1887, Kegan Paul, Trench), pp. 177–8.'

[4] e.g. in the opening passage of his work, quoted in the present Study, IV. iv. 58.

[5] Mr. Martin Wight points out that 'the same conception is artlessly revealed by Dr. Arnold, when discussing his plans for a course of lectures after having been appointed to the Chair of History at Oxford:

"I had thought of trying to do for England what Guizot began so well for France: to start with the year 1400, and make the first year's course comprise the 15th century. My most detailed historical researches happen to have related to that very century, and it gives you the Middle Ages still undecayed, yet with the prospect of daybreak near. I could not bear to plunge myself into the very depths of that noisome cavern, and to have to toil through centuries of dirt and darkness."—Letter to Stanley, 29th September, 1841, in A. P. Stanley: *Life & Correspondence of Thomas Arnold*, 11th edition (London 1880, Murray), vol. ii, p. 239.'

'Greek and Roman society was built on the conception of the subordination of the individual to the community, of the citizen to the state; it set the safety of the commonwealth, as the supreme aim of conduct, above the safety of the individual whether in this world or in a world to come. Trained from infancy in this unselfish ideal, the citizens devoted their lives to the public service and were ready to lay them down for the common good; or, if they shrank from the supreme sacrifice, it never occurred to them that they acted otherwise than basely in preferring their personal existence to the interests of their country. All this was changed by the spread of Oriental religions which inculcated the communion of the soul with God and its eternal salvation as the only objects worth living for, objects in comparison with which the prosperity and even the existence of the state sank into insignificance. The inevitable result of this selfish and immoral doctrine was to withdraw the devotee more and more from the public service, to concentrate his thoughts on his own spiritual emotions, and to breed in him a contempt for the present life which he regarded merely as a probation for a better and an eternal. The saint and the recluse, disdainful of earth and rapt in ecstatic contemplation of heaven, became in popular opinion the highest ideal of humanity, displacing the old ideal of the patriot and hero who, forgetful of self, lives and is ready to die for the good of his country. The earthly city seemed poor and contemptible to men whose eyes beheld the City of God coming in the clouds of heaven.

'Thus the centre of gravity, so to say, was shifted from the present to a future life, and, however much the other world may have gained, there can be little doubt that this one lost heavily by the change. A general disintegration of the body politic set in. The ties of the state and of the family were loosened: the structure of society tended to resolve itself into its individual elements and thereby to relapse into barbarism; for civilisation is only possible through the active cooperation of the citizens and their willingness to subordinate their private interests to the common good. Men refused to defend their country and even to continue their kind. In their anxiety to save their own souls and the souls of others, they were content to leave the material world, which they identified with the principle of evil, to perish around them. This obsession lasted for a thousand years. The revival of Roman Law, of the Aristotelian philosophy, of ancient art and literature at the close of the Middle Ages marked the return of Europe to native ideals of life and conduct, to saner, manlier views of the world. The long halt in the march of civilisation was over. The tide of Oriental invasion had turned at last. It is ebbing still.'[1]

[1] Frazer, Sir J. G.: *The Golden Bough: Adonis, Attis, Osiris: Studies in the History of Oriental Religion*, 2nd ed. (London 1907, Macmillan), pp. 251–3. The judgement expressed in this passage is qualified, without being retracted, by the author in the following footnote:

'To prevent misapprehension I will add that the spread of Oriental religions was only one of many causes which contributed to the downfall of ancient civilisation. Among these contributory causes a friend, for whose judgement and learning I entertain the highest respect, counts bad government and a ruinous fiscal system, two of the most powerful agents to blast the prosperity of nations, as may be seen in our own day by the blight which has struck the Turkish Empire. It is probable, too, as my friend thinks, that the rapid diffusion of alien faiths was as much an effect as a cause of widespread intellectual decay. Such unwholesome growths could hardly have fastened upon the Graeco-Roman mind in the days of its full vigour. We may remember the energy with which the Roman Government combated the first outbreak of the Bacchic plague.'

The passage reappears in the third edition of *The Golden Bough*, Part IV: 'Adonis, Attis, Osiris', vol. i, pp. 300–1 (London 1914, Macmillan, preface dated January 1914). The view expressed in it is cited, and accepted without question as a satisfactory state-

It was indeed still ebbing when the present lines were being written on the 4th March, 1948, and, in the act, the present writer was wondering what that gentle scholar would have had to say, if he had been revising *The Golden Bough* for a fourth edition, about some of the ways in which Europe's return 'to native ideals of life and conduct' had manifested itself during the forty-one years that had now passed since the first publication of this provocative passage in A.D. 1907.[1] In the light of the portentous events of this latter-day chapter of Western history, Frazer and his like-minded contemporaries had proved to be the last generation of Western neo-pagans of a rational, unenthusiastic, tolerant school that had first emerged in the Italy of the *Quattrocento* and that had captivated the Transalpine Western World in and after the closing years of the seventeenth century of the Christian Era. By A.D. 1952 they had been swept off the field by demonic, emotional, violent-handed successors who had suddenly emerged, unheralded, out of the unplumbed deeps of a secularized Western Society. The words of Frazer had been re-uttered by the voice of Alfred Rosenberg with a different ring. Yet this startling change in the application of a Western neo-pagan doctrine must not blind us to the truth that Rosenberg and Frazer were both propounding an identical Gibbonian thesis.

In dealing with this thesis in an earlier part of this Study,[2] we have been content to argue that Gibbon was mistaken in his view of the date at which the Hellenic Civilization reached and passed its zenith, and that in truth it had inflicted mortal wounds on itself long before the appearance, above its horizon, of Christianity or any of the other higher religions with which Christianity eventually competed for the conquest of a moribund Hellenic World. It is, indeed, indisputable that the Hellenic achievement of parochial self-government and the Hellenic virtue of parochial patriotism had by that time been discredited and extinguished through being misdirected and misused by their own authors and exponents. When, in the fifth century B.C., the supreme social need of the Hellenic World had come to be the achievement of political unity,[3] the characteristic features of Hellenic public life had become the bane, instead of the glory, of the Hellenic Civilization; and, though, even after these parochial patriotisms had brought the Hellenic Society to its breakdown in the outbreak of the Atheno-Peloponnesian War, the Hellenic peoples had continued, for four more terrible centuries, to sacrifice the pursuit of true prosperity and true happiness on the altars of traditional political idols, they had been weaned from this idolatry at last when it had demanded of them the immolation, not merely of 'the good life', but of life itself.

Augustus could never have established his oecumenical peace if the public feeling of the Hellenic Society of his day had not been over-

ment of the truth, in a note on 'the Importance of Palestine in the World of Religion' which appears in the official report on the Census of Palestine in 1931 (Mills, E.: *Census of Palestine, 1931* (Alexandria 1933, Whitehead Morris, 2 vols.), vol. i, p. 79).

[1] This passage is not to be found in the sections on Adonis, Attis, Osiris in the first edition of *The Golden Bough*, vol. 1 (London 1890, Macmillan), chap. iii, sections 4, 5, and 6, pp. 278–320.

[2] In IV. iv. 58–63.

[3] See IV. iv. 61–3 and 206–14.

whelmingly in favour of his policy.[1] By Augustus's time there was nobody left in the Hellenic World except the Roman senatorial aristocracy who would still have preferred retaining self-government to getting rid of social disorders, and nobody at all who would still have preferred retaining parochial sovereignty to getting rid of wars. The sufferings that the Hellenic Society had inflicted on itself had produced this revolutionary change in its outlook without the intervention of any external agency. In a post-mortem inquiry into the causes of the death of Hellenism, this reading of Hellenic history, if correct, acquits Christianity and the other higher religions that, in the next chapter of the story, were Christianity's competitors for the spiritual conquest of Hellenic souls. These 'Oriental faiths' were filling a spiritual vacuum, not creating one; and the same verdict emerges from an examination of the role of the Mahāyāna—an 'Occidental faith'[2] from the Sinic World's geographical standpoint—in the closing chapters of the history of a disintegrating Sinic Civilization.[3]

The issue, however, is too important to allow us, at this stage of our inquiry, to dismiss it when we have recapitulated our argument that the Frazerian view is in fact confuted by the principal relevant passages of history up to date. This *argumentum ex Cliûs silentio* is not enough. Higher religions might not have caused the deaths of civilizations in the past, yet this tragedy might still be a possibility. To get to the bottom of the issue, we must carry our inquiry from the macrocosm into the microcosm, from the facts of past history to the abiding characteristics of Human Nature.

Even if Frazer may be wrong in his interpretation of the past historical facts with which he seeks to put his thesis to the proof, we have to ask ourselves whether he may be right, nevertheless, in his contention that the higher religions are essentially and incurably anti-social. When there is a shift in the focus of human interest and energy from the ideals aimed at in the civilizations to those aimed at in the higher religions, is it true that social values, for which the civilizations claim to stand, are bound to suffer? Are spiritual and social values antithetical and inimical to one another? Is the fabric of civilization undermined if the salvation of the individual soul is taken as being the supreme aim of life? Frazer answers these questions in the affirmative; and, if his answer were right, it would mean that human life was a tragedy without a catharsis. The writer of this Study believed that Frazer's answer was not right; for, in his belief, it was based on a fundamental misunderstanding of the nature of the higher religions and the nature of souls or personalities.

In earlier passages of this Study it has been contended that Man is neither a selfless ant nor an Ishmaelitish Cyclops,[4] but a social animal[5] in whose nature there is not a Frazerian 'pre-established disharmony'

[1] For the gratitude that Augustus's work evoked in the hearts of his contemporaries see V. v. 648 and 649, n. 1; V. vi. 181, n. 3; and p. 41, with n. 2, above.

[2] When once we have parted company with sanity by reading emotional connotations of comparative moral and cultural values into the points of the compass, 'Occidental' will serve just as well as 'Oriental' for a term of abuse.

[3] See IV. iv. 65–66.

[4] See III. iii. 217–22.

[5] See I. i. 173, n. 3, and 454, n. 3; III. iii. 223–30.

between the individual and Society. It would be nearer the truth to say that this supposed antithesis is illusory; for the individual can only express and develop his personality through relations with other personalities, while, conversely, Society is nothing but the common ground between one individual's network of relations and another's, and it has no existence except in the activities of individuals who, for their part, cannot exist except in Society. Nor, again, is there any 'pre-established disharmony' between the individual's relations with his fellow men and his relation with God. In the spiritual vision of Primitive Man there is manifestly a solidarity between the tribesman and his gods[1] which, so far from alienating the human members of a primitive society from one another, is perhaps the strongest of all social bonds between them. The workings of this harmony between Man's duty to God and his duty to his neighbour have been explored and illustrated at the primitive level by Frazer himself, and disintegrating civilizations had borne witness to it when they had sought a new bond for Society in the worship of a deified Caesar. Is the harmony converted into a discord by 'the higher religions,' as Frazer contends? In theory and in practice alike, the answer would appear to be in the negative.

On an *à priori* view (to start from that approach) personalities are not conceivable except as agents of spiritual activity; and the only conceivable scope for spiritual activity lies in relations between spirit and spirit. In seeking God, Man is performing a social act; and, if God's Love has gone into action in This World in the redemption of Mankind by Christ, then Man's efforts to make himself less unlike a God who has created Man in His own image[2] must include efforts to follow Christ's example in sacrificing himself for the redemption of his fellow men. Seeking and following God in this way that, in a Christian's belief, is God's way, is, in a Christian's eyes, the only true way for a human soul on Earth to seek salvation. The antithesis between trying to save one's own soul by seeking and following God and trying to do one's duty to one's neighbour is therefore false.

> 'Thou shalt love the Lord thy God with all thy heart and with all thy soul and with all thy mind. This is the first and great commandment. And the second is like unto it: Thou shalt love thy neighbour as thyself. On these two commandments hang all the Law and the Prophets.'[3]

The two activities are indissoluble because 'he that loveth not his brother whom he hath seen, how can he love God whom he hath not seen?'[4] The Christian soul that is truly seeking to save itself by loving God in God's way is as fully social a being as the bee-like Spartan who saves his personal honour by dying for his hive at Thermopylae; only the Christian soul on Earth is enrolled in a different society from the Spartan hive or the Roman Leviathan. He is a citizen, not of a secular commonwealth, but of the Kingdom of God, and therefore his paramount and all-embracing aim is, not to identify himself with the genius of an earthly city, but to attain the highest degree of communion with,

[1] See V. vi. 13.
[2] Gen. i. 26 and 27; v. 1; ix. 6.
[3] Matt. xxii. 37–40.
[4] 1 John iv. 20.

and likeness to, God Himself; his relations with his fellow men are consequences of, and corollaries to, his relations with God; his standard for his attitude towards his fellows will be his intuition of God's attitude towards Man; and his way of loving his neighbour as God loves Man will be to try to help his neighbour to win what the Christian is seeking for himself—that is, to come into closer communion with God and to become more godlike.

If this is a soul's recognized aim for itself and for its fellow souls in the Christian Church Militant on Earth, then it is evident that under a Christian dispensation God's will *will* be done on Earth as it is in Heaven to an immeasurably greater degree than in a secular mundane society. It is also evident that, in the Church Militant on Earth, the good social aims of the mundane societies will incidentally be achieved very much more successfully than they ever have been or can be achieved in a mundane society which aims at these objects direct, and at nothing higher. In other words, the spiritual progress of individual souls in this life will in fact bring with it much more social progress than could be attained in any other way. It is a paradoxical but profoundly true and important principle of life that the most likely way to reach a goal is to be aiming not at that goal itself but at some more ambitious goal beyond it. This is the meaning of the fable in the Old Testament of Solomon's Choice[1] and of the saying in the New Testament about losing one's life and finding it.[2]

> Ah, but a man's reach should exceed his grasp,
> Or what's a heaven for?[3]

This exposition of the harmony between the conception of Man's duty to God and the conception of his duty to his neighbour has been made in terms of Christianity, but it could be translated into terms of Mithraism or of the worships of Cybele and Isis, which competed with Christianity for the captivation of the Hellenic World, or into terms of the Mahāyāna, which did captivate the Sinic World as Christianity captivated the Hellenic. The essence of Christianity is the essence of the higher religions as a class, though in different eyes these different windows through which God's light shines into Man's soul may differ in the degree of their translucency or in the selection of the rays that they transmit. When we pass from theory to practice, we shall learn most from the histories of Christianity and the Mahāyāna, which went on living and working after their competitors had fallen by the way.

The harmony which Frazer denies is exemplified in practice in the lives of the Christian anchorites—a Saint Antony in his desert in Egypt or a Saint Symeon on his pillar in Syria—in an age when the Roman Empire, and the Hellenic Society embodied in it, were approaching their final dissolution. It is manifest that, in insulating themselves physically from their fellow men, these saints were entering into a far more active relation with a far wider circle than any that would have centred round them if they had remained 'in the World' and had spent their lives in

[1] 1 Kings iii. 5–15.
[2] Matt. x. 39 and xvi. 25; Mark viii. 35; Luke ix. 24 and xvii. 33; John xii. 25.
[3] Browning, R.: *Andrea del Sarto*, ll. 97–98.

some secular occupation. They swayed the world from their retreats to greater effect than the Emperor in the city or than the master of the soldiers in the cantonment, because their personal pursuit of holiness through seeking communion with God was a form of social action that moved their fellow men more powerfully than any secular social service on the military or the political plane. The anchorites were recognized by their contemporaries to be pursuing the highest social aim on behalf of all Mankind with complete single-mindedness and disinterestedness; and this spectacle of their self-realization through self-surrender struck their contemporaries' imaginations and touched their hearts and thereby played its part in the forging of a social bond of a spiritual order which held firm when Society dissolved on the political and economic levels.

'It has sometimes been said that the ascetic ideal of the East Roman was a barren withdrawal from the world of his day; the biography of John the Almsgiver[1] may suggest why it was that the Byzantine in his hour of need turned instinctively for aid and comfort to the ascete in the full assurance of his sympathy and succour. . . . One of the outstanding features of early Byzantine asceticism is its passion for social justice and its championship of the poor and oppressed.'[2]

The anchorites' concern and travail for the welfare of their fellow men would still have been recognized without question by their contemporaries if the anchorites themselves had never departed from their chosen and approved way of performing the *opus Dei*. But there were occasions on which the anchorites showed their love for Man and their humility towards God by breaking the régime of insulation that they had imposed on themselves and returning to the World to intervene in a secular crisis.

Thus[3] in A.D. 475–6 Saint Daniel the Stylite, at the instance of the emissaries of the Orthodox Patriarch of Constantinople, consented to descend from his pillar at Anaplus, up the Bosphorus, in order to save Orthodoxy from the Monophysite proclivities of the usurping Emperor Basiliscus.[4] The mere news of the holy man's epiphany in the cathedral church of the Apostles in the Imperial City frightened the Emperor into evacuating his own capital and retreating to the imperial palace at the seventh milestone. It was indeed a crushing indictment of his conduct of public affairs that the report of his people's affliction should have moved the saint to re-emerge from a physical isolation in which, by

[1] John the Almsgiver was Orthodox Patriarch of Alexandria from A.D. 611 to A.D. 619. During these years Syria was under Persian military occupation while Egypt was still in Roman hands, and the Patriarch had to cope with an influx of Syrian refugees.

[2] Dawes, E., and Baynes, N. H.: *Three Byzantine Saints* (Oxford 1948, Blackwell), pp. 198 and 197.

[3] An English translation of the original Greek text narrating the following story will be found in Dawes and Baynes, op. cit., pp. 49–59. The anonymous author was one of the Saint's personal attendants.

[4] Monophysitism versus Orthodoxy was a secular as well as a religious issue at this date, since Monophysitism was becoming the theological expression of the resurgent national consciousness of the non-Hellenic peoples of the eastern provinces of the Roman Empire—particularly the Copts, Syrians, and Armenians—as against the Orthodoxy of the 'Melchite' Greek-speaking supporters of the Roman Imperial régime (see I. i. 91 and 155; II. ii. 76, 286–7, and 374; IV. iv. 325–6 and 593, n. 3; and V. v. 127).

that time, he had been living already for twenty-four years[1] and which was to have lasted unbroken till his death. Working spiritual acts of psychical and physical healing on his way, Saint Daniel led the clergy and people of Constantinople to beard the truant prince in his suburban asylum; and, when the guards refused the crowd admission to the imperial presence, the saint directed the people to follow him in the scriptural symbolic act of shaking the dust of the palace precincts off their garments—which they did with such a thunderous reverberation that most of the guards on duty were moved to desert their imperial master and follow in the stylite's train. In vain the Emperor sent messages after the departing saint to beg him to return to the Hebdomon; in vain he returned to Constantinople himself and besought Daniel to visit him in his palace there. In the end the Emperor was constrained to present himself before the Saint in the Cathedral and prostrate himself at his feet; and a public profession of Orthodoxy was the price that he eventually had to pay in order to save his throne by setting Daniel at liberty to resume his station on his pillar-top.

This was the sole occasion on which Saint Daniel issued from his physical seclusion during a period of forty-two years (A.D. 451–93) which saw the Roman Empire founder in the West while in the East it escaped shipwreck under the spiritual pilotage of the stylite's 'distant control'.

'For three and thirty years (A.D. 460–93) he stood for varying periods on the three columns. . . . During these he was deemed worthy to receive "the prize of his high calling";[2] he blessed all men, he prayed on behalf of all, he counselled all not to be covetous, he instructed all in the things necessary to salvation, he showed hospitality to all, yet he possessed nothing on Earth beyond the confines of the spot on which the enclosure and religious houses had been built.'[3]

On the face of it, Saint Daniel's return to the World in order to rescue his fellow men from political oppression is the same story as the return of Purun Baghat[4] to give warning, to the village below this Hindu hermit's cave, of an impending landslide that would otherwise have engulfed the villagers unawares. The point is, indeed, the same in the legend of the Christian saint and in the Western storyteller's version of a Hindu theme. The historic Christian and the imaginary Hindu hermit each rises to his highest spiritual flight by breaking away, for the love of God and Man, from a settled course of physical withdrawal from the World along which he had been seeking spiritual perfection. Yet, though both responded in the same way to the same illumination, there is a difference between their spiritual histories in the crucial point of the relation of the new light that had dawned on them to their previous spiritual outlook. The Christian saint had been led into his physical retreat from the World by the same love of God and Man that eventually moved him to descend from his pillar, whereas the Hindu sage, when

[1] For the first nine years of these twenty-four, Saint Daniel had immured himself in an ex-pagan temple; for the last fifteen he had marooned himself on the top of a pillar.

[2] Phil. iii. 14.

[3] Dawes and Baynes, op. cit., pp. 70–71.

[4] Kipling, Rudyard: 'The Miracle of Purun Baghat' in *The Second Jungle Book* (cited in III. iii. 190–1).

he yielded to the impulse of love and pity that sent his feet hastening down the mountainside from the cave to the village, was not fulfilling his philosophy but was flying in its face—and who can say whether he would have brought himself to make this sacrifice 'in real life', if he had been an historical character authentically brought up in a philosophical tradition inherited by Hinduism from a Primitive Buddhist School, instead of having been created, as he was, by the imagination of a Western man of letters brought up in the religious tradition of Christianity?

The truth is that Frazer's strictures, which miss their mark when he directs them against the saints, find a legitimate target in the philosophers, be they of the Indic or of the Hellenic school, who cultivate a detachment in which the withdrawal leads to no return.[1] The Hinayanian, Stoic, and Epicurean ideal of the sage goes astray through casting Man for a superhuman role of godlike self-sufficiency and thereby condemning the adept to seek a way out of an impossible position by restricting himself to a sub-human performance. This philosophy attempts to make of Man, not a saint inspired by God's grace, but a very god in himself; and, since this is too heavy a burden for a human soul to bear, the philosopher cannot make even a pretence of carrying it off unless he lightens his self-imposed load by casting out his God-given feelings of love and pity for the rest of God's creatures.[2]

It is true that, when we diagnose the causes of the breakdown of the Hellenic and the Indic Civilization, the philosophers, too, must be acquitted. It can be demonstrated that, though they made their appearance earlier than the saints, they too did not appear till after the civilization had dealt itself a mortal wound, and that they too did not make a spiritual vacuum but sought, like the missionaries of the higher religions after them, to fill one that had already been made by a parochial patriotism which had begun by claiming the citizen's entire allegiance and had ended by discrediting the civic virtues through the evil which it had led men to do in their name. If, however, we were to put Philosophy on trial, not for historic sins against Society imputable to her account, but for latent anti-social potentialities in her doctrines, ideals, and êthos, we should find her more vulnerable than Religion to Frazer's indictment.[3] Philosophy's most insidious offence is to refashion Man's ideal of God in the human sage's image. In place of a homicidal God-the-tribesman she has nothing better than a stony-hearted God-the-isolationist[4] to offer to souls that have wearied at last of the never-ending holocausts exacted by a hydra-headed idol.

No doubt we should also find that many would-be saints—like the pilgrim in Tolstoy's tale who persisted in his journey to Jerusalem without letting the love of God side-track him, like his companion, into helping a neighbour in need[5]—had sinned against their own ideal by falling into the unsocial practice of the philosophers. To detach oneself spiritually from the World is an easier option than the travail of sharing

1 See V. vi. 132–48.
2 See the passages quoted from Edwyn Bevan in V. vi. 146–7 and 151–2.
3 See further pp. 515–16, below.
4 This idea of God is illustrated in the passages of Hellenic and Indic literature that have been quoted in V. vi. 144–6.
5 See Tolstoy, Leo: *Two Old Men.*

God's love for the World and participating in His work of transfiguring it; and in the Hellenic World the higher religions found Philosophy already in the field, with an established tradition and prestige, on the wait to captivate souls in whom the flame of divine love was burning low. Many, perhaps a majority, of the aspirants to sainthood fell by the wayside; yet the few who did live up to the Christian ideal in some measure sufficed to secure the survival of a Christian society when Roman hands failed to save an Hellenic Civilization from the final consequences of its own past suicidal acts. It looks as if the spirit of the higher religions, so far from being a social cancer, were the bread of social, as well as spiritual, life.

(II) CHURCHES AS CHRYSALISES

(*a*) THE GROUNDS FOR THE CHRYSALIS CONCEPT

In the preceding chapter we have joined issue with Celsus and Rutilius and with the exponents of their thesis in our Western World in its modern age. We have contested the view that churches are cancers which eat the living tissues of a civilization away; yet we may still agree with Frazer's dictum, at the close of the passage which we have taken as our text,[1] that the tide of Christianity, which had flowed so strongly in the last phase of Hellenic history, had been ebbing in these latter days, and that the post-Christian Western Society that had emerged was one of the same order as the pre-Christian Hellenic Civilization. This observation opens up a second possible conception of the relation between universal churches and civilizations. On this view the churches present themselves, not as the sinister destroyers of civilizations, but as their useful humble servants. This role is assigned to the Catholic Christian Church—in contrast to the spirit of a gnostic form of Christianity that had gravitated towards the standpoint of the philosophies of Detachment—in a passage from the pen of a Modern Western scholar which has been quoted at a previous point in this Study[2] without its significant concluding sentence.

'The old civilisation was doomed, but this religious Nihilism puts nothing in its place. To the orthodox Christian, on the other hand, the Church stood, like Aaron, between the dead and the living, as a middle term between the things of the Next World and of This. It was the Body of Christ and therefore eternal; something worth living for and working for. Yet it was in the World as much as the Empire itself. The idea of the Church thus formed an invaluable fixed point, round which a new civilisation could slowly crystallise.'[3]

On this view, universal churches have their *raison d'être* in keeping the species of society known as civilizations alive by preserving a precious germ of life through the perilous interregnum between the dissolution of one mortal representative of the species and the genesis of another. In this repetitive process of the reproduction of civilizations, which is assumed to have an absolute value as an end in itself, the

[1] See p. 384, above. [2] In V. vi. 157.

[3] Burkitt, F. C.: *Early Eastern Christianity* (London 1904, Murray), pp. 210–11.

churches are useful and perhaps necessary, but secondary and transitional, phenomena. A church serves as egg, grub, and chrysalis between butterfly and butterfly. The writer of this Study had to confess that he, too, had been satisfied for many years with this rather patronizing view of the churches' role and nature;[1] and he still believed that this conception of churches as chrysalises, unlike the conception of them as cancers, was true as far as it went; but he had come to believe that this was so small and unrepresentative a facet of the whole truth about universal churches as to be utterly misleading if it was mistaken for the whole of which it was in reality a minor part. It may be convenient at this point to explore, by an empirical survey, how far this partial truth—if such indeed it is—will carry us, and then to take the limit reached in this inquiry as a starting-point for seeking a standpoint that will yield a more enlightening perspective.

If we cast our eye over the civilizations that were still alive in A.D. 1952, we shall see that every one of them had in its background some universal church through which it was affiliated to a civilization of an older generation. The Western and Orthodox Christian civilizations and the offshoot of Orthodox Christendom in Russia were affiliated through the Christian Church to the Hellenic Civilization; the Far Eastern Civilization and its offshoot in Korea and Japan were affiliated through the Mahāyāna to the Sinic Civilization; the Hindu Civilization was affiliated through Hinduism to the Indic; the Iranic and the Arabic through Islam to the Syriac. All the eight then extant civilizations had churches for their chrysalises, and the seven then extant fossils of extinct civilizations were all preserved in ecclesiastical integuments. This was true alike of Jewry, a fossil of an extinct Syriac Civilization that had come to be dispersed throughout the World; of the Parsee, Nestorian, and Monophysite fossils of the same extinct Syriac Civilization in South-Western Asia and India; of the Jain fossil of the Indic Civilization in India; of the Hinayanian Buddhist fossils of the Indic Civilization in Ceylon, Burma, Siam, and Cambodia; and of the same civilization's Tantric Mahayanian Buddhist fossils in Tibet, Mongolia, and the Soviet Union.[2] Even the Buddhist fossils, which were not scattered in diasporà but possessed national homes of their own in physical fastnesses or in 'geopolitical' *intermundia*, might have been ground to powder, long since, by the mighty living civilizations around them, but for the consolidation of their texture by the 'social cement' of a highly and peculiarly institutionalized religion.

[1] In a spiritually sensitive soul, the same interpretation of the historical facts may, of course, breed a mood of melancholia instead of complacency:

'As Classical Civilisation collapsed, Christianity ceased to be the noble faith of Jesus the Christ: it became a religion useful as the social cement of a world in dissolution. As such, it assisted at the rebirth of Western European Civilisation after the Dark Ages. It has endured to be the nominal creed of clever and restless peoples who are ceasing to give even lip-service to its ideals. As to its future, who can prophesy?' (Barnes, E. W.: *The Rise of Christianity* (London 1947, Longmans Green), p. 336).

[2] In A.D. 1952 the Buriat community still survived in Transbaikalia, though the Calmuck community that had tenanted the pasturelands between the lower reaches of the Volga and the Don since the seventeenth century of the Christian Era (see III. iii. 397) was reported to have been liquidated as a punishment for disloyalty to the Soviet Union at the time of the German invasion during the General War of A.D. 1939–45.

In these fossil communities the chrysalis church had preserved an elsewhere extinct civilization in a state of suspended animation, without having succeeded in inducing a new civilization to germinate within its protective but restrictive sheath. To investigate the process by which a new civilization does affiliate itself to a predecessor through the agency of a church, we must concentrate out attention on the living civilizations. On a synoptic view of the antecedents of these, we shall find ourselves able to analyse the process of transition to them from their predecessors into three phases which, from the standpoint of the chrysalis church, we may label 'conceptive', 'gestative', and 'parturient'.

The conceptive phase of the transmissionary role of a universal church sets in when the church seizes an opportunity that is offered to it by the secular social environment in which it arises.

This environment is the universal state which a disintegrating civilization throws up, at an advanced stage of its decline, in an effort to arrest the fatal process. By the time when this rally is achieved, and not least in the very act of achieving it, the ailing secular society, partly unintentionally and partly deliberately, has put out of action many of the master institutions of its phase of growth—above all, the parochial states which, while the society was still in health, gave such scope for variety in the exercise of its creative powers, and this not only in the political and economic fields, but in the visual arts, literature, and other provinces of culture. The universal state could not arise until its parochial predecessors had decimated their own ranks by recurrent fratricidal wars, and until the weakened survivors had exhausted their credit of affection and loyalty in the hearts of citizens on whom they had been calling for never-ceasing and ever-increasing sacrifices; and, after establishing itself, it could not secure its position against the threat of a recrudescence of international anarchy without curbing the remnant of parochial sovereignty and sapping the remnant of self-government. In this situation the sorely tried populations that have been united politically at last within the universal state's frontiers find themselves torn between conflicting feelings which they cannot reconcile. Their dominant emotions are a thirst for peace and quiet and a grateful acquiescence in the oecumenical régime that has brought them these long-desired blessings, and this general attitude of mind is the psychological foundation of the parvenu imperial government's rule. But the sense of relief is traversed and tempered by a sense of frustration; for Life cannot preserve itself by bringing itself to a halt; the stream of psychic energy known in the language of a Modern Western school of Psychology as *libido* continues to well up out of its springs in the subconscious depths; and, as the universal state settles down and its subjects begin to recuperate from their exhaustion, while the memory of the preceding Time of Troubles begins to fade, they suffer more and more discomfort from the choking up of the ancient institutional outlets for the flow of the human 'social animal's' life-force.[1]

[1] The discomfort is apt to be at its maximum in the universal state's capital city, 'quo cuncta undique atrocia aut pudenda confluunt celebranturque' (Tacitus: *Annals*, Book XV, chap. 44).

This is a psychological need for which the universal state itself does not provide; for its *raison d'être* is the negative one of re-establishing control over destructive forces that have got out of hand; and, so far from being concerned to open up innocuous alternative channels for activity, it tends to look askance at all new manifestations of Life as so many more openings for fresh outbreaks of the demonic spirit of Anarchy. In this situation a nascent universal church may make its own fortune by doing for a stagnant secular society the service that is now its most urgent need; for it can open up new channels for the baulked spiritual energies of Mankind without asking the imperial government's leave and sometimes, still more effectively, in defiance of its veto. In the Roman Empire,

'The victory of Christianity over Paganism . . . furnished the orator with new topics of declamation and the logician with new points of controversy. Above all, it produced a new principle, of which the operation was constantly felt in every part of Society. It stirred the stagnant mass from the inmost depths. It excited all the passions of a stormy democracy in the quiet and listless population of an overgrown empire. The fear of heresy did what the sense of oppression could not do; it changed men, accustomed to be turned over like sheep from tyrant to tyrant, into devoted partisans and obstinate rebels. The tones of an eloquence which had been silent for ages resounded from the pulpit of Gregory. A spirit which had been extinguished on the plains of Philippi revived in Athanasius and Ambrose.'[1]

This passage from the pen of a Modern Western historian is as truthful as it is eloquent, but its theme is the second chapter in the story. At this stage the opening of new channels by the Christian Church did indeed release intellectual and political energies that had been dammed back so long that their currents had been flowing in reverse into the Dead Sea of Archaism.[2] But this chapter followed a previous, and more critical, stage in the encounter between universal church and universal state in which a head-on collision between them had given ordinary men and women a fresh opportunity for making a supreme sacrifice that had been the glory and the tragedy of Society in the age of parochial sovereignty and fratricidal warfare.

The essence of the institution of the parochial state is the custom that calls on its citizens to give their lives for it in war, and this demand is psychologically possible so long as their country fills the whole of their mental horizon and appears to embrace the sum of things human and divine. This pretension of a state to be the Universe, preposterous though it be, only ceases to command assent and obedience when the last of the contending parochial states of a disintegrating society have been annihilated and replaced by a single universal state which, at the beginning, commands the loyalty of no more than that fraction of its population that constitutes the imperial people, and when concurrently the people's religious devotion is transferred from cults with local roots to higher

[1] Macaulay, Lord: 'History', in *Miscellaneous Writings* (London 1860, Longmans Green, 2 vols), vol. i, p. 267. Compare the passage, describing how Religion filled a psychological vacuum in the Achaemenian Empire, that has been quoted from Eduard Meyer in V. vi. 29–33.

[2] See V. vi. 49–97.

religions with a message for all Humanity.[1] Under the pagan Roman Empire in the Age of the Principate, no one, as we have seen,[2] except a handful of professional soldiers, recruited by voluntary enlistment, was called upon to die for an oecumenical polity, but the Roman Government itself was unable to prevent civilians of the most 'unmartial' social antecedents from sacrificing their lives as martyrs to the cause of the Christian Church. This state of affairs—so rare up to date in the Age of the Civilizations—in which the object for which men and women were prepared to give their lives was a church and not a state,[3] might foreshadow the future relation between Politics and Religion in a coming age that had not yet emerged above the historical horizon of the writer's generation.

Thus, in this 'conceptive' phase of the encounter between a universal church and a universal state, the church receives into itself the energies that the state can neither utilize nor liberate, and creates new channels along which these can find vent. The 'gestative' phase that follows is distinguished by a vast increase in the church's range of creative action. The outlets already found by the church for energies with which the

[1] See Eduard Meyer, loc. cit. [2] On pp. 342–4, above.

[3] The foregoing account of the conceptive phase of the transmissionary role of a church has drawn the following comment from Mr. Martin Wight:

'An interesting point emerges here, which the reader would like you to develop. You illustrate the conceptive phase only from Christian history. Does this mean that there is not comparable evidence from the other higher religions?

'Is it correct to say that the characteristic mark of the conceptive phase is *sanguis martyrum semen ecclesiae*? If so, then there are *a priori* reasons for expecting the conceptive phase to have a peculiar importance in the history of Christianity, if not actually to be peculiar to Christianity. 1. Christianity is the only higher religion whose Founder consummated his mission by being himself martyred. Is it also the only one whose Founder emphasised martyrdom as the likely fate and the supreme test of fidelity for his followers?—Anyway, to share the sufferings of Christ has always had a central place in the tradition of Christian devotion (cp. Matt. x. 17–22 and 39, Mark x. 39, John xvi. 2, Rom. viii. 17, Rev. vi. 9–11), and the will-to-martyrdom was probably greater among Early Christians than among the early adherents of other higher religions. 2. Christianity has always made more exclusive claims than the other higher religions (except Islam), and consequently made it peculiarly difficult for the universal state in which it arose to be tolerant towards it (cp. V. vi. 46–47).

'In other places in this Part you refer to what might be evidence for or against an occurrence of the conceptive phase in the other churches. Islam did not grow up within a universal state but conquered one from outside, so that its seed was not the blood of the martyr but the sword of the warrior: the conceptive phase, if any, must therefore have taken a different form (see p. 411, n. 4, below), and the subsequent retroactive persecution by the new church of the residual pre-higher-religion minority was less severe than in the case of Christianity (cp. p. 400, below). The two Indic religions have been inherently tolerant (see pp. 438–9, below). Does this mean that Hinduism established itself without any need of *sanguis martyrum*? As for the Mahāyāna, it permeated the Far Eastern Society with only "occasional bouts of repression" (see p. 405; cp. pp. 541–2). "These persecutions", says C. P. Fitzgerald, "never resembled those so familiar from Western religious history. There were no burnings, no torture or massacre of the faithful. At most the authorities ordered the destruction of some or all of the monasteries, and forced nuns and monks to return to family life, sometimes by the expedient, repugnant to all good Buddhists, of mating the monks and nuns themselves" (*China, A Short Cultural History*, p. 276). Is this a valid generalisation?

'The question is twofold: 1. Has *sanguis martyrum semen ecclesiae* been true on the whole only of Christianity? For if so, it seems to give the conceptive phase a deeper significance for the Christian Church than for the others. 2. If so, what have been the marks of the conceptive phase for the others?'

In the opinion of the writer of this Study the answer to the first of these two questions is in the affirmative, while the answer to the second is that, in the histories of the other higher religions, as in the history of Christianity, the essential mark of the conceptive phase is to be found in a transfer of spiritual energy from secular to religious channels.

universal state has been unable to cope are equivalents, as we have seen, of secular institutions and activities which had been creative in a civilization's growth phase but destructive in its Time of Troubles and incompatible with the rest-cure of an oecumenical polity. In the next chapter of the story the secular oecumenical institutions which the universal state has built up go the same way as the secular parochial institutions that they have supplanted. After having come into existence to meet a social need, they become a social incubus by clinging to existence after they have ceased to fulfil their purpose; and at this point the church intervenes again. She uses the achievements and experience of the now declining universal state for building new oecumenical institutions of her own, and draws into her service for this purpose men of mark who have failed to find scope for their genius as public servants of the secular imperial power in its tragi-comic last phase of paralysis and ineptitude.

We have studied this process of spoiling the Egyptians already in our survey of the beneficiaries from imperial installations, currencies, and corporations,[1] and we need not recapitulate our findings. We may pass on now to observe that the new shapes into which the church recasts the borrowed secular institutions prove capable of surviving a social interregnum in which the declining universal state goes to pieces, carrying with it the moribund secular civilization of which it is a political embodiment. What is more, this ability of the church to ride the storm is apprehended intuitively by the mass of Mankind, who by this time have a presentiment of the secular society's doom and are anxiously looking for a raft on which they may take refuge from the sinking ship. The transition to the 'gestative' from the 'conceptive' phase of the church's service as a chrysalis is signalized by a spate of mass-conversions.

The speed and scale of such religious landslides appear, as might be expected, to be proportionate to the degree of the pressure exerted on the disintegrating civilization by the barbarian aggressors who are the church's competitors for this derelict heritage.

In another context[2] we have already observed that in a moribund Sinic World the Mahāyāna began to make appreciable progress after the collapse of the Han Empire towards the close of the second century of the Christian Era and its replacement in the third century by the indigenous successor-states known as 'the Three Kingdoms'. When, however, in the fourth century of the Christian Era the North was overrun and occupied by Eurasian Nomad war-bands, while the regions south of the watershed between the Yellow River and the Yangtse Basin succeeded in keeping these alien invaders at bay, there was a sudden sharp differentiation in the fortunes of the Mahāyāna in these two now politically differentiated areas. In the North the Mahāyāna now captivated an overwhelming majority of the population—no less than 90 per cent., even according to the testimony of unsympathetic historians of the Confucian School. In the South, where the sense of insecurity was less acute, the new higher religion never succeeded in either absorbing or erasing the old secular culture. Though the strength

[1] On pp. 80–379, above. [2] On pp. 370–2, above.

of the hold which the Mahāyāna obtained there too is attested by the devotion to it of so cultivated a ruler as Liang Wuti (*imperabat* A.D. 502–49), the tradition of Confucian scholarship and administration succeeded in maintaining in the South a base of operations from which it eventually reasserted itself throughout the domain of a nascent Far Eastern Society.

In a moribund Hellenic World the sudden mass-conversion of the northern provinces of the Han Empire to the Mahāyāna in the fourth century of the Christian Era had its counterpart in the similar conversion of the western provinces of the Roman Empire to Catholic Christianity in the fifth century, when these provinces were being overrun by Nomadic or Nomadicized barbarians from the Eurasian Steppe and by sedentary barbarians from the North European forests. The religious landslide that was precipitated here at this date by a similar political and social crisis was the more remarkable considering that the Christian Church had won the bulk of its converts in the eastern and central provinces of the Empire during the first three centuries of its history; and, though Constantine's manifesto in favour of Christianity on the eve of the Battle of the Milvian Bridge indicates that, by A.D. 312, Christianity was already a force to be reckoned with in the western regiments of the Imperial Army,[1] it seems not to have become anything more than a minoritarian religion among the civil population in the West till the close of the fourth century. In these backward western provinces at this time the peasantry and gentry were falling more and more under the influence of the great landowners of the Senatorial Order, and these western provincial *viri senatorii* were influenced in their turn by the metropolitan senatorial nobility in Rome, who were 'die-hard' devotees of Paganism.[2] Among the Gallic Roman grandees and their retainers the revolutionary change of religious outlook within the century that embraces the lifetimes of Rutilius Namatianus and Sidonius Apollinaris is no doubt to be explained by the deeply disquieting effect of the successive waves of barbarian invasion that swept across Gaul between the breach of the Rhine frontier by the Vandals and their comrades in A.D. 406 and the overthrow of the no longer unmitigatedly barbarous Visigoths by the still portentously unreclaimed Franks in A.D. 507.

In a moribund Syriac World in the time of the Caliphate the barbarian pressure that evoked the sharpest anxiety and apprehension was the onset of the Eurasian Nomad Turks, and the exposed area consisted of the provinces of the Caliphate, from Khurāsān to Farghānah inclusive, that lay to the north-east of the central desert of Iran and of the narrow passage at the Caspian Gates between the north-western edge of the desert and the belt of mountains, forest, jungle, and swamp that extended, on the other side of the fairway, to the shores of the Caspian Sea. In the light of the episodes of Hellenic and Sinic history which we have noticed above, it is not surprising to catch glimpses of mass-

[1] See p. 341, above. N. H. Baynes, in his *Constantine the Great and the Christian Church* (London 1929, Milford), p. 4, estimates that Christianity was professed by perhaps one-tenth of Constantine's subjects at this date.

[2] See V. vi. 88–89.

conversions to the orthodox Sunnī form of Islam in these outpost provinces of the Caliphate from the turn of the eighth and ninth centuries of the Christian Era onwards.

Already in the Umayyad Age, when Khurāsān was still the north-east frontier province of the Caliphate, before the definitive conquest of Transoxania, the local Iranian population had been quick to fraternize with its Arab conquerors in the common interest of fending off the barbarians; and the Iranian clients whom the Arab frontier garrisons enlisted in their ranks seem to have become converts to Islam as a matter of course.[1] After the definitive incorporation of Transoxania in the Caliphate and the subsequent turn of the tide of war in the barbarians' favour under the ʿAbbasid régime, the process gathered momentum. The conversion of Sāmān, a member of the local Iranian nobility at Bālkh, from Zoroastrianism to Islam, towards the end of the eighth century of the Christian Era,[2] was the first step towards the establishment of a Samanid successor-state of the ʿAbbasids that took over from its nominal suzerains a wardenship of the north-eastern marches which the ʿAbbasids themselves had become too feeble to administer effectively any longer from their distant headquarters at Baghdad.[3]

The example set by Sāmān's conversion to Islam was widely followed by his descendants' subjects,[4] and, when the Samanids in their turn collapsed after having held the fort for 180 years (A.D. 819–999), and the long-dammed-back flood of barbarian invasion at last broke through, the final stage in the process of conversion went with a run. There were few Zoroastrians left in Khurāsān, and few followers of the Mahāyāna in Transoxania or Afghanistan, by the time when the utterly barbarous Mongols broke in at the heels of the more amenable Turks. This last and most devastating wave of Eurasian Nomad invaders almost obliterated the remnants of the ancient culture in the dominions of the Samanids' Turkish successors the Khwārizm Shāhs; and, if a common Islam, which by that time had superseded the previous sectarian faiths, had not inspired the survivors of the sedentary population between the Jaxartes and the Caspian Gates to present a united front to their alien oppressors, the Syriac Civilization might have perished without a successor. The Iranic Muslim Civilization, which arose out of the ruins of the Syriac Civilization and which succeeded in taking the savage Mongol conquerors captive, unmistakably owed its existence to an Islamic chrysalis.[5]

The conversion to Islam of the Zoroastrian and Buddhist subjects of an empire in which Islam was the hall-mark of the imperial people was not, however, so remarkable as the conversion of the unconquered Zoroastrians of Daylam and Tabaristān, who, in their fastness between the Elburz Range and the Caspian Sea, had preserved their freedom when all the rest of the Sasanian Empire had capitulated to the Primitive

1 See V. v. 450, and pp. 140–1, above.

2 See Arnold, Sir Thomas: *The Preaching of Islam*, 2nd ed. (London 1913, Constable), p. 210.

3 See II. ii. 142.

4 According to Arnold, op. cit., p. 214, the decisive date in the conversion of Transoxania to Islam was the reign of the ʿAbbasid Caliph Muʿtasim (*imperabat* A.D. 833–42).

5 See II. ii. 142, 144–50, and 446–52; and pp. 256–7, above.

Arab Muslim armies.[1] Their retention of their ancestral Zoroastrian faith had been the symbol of the successfulness of their resistance; yet in the course of the ninth and tenth centuries of the Christian Era they abandoned Zoroastrianism in favour of Islam on their own initiative. A landmark in this process was the voluntary conversion of the independent prince Karīm b. Shahriyār of the Qābūsī House at the turn of the eighth and ninth centuries of the Christian Era; and there were subsequent mass-conversions in Daylam in A.D. 873 and in both Daylam and Tabaristān *circa* A.D. 912.[2] It is true that these converts in the Caspian Provinces advertised their independence, even in the act of conversion, by adopting Islam in its heretical Zaydī Shiʿite form;[3] yet, even so, this act was a striking manifestation of a desire for solidarity with the rest of their society on the part of a people whose traditional parochialism was inspired and abetted by the physical isolation of their habitat.

In a disintegrating Indic World the effacement of Buddhism by Hinduism seems to have been accomplished by insensible degrees and to have been in progress from perhaps as early as the second century B.C. until as late as the seventh century of the Christian Era—even if we leave out of account the survival of Buddhism in Bengal, where, in the Tantric version of the Mahāyāna, it persisted for some six centuries longer, till the rising tide of Hinduism engulfed its rival here too, thanks to the destruction of the Tantric Buddhist culture in Bengal by the Muslim invaders of the Ganges Valley at the close of the twelfth century of the Christian Era. Yet we can date within narrower chronological limits the period in which, in the Indic World as a whole, Hinduism decisively gained the upper hand. This happened under the Guptan Rāj, which provided the Indic World with an effective universal state (an avatar of the Mauryan Rāj) from the last decade of the fourth century till the third quarter of the fifth century of the Christian Era.[4] It is perhaps no accident that the Guptan 'Indian Summer', in which Hinduism definitively established itself as the universal religion of a disintegrating Indic Society, was also the eve of the Hun and Gurjara Eurasian Nomad barbarian invasions of Hindustan. At any rate it would appear[5] that Hinduism in North-Western India, like Islam in North-Eastern Iran, Catholic Christianity in Western Europe, and the Mahāyāna in Northern China, gave a new civilization the possibility of coming to birth by holding together the conquered subjects of a fallen universal state and taking their barbarian conquerors captive.

Hinduism in India and the Mahāyāna in the Far East share with one another the honourable distinction of having achieved their sweeping spiritual conquests of human souls without resorting to the use of physical violence to supplement their preaching. By contrast, in both the ʿAbbasid Caliphate and the post-Diocletianic Roman Empire the mass-conversions of a majority of the population to the prevailing higher religion were accompanied by manifestations of exasperation with a residual minority whose obstinate loyalty to its ancestral faith was

[1] See II ii. 446–7.

[2] See Arnold, op. cit., p. 210.

[3] See I. i. 354 and II. ii. 448.

[4] See I. i. 85.

[5] See I. i. 85, n. 2.

cheating Mankind of a unity in which it was ardently longing to find strength. In the Caliphate this exasperation vented itself in spasmodic popular outbreaks of persecution;[1] but these were never pressed home—as is witnessed by the fact that the persecuted non-Muslim religious minorities were still in existence *in situ* at the time of writing, not much less than a thousand years after the date at which they had first begun to feel the breeze of Muslim intolerance.

In the Roman Empire Christian intolerance took the grimmer form of a systematic official repression of all non-Christian religions except Judaism; and this policy was persistently enforced till it resulted in the *Gleichschaltung* that was its objective.[2] It is significant that this sinister departure from the Constantinian *modus vivendi* between Christianity and Paganism was made in A.D. 382, four years after the Roman military disaster at Adrianople,[3] and that the author of the new militant policy was Theodosius I, who was striving to save the Empire from immediate dissolution. When the news of the great catastrophe of A.D. 378 reverberated through the Roman World, a panic-stricken population—faced with an imminent prospect of seeing the familiar secular social framework of its life fall in ruins about its ears—instinctively closed its ranks round the standard of an oecumenical religious organization that gave promise of being able to weather the storm; and this flustered majority turned with savage resentment upon a minority of archaistic-minded grandees and backward peasants who, as the rest of Mankind saw it, were wantonly thwarting Mankind's one hope of social as well as spiritual salvation.

If the foregoing analysis is correct, the transition to the 'gestative' from the 'conceptive' phase of a church's service as a chrysalis is marked by an increase in the impetus of the flow of vitality without any change in its direction. In both these phases a current of psychic energy that can no longer find vent through the choked or shattered institutional channels of a disintegrating civilization is flowing into alternative channels newly opened for it by the church. In the 'conceptive' phase the church is absorbing energy, released by the atrophy of the disintegrating civilization's previous parochial institutions, for which a universal state has failed to provide an outlet; at the transition from the 'conceptive' to the 'gestative' phase the church goes on to absorb the residual energy of the moribund secular society for which the universal state did provide an outlet until its own collapse. In this second phase the church is freighted with all the heritage and all the potentialities of Mankind; and, carrying with it this inestimably precious cargo, it embarks on its perilous passage across the gulf that opens beneath its feet when the fabric of the dead civilization finally dissolves into a social vacuum.

In the quaint but expressive imagery of Islamic Mythology, we may liken the church, in this heroic phase of its history, to the avatar of the Prophet Muhammad as a ram who sure-footedly crosses the bridge—

[1] See V. v. 678, n. 2, and V. vi. 205. The subject is dealt with in greater detail in Tritton, A. S.: *The Caliphs and their Non-Muslim Subjects* (London 1930, Milford), especially chaps. 4 and 9, and in Browne, L. E.: *The Eclipse of Christianity in Asia from the Time of Muhammad till the Fourteenth Century* (Cambridge 1933, University Press).

[2] See IV. iv. 226–7.

[3] See IV. iv. 440–3.

narrow as a razor's edge—which is the only avenue of access to Paradise just because it spans the yawning gulf of Hell. Sinners and unbelievers who hazard the dizzy adventure on their own feet infallibly fall into the abyss; the only human souls that find their way across are those which, as a reward for their virtue or for their faith, are permitted to cling to the miraculous ram's fleece in the conveniently portable shape of beatified ticks.[1] When the crossing has been duly accomplished, the 'gestative' phase in the church's transmissionary service is succeeded by the 'parturient' phase, and at this second transition the tide in the flow of spiritual energy turns and the roles of church and civilization are reversed. In the 'conceptive' phase the church was drawing vitality from an old civilization within whose framework the church had sprung up; in the 'parturient' phase the church gives out vitality to a new civilization that has been conceived in the church's womb. We can watch this creative energy that has been confined within ecclesiastical bounds during the social interregnum flowing out again, under religious auspices, into secular channels on the economic and political, as well as the cultural, plane of social life.

On the economic plane at the time of writing, by far the most impressive existing legacy of a 'parturient' universal church to an emergent civilization was to be seen in the economic prowess of a contemporary Western World. By that date a quarter of a millennium had passed since a new secular society had completed a long-drawn-out process of extricating itself from the chrysalis of the Western Catholic Christian Church, and seven centuries since the first audacious anti-clerical stroke had been struck by the *Stupor Mundi* Frederick II Hohenstaufen.[2] Yet the marvellous and monstrous apparatus of Western technology, whose mechanical tentacles were now holding the whole globe in their grip, was a monument of the economic genius of an ecclesiastical Frankenstein; for, when the history of this unprecedented and peculiar Western economic achievement was traced back, it turned out to have originated as a by-product of Western Christian monachism.[3] The psychological foundation of this mighty material edifice was a belief in the duty and

[1] An inquiry into the origins of this Islamic myth might carry us far afield and give us light on obscure tracts of religious history. The bridge is manifestly the 'Chinvat Bridge' of Zoroastrian Eschatology (see Nyberg, H. S.: *Die Religionen des Alten Iran* (Leipzig 1938, Hinrichs) (Mitteilungen der Vorderasiatisch-Aegyptischen Gesellschaft (E. V.), 43 Band), pp. 179–86). Is the ram the Cyclops' ram under whose belly Odysseus, clinging to the fleece, passed safely out of the mouth of the Cyclops' cave without being detected by the blinded monster's groping hands? And is this the same ram on whose golden fleece Phrixos safely rode the waves of the Hellespont when his sister Hellê fell off in mid-course and gave her name to the waters in which she perished?

[2] For the historical significance of the Emperor Frederick II, see pp. 440, 446, and 537–9, below, and IX. viii. 394–5.

[3] Mr. Martin Wight comments: 'This is true not only on the social level on which you are discussing it. Is it not more profoundly true on the intellectual level? For does not a Modern Western Science rest on the foundations of a Christian theology and take for granted a Christianised World? "The pre-suppositions that go to make up this 'Catholic Faith', preserved for many centuries by the religious institutions of Christendom, have as a matter of historical fact been the main or fundamental presuppositions of Natural Science ever since" (Collingwood, R. G.: *An Essay on Metaphysics* (Oxford 1940, Clarendon Press), p. 227. Compare Berdyaev, N.: *The Meaning of History* (London 1936, Bles), p. 117, and Polanyi, M.: *Science, Faith and Society* (London 1946, Oxford University Press). Compare also the quotation from Gilson on p. 514, below, which makes the same point).'

dignity of physical labour; and this attitude—which was a revolutionary departure from the Hellenic contempt for labour as something vulgar and servile[1]—would not have established itself if it had not been hallowed through being inculcated in Saint Benedict's Rule as a means, not of conjuring into existence a titanic 'commonwealth of swine',[2] but of providing for aspirants to citizenship in a 'commonwealth of God' a discipline in the life of This World that would be propitious for their spiritual endeavours. On this immaterial foundation the Benedictine Order planted the agricultural groundwork of Western economic life, and this groundwork gave the Cistercian Order a basis for the industrial superstructure which their silent activity erected over their monastic folds and fields, until the cupidity that this monk-built Tower of Babel aroused in the hearts of its builders' secular neighbours reached a pitch at which they could no longer keep their hands off it. A spoliation of the monasteries was one of the origins of a Modern Western capitalist economy.

When we pass from the economic to the political plane, we see churches calling into existence new 'commonwealths of nations' and providing the statesmen and administrators required for the government of secular polities.

In a different context[3] we have watched the Papacy giving a new political form to a Medieval Western Christendom by moulding it into a *Respublica Christiana* that promised to enable Mankind to enjoy simultaneously the benefits of both parochialism and oecumenicalism without having to suffer from the characteristic drawbacks of either of these hitherto antithetical dispensations. In bringing new communities into the comity of Western Christendom with the political status of independent kingdoms, the Papacy was bringing back into the political life of Mankind the multiplicity and variety that had been so fruitful in the growth stage of the antecedent Hellenic Civilization, while the political disunity and dissension that had brought the Hellenic Society to ruin and its political parochialism into disrepute were to be exorcised, in this new attempt to solve an old problem, by a recourse to the oecumenical authority which the Papacy had inherited from the Roman Empire. The secular parochial princes of a Western Christian World were to dwell together in unity[4] under the presidency of an ecclesiastical shepherd; and, for the exercise of these political responsibilities, the Pope had sanctions at his command which had been lacking in the Delphic Amphictyony. In the eyes of the subjects of a Medieval Western Christian prince, their ruler's title to their obedience rested on the recognition of his legitimacy by the Apostle at Rome, and the power to bind implied the power to loose.[5]

In a previous Part of this Study[6] we have observed the tragic breakdown of this Medieval Western Christian ecclesiastico-political experiment, and the course of our inquiry will lead us back to this tragedy

[1] See IV. iv. 239–41.

[2] Plato: *Respublica*, 369B–372D, cited in the present Study in II. i. 193, n. 1, and II. ii. 23, n. 2. See further XII. x. 523, 612, and 604–14.

[3] In IV. iv. 351–2, 378–9, and 518–20.

[4] Ps. cxxxiii. 1.

[5] Matt. xvi. 19 and xviii. 18.

[6] In IV. iv. 533–84.

again. At this point we have merely to take note of it as one illustration of the political role of a church in its 'parturient' phase, and to observe the corresponding role played by the Brahman ecclesiastical fraternity in the political articulation of a nascent Hindu Society when the Brahmans conferred legitimacy on Rājput dynasties descended from Hun and Gurjara Eurasian Nomad founders of barbarian successor-states in the former domain of the Guptan Empire by discovering irreproachable genealogies for these casteless interlopers, who could never have passed themselves off as kshatriyas without the aid of the Brahmans' intellectual dexterity and religious prestige.[1]

When we pass on to examine the Christian Church's political role in Orthodox Christendom and the Mahāyāna's in the Far East, we see the church's field of activity being circumscribed in both these societies by the evocation of a ghost of the antecedent civilization's universal state—the Sui and T'ang renaissance of the Han Empire in the main body of the Far Eastern Society, and the East Roman renaissance of the Roman Empire in the main body of Orthodox Christendom.[2] In these circumstances in the Far East the participation of the Mahayanian clergy in secular public life never became more than a passing phase in a particular region. The prospects opened up by their employment in the fourth and fifth centuries of the Christian Era as civil servants in the barbarian successor-states of the Han Empire in its northern provinces, in place of Confucian civil servants who were unwilling to serve a barbarian régime,[3] were decisively closed when, in A.D. 589, the South of a nascent Far Eastern World was united politically with the North and when, in the next generation, the Confucian scholar-administrators were enticed by T'ang T'ai Tsung out of their southern citadel to take over the administration of an avatar of the oecumenical empire of the Han.[4] In Orthodox Christendom the Christian Church's field of political activity had promised in the seventh century of the Christian Era to become what it eventually did become in the West; but in the event the Oecumenical Patriarch Sergius (*fungebatur* A.D. 610–38) proved not to have been the harbinger of an Orthodox Christian counterpart of the Medieval Western Papal ascendancy. In Orthodox Christendom this promise failed to materialize owing to the Emperor Leo Syrus's success in organizing the East Roman Empire in the eighth century and to the re-emergence in the ninth century of a classically educated Christian laity capable of conducting a complicated civil administration without the Church's assistance.[5]

In these altered political and cultural circumstances the fate of the Christian Church in Orthodox Christendom was more ironical than that of the Mahāyāna in the Far East. In the Far Eastern Society from T'ang T'ai Tsung's day onwards the Mahāyāna found a new place for itself as one among a number of religions and philosophies existing side by side and catering, without any mutual exclusiveness, for the divers

[1] See Smith, V. A.: *The Early History of India*, 3rd ed. (Oxford 1914, Clarendon Press), pp. 407–15.
[2] See pp. 19–21, above, and X. ix. 16 and 15.
[3] See pp. 370–2, above, and X. ix. 20.
[4] See pp. 370–2, above, and X. ix. 20.
[5] See IV. iv. 344–6.

spiritual needs of the same public; and, just because the Mahāyāna did offer spiritual sustenance that was not to be obtained either from a vulgar Taoism or from an academic Confucianism, it unobtrusively continued to permeate the life of the Far Eastern Society in spite of occasional bouts of repression to which it was subjected by Gallio-like emperors at the instigation of envious-hearted Confucian counsellors.

The continuing importance of the Mahāyāna in this unofficial guise is attested by the part that it played in the cultural conversion of Korea and Japan to the Far Eastern way of life—a part that bears comparison with the role played by the Christian Church in the attraction of Hungary, Poland, and Scandinavia into the orbit of Western Christendom. A comparable role was played by the Eastern Orthodox Christian Church in planting an offshoot of the Orthodox Christian Civilization in the soil of Russia; but in Orthodox Christian history this achievement was exceptional; for, although, to outward appearance, the Christian Church in the main body of Orthodox Christendom had suffered less than the Mahāyāna in the main body of the Far Eastern World from an Hellenic political and cultural renaissance that lacked the self-assurance and the driving-force of the Sinic renaissance in the Age of the T'ang, it had been manœuvred, as a consequence, into a more invidious position. It would have been happier for the Church to have been disestablished than to be kept in harness, as she was, as the handmaiden instead of the Egeria of a ghost of the Roman Empire; for, in her new official status of subjection to the East Roman state, the Church brought, not peace, but a sword[1] into the international life of an expanding Orthodox Christendom.

The disastrous effect of the Orthodox Church's constitutional position on the relations between the East Roman Empire and Bulgaria after Bulgaria's conversion has been examined in some detail in another context,[2] and we have also noticed how the ascendancy, of which the Church was disappointed in Orthodox Christendom in the auspicious hour when the new society was in growth, was thrust upon the Church out of due time and beyond due measure after the Orthodox Christian Civilization had prematurely broken down in consequence of the monstrously disproportionate over-development of a renascent state that had established its own ascendancy over the Church.[3] When the main body of a broken-down Orthodox Christian Society found itself constrained, as the penalty for its political failure, to accept an indispensable universal state at alien hands, and Greeks and Bulgars were forced into political parity at last as fellow *ra'īyeh* of an Ottoman shepherd, the Oecumenical Patriarch Gennadius and his successors were invested *de jure* by the statesmanship of Sultan Mehmed Fātih with the political authority that had once devolved *de facto* on the Oecumenical Patriarch Sergius at the Roman Empire's nadir in the days of Heraclius. During the period between the Ottoman conquest of Constantinople in A.D. 1453 and the impact of the West at the turn of the eighteenth and nineteenth centuries of the Christian Era, the main body of Orthodox Christendom survived in a state of suspended animation as a *millet* of

1 Matt. x. 34; cp. Luke xii. 51.

2 In IV. iv. 379–405.

3 See IV. iv. 352–71.

the Ottoman Empire with the Oecumenical Patriarchate as its *millet bashy*.[1] In this role the Church was once again serving the Orthodox Christian Civilization as a protective ecclesiastical integument, but this time it was not a chrysalis fostering a germ of new life but a napkin enfolding a buried talent.[2]

While there was no doubt about the part played by the Christian Church in the West in calling a new commonwealth of parochial states into existence at and after the close of the first chapter of Western history in the eleventh century of the Christian Era, it was still, at the time of writing, a debatable question whether—and, on an affirmative answer, to what extent—the church was also the source of the parliamentary representative institutions which began, in the second chapter of Western history, to take shape in a number of Western parochial states. It had been affirmed and denied that these parochial secular rudiments of representative government had been derived from the regional conferences of bishops or had been copied from the oecumenical constitutions of monastic orders. Whatever the truth might be on this point, an historian might feel more confidence in ascribing an ecclesiastical origin to the institutions of self-government in the city-states of the Medieval Western World;[3] for it was certain that on the secular plane the civic self-government that had once been the distinctive political feature of the Hellenic Civilization did not survive the post-Diocletianic Age, and was indeed already wilting as far back as the early days of an Antonine 'Indian Summer'—to judge, among other evidence, by the correspondence that passed between the Younger Pliny and the Emperor Trajan when Pliny was governor of the province of Bithynia. By that date a vitality which was no longer finding a satisfactory outlet in secular civic life was flowing into the self-government of the local Christian communities in the municipal cells composing the Roman body politic;[4] and, though, in the stress of the social interregnum following the dissolution of the Roman Empire in the West, ecclesiastical institutions of local self-government went the same way as their secular patterns, the authoritarian influence exerted on elections of bishops by the incumbents of neighbouring sees and by the secular arm never wholly eradicated the memory of the historical fact that the election of a bishop was traditionally the prerogative of the clergy and people of the diocese. In so far as the development of local self-government in the city-states of a Medieval Western Christendom was due to the stimulus of memories of a similar dispensation in the past, the creative reminiscence was a recollection of an ecclesiastical self-government in the Roman Imperial Age rather than of a previous secular self-government which had passed its zenith as far back as the beginning of the Hellenic Time of Troubles in the fifth century B.C.

[1] See IX. viii. 184–6.

[2] Matt. xxv. 14–30; Luke xix. 12–27.

[3] This Medieval Western renaissance of the Hellenic institution of the city-state is examined further in X. ix. 645–8.

[4] This underlying connexion between the two phenomena in Bithynia that caused Pliny the greatest concern—the decay of civic institutions and the spread of Christianity—does not seem to have been apprehended by either the conscientious governor or the level-headed emperor.

When we turn to consider the enlistment of ecclesiastical dignatories in the service of secular governments as statesmen and administrators, we find a sharp divergence between the course of Western and Hindu history on the one side and Orthodox Christian and Far Eastern history on the other.

In Western Christendom at moments of acute political and social crisis—as, for instance, when the Roman Empire was dissolving there in the fifth century of the Christian Era, or after the collapse of the Carolingian Empire in the ninth century—bishops were sometimes constrained by the importunity of their harassed flocks to take over the political as well as the ecclesiastical government of their dioceses. In the fifth century of the Christian Era this burden was thrust upon the shoulders of Apollinaris Sidonius by his Auvergnat compatriots on the eve of the annexation of Auvergne by the Roman Empire's Visigothic successor-state; and the elected magistrates who governed the city-states of Northern Italy from the eleventh century onwards seem to have been the direct political heirs, not of Carolingian counts, but of the local bishops who had stepped into the breach when an over-centralized Carolingian administration had broken down. On the Italian side of the Alps the only local bishop, apart from the Pope, who retained this temporal authority during the later Middle Ages was the Bishop of Trent, on the outermost fringe of the North Italian city-state cosmos. In the less precocious Transalpine regions of Western Christendom prince-bishoprics survived until far into the Modern Age. Within the shrunken confines of 'the Holy Roman Empire' the ecclesiastical principalities of Trent, Salzburg, Passau, Würzburg, Mainz, Trier, Köln, Münster, and Liége—to mention only a few of the most illustrious —were not swallowed up by their secular neighbours till A.D. 1803; and even in the Kingdom of England, where the development of an effective central government had been brought on at an exceptionally early date by the Danish invasions and by the Norman Conquest, the Bishop Palatine of Durham did not lose the last vestiges of the attributes of temporal sovereignty until A.D. 1836.[1]

As the counsellors and ministers of secular rulers, the ecclesiastical dignatories of Western Christendom had had a longer and more continuous career of political activity than as temporal rulers in their own right. It was not, perhaps, surprising to see the government of a barbarian successor-state of the Roman Empire, such as the Visigothic Kingdom in the Iberian Peninsula in the seventh century of the Christian Era, virtually falling into the hands of the local bishops in council. It was more remarkable that, a thousand years later, after the beginning of the Modern Age, when a Transalpine Western Christendom, in the train of a Medieval Italy, had equipped itself with an educated laity, the secular sovereigns of a sixteenth-century England and Castile and a seventeenth-century France should still have been so prone as they were to place their governments in ecclesiastical hands. The bare recital of the names Wolsey, Ximenes, Adrian, Richelieu, Mazarin is enough to remind us of the prominence of ecclesiastics in the political life of the

[1] An Act of Parliament separating the Palatinate jurisdiction from the See of Durham and vesting it in the Crown was passed at Westminster on the 21st June, 1836.

Western World in its Early Modern Age; and the list runs over into a self-consciously secular-minded eighteenth century. In a post-Hapsburg Spain an offshoot of the House of Bourbon burnt its fingers by placing itself in the venturesome hands of a Cardinal Alberoni; in a Bourbon France an archbishop of Toulouse, Étienne-Charles Lomérie de Brienne, was the last prime minister of an expiring *Ancien Régime* before Louis XVI recalled Necker and convened the States-General; and in a post-Bourbon France a Napoleon appointed at his Minister for Foreign Affairs a revolutionary politician who had served his apprenticeship as a bishop under the *Ancien Régime*. A procession of ecclesiastical statesmen that is headed by a fifth-century Roman *vir senatorius* who ended his career as bishop of Auvergne is closed by an eighteenth-century French diplomatist who began his career as bishop of Autun. From the days of Sidonius to those of Talleyrand inclusive, the 'parturient' phase of the Christian Church's service as a chrysalis was drawn out, in Gaul, over a span of more than twelve hundred years.

In the Hindu World the political record of the Brahman Caste was no less impressive. The new commonwealth of parochial states which the Brahmans had conjured up in the eighth century of the Christian Era out of the post-Guptan social interregnum soon fell into a fratricidal warfare, and in the twelfth century this breakdown opened a breach for the entry of successive waves of alien invaders;[1] yet, through all subsequent vicissitudes of Hindu political fortunes, the Brahmans managed to make their services as secular administrators indispensable under the most diverse régimes. When a disintegrating Hindu Civilization entered into its universal state, Brahman agents—from junior clerks upwards to ministers of state—were employed by the Mughal Rāj and the British Rāj in succession. Akbar ruled India through the agency of Mahēsh Dās (*alias* Rājā Bīrbal), and in A.D. 1952 a Kashmīrī Brahman, Jawaharlal Nehru, was serving as the first Prime Minister of the British Rāj's newly established Hindu successor-state.

When we turn to the histories of the Orthodox Christian and Far Eastern civilizations, the picture changes. In the main body of Orthodox Christendom the Oecumenical Patriarch Sergius's effective intervention in secular politics in the reign of the Emperor Heraclius (*imperabat* A.D. 610–41) was, as we have seen, a flash in the pan; thereafter, the Oecumenical Patriarchate went into a political eclipse that lasted for more than eight hundred years; and, even when Mehmed the Conqueror found it convenient to turn this ancient Orthodox Christian ecclesiastical institution to the political account of an alien régime, he entrusted Gennadius with the management, not of the Ottoman Empire itself, but merely of its largest subject community, the *Rūm Milleti*. In the seventeenth and eighteenth centuries of the Christian Era the Ottoman Government did bring itself to employ unconverted Greeks as ministers of state,[2] and it recruited these Dragomans of the Porte and Dragomans of the Fleet from the Patriarchal côterie in the Phanar at Constantinople; but these Christian Greek Ottoman high officials were invariably laymen. In a nascent Far Eastern Society the Mahayanian clerical administrators

[1] See IV. iv. 99. [2] See II. ii. 222–8.

in the service of the barbarian successor-states of the Han Empire in the North played a political part not unlike that of the Catholic Christian bishops in Visigothic Spain; but, unlike their Western Christian counterparts, they had no successors. No Buddhist Richelieu found service with the Ming and no Buddhist Talleyrand with the Manchus.

The picture changes again, however, when we pass from the political to the cultural plane; for a Mahāyāna which was driven out of the Far Eastern political arena so decisively by a resurgent Confucian School of scholar-administrators in the Age of the T'ang reasserted itself in the intellectual field in the Age of the Sung. The five Far Eastern philosophers, culminating in Chu Hsi,[1] who, in the course of the eleventh and twelfth centuries of the Christian Era, created a new system of metaphysics and ethics in the belief that they were rediscovering the original meaning of the Confucian Classics, owed less to the authentic Confucian canon than to a Mahayanian *Weltanschauung* which by their day had so subtly permeated the intellectual atmosphere of the Far Eastern World that it could govern the thought of minds that were set upon ignoring or repudiating it.[2]

This enduring intellectual potency was part of the heritage of the Mahāyāna from a Primitive Buddhist school of philosophy of which this higher religion was a metamorphosis.[3] In contrast to the Mahāyāna, Christianity had started life without any philosophical system of its own, and had subsequently found itself constrained to attempt the *tour de force* of presenting its faith in the alien intellectual terms of the Hellenic schools in order to commend itself to the intellectually cultivated upper stratum of the Hellenic Society.[4] In Western Christendom this Hellenic intellectual alloy in Christian thought became overwhelmingly dominant after it had been reinforced in the twelfth century by the 'reception' of Aristotelianism into a Western Christian theology;[5] and, though the Christian Church did make a most effective contribution to intellectual progress in the West by founding and fostering the Western universities,[6] it was not in the intellectual so much as in the artistic sphere that the cultural influence of Christianity on the Western Civilization made itself felt. In the West, the liturgy of the Christian Church was one of the roots of a secular literature[7]—first in the Latin that was the sacred language of the Church in the domain of the Patriarchate of Rome,[8] and thereafter in a galaxy of living vernacular tongues that burst out of their Latin swaddling clothes in the twelfth century as buds break into flower in spring.[9]

[1] See II. i. 202–3.

[2] See, for example, Fung Yu-lan: *A Short History of Chinese Philosophy* (New York 1948, Macmillan), pp. 254 and 268. In the present study the Neoconfucian renaissance of the Confucian philosophy is examined further in X. ix. 40–45.

[3] See V. v. 133–6.

[4] See V. v. 366–7 and 539.

[5] See X. ix. 45–48.

[6] See IV. iv. 527.

[7] Another root of the secular literature of the Western World was the heroic poetry inspired by the experiences of the Western Christian barbarian invaders of the Andalusian Umayyad Caliphate in the Iberian Peninsula (see V. v. 259–61).

[8] The renaissances of an extinct Hellenic secular literature—in a Latin dress in Western Christendom and in a Greek dress in Orthodox Christendom—are examined further in X. ix. 60–67.

[9] There was no such flowering of a new vernacular in the main body of Orthodox

(b) THE INADEQUACY OF THE CHRYSALIS CONCEPT

We have now perhaps carried our analysis far enough to warrant the conclusion that, in each of the eight cases that have been the subject of our inquiry so far, a church had in fact served as a chrysalis which had absorbed energy emitted by a disintegrating civilization and then, in the fullness of time, had transmitted this store of energy to another civilization that had germinated in the transmissionary church's womb. If this conclusion is correct, the conception of a church as a chrysalis is borne out by the phenomena in so far as we have considered them up to this point; but we have still to ask ourselves two questions: First, does the transition from an 'apparented' to an 'affiliated' civilization invariably take place by way of a chrysalis church? And, second, even in a case in which a church has demonstrably served as an instrument for furthering the process of the reproduction of civilizations, does it follow that this service is the be-all and end-all of the church by which it has been rendered? Can we be sure that this is as important an event in the history of the chrysalis church as it manifestly is in the history of the emergent civilization? Its importance for the church itself must be outstanding if we are to be justified in taking this service as the key to the church's historical function and significance. Yet it is conceivable that, in the church's history, this may be a minor episode, if not a major aberration. Evidently our inquiry is not yet at an end. We must carry our analysis further.

If we examine more closely our eight cases in which the transition from an 'apparented' to an 'affiliated' civilization had been made by way of a chrysalis church, we shall see that in all of them the 'affiliated' society had been a civilization of the third generation and the 'apparented' society one of the second generation.[1] The Western Civilization and the Orthodox Christian, both in its main body and in its Russian offshoot, are affiliated to the Hellenic, which in its turn is affiliated to the Minoan. The Iranic and Arabic Muslim civilizations are affiliated to the Syriac, which is affiliated to the Minoan, as the Hellenic is. The Hindu Civilization is affiliated to the Indic, which in its turn is undoubtedly affiliated to the so-called 'Indus Culture', whether this is to rank as a distinctive civilization in its own right, or whether it is to be classified as an offshoot or a colonial version of the Sumeric Civilization.[2] Moreover, the progress of archaeological discovery, which had brought a not merely buried but also forgotten 'Indus Culture' to light within the lifetime of the writer of this Study, had subsequently verified and vindicated the Sinic tradition that there had been a 'Shang Culture' in the Yellow River Basin before

Christendom; for here the renaissance of Hellenism was as potent, and as blighting, in literature as it was in philosophy (see X. ix. 73–75). The spark of medieval Greek epic poetry that was struck out by the border warfare between the East Roman Empire and the 'Abbasid Caliphate did not kindle a flame; and the heroic poetry of the Russian barbarian invaders of a crumbling Khazar Empire and the Greek and Serb barbarian invaders of a crumbling Ottoman Empire was likewise abortive (see V. v. 252–9, 288–9, and 296–301). Since the Comnenian Age the vernacular literature of Orthodox Christendom had sprung, not from native roots, but from exotic Western slips and cuttings.

[1] See the table in I. i. 131–2.

[2] See I. i. 104–9.

the rise of a Sinic Civilization there in the Chóu Age;[1] and by the year A.D. 1952 the disinterment of this buried but never forgotten pre-Sinic Shang Culture had been carried far enough to warrant a student of History in concluding that the Far Eastern Civilization, both in its main body in China and in its offshoot in Korea and Japan, resembled its living contemporaries in being a civilization of the third generation—seeing that the Sinic Civilization, to which the Far Eastern was affiliated, had now proved to be affiliated in its turn to an antecedent Shang Culture which could no longer be dismissed as being merely legendary.[2] This impressive uniformity suggests that the reproduction of civilizations through the agency of chrysalis churches may be a special feature of the transition from civilizations of the second generation to those of the third.

If we test this conclusion by reckoning the generations from the standpoint, not of the 'apparented' and 'affiliated' civilizations, but of the chrysalis churches, we shall find ourselves arriving at the same uniform result; for the four churches—Christianity, Islam, Hinduism, and the Mahāyāna—which served as chrysalises in the eight cases of reproduction that we are examining, had been, every one of them, the creation of the internal proletariat of a civilization of the second generation. Christianity and the Mahāyāna stood in this relation to a disintegrating Hellenic Society,[3] Islam to a disintegrating Syriac Society,[4] Hinduism to a disintegrating Indic Society. Moreover, in the two churches—namely Christianity and the Mahāyāna—in which the creative spark of life had been derived from a source outside the society by whose internal proletariat the church had been established,[5] this alien source had likewise been a civilization of the second generation. Christianity had been inspired by the Syriac, and the Mahāyāna by the Indic, Civilization; and the Syriac and Indic societies, like the Hellenic Society within whose social framework Christianity and the Mahāyāna both grew up, were civilizations of the second generation.

Not all civilizations of the second generation, however, had become apparented to civilizations of the third generation through a chrysalis church. The achievement of this by the Indic Society, for instance, had not been emulated by any of its three sister civilizations. The abortive

[1] The place of this Shang Culture in the history of the civilizations is examined further in X. ix. 375, 694, n. 3, and 696, n. 1.

[2] This confirmation of a Sinic tradition through the disinterment of material remains that the Shang Culture had deposited during the last phase of its history was an archaeological addition to historical knowledge which, in bringing to light a previously unauthenticated 'cycle of Cathay', called for a change in the classification in previous Parts of this Study. In the table in I. i. 131 the Sinic Society should be transferred from the group of societies unrelated to earlier societies (e.g. the Minoan, Sumeric, and Mayan) to the group of 'infra-affiliated' societies (e.g. the Indic, Hittite, Syriac, and Hellenic); in the table on p. 133 in the same context the Sinic Society should be transferred from the second to the fourth line. In II. i. 318–21 the genesis of the Shang Culture, not the genesis of the Sinic Civilization, should be equated with the human response to the physical challenge of the Middle and Lower Yellow River Basin.

[3] For the relation of the Mahāyāna to the Hellenic Civilization, see V. v. 134–5, 361–3, 371, and 482–3.

[4] Islam was given its historic form by the Syriac internal proletariat, though the Arabian social milieu in which the Founder lived and died was a section of the external proletariat of the Hellenic World (see II. ii. 287–8; V .v. 127–8 and 672–8).

[5] See I. i. 57.

First Syriac, Hittite, and Babylonic societies all passed away without generating successors; and, though the internal proletariat of the Babylonic Society did succeed in creating two higher religions—Judaism and Zoroastrianism—these embryonic universal churches both missed fire through being diverted to serve the militant political purpose of championing the Syriac Civilization, from which they had derived their inspiration, against an intrusive Hellenism.[1] Thus, even in the transition from the civilizations of the second to those of the third generation, the epiphany of a chrysalis church is not an invariable feature; and, if we now extend our survey first backwards in time behind the second generation and then forwards beyond the third generation, we shall find the picture changing. In the affiliation of the Hellenic and Syriac civilizations to the Minoan Civilization, and of the Indic Civilization to the Sumeric or to the Indus Culture, there is no trace of any chrysalis church performing the service which was rendered by Christianity, the Mahāyāna, Hinduism, and Islam in the next chapter of the story, when the Hellenic, Sinic, Indic, and Syriac civilizations in their turn reproduced their kind in a third generation.

In an earlier passage[2] we have considered the possibility that Orphism might be a vestige of an almost obliterated universal church, emanating from a Minoan internal proletariat, which then would have done for a nascent Hellenic Civilization what Christianity was to do in the next generation for the Orthodox Christian and Western civilizations. But on second thoughts[3] we have inclined to the view that Orphism was not a legacy inherited by the Hellenic Society from a Minoan past but was an artificial and somewhat academic product of Hellenism itself in the Achaemenian Age when, on this view, Orphism was self-consciously manufactured by sophisticated Hellenic souls which had been made aware of a spiritual void in their own social heritage by a sudden revelation, through the conductive medium of the Achaemenian Empire, of the spiritual riches of Syriac religion and Indic philosophy.

If we turn from an almost unknown Minoan to a rather less obscure Sumeric history in its disintegration phase, a glimmer of light here enables us just to discern the emergence of the rudiments of a higher religion from an idolatrous worship which the inventors of Agriculture had paid to their own astounding handiwork.[4] The worship of a god who dies for his worshippers, and of a goddess who is the dying god's mother and also his bride, seems to have been communicated by a disintegrating Sumeric Civilization not only to its Hittite and abortive Syriac successors and to its Egyptiac neighbour but to barbarian and primitive peoples beyond the pale of Civilization up to the extreme north-western bounds of the Old World.[5] This Sumeric worship of

[1] See V. v. 117–26.
[2] In I. i. 95–100.
[3] See V. v. 82–87 and 697–8 and X. ix. 738–40.
[4] See III. iii. 256–9.
[5] See I. i. 115, n. 1, and V. v. 149–50. Henri Frankfort, in *Kingship and the Gods* (Chicago 1948, University of Chicago Press), pp. 286–94, sets out to disprove Sir James Frazer's assumption—which has been followed in the present Study throughout, and especially in V. v. 147–52—that the worships of Tammuz, Adonis, Osiris, and Attis are so many variants of a single religion. To the present writer's mind, Frankfort's

Tammuz and Ishtar had perhaps been the first institutional embodiment of a new spiritual insight that was so deep and significant that it was still to be found at the heart of the higher religions that were living and working in the *Oikoumenê* in the twentieth century of the Christian Era. Ishtar—the goddess who was at the same time 'virgin, mother and queen'[1]—lived for followers of the Mahāyāna in Kwanyin as well as for Christians in Mary, while Tammuz lived in Amitabha as well as in Husayn and in Christ.[2] The inchoate Sumeric higher religion which was eventually to bear this precious spiritual fruit does not, however, seem to have lent itself in its infancy to the mundane social task of serving as a chrysalis in the transition from a Sumeric to a Hittite or an abortive First Syriac Civilization. When the curtain rises on a Hittite World whose infancy was still obscure to historians in A.D. 1952, we find the gods of the 'apparented' Sumeric Society sharing the field with the gods of the north-western barbarians who had brought a new civilization to birth by overrunning the Anatolian provinces of a dissolving Sumeric Empire of the Four Quarters.[3] The Anatolian cult of Ishtar had to wait until the Hittite Civilization, in its turn, had gone down to Sheol before the introduction of the Sumeric goddess into the Hellenic World under the name of Cybele by a Hittite contingent of the Hellenic internal proletariat enabled her worshippers to compete with those of Isis, Mithras, and Christ for the privilege—or *corvée*—of providing a chrysalis for the transition from a declining Hellenic Civilization to successor societies of the same species.

In the Egyptiac World, where the Sumeric pair of divinities acclimatized themselves under the names Osiris and Isis, their worshippers did, if Breasted is right,[4] come within an ace of creating a proletarian church which might have conjured a new civilization out of the social interregnum that followed the break-up of 'the Middle Empire'. But this denouement, which would have anticipated by a whole generation the performance of the chrysalis role by Christianity, the Mahāyāna, Hinduism, and Islam, was prevented at the last moment by an *union sacrée* between the hitherto mutually antipathetic and hostile religions of the Egyptiac internal proletariat and dominant minority against the alien religion of the intrusive barbarian Hyksos; and, in consequence, the Egyptiac Civilization was able to double the natural term of its life, at the cost of renouncing the possibility of reproducing its kind.

It thus appears that the intervention of a church in the role of chrysalis,

arguments against the Frazerian view are less convincing than those in favour of it, which are summarized as follows by Frankfort himself with admirable candour:

'One must start by conceding that it is possible to recount a myth of a dying god which contains features common to the myths of Egypt, Mesopotamia and Syria. His story would run like this: The god was killed by an enemy in the guise of a boar (Adonis) or symbolised by the boar (Osiris, Marduk). Moreover, the god's body floated upon the water, or he was said to have drowned (Osiris, Tammuz), or his blood stained the water of a river (Adonis). His death brought about the stagnation of all natural life; a goddess bewailed him and set out to retrieve him. The god was found and liberated, sometimes with the aid of his son (Osiris, Marduk, Enlil). With his resurrection, Nature, and especially all vegetation, revived. . . . Furthermore, it has been maintained that the names of Osiris and Assur, and the epithet "Asaru" borne by Marduk, may be derived from a common root' (Frankfort, op. cit., pp. 287 and 293).

1 Goethe: *Faust*, Part II, ll. 12102–3.

2 See V. vi. 276.

3 See V. v. 266.

4 See I. i. 140–3 and V. v. 150–2.

which was a normal occurrence in the transition from civilizations of the second generation to their successors in the third generation, had never occurred in the corresponding transition to the second generation from the first. No such phenomenon had attended the exits of either the Sumeric and Egyptiac or the other primary civilizations, namely the Minoan, the Andean, and the Mayan; and, in passing, we may note that, so far as we know, the New World had never given birth to any indigenous higher religion in any chapter of the history of civilizations there.

If we now extend our survey in the opposite direction in Time, and review the latter ends of the civilizations of the third generation, we shall find that in this chapter of the story too, down to the time of writing, there had been no examples, and few auguries, of a repetition of the process of reproduction by way of chrysalis churches. This difference from the preceding chapter was not due to an absence of those circumstances that had been the predisposing conditions when the Christian Church, the Mahāyāna, Hinduism, and Islam had been created by the internal proletariats of disintegrating civilizations of the second generation; for, whatever might be the state of the Western, Iranic Muslim, and Arabic Muslim societies in the twentieth century of the Christian Era,[1] each of the five other surviving civilizations had by that time given unmistakable proof of being in disintegration by having entered into a universal state; yet these five civilizations, between them, had failed to produce a crop of higher religions that could compare with their predecessors' religious harvest at a corresponding stage in their history, and the balance is not redressed if we add to the catalogue the meagre symptoms[2] in a Western World whose disintegration could not, in A.D. 1952, yet be taken for granted.

Of the rudiments of higher religions that had been thrown up by one or other of the eight civilizations that were still alive in the sixth decade of the twentieth century of the Christian Era, some had stultified themselves by going into politics and resorting to violence, while others, which had refrained from stultifying themselves in this way and had persisted in a gentle course, had then after all stultified themselves nevertheless by falling into the trap that had once ensnared the Osirian Church in the Egyptiac World. These persistently gentle religions had carried their practice of non-violence to the point of depriving themselves of their *raison d'être* by becoming reconciled to a dominant minority whose failure to save society had called them into existence to stand in the breach. These miscarriages have come to our notice already in our survey of internal proletariats and their works,[3] and in this place we have merely to remind ourselves of episodes that have been touched upon already there.

An outstanding example of self-stultification through resort to force was presented in Hindu history by Sikhism,[4] a would-be synthesis of Hinduism with Islam which had started by practising fraternity as a corollary to its preaching of monotheism, had gone astray through allow-

[1] The prospects of the Western Civilization are discussed in XII. ix. 406–644.
[2] See V. v. 188. [3] See V. v. 58–194. [4] See V. v. 106.

ing itself to become the sectarian faith of militant founders of a successor-state of the Mughal Rāj, and had come eventually to be little more than the distinctive mark of a community that had virtually become another Hindu caste. The more romantic fate of perishing with the sword that they had misguidedly drawn had been suffered in China under the Manchu Empire by the T'ai P'ing[1] and in the main body of Orthodox Christendom under the Ottoman Empire by the followers of Sheykh Bedr-ed-Dīn and thereafter by the adherents of a resurgent Imāmī Shiʿism,[2] while the Bektāshī movement had steered clear of this particular wrong turning, only to sacrifice its oecumenical mission for the sake of becoming, first a regimental badge for the Ottoman Janissary Corps, and afterwards a national heterodoxy for Albanian barbarians[3] whose war-bands had just missed their manifest destiny of entering into the heritage of an Ottoman Empire in dissolution.[4]

In the Western World an ideal of social justice had lured a Christian sect into seeking to anticipate God's work by drawing the sword when the militant wing of the Anabaptist movement had seized the Tyrolese city of Brixen in A.D. 1528 and the Westphalian city of Münster in A.D. 1534;[5] and it was the same impatience to put down the mighty from their seat and to exalt the humble and meek[6] that had found vent, in a semi-Westernized Russia in A.D. 1917, in a similar recourse to violence in which a band of militant Marxists had seized, not one city, but an empire, and had victoriously maintained their hold on their huge prize against the hostile world in arms to which their Anabaptist forerunners had quickly succumbed. Like a latter-day Mahayanian Buddhism, this latter-day Marxian Communism could neither be classified correctly nor understood aright as anything but a religion; for, though Marxism, too, was a metamorphosis of a philosophy, and though its exponents vehemently denounced and repudiated Religion in general and Christianity in particular, the Marxian myth, faith, and hope all betrayed their Christian origins,[7] and the Marxian mission to preach the gospel to every creature[8] ran true to type by stultifying itself, as other once oecumenical-minded religious movements had stultified themselves in their day, when it enlisted in the service of a secular state.

In a previous Part of this Study, written before the General War of A.D. 1939–45,[9] it has been suggested that, in a Westernizing World which

[1] See V. v. 107.
[2] See V. v. 111.
[3] See V. v. 295.
[4] See IV. iv. 76–77.
[5] See V. v. 167 and 170. Mr. Martin Wight points out that, in the history of Western Christendom, 'the first violent Christian social revolutionaries to make a big stir were the Bohemian Taborites of the early fifteenth century, and' that 'the tradition to which they and the Anabaptists belong can be traced back to the Patarines of Milan. It goes back ultimately, perhaps, to such primitive Christian Futurists as the Montanists and the Circumcelliones, whose centre of interest, however, was not social justice on This Earth so much as apocalyptic expectation or personal salvation.' Mr. Wight also points out that Reinhold Niebuhr 'has something like' the 'distinction between "violent" and "gentle" reactions in an internal proletariat in his distinction between "hard utopians" and "soft utopians" among Christian sectaries'. See his *Faith and History* (New York 1949, Scribner), pp. 205–13.
[6] Luke i. 52.
[7] See V. v. 177–9. For a further discussion of the affiliation of Marxism to Christianity, see Toynbee, A. J., and Boulter, V. M.: *Survey of International Affairs, 1933* (London 1934, Milford), p. 121, n. 2, and *Survey, 1934* (1935), p. 355, n. 3, and p. 373.
[8] Mark xvi. 15.
[9] See V. v. 179–85.

at that time, on the political plane, was still a house of many mansions, Marxism might be heading towards the prosaic destination that Sikhism, Imāmī Shīʿism, and Bektashism had each already reached in becoming the national religion of a parochial state. By the year A.D. 1952 Mankind had seen the number of Great Powers in the World reduced to no more than two through the cumulative effect of two world wars in one lifetime,

> in dubioque fuere utrorum ad regna cadendum
> omnibus humanis esset terrâque marique.[1]

Communism, now dominant by force over one of two political spheres between which the World had come to be partitioned, now appeared to be playing for the supreme stakes of world power or downfall; yet in essence its prospects were unchanged; for the compromising subservience to the Soviet Union, into which the Communist Movement had fallen during the inter-war years as a result of its brilliant politico-military success in seizing and holding the Russian Empire by force, had been confirmed and intensified by the outcome of the Second World War. This picture had not been changed in its essence by the capture of China in A.D. 1948–9, which had been another brilliant politico-military success in Communism's career; for this had only harnessed Communism to a second Great Power and thereby given Communism the role of serving as the ideological expression of a temporary coincidence between Chinese and Russian political interests. If the Soviet Union was destined to provide a Westernizing World with its universal state, no doubt Communism would be rewarded for its alliance with the state which, in that event, would be the single surviving Great Power. The Soviet Union's established 'ideology' would then be imposed on the World as its official faith; but, whatever might or might not be the Soviet Union's prospects of attaining world-wide dominion, it could be forecast with confidence, in the light of the historical precedents,[2] that Communism's reward, if it were ever to be won, would prove to be Dead Sea fruit; for the Human Heart is the only realm on Earth in which a religion can reign, and nothing so surely alienates the Heart as an attempt to force an entry into it by breaking the will with the bludgeon of political coercion.

This completes our tale of the new religions, thrown up by the surviving civilizations, that appeared in A.D. 1952 to have compromised their spiritual prospects by going into politics and resorting to force. The alternative snare, into which the meek are prone to fall, of coming to terms with an unregenerate dominant minority and allowing themselves to be drawn into its ranks and insensibly influenced by its êthos appeared, by the same date of observation, to have entangled most of the rest of the nascent new higher religions that might otherwise perhaps have been capable of providing chrysalis churches if the process of the reproduction of civilizations was to repeat itself by that means.

The popular adaptations of the Mahāyāna which had sprung up among the internal proletariat of a Japanese offshoot of the Far Eastern

[1] Lucretius: *De Rerum Natura*, Book III, ll. 836–7, quoted in V. vi. 135 and in XII. ix. 484.

[2] For these, see V. v. 646–712.

Society during its Time of Troubles[1] had in the subsequent universal state been fused by a severely authoritarian Tokugawa régime into a spiritual amalgam with an exotic Confucianism and an archaistic Shinto;[2] and in this Japanese syncretism the popular hope of salvation by faith in the power of a compassionate-hearted Amida had been swallowed up in the philosophic self-discipline of a dominant minority and the primitive self-worship of an artificially insulated fraction of Mankind. In the Hindu World an attempt, in the shape of the Brahmō Samāj, at a synthesis between Hinduism and Christianity[3] had been diverted, not by the flagrant militancy that had been the bane of the Hindu-Muslim Sikh Khālsā, but by the more insidiously corrupting attractions of an exotic middle-class Western way of life under a British Rāj. In the Western World itself the same ironic spiritual penalty for social virtue had overtaken the non-militant Mennonite and Moravian Anabaptists[4] and their kindred spirits in the Society of Friends[5] during the lull between the Wars of Religion and the Wars of Nationality.[6] In that liberal and utilitarian age the epigoni of Elizabethan and Jacobean saints and martyrs had been captivated by a Georgian and Victorian prosperity and respectability; and the anaesthetic spiritual atmosphere of a bourgeois 'commonwealth of swine'[7] had stilled the pricks, and thereby blunted the creativity, of an ancestral faith in which the spark of divine fire had first been kindled by tribulation. In the United States the fascinating mirage of a middle-class Earthly Paradise which had been conjured up there at the North and in the West since the Civil War of A.D. 1861–5 seemed to be exerting an effect even on the *anima naturaliter Christiana* of an 'under-privileged' Negro minority, still battened down in the sump of an alien society, whose traditional rendering of the religion which their forefathers had received from their White masters had been inspired by the agonizing experiences of deracination and enslavement.[8]

When we have discounted the prospects of those living higher religions whose adherents had turned either savage or soft, we are left with a couple of heterodox versions of Islam—the Bahā'īyah and the Ahmadīyah[9]—as the only competitors still in the field, midway through the twentieth century of the Christian Era, for the role of supplying the Western Civilization with a chrysalis church.

These negative findings of our inquiry did not, of course, prove conclusively that History was not going to repeat itself in this case. Within the lifetime of the writer and his readers the rational and comfortable life that had been lived by a privileged minority in the leading countries of the West in the eighteenth and nineteenth centuries of the Christian Era had been shown, by the shattering cumulative effect of two world wars in one lifetime, to have been something local, transitory, and exceptional, and not the dawn of a mundane millennium for which its

1 See V. v. 99–103. 2 See V. vi. 88–93. 3 See V. v. 106.
4 See V. v. 168–70 and 171–3. 5 See V. v. 168 and 172–3.
6 For the rhythm of rout-rally-rout in the modern chapter of the history of the Western Civilization, see V. vi. 312–21.
7 Plato: *Respublica*, 369 B–372 D.
8 See II. ii. 218–20 and V. v. 191–3. 9 See V. v. 174–6.

dazzled beneficiaries had mistaken it. If the advent of prosperity had banked down the fires of religion, the recurrence of adversity might fan them into flame again. And, even apart from the change of outlook which the catastrophes of the twentieth century had brought in their train, it was manifestly still too early to make any confident prophecy about the religious destinies of the Western World. Denizens of that world half-way through that century were not in a position to tell whether the Western Civilization was already in disintegration or was still in growth. Even if it should prove to have already broken down, the one thing certain about its condition was that it had not yet entered into a universal state; and, even if it should prove to have been, at that moment, so far gone in decline as to be on the verge of political unification under a *pax oecumenica*, a comparison with the situation in other societies of the same species at a corresponding stage of their history would suggest that the contemporary observer was most unlikely to be able to foresee the shape of spiritual things to come. In the Hellenic World on the eve of the Augustan Peace, in the lifetime of Cicero (*vivebat* 106–43 B.C.) and Julius Caesar (*vivebat* 100–44 B.C.), who could have cast the horoscope of a still unborn heterodox offshoot of Judaism? And, in the Sinic World in the generation before Ts'in She Hwang-ti's, who could have guessed the role that was to be played in the last chapter of Sinic history by a Mahayanian church which at that date had still to arise out of a Primitive Buddhist philosophy through an encounter between three occidental civilizations whose very existence was unknown to the Sinic World of the third century B.C.?

In the light of these historical parallels it would have been rash in the twentieth century of the Christian Era to pronounce dogmatically that the Bahā'ī and Ahmadī movements—exotic and insignificant though they might appear to be at this time—were incapable of playing, in a later chapter of Western history, the role of Christianity in Hellenic history and of the Mahāyāna in Sinic. It would have been rasher still to declare that this part would not be played by some religion that, in the sixth decade of the twentieth century, was still unborn. In and after the General War of A.D. 1939–45 the social scourge and personal catastrophe of deracination had smitten the Western World, for the first time in its history, with a violence that was comparable, scale for scale,[1] with its

[1] The mass movements of deportation, flight, and expulsion in the vast areas in Europe, Russia, and China that came under the power of hostile foreign invaders during these years, at one stage or another of the war and its aftermath, were the most conspicuous but perhaps not the most significant features in the picture. We have also to bear in mind that the soldiers in the invading and the liberating armies were separated from their homes and families for years on end as both combatants and prisoners of war. In countries that were bombed without being invaded, there was a vast exodus of children, industrial workers, and civil servants from the cities to the countryside. And even the United States, which was unique among the major belligerents in remaining exempt from the direct devastation produced by military operations, was far from being exempt from the malady of deracination and its psychological effects. Apart from the temporary uprooting of the millions of young Americans who served in the armed forces in Africa, Europe, Asia, and the Pacific, the enormous industrial war effort of the United States was achieved at the cost of a general post of industrial workers over the vast area of the Continental United States, and even the rural population of previously stagnant agricultural areas was drawn into this war-time economic vortex. In 'the Old South', for example, the war of A.D. 1941–5 produced a radical agrarian revolution that was economic, social, and personal at the same time. In this great region in the course

ravages in the Babylonic and Syriac worlds in the eighth, seventh, and sixth centuries B.C. and in the Hellenic World in the last two centuries before the beginning of the Christian Era; and an experience of tribulation which had been so potent in its spiritual effects in each of these other two cases was perhaps unlikely to be altogether barren of similar consequences in the history of the Western Civilization. Yet, even when the wary historian had made these circumspect reservations, he would still have to report that, within his limited range of vision, there was at any rate no positive indication that History was going to repeat itself in this case by producing another generation of civilizations through the agency of another generation of chrysalis churches.

We have now perhaps carried our survey as far as our knowledge and understanding allow in either direction from our point of departure, which was the service rendered by churches as chrysalises in the transition to the eight still living civilizations from their four progenitors. In the perspective which this reconnaissance has opened up for us, one conclusion seems clear. This chrysalis-church mechanism for the reproduction of civilizations had been the exception, not the rule. Though this species of human society that we call 'civilizations' had been in existence, up to date, for no longer than some five or six thousand years, societies of this species had reproduced themselves at least twice over already, and might repeat the performance again for all that a twentieth-century Western student of History could tell; but it was only in the genesis of one out of these successive litters of civilizations that the process of reproduction had taken this particular form. A previous litter had been produced without the aid of chrysalis churches, and there was no reason for supposing that subsequent litters might not be produced without it likewise. Chrysalis churches were evidently not a necessity of life for the species of society known as civilizations; and this observation suggested that, conversely, the species of society known as churches could not have come into existence simply in order to perform this service. While History testified that the four living churches had in fact performed this service on one occasion, it also indicated that this episode in the careers of these churches might have been incidental and perhaps even accidental. If this was the truth, it signified that the historic role of these churches as chrysalises for civilizations told a historian no more than their fabulous role as cancers told him about the essence of their nature, mission, and prospects. In our search for this ultimate objective of our inquiry, we have once again drawn blank. If we are to continue our investigation, we must make a fresh start from quite a different premiss.

of these few years, man-power and horse-power were largely replaced by machine-power, and the less competent or less fortunate of the former inhabitants were uprooted from the land and swept up into the cities. The consequent immediate increase in economic efficiency and productivity was calculable and gratifying; the ultimate psychological and moral costs were obscure and redoubtable.

(III) CHURCHES AS A HIGHER SPECIES OF SOCIETY

(a) A REVISION OF OUR CLASSIFICATION OF SPECIES OF SOCIETY

A Reversal of Roles

In our inquiry into the relation between churches and civilizations up to this point, we have tacitly worked on the assumption that in the interplay between societies of these two species the civilizations had been the protagonists and that the role of the churches, whether usefully subsidiary or obnoxiously corrosive,[1] had, on either interpretation, been secondary and subordinate. Now that our operations on these lines have proved fruitless, let us try the effect of reversing our point of view. Let us open our minds to the possibility that the churches might be the protagonists and that vice versa the histories of the civilizations might have to be envisaged and interpreted in terms, not of their own destinies, but of their effect on the history of Religion.

As our opening operation in this alternative line of inquiry, let us combine our previous tables of higher religions[2] and civilizations[3] into a single conspectus and see what conclusions this visual presentation of our problem yields us on our new working hypothesis.

The order in which the representatives of three species of human society are set out in the resultant new table[4] is in the first place a chronological one. The primitive societies, as we have noticed in another context,[5] must be actually older than Mankind itself; for, if the pre-human progenitors of the Human Race had not already become social animals, it is hard to imagine how they could have been transfigured into human beings.[6] After Man had become human, he continued to live

1 A third variation on this assumption, in which the role attributed to the churches is ineptly conservative, is examined on pp. 692–700, below.

2 See the table in vol. vi, on p. 329.

3 See the tables in vol. i, on pp. 131–3 and 186.

4 Table IV, folding out opposite p. 772, below.

5 In I. i. 173.

6 The original draft of this sentence ran: 'if the pre-human progenitors of the Human Race had not already become social animals, it is hardly conceivable that they could have achieved the still more difficult feat of turning into human beings.' In this form the passage provoked a challenge from Mr. Martin Wight which led the writer to substitute the present text. Mr. Wight's challenge, however, cuts too deep to be parried by any mere change of words; and the writer would not be dealing frankly with his readers if he did not quote it in full and did not attempt to answer it explicitly.

'This', Mr. Wight comments with reference to the original draft, 'is difficult to follow because the reader is not clear what you regard as the specific differentiae of Man. At several places below you use traditional language in this connexion, saying that Man is "made in God's image" (p. 469, below), possesses a "moral faculty" (p. 470), and is the sole vehicle of "spiritual values" (p. 562, below). Such language suggests that Man was created by God, viz. that at some point in the evolutionary biological process (if we accept that hypothesis) God created a creature different in kind from what went before by endowing it with a soul. See in this connexion the "Platonic myth" in C. S. Lewis: *The Problem of Pain* (London 1940, Centenary Press), pp. 65–68. Now, on such a view, the sociality of Sub-Man is irrelevant. To endow a single individual with a soul, i.e. to make him "in God's image", and then to give him "an help meet" (Gen. ii. 20), was quite enough to start the Human Race. Incidentally the quotation from Eduard Meyer in I. i. 173, n. 3, does not seem to clinch the matter. Speech is "the first thing that makes Man human" certainly, and obviously it cannot have been "fashioned" in the "relation of parents to children", in the sense that the languages of hunting, agriculture or ship-in primitive societies for hundreds of thousands of years before the first civilizations made their appearance; and the first civilizations were considerably older than the first higher religions. Even the rudiments of higher religions did not appear till some of the civilizations of the first generation were already disintegrating, while the rise of fully-fledged higher religions was subsequent to the breakdown of civilizations of the second generation. Thus our series is a chronological sequence; but it is also a genealogical tree; for the primary civilizations must have been derived from the primitive societies through mutations achieved in response to challenges from the physical environment;[1] the first rudiments of higher religions were derived from the primary civilizations through their internal proletariats; the secondary civilizations were derived from the primary civilizations either through the primary civilizations' dominant minorities or through their external proletariats; the fully-fledged higher religions were derived from the secondary civilizations through their internal proletariats;[2] the tertiary civilizations

building imply wider social groups; but why cannot speech have *begun* within the family? Meyer seems to beg the question.

'But when you speak of Sub-Man as "achieving" the "difficult feat of turning into human beings", you imply something quite different: an evolutionary pulling-oneself-up-by-one's-own-bootstraps. The reader is entitled to ask: "Did Man make himself? Or did God create him?" There can be no conflation of the two views that does not give the second an absolute logical and historical priority.'

So clear and so crucial a question required the clearest and frankest answer that the writer could give. His own belief was that there was nothing in the Universe known to Man that had made itself. All things—human and non-human, animate and inanimate—were 'creatures' in the sense that they had been brought into existence, were kept in existence, and were changed or disbanded by a divine Power and a divine Purpose that were not their own and that, though manifested in and through them, were also always and everywhere outside them and always and everywhere independent of them. At the same time the writer believed that the Creator's purpose and method was, at all stages and levels of creation, to take His creatures into partnership with Himself and to give them the utmost opportunity of sharing in His work. This seemed manifest in the Human Nature with which God had endowed His creature Man; and the writer believed that, in this respect, Man was not a 'sport' (in the naturalist's usage of the word) but was, on the contrary, a type of all creation which gave an insight into the character and aim of all God's work. On this view, both the soul in Man and the sociality of Sub-Man would be gifts given by God to a creature that had responded to a challenge from God to embrace a God-given opportunity of becoming more godlike.

As for the writer's use of the traditional language, on which Mr. Wight legitimately lays his finger, he might say, for his readers' information, that his regular and deliberate practice was to continue to employ traditional language unless and until he could find new words that seemed to him to express his meaning more clearly and more exactly. In the writer's day the resources of language were still utterly inadequate.

1 See II. i. 302–30.

2 In virtue of their all thus standing on the same line in the same genealogical table, the fully-fledged higher religions—as distinct from the rudiments of higher religions discernible in such refinements upon a primitive Nature-worship as the cult of Tammuz and Ishtar—might be regarded as being 'philosophically contemporary' with one another. When, however, the dates of their respective epiphanies were entered on a single time-chart, it proved that their common chronological 'locus' was not a single generation or even a single century, but was an aeon of the order of not less than two millennia.

This comparatively wide chronological spread of the age which had seen the higher religions make their appearance on Earth was due to several causes. In the first place the civilizations of the second generation did not all emerge at the same moment. The emergence of the Babylonic, Hittite, and Indic civilizations might be dated tentatively in the fourteenth century B.C., the emergence of the Syriac and the Hellenic in the twelfth century B.C., the emergence of the Sinic in the twelfth or in the eleventh according to our choice between the two variant versions of a traditional Sinic chronology. In the second place the durations of their growth-phases were unequal. The Syriac Civilization broke down after Solomon's death *circa* 937 B.C., the Indic perhaps at some date in the eighth century B.C., the Sinic in 634 B.C., the Hellenic in 431 B.C. In the third place the

were derived from the secondary through higher religions providing chrysalis-churches; and the internal proletariats of disintegrating tertiary civilizations had been creating the rudiments of higher religions of a new generation—rudiments, whose genesis was, at the time of writing, an accomplished fact, though their prospects were still obscure. Let us now apply to this serial order of societies, which is both chronological and genealogical, our new experimental procedure of viewing the histories of civilizations in terms of the histories of higher religions.

On this view, we shall have first of all to revise our previous tacit and uncritical assumptions about the *raison d'être* of civilizations. We shall have to think of the civilizations of the second generation as having come into existence, not in order to perform achievements of their own, and not in order to reproduce their kind in a third generation, but in order to provide an opportunity for fully-fledged higher religions to come to birth; and, since the genesis of these higher religions was a consequence of the breakdowns and disintegrations of the secondary civilizations, we must regard the closing chapters in the secondary civilizations' histories—chapters which, from their standpoint, spell failure—as being their justification for existence and their title to significance. In the same line of thought, we shall have to think of the primary civilizations as having come into existence, in their day, for the same purpose. Unlike their successors in the second generation, these pioneer civilizations failed to fulfil their *raison d'être* directly by bringing higher religions to birth. The rudimentary higher religions that their internal proletariats did create—the worship of Tammuz and Ishtar and the worship of Osiris and Isis—did not come to flower. Yet, in spite of this immediate failure, the primary civilizations accomplished their mission indirectly

disintegrations of the Syriac and the Indic civilizations were protracted by the Hellenic Civilization's forcible intrusion upon them. The disintegration of the Indic Civilization took some 1,500 years (*circa* 725 B.C.–A.D. 775) and that of the Syriac some 2,200 years (937 B.C.–*circa* A.D. 1275), as against the 1,100 years taken by the same process of disintegration in Sinic history (634 B.C.–*circa* A.D. 475) and in Hellenic history (431 B.C.–*circa* A.D. 675).

The total span of the period during which the higher religions were making their epiphanies in the internal proletariat of one or other of these four disintegrating civilizations thus ran from the tenth century B.C. to the thirteenth century of the Christian Era; and, in dating this period, which he labels 'the Axis Age' (*die Achsenzeit*), *circa* 800–200 B.C., Karl Jaspers (*Vom Ursprung und Ziel der Geschichte* (Munich 1949, Piper), p. 19) is excluding from it the epiphanies of Christianity, the Mahāyāna, Hinduism, and Islam. It would be a still greater mistake to try to confine 'the Axis Age' to the single generation (*florebat circa* 500 B.C.) of Confucius, Lao-tse, the Buddha, Deutero-Isaiah, and Pythagoras; for, while it was true that these seers were all contemporary with one another and were also all outstanding representatives of the philosophers and the prophets of the Age of the Disintegration of the Civilizations of the Second Generation, it was not true that they were all representatives of the same phase of the identical experience to which they were all responding; for a merely chronological contemporaneity does not necessarily carry with it the 'philosophic contemporaneity' which consists in living in a corresponding phase of experience and not in living at the same date. Confucius and the Buddha were, perhaps, approximately contemporary with one another in the philosophical as well as in the chronological sense, considering that the Sinic and the Indic Civilization appear to have broken down at dates that were perhaps not more than a hundred years apart. On the other hand the breakdown of the Hellenic Civilization had not yet occurred in Pythagoras' day, and the philosophic contemporaries of the Buddha and Confucius in Hellenic history were not their chronological contemporaries Pythagoras and the fathers of Orphism, but a Zeno and an Epicurus who, on a chronological time-chart, were to make their appearance some two hundred years later than their 'philosophic contemporaries' in the Sinic and the Indic World.

by giving birth to secondary civilizations out of whose breakdown and disintegration the fully-fledged higher religions did eventually arise. We were feeling our way towards this revised view of the significance of the histories of the civilizations, and towards this inverted valuation of the growth-chapters and the disintegration-chapters of the story, when we were making our survey of universal states and were discovering that these master-institutions of civilizations in decline were apt to be barren in so far as they worked for themselves and fruitful only in the service of alien beneficiaries.[1] We have now to apply this finding comprehensively to the histories of civilizations from beginning to end.

Revelation through Tribulation

On this showing, the successive rises and falls of the primary and the secondary civilizations are an example of a rhythm—observed in other contexts[2]—in which the successive revolutions of a wheel carry a vehicle, not on the repetitive circular course that the revolving wheel itself describes, but in a progressive movement towards a goal. And, if we ask ourselves why the descending movement in the revolution of the wheel of Civilization should be the sovereign means of carrying the chariot of Religion forward and upward, we shall find our answer in the truth that Religion is a spiritual activity, and that spiritual progress is subject to a 'law' proclaimed by Aeschylus in the two words *πάθει μάθος*, and by the author of the Epistle to the Hebrews in the verse: 'Whom the Lord loveth He chasteneth, and scourgeth every son whom He receiveth.'[3]

If we apply this intuition of the nature of spiritual life to a spiritual endeavour that culminated in the flowering of Christianity and her sister higher religions the Mahāyāna, Islam, and Hinduism, we may discern in the passions of Tammuz and Attis and Adonis and Osiris a foreshadowing of the Passion of Christ, and may find in Christ's Passion a crowning experience in the spiritual travail of legions of human souls in successive failures of the secular enterprise of Civilization.

Christianity itself had arisen out of spiritual travail that was a consequence of the breakdown of the Hellenic Civilization; and this was the latest chapter in a longer story; for Christianity had Jewish and Zoroastrian roots, and these roots—altruistically fertile in a stem that had been grafted on to them—had sprung from the earlier breakdown of two other civilizations of the second generation, the Babylonic and the Syriac, which had become locked together, in an embrace that was both deadly and fruitful, in the course of their simultaneous disintegration.[4] The living waters of Zoroastrianism had flowed into the stream of Judaism—to find their way thence, in the fullness of time, into the river of Christianity[5]—within the framework of an Achaemenian Empire that had provided the Syriac World with its universal state; and Judaism

1 See Part VI, *passim*, above.

2 See IV. iv. 34–38 and V. vi. 324–5.

3 Aeschylus: *Agamemnon*, ll. 177–8, and Heb. xii. 6, quoted in I. i. 169, n. 1, and in II. i. 298. For the working of this spiritual 'law', see further p. 425, n. 4, below.

4 See V. v. 117–22.

5 The contributions of Zoroastrianism to Christianity have been touched upon in V. vi. 43–44.

and Zoroastrianism alike had been the spiritual fruit of the tribulation of a preceding Time of Troubles. The kingdoms of Israel and Judah, in which the well-springs of Judaism were to be found, had been two of the many warring parochial states of the Syriac World in its ages of growth and disintegration; and the premature and permanent overthrow of these mundane commonwealths, and extinction of all the political hopes which had been bound up with their existence as independent polities, were the experiences that had brought the religion of Judaism to birth and had evoked the highest expression of its spirit in the elegy of the Suffering Servant that had been indited in the sixth century B.C. during the last throes of a Syriac Time of Troubles, on the eve of the foundation of the Achaemenian Empire by Cyrus.[1]

This was not, however, the beginning of the story of progressive spiritual experience of which Christianity was the climax;[2] for the Judaic root of Christianity had a Mosaic root of its own, and this pre-prophetic phase of religion in Israel and Judah had been the outcome of a previous secular catastrophe, the break-up of 'the New Empire' of Egypt.[3] Whether or not there was any truth in the Israelites' tradition that, in the militantly expansive chapter of Egyptiac history following the expulsion of the Hyksos, the Hebrews had been temporarily conscripted into the Egyptiac internal proletariat, it was certain that they had filtered into the Egyptian dominions in Syria as barbarians from the North Arabian Steppe during an age in which Syria was being annexed to a disintegrating Minoan World through a mass-migration of refugees from the Aegean 'Isles of the Sea'.[4] The Israelites themselves believed that this Egyptiac episode in their history had been preceded by a Sumeric initiation, in which Moses' forefather and forerunner Abraham had received a revelation and a promise from a divinity that was the One True God, and had been led by this divine guidance to extricate himself from the doomed imperial city of Ur, as Christian, in *The Pilgrim's Progress*, fled betimes from the City of Destruction. According to the tradition the enlightenment of Abraham was the first act in God's manifestation of Himself to a Chosen People; and the secular historical background against which this opening of a spiritual drama was set was the break-up of an 'Empire of the Four Quarters' which had been the final embodiment of a disintegrating Sumeric Civilization. Thus the first step in a spiritual progress which was to culminate in Christianity was traditionally associated with the first instance, known to historians, of the collapse of a universal state, which is the supreme catastrophe for a secular civilization.

Though a twentieth-century Western historian did not know whether 'Abraham' and 'Moses' were 'historical characters', the answer to that question was not of capital importance, since it could be taken as certain that their names stood for authentically historical stages of religious experience. The human beings who 'learnt through suffering' in the last agonies of the Sumeric and Egyptiac civilizations were precursors of Prophets of Israel and Judah who were enlightened, in their turn, by

[1] See V. vi. 120–30.
[2] See V. v. 119, n. 4.
[3] See V. vi. 39 and 43.
[4] See I. i. 92–94 and 100–3 and V. v. 611.

the tribulations of a Babylonic and Syriac Time of Troubles,[1] and all these men of sorrows were precursors of Christ. The successive sufferings through which they won a progressive enlightenment stood out, on a retrospective view, as Stations of the Cross in anticipation of the Crucifixion.[2]

In this perspective, Christianity could be seen to be the climax of a continuous upward movement of spiritual progress which had not merely survived successive secular catastrophes but had drawn from them its cumulative inspiration. To judge by this momentous historical instance, the circumstances favourable to spiritual and to secular progress are not only different but are antithetical;[3] and this 'law'—if we have stumbled here upon a 'law' governing the relations between mundane life and Religion—is not a paradox.[4] Spiritual and secular ideals are at variance; they are perpetually striving with one another for mastery over human souls; and it is therefore not surprising that souls should be deaf to the call of the Spirit in times of secular prosperity, and sensitive to the neglected whisper of the still small voice[5] when the vanity of This World is brought home to them by secular catastrophes and when their hearts are softened by the sufferings and sorrows that these catastrophes inflict. When the house that Man has built for himself falls in ruin about his ears and he finds himself standing again in the open at the mercy of the elements, he also finds himself standing again face to face with a God whose perpetual presence is now no longer hidden from Man's eyes by prison walls of Man's own making. If this is the truth, the interregna which punctuate secular history by intervening between the submergence of one civilization and the emergence of a successor may be expected to have, as their counterparts in religious history, not breaches of continuity or pauses in the pulsation of life, but flashes of intense spiritual illumination and bursts of fervent spiritual activity.[6]

The Higher Religions' Consensus and Dissension

On this reading, the history of Religion appears to be unitary and progressive by contrast with the multiplicity and repetitiveness of the

[1] 'The example of Judaism shows that a political catastrophe can actually give a mighty impetus to religious development' (Meyer, E.: *Geschichte des Altertums*, 4th ed., vol. i, Part I (Stuttgart and Berlin 1921, Cotta), p. 156).

[2] See Luke xvi. 16; Acts x. 43 and xxvi. 22; Heb. i. 1–2.

[3] On this question see, further, pp. 701–15, below.

[4] 'Perhaps there lies an historical law here, still incompletely revealed to us, which transcends even the might of Rome and of Christianity. Augustine may have had an intimation of it; for, having said that God brought the great empire into being in order that His revelation might be the more easily comprehended and diffused, he might logically have added that God was now bringing about its dissolution in order that Man, confronted by the contrast between his aspirations and his achievements, might the more fully perceive that inner must precede outer reformation' (Pickman, E. M.: *The Mind of Latin Christendom* (London 1937, Oxford University Press), p. 148).

[5] 1 Kings xix. 12.

[6] 'Times of transition, in which the old order is breaking up and new rules of life are taking shape—times in which nothing remains secure—are the very times in which the religious life displays the most intense activity. . . . [The personalities of religious reformers] make their appearance in the greatest numbers and do their work with the greatest effect in times of ferment, in which the life has gone out of the old order and

histories of civilizations; and this contrast in the Time-dimension presents itself in the Space-dimension as well; for Christianity and the other higher religions that, in the twentieth century of the Christian Era, were living side by side, in an *Oikoumenê* which had recently become coextensive with the whole habitable and traversable surface of the planet, had a closer affinity among themselves than coeval civilizations had been apt to have with one another.[1]

This affinity was conspicuously close as between Christianity and the Mahāyāna, which shared the same vision of God[2] as a self-sacrificing saviour, and owed this penetrating common insight into God's nature to a common Syriac inspiration within a common Hellenic framework. While, in an Hellenic universal state provided by the Roman Empire, a proletarian religion sprung from Judaism was being translated into terms of Greek philosophy, the inverse process of converting an Indic philosophy into a proletarian religion was being carried out, at the opposite extremity of a Hellenizing World, in the Kushan successor-state of Bactrian Greek empire-builders who had 'abolished the Hindu Kush';[3] and the uniform influence of these convergent experiences on the two religions was manifest eighteen hundred years later. As for Islam and Hinduism, we have noticed in other contexts that they had allowed themselves to be used for the compromising secular purpose of expelling an intrusive

new ideas are seeking to break through' (Meyer, E.: *Geschichte des Altertums*, 4th ed., vol. i, Part I (Stuttgart and Berlin 1921, Cotta), pp. 126–7 and 151).

This would appear to be the answer to a question which had been raised by Karl Jaspers in *Vom Ursprung und Ziel der Geschichte* (Munich 1949, Piper), pp. 19–42: 'Erster Teil, 1. Die Achsenzeit'): Why was it that like-minded philosophies and, at their heels, like-hearted higher religions had made simultaneous epiphanies at three points in the *Oikoumenê*—in the Sinic World, the Indic World, and the Syriac and Hellenic worlds according to the terminology used in the present Study—independently of one another (p. 33)? After rightly rejecting, as inadequate, the suggestion that a new *Weltanschauung* was propagated by commercial intercourse (p. 39), or that it was an identical reaction to the identical experience of antecedent Eurasian Nomad invasions (pp. 37–38), Jaspers points out that each of these epiphanies occurred in a society that was articulated politically into a host of warring parochial states (pp. 23 and 39), and that 'what had begun by being freedom of movement turned in the end into anarchy' (p. 24). An identical spiritual response to the challenge of this identical tragic social experience would be the explanation of the identity of mind and heart in philosophies and religions which made their appearance simultaneously in several societies that were still insulated from one another at the time. This common tragic experience of the failure of a secular civilization would account for the common êthos which Jaspers portrays with a masterly touch.

'The new feature of the Axis Age, which displays itself in all three worlds alike, is that Man becomes conscious of the Universe, of himself, and of his own limitations. He realises the awfulness of the World and his own impotence. He asks himself radical questions. Finding himself on the edge of the abyss, he strives for liberation and redemption. While he consciously comprehends his limitations, he sets himself the highest goals. He becomes aware of the Absolute both in the depths of his selfhood and in the clarity of the Transcendent' (p. 20).

[1] The points of likeness and difference between the four higher religions that were alive in this age are examined further, on pp. 716–36, below.

[2] In theory a bodhisattva was, not a god, but a spiritual athlete who had arrived at the brink of *Nirvāna* where it was within his power at any moment to escape from the sorrowful wheel of existence, of which the motive-power is *libido* and the momentum is *karma*. In an inverted Christian terminology the bodhisattva could be described as a bondsman of immortal life who had won, but had generously forborne to exercise, the right to put on mortality and so to bring to pass the saying that is written: 'Life is swallowed up in victory' (1 Cor. xv. 53–54). In practice, however, the Mahayanian bodhisattvas were worshipped by their devotees as very gods. (See V. vi. 148 and 164, n. 3, and pp. 482–3, below.)

[3] See V. v. 139–40, and pp. 471 and 478, below.

Hellenism from the Syriac and from the Indic World respectively; but this was not the last word that remained to be said about them; for, notwithstanding this mundane role of theirs in an encounter between civilizations, they too reflected insights into the nature of God which gave them a distinctive meaning and mission of their own on the spiritual plane. Islam was a reaffirmation of the unity of God against an apparent weakening in Christianity's hold on a vitally important truth which had been won for Mankind by Judaism; Hinduism re-affirmed the personality of God—at any rate on the plane of reality on which God reveals Himself as an object of devotion for a human worshipper—against an apparent denial of the existence of personality in the Primitive Buddhist system of philosophy.[1] An exponent of the Mahāyāna might protest that this denial was no part either of Siddhārtha Gautama's original teaching or of latter-day Mahayanian practice, and an exponent of Christianity might protest that the Christian doctrine of the Trinity was an enunciation of the sociality of God which left the recognition of God's unity intact. Yet, in maintaining that a synthesis of all the essential truths about God was to be found in his own religion, neither the Christian nor the Buddhist would deny that the Muslim and the Hindu were alertly alive to certain aspects of the truth—even if they might appear, in Christian and Mahayanian eyes, to be blind to others.

After agreeing with the follower of the Mahāyāna in this verdict on the rival claims of the Muslim and the Hindu, a Christian might go on to maintain that there was one aspect of the truth that was revealed in Christianity alone.[2] While Islam, Hinduism, and the Mahāyāna shared with Christianity the vision of God as Man's lord, and the Mahāyāna shared with her the vision of Him as Man's saviour, Christianity was unique (so the Christian might contend) in revealing God to Man as Man's father and brother.[3]

[1] See V. v. 134–8.

[2] Cassian, the Christian spiritual pioneer who, after the turn of the fourth and fifth centuries of the Christian Era, migrated from his birthplace at the eastern extremity of the Latin-speaking world in the Dobruja (see IV. iv. 326, n. 2) to the western extremity of the Greek-speaking world at Marseilles in order to sow seeds of Egyptian monasticism in the soil of a Gaul that was being relieved of the economic incubus of the Roman Imperial régime at the price of becoming the political prey of barbarian conquerors, depicted the aspiring Christian soul's way of ascent towards the *Visio Beatifica* as a spiritual ladder; and the lower rungs, as described by him, can be identified with the ideals of non-Christian religions that, in the previous generation, had been Christianity's rivals for the captivation of Hellenic souls. 'This ladder roughly reproduces that chronological way by which Augustine climbed: the lower third, with its repudiation of matter and the flesh, is Manichaean; the middle third, with its hope that, through virtuous living and a concentration on the supersensuous, Man can resume his spiritual nature, is Neoplatonic; the last third, with its indifference to both matter and spirit, provided the joy comes of loving a God whose might is only equalled by His mercy, is Christian. It is this love and joy that is the gift of grace' (Pickman, E. M.: *The Mind of Latin Christendom* (London 1937, Oxford University Press), p. 476).

[3] In this divination of the presence of 'a friend behind the phenomena', Christianity had been anticipated by the Stoic school of Hellenic philosophy, but the Stoic's intellectual apprehension of this amazing truth about the relation between God and Man had not the same power as the Christian revelation to move men's hearts. 'Man finds God in helping his neighbour' (*Deus est mortali iuvare mortalem*) has the same meaning as 'God is Love', but the philosopher's prose lacks the fire of the Evangelist's poetry. For this Stoic intuition of the nature of God, see Murray, Gilbert: 'The Stoic Philosophy', in *Essays and Addresses* (London 1921, Allen & Unwin), pp. 99 and 103–4. 'A friend behind the phenomena' is a phrase of Edwyn Bevan's. 'Man's true God is the helping of Man' is quoted from an unnamed Stoic source by Pliny: *Naturalis Historia*, Book II, chap. 7 (5), §18.

So the All-Great were the All-Loving too—
So through the thunder comes a human voice
Saying: 'O heart I made, a heart beats here!
'Face, my hands fashioned, see it in myself!
'Thou hast no power nor mayst conceive of mine,
'But love I gave thee, with myself to love,
'And thou must love me who have died for thee.'[1]

This claim that Christianity made to pre-eminence over her sister religions (a claim that was, of course, echoed in counter-claims of theirs) was a crux for an historian brought up in a Christian tradition.

The personal *tour de force* which an historian has to attempt if he is to perform his professional service for his fellow human beings is to correct, by imagination, the bias inherent in the standpoint at which he has been placed by the historical accidents of his birth and upbringing, in order to see and present the flux of human life *sub specie aeternitatis*. But human attempts to see human affairs through God's eyes must always fall infinitely short of success; and, while it is difficult enough for the historian to correct his political bias as a citizen of a state and his cultural bias as a member of a society, the hardest of all the feats of imagination that are required of him is to see beyond the *Weltanschauung* of an ancestral higher religion. If he turns savage against it and tries to break out of its confines by force, the faith of his fathers revenges itself upon him by becoming a veritable prison-house whose magic walls pen the ex-Christian atheist and the still Christian believer together in a common mental captivity which is palpable to a non-Christian looker-on. With this warning to himself and his readers, the writer of this Study will venture to express his personal belief that the four higher religions that were alive in the age in which he was living were four variations on a single theme, and that, if all the four components of this heavenly music of the spheres could be audible on Earth simultaneously, and with equal clarity, to one pair of human ears, the happy hearer would find himself listening, not to a discord, but to a harmony.[2]

[1] Browning, Robert: *An Epistle containing the Strange Medical Experience of Karshish, the Arab Physician.*

[2] A searching Christian criticism, not only of this passage, but of the whole of this Part of the present Study, by Mr. Martin Wight has been printed, with its author's consent, as an annex to this chapter on pp. 737–48, below. In the present writer's belief, Mr. Wight's exposition of the historic Christian standpoint regarding the relation between Christianity and the other higher religions was not merely correct; it also appeared to him to go to the heart of the matter; and the writer therefore agreed with Mr. Wight's conclusion that his 'solution of the problem of the relationship between Christianity and the higher religions fails to be in Christian terms' if the interpretation of the word 'Christian' was to be confined, as the Christian Church was, no doubt, historically and juridically entitled to confine it, to the sense in which the word had been used in the Church's own authoritative statements of its position. If the writer were to be asked: 'Do you believe or disbelieve that Christianity or any other higher religion is an exclusive and definitive revelation of Spiritual Truth?' his answer would be: 'I do not believe this. I believe that any such claim is an error which is at the same time a sin. In claiming to possess a monopoly of the Divine Light, a church seems to me to be guilty of hybris. In denying that other religions may be God's chosen and sufficient channels for revealing Himself to some human souls, it seems to me to be guilty of blasphemy. If it is inadmissible to call oneself a Christian without holding these tenets, then I am not entitled to call myself a Christian; I must call myself a Symmachan (see p. 442, below). Symmachus's confession of faith—"The heart of so great a mystery can never be reached

This belief is declared—in terms that, no doubt, betray the inevitable bias and limitations of an hereditary Christian standpoint—in a passage from the pen of a leader of Christian thought and action in the generation of the wars of 1914 and 1939 whose untimely death had been a grievous loss to his contemporaries.

'All that is noble in the non-Christian systems of thought or conduct or worship is the work of Christ upon them and within them. By the Word of God—that is to say, by Jesus Christ—Isaiah and Plato and Zoroaster and [the] Buddha and Confucius conceived and uttered such truths as they declared. There is only one divine light; and every man in his measure is enlightened by it. Yet . . . each has only a few rays of that light, which needs all the wisdom of all the human traditions to manifest the entire compass of its spectrum.'[1]

A Muslim, Buddhist, or Hindu who found this Christian formulation unacceptable would confess to the same belief in terms of his own faith if he had reached the same degree of insight as the writer of those words. A Buddhist or a Hindu mystic would report that his Christian or Muslim fellow spiritual pioneer, who had likewise pierced the barriers of time and place and historical accident, had been driven by a still unextinguished demon of Desire into trying to push on beyond the goal of *Nirvāna* in which the Indic pilgrim had entered into his rest, while the Muslim or the Christian pilgrim would report that his Hindu and Buddhist fellow travellers had mistaken a spiritual station for a spiritual terminus. Yet both parties of explorers would bring back to their fellow men an identical report of the first stage, at least, of their journey.[2]

Dare we discern in this partial consensus of the elect the glimmer of a dawn, heralding a spiritual sunrise? 'The elders obtained a good report'[3] by faith. But such faith—which 'is the substance of things hoped for, the evidence of things not seen'[4]—would be ill-inspired if it were to tempt a student of History in the writer's generation to evade a question that was raised—and this immediately and insistently—by any sanguine forecast of the spiritual future of Mankind on Earth. Why was it that, at least in the Judaistic churches,[5] Man's glimpse of the unity of revelation

by following one road only"—is an article in my creed which neither my head nor my heart will allow me to abandon.'

As the writer saw it, Symmachus's challenge to Ambrose was still awaiting its answer after the passage of more than fifteen and a half centuries. The repressive use of physical force, which had been a Christian Roman Imperial Government's retort to Symmachus, had, of course, been no answer at all.

[1] Temple, William: *Readings in Saint John's Gospel*: First Series, chaps i–xii (London 1939, Macmillan), p. 10.

[2] See V. vi. 171–2, where it has been argued that *Nirvāna* lies on the same road that leads on to the *Civitas Dei*, and V. vi. 143, n. 3, where the reader's attention has been drawn to the difference between an Hellenic-Indic and a Christian-Islamic kind of mystical experience. This difference is underlined by Mr. Martin Wight in a comment on the original draft of the present passage:

'There seem to be two kinds of mystic, one of whom attains the annihilation of personality, the other the fulfilment of personality in the Vision of God. They have nothing in common except that both, from the ordinary man's point of view on the plain, are well above the snow-line. The first kind, in Christian eyes, is pantheistic and heretical, e.g. Eckhart; the second kind is illustrated by Saint John of the Cross. Cp. below, p. 729.'

[3] Heb. xi. 2.

[4] Heb. xi. 1.

[5] 'Surely it is a characteristic difference between Hinduism and the religions of the Judaic tradition that Hinduism does *not* make this exclusive claim. Cp. V. vi. 47–48. "Hinduism", says Radhakrishnan, "seeks the unity of religion not in a common creed

had been confined, hitherto, to a few rare spirits, whereas the ordinary outlook had, unhappily, been the opposite? In the official view of each of the Judaistic higher religions the light that shone through its own private window was the only full light, and all its sister religions were sitting in twilight, if not in darkness; the same standpoint was maintained by each sect of each religion against all its sister sects; and this uniform refusal of diverse denominations and churches to recognize what they had in common and to admit one another's claims gave occasion for the agnostic to blaspheme.

'These professedly higher religions', the agnostic could point out, 'all claim to be complete and final revelations of spiritual truth and prescriptions for the right conduct of life. They all bring forward the same considerations in support of their claims; and, whatever one may think of their arguments, their consensus is so impressive that the most sceptical mind might feel some trepidation at the prospect of having to enter into a disputation with such a troop of advocates of a common thesis. Fortunately, though, for the poor agnostic, the angelic doctors have exempted him from this intellectual ordeal. Withough waiting for their common adversary to put the Devil's case, they have each done the Devil's work for him by repudiating the claims of their brethren. In their animus against one another they have never (*mirabile dictu*) paused to consider that, in refusing recognition to one another's claims, they are each cutting the ground from under his own feet. The truth is that their pretensions are identical; and so they stand or fall together. In electing to fall by their own act, they have stripped themselves of their disguise and exposed themselves in their true colours.

'In their self-inflicted nakedness, they have revealed themselves as being primitive tribal religions, which are exceptional in nothing but the magnitude of their spiritual pretensions and of their geographical domains. Whereas the worship of an Athena Poliûchus or a Fortuna Praenestina had a range of no more than a few miles' radius from the local shrine of the tribal goddess, Christianity and Islam and Hinduism and the Mahāyāna can boast of hundreds of millions of adherents occupying whole continents and overflowing to the opposite shores of oceans. Yet, huge though these latter-day ecclesiastical empires are, they too are still parochial.

'Their parochial patriotism is betrayed in their institutions and in their rites. Is not tribalism inherent in the very notion of a "holy land" or a pilgrimage-resort?[1] How can the presence of a hypothetically infinite

but in a common quest" (*The Hindu View of Life* (London 1927, Allen & Unwin), p. 58). Is the Mahāyāna equally non-exclusive? (cp. below, pp. 438–9).'—Martin Wight.

Sir Charles Eliot, in his *Hinduism and Buddhism* (London 1921, Arnold, 3 vols.), points out that, 'more than any other religion, [Hinduism] is a quest of truth and not a creed which must necessarily become antiquated' (vol. i, p. xci). This passage also has a bearing on the argument on pp. 438–9, below.

1 'The agnostic here runs the risk of misrepresenting his opponents. It is true that the practice of pilgrimage can sink to the superstitious level of supposing that God "makes Himself felt more palpably" in the holy place than elsewhere, but its original and uncorrupted purpose is to acquire merit by making an act of devotion or expiation.'—Martin Wight.

'Catholic pilgrimages are made, not because God is more here than there, but because people—being what human beings are—associate places with deeds and so stir them-

and eternal God be supposed to make itself felt more palpably in Palestine than in Alberta, or in the Hijāz than in Eastern Bengal? Is not this geographical fantasy of the Scribes and Pharisees confuted by the spiritual vision of a poet whose inward eye can see Jacob's ladder pitched between Heaven and Charing Cross, and Christ walking on the water, not of Gennesareth, but of Thames? Is not this poet a true seer in divining that God dwells in no strange land? And what doth it profit a man to make the pilgrimage to Rome or Jerusalem, Mecca or Karbalā, Benares or Bodh Gaya? Is the pilgrim exempt from the psychological law that "caelum, non animum, mutant qui trans mare currunt"?[1] Has not the truth about the virtue of going on pilgrimage been told by Tolstoy in his Tale of *Two Old Men*? Does not God's true servant do God's will if he tarries to play the Good Samaritan in an Ukrainian village better than if he ruthlessly shuts his ears to a human cry of distress and pushes on to witness the magic rekindling of the sacred fire in the Church of the Holy Sepulchre? And what about the provincialism of "the higher religions'" rituals? Does not Christianity proclaim itself to be, not a religion for all Mankind, but merely a local Mediterranean cult, when it insists that its crucial sacrament is only efficacious if it is celebrated with bread and wine? On this point of ritual practice there is a rigid conformity between the divers Christian denominations that wrangle with one another over the nature and the significance of the rite. How can a sacrament that is thus indissolubly associated with the regional diet of *Homo Mediterraneus* be expected to serve as a means of grace for the rice-eating majority of Mankind, in continents where the vine does not grow, and in archipelagos that know no name for bread?[2]

'The truth is that these would-be world religions are serfs of tribalism, *ascriptae glebae*. The vast majority of their supporters adhere to them for the same primitive reason for which the Athenians adhered to Athena Poliûchus and the Praenestines to Fortuna Praenestina—not because the worshipper has been personally convinced, after a searching and impartial scrutiny of all the alternative religions, that this particular religion is true and right, but because this particular religion happens to be prevalent, short of being officially "established", in the place at which the worshipper happens to have been born, at the date at which his birth happens to have taken place. "Fato Metelli Romae consules fiunt."[3]

'You, Thomas,' our agnostic might point out *ad hominem*, 'are a Christian of the Orthodox Faith because you happen to have been born at Damascus in the fourth century of the Christian Era; if you had been born there a hundred years later, you would certainly still have been a

selves to greater fervour. Saint Thomas More was as much against an excess in the practice of pilgrimage as Tolstoy was. I do not think your remarks just at this point.'—Comment by a Catholic friend of the writer's.

1 Horace: *Epistulae*, Book I, Ep. xi, l. 27.

2 The writer of this Study vividly remembers how forcibly his own provincialism was borne in upon him when —landing in Japan in the autumn of A.D. 1929, and making his way up country from Nara to Koya San, the Mahayanian Olympus—he found himself compelled to ask for an unobtainable form of food in Portuguese, because, in the Japanese language, there was no indigenous word for 'bread'.

3 Naevius, C.: *Bellum Pœnicum*.

Christian, but probably a Monophysite—while a birthday a hundred years later still in the same birthplace might have changed your faith to Islam and your name to Ahmad. If you are thus born a Muslim at Damascus in the second century of the *Hijrah* you will find yourself a Sunnī; but get yourself born eight hundred years later at Tabrīz—or, indeed, no more than three hundred years later, no farther afield than the Lebanon—and you will find yourself an Imāmī Shīʿī. Get yourself born at Amsterdam in A.D. 1500 and you will find yourself a Roman Catholic; wait to be born in the same Dutch city in A.D. 1600 and you will turn out to be a Protestant; but, if the stork who is delivering you to your parents slightly mistakes his direction and deposits you on the right date at the wrong address, you will be born in A.D. 1600 a Roman Catholic still if he has landed you at Antwerp, but a Tantric Mahayanian Buddhist if the bird has gone so far astray as to make Lhasa your birthplace.[1] In fact, as certain also of your own apologists have said (if you will pardon my paraphrase of a celebrated passage in one of your own scriptures):[2] "Un méridien décide de la vérité."[3]

1 The geographical distribution of the conflicting views on the controversial issue of Predestination versus Free Will in the west of the Roman Empire during the first half of the fifth century of the Christian Era is a striking illustration of an apparent predetermination of theological tenets by the theologically irrelevant accident of the theologian's domicile.

'Very securely, one may move north from [Africa and] Manichaean and Augustinian fatalism to Italy and prevenient grace, to Gaul and grace for merit, to Britain and merit without grace. Was the cause racial instinct, intellectual disposition, maturity of civilisation, climate or mere chance? We do not know' (Pickman, E. M.: *The Mind of Latin Christendom* (London 1937, Oxford University Press), p. 442).

2 Acts xvii. 28.

3 'On ne voit rien de juste ou d'injuste qui ne change de qualité en changeant de climat. Trois degrés d'élévation du pôle renversent toute la jurisprudence, un méridien décide de la vérité; en peu d'années de possession, les lois fondamentales changent; le droit a ses époques, l'entrée de Saturne au Lion nous marque l'origine d'un tel crime. Plaisante justice qu'une rivière borne! Vérité au deçà des Pyrénées, erreur au delà' (Pascal, Blaise: *Pensées*, No. 294 in Léon Brunschvicg's arrangement).

The institution which, in this famous passage, Pascal is discrediting by making an exposure of its geographical relativity is, of course, not Religion, but Law. The same critique can, however, be directed with the same devastating effect against Theology, as indeed it has been directed in other contexts by Pascal himself:

'Pour le choix de la condition et de la patrie, le sort nous le donne. C'est une chose pitoyable de voir tant de Turcs, d'hérétiques, d'infidèles, suivre le train de leurs pères, par cette seule raison qu'ils ont été prévenus chacun que c'est le meilleur' (No. 98).

'On a beau dire, il faut avouer que la religion chrétienne a quelque chose d'étonnant. "C'est parce que vous y êtes né", dira-t-on. Tant s'en faut; je me roidis contre, pour cette raison-là même, de peur que cette prévention ne me suborne. Mais, quoique j'y sois né, je ne laisse pas de le trouver ainsi' (No. 615).

There is an admirable candour and sincerity in this last passage, in which the critic is applying his critique of the geographical relativity of human institutions to his own ancestral faith. An agnostic John Stuart Mill did not have to exercise the same high virtues in making the same point:

'The World, to each individual, means the part of it with which he comes in contact: his party, his sect, his church, his class of society; the man may be called, by comparison, almost liberal and large-minded to whom it means anything so comprehensive as his own country or his own age. Nor is his faith in this collective authority at all shaken by his being aware that other ages, countries, sects, churches, classes and parties have thought, and even now think, the exact reverse. He devolves upon his own world the responsibility of being in the right against the dissentient world of other people; and it never troubles him that mere accident has decided which of these numerous worlds is the object of his reliance, and that the same causes which make him a Churchman in London would have made him a Buddhist or a Confucian in Pekin' (Mill, J. S.: *On Liberty*, chap. 2 (p. 80 in the Everyman edition)). The writer's attention was drawn to this passage by Mr. Martin Wight.

The Causes of the Dissension and the Prospects of Transcending it

The words that we have put into the mouth of our imaginary *advocatus diaboli* were true to fact, and the facts were surprising, because it was also true that this provincialism, of which the higher religions stood convicted in practice, was the antithesis of the revelation which was their common essence. The higher religions had revealed a new insight into the nature of God which carried with it, as its necessary corollary, a new view of the relations of human beings with one another. If God is One, He cannot be either Athena Poliûchus or Fortuna Praenestina or any other of the innumerable local godlets who had been these two city-goddesses' neighbours and rivals; and He must have 'made of one blood all nations of men for to dwell on all the face of the Earth'.[1] If God is Love, he cannot be 'a man of war',[2] and the Psalmist errs and sins in singing 'blessed be the Lord my strength which teacheth my hands to war and my fingers to fight'.[3] If God is not contained in any of His creatures, then Man's corporate self-worship of himself is idolatry, even if this worship is paid, not to a parochial and militant Athena Poliûchus, but to an oecumenical and pacificatory Dea Roma. Moreover, the higher religions did not merely stand for these truths; they had put them into action. Their entry into the World had been an epiphany of God and at the same time a liberation of Man. It had freed Man from his previous bondage to his own corporate self.[4] In the spiritual power of the higher religions, Man had been able to overcome the political barriers between parochial states and even the cultural barriers between parochial civilizations.[5] How had the churches come to reimpose on their adherents the very bonds from which they had once set them free?

One answer to this perplexing question was perhaps to be found in the fact that the higher religions' ability to convert souls had been limited by Man's inability to learn except through suffering, so that the missionary's labour of love had had to wait upon the conqueror's work of destruction. In doing the Devil's work for the ephemeral aggrandisement of his fatherland and the trivial satisfaction of his own petty personal ambition, the conqueror is doing God's work without either willing or knowing it;[6] for, in destroying the political liberty of his corporate victims the deified parochial states, he is unintentionally and unconsciously bringing religious liberty to souls that, in the days of their own country's perversely lamented sovereign independence, were fast bound in the misery and iron[7] of spiritual servitude to a religion of corporate self-worship. When the conqueror strikes down a deified parochial state, his stroke does not simply enlarge the scale of social life by incorporating a statelet into an empire; it simultaneously transmutes the

[1] Acts xvii. 26.

[2] As Moses chants in Exod. xv. 3.

[3] Ps. cxliv. 1.

[4] On this point see Meyer, E.: *Geschichte des Altertums*, 4th ed., vol. i, Part I (Stuttgart and Berlin 1921, Cotta), pp. 155–6.

[5] See V. v. 527–68, *passim*, and V. vi. 1–49, *passim*.

[6] 'Nun gut, wer bist du denn?'—'Ein Teil von jener Kraft
'Die stets das Böse will und stets das Gute schafft.'
Goethe: *Faust*, ll. 1335–6, quoted in II. i. 282.

[7] Ps. cvii. 10.

structure of social life by splitting the primitive social atom and accomplishing, in this blind act of social alchemy, that momentous separation of the Church from the State which gives individual souls their opportunity to 'seek the Lord if haply they might feel after Him and find Him'.[1]

When the parochial state has been liquidated by the force of a conqueror's arms, its former citizens are converted on the political plane into subjects of the empire that this conqueror is building; but they are not thereby converted automatically into worshippers of the imperial gods. Superstition or policy or a subtle combination of the two considerations usually deters the victorious war-lord from giving this further turn to his screw. In consequence, the subjects of a parvenu oecumenical régime are apt to find themselves free to follow any religion that they may choose; and, while some of them will now voluntarily abandon the worship of hereditary parochial divinities who have disconcertingly proved to lack either the inclination or the strength to preserve their former temporal power inviolate against the gods and men of the victorious empire,[2] it is rare for these sheep without a spiritual shepherd to take their religious cue from the turn of political events by voluntarily transferring their ecclesiastical allegiance to the high god of the Imperial Power that has robbed the former parochial states of their political liberty.[3] When, for example, Rome conferred freedom of religious choice on Spartan and Athenian souls by converting them from citizen-devotees of a deified Sparta and Athens into Rome's political subjects, their liberated hearts were captivated, not by Divus Caesar or by Dea Roma, but by Cybele, Isis, Mithras, and Christ.

This religious and ecclesiastical effect of a military and political cause was divined by Deutero-Isaiah at a turning-point in history[4] when Cyrus was setting himself to build into an Achaemenian Empire the political debris of Syriac and Babylonic parochial states which had been previously broken in pieces[5] by an Assyrian battering-ram. The Judaean prophet was correctly interpreting the political empire-builder's unconscious religious mission in 'the voice of him that crieth in the wilderness: Prepare ye the way of the Lord; make straight in the desert a highway for our God.'[6] An access to the hearts of Mankind was indeed being opened for Judaism by the flying columns of Cyrus's army that were sweeping up Judah's destroyer, the Neo-Babylonian Empire, into the net of an Achaemenian universal state which was to dwarf, not only this Babylonian successor-state of the Assyrians, but the Assyrian Power itself at its short-lived apogee. Yet the Achaemenian Empire, like every other 'universal state' up to date, had been 'universal' in the psychological sense of being oecumenical-minded without also being universal in the literal sense of having actually inherited the Earth;[7] for hitherto the military conquerors' salutary achievement of breaking down

[1] Acts xvii. 27.
[2] See the illuminating passage quoted from Eduard Meyer in V. vi. 30, ll. 15–17, and the references ibid. (vol. vi, p. 33, n. 1) to two other passages in which the same author recurs to this theme.
[3] See V. vi. 36–38.
[4] See p. 424, above.
[5] Ps. lxxii. 4.
[6] Isa. xl. 3.
[7] Matt. v. 5.

barriers, far though it had gone if measured by the extreme degree of the previous disunity of Mankind, had never been literally world-wide. During the five or six thousand years that had seen the rises and falls, up to date, of the species of society that we have labelled 'civilizations', even the most devastatingly successful of the would-be world conquerors had fallen ludicrously short of their vainglorious aim. Alexander's Macedonians had refused to cross the Hyphasis and had never seen the Tiber;[1] and the Mongols, who had once marched simultaneously on China and Hungary from opposite gates of the Khāqān's camp, had gained no foothold in India or in Western Christendom and had been repulsed with ignominy from the thresholds of Egypt[2] and Japan.[3]

Against this historical background there might be some significance in one feature of a Modern Western secular civilization which was historically unprecedented, though intrinsically superficial. While other civilizations too had burst their bounds and had incorporated into their own body social the domains of neighbouring societies either entire or in part, the Western Civilization had been unique in establishing for itself a literally world-wide dominion. At the turn of the fifteenth and sixteenth centuries of the Christian Era a society which, till then, had been leading an obscure and undistinguished existence in Ultima Thule, at the extreme north-western corner of the habitable zone of the Old World, had suddenly and surprisingly launched out upon the oceans[4] and taken in the rear its Orthodox Christian and its Arabic and Iranic Muslim rivals—who had been pressing hard upon Western Christendom overland since the failure of her medieval attempt to expand at their expense across the Mediterranean in 'the Crusades'.[5]

In the course of the four and a half centuries that had passed since the launching of the Western oceanic voyages of discovery down to the time of writing, a post-da Gaman Western Civilization had become as world-wide as the high seas in which it had found its medium of expansion. Along these ubiquitous oceanic waterways it had propagated itself over the entire traversable and habitable surface of the globe, and had drawn into its net all other surviving civilizations as well as all surviving primitive societies. The social and psychological phenomena arising from these encounters between the Western Society and its contemporaries were not, of course, new departures.[6] They could all be illustrated from the histories of previous encounters of the kind, in which the operations had been on a less than world-wide scale—such, for example, as the impact of the Hellenic Civilization on the Syriac, Egyptiac, Babylonic, Hittite, Indic, and Sinic civilizations in the chapter of Hellenic history that had been opened by the conquests of Alexander

1 This unfulfilled possibility of Hellenic history has been discussed by Livy in a famous passage (Book IX, chap. 16, *ad fin.*, to chap. 19, inclusive). Cp. Tarn, W. W.: *Alexander the Great* (Cambridge 1948, University Press, 2 vols.), vol. ii, pp. 396–7.

2 See I. i. 350 and IV. iv. 446–7.

3 See IV. iv. 93 and V. vi. 310, n. 2.

4 See Toynbee, A. J.: 'The Unification of the World and the Change in Historical Perspective' in *Civilisation on Trial* (New York 1948, Oxford University Press), pp. 62–96, and the present Study, IX. viii. 217–18 and XII. ix. 465–72.

5 See I. i. 38 and IX. viii. 346–63.

6 These phenomena are examined in Part IX, *passim*.

the Great. Such older illustrations were, indeed, more illuminating than the Modern Western instance for a twentieth-century Western historian, since in the earlier cases the end as well as the beginning of the story was already known. The unique feature in the Modern Western case was the prospect that, in a World which had now been brought together on a literally world-wide scale within a Western social framework, the familiar social and economic consequences of unification might make themselves felt in the relations between the living higher religions.

In the histories of other civilizations, as we have seen,[1] the process of unification had translated itself, sooner or later, into a political form; the resultant universal states had developed a high degree of 'conductivity'; and the higher religions had been the principal beneficiaries of this characteristic property of their political hosts. One of the fateful questions that were exercising Western minds in A.D. 1952 was whether, in a Westernizing World, History was going to repeat itself in this respect. This question concerning the prospects of the Western Civilization is examined in a later part of this Study;[2] and the considerations there submitted need not be anticipated at this point except in so far as to say that, at this date, political unification seemed likely to be the destiny of the Western Society, too, in the near future—without its being possible to forecast whether an identical and perhaps inevitable goal would be reached along the familiar road of internecine fratricidal warfare, culminating in a 'knock-out blow', or by the unprecedented method of co-operation on a constitutional basis inaugurated by peaceful agreement. On either alternative the spiritual atmosphere of a politically unified world would be likely to have much the same effect on higher religions exposed to it.

In cases in which—on a less than world-wide scale, and by the barbarous method of military conquest—the citizens of a throng of parochial states and the children of a number of different civilizations had been brought into political union, the effect on the religious plane had been, as we have observed, to transfer Religion from the field of automatic social heritage to the field of free personal choice. In the language of Natural History, this change in the social environment had given Religion the opportunity to achieve a spiritual mutation which had lifted it, so to speak, out of the Vegetable into the Animal Kingdom. Whereas Primitive Religion had been rooted in the soil of some parochially earth-bound tribe, the higher religions were volatile. As the Roman poet Ennius could look forward to living, after his own physical death, on the lips of every Latin-speaker that recited his poetry,[3] so the higher religions could live in every human heart that opened itself to their revelation; and, conversely, for the Soul, Religion could cease to be an accident of birth and become a matter of choice—the most momentous choice that life in This World could present.

[1] In Part VI, *passim*.

[2] In Part XII. D, *passim*, in vol. ix, pp. 473–560.

[3] Nemo me dacrumis decoret, nec funera fletu
Faxit. Cur? Volito vivu' per ora virum.

Were similar circumstances likely to produce similar effects in the world-wide society which the Western Civilization had been bringing into being during the most recent chapter of its history? Some effects of the kind were already discernible, for the higher religions had not waited for the political unification of the World, but had started on their missionary journeys again in the wake of the Modern Western pioneer mariners. Saint Paul, who had once sailed two-thirds of the length of the Mediterranean from Caesarea to Puteoli, had taken ship again fifteen hundred years later from an Andalusian port to fulfil a prophecy of his Cordovan contemporary Seneca[1] by crossing the Atlantic and winning a New World for Caesar's pontifical heir at Rome; and in an age in which the caravel had been superseded by the steamship and the aeroplane it could be foreseen[2] that the other higher religions would emulate the example, set by Irish and Syrian Christian missionaries in the sixth century and by Roman Catholic Christian missionaries in the sixteenth century of the Christian Era, of going into all the World and preaching the Gospel to every creature.[3]

What would be the outcome of a new outburst of simultaneous missionary activities in a single field—this time, on a world-wide range? The histories of the corresponding activities within the less than world-wide frameworks of the Achaemenian, Roman, Kushan, Han, and Gupta empires (to cite only the most conspicuous of the earlier oecumenical mission fields) showed that the outcome might be either of two alternatives. The plurality of higher religions and philosophies might either be reduced to unity by the victory of one of them over all its competitors, as had happened in the Hellenic and Syriac worlds, or alternatively the competing religions might reconcile themselves to living and letting live side by side, as had happened in the Sinic and Indic worlds. The two denouements were not quite so different as would appear on the surface; for, in the cases in which the competition had gone on to the bitter end, the victorious religions had found themselves constrained to purchase their victory at the price of adopting from their discomfited rivals all elements—important or trivial, good or bad—which the souls whose ecclesiastical allegiance had been at stake were obstinately reluctant to give up.[4] In the pantheon of a triumphant Christianity, the figures of Cybele and Isis reasserted their power in the transfiguration of Mary the mother of Jesus into the Great Mother of God,[5] and the lineaments of Mithras and Sol Invictus were visible in a militant presentation of Christ. Similarly, in the pantheon of a triumphant Islam, a banished God Incarnate stole back into an empty place in hungry hearts in the guise of a deified ʿAlī, while a forbidden idolatry reasserted itself in the Founder's own act of consecrating the fetish-worship of the Black Stone in the Kaʿbah at Mecca.

1 Seneca: *Medea*, ll. 375–9, quoted in II. i. 263, n. 1.

2 On this point see pp. 105–8, above.

3 Mark xvi. 15.

4 On this point, see further pp. 457, 467, and 716–36, below.

5 Eastern Orthodox and Western Catholic Christians did not, of course, admit that the honour paid by them to the Theotókos amounted to the apotheosis from which it was indistinguishable in Muslim, in Eastern Iconoclast Christian, and in Western Protestant Christian eyes (see further pp. 457, 467, and 716–36, below).

'All religions, without exception, in order to overcome the obstacles that retard their progress, have had to come to terms with the forces that they have been combating, and to succumb to some extent to the very evils against which it has been their mission, and indeed their *raison d'être*, to wage war. . . . This law holds good for all the great [ways of life] that have been evolved by Man, and, above all, for Islam. Though Islam came into being in order to give the Arabs a religion and to raise them out of a particularly crass form of idolatry, it was compelled to purchase its triumph at the price of taking political form and substance and turning itself into a theocracy. It was only then, when it had absorbed, in a diluted and modified form, the very elements which, in the beginning, it had been its special mission to suppress, that Islam found itself able to start the work of moral and religious reform in the Arabian Peninsula and in a large part of [the rest of] the medieval world.'[1]

Even the victors in a religious war *à outrance* have found themselves constrained to adopt their defeated adversaries *sub rosâ* as members of their own household. Nevertheless, the difference between the two alternative denouements to a competition between higher religions is morally momentous; and the children of a twentieth-century Western Civilization could not be indifferent about the prospects in their own case.

Which of the two alternatives was the more likely to be the destiny of a Westernizing Modern World? In the past, intolerance had gained the mastery where higher religions of Judaic origin had been in the field,[2] while 'live and let live' had been the rule where the Indic êthos had been paramount. Which of these two spirits was going to prevail in a Westernizing World in the coming chapter of its history? The Judaic vein in Christianity and Islam? Or the Indic vein in the Mahāyāna and

[1] Caetani, L.: *Studi di Storia Orientale*, vol. iii (Milan 1914, Hoepli), p. 139. In the Prophet Muhammad's career the classical example of a compromise with the primitive practices of the pre-Islamic 'Times of Ignorance' is his deal with the Quraysh in A.H. 9 (see ibid., pp. 270–3). In exchange for a genuine acceptance of the sovereignty of the Medinese theocracy and a nominal acceptance of Islam, Muhammad assured to the Quraysh the continuance of their profits from their management of the sanctuary of the Ka'bah by incorporating into Islam, virtually intact, the pagan rites of the annual pilgrimage to Mecca. In this case the practical consecration of a theoretically execrated pagan past was unusually deliberate.

[2] The melancholy historical fact that the transition from a pagan parochialism to a Christian universalism was accompanied by a change of religious climate from tolerance to intolerance has been noticed in IV. iv. 226–7. The following comment on the same phenomenon from the pen of Eduard Meyer (*Ursprung und Anfänge des Christentums*, vol. iii (Stuttgart and Berlin 1923, Cotta), p. 633) is bitter yet not unjust:

'The accepted basis of association is no longer the natural community based on kinship and neighbourhood, but a unanimity of feeling and of creed which is supposed to proceed from a common conviction—though in reality it often boxes the compass by turning into a merely external assent. This is the outlook which now at once asserts itself everywhere and which has continued to dominate the succeeding millennia. A state which had been the natural outgrowth of the practical conditions of earthly life, and which had provided complete freedom for the individual to think his own thoughts, is now replaced by the ideal of a supernatural church, guided by God, which ruthlessly suppresses and eradicates any departure from orthodoxy—even if it is only a question of a single word. To protect the Church, and to impose her unity on all Mankind, now becomes the most important—and, in the last analysis, the only true—task of the State. There has been no religion in which this fanaticism—this persecution of all heterodox opinions without regard for the consequences and without shrinking from any crime—has been, and remained, so dominant as it has in Christianity in all its manifestations. This is a signally glaring example of the operation of the law that an idea, in translating itself into reality, boxes the compass by turning into its own antithesis.'

Hinduism? The historical precedents suggested that the answer to this question might be determined by the nature of the alien adversaries whom the higher religions would find in their path at this point.

Why did Christianity, which appeared to have taken a decisive new departure from Judaism by recognizing and proclaiming that God is Love, readmit the incongruous Israelitish concept and service of 'the Jealous God' Yahweh[1] without heeding Marcion's prophetically warning voice? This partial spiritual regression, from which Christianity had suffered grievous spiritual damage ever since, was the price that Christianity had had to pay for her victory in her life-and-death struggle with the worship of Caesar.[2] This religious war had to be fought—and fought to a finish—because Man's corporate worship of Humanity in the shape of an oecumenical commonwealth was the most insidious form of idolatry that the worshippers of the One True God could have encountered. Compromise was impossible—all the more so because this Caesar-worship stood for an ideal that was noble and beneficent within the range of its own lights. The Great Romano-Christian religious war was impossible to avoid, and, once started, it could have no end short of unconditional surrender on the part of one or other belligerent. In this tragic conflict it was in vain for Christians to inscribe 'God is Love' on their war-flag. Love had to cede the high command to Jealousy if defeat was to be inflicted upon Caesar; and the restoration of peace through the Church's victory did not dissolve, but, on the contrary, confirmed, the incongruous association of Yahweh with Christ; for in the hour of victory the intransigence of the Christian martyrs degenerated into the intolerance of Christian persecutors who had picked up from the martyrs' defeated pagan opponents the fatal practice of resorting to physical force as a short cut to victory in religious controversy.[3]

This early chapter in the history of Christianity was ominous for the spiritual prospects of a twentieth-century Westernizing World, because the worship of Leviathan, on which an infant Christian Church had inflicted a defeat that had appeared to be decisive, had afterwards been conjured back from limbo to haunt both Eastern Orthodox and Western Christendom.[4] In the Orthodox Christian World a ghost of the Roman Empire had been successfully resuscitated as early as the eighth century of the Christian Era[5] and had survived the catastrophe which it had brought upon the main body of Orthodox Christendom in the tenth century[6] to become the master institution of an offshoot of Orthodox Christendom in Russia.[7] In the Western World an Austrasian Charlemagne's fortunate failure to emulate the political achievement of a Leo Syrus had been eventually frustrated by the sinister emergence of a totalitarian type of state in which the Modern Western genius for organization and mechanization had been enlisted, with diabolic ingenuity, for the purpose of enslaving souls as well as bodies to a degree

[1] See V. vi. 38–49.
[2] This point has been touched upon already on pp. 75–76, above.
[3] See IV. iv. 226–7 and V. vi. 88–9.
[4] See pp. 445–6 and 478–9, below.
[5] See IV. iv. 340–53 and X. ix. 15.
[6] See IV. iv. 377–404 and X. ix. 15.
[7] See pp. 31–40, above.

which had not been within the power of even the worst-intentioned tyrants at other times and in other societies.

Moreover, these two monstrous growths of resurgent Caesar-worship had cross-fertilized one another. The tradition of autocracy, which Hitler, Mussolini, and Napoleon had ultimately derived—through eighteenth-century Transalpine 'enlightened monarchs' and fourteenth-century Italian despots—from the Holy Roman Emperor Frederick II Hohenstaufen,[1] had been conveyed to this official successor of Charlemagne by the political atmosphere of his Kingdom of the Two Sicilies, which was a successor-state of Leo Syrus's East Roman Empire.[2] In later chapters of the melancholy history of the relations between Western and Orthodox Christendom, this inauspicious loan was repaid with interest, twice over, when first Peter the Great, and after him the Bolsheviki, envenomed the native Byzantine autocratic tradition of Muscovy by doctoring it with the latest brews of Modern Western political alchemy.[3]

In Western souls at the time of writing, this appalling renaissance of a demon that had afflicted the declining years of the apparented Hellenic Society was 'projected' (in the language of the psychologists) upon its contemporary manifestation in the Russian World in the shape of the Soviet Communist régime; but the terror which Russian Communism was inspiring in Western hearts betrayed their awareness that the Western World was also favourable soil for the tares of totalitarianism. It looked as if, in a Modern Westernizing World, the war between God and Caesar might have to be waged once again; and it also looked as if, in that event, the morally honourable yet spiritually perilous role of serving as the church militant would once again fall upon Christianity.

Of the four living higher religions, the Mahāyāna and Hinduism were disqualified for undertaking this grim task by the spirit of tolerance that was a characteristic virtue of each of them, while Islam, which was armed with the necessary intolerance in ample measure, would be seriously embarrassed, in a *jihād* against Leviathan, by its Founder's *hijrah* from a prophet's bed of thorns to a prince's curule chair.[4] In these circumstances it could be foreseen that, if the battle were joined again between God and Caesar, the Christian Church would again be the protagonist on God's behalf, and might again have to pay the spiritual price that is exacted by militancy even in just wars waged for good causes. The price paid by Western Christendom for the Primitive Church's victory in a three-hundred-years' war against Caesar-worship had been a fourteen-hundred-years-long service of a God who resembled the God of Joshua more closely than the God of Jesus;[5] and, when at last the archaic image of Yahweh 'the man of war'[6] had lost its hold on Western hearts, the

[1] See p. 402, above, and pp. 446 and 537–9, below, and IX. viii. 394–5.

[2] See pp. 538–9, below, and X. ix. 9–10.

[3] This traffic in the diabolically wonder-working talisman of totalitarianism will remind Robert Louis Stevenson's readers of his story *The Bottle Imp*.

[4] See III. iii. 466–72, and p. 493, below.

[5] Mr. Martin Wight comments on this passage: 'This seems incompatible with the description of the Church, on p. 563, below, as "an incomparably effective institution" for preserving the Christian revelation'. The writer's answer is that institutions preserve revelations 'in cold storage'.

[6] Exod. xv. 3, quoted on p. 433, above.

consequent spiritual vacuum had remained a waste land tenanted only by the barren spirits of scepticism and cynicism.[1] Christians born into the twentieth century of the Christian Era had to reckon with the possibility that a second war with Caesar-worship might cost the Christian Church a second set-back of the kind, before she had recovered from the first. Yet, if they had the faith to believe that, in the end, the revelation of God as Love incarnate in a suffering Christ would turn stony hearts into hearts of flesh,[2] they might venture to peer into the prospects for Religion in a politically united world that would have been liberated by the Christian revelation from the worship of Yahweh as well as from the worship of Caesar.

A reconciliation, on Christian initiative, between hitherto exclusive-minded religions was not a chimaerical hope to cherish; for Mankind had already had an earnest of its fulfilment in the first chapter of the history of the impact of a Modern Western Christendom upon the rest of the World. In the sixteenth and seventeenth centuries of the Christian Era the Jesuit missionaries had aspired to attract the Hindus and Buddhists and Shintoists and Confucians of India and Japan and China, in their millions, into the fold of the Roman Catholic Christian Church; and they had entered upon the gigantic task that they had set themselves in a spirit of charity which might have blessed their endeavours if they had not eventually been frustrated by the intervention of higher ecclesiastical authorities. Instead of dwelling on the points of difference between the existing religions and philosophies of the non-Christian majority of Mankind and their own Catholic Christian faith, the Jesuits had dwelt on the points of likeness, and, from this angle of spiritual vision, they had been able to approach these alien faiths with sympathy, understanding, and reverence instead of animus, prejudice, and scorn.

This Christian charity was remarkable in an age when Christianity was still glowing with a militancy that had been kindled in the hearts of the Early Christian martyrs, and when, in Western Christendom, this fire had been stirred into a fiercer flame by the recent schism between Catholics and Protestants. It is, indeed, more surprising that the Jesuit missionaries of the Early Modern Age should have been capable of that degree of charity and insight than that the Vatican, at the prompting of rival missionary orders, should have condemned and banned the Jesuit line of approach as a theologically illegitimate condonation of pagan practices and beliefs.[3] In the eyes of a latter-day Western Christian historian, looking back on this incident in the Time-perspective of the quarter of a millennium that had since elapsed, those truly Christian-minded early Jesuit missionaries seemed to have been, not out of their reckoning, but before their time. In his outlook, the future lay with the spirit of Matteo Ricci, the Jesuit father who had also been a Confucian litteratus, and whose childlike Christian charity had not been smothered by his formidable intellectual freight of Christian theological and Sinic

[1] See IV. iv. 142–3, 150, 184–5, 225, and 227–8; V. v. 669–72; and V. vi. 316–8.
[2] Ezek. xi. 19.
[3] For the Jesuits' missionary enterprise and its condemnation as being a kind of theological 'appeasement', see I. i. 346; V. v. 365–7, 539, and 700.

philosophical erudition. Charity is the mother of insight, and in A.D. 1952 there was still time for Saint Ambrose, sitting at Father Ricci's feet and praying for the spiritual welfare of a twentieth-century oecumenical commonwealth of literally world-wide extent, to perceive and confess that the moral victor in A.D. 384 had been, not the politically triumphant Christian advocate of intolerance, but his politically defeated pagan opponent.[1] It had been Symmachus, not Ambrose, who had had the last word on a question that had been at issue in their world in the fourth century of the Christian Era, and that was at issue still in the twentieth century throughout a now literally world-wide *Oikoumenê*. Is uniformity or diversity more blessed in the practice and presentation of Religion? Symmachus assuredly divined and proclaimed the truth when he pleaded that 'the heart of so great a mystery can never be reached by following one road only'.[2]

The Value of Diversity

Uniformity is not possible in Man's approach to the One True God because Human Nature is stamped with the fruitful diversity that is a hall-mark of God's creative work,[3] and psychologically diverse human souls need different lenses for seeing, through a glass,[4] a Beatific Vision in which, if we could see God face to face, we should find that there 'is no variableness, neither shadow of turning'[5]—as we must believe by faith, here and now, since God's ineffable brightness is never revealed, utterly unveiled, to the naked eye of Man's frail spirit in its passage through This World. 'The true light, which lighteth every man that cometh into the World',[6] has to be received by every creature according to the particular lights with which the Creator has endowed it. To enable human souls to receive the divine light is the purpose for which Religion exists, and it could not fulfil this purpose if it did not faithfully reflect the diversity of God's human worshippers. On this showing, it might be surmised that the way of life offered, and the vision of God presented, by each of the living higher religions might prove to correspond to one of the major psychological types whose distinctive lineaments were gradually being brought to light by twentieth-century Western pioneers in a new field of human knowledge.[7] If each of these religions did not genuinely satisfy some widely experienced human need, it is indeed hardly conceivable that each of them should have succeeded, as each had done, in securing the allegiance of so large a portion of the Human Race. 'Every good gift and every perfect gift is from above, and cometh down from the Father of lights';[8] and, if the followers of the living higher religions were to recognize reciprocally the common

1 For the contest between Ambrose and Symmachus, see V. vi. 88–89.

2 'Uno itinere non potest perveniri ad tam grande secretum' (Symmachus, Q. Aurelius: *Relatio Tertia*).

3 The old order changeth, yielding place to new,
And God fulfils Himself in many ways,
Lest one good custom should corrupt the World.
Tennyson: *The Passing of Arthur*.

4 1 Cor. xiii. 12. 5 James i. 17. 6 John i. 9.

7 A tentative interpretation of the four living higher religions in terms of the scheme of psychological types propounded by C. G. Jung will be found on pp. 716–36, below.

8 James i. 17.

origin of all these gifts of God,[1] they might win a life-giving liberation from the self-stultifying impulse that had moved them to thwart themselves by thwarting one another from fulfilling their common destiny.

This destiny, to which assuredly they had been called if the call had truly come from God, was that they should each go into all the world[2] without conflicting with one another. Their spiritually regressive political vested interest of serving as tribal religions for regimented continents would then be relinquished in order to free each of them for fulfilling a world-wide mission of revealing God to individual souls which would have chosen this particular communion in the light of their personal needs and capacities instead of having inherited it through the accident of birth. In that hour of reconciliation through enlightenment,

'the wolf . . . shall dwell with the lamb, and the leopard shall lie down with the kid; and the calf and the young lion and the fatling together; and a little child shall lead them'.[3]

In this light the diversity of the living higher religions would cease to be a moral stumbling-block and would reveal itself as a necessary corollary of the diversity of the Human Psyche. It was a necessity if there was truth in the Christian intuition that God is Love; for Love seeks to draw all men unto Him;[4] and His desire to beatify all His creatures by bringing them into communion with Himself would perforce remain unfulfilled if one road only were open for approaching the great mystery; for in that case the common goal of all men's endeavours would be attainable only by one arbitrarily favoured fraction of Mankind that happened to be psychologically equipped for following this particular spiritual path. Any such conclusion had been rejected by the Christian Church itself when it had expressed its intuition that God is Love in a doctrine that the door of salvation stands open for all men, including those outside the Christian Church's fold. A Symmachan-minded disciple of C. G. Jung who had retained the Christian vision of God's nature from a Christian upbringing would hold that, if the revelation of the One True God is to be accessible to all men, it has to be diffracted; but in holding this he would be holding, in common with his Christian predecessors and contemporaries, that the different rays that reach and illumine diverse souls are radiations of one light from one source.

'There are diversities of gifts, but the same Spirit. And there are differences of administrations, but the same Lord. And there are diversities of operations, but it is the same God which worketh all in all. But the manifestation of the Spirit is given to every man to profit withal.'[5]

This necessary diffraction of the divine light in its manifestation to diverse souls is a challenge to the recipients, like God's other dispensations to His creatures. It is a stumbling-block for them as well as an

[1] 'Part of the Christian answer to this argument (inasmuch as Christianity makes exclusive claims) is contained in the simile of "veils differing from one another in their degree of opaqueness" which you use below, on p. 461.'—Martin Wight.

[2] Mark xvi. 15.

[3] Isa. xi. 6.

[4] John xii. 32.

[5] 1 Cor. xii. 4–7.

opportunity; for diversity can breed a destructive discord as well as a creative harmony. The catastrophe that Phaethon brought upon himself by attempting to drive the four-horse chariot of his Father Helios might not have overtaken the unfortunate demigod if the heavenly vehicle had been a one-horse shay. In the relations between the living higher religions in the twentieth century of the Christian Era the heavenly harmony that was audible to the ear of faith was being mocked, as we have seen, by a hideous discord that was the official order of the day; and faint hearts might doubt whether this very present hazard of the ordeal of diversity were indeed worth the bare chance of winning the possible prize. The answer was that the hazardously aspiring unity-in-diversity of a harmony has in it virtue that is not to be found in a safely pedestrian unison. The one-horse shay is a safe form of conveyance just because it is incapable of mounting to the zenith. The quadriga may bear Phaethon heavenward to a height from which a fall spells death; yet, by the same token, it—and no vehicle of lesser power—can carry Helios in triumph from horizon to horizon.

What, midway through the twentieth century of the Christian Era, were the omens for Man's air-borne religious quest? The last chapter had ended on an inauspiciously discordant note; yet, if any credit could be given to the findings of a tentative reconnaissance into the future, there were grounds for hope that, in the next chapter, the diversity of religions might resolve itself into a harmony in which the unity of Religion would be made manifest. In the light of this prospect, an anxious observer need not be unduly dismayed to see the mettlesome chariot-horses pulling restively against one another. On the longer view that was visible to the eye of faith, it could be forecast that the driver would master his team and that the chariot would continue to mount on the heavenward course that it had been following continuously since before Abraham was.[1]

The Role of the Civilizations

If this view of the prospects of Religion were to carry conviction, it would open up a new view of the role of the civilizations. If the movement of the chariot of Religion was continuous in its rise and constant in its direction, the cyclic and recurrent movement of the rises and falls of civilizations might be not only antithetical but subordinate. It might, as we have surmised,[2] serve its purpose, and find its significance, in promoting the fiery chariot's ascent towards Heaven by periodic revolutions on Earth of 'the sorrowful wheel' of birth-death-birth.

In this perspective the civilizations of the first and second generations might justify their existence,[3] but those of the third generation would

[1] John viii. 58. [2] On pp. 423–5, above.

[3] On this view the rises and falls of the civilizations of the first and second generations would be a valuable, and perhaps indispensable, stage of human experience between the primitive societies and the higher religions; for, if learning comes through suffering, the experience of a civilization would have an educative effect which the experience of a primitive society could not provide. One of the obvious specific differences between civilizations and primitive societies was the immense disparity in the mass and weight of their respective corporate power (see I. i. 148–9). In consequence, there was, for good

cut a disconcertingly poor figure. If civilizations were the handmaids of Religion, and if the Hellenic Civilization had served as a good handmaid to Christianity by bringing this higher religion to birth before that civilization had finally fallen to pieces, then the civilizations of the third generation would appear to be 'vain repetitions' of the heathen.[1] If, so far from its being the historical function of higher religions to minister, as chrysalises, to the cyclic process of the reproduction of civilizations, it was the historical function of civilizations to serve, by their downfalls, as stepping-stones for a progressive process of the revelation of always deeper religious insight,[2] then the societies of the species called civilizations would have fulfilled their function when once they had brought mature higher religions to birth; and, on this showing, a Western post-Christian secular civilization might at best be a superfluous repetition of the pre-Christian Hellenic Civilization, and at worst a pernicious backsliding from the path of spiritual progress. The one conceivable historical justification for its otherwise inauspicious existence would be the possible future service that it might inadvertently perform for Christianity and her three living sister religions by unintentionally providing them with a mundane meeting-ground on a literally world-wide range,[3] by bringing home to them the unity of their own ultimate values and beliefs, and by confronting them all alike with the challenge of a recrudescence of idolatry in the peculiarly vicious form of Man's corporate worship of himself.[4]

Meanwhile, in a secularized Western World in the twentieth century of the Christian Era, symptoms of spiritual backsliding were unmistakably manifest. The recrudescent worship of Leviathan was a religion to which every latter-day Westerner paid some measure of allegiance; and this Modern Western renaissance of the tribal religion of the Hellenic World in its unregenerate days,[5] before it had been purified from the sin of parochialism in the furnace of suffering, was, of course, sheer idolatry. Communism, which was another of Western Man's latter-day religions, had the merit of being a leaf taken from the book of Christianity, but it was a leaf taken in vain through being torn out and misread;[6] and Democracy, which was another leaf from the book of Christianity, had also been torn out and, while perhaps not misread, had certainly been half-emptied of meaning by being divorced from its Christian context and being secularized. Perhaps the most ominous symptom of all was that, for a number of generations past, people in the Western World had been living on spiritual capital—clinging to Christian practice without holding Christian beliefs. This was ominous because practice

or evil, an immensely greater 'drive' behind human acts which had a civilization for their social setting; and, in consequence of this in turn, the catastrophes caused by the mismanagement of a civilization's corporate power were likely to make a deeper and more lasting impression on the Soul than their counterparts in primitive life.

1 Matt. vi. 7.

2 That men may rise on stepping-stones
Of their dead selves to higher things.
Tennyson: *In Memoriam* (quoted in IV. iv. 261).

3 See p. 437, above.

4 See pp. 439–41, above; pp. 478–9 and 524–5, below.

5 This renaissance is discussed further in X. ix. 7–8.

6 See V. v. 581–7, and pp. 534–5, below.

unsupported by belief is a wasting asset, as Western Man in this generation had discovered to his dismay.

If this self-criticism was just, the children of the Western Civilization must revise the whole of their current conception of recent history; and, if they could make the effort of will and imagination to think this ingrained and familiar conception away, they would arrive at a very different picture of the historical retrospect. Westerners of the writer's generation not only took it for granted that the Christian Church had served its turn in bringing a new civilization to birth in the West; they looked upon this new civilization as having been immature so long as it had remained under Christian auspices; and, after having waited with impatience for it to get through its medieval Christian childhood, and having joyfully greeted the repudiation of its Christian origins with which it had celebrated its coming of age,[1] they had focused their attention on the rise of a Modern Western secular way of life. As they followed that rise, from the first premonition of it in the genius of Frederick II Hohenstaufen,[2] through the renaissance of Hellenic culture in an Italian cradle, to the Transalpine eruption of Democracy and Industrialism under the pagan auspices of a modern scientific technique, they thought of this secular movement as being the great new event in the World which demanded their attention and deserved their admiration. If they could bring themselves to think of it, instead, as being one of the 'vain repetitions' of the heathen—an almost meaningless repetition of something that the Hellenes had done before them, and done supremely well[3]—then the greatest new event in the historical background of a Modern Western Society would be seen to be a very different one. The greatest new event would then not be the monotonous

[1] See I. i. 34.

[2] See pp. 402 and 440, above; pp. 537–9, below; and IX. viii. 394–5.

[3] In a previous passage of this Study (in II. ii. 355–7) we have noticed the 'family likeness' between the Hellenic Civilization and the abortive Scandinavian Civilization. The Scandinavian, like the Hellenic, was distinguished by a precocious freshness and originality and a precocious clarity and rationalism, and we have ascribed these distinctive qualities, which the two civilizations display in common, to a similarity in the circumstances in which they came to birth. While either was affiliated to an antecedent civilization, the affiliation was, in either case, through the antecedent civilization's external proletariat, and this was a looser link than the alternative form of affiliation through a chrysalis church provided by the antecedent civilization's internal proletariat. In the same context (ibid., pp. 357–60) we went on to observe that this thesis appeared to be borne out by the confusion and obscurity into which Scandinavian minds fell after an abortive pagan Scandinavian Society had been absorbed into the alien body social of Western Christendom and had thereby been condemned to wrestle with the impossible task of reconciling an exotic Helleno-Syriac culture with its own native pagan Scandinavian cultural heritage. The impossibility of this mental *tour de force* is vividly illustrated by the incongruousness of the catalogue of the books in the library of a fourteenth-century Icelander, Hauk Erlendsson (see ibid., pp. 358–9).

This evidence suggests that, for the flowering of a secular culture, the most favourable field is a civilization of the second generation that is affiliated to a predecessor through barbarian intermediaries, and not a civilization of the third generation that is affiliated to a predecessor through a chrysalis church. If this was the truth, the neo-pagan civilizations of the third generation seemed likely to prove themselves to be a lower form of society than the palaeo-pagan civilizations of the second generation and the first. In that event, a civilization of the second generation that had helped to bring to birth something higher than itself in serving as an overture to a church would prove to have lapsed into bringing to birth something lower than itself if, in the next chapter of the story, the adolescent church were checked, and perhaps even blighted, in its growth by the outbreak of a new secular civilization. (On this point see, further, pp. 533–44, below.)

rise of yet another secular civilization out of the bosom of the Christian Church in the course of these latter centuries; it would still be the Crucifixion and the Crucifixion's spiritual consequences.

On this view, students of History would likewise have to revise the current Western conception of the service of Christianity and the other higher religions as chrysalises. They must conclude that, in assisting civilizations of the second generation to reproduce themselves in a third generation, the higher religions had responded to the call *noblesse oblige* at a cost which, at its lightest, would amount to an unprofitable digression from their own proper path and postponement of their entry upon their own true calling, while at its heaviest it might drag them down to the tragic ending of *Beauchamp's Career*. It would be a supreme tragedy, on the face of it, if a fully-fledged higher religion were to compromise its own future for the sake of bringing a civilization of the third generation to birth, because it would be sacrificing itself to secure the reproduction of a secular institution which was not only intrinsically inferior to its religious chrysalis but was now also superfluous in virtue of the faithful fulfilment, by civilizations of a preceding generation, of their specific mission of giving the higher religions an opportunity of coming to flower. The civilizations would be in the same relation to the higher religions as the primitive societies to the civilizations. When the primitive societies had succeeded in giving birth to civilizations, they had performed their task and exhausted their mandate, and, in the new chapter thereby opened in the history of Mankind, no civilization had ever sacrificed itself for the perversely anachronistic purpose of assisting the surviving primitive societies to reproduce their outmoded kind. Why should higher religions perform unprecedented acts of self-sacrifice in order to bring into the World a new litter of outmoded civilizations? If there were any justification for this folly, it would not be found in reason but in the intuition that 'God hath chosen the foolish things of the World to confound the wise'.[1] A church which stepped aside from its course and forbore to press forward towards its goal, in order to minister to a dying civilization and to nurse an infant civilization in its cradle, might save its life—if it did save it—by losing it for Christ's sake and the Gospel's[2]—like the pilgrim in Tolstoy's tale[3] who won God's grace when he earned his obtusely pharisaical travelling companion's contempt by fulfilling his pilgrimage in the spirit at the sacrifice of the letter.

In submitting to serve as chrysalises for civilizations, the living higher religions might indeed have compromised their own future if it were true that this service was their *raison d'être*. In tiding over the interregna between civilizations of the second and third generation and duly bringing civilizations of a third generation to birth, the living higher religions would then have exhausted their mandates, and, while there might be no reason to expect that the latest crop of civilizations would not eventually go the way of their predecessors, there would be still

[1] 1 Cor. i. 27, quoted in IV. iv. 249 and in V. vi. 150.
[2] Matt. x. 39 and xvi. 25; Mark viii. 35; Luke ix. 24 and xvii. 33; John xii. 25.
[3] *Two Old Men*, cited on p. 391, above.

less reason to expect that the higher religions which had brought them to birth would live to survive, or even witness, their demise. On the hypothesis that higher religions come and go for the convenience of falling and rising civilizations, we should expect to see the civilizations of the third generation providing, as providently as their predecessors, for the propagation of their species by conscripting new religions to serve as new chrysalises for tiding over new interregna and bringing a new generation of civilizations to birth.

Candidates for this *corvée* were in fact, as we have seen, in the field in the shape of rudiments of secondary higher religions that had been created by the internal proletariats of living non-Western civilizations which had latterly been enmeshed in an expanding Western Society's world-encompassing net; but there was no warrant for expecting to see History repeat itself by casting this new batch of religions for this old role if the truth lay, not in the chrysalis theory, but in its converse. If the truth was that Religion is the true end of Man, and that civilizations have their *raison d'être* in ministering to spiritual progress, then, once again, a civilization might break down, but the replacement of one higher religion by another need not be a necessary consequence. So far from that, it might be augured that, if a secularized Western Civilization were to break down in its turn after having swept all its contemporaries into its net, the living higher religions would not only survive but would grow in wisdom and stature as the result of a fresh experience of secular catastrophe. The spiritual insight that they might gain through further suffering might lead them, as we have suggested, to a mutual recognition of their own essential unity in diversity. As for the rudiments of secondary higher religions which were visible in the twentieth century of the Christian Era in the oecumenical landscape, these might be drawn back into the main stream of Mankind's religious life, to make creative contributions to its flow in this reach of the river, or they might drain away into the desert and lose themselves in its sands; but there was no reason—if the assiduous provision of chrysalises were not assumed to be Religion's *raison d'être*—for expecting to see these secondary higher religions supplant Hinduism, Christianity, Islam, and Buddhism as these four living higher religions themselves had supplanted the paganism of Primitive Mankind.

If we now look again at our table, we shall see that the serial order in which the societies are there displayed is not only chronological and genealogical but is also qualitative. In the light of our intervening investigation, the order reveals itself as an ascending scale of values in four degrees:

4. Higher Religions.
3. Secondary Civilizations.
2. Primary Civilizations.
1. Primitive Societies.

In this new value-scale, two of our three familiar species of human society, the higher religions and the primitive societies, reappear, with their identities unchanged, at the top and the bottom of the ladder. The third species, on the other hand, has lost an identity with which we have credited it since our judgement, at an early stage in this Study, that all civilizations are philosophically equivalent.[1] This judgement is assuredly true as far as it goes; and it has not played us false so long as we have been dealing with the civilizations themselves, in their geneses, growths, breakdowns, and disintegrations, as the ultimate objects of our inquiry. Now, however, that our Study has carried us to a point at which the civilizations in their turn, like the parochial states of the Modern Western World at the outset of our investigation, have ceased to constitute intelligible fields of study for us and have forfeited their historical significance except in so far as they minister to the progress of Religion, we find that, from this more illuminating standpoint, the species itself has lost its specific unity. In our new list of societies arranged in a serial order of ascending value, the primary and secondary civilizations appear as separate categories, differentiated from one another and located on different qualitative levels by the difference in value between their respective contributions to the achievement of bringing the higher religions to flower. As for the civilizations of the third generation, they are now right out of the picture.

(*b*) THE SIGNIFICANCE OF THE CHURCHES' PAST

In coming to the conclusion reached at the close of the preceding chapter, we are merely applying to all eight of the living civilizations a judgement which the children of the Western Civilization in its latest phase had confidently passed upon their own society's seven sisters. In diagnosing the symptoms of breakdown and dissolution in the present state of these seven other civilizations of the third generation, a student of History midway through the twentieth century of the Christian Era was not flying in the face of current opinion in the West; for, even after having run into two general wars in one lifetime and having been kept, by the aftermath of the second war, in haunting fear of the advent of a third, Western Man had not yet been cured of his conviction that he was 'not as other men are';[2] and so he still saw nothing paradoxical or questionable in the proposition that the Western Civilization was the only society of its kind that still had a future. On this Modern Western view, on which a latter-day secularized Western Civilization was the climax of human achievement, the other living civilizations were put out of court automatically, while the extinct civilizations could not hope to be awarded even a posthumous patent of nobility except in so far as their advocates could prove that they had had some hand in making the Western Civilization what it had come to be. In an intellectual milieu in which this was accepted as a reasonable view, there should have been nothing very shocking in the alternative suggestion that a rather larger number of the extinct civilizations had 'made good', and that all eight, instead of seven, of the living civilizations were 'on the shelf'. Yet, even so late in the Western Civilization's day as the year A.D. 1952, this variation on the conventional Western view could hardly

[1] See I. i. 175–7.

[2] Luke xviii. 11.

be suggested in Western circles without raising an uproar there; for, even if the traditional Western rationalist, in an elegiac mood, were to acquiesce in seeing the Western Civilization deposed from the place of honour in the moving picture of human progress up to date, he would be moved to indignation and mockery at the notion of assigning the vacated place to Religion.

'This mountebank', the affronted Western rationalist would exclaim, 'is trying to pass off, as the last word in wisdom, one of the most naïve of all the commonplaces with which the professional apologists of the so-called "higher religions" have sought to impose upon Mankind ever since an apology was first called for by the simultaneous social triumph and moral bankruptcy of these extraordinary ecclesiastical institutions that the apologists have undertaken to defend. The fallacy in this commonplace has been exposed already a thousand times over in as many years. The trick, whether performed disingenuously or in childish good faith, is, after all, a simple one. You have merely to ascribe to a church the virtues preached in the scriptures attributed to the church's founder, and your church inevitably takes the highest place on the ladder. The trick, however, is as easy to unmask as it is to play. To unmask it you have merely to re-direct the observer's attention from the alleged ideals of the church's founder to the current practice of the church as it can be observed at first hand in the observer's own day. Look around you. Behold Christianity, the Mahāyāna, Islam, and Hinduism not as they claim to be but as they are, and your judgement of relative values will register a very different result. Call the insight of the prophets a flash if you will, so long as you admit that it has been a flash in the pan.'

This line of attack on the living higher religions may be illustrated by quotations from the works of a pioneer Western rationalist of the generation that had seen the end of the Wars of Religion and a latter-day follower of the same school who had lived to see the onset of the Wars of Ideology.

In an appeal addressed by Bayle to his Roman Catholic countrymen and contemporaries, the *déraciné* French philosopher pleads:

'Je voudrais que vous entendissiez ceux qui n'ont d'autre religion que celle de l'équité naturelle. Ils regardent votre conduite comme un argument irréfutable, et lorsqu'ils remontent plus haut et qu'ils considèrent les ravages et les violences sanguinaires que notre religion catholique a commises pendant six ou sept cents ans par tout le monde, ils ne peuvent s'empêcher de dire que Dieu est trop bon essentiellement pour être l'auteur d'une chose aussi pernicieuse que les religions positives; qu'il n'a révélé à l'homme que le droit naturel, mais que des esprits ennemis de notre repos sont venus de nuit semer la zizanie[1] dans le champ de la religion naturelle, par l'établissement de certains cultes particuliers, qu'ils savaient bien qu'ils seraient une sémence éternelle de guerres, de carnages et d'injustices. Ces blasphèmes font horreur à la conscience; mais votre Église en répondra devant Dieu.'[2]

Frazer, writing more than two hundred years later, can venture to go

[1] Matt. xiii. 25.

[2] Bayle, P.: *Ce que c'est que la France Toute Catholique sous le Règne de Louis le Grand* (Saint-Omer 1686, Lami).

farther with himself and with his readers. While Bayle professes to be distressed at finding that the perversion of Religion should have given her enemies an occasion to blaspheme, Frazer professes partially to condone the perversion by presenting, in the ironical form of an apologia, a radical criticism of Religion itself. He offers the devastating suggestion that a cynical adulteration of the pure milk of the word may have saved the lives of a flock that would probably have starved if it had been forced to remain for very long on so etherial a diet.

'Taken altogether, the coincidences of the Christian with the heathen festivals are too close and too numerous to be accidental. They mark the compromise which the Church in the hour of its triumph was compelled to make with its vanquished yet still dangerous rivals. The inflexible Protestantism of the primitive missionaries, with their fiery denunciations of heathendom, had been exchanged for the supple policy, the easy tolerance, the comprehensive charity of shrewd ecclesiastics, who clearly perceived that if Christianity was to conquer the World it could do so only by relaxing the too rigid principles of its Founder, by widening a little the narrow gate which leads to salvation.

'In this respect an instructive parallel might be drawn between the history of Christianity and the history of Buddhism. Both systems were in their origin essentially ethical reforms born of the generous ardour, the lofty aspirations, the tender compassion of their noble Founders, two of those beautiful spirits who appear at rare intervals on Earth like beings come from a better world to support and guide our weak and erring nature.[1] Both preached moral virtue as the means of accomplishing what they regarded as the supreme object of life, the eternal salvation of the individual soul, though by a curious antithesis the one sought that salvation in a blissful eternity, the other in a final release from suffering, in annihilation. But the austere ideals of sanctity which they inculcated were too deeply opposed not only to the frailties but to the natural instincts of Humanity ever to be carried out in practice by more than a small number of disciples, who consistently renounced the ties of the family and the state in order to work out their own salvation in the still seclusion of the cloister. If such faiths were to be nominally accepted by whole nations or even by the World, it was essential that they should first be modified or transformed so as to accord in some measure with the prejudices, the passions, the superstitions of the vulgar. This process of accommodation was carried out in after-ages by followers who, made of less etherial stuff than their masters, were for that reason the better fitted to mediate between them and the common herd. Thus as time went on the two religions, in exact proportion to their growing popularity, absorbed more and more of those baser elements which they had been instituted for the very purpose of suppressing.

'Such spiritual decadences are inevitable. The World cannot live at the level of its great men. Yet it would be unfair to the generality of our kind to ascribe wholly to their intellectual and moral weakness the gradual

[1] 'The historical reality both of [the] Buddha and of Christ has sometimes been doubted or denied. It would be just as reasonable to question the historical existence of Alexander the Great and Charlemagne on account of the legends which have gathered round them. The great religious movements which have stirred Humanity to its depths and altered the beliefs of nations spring ultimately from the conscious and deliberate efforts of extraordinary minds, not from the blind unconscious cooperation of the multitude. The attempt to explain History without the influence of great men may flatter the vanity of the vulgar, but it will find no favour with the philosophic historian.'

divergence of Buddhism and Christianity from their primitive patterns. For it should never be forgotten that by their glorification of poverty and celibacy both these religions struck straight at the root not merely of civil society but of human existence. The blow was parried by the wisdom or the folly of the vast majority of Mankind, who refused to purchase a chance of saving their souls with the certainty of extinguishing the species.'[1]

The verdict on the record of the churches which Bayle has presented as an indictment, and Frazer, more insidiously, as a defence, might be put in still stronger terms than those here employed by either of these two distinguished rationalists. The ecclesiastics who had betrayed or fulfilled their trust by bringing the churches back to Earth seemed almost to have gone out of their way to fly in the face of the founders by sinning against their principal precepts as recorded in scriptures that had been canonized by the ecclesiastics themselves. The Christian Church, for example, was open to the charge of having denied Christ by appropriating the priestcraft and pharisaism of the Jews, the polytheism and idolatry of the Greeks, and a championship of vested interests that was the legacy of the Romans; and the outcome might be described as an institution whose practice was the exact inverse of a vision which had seen God as a spirit who was to be worshipped in spirit and in truth[2] in a communion of saints in which the social schism between classes and states was to be healed by a union of hearts under the reign of Love.[3] The Mahāyāna and Hinduism, as they presented themselves in the writer's day, were not less vulnerable to criticism, while of Islam it might be said with sorrow that the Founder himself had betrayed his own ideals in his own lifetime by becoming the successful ruler of an aggressive state.[4] The final judgement on Religion which a rationalist line of attack implies is Lucretius's judgement on the Universe:

> Nequaquam nobis divinitus esse paratam
> Naturam rerum; tantâ stat praedita culpâ.[5]

And the immediate answer to both judgements is a suspensive 'Wait and see!'

The weak point in the rationalist argument was, in fact, its blindness to the implications of a Time-scale, recently established by the discoveries of a Modern Western Science, which, in a different context, the rationalist himself had eagerly turned to account as an engine for breaching the curtain-walls of religious orthodoxy.

The rationalist had legitimately pointed out that the seventeenth-century Protestant Christian chronologist Archbishop Ussher's reckoning[6] that the World had been created at 6.0 p.m. on the evening before the 23rd October, 4004 B.C., Old Style, and the Primitive Christian expectation that the last Trump might sound any day were both incompatible with the evidence that had since come to light about the

[1] Frazer, Sir J. G.: *The Golden Bough: Adonis, Attis, Osiris: Studies in the History of Oriental Religion* 2nd ed. (London 1907, Macmillan), pp. 260–1.
[2] John iv. 24.
[3] 'Where there is neither Greek nor Jew, circumcision nor uncircumcision, barbarian, Scythian, bond nor free; but Christ is all, and in all' (Col. iii. 11).
[4] See III. iii. 466–72.
[5] Lucretius: *De Rerum Natura*, Book V, ll. 198–9.
[6] See p. 299, above, and XI. ix. 178.

age of the Earth up to date and about the probable prospects of life on its surface. This planet, though not an old inhabitant of the stellar—or nebular—universe, had been in existence already, it would now appear, for some two thousand million years; Life had already existed on Earth for at least five hundred million years, and perhaps eight hundred million; Human Life had existed for at least six hundred thousand years, and perhaps one million; and the lengths of time during which the Earth's surface had been tenanted by divers orders of living creatures so far were all infinitesimally short compared with the aeons during which the Earth seemed likely to continue to be habitable in the future. These aeons of possible existence ahead of Life on Earth might run into millions of millions of years.[1]

This modern scientific Time-scale was brought into action by the ex-Christian Western rationalist against the contemporary Christian Western traditionalist in order to explode a traditional chronology; but the rationalist had failed to perceive that, in allowing himself this line of attack on his adversary, he had implicitly denied himself another line which implied an acceptance of the traditional chronology at its face value. The rationalist found fair game in a chronology which, should the Last Trump sound tomorrow, would have packed the World's history, from beginning to end, within a span of less than six thousand years; yet he was apt in the same breath to assert that there was nothing to be hoped for from a religion that had been in existence now for more than nineteen hundred years without having produced its promised change for the better. This arrow might well transfix the conscience of a traditionalist Christian in whose belief these 1,952 years amounted to nearly one-third of the total life-span of the World up to date; but the rationalist was logically debarred from shooting this shaft unless he first renounced his own Time-perspective and accepted his traditionalist victim's chronological tenets; for, on the rationalist's own reckoning, a period of nineteen or twenty centuries,[2] so far from being 'a long time',

[1] The figures here given are based on Zeuner, F. E.: *Dating the Past* (London 1946, Methuen), whose estimates for the age of diverse orders of life are higher, as will be seen, than those suggested, on the authority of Sir James Jeans, in I. i. 173, n. 2.

[2] The age of Christianity up to date would have to be reckoned at something between twenty-one and twenty-two centuries if we were to carry the reckoning back behind the Ministry of Jesus to include the experience of the internal proletariat of the Hellenic World during two preceding centuries of tribulation (see I. i. 40–42 and V. vi. 289). Yet, even if we were to trace the origins of Christianity as far back as the Passions of Kings Agis IV and Cleomenes III of Sparta in the third century B.C. (see V. vi. 376–539), the length of Christianity's life up to date would not have been appreciably increased on the Modern Western scientific Time-scale. The maximum reckoning was approximately the same for Christianity and for the Mahāyāna; for, though the process of the Mahāyāna's evolution was obscure, and it would have been difficult to pick out any single event that might stand for the beginning of it, even symbolically, it seemed clear that this metamorphosis of a primitive Buddhist philosophy had not begun till after the time of the Mauryan Emperor Açoka (*imperabat* 273–232 B.C.). The origins of Hinduism could be traced back to about the same date if the distinctive note of Hinduism was held to lie in the personal relation between the god and his devotee (see V. v. 138, and p. 427, above). If, however, the criterion was to be the first appearance, not of *Bhakti*, but of a distinctively Hindu theology, the founder of Hinduism would be Šankara (*florebat circa* A.D. 800) and Hinduism would have to be reckoned as being younger even than Islam, which did not come to birth till the beginning of the Prophet Muhammad's ministry *circa* A.D. 609.

Mr. John Lodge comments: 'But the Vedānta, as expounded by Šankara, is based on

was no more than the twinkling of an eye. It was, in fact, so infinitesimally short that, if we offered our rationalist a whole blank folio page and asked him to plot out on it his scientific chronology to scale, he would not find room to make the span of two thousand years visible within that compass even under the lens of the most powerful microscope.

'The history of Man is immensely, incalculably old: the latest discoveries of human remains in deep geological strata in various parts of the World, corroborated by the latest conclusions of Biology, are now sufficient to prove with certainty that Man has existed for hundreds of thousands, and perhaps for millions, of years. Out of this fact there springs a singular thought: The *historical* period, extending over the last five or six thousand years, is virtually a nothing, a flash (*lampo*), when confronted with the incommensurably longer past. Indeed, when we reflect upon the rapidity with which Time flies, and upon the painfully ephemeral nature of our wretched existence, it is not difficult to reach the conviction that even the most remote historical events known to us—the foundation of the Roman Empire, the Battle of Marathon, and, no less than they, the victory of Sesostris, Pharaoh of Egypt, over the Hittites in Syria eighteen centuries before the beginning of the Christian Era—are events of yesterday that are separated from us merely by an interval of time that is infinitesimal by contrast with the boundless vista of our geological past.'[1]

Yet, in defiance of self-consistency, the rationalist did take issue with the traditionalist on a ground that tacitly assumed the validity of the traditional Time-reckoning; and, to a detached observer of this nineteenth-century Western controversy, the points of agreement between the parties would appear more significant than the differences. For both of them it was an axiom that the Church as she was in their day gave the measure of the Church as she ever would be, world without end; and their quarrel arose over the difference in their subsequent value-judgements on the basis of their common factual premiss. In the traditionalist's eyes the Church's supposed immutability in her present shape was a glorious evidence of her divine origin and mission, while in the rationalist's eyes it was a damning confutation of the Church's extravagant claims; but the disputants agreed in their reading of the facts from which they drew these opposing conclusions, and, on the testimony of a Modern Western Science, their common reading was wrong.

The rationalist's error may be likened to the saucy townsman's when

the *Upanishads*, which go back before 500 B.C., and on the Vedic hymns, which go back before 1000 B.C. The so-called "Song of Creation" (*Rigveda* x. 129) is essential Hinduism.' The writer's answer would be that Šankara and his successors relieved Hinduism, in practice, of the incubus of the Indic Scriptures by professing to place these on a pedestal high enough to remove them conveniently out of the way.

[1] Caetani, L.: *Studi di Storia Orientale*, vol. i (Milan 1911, Hoepli), p. xiv.

Mr. Martin Wight comments: 'This passage from Caetani echoes Tacitus's discussion of chronological relativity in his *Dialogus de Oratoribus*, chap. 16, which you cite in V. vi. 80, but in a different connexion. Caetani's "historical period" of five or six thousand years corresponds to Tacitus's historical period of 1,300 years going back to Ulysses and Nestor; Caetani's "modern" period (implied but not mentioned in this passage) would correspond with Tacitus's period of "not much more than 300 years" going back to Demosthenes; and Caetani's "boundless vista of our geological past" corresponds with the *magnus et verus annus* which Tacitus derived from Cicero. J. B. Bury (*The Ancient Greek Historians* (London 1909, Macmillan), p. 254) seems to think that Tacitus was the first person who apprehended the relativity of the historical Time-scale in this way.'

he visits his country cousin and watches him sowing his seed. 'This seed has come to nothing', says the townsman as he inspects the field the day after the sowing and sees nothing there but bare soil; 'this seed has come to nothing', he repeats with still greater assurance when, revisiting the field next spring, he finds stalk and leaf with no grain in the ear. The townsman's egregious error arises from simple ignorance of the time that Life takes to bring her work of creation from seed to harvest.

The Christian traditionalist's error may be likened to the guileless Nubian's when, squatting on the desert bank of the Nile in flood, he watches the mighty brown stream swirl past him on its way from the Abyssinian Highlands to the Mediterranean Sea. The Nubian insists that this muddy mixture is pure water, and you cannot convince him of his error by ocular demonstration; for, if you pass a sample through a filter and show him the clear liquid that comes out, he tells you that this anaemic fluid is no longer water at all. 'You have robbed it', he declares, 'of all the goodness that makes water the life-giving elixir that it is.' In identifying the muddy mixture with water, our Nubian has, of course, come within an ace of arriving at the truth, if more than ninety-nine and a half per cent. of the brew in truth consists of water and less than the half of one per cent. consists of water-borne soil;[1] his error lies in stubbornly asserting that the complement of mud is not an accretion but is the water's very essence.

Our Nubian's stubbornness might relax if his vision could be expanded. Suppose that, instead of being earth-bound on his patch of river-side desert somewhere between the sixth and the first cataract, he could soar up aloft in an aeroplane, survey the basin of the Nile from Lake Tana to Rosetta, and follow from beginning to end the whole course of the natural phenomenon of which he now apprehends no more than a single phase. The truth might then dawn upon his understanding.

The truth is that the life-giving rain from Heaven comes down in such a mighty spate that, when the Monsoon discharges itself against the Abyssinian mountains and turns, on Earth, into a mighty rushing flood, it scours out the rock into gorges and carries away and along with it all manner of debris and flotsam which will fructify the seeds of vegetation if and when the water can deposit this freight as sediment. But the river cannot drop its load till its heaven-sent impetus abates, and on the Nubian stage of its long purificatory pilgrimage it is still flowing so fast that it has not yet rid itself of any of its earthy encumbrance. So it flows past the eyes of the awestricken Nubian onlooker in a thick brown stream, leaving his land unfertilized and barren. Any crop that the poor Nubian reaps is not a gift of the Nile but is a trove from some casual gust of rainfall that has momentarily moistened the dry bed of a tributary wadi.[2] The hurrying river passes Nubia by. It is only when it reaches the favoured land of Egypt that its pace slackens

1 'The maximum silt content by weight usually found in the Nile where it enters Egypt is about 4000 parts per million, and the average from August to October about 1500 parts per million' (Hurst, H. E., and Phillips, P.: *The Nile Basin*, vol. v: 'The Hydrology of the Lake Plateau and Bahr el Jebel' (Egyptian Ministry of Public Works, Physical Department, Paper No. 35 (Cairo 1938, Schindler), p. 19).

2 See II. i. 308–9.

enough to allow it to begin to disburden itself. From now onwards, mile by mile, the water converts its suspended alluvium into fertile fields and, in the creative act, progressively liberates itself, until, as it leaves the utmost fringe of the Delta behind it and breasts its way out to sea, it has become once again as clear and transparent as it was when it was falling from the sky on its way to furrow a contaminating yet fructifying Mother Earth. From the steeps of Semyen to the coasts of Cyprus may seem a long road; but all distances are comparative, and the breadth of half a continent is not really long compared to the circumference of the globe; nor is the labour of carrying its freight of earth so far an unduly heavy price for the river to pay for the boon of winning a bed; for, if the teeming water's first mighty impact on the Earth had not ploughed out the *cañon* from which its tardily deposited water-borne spoil derives, who knows whether the flood would ever have made history by turning into the Nile? Who knows whether it might not have surged back, uncreative and unsung, over the wastes of the Ogaden into the abyss of its parent Indian Ocean?

The heart of the matter is the truth to which the Nubian spectator is blind. The truth is that, so long as the alluvium is held in suspense, the alluvium itself remains unfertile and the water remains impure. It is only when the flotsam is able to sink from the intellectual surface of the psychic stream to the well-springs of lowly folk-lore and lofty poetry in the Psyche's intuitive and emotional depths that this sediment can fertilize the Psyche and that, in virtue of this fruitful disentanglement of two fortuitously intermingled elements, the heavenly water of spiritual life can regain its original purity. In the Roman Catholic Church this truth had been perceived by the Modernists;[1] but their insight had drawn down upon their heads the thunderbolt of a Juppiter in Agro Vaticano[2] who, with his gaze fixed on the Past and averted from the Future, seemed oblivious—though his hand still held the keys—of his previous local avatar in Ianiculo as the genius who had the power to open the door because he had the vision to look before and after.[3]

[1] 'Evolvi . . . ac mutari dogma non posse solum sed oportere, et modernistae ipsi perfracte affirmant, et ex eorum sententiis aperte consequitur. . . .' (*Litterae Encyclicae SS. D. N. Pii P.P. X*: 'Pascendi dominici gregis. . . .' (8th September, 1907)).

[2] 'Si quis dixerit fieri posse ut dogmatibus ab Ecclesia propositis aliquando secundum progressum scientiae sensus tribuendus sit alius ab eo quem intellexit et intelligit Ecclesia, anathema sit' (Concilium Vaticanum, 1869–70, Sessio III (24 Aprilis, 1870), canones: 4. *De Fide et Ratione*, Canon 3).

[3] While the extremeness of the conservatism of the Papacy was manifestly due to the relative vastness and antiquity of the particular Christian ecclesiastical institution that was administered from the Vatican (see pp. 549–50, below), this latter-day Roman Catholic conservatism was in itself only an exaggeration of a trait which had been characteristic of the Christian Church since its infancy and which had persisted in divers degrees in all the denominations between which the Church had come to be divided. Four reasons for this conservatism of Christianity in general, and of Western Christianity in particular, have been suggested by Canon B. H. Streeter:

(i) The Church among the Gentiles was a missionary church which had hardly set to work before it found itself cut off from its base of operations owing to the rejection of Christianity by Jewry. This breach with a contemporary Jewry, which, in a sense, made the Gentile Christian Church's fortune by making it into *the* Christian Church *sans phrase*, had the further effect of making the Church meticulous in maintaining continuity, on its own account, with a Jewish past from which, on its own view, it derived both credentials and inspiration that it could not afford to lose.

(ii) A Christian tradition had no sooner begun to take shape than it was constrained

The legacy of the Past to the Present was indeed as precious as it was conspicuous. 'Before Abraham was, I am';[1] and, since it was not credible that God should have shown no glimmer of His light to Man before a revelation to 'Abraham' that was the traditional first epiphany of that ray of progressive enlightenment which had culminated in Christianity, students of History must also recognize true gleams of divine light in religious rites and symbols, older than Abraham's day, that had been caught up and carried along in the latter-day Christian stream.[2]

'The calling of Abraham' itself might be an echo of one of the spiritual experiences of a disintegrating Sumeric Civilization if the spiritual meaning of the story was the establishment of a personal relation between the worshipper and the genius of his household,[3] for this is a revelation of God's nature to which the human heart and mind are attuned when the corporate political aspect of Religion—the worship of a deified parochial or universal state—is discredited by the collapse of the mundane society whose will to live is reflected in it.[4] We have already noticed another fruit of Sumeric spiritual experience which had likewise been garnered by Christianity, though this without recognition of the Sumeric source. The Passion of Christ, as we have seen, had been foreshadowed in a Passion of Tammuz in which the death of one god, made manifest in the ἐνιαυτὸς δαίμων,[5] had been celebrated under the divers names of Adonis, Osiris, Attis, Zagreus, Balder, as the rite had radiated over the face of the Earth. The Queen of

to freeze itself hard in order to save itself from being liquidated by Gnostic and other alien influences (on this point, compare the passage quoted from Bishop E. W. Barnes on p. 465, below).

(iii) In the West, from the fifth century of the Christian Era onwards, the Christian Church was drawn into playing the role of serving as a chrysalis for the genesis of a new Western Christian Civilization out of the moribund body social of an old Hellenic Civilization (on this point see the present volume, pp. 392–419, above).

(iv) In the West, in the fourteenth and fifteenth centuries of the Christian Era, the Christian Church was drawn into participation in a backward-looking renaissance of the Hellenic Civilization to which the Western Christian Civilization was affiliated (on this point see the present volume, pp. 538–44, below).

The foregoing considerations are set out, under the cross-heading 'The Conservatism of the Church', in an essay on 'Christ the Constructive Revolutionary' on pp. 348–52 of a symposium entitled *The Spirit* (New York 1919, Macmillan).

Mr. Martin Wight comments: 'The conservatism of modern Christianity has another cause which is not mentioned here. As a post-Christian Western Civilization developed out of Western Christendom from the seventeenth century onwards, the Church, rightly fearing the spread of secularism and the reversion to neo-paganism, wrongly identified the Faith with the social system that was passing away. Thus, while conducting an intellectual rearguard action against "liberal", "modernist", and "scientific" errors, it incautiously fell into a posture of political Archaism, supporting feudalism, monarchy, aristocracy, "capitalism", and the *ancien régime* generally, and became the ally and often the tool of political reactionaries who were as anti-Christian as the common "revolutionary" enemy. Hence the unedifying political record of modern Christianity: in the nineteenth century it allied itself with monarchism and aristocracy in order to denounce liberal democracy; in the twentieth century it allies itself with liberal democracy in order to denounce totalitarianism. Thus it had seemed, ever since the French Revolution, [always] to be one political phase behind the times. This, of course, is the gist of the Marxist criticism of Christianity in the Modern World. The Christian answer would perhaps be that, when the Gadarene swine of a disintegrating civilization are engaged in their headlong downward rush, it may well be the Church's reponsibility to keep as far as possible to the rear of the herd and direct the eyes of as many as possible backwards up the slope.'

[1] John viii. 58.

[2] On this point, see further pp. 764–5 and 766–7, below.

[3] See V. vi. 39, n. 3.

[4] See V. v. 529–32 and V. vi. 14–16.

[5] See III. iii. 256–9.

Heaven who was the virgin mother and spouse of the dying god had been adored as Ishtar, Ashtoreth, Isis, Cybele, Britomartis, and Inanna on her way to being adored as Mary.[1] In the sacrifice of the Mass, Christians were still partaking of the sacrament of all the pagan mysteries.

The travail of Christ Incarnate for the salvation of Mankind had been foreshadowed in the labours of Gilgamesh, Hêraklês, Prometheus, and the 'culture heroes' of a Sinic mythology,[2] and the Incarnation had been no stumbling-block to the imagination of an Hellenic World which had added the revolutionary worship of Caesar to a traditional worship of the Olympians. In the Olympians the mundane society that was Christianity's first mission-field was already familiar with the spectacle of divinity in human form—though, through the dark glass of a barbaric Achaean mythology, the many gods into whom the One True God's image was here diffracted showed themselves prone to all human moral infirmities and free merely from all human physical limitations.[3] In Divus Augustus the potential converts of the first Christian missionaries had already acknowledged an incarnation of the Godhead in a living human being whose mortal mother was fabled to have been got with child by an immortal sire;[4] and this divine deed, which must shock the sensibilities of a philosophic soul as a vulgar moral transgression when it was attributed to an Olympian, was to shine, in the self-revelation of a God whose power was love and whose Godhead was as wholly present in the Son as in the Father, as a voluntary evacuation (*κένωσις*) of His own divinity which was a supreme act of self-sacrifice for the redemption of His fallen creatures.

The tableau of Mother and Child among the gentle cattle in the stable at Bethlehem, which symbolized Christ's act of *κένωσις* in the imagery of the Christian Faith, had been anticipated in the tableau of a Minoan *πότνια θηρῶν* surrounded by her *comitatus* of beasts of the field.[5] The lamb who had been moved to prophesy by the agony of an Egyptiac Time of Troubles had been a prototype of the lamb who was Christ;[6] and the Sumeric fish-god Ea—incarnate in the fish whose presence had hallowed the tanks of latter-day shrines at Mambij and Ascalon[7] and Brusa[8]—had been a prototype of the Christ whose epiphany as a fish had been ingeniously explained away as a play upon the initial letters of his style and title in Greek.[9] The dove that became

1 See V. v. 81–82 and 148–50, and p. 437, above, and pp. 467, below.

2 See V. vi. 266–7.

3 'Mr. Gladstone, in his essay on "The Place of Ancient Greece in the Providential Order", has a very interesting discussion of the character and attributes of Apollo, seeing in him a precursor of Christ. "In his hands we find numerous functions of such rank and such range that we cannot understand how they could pass to him from Zeus the supreme deity until we remember that they are the very functions assigned by a more real and higher system to the Son of God: the true Instructor, Healer, Deliverer, Judge and Conqueror of Death, in whom the power and majesty of the Godhead were set forth to the World" (Gladstone, W. E.: *Gleanings of Past Years*, vol. vii (London 1879, John Murray), p. 49).'—Martin Wight.

4 See V. vi. 267–8 and 269, n. 1.

5 See III. iii. 260–1.

6 See IV. iv. 409–11.

7 The temples of Atargatis at Mambij and Ascalon (Meyer, E.: *Geschichte des Altertums*, vol. iii (Stuttgart 1901, Cotta), p. 137).

8 The Ulu Jāmy'sy (Great Mosque) at Brusa.

9 *Ἰησοῦς Χριστὸς Θεοῦ Υἱὸς Σωτήρ = ΙΧΘΥΣ.*

the Holy Spirit descending on Jesus at His baptism in Jordan had hovered in ages past round the fane of Aphrodite as Paphos.[1] The stone[2] on which the Church of Christ was built had made its earliest advent to Rome, not in the first century of the Christian Era, but in 204 B.C. as the baetylus of a Pessinuntine Cybele, and the Roman Catholic Church was not the only surviving religious edifice that rested upon it; it was also embedded in the foundations of the Ka'bah at Mecca.[3]

Man's worship of forces of Nature, less amenable than stocks and stones, that mocked his audacious efforts to harness and exploit his fellow creatures, had given Man an inkling of the One True God's transcendent power. A sky god and a volcano *jinn* had lent their potency to quicken Israel's overwhelming sense of the omnipotence of the Living God Yahweh;[4] and an ancestral worship of a Sun in which a maturing Scientific Mind had correctly discerned the physical source of terrestrial energy and life had initiated Constantine into the secret that God's power is the power of love[5] when he had seen the Cross flame out athwart the Aton.[6]

In their handling of this spoil that had been carried in suspense in the current of Christianity, the traditionalists and the rationalists had played into one another's hands once again. The same historic rites and symbols that the traditionalists had defended tooth and nail, in the forms in which Christianity happened to have adopted them, as essential and inalienable elements of Christian practice and belief, had been denounced by the same Christian controversialists, with reckless inconsistency, in the unmistakably kindred forms in which they were to be found in other faiths and worships. The resemblance was indeed so striking that the Christian traditionalists had been unable to ignore it; but, instead of allowing themselves to apprehend the simple truth that it was a family likeness, they had concocted the ingenious alternative explanation that it was devil's work. The Devil and his angels had put into circulation counterfeit copies of the institutions of the Church in order to mislead Mankind into rejecting the One True Faith.

In thus branding the pagan mysteries as frauds, the Christian traditionalists had delivered themselves into the hands of their ex-Christian rationalist adversaries. The Higher Criticism could demonstrate incontrovertibly that the genetic relation between corresponding rites and symbols was the inverse of what the traditionalists alleged. So far from the pagan forms being counterfeits of the Christian, the Christian could be shown to be derivatives of the pagan; and, therewith, the Christian traditionalists were hoist with their own petard; for they themselves were unescapably 'on record' as having declared these

[1] See V. vi. 362.

[2] 'Stone' is the authentic meaning of the masculine Greek word πέτρος, not 'rock', which is the meaning of the collective feminine πέτρα.

[3] See V. v. 685–8, and pp. 465 and 466, below.

[4] See V. vi. 38–45.

[5] See V. v. 691–4 and V. vi. 24–25.

[6] This intuition that the divinity embodied in the Sun was identical with a Dead and Risen Christ enabled Constantine to fulfil Ikhnaton's unfulfilled mission of becoming the One True God's oecumenical bishop. Ikhnaton had failed to take the literally crucial step of identifying the Aton with Osiris—perhaps because a nascent Osirian Church had already been blighted by being drawn into an unholy alliance with the barefacedly political religion of Amon-Re (see I. i. 143–5).

elements of religion to be a sham and a delusion in their pagan version, and the words could be taken out of their mouths to pronounce the same judgement on their own holy of holies. On the Christians' own confession, so the neo-pagans could declare, a religion which had adopted and cherished these crude primitive rites and symbols stood convicted of having the lie in its soul.

This was a fair shot[1] in the not illegitimate warfare that the neo-pagans waged against the Christian traditionalists; and in that battle it was also a knock-out blow. From the rigorously exclusive traditionalist Christian standpoint the Higher Criticism's argument was unanswerable. Since the days of the Fathers of the Church, however, there had been other Christians who had acknowledged Christianity's pagan ancestry, and these could still hold the field and turn the argument's edge against its neo-pagan authors. In contrast to the Christian traditionalists, the Christian evolutionists[2] had started, not from the negative premiss that pre-Christian paganism was false, but from the positive premiss that Christianity was true; and they could therefore accept with impunity a recognition of the truth that the resemblances between Christianity and pre-Christian paganism were due to Christianity's indebtedness to a pagan past. The Christian evolutionist's inference from this would be, not that there was no truth in Christianity, but that the truth which was in Christianity had already been aglow in paganism for ages before it had burst into a Christian flame. The enlightened Christian would not only accept this new perspective without hesitation or embarrassment; he would give glory to a God who 'is' before Abraham 'was', for having revealed some glimmer of His light to Man before Abraham's day.

This was not the last word, however; for, if the Christian evolutionist was in a posture to stand his ground and to return the neo-pagan's fire after the Christian traditionalist's batteries had been silenced, he must be on guard against ranging himself under the Christian traditionalist's standard and thereby nullifying his own Christian victory. Transposing our simile of the flow of a river into terms of a simile of the radiation of light, we must be ever alert to distinguish between the eternal source of light and its transient manifestations. 'No man hath seen God at any time';[3] we apprehend God's existence and divine His nature thanks to the Creator's revelation of Himself through His works;[4] but God's

[1] Mr. Martin Wight comments: 'The reasoning of this paragraph does not carry conviction. Whatever [a] Higher Criticism can demonstrate, it has nothing to say to the question whether the pagan rites are diabolical in origin. The fact that pagan theophagy is historically and anthropologically prior to the Eucharist does not in the least affect the Christian's assertion that pagan theophagy is false while the Eucharist is the real thing. Genetic relationships are irrelevant to teleology—though, of course, most Christians today, and many Christians at all times, would say that these pagan rites were (or are) adumbrations of and preparations for the real thing rather than diabolical counterfeits. The dual interpretation of non-Christian religions either as demonic or as a *praeparatio evangelica* goes back to the earliest days of the Church.'

[2] The word 'evolutionists' is, of course, used in the present context in its generic meaning, without any intention of importing into it the specific associations attaching to its use in hypotheses and controversies precipitated by the Modern Western science of Biology.

[3] 1 John iv. 12.

[4] Mr. Martin Wight justly comments: 'For a Christian, through Christ.' It was the Christian Faith that God had made one unique direct revelation of Himself to Mankind on Earth in tbe incarnation of the Second Person of the Trinity as Christ Jesus, and this Christian belief was in contradiction with the statement that has just been quoted from

works are not only windows through which the heavenly light is made visible to the eye of the Human Soul on Earth; they are at the same time veils through which the radiance is dulled to a degree at which the Soul's eye can receive it without being blinded; they are partly opaque as well as partly translucent, and they never reveal to us more than a local aspect of God's omnipresence or a temporary aspect of His eternity.[1] In the rudimentary theology of a North American Indian tribe, these elusive epiphanies of God had been described in the vivid imagery of the primitive imagination:

'Everything, as it moves, now and then, here and there, makes stops. The bird as it flies stops in one place to make its nest, and in another to rest in its flight. A man, when he goes forth, stops when he wills. So the god has stopped. The Sun, which is so bright and beautiful, is one place where he has stopped. The Moon, the stars, the winds he has been with. The trees, the animals, are all where he has stopped, and the Indian thinks of these places and sends his prayers there to reach the place where the god has stopped and to win help and a blessing.'[2]

This intuition that God's works are God's stopping places had been the inspiration of Goethe's greatest poem[3] and Bergson's greatest philosophical work.[4] The error of idolatry lies in mistaking the creature for the Creator, and the sin of it lies in worshipping the creature in the Creator's stead.[5] Man has thus idolized the productive and destructive forces in Non-Human Nature—cow and bull, field and mountain, sun and storm—and the corresponding antithetical forces in Man himself: the key roles, gracious or forbidding, in the drama of human life—motherhood, fatherhood, kingship, self-sacrifice—and a Leviathan that is the appalling projection of a demonic corporate human power. Yet any veil through which God's light dimly shines is an intimation of God that is not God Himself, though one veil may differ from another in the degree of its opaqueness. Moreover there is veil behind veil, and the

the New Testament. Yet, if the Christian Church had apparently revoked the Johannine declaration that 'no man hath seen God at any time', a Christian would not dispute the proposition that 'no man hath seen God at any time except in "the incarnation of Our Lord Jesus Christ" '; he would hold that Christ's human nature, from which His divine nature was never dissociated at any time during its direct revelation to human beings, was one of the works of the God who had incarnated Himself in this human nature as Christ Jesus; and—holding also, as he must, that 'although he be God and man, yet He is not two, but one Christ'—he must hold Christ to be 'inferior to the Father as touching His manhood' while 'equal to the Father as touching His Godhead'. Thus, according to the Christian Faith, God, in Christ incarnate, had revealed Himself 'in association with' one of His works, though not in this case solely 'through' it, since, according to the Christian Faith, this unique revelation was a direct self-revelation of the Godhead.

1 This is T. S. Eliot's theme in *The Rock*, Chorus X, beginning 'O Light Invisible, we praise Thee! Too bright for mortal vision', with its refrains in the words of the liturgy of the Holy Communion, and with its conclusion:

'And when we have built an altar to the Invisible Light, we may set thereon the little lights for which our bodily vision is made,
'And we thank Thee that darkness reminds us of light.
'O Light Invisible, we give Thee thanks for Thy great glory.'

2 Quoted by Fletcher, A. C., in *Reports of the Peabody Museum of American Archaeology and Ethnology*, vol. iii, 1880–6 (Cambridge, Mass. 1887, Peabody Museum), p. 276, n. 1.

3 For this theme in Faust, see II. i. 271–98.

4 Bergson, H.: *Les Deux Sources de la Morale et de la Religion* (Paris 1932, Alcan).

5 See IV. iv. 261–2.

Soul's approach on Earth towards the Beatific Vision and the Communion of Saints is made by stripping away one revealing-obscuring veil after another, as far as Man's spiritual insight can penetrate and as fast as his Soul's eye can accustom itself to the increase in the degree of the radiance that the removal of each successive veil brings with it.[1] A veil between the Human Soul and God is removed when the creature in which this veil consists is mastered—and, in the act of being mastered, is exorcised—by the Human Intellect; and this is why 'the discovery of new means by which Consciousness is enabled to extend its range of objectives has always been the decisive factor in the history of human development'.[2]

This is the way of Life; but it is a hard way, because the stepping-stones are stopping-places and the pilgrim's progress is a *tour de force*. The Soul in search of God has 'to make a movement out of something which, by definition, is a halt',[3] and she has to see through the ambivalence of windows that are veils. Each veil becomes suffused with light in the act of obstructing the light's passage from its source to the eye. How can we believe that this rose-flushed or that opal-tinted cloud owes its glow and colour to a glory that is not in, but is beyond, the cloud itself? And, even if our minds do become convinced of the truth of this hardly credible proposition, how can out hearts bear to discard a thing of beauty that has been a joy, and at which we have learnt to gaze without being dazzled? Can it not be a joy for ever? Is it not sacrilege to discard it? Is it not madness? Man is prone to idolatry because he is always tempted to play truant from his God-given task of a never-ending search for God by seeking rest in a finite object of worship, and this, in the imagery of a seventeenth-century English poet, was the reason why God 'made a stay' in pouring his blessings on Man when rest alone remained to bestow upon him.

> For if I should (said he)
> Bestow this jewel also on my creature
> He would adore My gifts instead of Me,
> And rest in Nature, not the God of Nature;
> So both should losers be.[4]

Here is the crux in the way of Man's approach to God; and, because of it, each spiritual step in advance has to be paid for, like all true gains, by a painful sacrifice. We have to throw away a treasure of the highest value so far known to us in order to purchase another treasure whose value, before we have grasped it, we can only take on faith as being higher still.[5] This Pilgrim's Progress requires an ascetic ruthlessness as

[1] Mr. Martin Wight comments: 'This is the Christian's answer to your assertion above, on pp. 442–3, of the spiritual equivalence of the four higher religions: "God, who at sundry times and in divers manners spake in time past . . . by the Prophets [and by the pagan precursors], hath in these last days spoken unto us by His Son" (Heb. i. 1–2).'

[2] Baynes, H. G.: *Mythology of the Soul* (London 1940, Baillière, Tindall, & Cox; 1949, Methuen), p. 309. The quotations from this book have been made with the permission of the publishers.

[3] Bergson, op. cit., p. 251, quoted in III. iii. 235.

[4] Herbert, George: *The Pulley*.

[5] 'This is moving and, from the Christian point of view, true. It is the demand which God made on Abraham when He called him to abandon the "other gods" whom his

well as a sanguine hope and valour; and faint souls that flinch from the ordeal seek to justify their failure to themselves by enlarging on the negative aspect of the spiritual feat that is demanded of them, and closing their eyes to the spiritual gain of which this sacrifice is the inexorable price.

'Prometheus, the cultural innovator who stole the fire of the Gods, is the prototype for all time of the daring hero-criminal who challenges the primordial images, the immemorial gods of the Unconscious, in order to place more power—i.e. knowledge—in the hands of Consciousness. . . . The guilt of Prometheus (which is also the guilt of the psychological innovator and pioneer) consists in the fact that he transferred from Heaven (i.e. the realm of primordial images) energy which had been latent in the Unconscious since the World began, bringing it under the control of Consciousness.'[1]

Hence the paradox that some of the greatest advances in the Soul's approach to God that have been made, at divers times and places, by saints and seers, have been anathematized as appalling backslidings—and this in good faith—by men of common clay who could not 'make the grade'. An Hellenically cultivated Pompey was dumbfounded at finding no material object of worship whatsoever inside the Holy of Holies of the Temple of Yahweh at Jerusalem when he forced his way in under the stimulus of a curiosity that had been whetted by the provocative self-confidence of a Jewish community's claim to be the only rightly guided worshippers of the One True God. In the next age of Hellenic history a now rather more pious pagan public discovered to its horror that the harmless-looking adherents of a new sect called Christians were 'atheists' who rejected everything that their pagan neighbours held sacred,[2] while pious Jews, for their part, execrated the Christians as libertines who had betrayed the faith of their fathers by admitting Gentiles into religious communion with Christian Jews and by exempting these uncircumcised proselytes from the duty of observing the Mosaic Law.

This was the historical background against which students of history midway through the twentieth century of the Christian Era had to view the state of Christianity and the other living higher religions in their day; and the conclusion to be drawn seemed to be in sharp contradiction with both the rationalist and the traditionalist position. The flotsam scoured out from older strata of religious experience and carried along in suspense in a Christian, Mahayanian, Hindu, or Islamic stream was no evidence that the water with which it was mingled was not the true living water from Heaven; but the water was given a clean bill of health in virtue of the finding that its load of fertilizing mud was only a temporary accretion; and this finding, which disposed of the rationalist's indictment of the muddiness of the stream, was at the same time fatal to the traditionalist's defence of it on the ground that the mud was of the

father Terah served (Joshua xxiv. 2); on Saul before he could become Paul; and on Augustine; and it is the demand which is made, in principle, on the adherent of every other higher (and lower) religion.'—Martin Wight.

[1] Baynes, op. cit., pp. 310 and 316.

[2] See V. vi. 536, and p. 491, below.

water's essence. The waters dropped by the Monsoon could not have become the Nile without scooping up the Abyssinian silt and carrying it along with them; but it was equally true, and true for the same reason, that the Nile could not be what it was without depositing its load sooner or later and eventually flowing out to sea in a stream as pure as the rain that had originally fallen from Heaven.

A Christian Father, Justin Martyr, writing his *First Apology* in the second century of the Christian Era, had not shrunk from pressing his argument against his pagan adversaries by drawing attention to a parallelism between the virgin births ascribed to Jesus and to Perseus, between the miracles of healing ascribed to Jesus and to Aesculapius, and between the alleged resurrection of Jesus and the apotheosis of Ariadne and the Caesars;[1] and the illuminatingly charitable distinction between the essence of a religious revelation and the accidents of the time and place in which it has come into the World, which a Christian 'evolutionist' might have derived from the polemical argument of a Christian 'fundamentalist', had been drawn by an eminent Modern Western Islamic scholar in an appreciation of the character and career of the Prophet Muhammad.

'Certainly Muhammad was guilty of errors, some of which were involuntary, but others not; besides these, he also perpetrated not a few acts that would be classified by us to-day as common crimes inspired by the basest of human passions; but it will be the task of future generations of historical critics to elucidate how far, in all this, the Prophet's personal responsibility is engaged, and to what extent his acts are, on the contrary, to be regarded as being an impersonal expression of the specific conditions of a society that was still in a primitive stage of development. Our own belief is that the errors and defects discernible in the Prophet, and in the religious system that he created, are to be attributed to the society in which he lived. To this society Muhammad was superior in many respects, but in others he was its native child and, as such, was necessarily a party to all its vices, imperfections and prejudices.'[2]

The Prophet Muhammad, as we have seen,[3] did deliberately compound with a pre-Islamic Arabian paganism, when he consented to adulterate the purity of his 'Religion of Abraham' by alloying it with the

[1] Justin Martyr's standpoint is described by Mr. Martin Wight as follows: 'Justin was the reverse of an "evolutionist"; he was an exclusivist or universalist, believing that the Christian Revelation is exclusively true and makes demands on the entire Human Race. He believed in the demonic character of pagan religion, especially where it imitated the Christian mysteries: see his discussion of the Mithraic mysteries as a diabolical travesty of the Eucharist, *Dialogus cum Tryphone*, ch. 70, and *First Apology*, ch. 66. In the passage that you cite he is not drawing parallels between Christian and pagan miracles; he is arguing with polemical irony: Who are you pagans to sneer at our belief in a virgin birth—what about Perseus? Or to find the miracles of healing incredible—what about Aesculapius? Or to find the Resurrection and Ascension ridiculous—"we propound nothing different from what you believe about those whom you consider to be the sons of Zeus . . . [and] the emperors . . . whom you deem worthy of deification, and on whose behalf you produce somebody to swear that he has seen the burning Caesar ascend to Heaven from the pyre" (*First Apology*, ch. 21). Justin makes the natural and reasonable assumption—for a Christian—that, in so far as pagan myths are true, they foreshadowed and find their fulfilment in Christ, but that, in so far as they described gods who are engaged in every kind of crime and vice, they are the work of the Devil.'

[2] Caetani, L.: *Studi di Storia Orientale*, vol. iii (Milan 1914, Hoepli), p. 295.

[3] On pp. 437–8, above.

local cult of the Black Stone embedded in the wall of the Kaʿbah at Mecca and with the regional practice of an annual pilgrimage to this Hijāzī shrine.[1] Yet this conciliatory concession to the prejudices and interests of his stiff-necked clansmen the Banu Quraysh was a venial sin against the Prophet's own Heaven-sent lights which left untarnished the sincerity and strength of will which Muhammad consistently displayed in resisting a perpetual temptation to compromise with the two mortal sins of Polytheism and Idolatry that were rampant not only in the Arabian paganism but also in the Hellenic Christianity of Muhammad's day; and in Christianity likewise, in spite of all the Christian Church's lamentable shortcomings and backslidings, there had always been a tendency for the living waters to defend their purity by refusing to pick up and carry the sullying soil that they had found in their path.

'The temptation to form tacit alliances with other religious movements, in some ways remarkably similar, must have been strong. Such an alliance would, however, have meant the ultimate repudiation of all that was most characteristic in the teaching of Jesus. Because Christianity refused compromise with other faiths, it survived to become, until practically our own time, the nominal, and not wholly ineffective, religion of Europe. Whether, by re-affirming the teaching of Jesus in its undeviating severity, Christianity can resume its hold on the hearts and minds of men, is a question of great importance as regards the ultimate fate of European Civilisation.'[2]

How were souls in search of God to disengage the essence of Religion from the accidents? Doubtless Time would show; for the expectation of human life on Earth (supposing that Man did not use his swiftly increasing technological command over Physical Nature to annihilate himself) was unimaginably long, and, in the course of those future aeons, the living waters would assuredly have time to purify themselves, like the Nile in its vastly briefer passage from Lake Tana to the sea. Time would show; but, in the life of the Spirit, operations are never impersonal or automatic; and, if this salutary purification were indeed eventually to be accomplished, this would be the achievement of individual souls. At any moment in its personal pilgrimage through life on Earth, a soul might be challenged by God to discriminate between the silt and the water, between the light and its reflection, by trial and error at the Soul's own peril; 'and narrow is the way which leadeth unto Life, and few there be that find it',[3] for, on the spiritual even more conspicuously than on the physical plane, it is impossible to live without living dangerously.

(c) THE CONFLICT BETWEEN HEART AND HEAD

Essence and Accidents

How, in an *Oikoumenê* that was being united on a literally world-wide range within a Western framework, were Christians, Buddhists, Muslims, and Hindus to make further progress in disengaging the essence of Religion from the accidents? The only way open to these fellow seekers after spiritual light was the hard road of spiritual travail along which

1 See p. 466, below.

2 Barnes, E. W.: *The Rise of Christianity* (London 1947, Longmans Green), p. 296, apropos of the eucharistic doctrine expounded in 1 Cor. x. 16–21.

3 Matt. vii. 14.

their predecessors, with God's help, had arrived at the degree of religious enlightenment represented by the living higher religions at the stage in which they found themselves at this crucial moment in Mankind's history. By comparison with the stage embodied in Primitive Paganism, the state of relative enlightenment to which the adherents of the higher religions had attained by a date midway through the twentieth century of the Christian Era manifestly represented a marvellous spiritual advance; yet, marvellous though it might be, they had now become aware that they could no longer go on living parasitically on God's past mercies to their forefathers and on their own forefathers' past spiritual endeavours to win a fuller vision of God, and a closer communion with Him, for themselves and for their children. They knew that they could no longer rest on their predecessors' spiritual labours because, in their generation, they were being racked by a conflict between heart and head which they could not leave unresolved with impunity, and which could be resolved only by a fresh spiritual move forward.

As the pilgrims girded themselves to take the hard road again, they might draw some encouragement from divers past successes of Mankind in discarding veils which had served as windows in their time. In default of fuller light, there had been a glimmer of spiritual enlightenment in the faint translucency of Man's vision of God through the animal creation.[1] In the demonic physical energies of untamed wild beasts Man had caught a glimpse of a divine power surpassing Man's own strength; in the hunter's game and in the shepherd's flock he had caught a glimpse of God's beneficence as the giver and sustainer of life; and a primitive worship of God in animal form had lived on to play a leading role in the religion of the Egyptiac Civilization. Yet, in the World as it was in A.D. 1952, this dim 'theriomorphic' vision of God, though still a living reality for unsophisticated souls at the lower levels of Hinduism, was on the whole on the wane. In the Christian consciousness the lamb, the dove, and the fish stood, not for literal likenesses of God, but for poetic images of His ineffable nature—just as the rock on which the Church was built according to the Roman Catholic Christian belief was not a literal stone like the stone that had once embodied the Emesan divinity Elagabalus or the stone that still supported the wall of a Meccan Kaʿbah.

There were, however, some relics of past stages of enlightenment which might not prove so easy to purge away. The Muslims, who had resolutely rejected all visual representations of God in the physical likeness of living creatures, including 'the human form divine', had not yet summoned up the resolution to break with that older and cruder phase of idolatry which had been embedded in Islam by the founder Muhammad himself—against the grain of his own prophetic mission—when he had given his sanction to the adoration of the Black Stone as part of a compromise with the vested interests of an *ancien régime* at Mecca.[2] Even the puritanical Wahhābī reformers, who had twice entered Mecca

[1] See p. 461, above.

[2] This perhaps trivial but hitherto indelible blemish upon the purity of Islam has been noticed on pp. 464–5, above.

as conquerors pledged to purge Islam of idolatrous accretions, had left the Black Stone untouched both in A.D. 1804 and in A.D. 1924. To Christian minds the Muslims' reluctance to part with the Black Stone seemed a quaint anachronism in glaring contradiction with the abhorrence of idolatry and devotion to monotheism that were the twin beacon-lights of Islam; and, conversely, Muslim minds found stumbling-blocks in the idolatry and the polytheism which, as they saw it, were still being practised by Christians, as well as by Buddhists and Hindus. In Muslim eyes the Christians' persistent idolatry betrayed itself in the visual representation of God in the forms of a man, a bird, and an animal, and their persistent polytheism in their doctrine of the Trinity and their cults of the saints, while in a Protestant Christian's eyes the sacrament of the pagan mysteries survived in the Catholic 'Sacrifice of the Mass', and the worship of the Great Mother had been withdrawn from Ishtar, Astarte, Isis, Cybele, and Inanna only to be paid, by Catholic devotees, to the same Mother of God under the name of Mary.[1]

Of all the veils through which the vision of God had been transmitted and at the same time obscured, the hardest for Muslims as well as for Hindus, Christians, and Buddhists to discard would be their representation of God to themselves in the likeness of Man.

It might be true that the corporeal version of 'anthropomorphism' was as obsolete as 'theriomorphism' and fetish-worship. The vision of divinity incarnate in the physical likeness of men and women of flesh and blood—a vision that had found its most attractive expression in Hellenic poetry and art—was not accepted by the adherents of any of the higher religions as a revelation of the ultimate nature of God. In terms of Christian theology the incarnation of God in Jesus Christ had been an 'emptying' (κένωσις)[2] of God's own ultimate nature; and God's voluntary act of thus 'emptying' Himself in order to be born a man had been God's supreme self-humiliation and self-sacrifice for Man's sake—a sacrifice entailing but transcending the death on the Cross through which God Incarnate had fulfilled His Mission on Earth. Yet, when Christians sought to know God, their conception of God was still 'anthropomorphic' in being in terms of the feelings, will, and intellect of a human personality—in terms, that is, of elements of conscious human psychic life which they had never encountered at first hand except in association with human bodies. And, when Hindus sought to know God, they eliminated from their conception of God both the physical body and the conscious surface of the Psyche, only, it would seem, to identify deity (*brahman*) with the impersonal subconscious psychic depths (*ātman*) that underlie the personal conscious surface of a human soul.[3] This psychic anthropomorphism was perhaps one of the inescapable limitations of Human Nature, since human beings were

[1] See pp. 437 and 457, above, and p. 717, below. Catholic Christians, of course, did not admit the Protestant allegation that their adoration of Mary amounted to the worship of a goddess. According to the Catholic Christian doctrine, Mary was one of God's creatures, and the qualities that Catholics adored in her were gifts to her from her Creator.

[2] Phil. ii. 7 (R.V.).

[3] See pp. 497–8 and 725, with n. 1, below.

incapable of conceiving of God's nature except in images drawn from, and therefore inevitably bounded by, human experience. Yet a necessary limitation might be a potential source of errors into which the Human Spirit need not fall and into which it could not allow itself to fall with impunity.

One of Man's fundamental and perennial errors—an error that is both an intellectual and a moral lapse—is to idolize discoveries of his own making that enhance his power. About half-way through the last millennium B.C., Indic minds had discovered the Subconscious Psyche and Hellenic minds the Reason, and their idolization of these discoveries had been taken over, and carried along down-stream, by Hinduism and Christianity respectively. In the twentieth century of the Christian Era, Western minds, by an experimental method of scientific inquiry which they had forged for themselves in a Modern Age of Western history, had arrived independently at that discovery of the Subconscious which Indic minds had attained by intuition some 2,500 years earlier; and in the year A.D. 1952 a student of History might guess that the Western World, after having followed an Hellenic philosophy hitherto in worshipping a false 'God the Reason', would now veer about and follow an Indic philosophy in worshipping an equally false 'God the Subconscious'. This nascent new religion of the West had been portended in Mr. Aldous Huxley's exposition of a 'Perennial Philosophy',[1] and it was assuredly salutary for Western thinkers to recognize that the Anaxagorean deification of human intelligence, like the Homeric deification of human flesh and blood, was an inadequate representation of the Godhead, and that Indic sages had made momentous discoveries in the spiritual sphere to which Hellenic philosophers and Western scientists had been blind. The mistake that an unnerved Western rationalist might be in danger of making would lie in overlooking the truth that, in identifying the human subconscious psyche with God, the Indic sages had fallen into the same 'perennial error' as the Hellenes who had found God in the human reason or in the human body.

The truth is that Anthropomorphism, even in its most etherial expressions, is a form of idolatry if idolatry is to be defined as a worship of the creature instead of the Creator;[2] and this worship of God in the image of Man—unlike the worship of God in an animal or in a stone—is also vitiated by the intellectual error and moral failing of 'the egocentric illusion'. At an earlier point in this Study[3] we have observed how this illusion had tempted the representatives of parochial and ephemeral secular societies to imagine that their own particular civilization, in the particular phase in which it had happened to find itself in their day, was the consummation of human history. The same illusion can be detected in Man's anthropomorphic conception of God; and the fallacy in it has been exposed with a devastating finality, apropos of this far

[1] Huxley, A.: *The Perennial Philosophy* (London 1946, Chatto & Windus).

[2] For this definition, see IV. iv. 261–2. A Christian, of course, would maintain that he was not worshipping a creature in worshipping Christ Jesus, for he would say that in Christ he was worshipping God and not the human nature in which God was incarnate and in which the Christian would see one of God's works of creation.

[3] In I. i. 158–64.

more momentous issue, in the satirical verse of the Hellenic philosopher Xenophanes:

'The Aethiopians say that their Gods are snub-nosed and black-skinned, and the Thracians that theirs are blue-eyed and red-haired. If only oxen and horses had hands and wanted to draw with their hands or to make the works of art that men make, then horses would draw the figures of their Gods like horses, and oxen like oxen, and would make their bodies on the model of their own.'[1]

There is, no doubt, a sense in which it is true that 'God created Man in His own image'[2]—though in the same sense this is also true in some measure of each of God's other works of creation, since all are windows that reveal their Creator, besides being veils that conceal Him—but, when Man is tempted by his awareness of his own God-given likeness to his Maker into setting himself up as the measure of all things,[3] including the God whose image is dimly revealed through the dark glass of Human Nature,[4] Man can be acquitted of the sin of hybris only on the plea that he labours under an invincible ineptitude. In his continuing search for God, Man is called upon to transcend Anthropomorphism; but, in attempting to respond to this challenge from his Maker, Man is confronted by a crux inherent in the paradoxical ambivalence of Human Nature.

Anthropomorphism seems likely to be harder for Man to transcend than any other form of idolatry because Man is the highest of God's creatures that is known to Man, and therefore, in so far as our knowledge of God Himself is derived from our knowledge of His creation, the image of God that is presented by Man is the least opaque fragment of the glass through which we see God darkly.[5] Yet, in the act of becoming aware of his position at what appears to be the apex of God's creation, Man is caught between Scylla and Charybdis. He is lost if the relative sublimity of his station turns his head; for, when he allows himself to be overcome by the dizziness of pride, he falls crashing down from his pinnacle; and, in his exposure to this danger, he is less happily placed than his humble servant the dog, who is immune against the sin of pride thanks to an overwhelming awareness of his own inferiority to the mysterious fellow creature that has domesticated him. Yet Man's undoglike capacity to fall is a measure of the height on which God has set him; for Man is the highest of God's creatures known to Man in virtue of his knowledge of good and evil and of his power to choose between them; and he is the best of God's creatures because it is in his

1 For the original Greek text of this passage, which has been quoted already at the head of the opening chapter of this Study, see I. i. 1, n. 1.

2 Gen. i. 27.

3 The dictum is ascribed to the Hellenic philosopher Protagoras.

4 This temptation is likely to be particularly insidious in its attack on human souls which believe that God has created in His own image Man alone among all His works; and Mr. Martin Wight points out that this is the traditional Christian doctrine. 'God's creation of Man in His own image means that God created Man with a rational faculty which can reciprocate God's love and with an immortal soul which can be freely dedicated to God's glory; and here is the specific difference between Man and God's other works of creation. These are His handiwork and to that extent "reveal" Him; they are not in any sense "in His image".'

5 1 Cor. xiii. 12. See p. 467, above.

power to be the worst, as well as the best, of them all. This moral faculty is the distinctive feature of Human Nature that makes it a less imperfect image of the Godhead than any other of the works of God. Man's farthest reach in his effort to comprehend God's nature is to attribute to his Creator the moral power with which Man himself is conscious of being endowed; but, in reaching this limit of his powers of comprehension, Man becomes aware of the infinity of the distance by which he still falls short of his spiritual goal; and, whether this crushing experience moves him to humble himself like Job, or to sneer like Mephistopheles, or to hover between the two moods like Pope, he will acknowledge the truth of the words that are put into God's mouth by Deutero-Isaiah:

'My thoughts are not your thoughts, neither are your ways My ways, saith the Lord. For, as the Heavens are higher than the Earth, so are My ways higher than your ways, and My thoughts than your thoughts.'[1]

This was the challenge that confronted the followers of the historic higher religions in a world in which they had suddenly been brought to close quarters with one another and with a Modern Western Science owing to the rapid spread of a secularized Western Civilization over the whole habitable and traversable surface of the planet. In the year A.D. 1952 the living generation of Mankind did not yet know how they were going to negotiate this next stage of their present 'climbers' pitch';[2] still less did they know whether they would succeed in scaling it; but they could see that they stood no chance of succeeding unless they could settle their latter-day conflict between Heart and Head, and that therefore a sincere and earnest attempt to recapture a lost spiritual harmony was an indispensable prelude to grappling with the formidable precipice that towered above them.

The Origin of the Conflict

In order to settle a conflict, one must understand how it has arisen, and fortunately the origin of the current conflict between Heart and Head was not obscure. It had been precipitated by the impact of a Modern Western Science on Christianity and the other living higher religions; and this impact had resulted in conflict because it had overtaken the religions at a stage in their course at which they were still carrying along with them, suspended in their rolling stream, the silt that they had picked up in the process of scouring their channels out of the flanks of the archaic mountains on which their head-waters had been discharged by the rain-laden Monsoon.

This was not the first instance of an encounter between Religion and Rationalism that was known to History. At least two previous instances were on record. To recall first the more recent of the two, we may remind ourselves that the four living higher religions had each encountered—and each in this instance succeeded in coming to terms with—an older version of Rationalism in an earlier chapter of each religion's history. The now orthodox theology of each of them had been the

[1] Isa. lv. 8–9. [2] For this simile, see II. i. 192–4.

product of an accommodation with an established secular philosophy which the rising religion had found itself unable to reject, or even to ignore, because this school of thought had governed the mental climate, and had commanded the intellectual allegiance, of a cultivated minority in the society that had at that time been the church's mission field. Christian and Islamic theology was a presentation of Christianity and Islam in terms of Hellenic philosophy, and Hindu theology was a presentation of Hinduism in terms of Indic philosophy, while the Mahāyāna was a particular school of Indic philosophy which had exempted itself from the ungrateful task of having to give an intellectual veneer to a parvenue religion by the master-stroke of transforming itself into a religion with a popular appeal, without ceasing to be an esoteric philosophy as well. That was not, however, the first chapter in this story; for the philosophies that were already hard-set static systems of ideas by the time when the rising higher religions had to reckon with them had once been dynamic intellectual movements; and in this youthful stage of life and growth—which was comparable to the growth-stage of a Modern Western Science since its birth in the seventeenth century of the Christian Era—the Hellenic and Indic philosophies had had encounters with the pagan religions which the Hellenic and Indic civilizations had inherited from Primitive Man.[1] There had been a similar encounter between a primitive paganism and a philosophical enlightenment in the Sinic World in a corresponding phase of Sinic history.

At first sight it might look as if these two precedents were reassuring. If Mankind had survived two past encounters between Religion and Rationalism, was not that a good augury for the outcome of a current spiritual conflict? The answer was that in the first of these two previous encounters the current problem had not arisen, while in the second encounter, in which it had arisen, the problem had received an apparent solution which had been so efficacious in keeping the peace in its own time and place that it had survived to become the crux of the problem confronting a twentieth-century Westernizing World.

In the encounter between a dawning philosophy and a traditional paganism there had been no problem of reconciling Heart and Head because there had been no common ground on which the two organs could have come into collision. The pith of Primitive Religion is not belief but action, and the test of conformity is not assent to a theological creed but participation in ritual performances. For the vast majority of the faithful, the correct and alert execution of their ritual duties is the alpha and omega of Religion; primitive religious practice is an end in itself, and it does not occur to the practitioners to look, beyond the rites which they perform, for a truth which these rites convey. The truth is that the rites have no meaning beyond the practical effect which their correct execution is believed to have upon the human performers'

[1] This primitive religious heritage had come to the Hellenic and Indic civilizations through Achaean and Aryan barbarians who had broken into the domains of the antecedent Minoan Civilization and Indus Culture, to which the Hellenic and Indic civilizations were respectively affiliated (see Table IV folding out opposite p. 772, below).

social and physical environment. The so-called 'aetiological myths', which purport to explain a traditional practice's historical origin, are not taken as statements concerning matter of fact that can be labelled 'true' or 'false'; they are taken in the spirit in which, in a more sophisticated state of society, a child takes a fairy-story or a grown-up person takes poetry. Accordingly, when, in this primitive religious setting, philosophers arise who do set out to make a chart of Man's environment in intellectual terms to which the labels 'true' and 'false' apply, no collision occurs so long as the philosopher continues to carry out his hereditary religious duties—and there can be nothing in his philosophy to inhibit him from doing this, because there is nothing in the traditional rites that could be incompatible with any philosophy.

Awkward situations do, no doubt, occasionally arise, as when, in a ritually conservative Athens, the intellectually adventurous Ionian philosopher Anaxagoras of Clazomenae (*vivebat* 500–428 B.C.) got into trouble for having made public his opinion that the heavenly bodies were not living gods but inanimate material objects. A more celebrated case was the prosecution, conviction, and judicial murder of Socrates by his Athenian fellow countrymen in 399 B.C. on three charges,[1] of which the second was that Socrates did not pay due worship to the gods who were the official objects of worship at Athens,[2] and the third was that he paid worship to other divinities who were strange gods.[3] Yet it may be doubted whether legal proceedings involving Anaxagoras would have been taken, some twenty years after the Clazomenian philosopher had ceased to reside in Athens, if these had not served the current political purpose of 'smearing' Pericles; and it may equally be doubted whether Socrates would have suffered the death-penalty that Anaxagoras escaped if Socrates' attitude towards religion had been all that his enemies had had against him. Socrates was—and remained to the last—a scrupulous performer of his ritual duties; and, on the religious counts, Aristophanes' malicious caricature of him in *The Clouds* might have remained the limit of the penalty exacted from him, if he had not also been under fire in 399 B.C. on another count—the political charge of 'corrupting the young'—which, significantly, figured first in the indictment. Socrates was the victim, not so much of conservative Athenian religious fanaticism,[4] as of democratic Athenian resentment over the final defeat of Athens in the long-drawn-out Atheno–Peloponnesian war and democratic Athenian vindictiveness towards a fascist-minded Athenian minority who had seized the opportunity opened to them by the discrediting of the democratic régime through military defeat in order to overthrow the democratic constitution. Socrates' past personal association with Critias, the moving spirit among 'the Thirty Tyrants', was the offence that the restored democratic régime could neither forget nor forgive. It was Politics, not Religion, that cost Socrates his life.

[1] Plato: *Apologia Socratis*, 24 B.

[2] *Θεοὺς οὓς ἡ πόλις νομίζει οὐ νομίζοντα* (Plato, loc. cit.).

[3] *ἕτερα δὲ δαιμόνια καινά* (Plato, loc. cit.).

[4] The part played by 'Zealotism' in the prosecutions at Athens, during and after the Great Atheno–Peloponnesian War, of Anaxagoras (? *in absentia* and not *nominatim*), Aspasia, Protagoras, Diagoras, Alcibiades, and Socrates is discussed in IX. viii. 581, n. 3.

Where the issue was not confused, as it was in Socrates' case, by political animus, Philosophy and Primitive Religion encountered one another without colliding. The death of Socrates was an exception to a rule of which the life of Confucius was a classical example. Confucius reconciled a conservative reverence for the traditional rites of primitive Sinic religion with a new moral philosophy of his own making by presenting his personal ideas as the meaning which the rites had been intended to convey. Fortunately for himself, Confucius found no Sinic Critias to be his political pupil in his own lifetime; and—thanks to this failure, which was the great disappointment of his life—he died peacefully in his bed. Confucius's attitude and experience were characteristic of the normal relations between Philosophy and Primitive Religion; but a new situation arose when the higher religions came on the scene.

The higher religions did, indeed, sweep up and carry along with them a heavy freight of traditional rites that happened to be current in the religious milieux in which the new faiths made their first appearance; but this religious flotsam was not, of course, their essence. The distinctive new feature of the higher religions was that they based their claim to allegiance, and their test of conformity, on personal revelations received by their prophets;[1] and these deliveries of the prophets were presented, like the propositions of the philosophers, as statements of fact, to be labelled either 'true' or 'false'. Therewith, Truth became a disputed mental territory; for thenceforward there were two independent authorities—on the one hand prophetic Revelation and on the other hand philosophical or scientific Reason—each of which claimed sovereign jurisdiction over the Intellect's whole field of action; and, when once the hypothesis that the spheres of Revelation and Reason were even partially coincident had been accepted—and both parties did accept this as axiomatic—it became impossible for Reason and Revelation to live and let live on the auspicious precedent of the amicable symbiosis of Reason and Ritual. 'There is a peculiar agony in the paradox that Truth has two forms, each of them indisputable, yet each antagonistic to the other.'[2] In this new and excruciating situation, there were only two alternative possibilities. Either the two rival exponents of a supposedly one and indivisible Truth must convert their rivalry into a partnership by agreeing that their expositions were mutually consistent, or, finding themselves unable to agree, they must decide the ownership of an apparently unpartitionable disputed territory in an ordeal by battle that would have to be fought out until one or other party had been driven right off the field.

In the encounter between Hellenic and Indic philosophy and Christian, Islamic, Buddhist, and Hindu revelation, the parties did manage to arrive at a peaceful accommodation in which Philosophy tacitly consented to suspend the exercise of rational criticism against the

[1] This was true in some degree—in practice even if not in theory—of the 'Indistic' higher religions as well as the 'Judaistic'. *Ipse dixit* came to be a criterion of truth, not only for the followers of Jesus and Muhammad, but also for the followers of Siddhārtha Gautama and of the philosophic prophets of a post-Buddhaic Hinduism.

[2] Gosse, E.: *Father and Son*, chap. 5.

deliveries of Revelation in exchange for being allowed to reformulate the prophets' message in the sophists' language.[1]

'The reception of the philosophical theology of the Greeks into the Church, so far as it was commensurable with Christianity, and the development of a Christian theology and dogma did not serve only apologetic purposes. The Greek mind was either not able to adapt the Christian faith in another way, or at least this was the specifically Hellenic way of adapting it to their culture. Nothing is so characteristic of the Greeks, says Saint Gregory of Nyssa, one of the outstanding Christian Platonists of the fourth century, as the belief that the essence of Religion lies in the dogma.'[2]

We need not doubt that this compromise was made in good faith on both sides, but we can see clearly in retrospect that it was not based on any genuine solution of the problem of what the relation is between Truth in the scientific sense and Truth in the prophetic usage of the word. The would-be reconciliation of the two kinds of Truth in terms of a new mental discipline called Theology was no more than verbal, and the formulae that were consecrated in the creeds were doomed to prove impermanent[3] because they left the equivocal meaning of Truth still as ambiguous as they had found it. Thus a problem which had first come

[1] As the writer saw it, the achievement of this verbal accommodation accounted for the historical fact, to which Mr. Martin Wight draws attention, that Early Christianity quarrelled with Hellenic philosophy, not 'because of its implicit rationalism, but because of its pagan religious overtones, which culminated when Julian turned Neoplatonism into a pagan substitute for Catholic Christianity'. The writer agreed with Mr. Wight's contention that 'the first seven centuries of Christian history were a contest, not between Reason and Revelation, but between Paganism and Revelation', but he would account for this by submitting that, from the beginning, there had been a latent conflict which had been suppressed without being genuinely resolved and therefore without being permanently eliminated; and, in his eyes, this would be the historical explanation of the fact, pointed out by Mr. Wight, that 'the contest between Reason—in the sense of an emancipated sovereign Reason—and Revelation grew up within the bosom of Christendom. There are hints of it in the histories of Erigena and Abelard, and then it burst forth in the débacle of Christendom with Giordano Bruno, Bacon, Descartes and Hobbes.' The writer of this Study would not dissent from this, but he would agree only on grounds different from Mr. Wight's with Mr. Wight's thesis that 'this Modern Reason seems to be a very particular historical phenomenon: it is only dimly prefigured in the Ionians; its tone of authority and its universalist claims are something quite new, and they betray their origin—it is in fact (like its identical twin-brother Science and its half-brother, by a Jewish mother, Marxism) one of the parricidal offspring of Christianity'. The writer of this Study would agree that a post-Christian Western rationalism had inherited from Christianity a Judaic fanaticism and intolerance in its feelings and its conduct towards its adversaries, but he would not agree that there was any intrinsic difference on the intellectual plane between an uncompromising post-Christian Western rationalism and a pre-Christian Hellenic rationalism which had eventually betrayed its own principles by negotiating a verbal compromise with Christianity. As he saw it, it was in the nature of Rationalism, at all times and places, to follow the argument whithersoever it might lead, without being willing to allow its pursuit of intellectual truth to be arrested by any non-intellectual considerations.

[2] Jaeger, W.: *Humanism and Theology* (Milwaukee 1943, Marquette University Press), p. 60, citing *Gregorii Nysseni Opera*, edited by Jaeger, W., vol. ii (Berlin 1922, Weidmann), p. 271, 19.

[3] Mr. Martin Wight comments: 'By "impermanent", do you mean "not universally accepted"? That, of course, they are and probably always will be. But their *permanence* seems to be one of the most remarkable things in the history of the Human Intellect: they are still recited, with whatever differences of superstition or incomprehension, by perhaps a quarter of the Human Race, and the churches have never thought that the basic work of hammering out these formulae needs to be re-done or even revised.' If this was the churches' view, the writer's expectation was that it was likely to be proved untenable in the event.

to light when the now extinct Hellenic and Indic civilizations in their decline had encountered the now still living higher religions in their rise, had been passed on, unsolved, to confront a Westernizing World in the twentieth century of the Christian Era; and this legacy bequeathed to the then living generation by its predecessors was a grievous one. Those predecessors had not only failed to find an intellectual and emotional solution of the problem for themselves;[1] the verbal accommodation which they had handed down to Posterity had made it harder for souls born in a later generation to solve the problem, now that they, in their turn, were faced with it, than it would have been for them if their predecessors had shirked the issue and had refrained from meddling.

The true solution could not be found until it had been recognized that the same word Truth, when used by the philosophers and men of science and when used by the prophets, does not refer to the same realities, but is a homonym for two different forms of experience. Scientific truth and prophetic truth are experiences on different planes, as are scientific truth and ritual observance.

'What kind of a truth is it . . . which is revealed to Faith? It is not truth in the sense of knowing something, but in the sense of a divine-human personal encounter. God does not reveal this and that; He does not reveal a number of truths. He reveals Himself by communicating Himself. It is the secret of His person which He reveals, and the secret of His person is just this, that He is self-communicating will: that God is Love. . . . If it is true that the word of God is the truth, we have first to distinguish between Truth in the singular, which means God, and truths in the plural, which are truths about the World. As God is the Creator . . . and the World is His creation . . . so there are also two kinds of truths: God-truth and world-truths. It is one of the great tragedies of Christian history that this distinction has not been carried through.'[2]

When this difference had been recognized—and only then—it might begin to be possible for pilgrim souls to feel their way towards an angle of spiritual vision from which the real nature of the relation between these diverse kinds of experience would become apparent.

'Even that which we know by God's revelation, we know only in part.[3] It is absolute truth merely in so far as it is God's word; formulated by us as our knowledge, it at once becomes part in the whole weakness and imperfection of our human condition. God's revelation identified with human dogma is the transformation of God-truth into world-truth.'[4]

This verbal reconciliation of scientific truth and prophetic truth in terms of Theology had placed an unnecessary additional stumbling-block in the pilgrim's anyway arduous path; and this theological stumbling-block was a formidable one because it drove Science and Religion into

[1] Mr. Martin Wight comments: 'What would a genuine solution be? They [the creeds] are attempts to make statements about the Incomprehensible within the limits of human language. They have never claimed to be anything but approximations.' The writer's comment on this would be that the Intellect is deluding itself when it imagines that it has arrived at even approximations between incommensurables.

[2] Brunner, Emil: *Christianity and Civilisation*, first part (London 1948, Nisbet), pp. 37 and 35. Cp. eundem: *The Divine-Human Encounter* (English translation: London 1944, S.C.M. Press), *passim*.

[3] 1 Cor. xiii. 9.

[4] Brunner, op. cit., first part, pp. 41–42.

a conflict in which either combatant found himself constrained to make the desperate choice of surrendering to his opponent ground which he knew to be his own legitimate territory, or else capturing the entire field of Truth for himself and denying his opponent any *locus standi* there at all.

This conflict had been bound to break out sooner or later as a result of the foregoing verbal accommodation; for, when once the truth of Revelation had been formulated verbally in terms of the truth of Science, Science could not forever forbear to criticize a body of doctrine that purported now to be true in the scientific sense; and in fact, since the seventeenth century of the Christian Era, a Modern Western Science had broken the truce with Christian doctrine into which the Hellenic philosophy had entered in the fourth and fifth centuries when it had lent its services for the freezing of Christian orthodoxy in the mould of the creeds. On the other side, Christianity, when once its doctrine had been formulated in rational language, could not forbear, for its part, to claim authority over other provinces of knowledge which were really Reason's legitimate domain; and, when in the seventeenth century a Modern Western Science cast off the spell of Hellenic philosophy and began to break new intellectual ground, the first impulse of the Roman Church was to issue an injunction against the aggression of an awakening Western intellect upon the Church's old Hellenic intellectual ally—as if the geocentric theory of Astronomy, which was an Hellenic endorsement of a Babylonic hypothesis, had been an article of the Christian faith, and Galileo's correction of Ptolemy had been a theological heresy.

Possible Alternative Outcomes

By the year A.D. 1952, this war between Science and Religion in the soul of Western Man had been raging with increasing fury for three hundred years without having yet reached a decision. It could no longer continue to be waged with impunity, and of three conceivable alternative outcomes—the discrediting of Religion, the capitulation of Science, and a peace based, not on a verbal formula, but on a genuine reconciliation of the two points of view—either of the first two would manifestly be disastrous.

Towards the close of the two and a half centuries between the ending of the Wars of Religion and the outbreak of the general war of A.D. 1914–18, the discrediting of Religion might have seemed to be the most probable denouement. By that time the ecclesiastical authorities had come to be in much the same state of mind as the Governments of Great Britain and France after Hitler's destruction of the remnant of Czechoslovakia on the 15th March, 1939. For more than two hundred years the churches had been seeing Science capture from them one province of knowledge after another. Astronomy, Cosmogony, Chronology, Biology, Physics, Psychology had each in turn been reconstructed by Science on revolutionary lines that were incompatible with established religious teaching on these subjects; and no end of these losses was in sight. The conquest of one province, so far from contenting the aggressor, had, each time, led him on to attack another. The appetite of Science for aggression appeared to be insatiable, and the churches had come to feel that they could no longer afford to practise 'appeasement'. Their only remaining hope of saving themselves from utter rout now lay, as they saw it, in a complete intransigence. They must hoist the signal 'My doctrine, right or wrong', and must refuse to surrender even the shakiest outworks of their Maginot Line. They must not abandon one single further tenet, however unimportant or however indefensible. They must insist that their prophetic truth was Truth in the scientific sense, and that the silt which they had scoured out of the archaic rocks of Primitive Religion was of the essence of their own living waters and was not an extraneous impurity that could and should be dropped.

This 'die-hard' spirit had asserted itself in the course of the nineteenth century of the Christian Era. In the ranks of the Roman Catholic Church it had found expression in the decrees of the Vatican Council of A.D. 1869–70 and in the anathema pronounced against Modernism in A.D. 1907;[1] in the domain of the Protestant Churches of North America it had entrenched itself in 'the Bible Belt'; and this reaction had not been confined to those fractions of Christendom that constituted the home territory of the Western World; for by this time the wave of Westernization was sweeping over the whole face of the planet, and Western Science—which was both the force behind the wave and the rider on its crest—was impinging upon all branches of all the higher religions. Under this ubiquitous pressure the 'Zealot' mood[2] was manifesting itself in Orthodox as well as in Western Christendom, and it was simultaneously on the war-path in the Islamic World, where the first stirrings of a Westernizing movement under the stimulus of the disastrous ending of the Great Russo-Turkish War of A.D. 1768–74 had provoked, in retort, the militantly archaistic movements of Wahhabism, Idrisism, Sanusism, and Mahdism in the fastnesses of the Arabian and North African deserts.

This 'die-hard' reaction of the churches to the victorious advance of Science was not unnatural, but it was unfortunate and it was ominous; for it was a symptom, not of self-confidence, but of the loss of it, and indeed the disarray into which their own camp had fallen by this time could not fail to rack the ecclesiastical authorities' nerves. A decay of belief in the churches' doctrines, and a still more deadly loss of faith in their mission and slackening of loyalty to their cause, had revealed itself first within the small circle of a sophisticated minority in the Western World which had been disillusioned by the Wars of Religion.[3] By the turn of the nineteenth and twentieth centuries this spirit of scepticism and indifference had spread in the West among the masses and had also flowed out of the West into the domains of the other surviving civilizations, where a nineteenth-century French type of Rationalism with an anticlerical tinge was becoming the standard *Weltanschauung* of the

[1] See p. 456, n. 2, above.

[2] For 'Zealotism' as one of two alternative psychological reactions to the impact of an alien cultural influence, see IX. viii.580–623.

[3] See the references on p. 441, n. 1, above.

Westernizers. In fact, at the opening of the twentieth century it looked as if the higher religions were riding for a fall.

This prospect that the higher religions might irretrievably lose their hold upon the allegiance of Mankind boded evil; for Religion is manifestly one of the essential faculties of Human Nature. No individual human being and no human community is ever without a religion of some kind; and, when people are starved of Religion, the desperate spiritual straits to which they are reduced by being deprived of this necessity of life can fire them to extract grains of religious consolation out of the most unpromising ores. The classical example of this, up to date, was the astonishing metamorphosis by which the religion of the Mahāyāna had been conjured out of the forbiddingly impersonal philosophy that had been the first attempt of the disciples of Siddhārtha Gautama to formulate the message of the Buddha. In a Westernizing World in the twentieth century of the Christian Era the beginnings of a similar metamorphosis of the Western materialist philosophy of Marxism were perhaps discernible in Russian souls that had been deprived of their traditional religious sustenance.

When Buddhism had been converted from a philosophy into a religion, a higher religion had been the happy outcome; but, if the higher religions themselves were to be driven off the field, it was to be feared that lower religions would swiftly occupy the abhorrent vacuum.

In a world on which the higher religions had been losing their hold there were in A.D. 1952 many people who had been finding substitutes for lost higher religions in 'ideologies', and in several countries the converts to these new mundane faiths had been strong enough to seize control of the government and to use the whole power of the state to impose their own doctrine and practice on their fellow countrymen. By these methods Communism had been established in Russia, Fascism in Italy, National Socialism in Germany. But these flagrant examples of the recrudescence of Man's ancient worship of himself in the panoply of his corporate power gave no measure of the actual prevalence of this spiritual malady. The most serious symptom was that, in professedly democratic and professedly Christian countries, whose complacent citizens were congratulating themselves that they were not as other men were,[1] or even as this Fascist or this Communist, four-fifths of the religion of five-sixths of the population in these countries likewise was, in practice, by this time, the primitive pagan worship of the bee-hive by the bee and of the ant-heap by the ant.[2] This recrudescent idolatry was not redeemed by being concealed under the fine name of patriotism;[3] and, indeed, in this unacknowledged cult of it, its influence was more insidious than in the naked Fascism and Communism at which the

[1] Luke xviii. 11.

[2] See pp. 439–40 and 445–6, above, and pp. 520–1, below.

[3] The termite can idolize the termitery at the cost of condemning its kind to the fate of Lot's wife; but the human soul that idolizes a Corporate Humanity instead of worshipping God condemns itself, not to self-petrifaction, but to self-destruction. The corporate-self-worshipping human social animal wrecks the fabric of a sociality without which Man cannot survive, in this godless attempt to perfect it. When Man seeks to become a bee in the bee-hive, he turns himself into an Ishmael in the arena, where 'his hand will be against every man, and every man's hand against him' (Gen. xvi. 12).

Christian democratic pharisee pointed his reproving finger, or than in the still franker form in which the same idolatry had been practised in the Hellenic World in the cults of Athena Poliûchus, Tyche Antiocheôn, Fortuna Praenestina, Dea Roma, Divus Caesar.[1]

This corporate self-worship was perhaps the most vicious of all the lower religions that were surging in to take the higher religions' vacated place, but it was far from being either the only revenant or the most primitive of these haunting ghosts. In the twentieth century of the Christian Era all the surviving primitive societies and all the hardly less primitive peasantries of the non-Western civilizations—the muzhiks, the ryots, and the coolies who, in their hundreds of millions, amounted to three-quarters of the living generation of Mankind—were being conscripted into the Western Society's swollen internal proletariat;[2] and, in the light of all the historical precedents, the ancestral religious practices through which this host of humble new recruits would continue to seek satisfaction for their own religious needs seemed likely to find their way into the empty hearts of the proletariat's sophisticated masters.

On this showing, a crushing victory of Science over Religion would be a disaster, for, if Science should succeed in expelling the higher religions from the human heart, she would not be able to prevent the lower religions from taking their place.

> 'When the unclean spirit is gone out of a man, he walketh through dry places, seeking rest; and, finding none, he saith: I will return unto my house whence I came out. And, when he cometh, he findeth it swept and garnished. Then goeth he and taketh to him seven other spirits more wicked than himself, and they enter in and dwell there; and the last state of that man is worse than the first.'[3]

The same disastrous set-back would likewise be the nemesis of a crushing victory of Religion over Science; for Reason, as well as Religion, is one of the essential faculties of Human Nature, and the historical precedents indicated that, when a higher religion routs an intellectual enlightenment, it pays the penalty of degenerating into a lower religion. Religion cannot deny scientific truth, or suppress free and disinterested scientific inquiry, with impunity. When Religion commits this crime, the society that is the victim of it becomes petrified; for a civilization that allows itself to be castrated intellectually is allowing itself to be deprived of part of its creative faculty—in which intellectual creativity is an essential element.

In the histories of other civilizations known to latter-day Western students of History, there were notorious examples of this calamity. When the Hellenic philosophy had capitulated to Christianity in the fourth and fifth centuries,[4] and to Islam in the ninth and tenth centuries, of the Christian Era, and when the Sinic philosophy had capitulated

[1] See I. i. 443–4. [2] See V. v. 153–4.

[3] Luke xi. 24–26; cp. Matt. xii. 43–45.

[4] For an explanation of this portent, see the passage quoted from Edwyn Bevan in V. v. 558–9. Mr. Martin Wight comments: 'The passage quoted from Edwyn Bevan simply makes the point that Philosophy capitulated because it was inadequate to human needs, and implies that the capitulation was good and necessary.'

to the primitive religions of a swollen Sinic internal proletariat during the last two centuries B.C.,[1] the victorious religion had in each case paid for its victory by suffering a set-back that had been not merely an intellectual but a moral and a spiritual reverse as well.[2] In the Western World at the close of the nineteenth century of the Christian Era the triumphantly militant men of science would have laughed to scorn any suggestion that they, in their turn, might be on the eve of making a similar surrender, and the 'die-hard' defenders of the integrity of traditional religion would have been almost equally surprised, in their heart of hearts, to receive tidings of the imminence of this miraculous reversal of roles at this stage of their long losing battle against their aggressive rationalist opponents; yet, only fifty years later, the outlook and temper of the men of science had in fact already changed to an astonishing degree as a result of the shattering experience of two world wars.

During the quarter of a millennium ending in August 1914 the Western man of science—surveying the world around him, believing that he had made it,[3] and never doubting that it was very good[4]—had been buoyed up by the naïve conviction that he had only to go on churning out fresh scientific discoveries, and leaving it to his technological and commercial executants to apply these discoveries in any way that might please them, in order to ensure that the World should go on growing better and better. The pace of scientific, technical, and economic progress was accelerating, and no limit was in sight. The scientist's observation of the current phenomena was not incorrect, but his interpretation of them was vitiated by two fundamental errors.

The scientist was mistaken in attributing the relative well-being of the eighteenth-century and nineteenth-century Western World to his own intellectual achievements; and he was mistaken in assuming that this

[1] See the passages quoted from Dr. Hu Shih in V. v. 549 and 555–6. Mr. Martin Wight comments: 'In so far as the Sinic philosophy capitulated, was it not rather to the Mahāyāna—at any rate in the long run—than to the primitive religions of the internal proletariat?'

[2] Mr. Martin Wight comments: 'The examples that you give do not bear out your thesis. (i) It seems rather question-begging to adduce the Hellenic philosophy of the fifth to tenth centuries of the Christian Era as an instance of "an intellectual enlightenment": most people would regard it as an instance of the moribundity of a particular philosophical tradition, reflecting the moribundity of a particular civilization—and this would be consonant with your general view of a philosophy as the expression of a Dominant Minority. "An intellectual enlightenment" usually means a creative phase, like the Ionian philosophy of the sixth–fifth centuries B.C. or the Aufklärung of the eighteenth century of the Christian Era. Actually the three examples that you give are all examples of a philosophy giving up the ghost in the last stages of the decadence of a civilisation—and would it not be natural to regard this as a regular feature of that process, wherein (as you have argued throughout) the higher religion inherits the past and transmits it to the future? (ii) Did Christianity in the fifth century of the Christian Era, and Islam in the tenth, "pay the penalty of degenerating into a lower religion"?'

The writer would accept Mr. Wight's contention that each of the three philosophies cited in this passage had exhausted its creative powers long before the free exercise of its now traditional and conventional mode of thought was suppressed by a higher religion; but he would also contend that in each case the repressive higher religion inflicted—as the historical sequel in each case shows—a deep spiritual injury on itself in the act of suppressing even a moribund intellectual activity.

[3] This belief was advertised, as late as A.D. 1936, by an eminent latter-day Western archaeologist, Mr. V. Gordon Childe, in the title of his book *Man Makes Himself* (London 1936, Watts). See p. 541, n. 2, below.

[4] Gen. i. 13.

recently achieved well-being was going to persist *in saecula saeculorum* and to increase *ad infinitum*. A Modern Western Science had been, not the author, but merely the beneficiary, of the lull between the dying down of the storm of the wars of religion and the rising of the storm of the wars of nationality—a new tempest which had breathed its first ominous gust in the American Revolutionary War, and had blown half a gale in the wars of the French Revolution and Napoleon, before it had burst on the World in its full fury in the general wars of A.D. 1914–18 and A.D. 1939–45.[1] The breathing-space between these two paroxysms in the recent course of Western history had been the achievement, not of eighteenth-century and nineteenth-century Western scientists, but of seventeenth-century Western statesmen who had come to the conclusion that the wars of religion were leading nowhere but towards destruction and that this senseless barbarity ought to be stopped. These statesmen had duly brought the wars of religion to an end, but their work had been ephemeral because it had been performed in a cynical spirit, on the strength of a mistaken diagnosis of Human Nature. The spiritual truce that had reigned from the close of the seventeenth century to the opening of the twentieth had been founded on the false assumption that Religion, so far from being one of the essential faculties of the Soul, was a relic of savagery which a civilized society had now learnt, by bitter experience, to discard once for all. The psychic energy released from the baneful service of this supposed anachronism was henceforward to be led into the channels of Science and Technology, where its free flow was expected to prove, not merely harmless, but positively useful.

Before the twentieth century had run half its course, the falsity of these beliefs and expectations about their society's situation and prospects had been demonstrated to Western men of science by the shattering effect of two catastrophic world wars in one lifetime on the society of which they were members and on the intellectual activity which was their own vocation. The scientists had seen their society driven once again along the road leading towards destruction; they had seen their own inventions and abilities conscripted, without their leave being asked, in order to speed the World on this fatal course; and their political impotence and moral responsibility had both been brought home to them, in the last act of the Second World War, by the dropping of the atom-bombs on Hiroshima and Nagasaki. The discovery of the structure of the atom, which was the supreme achievement, up to date, of Western Science, and the working-out of the 'know-how' for disintegrating atoms on a scale that would produce effectively devastating results, which was the supreme achievement, up to date, of Western Technology, had been used to arm Man with an annihilating weapon before he had got rid of the institution of War; and this appalling application of Physical Science had cut the scientists to the heart and at the same time confronted them with a moral dilemma.[2]

[1] See IV. iv. 141–85; V. v. 160–1 and 668–72; V. vi. 316–21.

[2] See, for example, the presidential address on 'The Ethical Dilemma of Science' that was given by Professor A. V. Hill to the British Association on the 3rd September, 1952.

In a world which had not yet got rid of War, atomic research itself, as well as its practical application in the manufacture of annihilating weapons, threatened to be a desperately dangerous occupation for human minds and hands unless and until it were to be brought under the undivided political control of some single world authority. Pending the attainment of this supremely difficult international objective, it would inevitably remain under the political control of individual Great Powers that possessed the secret and that commanded the resources to turn it to military account. Political control of atomic research was thus morally desirable in one form, and practically inevitable in some form or other; but this would mean the end of the liberty to conduct research, and to make public the results of his labours, at his own discretion, which the Modern Western man of science had enjoyed for the last quarter of a millennium. In the seventeenth century, Science had wrested this liberty from the Church, and now, in the twentieth century, she was to forfeit it to the State. The prospect was disconcerting, for the right of free inquiry and publication was Science's palladium. It was the breath of her nostrils; it was the key to her unprecedented performance in the Western World in the Modern Age; and, most important of all, it was a moral principle of which she was the recognized trustee on behalf of Mankind at large, beyond the narrow ranks of the small minority represented by the professional scientific workers.

In this situation, an inclination to capitulate was already revealing itself, midway through the twentieth century, among physical scientists and other intellectual workers in a now battered and disillusioned Western World. Some had been crushed by the adversity which had overtaken their own intellectual avocation; others had had their hearts broken by the tribulations that had overtaken Mankind, their country, their family, and themselves; others had yielded to political pressure or coercion; others had been infected with the 'second childhood' that was rife in a 'Brave New World' around them; while others—and this was the most significant and most dangerous case—lacked the fortitude to bear patiently the spiritual distress of having lost a traditional religion without having gained a new one to take its place.[1] These weaker vessels were seeking an intellectual *Nirvāna* by embracing either another traditional religion, carrying a still heavier load of archaic silt than the faith of their fathers, or else one of the new mundane 'ideologies'. Either of these alternative spiritual refuges offered the fugitive what he was seeking; for he was fleeing from a no longer bearable intellectual liberty and was seeking asylum in a spiritual prison-house.

This failure of nerve was *la trahison des clercs*;[2] and the error was one both of conduct and of judgement. If *noblesse oblige*, it is unworthy of the intellectual leaders of Mankind not to stand their intellectual ground when they find themselves out in the cold or marooned in the wilderness. Their high intellectual calling cannot be practised if its votaries cannot

[1] In deploring contemporary reversions to traditional religions when these were the fruit, not of conviction, but of distress, the writer would not deny that there were also contemporary reconversions that had the virtues of being disinterested and being sincere.

[2] Benda, J.: *La Trahison des Clercs* (Paris 1927, Grasset), quoted in IV. iv. 302.

rise to the legendary moral strength of Moses and the bodhisattvas. Moses had not quailed when he had been condemned to wander in the wilderness for forty years in atonement for sins that had been not his own but Israel's, and then to die without being granted more than a Pisgah sight of the Promised Land. The bodhisattvas had become the heroes of the Mahāyāna, and had eclipsed the arhats in the hearts and minds of their devotees,[1] because at the supreme moment when, in virtue of aeons of spiritual effort, they had attained the verge of *Nirvāna* and need only take the last final step in order to enter into their rest,[2] they had risen to a sublime height of unselfishness in condemning themselves, uncoerced and unprompted, to postpone their release from selfhood for aeons upon aeons more, in order to pilot their fellow beings along the arduous road, leading to salvation from the sorrowful wheel of existence, which the bodhisattvas themselves had travelled, in advance of their flock, to within a hair's breadth of journey's end.[3]

The heroic self-control of the bodhisattvas was the example which the intellectual leaders of Mankind needed to take to heart in a Westernizing World in the twentieth century of the Christian Era, because the hope of finding a second-best Promised Land just round the corner, in the *cañon* of Edom or in the mountains of Moab, was as illusory as the temptation to slink back to the flesh-pots of Egypt was craven-hearted. It was an illusion because Religion, once lost, whether the loss of it has been the loser's fault or no, can never be whistled for, like a dog, to come back obediently to heel at Man's convenience. If the wanderer in the wilderness is eventually to reach the authentic Promised Land, he must have the endurance to stay the course; and, in the West midway through the twentieth century of the Christian Era, it was uncertain how the men of intellect were going to take their ordeal.

Thus, after three hundred years of spiritual warfare in the West between Science and Religion, it was impossible to guess which way the decision would fall if the outcome was to be a decisive one. Both combatants were in danger of collapsing; and the only prophecy that could be made with any assurance was that, if their discomfiture were not simultaneous, the overthrow of the first to collapse would not spell victory for the momentary survivor. Whichever way the battle might eventually go, the real victor would be a *tertius gaudens* in the shape of a host of primitive religions that were hovering round the battlefield on the wait for an opportunity to reoccupy a spiritual kingdom over which they had reigned unchallenged for hundreds of thousands of years before the advent of either Reason or Revelation.

A Demarcation of Spheres

This threat of a calamitous spiritual regression in the event of a fight to a finish between Science and Religion was an urgent warning of the need for a peace by agreement; but, if the peace was to be lasting, the agreement must be genuine, as had been demonstrated by the sequel to the diplomatic accommodation that had been made—in words but not

[1] See V. vi. 148, and p. 426, n. 2, above. [2] Ps. xcv. 11.
[3] See V. vi. 164, n. 3, and p. 426, n. 2, above, and IX. viii. 628 and XII. ix. 633, below.

in deed—between a Christian revelation and an Hellenic philosophy in the fourth and fifth centuries of the Christian Era.[1] This untoward precedent indicated that it was not enough that the parties should agree about the facts; their agreement with one another, if there was to be any virtue in it, must also tally with reality.

This last point may be illustrated by picturing a pair of Oklahomans travelling, on the last lap of their first journey to the East, on the Pennsylvania Railroad between Newark and New York. The two provincial travelling companions have different interests in life; one of them is technological-minded, the other political-minded; but both are patriots. As their train cuts its way across the dismal reed-beds of the Jersey marshes, they see out of the coach-window a remarkable engineering enterprise in full swing. A section of the marshes is being filled in to make a site for a new factory or power-station or what-not, and this arresting spectacle moves either spectator to ejaculate the first thought that comes into his head. 'My goodness,' exclaims the Oklahoman technocrat, 'if they go on at this pace they will soon have filled in the Atlantic, and that will teach Joe Stalin what Uncle Sam can do!'—'Good gracious,' exclaims the Oklahoman politician at the same instant, 'if they go on at this pace they will soon have filled in the Atlantic, and

[1] A Catholic friend of the writer's comments: 'The Church never considers any philosophy more than an approximation to the truth, and would discard Aristotle to-morrow if it found a philosophy that went deeper into reality.' The writer would not dispute his friend's contention that this was the Christian Church's theory of the terms on which it had made use of an Hellenic philosophy for the formulation of a Christian theology; he would simply note that, in practice, the Church was still treating this Hellenistic theology as the orthodox, official, and obligatory presentation of the Christian Faith fifteen or sixteen hundred years after the epoch in which Christianity had originally been translated into this Hellenic philosophical language. Notable attempts, made in the Early Modern Age of Western history by missionary members of the Society of Jesus, to retranslate Christianity into the alternative language of a post-Buddhaic Hindu philosophy and a Confucian philosophy had eventually been quashed (see V. v. 365–7). Yet, if the Christian Church, as an institution, thus remained enmeshed in an Hellenistic theology of its own weaving, the greatest of all Western Christian theologians lived, in his personal religious life, to become aware of the limitations of theology through attaining the experience of transcending them.

'Item dixit idem testis, quod, cum dictus Fr. Thomas celebraret Missam in dictâ capellâ S. Nicolai Neapoli, fuit mirâ mutatione commotus, et post ipsam missam non scripsit; neque dictavit aliquid, imo suspendit organa scriptionis in tertiâ parte Summae in Tractatu de Poenitentiâ: et, dum idem Fr. Raynaldus videret, quod ipse Fr. Thomas cessaverat scribere, dixit ei: Pater, quomodo dimisistis opus tam grande, quod ad laudem Dei et illuminationem mundi coepistis? Cui respondit dictus Fr. Thomas: Non possum. Idem vero Fr. Raynaldus timens, ne propter multum studium aliquam incurrisset amentiam, instabat semper, quod idem Fr. Thomas continuaret scripta, et similiter ipse Fr. Thomas respondit: Raynalde, non possum, quia omnia, quae scripsi, videntur mihi paleae' (Statement by Dominus Bartholomaeus de Capuâ, logotheta et protonotarius regni Siciliae, in the *Processus Inquisitionis Factae super Vitâ, Conversatione, et Miraculis recol. mem. fr. Thomae de Aquino*, printed in *Acta Sanctorum*, Martii, Tom. I, pp. 712*f*–713*a*).

'Unde post aliquam horam ivit socius ad Magistrum, et, trahens ipsum per cappam fortiter, quasi a somno contemplationis ipsum ultimo excitavit. Qui suspirans dixit: Raynalde fili, tibi in secreto revelo, prohibens ne in vitâ meâ alicui audeas revelare. Venit finis scripturae meae, quia talia sunt mihi revelata, quod ea, quae scripsi et docui, modica mihi videntur, et ex hoc spero in Deo meo quod, sicut doctrinae, sic cito finis erit et vitae' (Evidence given during the Process by the Prior of the Convent at Benevento, extracted from the life of Saint Thomas by Giulielmus de Thoco, O.P., and printed ibid., p. 674*c*).

A spirited English version of these two passages, with characteristic comment, will be found in Bridges, Robert: *The Testament of Beauty*, Book I. ll. 465–500, particularly the last seven lines, which literally translate from 'Qui suspirans dixit' to the end.

then what will become of America's security? Why, the Red Army will be able to march on Oklahoma dry-shod!' Agreeing about the facts, and never suspecting that their identical reading of them may be wrong, the two unsophisticated wayfarers fall to quarrelling, as their train drives into darkness under the Hudson, over the question whether the imminent abolition of the Atlantic is going to be a good thing or a bad thing. They could have spared themselves their quarrel if they had had the imagination to realize that the marshes and the Ocean were incommensurable, and that the integrity of the Atlantic was no more in danger from those forceful and efficient Yankee engineers with their bulldozers than if they had been little children armed with toy spades and buckets. In transforming a patch of the morass into solid earth the engineers had been doing a creditable job, but they had not been miraculously achieving the impossible. They had, in fact, been doing an economic service to their country without jeopardizing her military security. But Man does not find it easy to imagine what he has not experienced, and we have to bear in mind that our pair of rustic Oklahomans have never set eyes on the Atlantic, not to speak of crossing it. If they had ever sailed on its waters or sounded its depths, it would not have occurred to them to think of the Ocean as an annex to the Jersey marshes.

The application of our parable to a current Western spiritual crisis is, of course, to be found in the suggestion that, if only the men of science and the religious authorities could agree in seeing the facts as they were, instead of agreeing in making an identical mistake about them, they might come to agree over the hitherto controversial question whether the facts were to be welcomed or were to be deplored. Either party might then arrive at a just self-confidence in estimating its own prowess and a just humility in recognizing its own limitations, and this psychological reorientation might enable them both to serve God and Man by overcoming their discord and working together in harmony.[1]

Science need abandon neither her belief in her mission to give Man an ever-increasing command over Non-Human Nature nor her confidence in her ability to go on winning successes in her own proper field. It could, indeed, be predicted that, with her marvellous enterprisingness and resourcefulness, she would go on reclaiming, for Man's benefit, one patch after another of Non-Human Nature's sterile and formidable slough, but the date could not be foreseen by which she would have converted the whole of this waste land into productive turnip-fields and remunerative building-lots, and the time would never come when she would have made dry land out of the Ocean. It was at this point that a saving humility—the sovereign prophylactic against the fatal sin of

[1] A belief that there is no ground for a collision between Faith and Science is attributed to the Modernists by Pope Pius X in his encyclical 'Pascendi dominici gregis' of the 8th September, 1907:

'Fides . . . id unicè spectat, quod scientia incognoscibile sibi esse profitetur. Hinc diversum utrique pensum: scientia versatur in phaenomenis, ubi nullus fidei locus; fides e contra versatur in divinis, quae scientia penitus ignorat. Unde demum conficitur, inter fidem et scientiam nunquam esse posse discidium: si enim suum quaeque locum teneat, occurrere sibi invicem numquam poterunt, atque ideo nec contradicere.'

hybris—might usefully steal over the giantess's mind while she was rejoicing to run her course.[1]

Man's Intellect is always in danger of being dazzled by its own triumphs through overlooking the sobering truth that, by comparison with the Soul, the Intellect has an easy task. The field within which the Intellect makes its conquests is relatively narrow, and the objects with which it deals are relatively tractable. A triumphant Modern Western Science and Technology should reflect and confess that, before the expiration of the Upper Palaeolithic Age, Man's Intellect had already fulfilled the essence of its modest task of making Man 'the lord of Creation' by taking delivery of God's gift to Man of 'dominion over the fish of the sea and over the fowl of the air and over the cattle and over all the Earth, and over every creeping thing that creepeth upon the Earth'.[2]

'The evidence derived both from a study of fossil remains and from a study of primitive races leads to the conclusion that the evolution of human intellectual capacity early reached a relatively advanced stage. . . . It would seem that the major part of the progress in the evolution of the intellectual faculties had been accomplished far back in Palaeolithic times. Those living races which, with all due reservations and qualifications, may be held to represent in mental and bodily characters Palaeolithic races, differ from Modern European Man rather in disposition than in intellect. And it is important to note that it is in the growth of the Intellect rather than in the growth of the other mental faculties that Modern Man is distinguished from his pre-human ancestor. . . . An inquiry into the forces which we must assume to have been at work shows that intellectual capacity was more favoured in the intermediate stage than after Primitive Society had come into being. . . . Within this period, Man descended to the ground, spread, if not into every continent, at least far over the surface of the World, and came to dominate all other living organisms as no species had ever done before. Clearly he was enabled to achieve this result by his [already attained] intellectual powers and by them alone.'[3]

From that stage upwards in the ascending and accelerating course of Man's scientific and technological progress, Man had never lacked the necessities of material life; all subsequent additions had been superfluities; and these superfluous increments of material wealth and power had not been blessings in themselves; they had been searching tests of Man's character, proving themselves blessings if he used them for good, and curses if he used them for evil.[4] Such double-edged material gifts had been challenges to Man's spiritual nature; and the challenge had become more formidable with each fresh scientific and technological advance, because each had added momentum to the material 'drive' that goes into Man's moral acts, whether good or bad. Man's apparently boundless ability in mastering his material environment had thus played, in Man's spiritual life, the part played by Mephistopheles in Faust's;[5]

[1] Ps. xix. 5. [2] Gen. i. 26.

[3] Carr-Saunders, A. M.: *The Population Problem* (Oxford 1922, Clarendon Press), pp. 405 and 399.

[4] An admirable presentation of this point will be found in Brunner, Emil: *Christianity and Civilisation*, first part (London 1948, Nisbet), pp. 8–70.

[5] See II. i. 271–99.

and in this sense only—and it was a negative sense which was at the opposite pole from Marx's—Man's economic progress had been the key to human history.

The truth is that the command over Non-Human Nature, which the Intellect has in its gift, is of almost infinitely less importance to Man than his relations with himself, with his fellow men, and with God. But 'Abstract Reason does not tend to communion, but to unity. In thinking I am related to general truth, to ideas, but not to the Thou of my neighbour';[1] and Man's Intellect would never have had a chance of making Man the palaeolithic Lord of Creation, and never even a possibility of achieving its own existence, if Man's pre-human ancestor had not been endowed with the capacity for becoming a social animal, and if Primitive Man had not risen to this spiritual occasion so far as to school himself in those rudiments of sociality that are the Intellect's indispensable conditions for performing its co-operative and cumulative work.[2] And, when once Man's Intellect had given him dominion over Non-Human Nature on the face of this planet to a degree that made it certain that Man would be able to keep the Human Race in existence here so long as the physical conditions might continue to allow of the possibility of mammalian life, Man's command over Non-Human Nature ceased, from that time onwards, to have significance apart from providing a test of Man's capacity, and a gauge of his success or failure, in the spiritual field. From that time onwards at any rate, if not from the first moment at which Man's pre-human ancestor had become human, Man's intellectual and technological achievements had been important to him, not in themselves, but only in so far as, by penalizing his moral failures and rewarding his moral successes, they had forced him to face, and grapple with, moral issues which otherwise he might have managed to go on shirking. They had driven him through dry places, seeking rest and finding none,[3] as Io was goaded by the ceaseless stings of Hera's gadfly.

Through its unprecedented achievements on its own plane a Modern Western Science had indeed raised moral issues of profound importance, but it had not solved any of these moral problems and had not even made any contribution towards solving any of them, because it had not added anything to Man's knowledge of Man and God, or to his insight into how to deal with either of them. 'The most important questions that Man must answer are those for which scientific knowledge is not enough.'[4] 'The possession of Reason, of intellectual activity as such, is no guarantee of Truth, Goodness, and true Humanity. The principle of the truly human, of Goodness and Truth, is higher than Reason.'[5] In spiritual insight and action the higher religions still remained the pioneers; and their unique achievement in this crucial field put them in a light to which a Modern Western Science ought to open its eyes. For

[1] Brunner, op. cit., first part, p. 94.
[2] This aspect of Man's intellectual life is examined further in X. ix. 697–704.
[3] Matt. xii. 43.
[4] Burgmann, Bishop E. H.: *The Church's Encounter with Civilisation* (London 1948, Longmans), p. 19.
[5] Brunner, op. cit., first part, p. 69.

a quarter of a millennium, reckoning back from the year A.D. 1952, a Modern Western rationalism had been deriding traditional religion for its reluctance to drop the flotsam of primitive rites and myths that it had still been carrying along in its current,[1] and this attack had been justified in so far as the ecclesiastical authorities had continued to insist on explaining traditional practices, and formulating traditional beliefs, in the antiquated intellectual terms of an ephemeral Hellenic or Indic exposition of Philosophy.[2] But, in passing this just judgement on the theologian, the rationalist was exposing himself to the stricture of the Gospels:

'Why beholdest thou the mote that is in thy brother's eye, but considerest not the beam that is in thine own eye? Or how wilt thou say to thy brother: Let me pull out the mote out of thine eye; and, behold, a beam is in thine own eye? Thou hypocrite, first cast out the beam out of thine own eye, and then shalt thou see clearly to cast out the mote out of thy brother's eye.'[3]

It was not only the fact that, on the spiritual plane, where one inch gained is of greater consequence for Mankind than a mile gained in supererogatory additions to Man's command over Non-Human Nature, traditional religion was still holding the lead; it was also the fact that, in the latest chapter of Western history, in which a Modern Western Society had placed her destinies in Science's hands, she had been as sensationally unsuccessful in things human and divine as she had been sensationally successful in things material. The exercise of humility that was required of a Modern Western Science was, not to lose confidence in her prowess within her own field, but to recognize the bitter truth that, in spite of all her intellectual achievements—past, present, and future—she was spiritually impotent, and that Socrates had taken the right turning at that critical point in his life at which he had abandoned the study of Physical Science in order to seek communion with the spiritual power that informs and governs the Universe.[4] The Hel-

[1] See the passage from Butler's *Analogy*, quoted in V. v. 670, n. 3.

[2] Mr. Martin Wight comments: 'What is the criterion of obsoleteness in Philosophy? Plato and Aristotle are the two philosophers who have been drawn upon by Christianity most—are they obsolete? In what sense is the Logos doctrine antiquated, in which the Aeschylean doctrine of πάθει μάθος is not? If one thinks of a moral or intellectual tradition, not in the physico-geographical terms of a silt-laden river, but in the perhaps more accurate and appropriate biological terms of ontogenesis or of a tree putting on rings, then very little (if anything) is seen as antiquated or ephemeral: everything takes its place in a tradition that steadily develops and becomes richer, the new reflecting back upon and giving fresh meaning to the old. This figure of organic growth is the Biblical one (Eph. iv. 13–16).'

The writer of this Study would agree that Man's intellectual equipment is a cumulative heritage that is perpetually being enriched by a continuing process of growth; and, for this very reason, he would submit that each successive stage of Man's intellectual achievement is as ephemeral as the girth of a tree in any particular year, whereas a flash of spiritual insight, like Aeschylus's perception that learning comes through suffering, is perennial because it is complete and perfect in itself. This point is examined further in X. ix. 697–704.

[3] Matt. vii. 3–5; cp. Luke vi. 41–42.

[4] The story of Socrates' conversion is told by Plato, ostensibly in Socrates' own words, in *Phaedo*, 96–97, quoted in III. iii. 186–7.

'This was the line taken by Socrates; and, after him, the school of Aristippus of Cyrene, and later on the school of Aristôn of Chios, took up the position that Philosophy ought to confine itself to Ethics, on the ground that Ethics were both a feasible and a useful field of inquiry, in sharp contrast to a Physical Science which [according to this

lenic philosopher's momentous choice had indeed been approved by a Modern Western Christian man of science:

'La science des choses extérieures ne me consolera pas de l'ignorance de la morale au temps d'affliction; mais la science des mœurs me consolera toujours de l'ignorance des sciences extérieures.'[1]

In its pursuit of the audacious task for which it has been equipped and commissioned by its Creator, the Human Intellect is indeed perpetually courting the nemesis that is visited upon the sin of hybris.

'It is as true to-day as ever that the Promethean man who thus disturbs afresh the primordial balance of Nature will have to pay for his impiety. Yet he cannot forswear the principle he serves. . . . Never before in the history of Man has the pride and power of the Intellect as a means of superiority over Nature been so proudly asserted as it is to-day. . . . The development of . . . the Scientific Intellect . . . has, more than any other single cause, served to repress the intuitive science of Antiquity which gave ear to the voice of dreams and which honoured the wisdom that tried to discern naturally revealed truths rather than the capacity to accumulate data.'[2]

From the same angle of vision, we can see the points in which humility and self-confidence were required of the higher religions. The ecclesiastical authorities ought to be confident about the essence, and humble about the accidents, of the faiths of which they were the momentary trustees.

Religion ought to be prepared to surrender to Science every province of intellectual knowledge, traditionally within Religion's field, to which Science might succeed in establishing a title.[3] A just humility would

school of thought] was in the first place incomprehensible, while in the second place it could never be of any use even if it could be brought into focus. Physical Science would always leave us just where we were, even if it were to carry us aloft, higher than Perseus, "above the face of the deep and above the Pleiads", to give us a direct physical vision of the whole Cosmos and the nature of Reality, whatever that may be. This scientific enlightenment would not make us any wiser or juster or braver or better, not to speak of its not endowing us with the blessings of strength and beauty and wealth, which are essential for happiness' (Eusebius: *Praep. Evang.*, xv. lxii. 7 (p. 854 c), reprinted in von Arnim, J.: *Stoicorum Veterum Fragmenta*, vol. i (Leipzig 1905, Teubner), No. 353).

[1] Pascal, Blaise: *Pensées*, No. 67, according to Brunschvicg's arrangement.

[2] Baynes, H. G.: *Mythology of the Soul* (London 1940, Baillière, Tindall, & Cox; 1949, Methuen), pp. 316, 310, 317. Cp. pp. 485–6 and 631–2.

[3] Mr. Martin Wight comments: 'But it is just over this establishment of a title that agreement is so difficult to reach. What is Religion to do when a Freudian or a Behaviourist Psychology asserts a title to the province of Moral Philosophy? The history of the past three centuries has abundantly shown that Science like every other field of human activity—like Religion itself—is inherently encroaching: it tends constantly to transform itself into the autonomous creed "claiming sovereign jurisdiction over the whole field" of which you speak on p. 473 above; and is Religion not to defend its own truths? Surely there is here an ineluctable warfare arising out of the Faustian nature of the Western tradition (if not of Man himself), and at best this warfare can only be keyed down to what von Hügel, who grappled with this problem more profoundly perhaps than any other Modern English philosopher, used to call a "costing and fruitful tension".'

The writer of this Study would agree that there was bound to be a tension between Religion and Science, if only because of Science's empirical method of inquiry by a process of trial and error. It was the intellectual glory of a Modern Western Science that it was always willing to put its successive hypotheses to the test of a free and unfettered examination, and to modify or even abandon any hypothesis that might be impugned by the progress of thought and discovery. This intellectual honesty, which was a point

require Religion to confess that, if it was true that on the spiritual plane Science was impotent, it was also true that on the intellectual plane Religion was a babe who was childishly prone to err.[1] A just moral probity and self-respect would require Religion to refrain from putting any stumbling-block in Science's way when Science was practising her own sovereign virtue of intellectual honesty by following the argument faithfully whithersoever it might lead. And a just self-confidence would require Religion to comprehend and proclaim that she could go on surrendering to Science one province of intellectual knowledge after another without impairing her own essence or diminishing the infinity of the Kingdom of God—any more than the volume of the Atlantic could be diminished by successive achievements of American civil engineers in the progressive reclamation of the Jersey marshes. Religion could afford to lose the marshes so long as she retained the Ocean; and, more than that, she would not only suffer no appreciable loss; she would win an appreciable gain by getting rid of an alien slime which, on her hands, was nothing but an encumbrance and a defilement.

Religion's traditional dominion over intellectual ground had been an historical accident, and this accident had been as detrimental to the true interests of the provisional occupier of the vacant slough as to those of the tardily appearing rightful owner. On the Time-scale of the age of the Human Race the Intellect's achievement of making Man the Lord of Creation had been a relatively recent event. In the practical sphere, as we have observed,[2] this had not been achieved until the Upper Palaeolithic Age, and in the theoretical sphere it had not been achieved until the emergence of the civilizations of the first generation. Down to

of honour among Western scientists, was perhaps the chief single cause of their astonishing success; and this admirable empirical method of inquiry, which the men of science followed, manifestly absolved the layman from any intellectual obligation to accept a new scientific hypothesis unless and until it had established its title by surviving the ordeal of being put to the proof in an exhaustive debate among the scientists themselves. The history of a Modern Western Science over a span of some three hundred years, reckoning back from the year A.D. 1952, did, however, indicate that the empirical scientific method of inquiry usually resulted in course of time in producing agreed and assured additions to scientific knowledge; and at this stage the layman who, up to this point, had been justified in suspending judgement would no longer be justified in rejecting Science's considered and tested findings.

The heliocentric hypothesis proposed by a Modern Western astronomy was a classic example of a new scientific theory which had established its title after the authorities responsible for the policy of the Christian Church had committed themselves to a rejection of it. They would have been better advised if they had merely suspended judgement until a final verdict had been pronounced in the court of Science, within whose intellectual jurisdiction the trial of this hypothesis unquestionably fell; and it should have been relatively easy for the ecclesiastical authorities to leave the last word to the scientists in an astronomical province of scientific inquiry which was manifestly rather remote from the realm of spiritual affairs. The same principles, however, would apply with no less force in a province in which questions of moral conduct were involved, as they were in Science's new province of Psychology. In an encounter with a new psychological hypothesis, as in an encounter with a new astronomical hypothesis, Religion would be justified in suspending judgement so long as the hypothesis was on trial in the court of Science, but it would not be justified in rejecting Science's considered judgement on any point of scientific fact.

[1] This proposition had been pilloried by the Sacred Office in Rome, in the Decree 'Lamentabili' of the 3rd July, 1907, as the fifth point in a catalogue of errors imputed to the Modernists:

'Cum in deposito fidei veritates tantum revelatae contineantur, nullo sub respectu ad Ecclesiam pertinet iudicium ferre de assertionibus disciplinarum humanarum.'

[2] See pp. 486–7, above.

those comparatively recent dates the technical and speculative activities over which the Intellect had not yet asserted her mastery had been fumblingly performed by her, blindfold, under the aegis of Religion and in Religion's name. Primitive Man's success or failure in hunting, in agriculture, in navigation, had to be an affair of the Heart in default of the Head; and this responsibility of Primitive Religion in a field that was not Religion's own had been taken over from their predecessors by the higher religions when the heavenly waters of Revelation had descended upon the Earth and scooped up the soil from the *cañons* that they had scoured out to make beds for mighty rivers. If we ask ourselves whether, on balance, Religion had lost or gained, in terms of her own intrinsic values, by subsequently relinquishing to Science the intellectual provinces of Cosmogony, Astronomy, Geology, and Biology, we shall answer unhesitatingly that she had been the spiritual gainer, and that she had been threatened with spiritual loss only in so far as she had been tempted to convert herself from an unintentional trespasser into a wilful usurper by resisting Science's legitimate claims.

Religion had been the gainer by parting with her dominion over these works of God's creation because, for Religion, this is obnoxious lumber. Religion's task is to lead Man towards his true end of worshipping God and entering into communion with Him, and Man is always apt to miss his goal by turning aside to worship the creature, through whom God is both manifested and obscured, instead of worshipping the Creator Himself.[1] When Religion associates the works of God with their Maker as objects of worship, she is encouraging a spiritual infirmity to which Man is prone instead of helping him to overcome it; and, in view of this, she ought humbly to confess that, so far from doing her an injury, Science is doing her a service in wresting from her, even against her will, the intellectual flotsam that ever threatens to defeat Religion's purpose by becoming an object of idolatry.[2] For the adherents of a traditional Christianity it had always been evident that the Jewish and Christian iconoclasts of the last two centuries B.C. and the first three of the Christian Era, who had been branded as 'atheists' by their contemporaries,[3] had in reality been the liberators of Religion from the idolatrously worshipped ritual impedimenta of an Hellenic paganism. On the same showing, the ecclesiastical authorities of a later day ought to recognize with humility that a Modern Western Science was likewise a liberator

[1] See pp. 460–3, above.

[2] 'We ask . . . why Copernicanism has shaken the Christian Church and theology to such a degree that even in the beginning of the eighteenth century the government of the Canton of Zürich strictly prohibited the discussion of this theory. . . . Copernicanism had this effect because the Church did, and had done for centuries, what it should not have done. The Church had mixed up truth-of-God with world-truth. It had established and dogmatically canonised the Biblical world-picture of Antiquity, which, because of its origin, we call the Babylonian world-picture, with its three storeys: the flat plate of the Earth; above it and on the same axis, so to speak, the Sky or Heaven; below it the Underworld. This ancient world-picture is merely the vessel in which the divine revelation is given to Man, but has itself nothing to do with that revelation. The Church and its theology therefore were forced by Science to withdraw from a realm which was not theirs. Natural Science has helped the Church to understand its own truth and essence better than it had understood them in the course of preceding centuries' (Brunner, E.: *Christianity and Civilisation*, first part (London 1948, Nisbet), p. 83).

[3] See V. vi. 536, and p. 463, above.

from the idolatrously worshipped theological impedimenta of the higher religions.

A Christian Church which had taken it so hard when a Modern Western Science had relieved it of the load of an outworn Babylonic astronomy might be expected to feel a far more vehement distress, resentment, and impulse towards contumacy if it were to be summoned to stand and deliver the hard-set theology in which a living original Christian faith had been petrified in the act of being translated into terms of an Hellenic philosophy.[1] Yet this Hellenic philosophical terminology itself bore witness to its own contingency and relativity in its presentation of a doctrine which was a Christian theology's central and distinctive mystery; for the Greek word πρόσωπα—correctly rendered in Latin as *personae*—which had been used by the Nicene Fathers[2] to describe the three persons of a Triune Godhead, signified the masks worn by the actors on an Hellenic stage; and masks are only another name for veils that perform to a consummate degree the veil's ambiguous function of concealing a countenance by reproducing a simulacrum of its features in an alien substance.[3] In the year A.D. 1952 it might be augured that, in carving out for itself a new province labelled Psychology, a post-Modern Western Science would be imposing upon Christianity the most painful and at the same time perhaps most beneficent of all its acts of liberation by stripping away from a Christian theology some of those anthropomorphic veils that had proved in the past to be the most tenacious of all the barriers between the Human Soul and its Maker.[4] In performing for Christianity this excruciating service, Science, so far from depriving the Soul of God, would assuredly prove to have brought the Soul one step nearer towards the infinitely distant goal of the journey back towards its Maker on which every creature is perpetually travelling all the days of its pilgrimage on Earth.[5]

Such were the gains that Science might be expected to continue to confer upon a reluctant Religion as a result of successive extensions of the bounds of Science's own domain. It was only human that the authorities who had inherited a responsibility for the churches' traditional organization should wince and repine at acts of liberation and enlightenment when these were imperiously imposed upon them by a Science which was not under their control; yet it was certain that the Soul's spiritual progress and profit could never be purchased at the cost of any set-back or loss to the Soul's Creator; for Science's enlargement of her intellectual client kingdom can never abate, by one jot or tittle, the absoluteness of God's eminent domain.

The gain to Religion from surrendering provinces that were not legitimately hers could be measured by the loss that she had invariably suffered through reacquiring them. In a twentieth-century Westernizing World there was no serious prospect of Religion's emulating past pyrrhic victories of hers by reasserting her dominion over lost provinces of

[1] See pp. 470–1 and 473–4, above.
[2] Together with their more frequently used term ὑποστάσεις.
[3] The role of God's creatures as veils which both reveal and conceal God's countenance has been touched upon on pp. 460–3, above.
[4] See pp. 469–70, above.
[5] 'To Him return ye every one' (Qur'ān x. 4).

intellectual theory, such as Astronomy, but there were conspicuous historical examples of Religion's having stultified and sterilized herself by backsliding into politics. In contrast to Primitive Religion, in which the worship of the human ant-heap by human ants had been inextricably entangled with Man's worship of God, the higher religions had shaken themselves free of politics at their birth;[1] for their earthly parents had been prophets who had broken through the barrier of Man's idolatrous corporate self-worship that had intervened between the Soul and God under the previous pagan religious dispensations. This had been the strait gate[2] through which the prophets had led their followers into a new vista of spiritual life, and its reclosure had invariably had disastrous spiritual consequences. The classic case had been the tragic counter-transfiguration of Muhammad from a prophet without honour in his own country[3] into the successful ruler of a rival oasis-state.[4]

This was perhaps the only instance in which a higher religion had been politically debauched by its own founder; but the tragedy of Islam since the *Hijrah*—which Muslims had taken, with characteristic political-mindedness, as the initial date for their distinctive ecclesiastical era[5]—had also been the tragedy of other higher religions at later stages in their careers.[6] We have seen the same blight overtaking Judaism and Zoroastrianism when they went into political action against the Hellenic conquerors of the Syriac World; overtaking Imāmī Shiʿism when it was mobilized by the Safawīs as a mundane weapon against the Ottoman and Uzbeg Powers; overtaking Sikhism when it turned militant against the Mughal Rāj; overtaking a Medieval Western Christianity when it incarnated itself in a *Respublica Christiana*;[7] and overtaking the modern Protestant variation of the same Western Christianity in so far as it allowed itself to become the established religion of this or that secular parochial successor-state of the abortive ecclesiastical commonwealth of Pope Gregory VII and Pope Innocent III.

Politics was the province of mundane practical affairs in which the higher religions had implicated themselves with the most conspicuously disastrous results; but other provinces could furnish further illustrations. A censorious Christian critic might point out that Islam had been saddled by her founder not only with the political incubus of the Temporal Power but with the social incubus of Polygamy[8] and the ritual incubus of the adoration of the fetish animating the Black Stone; and a censorious Muslim critic might retort by counter-charges in kind against Christianity and the other living higher religions. If it was true that Polygamy had been picked up by Islam from the social heritage of 'the Times of Ignorance' in a barbarian Arabia, was it not also true that

[1] See p. 433, above. [2] Matt. vii. 13; Luke xiii. 24.
[3] Matt. xiii. 57; Mark vi. 4; Luke iv. 24; John iv. 44.
[4] See III. iii. 466–72, and p. 440, above. [5] See p. 298, above.
[6] See V. v. 646–712, *passim*. [7] See IV. iv. 512–84.
[8] An apologist for Islam might reply, in defence, that an unlimited polygamy had been the established practice in the social environment into which the Prophet had happened to be born, and that he had reformed this existing social institution, so far as the weakness of the flesh would allow, by restricting the number of a man's lawful wives to four (making a personal exception for himself, and allowing to everybody any number of concubines). This apology would raise the question whether it is expedient to reform an undesirable custom at the price of consecrating it.

the likewise undesirable social institution of Caste had been picked up by Hinduism from the Indic Civilization,[1] and the idolatrous rite of image-worship[2] by the Mahāyāna from Hinduism and by Christianity from Hellenism? And (our Muslim critic might add) was not the Eucharist itself, which was the distinctive and fundamental sacrament of the Christian Church, a relic of Man's pre-Christian worship of his domesticated food-supply?[3]

These stones that lay so ready to the hand of a polemical champion of each of the higher religions, if he chose to put his own glass windows in jeopardy by breaking his neighbour's, were so many mutual danger-signals which ought to move the ecclesiastical authorities in all the churches to show the humility that was required of them; and the requirement was that they should humbly renounce dominion over provinces of practical life, and likewise of intellectual theory, in which Religion had no legitimate title to lay down the law.

A Common Endeavour

If Religion and Science could each acquire humility, and retain self-confidence, in the spheres in which, for each of them, self-confidence and humility were respectively in place, they might then find themselves in a mood that would be propitious for a reconciliation; but a propitious state of feeling, though it is an indispensable condition for successful action, is not an effective substitute for action itself; and, if a reconciliation was to be achieved in deed, the parties must seek it through some joint endeavour.

This psychological truth had been recognized in the past by the parties to the encounters between Christianity and an Hellenic philosophy and between Hinduism and an Indic philosophy. In both these encounters, as we have seen, a conflict had been arrested by the pacificatory act of giving theological expression to religious ritual and myth in philosophical terminology; and the impulse to take action had in itself been well inspired; but, as we have also seen, the particular line of action actually taken had, in both these cases, been an aberration which had failed to bring a true and lasting peace because it had taken its cue from a false diagnosis of the relation between spiritual and intellectual truth. It had proceeded on the mistaken assumption that spiritual truth could

[1] See IV. iv. 229–32.

[2] The votaries of religions which had admitted the use of images into their liturgy might contend—as, indeed, they had contended—that images could be used as aids to the worship of God without becoming objects of worship in themselves. The iconoclast's reply would be that this was a theoretical possibility which had seldom been achieved in practice.

[3] A Christian apologist might reply, in defence, that this antique rite of communion with a god incarnate in material food produced by human labour had been the established practice in the social environment in which Christianity had happened to arise. It had survived there as the fundamental sacrament in the worship of Tammuz and his doubles, Adonis and Osiris, and in the Hellenic mysteries of Zagreus, Triptolemus, and Dionysus. Christianity had etherialized this existing ritual institution, as far as the weakness of the flesh would allow, by transfiguring its originally material meaning into a spiritual one. The abortive higher religions from which this sacrament had been taken over by Christianity had already travelled some distance along this road. And was this not the only known avenue to spiritual enlightenment? Were not Man's highest spiritual ideas all imaginative applications of familiar material facts to the mysterious realities of the Spiritual Universe?

be formulated in intellectual terms. In a twentieth-century Westernizing World the Heart and the Head would be well advised to take warning from this historic failure of a previous attempt of theirs to achieve a reconciliation on erroneous lines.

Even if it were psychologically feasible, by agreement, to discard the classic theology of the four living higher religions and to substitute for it a new-fangled theology expressed in terms, not of an Hellenic or an Indic philosophy, but of a Modern Western Science, a successful achievement of this *tour de force* would merely be a repetition of a previous error which would invite the same nemesis. A scientifically formulated theology (if such could be conceived) would be as unsatisfying and as ephemeral as the philosophically formulated theology that was hanging like a millstone round the necks of Buddhists, Hindus, Christians, and Muslims in the year A.D. 1952. It would be unsatisfying because the language of the Intellect is an inadequate medium for conveying the insight that the Soul acquires when it has been 'caught up to the third heaven' and has 'heard unspeakable words, which it is not lawful for a man to utter.'[1] It would be ephemeral because it is one of the virtues of the Intellect not to rest on its oars but ever to be striving to increase its knowledge of the Truth on its own level and to re-articulate the whole body of existing intellectual knowledge in the light of each new acquisition. In a Western World the writer's generation had seen the entire *corpus intellectuale* of Modern Western scientific thought subjected to a revolutionary reorganization as a result of the two discoveries of the theory of relativity and the structure of the atom. A theology expressed in terms of some current system of philosophy or science that was bound, *ex officio*, to be superseded,[2] would stand con-

[1] 2 Cor. xii. 2 and 4.

[2] In this passage, as elsewhere in this Study, the writer linked Philosophy with Science, because he believed that every system of philosophy was a *Weltanschauung* derived from the body of scientific knowledge current at the time and place at which the particular system of philosophy had been formulated. Believing this, he believed that philosophies changed, and were bound to change, in response to changes in the field of Science. This belief in the dependence of Philosophy on Science is challenged by Mr. Martin Wight. 'Modern Science', he comments, 'proceeds by the elaboration, testing and discarding of hypotheses; Philosophy does no such thing—least of all does Metaphysics. Thus Newton's hypotheses have now been replaced by Einstein's, because the latter explain observed phenomena more satisfactorily; but there is no sense in which Kant has replaced Plato, or Bergson has replaced Anselm. Their relationship with one another is not a relationship of progress and supersession, but of facets of a single truth, soundings in a single ocean, portraits of a single sitter. Your own copious quotation from Plato in this Study is evidence that philosophies are not "bound *ex officio* to be superseded". "The bickerings of philosophic sects are an amusement for the foolish; above these jarrings and creakings of the machine of thought there is a melody sung in unison by the spirits of the spheres, which are the great philosophers. This melody, *philosophia quaedam perennis*, is not a body of truth revealed once for all, but a living thought whose content, never discovered for the first time, is progressively determined and clarified by every genuine thinker" (Collingwood, R. G.: *Speculum Mentis* (Oxford 1924, Clarendon Press), p. 13). There is no important sense in which Theology expresses itself in terms of "some current system of science": Paley's God the Watchmaker, Whitehead's God the mathematician, and the Modernist churchman's God the evolutionary force, if they would be examples of what you mean, are not serious or significant contributions to Theology. But the association between Theology and Metaphysics is, of course, extremely close; Theology must always borrow its expression in part from the imperishable armoury of philosophical equipment; and every great theologian, even if he seems as revolutionary as Aquinas *vis-à-vis* Augustine, or Luther *vis-à-vis* Aquinas, or Calvin *vis-à-vis* Luther, or von Hügel *vis-à-vis* official Neo-Thomism, or Karl Barth *vis-à-vis*

demned to as swift a collapse as the house that a foolish man built upon the sand.[1]

What then, should the Heart and Head do to be reconciled in the light of the monumental failure of their previous attempt to build a common platform for themselves in the shape of Theology? Was there any opening in the Westernizing World of A.D. 1952 for a combined operation in a more promising direction? At that date the imagination of Western Man was still obsessed by the mounting triumphs of Physical Science, which had recently been crowned by the supreme intellectual achievement of dissecting the structure of the atom. Yet, if it were true, as has already been suggested in this chapter, that a mile gained in the progress of Man's control over Non-Human Nature is of less importance to him than an inch gained in the enhancement of his capacity to deal with himself and with his fellow men and with God, then it was conceivable that, of all Western Man's achievements in the twentieth century of the Christian Era, the feat that would loom largest in retrospect in the epimethean view of Posterity might be the breaking of new ground in the field of insight into Human Nature.

That century was witnessing the ironical spectacle of Man standing appalled in face of his latest intellectual success, and the prospect that was terrifying and dispiriting him had been conjured up, not by anything in his newly won mastery of the atom, but by something in his age-old experience of himself. This experience told him, in accents too forcible to be ignored, that he could not trust himself to refrain from using the 'know-how' of the technique for splitting the atom for his customary purpose of forging a weapon to wield against his fellow men, and his scientific knowledge told him no less plainly that, when a weapon of this unprecedented potency had fallen into an unregenerate Humanity's hands, the wages of the sin of War might be the death of the Race.[2] Where, in these appalling circumstances, was Man to look for access to the life that is the gift of God?[3] A gleam of light might be caught in a passage from the shrewd pen of a contemporary English poet.

> No more across the Ocean ships return
> Fresh from the ends of Earth, the globe astern,
> Homeward for Europe's tiny corner bound,
> Tense with the tidings of a world new-found . . .
> Yet even so, in spite of every change,
> One world remains where Fancy still may range,
> Remote, mysterious-sea'd, uncertain-shored,
> And only recently by men explored.

Classical Lutheranism, can be seen in retrospect as having taken his place in a melody sung in unison, and as a contributor to *theologia quaedam perennis*.'

The writer would agree, of course, that Theology was an expression of Religion in terms of Philosophy, and this was the vice of Theology as he saw it, because he believed, with Collingwood, that Philosophy (like Science) 'is progressively determined and clarified', and therefore also believed that each successive formulation of Philosophy, as well as Science, was ephemeral. The great philosophers had been great in virtue of being also poets and prophets; and it is Plato the poet and prophet, not Plato the philosopher, whose imperishable words are copiously quoted in this Study.

1 Matt. vii. 24–27; Luke vi. 47–49.

2 Rom. vi. 23.

3 Ibid.

A world of phantom shapes, fear-haunted mists,
Sailed not by seamen but psychologists,
Without Equator, latitude or Pole,
The veiled, vague chaos of the human soul.[1]

The sudden entry that had been made by the Western scientific mind into this realm of Psychology during the generation in which those lines had been written had been a by-product of two world wars waged with weapons that were capable of producing shattering effects on the Psyche, though their ravages were only the child's play of a pre-atomic Western Science. Thanks to the unprecedented clinical experience provided by these mental derangements that had been inflicted by two collective Western crimes, the Western Intellcct had descried the subconscious depths of the Psyche and, in the act, had acquired a new conception of itself as a will-o'-the-wisp hovering over the surface of this unplumbed psychic abyss.[2]

Considering Man's proneness to identify with God Himself any work of God that Man, in the exercise of his puny prowess, has newly discovered or newly mastered,[3] it could be augured that the Modern Western scientific mind, after having followed the Hellenic school of philosophy for three Cartesian centuries in mistakenly identifying God with the conscious rational superstructure of the Psyche, might be led astray by its portentous discovery of a psychic underworld into exchanging an Hellenic error for an Indic one and following in turn the Indic school in mistakenly identifying God with the Psyche's subconscious irrational abyss.[4] Yet it would be as vain for Science to hope to find God in the Subconscious as it would be needless for Religion to fear to lose Him there.

'Behold, the Lord passed by, and a great and strong wind rent the mountains and brake in pieces the rocks before the Lord; but the Lord was not in the wind; and after the wind an earthquake, but the Lord was not in the earthquake; and after the earthquake a fire, but the Lord was not in the fire.'[5]

Nor, again, had the Lord ever been in—in the sense of being contained in, and so being identical with—the Earth from which He had given Man his sustenance, or in the Sky from which He had sent him rain, or in the Sun from which He had blessed him with light and warmth, or in the fire that Man had kindled, or in the crop that he had

1 Skinner, Martyn: *Letters to Malaya, III and IV* (London 1943, Putnam), pp. 41 and 43.

2 In making its own discovery of the realm of Psychology a Modern Western Science might prove not to have been the first Western explorer in this field; it might prove to have been merely rediscovering a realm that had already been explored and mapped in the confessional manual of a Medieval Western Christian Church.

3 See pp. 460–3 and 468–9, above, and p. 725, n. 1, below.

4 In the exultation of their intellectual conquest of the psychic realm of the Subconscious, the pioneers of the twentieth-century Western school of Psychology were apt to cry

We were the first that ever burst
Into that silent sea,

without pausing to consider that Indic minds, following an intuitive line of approach, had anticipated them by some twenty-five centuries. See further, p. 725 with n. 1, below.

5 1 Kings xix. 11–12.

raised, or in the flock that he had bred, or in the tribe whose union had been his strength, or in any mansion of Man's own Psyche—either on its conscious surface or in its subconscious depths.

Twentieth-century Western minds were well enough aware that Man's Reason would serve him, with an unmoral impartiality, for good and evil purposes alike; but, in the exhilaration of their new discovery of the Subconscious, they perhaps needed a seventeenth-century mentor to remind them that this infant prodigy was likewise morally ambivalent.

'Le Cœur aime l'Être Universel naturellement et soi-même naturellement, selon qu'il s'y adonne; et il s'adurcit contre l'un ou l'autre à son choix.'[1]

The Subconscious is indeed a child, a savage, and a brute beast which is at the same time also wiser, more honest, and less prone to error than the Conscious Self. The Subconscious is one of those statically perfect works of creation that are the Creator's 'stopping places',[2] whereas the Conscious Human Personality is an infinitely imperfect approximation towards a Being of an incommensurably higher order, who is Himself the maker of both these diverse but inseparable organs of the Human Psyche. Yet even the least ungodlike of God's creatures falls as immeasurably short of the divine stature of its Maker as the broadest span of the Jersey marshes falls short of the breadth of the Atlantic Ocean; and, when the Human Spirit has both caught the light of Human Consciousness and explored the darkness of the Human Psyche's subconscious depths, it is still as far as ever from having beheld the Beatific Vision of a Creator whose infinite being is never confined to any of His momentary stopping places, and whose ubiquitous presence always reveals itself behind and beyond each of His innumerable works.

'Whither shall I go then from Thy spirit? Or whither shall I go then from Thy presence?

'If I climb up into Heaven, Thou art there; if I go down to Hell, Thou art there also.

'If I take the wings of the morning and remain in the uttermost parts of the sea,

'Even there also shall Thy hand lead me, and Thy right hand shall hold me.

'If I say "Peradventure the darkness shall cover me", then shall my night be turned to day.

'Yea, the darkness is no darkness with Thee, but the night is as clear as the day; the darkness and light to Thee are both alike.'[3]

If Western minds in the twentieth century of the Christian Era were to have discovered the Subconscious merely to find in it a new object for idolatrous worship,[4] they would be placing a fresh barrier between themselves and God[5] instead of seizing a fresh opportunity to draw

[1] Pascal, Blaise: *Pensées*, No. 276, according to Brunschvicg's arrangement.
[2] See p. 461, above. [3] Ps. cxxxix. 6–11, as in *The Book of Common Prayer*.
[4] See pp. 460–3 and 468–9, above, and p. 725, n. 1, below.
[5] The worship of the Subconscious would be an impoverishment of the vision of God as Christus Patiens. An incarnate god identified with the subconscious element in the Human Psyche would lose his full humanity and become non-moral (like the Hindu gods and the Olympians) in becoming impersonal (like the deified forces of Nature and their summation in the perfunctory God of the Philosophers).

nearer to Him. The opportunity was there; for, at each previous discovery or mastery of a formerly unknown or untamed creature which Man had duly recognized as being, not the Creator, but another masterpiece of His handiwork, Man had, in the intellectual act of spiritual liberation, won a possibility of learning more about God as well, and of thereby entering into closer communion with Him. Man had always been thus rewarded for this lawful exercise of a dominion over his fellow creatures which had been conferred on Man by a Godhead who was both their creator and his; and an Alexandrian Hellenic philosopher of the allegorizing school—a Jewish Philo or a Greek Hypatia—might have found an intimation of this truth in the aetiological myth of Jacob's wrestling-match with the *jinn* at Peniel[1] and in the fairy-story of the kidnapping of Proteus on Pharos by Menelaus and his men.[2]

'With a shout we threw ourselves upon him and pinioned him in our arms; and, sure enough, the old fellow started to play his sly tricks. First of all he turned himself into a lion with bushy mane, and next into a serpent, a leopard and a mighty boar; and, before he had finished, he had changed into drenching water and into the towering foliage of a tree. But all the while we held on like grim death without relaxing, till at last the uncanny old fellow grew tired of it.'[3]

When Proteus was convinced, at last, that he could not wriggle out, he resumed his original form and gave Menelaus the information that he wanted;[4] and Jacob's mysterious antagonist likewise gave Jacob the blessing for which Jacob asked when the *jinn* was convinced that his human adversary had the strength to hold him, if he chose, till they were overtaken by the breaking of the day. A Philo might have interpreted the *jinn* as a symbol of Nature's potency, with which Man cannot venture to grapple without risk to his own integrity; an Hypatia might have interpreted Proteus as a symbol of the same Nature's infinite variety; but both, if they had struck out this particular line of interpretation,[5] would have declared, with one accord, that it was Nature, not the

[1] Gen. xxxii. 24–32. [2] *Odyssey*, Book IV, ll. 351–570.

[3] Ibid., 454–60.

[4] The price that Man has to pay for this acquisition of a scientific knowledge of Nature is eloquently appraised by a writer in *The Times Literary Supplement*, 17th August, 1951, p. 514:

'Primitive Man, it is to be supposed, did not feel lonely in his environment: however cruel and terrifying it might sometimes be, it was at least something akin to himself, something he could intuitively understand—could influence and propitiate. But on Modern Man the gates of Eden have closed. The more he knows of the world around him the less he understands it. Nature is no longer kind or unkind, no longer amenable to human persuasion, but a soulless problem in higher mathematics; and there are times when one re-echoes in an even deeper sense Wordsworth's lament:

Great God! I'd rather be
A pagan suckled in a creed outworn—
So might I, standing on this pleasant lea,
Have glimpses that would make me less forlorn;
Have sight of Proteus rising from the sea,
Or hear old Triton blow his wreathèd horn.'

[5] Philo does not, in fact, take this line in any of the seven passages in which he offers a symbolic interpretation of this episode of the Book of Genesis (chap. xxxii, vv. 24–32), according to the index of passages, cited by him from the Old Testament, that is to be found in vol. vii of Cohn, L., and Wendland, P.: *Philonis Alexandrini Opera Quae Supersunt* (Berlin 1896–1926, Reimer, 7 vols.). The passages in question are: *De Ebrietate*, chap. 20 (Cohn and Wendland's edition, vol. ii, p. 185, ll. 11–13); *De Mutatione Nominum*,

God of Nature,[1] that was at grips with the human hero of a philosophic folk-tale. Hypatia would have appealed to the unimpeachable testimony of Proteus' own daughter Eidothea, as evidence that this immortal oracle of exact science was not the Lord God Poseidon, but was merely Poseidon's underling, 'the Old Man of the Sea';[2] and Philo would have pronounced Jacob to have been in error in inferring, from his antagonist's refusal to reveal his name, that he had 'seen God face to face'.[3] Had not Jacob confuted his own conjecture by living to tell the tale and putting it on record that his life had been preserved? For had not God Himself said to Moses: 'Thou canst not see My face, for there shall no man see Me and live'?[4]

The Fundamental Unity of Truth[5]

If Science and Religion could seize their opportunity of drawing nearer to God by jointly seeking to comprehend God's protean creature the Psyche in its subconscious depths as well as on its conscious surface, what would be the rewards that they might expect to win if success were to crown such a joint endeavour? In this spiritual adventure the prize would indeed be splendid and the hope indeed be great;[6] for the Subconscious, not the Intellect,[7] is the organ through which Man lives his spiritual life for good or evil. It is the fount of Poetry, Music, and the Visual Arts, and the channel through which the Soul is in communion with God when it does not steel itself against God's influence. In this enthralling voyage of spiritual exploration the first objective would be to seek insight into the workings of the Heart; for 'le Cœur a ses raisons que la Raison ne connaît point.'[8] The second objective would be to explore the nature of the difference between rational truth and intuitive truth, in the belief that each of them is genuine Truth—though each only in its own sphere, and only as far as it goes. The third objective

chap. 2 (vol. iii, p. 159, ll. 7–8); chap. 5 (vol. iii, p. 164, ll. 14–15); chap. 35 (vol. iii, p. 188, l. 24); *De Somniis*, Book I, chap. 14 (vol. iii, p. 222, l. 2); chap. 21 (vol. iii, p. 233, l. 5); *De Praemiis et Pœnis*, chap. 8 (vol. v, p. 346, l. 17).

[1] Herbert, George: *The Pulley*, quoted on p. 462, above.

[2] *Odyssey*, Book IV, ll. 384–7.

[3] Gen. xxxii. 29–30.

[4] Exod. xxxiii. 20.

[5] Robert Bridges, in *The Testament of Beauty*, Book I, ll. 148–61 and *passim*, has expressed what the writer of this Study is trying to say here.

[6] Plato: *Phaedo*, 114 C, quoted in V. vi. 168.

[7] The thesis that Man has become *Homo Sapiens* incidentally to becoming *Homo Faber* has been propounded by Henri Bergson in *L'Évolution Créatrice* (24th ed.: Paris 1921, Alcan), chap. 2, pp. 163–79:

'L'instinct est, par excellence, la faculté d'utiliser un instrument naturel organisé. . . . Mais l'intelligence est la faculté de fabriquer des instruments inorganisés, c'est-à-dire artificiels. . . . Nous tenons l'intelligence humaine pour relative aux nécessités de l'action. Posez l'action, la forme même de l'intelligence s'en déduit. . . . Partons donc de l'action, et posons en principe que l'intelligence vise d'abord à fabriquer. . . . Notre intelligence, telle qu'elle sort des mains de la nature, a pour objet principal le solide inorganisé. . . . Elle est la vie regardant au dehors, s'extériorisant par rapport à elle-même, adoptant en principe, pour les diriger en fait, les démarches de la nature inorganisée. De là son étonnement quand elle se tourne vers le vivant et se trouve en face de l'organisation. Quoi qu'elle fasse alors, elle résout l'organisé en inorganisé, car elle ne saurait, sans renverser sa direction naturelle et sans se tordre sur elle-même, penser la continuité vraie, la mobilité réelle, la compénétration réciproque et, pour tout dire, cette évolution créatrice qui est la vie. . . . L'intelligence est caractérisée par une incompréhension naturelle de la vie.'

[8] Pascal, Blaise: *Pensées*, No. 277, according to Brunschvicg's arrangement.

would be to seek to strike the underlying rock of fundamental Truth on which rational and intuitive truth alike must be founded. And the final objective, in striving to strike rock-bottom in the psychic cosmos, would be to attain to a fuller vision of God the Dweller in the Innermost. In the present Study we cannot aspire to do more than follow our pair of explorers—if Science and Religion can be imagined as setting out hand in hand—on the first stages of this new quest for the *Visio Beatifica*.[1]

The warning, so unfortunately ignored by well-intentioned theologians, that 'it hath not pleased God to give His people salvation in dialectic',[2] is one of the refrains of the Gospels:

> 'Jesus said: Suffer little children, and forbid them not, to come unto me; for of such is the Kingdom of Heaven. . . . Verily I say unto you: Except ye be converted and become as little children, ye shall not enter into the Kingdom of Heaven. Whosoever, therefore, shall humble himself as this little child, the same is greatest in the Kingdom of Heaven. And whoso shall receive one such little child in my name, receiveth me. But whoso shall offend one of these little ones which believe in me, it were better for him that a millstone were hanged about his neck and that he were drowned in the depth of the sea.'[3]

From the standpoint of the Reason, the Subconscious is indeed a childlike creature, both in its humble-minded attunedness to God, which the Reason cannot emulate, and in its undisciplined inconsequence, which the Reason cannot approve.

> 'The wind bloweth where it listeth, and thou hearest the sound thereof, but canst not tell whence it cometh and whither it goeth.'[4]

Conversely, in the sight of the Subconscious, the Reason is a heartless pedant who has purchased a miraculous but superfluous command over Nature at the sinful price of betraying the Soul by allowing her primordial vision of God to fade into the light of common day.[5] 'Thou madest him to have dominion over the works of Thy hands; Thou hast put all things under his feet';[6] yet what an insignificant fragment of God's creation it is that the Reason manages to catch in the clumsy crab-claws

1 Mr. Martin Wight comments: 'These three objectives of "seeking insight", "exploring the difference between rational truth and intuitive truth", and "seeking the underlying . . . fundamental truth" appear to the reader to be objectives in which, as with all human objectives, the Intellect and the Intuition are equally concerned. If this supposed reconciliation between "Reason" and "the Subconscious" means anything at all, it is a reconciliation that must be purveyed or communicated to Mankind in general in some systematized and stated formulation; such a formulation is the proper work of Reason itself; and it will be open to all the criticisms that you level against Theology.'—'Indeed it will', would be the present writer's reply, 'and that is why I have set my face (see pp. 494–5, above) against the precipitation of a new theology through a fresh attempt to formulate in the language of Reason the truths of Poetry and Prophecy. I do not accept your postulate that a reconciliation between Reason and the Subconscious must be communicated by the Reason in some systematized formulation. Plato, for example, scrupulously refrained from attempting this. He yokes Reason and Intuition to his winged chariot side by side, without ever trying to disguise either one of them in any trappings that belong to the other. In my belief it is because he drives this pair of horses in double harness that he succeeds in flying so high. I appeal to Plato's example.'

2 Ambrose: *De Fide*, Book I, chap. 5, § 42, quoted in V. v. 564.

3 Matt. xix. 14 and xviii. 3–6; cp. Matt. x. 42; Mark ix. 37 and 42 and x. 14–15; Luke x. 48, xvii. 1–2, and xviii. 16–17.

4 John iii. 8.

5 Wordsworth: *Intimations of Immortality from Recollections of Early Childhood.*

6 Ps. viii. 6.

of its categories within the wavering framework of Space-Time! 'There are more things in Heaven and Earth,' exclaims the Subconscious to the Reason, 'than are dreamt of in your philosophy';[1] and she thanks and praises God for having given to her lowly self the mission of defending what the Reason has abandoned.

> 'Out of the mouths of babes and sucklings hast Thou ordained strength because of thine enemies, that Thou mightest still the enemy and the avenger.'[2]

Yet in truth the Reason is not, of course, the enemy of God, any more than the realm of the Subconscious is, in truth, out of Nature's bounds; for the Reason and the Subconscious alike are God's creatures. Either has its own appointed field and task, and they need not scandalize one another if they cease to trespass.[3] Theology, which is the Reason's misguided attempt to state intuitive truth in terms of intellectual truth, is the counterpart of magic, which is a misguided attempt of the Subconscious to usurp the Reason's task of establishing Man's dominion over Non-Human Nature. These reciprocal trespasses are no doubt partly traceable to a hybris which is one of the symptoms of Original Sin, and which can only be kept in check by an unceasing spiritual travail; but there was another cause of confusion which the Reason and the Subconscious, between them, had it in their power to remove by co-operation.

Owing to the poverty of Man's mental equipment up to date, these two departments of the Psyche had been constrained to use one language to express two kinds of truth relating to different aspects, planes, and dimensions of Reality; and here lay the remediable cause of the insoluble and estranging verbal controversies that had arisen between Science and Religion over, for example, the Real Presence of a *Latens Deitas* in the consecrated elements of bread and wine in the rite of the Eucharist and over the Virgin Birth of a God Incarnate who had been conceived by the Holy Ghost. In a Hellenizing World in the first century of the Christian Era there was a traditional usage of words for describing the spiritual experience of the Soul's communion with God in and through the rite of sacramental eating and drinking. The God who

> 'bringeth forth grass for the cattle and green herb for the service of men, that He may bring food out of the Earth, and wine that maketh glad the heart of Man, and oil to make him a cheerful countenance, and bread to strengthen Man's heart',[4]

was traditionally described as animating these His creatures when they were eaten by Man in a rite in which Man's aim was to commune with his Maker. In the same world in the same age there was another traditional usage of words for describing the spiritual experience of

[1] Shakespeare: *Hamlet*, Act I, scene v, l. 162.

[2] Ps. viii. 2, as in *The Book of Common Prayer*.

[3] A Catholic friend of the writer's comments: 'Science should have its own field to itself and should recognize that the laws which it finds are God's laws and that He can do with them as He wills. While Science and Revealed Truth are on different planes they will not contradict one another; each can safely affirm what is certainly truth in its own sphere with no fear that they will be at variance. In the past, both Science and Religion have exceeded their limits.'

[4] Ps. civ. 14–15.

encountering a man through whose personality God's light streamed into his fellow men's souls, not darkly, as through a glass,[1] but undimmed, as through an open window. Such a human soul divine (θεῖος ἀνήρ),[2] whose appearance in This World had given light to them that sat in darkness and in the shadow of death,[3] was traditionally described as being a Son of God by a human mother.[4]

Does not this mythological use of language aptly express the truth of the Heart?[5] And, if it does so, is not this the most important of the alternative uses to which words can be put? Which is the more significant truth about bread and wine? The spiritual truth that, in the Eucharist, they bring the Soul into communion with God? Or the scientific truth that they keep a physical organism alive in virtue of such-and-such tissue-repairing and such-and-such energy-giving ingredients? And which is the more significant truth about the birth of a new man into the World?[6] The spiritual truth that, through the tender mercy of our God, the dayspring from on high hath visited us?[7] Or the scientific truth that an embryo has been conceived in such-and-such a way by sexual intercourse, and has passed through such-and-such physical metamorphoses between conception and birth? In the realm of spiritual values, bread and wine exist for the sake of the Eucharist, not of the food-supply, and conception and birth take place for the sake of the Incarnation, not of man-power. And, if Science, using the same words in a different sense of her own, declares that the spiritual usage of them is, if literally intended, untrue, and, if symbolically intended, unscientific, Religion can have the last word if she is content to retort that, for her, the scientific meaning is trivial and irrelevant. She does not expose her mythological expression of spiritual truth to any damaging scientific attack unless she stakes the perverse theological claim that her truths are true in the scientific sense as well as in the spiritual.[8]

The first step towards a reconciliation between Religion and Science would be a mutual recognition that either of them has a truth of her

[1] 1 Cor. xiii. 12.

[2] See Bieler, L.: Θεῖος Ἀνήρ (Vienna 1935–6, Höfels, 2 vols.).

[3] Luke i. 79.

[4] For the myth of the encounter between the Virgin and the Father of her Child, see II. i. 271–2; V. vi. 267–75; and p. 464, above.

[5] This question appears to the writer to be answered in the affirmative in the following comment by a Catholic friend of his: 'The revealed truths of the Christian Faith are in some respects about things that we could not know [solely by the light of our human intellectual powers]: Grace, the Trinity, Redemption. A full comprehension of these truths is beyond the powers of our intelligence, and part of their meaning can only be understood in the way of analogy. This will continue to be so as long as men are men. Only God can lift us out of the use of images, for that is our way of knowing. We must not forget the poets, who are among the greatest of men; their way is the way of symbolism throughout. The danger of this way is that the image may be mistaken for the reality behind. The right way of meeting this danger is, not to throw the image away, but to use it only as a means.'

[6] John xvi. 21.

[7] Luke i. 78.

[8] 'All religious propositions are symbolic, but come to be taken literally. For literal language and the language of fact are identical. This is everywhere the trap which lies in the path of the religious consciousness. It mistakes its own utterances for literal statements of fact. Its doom is then sealed. For always in the end it turns out that the alleged facts are not facts, but fictions. And the discovery of this, whether by Science, or Philosophy, or merely by Common Sense, is the triumph of Scepticism' (Stace, W. T.: *Time and Eternity* (Princeton 1952, University Press), p. 132).

own which cannot be taken in the sense of the other truth on the strength of the verbal accident that the same language has to be used for conveying these two different meanings. This would be the first step, but it could not be the last, for, if Truth were not reducible to unity, God would not be accessible to Man; and this would be in contradiction with Man's experience.[1] Moses did not see God's face on Mount Sinai, yet he did come down from the mount with the tables of testimony in his hand;[2] Elijah did not feel God's presence in the wind or in the earthquake, nor did he see it in the fire, yet he did hear the still small voice[3] which spoke to him after the fire and the earthquake and the wind had expended themselves. If Truth is ultimately one, and if the diversity of spiritual and scientific truth should prove not to be reducible to unity by the naïve method of trying to interpret one of the two in the sense of the other, the ultimate unity must be sought on some third plane—distinct from both the planes of truth so far known to Mankind.

This hypothetical underlying unitary truth had so far been beyond the range of Man's spiritual vision; and it seemed unlikely that he would even begin to apprehend it till he had advanced much farther than he had progressed so far in his understanding of both the Reason and the Subconscious. At a date which was perhaps less than six thousand years removed from the date of the first emergence of the earliest of the civilizations, Man was still barely on the threshold of his knowledge of himself; and this dark jungle would be harder for Man's intelligence to penetrate than the great open spaces of Non-Human Nature where the Intellect found itself at home[4] and where in the past it had overrun one province after another in a continual succession of sweeping conquests. Nor, in the field of self-knowledge, would the utmost intellectual prowess avail by itself to bring Man to his objective; for spiritual truth cannot be divined except through spiritual experience, and the dumb Heart cannot express what it has learnt through suffering till the liberating word is uttered by a prophet inspired with the gift of tongues. But neither the revealing experience nor its prophetic interpretation could be whistled for at the convenience of a hard-pressed generation; and, pending the fuller enlightenment which might come to Man in God's time, but which was not at Man's command, a belief in the existence of bed-rock Truth must rest on the faith which 'is the substance of things hoped for, the evidence of things not seen'.[5] The grounds for this faith which passes understanding could be indicated in a simile.

Elemental truths might be likened to high buildings whose weight is so crushing that the structure cannot stand without being founded on rock. When, standing on the heights overlooking Sandy Hook, we see on the horizon the sky-line of New York, we can confidently infer from

[1] 'If one sticks to the "commonsense" attitude, of course it seems purely pedantic and sophistical to discuss the relation of poetical to historical truth, but no one can have done more than a trifle of philosophical thought without discovering that there is such a thing as poetic truth, that it is not the same as historical truth, and that the relating of the two is an extremely complicated matter' (William Temple, in a letter quoted in Iremonger, F. A.: *William Temple, Archbishop of Canterbury* (London 1948, Cumberlege), p. 466).

[2] Exod. xxxiii. 23 and xxxiv. 29.

[3] 1 Kings xix. 12.

[4] See pp. 500–1, above.

[5] Heb. xi. 1.

our first glance the presence of rock at the distant sky-scrapers' base. On Manhattan Island the rock on which these giant towers are founded crops out on the surface, visible to the eye when we view the *terrain* at close quarters. But what about the high buildings in Chicago? On the shore of Lake Michigan the visible surface of the Earth is composed, not of solid rock, but of softer substance—alluvium or gravel or clay—yet the buildings there tower up to heights that rival the altitudes of their sisters in New York. What is the secret of the Chicagoan architects' apparent achievement of the impossible feat of building Towers of Babel on the sand? The secret is that these high buildings in Chicago rest, not on the visible surface soil—which would indeed be incapable of supporting them—but on concrete piles which are driven down through softer strata till they strike the rock, at whatever depth it may lie. The depth is variable, for the invisible rock underlying Chicago, like the visible rock that crops out in New York, is capriciously irregular in its configuration, so that one pile may strike it at no more than 20 feet below the surface, and another at no more than 70 feet, while a third may have to probe down no less than 200 feet before finding rest for the sole of its foot.[1] In the imagery of this simile, Truth might be likened to a house of many mansions with a rock-based pile supporting each. The buried pinnacle of rock on which rational truth is founded may be situate not very far below the surface, while spiritual truth may be based on the rock-bottom of an abyss; but, however great the difference in the level may be, the foundations of both kinds of truth alike go down to the rock, and at either level it is the same rock, living yet invisible, that bears the weight on its atlantean shoulders.[2]

If the eye of Faith could thus divine the presence of a Unitary Truth founded on the rock but buried deep below the surface, how were the Heart and the Head to pursue their common enterprise of striving to reach and grasp this hidden treasure? Two points, at least, could be taken as certain: the characteristic and peculiar gifts of both organs must be brought into play if the quest was to have any prospect of success, and this indispensable co-operation would only be possible in virtue of the constant exercise of a mutual charity; 'for we know in part and we prophesy in part,'[3] but 'charity never faileth'.[4]

The relation between the two organs of the Psyche might be likened to that between a human herdsman and a powerful and wayward yet domesticable and serviceable animal. Neither man nor beast can truly afford to do without his fellow creature; for the beast remains an aimless wanderer in the wilderness so long as he does not accept human guidance, while the man remains a puny plaything of Nature so long as he

[1] Gen. viii. 9.

[2] Mr. Martin Wight justly comments: 'This conclusion, and the simile in which it is expressed, is, of course, at odds with the New Testament, whose writers were compelled to assert that the rock had once for all cropped above the surface on the historical soil (1 Cor. x. 4) and had provided the foundation for the building of the Kingdom of God (Eph. ii. 20)—that the Eternal had once for all irrupted into the temporal, the Meta-historical into the historical—and that the "hypothetical underlying unitary truth", which you project "at present beyond our range of vision" (p. 504, above), had once for all appeared in human flesh: "I am . . . the Truth" (John xiv. 6).' Yet the scientific truth explored by the Reason is, in fact, independent of the spiritual truth revealed in Christ.

[3] 1 Cor. xiii. 9.

[4] 1 Cor. xiii. 8.

does not command the beast's services. How are they to co-operate? They will never succeed so long as either imagines that he can dominate the other by sheer force; for the Subconscious, like some camel, mule, or goat, is merely stung into a maliciously obstinate contrariness by a touch of the whip, while, conversely, if the Subconscious wantonly takes the offensive against the Reason in seeking to overwhelm it by some demonic exertion of its own brute strength, it is apt not to break the Will but to steel it. In the everlasting intercourse between the two members of this indissoluble pair of psychic partners, aggression on either side can produce nothing but a mutual frustration. When Mithras has slain his bull, he still has the carcass on his hands and the murder on his conscience. A better way is indicated in a Zen Mahayanian Buddhist parable of the drama of the Soul that is presented in visual form in divers versions of 'the Ten Oxherding Pictures'.[1] In this encounter between beast and man the victory is won in the end not by Hêraklês' muscles but by Orpheus' music.

Riding on the animal, he leisurely wends his way home;
Enveloped in the evening mist, how tunefully the flute vanishes away!
Singing a ditty, beating time, his heart is filled with a joy indescribable!
That he is now one of those who know, need it be told?[2]

(*d*) THE PROMISE OF THE CHURCHES' FUTURE

1. *Man's Fellowship with the One True God*

If a generation born into the twentieth century of the Christian Era might dare to look forward to a day when Heart and Head would have been reconciled by a unison of charity, insight, and faith, they might also hope to persuade Heart and Head to concur in a reading of the significance of the Churches' past; and, if our findings on that point were agreed, they would provide a starting-point for entering on the last stage of our inquiry into the relation between churches and civilizations. After having found that churches are not cancers, and that they are no more than incidentally chrysalises, we have been looking into the alternative possibility that they may be a higher species of society. We cannot give our verdict on this issue without asking ourselves what light the significance of the churches' past may throw on the promise of their future.

In embarking upon this necessary yet hazardously speculative quest, we may take courage from a consideration that has already emerged.[3] The chronological 'yardstick' that gives the true measure of the churches' past and future is the Time-scale established by a Modern Western Physical Science; and on this Time-scale the species of human society that we have called the higher religions was, at the time of writing, still extremely young. This meant that, in comparing the value of the higher religions with the value of the civilizations and the primitive societies, students of History midway through the twentieth century of the

[1] See Suzuki, Daisetz Teitaro: *The Ten Oxherding Pictures* (Kyoto 1948, Sekai Seiten Kanko Kyokai).

[2] Op. cit., English translation of the poem accompanying Picture No. 6 in the first of the two versions of the series that are reproduced in this brochure.

[3] On pp. 452–5, above.

Christian Era were entitled, in judging the youngest of the three species, to take account of its potentialities as well as its already harvested achievements. Their inevitably tentative judgement on this basis might be confuted by the future course of events; for of course there was no guarantee in the mere effluxion of Time that promise would be fulfilled in performance. Manifestly, error lay in wait here to ensnare observers born into this generation; yet, considering the circumstances, they must reckon themselves less likely to err by counting chickens before they were hatched than by pronouncing the eggs to be addled before there had been time for incubation.

After giving ourselves this encouragement, tempered by this warning, let us ask ourselves what was the feature in a church which differentiated it from both a civilization and a primitive society and which led us to classify churches as a distinct, and higher, species of the genus in which all these three types of society were embraced. The distinguishing mark of churches was not their inclusion of dead and unborn, as well as living, human members, for a membership transcending the living generation was a feature that was common to all species; nor was the distinguishing mark of churches their inclusion of divine as well as human members, for all species of society had in common this feature likewise. The distinguishing mark of the churches was that they all had as a member the One True God—for this feature was shared by the churches with no other species of society but was common to all the churches alike, whether they regarded the personal aspect of the Godhead, through which He enters into a relation of fellowship with His creature Man, as a revelation of His essence or as an avatar, manifested to Man in a form which Man can grasp, of an Ultimate Reality that is beyond Personality. This human fellowship with the One True God, which had been approached in the primitive religions and been attained in the higher religions, gave to these certain vital virtues that were not to be found in either primitive societies or civilizations. It gave power to overcome the discord which was one of the inveterate evils of Human Society; it offered a solution of the problem of the meaning of History; it inspired an ideal of conduct which could be an effectively potent spiritual stimulus for the superhuman effort of making Human Life possible in This World; and it availed to exorcize the peril that was inherent in mimesis when this was oriented, not towards the One True God, but towards one of Man's fellow human creatures.

2. *The Promise of Overcoming Discord*

Discord is inveterate in Human Life because Man is the most awkward of all things in the World that Man is compelled to encounter; and Man has to face Man on two fronts: in the macrocosm as his neighbour and in the microcosm as himself.

'Of all tools used in the shadow of the Moon, men are most apt to get out of order';[1] and the source of this trouble becomes manifest when we put together the two facts that Man is a social animal and that Man is endowed with free will. The combination of these two elements in the

[1] Melville, H.: *Moby Dick*, chap. xlvi.

nature of Man—and both are key-elements in Human Nature—means that in any society consisting exclusively of human members there will be a perpetual conflict of wills; and this human conflict is bound to be more terrible than the blind struggle for life among non-human animals, because 'human passions are always characterised by unlimited and daemonic potencies of which animal life is innocent'.[1] Man is indeed always and everywhere the Faust that has been taken as the type of Western Man by the intuitive genius of Spengler; and, when a Faustian insatiability betrays Man's likeness to his Maker by grasping at infinity, this impact of Man's explosive vein of godlikeness upon his hidebound animal nature must produce some spiritual revolution or enormity[2] if it is not graced by the miracle of conversion.

Man's conversion is necessary for Man's salvation because his free and insatiable will gives him his spiritual potentiality at the risk of alienating him from God. This risk will not have beset a pre-human social animal not blessed—or cursed—with a spiritual capacity for rising above the level of the Subconscious Psyche; for the Subconscious Psyche enjoys the same effortless harmony with God that its innocence assures to every non-human creature.[3] This negatively blissful Yin-state, in which the Psyche 'was without form and void, and darkness was upon the face of the deep',[4] was broken up when human consciousness and personality were created through a Yang-movement in which 'the spirit of God moved upon the face of the waters'[5] 'and God divided the light from the darkness'[6] 'and divided the waters which were under the firmament from the waters which were above the firmament';[7] for Man's Conscious Self, which can serve as God's chosen vessel for the achievement of a miraculous spiritual advance if it seeks and finds that harmony with its Creator which the Subconscious possesses *ex officio naturae*, can also condemn itself to a lamentable fall if its awareness of being made in God's image intoxicates it into idolizing itself. This suicidal infatuation (*ἄτη*) which is the wages of the sin of pride (*ὕβρις*)[8] is a spiritual aberration to which the Soul is perpetually prone in the unstable spiritual equilibrium which is of the essence of Human personality;[9] and the Self cannot escape from itself by a spiritual regression into the Yin-state of *Nirvāna*. The recovered Yin-state in which salvation is to be found by Man is the peace, not of nerveless self-annihilation, but of taut-strung harmony. Psyche's task is the *tour de force* of recapturing a childlike virtue after having 'put away childish things'.[10]

[1] Niebuhr, R.: *The Nature and Destiny of Man*, vol. i (London 1941, Nisbet), p. 191. Compare p. 268.

[2] For the 'revolutions' and 'enormities' that are alternative possible disastrous outcomes of putting new wine in old bottles, see IV. iv. 133–7.

[3] For this sense in which the Subconscious is nearer to God than the Conscious Self, see pp. 498 and 501–2, above.

[4] Gen. i. 2.

[5] Gen. i. 2.

[6] Gen. i. 4.

[7] Gen. i. 7.

[8] See IV. iv. 245–61.

[9] This inevitable exposure of a 'high-powered' human personality to the risk of a spiritual disaster, from which the 'low-powered' pre-human Subconscious Psyche is exempt, is a spiritual analogue of the perilousness of a road on which mechanically propelled vehicles have replaced horse-carts and wheel barrows (see III. iii. 209–12). The self-discipline that is called for in the Soul if it is to find salvation is the counterpart of the traffic-control that is required in order to make a speedway safe for life and limb.

[10] 1 Cor. xiii. 11.

'Except ye be converted and become as little children, ye shall not enter into the Kingdom of Heaven';[1] but the Self has to achieve its childlike reconciliation with God by the manful exertion of a god-given will to do the will of God and thereby evoke God's grace.

If this is Man's way of salvation he has a rough road to tread; for the mighty act of creation that has made Man *Homo Sapiens* has, by the same stroke, made it mortally hard for Man to become *Homo Concors*, and a social animal that is an accomplished *Homo Faber* must co-operate or perish. The disastrous social consequences of an unresolved moral contradiction which the theologians had called Original Sin were written large on the pages of History.

In virtue of Man's innate sociality, every human society is potentially all-embracing. In a previous context[2] we have observed that every civilization had demonstrably radiated its influence over all the rest of Mankind; and the feebler radiation of the primitive societies, which is less easy to detect, is not likely to have been less ubiquitous. This constant mutual interpenetration of social influences makes any society unstable and provisional so long as it falls short of being world-wide (as all societies of every species had hitherto fallen short in fact); but here the egocentric pull of every individual human will comes contradictorily and obstructively into play. Down to the year A.D. 1952 no human society had ever yet become literally world-wide on every plane of social activity. A secularized Modern Western Civilization had latterly attained to virtual universality on the economic plane without having achieved any comparable political or cultural success;[3] and, after the shattering experience of two world wars in one lifetime, it was uncertain whether an indispensable and perhaps inevitable political unification of the World could come to pass without that grimly familiar 'knock-out blow' that had been the traditional price of oecumenical unity in the histories of civilizations of a less than literally world-wide extent.[4]

In the past this price had always proved prohibitively high; for civilizations which had arrived at political unity by this road had inflicted mortal wounds on themselves in the process; and the unification of a Westernizing World by the familiar method of military force was likely to wreak damage of an unprecedented degree of severity owing to the keying-up of the material 'drive' behind War through the triumphs of a Modern Western Technology.[5] The relentless advance of Man's command over Non-Human Nature, since the date in the Palaeolithic Age when his technological prowess had made him lord of all creation except himself,[6] had indeed been steadily accentuating the pressure of its challenge to Man to build for himself a society embracing the entire Human Race. But the ever-increasing urgency of this necessity had been obstinately ignored by the defiant egotism of human wills, and the efforts of civilizations to advance towards the goal of universality had been mocked by their proclivity to fall asunder on the political

1 Matt. xviii. 3 (see IV. iv. 248–9, and pp. 501–2, above).
2 In II. i. 187.
3 See I. i. 35–36.
4 This grave question is considered further in XII. ix. 524–36.
5 See IV. iv. 141–55.
6 See pp. 486–7, above.

plane into sovereign parochial states whose fratricidal warfare had been perhaps the most frequent cause of the breakdowns and disintegrations of civilizations up to date.[1] This self-inflicted calamity had overtaken the Western Civilization in its turn in its Modern Age, when the failure of the medieval attempt to establish a Papal *Respublica Christiana* had discredited the ideal of an oecumenical unity resting on the supremacy of the Church over the parochial states,[2] and when the success of the recent expansion of the West over the rest of the World had relieved the West from the pressure of hostile neighbour societies which had almost mechanically held a Medieval Western Christendom together.[3]

The truth is that the unity of Mankind cannot be achieved either by stitching together local communities into a pantheon of tribal deities presiding over a terrestrial conglomeration of parochial states, on the pattern of Cyrus's 'Kingdom of the Lands',[4] or by purging Society of its primitive divine participants and making Humanity itself the Absolute, as had been attempted by Humanists of a Modern Western school.[5] In another context[6] we have already taken note of the paradoxical but profound truth that the most likely way to reach a goal is to be aiming not at that goal itself but at some more ambitious goal beyond it. The unity of Mankind can be achieved only as an incidental result of acting on a belief in the unity of God,[7] and by seeing this unitary terrestrial society *sub specie aeternitatis* as a province of a Commonwealth of God which must be singular, not plural, *ex hypothesi*.[8]

This is the necessary condition because, without a harmony of wills, Society cannot maintain itself even on the most narrowly restricted tribal range, not to speak of its becoming world-wide, and the only society in which there can be a harmony of wills is one in which two or three—or two or three thousand million—are gathered together in God's name with God Himself in the midst of them.[9] In a society including the One True God as well as His human creatures, God plays a unique part. He is a party to the relation between each human member and Himself; but in virtue of this He is also a party to the relation between each human member and every other human member, and through this participation of God, breathing His own divine love into human souls, human wills can be reconciled.[10]

The great gulf fixed[11] between 'the open society' of the Commonwealth of God and 'the closed society' that is exemplified not only in primitive societies but in civilizations, and the spiritual leap without which this gulf cannot be crossed, had been pictured by a Modern Western pioneer philosopher in a passage, referred to in an earlier context,[12] which calls for quotation here.

[1] See XII. ix. 441–6.
[2] See IV. iv. 576–84.
[3] See I. i. 33–34.
[4] See V. v. 529–34 and V. vi. 15.
[5] See V. vi. 8.
[6] On p. 388, above.
[7] See V. vi. 9–16.
[8] On this point see further pp. 558–9, below.
[9] Matt. xviii. 20.
[10] This reconciliation is not, of course, automatic, and indeed the intervention of the One True God in Man's struggle with himself for the attainment of social unity is a challenge which may evoke in response, not love, but a hate-inspired intolerance (see IV. iv. 222–9, and pp. 430–1, above).
[11] Luke xvi. 26.
[12] In V. vi. 12.

'L'homme [a] été fait pour de très petites sociétés. Que telles aient été les sociétés primitives, on l'admet généralement. Mais il faut ajouter que l'ancien état d'âme subsiste, dissimulé sous des habitudes sans lesquelles il n'[y] aurait pas de civilisation. . . . Le civilisé diffère surtout du primitif par la masse énorme de connaissances et d'habitudes qu'il a puisées, depuis le premier éveil de sa conscience, dans le milieu social où elles se conservaient. Le naturel est en grande partie recouvert par l'acquis; mais il persiste, à peu près immuable, à travers les siècles. . . . Le naturel est indestructible. On a eu tort de dire: "Chassez le naturel, il revient au galop",[1] car le naturel ne se laisse pas chasser. Il est toujours là. . . . Habitudes et connaissances sont loin d'imprégner l'organisme et de se transmettre héréditairement, comme on se l'était imaginé. . . . Refoulé, impuissant, [l'ancien état d'âme] demeure pourtant dans les profondeurs de la conscience . . . [et] il se maintient en fort bon état, très vivant, dans la société la plus civilisée. . . . Nos sociétés civilisées, si différentes qu'elles soient de la société à laquelle nous étions immédiatement destinés par la nature, présentent d'ailleurs avec elle une ressemblance fondamentale. Ce sont en effet, elles aussi, des sociétés closes. Elles ont beau être très vastes en comparaison des petits groupements auxquels nous étions portés par instinct . . . elles n'en ont pas moins pour essence de comprendre à chaque moment un certain nombre d'individus, d'exclure les autres. . . . Entre la nation, si grande soit-elle, et l'humanité, il y a toute la distance du fini à l'indéfini, du clos à l'ouvert. . . .

'De la société close à la société ouverte, de la cité à l'humanité, on ne passera jamais par voie d'élargissement. Elles ne sont pas de même essence. . . . La différence entre les deux objets est de nature, et non plus simplement de degré. . . . Qui ne voit que la cohésion sociale est due, en grande partie, à la nécessité pour une société de se défendre contre d'autres, et que c'est d'abord contre tous les autres hommes qu'on aime les hommes avec lesquels on vit? Tel est l'instinct primitif. Il est encore là, heureusement dissimulé sous les apports de la civilisation; mais aujourd'hui encore nous aimons naturellement et directement nos parents et nos concitoyens, tandis que l'amour de l'humanité est indirect et acquis.

'A ceux-là nous allons tout droit, à celle-ci nous ne venons que par un détour; car c'est seulement à travers Dieu, en Dieu, que la religion convie l'homme à aimer le genre humain; comme aussi c'est seulement à travers la Raison, dans la Raison par où nous communions tous, que les philosophes nous font regarder l'humanité pour nous montrer l'éminente dignité de la personne humaine, le droit de tous au respect. Ni dans un cas ni dans l'autre nous n'arrivons à l'humanité par étapes, en traversant la famille et la nation. Il faut que, d'un bond, nous nous soyons transportés plus loin qu'elle et que nous l'ayons atteinte sans l'avoir prise pour fin, en la dépassant. Qu'on parle d'ailleurs le langage de la religion ou celui de la philosophie, qu'il s'agisse d'amour ou de respect, c'est une autre morale, c'est un autre genre d'obligation, qui viennent se superposer à la pression sociale.'[2]

There can be no unity of Mankind without the participation of God; and, conversely, when the heavenly pilot is dropped by an insensately self-confident human crew, Society inevitably falls into a Time of Troubles—as has been testified, with an impressive conviction, by an

[1] 'Naturam expelles furcâ, tamen usque recurret' (Horace: *Epistulae*, Book I, Ep. x, l. 24).

[2] Bergson, Henri: *Les Deux Sources de la Morale et de la Religion* (Paris 1932, Alcan), pp. 24–25, 27–28, 288, 293, 297.

accomplished and sceptical Modern Western statesman in the light of the political experience of a lifetime ending in the failure of his attempt to engineer the restoration of a pre-Revolutionary *ancien régime.*

'La décadence des empires va toujours de pair avec les progrès de l'incrédulité. La foi religieuse, qui est la première des vertus, est précisément pour cela la plus grande des forces. Elle seule règle l'attaque et rend la résistance invincible. La foi ne peut pas diminuer chez une nation sans entraîner l'affaiblissement de cette dernière; or, la chute des états ne suit pas une progression arithmétique comme la chute des corps, elle ne tarde pas à conduire au néant.'[1]

In this prophetic passage, Metternich was foreboding the 'revolution of destruction' which had duly overtaken the Western World in a subsequent generation. The suffering and shame which Western Man had brought upon himself by the sin of 'totalitarianism'[2] had been a painful revelation of the truth that human beings cannot live without worshipping something. When they repudiate the worship of the One True God, they swiftly relapse into a worship of Leviathan.

3. *The Promise of Revealing a Spiritual Meaning in History*

When Man is out of fellowship with God, he not only lapses into a discord which is at variance with his innate sociality; he is also tormented by a tragic crux which is inherent in his being a social creature, and which therefore presents itself the more sharply, the better he succeeds in living up to the moral requirements of his social nature, so long as he is seeking to play his part in a society of which the One True God is not also a member. This crux is that the social action in which a human being fulfils himself immensely exceeds in its range, in both Time and Space, the limits of an individual's life on Earth. *Ars longa, vita brevis*[3] is a truth that is true of all the social activities of *Homo Faber*. This discrepancy is manifest in primitive societies, and it makes itself felt overwhelmingly in civilizations. Even in the most narrow-verged society the ablest, most energetic, and most fortunate individual cannot influence, or even survey, the action in which he is concerned beyond the close-drawn limits of a horizon which embraces no more than a fraction of the human actor's minimum field of action. Thus history, seen solely from the standpoint of each individual human participant in it, is 'a tale told by an idiot, signifying nothing'.[4] But this apparently senseless 'sound and fury' acquires spiritual meaning when Man catches in History a glimpse of the operation of a One True God who is both transcendently infinite and intimately loving, and who has the power and the will to take up His human creatures into His own range of action and mode of existence,[5] in so far as they respond to His challenging call

[1] Metternich, Le Prince de: *Mémoires*, vol. viii (Paris 1884, Plon-Nourrit), pp. 606–7. This passage, which was written in A.D. 1858, was brought to the notice of the writer of this Study by his friend and colleague Sir Charles Webster.

[2] The twentieth-century Western totalitarian states were 'enormities' in the sense in which the word has been used in IV. iv. 135.

[3] *Ὁ βίος βραχὺς, ἡ δὲ τέχνη μακρὴ, ὁ δὲ καιρὸς ὀξὺς, ἡ δὲ πεῖρα σφαλερὴ, ἡ δὲ κρίσις χαλεπή* (Hippocrates: *Aphorisms*, i. 1).

[4] Shakespeare: *The Tragedy of Macbeth*, Act III, scene ii, ll. 22–23.

[5] The sense in which Man can transcend the dimensions of Space and Time by enter-

to act in This World as partners in His divine work. 'God is not the God of the dead . . . but the God of the living . . . for all live unto Him.'[1] 'For He became man in order that we might be made God.'[2]

'If it is true that the existence of each individual goes on elsewhere in the Unseen World after he has passed from the stage of This World, there is a curious difference in the value which each individual life here has, according as it is considered in the one or the other of its two contexts. Looked at in its earthly context, it is something which is over in a moment, and counts for almost nothing in comparison with the relatively permanent things on this planet.

Time, like an ever-rolling stream,
Bears all its sons away;
They fly forgotten, as a dream
Dies at the opening day.

Even of our own great-grandfathers few of us know more than the names, and perhaps the place where they mostly lived. England, which abides, is important, but the individual Englishmen are creatures of a day, and perish like summer flies. . . .

'But when we look at the individual life in its other context, the relative importance of things is reversed. Human life may continue on this planet for another million years, but, sooner or later, it must come to an end. From this standpoint it is England which is destined to pass away, and it is the individual whose existence continues for ever. The actor who was on the stage for a brief ten minutes was a transitory appearance, looked at in relation to the play, but the life of the actor goes on long after the play is over.'[3]

Thus, while a civilization may be a provisionally intelligible field of study,[4] the Commonwealth of God is the only morally tolerable field of action; and membership in this *Civitas Dei* on Earth is offered to human souls by the higher religions; for, though these divers earthly embodiments of the *Civitas Dei* are, each of them, only partial and imperfect, they do all faithfully represent their original in offering Man membership in a society in which he will find himself in fellowship with God seen through a less dark glass than that which the primitive religions interpose. It was noteworthy that the two 'Indistic' higher religions—committed, though they were, to a philosophy which dismissed the phenomenal life of consciousness and action in This World as an illusion and condemned this illusion as an evil—had nevertheless conceded that an ultimately impersonal Reality manifests itself to Man in personal forms with which he can enter into communion, and they had

ing into communion with God is discussed further—with all diffidence in seeking to approach so great a mystery—on pp. 756–8, below.

[1] Matt. xxii. 32; Mark xii. 27; Luke xx. 38.

[2] *Αὐτὸς γὰρ ἐνηνθρώπησεν ἵνα ἡμεῖς θεοποιηθῶμεν.*—Athanasius: *Oratio de Humanâ Naturâ a Verbo Assumptâ et de Eius per Corpus ad Nos Adventu*, chap. liv (Migne, J.-P.: *Patrologia Graeca*, vol. xxv, col. 192), following Irenaeus: *Contra Haereses*, Book III, chap. xix, § 6: *Εἰ μὴ συνηνώθη ὁ ἄνθρωπος τῷ Θεῷ, οὐκ ἂν ἐδυνήθη μετασχεῖν τῆς ἀφθαρσίας.*

[3] Bevan, Edwyn: *Our Debt to the Past* (London 1932, British Broadcasting Corporation), pp. 10–11. Cf. eundem: *The Kingdom of God and History* (London 1938, Allen & Unwin), p. 57; *Christians in a World at War* (London 1940, S.C.M. Press), pp. 95–96.

[4] See I. i. 17–50, and pp. 1–2, above.

brought these personal gods and bodhisattvas within Man's reach on Earth in recurrent terrestrial epiphanies (*avatars*). It was also noteworthy that Islam, which shared with Christianity the Judaic vision of an Ultimate Reality that is a Personal God, but parted company with Christianity in reaffirming Judaism's uncompromising insistence on God's 'otherness' from Man and on His undifferentiated unity, had been drawn, after all, into an approach towards the Christian view by Man's deep need for God's fellowship. As Saint Athanasius had divined, God had to come down to Man's level in order to raise Man to His; and a religion which, in vindicating God's unity, had denied the divinity of Christ, had been constrained to find an equivalent for Christ's crucifixion in the martyrdoms of ʿAlī, Hasan, and Husayn, and even (in an extreme form of the Shīʿah) to transfigure these human heroes into incarnations of the Godhead.[1]

Man's fragmentary and ephemeral participation in terrestrial history is indeed redeemed for him when he can play his part on Earth as the voluntary coadjutor of a God whose mastery of the situation gives a divine value and meaning to Man's otherwise paltry endeavours; and this redemption of History is so precious for Man that, in a secularized Modern Western World, a crypto-Christian philosophy of History had been retained by would-be ex-Christian rationalists.

'Because they put faith in the Bible and the Gospel, in the story of creation and in the announcement of the Kingdom of God, Christians were able to venture on a synthesis of the totality of History. All subsequent attempts of the same kind merely replaced the transcendent end that assured the unity of the mediaeval synthesis by various immanent forces that served as substitutes for God; but the enterprise remained substantially the same, and it was the Christians who first of all conceived it: namely, to provide the totality of History with an intelligible explanation, which shall account for the origin of Humanity and assign its end. . . .

'The whole Cartesian system is based on the idea of an omnipotent God who, in a way, creates Himself and therefore, *a fortiori*, creates the eternal truths, including those of mathematics, creates also the Universe *ex nihilo*, and conserves it by an act of continuous creation, without which all things would lapse back into that nothingness whence His will had drawn them. . . . Consider the case of Leibnitz. What would be left of his system if the properly Christian elements were suppressed? Not even the statement of his own basic problem—that, namely, of the radical origin of things and the creation of the Universe by a free and perfect God. . . . It is a curious fact, and well worth noting, that, if our contemporaries no longer appeal to the *City of God* and the Gospel as Leibnitz did not hesitate to do, it is not in the least because they have escaped their influence. Many of them live by what they choose to forget.'[2]

4. *The Promise of Inspiring an Effective Ideal of Conduct*

A human being who, in this life, breaks the bounds of Time and Space by entering into communion with God is transfigured, if the communion becomes habitual, from a savage into a saint.

[1] See pp. 718–19, 731–2, and 733–4, below.

[2] Gilson, E.: *The Spirit of Mediaeval Philosophy*, English translation (London 1936, Sheed & Ward), pp. 390–1 and 14–17.

'Le sauvage qui est en nous et qui fait notre étoffe première doit être discipliné, policé, civilisé, pour donner un homme. Et l'homme doit être patiemment cultivé pour devenir un sage. Et le sage doit être éprouvé pour devenir un juste. Et le juste doit avoir remplacé sa volonté individuelle par la volonté de Dieu pour devenir un saint. Et cet homme nouveau, ce régénéré, c'est l'homme spirituel, c'est l'homme céleste, dont parlent les Védas comme l'Évangile, et les Mages comme les néo-platoniciens.'[1]

Such sainthood is indispensable for the maintenance of societies—even those of the pettiest and simplest and lowest kind—because even the minimum of unselfishness and determination and courage and vision that is required for making social life possible on Earth far exceeds the range of the natural altruism of a social animal.

I will not cease from mental fight,
Nor shall my sword sleep in my hand,
Till we have built Jerusalem
In England's green and pleasant land,[2]

is a resolution that can be taken only by a soul that, through eyes enlightened by communion with God, sees This World consecrated and illumined by God's indwelling presence. And the courage to abide by this resolution, in the face of disappointment and defeat, can be kindled only by a vision of the invincible action of God which reduces to insignificance the fickle fortunes of a desperate human battlefield.

For while the tired waves, vainly breaking
Seem here no painful inch to gain,
Far back, through creaks and inlets making,
Comes, silent, flooding in, the main.

And not by eastern windows only,
When daylight comes, comes in the light;
In front the Sun climbs slow, how slowly!
But westward, look, the land is bright.'[3]

This ideal of conduct is inspired by the saint's communion with God, and there is no effective alternative stimulus. The ideal of the sage breaks down because it tries to make Man become, not a saint inspired by the grace of a God who is Love, but a very god in himself in virtue of his own spiritual prowess; and for Human Nature this, if it were an attainable goal, would prove an intolerable burden. The moral impracticability of the enterprise is betrayed by the spiritual sterility of the aim. The Stoic or Epicurean philosopher seeks to be an isolationist God Incarnate; the Hinayanian arhat schools himself for the self-annihilation of the Buddha, not for the self-sacrifice of Christ. Such attempts at a withdrawal from the suffering and sorrow of This World without a return cannot bring salvation to Man because they are not truly godlike.[4]

This breakdown of a nobly austere Hellenic and Indic ideal of 'en-

[1] Amiel, H. F.: *Fragments d'un Journal Intime*, new edition by Bouvier, B. (Paris 1927, Stock; Geneva 1927, Georg, 2 vols.), vol. i, pp. 290–1.
[2] Blake, William: *Jerusalem.*
[3] Clough, Arthur Hugh: *Lines Written on the Bridge of Peschiera.*
[4] See V. vi. 132–48, and pp. 391–2, above.

lightened self-interest' proclaimed the bankruptcy of its basely self-indulgent Modern Western caricature; and the writing on the wall of this Circaean 'City of Swine' was clear to read even before the outbreak of a Second World War.

'In A.D. 1933 the state of the World already afforded a crushing refutation of the creed of Humanism which had inspired the march of Western Civilisation for more than four hundred years and which had received its definitive formulation in nineteenth-century England in the apotheosis of "Enlightened Self-Interest".

'The enthronement of this nakedly pagan goddess is announced—to take one out of many examples at random—in the following sentence of a pamphlet which was published by the Society for the Promotion of Christian Knowledge, and which went into its twelfth edition in A.D. 1850:

> "It is curious to observe how, through the wise and beneficent arrangement of Providence, men thus do their greatest service to the public when they are thinking of nothing but their own gain."[1]

'While formally ascribing to Divine Providence the ultimate credit for this newly discovered beneficence of the Old Adam, the votaries of Enlightened Self-Interest were unavowedly replacing Christianity by a worship of unregenerate Human Nature. And the lie direct, which, in the name of Deism, is given in this passage to the teachings of the New Testament and to the doctrines of the Christian Church, seemed unanswerable in the particular time and place in which the pamphlet was written and disseminated. In mid-nineteenth-century England the uncompromising denunciations of economic acquisitiveness in the New Testament were reverentially but unhesitatingly explained away as Oriental hyperboles, and the ecclesiastical ban upon usury was openly laughed to scorn as a superstition, because the superiority of the children of This World over the children of Light, in practical wisdom, seemed conclusively demonstrated in the eyes of those in authority in that generation. On the other hand in the year 1933, which saw the failure of the World Economic Conference and the World Disarmament Conference, the nineteenth-century proposition seemed as ludicrous a paradox as the Christian view of life, and of human relations, had seemed in the Western World of A.D. 1850. In Victorian England, as in Periclean Athens and in Medicean Florence, Humanism had seemed sufficient unto itself, because Man was then experiencing the momentary sensation of being triumphantly master of his own fate through the power of his own ἀρετή or *virtù* or science, without needing the intervention of God either to chasten or to inspire him. By the year 1933 it was once more manifest that, "when they" were "thinking of nothing but their own gain", men were not only quite incapable of serving the public, but were even impotent to manage their own personal affairs to their own personal advantage. So far from being the great constructive driving-force in social life, the myopic pursuit of selfish personal interest was shown to be doomed, *a priori*, to miss its mark. Self-interest had proved, once more, to be a target of human aims on which direct hits could never be registered. This object of human desires could only be attained incidentally by people who stumbled across it on their road towards a transcendental goal of endeavour; and it followed that, if and when self-interest, private or social, was ever successfully

[1] *Easy Lessons on Money Matters for the Use of Young People*, 12th ed. (London 1850, S.P.C.K.), quoted by J. M. Keynes: *Essays in Persuasion* (London 1931, Macmillan), p. 85.

realised in this fortuitous way, it would turn out to be something with no recognisable likeness to the earthly paradise of *Homo Economicus.*

'Thus, as so often before, the so-called paradoxes of Christianity were proved to be truisms, while the children of This World were numbered once again among "the silly people who do not even know their own silly business". They were, in fact, most ludicrously convicted, in this chapter of history, of having sacrificed their own substantial interests to an academic dream. For the histories of the World Disarmament Conference and the World Economic Conference completed the proof that "Enlightened Self-Interest", so far from being an automatic, self-regulating psychological mechanism for making all things work together for Man's good, was nothing more than an intellectual abstraction which had no counterpart at all in the realm of practical life.'[1]

The association of the words 'enlightened' and 'self-interest' is, indeed, a *contradictio in adjecto* when 'enlightenment' is taken to mean a blindness to everything supernatural and superhuman in Man's vision of the Universe. In such a *Weltanschauung*, in which the Heavenly Light has been 'blacked out', 'enlightenment' does not lead even to the common-sense conclusion that the interest of the individual is inseparable from 'the greatest good of the greatest number'. Within the narrowing moral horizon of a godless universe, in which piety towards the dead has become inept, and providence for the unborn quixotic, a concern for the living generation of his fellow men also ceases to be within the individual's moral capacity. Thus, paradoxically, pure rationalism applied as a rule of conduct leads to the conclusion that the only 'realistic' course is to abandon Society to the irrational play of Chance; and this philosophy of prosaic despair begets a policy of monochronistic hedonism: 'Let us eat and drink; for to-morrow we die.'[2] *Brevis hic est fructus homullis.*[3]

Thus a society whose ever more complicated structure depends for its maintenance upon planning on the grand scale may lose the indispensable minimum of moral virtue at the moment when it has attained the requisite degree of intellectual capacity.[4] It is, no doubt, emotionally abhorrent, as well as intellectually inept, to make irrevocable sacrifices in the hope of unguaranteed rewards; and, since, in terms of wordly results, every human endeavour may be proved by the event to be so much labour lost, Man would paralyse his powers of action altogether if he were ever to succeed in devaluing to zero the moral reward that is intrinsic in doing right, whatever the material consequences. Action is creation; and this godlike activity is possible for God's creatures only in so far as they surrender their wills to their Maker and thereby consecrate their action to the service of an actor whose plan is not subject to the miscarriages that so often overtake the best laid schemes of mice and men. The surrender of Man's will to God was the first and last commandment of a religion whose Founder had chosen this watchword

1 Toynbee, A. J., and Boulter, V. M.: *Survey of International Affairs, 1933* (London 1934, Milford), pp. 4–5.
2 1 Cor. xv. 32. Cp. Luke xii. 19 and Eccles. ii. 24.
3 Lucretius: *De Rerum Natura*, Book III, l. 914.
4 See IV. iv. 184–5.

to be its name; and *islām* was offered for love's sake in the prayer of Saint Ignatius Loyola:

'Suscipe, Domine, universam meam libertatem; accipe memoriam, intellectum et voluntatem omnem. Quidquid habeo vel possideo, mihi largitus es; id tibi totum restituo, ac tuae prorsus voluntati trado gubernandum. Amorem tui solum cum gratiâ tuâ mihi dones, et dives sum satis, nec aliud quidquam ultra posco.'[1]

The evaporation of this prayer out of a desiccated heart had deprived a Modern Western *Homo Economicus* of the faculty which his Nazi Western adversary had aptly labelled *Aktionsfähigkeit*. The self-same 'enlightened self-interest' that had given him the technical skill to build a liner or a sky-scraper or a wireless station or an atom bomb plant had robbed him of the moral power to act on the unselfseeking motives, and to take the long views, which his marvellous technique required of him in order to allow it to bear fruit. An eighteenth-century English Whig landowner, who had put his treasure into the founding of a family, would plant avenues which even his grandchildren would not live to see with the eye of the flesh in the glory of the timber's full-grown stature. A twentieth-century Ministry of Agriculture planted soft wood to replace the hard wood that it felled; and, in this greediness for quick returns, it was advertising its disbelief in its own immortality, however loudly it might shout *Le Roi est mort! Vive le Roi!* The business men who had taken over from the landowners the management of a British Conservative Party had restricted the horizon of politics to the range of their own myopic commercial vision. *Après moi le déluge*, if business is booming today.

In June 1936, at a moment when the Western World was faced with a choice between checkmating Italy's aggression against Abyssinia and condemning itself to wage a Second World War, a British statesman-manufacturer who gave the *coup de grâce* to collective security betrayed an utter unawareness of the issue that was at stake. In Neville Chamberlain's eyes at that juncture, Great Britain's stand in support of the Covenant of the League of Nations was not a far-sighted attempt to avert a political catastrophe by upholding a moral principle; it was a perverse freak of pedantry which, by making bad blood between Great Britain and Italy, threatened to check the incipient recovery from the great depression that had afflicted the Western World in the opening years of that decade. This transitory return of economic prosperity was, for Chamberlain, the supreme reality that dominated his field of vision. 'The National Government . . . was able to point to a recovery which

[1] In *The Spiritual Exercises of Saint Ignatius*, edited by Rickaby, S. J., Joseph (London 1915, Burns & Oates), p. 209, the original Spanish text is given with the following English translation:

'Tomad, Señor, y recibid toda mi libertad, mi memoria, mi entendimiento, y toda mi voluntad, todo mi haber y mi poseer: vos me lo distes; á vos, Señor, io torno, todo es vuestro, disponed á toda vuestra voluntad. Dadme vuestro amor y gracia, que esta mi basta.'

'Take, O Lord, and receive all my liberty, my memory, my understanding, and all my will, all I have and possess: you have given it to me; to you, O Lord, I return it; all is yours; dispose of it entirely according to your will. Give me your love and grace, because that is enough for me.'

exceeded that of any great industrial nation in the World.... All around to-day were signs that the national prosperity was still mounting.' This was the leading note of an after-dinner speech, delivered by Chamberlain on the 10th June, 1936, in which he expressed the opinion that the continuance of economic sanctions against Italy on behalf of her victim, Abyssinia, was 'the very mid-summer of madness',[1] and of another address, delivered on the 27th of the same month, in which the same speaker asked whether a political opponent of his would 'suggest ... that we should expose our people to the risk of those horrors which so shocked us when they were applied to Abyssinia?'[2]

> The Youth, who daily farther from the East
> Must travel, still is Nature's priest,
> And by the vision splendid
> Is on his way attended;
> At length the Man perceives it die away,
> And fade into the light of common day.[3]

And, 'where there is no vision, the people perish'.[4] The epigoni of the paladins push their 'realism' to a point at which 'enlightened self-interest' spells an unheroic self-immolation—in the craven spirit of those Egyptian fallāh-conscripts who, with rifles grounded and bayonets unfixed, used to kneel in orderly ranks with their throats meekly uplifted for the Sudanese Mahdist warrior to cut at his ease.

These poor creatures allowed themselves to be massacred for lack of even that modicum of public spirit that was needful for saving their own skins;[5] their Mahdist adversary conquered in virtue of a visionary willingness to die for his leader and his faith; and, when this Sudanese strong man armed was overcome physically by a stronger than he,[6] his vision did not fail him. The 2nd September, 1898, which saw the annihilation of the hosts of the Khalīfah of the Mahdī Muhammad Ahmad at Omdurman, 'was the last day of Mahdism, and the greatest'.[7] The virtue of the barbarian who dies fighting for his tribe against hopeless odds—undismayed by the calculation that, on an 'enlightenedly self-interested' reckoning, he is sacrificing his life in vain—was exhibited on that day by the aged standard-bearer who charged a battalion armed with magazine rifles,[8] and by the three survivors out of thirty thousand dead who stood facing three thousand victors, with their arms round the staff of their flag, till Death claimed them likewise.[9] The same spirit was shown thirty-seven years later by the Amhāra when, in A.D. 1935, they ran to meet certain defeat and death at the hands of a Western aggressor

1 See Toynbee, A. J. and Boulter, V. M.: *Survey of International Affairs, 1935* (London 1936, Milford), vol. ii, pp. 462–4.
2 See op. cit., p. 446.
3 Wordsworth: *Intimations of Immortality from Recollections of Early Childhood.*
4 Prov. xxix. 18.
5 By contrast, it was observed that the Spartans usually came off with comparatively light casualties, just because they went into battle with an exceptionally strong determination to lose their lives rather than survive with dishonour (see the passage quoted from Xenophon in III. iii. 63).
6 Luke xi. 21–22; cp. Matt. xii. 29; Mark iii. 27.
7 Steevens, G. W.: *With Kitchener to Khartum,* 10th ed. (Edinburgh and London 1898, Blackwood), p. 204.
8 See ibid.
9 See ibid., pp. 282–3.

whose armoury had been reinforced, since the turn of the century, by the invention of aircraft and of poison-gas.

> κεῖνοι μέν, γυμνοὶ καὶ βάρβαροι ἄνδρες ἐόντες,
> ὄργανα φρικώδους οὐκ ἐφοβοῦντ' Ἄρεως,
> ἀλλ' αὐτοσχεδίῃ, ἔτ' ἐλεύθεροι, οὔ τι τρέσαντες,
> εἰς Ἀΐδην καλῶς μαρνάμενοι κάτεβαν.
> ἡμεῖς δ' οἱ μεγάλοι καὶ καρτεροί, οἱ σοφοί; ἡμῖν
> τῶν αὐτῶν ὀδυνῶν γευσαμένοισι θανεῖν
> μοῖρ', ἀλλ' οὐ θάνατον τὸν Ἀρήϊον· οὔποτε τοῖον
> τοῖς ἐπιορκοῦσιν δῶρον ἔδωκε Θεός.[1]

In a Modern Western social milieu in which the *reductio ad absurdum* of an 'enlightened self-interest' seemed to be extinguishing the vision without which Society cannot endure, the writer's generation had lived to see the example of a primitive barbaric virtue inspire a demonic Neo-Paganism. Fascism and Nazism had been formidable, in their brief hour, in so far as they had succeeded in winning the allegiance of good characters and in appealing to the better side of bad characters; and the touch of moral attractiveness, which was their strength, was due to their melodramatic repudiation of the *laisser-faire*, the utilitarianism and the *surtout pas de zèle* that had been the pedestrian principles of a commercial-minded age of Western history. This militant totalitarianism,[2] aping the tribalism of Primitive Man, had, of course, been only a pathological exaggeration of a parochial patriotism, caught by the West from a resurgent Hellenism[3] at the dawn of the Modern Age of Western history,[4] which, since this renaissance, had gradually come to be perhaps four-fifths of the effective religion of five-sixths of the people of the

[1] These Greek verses were first published in *The Times*, under a letter from the writer of this Study, on the 22nd April, 1936. The following translation, by G. M. Gathorne Hardy, appeared in *The Times*, under a letter from him, on the 25th of the same month:

> Without our arms or art, these men could dare
> War's utmost frightfulness, since men they were,
> And, in close fight, to death untrembling passed,
> Still freemen, battling nobly to the last.
> But we, whose science makes us strong and great,
> Are doomed to share the tortures of their fate,
> Yet not their soldier's grave; the gods in scorn
> Withhold that privilege from men forsworn.

[2] See pp. 439–40, above.

[3] See X. ix. 7–8.

[4] This reversion, in a Modern Western World, to the principal cult of Hellenic paganism had generally carried with it, as its corollary, an avowed or tacit repudiation of Christianity. At certain times and places, however, this Western Neo-Paganism had had the hardihood to try to turn Christianity to its own account by treating it as if it were an ancestral pagan religion which it was convenient to preserve as an integral part of the social heritage of the secular community—as, in the Athenian city-state, the worships of Demeter and Dionysus and All Souls had been associated with the corporate self-worship of Athena Poliûchus as part-and-parcel of a totalitarian communal life in which there was no distinction between Church and State. This had perhaps been the prevalent attitude towards Christianity in Modern Italy during the century immediately preceding the Counter-Reformation; and, in the same spirit, the Modern French bourgeoisie had shown signs, in the nineteenth century, of reverting to a worldly-wise Catholicism from an 'enlightened' anti-clerical agnosticism. This latter-day movement in France was sketched in A.D. 1929 in the following terms, in a private letter to the writer of this Study, by an eminent French student of French life and politics:

'In my opinion, the renaissance of French Catholicism is closely bound up with the evolution of the French bourgeoisie itself. In 1848 the bourgeois took fright at the Revolution. Until then they had been, at bottom, Voltairians (though this did not

Western World.[1] The hold gained by this Neo-Hellenic corporate self-worship on a majority of ex-Christian hearts was due to its power of inspiring its votaries to give their lives on its behalf. Under the ashen deposit of 'enlightened self-interest' this fire lay hidden, yet unextinguished, in the hearts of Neville Chamberlain's countrymen; and Winston Churchill was able to blow it into sudden flame when the Fascist Powers scattered the ashes, to their own undoing, by assault and battery. When, in the summer of A.D. 1940, a Modern Western 'nation of shopkeepers' woke up to find itself with its back to the wall, it upset all Hitler's calculations, and thereby doomed him to ultimate defeat, by emulating the antique virtue of the Sudanese at Omdurman and the Abyssinians at Lake Ashangi.[2]

This unconsciously far-sighted folly that could move men to die for their country showed that the Modern Western cult of patriotism—whether in the Apollinean democratic or in the Dionysiac totalitarian vein—was in truth a religious revival in the spiritual vacuum left in human hearts by the evaporation of a higher religion. But the tragedy

prevent them from holding that "religion is wanted for the people"). Towards 1848 they began to say to themselves: "The *curé* is the best support of the *gendarme*." Thus they tended to become Catholics out of social apprehension; but these were Catholics without conviction. Their children, brought up in the Church, accepted the Catholic religion in another spirit towards the end of the century. The younger generation was suffering from the excessive individualism of the age; it sought in the Church a moral armour against anarchy. This Catholicism was of a higher kind, but it was not yet really religious; it was a political Catholicism to a large extent. On the eve of the War (that is, since about 1907) a new phase set in. The younger people, tired of pure intellectualism, found vent in action, in sport. They felt the approach of the War and prepared themselves for meeting it. Their Catholicism took the form of an affirmation of faith, of action, of devotion to their country.'

This movement was carried to extremes by the moving spirit of *L'Action Française*, Charles Maurras, who 'explicitly commended the Catholic Church on the ground that it had de-Christianized Christianity and had thus laid the foundations for a Neo-Paganism devoted to the cult of the sovereign national state'. This audacious attempt 'to press a church which was supra-national in the essence of its being into the service of a militant nationalism which claimed an ultimate and absolute value for itself' drew down upon Maurras' head, in January 1914, a condemnation of his journal, together with several books from his pen, by the Second Congregation of the Index at the Vatican; but, in confirming this decree, Pope Pius X forbore to make it public, in deference to representations from eminent French Catholics who had 'welcomed Monsieur Maurras' left-handed benediction of their faith on the calculation that the force of his personality and the charm of his literary style would propagate the faith in certain quarters in France, particularly among the younger generation, where it had little prospect of regaining a footing under any other auspices'. After a delay that was partly due to the dossier's having been temporarily mislaid in the Vatican archives, the decree of January 1914 was confirmed by Pope Pius XI on the 29th December, 1926, and was published early in 1927. (See Toynbee, A. J., and Boulter, V. M.: *Survey of International Affairs, 1929* (London 1930, Milford), pp. 480–1, 483–4, 487–8).

This exploitation of a Catholic Christianity for pagan political purposes was, of course, only one of a number of diverse movements in the life of a nineteenth-century French Catholicism which was at the same time giving birth to great philosophers, great missionaries, and great saints (see IV. iv. 582).

[1] See p. 478, above.

[2] Churchill's decision in August 1940 to send powerful reinforcements from the British Isles to the British armies in the Middle East at a moment when the Battle of Britain was at its height in the air, when the victorious German armies were massed along the continental shores of the Channel, and when Great Britain was hourly expecting to be invaded on the ground by an enemy against whom she was momentarily defenceless, was an act of imaginative courage that is worthy to rank with the three great Roman deeds that have been compared with one another in this Study in a passage (III. iii. 269) written about six years before the outbreak of the General War of A.D. 1939–45.

of this Neo-Paganism was that its blinkered idealism only availed to replace its self-sacrificing votary's foot on the lowest rung of a ladder which had been scaled, to the summit, by the martyr, the bodhisattva, and the saint whose lead the neo-pagan's forefathers had once followed. A reinstituted worship of Leviathan is not the happy substitute that Frazer holds it to be[1] for the neglected worship of a One True God.

The only heart in which self-interest is truly 'enlightened', and therefore practically effective as a motive for action, is the heart of the saint who identifies his self-interest with the service of God and who therefore sees the field of action from God's angle of vision. He surveys the field from a height at which the authentic lineaments of the everlasting hills are not obscured by the mirage of uncertainty which pervades the landscape when it is regarded from the pedestrian human level. The saint is not paralysed by a horror of seeking unguaranteed rewards at the cost of irrevocable sacrifices, because he is convinced that the standpoint from which human action appears to be the unprofitable pursuit of a will-o'-the-wisp is one that gives a falsifyingly fragmentary vision of Reality. Such godlike enlightenment inspired the confidence and fortitude that Jesus and Socrates and More displayed when they forbore to embrace opportunities held out to them for saving their lives at the price of compromising the truth which it was their mission to proclaim.

'After this, as the duke of Norfolk and Sir Thomas More chanced to fall in familiar talk together, the duke said unto him: "By the mass, Master More, it is perilous striving with princes. And therefore I would wish you somewhat to incline to the King's pleasure; for by God's body, Master More, *Indignatio principis mors est.*"

' "Is that all, my Lord?" quoth he. "Then in good faith is there no more difference between your Grace and me, but that I shall die today and you tomorrow." '[2]

. . . . .

'When Sir Thomas More had continued a good while in the Tower, my Lady, his wife, obtained license to see him; who, at her first coming, like a simple ignorant woman, and somewhat worldly too, with this manner of salutation bluntly saluted him:

' "What the good year, Master More", quoth she, "I marvel that you, that have been always hitherto taken for so wise a man, will now so play the fool to lie here in this close filthy prison, and be content thus to be shut up amongst mice and rats, when you might be abroad at your liberty, and with the favour and goodwill both of the King and his Council, if you would but do as all the bishops and best learnèd of this realm have done. And, seeing you have at Chelsea a right fair house, your library, your books, your gallery, your garden, your orchard, and all other necessaries so handsome about you, where you might in the company of me your wife, your children, and household, be merry, I muse what a God's name you mean here still thus fondly to tarry."

'After he had a while quietly heard her, with a cheerful countenance he said unto her: "I pray thee, good Mistress Alice, tell me one thing."

[1] See the passage quoted on pp. 383–4, above.

[2] Roper, William: *The Life of Sir Thomas More*, edited by E. V. Hitchcock (Early English Text Society, original series No. 197, London 1935, Oxford University Press), pp. 71–72, as quoted with modernized spelling in R. W. Chambers, *Thomas More* (London 1935, Cape), p. 300.

' "What is that?" quoth she.

' "Is not this house", quoth he, "as nigh heaven as mine own?"

'To whom she, after her accustomed homely fashion, not liking such talk, answered, "Tilly vally, Tilly vally".

' "How say you, Mistress Alice", quoth he, "is it not so?"

' "Bone deus, Bone deus, man, will this gear never be left?" quoth she. . . . So her persuasions moved him but a little.'[1]

'The time has come', in the words ascribed to Socrates at the close of an address to his judges which was nominally a defence but was actually a refusal of a possible avoidance of the death-penalty, 'the time has come for us to go—I, Socrates, to my death, and you to carry on with your lives. Which of these two destinations is the better? That is a riddle which can be read by God alone.'[2]

τίς οἶδεν εἰ τὸ ζῆν μέν ἐστι κατθανεῖν
τὸ κατθανεῖν δὲ ζῆν κάτω νομίζεται;[3]

No human being in this life can answer this question in terms that will guarantee to him, as his dividend, the maximum of worldly advantage; but a Socrates can answer it, in terms that will ensure his own condemnation to death, in the strength of his communion with a God from whose love 'nor height nor depth nor any other creature shall be able to separate us'.[4]

In the light of the truth that a goal can often best be reached by aiming, not at it, but at some more ambitious goal beyond it,[5] we can now see the explanation of the paradox that, by striving single-mindedly to act as good citizens of the *Civitas Dei*, the saints succeed incidentally in saving the situation for social life in This World within the vastly larger framework of their own spiritual field of activity.[6] Even a mundane law and order can be effectively established on Earth only on the model of a building that 'we have from God—a house not made with hands, eternal in the Heavens'.[7]

5. *The Promise of Exorcizing the Perilousness of Mimesis*

The Achilles' heel in the social anatomy of a civilization is, as we have seen,[8] its dependence on mimesis as a 'social drill' for ensuring that the rank-and-file of Mankind shall follow their leaders. In the change over from a Yin-state into a Yang-activity which takes place at the genesis of a civilization through a mutation in the character of a primitive society, the rank-and-file transfer their mimesis from the ancestors[9] to creative human personalities of the living generation;[10] but the avenue

[1] Roper, ed. Hitchcock, pp. 82–84, as quoted with modernized spelling in Chambers, pp. 25–26.

[2] Plato: *Apology*, 42A.

[3] Euripides: *Polyeidus*, fragment 2.

[4] Rom. viii. 39.

[5] See pp. 388 and 510, above.

[6] On this point see III. iii. 267–9. The spiritual peril to which a terrestrial embodiment of the *Civitas Dei* exposes itself by such incidental mundane achievements is examined on pp. 545–8, below.

[7] 2 Cor. v. 1.

[8] In III. iii. 245–8 and IV. iv. 119–33.

[9] 'The mass of Mankind plods on, with eyes fixed on the footsteps of the generations that went before, too indifferent or too fearful to raise their glances to judge for themselves whether the path on which they are travelling is the best, or to learn the conditions by which they are surrounded and affected' (Galton, Francis: *Hereditary Genius* (London 1869, Macmillan), p. 197).

[10] See II. i. 192.

thereby opened for a social advance may end in a *ianua leti*,[1] since no human being can be creative except within limits, and even then no more than precariously, and, when an inevitable failure has bred an equally inevitable disillusionment, the discredited leader is apt to resort to force in order to retain an authority that is morally forfeit. In the *Civitas Dei* this peril is exorcized by a fresh transfer of mimesis—this time from the limitedly and precariously creative human personalities who are the ephemeral leaders of mundane civilizations to a God who is the source of all human creativity and whose own divine creativity is infinite.

This mimesis of God can never expose human souls that devote themselves to it to those disappointments and disillusionments that are apt to attend the mimesis of even the most godlike human beings, and that produce, when they do arise, that moral alienation of a restive proletariat from a now merely dominant minority which is one of the symptoms of social decline and fall. The communion between the Soul and the One True God cannot thus degenerate into the bondage of a slave to a despot, for in each of the higher religions, in diverse measure, the vision of God as Power is transfigured by a vision of Him as Love; and the presentation of this Loving God as a Dying God Incarnate is a theodicy which makes the imitation of Christ immune against the tragedy inherent in any mimesis that is directed towards unregenerate human personalities.

In the story of Christ's temptation in the wilderness at the beginning of His Ministry,[2] and of His Passion at the close of it,[3] He is presented in the Gospels as refusing, at the price of the Cross, to exercise a spiritually sterile option of imposing His divine will by an act of power. Let a renegade Dionysus indulge an ungodlike lust for human glory by conquering all the Kingdoms of the World,[4] and an unedifying animus against his pitifully unsuspecting human persecutor by dealing him, out of the blue, a blasting blow. A divinity who subjugates India and takes his revenge on Pentheus[5] demonstrates his power of taming men's bodies at the cost of alienating their feelings, while a God who suffers death on the Cross draws all men unto Him.[6]

'The story of the Temptations is, of course, a parable of His spiritual wrestlings. . . . It represents the rejection, under three typical forms, of all existing conceptions of the Messianic task which was to inaugurate the Kingdom of God. Should He use the power with which, as Messiah, He is endowed to satisfy the creature wants of Himself and His human brethren, so fulfilling the hope of a "good time coming" which prophets had presented in the picture of the Messianic Banquet—(cf. e.g. *Isaiah* xxv, 6)? Should He be a Caesar-Christ, winning the kingdoms of the World and the glory of them by establishing an earthly monarchy and ruling from the throne of David in perfect righteousness—(cf. e.g. *Isaiah* ix, 6, 7)? Should He provide irresistible evidence of His divine mission, appearing in the Temple courts upborne by angels, so that doubt would

[1] Lucretius: *De Rerum Natura*, Book I, l. 1112; Book V, l. 373.
[2] Matt. iv. 1–11; Mark i. 12–13; Luke iv. 1–13.
[3] Matt. xxvi. 53; John xviii. 36; xix. 11.
[4] Matt. iv. 8; Luke iv. 5.
[5] See V. vi. 265–6.
[6] John xii. 32.

be impossible—(cf. e.g. *Daniel* vii, 13, 14 and *Enoch*)? Every one of these conceptions contained truth. When men are obedient to the Kingdom of God and His justice, everyone will have what he needs for food and clothing (*St. Matthew* vi, 33). The Kingdom of God is the realm of perfect justice where God's righteous will is done (*St. Matthew* vi, 10). The authority of Christ is absolute and can claim the support of the hosts of Heaven (*St. Matthew* xxviii, 18; xxvi, 53). Yet, if any or all of these are taken as fully representative of the Kingdom and its inauguration, they have one fatal defect. They all represent ways of securing the outward obedience of men apart from inward loyalty; they are ways of controlling conduct, but not ways of controlling hearts and wills . . . and the Kingdom of God, who is Love, cannot be established in that way.'[1]

In the imitation of Christ, this God who is Love draws the Soul towards Himself by evoking a love that is a response in kind to His; and because, in this communion of loves, there is no alloy of coercion, a travail in the Soul which begins as an exercise of mimesis bears fruit in a reception of grace, through which the Soul is enabled to partake of the inward spiritual qualities whose outward visible manifestations it has taken as its rule of life. Instead of ending in frustration, disillusionment, and strife, 'imitation' (μίμησις) here flowers into an 'assimilation' (ὁμοίωσις) of Man's nature to God's.[2] The 'light caught from a leaping flame', which was imparted to Plato's disciples 'by strenuous intellectual communion and intimate personal intercourse' with the Master,[3] now reappears as the gift of the Holy Spirit at Pentecost;[4] but, instead of being an esoteric initiation within the sanctum of an Academy which none but a properly qualified mathematician may enter,[5] the pentecostal fire is a grace that God can give to any human soul that truly seeks it.[6]

1 Temple, William: *Readings in St. John's Gospel*: First Series, Chapters i–xii (London 1939, Macmillan), pp. xxvi–xxvii.

2 See Plato, *Theaetetus*, 176A–E, quoted in V. vi. 165, n. 6, and Athanasius, *De Incarnatione*, chap. liv, § 3, quoted on p. 513, n. 2, above.

3 Plato's Letters, No. 7, 341B–E, quoted in III. iii. 245.

4 Acts ii. 1–4.

5 Μηδεὶς ἀγεωμέτρητος εἰσίτω is said to have been inscribed over the entrance to Plato's institute of philosophy at Athens (Tzetzes: *Chiliades*, Book VIII, l. 973).

6 See V. vi. 165–6.

B. THE ROLE OF CIVILIZATIONS IN THE LIVES OF CHURCHES

(I) CIVILIZATIONS AS OVERTURES

IF the foregoing inquiry has convinced us that the churches embodying the higher religions are diverse approximate projections on Earth of one and the same *Civitas Dei*, and that the species of society of which this Commonwealth of God is the sole and unique representative is of a spiritually higher order than the species represented by the civilizations, we shall be encouraged to go farther in our experiment[1] of inverting the assumption, on which we have tacitly proceeded in previous Parts of this Study, that, in the relation between churches and civilizations, the civilizations' role is dominant and the churches' role subordinate. Instead of dealing with churches in terms of civilizations, as hitherto, we shall boldly make the new departure of dealing with civilizations in terms of churches. If we are looking for a social cancer, we shall find it, not in a church which supplants a civilization, but in a civilization which supplants a church; and, if we have thought of a church as being a chrysalis through which one civilization reproduces itself in another, we shall now have to think, inversely, of the 'apparented' civilization in this genealogical series as being an overture to the epiphany of a church, and of the 'affiliated' civilization as being a regression from this higher level of spiritual attainment.

This finding answers a question which, in an earlier context,[2] we have been led to raise through noticing an apparent inconsistency in Plato's reading of one of the riddles of human destiny. Which, we have asked ourselves, are the true catastrophes: the breakdowns of civilizations or their births? Our answer now will be that the birth of a civilization is a catastrophe if it is a regression from a previously established church,[3] while the breakdown of a civilization is not a catastrophe if it is the overture to a church's birth.

The second of these two interdependent conclusions is, as will be seen, an application to the life of a civilization as a whole, in all chapters of its history and on all planes of its activity, of a truth that has already impressed itself on us in our study[4] of the political institution in which a disintegrating civilization is apt to embody itself in the penultimate rally before its final dissolution. We have seen that universal states succeed in being creative in so far as they serve beneficiaries other than themselves, and that the beneficiaries of universal states who have made the most fruitful use of their secular benefactors' services have been the churches. We can now see that, in discharging this creative mission of helping churches to come to birth, universal states are acting not simply on their own account but as representatives and agents of the

[1] See p. 420, above. [2] In IV. iv. 585–8.
[3] On this point see the passage quoted from Metternich's memoirs on p. 512, above.
[4] In VI, *passim*, but especially in Parts A and B, on pp. 1–52, above.

civilizations embodied in them; and, while their official mandate—which is to avert, and not merely to postpone, the dissolution of a disintegrating society—may be an inherently impracticable task, they may find compensation for a perhaps inevitable failure here in the magnificent success of enabling a dying civilization to complete the fulfilment of its historical *raison d'être*.

If we take, as a test case for the verification of this thesis, the genesis of the Christian Church, and cite the tenuous yet significant evidence afforded by the transference of words from a secular to a religious meaning and usage, we shall find this philological testimony supporting the view that Christianity is a religious theme with a secular overture, and that this overture consisted, not merely in the Roman political achievement of an Hellenic universal state, but in Hellenism itself, in all its phases and aspects.

The Christian Church is indebted for its very name to the technical term employed, in the city-state of Athens, to denote the general assembly of the citizen-body when it was meeting to transact political, as distinct from judicial, business; but, in thus borrowing the word *ecclesia* (ἐκκλησία), the Church gave it a dual meaning which was no part of the original Attic usage but was the reflection of a new political order, in which Athens and all other surviving city-states of a disintegrating Hellenic World had been incorporated into the Roman Empire without losing their identities as units of local government and life on the municipal level. In Christian usage, *ecclesia* came to mean both a local Christian community[1] and the church universal.

When the Christian Church, local and universal, came to be articulated into the two ecclesiastical classes of 'laity' and 'clergy', and when the 'clergy', in turn, came to be graded into a hierarchy of 'orders' in an ascending scale of dignity and authority, culminating in the 'order' of 'bishops', the requisite terms of ecclesiastical administrative art were likewise borrowed from an existing secular Greek and Latin vocabulary.

The 'laity' of the Christian Church was suggestively designated by an archaic Greek word (λαός) which denoted the people as distinct from those in authority over them, with a connotation of amenability to the word of command. In the vocabulary of the Homeric Epic the word had been used of the naïvely loyal *comitatus* of a barbarian war-lord; in a post-Alexandrine Age of Hellenic history it had been revived to serve as a technical term for the naïvely submissive labour force on one of the large-scale agricultural estates which the Hellenic conquerors of the Achaemenian Empire had taken over from a dispossessed Persian landed aristocracy.[2] The ambivalency in the *nuance*, half-heroic and half-servile, which the word had thus come to acquire by the date of the beginning of the Christian Era, aptly fitted the 'laity' of a church which, on its own spiritual plane, was both militant and authoritarian.

By contrast, the 'clergy' took its name from a Greek word (κλῆρος)

[1] When the 'outdoor' Hellenic Civilization gave place to the 'indoor' Orthodox and Western Christian civilizations, the word *ecclesia*, in its local meaning, came to be applied, not only to the local Christian community, but to the parochial building in which it assembled for congregational worship.

[2] For this Persian landed aristocracy, see pp. 123–4, above.

whose general meaning of 'lot' had been specialized in a juridical sense to mean an allotted share of an inherited estate, and in a political sense to mean an allotted share of a conquered territory. This political usage, which had been borrowed from Spartan conquerors in the Peloponnese[1] by Athenian conquerors in the Archipelago and Macedonian conquerors in Egypt and South-Western Asia, had given the word a rather unfortunate connotation by the time when the Christian Church began to work out its ecclesiastical organization. The Church adopted the word, nevertheless, to mean the portion of the Christian community that God had allotted to Himself to serve Him as His professional priesthood.[2]

As for the 'orders' (*ordines*) of clergy in the Christian ecclesiastical hierarchy, they took their name from the politically privileged classes in the Roman body politic, which were known as *ordines* both collectively and severally (*ordo senatorius*, *ordo equestris*), to distinguish them from the common run of Roman citizens.

The members of the highest order in the Christian hierarchy came to be known as 'overseers' (ἐπισκόποι), and the initial preposition, as well as the literal meaning, of this compound Greek word are likewise to be found in the title (ἔφοροι) which had been given in the Spartan body politic to the members of a board of supreme executive officers who were appointed by election but were constitutional despots during their term of office.[3]

The Christian Church's sacred book—taken over from the Jews and eventually augmented by the addition of an exclusively Christian 'New Testament' to supplement and retrospectively reinterpret 'the Old Testament' of Jewish origin—was presented by the Church as its credentials in the belief that this was the authentic Word of God Himself. In so far as the Bible was not referred to as 'the Books' (τὰ βιβλία) *par excellence*, it was designated by a term long since current in the vocabulary of the Roman inland revenue. In the fiscal terminology of a post-Hannibalic Roman Commonwealth the word *scriptura* signified the tax payable for the right to graze cattle on the public lands in the devastated areas in the South of Italy, because an entry in the official register, certifying that a would-be grazier had duly paid his tax, was the warrant that authorized him to make use of the public pasturelands. The Greek equivalent of the Latin *scriptura* was γραφή, and in a latter-day Kingdom of Greece at the time of writing there was a district in the Southern Pindus, between the plains of Thessaly and the west coast, which was still known as the Agrapha because the agents of an Ottoman inland revenue—and an East Roman inland revenue in an earlier age—

[1] See III. iii. 53, 57, and 68.

[2] 'The following seems to be the sequence of meanings by which the word κλῆρος arrived at this peculiar sense: (i) the lot by which the office was assigned [as in Acts i. 26]; (ii) the office thus assigned by lot [as in Acts i. 17]; (iii) the body of persons holding the office' (Lightfoot, Bishop J. B., in his edition of Saint Paul's Epistle to the Philippians, 7th ed. (London 1882, Macmillan), p. 247). This usage cannot be traced back to the Old Testament; for, though, according to Num. xviii. 20, God is the κληρονομία of Aaron, and, according to Deut. xviii. 2, He is the κλῆρος of the Levites, 'the Jewish priesthood is never described conversely as the special "clerus" of Jehovah, while on the other hand the metaphor thus inverted is more than once applied to the whole Israelite people' (Lightfoot, op. cit., p. 246).

[3] See III. iii. 56.

had never succeeded even in inscribing in their registers, not to speak of actually collecting, the taxes due from the wild highlanders in this mountain fastness. As for the two 'testaments' of which the Christian scriptures consisted, they were called διαθῆκαι in Greek and *testamenta* in Latin because they were thought of as being the equivalents of legal instruments in which God had declared to Mankind, in two instalments, His 'will and testament' for the ordering of Human Life on Earth.

The 'training' (ἄσκησις) to which a spiritually ambitious *élite* in the Early Christian Church subjected itself took its name from the physical training of athletes for the Olympian and other international athletic contests that were one of the characteristic expressions of the Hellenic culture; and, when, in the fourth century, training to be an anchorite (ἀναχωρητής) took the place of training to be a martyr in the psychological warfare of a Christian Church which had now made its peace with the Roman Imperial Government, the action of this new-model Christian athlete, whose ordeal was to endure the solitude of the desert instead of facing the publicity of the criminal court, came to be designated by a Greek term taken from the technical administrative vocabulary of the country that bred the pioneer Christian hermits. In Augustan Egypt 'anachôrêsis' (ἀναχώρησις) had meant withdrawal from productive economic activities in protest against the exactions of the taxation-authorities;[1] in Diocletianic Egypt the same word came to mean withdrawal from the World in protest against mundane human wickedness.[2]

When these solitaries (μοναχοί) had the courage to act on the lessons of their spiritual experience, in common-sense defiance of the literal meaning of their name, by subjecting themselves to the spiritual discipline of leading a common life together without surrendering the spiritual freedom won by withdrawal from the rest of the World, this creative contradiction in terms—a society of solitaries—took its Latin name from a word which, in its previous secular use, had combined the two meanings of a quarter sessions and a chamber of commerce.[3]

When the originally informal proceedings at the periodic meetings of each of the local Christian communities crystallized into a hard-and-fast ritual, this religious 'public service' (λειτουργία) took its name from the nominally voluntary *corvées* which, in a democratic Athenian Commonwealth in the fifth and fourth centuries B.C., had been euphemistically

[1] 'So early as A.D. 20 we hear of the flight (*anachôrêsis*) of tax-payers' (Bell, H. I.: *Egypt from Alexander the Great to the Arab Conquest* (Oxford 1948, Clarendon Press), p. 77).

[2] We have observed in an earlier context (on pp. 388–91, above) that this withdrawal of the anchorites was not anti-social either in intention or in effect. The anchorites influenced, aided, and, in great emergencies, sometimes actually governed a tottering Hellenic World with a moral authority which they would never have commanded if they had not proved the sincerity of their disinterestedness by insulating themselves physically from their fellow men.

[3] The provinces into which the Roman Commonwealth had organized its subject territories had been mapped out into districts corresponding to the principal cities which each province contained; and it had been customary for the provincial governor to go on circuit round these 'county towns', to transact judicial and other public business. During his stay in each 'county town' he expected the leading Roman citizens, resident in that district, to hold a rendezvous with him there to serve as his assessors in court and to assist and advise him in other ways. This rendezvous was known as a *conventus*, and the name came thence to be applied both to the standing organization of Roman residents in each district and to the geographical area itself.

known by that name in order to gloze over the truth that they were virtual surtaxes under the guise of 'benevolences'.

In the Christian liturgy the crucial rite was a Holy Communion in which the worshippers achieved a living experience of their fellowship in and with Christ by partaking together of the 'sacrament' (*sacramentum*) of eating bread and drinking wine. This Christian 'sacrament' took its name from a pagan Roman rite in which a new recruit was 'sworn in' to the fellowship of the Roman Army.[1] The Holy Communion which this common participation in the Christian sacrament consummated took its name from a word which, in the previous mundane usage of both its Greek original (*κοινωνία*) and its Latin translation (*communio*), had signified 'participation' of any kind, but, first and foremost, participation in the membership of a political community, for which the current term was coined, in both languages, out of the same verbal metal (in Greek *κοινόν*; in Latin *commune*).

One of the features of the Christian liturgy was a recurrence of its ritual in both annual and weekly cycles. The Christian liturgical week was modelled on a Jewish prototype; and, though the Christian copy had been differentiated from the Jewish original by making the first day of the week the holy day instead of the seventh, the Christian adaptation still followed the pristine Jewish dispensation in retaining the Jewish name for the eve of the Sabbath. In the Greek Christian vocabulary, Friday continued to be called 'the preparation' (*παρασκευή*)—in accordance with a Jewish usage in which this elliptical term explained itself. In the psychological atmosphere of a post-Exilic Judaism, in which a stateless diasporà maintained its *esprit de corps* by a common devotion to the keeping of the Mosaic Law, 'the preparation' *sans phrase* could mean nothing but 'the preparation for the Sabbath'. By analogy it is evident that the inevitable connotation of the word would be, not a liturgical, but a political one in the psychological atmosphere of a pre-Alexandrine Athenian sovereign city-state whose citizens worshipped their own then still potent corporate political power under the name of Athena Poliûchus. In the usage of Thucydides, writing for an Athenian public for whom politics were the breath of life, and whose political-mindedness was being accentuated in the historian's generation by the military ordeal of the Great Atheno-Peloponnesian War, the word *παρασκευὴ* could be used as elliptically as it was afterwards to be used in the Septuagint to convey, just as unmistakably, an entirely different meaning. Thucydides uses the word to signify what a generation of Englishmen, overtaken unawares by a world war in the year A.D. 1914, learnt ruefully to take to heart as 'preparedness' when they found themselves within an ace of defeat owing to their pre-war neglect to emulate the Germans in building up a stock of armaments to stand them in good stead in a fight for their national existence.

The customary preparation for the congregational performance of the Christian liturgy was, in a Western Christian town or village, the ringing

[1] In the Latin-speaking Church the word *sacramentum* was used from the beginning in the two meanings of sacrament and military oath, according to Harnack, A.: *Militia Christi* (Tübingen 1905, Mohr), pp. 33–34.

of a bell; and in a pagan Hellenic walled city this had likewise been a familiar sound with a well-established mental association. Yet a citizen of an Hellenic city-state—if his ghost could walk in some latter-day Western town on a Sunday morning—would never suspect that the sound that was filling the air was a summons to religious worship; for, to his mind, the ringing of a bell would conjure up the utterly different mental vision of a military patrol going its rounds along the city wall to inspect the sentries.

The change of usage from a secular to a religious meaning can be illustrated by other instances. The 'transgression' (παράβασις) which had been a term of art in the Attic 'Old Comedy', in the physical meaning of a parade of the chorus from one side of the theatre to the other, had come to mean, in Christian language, a figurative 'side-step' in the spiritual sense of a sin. Edification (*aedificatio*) had similarly come to mean the figurative 'building up' of virtue in the Soul in place of its original meaning of the construction of a material edifice in brick or stone. The Greek word πνεῦμα, with its Latin equivalent *spiritus*, had come to mean 'spirit' instead of 'breath', and the Greek word σωτὴρ to mean a saviour, not of Society, but of the Soul.[1]

The evocation of an inspiringly spiritual meaning out of a crassly material one is an example of a process which, in an earlier context,[2] we have learnt to know as 'etherialization'[3] and to recognize as a symptom of growth. Our foregoing survey of the etherialization of the Greek and Latin vocabulary, in the course of its transference from pagan to Christian use,[4] has been brief, casual, and nothing like exhaustive; yet,

[1] See V. vi. 175–278. [2] In III. iii. 174–92.

[3] A comic instance of etherialization-under-misapprehension was recounted to the writer of this Study in A.D. 1928 when he was on a visit to the city of Kovno, which was at that time the *de facto* capital of a sovereign independent Republic of Lithuania. Standing on the bank of the Niemen and gazing across the river's broad expanse, he noticed, on the farther shore, a three-story brick building, with a tower at one end, which looked as if it were new and which made a prominent mark in the landscape. 'Oh, that,' said his cicerone, 'is our brand-new national grain elevator. We are proud of its efficiency; but the peasants who come into the city to market from this side of the river venerate it for a droll reason which I will explain. As these peasants never have any occasion to cross the river, they have never seen that building from nearer than this, and from this distance it looks to them like a church, though as a matter of fact it has been built on the most up-to-date American pattern for a grain elevator, and, if its architecture does have an ecclesiastical air, the effect is quite undesigned. The peasants, though, would never think of that. In fact, it would never occur to them that such a large, handsome, and expensive building as this could be put up for any purpose except the glory of God; so, for the peasants, that imposing pile is now "the church of Saint Levatorius". How did they coin the name, you ask me? Well, you see, that name was pretty well inevitable. When the peasants asked what the building was, they were told, of course, "elevator"; and of course they took it for granted that this was the name of the supposed church's patron saint. So they added a Homeric termination (you realize, I hope, that Lithuanian is the best preserved of all the living Indo-European languages) and dropped the initial "e". That makes "Levatorius". And could any saint have a more convincingly appropriate name? Isn't it a saint's first business to give his protégés' souls a helping hand upwards on their way to Heaven—to serve, in fact, as a spiritual "elevator", if it isn't unpardonable blasphemy to describe traditional Christian aspirations in the telling terms of modern economic apparatus?'

[4] The evidence of language, which testifies to the part played by Christianity in the etherialization of the Hellenic culture, also reveals that, in this work of semantic metabolism, Christianity had been anticipated by Greek philosophy. For example, the 'self-sufficiency' (αὐτάρκεια) which, in a pre-Alexandrine Age, had been the economic objective of sovereign city-states, whose governments approached economics from the standpoint of politics and war, thereafter became the moral ideal of a sovereign Stoic

even so, the handful of Greek and Latin words whose history we have been following range so wide and cut so deep in their interpretation of life as to indicate that Hellenism was an authentic *praeparatio evangelii*, and that, in looking for the *raison d'être* of Hellenism in its service as an overture to Christianity, we have at any rate set our feet on a promising line of inquiry. In this perspective it looks as if a civilization that brings a church to birth and perishes in the creative act does not stultify itself by perishing, but, on the contrary, justifies its existence by carrying out its historical mission at the cost of its own life. The egg-shell has to be broken for the chicken to be hatched, and the mould has to be broken in order to disengage the metal casting; but this sacrifice of the means for the accomplishment of the end is not the brand of failure; it is the seal of success. The egg-shell that remains unbroken is the shell of an addled egg which has miscarried in its purpose of bringing a new creature to life; the casting-mould that remains unbroken is the mould that has been scrapped either because its own pattern has proved faulty or because the injected molten metal has proved base. On the same showing, when the life of a civilization has served as the overture, not to the miscarriage of an abortive church,[1] but to the birth of a living church that has 'shot up and thriven'[2] and 'grown in wisdom and stature',[3] the death of the precursor civilization is not a disaster but a triumph. What looks, on first view, like wasteful incompetence or

sage who towered, politically naked and therefore spiritually free, above the ruins of a city-state sovereignty that had collapsed under the blows of Macedonian war-lords (for this moral autarky of the post-Alexandrine school of Greek philosophy, see V. vi. 132–48 and 149–54). We may also remind ourselves that the word 'organ' (ὄργανον) had been adapted by Aristotle to mean a mental instead of a physical tool before, in Christian usage, it relapsed into meaning a physical instrument with the special function of making music in church.

[1] The number of abortive churches has, as we have seen, been large by comparison with the number of those that have been born alive and have grown unwarped. The rudimentary churches created by the internal proletariats of the civilizations of the first generation all failed to come to flower (see opposite Table IV, p. 772, below); and, among the four churches that were alive at the time of writing, those two—namely the Christian Church and the Mahāyāna—to which the Hellenic Civilization had served as an overture were survivors of not less than seven competitors—if we enumerate, as their unsuccessful rivals, the worships of Cybele and Isis, Mithraism and Manichaeism, and the popular religion which was a metamorphosis of the Neoplatonic philosophy. If any or all of these five failures had been successes, Hellenism would no doubt have served as an overture to them as effectively as it did in fact perform that service for Christianity and the Mahāyāna.

These five abortive churches had been defeated in a competition to be the chosen vessel for playing a church's authentic role. There had been other churches, as we have also seen, which, with this spiritual opportunity open to them, had committed spiritual suicide by going into politics. Cases in point were the syncretistic Egyptiac Church which had owed its foundation, in the reign of Thothmes III, to a Pharaonic act of state, and whose *ex officio* pontiff Hrihor, the Chief Priest of Amon-Re of Thebes, had tried to step into Pharaoh's shoes when the New Kingdom had sunk to its nadir; Zoroastrianism, Judaism, Nestorianism, and Monophysitism, which had allowed themselves to be used by a submerged Syriac Civilization as weapons in its warfare against a dominant Hellenism; and Imāmī Shi'ism and Sikhism, which had invested their spiritual treasure in the perverse political enterprise of founding a mundane empire. Islam alone had partially succeeded in retrieving a false step into which it had been led in its infancy by its Founder. When a church thus sells its birthright for a mess of potage it can no doubt sterilize a precursor civilization's creative work, and thereby posthumously render that civilization's death of no avail; but, in such an event, the true failure is, not the precursor civilization's dissolution, but the beneficiary church's repudiation of a heritage that has been bequeathed to it at so great a price.

[2] Herodotus, Book I, chap. 66.

[3] Luke ii. 52.

wanton sabotage turns out to have been a *chef-d'œuvre* of the craftsman's art.

In the shipyard, idly talking,
At the ship the workmen stared:
Someone, all their labour balking,
Down her sides had cut deep gashes:
Not a plank was spared.[1]

King Olaf, who has come to feast his eyes on the new craft to which his master-builder, Thorberg Skafting, was to have put the finishing touches, is enraged at the havoc and dumbfounded to hear, from the lips of the master himself, that the hand which has laboured all night to do this thing is Thorberg's own. But this at first sight insensate act takes on the very opposite complexion when, before the King's eyes, the craftsman finishes and vindicates his work by chipping and smoothing the cruelly-gashed planking into lines of a fineness that no shipwright has ever before achieved.

Our test case of the relation between the Hellenic Civilization and Christianity has been summed up, with an admirably judicial precision, by an American scholar writing between the two World Wars:

'Because the greatness of Christianity was not temporal but spiritual, its triumph boded ill for the State. Its final victory was only gained in the later fourth century; in the early fifth the western half of the Empire collapsed, and it is undeniable that the victory contributed to that fall. To the Christians the Empire lived in sin and must die before it could be re-born. It is true that many of them mourned the fall and hoped, and even prayed, that it might be averted; on the other hand few troubled to raise a temporal hand to forestall it. Already the cloud of predestination was darkening the bright new teleological sky: the natural wish to save the State into which they have been born must, like other temporal inclinations—to friendship, self-respect and prosperity—be repressed; for God was apparently ordaining otherwise, and men could only submit humbly to His will. On the other hand it is equally impossible to maintain that Christianity was a symptom of decadence. Ambrose, Augustine, and Bossuet were here more nearly right than Gibbon.[2] For these three said that Rome had come into being in order that out of it Christianity might spring; and this, because it respects the law of cause and effect, is an evolutionary conception at bottom. . . . Ambrose and Augustine had each, in his own way, outgrown Ancient Civilisation as he found it; each had learnt that Man was in fact something more than Antiquity had supposed.'[3]

(II) CIVILIZATIONS AS REGRESSIONS

We have been trying to see how History looks if we break with our Modern Western habit of viewing the histories of churches in terms of the histories of civilizations and adopt, instead, the inverse standpoint; and this essay in a reorientation of our historical outlook has led us, in the preceding chapter, to think of the civilizations of the second genera-

[1] Longfellow: *The Saga of King Olaf*, xiii: 'The Building of the Long Serpent.'

[2] See IV. iv. 58–63, and pp. 696–8, below.—A.J.T.

[3] Pickman, E. M.: *The Mind of Latin Christendom* (London 1937, Oxford University Press), pp. 133–4.

tion as overtures to the living higher religions, and consequently to regard those civilizations, not as failures branded as such by their breakdown and eventual disintegration, but as successes in virtue of their service in helping these higher religions to come to birth—a service which they were able to perform in the strength of their suffering, and which they might never have had an opportunity of performing if they had not fallen into adversity. On this analogy the civilizations of the third generation are presumably to be thought of as regressions from the higher religions that had arisen out of the preceding civilizations' ruins; for, if the mundane miscarriage of those now defunct civilizations ought to be judged to have been redeemed by its auspicious spiritual sequel, then the mundane achievement of the living civilizations in breaking out of their ecclesiastical chrysalises and setting out to live a new secular life of their own ought likewise to be judged on the criterion of its effect on the life of the Soul; and this effect had manifestly been an adverse one.

If we take, as a test case for the verification of this thesis, the eruption of a Modern Western secular civilization out of a Medieval Western *Respublica Christiana*, we may find it illuminating to begin, on the lines of our inquiry in the preceding chapter, by citing the evidence of words, sounds, and acts that had undergone a change of meaning and usage. The change that we were studying in our review of civilizations as overtures to churches was a change from a secular significance to a religious. In a review of civilizations as regressions from churches, the tell-tale change would be a change from a religious significance to a secular one. In taking note of such changes in the particular case of the transition to a secular Modern Western Civilization from a Medieval Western Christian Commonwealth, it will be convenient as far as possible to survey the fortunes of the same words, sounds, and acts in the order that we have followed in tracing the antecedent transition to Christianity from a pagan Hellenism.

In a secularized Modern Western World the 'cleric', whose designation once proclaimed him to belong to that portion of the Christian community that God had allotted to His own special service, had had to surrender his title to the 'clerk' who in England performed the minor office work in a government department or private business concern, and in America served behind the counter in a store.

The Christian Holy Communion, in which the communicants experienced their fellowship in and with Christ, had been implicated in a struggle for equality of rights which, in itself, had been a legitimate quest for justice, but which, at each successive stage in a history that had now run through many chapters, had been waged in ever grosser terms for an ever more material stake. In Bohemia in the fourteenth century of the Christian Era the battle for equality had been opened on sacramental ground; the issue had been between the laity and the clergy; and the stake had been communion in both kinds, which the Utraquists had demanded for the laity as against a clergy which had come to reserve the cup as a privilege for clerks in holy orders. In Holland and England in the Early Modern Age of Western History, and in the Western World as a whole after the outbreak of the French Revolution, the battle for equality, which by then had long ceased to be fought at the altar rails, had found a new field in a political arena, where the bourgeoisie now demanded a share in the political power that had been exercised under the *ancien régime* by oligarchies, aristocracies, and monarchies. In the twentieth century the industrial working class of a Western Society that had now become literally world-wide was demanding equality in the distribution of economic wealth of which the lion's share had been appropriated by the middle-class authors of an eighteenth-century and nineteenth-century industrial revolution. In this twentieth-century class-war, which was being fought for an economic stake, the militant movement on the anti-bourgeois side had adopted the name 'Communism' to signify that it was fighting for a 'commune' in which there should be a community of worldly goods. Communion in this kind, not communion in the body and blood of Christ, was the connotation that this Latin word had come to have in secular twentieth-century Western minds. The twentieth-century Communists had travelled far indeed from the battle-ground of their fourteenth-century Utraquist forerunners. And, though, in their obsession with a legitimate struggle for economic justice, they had raised the emotional temperature of a political 'ideology' to a religious heat, the authentic leaf that they had torn out of the book of Christianity[1] was as unedifying out of its context as it was salutary in itself.

The change of values registered in this change in the meaning of a talismanic word was a consequence of perversity among the clergy as well as the laity of Medieval Western Christendom. The vanity of a lust for power, that had betrayed the priesthood into turning the eucharist into an esoteric incantation in a liturgical language which had long since ceased to be the living mother tongue of any of their congregations, was exposed in the meaning that had been given to the unintelligible Latin operative words in the Mass in the vocabulary of an alienated English-speaking Christian people. An epoch-making chapter of psychological as well as linguistic history was summed up in the contemptuously blasphemous distortion of *Hoc est Corpus* into 'hocus-pocus'.

This desecration of the Christian sacrament was advertised in a change in the meaning, not only of gabbled ritual words, but of rhythmic instrumental music. The ringing of a bell, which, in Christian ears, had traditionally been associated with a church bell calling the congregation to worship or announcing to them that the operative act in the Sacrament of the Mass had just been consummated by the officiating priest, had come in a twentieth-century North America to be associated with the matter-of-fact business of everyday life. A tolling bell there now signified the approach of a locomotive that was warning the public to beware, not of losing their souls, but of getting themselves run over; a buzzing bell was associated with the mental alertness of an efficient bell-boy in an hotel, who would present himself expeditiously at the door of Room No. 666 as soon as the momentary occupant had pressed the button that set the right bell ringing in the bell-captain's lair.

[1] See V. v. 581–7, and p. 445, above.

The Greek word (πνευματικός) that had been consecrated by Christianity to signify 'spiritual' had been 'released', in the Modern Western vulgar tongues, from its traditional service of conveying 'the wind' that 'bloweth where it listeth',[1] to provide the missing name for the ingenious new Western invention of imprisoning compressed air within 'pneumatic' rubber tires.

The Latin word 'conversion' had likewise been converted from an otiose religious to a practical secular use. This ancient word still 'rang a bell' in Modern Western minds, but in these latter-day mental bell-rooms its associations were no longer with the conversion of souls; in Western Man's swept and garnished house the word would suggest to an industrialist the conversion of coal or falling water into 'power'; to a financier it would suggest the conversion of the rate of interest on a loan to a lower rate than that originally guaranteed to a confiding investor; while to a police detective it would suggest the misappropriation of funds by a financier who had gone beyond the limits of the considerable discretion that the Law allowed him. In this last-mentioned usage, 'conversion' conveyed its meaning to modern Western minds *sans phrase qualifiante*—a nice point of language which distinctly indicated that funds were the commodity in which Modern Western Man had re-invested the treasure that his Christian forebears had once placed in souls.

In the Christian dispensation, 'conversion' had opened the door for 'salvation', but in a Modern Western secular usage this Latin word, too, had been 'released', like its old companion, from its traditional association with souls to serve more practical purposes. 'Salvage' had come to mean the rescue, not of an erring sinner, but of a foundering ship, and what was 'salved' in a twentieth-century Western World was, not a soul by the spiritual ministrations of a priest whose 'cure' was of that kind, but a body by the physical application of an ointment purchased in a shop, while what was 'saved' was, not the soul that had found its way to Heaven, but the money that had been deposited in the bank.

'Salvator'—the substantive coined by the Latin Christian Father Tertullian, at the turn of the second and third centuries of the Christian Era, to represent the Greek word σωτὴρ in its application to Christ[2]—had so far escaped the desecration suffered by the verb from the same Latin root; for, even in ex-Christian Western minds, the predominant association of the word 'Saviour' was still with 'Our Lord'. But in its older Latin rendering, which had been 'conservator', the key word of Christianity had not been spared by sacrilegious hands. In being applied to the 'conservator' of some national museum or public park, or a member of 'The Thames Conservancy Board', the word had been 'converted' to a respectably illicit use; and the American usage of the adjective in the phrases 'a conservative estimate' and 'a conservative figure' could also perhaps pass muster—however great the gulf might be between the caution that was the virtue of a reputable business man and the love that had moved God to become Man in order to become Man's Saviour. It would be difficult, however, to whitewash the political application of the

[1] John iii. 8. [2] See V. vi. 374, n. 3.

term which was its most familiar usage in a twentieth-century Western World; for in this context a 'conservative' meant the supporter of a political party whose *raison d'être* was the defence of material vested interests.

As twentieth-century Western students of History watched 'holy day' contracting into 'holiday', and 'the Christmas holidays' bringing with them a commercially profitable boom in retail trade instead of a spiritually regenerating reminder of Man's salvation through God's incarnation, they would realize that they were being carried away by a process of 'dis-etherialization' which was the inverse of what had happened when pagan Hellenic words had been converted to Christian uses; and the same tale was told by the lapse of the word 'news' from meaning 'the good news' (εὐαγγέλιον) of the Gospel to meaning the uninspiring output of a commercial newspaper press. In New Mexico the 'know-how' which there had once signified the innocent craft of Zuñi priests[1] had come to signify a lethal technology of atomic warfare that had been worked out at Los Alamos. But words and bell-peals were not the only evidence for the 'conversion' of spiritual treasures into worldly goods by an egocentric Western human nature. This mis-appropriation was also attested by positive and historic political acts.

'Frederick II had been the ward and pupil of the great Innocent, founder of the Church as a state. He was an intellectual man, and we need not wonder to find in his conception of Empire a reflection of the Church. The whole Italian-Sicilian State which the Popes coveted as their Patrimony of Peter became, as it were, the Patrimony of Augustus for this gifted monarch, who sought to release the secular and intellectual powers that were fused into the spiritual unity of the Church[2] and to build a new empire based on these.'[3]

In an earlier part of this Study[4] we have briefly followed the course of an internecine struggle—waged without compromise between the belligerents and without mercy for a Medieval Western Christian body social that their strife was rending asunder—which a victorious Papacy pushed to the point of 'unconditional surrender'. But this was one of those Pyrrhic victories in which the victor appears, in retrospect, to have been a *felo de se*,[5] while his victim proves to have been inextirpably hydra-headed.

'Let us grasp the full significance of Frederick's Italian-Roman State: a mighty pan-Italian seignory, which for a short time united in one state Germanic, Roman and Oriental elements—Frederick himself, Emperor of the World, being the Grand Signor or Grand Tyrant thereof, the first and last of these princes to wear the diadem of Rome, whose Caesarhood was not only allied with German kingship like Barbarossa's but with Oriental-Sicilian despotism. Having grasped this, we perceive that all the tyrants of the Renaissance, the Scala and Montefeltre, the Visconti, Borgia,

[1] See Benedict, Ruth: *Patterns of Culture* (Cambridge, Mass. 1934, Riverside Press), p. 96.

[2] See pp. 402 and 446, above, and IX. viii. 394–5.—A.J.T.

[3] Kantorowicz, E.: *Frederick the Second, 1194–1250*, English translation (London 1931, Constable), pp. 561–2.

[4] In IV. iv. 560–7.

[5] IV. iv. 567–71.

and Medici, are down to the tiniest features the sons and successors of Frederick II, the diadochi of this "Second Alexander".'[1]

Nor was this the end of the monstrous proliferation of hydra heads from Frederick's mortal coils; for the North Italian city-state despotisms[2] that were multiple replicas of Frederick's abortive oecumenical Caesaro-papacy reproduced themselves, in their turn, on the nation-state scale, in the Transalpine and Transmarine outer circle of an Italianized Western World at the opening of the so-called Modern Age of Western history;[3] and these epigoni of the diadochi of Frederick the frustrated despoiler of Pope Innocent III were the successful despoilers of Innocent's successors[4] when a golden opportunity was offered to them by the folly of a Martin V and a Eugenius IV in crowning Innocent IV's pyrrhic victory over Frederick's natural heirs[5] with a not less pyrrhic victory over the Conciliar Movement.[6] A scrutiny of the fundamental political and economic institutions of a secular Modern Western Society reveals that these were plunder from the Papal constitution of a Medieval Christian Commonwealth[7]—like the desecrated altars and dislocated drums of columns that had been built into acropolis-walls at Athens and at Ankara, or like the marble shafts, robbed from ruined temples, that supported the roofs of post-Hellenic basilicas and mosques. With silent eloquence these spoils proclaimed the Christian origin of a Western Civilization that had forfeited its title to its Christian name.[8]

If, in this sense, the secular civilization of the Modern Western World was an emanation of the spirit of Frederick II Hohenstaufen, what had been the source of the demonic power in virtue of which a would-be empire-builder who had been frustrated in his own lifetime had succeeded in producing this amazing posthumous effect? The riddle receives its answer when we remind ourselves of the reason why the Emperor Frederick II came so much nearer than his grandfather Frederick I to achieving their dynasty's arch-ambition. The abiding aim of the Hohenstaufen line was, within Ottonian bounds, to make a belated reality of an abortive Carolingian attempt to revive the Roman Empire in Western Christendom as it had been revived in Orthodox Christendom, two generations before Charlemagne's day, by the genius of Leo Syrus. What was it that nerved Frederick I Hohenstaufen to ignore the twin portents of Charlemagne's and Otto I's successive fiascos? What motive impelled him to make a third essay in an enterprise in which his two greatest predecessors had so signally failed? And what was it that gave his grandson the hardihood to renew the struggle in which his

1 Kantorowicz, op. cit., pp. 493–4.
2 See III. iii. 354–7.
3 See III. iii. 300–1, 305, and 357–63; IV. iv. 198–200; and IX. viii. 363 and 395.
4 See IV. iv. 576–8.
5 See ibid. 566–8.
6 See ibid. 571–6.
7 See ibid. 539–43. Mr. Martin Wight comments: 'The most striking instance of this that I have come across is that the Papacy "invented", not only diplomacy and international finance, but also the National Debt.

'"The system of exchanges adopted in the Middle Ages originated chiefly in the nature of the papal revenues, which, due from all parts of the World, were to be transmitted to the Curia from every separate country; but it is equally worthy of remark that the system of national debt by which we are even now enveloped, and which maintains so important an influence on the operations of commerce, was first fully developed in the States of the Church" (Ranke, *History of the Papacy*, Bk. iv, § 2, *ad init.*).'

8 See I. i. 32–34.

grandfather, in his turn, had been worsted? The grandfather had been inspired by the Caesaro-papal 'absolute' conception of the Imperial prerogative[1] that had been enshrined in the Justinianean *Corpus Iuris*[2] of a latter-day Constantinopolitan Roman Empire; for, in the Western Christendom of Frederick I's day, this treasure, which had recently been disinterred at Bologna,[3] had still been an exciting new discovery.[4] The grandson was inspired by the more vivid and convincing experience of inheriting the throne of the Sicilian 'successor-state' of an East Roman Empire[5] in which Leo Syrus and his successors had succeeded[6] in reasserting the Constantinian Roman Imperial ideal of 'Caesaro-papism' in the 'real life' of public administration, and not just in the lecture rooms of academic professors of a rediscovered Justinianean *Summa*.

It will be seen that the monstrous birth of a Modern Western secular civilization from the womb of a Medieval Western *Respublica Christiana*, which had been made possible by the mistakes and sins of the Medieval Western Church, was made practicable by the renaissance of the Hellenic institution of an 'absolute' state in which Religion had been a department of Politics. It will also be seen that, in Western Christendom, this renaissance of Hellenic political 'absolutism' was not achieved without external aid. Charlemagne's native Western attempt to revive the Roman Empire had been a fortunate failure; Frederick II Hohenstaufen's audacious repetition of Charlemagne's enterprise was a sinister posthumous success because the *Stupor Mundi Occidentalis* was able, in his Sicilian hereditary dominions, to draw upon the credit of East Roman statesmen who had duly performed the feat—an enterprise beyond Charlemagne's powers—of resuscitating the Constantinian Roman Imperial régime.

When a civilization of the third generation breaks its way out of a body ecclesiastic, is a renaissance of the 'apparented' civilization of the second generation the invariable and indispensable means by which this unhappy delivery is accomplished? If we look at the history of the Hindu Civilization, we shall find there no parallel to the resuscitation of an

[1] See IV. iv. 347–50. [2] See pp. 265–8, above.

[3] After the irruption of the Lombards into Italy in A.D. 568, Bologna had been the north-westernmost outpost of a Constantinopolitan Roman Empire *in extremis* for the best part of two centuries before its incorporation into the body social of Western Christendom through the conquest of the Exarchate of Ravenna by the Lombards in the course of the quarter of a century ending in A.D. 751.

[4] See IV. iv. 557. The renaissance of a Justinianean Roman law in a Medieval Western Christendom is examined further in X. ix. 30–31.

[5] Frederick's 'Oriental-Sicilian despotism', as Kantorowicz calls it, was, of course, a 'successor-state', not only of the East Roman Empire, but of the Arab Caliphate as well, since the greater part of the East Roman dominions west of the Straits of Otranto which Frederick's Norman predecessors had conquered in the eleventh century of the Christian Era had previously been reconquered by the East Romans from North-West African Arab *conquistadores* who, in the ninth and tenth centuries, had overrun a Lombard Apulia and an East Roman Sicily (see IV. iv. 343–4, 356–7, and 401–2). In Sicily the descendants of the Arab conquerors had not been dislodged by a Norman military conquest that had deprived them of their political ascendancy in the island; and they exercised a potent cultural influence over their new Western Christian barbarian masters. In its political aspect, this Arab influence was in harmony with the Byzantine, since the imperial tradition of the Caliphate, like that of the East Roman Empire, had descended through a Constantinian, Diocletianic, and Sasanian channel from an Achaemenian fountain-head.

[6] See IV. iv. 346–7, 352, and 592–693.

'absolute' Hellenic polity which was achieved first in Orthodox Christendom by native political genius, and then in Western Christendom on the strength of a Byzantine *fait accompli*. Hindu history records no corresponding revival of the Empire of the Mauryas or the Empire of the Guptas. When we turn, however, from India to China, and look at the history of the Far Eastern Civilization in its homeland, we do here find an unmistakable and striking counterpart of the Byzantine revival of the Roman Empire in the Sui and T'ang revival of the Empire of the Han.[1]

This Far Eastern renaissance of the universal state of an antecedent civilization is, indeed, the classic case; for by comparison even with the East Roman Empire, not to speak of 'the Holy Roman Empire', the Sui and T'ang Empire stands out as a solid success; and this success was due, as we have seen,[2] to a command of the administrative means required for achieving the political objective. Not only the political tradition but the administrative personnel of the Han Empire had survived the interregnum between the dissolution of the Sinic Civilization and the emergence of its Far Eastern successor. It had found asylum in the great cultural citadel which a disintegrating Sinic Civilization had provided for itself by expanding southwards up to the southern watershed of the Yangtse Basin and over it to the seaboard. The Confucian civil servants who reappeared in strength towards the close of the sixth century of the Christian Era, to administer a politically reunited South and North of China as a resuscitated Sinic universal state, surpassed their eighth-century Byzantine equivalents in cultivation and efficiency, as well as in numbers, in the measure in which the sub-continental citadel of Sinism between the Hwangho–Yangtsekiang watershed and the south coast of China surpassed in extent the ring-wall of the city of Constantinople, which was Hellenism's narrow-verged citadel during the interregnum between the dissolution of the Hellenic Civilization and the emergence of an Orthodox Christendom. As for Charlemagne's abortive 'Holy Roman Empire', the administrative reason for its failure[3] was that, in the West in Charlemagne's day, there was not even an exiguous remnant of the former Roman civil service for a would-be empire-builder to enlist.

In the light of this disparity in the amount and in the value of the initial assets in these three different undertakings, it is not surprising that the renaissance of the Sinic Civilization in the Far Eastern World should have gone farther than the renaissance of Hellenism in either a Western or an Orthodox Christendom. For the purposes of our present inquiry it is significant that the civilization of the third generation in whose history the renaissance of its predecessor of the second generation had been carried to the greatest lengths should likewise have been the most successful in its generation in shaking itself free from the trammels of the church which its predecessor had brought to birth.

[1] See pp. 19–21, above.

[2] On pp. 370–2, above. See further X. ix. 20 and 665–7.

[3] There was, of course, an economic reason as well (see II. ii. 345; IV. iv. 322–3 and 490).

The Mahayanian Buddhism that had bidden fair to captivate a moribund Sinic World as thoroughly as a moribund Hellenic World had been captivated by Christianity had reached its zenith in the Far East at the nadir of the post-Sinic interregnum;[1] but it had swiftly declined thereafter to a level of nonentity to which Christianity had never yet sunk either in Orthodox Christendom or in the West.

On this showing, we must conclude that the 'renaissance' of a dead civilization spells a 'regression' from a living higher religion, and that, the farther the revival is pushed, the greater the backsliding will be; but we may still be challenged to show why, even if this inverse variation were to prove to be a 'law' of History, it should be deplored as a catastrophe rather than be applauded as a triumph. Our judgement must indeed seem paradoxical to a Far Eastern Confucian civil servant or to a Western rationalist technician who believed in his heart that 'Man makes Himself'[2] and that, in Man's competent conduct of Mankind's proper business,[3] the episode of the rise and fall of the higher religions had been a disturbing and discreditable interlude.

The reply to this challenge is *Respice finem*; for renaissances, as we shall see when we study them more closely,[4] are apt to unfold themselves progressively by resuscitating elements of the life of the 'apparented' civilization in a chronological order that is the inverse of their historical sequence in their original appearance. A process of resuscitation which starts with the revival of a universal state that had been the last achievement of the antecedent society's dominant minority goes on to resuscitate the philosophy in which an imperial civil service had been schooled, and thence to resuscitate the styles of politics, architecture, sculpture, and literature that, in the history of the 'apparented' civilization, had been in vogue in earlier ages, until the pageant of a dead civilization's history has been dramatically re-deployed in reverse order on a living civilization's stage. This evocatory exercise of the imagination is manifestly bound to expose those souls that indulge in it to a risk of derangement through being distracted by a pursuit of incompatible ideals.

In Far Eastern history the tension produced by this inner psychic discord had from time to time sought relief in the outward form of a persecution of adherents of the Mahāyāna—or, at any rate, of followers of the Buddhist monastic way of life—by the secular public authorities at the instigation of the champions of Confucianism. The most extensive and persistent of these persecutions had occurred, as might be expected, during the second and less prosperous chapter of the T'ang Dynasty's three-centuries-long tenure of power—at a time when the Confucian scholar-administrators were beginning to feel less secure in the saddle and therefore less inclined to go on tolerating the persistence in their midst of a parvenu alien religious life which was a standing

[1] See Eliot, Sir Charles: *Hinduism and Buddhism* (London 1921, Arnold, 3 vols.), vol. iii, pp. 251–9.

[2] *Man Makes Himself* was the title of a book published in A.D. 1936 by a distinguished Western archaeologist, V. G. Childe (see p. 480, n. 3, above).

[3] Pope: *An Essay on Man*, Ep. ii, l. 2.

[4] In Part X, *passim*, in vol. ix.

challenge to the restored Confucian régime. These major persecutions had been inflicted in A.D. 845 and subsequent years.[1] But, even before the evocation of a ghost of the Sinic universal state by the Sui Dynasty in A.D. 589, there had been a persecution of the kind in A.D. 446[2] in a To Pa Eurasian barbarian 'successor-state' of the defunct Han Empire in Shansi which had sought to disguise its vulgar origin under the archaizing name of 'Wei'. At first sight it is surprising to find the Mahāyāna exciting the hostility of an ex-barbarian Power which had won its certificate of cultural respectability, and thereby made its political fortune, through its own conversion to the Mahāyāna in the preceding chapter of its history.[3] On a closer view we can see that the revulsion against the Mahāyāna which declared itself in 'Wei' in A.D. 446 in an act of political coercion was the reverse side of a renaissance of the pre-Buddhist pagan Sinic culture which, in the 'Wei' Principality, reached its climax in the last decade of the fifth century of the Christian Era in the pedantically thoroughgoing Sinomania of the 'Wei' prince Hiao Wên-ti.[4]

In the Western World, in contrast to the course of the corresponding renaissance in Orthodox Christendom and in the Far East alike, the universal state of the antecedent civilization had never been successfully resuscitated; the failure had been most signal when Frederick II Hohenstaufen had drawn upon Leo Syrus's Byzantine achievement in a last attempt at retrieving Charlemagne's Austrasian failure; and, in consequence, the political renaissance here had cut its way back behind the oecumenical last act of Hellenic political history till, in the hands of Frederick II's fourteenth-century Italian diadochi and sixteenth-century Transalpine epigoni, it had arrived at a resuscitation of the parochial patriotism which had been both the strength and the weakness of the Hellenic Civilization at the culmination of its growth and on the eve of its breakdown. 'There is high tension and hard encounter between the Christian Faith and any form of civilization';[5] and Modern Western Man's attempt to combine an ancestral Christianity with a resuscitated Hellenic idolization of a parochial political community had set up a tension in Western souls which had become all but intolerably high by the middle of the twentieth century.

'Europe's infatuation for the Greeks and Romans dates from the sixteenth century, when she began her great political and military reorganisation. She admired them in all things—even those arts in which the Middle Ages had excelled them—because they taught her how to organise armies, how to wage wars, and how to build up great states.'[6]

From the sixteenth century onwards the West had been seeking all the time to realize simultaneously a pagan Hellenic ideal of political

[1] See Eliot, Sir Charles: *Hinduism and Buddhism* (London 1921, Arnold, 3 vols.), vol. iii, pp. 267–8, and Franke, O.: *Geschichte des Chinesischen Reiches*, vol. ii (Berlin 1936, de Gruyter), pp. 496–8 and 572.

[2] See Eliot, op. cit., vol. iii, p. 252, and Franke, op. cit., vol. ii, pp. 203–4.

[3] See V. v. 356, with n. 6.

[4] See V. v. 477–8.

[5] Burgmann, Bishop E. H.: *The Church's Encounter with Civilisation* (London 1948, Longmans), p. 18.

[6] Ferrero, G.: *Peace and War*, English translation (London 1933, Macmillan): 'Paganism and Christianity', p. 194.

absolutism which, in the course of Hellenic history, had eventually choked the seeds of an Hellenic ideal of individual liberty, and a Christian ideal of individual liberty which was a corollary of a Christian belief in the value of every human soul in the sight of God;[1] and each of these two incompatible movements had been carried to a climax in the French Revolution.[2]

'We live in a state of permanent disharmony. The family, social life, manners and morals bear the stamp of Christianity; politics and war draw their inspiration from the classic and pagan tradition; law, literature, philosophy, art, and history are subjected to the competing influence of both. . . . What is the State? An end or a means? . . . Paganism and Christianity have each given a clear and definite answer. Paganism said that it was an end; Christianity replied that it was a means.'[3]

[1] Mr. Martin Wight comments on the original draft of this passage: 'Paganism came nowhere near the combination of political fanaticism and spiritual coercion which is the essence of a Modern Western "totalitarianism", for these are characteristic of a post-Christian Neo-Paganism—of the transfer of the religious "drive" and exclusive claims of Christianity to a debased secular creed, as you suggest on p. 554, below—which is indeed the supreme evidence, up to date, of a civilization of the third generation being a regression. Conversely it is very disputable whether Christianity can make an exclusive claim to the ideal of individual liberty. It certainly provided the milieu in which the Hellenic seed of individual liberty was able to germinate and come to flower in the Western Civilization; but in Eastern Christendom it did the reverse, and provided the milieu for the flowering of the older bulb of sacred monarchy, in which the unbiased reader of the Old and New Testaments and of the Fathers would be much more likely to see the natural political expression of Christianity than he would be likely to see it in any form of individual liberty. Christianity, in fact, seems capable of accommodating itself to any political régime: all that it asserts is that every political régime must be *responsible* to God, or (as Ferrero says) that the state, whether monarchic or democratic, is a means, not an end.

'Indeed, are you not here evading the question whether "the ideal of individual liberty" is not precisely a feature of Modern Western secular civilization, i.e. of regression? Western Christendom, like Eastern Christendom, knew nothing of "individual liberty" except marginally in the Medieval Western city-state cosmos.'

The writer's answer to Mr. Wight's question would be that, in his belief, the Modern Western—in contrast to the Medieval Western—ideal of individual liberty on the secular plane had been derived from a Christian, not from an Hellenic, source. As he saw it, the Late Modern Western ideals of political and economic liberty were secularized versions of an Early Modern Western ideal of religious liberty for the individual conscience, and this ideal of liberty on the plane of religious practice and conviction had been inspired by the Christian belief in the value of every human soul in the sight of God, inasmuch as this belief could be taken to imply that no human authority—neither a church militant on Earth nor any secular potentate—had a right to intervene between an individual human soul and the God who had created it and had undergone an Incarnation and a Crucifixion for its sake. The writer agreed that this deduction from a universal and unquestioned Christian belief about the relation between human souls and God had not been drawn in Western Christendom before the Early Modern Age and had not been drawn in any of the other Christendoms independently at any time; but he would submit that it was a legitimate deduction and that, whether or not its legitimacy were admitted by other students of History, the deduction had at any rate been made in an Early Modern Western Christendom as a matter of historical fact.

While the writer of this Study thus held that the Modern Western ideal of individual liberty had a Christian root, he would agree that its severance from its Christian root, and its 'counter-transfiguration' into a secular ideal of individual liberty on the political and economic planes, had indeed been symptoms of regression; and in his view this secularized version of a Christian ideal was not only regressive; it was also untenable. In repudiating a religious sanction for individual liberty which had been provided by a Christian belief in the value of each and every soul in the sight of God, a post-Christian Modern Western *homo democraticus* had reduced his pretension to individual liberty *ad absurdum*; for the claims that were now being put forward by this *homunculus* merely in his own right, and no longer in God's name, could not stand against the claims of a totalitarian state to sacrifice the individual liberty of any and every *homunculus* on the altar of an idolized corporate humanity, the great beast-god Leviathan.

[2] See Ferrero, op. cit., pp. 196–7.

[3] Ibid., p. 199.

The spiritual weapons, plucked from an Hellenic charnel house, with which Modern Western Man had brought to the ground the Hildebrandine *Respublica Christiana* had been as destructive as the material weapons with which Cromwell's soldiers had once shattered the west window of Winchester Cathedral.

'When ye shall see the abomination of desolation, spoken of by Daniel the Prophet, standing where it ought not (let him that readeth understand), then let them that be in Judaea flee to the mountains.'[1]

Nevertheless, there is a bow in the cloud.[2] At Winchester, on the morrow of the Puritan iconoclast's deed, it must have looked as if a mighty work of Medieval Christian art had been utterly destroyed; and in truth it had been damaged beyond all possibility of reinstatement in its inimitable medieval pattern. Yet the broken and scattered fragments were pieced together again, by the piety of a later generation, in a labour of love that—sheer disorder though it might have suggested to the eye of the original artificer—was in truth a new pattern,[3] fraught with unpremeditated beauty and letting in unforeseen light in the sight of eyes open to the self-revelation of a God who makes all things new.[4] A boy once watched, spell-bound, while this miracle of creation conjured out of destruction[5] was being lit up by the level radiance of a setting summer sun; and a man could catch a glimpse of the spiritual meaning of this visual allegory as he recalled it in his mind's eye in after-life, in the light of his generation's experience of a forty years' wandering in the wilderness. If the same sunlight could thus shine again through the same glass in a new pattern offering a fresh vision, might not the eternal and unchanging incorporeal light of the Beatific Vision again illuminate men's souls in a society that had been broken and remade by the sufferings of a Time of Troubles?

[1] Mark xiii. 14; cp. Matt. xxiv. 15–16.

[2] Gen. ix. 12–17.

[3] See Bergson's exposition of the relativity of the concept of disorder in the passage quoted from *L'Evolution Créatrice*, 24th ed. (Paris 1921, Alcan), pp. 239–55, in V. v. 419, n. 5.

[4] Rev. xxi. 5.

[5] The Destroyer's unintentional and unwilling service to the Creator has been illustrated in II. i. 271–99.

C. THE CHALLENGE OF MILITANCY ON EARTH

(I) CAUSES OF REGRESSION

IN the preceding chapter we have observed that a secular civilization that breaks out of a body ecclesiastic is apt to win its way with the aid of elements in the life of an antecedent civilization that it brings back to life; but, if we have seen here how an insurgent civilization takes advantage of its opportunity, we have still to see how the opportunity arises; and evidently this 'beginning of evils'[1] is to be looked for, not in the resourcefulness of the erupting civilization, but in some weak point, or false step, of the church at whose cost the eruption is achieved.

One formidable crux for a church is manifestly inherent in a church's *raison d'être*. A church is militant on Earth for the purpose of winning, or recapturing, This World for the *Civitas Dei* not by extinguishing life on Earth but by transfiguring it;[2] and this means that a church has to deal with secular as well as spiritual affairs and to organize itself on Earth as an institution, since this was the only method so far discovered by Man for managing mundane human relations on any scale beyond the narrow range of direct personal intercourse between one human being and another.[3] The gross institutional integument with which a church thus finds itself compelled to clothe its etherial nakedness, in order to do God's business in a recalcitrant environment, is as incongruous with a church's spiritual nature as the alien shell that is appropriated by a hermit crab; and it is not surprising to see disaster overtaking a terrestrial outpost of the Communion of Saints which, in This World, cannot do its own proper spiritual work without being drawn into grappling with secular problems and finding itself forced to attack these with institutional tools.

The most celebrated tragedy of the kind is the history of the Hildebrandine Papacy; and in another context[4] we have observed how Hildebrand was dragged over the precipice by an apparently inevitable concatenation of causes and effects. He would not be a true and loyal servant of God if he did not throw himself, with all his might, into the spiritual task of trying to reclaim the Western Christian clergy from the sexual and financial corruption in which they were wallowing in his day; he could not reform the clergy if he did not effectively organize the Church; he could not effectively organize the Church without vindicating her lawful authority over the clergy in matters ecclesiastical; he could not do this without arriving at a demarcation between the respective jurisdictions of Church and State; and, since the field of the Western Christian clergy's activity in Hildebrand's day included some ground that was indisputably secular, and much ground that was debatable, besides the ground that was admittedly ecclesiastical, Hildebrand was led, by

[1] Thucydides, Book II, chap. 12.
[2] See V. vi. 149–68.
[3] See III. iii. 223–30.
[4] In IV. iv. 552–4.

a sequence of steps in which each step seemed to be necessitated by the preceding one, from inspiring a spiritual revival in Christian souls to engaging in a conflict with 'the Holy Roman Empire' which carried the Church right into the arena of power politics and was fought out, by force of arms, in successive rounds of ever-increasing intensity and embitterment, over a period of two centuries, with eventual results that were disastrous alike for a Medieval Western Christendom's two master institutions, the Papacy and the Empire, and, worst of all, for Western Christendom itself.

This tragedy of the Hildebrandine Western Church is a prominent, though by no means unparalleled, example of spiritual regression precipitated by a church's becoming entangled in mundane affairs and committed to secular modes of action unintentionally, and indeed against its will, as an incidental consequence of its doing its own business. There is, however, another broad road leading to the same spiritually destructive worldliness which is more frequented, more characteristic, and more insidious. A church incurs the risk of falling into a spiritual regression in the very act of living up to its own standards by striving sincerely to do God's will on Earth. For the will of God is partially expressed in the righteous social aims of the secular mundane societies, and these mundane ideals are apt to be achieved incidentally in a religious society very much more successfully than they ever have been, or can be, achieved in a mundane society which aims at these objects direct, and at nothing higher. This is a necessary consequence of one of the laws of life that we have observed in other contexts[1]—the principle that the most likely way to reach a goal is to be aiming, not at that goal itself, but at some more ambitious goal beyond it—and, in the history of the Church Militant on Earth, two classic examples of the working of this law were the achievements of Saint Benedict and of Pope Gregory the Great.[2]

Both these saintly souls were bent upon the spiritual aim of promoting the monastic way of life in the West, and Gregory was also devoted to the further purpose—as unworldly as the other—of giving light to them that sit in darkness[3] by bringing the heathen within the Christian Church's fold. Yet, as a by-product of their spiritual work, these two unworldly men of action performed economic prodigies that were beyond the powers of secular statesmen. Gregory incidentally saved from starvation the urban proletariat of Rome at a moment when the Constantinopolitan Government of an expiring Roman Empire was quite incapable of doing its duty by a derelict imperial city which, at the turn of the sixth and seventh centuries, was an exposed Western outpost of a once oecumenical Power whose frontiers had contracted till its centre of gravity now lay in Anatolia. And Gregory not only responded to the urgent challenge of an immediate economic emergency within the walls of the city that was the seat of his bishopric; in the same power of the same spirit, he and his hero Benedict between them laid, without intending it or knowing it, the firm religious foundations on which the

[1] See pp. 388 and 510, above.
[2] See III. iii. 265–9 and IV. iv. 184–5.
[3] Luke i. 79.

immense edifice of a Medieval and a Modern Western economic life was subsequently erected. This incidental economic handiwork of two single-minded servants of God would be praised by Christian and Marxian historians alike with united voices, albeit with discordant minds. Yet, should these praises become audible to Benedict and Gregory in an Other World, these saints would assuredly recall, with a pang of misgiving, their Master's saying: 'Woe unto you when all men shall speak well of you';[1] and their misgiving would certainly turn to anguish if they were enabled to revisit This World and to see with their own eyes the ultimate moral consequences of the eventual economic effects of their immediate spiritual endeavours during their life on Earth.

The disconcerting truth is that the incidental material fruits of the spiritual labours of the *Civitas Dei* on Earth are not only certificates of its spiritual success; they are also snares in which a spiritual athlete who has been touched by the sin of pride, or has perhaps merely rested sluggishly on his oars,[2] may be trapped more diabolically than an impetuous Hildebrand is ruined by the spiritual disaster of entanglement in politics and war. In the medieval chapter of the Benedictine story, the Cistercian spiritual pioneers who founded their abbeys in a wilderness among the foothills of the Yorkshire Moors could hardly have foreboded that, in sacrificing themselves by seeking out this forbidding material environment, they were imperilling their successors' souls.

Was not the physical hardship of marooning themselves in this bleak landscape almost beyond endurance, even for a mortified monk? Was it not an edifying spiritual exercise to undertake, in faith, the humanly impossible task of making the desert rejoice and blossom as the rose?[3] How could they have foreseen that they were giving the initial impetus to a wool industry and a metallurgical industry that would go from strength to strength till, seven hundred years from then, these economic exercises of aspirants to a spiritual prize would make England 'the workshop of the World'? How could they have foreseen that, within only three hundred years, a mounting material wealth that was the almost inevitable reward of spiritual virtue would be tempting their abbots to break their rule, in the spirit and even in the letter, by building massive meat-kitchens in their abbatial quarters as a witness against themselves? Or that, within four hundred years, the discredit brought upon the Order by such conspicuous sins against its professed ideals would be seized upon by a covetous laity as an excuse for despoiling the monasteries as Israel had spoiled the Egyptians? The unfolding tale had taught Posterity that material riches which can be harvested with impunity by saints who neither seek them nor value them nor notice them may be the undoing of clerics of common clay who covet them for their own sake and pursue them to the neglect of their spiritual calling.

'The gulf which appeared between abbot and convent was largely caused by the accumulation of wealth. As time went by, the estates of the

1 Luke vi. 26.
2 For these two alternative ways of incurring nemesis, see IV. iv. 245–61.
3 Isa. xxxv. 1.

monasteries became so enormous that the abbot found himself almost fully occupied in the administration of his lands and in the various responsibilities which this entailed. A similar process of division of estates and duties was taking place at the same time among the monks themselves. . . . Each monastery was divided into what were practically separate departments, each with its own income and its own special responsibilities. The officer in charge of each department was known as an 'obedientiary'. To him certain sources of income were assigned; he had his own household and servants; and the burden of his office was such as to occupy a very large part of his time. . . . Any monk of average intelligence and ability could count on receiving some form of office in due course, and . . . would spend a good many years of his monastic life in the administration of his department. . . .

'As Dom David Knowles says: "Save in monasteries such as Winchester, Canterbury and Saint Albans, where strong intellectual or artistic interests existed, business of this kind was the career which absorbed all the talent of the house". . . .[1] For such as had administrative gifts, but were not blessed with any property on which to exert them, the monasteries, with their vast estates, offered much scope.'[2]

Of such it is written that 'he . . . that received seed among the thorns is he that heareth the word; and the care of This World, and the deceitfulness of riches, choke the word, and he becometh unfruitful'.[3] Yet the monk who has fallen out of the running in the race for a spiritual crown by degenerating into a successful man of business does not exemplify the most deadly form that spiritual regression can take. The worst temptation that lies in wait for citizens of the *Civitas Dei* in This World is neither to plunge into politics nor to slide into business but to idolize the terrestrial institution in which a Church Militant on Earth is imperfectly though unavoidably embodied. If *corruptio optimi* is *pessima*, an idolized church is the one idol that is more pernicious than the idolized human ant-heap that men worship as Leviathan.[4]

A church is in danger of lapsing into this worst of all forms of idolatry in so far as she lapses into believing herself to be, not merely a depository of truth, but the sole depository of the whole truth in a complete and definitive revelation of it.[5] For the value of a vessel is proportionate to the value of its contents, and, if the contents are believed to be inestimably precious, the guardians of the vessel may rate so high the adventitious sacrosanctity of a paltry alabaster box that, rather than break it, they may sacrilegiously refrain, when their testing time comes, from using the spikenard for the divine purpose for which it has been entrusted to their keeping by God.[6] The idolization of an ecclesiastical institution may be the outcome of a laudably prudent determination to preserve a divinely revealed truth by making sure that its earthly integu-

1 Knowles, Dom David: *The Monastic Order in England, 943–1216* (Cambridge 1940, University Press), p. 438.

2 Moorman, J. R. H.: *Church Life in England in the Thirteenth Century* (Cambridge 1945, University Press), pp. 279–80, 283, 353.

3 Matt. xiii. 22. Cp. Mark iv. 18–19; Luke viii. 14.

4 The idolization of institutions has been discussed in IV. iv. 303–423.

5 See Niebuhr, Reinhold: *Faith and History* (New York 1949, Scribner), pp. 238–40 and 242.

6 Mark xiv. 3–9. Cp. Matt. xxvi. 6–13; Luke vii. 36–50; John xii. 1–9.

ment shall be tough enough to outlast any mundane institution that might jeopardize the revelation by crushing its container. Yet, if the maker of the iron vessel falls down and worships his handiwork when it has duly proved itself more than a match for the colliding vessel of clay, it were better for him that he should never have purchased this material security for his spiritual treasure at so ruinous a moral cost.

A church is prone to set her feet on this easiest and sheerest of all the descents of Avernus when she has suffered some heavy blow, and particularly prone if the stroke has been struck by the members of her own household—who are proverbially a man's most grievous foes,[1] though their intimacy with their victim also makes them his shrewdest critics. The classic exemplar of this perhaps least readily retrievable form of regression had been the Counter-Reformational Tridentine Roman Catholic Church as non-Catholics saw her.[2] For four hundred years already, down to the time of writing, she had been standing on guard, in a posture that was as rigid as her vigilance was unrelaxing, massively armoured with the helmet of the Papacy and the breastplate of the hierarchy, and continually presenting arms to God in the recurrent rhythm of an exacting liturgy. In justification of her stand, this steel-clad figure could quote Scripture:

> 'For we wrestle not against flesh and blood, but against principalities, against powers, against the rulers of the darkness of This World, against spiritual wickedness in high places. Wherefore take unto you the whole armour of God, that ye may be able to withstand in the evil day, and, having done all, to stand.'[3]

The subconscious purpose of this heavy institutional panoply in which the Tridentine Church had encased herself was assuredly a determination to outlast the very toughest of the contemporary secular institutions of This World—above all, the upstart civilizations of the third generation. In the twentieth century of the Christian Era a Catholic critic of the Reformation could argue with force, in the light of four hundred years of Protestant history, that a Protestant impatience of even the lighter equipment of pre-Tridentine Catholicism had been premature. Yet that verdict, even if cogent, would not prove either that the casting off of impedimenta would always be a mistake or that the Tridentine multiplication of them had not also been an error. Institutional armour is possibly an indispensable means of survival for a Church Militant on Earth, but it is none the less certainly a mundane embarrassment which makes the Church Militant by that much spiritually inferior to the Kingdom of Heaven, where 'they neither marry nor are given in marriage, but are as the angels',[4] and where each individual catches God's spirit from personal communion with Him, 'like light caught from a leaping flame'.[5]

The awe inspired by the spectacle of Tridentine Catholicism in the heart of a twentieth-century Christian observer of a different persuasion

[1] Matt. x. 36, following Micah vii. 6.

[2] Catholics, of course, did not admit that their devotion to their church amounted to an idolization of her.

[3] Eph. vi. 12–13.

[4] Mark xii. 25.

[5] Plato's Letters, No. 7, quoted in III. iii. 245, and on p. 525, above.

was tempered by reminiscences of an Assyrian 'corpse in armour' standing magnificently but not invincibly at bay in the breach at Nineveh in 612 B.C.[1] and of long since extinct giant reptiles which had 'swelled and hardened up to their doom'[2] by assiduously reinforcing their carapaces, plate upon plate, till they had condemned themselves to stagnate 'awash in pools where water would bear some of their otherwise crushing weight.'[3] In the museums of a latter-day Western World the fossilized bones of the dinosaurs and the cap-à-pie steel carapaces of fifteenth-century Western men-at-arms bore concordant witness that 'there is no armour against Fate';[4] and the same truth was advertised in the spectacle of a derelict Great Wall of China and of desolate termite-built towers of Babel that would surpass the Great Pyramid in massiveness and the Empire State Building in height if translated into human dimensions, scale for scale.[5]

> 'A social pattern no longer open to change has, in fact, quite unconsciously signed its own death warrant. Just at the very moment when the system seems most perfected, when the structure seems most complete, and when inner peace and harmony seem to give the way of life a kind of perfection, the cracks in the structure make their appearance, the fission becomes evident, and the changes so long resisted precipitate a cataclysm.'[6]

The verdict[7] upon the idolization of an institution, ecclesiastical or secular, is: 'Whosoever will save his life shall lose it.'[8]

We have now laid our finger on some of the causes of regression from higher religions to vain repetitions of secular civilizations, and in each case we have found that the calamity is precipitated, not by a *saeva necessitas*[9] or any other external force, but by an 'Original Sin' which is innate in a terrestrial Human Nature.[10]

1 See IV. iv. 484.

2 Heard, Gerald: *The Source of Civilisation* (London 1935, Cape), p. 71, quoted in IV. iv. 427.

3 Heard, op. cit., loc. cit.

4 Shirley, James: *Death the Leveller*.

5 See III. iii. 107–8.

6 Tannenbaum, F.: *Slave and Citizen: The Negro in the Americas* (New York 1947, Knopf), pp. 108–9.

7 Mr. Martin Wight comments: 'A Roman Catholic critic would reply to you here, in words that you so often quote, "Respice finem". The whole of the foregoing passage is anticipation: it has not yet come true. Is it not the fact that the Roman Church is incomparably more vigorous and influential in the twentieth century than at any time since the Council of Trent? Whereas in 1870 it inscribed the Infallibility of the Pope among its dogmas, at the apparent nadir of its fortunes, as an act of defiance, in 1950 it was able still further to scandalize a secular Western World by adding the dogma of the Assumption of the Virgin as an act of self-confidence. Is it not equally likely, at the time of writing, that the Roman Church in its Tridentine panoply will be the only Western institution capable of challenging and withstanding the neo-pagan totalitarian Communist state, and is not this borne out by the particular fear and hatred with which Moscow regards the Vatican? If this be so, the figure of the dinosaur's carapace will be less apt than that of a long and successfully sustained siege, and the Tridentine phase of Catholic history may appear in retrospect like the Churchillian phase of British history from the fall of France to D-Day. You prejudice the outcome. "Respice finem".'

A Catholic friend of the writer's comments on the same passage: 'The odd thing about the post-Tridentine and twentieth-century Catholicism, surely, is its eternal youth—the wonderful sprouting of new orders and congregations of both religious and lay folk: the "Jocists", the Grail, the "Pays de Mission" priests in the banlieue of Paris, the Society of the Divine Word (Pater Schmidt and the Chinese cardinal). Even at the time of the Counter-Reformation itself there had not been such a flourishing of mystics.'

8 Luke ix. 24. Cp. Matt. xvi. 25 and x. 39.

9 See IV. iv. 7–39.

10 See IV. iv. 120.

(II) THE BOW IN THE CLOUD

(a) AUGURIES OF SPIRITUAL RECOVERY

If regressions from higher religions are effects of Original Sin, are we driven to conclude that, since Original Sin is reborn into This World at the birth of every new-born child,[1] such regressions are inevitable? If they are, this would mean that the challenge of militancy on Earth was so prohibitively severe[2] that no church would ever be capable of standing up to it in the long run; and that conclusion, in turn, would drive us back towards the view that the churches are good for nothing better than to serve as ephemeral chrysalises for vainly repetitive civilizations.[3] Is this the last word? Before we resign ourselves to a suggestion that God's inflowing light is doomed to be perpetually overwhelmed by an uncomprehending darkness, let us cast our eyes back once again over the series of spiritual illuminations brought into the World by the epiphanies of the higher religions; for these chapters of past spiritual history may prove to be auguries of spiritual recovery from the regressions to which a Church Militant is prone.

We have noticed[4] that the successive milestones in Man's spiritual advance that are inscribed with the names of Abraham, Moses, the Prophets, and Christ all stand at points where a surveyor of the course of secular civilization would report breaks in the road and breakdowns in the traffic; and the empirical evidence has given us reason to believe that this coincidence of high points in Man's religious history with low points in his secular history may be one of the 'laws' of Man's terrestrial life. If so, we should expect also to find evidence of the working of a converse 'law' that the high points in secular history coincide with low points in religious history, and that the religious achievements that accompany mundane declines and falls are therefore not merely spiritual advances but are also spiritual recoveries. They are, of course, presented as recoveries in the traditional version of the story.

'The call of Abraham', for example, which the recent discoveries of our Modern Western archaeologists have enabled us to locate, in our chart of secular history, as a spiritual accompaniment to the secular catastrophe of the downfall of the Empire of Sumer and Akkad, is presented in the Hebrew legend as a sequel—which was God's opening move for the redemption of Mankind from the consequences of the Fall of Adam—to a defiance of God by the self-confident builders of a mundane Tower of Babel.[5] The mission of Moses which, in the same secular chart, appears as an accompaniment of the comparable secular calamity of the break-up of 'the New Empire' of Egypt, is presented in the legend as a move to rescue God's Chosen People from a spiritually unpropitious enjoyment of the flesh pots of Egypt in her heyday by

1 'Ethics, like backbones, come out of non-existence into existence *de novo* in each individual development' (Huxley, Julian: *Evolutionary Ethics*, the Romanes Lecture, 1943, reprinted in Huxley, T. H. and J.: *Evolution and Ethics, 1893–1943* (London 1947, Pilot Press), p. 107.

2 See II. ii. 260.

3 This view has been examined on pp. 392–419, above.

4 On pp. 423–5, above; see also pp. 701–2 and 762, below.

5 Gen. xii. 1–6, against the background of Gen. xi.

exposing them to the spiritually fortifying experience of hungering and thirsting in the wilderness.[1] The Prophets of Israel and Judah, whose *floruit* is located by the secular historian in the Time of Troubles of a broken-down Syriac Civilization, were moved by a compelling concern (which, in their own belief, was a divine command) to preach to their countrymen a repentance from the spiritual backslidings into which Israel had lapsed when he had broken out of the wilderness into a land flowing with milk and honey which had not yet been blighted by Assyrian militarism. The Ministry of Christ, whose Passion, as a secular historian sees it, is fraught with all the anguish of an Hellenic Time of Troubles, is presented in the Gospels as an intervention of God Himself for the purpose of extending to the whole of Mankind a covenant previously made by God with an Israel whose epigoni in Jesus' generation had alloyed their spiritual heritage with a Pharisaic formalism, a Sadducaean materialism, an Herodian opportunism, and a Zealot fanaticism.

On this showing, four blazing outbursts of spiritual illumination had been sequels to spiritual eclipses besides having been accompaniments of mundane disasters, and we may surmise that this sequence of spiritual recoveries had been something more than a happy chapter of accidents. In another context[2] we have observed that physically hard environments are apt to be the nurseries of mundane achievements, and, on this analogy, it is to be expected that spiritually hard environments will have a correspondingly stimulating effect in the field of religious endeavour. A spiritually hard environment may be defined as being the atmosphere of 'the city of swine'[3] in which the Soul's spiritual aspirations are swamped by material well-being. This Circe's magic is too much for the general run of Mankind; and in such adverse spiritual circumstances a majority is apt to find its way, like Odysseus' shipmates, into the sorceress' pigsties. Yet all is not lost; for the miasma of worldly prosperity that stupefies the mass will provoke spiritually sensitive and strenuous souls into an utter defiance of the charms of This World. Even on the relatively low level of barbarian virtue, the fortitude of a single hero may avail, as Odysseus showed, to save the situation; and at the level of the higher religions the failure of the priest is the signal for the prophet.

We have noticed, in passing,[4] the classic case of the early Christian martyrs who bade defiance to the bourgeois comfort and security of a Trajanic, Hadrianic, and Antonine Age by insisting on sacrificing their lives for a moral punctilio. Their spiritual heroism outraged pagan contemporaries who would fain have made believe that a transient 'Indian Summer' was not October but June, yet were uneasily aware that the Christian martyrs' apparently fantastic *contemptus mundi* was inspired by a devastating insight. The same insight was displayed by Saint Francis of Assisi when he revolted, in disgust and alarm, against the empty life of luxury that his purse-proud father had provided for him,

[1] See II. ii. 24–25. [2] In II. ii. 31–73.
[3] Plato: *Respublica*, 369B–372D, cited in II. i. 193, n. 1, and II. ii. 23, n. 2.
[4] In IV. iv. 60–61.

and raised the rebel standard of Holy Poverty against a bourgeois prosperity that, in the Medieval Western Christendom of his day, was still only in its budding infancy. Saint Francis' father was the prototype of the commercially successful Western business man who was to inherit the Earth in the course of the next seven centuries; and, in an epoch in which *Homo Economicus Occidentalis* was thus going from strength to strength, it exasperated him to hear the Franciscan repetition of Saint Gregory's cry: 'Behold, the World that commands our love is fugitive!'[1] Yet, some eight hundred years after Pietro Bernardone's day, the apparently boundless vista of material progress, that had displayed itself as alluringly as ever to a twelfth-century Umbrian clothier's nineteenth-century English and American successors, had been effaced by the grimly different prospect that Saint Gregory had once depicted.

'To-day there is on every side death, on every side grief, on every side desolation; on every side we are being smitten, on every side our cup is being filled with draughts of bitterness. Yet the lusts of the flesh so blind our spirit that even a world that has turned bitter still charms us. We pursue it as it flees from us; we cling to it as it collapses; and, since we cannot arrest its collapse, we are sinking with it while we hold on to it in its fall. Once upon a time this world could hold us by its sheer attractiveness; to-day this poor world is so riddled with such fearful afflictions that the World itself now drives us into the arms of God.'[2]

Saint Gregory had divined that souls alienated from God by mundane prosperity might be reconciled to God by the agony of seeing an earthly paradise turn to dust and ashes. As the light of common day faded away into the darkness of night, the clouds of glory might shine out again. Was the experience of sixth-century Rome an augury for a twentieth-century world? In the twelfth-century springtime of Western mundane prosperity the vision of Saint Francis had been out of range of the spiritual capacity of *l'homme moyen sensuel*, as the vision of the martyrs Nereus and Achilles had been in the second-century 'Indian Summer' of Hellenism. But might not the pelting blows of mundane adversity avail to strike the scales from off the eyes of the grandchildren of Silas Lapham,[3] as dumb sermons in stones had once opened the eyes of Gregory's congregation to the truth which the pastor of their souls was preaching to them among the ruins of Imperial Rome? If the Palaeo-Paganism of the aeon of human history before the epiphany of the higher religions had never been able to extinguish a spark of True Religion that lay smothered in pagan souls,[4] and if the crashing fall of the civilizations of the second generation had stimulated this long-hidden spiritual fire to burst out into a blazing flame, was it likely that a latter-day Neo-Paganism would be capable of putting out the conflagration?

This 'vain repetition of the heathen'[5] lacked the stability and the

1 'Ecce mundus qui diligitur fugit' (Saint Gregory the Great: 'Sermo Habita ad Populum in Basilicâ Sanctorum Nerei et Achillei, Die Natalis Eorum', in *Homiliae Quadraginta in Evangelia*, No. xxviii (Migne, J.-P.: *Patrologia Latina*, vol. lxxvi, col. 1212), from which other sentences have been quoted in IV. iv. 60–61).

2 Saint Gregory, op. cit., partly quoted already in loc. cit.

3 Howells, W. D.: *The Rise of Silas Lapham*, reprinted in 'The World's Classics' series (London 1948, Cumberlege); first published at Boston, Mass., in A.D. 1884.

4 See pp. 759–68, below.

5 See pp. 446–7, above.

staying-power of its palaeo-pagan prototype, in the measure in which it surpassed a Palaeo-Paganism in driving-force; and in this last respect the difference between these two generations of Paganism was great indeed. The Neo-Paganism was a high-powered enormity[1] charged with the spiritual potency of higher religions whose place this Abomination of Desolation had sought to usurp; and this spiritual force was much greater than that of a pristine pagan Human Nature; for, if it is true that 'human passions are always characterised by unlimited and demonic potencies of which animal life is innocent',[2] this is true *a fortiori* of human passions reinforced by a powerful higher religious inspiration.

On the morrow of a Second World War, this daemonic goad was threatening to drive a Westernizing World into the supreme public crime and catastrophe of physical self-destruction through a third world war waged with atomic weapons; but this appalling prospect was merely the unveiling of a goal towards which a secularized Western Society had been heading ever since it had erupted out of a medieval *Respublica Christiana*. This terminus of the broad road along which he was travelling had not caught the eye of Modern Western Man during the deceptive interlude of prosperous mundane progress that had begun with the ending of the Western Wars of Religion and had continued until August 1914. Secular-minded Westerners who had lived and died in those halcyon generations had imagined that their utilitarian version of Neo-Paganism, in which all 'enthusiasm' was anathema, was the impregnable essence of their agnostic faith, whereas in reality this low temper was no more than a temporary reaction against the effervescent ferocity of the Wars of Religion. In the Western 'Age of Reason' this ferocity had been driven underground without being eradicated from Western souls; and it was to erupt again, with a force accumulated through a long repression, in the ensuing 'Age of the Wars of Nationality and Ideology'.

After a Second World War a world that was being secularized in the process of being Westernized was faced with a choice between two alternative possibilities. One possibility was that the vicious momentum of a Neo-Paganism that had run away headlong with the bit between its teeth might carry a Westernizing World over the precipice that had been the bourne of all other civilizations known to History; and in that event the flame of Religion might flare up again out of the wreckage as it had once burst out of the ruins of a Hellenized World. The other possibility was that neo-pagan souls might be smitten with a creative contrition, as well as with an unnerving dismay, by the revelation of the destructive powers and impulses which their reactionary religion had evoked in them, and that they might seek salvation—and haply find it—by turning again to the divers higher religions in which their fathers had received partial revelations of the Beatific Vision.[3] In the catastrophic event, Man would be relieved of further spiritual responsibility at the cost of

[1] The particular sense in which the word 'enormity' is used in this Study has been defined in IV. iv. 133–7.

[2] Niebuhr, R.: *The Nature and Destiny of Man*, vol. i (London 1941, Nisbet), p. 191, quoted on p. 508, above.

[3] See pp. 442–3, above, and pp. 716–36, below.

physical annihilation; but if he took the alternative and less melodramatic course he would have to abide a bout of those perplexing and tormenting questions that are the salt of spiritual life.

In returning to Religion, would a neo-pagan soul be finding her way back out of the broad way that leadeth to destruction into the narrow way which leadeth unto life?[1] Or would she be merely burying herself in a blind alley? Should she hearken to a voice saying, 'See, I have set before thee this day life and good, and death and evil',[2] and to an oracle declaring 'Except a man be born again, he cannot see the Kingdom of God'?[3] Or should she be influenced by the jibes of Mephistopheles pointing out that, whether or no a man can enter the second time into his mother's womb and be born,[4] a baby kangaroo is certainly not entering into the Kingdom of God[5] when it creeps back into the cosy physical *Nirvāna* of its mother's pouch. Was the still small voice luring the Soul into a sluggard's *Faulbett*,[6] or was it calling it to Eternal Life? That was the fateful question to which Mankind would have to find its answer, if Mankind survived.

(*b*) POSSIBILITIES OF SPIRITUAL GROWTH

Would a return to Religion be a signal spiritual advance? Or would it be an abject and inept attempt at an impossible evasion of the hard facts of Life as we know it? Our answer to this question will partly depend on our estimate of the possibilities of spiritual growth in This World.

In a previous chapter[7] we have touched upon the probability (as it appeared to be on the morrow of a Second World War) that the literally world-wide expansion of a secular Modern Western Civilization would translate itself into political form at no distant date through the establishment of a universal state which would fulfil at last the ideal of a polity of this species by embracing the entire habitable and traversable surface of the planet in a commonwealth that would have no physical frontiers because it would have no neighbours. In the same context[8] we have considered the possibility that, within some such literally oecumenical mundane framework, the respective adherents of the living higher religions might come to recognize that their once rival forms of worship were so many alternative approaches to the One True God along avenues offering divers partial glimpses of an identical Beatific Vision. The differences between the divers religions, and between the divers sects of each religion, which had so long been stumbling-blocks for faith and targets for the sceptic's arrows, might then prove to correspond to differences between divers psychological types of Human Nature which required a diversity of spiritual means and methods if they were to arrive at an identical spiritual goal.[9] We threw out the idea that, in this light, the historic living churches might eventually give expression to the unity in their diversity by growing together into a single terrestrial

1 Matt. vii. 13–14. Cp. Luke xiii. 24.
2 Deut. xxx. 15.
3 John iii. 3.
4 John iii. 4.
5 John iii. 5.
6 Goethe: *Faust*, l. 1692, quoted in II. i. 281.
7 On pp. 433–6, above.
8 On pp. 436–42, above.
9 This possibility is discussed on pp. 716–36, below.

Church Militant. Supposing that this were to happen, would it mean that the Kingdom of Heaven would then have been established on Earth? In a Westernizing World in the twentieth century of the Christian Era, this was an inevitable question, because some kind of earthly paradise was the goal of most of the current secular ideologies. If this question were to be answered in the affirmative, that would, in the writer's belief, be a misconception which would give Mephistopheles an opening for sarcasm and Mankind an occasion for disillusionment. In the writer's belief, however, the true answer was in the negative, and this for several reasons.

One manifest reason was exhibited by the nature of Society and the nature of Man. Society is nothing but the common ground between the fields of action of a number of personalities;[1] and human personality, at any rate as we know it in This World, has an innate capacity for evil as well as for good. This meant, as we have often observed,[2] that, in any terrestrial society, unless and until terrestrial Human Nature should undergo a moral mutation which would make an essential change in its character, the possibility of evil, as well as of good, would be born into the World afresh with every child, and would never be wholly ruled out as long as that person remained alive. The challenge, ordeal, struggle, and drama of Man's spiritual life repeat themselves in the experience of each single soul—in contrast to the impersonal accumulation and transmission, from one generation to another, of Man's scientific knowledge and technical 'know-how'.[3] This was as much as to say that the replacement of a multiplicity of civilizations and a diversity of higher religions by a single Church Militant on Earth would not have purged Human Nature of Original Sin; and this moral limitation on the possibility of perfection in This World had a political implication which limited the possibility still further. So long as Original Sin continued to be an element in terrestrial Human Nature, there would always be work in This World for Caesar to do; and, since the labourer is worthy of his hire,[4] and thankless tasks command high salaries, there would still be Caesar's things to be rendered to Caesar, as well as God's things to God.[5] Human Society on Earth would not be able wholly to dispense with institutions; and, since institutions are relations between human beings that extend beyond the narrow range of a direct personal intercourse in which love can make regulation superfluous,[6] an institution can never be founded entirely on the voluntary basis of the individual's will to make it work. If it is to be a going concern, it must be reinforced by habit and be backed, in the last resort, by the sanction of force. In fact, institutions are perfect reflections of the moral imperfection of Human Nature; and these social products of Original Sin would always have to be administered by a secular arm.

A state of society in which this secular power would be subordinated to the ecclesiastical would be a higher and a happier dispensation than a 'Caesaro-papal' absolute régime in which there would be no dis-

[1] See III. iii. 217–48.
[2] e.g. in IV. iv. 120, and on p. 551, above.
[3] See X. ix. 697–704, below.
[4] Luke x. 7. Cp. Matt. x. 10.
[5] Matt. xxii. 21.
[6] See I. i. 454–5.

tinction between the Church and the secular community; but to subordinate the secular power would not be to eliminate it; and, if the Church did seek to eliminate the State altogether, she would be defeating her own highest purposes; for Caesar *gleichgeschaltet* would live on underground in the constitution of his ecclesiastical supplanter, and a prison-house of totalitarianism that had been broken open by the Church's emancipation from the State would be reconstituted through the Church's false step of usurping the State's place instead of being content simply to vindicate her own. In looking into the causes of regression,[1] we have seen the Hildebrandine Church drawn into the arena of power politics—with tragic consequences for Western Christendom as well as for the Church herself—merely through a dispute over the line of demarcation between the ecclesiastical and the secular domain; and we have seen the Tridentine Church exposing herself to a risk of incurring the doom of Lot's wife through putting too much of her treasure into her concern to save her life as a terrestrial institution.[2]

The historic tragedy that had overtaken a Medieval Western Christian Church as the penalty for fighting Caesar with mundane weapons gave some inkling of the fate that a church would bring upon herself if she were to go to the length of stepping outright into Caesar's blood-empurpled shoes; and so, even if a united and concordant Church Militant were to have won a fully world-wide allegiance and to have entered into the heritage of the last of the civilizations, the Church on Earth would not be a perfect embodiment here on Earth of the Kingdom of Heaven. The Church on Earth would still have sin and sorrow to contend with as well as to profit by as a means of grace in a world where learning comes through suffering, and she might find herself unable, for a long time to come, to divest herself entirely of her historic panoply of ecclesiastical institutions. Some residue of her ancient institutional armaments would remain indispensable to her so long as she had to go on struggling for mundane survival; but a still necessary incubus would none the less inevitably still weigh her down—as

[1] On pp. 545–50, above.

[2] Mr. Martin Wight comments: 'On p. 549, above, your criticism of the Tridentine Church is that it has encased itself in "institutional armour". But institutional armour is not a weapon peculiar to Caesar: as you say above on p. 545, a church has to act and exist institutionally as well as a secular society. To this extent, therefore, the Church is not "fighting Caesar with his own weapons" in the implied sense of weapons to which she is not herself entitled. But further: the characteristic weapons of the Tridentine Church have been: (i) the tightening up of dogma, from the Creed of Pius IV down to the definition of 1950; (ii) the Holy Office and the Index, for the suppression of heresy; (iii) the founding of new orders [of religious], of whom the Jesuits (though chronologically they are just pre-Tridentine) are the most important. Now, none of these were "Caesar's weapons". Indeed the relationship is exactly the reverse: (ii) and (iii) are weapons which have made such a strong impression on Caesar that in his new totalitarian mood he has set about imitating them for his own purposes, in the shape of secret police, censorship, storm-troopers, and stakhanovites. It is therefore rather a case of Caesar fighting the Church with the Church's weapons (compare what you say above, on p. 554). And, if you reply that the Church had no business to use weapons like the Inquisition and the Index in the first place, that is a point certainly on which Christians will legitimately differ (and I will tend to agree with you); but are not (i) and (iii) the appropriate, indeed the ultimate, weapons of any Church?'

As regards (i), the writer of this Study would refer to what he has said about Theology in previous chapters of this Part.

Christian was oppressed, till an advanced stage of his painful pilgrimage, by the burden of sin that still lay bound upon his back.

A socially victorious Church Militant, contemplating this forbidding prospect, might hear the insidious voice of Mephistopheles whispering 'defeatism' in her ear. 'I suspect you are beginning to realize,' the tempter might insinuate, 'that your victory is an illusion. It could never, of course, have been anything else; for, after all, you had set yourself, hadn't you, an impossible task. "Thy Kingdom come! Thy will be done in Earth as it is in Heaven!" Why, that is the very definition of just what is inherently unattainable. Who lives in Rome must do as Rome does; and in This World, which is Mankind's concentration camp, there are only two alternative practicable courses of action for Man to choose between (a prisoner is lucky to have a choice, even if only between two extremes). Man can either put the whole of his treasure in This World, or can withdraw his last farthing from his terrestrial banking account. Bet your life on This World, and you can throw yourself wholeheartedly into the satisfying enterprise of turning a prison-yard into an earthly paradise; give up This World as a bad job, and you can detach yourself from mundane entanglements with a no less satisfying singleness of mind. In either of these directions there is an open road, but surely you can see that there is no middle course. If you had paid more attention to History, you would have observed that the whole of this very tricky *terrain* had been reconnoitred long ago by earlier pioneers. The way of detachment has been surveyed—yes, and traversed too—by Epicurean, Stoic, and Buddhist philosophers; the trail leading towards an earthly paradise has been blazed by those practical men of action who have discovered the secret of tapping organized collective human power. The facts are public knowledge, yet you have light-heartedly ignored them. What levity! What impudence! You have been just asking for disillusionment. No wonder you are down in the mouth!'

In this Mephistophelian attack on the ideal of a Church Militant on Earth the one true statement is that the topic is familiar ground. We have explored it already[1] in surveying the alternative ways of life—the ways of Archaism, Futurism, Detachment, Transfiguration—that present themselves to souls challenged by the disintegration of a mundane society, and we have discovered that there is no salvation for the Soul in seeking either an earthly paradise or a *Nirvāna*. Salvation is to be sought and found in a transfiguration of This World by an irradiation of the Kingdom of God—an intellectual paradox which is an historical fact. The truth is that This World is neither a kingdom for Leviathan nor an irreclaimable spiritual wilderness, but a province of the Kingdom of God. It is a rebellious province which has been betrayed by the sin of pride into ungratefully and unlawfully declaring its independence and has thereby brought upon itself the self-imposed penalties of misrule and distress; but this act of rebellion has neither invalidated God's sovereignty nor alienated His love, and He is concerned to re-inaugurate His rule—not because He has any need of this insignificant province's products and revenues, but because His compassion for His creatures

[1] In V. vi. 49–168.

makes Him yearn to redeem them from their self-inflicted sin and suffering.

'How think ye? If a man have an hundred sheep, and one of them be gone astray, doth he not leave the ninety and nine, and goeth into the mountains, and seeketh that which is gone astray? And, if so be that he find it, verily I say unto you, he rejoiceth more of that sheep than of the ninety and nine which went not astray. Even so, it is not the will of your Father which is in Heaven that one of these little ones should perish.'[1]

The human shepherd has to rescue his lost sheep by an act of power in which the dumb animal plays a purely passive part; but God's human flock has gone astray, not by innocent misadventure, but by a rebellious act of will which a repressive act of power could override but not reverse. Man's rebellion against God can only be extinguished by a conversion of the rebel's heart.

'I say unto you that . . . joy shall be in Heaven over one sinner that repenteth, more than over ninety and nine just persons which need no repentance.'[2]

God's province in This World has to be reclaimed by a divine king who wins the sinner's heart by becoming incarnate and by dying for him on the Cross; and Christ's work has to be followed up by representatives of a Church Militant that is in the World yet not of it.

'The direct identification of the Church, as an organised institution taking its part in the process of history, with the Kingdom of God . . . is just as bad theologically as the view which regards the Church as a mere instrument in preparation for the Kingdom of God. The only wholesome view is one which regards it as being constituted as the Church by the powers of the Kingdom of God within it, and yet as being always composed of people still citizens of This World, so that those powers manifest themselves partially and fitfully, and the historical Church is a mixed body.'[3]

In mundane history the device of dual citizenship had been a stroke of genius that had made unity in diversity practical politics at the cost of putting an exacting psychological strain on the citizen who had to reconcile his two allegiances. This had been the *arcanum imperii* of the Roman Commonwealth and of every parochial federal state in the Hellenic and in the Western body social. In the divine government of the *Civitas Dei* the same method had been used for the higher purpose of bringing back a dissident province into conformity with God's will through a voluntary return of rebel souls to their pristine allegiance; and the tension was proportionately greater in the souls of God's human agents who, in order to do His will by serving Him in His work of reclamation through love and not through force, had to live, so long as they were on duty in this arduously pacific campaign, as citizens of This World and of the *Civitas Dei* simultaneously.

The citizen of This World who has deliberately repudiated his

[1] Matt. xviii. 12–14. [2] Luke xv. 7.

[3] William Temple in a letter, written in August 1943, that is quoted in Iremonger, F. A.: *William Temple, Archbishop of Canterbury* (London 1948, Cumberlege), p. 420.

allegiance to God, or has never been aware of being the lawful subject of a heavenly sovereign, can make the best of This Life under the consoling illusion that he is living in the best of all possible worlds; but the citizen of This World who is loyal to his higher allegiance is bound in consequence to feel—and to suffer through feeling—that, in working for God in This World during a spiritual Time of Troubles that is coeval with terrestrial history, he is living and breathing in an element that is not native to his soul—like a diver working at sea-bottom on the salvaging of a foundered ship, or like the denizen of a Mediterranean *dólina*[1] who, in the fantasy of a Platonic myth, one day finds his way up to the true surface of the Earth.

'In my belief the Earth is of a vast order of magnitude, and only a tiny fraction of it is accounted for by the habitat of those of us who live between the Straits of Gibraltar and the eastern end of the Black Sea (τοὺς μεχρὶ Ἡρακλείων στηλῶν ἀπὸ Φάσιδος). We live round this [Mediterranean] sea like ants or frogs round a pond; and no doubt there are many other human societies living in many other similar localities in other parts of the World. All over the World there must be many such *dólinas* of divers forms and sizes, in which water, fog and air have collected. The Earth itself, though, stands clear in that clear sky which contains the stars and which goes by the name of Aether in the standard vocabulary of the astronomers. The *colluvies* that is perpetually collecting in the Earth's *dólinas* is the Aether's sediment. We denizens of the *dólinas* imagine, in our ignorance, that we are living on the Earth's surface, as some denizen of the bottom of the Sea might imagine that he was living on the Sea's surface and might suppose that the Sea was the Sky because he could see the Sun and the rest of the stars through the water. I am assuming, of course, that he is too sluggish and feeble ever to have been able to reach the surface, emerge, poke his head out of the Sea into our habitat, and behold how much clearer and lovelier this is than his own; I am also assuming that he has never heard of our habitat at second hand. Well, we are in precisely the situation of my imaginary inhabitant of the Sea. Living, as we live, in a *dólina*, we imagine ourselves to be living on the Earth's surface, and we call the Air the Sky, under the illusion that this Air is the medium—which can only be the Sky—through which the stars are travelling in their courses. The reality, though, is the same in our actual case as in my imaginary one. We are too feeble and sluggish to be capable of making our way out into the stratosphere; but, if anyone *could* reach its upper limit—for instance, by contriving to fly—and could then poke his head out, he would see the counterpart of what fish see here when they poke their heads out of the Sea and behold our habitat. If he had the stamina to endure this beatific vision, he would recognise that these are the true Sky and the true Light and the true Earth.'[2]

This Platonic conceit is an apt simile of Life on Earth. An earth-bound citizen of This World is the unsuspecting prisoner of his inferior habitat; an involuntary citizen of This World who is at the same time a conscious and active citizen of the *Civitas Dei* is like the fish which has put its head out into the Air or the flying man who has put his head

[1] The Serbo-Croat name for a precipitous-sided depression produced by the decomposition of limestone. The same formation can be seen by an English student of geology, nearer home, in the limestone country in Westmorland, and, farther afield, in the *cenotes* of Yucatan.

[2] Plato: *Phaedo*, 109.

out into the Aether. The soldier serving in the Church Militant on Earth knows that This World is a spiritual battlefield that is not his spiritual home.

'It is written of Cain that he founded a commonwealth; but Abel—true to the type of the pilgrim and sojourner that he was—did not do the like. For the Commonwealth of the Saints is not of This World, though it does give birth to citizens here in whose persons it performs its pilgrimage until the time of its kingdom shall come—the time when it will gather them all together.'[1]

If we adopt this Augustinian Platonic *Weltanschauung* as our own and attempt, in the light of it, to envisage terrestrial history *sub specie aeternitatis*, what significance shall we find in the idea of progress in This World?

In the Age of the Civilizations, progress, in so far as human minds had entertained this idea at all, had often been identified with the progressive improvement of some terrestrial institution: a tribe, a city-state, an empire, a church, a system of knowledge or 'know-how', a school of art, a code of morals. If this conception of the meaning of progress were credible to the pilgrim-citizens on Earth of the *Civitas Dei*, they would indeed be of all men most miserable,[2] since they are aware that, in a terrestrial life infected with Original Sin, neither souls nor institutions can carry progress to perfection, and are also aware that, whatever may be the ultimate destiny of souls, institutions are earth-bound creations of Man in an imperfect world whose limitations they can never transcend.[3] We have seen, in fact, that the idolization of institutions is an intellectual and spiritual error that entails the nemesis of social disaster, and that the self-inflicted penalty for this perversity is the greater, the nobler the institution that is sacrilegiously taken as a substitute for the One True God.[4] The last word on all institutions had been pronounced in the verdict on one master-institution which the Gospel attributed to Christ: 'And he said unto them: The Sabbath was made for Man, and not Man for the Sabbath.'[5] Man was not made for the Sabbath or for any other institution because Man was made for God. 'Thou hast made us for Thee, and our heart is unquiet until it finds rest in Thee.'[6] The touchstone of the value of an institution is whether it helps or hinders Man to find his way back to his Maker, and an institution will become an obstacle to Man's true end of glorifying God and enjoying Him forever if it is taken as being an end in itself instead of being used as the mere means that is all that it truly is.

But, if institutions are means and not ends, what is the significance and the purpose of the social heritage, far transcending the temporal and spatial limits of any single human life on Earth, which institutions

[1] Saint Augustine: *De Civitate Dei*, Book XV, chap. 1, quoted in V. vi. 366.

[2] 1 Cor. xv. 19.

[3] If the writer of the Book of Revelation had been the denizen, not of a circum-Mediterranean Roman Empire, but of a twentieth-century Westernizing World, his wishful thought in chapter xxi, verse 1, would assuredly have been 'there were no more institutions' instead of 'there was no more sea'.

[4] See IV. iv. 303–423, and pp. 548–9, above.

[5] Mark ii. 27.

[6] 'Fecisti nos ad Te, et inquietum est cor nostrum donec requiescat in Te' (Saint Augustine: *Confessions*, Book I, chap. 1).

embody, preserve, and transmit? All men of good will feel that it is God's will that, in their transit through This World, they should spend themselves in labouring for other human beings, living in distant places or destined to be born at remote future dates, whom they will never meet in the flesh; their only means of serving these unknown brethren of theirs is to make their mark for good on Man's social heritage by leaving some institution better than they found it; and they not only feel that this terrestrial duty is compatible with their allegiance to the Kingdom of God; they feel that they would be traitors to the *Civitas Dei* if they held back from playing their part in establishing its rule in the form of a terrestrial Society in an imperfect world through which they are making their brief pilgrim-passages. Is there any solution of this apparent contradiction?

A first step towards resolving it is to remind ourselves that in This World, as in the rest of the Kingdom of God, all spiritual reality, and therefore all spiritual value, resides in persons; for this means that a social heritage which alienates souls from God and leads them to disaster, when it is idolized as an end in itself, has a legitimate use and a genuine value in so far as it is dedicated to a beneficent service for individual human beings in their brief lives on Earth. Improvements in this social heritage, which register social 'progress', are to be estimated and valued according to their effect in increasing the possibilities for individual human beings in This World to live good lives. In taking this as the criterion of progress, the adherents of the higher religions will have the suffrages of any pagans who are innocent of Leviathan-worship; but, whereas a good pagan will work for an improvement in material opportunities for individual human beings through an enrichment of the social heritage in terms of mundane values, the pilgrim-citizen on Earth of the Kingdom of God will work to enrich the social heritage in terms of spiritual values in the hope of thereby helping God to create opportunities for souls to come nearer to doing His will during their transits through This World.

Servants of God will be aware that spiritual progress, in this sense, will incidentally bring mundane progress in its train. 'Seek ye first the Kingdom of God and His righteousness, and all these things shall be added unto you.'[1] They will also be aware that, on the principle of Solomon's Choice, the mundane progress that will be made in this incidental way will be far greater than the utmost that could be attained by aiming direct at a mundane goal.[2] But they will never lose sight of the truth that, in praying for progress in This World in the words 'Thy Kingdom come, Thy will be done in Earth as it is in Heaven', they are praying for a progressive increase in the means of grace within the reach of souls during their service in a Church Militant on Earth that will never be a perfect embodiment of the Kingdom of Heaven—though, in this refractory terrestrial province, it is the Kingdom's lawfully commissioned and effectively serving representative. The Lord's Prayer, prayed with this intention, gives an answer, in the form of a spiritual act, to our perplexing question how, if spiritual progress in Time in

1 Matt. vi. 33. Cp. Luke xii. 31.

2 See pp. 388, 510, and 546–8, above.

This World means progress achieved by individual souls during their brief passages through This World to the Other World, there can be at the same time such a thing in This World as spiritual progress taking place over a Time-span far longer than that of individual lives on Earth—a span running into the thousands of years that had been taken by the historical development of the higher religions from the rise of Tammuz-worship and the generation of Abraham to the Christian Era.

This historical evidence for progress did not necessarily invalidate the Christian view that there was no reason to expect any change in unredeemed Human Nature so long as human life on Earth went on. It was conceivable that, till the face of this planet should cease to be physically habitable by Man, the endowment of individual human beings with natural goodness, and their infection with Original Sin, might remain about the same, on the average, as they had always been so far as human knowledge went. The most primitive societies known to Modern Western anthropologists in the life or by report[1] presented examples both of natural goodness and of innate wickedness that were on a spiritual par with those presented in the histories of the highest mundane civilizations and highest religious societies that had yet come into existence. There had been no perceptible variation in the average sample of Human Nature in the past; there was no warrant in the evidence of History for expecting any great variation in the future either for better or for worse. The likewise Christian hope of a spiritually new species of personality, of which the first-fruits[2] had already been manifested in Christ and in the Saints, might never receive fulfilment in a regeneration of Mankind in the mass—even in the vastly prolonged possible aeon of life on Earth which was the scientific setting of this Christian hope in the minds of latter-day Western philosophers.[3] Yet, even if this hope of a future spiritual mutation of terrestrial Human Nature, which was authorized by Christian doctrine and by a post-Christian Western scientific *Weltanschauung* alike, were never to be realized, the past history of religious revelation would still bear witness that an unregenerate Human Nature was nevertheless a field in which there might be spiritual progress in Time extending over an unlimited number of successive generations of Human Life on Earth; for this history bore witness to the opportunity that, in despite of the spiritual imperfection of Human Nature, was offered to souls, by way of the learning that comes through suffering, for attaining to a closer communion with God, and becoming less unlike Him, during their brief individual transits through this mortal life.

What Christ, with the Prophets before Him and the Saints after Him, had bequeathed to the Christian Church, and what the Church, by virtue of having been fashioned into an incomparably effective institution, had succeeded in accumulating, preserving, communicating, and transmitting to successive generations of Christians, was a growing fund of illumination and of grace: 'illumination' in the sense of a

1 Pater W. Schmidt's views on the religion of Primitive Man are touched upon on pp. 759–68, below.

2 1 Cor. xv. 20; Col. i. 18.

3 See III. iii. 232–5, and p. 453, above.

'revealed discovery' of the true nature of God and the true end of Man in both This World and the Kingdom of Heaven, and 'grace' in the sense of an 'inspired will' to attain to a closer communion with God in the *dólina* of This World. The founders of the other living higher religions, and the followers of their founders, had made their divers contributions, in diverse measure, to the growing spiritual heritage of Mankind on Earth. In this matter of increasing spiritual opportunity for souls in their passages through this earthly life, there was assuredly an inexhaustible possibility of progress in This World.

If we accept this interpretation of the meaning of 'progress', it raises one last question. Were the spiritual opportunities given by Christianity and the other higher religions indispensable conditions for a soul's 'salvation' through a saving conformation of its personal will to God's will in the course of the soul's passage through Life on Earth?

If the answer to this question were in the affirmative, then the innumerable generations of men who had never had access to the illumination and grace conveyed by Christianity and the other higher religions would have been born and have died without a chance of the salvation which is the true end of Man and the true purpose of Life on Earth. Such a sacrifice of past generations for the sake of Posterity might be conceivable, however repugnant, if we believed that the true purpose of Life on Earth was, not the preparation of souls for another life, but the establishment in This World of an ant-like human society whose improvement was an end in itself without regard to the spiritual, or even material, welfare of 'man-power' whose *raison d'être* was to furnish fodder for Mars' war-machine and fuel for Moloch's furnace. If progress were to be taken as meaning the social progress of Leviathan and not the spiritual progress of individual souls, then it would be, perhaps, conceivable that, for the gain and glory of an inhuman body social, innumerable earlier generations should have been doomed to live a lower life in order that a higher life might subsequently be lived by successors who had entered into their labours in order to be sacrificed in their turn on the altar of an idolized collective human power that, on this view, would be the paramount end to which all human lives were, and ought to be, equally subservient. This nightmare view of human destinies might be conceivable on the hypothesis that individual souls existed for the sake of Society, and not for their own sake or for God's, but such a belief is not only repugnant but is inconceivable as well when we are thinking in terms of the history of Religion, in which the progress of individual souls through This World towards God, and not the progress of Society in This World, is the end in which the supreme value is found. Worshippers of the One True God who believed that He had revealed His power to Man as being a self-sacrificing love could not consistently believe that God's method, unfolded in Man's history, of imparting illumination and grace to men on Earth in successive instalments, beginning at a very recent date in the terrestrial history of the Human Race, and even then vouchsafed only gradually in the course of generations and centuries, could have entailed the consequence that the vast majority of souls born into This World so far, who had had no share in this spiritual opportunity, had, on that account, been spiritually lost.

If we believe that the true end of Man is 'to glorify God and fully to enjoy Him for ever',[1] we must believe that this glorious opportunity of attaining to communion with God and beholding the Beatific Vision had been open to every creature that had ever been raised by God to the spiritual stature of Humanity. A human being may be defined as a personality with a will of its own capable of making moral choices between good and evil, and it was impossible to believe that Man's Creator, who had manifested His power as Love Incarnate, would ever have endowed any human creature with the capacity to alienate himself from God by willing evil without also placing within his reach means of grace sufficient to enable him to reconcile himself with God by willing 'Thy will be done'. God's provision of effective means of salvation for human souls on Earth did not have to wait for God's progressive self-revelation; for the altar dedicated 'to the Unknown God' which caught Saint Paul's eye at Athens had always been visible in every pagan human heart to the eye of a God whose own merciful providence had placed it there.

'God that made the World and all things therein . . . hath made of one blood all nations of men for to dwell on all the face of the Earth . . . that they should seek the Lord if haply they might feel after Him and find Him—though He be not far from every one of us.'[2]

The spiritual operation of the grace of an Unknown God on souls ignorantly worshipping Him might be likened to the physical effect of the Gulf Stream on the material life of Man on the Atlantic seaboard of Europe. The genial climate that an ever-flowing Gulf Stream was perpetually bringing with it had made it possible for Primitive Man to work his way along the Atlantic Riviera of the Old World, from Gibraltar to the North Cape, up to latitudes in which, beyond the range of the Gulf Stream's influence, he would have found himself unable to gain any foothold at all; and thereafter, in the medieval phase of Western history, the same still unknown physical benefactor had made it also possible for a life that was not just bare life, but a good life,[3] to be lived in the same high latitudes by Man in process of civilization. All these human beneficiaries of the Gulf Stream had lived and died in ignorance of the Gulf Stream's existence, not to speak of its provenance. Yet the denizens of European coastlands that would have been uninhabitable, if they had not been laved by a current making across the Atlantic from the Gulf of Mexico, did not have to wait to benefit from its effect until they had detected its operation and traced it to its source as a consequence of their tardy discovery of the New World. Their ignorance did not impair the effectiveness of the Gulf Stream's operation during the aeons in which they supposed (so far as they thought about their situa-

[1] Answer to Question 1 in the Larger Catechism agreed upon by the Assembly of Divines at Westminster with the Assistance of Commissioners from the Church of Scotland . . . and approved Anno 1648 by the General Assembly of the Church of Scotland.

[2] Acts xvii. 24 and 26–27.

[3] See Aristotle: *Politics*, Book I, chap. 1, § 8.

tion at all) that they were living at the World's End—in their unawareness of the presence, on the farther side of a temporarily estranging sea, of another hemisphere whose unsuspected radiation, through the medium of the intervening Ocean, was the one thing that, all this time, had been making life possible for them in their northerly habitat. If the goodness of God's creatures reflected the goodness of God Himself, believers in God might feel confident that the children of the age-long 'Days of Ignorance' would be mustered in the Communion of Saints, in fellowship with the heirs of a latter-day Promise, at the time when the Kingdom of God would gather all its pilgrim-citizens together[1]—a time which is Now in the Eternity of I AM.[2]

But, if men on Earth had not had to wait for the recent advent of progressively revealed higher religions in order to become eligible, during their lives on Earth, for being received into the Kingdom of Heaven, then what difference had the advent on Earth of the higher religions really made? The difference—and it was a momentous one—surely was that, under the new dispensation, a soul which did make the best of its spiritual opportunities in This Life would be advancing farther towards communion with God and towards likeness to God under the conditions of life on Earth than had been possible for souls that had not been illuminated, during their pilgrimage on Earth, by the light of the higher religions. A pagan soul, no less than a Christian, Buddhist, Muslim, or Hindu soul, would have ultimate salvation within its reach; but a soul which had been offered, and had opened itself to, the illumination and the grace that the higher religions conveyed, would, while still in This World, be more brightly irradiated with the light of the Other World than a pagan soul that had attained salvation, with God's help, through making the best, in This World, of the narrower opportunity here open to it during its earthly pilgrimage. The soul that had lived on Earth under the new dispensation could attain, while still on Earth, a greater measure of Man's greatest good in This Life than could be attained by any pagan soul in this earthly stage of its existence.

This enlargement of the spiritual opportunity offered to souls for spiritual progress in This World during their transits from birth to death had been the aim, the effect, and the test of the historical progress of Religion in This World as manifested in the epiphany of the higher religions. Their pacific conquests might, and almost certainly would, bring with them incidentally an immeasurable improvement in the material, as well as the spiritual, welfare of individual human beings during their lifetimes on Earth; but a spiritual progress in This World was the boon for which Christians were asking when they prayed 'Thy will be done in Earth as it is in Heaven'; and a salvation that was within reach of all men of goodwill—sons of ignorance as well as witting heirs of the Promise—who made the most of their spiritual opportunities on Earth, however narrow these opportunities might be, was the grace for which Christians were asking when they prayed 'Thy Kingdom come'.

In praying this prayer, they were not asking for a millennial mundane

[1] Saint Augustine, quoted on p. 561, above.
[2] Exod. iii. 14; John viii. 58.

felicity in an earthly paradise that had been more aptly named 'the City of Swine'[1]—though it was certain that even a distant approximation to the establishment of the Kingdom of Heaven on Earth would have the incidental effect of ridding terrestrial human life of the ordinary social evils—the scourge of war and the cancer of class-conflict—which, down to the time of writing, had been the bane of Man in Process of Civilization. In praying 'Thy Kingdom come, Thy will be done', Christians were asking, not for social welfare, but for spiritual trouble that would remain unabated even if all current social problems were to be solved.

This truth had been made manifest in an apparent paradox in the lives of the Saints. It was notorious that saints suffered from an acute and painful sense of sin with which *l'homme moyen sensuel* was not afflicted, and that this conviction of their own sinfulness was apt to increase *pari passu* with their spiritual progress. The explanation, of course, was not that the Saints were in fact more sinful than ordinary sinners, and not that the Saints simulated—out of over-scrupulosity, affectation, or hypocrisy—a conviction of sinfulness which they did not genuinely feel. Their judgement on themselves was utterly sincere and was also fully justified; for, high though their spiritual performance might tower above the level attained by the rest of Mankind, their standard of spiritual endeavour dwarfed the ordinary human standard to a far higher degree. The gap between ideal and achievement was, indeed, of a different order of magnitude in the Saints and in other human souls on Earth; for, in catching a glimpse on Earth of the Beatific Vision, the Saints had taken the measure by which the highest flights of terrestrial Human Nature fell short of God's perfection. The Saints' superhuman intuition of their own unworthiness of God was the seal of their sainthood and the inspiration of their spiritual prowess; but it was also the source of a spiritual agony which the unsaintly majority of Mankind could never experience.

The Saints were 'the successors of the Christ of the Gospels, who imitate[d], with an originality of their own, though this only imperfectly, what He [had been] to perfection';[2] and the agony that was their portion had been suffered, *a fortiori*, by their Master.

> 'Then came to Him the mother of Zebedee's children with her sons, worshipping Him and desiring a certain thing of Him. And He said unto her: What wilt thou? She saith unto Him: Grant that these my two sons may sit, the one on Thy right hand and the other on the left, in Thy kingdom. But Jesus answered and said: Ye know not what ye ask. Are ye able to drink of the cup that I shall drink of, and to be baptised with the baptism that I am baptised with?'[3]

If God and Man were united in one person, the tension between the two natures would be so ineffably severe that a crucified man would be the only kind of man that an Incarnate God could be. So great is the

[1] Plato: *Respublica*, 369B–372D, cited in II. i. 193, n. 1, and II. ii. 23, n. 2.

[2] 'Les continuateurs et les imitateurs originaux, mais incomplets, de ce que fut complètement le Christ des Évangiles' (Henri Bergson, in a saying published in Lou Tseng-tsiang, Dom Pierre Célestin: *Ways of Confucius and of Christ* (London 1948, Burns Oates), p. 115).

[3] Matt. xx. 20–22; cp. Mark x. 35–38.

cost of 'the creation of a new species composed of one unique individual'.[1] Creation spells agony because learning through suffering is the only means of spiritual transfiguration.

At this cost, can any human being be made a son of God in the course of his passage through a world which is 'une machine à faire des dieux'?[2] Perhaps the spiritual achievement manifest in a transfigured soul on Earth 'could not have been attained all at once for the aggregate of Mankind'.[3] Certainly the transfigured soul's 'desire is with God's help to complete the creation of the Human Species and to make of Humanity what it would have been from the beginning if it had been capable of constituting itself definitively without the help of Man himself'.[4] But, since Man cannot become what God wills him to be save by willing God's will with a will of his own, we cannot conceive of Man in This World overcoming sin through a mutation of Human Nature that would render the Soul incapable of sinning; for without a capacity for sin there can be no freedom of moral choice and no possibility of learning through suffering; and a creature that could neither choose between right and wrong nor make spiritual progress through the spiritually perilous exercise of moral responsibility would be less, not more, than human and less capable of becoming godlike than Man was as men knew him in their sinful selves. A proneness to sin—*O felix culpa*[5]—was the spiritual price that Life had paid for becoming human, as mortality was the physical price that it had paid for an organic evolution beyond the limitations of the amoeba. The creation of the Human Species would be completed in a terrestrial Communion of Saints who would be free from sin, not because they would be incapable of it, but because each soul, in its passage through This Life, would be co-operating with God, at the cost of sore spiritual travail, in transfiguring its human nature with the help of God's grace; and, since without God's help this spiritual achievement was beyond the power of Man, the means of grace obtained, accumulated, transmitted, and increased in the spiritual warfare of the Church Militant on Earth was the pearl of great price in Man's social heritage—the earnest of a hope, given to Man by God, that Sin, like Death, might be, not expunged, but conquered.

[1] Bergson, H.: *Les Deux Sources de la Morale et de la Religion* (Paris 1932, Alcan), p. 96, quoted in III. iii. 232.

[2] Bergson, op. cit., p. 343 (the closing words of the book).

[3] Bergson, op. cit., p. 97, quoted in III. iii. 232.

[4] Bergson, op. cit., p. 251, quoted in III. iii. 234.

[5] 'O mira circa nos tuae pietatis dignatio! O in[a]estimabilis dilectio caritatis! Ut servum redimeres, Filium tradidisti! O certe necessarium Adae peccatum, quod Christi morte deletum est! O felix culpa, quae talem ac tantum meruit habere Redemptorem!'—The 'Exultet' for Holy Saturday in the *Missale Romanum*. The text in use at the time of writing was identical with the earliest version extant, as given in three Gallic sacramentaries that were used by Alcuin (*decessit* A.D. 804). See Duchesne, L.: *Christian Worship, Its Origin and Evolution*, English translation, 2nd ed. (London 1904, S.P.C.K.), pp. 251–6.

ANNEXES

VI. A, ANNEX

TABLE OF TYPES OF ENDINGS OF UNIVERSAL STATES

Type I

(Illustrated in the histories of the Yucatec, Arabic Muslim, Hittite, Central American, Chibcha Andean, Hindu, and main Orthodox Christian civilizations)

Act I: The breakdown of the civilization, precipitating a Time of Troubles.

Act II: The successful invasion of the disintegrating civilization by an alien society before the disintegrating civilization has succeeded in stemming its Time of Troubles by establishing an indigenous universal state.

Act III: One or other of two alternative sequels:

A. A direct incorporation of the social tissue of the invaded civilization into the aggressive civilization's body social (the fate suffered by the Yucatec Civilization at the hands of the Mexic,[1] by the Arabic Muslim at the hands of the Iranic Muslim,[2] and perhaps also by the Hittite at the hands of the external proletariat of the Minoan World as an incidental effect of a post-Minoan Völkerwanderung[3]).

B. A utilization—unintended on both sides, yet effective nevertheless—of the aggressive alien civilization's act of aggression in order to provide the invaded society with a universal state of alien workmanship in lieu of one made by its own hands (the *tour de force* achieved by the Central American Civilization, which found its universal state in the Spanish Viceroyalty of New Spain;[4] by the Chibcha province of the Andean World,[5] which found its universal state in the Spanish

[1] See I. i. 123–4; IV. iv. 105–6; V. v. 42 and 89.

[2] See I. i. 68–72, 119, 124, and 387–8; II. ii. 77 and 392; and IV. iv. 112–13. The Arabic Civilization had, however, latterly re-emerged from the body of the Iranic Civilization, like Jonah from the belly of the whale (see IV. iv. 113–14 and 115), and seemed to be moving, like the Iranic Civilization from which it had extricated itself, towards incorporation into the body social of the Western Civilization.

[3] See I. i. 93 and 114; II. ii. 79; IV. iv. 108–12.

[4] See I. i. 120; IV. iv. 105–6; V. v. 357 and 525.

[5] The Chibchas' domain lay within the latter-day frontiers of the Latin American Republic of Colombia (see IV. iv. 103). Like their southern neighbours the Karas in what was to become the domain of the Republic of Ecuador, the Chibchas were, culturally as well as geographically, on the fringe of the Andean World. Though by the time of the Spanish conquest in the sixteenth century of the Christian Era the Chibchas had become masters of the goldsmith's art, and had even established a monetary currency of gold disks (see Joyce, T. A.: *South American Archaeology* (London 1912, Lee Warner), pp. 40–41 and 24), they appear still to have been ignorant of the much more important art of irrigation (see op. cit., p. 39), which was the economic basis of the Andean Civilization in its birthplace in the valley-bottoms along the Peruvian coast (see I. i. 121, 122, 322–3, and 334; II. ii. 34). The Chibchas revealed their cultural inferiority

Viceroyalty of New Granada; by the Hindu Society, which found its universal state first in the Mughal Rāj and then in the British Rāj;[1] and by the main body of the Orthodox Christian Society, which found its universal state in the Ottoman Empire[2]).

Act IV: One or other of two alternative sequels to Alternative *B* in Act III:

A. A direct incorporation of the submerged society into the body social of the alien society that has provided it with its universal state, through the break-up of this universal state into 'successor-states' that gain admission to the comity of states into which the incorporating society's body politic is articulated. (At the time of writing this seemed[3] to be the destiny of the Central American and Chibcha Andean societies since the conversion of the corresponding portions of the former Spanish Empire into the Republics of Mexico and Colombia. At the same date it looked as if the Hindu Society would go the same way, now that, in A.D. 1947, a Hindu universal state, which had found its second avatar in the British Rāj, had broken up into two 'successor-states'—the Indian Union and Pakistan—both of which had shown their desire to be members of a Western comity of states by remaining within the British Commonwealth and joining the United Nations Organization.)

B. A break-up of the alien universal state—producing a perceptible social interregnum occupied by rudiments of the normal creative achievements of the internal and the external proletariat (the triumph of a universal church and a Völkerwanderung), but overtaken and overlaid, before these rudiments have had time to develop, by the incorporation of the mortal remains of the defunct universal state into the body

to their contemporaries in the heart of the Andean World by their persistence in the practice of human sacrifice, after this had been almost completely suppressed within the bounds of the Inca Empire (see Joyce, op. cit., pp. 28–29 and 162)—an indigenous Andean universal state under whose rule the Chibchas, unlike the Karas, had not been brought. In the Chibcha province of the Andean Civilization, as in the rest of its domain, this civilization was already in decline by the time when the Spanish *conquistadores* arrived on the scene; but, while in other parts of the Andean World a universal state had already been established by the Incas, the Chibcha province, like the Central American World, was then still in its Time of Troubles. The Spaniards found the peoples of what was to be Colombia, like those of what was to be Mexico, in the throes of a destructive fratricidal warfare among the local states, with the local principality of Bogotá winning its way towards a regional domination such as was all but achieved in Central America by the Aztec principality of Tenochtitlan (see Joyce, op. cit., pp. 13–17). In both cases, the imminent universal state was provided by the alien invaders after they had overthrown the native militarists on the eve of their final triumph.

[1] See II. ii. 77 and 131; IV. iv. 96–98; V. v. 53, 54, and 304–5.

[2] See II. ii. 77 and 177; III. iii. 27; IV. iv. 2, 68, 76, and 346, n. 2 (on p. 347); V. v. 105 and 107; V. vi. 298–300.

[3] This tentative form of expression seemed advisable in this case in view of the recent re-emergence of the Arabic Muslim Society as a separate social entity after no less than three hundred years of incorporation in the body social of the Iranic Muslim Society under the Ottoman régime (see IV. iv. 113–14). Indeed, the revolution that broke out in Mexico in A.D. 1910 and that was still in progress at the time of writing might prove to have marked the beginning of a similar re-emergence of the Central American Civiliza- from the body social of the Western Society, into which it had been incorporated by force of Spanish arms at about the time when the 'Osmanlis had been successively conquering 'Irāq, Syria, Egypt, the Yaman, and the Barbary States. Moreover, the upheaval that was already taking place in Mexico might prove to be merely the first of a series which might eventually extend into part or the whole of the domain of the Andean Civilization as well (notwithstanding the contrary view expressed in IV. iv. 80–81).

social of another alien civilization. (This seemed at the time of writing to be the destiny of the Orthodox Christian population that had once constituted the Ottoman Millet-i-Rum. The first step taken by all the Orthodox Christian 'successor-states' of the Ottoman Empire had been to organize themselves on the basis of a Modern Western nationalism and to seek admission to the Western comity of states.)[1]

Type II

(Illustrated in the histories of the Andean, Babylonic, Syriac, and Indic civilizations, the Western medieval city-state cosmos, and the Far Eastern Civilization in Japan)

Act I: The breakdown of the civilization, precipitating a Time of Troubles.

Act II: The foundation of an indigenous universal state (the Empire of the Incas in Andean history, the Neo-Babylonian Empire in Babylonic history, the Achaemenian Empire in Syriac history, the Mauryan Empire in Indic history, the Napoleonic Empire in the history of the Western medieval city-state cosmos,[2] the Tokugawa Shogunate in the history of Japan).

Act III: The overthrow of the indigenous universal state, through the successful intrusion of an alien civilization, before the exhaustion of the rally which the foundation of the indigenous universal state has inaugurated (the overthrow of the Inca Empire by Spanish *conquistadores* from Western Christendom; of the Neo-Babylonian Empire by the Achaemenian agents of the Syriac Civilization; of the Achaemenian and Mauryan Empires by Macedonian conquerors from the Hellenic World; of the Napoleonic Empire by the ferment of Modern Western political ideas of which the French empire-builders themselves were the principal disseminators; of the Tokugawa Empire by the impact of a Western Civilization equipped with the armaments of the Industrial Age).

Act IV: One or other of three alternative sequels:

A. A direct absorption of the invaded society into the intrusive alien society's body social (the fate of the Western medieval city-state cosmos, which was reabsorbed into the main body social of the Western Civilization as a result of the Napoleonic Empire's meteoric rise and fall).

B. A utilization of the aggressive alien civilization's act of aggression in order to replace the invaded society's overthrown indigenous universal state with an alien substitute and thereby allow the universal state phase of the history of the invaded society to complete its course. (The universal state phase of Babylonic history, begun under the indigenous

[1] For this ending of the Ottoman Empire, see IV. iv. 76–78 and 188–9; V. v. 294–302 and 520.

[2] For this historical function of the Napoleonic Empire, see V. v. 619–42.

Neo-Babylonian Empire, was continued under the alien Achaemenian Empire and was completed under the alien Seleucid Monarchy;[1] the universal state phase of Andean history, begun under the indigenous Empire of the Incas, was completed under the alien Spanish Viceroyalty of Peru.[2])

C. Persistent and eventually successful efforts on the part of the invaded civilization to expel the intrusive civilization from the whole of its domain (the eventual expulsion of Hellenism from both the Syriac World and the Indic World).[3]

Act V: Sequels to the alternative courses *B* and *C* in Act IV:

A. The sequel to Act IV, Alternative *B*, appears to be the incorporation of the invaded society into the body social of an intrusive society that has provided it with a continuation of its indigenous universal state. (The inheritance of the mortal remains of the Babylonic Society was contested between the Syriac and the Hellenic Society, and in this contest the Syriac Society was the victor;[4] the remains of the Andean Society appeared to have been incorporated into the body social of the Western Society since the conversion of the Spanish Viceroyalty of Peru into the Republics of Bolivia, Peru, and Ecuador.[5])

B. The sequel to Act IV, Alternative *C*, is the reintegration and resumption of the indigenous universal state that has been overthrown before the completion of its course by the irruption of an intrusive alien civilization (the resumption, in the Syriac World, of the Achaemenian Empire in the new shape of the Arab Caliphate;[6] the resumption, in the Indic World, of the Mauryan Empire in the new shape of the Guptan Empire[7]).

Act VI: The sequel to Act V, Alternative *B*: A break-up, in due course, of the reintegrated indigenous universal state, producing a social interregnum occupied by the normal creative achievements of the internal and external proletariats: the triumph of a universal church and a Völkerwanderung (mass-conversions to Islam and inroads of Eurasian, Afrasian, and Western Christian barbarians at the break-up of the Arab Caliphate;[8] mass-conversions to Hinduism and inroads of Eurasian barbarians at the break-up of the Guptan Empire[9]).

[1] See V. v. 123 (especially n. 2) and 370.

[2] See I. i. 120; IV. iv. 79–80 and 103.

[3] See I. i. 75–77 and 85–86; II. ii. 285–8 and 371–2; V. v. 125–8; V. vi. 210–11.

[4] See I. i. 79–81 and V. v. 370.

[5] See I. i. 119 and V. v. 524–5. At the time of writing this opinion could be no more than tentative, for the reasons given above on p. 570, n. 3. The then still apparently sluggish native peasantry of Bolivia and Peru might prove one day to be charged with the same explosive force that had already erupted from a corresponding social stratum in Mexico.

[6] See I. i. 76–77. The Achaemenian Empire had an abortive alien heir in the shape of the Seleucid Monarchy, and the Arab Caliphate an abortive indigenous precursor in the shape of the Sasanian Empire.

[7] See I. i. 85–86. The Mauryan Empire had a succession of abortive alien heirs in the shapes of the Bactrian Greek Empire and the Kushan Empire, and the Guptan Empire an abortive precursor in the Andhra Empire.

[8] See I. i. 72; V. v. 128 and 242–8.

[9] See I. i. 85; V. v. 137–8 and 276–9.

Type III

(Illustrated in the histories of the Hellenic, Sinic, Sumeric, and Russian Orthodox Christian civilizations).[1]

Act I: The breakdown of the civilization, precipitating a Time of Troubles.

Act II: The foundation of an indigenous universal state (the Roman Empire in Hellenic history, the Ts'in and Han Empire in Sinic history, the Empire of Sumer and Akkad in Sumeric history, the Union of Muscovy and Novgorod in Russian history).

Act III: A collapse of the indigenous universal state as the result of a fresh collapse of the disintegrating society (the collapse of the Roman Empire in the third century of the Christian Era;[2] the collapse of the Prior Han Dynasty just after the beginning of the Christian Era;[3] the downfall of Ur-Engur's (*alias* Ur-Nammu's) dynasty *circa* 2026 or 1962 B.C.;[4] the bout of anarchy in the early years of the seventeenth century of the Christian Era which is known as 'the Time of Troubles' in the Russian historical tradition[5]).

Act IV: A restoration of the prostrate indigenous universal state by one or other of two alternative means:

A. By self-help (the restoration of the Roman Empire by Illyrian marchmen, of the Han Empire by the Posterior Han Dynasty, of the Empire of Sumer and Akkad by Amorite marchmen).[6]

B. By self-help reinforced by the reception of an alien civilization. (The restoration, by the new dynasty of the Romanovs, of an empire which the House of Rurik had failed to save from collapse, corresponds to the restoration of the Prior Han Empire by the Posterior Han;[7] the new feature is the subsequent reception of the Western Civilization by Peter the Great in order to enable the restored Russian universal state to hold its own in a Westernizing World.)

Act V: Sequels to the alternative courses *A* and *B* in Act IV:

A. A break-up, in due course, of the restored universal state, producing a social interregnum occupied by the normal creative achievements of the internal and external proletariats: the triumph of a universal church and a Völkerwanderung (mass conversions to Christianity and inroads of North European, Eurasian, and Afrasian barbarians at the break-up of the Roman Empire;[8] mass-conversions to the Mahāyāna and inroads of Eurasian barbarians at the break-up of the Han

[1] It seemed probable, in the light of the information accessible at the time of writing, that the endings of the Minoan and the Mayan universal states likewise conformed to this type, but the evidence was still insufficient to warrant more than a tentative opinion in either case.

[2] See IV. iv. 8; V. v. 219 and 649–50; V. vi. 207 and 291.

[3] See V. vi. 295.

[4] See V. vi. 297, and the Note on Chronology, x. 171–2 and 212.

[5] See V. vi. 311.

[6] For references to previous passages touching on these restorations, see nn. 2, 3, and 4 on this page.

[7] See V. vi. 311–12.

[8] See I. i. 41–42 and 62–63; V. v. 80 and 220–2.

Empire;[1] inroads of Eurasian barbarians and Kassites and Hittites at the break-up of the Empire of Sumer and Akkad[2]).

B. A break-up, in due course, of the restored universal state, producing a perceptible social interregnum, but overtaken and overlaid, before the interregnum has had time to produce its normal phenomena, by a further stage of the progressive incorporation of the dissolving society into the alien society to which it has been deliberately assimilating itself since the restoration of its universal state (the decay and downfall of the Tsardom, after the exhaustion of the tonic of eighteenth-century Western 'enlightened Monarchy', and its prompt replacement by the Union of Soviet Socialist Republics as a vehicle of the nineteenth-century Western social gospel of Marxism).[3]

Type IV

(Illustrated in the history of the Egyptiac Civilization)

Act I: The breakdown of the civilization, precipitating a Time of Troubles (at some time between the end of the Fourth Egyptiac Dynasty *circa* 2500 B.C. and the fall of the Sixth Dynasty *circa* 2200 B.C.).

Act II: The foundation of an indigenous universal state (the Egyptiac 'Middle Empire').[4]

Act III: A break-up, in due course, of the universal state, producing a social interregnum occupied by the normal creative achievements of the internal and external proletariats: the triumph of a universal church and a Völkerwanderung (mass conversions to the Osirian Church[5] and the occupation of Lower Egypt by the Hyksos barbarians[6]).

Act IV: A premature termination of the social interregnum, before it has run its normal course, and before the dissolution of the moribund

[1] See I. i. 88; V. v. 140 and 272–4.

[2] See I. i. 105–6 and 111; V. v. 263–4.

[3] The decay of the Tsardom might be dated from the failure of the reforms, carried out in the eighteen-sixties, to bring and keep Russia abreast of the Western World. This failure was brutally but effectively proclaimed in the assassination of the Tsar-Liberator Alexander II in A.D. 1881; and the consequent reversion of the Imperial régime to a policy of repression in the tradition of Tsar Nicholas I was powerless to avert the downfall of the Tsardom in A.D. 1917; but the long impending interregnum had no sooner arrived than it was brought to an end by the establishment of the Soviet régime. In one aspect, this régime unmistakably represented a further step in the process of Westernization. Under the inspiration of a Western 'ideology' the Russian Communists ploughed deep where Peter the Great's hoe had merely scratched the surface of the ground. Peter had been content with Westernizing his professional soldiers and administrators; the Communists set themselves to Westernize the masses by making them literate and training them in a Modern Western industrial technique. At the same time, the policy of the Russian Communists was equivocal. Though Marxism was a Western creed, it was a revolutionary one which, in its Western homelands, was directed against the Western *ancien régime*; and on Russian ground and in Russian hands it might be brought to bear, not merely against the latest phase of the Western Civilization, but against the West as such, in all its manifestations, as the Western Romantic movement had been turned to account, in the nineteenth century, by the Russian Slavophils (for this ambiguity in the policy and character of Russian Communism, see III. iii. 200–2 and 364–5; V. v. 181–7; and IX. viii. 133–6 and 807–8).

[4] In the course of the Middle Empire we can descry a slight and transient crisis between the decease of the Twelfth Dynasty and the subsequent series of soldier emperors (see V. vi. 207).

[5] See I. i. 140–4 and V. v. 149–50.

[6] See I. i. 105, 106, and 137, and V. v. 266.

society has had time to work itself out, by a sudden fanatical restoration of the indigenous universal state (the Egyptiac 'New Empire').

Act V: The maintenance of the restored universal state—and, with it, of the reanimated civilization—for a term comparable in length to the reanimated civilization's original span of life. (In Egyptiac history, the restored universal state displayed an extraordinary tenacity:[1] When the Eighteenth Dynasty, which had founded 'the New Empire' in the sixteenth century B.C., lost its impetus after a run of more than two hundred years, its task was taken over in the fourteenth century B.C. by a series of soldier emperors[2] reminiscent of those that, in the history of the original Egyptiac universal state, had taken over the Twelfth Dynasty's task in the eighteenth century B.C. When the régime of the soldier emperors of the Nineteenth and Twentieth Dynasties, after having kept 'the New Empire' in being for another two hundred years, was eventually worn out,[3] in its turn, by its own superhuman efforts expended in victoriously stemming, first the Hittite assaults upon the dominions of the Empire in Syria,[4] and then the avalanche of barbarian invaders that descended upon the northern borders of Egypt itself in the post-Minoan Völkerwanderung,[5] the ecclesiastical power stepped into the breach laid open by the ultimate collapse of the secular power, and thereby tided the restored Egyptiac universal state over a critical moment in its history.[6] Some three hundred years later, a persistent, and all but successful, attempt to re-establish the restored Egyptiac universal state, up to the frontiers once attained by it under the Eighteenth Dynasty, was made by the Ethiopian marchmen of the Egyptiac World from Napata;[7] and, in the long series of successive alien dominations over the northern half of the Egyptiac World, for which the failure of the Napatan adventure in the seventh century B.C. opened the way, it proved impossible for any alien invader to keep his seat for long unless he could bring himself to overcome or dissemble his pride as a conqueror and his contempt for the conquered so far as to be willing to sit on the throne of the Pharaohs in the guise and insignia of a legitimate wearer of the Double Crown.[8] Thus the simulacrum, at least, of the restored Egyptiac universal state—and, with it, the substance of the Egyptiac culture—was maintained until the conversion of both the inhabitants of the Nile Valley and the Roman Imperial Government to the Syro-Hellenic syncretistic religion of Christianity;

[1] See I. i. 137–9. [2] See II. ii. 113. [3] See IV. iv. 422.

[4] See I. i. 113–14; II. ii. 113; and IV. iv. 110–11.

[5] See I. i. 93 and 100–1; II. ii. 113; IV. iv. 85 and 422; V. v. 237, 269, 290, and 352; and V. vi. 207.

[6] See II. ii. 116, n. 1; IV. iv. 421 and 515–17; p. 190, n. 1, above; and p. 692, below.

[7] See II. ii. 116 and V. v. 268.

[8] The Ptolemies and their successors the Roman Emperors had the intuition to conceive of this policy and the tact to put it into effect; and at Constantinople in the fifteenth century of the Christian Era, during the last phase of a Palaeologan restoration of an East Roman Empire which had been a restoration of the Roman Empire, the Egyptiac Double Crown was brought out of a lumber room to lend a show of dignity to a shadow emperor's head (see XIII. x. 51–52). The Assyrians made no attempt at conciliation. The Achaemenidae never succeeded in retrieving the effects of Cambyses' personal breach, in his treatment of a conquered Egypt, of the Dynasty's rule of considerateness for the traditional institutions of their subjects (see V. v. 704, n. 2, and 705, n. 2).

and this conversion, through which the dissolution of the Egyptiac Society was at last consummated, was separated by a Time-span of more than two thousand years[1] from the date in the sixteenth century B.C. at which an Egyptiac Society, at that time apparently *in extremis*, had been given its surprising new lease of life by the sudden uprising of Amosis against the Hyksos.)

Type V

(Illustrated in the history of the Far Eastern Civilization in China)

Act I: The breakdown of the civilization, precipitating a Time of Troubles.

Act II: The foundation of a universal state by intrusive barbarians with a tincture of alien culture (the imposition of a universal state on the Far Eastern Society in China through the completion of the conquest of the Sung dominions by the Mongols[2] in A.D. 1280).

Act III: A sudden fanatical replacement of the semi-alien universal state, before it has run its normal course, by an indigenous universal state (the expulsion of the Mongols from China by the Ming[3]).

Act IV: The maintenance of the universal state—and, with it, of the civilization—beyond the term at which it might have been expected to give place to an interregnum, through the transfer of the universal state from enfeebled indigenous to vigorous barbarian hands instead of its breaking up and being replaced by a bevy of barbarian successor-states (the transfer of rule over an undivided China from the Ming Dynasty to the Manchus in the seventeenth century of the Christian Era).

Act V: The transformation of the unexpired universal state into one of the parochial states of an alien society (the admission of China to the Western comity of states after the Chinese Revolution of A.D. 1911[4] and the subsequent transfer of her cultural allegiance from the Western Civilization to the Russian[5]).

[1] See I. i. 139.

[2] For the tincture of Far Eastern Christian culture which the Mongols had acquired before their conquest of China, see II. ii. 237–8; III. iii. 451; V. v. 309 and 348.

[3] See II. ii. 121; V. v. 3–4, 54, and 348.

[4] As was signified in the symbolism of the flag which the Chinese Republic devised for itself, this successor of the Manchu Empire claimed to be the heir of the latter in its capacity of universal state, though at the same time the Revolution of A.D. 1911, in which the Republic came to birth, was an indigenous Chinese uprising against barbarian rule—partly in the tradition of the uprising against the Mongols which had brought the Ming Dynasty into power four and a half centuries earlier, and partly under the inspiration of the alien political creed of Western nationalism.

[5] Whether the incorporation of the main body of the Far Eastern Society into the body social of a Communist World was to be the last chapter of its history, or whether it might one day extricate itself again and re-enter on a distinct life of its own, was a question that, at the time of writing, seemed likely to remain inscrutable for a long time to come.

VI. B (i), ANNEX

THE ROLE OF THE BYZANTINE ELEMENT IN MUSCOVY'S HERITAGE

WHILE the writer was revising his draft of the chapter to which this Annex attaches, he had the benefit of comments and criticisms from B. H. Sumner, the Warden of All Souls College, Oxford, and from Prince Dmitri Obolensky, the Reader in Russian and Balkan Medieval History in the University of Oxford, on the question of the degree to which the course of Muscovite History was affected by the influence of the Byzantine element in the Russian Orthodox Christian cultural heritage.

B. H. Sumner's opinion on this question is set out in the following passages of a letter of his, dated the 25th January, 1951, to the writer of this Study:

'I find the build-up and development of the Muscovite state in the fifteenth and sixteenth centuries very difficult to analyse, but, from what I have read of those two centuries from the Russian side, I should say that the most effective and practical influences in building up centralized administration and government came from autochthonous Russian developments of the semi-feudal conditions of Moscow and the other Russian principalities (shot through with a strong nationalist colouring), combined with some Tatar influence, but with little Byzantine influence. I do not think, for instance, that either Ivan the Great or Ivan the Terrible regarded themselves as successors of the Byzantine emperors, or that they and their civil servants, *boyars*, diplomats, &c., had any idea of "oecumenical" pretensions. It is true that Ivan the Terrible, for instance, claimed to be Tsar "Autocrat", Gosudar, and appointed by God, combining plenitude of power both *vis-à-vis* his subjects and as against any other states, but he never claimed to be the successor of the *Basileus*, or to be "oecumenical' or "Tsar of the Orthodox Christians of the whole World" (that was the expression used by the Patriarch of Constantinople in a letter to Ivan in A.D. 1561, but not by Ivan). I don't think that it could be held that Ivan the Great and Ivan the Terrible and the civilians in Russia held that there had been any *translatio imperii*, or made any claim over all Christians or all Orthodox.

'Such claims, implicitly or explicitly, had appeared from the end of the fifteenth century onwards, bound up with the idea of Moscow as the Third Rome, but, at any rate at that time, this idea, which admittedly had its origins in writings of certain monks, continued to be confined to certain ecclesiastical circles in Russia, with occasional echoes from Constantinople. It is striking, I think, that the official historiography of the sixteenth century in Russia, which was built up by the Tsars, does not lean at all towards Byzantium: both in the chronicles and in Russian diplomacy of the time the emphasis is all on the heritage of Kiev, not at all on the heritage of Byzantium. That, of course, was because of the continuous struggle for the Russian western lands against Lithuania-Poland.

'From about A.D. 1470 onwards, for more than a century, Moscow had a whole series of overtures, either from Rome or from the Emperor, or both, linking together an anti-Turkish alliance, re-union of churches, recognition of Moscow as the heir of the Byzantine Empire, and elevation of the Metropolitan of Moscow to the patriarchal dignity. It is, I think, significant that the Russians in reply were always silent as regards the inheritance of the Byzantine Empire, or coronation of the Tsar as "the Christian Tsar". What the Russians were interested in was their claims against Lithuania-Poland and their struggle for an exit to the Baltic, and not the Balkans or the Ottomans: hence the failure of Western overtures for an anti-Turkish alliance and of Western attempts to win the Russians for this by dangling before them the lure of the Byzantine heritage.

'Thus, the conception of Moscow as "the Third Rome", or of Muscovy as the inheritor of the "oecumenical" role of Byzantium, was, in my view, of no practical importance and of very little theoretical or emotional importance among the governing class in Muscovy in the late fifteenth, sixteenth, and seventeenth centuries. Its appeal was in the main limited to certain ecclesiastical circles in Muscovy—and, in a sense, to needy Orthodox in the Ottoman Empire in quest of money from Moscow. It is quite true that the idea of Muscovy as the sole possessor of the pure Orthodox Christian faith after the Council of Florence and the capture of Constantinople was a stock-in-trade element in Muscovite national pride during these centuries, and it fostered Muscovite exclusiveness and xenophobia. But this line is not the same as stepping into the shoes of Byzantium by aspiring to an "oecumenical" role.

'Much later, when the Russians had advanced far southwards and were strong enough to challenge the Turks, then the idea of the liberation of the Orthodox, and sometimes that of some form of resurrected Orthodox empire at Constantinople, became prominent, and increasingly so in the nineteenth century. Even so, I think that the influence of the messianic ideas of the Slavophils and Dostoievsky and their typicalness can be exaggerated, and that the "oecumenical" and messianic elements in Russian nineteenth-century thought ought not to be read back into earlier centuries as being then powerfully creative and proof of a strong and continuous Byzantine heritage.'

In a note communicated to the writer of this Study on the 1st June, 1951, Prince Dmitri Obolensky expresses the same view.

'Neither the successive Russian governments of the sixteenth century nor, on the whole, contemporary Russian writers and historians seem to have taken the theory of "Moscow the Third Rome" very seriously; for the Muscovite rulers from Ivan III onwards, Moscow was much more the "Second Kiev" than the "Third Rome". I would agree here with Humphrey Sumner. Some recent historians have, rightly, it seems to me, "played down" the importance of the theory of "Moscow the Third Rome" in the development of Russian sovereignty. See, for example, G. Olšr: "Gli ultimi Rurikidi e le basi ideologiche della sovranità dello Stato russo", in *Orientalia Christiana Periodica*, vol. xii, Nos. 3–4 (Rome, 1946), pp. 322–73.'

It will be seen that Sumner and Obolensky agree in making three points: In the first place, the concept of 'Moscow the Third Rome' was an academic idea which was never taken very seriously outside ecclesiastical circles; secondly, the architects of a Muscovite autocracy were indebted to the institutions of the East Roman Empire for little except certain external forms and ceremonies; thirdly, the statesmen in control of Muscovite policy showed themselves unwilling to sacrifice the interests of their own Russian Orthodox Christendom to those of an Ottoman Orthodox Christendom which was sundered from Russia by the double barrier of the Eurasian Steppe and the Black Sea. None of these three points would be contested by the present writer; but he would point out, in his turn, that none of them is incompatible with the thesis that the extinction of the last glimmer of the East Roman Empire in A.D. 1453 had an important and enduring psychological effect on Russian souls,[1] and that this effect consisted in the implantation in them of a feeling that Muscovy, as the now sole surviving Orthodox Christian Power of any consequence, had inherited from the East Roman Empire both the mission of preserving intact the purity of the Orthodox Christian Faith and the high destiny which this onerous mission carried with it *ex officio*.

It will be noticed that Sumner, in the passages quoted above, equates the ideological legacy of the East Roman Empire with a pretension to an oecumenical authority. As the present writer sees it, the idea for which the East Roman Empire had stood, first and foremost, in its own people's minds was the guardianship of Christian Orthodoxy rather than the possession of a title to world-wide dominion. He would, however, go on to contend that, in fact, the second of these two pretensions was logically latent in the first, since it would be difficult for a people to believe that God had singled them out to be the unique heralds of His Truth on Earth without also believing that He had likewise singled them out to be His instruments for propagating this Truth eventually throughout the *Oikoumenê*. It was, for example, an article of orthodox Jewish belief among a politically impotent Jewish diasporà that the extinct Kingdom of David would eventually be restored by the Messiah, not in its historic form as a parochial state, but with a dominion that would be coextensive with the *Oikoumenê*. The writer would therefore take issue with Sumner's contention that the idea of being the sole possessor of the pure Orthodox Faith does not carry with it an aspiration to an oecumenical role; and he would have consulted his friend and mentor further on this point if, by the date when he was revising the present Part of this Study for the press, Humphrey Sumner's friends and fellow historians had not suffered an irreparable loss in this saintly scholar's untimely death.

[1] This psychological effect of the concept of 'the Third Rome' is, however, also questioned by Prince Obolensky:

'I do not wish to minimize the importance of the religious factor in the resistance offered by the seventeenth-century Russian conservatives to the infiltration of Western ideas and customs: some of them at least seem to have regarded Russia as a guardian of the Orthodox faith against the heretical West. But I doubt whether the theory of "Moscow the Third Rome" had much to do with this attitude, except possibly among the "Old Believers". Except in some ecclesiastical, and particularly monastic, circles, this theory does not seem to have made much headway in Russia. . . . [It] does not seem to have been sufficiently accepted to justify the view that future generations of Russians were moved by it to resist the impact of Western culture upon their way of life.'

VI. C (ii) (*c*) 3, ANNEX

THE ADMINISTRATIVE GEOGRAPHY OF THE ACHAEMENIAN EMPIRE[1]

The Spirit and Policy of the Achaemenian Régime

IN the chapter to which this annex attaches,[2] we have taken note of the easy-going spirit that was characteristic of the Achaemenian régime.

This êthos accounts for the speed and facility with which the Achaemenian Empire was created by Cyrus II and extended by Cambyses II, and for the comparable speed with which it was less easily re-established and farther extended by Darius I. Achaemenian rule was accepted by the stricken peoples of the Syriac and Babylonic worlds because it offered them the 'rest cure' that they needed after their sufferings from the last and worst bout of Assyrian militarism (*saeviebat* 745–609 B.C.),[3] from a contemporaneous Eurasian Nomad Völkerwanderung, and from the subsequent wars between the fallen Assyrian Power's successor-states; and the widespread *émeute* which broke out in 522 B.C. on receipt of the news of the assassination of the reigning emperor by Darius and his accomplices was an exception that proved the rule of normal acquiescence in the Achaemenian régime. It is true, as we shall see, that the terrible year 522–521 B.C. brought with it a change for the worse in the political êthos and structure of the Achaemenian Empire which was never afterwards retrieved. It is also true that, throughout the age of Achaemenian dominion, there were marked differences in the degree of the acquiescence of the divers subject peoples. The Egyptians and the Babylonians—conscious, as they were, of the antiquity of their distinctive cultures and the recentness of their own latest spells of imperial power—persistently felt, and repeatedly acted upon, a hostility towards their Persian masters which was not shared by the Babylonians' former victims the Jews and the Phoenicians.[4] On the whole, however, the Achaemenian régime met with remarkably little resistance and succeeded in maintaining itself for more than two hundred years at the cost of an impressively slight exertion of force.

This success is largely explained by a policy of *laisser faire* which stood

[1] This amateur essay owes more to Professor Roland G. Kent and Professor George G. Cameron than the writer can easily convey to the reader. It could not have been undertaken at all without the foundation provided by their published work, and the writer might not have had the temerity to print it if these two scholars had not generously spent much time and trouble in reading and commenting on the first draft. While, of course, no responsibility whatsoever attaches to either of them for misstatements of fact and errors of judgement that have still not been eliminated by the writer, with the aid of their comments, in the version here published, the reader would hardly be able to appreciate the magnitude of the writer's debt without seeing with his own eyes the corrections, and better still, the omissions, that were made on the original typescript when it was being revised with these invaluable comments at the writer's elbow.

Before this page was in first proof, the World had lost a great scholar through Professor Kent's death.

[2] VI. C (ii) (*c*) 3, pp. 178–9, above.

[3] See IV. iv. 473, n. 3.

[4] See V. v. 123.

out in welcome contrast to the policies of Assyria and of a Neo-Babylonian Empire that had followed in the Assyrians' footsteps.

Ever since Assyria had won her fight for her existence against the Aramaean invaders of Mesopotamia at the turn of the second and the last millennium B.C.,[1] she had not been content simply to rule the territories which she annexed progressively to her ancestral domain; she had sought to assimilate them as well; and the rigour with which she stamped her impress even on her latest, most ephemeral and most outlying territorial acquisitions is attested by the survival there of the *Assyrium nomen* long after it had been forgotten on the sites of Nineveh, Calah, and Asshur itself.[2] Though the Assyrian records known to Western scholars in the twentieth century of the Christian Era did not bear witness to any extension of a short-lived Assyrian hegemony in South-Eastern Anatolia any farther north-westward than the principality of Khilakku (*Graecè* Kilikia, *Latinè* Cilicia) astride the southernmost bend of the River Halys, the Assyrian name must have been associated with the 'White Syrian' inhabitants of the north coast of Anatolia, round the mouths of the rivers Halys, Iris, and Thermodon,[3] at the time when, in the course of the seventh century B.C., the Hellenic explorers and colonizers of this coast had pushed that far eastwards.[4] In this quarter, it is true, the Assyrian name did not survive for long; but in Western parlance in A.D. 1952 it was still current in 'Syria', where the Persians and the Hellenes had successively taken over from the Neo-Babylonian régime the name 'Assyria' to denote a country which had always been vehemently recalcitrant to Assyrian rule, and whose coastline was occupied by peoples bearing the famous names 'Phoenicians' and 'Philistines'.

In Syria, at any rate (though not, as far as was known, in Pontic Cappadocia), one of the means by which the Assyrians had thus succeeded in stamping their name on countries and peoples that execrated their domination and abhorred their culture had been a systematic obliteration of previous political landmarks and substitution of an arbitrarily mapped out network of Assyrian provinces; and, at the opening of the last paroxysm of the *terror Assyriacus*, this administrative engine of 'Assyrianization' had been keyed up by Tiglath-Pileser III (*accessit* 746 B.C.). The twenty-four provinces into which the Assyrian Empire had been articulated within its frontiers as these had stood at Tiglath-Pileser's accession had been redistributed, by 745 B.C., into twice as many departments,[5] and thereafter additional departments on the new scale had been created *pari passu* with the further expansion of Assyrian rule south-westward into Syria, eastward on to the western rim of the Iranian Plateau, and south-eastward into Babylonia. In instituting and extending this new close-meshed system of local administration, Tiglath-Pileser III and his successors were pursuing the same aim as the post-Revolutionary French conquerors of Northern

[1] See II. ii. 134–5.
[2] See IV. iv. 469–72.
[3] See Herodotus, Book II, chap. 104.
[4] See IX. viii. 432, n. 2.
[5] See Forrer, E.: *Die Provinzeinteilung des Assyrischen Reiches* (Leipzig 1920 Hinrichs), pp. 5, 10–11, and 49–50.

Italy, the Low Countries, the Rhineland, and North-Western Germany. The Assyrian Empire, like the Napoleonic Empire, was attempting permanently to assimilate and absorb the annexed territories into its own body politic.

This Assyrian policy of assimilation was the background and foil against which an antithetical policy was inaugurated by the Achaemenidae. Cyrus II and his successors sought to reconcile their subjects to their rule by keeping down to a minimum the Achaemenian Imperial Government's interference with existing habits and customs; and, on the plane of administrative geography, this policy took the forms of permitting a maximum amount of local self-government and refraining from more than a minimum amount of change in those *ci-devant* frontiers between sovereign states that had now become boundaries between Achaemenian viceroyalties ('satrapies').[1] So long as their subjects kept the peace and paid their taxes, the Achaemenidae were content to leave them to live as they pleased in other respects; and they were slow to anger, even when they had to deal with inveterate rebels. Herodotus was rightly much impressed by their generosity in reinstating the sons of both the two insurgent Egyptian client princes Inarôs and Amyrtaeus on the thrones that their fathers had forfeited—'regardless of the fact that no one had given more trouble than Inarôs and Amyrtaeus had to the Persian Imperial Government.'[2]

This Achaemenian policy of *laisser faire* was, however, to some extent frustrated by the recalcitrance of certain of the beneficiaries. While the unwaveringly loyal Phoenician city-states along the coast of Syria were rewarded by being invested with miniature empires—*imperia Punica in imperio Persico*—astride one of the vital lines of Achaemenian communications,[3] the persistently refractory Hellenic city-states along the west coast of Anatolia had to be held through the agency of local despots, acting in the Achaemenian interest, whom their subjects regarded as 'quislings'; and a corresponding discrimination was forced upon the Achaemenian Imperial Government in their policy towards the viceroyalties that were the largest units of regional administration within this universal state. The Neo-Babylonian Empire, which Cyrus had swallowed whole, was subsequently broken up into two taxation districts[4]—one consisting of Babylonia itself and the other of the ex-Assyrian territory that had fallen to the Neo-Babylonian Empire's share when Nabopolassar had partitioned the Assyrian dominions with his Median ally; and Herodotus's gazetteer of Darius I's taxation districts—muddled though it is here and there—brings some skeletons out of an Imperial cupboard which the draftsmen of the official inscriptions had been careful to leave unopened. Herodotus's information makes it evident, as we shall see, that three of the original viceroyalties—an Armenia that had perhaps been taken into partnership by the founder of the Median Empire, a Media that had undoubtedly been taken into

[1] The Old Persian word 'khšathrapāvan' (*Graecè* 'satrapês') signified 'protector of the kingdom' (Kent, *Old Persian: Grammar, Texts, Lexicon* (New Haven, Conn. 1950, American Oriental Society), p. 181).

[2] Herodotus, Book III, chap. 15.

[3] See V. v. 123, n. 2.

[4] See further pp. 657–8, below.

partnership by the founder of the Achaemenian Empire, and a Persia that had become, and still remained, the reigning imperial country—had each been partitioned in Darius I's new division of the Empire into taxation districts; and we may guess that this dissection of these great political units into a larger number of smaller fiscal units had been carried out as a precaution against any repetition of the all but lethal stabs which the usurping scion of the Ariaramnan branch of the Achaemenidae had received from Armenians, Medes, and Persians alike in the anarchic first year of his reign. On the evidence supplied by Herodotus, we can see that, for fiscal purposes, Media had been partitioned into four divisions;[1] Armenia into three;[2] and Persia into two.[3] Conversely, Herodotus reveals that one loyal viceroyalty had been given a territorial reward—though one of dubious value. The rebellious Medes who had been deported to islands in the Persian Gulf and three rebellious Persian tribes, the Yautiyā (*Graecè* Outioi) and the Mačiyā (*Graecè* Mykoi) in Lāristān and the Asagartiyā (Sagartioi) in Kirmān, who had been degraded to the status of subject peoples burdened with a penally heavy tribute, had all been attached to the loyal viceroyalty of Harahvatiš (written Harauvatiš: *Latinè* 'Arachosia').[4] The official lists indicate that the Viceroyalty of Harahvatiš had been further enlarged by the transfer of Zrāka from the Viceroyalty of Parthava, and that the loyal viceroyalty of Bākhtriš (*Latinè* Bactria or Bactriana) had been rewarded by being allowed to retain a sub-empire which included not only the administration of Suguda or Sugda (*Latinè* Sogdiana), north-east of the Oxus, but a supervision over the Achaemenian Empire's independent allies the Sakā Haumavargā (*Graecè* Sakai Amyrgioi), north-east of the Jaxartes, in Farghānah.[5]

The grounds for these inferences from the information furnished by Herodotus are discussed below, and the conclusions are mentioned, by anticipation, at this point simply to illustrate the historical fact that in certain cases the Achaemenian Imperial Government found itself compelled by *force majeure* to depart from its standing policy of respecting the traditional boundaries between viceroyalties. In the course of the Achaemenian Empire's history, both the areas and the number of the viceroyalties are known to have varied. They might be—and perhaps usually were[6]—larger than taxation districts, or they might be smaller, as was, for example, the viceroyalty of Karkā (*Latinè* Caria) that was separated from Yauna (*Latinè* Ionia) eventually—perhaps after the suppression of the Ionian Revolt of 499–491 B.C.—if we may draw this inference from the absence of the name Karkā in the three earliest, and its presence in the three latest, of the official lists of countries under Achaemenian sovereignty or suzerainty. On the other hand it is to be

[1] See further pp. 602–4 and 623–32, below.
[2] See further pp. 604–11 and 660, below.
[3] See further pp. 620–3 and 637–41, below.
[4] See further pp. 602–3 and 637–41, below.
[5] See further pp. 644–8, below.
[6] See Junge, P. J.: 'Satrapie und Natio: Reichsverwaltung und Reichspolitik im Staate Dareios' I' (*Klio*, vol. xxxiv (Neue Folge, vol. xvi, Heft 1/2) (Leipzig 1942, Dieterich), pp. 1–55, especially p. 5, n. 5).

presumed that the boundaries of the taxation districts remained relatively constant throughout,[1] since any variation of these would inevitably have thrown into confusion the records, kept in the Imperial Ministry of Finance, which were the key to an effective maintenance of the Imperial taxation system. In the administrative geography of the Achaemenian Empire the two sets of permanent units must have been these taxation districts and the communes, exercising local self-government, out of which each taxation district was built up.

In his gazetteer of the Achaemenian taxation districts,[2] Herodotus makes it clear that, in his belief, these had been instituted by Darius I at the beginning of his reign,[3] at a date at which he had not yet overstepped the north-west frontier along the coastline of the mainland of Anatolia which he had inherited from his predecessors. Herodotus believed that, within these limits (which included Darius's own conquests in the Indus Basin), the Achaemenian Empire had originally been dissected by Darius into twenty taxation districts, and that two more—'the Isles' and 'the Peoples of Europe as far as Thessaly'—had subsequently been added before the recession of the North-West Frontier as a result of the disastrous outcome of the campaigns of 480–479 B.C. Herodotus was aware that the Achaemenian Empire also embraced one partially tax-paying non-subject principality, Cilicia, which he has included in his list of the twenty taxation districts as his Number 4, and some tax-free countries besides. The chief of these was Pārsa (*Graecè* Persis)[4]—or, more accurately, the remnant of Pārsa whose denizens had retained the privileged status of being the imperial people after the civil war between Persian and Persian in the South-East during the terrible year 522–521 B.C. The other three non-tax-paying peoples known to Herodotus were, all of them, transfrontier allies: the Ethiopians marching with the southern frontier of the Viceroyalty of Egypt; the Arabs whose autonomous territory included a short strip of coast at the south-east corner of the Mediterranean,[5] and 'the Colchians and adjoining peoples, as far as the Caucasis Range', on the north.[6]

This distinction in status between the imperial people, its allies, and its subjects may perhaps have counted for something on the political plane. Cilicia, for example, is not included in any official Achaemenian list of the peoples of the Empire, and Pārsa is tactfully omitted from the list of tax-paying subject countries in Darius's inscription 'Persepolis *e*' and is still more tactfully differentiated from them in his 'Susa *e*' and in his 'Naqš-i-Rustam *a*'. But on the fiscal plane in any case it looks as

[1] On this see Junge: 'Satrapie' (ibid., pp. 4–5); eundem: 'Hazarapatiš' (ibid., vol. xxxiii (Neue Folge, vol. xv) (Leipzig 1940, Dieterich), pp. 30–38, especially p. 32, n. 1).

[2] Herodotus, Book III, chaps. 89–97.

[3] The text of the Behistan Inscription was not one of the Achaemenian official documents that had come into Herodotus's hands (though a copy of it was in the archives of so remote a community as the Jewish military colony at Elephantinê on the southern frontier of the Viceroyalty of Egypt); and Herodotus was not aware of the year of anarchy between Darius's assumption of the Imperial Crown and his effective assertion of his authority throughout the Achaemenian dominions.

[4] See Herodotus, Book III, chap. 97.

[5] See ibid., chaps. 4–9.

[6] These peoples are all entered in the list of non-tax-paying peoples in Book III, chap. 97; but in Book III, chap. 88, the Arabs are declared to be the only free allies of the Empire. Herodotus was unaware of the status of the Amyrgian Sakas.

if the distinction were little more than a formality, considering that the 'free' peoples, including the Persians themselves, were constrained to bring the Emperor annual gifts that were no more voluntary than the 'benevolences' exacted by King Henry VII of England, while on the other side the avowedly tax-paying subjects appear (to judge by the official bas-reliefs) to have paid their taxes, including those discharged in the precious metals, in kind (i.e. in the form of gold and silver vases) and not in coin. Moreover, all parts of the *Oikoumenê* that lay within economic range of the Achaemenian Imperial Government, including distant regions that were completely independent of it politically, were affected economically by the annual non-return journey of appreciable quantities of the precious metals to the Imperial treasuries at Susa, Ecbatana, and Persepolis. This one-way flow persisted for some two centuries, until the accumulated hoards were suddenly thrown into circulation again by Alexander.

The Extant Sources of Information

The information about the administrative geography of the Achaemenian Empire that was accessible to Western scholars in A.D. 1952 was all derived ultimately from Achaemenian official sources; but it had come through two separate channels: official documents inscribed by the Achaemenian Government itself and facts and figures, doubtless originally emanating from Achaemenian official documents, which had been obtained, and incorporated into his own work, by the Hellenic historian Herodotus. Either of these two sets of statements could be used as a check upon the other; and this was fortunate, since neither authority was satisfactory in and by itself. Herodotus—or the intermediaries through whose hands his information had reached him—had obviously misunderstood, wrongly presented or erroneously emended some of the official material on which the Herodotean account of Achaemenian administrative geography was based; yet, in virtue of being a private person who had ceased to be an Achaemenian subject and who had no official axe to grind, Herodotus had conveyed to his readers information which the Achaemenian Government had taken care not to impart in its official inscriptions. Conversely, these official inscriptions, while they certainly did not tell the whole truth that the Herodotean picture revealed, were presumably free, so far as they went, from the misunderstandings and errors into which Herodotus had fallen.

In Table V, folding out opposite page 772, the names of countries and peoples given in the six official lists are set out on the left-hand side[1] and the corresponding names given by Herodotus on the right-hand side. The interpretation of the information, coming from these divers sources, which has determined the arrangement of the names in this table is explained and discussed in the remainder of the present Annex.

1 In handling the names given in the six official lists, the present writer has taken for his guides two papers by experts: R. G. Kent's 'Old Persian Texts, IV: The Lists of Provinces', in the *Journal of Near Eastern Studies*, vol. ii, January–October 1943 (Chicago 1943, University of Chicago Press), pp. 302–7, and G. G. Cameron's 'Darius, Egypt and "the Lands beyond the Sea"', ibid., pp. 307–13. Without these guides, he would have been incapable of embarking on his own present amateur essay.

The official information that had come into Modern Western hands direct consisted of six lists—five inscribed by Darius I and one by Xerxes—of *dahyāva* (countries represented on the throne-bearer reliefs by male figures displaying the characteristic physique, style of hair-dressing, and costume of their respective peoples) over which Darius I and Xerxes claimed to be bearing rule. The documentary monuments in which these lists occurred were Darius I's record of the events of the first year of his reign on the cliff at Behistan, overlooking the Great North-East Road from Babylon via Ecbatana and the Caspian Gates to the Oxus-Jaxartes Basin ('DB'); Darius's inscription *e* at Persepolis ('DPe'); Darius's inscription on the stelae that he erected in Egypt along the ship canal that he dug to connect the Indian Ocean with the Mediterranean from Suez via the Wady Tumilat and the Nile ('DZd'); Darius's inscription *e* at Susa ('DSe'); Darius's inscription on his tomb cut into the cliff at Naqš-i-Rustam ('DNa');[1] and Xerxes' inscription *h* at Persepolis ('XPh'). Of these six lists, 'DB', 'DSe', 'DNa', and 'XPh' were inscribed in three languages: Old Persian, Elamite, and Babylonian; 'DPe' was inscribed in Old Persian only; the inscription on the stelae at Suez was in Egyptian hieroglyphic characters, into which it had been transcribed from Aramaic. Inscription 'DNa' was accompanied by a bas-relief—to which the inscription called the reader's attention —in which the thirty peoples, including the Pārsā, whose names were recited in the list, were delineated, as throne-bearers, in the order of their mention in the list and with their names attached to them;[2] and this set of figures was repeated at Persepolis in a tripylon dating from the end of Darius I's reign and again in 'the Hall of the Hundred Columns' dating from the end of Xerxes' reign.[3]

The six lists contain between them thirty-two names, including Pārsa. Twenty-one of the thirty-one names other than Pārsa occur in all six lists (though not in the same order in each list) namely (to cite them in the order of the earliest document, 'DB'): Hūja (written Ūvja), Bābiruš, Athurā, Arabāya, Mudrāya, Sparda, Yauna, Māda, Armina (*alias* Arminiya), Katpatuka, Parthava, Zrāka, Haraiva, Hvārazmīy or Hvārazmiš (written Uvārazmīy or Uvārazmiš), Bākhtriš, Suguda (*alias* Sugda), Gādāra, Saka, Thataguš, Harahvatiš (written Harauvatiš), Maka. Four lists out of the six—i.e. all except 'DB' and 'DPe'—divide one of these twenty-one common units, namely the Sakā, into two groups. 'The

[1] There were four rock-tombs, in all, at Naqš-i-Rustam (see Kent, *Old Persian*, p. 109).

[2] 'The inscriptions identifying the throne-bearers on DN are mostly illegible; most of those on the other tomb at Naqš-i-Rustam displaying throne-bearers, which may be the tomb of Artaxerxes II or III, are still decipherable.'—Professor Roland G. Kent.

[3] See Junge, P. J.: 'Satrapie und Natio', p. 22. According to Junge, ibid., p. 24, this set of figures of throne-bearers was not identical with the set of figures of tax-payers, supplemented by a set of figures of present-bringers, representing the Persian nobility of Hūja (where there was a Persian population in the districts of Parsuwaš, *alias* Parsawaš, and Anšan) and Pārsa and the Median nobility, of which a complete specimen had been preserved in a relief in Darius's apadāna dating from the last years of Darius's reign. According to the same authority (p. 25), the set of figures representing the tax-payers omitted the Sakā Haumavargā, the Hvārazmiš, 'the Sakā beyond the Sea' (i.e. the Scyths in the Great Western Bay of the Eurasian Steppe), the Dahā and the Thatagu[?d or v]iyā.

Hauma-(?)drinking Sakā' (Sakā Haumavargā)[1] are distinguished from 'the Pointed-Hood Sakā'[2] (Sakā Tigrakhaudā) in 'DSe', 'DNa', and 'XPh', and 'the Sakā of the Marshes' from 'the Sakā of the Plains' in Darius I's Egyptian list 'DZd'.[3] Gādāra and 'those in the Sea', both mentioned in all the other five lists, are omitted from 'DZd', whether by inadvertence or through lack of space.[4] Hīduš, which had evidently not yet been annexed at the date at which 'DB' was inscribed, appears in all five subsequent lists. 'Those beyond the Sea' (i.e. the peoples of Thrace, perhaps also including some of the Nomad Scyths on the north bank of the Lower Danube) are not mentioned in either 'DB' or 'DE', but appear in all four subsequent lists. 'DSe', 'DNa', and 'XPh' all also add Skudra, Putāyā, Kūša, and Karkā.[5] 'XPh' alone adds the Dahā and the Ākaufačiyā as well, but none of these three latest lists includes Asagarta,[6] which is named in 'DPe' only.[7]

1 'The hauma-, of course, is identical etymologically with Sanskrit soma-, and the *Avesta* and the *Rigveda* agree as to its use. In the *Avesta* it is the name of a plant, which may have been of the milkweed type, and of the juice which was pressed out from it, the juice then being allowed to ferment and develop intoxicating properties, after which it was used as a drink by the priests—or perhaps by other persons also. There is no identified Indo-European root from which varga can come. The resemblance to Greek ϝergon is unfortunately misleading, since that goes back to a *werg- with a palatal g that gives Iranian z, as in Avestan varəz, and O.P. d, as in Arta-*vard*-iya. The *werg- in haumavarga- must have had a velar or labiovelar g at an earlier stage. The hauma being a liquid, this varga- may mean "pressing out" or "preparing" or "using" or "consuming" —the last word covering "eating and drinking".

'If Greek Aspourgianoi (your p. 644, n. 5) represents Iranian aspa-vargā, the latter need not mean "horse-eaters", but might be kumīz-drinkers, i.e. drinkers of fermented mare's-milk. Then we could re-establish "hauma-drinking" for haumavargā.'—Note by Professor Roland G. Kent.

'Pressing out', which is one of the alternative possible meanings of varga- that are suggested above by Professor Kent, might perhaps be used both for milking a mare and for squeezing the juice out of a plant. If this is its meaning, 'aspavargā' would be an Iranian equivalent of the Homeric Greek ἱππημολγοι.—A.J.T.

2 The shape of 'the Pointed-Hood Sakā's' distinctive headgear was known from the portrayal of their prince, Skunkha, on Darius's Behistan relief. The twentieth-century English word that would most naturally have been used to describe it was not 'hood' but 'cap'. The word 'hood' has been applied to it in this Study because there seemed to the writer to be indications that the Medieval and Modern Western hood was ultimately derived from the Sakā Tigrakhaudā's head-dress (see XIII. ix. 53–55). The writer did not possess the philological knowledge to be able to judge whether Skunkha's 'khauda' was to be identified with a Western scholar's hood etymologically as well as genetically, or whether this Old Persian word was represented by the New Persian 'khūd', meaning helmet by itself and cock's-comb in the compound 'khūd khurūs'.

3 Though, on the face of it, it seems unlikely that the same Achaemenian emperor Darius should divide the same people into two groups on different lines in different official inscriptions, it cannot be demonstrated that these two formulas for dividing the Sakā into two are equivalent to one another.

4 Lack of space is A. T. Olmstead's explanation in his *History of the Persian Empire* (Chicago 1948, University of Chicago Press), p. 149.

5 The plural of the ethnikon, standing for the name of the country.

6 Asagarta is mentioned four times, and the ethnikon Asagartiya twice, in the text of 'DB'.—Professor Roland G. Kent.

7 These discrepancies between the contents of the divers official lists enable us to arrange them in the chronological order of their successive redaction with one exception: we are left in doubt about the chronological relation between 'DPe' and 'DZd'. Both these lists are evidently later than 'DB' (on the assumption that the reason why Gādāra and 'those in the Sea', which appear in 'DB', are omitted in 'DZd' is simply lack of space or inadvertence, and not because these two peoples were not yet included in the Achaemenian Empire at the time when 'DZd' was composed). 'DPe' and 'DZd' are also both evidently earlier than 'DSe', 'DNa', and 'XPh'. The chronological relation between 'DZd' and 'DPe' themselves is, however, impossible similarly to establish from the internal evidence, because different items point to opposite conclusions. From the absence in 'DZd' of 'those beyond the Sea', who appear in 'DPe', as they do in all

It is not easy to make out on what principle, if any, the names included in these official lists have been selected. It is clear that they are only a selection from a larger list, since the names of several other countries—e.g. Marguš, Varkāna, the Yautiyā—are mentioned incidentally by Darius in his record of the events of the year 522–521 B.C. in associations which show that Marguš was embraced in the Viceroyalty of Bākhtriš and Varkāna in the Viceroyalty of Parthava, and that the Yautiyā were Persians. In the lists, however, Varkāna is never named, though Haraiva, which would appear to have had the same status as Varkāna within the Viceroyalty and Taxation District Parthava, is named in the lists invariably; and similarly Marguš is never named in the lists, though they invariably name Suguda, which, like Marguš, was a canton within the Viceroyalty and Taxation District Bākhtriš. Moreover, the peoples mentioned in Herodotus's gazetteer of the taxation districts, either by name or as the anonymous neighbours of other peoples who are mentioned by name, amount to seventy-three in all, according to the reckoning adopted in this Annex; and we have to conclude that Herodotus or his intermediary obtained from official Achaemenian sources about twice as many names as are mentioned in the Achaemenian official lists—even when we have allowed for Herodotus's several times repeated error of inserting the same people twice or three times over under different names which he had failed to recognize as being synonymous, and when we have also recognized the possibility that, in naming peoples included in taxation districts with seaboards on the Mediterranean, the Aegean, and the Black Sea, the Herodotean list may have supplemented its official source by adding other names that were household words in Hellas.[1]

The omission of the name of Cilicia in all six official lists, and the special treatment of Pārsa in three of them,[2] are features that would suggest in themselves that these lists were intended to be representative of the tax-paying subject population—each name standing either for a single taxation district or for a single viceroyalty[3]—but this explanation is ruled out by the inclusion of Arabāya, the Kūšiyā, the Ākaufačiyā, and the Sakā Haumavargā, since the Arabs, the African Ethiopians, and

the three latest lists, we might infer that 'DZd' was earlier than 'DPe', if the opposite conclusion were not just as strongly commended by the absence in 'DPe' of the Putāyā and the Kūšiyā, who appear in 'DZd' as they do in all the three latest lists likewise. Two further points of difference both also tell in favour of dating 'DPe' earlier than 'DZd'. 'DPe' mentions the Sakā without distinguishing between two varieties of them, whereas 'DZd' distinguishes two varieties—though we cannot be sure that its distinction between 'the Sakā of the Marshes' and 'the Sakā of the Plains' is identical with the distinction, made in the three latest lists, between 'Sakā Tigrakhaudā' and 'Sakā Haumavargā'. Moreover, the order of the names in 'DPe' indicates that Zrāka is still included in the Viceroyalty of Parthava, whereas the order in 'DZd' indicates that Zrāka has already been detached from Parthava and attached to Harahvatiš.

On this showing, 'DZd' has tentatively been placed after 'DPe' in the Table.

[1] On the other hand, such names as the Outioi in Herodotus' Taxation District No. 14, and the Dadikai and Aparytai in his No. 7, can have reached him only from Achaemenian official sources, though they do not appear in any of the official lists.

[2] See p. 584' above.

[3] Professor G. G. Cameron comments: 'The omission of Cilicia and special treatment of Pārsa indicate to me not a list of tax-paying subjects but simply a list of areas where there was a satrap'. But will not the imperial territory administered by satraps have been co-extensive with the imperial territory inhabited by tax-paying subjects, even though, within this total domain, the respective areas of particular satrapies and particular taxation districts did not coincide?

the Colchians are known from Herodotus, and the Sakā Haumavargā are known from other Hellenic sources,[1] to have been, not tax-paying subjects, but 'gift-bringing' allies. Moreover, while the number of the taxation districts seems unlikely ever to have risen from an original figure of twenty to as many as thirty-two, and the number of the viceroyalties, at its highest, will have fallen short of thirty-two *a fortiori*,[2] the four taxation districts into which Media had been partitioned on the testimony of Herodotus are all embraced, in all the official lists, under the single name 'Māda', while on the other hand the three components of the single viceroyalty of Bactria—namely the two subject peoples Bākhtriš and Suguda and the allied people known as the Sakā Haumavargā who were brigaded with them—are separately mentioned in all the official lists, each under its own name. The generally accepted view that Suguda was an integral part of the Viceroyalty of Bākhtriš rests on the fact that it is placed immediately after Bākhtriš in all six lists; and the same reasoning suggests that Haraiva was always included in the Viceroyalty of Parthava and that Zrãka was originally also attached to Parthava and was subsequently transferred, at least for a time, to the Viceroyalty of Harahvatiš.[3]

It is thus evident that the selection of names in the official lists is not the roll-call either of the viceroyalties or of the taxation districts or of either of these two sets of administrative units together with the 'externally associated' allies. At least nine names[4] out of a total of thirty-two that appear on one or other of the lists are those of countries which never, so far as we know, constituted either separate viceroyalties or even separate taxation districts; and there are at least two taxation districts in the Herodotean gazetteer—Nos. 17 and 19—which are not represented by any of the names in the official lists. None of this, however, is surprising, since we may feel sure that the purpose for which this selection of names was made by Achaemenian officials was not that of enabling twentieth-century Western scholars to reconstruct the Ariaramnan Achaemenian Empire's administrative geography. It is indeed manifest that the positive purpose of the lists, like that of the accompanying visual representations of throne-bearers, is to give the reader and spectator an impression of the Imperial Dynasty's and Imperial People's achievement in conquering and holding an empire of so vast an extent and so variegated a racial and cultural composition. This intention is indicated in 'DB' in the observations in §§ 7–9, which immediately follow the recital of the list and which are recapitulated more briefly in 'DNa', § 4, in the same context. The latter passage continues as follows:

'If you say to yourself: "How manifold were those lands that King Darius possessed", look at the representations of the throne-bearers, and then you will recognise—then verily you will know—that a Persian fight-

[1] See further pp. 644–5, below. [2] See further pp. 683–4, below.

[3] In both 'DB' and 'DPe' the three names Parthava-Zrãka-Haraiva appear consecutively in this order, and Haraiva is placed immediately after Parthava in 'DSe', 'DNa', and 'XPh', while in 'DZd', conversely, Haraiva is placed immediately before Parthava. On the other hand, Zrãka is placed immediately after Harahvatiš in 'DZd', and immediately before Harahvatiš in 'DSe' and 'DNa'. In 'XPh', Zrãka-Parthava-Haraiva are cited consecutively again in this order.

[4] Zrãka, Asagarta, Maka, Dahā, Hvārazmiš, Haraiva, Suguda, Thataguš, Putāyā.

ing-man's spear has pressed forward far—then verily you will know that a Persian fighting-man has given battle far from Pārsa.'

In short, the intention of the lists is to convey the fact that is more succinctly expressed in a boast inscribed on the foundation tablets of the apadāna at Persepolis and is reproduced in identical terms in an inscription found *in situ* at Ecbatana: the Achaemenian Empire extends 'from the Sakā who are beyond Suguda to the Kūšiyā, and from Hīduš to Sparda'.[1]

At the same time the circumspect compilers of the official lists did not allow their enthusiasm for advertising the extent and variety of the Achaemenian Empire to lead them into mentioning names that might have drawn attention to other facts which would have betrayed a damaging truth. The Ariaramnan branch of the dynasty that proudly reigned over this far-flung empire had learnt by the bitter experience of their anarchic inaugural year 522–521 B.C. that they could not depend on the loyalty of more than a minority even of the two imperial peoples, the Pārsā and the Mādā; and they had accordingly taken the precautions of partitioning them both for fiscal purposes, of degrading dissident Pārsā to the status of tax-paying subjects, and of deporting dissident Mādā to islands in the Persian Gulf. But, the more necessary these political precautions were held to be, the more inexpedient it would have been to draw attention to them; and the very frankness of the account in 'DB' of the rebellion of the Yautiyā Pārsā explains why this name of ill omen does not appear on any of the six official lists, though it is tactlessly included, in the Hellenized form 'Outioi', in Herodotus's recital of the peoples brigaded, in his taxation District No. 14, with the Harahvatiyā (disguised in the terminology of Herodotus's source as 'the Thamanaioi', signifying 'the borderers'). As for the no less tell-tale name 'Asagarta',[2] the imprudent mention of it in 'DPe' is never afterwards repeated. The official lists do, in fact, skilfully achieve the dual purpose of advertising the grandeur of the Ariaramnan Achaemenian Empire without exposing its seamy side to public view. But, of course, the more successful these lists are in achieving the combination of purposes which they were designed to reconcile, the harder they make it for the historian to wring out of them the truth for which he is seeking.

The information—drawn, at least in part, from Achaemenian official sources, though perhaps only at second or third hand—that has been incorporated by Herodotus into his history, is presented by him in what profess to be three official documents: a gazetteer of Darius's original twenty taxation districts;[3] an itinerary of the Achaemenian Empire's Great North-West Road,[4] associated by Herodotus with a map of the

[1] See Junge: 'Satrapie und Natio', pp. 15–16; Cameron, G. G.: 'Darius, Egypt and "the Lands beyond the Sea"', in *The Journal of Near Eastern Studies*, vol. ii, January–October 1943 (Chicago 1943, University of Chicago Press), pp. 307–13. The present reference is to p. 312, n. 31.

[2] Its historical associations were known to twentieth-century scholars, thanks to six mentions of it (four times in the place-name form and twice in the ethnic form) in Darius's narrative, in 'DB', of the events of the year 522–521 B.C.—a narrative that was as frank as the official lists of *dahyāva* were discreet.

[3] Herodotus, Book III, chaps. 89–96 (see p. 178, above).

[4] See p. 82, n. 1, above.

World, engraved on a brass plate, which the turn-coat 'quisling', Aristagoras of Miletus, is alleged to have brought with him on a mission to King Cleomenes I of Sparta in the hope of persuading Cleomenes to invade the Achaemenian Empire as a champion of the Imperial Government's malcontent Asian Hellenic subjects;[1] and a field-state of the expeditionary force with which Xerxes crossed the Dardanelles in 480 B.C.[2] The last two of these three alleged documents may be more or less authentic. A written statement of the order of battle of Darius III Codomannus's army at Gaugamela was, after all, captured on the field by the victors and has been reproduced, on the authority of Alexander's general Aristobûlus, by Arrian in his *Alexander's Expedition*;[3] and this order of battle corresponds to a field-state given by Arrian at an earlier point.[4] On the other hand the so-called gazetteer bears tell-tale marks of being an amateur compilation in which first-rate official information, drawn from more than one official source, has been used but, in being edited, has, here and there, been misinterpreted and also been 'scrambled' (no doubt, unintentionally).

The order in which the twenty taxation districts are placed by Herodotus—to consider this point first—cannot be the original order; for, as our six extant official lists of *dahyāva* testify, an official list drafted in the Imperial Chancery would normally have started, in a recital in which Pārsa was being omitted because it did not pay taxes, by naming Māda and Hūja (Ūvja), the two countries that shared with Pārsa the distinction of constituting the heartland of the Empire.[5] By contrast, Herodotus's gazetteer starts with Yauna, goes on to Sparda in Yauna's immediate hinterland, and then recites all the other districts with seaboards on the Black Sea or on the Mediterranean—Katpatuka, Cilicia, Syria, and Egypt—before penetrating into the interior of the Empire. Even then this Herodotean gazetteer does not mention Hūja (in Herodotus's terminology, 'the Kissioi'), Bābiruš (in Herodotus's terminology 'Assyria') or Māda until after it has made a flying leap to the Thatagu[?d or v]iyā (*Graecè* Sattagydai) in the Upper Indus Basin. The concentration of interest on the western seaboards of the Empire, where the Achaemenian dominions overlap with the eastern fringes of the Hellenic World, is likewise displayed in the order in which the gazetteer mentions the peoples embraced in a taxation district extending from the west bank of the Lower Halys to the Asiatic shore of the narrow seas connecting the Black Sea with the Aegean. We may presume that the most important of the cantons in this district was Katpatuka (*Graecè* Kappadokiê), since this is the only one of them that is mentioned in the Achaemenian official lists of *dahyāva*. Yet, instead of starting with the Cappadocians (*alias* 'White Syrians') and proceeding from east to west, the gazetteer, in its enumeration of the peoples in this taxation district, starts with

1 Herodotus, Book V, chaps. 49–54.
2 Ibid., Book VII, chaps. 61–99.
3 Arrian: *Expeditio Alexandri*, Book III, chap. xi, §§ 3–7.
4 In Book III, chap. viii, §§ 3–6.
5 Pārsa is placed at the head of all our six extant official lists. Māda is placed second in DZd, DSe, DNa, XPh, and third in DPe. Hūja is placed second in DB and DPe, and third in DZd, DSe, DNa, XPh. The one exception to this general rule of precedence is the placing of Media tenth in DB (i.e. in the place that Media occupies in Herodotus's gazetteer).

the Hellenic communities along the Asiatic shore of the Straits and proceeds thence from west to east till it arrives at the Cappadocians last of all.

It is perhaps conceivable that this drastic departure from the order of precedence observed in lists of *dahyāva* inscribed by the Imperial Government had been made in the provincial chancery of one or other of the three westernmost viceroyalties on the Asiatic mainland—Yauna, Karkā, or Sparda—before the list came into private Hellenic hands; but it would seem more likely that the provincial chanceries would have abode by the Imperial Chancery's practice, and that the violent change of order through which the western lands of the Empire have been given precedence over the heartland will have been the work of a private Hellenic man of letters—whether this was Herodotus himself or was some predecessor of his—who was concerned to adapt the Achaemenian official information that had come into his hands to the requirements of a book which was to be read to and by an Hellenic public and which must therefore present its picture of the Achaemenian Empire in a perspective calculated to commend it, not to Achaemenian, but to Hellenic eyes.

This officious Hellenic literary rearrangement of the official order of precedence of the Achaemenian Empire's lands and peoples has had its nemesis. It has caused Herodotus, or his unofficial Hellenic intermediate source, to lose his way in the maze of the Empire's vast interior as soon as he has had to let go of the alternative guide-rope which he has improvised for himself, after taking his starting-point in Yauna, by following the coastline of the maritime western lands, first north-eastward along the coast of the Black Sea and then south-eastward along the coast of the Mediterranean. Even this cue taken from Physical Geography for the filling of the first six of the twenty spaces in his blank form for a gazetteer of the Achaemenian taxation districts has already led the Hellenic amateur archivist into one error which would have involved him in difficulties in any case. It has led him to assign one of the twenty pigeonholes at his disposal to the principality of Cilicia; and, though, down to the time of writing, the researches of Modern Western archaeologists had not yet disinterred an official list of Darius's original twenty taxation districts, it could be taken as almost certain that Cilicia was not numbered among the twenty, considering that Cilicia was not included in any of the six already known lists of *dahyāva* and that, on this showing, we must conclude that Cilicia ranked juridically as a sovereign independent state in spite of the political fact that this state happened to be one of the Empire's 'gift-bringing allies'. But the Herodotean gazetteer is vitiated by a far more serious flaw than its abandonment of the official order of precedence and its inclusion of a nominally independent state in the list of imperial taxation districts: it has drawn its information from more than one source, and at least two of its sources reproduce respectively two administrative maps which are not merely different from one another but are actually incompatible and which therefore cannot both be delineations of one and the same network of geographical subdivisions of the imperial domain. In the Herodotean gazetteer there are instances of the same peoples figuring twice over because they have been attributed to two different taxation districts under two different names which Herodotus has not recognized as being the synonyms that they are in fact; there is at least one instance of the same territories figuring twice over because they have been assigned to two different administrative units which therefore cannot both have figured side by side on one and the same administrative map, though either of them may have figured simultaneously with the other on one of two different maps that will have been in force simultaneously for two different purposes; and there is also at least one instance of the same whole district figuring twice over under two different names. In consequence, Herodotus has found himself left with more names on his hands than he can find room for in his twenty pigeon-holes, and his desperate search for apparently vacant nooks and corners to house the surplus names has misled him into attributing geographically non-contiguous peoples to the same taxation district and, worse still, into introducing districts with overlapping frontiers on to what purports to be the same administrative map.

If we let our eye travel down Herodotus's list of his twenty taxation districts in the order in which he has presented them to us, we shall catch him adding to his embarrassments as he proceeds. After having reduced the number of the pigeon-holes at his disposal from the necessary twenty to nineteen by erroneously assigning one pigeon-hole to Cilicia, he goes on to reduce the number to eighteen by counting in Harahvatiš twice over, through a failure to detect that the Thamanaioi (*alias* Harahvatiyā) who occupy a pigeon-hole in one of his sources are identical with the Paktyes (*alias* Harahvatiyā) to whom he has already just assigned the pigeon-hole which, in another of his sources, the same Harahvatiyā occupy under this different name. A twentieth-century Western scholar could identify the habitat of Herodotus's Paktyes because their name—like that of Herodotus's Dadikai (Tajik) and Aparytai (Afridi)—was still borne by a living people. In the twentieth century of the Christian Era the North-East Iranian people whom foreigners knew as Afghans were still calling themselves 'Pakhtāna', 'Pashtāna', 'Pathān' in the divers dialects of their Iranian language;[1] and this survival of the name locates Herodotus's Paktyes in the Achaemenian *dahyāuš* that is named 'Harahvatiš' (eventually Hellenized as 'Arakhosia, *Latinè* Arachosia') in the official lists. But this same Harahvatiš is also represented by Herodotus's 'Thamanaioi', as we can verify by comparing Herodotus's gazetteer of Darius I's taxation districts with his field-state of Xerxes' expeditionary force, since the two peoples called Outioi and Mykoi who are grouped with the Thamanaioi in the gazetteer are grouped with the Paktyes in the field-state. It is natural enough that one and the same *dahyāuš* should have been known by three alternative names; for, while 'Harahvatiš' is the name of the country'[2] and 'Paktyes' is the proper name of the people inhabiting it, 'Thamanaioi' is a descriptive title. The sur-

[1] These were the plural forms; the corresponding singular forms 'Pakhtūn' and 'Pashtūn' were still closer to the Greek singular form 'Paktys'.

[2] The country seems to have taken this name from the river that was its lifeline (see A. V. W. Jackson in *The Cambridge History of India*, vol. i (Cambridge 1922, University Press), p. 321, n. 2; Olmstead, A. T.: *History of the Persian Empire* (Chicago 1948, University of Chicago Press), p. 46, n. 59).

vival, in a New Persian language, of the word 'dāmān',[1] meaning the skirt of a garment and, by analogy, a 'borderland' or 'march', tells us that 'Thamanaioi' means 'the borderers'; and Harahvatiš had, in fact, been the south-easternmost territory of the Achaemenian Empire until Darius had relegated it to the interior by annexing Sind and the country, corresponding in area approximately to a latter-day Makrān, which (though not named in any of the official lists) is included in Herodotus's gazetteer as his District No. 17, inhabited by Parikanioi and by Asiatic Ethiopians.

Thus, as a result of two mistakes—the assignment of one pigeon-hole (No. 4), instead of none, to the Cilicians, and the assignment of two pigeon-holes (Nos. 13 and 14), instead of one, to Harahvatiš in order superfluously to provide for both of Harahvatiš's two synonyms 'Paktyes' and 'Thamanaioi'—Herodotus ran through his twenty pigeon-holes without having disposed of all the names that had been thrust upon him by his divers sources. As we can see from the final shape of the gazetteer as he eventually published it, there were at least four names still on his hands after he had assigned his twentieth and last pigeon-hole to the Indoi. These four names were, first, a second set of Parikanioi, who were distinguished from the set already stowed by him in Pigeon-hole No. 17 by being bracketed, not with Ethiopians, but with Orthokorybantioi; second, these Orthokorybantioi who were bracketed with the still unhoused set of Parikanioi; third, the Armenians; fourth, the Sogdoi.

If Herodotus had only known it, two, at any rate, out of these four surplus names need not have worried him; for these two were already accounted for in the description of his District No. 12 which he had copied from one of his sources: 'the Baktrianoi as far as the Aiglai'. 'Aiglai', like 'Thamanaioi', is a descriptive title, if its meaning is 'allies';[2] and the people denoted by this title are the Sakā Haumavargā of the official lists who, in the foundation tablets at Persepolis and Ecbatana, are called 'the Sakā who are beyond Suguda',[3] i.e. the Sakā inhabiting the upper basin of the River Jaxartes (*alias* Sir Darya), which, at the time of writing, bore the name 'Farghānah'. This surviving name is manifestly derived from that of the Parikanioi whom Herodotus found associated with the Orthokorybantioi; these 'parikanioi' (the Avestan 'pairikās', meaning

[1] In the Kingdom of Afghanistan in the early decades of the nineteenth century there were at least two areas bearing the name 'dāmān', and one of these—the 'Damaun' that 'comprehends all the country between the Salt-range, the Solimauny Mountains, the Indus and Sungur in Upper Sind' (Elphinstone, M.: *An Account of the Kingdom of Caubul*, 2nd ed. (London 1839, Bentley, 2 vols.), vol. ii, p. 55) may well have been included within the bounds of the Achaemenian *dahyāuš* whose people Herodotus calls 'Thamanaioi' in his description of his Taxation District No. 14. Another 'dāmān' was to be found in the nineteenth century of the Christian Era at the opposite extremity of the Kingdom of Afghanistan, to the north of Kābul, in the direction of the Hindu Kush. The pleasantness of this land, and the unpleasantness of its inhabitants the Tajiks (Herodotus's 'Dadikai'), are described at first hand by Alexander Burnes in *Cabool, A Personal Narrative of a Journey to, and Residence n, that City in the Years 1836, 7 and 8*, 2nd ed. (London 1843, Murray), pp. 146–66, and by Burnes' companion Captain John Wood in *A Journey to the Sources of the River Oxus*, new ed. (London 1872, John Murray), pp. 110–16.

[2] See further pp. 644–5, below.

[3] See p. 590, above.

either 'sorcerers'[1] or 'fairy people' or 'fairy-worshipping people'[2]) are identical with the 'allies' ('Aiglai') of the Achaemenian Empire who were also officially known as 'Sakā Haumavargā'; the 'Orthokorybantioi', whom Herodotus had found bracketed with the 'Parikanioi' in one of his sources, are 'the Pointed-Hood Sakā' who are bracketed with 'the Hauma-(?)drinking Sakā' in the three latest of the six official lists;[3] and the Sogdoi, though not mentioned by name in the description of District No. 12, are included in it by implication, since a district which extended from Bactria as far as a Farghānah which was the habitat of the Empire's Hauma-(?)drinking Sakā allies could not have left the intervening country out, and this intervening country was Sogdiana. The Sogdoi had thus, after all, been provided for, and the Sakan Parikanioi had no right to a place in the gazetteer of taxation districts, since, like the Cilicians, they were, juridically, not tax-paying subjects of the Achaemenian Empire, but gift-bringing sovereign independent allies. In the formula 'as far as the Aiglai' the term 'as far as' was evidently being used in an exclusive, not in an inclusive, sense, and the couple of names 'Parikanioi-Orthokorybantioi' must have come into Herodotus's hands from a list, which like the six extant official lists, was not a gazetteer of taxation districts, but was a selection of *dahyāva* of divers status.

This satisfactory solution of half his residual difficulties must, however, have escaped Herodotus's notice; for the expedient by which he has sought to extricate himself is the unlucky one of stuffing the Parikanioi and Orthokorybantioi into Pigeon-hole No. 10, already assigned to Media, and stuffing the Sogdoi into Pigeon-hole No. 16, already assigned to the Parthoi, Areioi, and Khorasmioi. This desperate remedy has made nonsense of the gazetteer in two several ways: it has resulted in the Sogdoi and the Hauma-(?)drinking Sakā of Farghānah figuring in the gazetteer twice over in different contexts, and it has resulted in the attribution of non-contiguous peoples to the same taxation district. The Hauma-(?)drinking Sakā (who ought not to figure in any taxation district at all) appear in District No. 10 as 'Parikanioi', besides appearing as 'Aiglai' in the description of District No. 12; the Sogdoi appear in District No. 16 *nominatim*, besides being included by implication in District No. 12. On the point of non-contiguity, it is, of course, geographically inadmissible to brigade Sogdiana with Parthia, considering that the intervening territory—Marguš—is known, from the evidence of 'DB', to have been included in Bākhtriš; it is a geographical absurdity to brigade with Media 'the

[1] In the Avestan Iranian language the feminine singular 'pairikā' means 'witch'.—Professor Roland G. Kent.

[2] See Nyberg, H. S.: *Die Religionen des Alten Iran*, in *Mitteilungen der Vorderasiatischen-Ægyptischen Gesellschaft*, 43. Band (Leipzig 1938, Hinrichs), pp. 297, 314 seqq., 340, 469.

[3] In another context—in his field-state of Xerxes' expeditionary force—Herodotus catches an echo of the official distinction between the two branches of the Sakā, only to confound them with one another. After giving, in Book VII, chap. 64, a description of 'the Pointed-Hood Sakā'—he calls them 'Skythai wearing stiff upright pointed kyrbasiai' —he goes on to say that these particular Skythai were called Sakai Amyrgioi (i.e. Sakā Haumavargā) by the Persians. Herodotus did not notice that the Orthokorybantioi whom he had brigaded with the Medes in his gazetteer were the same people as 'the Pointed-Hood Sakā' of his field-state.

Pointed-Hood Sakā', who were separated from Media by the whole breadth of the Viceroyalty of Parthava, and *a fortiori* to brigade 'the Hauma-(?)drinking Sakā' with Media, since these were separated from Media not only by the Viceroyalty of Parthava but also by the sub-empire of Bākhtriš beyond that.

After having fallen into these errors as the price of disposing of three out of his four surplus names, Herodotus fell into another error in disposing of Armenia. The process of reasoning that led him to the manifestly erroneous conclusion that the Armenians were brigaded with Southern Afghanistan in one and the same taxation district may perhaps be reconstructed as follows.

As Herodotus was re-examining his divers materials in search of a vacant space in which Armenia could be stowed, we may conjecture that his eye caught, in one of his cahiers, an entry that had been transliterated into Greek 'Paktyïkê and Armenioi and the adjoining peoples as far as the Black Sea'; and here (if our guess is right) he fancied that he had found salvation; for 'Paktyïkos' is the Greek adjective corresponding to the Greek substantive 'Paktyes'; and the Paktyes already had a pigeon-hole of their own in District No. 13 (duplicating District No. 14, which had also been assigned by Herodotus inadvertently to the Paktyes under their *alias* 'Thamanaioi'). Now that the Armenians had proved to have been included in the same administrative area as the Paktyes, Herodotus's last difficulty will have seemed to him to have been overcome. He had only to replace 'Paktyes' by 'Paktyïkê and Armenioi and the adjoining peoples as far as the Black Sea' as the label for his District No. 13, and he would have completed his task of making all the names in his divers cahiers fit into the twenty pigeon-holes at his disposal. At this point it must have escaped his notice that the peoples adjoining the Armenians as far as the Black Sea could be none other than the Moskhoi, Tibarênoi, Makrônes, Mossynoikoi, and Mâres, to whom he had already assigned a separate pigeon-hole of their own (his District No. 19); and furthermore he cannot have been fully alive to the improbability of an apparent solution which was committing him to the thesis that peoples with a frontage on the Black Sea could have been included in the same taxation district as a people whose home lay at the eastern extremity of the Empire.

All the same, when he came to write his introductory note for his gazetteer as he was now presenting it, the awkwardness of this thesis seems to have forced itself upon his attention. The first sentence of the introductory note runs:

> 'When Darius had set up his viceroyalties and had appointed viceroys for them, he assessed taxes that were to be paid to him by single peoples in some cases and in other cases by syndicates in which a people's neighbours were brigaded with it.'

We may guess that this sentence was a correct statement of the truth, and that it was copied out by Herodotus verbatim from one of his sources; but, as he copied the word 'neighbours' (πλησιοχώρους), a misgiving must have assailed him. He must have recollected that, in the gazetteer as he had now edited it, the Armenians of Eastern Anatolia figured in the same district as the Paktyes of Eastern Iran. This must (he would have reassured himself) be correct, since one of his sources (as interpreted by him) had vouched for it; and, besides, he would find himself with the Armenians on his hands again if he were to reject this welcome solution now on second thoughts. All the same, he was bound to feel uncomfortable about a solution of a particular problem that was in flat contradiction with the general statement in one of his sources that all members of a taxation-syndicate were contiguous with one another. He could not leave it at that, considering that he had taken for the label of his Taxation District No. 13 a statement by one of his authorities that the Paktyes (whom he knew of as an East Iranian people) were syndicated with the Armenians and with peoples adjoining the Armenians who had a seaboard on the Black Sea. So Herodotus (if our reconstruction of his process of composition is correct) uneasily took up his pen again and amplified the introductory note by appending the following *contradictio in adjecto*:

'And in other cases he passed over the adjoining peoples and assigned the [non-contiguous] peoples on the farther side of [the peoples that he had passed over] to the same taxation district as the peoples [on the nearer side of them].'

This additional sentence, which makes the introductory note self-contradictory, was, we may suppose, extorted from Herodotus by his own previous manipulation of the contents of a gazetteer that he had compiled, at his peril, from more than one source;[1] but this does not mean that the entry 'Paktyïkê and Armenioi and the adjoining peoples as far as the Black Sea' had made nonsense in the original context out of which Herodotus had lifted it in order to substitute it for the entry 'Paktyes', taken from a different source, with which he had mistakenly assumed that an entry opening with the word 'Paktyïkê' must be identical. All that was the matter with the entry beginning 'Paktyïkê' was that it belonged to the political map of the Achaemenian Empire as this had been organized by Cyrus II after he had ousted Astyages from the throne of Media, and not to the fiscal map of the Empire as this had been organized by Darius I after the anarchic year 522–521 B.C. When it was retransferred to the political map, to which it properly belonged, from the fiscal map, into which Herodotus had mistakenly introduced it, this entry would make sense, as we shall see.[2]

Administrative Geography and Political History

The coexistence of two different administrative maps of the Achaemenian Empire—one fiscal and the other political—of which Herodotus has thus unwittingly preserved an indication in his gazetteer, throws light on a dark passage in the Empire's political history.

The constant ideal of the Achaemenian régime was to govern as far

1 A tentative reconstruction of the authentic list of Darius's original twenty taxation districts is presented in Table VI, folding out opposite p. 772, below.

2 On pp. 604–11, below.

as possible with the consent of the governed; and, while the originator of this ideal had been the founder of the Empire, Cyrus II, the restorer of the Empire, Darius I, showed—for example, by his policy in Egypt—that he too had taken the founder's ideal to heart. The difference between Darius's position and Cyrus's was one not so much of ideals as of possibilities of putting ideals into practice. The nemesis of Darius's assassination of a reigning emperor who, truly or falsely, had claimed to be Cyrus's son Smerdis had been the outbreak of the widespread *émeute* of 522–521 B.C., and the nemesis of this terrible year had been a grievous and irretrievable blow to the system, which Cyrus had created, fostered, and succeeded in bequeathing to his successors, of governing with the consent of at least a large minority of the governed.

Though Cyrus II's usurpation of Astyages' Median throne had not been either accomplished or maintained without bloodshed, Cyrus seems nevertheless to have managed to achieve the all-important political objective of sparing the Median imperial people's susceptibilities by saving their 'face'. He seems to have been able to avoid creating the impression either that the Medes were being ousted by the Persians or that the House of Cyaxares was being supplanted by the Cyran branch of the House of Achaemenes. He ascended the Median throne as a grandson of Astyages who had been substituted for his grandfather by the suffrages of a preponderant party among the Medes themselves, and he associated his own people—the men of Parsuwaš, Anšan, and Pārsa—with their imperial kinsmen the Medes on a footing, not of superiority, but of strictly equal partnership. The same fundamental policy of conciliation was likewise applied by Cyrus in the far more difficult case of his conquest of the Neo-Babylonian Empire. Thanks to the Babylonian priesthood's quarrel with Nabonidus, Cyrus was able to occupy the throne of Babylon as the Babylonian priesthood's champion and candidate. As for the peoples of Eastern Iran and North-Western India whom Cyrus appears to have brought under his rule between his enthronement in Media *circa* 556–550 B.C.[1] and his attack on the Neo-Babylonian Empire in 539 B.C., the speed and ease with which he established his authority over these vast tracts of territory was perhaps his reward for presenting himself there as a champion of Sedentary Civilization against Nomadism (a cause in which he eventually proved his sincerity by losing his life in its pursuit); for a majority of the sedentary peoples in the Oxus–Jaxartes Basin and the Indus Basin had suffered cruelly from Eurasian Nomad invasions within living memory.

Cyrus II's policy of governing as far as possible by consent was reflected in the structure of his administrative map. His normal practice seems to have been to respect the territorial integrity of the *ci-devant* empires that he had converted into viceroyalties within a universal state; and, during Cyrus's own reign, the Lydian Empire—where there was an abortive revolt shortly after the original conquest[2]—seems to have been

[1] The overthrow of Astyages by Cyrus II is dated 550–549 B.C. in the Babylonian Nabonidus-Cyrus Chronicle, 556–555 B.C. in another Babylonian historical document, according to Weissbach, F. H., s.v. 'Kyros', in Pauly–Wissowa: *Realencyclopädie der Classischen Altertumswissenschaft*, Neue Bearbeitung, Supplementband IV, cols. 1142–3.

[2] See Herodotus, Book I, chaps. 154–60.

the only one of Cyrus's territorial acquisitions which the conqueror found himself compelled to partition between two separate viceroyalties as the price of maintaining his hold upon it.[1] The former Neo-Babylonian, as well as the former Median, Empire was converted by Cyrus intact into a single viceroyalty; and in the North-East, on the Achaemenian Empire's most dangerous frontier, where the trans-frontier barbarians were the formidable Eurasian Nomads, a Viceroyalty of Bākhtriš that was a sub-empire in itself was either preserved by Cyrus or perhaps actually called into existence by him to serve as the Empire's principal anti-Nomad march.

In Herodotus's gazetteer of Darius's taxation districts the boldly generous Cyran political map has, for the most part, been replaced—and this, of course, correctly—by a cautiously repressive Darian fiscal map reflecting the usurper's reaction to his fearful ordeal in 522–521 B.C.

Darius's assumption of the Imperial Crown had—as we know from Darius's own record—been the signal for a widespread attempt to throw off the Achaemenian yoke (light though this had been so far) and to re-establish the pre-Cyran régimes in empires that Cyrus had deprived of their former sovereign independence. The Medes, for instance, who, in accepting Cyrus II, had been accepting as a legitimate heir to the Median throne a scion of the Cyran branch of the House of Achaemenes whose mother had been a Median princess, could have no such grounds for feeling any loyalty to a pretender, descended from the Ariaramnan branch of the Achaemenidae, who had no Median royal blood in his veins and who had won the imperial throne by assassinating a reigning emperor who had at least professed to be Astyages' great-grandson.

In A.D. 1952 there was no means of knowing for certain whether the Smerdis whom Darius had assassinated had indeed been the authentic son of Cyrus II or whether he had been the impostor that Darius asserts that he was;[2] and there was also no information about the previous

[1] See pp. 671–3, below.

[2] The following expert opinion has been given to the writer by Professor Roland G. Kent:

'I accept the account of a true Smerdis, son of Cyrus, and of a false Smerdis, the Magian Gaumāta, for several reasons. (1) The account of Darius himself on the Behistan Rock, and the account by Herodotus, agree in the essentials, though differing in details. (2) If Darius had slain the true Smerdis, son of Cyrus and brother of Cambyses II, and if the fact had been known widely enough to have resulted in the sundry uprisings related by Darius in his inscription, it is hardly conceivable that no hint of this should have come down in the literature, and especially that the inveterate gossip Herodotus, in all his lengthy account of the event, should have given no indication that there was a differing version. (3) Further, if Darius had had to justify his slaying of the real brother of Cambyses, he would have had at hand a much better account to set before the World, and a true account at that, better than what in that case would have been a cock-and-bull story about his having slain an impostor.

'When Darius slew (true or pseudo-) Smerdis, he needed no fanciful story to justify him. All that he had to say was that Smerdis' father had wrongfully deprived his (Darius's) grandfather Arsames of the throne of Persia (or Persis), and that he was avenging the wrong done to his line. Old Arsames was no longer physically able to reassume the sovereignty, so Darius took it for himself. He did not need to invent a pseudo-Smerdis, so why place himself in the position of a liar about the whole matter? Therefore, in view of the concurrent testimony of the Inscription of Behistan and of Herodotus, I believe that the true Smerdis had been murdered previously (unless he had died of natural causes just at that time) and that a Magian named Gaumāta had assumed his place and was presently killed by Darius and his helpers. Note that Darius

relations between the two branches of the House of Achaemenes—perhaps because there had never been a moment at which it had suited either branch to give publicity to facts which, it might be suspected, were to neither branch's credit. Supposing that the Smerdis whom Darius assassinated had been, and been known by Darius to be, the

lists his helpers on the inscription, and that the names agree, with but slight variations, with those given by Herodotus.'

A statement of the case for the contrary thesis that the reigning emperor whom Darius assassinated was the authentic Smerdis, the son of Cyrus II, is presented by A. T. Olmstead in his *History of the Persian Empire* (Chicago 1948, University of Chicago Press), p. 109, as follows:

'Darius claims that Bardiya [*Graecè* Smerdis], younger brother of Cambyses, was put to death by that brother. Yet there is complete disagreement between our sources as to the time, place, and manner of his murder. Darius puts the episode before the Egyptian expedition of Cambyses, Herodotus during it, and Ctesias after. The official version followed by Herodotus blames a certain Prexaspes for the actual murder, but there was doubt as to whether "Smerdis" was killed while hunting near Susa or was drowned in the Erythraean Sea. After the death of Cambyses, we are expected to believe, Prexaspes publicly recanted his story, informed the people of the secret murder of the "true" Bardiya, and then in repentance committed suicide. Deathbed repentances we all know as frequent devices of the propagandist; after a suicide, the dead man can tell no tales. Furthermore, the "false" Smerdis was false only in claiming to be the son of Cyrus; his actual name *was* Smerdis! The height of absurdity is reached when we are informed that so alike were the "true" and the "false" Smerdis that even the mother and sisters of the "true" Smerdis were deceived! Contemporary Aeschylus had no doubt that Mardos, as he calls him, was a legitimate monarch and that he was slain by the wiles, not of Darius, but of Artaphrenes, one of the "Seven" (Aeschylus, *Persae*, lines 774–7). . . . Last, but far from least, Darius so continuously insists that all his opponents—the "false" Bardiya in particular—are liars that we are convinced he "doth protest too much". It is significant that in Herodotus, Book III, chap. 72, Darius is made to give an elaborate defence of lying.'

The present writer, who was only an amateur in Achaemenian history, was not competent to judge between the authorities on points on which these disagreed with one another. On the issue here in question he would confine himself to recording that, in the first draft of the present passage, he had rashly ventured to opt for the view that Darius's victim had been the authentic Smerdis son of Cyrus II, and that he had been convinced of this as a result of several times rereading 'DB'. The impression made on his mind by Darius's ostensibly frank account of the dramatic events of the first year of his reign had been just the opposite of the impression that Darius himself, in 'DB', is manifestly striving to create. At each repetition of Darius's assertion that he alone is speaking the truth and that each of his rivals is a liar, one reader, at any rate, had come more and more strongly to suspect that Darius must have some portentous lie and crime on his own conscience; and he had actually concluded this now expunged passage in his first draft by quoting the line from Shakespeare, *Hamlet*, Act III, scene ii, on which Olmstead concludes his statement of the case for the prosecution. (This might, of course, have been a subconscious reminiscence of the passage, quoted above, in Olmstead's book, which the present writer had read several years back.)

On this last point, Professor R. G. Kent, in a note to the present writer, suggests that, in calling his rivals 'liars', Darius is using the word in the technical theological sense of subscribers to a false religious doctrine (i.e. to a religion other than Darius's own worship of Ahuramazda). Evidently this interpretation of the compound substantive 'lie-follower' (O.P. *draujana*) would be possible—though the non-technical translation 'liar', in the plain ordinary meaning of the word, would also be possible—in 'DB', §§ 63 and 64; on the other hand, in § 52 the verb 'he lied' (O.P. *adurujiya*) is used no less than nine times running to stigmatize the pretensions of Darius's defeated rivals. The same verb is used with the same plain meaning in § 11, with reference to the 'false' Smerdis' claim to be the authentic Smerdis; in § 16, with reference to Nidintu-Bel's claim to be Nebuchadrezzar the son of Nabonidus; and in § 49, with reference to the Armenian Arkha son of Haldita's claim to be Nebuchadrezzar the son of Nabonidus. As for § 10, the most natural interpretation of the sentence 'After that the Lie waxed great in the country, both in Persia and in Media and in the other provinces', is surely not that the worship of Ahuramazda receded before the advance of rival religions, but that there was a widespread disposition to accept, at its face value, the 'false' Smerdis' claim to be the true Smerdis, because (in the words of the last sentence but one before this sentence) 'when Cambyses slew Smerdis, it did not become known to the people that Smerdis had been slain'.

rightful owner of the name and in consequence the legitimate heir of Cyrus II, it was conceivable that, from the Ariaramnan branch's standpoint, Darius, in thus assassinating the true Smerdis, would have simply been taking a belated but justifiable revenge for an earlier *coup d'état*, whatever the date and circumstances of this might have been, which had resulted in the deposition of Darius's grandfather Aršāma, and exclusion of his father Vištāspa, from the throne of Pārsa, after Darius's great-grandfather Ariyāramna had ruled in Pārsa and had, perhaps, even exercised a suzerainty over his brother Cyrus I's appanage in Parsuwaš and Anšan as well.[1] This Ariaramnid point of view, however, was not calculated to appeal to the peoples who had acquiesced in the rule of the Cyran branch of the Achaemenidae.

These peoples might not much care whether the emperor whom Darius had murdered was or was not the genuine Smerdis son of Cyrus, or whether Darius had or had not been justified in murdering him, whatever his identity might be. A murder which, in Darius's eyes, would have been primarily an incident in a family quarrel if it was not the exposure and punishment of an imposture, as Darius himself declared it to be, was a sensational piece of news for the Cyran House's former subjects—above all, for those of them who were Medes—because it was conclusive evidence that the Cyran House had now become extinct, without having left any legitimate male heir to succeed to its title. If the Smerdis whom Darius had just murdered was not the authentic son of Cyrus, then either this impostor or Cambyses must previously have taken the authentic Smerdis' life; and, on either of these two alternative possible hypotheses, the Cyran House's subjects now found themselves absolved from their allegiance by the disappearance of the dynasty to which this allegiance had been owed. Unlike the death of Cambyses, the death of Darius's victim, whoever he might have been, had made it certain that there was now no surviving legitimate representative of the imperial line of Astyages and Cyrus II; and evidently this was why, in contrast to the first of these two successive pieces of sensational news, the second was followed by pronunciamientos of insurgents who claimed to be the legitimate representatives of dynasties that Cyrus II had deposed and superseded.

The gruesome fate of all these rivals of Darius's who fell into Darius's hands (as every one of them did, sooner or later) did not deter others from trying their luck in turn. The rendition to Darius of the Elamite pretender Āçina by the Elamites themselves was followed by the *pronunciamiento* of a second pretender to the Elamite throne in the person of Martiya. The overthrow of Nidintu-Bel, the pretender to the throne of Babylon, was followed by the *pronunciamiento* of a second

1 See Cameron, G. G.: *A History of Early Iran* (Chicago 1936, University of Chicago Press), pp. 212 and 214. In a letter to the present writer, Professor Cameron drew his attention to Sidney Smith's rejection of his thesis that Cyrus I of Anšan was under his brother Ariaramnes of Pārsa's suzerainty (see Smith, S.: *Isaiah, Chapters XL–LV, Literary Criticism and History* (London 1944, Milford), p. 122, n. 31, referring to p. 28). If the case for Cameron's thesis rests on the attribution of the title 'King of Kings' to Ariaramnes in 'AmH', it would, no doubt, be invalidated by Professor R. G. Kent's finding (see p. 622, n. 1 below) that 'AmH' was a forgery made by Artaxerxes II for a political purpose.

pretender, Arkha. The defeat, flight, capture, and execution of the Median pretender Fravartiš was followed by the *pronunciamiento* of a second Median pretender, Ciçantakhma. Moreover, the pretenders in Media, unlike those in Elam, were the leaders of a genuine national revolt, and this national revolt was not confined to the Medes themselves; the other peoples of the former Median Empire—the Northern Asagartiyā, the people of Varkāna, the Parthavā, and, above all, the Arminiyā—revolted likewise, and the Armenians seem to have given Darius more trouble than the Medes themselves. Most significant of all, Darius's title was disputed by some of his fellow Persians. Martiya, the second insurgent in Elam, was a Persian in nationality,[1] though he claimed to be a scion of the former Elamite royal family; and so was Vahyazdāta, the insurgent in Yautiyā, a country which Darius expressly describes as lying within the bounds of Pārsa.[2]

These facts, for which our authority is Darius himself, make it clear that some Persians, as well as most Medes, believed that the murder committed by Darius, if not a previous murder by some other hand, had extinguished the last legitimate representative of the houses of Cyrus I and Cyaxares which had been united in the persons of Cyrus II and his sons, and that they were therefore now morally free to make their own choice of a ruler, and certainly free from any obligation to accept Darius's claim to be Cyrus II's legitimate successor. This was why the death of Darius's victim in 522 B.C. had the same catastrophic effect as Nero's suicide in A.D. 69. The consequent certainty that now, at any rate, no authentic heir of the legitimate dynasty remained alive opened the flood-gates for an outburst of anarchy.

This is the background against which we have to read the Median portion of Herodotus's gazetteer of Darius's taxation districts. In this gazetteer, as we shall see,[3] Media is partitioned into four separate districts. Besides District No. 10, which is duly labelled 'Media' by Herodotus, there is his district No. 11, which appears to cover a strip of territory extending westward, between the Elburz Range and the Central Desert of Iran, from the narrow passage between them that was known as 'the Caspian Gates'. There is also Herodotus's District No. 18, which appears to cover the Basin of Lake Urmīyah, together with the former territory of Assyria to the east of the Tigris (annexed by Media when she had partitioned the Assyrian Empire with her Babylonian ally) and with the former kingdom of Urartu (annexed by Media subsequently). It is probable, too, that Herodotus's District No. 15 likewise is another fragment of Media, consisting of the steppe country round the lower courses of the rivers Aras and Kur, where they join one another before their common debouchure into the Caspian Sea. Finally, we find a detachment of Medes marooned, far from home, in the islands of the Persian Gulf, as one of the peoples included in Herodotus's District No. 14. The Median origin of these *déracinés* is revealed in the field-state of Xerxes' expeditionary force, in which their equipment and armament are described as being almost identical with those that the

1 See 'DB', § 22.

2 See 'DB', § 40.

3 On pp. 623–32, below.

Medes wore;[1] and their inclusion in District No. 14 is also significant, since these dissident Medes were interned there next door to the dissident Persian clan called the Yautiyā (Outioi). The south-western quarter of District No. 14 was, in fact, a prison for the most heinous of the Median and Persian offenders against Darius; and, as a further precaution, the prisoners there had been chained to the loyal Harahvatiyā (*alias* Paktyes, *alias* Thamanaioi) in Southern Afghanistan, who had been rewarded for their trustworthiness by being conscripted to serve as jailers.[2]

Herodotus's gazetteer of Districts Nos. 10, 11, 18, 15, and 14 thus informs us that Darius took the opportunity of his redivision of the Empire for fiscal purposes in order to insure himself against the risk of a fresh national insurrection in Media by breaking Media up for these purposes, besides deporting a portion of the Median people; but there are two other passages in Herodotus's work in which Media is credited with a much wider extension, at any rate towards the north, than can be attributed to the district labelled 'Media' and numbered '10' in the gazetteer of Darius's taxation districts. When Herodotus is indicating[3] the region of Media which was the home, according to the Cyrus legend, of the hero's bucolic foster parents, and again when, in quite a different context,[4] he is discussing the boundaries of 'Europe' and 'Asia', he makes Media march on the north with the country of the Saspeires, and these Saspeires with the Colchians, who have a seaboard on the Black Sea; and these two passages, while in harmony with one another, are incompatible with the administrative geography of the gazetteer; for, in the gazetteer, District No. 18, in which the Saspeires are included, also comprises the Matiênoi and the Alarodioi, and in A.D. 1952 it could still be discerned that the 'Alarodioi'—Herodotus's rendering of the ethnikon of 'Urartu', which was situated in the basin of Lake Van and along the middle and upper reaches of the valley of the River Aras—and the Matiênoi, who stamped their name on the basin of Lake Urmīyah, must have lain between the Saspeires—a people who had bequeathed their name to the canton of Isbir in the upper valley of the River Choroq—and the environs of Hamadān, to which the name 'Media' is confined in the gazetteer. This means that, in the two passages now in question, Herodotus is including in Media at least one district which is not included in Media in the gazetteer; and the explanation must be that these passages record the political boundaries of the Viceroyalty of Media as these had been established by Cyrus before Media had been partitioned by Darius for fiscal purposes in consequence of her insurrection in 522–521 B.C. Herodotus is here describing a Viceroyalty of Media which includes Urartu as well as the Basin of Lake Urmīyah between Urartu and the heart of Media round Ecbatana.

We can now also see that these two passages are not the only places in which Herodotus is writing in terms of a political map which is antecedent to—but on paper, at any rate, has not been superseded by—

1 Herodotus, Book VII, chap. 80.

2 See further pp. 622 and 640, below.

3 In Book I, chap. 110.

4 In Book IV, chap. 37.

Darius's precautionary partition, for fiscal purposes, of perilously large political units that Cyrus II had left intact. This officially surviving integral Viceroyalty of Media has a counterpart and neighbour in an officially surviving integral Viceroyalty of Armenia, and this is the geographical entity that has found its way into Herodotus's edition of the gazetteer of Darius's taxation districts in the formula 'Paktyïkê and Armenioi and the adjoining peoples as far as the Black Sea', which Herodotus has taken for the description of his Taxation District No. 13.

The region to which the name 'Armina' or 'Arminiya' had originally attached seems to have been the country—occupying the upper basin of the Tigris and extending thence farther north-westward into the north-west corner of the basin of the Euphrates, where the two arms of the Upper Euphrates unite—which the Assyrians had called 'Naïri'. The first wave of Assyrian settlers in Naïri—some of whom had been established in the reign of Shalmaneser I in the thirteenth century B.C. —had been submerged by the cataclysm of the Aramaean Völkerwanderung out of the North Arabian Steppe at the turn of the second and the last millennium B.C. Thereafter, Asshurnazirpal II had reasserted the Assyrian Crown's authority over dissident descendants of these Assyrian settlers in 882 B.C. and had annexed the Aramaean principality of Bit Zamani in 879 B.C. In this quarter the extension of Assyrian rule had been at its widest *circa* 799 B.C.; thereafter, the whole of Naïri except an isolated enclave round Amedi (*Latinè* Amida, *Arabicè* Diyār Bakr), the former capital of Bit Zamani, had been conquered from Assyria by Urartu; the south-western part of the lost Assyrian domain in Naïri (i.e. the province later known to post-Alexandrine Hellenic geographers as Sophênê) had then been reconquered by Tiglath-Pileser III in 739 B.C.; but the south-eastern part (*Graecè* Arzanênê) had remained a debatable territory;[1] and the eventual beneficiaries from a stubborn, long-drawn-out, and indecisive contest between Assyria and Urartu in this arena had been the Thracian-speaking followers of the Mushkian (i.e. Phrygian) war-lord Gurdi (*Graecè* Gordios).

In 695 B.C., Sennacherib had attempted, without success, to dislodge Gurdi's war-band from Til-Garimmu (*Hebraicè* Togarmah), astride the road leading south-eastward from Sivas in the upper basin of the River Qyzyl Irmaq (*Graecè* Halys) to Malatīyah (*Assyriacè* Meliddu) in the valley of the Tokhma Su (a west-bank affluent of the Upper Euphrates).[2] Upon the collapse of the Assyrian Power after the death of Asshurbanipal, the Mushkian invaders to whom Gurdi had bequeathed his name swooped down from the north-west towards the heart of Assyria till their path was crossed by Sagartian invaders swooping down from the north-east upon the same objective—if the Kardoukhoi whom Xenophon and his comrades encountered in the tangle of mountains —known to post-Alexandrine Hellenic geographers as Gordyênê—south of the River Bohtān (*Latinè* Centrîtês)[3] are to be identified with the descendants of Gurdi's men, and if the latter-day place-name Si'irt

[1] These vicissitudes in the history of Naïri are recorded in Forrer, op. cit., pp. 25–33 and 84–87.

[2] See ibid., pp. 80–81.

[3] See Xenophon: *Expeditio Cyri*, Book III, chap. v, § 14—Book IV, chap. iii.

(*Armeniacè* Sghert or Sgherd), borne by a town near the confluence of the River Bohtān with the Eastern Tigris, testified that the north-western branch of the Iranian-speaking Nomad Asagartiyā had once pushed their way that far westward from their previous habitat somewhere to the east or south-east of Lake Urmīyah.[1]

The seventh-century Median settlers in the metropolitan territory of Assyria east of the Tigris and the contemporary Phrygian settlers in the region known by the Assyrians as 'Naïri' and by the Achaemenidae as 'Armina' seem to have met at the south-eastern corner of the Upper Tigris Basin without falling out with one another.[2] By the time, in or after 585 B.C., when the course of the River Halys, from the point where it emerged from the Kingdom of Cilicia down to its mouth, was accepted by the Median and the Lydian Empire as the frontier between them, 'Armina' must already have been incorporated into the Median Empire; but the simultaneous insurrection of Armina and Māda against Darius in 522 B.C., and the strength of the resistance that the insurgents in Armina offered to Darius's forces, are facts which indicate that the previous relations between Armina and Māda had been friendly; and a clue to the grounds of this friendship is perhaps to be found in the title 'Paktyïkê and Armenioi and adjoining peoples as far as the Black Sea' which Herodotus has taken for his description of Darius's thirteenth taxation district—if we are right in seeing in this formula the description, not of any Darian taxation district, but of an integral Viceroyalty of Armenia which, like the integral Viceroyalty of Media, will have been established under the Median imperial régime of Cyaxares and Astyages; will have been maintained as a going concern under the Medo-Persian imperial régime of Cyrus II, Cambyses and a *soi-disant* Smerdis; and will not have been officially abolished by Darius I in being partitioned by him for fiscal purposes.

The formula suggests that the whole of the territory added to the Median Empire by Cyaxares to the west of Urartu, to the east of the Lower Halys, and to the north of a Kingdom of Cilicia which bestrode the middle course of the Halys in the neighbourhood of Mazaka, had been included by Cyaxares in a single viceroyalty; and, if this interpretation is correct, it would mean that Cyaxares had reconciled the Phrygian

[1] This identification is suggested by Herzfeld, E.: 'Zarathustra, Teil I', in *Archäologische Mitteilungen aus Iran*, Band I (Berlin 1929–30, Reimer), pp. 76–124, on p. 81, n. 1. Professor G. G. Cameron makes the following cautionary comment: 'This interpretation of "Kardoukhoi" as meaning "Gurdi's men", and, even more, the interpretation of Si'irt as being an echo of "Asagartiyā", is really playing with fire. I want more linguistic evidence.'

A derivation of the ethnikon 'Kardoukhoi' and the place-name 'Gordyênê' from the personal name 'Gurdi (Gordios)' is, indeed, impugned by the appearance of 'the wide-spreading Kurti warriors' in the annals of the Assyrian King Tukulti-Ninurta I, who reigned in the second half of the thirteenth century B.C. (see Luckenbill, D. D.: *Ancient Records of Assyria and Babylonia* (Chicago 1926–27, University of Chicago Press, 2 vols.), vol. i, pp. 143, 152, 164, 171), and in the record of the campaign in the accession year of King Tiglath-Pileser I (*regnabat* 1114–1076 B.C.) (see op. cit., vol. i, pp. 222 and 229). If these Kurti were one of the Phrygian hordes that overwhelmed the Empire of Khatti at the turn of the thirteenth and twelfth centuries B.C., the personal name of the seventh-century Phrygian war-lord Gurdi will have been derived from the ethnikon 'Kurti', not vice versa, and will have signified 'the Phrygian'.

[2] So far from clashing, they appear to have amalgamated; for the latter-day Kurds, who perhaps bore Gurdi's name, spoke an Iranian, not a Thracian, dialect.

settlers in Naïri-Armina to a voluntary acceptance of a Median overlordship by taking them into partnership with the Median imperial people and conferring on them a sub-empire covering the Median Empire's western marches. This would be a counterpart of the policy by which Cyrus II, in his day, appears to have reconciled the Bactrians to a Medo-Persian overlordship; and, in this case as in that, we can see that the two parties were bound to one another by a common interest which constituted a practical guarantee that the paramount Power's generosity would not be abused by the beneficiaries from it. Though the Phrygian invaders of Naïri-Armina and the Median invaders of Adiabênê might have been competitors in the scramble for the spoils of a defunct Assyrian Empire, they still had an abiding common interest in standing shoulder to shoulder against a surviving common enemy who remained formidable after Assyria had been annihilated.

This abiding common enemy was the Nomad Power which had erupted out of the Great Eurasian Steppe into South-West Asia before the end of the eighth century B.C. If we have been right in thinking that, at some date between 556 B.C.[1] and 539 B.C., Cyrus II took the Bactrians into partnership and entrusted to them the surveillance over their Nomad neighbours the Sakā Haumavargā in Farghānah, we may perhaps now go on to hazard the guess that, in making this settlement of his north-eastern frontier, he was following a precedent that had been provided for him by Cyaxares' settlement of his north-western frontier at some date between 610 and 585 B.C. We may guess that Cyaxares had taken into partnership the Phrygian settlers in the country which the Achaemenian lists of *dahyāva* call 'Armina', and that he had entrusted to them the surveillance over Nomad neighbours of theirs whose tribal name was Paktyes and who had established themselves in the sixth century B.C. within the bend of the Halys, in the country which the Achaemenian lists call 'Katpatuka'.[2]

If the Paktyes were one of the Eurasian Nomad peoples who, in and after the eighth century B.C., had erupted out of the Great Eurasian Steppe into South-West Asia through the gap between the Pamir Plateau and the south-east corner of the Caspian Sea,[3] it would not be

[1] See p. 598, n. 1, above.

[2] Professor G. G. Cameron makes the following comment: 'This is a fine theory and perhaps makes sense; but I want much more to go on than the name [Paktyikê standing for Paktyes]; I want more proof.'

[3] See III. iii. 400–1. In the writer's belief, all the Nomad hordes who had ever invaded South-West Asia had always come through this gap and had never come over or round the Caucasus. He would not, of course, deny that, at times, Nomad peoples in occupation of the Volga-Don steppe had made raids round the eastern end of the Caucasus Range into the Kur-Aras Basin and beyond, but he would deny that this route had ever given passage to permanent migrants. Herodotus's statement, in Book I, chaps. 103–4, that this was the route by which the Cimmerians, with the Scyths at their heels, had broken into South-West Asia (at the turn of the eighth and seventh centuries B.C.) was, in the writer's judgement, not derived from any authentic record of the event, but was merely an inference from the fact that, in Herodotus's day, the only extant Scyths known to Herodotus were domiciled in the Great Western Bay of the Eurasian Steppe. Herodotus was transporting his Scyths from there to Media by, not the shortest, but the shortest practicable, route; but his premiss that the Scyths living in his day on the Black Sea Steppe must have been the Scyths who had invaded South-West Asia two or three centuries earlier was, in the present writer's opinion, erroneous. It was, surely, more likely that, when the Scyths had erupted out of the Central Asian heart of the Eurasian Steppe,

surprising to find Eastern Anatolia subsequently occupied by one wing of a horde whose other wing had occupied Eastern Iran; for, throughout the four thousand years or so of Eurasian Nomad history, each successive wave that broke upon the northern escarpment of the Iranian Plateau tended to split into divergent streams following diverse lines of least resistance. While the left wing of a horde that had mounted the plateau would be inclined to head south-eastward for the plains of the Indus Basin, the right wing of the same horde would be inclined to sweep on westwards, along the corridor between the southern foot of the Elburz Range and the northern edge of the Central Desert of Iran, till it arrived at congenial pasture-lands in the basin of Lake Urmīyah and, beyond that, in the steppe country in the lower basin of the rivers Aras and Kur, adjoining the west coast of the Caspian Sea. From these temporary camping grounds a subsequent horde, following at the first horde's heels, might then drive these forerunners of theirs on again up the Aras Valley, either to entangle themselves in the mountain maze overhanging the south-east corner of the Black Sea[1] or, if they were more fortunate, to travel on still farther westward over the watershed between the basins of the Aras and the Qyzyl Irmaq (Halys) until eventually they debouched into the Anatolian Peninsula. This had been the story of the Sanskrit-speaking Nomad invaders of South-Western Asia in the eighteenth or seventeenth century B.C. whose left wing had descended upon the Indus Basin while their right wing had made its appearance in Azerbaijan, Mesopotamia, North Syria, Transcaucasia, and Anatolia under the name Mitanni and perhaps also as the 'mariannu'. [2] In a subsequent invasion of South-West Asia by Iranian-speaking peoples which had brought the Medes and Persians into Iran, the deployment of the invading war-bands had been remarkably symmetrical.

In this invasion—as its course can be reconstructed by inference from the eventual locations of the participants after they had come to rest—the Persians must have been in the van—in an échelon in which the Yautiyā and the Mačiyā formed the advance guard and the Pārsā proper the main body, with the Asagartiyā bringing up the rear—while the Medes, following close behind, must have split the Persian vanguard into a right wing, which was pushed by Median pressure north-west-

they had been split (as in the eleventh century of the Christian Era the Turks, and in the thirteenth century the Mongols, were to be split) by the Caspian Sea into two wings, one of which had made its way between the Caspian and the Pamirs into South-West Asia and India, while the other had made its way between the Caspian and the Urals into the Great Western Bay of the Steppe to the north of the Black Sea.

Professor Cameron queries: 'What drove the Hurri into Mesopotamia [in the seventeenth century B.C.] and later brought Urartu into increasingly bloody contact with Assyria? Must it not have been the pressure of new peoples from across the Caucasus?' The present writer sees no need for this hypothesis. Nomad invaders breaking in via the Caspian Gates and/or non-Nomadic Caucasian highlanders could surely have supplied the driving force, without its being necessary also to postulate a Nomad invasion via Derbend.

[1] In this mountain bunker, lost tribes whose names—Mâres, Sannoi, Skythênoi (Xenophon, op. cit., Book IV, chap. vii, § 18, and chap. viii), Sakasênoi, Taokhoi (ibid., chap. iv, § 18; chap. vi, § 5; chap. vii, §§ 1–14), Sirakes—revealed their provenance from the Eurasian Steppe, rubbed shoulders with others whose names showed that they had found their way into the same blind alley out of Anatolia. This was, for example, the provenance of the Tibarênoi (from Tabal) and of the Moskhoi (from Phrygia and, before that, from South-Eastern Europe).

[2] See the Note on Chronology in x. 199–202.

wards, and a left wing which the same Median pressure pushed away towards the south-east. When, in and after the ninth century B.C., first the Assyrian and then the Achaemenian records progressively bring to light the positions in which the divers participants in this Iranian Völkerwanderung had established themselves, we find the Medes in the centre, astride the Great North-East Road leading up from Babylonia on to the Iranian Plateau via Behistan, with the Yautiyā and the Mačiyā at the outer extremity of either flank, the Pārsā between the Yautiyā and the Medes, and the Asagartiyā immediately to the rear of the Pārsā. On the south-east flank the Yautiyā are in North-Eastern Lāristān, the Mačiyā in South-Western Lāristān, the Pārsā in Fars and in Lūristān (Parsuwaš), and the Asagartiyā in Kirmān. On the north-west flank, the right-wing fraction of the Yautiyā can be detected in the latter-day Armenian name Uti (*Graecè* Utênê),[1] which attached to a district between the Qārabāgh and the south bank of the River Kur in Transcaucasia. The right-wing fraction of the Mačiyā (*Graecè* Mykoi) can be detected in the name Mūqān, Mughkān, or Mūghān[2] which attached to the patch of steppe to the south of the confluence of the rivers Aras and Kur. The right-wing fraction of the Pārsā turn up in Parsua, which was the Assyrian name for a canton in the North-Western Zagros, somewhere to the south-south-east of the basin of Lake Urmīyah,[3] while the right-wing fraction of the Asagartiyā (*Assyriacè* Zikirtu) is located in the Assyrian records somewhere to the east or south-east of Lake Urmīyah.

This bifurcation into a westward-riding and a south-eastward-riding column was likewise to be the history of the Turkish-speaking Nomads who were to break upon the Iranian Plateau in the eleventh century of the Christian Era.[4] It would have been strange if the wave of Iranian-

[1] See Adontz, N.: *Histoire d'Arménie, Les Origines* (Paris 1946, Union Générale Arménienne de Bienfaisance), p. 308. In Strabo: *Geographica*, Book XI, chap. vii, § 1 (C 508) and § 8 (C 514), these north-western Yautiyā are called Ouitioi.

[2] See Le Strange, G.: *The Lands of the Eastern Caliphate* (Cambridge 1905, University Press), pp. 175–6.

[3] The evidence for the existence of this north-western Parsua, and for its location somewhere to the north of the Upper Zab [? i.e. the upper course of the Lesser Zab] is set out by Sidney Smith in *Isaiah, Chapters XL–LV, Literary Criticism and History* (London 1944, Milford), pp. 119–20 (notes 24 and 25, referring to p. 28). See also Forrer, op. cit., pp. 89–90, and Adontz, op. cit., pp. 100–3 and 366–9. The name of this Parsua, like the name Madai (Māda, Media), first occurs in the annals of Shalmaneser III. According to König, F. W.: *Älteste Geschichte der Meder und Perser* (Leipzig 1934, Hinrichs), p. 8, Parsua is first heard of in 844 B.C., Madai in 836 B.C. Cp. Cameron, G. G.: *A History of Early Iran* (Chicago 1936, University of Chicago Press), pp. 143–4.

[4] This instance is also a reminder of the fact (noticed on p. 606, n. 3, above) that the frontier of the Eurasian Steppe between the Pamir Plateau and the south-east corner of the Caspian Sea was not the only sector on which an erupting horde of Eurasian Nomads was apt to fan out in diverse directions in the course of its farther advance. In and after the eleventh century of the Christian Era the fanning out, as far afield as India on the left and Anatolia on the right, of the Turks who had crossed the frontier between the Pamirs and the Caspian was matched by a corresponding dispersion of their brethren who had simultaneously broken out of the heart of the Steppe into its Great Western Bay through the gap between the Caspian and the Urals. Some of these Turkish-speaking invaders of the Western Bay moved north-westward up the Volga towards Great Bulgaria (Qāzān); others moved south-westward into the Kuban; while others, advancing due westward, crossed first the Don and eventually the Carpathians, when a remnant of the Ghuzz (*alias* Cumans) found asylum on the Hungarian Alföld from the pursuing Mongols (see XIII. x. 54–55).

A simultaneous eruption north and south of the Caspian Sea was, indeed, normal.

speaking Nomads—this time Saparda, Cimmerians, Scyths, Paktyes, and Kaspioi (*Latinè* Caspii)—who broke upon the same plateau out of the same steppe in the eighth and seventh centuries B.C., had not splayed apart in the same two divergent directions; and the word 'Paktyïkê' in Herodotus's description of District No. 13 in his gazetteer is not the only piece of evidence that points to this conclusion. The tribal name of a detachment of the Paktyes established in Anatolia may also perhaps be detected in the place-names Paktyê, borne by a town at the neck of the Gallipoli Peninsula before the end of the sixth century B.C.,[1] and Paktyês, borne by a mountain near Ephesus,[2] and likewise in the personal name 'Paktyas' which, in Herodotus's history,[3] is borne by a Lydian whom Cyrus put in charge of Croesus's captured treasure, and who took this opportunity to place himself at the head of a Lydian insurrection against Achaemenian rule. It is also worth noticing that the Kaspioi, whom Herodotus locates in the corridor leading out of Khurāsān into Azerbaijan, as one of the peoples in his District No. 11, and in the lower basin of the rivers Aras and Kur, as one of the peoples in his District No. 15, appear in his field-state of Xerxes' expeditionary force in an association which suggests that there must have been another detachment of Kaspioi who, like the other wing of the Paktyes, were established somewhere in Eastern Iran.[4]

On this line of reasoning, we may interpret the 'Paktyïkê' in Herodotus's description of District No. 13 of his gazetteer as standing for Paktyes who were not the well-known bearers of the name in Eastern Iran, where it had survived down to the twentieth century of the Christian Era in the form Pakhtūn-Pakhtāna. The Paktyes whom Herodotus had found associated with the Armenians would not be these

In the fifth century of the Christian Era, for example, the Huns were invading the Indian and the European peninsula of Asia at the same moment, while in the seventh century B.C. the westward advance of detachments of Cimmerians and Scyths south of the Caspian into Anatolia was accompanied by a simultaneous westward advance of other detachments of the same two peoples north of the Caspian into the Great Western Bay of the Eurasian Steppe (where the passage of a band of Cimmerians, in advance of a pursuing band of Scyths, was attested by the name 'Cimmerian Bosphorus' by which the Straits of Kerch were known in Hellenic parlance).

It will be evident that, when a Nomad horde thus erupted north and south of the Caspian Sea simultaneously, and then fanned out both in the Great Western Bay of the Steppe and in South-West Asia, its extreme right and left wings might eventually come to rest at an enormous distance apart. On the map of the Old World in the twentieth century of the Christian Era, for example, the fanning out of the Bashkirds was commemorated by the survival of their name both in the Southern Urals and in South-Western Baluchistan; and in the light of this latter-day parallel it is not surprising to find the Boudinoi, whom Herodotus (Book IV, chaps. 21 and 108) locates within the timbered country north of the steppes east of the River Don (locates, that is, somewhere in the neighbourhood of Bashkiristan), also figuring (in Book I, chap. 101) as one of the tribes of the Medes under the name Boudioi, or again to find established on the banks of the River Kuban the right wing of the Sindoi whose left wing stamped this originally Eurasian Nomad people's name first on the River Indus and eventually on the whole Indian sub-continent.

1 See Herodotus, Book VI, chap. 36.

2 See Strabo: *Geographica*, Book XIV, chap. i, § 13 (C 636), and chap. i, § 39 (C 647).

3 Book I, chaps. 153–6.

4 This eastern wing of the Kaspioi is mentioned in Book VII, chapter 67, between the Gandaro-Dadican brigade on the one side and the Sarangian (*Persicè* Zrāka) contingent on the other side. The Persian commanders of the Gandaro-Dadican brigade and of the Caspian contingent are brothers. These Eastern Kaspioi, like the Eastern Paktyes, are described in this context as wearing *sisyrnai* (sheepskin coats). See pp. 635–6, below.

Pactyan denizens of Harahvatiš, to whom Herodotus had allotted both his District No. 13 under their own name and his District No. 14 under the descriptive title 'borderers' (Thamanaioi); the Armenians' Pactyan associates would be a western branch of the Pactyan horde who had established themselves in Eastern Anatolia and who must have been associated with, if not identical with, the intrusive Nomad occupants of the same territory who bore the name Cimmerians'.[1] The Greek adjectival form 'Paktyïkê' would be an Hellenic man of letters' rationalization of a plural form of the substantive 'Pakty-' taking the non-Indo-European plural ending in 'k' which was endemic in the region between the Caucasus and Mesopotamia;[2] and this plural 'Paktuk' would reappear in the second and third syllables of the name 'Katpatuka' which, like the name 'Armina', makes its first appearance in history in the Achaemenian lists of *dahyāva*. 'Katpatuka' would signify 'the Paktyes domiciled in Khatti', as distinguished from their brethren and homonyms who were domiciled in the South-East Iranian *dahyāuš* known as Harahvatiš.

If Cappadocia and the peoples along the north coast of Anatolia between Cappadocia and Colchis, exclusive of Colchis itself, had in truth been thus associated with Naïri-Armina in a single viceroyalty

1 A remnant of the Cimmerians who had swept westwards as far as the west coast of Anatolia in the seventh century B.C. appears to have survived in Cappadocia, to judge by the fact that the name by which Cappadocia was subsequently known in the Armenian language was Gamir (see Prášek, J. V.: *Geschichte der Meder und Perser* (Gotha 1906, Perthes, 2 vols.), vol. i, p. 148).

2 The acquisition of a plural ending in 'k' was one of the penalties entailed in settling within this area. This fate overtook the Armenian language and, among other substantives in it, the Armenians' own name for themselves; for 'Haik', as the Armenians called themselves, is the plural of a singular form 'Hay' which would appear to denote an inhabitant of the country, occupying the north-west corner of the Euphrates Basin, which the Hittites had once known as 'Hayasa' and which the Hellenic geographers were later to know as 'Armenia Minor'. Gurdi's war-band, likewise, became known (if there is any substance in our conjecture on p. 604, above) as 'Gordi-k' (*Graecè* Kardoukhoi) in the mountain bunker between the Rivers Bohtān (*Latinè* Centrîtês) and Tigris which brought their south-eastward *trek* to a halt and which came to be known, after them, as 'Gordyênê'. The Taokhoi whom Xenophon and his comrades encountered in the highlands in the hinterland of the south-eastern corner of the Black Sea were perhaps a lost tribe of Transcaspian Nomad Dahā who had acquired the same inevitable plural in 'k' after finding their way into this 'living museum' in which so many splinters of broken peoples silted up (though there was also a cape and a town called Taokhê and a canton called Taokhênê outside the 'k' area, along the coast of Fars (see Strabo: *Geographica*, Book XV, chap. iii, § 3 (C 728), and Ptolemy: *Geographia*, Book VI, chap. iv, §§ 2, 3, and 7)).

The Saparda, who had headed the Eurasian Nomads' seventh-century ride into Anatolia, in the van of the column in which the Paktyes, Cimmerians, Scyths, and Kaspioi followed behind them in échelon, reappeared as Sevordi-k some fourteen centuries later, when *circa* A.D. 750–60 they sacked an outpost which had been established at Bardha'ah by the Arab Muslim conquerors of the Sasanian Empire. The historical evidence bearing on this incident is discussed in Marquart, J.: *Osteuropäische und Ostasiatische Streifzüge* (Leipzig 1903, Dieterich), pp. 36–40, and in Macartney, C. A.: *The Magyars in the Ninth Century* (Cambridge 1930, University Press), pp. 87–90 and 174–6. These Modern Western students of the origins of the Magyars had been led astray by the Byzantine scholar-emperor Constantine Porphyrogenitus's erroneous assertion that these survivors of the Saparda who had invaded South-West Asia in the seventh century B.C. were a detachment of the Magyar horde. The form in which Constantine presents the Saparda's name—*Σάβαρτοι ἄσφαλοι*—is manifestly a transliteration of an Arabic original 'Sāwardīyah al-asfal', 'the lowland Sāwardīyah' in the plain between the Qārabāgh and the River Kur, as contrasted with 'the highland Sāwardīyah' somewhere else. Mas'ūdī's and Istakhrī's description of these descendants of the Saparda as being 'a kind of Armenian' is not so wide of the mark as Constantine's blunder.

by the policy of Cyaxares and Cyrus II, it would follow that Persia and Media were not the only political divisions of the Achaemenian Empire that Darius partitioned in his new fiscal map. Besides dividing Persia into two fragments, one of them now officially tax-paying and the other still nominally exempt, and Media into four fragments, Darius will also have divided Armenia into three by erecting the peoples between the northern boundary of Armenia Proper and the Black Sea coast of Anatolia into a separate taxation district, duly reported by Herodotus as his District No. 19, and by detaching Cappadocia from Armenia, at any rate for fiscal purposes, to constitute a taxation district—Herodotus's District No. 3—in which we find Cappadocia brigaded with a province, administered from Dascylium near the Anatolian coast of the Sea of Marmara, which had already been detached politically from Lydia.[1]

We are now perhaps in a position to take the full measure of the grievous change for the worse in the domestic life of the Achaemenian Empire which was the nemesis of Darius's assassination of the reigning emperor and usurpation of the Imperial Crown. Under the Cyran branch of the House of Achaemenes, as under the foregoing Median dynasty, the Empire had (if we have been right in our reconstruction of its history) been securely grounded on the paramountcy of a broad association of imperial peoples—the Medes, the Persians, the Armenians, and eventually also the Bactrians—who were bound to one another by their common enjoyment of a privileged status and their common loyalty to a dynasty by whose generosity this status had been conferred upon them.[2] A sadly different picture is presented in Herodotus's gazetteer of Darius's taxation districts; for, in spite of the errors and confusions, here and there, that we have been attempting to clear up, Herodotus's gazetteer does bring to light something that none of the six official lists of *dahyāva* betray. As a result of the revolts against Darius's assumption of the Imperial Crown which had broken out in 622 B.C. among the privileged paramount peoples of the Empire as well as among the subject peoples, Darius had found himself constrained to reduce to a dangerously narrow compass the once broad basis of voluntary support on which Cyaxares' and Cyrus II's régime had safely rested. Of the four former imperial peoples, the Bactrians alone had retained their previous position intact. The Persians had been partitioned most invidiously into a still privileged remnant of loyalists in Fars and a batch of dissident communities—the Yautiyā and Mačiyā in Lāristān and the South-Eastern Asagartiyā in Kirmān—who had been degraded to the ranks of their own former subjects. Media had been partitioned, for fiscal purposes, into four fragments—in addition to the

[1] This separate province, known in Hellenic parlance as 'Hellespontine Phrygia', must have been detached politically from Lydia already before the date of Darius's division of the Achaemenian Empire into taxation districts, since Herodotus testifies to its separate existence on the political map, not only in the first decade of the fifth century B.C., at the time of the Ionian Revolt (see Book VI, chap. 33), but already as early as the reign of Cambyses, when the governor of Dascylium, Mitrabates, was at loggerheads with the viceroy of Sardis, Orœtes, who had been Cyrus's appointee (see Book III, chaps. 120 and 126, and the present Annex, p. 671, below).

[2] On this point, see Herzfeld, op. cit., pp. 117–18.

deportation of the *déracinés* who had been marooned on the islands in the Persian Gulf. Armenia had been partitioned for fiscal purposes into three fragments.

No doubt Darius felt rueful about having to take these precautionary measures. They were a poor substitute for the goodwill that the House of Achaemenes had forfeited in consequence of the extinction of the Cyran branch and the transfer of the crown to the Ariaramnan branch through the assassination of a reigning emperor who had professed himself to be Cyrus's authentic son and Cambyses' legitimate successor. We know that Darius did his utmost retrospectively to justify his acts and to regularize his position. He published his own account of the obscure and controversial events of the year 522–521 B.C. on the cliff-face at Behistan in the three languages of the imperial capitals,[1] and arranged for the distribution of an Aramaic translation of the text, in a portable form, throughout his dominions.[2] He married two of Cyrus's daughters and one of his granddaughters whose father had admittedly been the genuine Smerdis,[3] whether the Smerdis whom Darius had assassinated had been the murderer's subsequent wife's father or an impostor. He also, as his inscriptions and bas-reliefs record, took care to employ Medes as well as Persians in posts of high confidence and responsibility.[4] In the light of these recorded evidences of Darius's general policy, we could have guessed—even without the help of the direct evidence that we have gleaned from Herodotus—that, in taking his precautions to make it impossible for an integral Persia, integral Media, and integral Armenia ever again to be carried away by an anti-Ariaramnan national movement, as each of these three great sub-empires had been carried away in 522–521 B.C., Darius would have taken pains to avoid any unnecessary provocation.

The straightforward way of guarding against the danger in Media and Armenia would have been simply to abolish the two sub-empires and to break each of them up into a number of smaller viceroyalties; but, as we have seen,[5] there are indications in Herodotus's work that, on the post-Darian map of the Achaemenian Empire, an integral viceroyalty of Media and an integral viceroyalty of Armenia still survived side by side with the smaller districts into which either of them had been dissected by Darius for fiscal purposes. This coexistence of an old political with a new fiscal map was revealed to us by an examination of inconsistencies in the Herodotean gazetteer which we traced back to a confusion in certain places between the two coexistent maps; and

1 See V. v. 499, n. 3.

2 'By the favour of Ahuramazda this inscription in other ways I made. In addition, it was in Aryan, and has been made on leather. . . . Afterwards this inscription was sent by me everywhere among the provinces; the people universally were pleased' ('DB', § 70, Professor R. G. Kent's translation in *Old Persian*, p. 132).

A well-thumbed fragment of the Aramaic translation had been retrieved by Modern Western archaeologists from the débris of the loyal Jewish military cantonment at Elephantinê (see Hoonacker, A. van: *Une Communauté Judéo-Araméenne à Éléphantine, en Égypte, aux vi^e et ve siècles av. J.-C.* (London 1915, Milford), p. 32).

3 See Olmstead, A. T.: *History of the Persian Empire* (Chicago 1948, University of Chicago Press), p. 109.

4 See Junge, P. J.: *Dareios I* (Leipzig 1944, Harrassowitz), pp. 129–30, with n. 13 to chap. 5.

5 On pp. 603–11, above.

the official preservation of Cyaxares' and Cyrus II's sacrosanct sub-empires is indeed what we should have expected *a priori*, for an official abolition of them would have been flagrantly impolitic. Besides keeping open the wounds unavoidably inflicted on the pride of high-spirited imperial peoples who had constrained Darius to subdue them by force of arms in 522–521 B.C., so drastic a precautionary measure as this would have advertised Darius's lack of confidence in the finality of a victory which had indeed been glorious just because it had been so hardly won. We shall therefore not be surprised to find that Darius officially respected the integrity of the Cyran viceroyalties, but at the same time we must not allow ourselves to be hoodwinked by Darius into imagining that the power of the dangerous viceroyalties was not broken in fact as a result of the partitioning of these particular viceroyalties into a larger number of smaller districts on Darius's new fiscal map.

Darius was not named 'the huckster'[1] for nothing, and his precocious appreciation of the potency of economics and finance in public affairs gave him the cue for solving his political problem of taking precautions without giving provocation by attracting attention to what he was actually doing. Darius was aware of the power of the purse; and he will have perceived that a viceroy—or some insurgent nationalist leader who might have disposed of a viceroy as Darius himself had disposed of Smerdis—would not find it easy to try conclusions with the Imperial Government when the control of revenue within his viceregal boundaries had been transferred from him to several district intendants of finance, each separately and directly responsible to the Imperial Chancery. Of course, in an empire in which most of the provinces were economically backward, and in which a money economy was still in its infancy, the power of the purse was modest if measured by twentieth-century Western standards; yet, combined with the weapon of secret intelligence, which the Central Government will have also acquired by setting up a new financial administrative network independent of the existing political administrative network, the separation of political and fiscal powers would greatly reduce a viceroy's capacity for making mischief. Darius must have perceived that his new network of taxation districts, operating unobtrusively behind the façade of an old network of viceroyalties, would be, *de facto*, the effective engine of imperial administration in a huckster-emperor's hands.

The local variations in the relation of the new fiscal map to the old political map are significant. The policy of breaking up, on the fiscal map, viceroyalties that were politically dangerous was applied, as we shall see, not only to Media and Armenia, but also to 'Babylon-cum-Beyond the River' ('Pahat Babili u Ebir-Nari'),[2] which was partitioned into the two taxation districts Bābiruš and Athurā, and to West Anatolia,

[1] 'Darius's assessment of tribute and other similar measures of his provoked the Persians into coining the *mot* that Darius was a huckster, Cambyses a despot and Cyrus a father—in allusion to Darius's vice of dealing in a huckster's spirit with all affairs of state, to Cambyses' vices of irritability and contemptuousness, and to Cyrus's virtue of gentleness and to the consequently invariable beneficence of his acts' (Herodotus, Book III, chap. 89).

[2] See Professor G. G. Cameron's observation quoted on p. 657, n. 3, below.

which was partitioned into the two taxation districts Sparda and Yauna, though in either of these two cases, likewise, the political viceroyalty appears to have been kept intact.[1] By contrast, the loyal Viceroyalty of Harahvatiš was enlarged politically by the addition of Zrãka,[2] and was still further enlarged on the fiscal map by the attachment to it, for taxing purposes, of the disaffected Persian cantons Asagarta, Yautiyā, and Maka, in Kirmān and Lāristān, to constitute the Herodotean Taxation District No. 14.[3] The loyal Viceroyalty of Bākhtriš, again, seems to have been left intact not only on the political map but also on the fiscal map, where it constituted the Herodotean Taxation District No. 12.[4]

It will be seen that Darius's policy was as adroit as any policy could be in the adverse circumstances with which the Ariaramnan usurper had condemned himself to have to contend; yet a sovereign who has acquired the nickname 'huckster' stands convicted of not being loved; and, for all that Darius could do, it was beyond his power, and beyond his successors' power, to put the Achaemenian Empire back on to the broader basis of consent and support on which it had rested in the auspicious Cyran initial chapter of its history. When Darius and Xerxes then proceeded to strain the weakened structure of their régime by embarking on an ambitious forward policy of incorporating the remainder of the Hellenic World, together with its Nomad hinterland on the Great Western Bay of the Eurasian Steppe, it is no wonder that they should have run into a catastrophe.

The Ambiguity of Homonyms

The foregoing general account of the administrative geography of the Achaemenian Empire must now be supplemented by some consideration of the evidence—partly anticipated in the preceding discussion—which was at the disposal of twentieth-century Western scholars seeking to identify and locate particular countries and peoples named in the extant sources of information, both official and Herodotean. One of the difficulties that beset an investigator in this field was the frequent occurrence of an identical name in more than one place on the map, and it may therefore be useful to face this fertile source of confusion before plunging into details.

The occurrence of these homonyms was confusing in two ways. In the first place it was apt to leave the investigator in doubt as to whether he was confronted with a single people or with two or more distinct and separate peoples bearing such-and-such a name. Cases in point were the uncertainty about the existence of a north-western detachment of Paktyes in Cappadocia (Katpatuka)[5] and of a south-eastern detachment of Kaspioi in Arachosia (Harahvatiš) or thereabouts.[6] In the second place it was not always possible, even where the recurrence of a name was not in doubt, to be sure that the recurrence was anything more than

[1] See pp. 657 and 678, below.
[2] See p. 589, with n. 3, above, and p. 637, below.
[3] See pp. 622 and 637, below.
[4] See p. 644, below.
[5] See pp. 608–10, above.
[6] See p. 609, above, and pp. 635–6, below.

a coincidence that was a phonetic accident of no historical significance.[1] In the third place, even if it could be demonstrated—or at least be shown to be probable—that the homonyms really were recurrences of the same name in the same language, it was not always possible to determine the recurrent name's character. On the one hand it might be a genuinely proper name, whose occurrence in different places was evidence that the two or more peoples bearing it were akin to one another and that they had reached their eventual locations from some common original centre of dispersion, however remote from one another might be the regions in which they had respectively come to rest at the end of their divergent migrations. A number of apparent examples of the fission and fanning out of Eurasian Nomad peoples in the course of their eruption out of the Steppe into the regions round about have come to our notice already in our discussion of the geographical distribution of the Paktyes.[2] We have, however, also already come across names that are manifestly not proper names but are descriptive epithets or labels which bear their meaning on their face and which in some cases are known to have been current side by side with genuine proper names which they had not driven out of currency. A classic example is the multiple nomenclature of one branch of the people whose proper name was Paktyes.[3] The south-eastern Paktyes lived, as we know, in a country that bore the proper name Harahvatiš (*Latinè* Arachosia) in virtue of being situated in the basin of a river which in the *Avesta* is called the Harahvaitī.[4] This *dahyāuš* is called exclusively by the name of the country in the official lists, and this place-name Harahvatiš (*ethnikon* Harahvatiyā) is duly reproduced in the Hellenized form 'Arakhôsia' (*ethnikon* Arakhôtoi) in the works of post-Herodotean Hellenic geographers. In Herodotus's work, on the other hand, the name 'Arakhosia' never occurs. In his field-state of Xerxes' expeditionary force, Herodotus calls the people of Arachosia by their national name 'Paktyes',[5] while in his gazetteer of Darius's taxation districts he calls them by their descriptive label 'thamanaioi', meaning 'borderers'.[6]

It is evident that the same title 'borderers' might have been conferred by the Achaemenian authorities, whether officially or informally, on half a dozen different peoples who would have had nothing in common with one another beyond their geographical location on one or other of

[1] In a cautionary comment, Professor G. G. Cameron recommends a prudent adherence to the hypothesis of a non-significant coincidence unless and until convincing evidence in favour of some other explanation presents itself. 'I feel', he writes, 'that there are passages in which you have leaned too heavily on homonyms. I believe, for example, that many town names go back to such primordial times that any attempt to deduce tribal, ethnic, or linguistic conclusions is hopeless. I am innately suspicious of such things. We thought, for example, that Arbela meant "the Four God City", and so it could have been interpreted in Semitic; but now earlier documents present us with Urbillum, which is by no means so explainable. The name, consequently, is pre-Semitic.' After receiving this wise and kindly caution, the writer of this Annex could not plead that he had not been warned.

[2] See pp. 606–9, above.

[3] See pp. 593–4, above.

[4] See Jackson, A. V. W., in *The Cambridge History of India*, vol. i (Cambridge 1922, University Press), p. 321, n. 2.

[5] See Herodotus, Book VII, chaps. 67 and (?) 86 (if 'Paktyes' is to be read here as an emendation for a repetitive 'Kaspioi').

[6] See Herodotus, Book III, chap. 93

the Achaemenian Empire's far-flung frontiers; and in this case an identical label would have been presumptive evidence, not that the peoples bearing it were akin, but, on the contrary, that they had nothing to do with one another. On a latter-day map of Iran and the regions round about, there were, as we have already noticed,[1] at least two 'dāmāns': one between the eastern escarpment of the Iranian Plateau and the west bank of the Indus, and the other at the southern approaches to the Hindu Kush in the basin of the Kābul River; and there was evidently no reason to suppose that there was any national affinity between these eastern and northern borderers of an Afghan Empire. In the administrative geography of the Achaemenian Empire the only borderers labelled, in the extant sources, with the word 'dāmān' were the Paktyes of Arachosia; but there was another word signifying 'border' in the Old Persian language which did occur in at least four places on the Achaemenian and Hellenic map of Iran, and this was 'paraitaka'.

One such 'paraitaka' was the first district of Media which Alexander found on his path in his twelve days' march in the spring of 330 B.C. from his winter-quarters in Persis (Pārsa, Fars) to Ecbatana (Hamadān),[2] and these indications locate this 'paraitaka' in the latter-day province of Ispahan.[3] This was evidently the border province of Media over against Persis, and that will have been the country of the Parêtakênoi who are cited by Herodotus in his list[4] of the tribes of the Medes. This 'paraitaka' between Media and Persis may also be the Partakka or the Partukka mentioned in the Assyrian King Esarhaddon's record of the Assyrian cavalry's operations on the Iranian Plateau, between the Zagros and the Central Desert, in 673 B.C.,[5] since on the same expedition the Assyrians also raided a country called Patush Arri, and this name is evidently identical with the name of the Pateiskhoreis who were one of the tribes of the Persians according to Strabo.[6] There was, however, another Median 'paraitaka', known to post-Herodotean Hellenic geographers and likewise included in Media by them,[7] though not mentioned by Herodotus,[8] near the intersection of the Great North-West Road and the Great

1 On p. 594, n. 1, above.

2 See Arrian: *Expeditio Alexandri*, Book III, chap. xix, § 2.

3 For this 'paraitaka' at the south-eastern extremity of Media, see further Strabo: *Geographica*, Book II, chap. i, § 26 (C 80); Book XI, chap. xiii, § 6 (C 524); Book XV, chap. ii, § 8 (C 723) and § 14 (C 726); chap. iii, § 6 (C 729); Book XVI, chap. i, § 17 (C 744).

4 See Herodotus, Book I, chap. 101.

5 See Cameron, G. G.: *A History of Early Iran* (Chicago 1936, University of Chicago Press), pp. 172–4. In spite of the similarity of their names, these two districts are not identical, since they are mentioned side by side (see Luckenbill, D. D.: *Ancient Records of Assyria and Babylonia* (Chicago 1926–7, University of Chicago Press, 2 vols.), vol. ii, pp. 519, 540, 566).

6 See Strabo: *Geographica*, Book XV, chap. iii, § 1 (C 727), cited by Cameron, ibid. Eserhaddon's record runs: 'Patush Arra, a district on the border of the salt desert, which lies in the land of the distant Medes, on the edge of Mount Bikni, the lapis lazuli mountain, the soil of whose land not one among the kings my fathers had trodden' (Luckenbill, op. cit., vol. ii, pp. 519, 540, [560], 567).

7 See, for example, Strabo: *Geographica*, Book XI, chap. xii, § 4 (C 522); Book XV, chap. iii, § 12 (C 732); Book XVI, chap. i, § 2 (C 736) and § 8 (C 739).

8 Herodotus's Parêtakênoi cannot have been the inhabitants of this western 'paraitaka', considering that, in his itinerary of the Achaemenian Empire's Great North-West Road in Book V, chaps. 49–54, Herodotus does not assign to Media any of the territory through which this road ran. According to the passage in Book V, chaps. 52–53, the road ran from 'Armenia' through 'Matiênê' into 'Kissia' (see pp. 629–30, below).

North-East Road.[1] There was a third 'paraitaka' on one of the borders of Sogdiana which cannot be located exactly from Arrian's narrative[2] of Alexander's operations there, and there was a fourth—the latter-day Sakastênê (Seistan)—astride the lower course of the River Hilmand between Zarangianê (Zrãka) and Arachosia (Harahvatiš).[3]

Obviously there was no more affinity between the inhabitants of these four 'paraitakas' in an Achaemenian Iran than there was in a Medieval Western Christendom between the inhabitants of the March of Ancona, the March of Brandenburg, Denmark, and Finmark, or between the inhabitants of the County Palatine of Durham, the quarter known as the Pallant within the walls of the city of Chichester, a Kur Pfalz astride the Rhine and an Ober Pfalz at the northern tip of Bavaria.

While 'borderers'—denoted by the synonyms 'parêtakênoi' and 'thamanaioi'—is one of the descriptive labels on the map of the Achaemenian Empire, another is 'pairikās', meaning people practising an objectionably distinctive religion. We have observed already[4] that this name, *Graecè* 'parikanioi', was one of several descriptive titles of an Iranian-speaking Nomad people, marching with Sogdiana in the upper valley of the Jaxartes (Sir Darya), whose national name had not been preserved. The Achaemenian imperial authorities, who had originally confounded this people with a host of others of their kind under the generic title 'Sakā' signifying 'Eurasian Nomads', appeared to have subsequently distinguished them from other Nomads by calling them alternatively 'Hauma-(?)drinking Sakā' ('Sakā Haumavargā'), in allusion to one of their religious rites, and 'the Allies' (the Herodotean 'Aiglai'), in allusion to their exceptionally favourable juridical relation with the Achaemenian Empire. But this particular people had no monopoly of being in a treaty relation with the Achaemenian Imperial Government or of drinking hauma or, again, of practising an objectionable religion;[5] and accordingly, when we find another people labelled 'parikanioi' in Herodotus's gazetteer, we cannot infer from the common name that these two peoples had anything in common beyond their common failure to win approval for their respective religions, whatever these may have been. This common label 'pairikās', rendered 'parikanioi' in Greek, was undoubtedly affixed to each of the two peoples to whom Herodotus applies it; for in A.D. 1952 the upper basin of the Sir Darya, which had once been the habitat of 'the Hauma-(?)drinking Sakā', still bore the name 'Farghānah', while the name of a place called Fārghān, 60 kilometres to the east of Tārum and 120 kilometres to the north of Bandar 'Abbās,[6] together with the name of the neighbouring Mount Furghun, attested the former presence of people labelled 'parikan' just

[1] See p. 210, n. 3, above.

[2] See Arrian: *Expeditio Alexandri*, Book IV, chap. xxi and chap. xxii, §§ 1–2.

[3] See Tarn, W. W.: *The Greeks in Bactria and India* (Cambridge 1938, University Press), p. 95, following Isidore of Charax: *Parthian Stations*, chap. 18.

[4] On pp. 594–5, above.

[5] For example, the Hellenes who burned their fathers' corpses and the Callatian Indians who ate their fathers' corpses (see Herodotus, Book III, chap. 38) were, no doubt, both alike stigmatized as 'pairikās' by devout Zoroastrian Persians who exposed their fathers' corpses to be devoured by carrion-eating birds and beasts.

[6] See Herzfeld, op. cit., p. 83.

where we should expect to find 'parikanioi' whom Herodotus presents in his gazetteer as yoke-fellows of the Asiatic Ethiopians in Darius's eighteenth taxation district.[1]

A third descriptive epithet that was rife in the Achaemenian Empire, side by side with 'heathens' and 'borderers', was 'highlanders'. 'Ākaufačiyā', which bears this meaning in Old Persian, figures as the name of the people of an Achaemenian *dahyāuš*;[2] and 'parvatā', which, like 'kaufa', was an Iranian word meaning 'mountain',[3] appears in Greek dress in Herodotus's ethnikon 'Aparytai' and in Ptolemy's ethnika 'Parouêtai' and 'Parautoi'.[4] Did one of the pre-Indo-European languages current on the plateaux of Anatolia, Armenia, and Iran have a word meaning 'hill country' which generated the name 'Tabal' in Assyrian records of the ninth, eighth, and seventh centuries B.C.?[5] In the Assyrian usage of this word there is an ambiguity; for, while it is used generically to signify the whole of the highlands of the Taurus and Antitaurus, it is also used specifically as the proper name for one particular principality in this region which bestrode the upper waters of the rivers of Cilicia in the country afterwards known to Hellenic geographers as Cataonia.[6] This variety of usage leaves us in doubt as to whether the Tibarênoi in the Herodotean Taxation District No. 19, towards the eastern end of the Black Sea coast of Anatolia, were just the local highlanders ('people of the tabal'), or whether 'Tibarênoi', as applied to them, is a proper name which informs us that these were descendants of refugees from the East Central Anatolian principality of Tabal who had taken refuge in this north-eastern fastness from assaults by Moskhoi falling upon them from the west or by Saparda, Paktyes, Cimmerians, and Scyths falling upon them from the east, or both. Similarly we are left in doubt as to whether the Mount Tabor above the headwaters of the River Jordan was named after the Mount Atabyrios in Rhodes by Philistine settlers on the coast on which they stamped their own name; or whether the two mountains are both called 'tabal' simply because 'tabal' means 'mount'. However that may be, it is easier to believe that the 'highlanders' (*Graecè* 'Tapouroi'; *Arabicè* 'Tabarī') who gave the name 'Tabaristan' to the country between the Elburz Range and the south coast of the Caspian Sea, bore the same name as the Tibarênoi of Anatolia because both peoples happened to live in a hill country, than it is to believe that the identity between the two names is evidence that the two peoples had a common ancestry; and the wisest course here is no doubt the third alternative of refraining, in default of positive evidence, from seeing in the resemblance between the two names 'Tibarênoi' and 'Tapouroi' anything more than an accidental coincidence.

There are at least three other cases in which corresponding doubts arise. Considering that the Iranian word 'dahā' (Sanskrit 'dasā') means 'brigand', how are we to know whether the 'dahā' (*Latinè* Dahae, Davi),[7]

1 See further p. 623, below.
2 See p. 668, below.
3 See p. 647, with n. 5, below.
4 See p. 647, n. 6, below.
5 Hence the 'Tubal' of Gen. x. 2.
6 See Forrer, op. cit., p. 73.
7 This ethnikon 'Davi' is implied in the personal name 'Dāvus', representing a Greek Dâos, which is borne by slaves in Latin translations of Attic comedies written in the third century B.C.

whom we find at divers points on our map bear an identical name in virtue of having a common ancestry, or whether they bear it merely as the stigma of a disreputable common profession? Again, considering that the word which appears in Hellenic dress as 'Amardos' or 'Mardos' seems to be merely a rendering of the Old Persian word 'martiya' meaning 'man', how are we to know whether the north-western neighbours of the Tapouroi in the Elburz Range who bore this name, and their homonyms in the North-Western Zagros (the latter-day Mardistan, east of Lake Van) and in Persis, were branches of a single people which had split, like its sister-peoples the Yautiyā, Mačiyā, Pārsā, and Asagartiyā,[1] in the course of travelling across the Iranian Plateau, or whether the only thing that the three bands of 'mardoi' had in common was that, in their common Iranian tongue, they had, all three, elected to style themselves 'the men' *par excellence* in allusion to their common pursuit of the same manly calling of robbery under arms?[2] In the third place we find ourselves at a loss to tell whether the Yaudheya whose habitat was in the borderland between the Panjab and Rājputāna were akin to the Yautiyā (Outioi) of Lāristān and to the Ouitioi of Transcaucasia, or whether the identity of these names tells us merely that the two peoples who bore them in India and in South-West Asia both took pleasure in calling themselves 'the warriors'.[3]

After this precautionary reconnaissance of some of the pitfalls graven across a scholar's path by the ambiguity of homonyms, we have now to hazard ourselves on this treacherous ground. The one slightly encouraging feature in a foolhardy enterprise is that there is manifestly some safety in numbers. Where we have only a single name to confront with a single name—for example 'Tapouroi' with 'Tibarênoi'—the hypothesis of an accidental coincidence is, no doubt, our most prudent recourse. But, where we have a pair of names to confront with a corresponding pair—for example the Greek 'Tibarênoi' plus 'Moskhoi' with the Assyrian 'Tabal' plus 'Mushki' (the Biblical 'Tubal' plus 'Mesech'), or, again, the Mount 'Tabor' plus River 'Jordan' of Palestine with the Mount 'Atabyrios' of Rhodes plus River 'Iardanos' of Crete—the hypothesis of sheer coincidence would seem less probable; and it would seem decidedly improbable where we have a four-in-hand on either side—as, for example, in the correspondence between the 'Yautiyā (Outioi)' plus 'Mačiyā (Mykoi)' plus 'Asagartiyā (Sagartioi)' plus 'Pārsā (Persai)' of South-Western Iran with the 'Ouitioi' plus 'Mūqān' plus 'Asagartiyā' plus 'Parsua' of North-Western Iran. In this last case, at any rate, we can confidently infer that our four associated pairs of homonyms are less likely to have been the product of Chance than to be the monument of an historical fission of each of four co-migrant peoples into two diverging wings.

1 See pp. 607–8, above.

2 This question is raised by Strabo in Book XI, chap. xiii, § 3 (C 523).

3 For the Yaudheya, see Rapson, E. J., in *The Cambridge History of India*, vol. i, p. 528, and de la Vallée Poussin, L.: *L'Inde aux Temps des Mauryas* (Paris 1930, Boccard), p. 16.

Notes on Names and their Locations

In the following discussion of outstanding questions of interpretation and identification, we shall follow the order in which the names of peoples and countries occurring in our sources have been entered in Table V, attached to this Annex, which folds out opposite p. 772. In each successive line we shall deal first with the Old Persian name in the left-hand column of the table, and shall then consider, in connexion with it, the Herodotean name or names that have been equated with it in the table, before proceeding to deal with the next Old Persian name in the left-hand column.

The *Pārsā* (*Graecè* Persai) who retained the status of a privileged imperial people in the Achaemenian Empire after its reorganization by Darius I were only a fraction of the Persian people. For one thing, they did not include the Nomad rearguard of the Pārsā who had become one of the tribes of the Achaemenian Empire's Central Asian Nomad subjects the Pointed-Hood Sakā (*alias* Massagetae); for these dilatory 'Parsioi' did not mount the northern escarpment of the Iranian Plateau till *circa* 130 B.C.[1] Nor did Darius's Pārsā or Herodotus's Persai include the right wing of the Pārsā, known to the Assyrians as Parsua, which, in the course of the original Medo-Persian occupation of Western Iran, had settled, together with the right wings of the three companion peoples—Yautiyā, Mačiyā, Asagartiyā—in Ardalan, in Azerbaijan, and still farther north and north-west, in the lower basin of the rivers Aras and Kur. Though a fourfold community of name would appear to testify to a common national origin, these north-western representatives of the four Persian peoples had all, no doubt, long since become Medes in their political feelings—as the north-western Asagartiyā, at any rate, showed by embarking on the forlorn hope of rising in revolt against Darius at the call of a leader claiming to be a descendant of Cyaxares after the revolt in Media Proper had been crushed and after the leader of that revolt had been captured at Ragā (Rayy) and been executed at Ecbatana.[2] It is more significant that the Pārsā (Persai) of our lists do not include even the whole of that portion of the Persian people that had been under the sovereignty of the House of Achaemenes (Hakhāmaniš) since the reign of Achaemenes' son Teispes (Čispiš, *regnabat circa* 675–640 B.C.).

The original patrimony of the House of Achaemenes had been the canton of Parsuwaš or Parsawaš (*Assyriacè* Parsumaš or Parsamaš) in the upper basin of the River Karkhah, to the south of Media and to the north of the plains of Elam (i.e. it had been the latter-day country of Lūristān).[3] Parsuwaš is mentioned in the Assyrian records as early as

[1] See Tarn: *The Greeks in Bactria and India*, pp. 292–4.

[2] See 'DB', §§ 32–33.

[3] This location of Parsuwaš, which is Cameron's, has been adopted in this Study, as against the view (advocated by Sidney Smith in his *Isaiah, Chapters XL–LV, Literary Criticism and History* (London 1944, Milford), p. 28) that Parsuwaš was not a separate and distinct country from Pārsa, and was not situated in Lūristān, but was identical with Pārsa and was therefore situated in Fars. On this view the appanage of the Cyran elder branch of Teispes' line was Anšan alone, not Anšan-cum-Parsuwaš, while the appanage of the Ariaramnan younger branch was a Pārsa with which Parsuwaš was identical. In the present writer's amateur judgement, Sidney Smith's identification of Parsuwaš with

815 B.C.,[1] and Achaemenes (*regnabat circa* 700–675 B.C.)[2] must have been on the throne when Parsuwaš sent a contingent to the army of the anti-Assyrian alliance, headed by Elam, which defeated Sennacherib at Halūlah.[3] Achaemenes' successor Teispes is described in later records as 'King of the city of Anšan',[4] which must have lain somewhere on the border between Parsuwaš, Elam, and Babylonia;[5] and it appears to have been in Teispes' reign (*circa* 675–640 B.C.) that the Achaemenian Dynasty achieved an immense extension of its dominions by adding to Parsuwaš and Anšan the whole left wing of the Persian group of Iranian peoples on the farther side of Elam in the latter-day provinces of Fars, Lāristān, and Kirmān.[6] Teispes must have found his opportunity as a *tertius gaudens* during the great Assyro-Elamite war that had broken out in 663 B.C. and that ended, after continuing for about a quarter of a century, in the destruction of Elam and the exhaustion of the Assyrian winners of a Pyrrhic victory.

Teispes divided these expanded dominions between his elder son Cyrus I (*regnabat circa* 640–600 B.C.), to whom he bequeathed the dynasty's patrimony in Parsuwaš and Anšan, and his younger son Ariaramnes, to whom he gave the dynasty's new acquisitions in the South-East. The fortunes of the elder branch of the house were depressed when, after the destruction of Elam, Cyrus I of Anšan was compelled by one of Asshurbanipal's generals to acknowledge Assyria's overlordship and to surrender one of his sons as a hostage;[7] but thereafter there was a dramatic reversal of fortunes which may have been a

Pārsa was less convincing than Cameron's location of it in Lūristān, and this for two reasons. In the first place a Parsuwaš with which Assyria came into military collision in the early years of the seventh century B.C. seems more likely to have lain in Lūristān than to have lain in Fars, on the farther side of Elam. In the second place it seems unlikely that, when Teispes was dividing his dominions between his two sons, he should have assigned to his younger son Ariaramnes his own hereditary patrimony Parsuwaš—as he will have done if Parsuwaš is identical with Pārsa—and have bequeathed to his elder son Cyrus I nothing more than his new acquisition Anšan. Teispes' partition of his dominions would be less difficult to account for on the view that he assigned to his elder son Cyrus I his own ancestral patrimony Parsuwaš in Lūristān, together with an Anšan that had been the earlier and the nearer of Teispes' two acquisitions, while he assigned to his younger son Ariaramnes his later and more distant acquisition Pārsa. It is geographically possible that Teispes, starting from Lūristān, should have pushed his way into Fars via Anšan in the north-west corner of the lowlands of Elam.

1 See Cameron: *A History of Early Iran*, p. 179.

2 See ibid., p. 179.

3 This battle is dated 692 B.C. by Cameron, loc. cit.; 691 by Sidney Smith in *The Cambridge Ancient History*, vol. iii (Cambridge 1925, University Press), p. 68.

4 See Cameron, op. cit., p. 180.

5 F. W. König, in his *Älteste Geschichte der Meder und Perser* (Leipzig 1934, Hinrichs), p. 9, locates Anšan somewhere not far from the district of Dêr, which lay in the north-east corner of Babylonia. Sidney Smith, in his *Isaiah, Chapters XL–LV*, p. 121 (note 27, referring to p. 28), identifies Dêr with the latter-day Badrah, just on the 'Irāqī side of the 'Irāqī–Persian frontier, east by south of Baghdad. This location of Anšan would appear to refute decisively Sidney Smith's statement, in op. cit., p. 28, that 'both Parsumaš and Anšan designate the province round Pasargadae'. In the immediately preceding sentence, Smith testifies that Anšan was 'known to the Babylonians from early Sumerian times'—i.e. from times when 'the province round Pasargadae', *alias* Pārsa, Persis, Fars, was far beyond the horizon of the Land of Shinar. This last point is made by Weissbach in P.-W., loc. cit., col. 1142. See also the present Study, p. 204, above.

6 See Cameron, op. cit., p. 212.

7 See Cameron, op. cit., p. 204. Sidney Smith argues, in *Isaiah, Chapters XL–LV* p. 122 (note 31 referring to p. 28), that this would have been *ultra vires* for Cyrus I if he had been already under the suzerainty of his brother Ariaramnes, as Cameron suggests that he was (see p. 601, with n. 1, above).

consequence of the sudden rise of the Median Power upon the collapse of Assyria after Asshurbanipal's death. The crown of Pārsa, which Ariaramnes had inherited from his father Teispes, was certainly never worn by Ariaramnes' grandson Hystaspês, the father of Darius I;[1] and, since we find a scion of the elder branch of the House of Achaemenes—Cambysês I (*regnabat circa* 600–559 B.C.), son of Cyrus I and father of Cyrus II—reigning over Pārsa as well as over Parsuwaš, with the title 'King of the City of Anšan', under the suzerainty of King Cyaxares of Media,[2] it seems possible that the deposition of the Ariaramnan branch of the Achaemenidae may have been a consequence of a Median act of intervention that had restored the Cyran branch's fortunes, though it is also possible that King Ariaramnes' son King Arsâmês may have retained the throne of Pārsa till he was ejected from it by Cambysês I's son Cyrus II as one of the moves in this empire-builder's career of self-aggrandizement.[3]

The only indication in Darius and Xerxes' official lists of *dahyāva* that the Pārsa to which these lists give the place of honour did not include the whole of the Persian territory which had been inherited by the successors of Teispes is the separate mention of Maka in all six lists and of Asagarta as well in 'DPe'. But we should not have known how to interpret the appearance of these two names in the official lists if the key had not been given to us by Herodotus's list of the peoples comprised in his Taxation District No. 14, in which we find not only the south-eastern Mykoi (Mačiyā) and the south-eastern Sagartioi (Asagartiyā), but also the south-eastern Outioi (Yautiyā),[4] attached to the Thamanaioi (i.e. the Paktyes in Arachosia)[5] and to the Sarangai (Zrāka).

1 'Cyrus the Great was a great-nephew of Ariaramnes, and a second cousin of Hystaspes father of Darius. I think we must credit Darius's statement that he was the ninth king of the Achaemenian line; and to me the reasonable way to enumerate them is Achaemenes, Teispes, Cyrus I, Cambyses I, Cyrus II, Cambyses II—then, turning to the other line, Ariaramnes, Arsames, Darius. Hystaspes was never King, since both he and his father Arsames were living when Darius won the throne (so DSf, §§ 12–15, and XPf, §§ 20–25), so that only Arsames could bear the royal title.'—Professor Roland G. Kent, in a note to the present writer.

The texts, with English translations, of two inscriptions found at Hamadān (Ecbatana), which purport to have been dictated by King Ariaramnes (AmH) and by his son and successor King Arsames (AsH) respectively, are published in Kent, R. G.: *Old Persian: Grammar, Texts, Lexicon* (New Haven, Conn. 1950, American Oriental Society), p. 116, with bibliographies on p. 107. See also Kent: 'The Oldest Old Persian Inscriptions', in the *Journal of the American Oriental Society*, vol. lxvi, No. 3, July–September 1946, pp. 206–12. Kent's conclusion is that 'the inscriptions of Ariaramnes and Arsames were inscribed in the time of Artaxerxes II, to do honour to the royal ancestors of Ariaramnes' line—apparently as a part of anti-Cyrus activity by Artaxerxes'.

2 See Cameron, op. cit., p. 218, and the present Study, p. 204, above.

3 'Cyrus II deposed Arsames from his throne, yet not in a bitter struggle, for Arsames retained his life and apparently his liberty, and was still living when his grandson Darius became ruler of the Empire after the death of Cambyses II, son of Cyrus the Great (so in DSf, §§ 12–15, and in XPf, §§ 20–25). Possibly there was some arrangement as to alternate overlordship [cf. Sidney Smith, *Isaiah, Chapters XL–LV*, p. 29.—A. J. T.], which Cyrus unilaterally abrogated—as is usually the case in such matters. Thus it resulted that Hystaspes, son of Arsames, never had a throne of his own, and is never called King in the O.P. inscriptions when Darius mentions him as his father, though Xerxes normally gives the title to his father Darius when he names him in the inscriptions.'—R. G. Kent, in *J.A.O.S.*, vol. lxvi, No. 3, pp. 210–11, following F. H. Weissbach, in P.-W., Supplementband IV, cols. 1132–44, s.v. 'Kyros', who points out in cols. 1141–2 that, in the Babylonian Nabonidus-Cyrus Chronicle, Cyrus II is called 'King of Anšan' shortly before 548 B.C., but 'King of Parsu' in 547 B.C. See also the present Study, p. 204, above.

4 See pp. 637–41, below.

5 See pp. 593–4, above, and p. 633, below.

Pārsa in the political and constitutional sense of the domain of a privileged Persian imperial people did not, as it emerged from the upheaval of 522–521 B.C., include either Lāristān or Kirmān on the one hand or Lūristān on the other. Not only the disaffected south-eastern Mačiyā, Yautiyā, and Asagartiyā, but also a Parsuwaš that had been the Achaemenian Dynasty's original patrimony, had now been degraded to the ranks of the Empire's tax-paying subjects. While two-thirds of what had formerly been Pārsa had now been attached to Harahvatiš, the whole of the former Parsuwaš had been merged in Hūja (the Viceroyalty of Greater Elam).

As for *Māda*, we should never have known from the non-committal mention of the name in all six official lists that it had been partitioned on the Darian fiscal map into the four fragments that the Herodotean gazetteer reveals to us.

One of these fragments, Herodotus's District No. 10, which he calls 'Media' *par excellence*, appears (as soon as we have stripped away an adventitious pair of remote Sakan peoples)[1] to be confined to the environs of Ecbatana (Hamadān) and to the upland section of the Great North-East Road to the south-west of Hamadān as far as the latter-day town of Kirmānshāh inclusive.

Another fragment of Media seems to be represented by Herodotus's District No. 11, embracing the countries of the *Kaspioi*, *Pausikai*,[2] *Pantimathoi*, and *Dareitai*. A key to the location of this district is perhaps to be found in the last of these four names, if we are right in interpreting it to mean the people living in the neighbourhood of the Caspian Gates.

'Duvarayā', the locative singular case of the Old Persian word meaning 'door', occurs in 'DB', § 32; and in the New Persian language the compound word 'dar-band' (meaning literally 'door-barrier') came to be the technical term for one of those fortified and garrisoned passes that played so important a part in the administrative as well as the strategic geography of the Ottoman Empire under this name, and of the East Roman Empire under the graecized Latin name 'Kleisoura' (i.e. 'clausura').[3] The Caspian Gates commanded one of the only two non-trans-desert roads between the main body of the Achaemenian Empire and its vast outlying territories on the farther side of the Central Desert of Iran. The road through the Caspian Gates from Māda to Parthava circumvented the north-western end of the desert; the road from Kirmān to Arachosia circumvented its south-eastern end; and in 522–521 B.C. both these strategic routes had proved to be of critical importance. The south-eastern route had carried the Yautiyan rebel Vahyazdāta's expeditionary force on its daring raid from Pārsa to the basin of the Kābul River; the north-western route would have brought the Median rebel Fravartiš's troops to the support of the insurgents in

[1] See pp. 594–5, above.

[2] The *Πανσίκαι καὶ Παντίμαθοι* of A[1] would appear to be the right reading. The *Πανσοὶ και Παντίμαθοι* of S looks like an attempt to rationalize a *Πανσὶ καὶ Παντίμαθοι* of RV which has arisen from a *Πανσίκαι Παντίμαθοι* of BCPA[c] which has arisen from the accidental omission of one of the two consecutive *και*'s of the correct text.

[3] See p. 82, n. 3, above.

Hyrcania (Varkāna) and Parthia (Parthava), who had raised the standard of revolt in Fravartiš's name, if they had not, like the North-Western Asagartiyā, waited to rise until after Fravartiš had been crushed.

As it turned out, Darius was able to detach troops to the aid of his father Hystaspes, the Viceroy of Parthava, from Ragā via the Caspian Gates, and this reinforcement decisively turned the tide;[1] but the incident served to illustrate the Caspian Gates' strategic importance, and Darius manifestly took both these lessons to heart. After the flames of rebellion had been stamped out, he made sure of his control over the Kirmān–Arachosia road by attaching Kirmān to the loyal viceroyalty of Harahvatiš. The security of the Caspian Gates must have concerned him equally, and the occurrence of the name Dareitai among the names of the peoples in Herodotus's eleventh district suggests that this district included the Caspian Gates within its boundaries. Ptolemy places 'the Dareîtis district' at the north-eastern extremity of Media, to the east of Rhagianê (the district round Ragā, *Graecè* Rhagai), with 'the Ouadassoi' in between.[2]

If the Dareitai are to be located at the Caspian Gates, this gives us a clue to the location of the three associated peoples. It is clear that they cannot have lain east of the Caspian Gates, since the immediately adjoining territories in that quarter were Hyrcania and Parthia in District No. 16. They are unlikely to have lain between the Elburz Range and the Caspian Sea, since there is no evidence that the south coast of the Caspian, west of Hyrcania, was ever under Achaemenian rule.[3] Therefore they are likely to have lain west of the Caspian Gates; and, if so, we can perhaps detect the imprint of the former presence of the detachment of Kaspioi that is here associated with the Dareitai in the latter-day place-name Qazwīn. We may also perhaps detect in Herodotus's Pausikai the Paesici or Pesticae who, in a Roman version of a post-

[1] See 'DB', §§ 35–37.

[2] See *Geographia*, Book VI, chap. ii, § 6.

[3] Professor G. G. Cameron, commenting on this passage, makes the point that, since Hyrcania was undoubtedly embraced in the Achaemenian Empire, it seems unlikely that the rest of the southern shore of the Caspian Sea will have remained independent. Where, he asks, were the Cadusians, if not here? Certainly the Cadusians were to be found in this coastal strip, at its north-western end, to the north of the Gêlai (see p. 631, below). But is there any evidence that the Cadusians were ever the Achaemenidae's subjects, or even their allies? We hear of inconclusive Achaemenian punitive expeditions into Cadusian territory, and of Cadusian troops serving in Achaemenian armies; but, after all, Continental European Greece was likewise invaded by Darius I and Xerxes, and Continental European Greek soldiers of fortune were hired by Xerxes' successors. Have we any warrant for assuming that Achaemenian authority was any more effective in Cadusia than it was in, say, Attica?

No doubt, at first sight it is not easy to give credence to a map in which Gīlān and Tabaristān (the latter-day Mazandarān) are depicted as lying outside the frontiers of an empire that encircles them by coming down to the shore of the Caspian on either side of them, round the mouths of the rivers Aras and Kur to the north-west and round the mouth of the River Atrak to the east, besides controlling a corridor of territory, connecting Western Iran with Khurāsān, between the southern face of the Elburz Range and the north-west corner of the Central Desert of Iran. A closer inspection, however, brings out the fact that this strip of territory is a natural fastness, where an invader who has managed to surmount or outflank the southern rampart of mountains will be baffled on the seaward slopes by forests and in the lowlands by jungles and swamps. It is perhaps relevant to recall that the Arab Caliphate, in its day, touched the shore of the Caspian round the mouths of the rivers Aras and Kur, and extended eastwards through the Caspian Gates across the Oxus to Farghānah, without succeeding in bringing Gīlān or Tabaristān under its rule (see II. ii. 447–8).

Alexandrine Hellenic gazetteer,[1] are associated with the Amardi, and whom this association would locate somewhere to the north-west of Qazwīn, in the upper part of the basin of the Safid Rud, above the gorge in which it breaks through the Elburz *en route* for the Caspian. This, in turn, would lead us to look for the Pantimathoi, who were the fourth people in this district, somewhere to the west of Qazwīn.

This is where the Assyrian records appear to locate the north-western branch of the Nomad Persian people named Asagartiyā (*Assyriacè* 'Zikirtu' and 'Zakruti'; *Graecè* Sagartioi),[2] whom Ptolemy likewise locates to the east of the Zagros;[3] and it is also just where we should expect to find a remnant of these north-western Asagartiyā surviving after the next eruption of Nomad peoples on to the Iranian Plateau from the Eurasian Steppe had sent a fresh stream of migrants pouring westward through the Caspian Gates into the basin of Lake Urmīyah and beyond it into the basin of the rivers Aras and Kur. The country between the two provinces of Ardalan and Qazwīn lay astride the habitual westward route of Eurasian Nomad Völkerwanderungen south of the Caspian Sea, but it was one of the most mountainous sections of this route and was therefore one in which no migrant Nomad people would linger by preference. It would therefore not be surprising to find a batch of Asagartiyā still entrenched here between one batch of Kaspioi just behind them, round Qazwīn, and another batch of Kaspioi just in front of them, to the north of Lake Urmīyah and in the lower valleys of the rivers Aras and Kur.

On a latter-day map, this country between Qazwīn and Ardalan was called 'Khamsah', which is the Arabic word for 'five', and we may perhaps venture to identify this name with that of the frontier fortress called 'Panziš' which the Assyrians built somewhere on the border between the independent territory of Asagarta and the Assyrian protectorate called Mannai in the relatively open southern part of the Urmīyah Basin, between the south end of the Lake and Parsua.[4] If Panziš is an Assyrian version of 'panča', which means 'five' in the Old Persian language, we may perhaps hazard the guess that 'Khamsah' may have been an Arabic translation of a previous local Iranian place-name, and that the five entities commemorated in this place-name may have been five tribes constituting the north-western branch of the Asagartiyā. A Eurasian Nomad horde was apt to be an association of constituent tribes; and hordes thus constituted would sometimes style themselves 'the so many so-and-so'—e.g. 'the ten [tribes of] Uigurs' (*Turcicè* 'Onugur') or whatever the number and the name might be—as a simple way of advertising their strength. The Pañchalas, who are associated with the Kurus in the legendary tradition of an archaic age of Indic history, were believed to have been a confederacy of five tribes who

1 In Pomponius Mela's *Chorographia*, Book III, chap. v, §§ 39 and 42. They reappear in Pliny's *Historia Naturalis*, Book VI, chap. xvii (xix), § 50.

2 See Cameron, op. cit., pp. 149–50; König, op. cit., p. 16; Herzfeld, op. cit., p. 82; Forrer, op. cit., p. 75; and the present Annex, p. 608, above.

3 Ptolemy: *Geographia*, Book VI, chap. ii, § 6.

4 For the site of Panziš, see Forrer, op. cit., p. 75; Adontz, op. cit., pp. 102 and 367. 'Panziš, the strong fortress that lies over against the lands of Zikirtu and Andia' (Sargon's record of his eighth campaign (714 B.C.) in Luckenbill, op. cit., vol. ii, pp. 150–1).

took their name from their number.[1] If the north-western Asagartiyā did style themselves 'the Five Tribes', the Old Persian word 'panča', meaning 'five', might perhaps account for the first two syllables of an old Persian compound proper name that makes its appearance in Greek dress as 'Pantimathoi'.

If these considerations carry any conviction, they indicate that Herodotus's Eleventh District was a chain of cantons, running west and east from the Asagartiyā in Khamsah through the Kaspioi round Qazwīn as far eastward as the Caspian Gates inclusive. It is noteworthy that neither the Herodotean gazetteer nor any of the Achaemenian official lists mention by name the Median district that had for its local capital the city of Ragā, in the neighbourhood of a latter-day Tehran, where the Median pretender Fravartiš had made his last stand.[2] Ragā will either have been included in the canton of the Kaspioi round Qazwīn, or else it will have been left out of the reckoning on account of its being an autonomous temple-state[3] like Jerusalem, Comana Cataoniae, and Comana Pontica.

Is another fragment of Media to be detected in Herodotus's District No. 15? This possibility is suggested by the fact that the two names here associated by Herodotus—the *Sakai* and the *Kaspioi*—recur on a post-Alexandrine Hellenic map side by side in the lower basin of the rivers Aras and Kur in two countries called Sakasênê[4] and Kaspianê. The Sakan contingent in this Herodotean pair of peoples stamped their name on a canton called 'Sakašayana' ('Saka-land') in the province of Utênê,[5] between the Qārabāgh highlands and the River Kur, whose name, as we have seen, commemorated the former presence of these Sakas' local forerunners, the north-western branch of the Yautiyā. In the field-state of the army assembled by Darius Codomannus at Gaugamela in 331 B.C., Sakesînai are brigaded with the Albanians, Cadusians, and Medes.[6] Sakasênê is cited by Strabo in association with Araxênê and with 'Matianê in Media';[7] and in this context both Sakasênê and Araxênê are described as being 'in Armenia'.[8]

The Armenia which Strabo, or his source, has in mind in this passage is evidently the Great Armenia that had eventually been brought into existence by the progressive expansion of a successor-state of the Seleucid Empire which, after the defeat of Antiochus III by the Romans in 190 B.C., had been founded by Artaxias, Antiochus's viceroy in one of the Seleucid Empire's two Armenian provinces.[9] Artaxias' Armenian king-

[1] See Keith, A. Berriedale, in *The Cambridge History of India*, vol. i, p. 118. These Pañchalas' Kuru associates were perhaps the left wing of an ex-Eurasian Nomad people whose right wing had given its name to the River Kur in Transcaucasia, to the north-west of Panziš.

[2] See 'DB', § 32.

[3] See Nyberg, H. S.: *Die Religionen des Alten Iran* (Leipzig 1938, Hinrichs), pp. 314 et seqq. and 342.

[4] The Sakapênê of Ptolemy: *Geographia*, Book V, chap. xiii, § 9.

[5] See Adontz, op. cit., p. 308. Utênê is Ptolemy's Otênê (see *Geographia*, Book V, chap. xiii, § 9).

[6] See Arrian: *Expeditio Alexandri*, Book III, chap. viii, § 4.

[7] See Strabo: *Geographica*, Book II, chap. i, § 14 (C 73); Book XI, chap. vii, § 2 (C 509). Cp. Book XI, chap. xiv, § 4 (C 528).

[8] Strabo, loc. cit. See also Book XI, chap. viii, § 4 (C 511).

[9] See ibid., Book XI, chap. xiv, § 5 (C 528) and § 15 (C 531).

dom did not acquire an exclusive title to the name 'Armenia' until Artaxias' descendant and successor Tigranes (*regnabat circa* 96–55 B.C.) had annexed the adjoining Armenian successor-state of the Seleucid Empire in the Upper Tigris Basin (*Graecè* Sophênê, *Assyriacè* Naïri).[1] But in his record of the details of the previous expansion of the kingdom founded by Artaxias, before its culmination in the reign of Tigranes, Strabo mentions[2] its acquisition from Media of 'the Phaunîtis' (?),[3] 'Basoropeda' (Vaspuragan) and Kaspianê. This Kaspianê must be the country of the Kaspioi whom Ptolemy[4] locates on the western edge of Media, adjoining Armenia (i.e. the Greater Armenia that had come into existence since 190 B.C.); and here the Kaspioi had bequeathed their name to 'the Caspian mountain range' which is Ptolemy's name for the watershed between the basins of lakes Van and Urmīyah along which he locates the boundary between the Armenia and the Media of his day, and at whose southern extremity he locates the meeting-point of Media and Armenia with Assyria.[5]

This ex-Median Kaspianê had also stamped its name on a canton called 'Kasbi-k' (i.e. 'Kaspioi'), which is mentioned by the Armenian historians Agathangelus and Faustus of Byzantium[6] as having been in existence in the third and fourth centuries of the Christian Era near the town of P'aitarakan in the angle between the rivers Aras and Kur just above their confluence. At an earlier date this Kaspianê must have occupied the whole of the steppe country in the lower basin of the rivers Aras and Kur from the northern rim of the basin of Lake Urmīyah on the south to the southern foothills of the Caucasus Range on the north; for in another passage Strabo records that Kaspianê extended north of the River Kur into the South-East Caucasian country called Albania.[7]

Even if it had not been expressly stated by Strabo, in a passage cited above, that Kaspianê had been part of Media before its annexation to Armenia, we could have inferred from the evidence presented by Herodotus that this Kaspianê astride the lower course of the River Aras must have been the home of one of the two or more detachments of the Kaspioi whom he mentions in his work; for Herodotus has no other name than 'Caspian' for the Caspian Sea (in contrast to the usage of the post-Alexandrine Hellenic geographers, who took to calling it 'the Hyrcanian Sea'); this Herodotean usage means that the section of the shore on which Herodotus's informants had access to this sea (and they had not only sailed on it but had coasted all round it, for they had discovered that it was landlocked)[8] must have been inhabited by people called 'Kaspioi'; and the only Kaspioi on record who unquestionably possessed

1 See ibid., Book XI, chap. xiv, § 15 (C 532).
2 See ibid., Book XI, chap. xiv, § 5 (C 528).
3 Cp. the 'Phavênê' of Book XI, chap. xiv, § 4 (C 528).
4 In his *Geographia*, Book VI, chap. ii, § 5.
5 See Book V, chap. xiii, §§ 3 and 4. Cp. § 6.
6 See Agathangelus: *A History of Tiridates the Great and of Saint Gregory the Illuminator's Preaching*, chap. 1, French translation, in Langlois, V.: *Collection des Historiens Anciens et Modernes de l'Arménie*, vol. i (Paris 1867, Didot), p. 115, col. 2; Faustus: *An Historical Library*, Book IV, chap. 50, and Book V, chap. 14, French translation, ibid., p. 267, col. 1, and p. 288, col. 2.
7 See Strabo: *Geographica*, Book XI, chap. iv, § 5 (C 502).
8 See Herodotus, Book I, chap. 203.

a seaboard on the Caspian Sea were the Kaspioi who had given their name to this once Median Kaspianê on the steppes round the mouth of the River Aras. Herodotus also knew that the River Aras flowed into the Caspian Sea at the end of a course running from west to east.[1] Considering the wildness of the peoples adjoining the Caspian Sea both in and after the Achaemenian Age, it is improbable that Herodotus's sources could have learned of the existence of the sea to which they gave the name 'Caspian', or could have ascertained that the River Aras debouched into it, unless this section of the shore of the Caspian Sea, together with a hinterland inhabited by Kaspioi, had been made accessible to geographers through its having been brought under Achaemenian rule. It seems legitimate to infer that the lower basin of the rivers Aras and Kur, as far as the adjoining section of the Caspian shore, must have been included within the Achaemenian Empire's frontiers; and, if this inference is justified, then this Kaspianê which was next-door neighbour to a Sacasênê seems the obvious location for the Kaspioi who are associated with Sakai in Herodotus's District No. 15.

The westernmost of the divers fragments of Media that figure in Herodotus's gazetteer in his District No. 18, 'the *Matiênoi*, *Saspeires* and *Alarodioi*'; and, as we have observed already,[2] the habitats of both the Alarodioi and the Saspeires are easy to identify. The Alarodioi are the people of the former Kingdom of Urartu, which extended over the basin of Lake Van and over the upper valleys of the Eastern Euphrates (Murād Su) and the Aras. The Saspeires are the inhabitants of the canton of Isbir, north of Urartu, in the valley of the River Choroq. It remains to locate the country named after the Matiênoi whom Herodotus associates with the Alarodioi and the Saspeires in the present context.

These easterly Matiênoi must have been a quite separate branch from those who, in the Achaemenian Age, were living within the bend of the Halys near the meeting-point between Cilicia, Cappadocia, and Phrygia;[3] and, unlike those Western Matiênoi, the Eastern Matiênoi seem by this time to have been extinct; for, in the field-state of Xerxes' expeditionary force, the Eastern Matiênoi do not appear, whereas their homonyms the Western Matiênoi, and their neighbours and associates the Alarodioi and the Saspeires, are all credited with contingents whose equipment is described and whose commanders are named The Alarodioi and Saspeires are brigaded under a single command and are both paraded in the same sub-Moschian equipment as the Kolkhoi.[4] In this context the absence of the Eastern Matiênoi from the muster-roll is conspicuous; and this indicates that in 480 B.C. they were no longer in the land of the living. On the other hand the presence of their name in the gazetteer indicates that at this time some country was still called after them.

[1] See Herodotus, Book IV, chap. 40. In all other passages in which Herodotus mentions a river 'Araxes' (i.e. in Book I, chaps. 202 and 205, and in Book III, chap. 36), he is confounding the Aras with the Oxus or the Jaxartes or both.

[2] See pp. 603–4, above.

[3] The evidence for the location of the Western Matiênoi is reviewed in the Note on Chronology in x. 201.

[4] See Herodotus, Book VII, chap. 79.

If the proper noun 'Matiênoi' in Herodotus's work stands for a place-name, and not for the name of a living people, in those passages in which Herodotus is not referring to the Western Matiênoi on the River Halys, this place-name is not always used to denote an area of identical extent. In the description of Darius's Eighteenth Taxation District the name designates only those portions of this district, whatever they may prove to have been, that were not embraced in either Urartu or Isbir. There are other passages, however, in which the region bearing the name of these apparently extinct Eastern Matiênoi manifestly stands, in Herodotus's mind, for 'a roof of the world' from which a number of the principal rivers of South-West Asia—the Aras, the Diyālah (Gyndes),[1] and the Lesser Zab[2]—flow out in all directions; and in these passages 'the Matiênoi' is evidently a comprehensive label for the whole of District No. 18, including the domains of the Alarodioi and the Saspeires.

On the map of the Great North-West Road, which Herodotus or his source had under his eye while he was writing the account of Aristagoras of Miletus's unsuccessful solicitation of Cleomenes I of Sparta on the eve of the Ionian Revolt of 499 B.C.,[3] the name 'Matiênoi' was applied to the ex-Assyrian territories (Mygdonia, Adiabênê, and Chalonîtis in the nomenclature of the post-Alexandrine Hellenic geographers) that had been annexed by Media in the Medo-Babylonian partition of Assyria in 610–609 B.C.;[4] and, since the rest of Herodotus's description of this map

1 See Herodotus, Book I, chaps. 189 and 202. When, in chap. 202, Herodotus writes that the Araxes and the Gyndes 'flow out of the Matiênoi', the river represented by his 'Araxes' is manifestly the Aras, though in the same context the same name 'Araxes' means, not the Aras, but the Oxus, when it is described as constituting the frontier between Cyrus's empire and the ranges of the Central Asian Nomad Massagetae, and when it is said to have forty mouths of which only one flows out into the Caspian Sea, while the rest lose themselves in swamps and lagoons (i.e. in the marshy borders of the Sea of Aral).

2 See Herodotus, Book V, chap. 52. In this passage, Herodotus mistakenly locates the source of the Greater Zab in his Armenia.

3 See Herodotus, Book V, chaps. 49–54.

4 In the detailed description of the Great North-West Road in Herodotus, Book V, chaps. 52–54, the text of the relevant passage in chap. 52, as it had reached the hands of Modern Western scholars, ran as follows:

'In Armenia there are fifteen stages of posting-stations, making 56½ parasangs, and among these stations there is a guard-house. Four navigable rivers flow through this country, which all have to be crossed by ferry: first the Tigris; then a pair that have the same name, though it is not the same river and does not rise from the same source; for the one that comes first in the itinerary rises among the Armenians and the one that comes second among the Matiênoi. The fourth of these rivers is called the Gyndes (Cyrus once distributed its waters into 360 channels). When one breaks out of this Armenia into the Matienian country, there are four stages; and when one passes out of this country into the Cissian country there are eleven stages, making 42½ parasangs, up to the River Choaspes—likewise navigable—on whose banks stands the city of Susa.'

In this text there were three things that must be wrong. In the first place a figure, giving the number of parasangs in Matiênê, must have dropped out, for this was the only country in the chart for which this entry was missing, and, in the text as it stood, the aggregate of the numbers of parasangs, given country by country with the exception of Matiênê, fell short, by 137, of the total number of parasangs given in chap. 53. In the second place, in the text as it stood, the aggregate of the numbers of posting-stages, given country by country, fell short, by 30, of the total number of posting-stages given in chap. 52. In the third place the text as it stood differed from all other known accounts of the boundaries of Armenia in including within them the navigable section of the course of the Greater Zab and *a fortiori* in including any part of the courses of the Lesser Zab and of the Diyālah.

These errors required one addition to the text and one transposition of sentences in order to make the whole description self-consistent and to eliminate the incorrect inclusion in Armenia of the courses of the Diyālah, the lesser Zab, and the lower

agrees with his gazetteer of Darius's taxation districts, it follows that, in the gazetteer as well as on the map, these ex-Assyrian territories were associated, under the name 'Matiênoi', with Urartu and Isbir.[1]

This conclusion raises the question of the geographical practicability of this administrative arrangement. What practicable route was there for maintaining communications between this fragment of Assyria and Urartu? And where was the common centre from which these two portions of Taxation District No. 18 could both be administered? The line of communications between the two territories cannot have been via the Great North-West Road; for this road, as Herodotus charts its course, ran north-westwards out of the ex-Assyrian territory embraced in 'the Matiênoi' into Armenia direct, without passing through Urartu *en route*. Nor can the line of communications between this ex-Assyrian territory and Urartu have run to the east of the River Tigris over the highlands of Gordyênê in the angle between the Tigris and the Centrîtês (Bohtān); for, when Xenophon and his comrades took that route in 401 B.C., they found no road; they had to fight every inch of their way across the mountains; and, when they had struggled through to the north bank of the Centrîtês, they found themselves, not in Urartu, but in 'Armenia' (or, more precisely, in Arzanênê).[2] Nor was there any

reaches of the Greater Zab; and, after these requisite emendations, the corrected text would read:

'In Armenia there are fifteen stages of posting-stations, making 56½ parasangs, and among these stations there is a guard-house. When one breaks out of this Armenia into the Matienian country, there are four [and thirty] stages, [making 137 parasangs]. Four navigable rivers flow through this country, which all have to be crossed by ferry: first the Tigris; then a pair that have the same name, though it is not the same river and does not rise from the same source; for the one that comes first in the itinerary rises among the Armenians and the one that comes second among the Matiênoi. The fourth of these rivers is called the Gyndes (Cyrus once distributed its waters into 360 channels). And when one passes out of this country into the Cissian country there are eleven stages, making 42½ parasangs, up to the River Choaspes—likewise navigable—on whose banks stands the city of Susa.'

On the outward journey from Susa, the road, after passing out of 'Cissia' into 'Matiênê', will have intersected with the Babylon-Ecbatana road (see p. 210, n. 3, above); then crossed first the Diyālah and next the Lower Zab to Arbela; crossed the Upper Zab to the site of Nineveh on the east bank of the Tigris; and crossed the Tigris at the crossing taken by the former Assyrian military road leading to Naïri (i.e. at or near the site of Nineveh, and not as far north as Bezabdê, where in 331 B.C. Alexander was to cross the Tigris in the opposite direction). The road will then have run through Nisibis (giving a wide berth to the Tigris gorge between the Tūr 'Abdīn highlands (Mount Masius), in the angle of the Tigris, and the highlands of Gordyênê on the farther side), and will finally have passed out of the Khabūr Basin into the Upper Tigris Basin—and simultaneously out of Matiênê into Armenia—between the Tūr 'Abdīn on the right hand and Mount Izalā on the left. This pass leading out of the Khabūr Basin into the Upper Tigris Basin was one of the positions at which the Armenian insurgents had brought Darius's flying columns to a halt in 522–521 B.C. (see 'DB', §§ 29–30).

The distance by road, as measured on a map that was up to date in A.D. 1952, from Mardīn via Diyārbakr, the head-waters of the Western Tigris and Kharpūt to the crossing of the Euphrates *en route* from Kharpūt to Malatīyah worked out at approximately 312½ kilometres, making about 52½ parasangs. Allowing for possible variations in the route and possible inaccuracies in both sets of measurements, this came sufficiently near to Herodotus's figure of 56½ parasangs for the Armenian section of the Great North-West Road to make it likely that the south-eastern terminal of this section was at or near Mardīn, considering that the north-western terminal is expressly stated by Herodotus to have been at the crossing of the Euphrates between Armenia and Cilicia.

[1] This group of *dahyāva* reappears in 'the Syspirîtis as far as Kalakhanê and Adiabênê' mentioned in Strabo: *Geographica*, Book XI, chap. iv, § 8 (C 503), and chap. xiv, § 12 (C 530).

[2] See Xenophon: *Expeditio Cyri*, Book III, chap. v, § 15; Book IV, chap. iii, especially IV. iii. 1.

other practicable south-and-north route anywhere between the east bank of the Tigris and the crest of the Zagros Range; for the upper valley of the Greater Zab is, not a passage, but a cul-de-sac, as a remnant of the Nestorian Christians were eventually to demonstrate by ensconcing themselves in this fastness.[1]

If the former metropolitan territory of Assyria was in truth associated with Urartu in one and the same taxation district on the Darian fiscal map of the Achaemenian Empire, these two territories' practical point of junction and seat of administration must have lain somewhere to the east of the North-Western Zagros in the basin of Lake Urmīyah. From the Urmīyah Basin there were practicable routes leading not only south-westward into Assyria but also westward into the basin of Lake Van and north-westward into the upper valley of the River Aras. The practicability of these lines of communication radiating from the Urmīyah Basin is attested by the long history of the warfare between Assyria and Urartu in this arena. The Assyrian name for this relatively open country was 'Mannai', which might be a contraction of a local name which was subsequently Hellenized as 'Matiênoi' by Herodotus or his source; and this location of Herodotus's eastern 'Matiênoi' is confirmed by the re-appearance of this name precisely here on the post-Alexandrine Hellenic map of South-West Asia.

We have already noticed[2] that, in a passage that occurs twice in Strabo's work, a 'Matianê in Media' is associated with Araxênê and Sakasênê, and Strabo elsewhere gives further indications which are in consonance both with these and with one another: Matianê is Media Atropatênê's northern neighbour;[3] the northern parts of Media extend from the Caspian Gates and Rhagai (Ragā) as far west as Matianê and Armenia;[4] the Matianoi, as well as the Medes, march, under the lee of the Parakhoathra Range, with the Kadousioi[5] (who are located along the west shore of the Caspian Sea, immediately to the north of the Gêlai, i.e. of Gīlān),[6] while, according to Ptolemy,[7] Martianê [*sic*][8] also marches with the [eastern] flank of Assyria along its whole length, and with the southern border of the Kaspioi who lie in Media.

These fragmentary pieces of evidence, taken together, locate the name 'Matianê' in the basin of Lake Urmīyah; and the lake itself is called 'Lake Martianê' by Ptolemy and 'Lake Mantianê' by Strabo in one passage.[9] We may conclude that the basin of Lake Urmīyah, as well as

[1] See II. ii. 257–8. [2] On p. 626, above.

[3] Strabo: *Geographica*, Book XI, chap. xiii, § 2 (C 523).

[4] Ibid., § 7 (C 525). In this statement Strabo is perhaps following Polybius, Book V, chap. 44, § 9, where the Matianoi are associated with the Kadousioi as two of Media's neighbours on the north.

[5] See Strabo, *Geographica*, Book XI, chap. viii, § 8 (C 514).

[6] See ibid., chap. vii, § 1 (C 508), and chap. viii, § 1 (C 510). Pliny identifies the Cadusii with the Gelae or Gaeli in a passage (*Historia Naturalis*, Book VI, chap. xvi (xviii), § 48) in which he mentions them in juxtaposition with the Matieni.

[7] *Geographia*, Book VI, chap. ii, § 5.

[8] 'The Old Persian word martiya meaning "man", which gives certain other place-names, is an easy source for a change of Mat- to Mart-.'—Note by Professor Roland G. Kent.

[9] Strabo: *Geographica*, Book XI, chap. xiv, § 8 (C 529). In this passage, Strabo locates his 'Lake Mantianê' in Armenia, but nevertheless it is clear that he is referring to Lake Urmīyah, since he mentions Lake Van ('Lake Arsênê, *alias* Lake Thôpîtis) in the next

the ex-Assyrian territory that had fallen to Media in the partition of 610–609 B.C., was associated with Urartu and Isbir in the Eighteenth Taxation District; that the administrative capital of the whole district lay somewhere in the Urmīyah Basin; and that on this account the whole of District No. 18 was sometimes called 'the Matiênoi' for short.

This usage would also be politically convenient, since the name of an extinct people would not awaken any such politically dangerous memories as might still come to life at the sound of the names 'Media' and 'Assyria'. The Eastern Mitanni had, in truth, been dead since the annihilation of their empire by the Hittites and the Assyrians in the fourteenth century B.C. In the last phase of its history this East-Mitannian Empire had been ruled from a capital somewhere in the basin of the River Khabūr in Mesopotamia. The survival of the name in the basin of Lake Urmīyah testified that this had been a previous station of the Mitanni on their westward trek from Central Asia via the Caspian Gates; and it is possible that, after moving their political headquarters down into the Khabūr Basin, they had still retained summer pastures in the Urmīyah Basin, like their Turkish-speaking Eurasian Nomad successors the Black Sheep Türkmens and White Sheep Türkmens in the fifteenth century of the Christian Era. The routes between Mesopotamia and the Urmīyah Basin across Adiabênê were under the control of the Mitanni when, at the height of their power, they exercised a suzerainty not only over Asshur but also over Arrapkha.[1]

If we now cast up the total of figures in Euboic talents which Herodotus gives for the four taxation districts into which the Viceroyalty of Media had been carved up, we shall see that Media had been penalized financially as well as politically; for the total comes to 1,000, and this is the figure which, in the Herodotean gazetteer, is the assessment on Babylonia, which was a much more populous and wealthy country in the Achaemenian Age than all four fiscal sections of Media added together. In order to be sure that these two figures were truly comparable, we should have, of course, to be sure, first, that (except for the payments in kind explicitly mentioned in this context) they both of them represented comprehensive valuations of imposts of all kinds, including the costs of maintenance of the Imperial Court and Imperial Standing Army during their alternating periods of residence at Ecbatana and at Babylon, and on this point we are in the dark. Yet, even allowing for this uncertain element in the comparison, it looks as if the Darian assessment on Media had been exceptionally heavy.

sentence. In this passage Strabo says that 'Mantianê' means 'ultramarine blue' (Kyanê); but this is actually the meaning of the Armenian word 'kapoit' which can be detected in the alternative name 'Kapauta' (corrupted into 'Spauta' in the extant text) which Strabo gives to Lake Urmīyah in Book VI, chap. xiii, § 2 (C 523). A comparison of XI. xiv, § 8 (C 529), with I. iii, § 4 (C 49), in which Strabo cites the fifth-century Lydian historian Xanthus's observation of geological phenomena indicating that areas which were now dry land had once been covered by the sea, shows that the 'salt lakes in Armenia and the Matiênoi and Lower Phrygia' which Xanthus had cited as evidence in support of his thesis must be respectively Lake Van, Lake Urmīyah, and the Tuz Gölü (*Graecè* Tatta) in Central Anatolia.

[1] See Götze, A.: *Hethiter, Churriter und Assyrer* (Leipzig 1936, Harrassowitz), pp. 98–99 and 116–17. Professor G. G. Cameron equates Arrapkha with the latter-day Kirkūk.

The *dahyāuš* called '*Hūja*' (written '*Ūvja*') in the official lists and '*Kissioi*' by Herodotus included the wild highland northern and north-western hinterland of Elam as well as the ancient seat of civilization in the lowlands; and both the official and the Herodotean name are taken from the hill-country and not from the plains. Hūja reappears in the Greek 'Ouxioi', the Arabic plural Ahwāz, and the New Persian place-name Khūzistān.[1] 'Kissioi' must stand for 'Kassites',[2] whose rearguard in the Zagros, marching with the south-eastern paraitaka of Media, lived on through the Achaemenian Age to give a rough reception to Antigonus when, after Alexander's death, the Macedonian war-lords were fighting over the division of the Achaemenian Empire's carcass.[3] In the absence of any indications to the contrary, we may take it that this Greater Elam, which constituted a single taxation district (the Herodotean District No. 8) on the fiscal map, also constituted, on the political map, a single viceroyalty.

In the South-Eastern Quarter of the Achaemenian Empire, the *Harahvatiš* (written *Harauvatiš*; *Graecè* Arakhosia) of the Achaemenian lists is, as we have seen,[4] the *dahyāuš* whose people Herodotus calls 'Thamanaioi' (signifying 'borderers') in his gazetteer and by their national name 'Paktyes' in his field-state.

Eastward, the Achaemenian Harahvatiš seems to have extended as far as the west bank of the Indus in a region which, in the nineteenth century of the Christian Era, was still known as 'the Dāmān' as well as 'the Darajāt'. At least, this seems to be the most convincing interpretation of Herodotus's statements that the city of Kaspatyros and the Paktyan country (i.e. Harahvatiš) marched with the northernmost and most warlike of the Indoi, who were sent to collect the gold from the Indian Desert,[5] and that the city of Kaspatyros and the Pactyan country had also been the point of departure from which Scylax of Caryanda and his shipmates had sailed down the Indus, out into the Indian Ocean, and up the Red Sea to an Egyptian port on a voyage of exploration on which they had been dispatched by Darius.[6] This interpretation of these two statements of Herodotus's is borne out by Eratosthenes' statement[7] that 'the Arakhôtoi' (i.e. the Viceroyalty of Harahvatiš), as well as the Paropanisadai (i.e. Gădara) to the north of them and the Gedrosians (i.e. Herodotus's Taxation District No. 18) to the south of them, extended eastwards as far as the west bank of the River Indus before Seleucus Nîcâtôr's cession of portions of these provinces to Chandragupta Maurya.

If Herodotus's 'Kaspatyros' is a less accurate Hellenic rendering than Hecataeus's 'Kaspapyros' for this Indus river-port's authentic name, Herzfeld may be right in reconstructing an original Sanskrit name

[1] See Le Strange, G.: *The Lands of the Eastern Caliphate* (Cambridge 1905, University Press), p. 232, and the present Study, p. 209, n. 3, above.

[2] It is noteworthy that the two names of the original patrimony of the House of Achaemenes and its Cyran branch in Lūristān and Pusht-i-Kuh—Parsuwaš and Anšan—have both been passed over in the official and in the Herodotean nomenclature alike.

[3] This incident has been noticed on p. 210, n. 3, above.

[4] On pp. 593–4, above.

[5] See Herodotus, Book III, chap. 102.

[6] See Herodotus, Book IV, chap. 44.

[7] Preserved in Strabo: *Geographica*, Book XV, chap. ii, § 9 (C 724).

'Kaśyapa-pura';[1] and, whatever the exact location of this river-port may have been, we may venture to interpret its meaning as 'the Caspians' city', and to see in it the entrepôt between an inland navigation in the Indus Basin and overland caravan routes between the Indus Valley and Eastern Iran via the passes through the Sulaymān Range.

In the early years of the nineteenth century of the Christian Era, when English observers were obtaining their first view of the eastern fringes of a then dissolving Afghan Empire, there was a busy seasonal migration through these passes between the Dāmān, along the west bank of the Indus, and both Qandahar[2] (in what had once been the heart of the Achaemenian *dahyāuš* Harahvatiš) and Kābul (in the former *dahyāuš* Gādāra); and we may guess that, in so conservative a quarter of the *Oikoumenê*, this traffic—in which trade was combined with the seasonal movement of flocks and herds between summer pastures on the Iranian Plateau and winter pastures in the Indus Valley[3]—had been carried on, year by year, ever since the Achaemenian Age. If the traffic was in truth already active in Darius's day,[4] this would have been the consideration that prompted 'the Huckster'[5] to explore the possibility of extending an already flourishing trade-route, on one section of which the goods were already water-borne, from the inland waterways of the Indus system out into the Indian Ocean and round Arabia to the Red Sea ports of the Egyptian province of his empire;[6] and, if Kaspapyros, wherever its exact site may have been,[7] was the river-port on which the

[1] See Herzfeld, op. cit., p. 94.

[2] The place-name 'Qandahar' seems to be neither a survival of the place-name 'Gādāra' nor a derivative from the personal name 'Alexander', but to stand for 'Gondophareia', the city of the Parthian Suren Gondophares (see Tarn, W. W.: *The Greeks in Bactria and India* (Cambridge 1938, University Press), p. 471), who was reigning in the first quarter of the first century of the Christian Era (see ibid., pp. 344 and 347).

[3] See the descriptions in Elphinstone, M.: *An Account of the Kingdom of Caubul and its Dependencies*, new ed. (London 1839, Bentley, 2 vols.), vol. i, pp. 378–88, and vol. ii, pp. 58–59; and Burnes, A.: *Travels into Bokhara* (London 1824, John Murray, 3 vols.), vol. ii, pp. 415–16.

[4] Tarn, in op. cit., p. 100, n. 3, points out that Darius I obtained ivory from Arachosia according to the inscription from the apadāna at Susa, line 43, and that Darius III Codomannus obtained elephants from it according to Arrian: *Expeditio Alexandri*, Book III, chap. viii, § 6, in the context of § 4.

[5] Herodotus, Book III, chap. 89, quoted on p. 613, n. 1, above.

[6] Darius—who, like Peter the Great, had a keen eye for natural resources, communications, commerce, and finance—is likely to have been as much excited as were the British empire-builders in the early nineteenth century of the Christian Era over the prospect of the profits to be made by developing the trade via the Indus waterway between Iran and the Oxus Basin on the one hand and the Indian sub-continent and the Indian Ocean on the other. A notion of the report that will have been submitted to Darius by Scylax may be obtained by reading Alexander Burnes' 'Report of the establishment of an Entrepôt, or Fair, for the Indus Trade', printed as Appendix I to his *Cabool*, 2nd ed. (London 1843, John Murray), on pp. 283–303. In the history of the Achaemenian, as in that of the British, Rāj, military conquest was the sequel to commercial exploration.

[7] Some light on the probable location of the historic entrepôt named Kaspapyros is thrown by Burnes' discussion, in the report cited just above, of the respective merits of divers alternative possible locations for a projected entrepôt for the Indus trade that was to be established under British auspices. After entering into a comparative consideration of the four entrepôts in the Indus Basin that were currently frequented by the Lohānī Afghan traders—Dera Ismā'īl Khan and Dera Ghāzi Khan in the Darajāt (Dāmān) on the west bank of the Indus, Multān near the south-east bank of the Lower Chenab, and Bahawalpur near the south-east bank of the Sutlej, not far above its confluence with the Chenab—and then proceeding also to consider Qalabagh, on the west bank of the Indus, as the northernmost feasible point, and Mithankot, likewise on the

traffic from Gădāra as well as the traffic from Harahvatiš converged,[1] we can see why Hecataeus[2] called it 'a Gandarian city' and why Herodotus located it in 'the Pactyan country', in spite of its being a Caspian foundation.

Hecataeus[3] also describes Kaspapyros as being 'a "shore" or "promontory" (*Graecè* "aktê") of the Scythians', and we have already seen reason[4] for numbering the *Kaspioi* among the Eurasian Nomad peoples who had broken out of the Steppe and mounted the Iranian Plateau, between the Caspian Sea and the Pamirs, in the eighth or seventh century B.C. While the right wing of these Caspii will have ridden on due west to bequeath their name first to the Caspian Gates and then to the Caspian Sea after they had been brought to a halt in the lower basin of the rivers Aras and Kur against the barriers of the Qarabagh and the Caucasus, the left wing will have swerved leftwards and ridden across Parthava, Haraiva, and Harahvatiš till they were brought to a halt against the barrier of the Sulaymān Mountains.[5] We shall probably not

west bank just below the confluence between the Indus and the united waters of the five rivers of the Panjab, Burnes opts for Dera Ghāzi Khan.

'It embraces not only the trade of the Punjaub and India, of Candahar and Cabool, but of the more remote capitals dependent on them, Herat and Bokhara. . . . From Bombay to Dera Ghazee the water communication is open, and from the Upper Indus the intercourse is equally available. In former times many roads led down upon this town from the west. Time and peace will, in all probability, again open these now forsaken lines; and thus will be concentrated in one point all the desirable means of approach' (op. cit., p. 287).

If ever a fragment of Scylax's report to Darius were to be recovered from the Achaemenian archives at Susa or Persepolis, it would not be surprising to find it anticipating the latter-day English explorer's words.

[1] The itinerary (originally recorded by the surveyors attached to Alexander's expeditionary force) of one route leading from the Caspian Gates to some point on the west bank of the Indus had been preserved in two versions: by Strabo in a couple of passages (*Geographica*, Book XI, chap. viii, § 9 (C 514), and Book XV, chap. viii, § 8 (C 723)) derived from Eratosthenes' work, and by Pliny (*Historia Naturalis*, Book VI, chap. xvii (xxi), §§ 61–62).

This route ran from the Caspian Gates via Hecatompylus in Parthia to Alexandria in Areia (Herat), and thence to Ortospana (Kābul) either direct, over the mountains, through Bactria, or alternatively in a southward loop via Prophthasia in Drangiana and the provincial capital of the Viceroyalty of Arachosia (? Qal'at-i-Gilzai). From Ortospana (Kābul) the route followed the valley of the Kābul River eastwards to the Indus. In both the passages in Strabo's *Geographica*, Ortospana (Kābul) is described as being 'the point of access to the junction of the three roads from Bactria ('Ορτόσπανα ἐπὶ τὴν ἐκ Βάκτρων τρίοδον)', but, of course, this description applies only for a traveller approaching Ortospana (Kābul) by the roundabout southern alternative route, since the direct route through the Bactrian hill-country would have brought the traveller to 'the junction'—i.e. to the twin cities Kāpiša and Kāniš, astride the confluence of the Panjshir and Ghorband tributaries of the Kābul River (see p. 640, with n. 2, below)—on his way to Ortospana.

[2] As quoted by Stephanus of Byzantium, s.v. 'Kaspapyros'.

[3] Apud Stephanum.

[4] On pp. 608–9, above.

[5] This hypothetical route of the South-Eastern Kaspioi in the Völkerwanderung of the eighth and seventh centuries B.C. was demonstrably followed by their fellow Sakā the Tūrā in the Völkerwanderung of the second century B.C. In the *Avesta* the Tūrā make their appearance, in company with the Airyā (? Alanoi), Sairimā (Sarmatai), Sāinavās (? Sannoi) and Dahā (Dahai), among the Iranian Nomad peoples on the Central Asian Steppe who gave Zarathustra a good reception when he made his *hijrah* (see Nyberg, op. cit., pp. 237, 249–51, and 297). A district of Khwārizm still bore the name Tūr in the Sasanian Age (see ibid., p. 251). The emergence, after the beginning of the Christian Era, of the legendary Turan patriarch Fryāna's name in the Hellenized form 'Phlianos' in the Hellenic city-state of Olbia on the Black Sea coast of the Great Western Bay of the Eurasian Steppe indicates that one detachment of the Tūrā had accompanied the Sarmatians in their westward trek north of the Caspian Sea (see ibid., pp. 237 and 251). Another detachment of Tūrā, however, must have mounted the

be far wrong if we locate these Eastern Kaspioi here, between the Eastern Paktyes in the Hilmand Basin to the west of them and the middle course of the River Indus to the east.[1]

In the Herodotean field-state—they do not figure in the gazetteer—the Eastern Kaspioi are mentioned immediately after the Gandarioi and the Daḍikai, who, in the gazetteer, figure in Taxation District No. 7, and the Caspians' commander is the brother of the commander of the Dadico-Gandarian brigade. On the other hand the Kaspioi are also associated with the Paktyes by being paraded, like these, in the *sisyrna*—the Greek name for the sheepskin or felt top-coat, *Pactyicè* 'pustīn', which in the early nineteenth century was still a distinctive feature in the national costume of the Western Afghans, and which Elphinstone[2] describes as

'a large cloak of well-tanned sheep-skin with the wool inside, or of soft and pliant grey felt. This garment is worn loose over the shoulders, with the sleeves hanging down, and reaches to the ankles.'

If the reader feels moved to ask how an ex-Central Asian people who had founded a city in the Indus Basin could have persisted, in their torrid new abode, in suffocating themselves under this ancestral article of arctic dress, the writer has a twofold rejoinder to make. He can point out that the Circassian refugees from the North-Western Caucasus who were settled by the Ottoman Government in Transjordan in the nineteenth century of the Christian Era showed a comparable conservatism in clinging to their ancestral costume; and he can quote Elphinstone's authority for the fact that, in the Dāmān in the same century, the *sisyrna* was still part of the Eastern Afghans' winter dress.

'Though their summer dress is nearly the same as that of India . . . and . . . even in winter they wear turbans, . . . at that season they also wear brown and grey woollen great coats and posteens.'[3]

On this showing, Herodotus's parade of the Eastern Kaspioi in *sisyrnai* is not incompatible with a location which would allow them to have been the founders of the river-port of Kaspa-pyros in the tropical lowlands of the Middle Indus Basin.

Iranian Plateau and then wheeled south-east; for in the 'Abbasid Age the name Tūrān was borne by a canton in Eastern Baluchistan in the neighbourhood of the latter-day Khanate of Qal'at (see Le Strange, op. cit., pp. 331–2), and in the twentieth century of the Christian Era a community of Tūrīs was still to be found alive among the Sulaymān Mountains in the upper valley of the Kurram River, immediately to the south of the Kābul Valley (Gădāra). These Tūrīs were said to have formerly been pastoral nomads who migrated twice a year between summer pastures in the Kurram Valley and winter pastures round Qalabagh on the west bank of the Indus north of the Salt Range (see Pennell, T. L.: *Among the Wild Tribes of the Afghan Frontier* (London 1912, Seeley Service), pp. 55–56). On their way from the Central Asian Steppe to the eastern edge of the Iranian Plateau, the Tūrā had bequeathed their national legend to a school of epic poetry that was to arise in their wake in the former Achaemenian *dahyāuš* Zrāka, on which the name Seistan was stamped by the hoof of the Saka horse *en route* (see V. v. 600–2).

[1] If W. H. Schoff, in his edition of *The Periplus of the Erythraean Sea* (London 1912, Longmans Green), p. 189, is right in deriving the latter-day name 'Kashmir' from an original Sanscrit compound 'Kāsyapa-mata' meaning 'home of the Kāsyapa', we may infer that another detachment of the Eastern Kaspioi lodged itself in Kashmir, and that the name of a forgotten people was posthumously interpreted as the name of a legendary pre-Gautaman Buddha in the hagiography of the Mahāyāna.

[2] In op. cit., vol. i, p. 313.

[3] Elphinstone, op. cit., vol. ii, p. 59.

While it thus seems possible that Darius's Harahvatiš may have extended eastward as far as the west bank of the River Indus, it is certain that, on the political map, the Viceroyalty of Harahvatiš in the later years of Darius I's reign extended westward to include *Zrăka*[1] in the latter-day Seistan, and that, on the fiscal map, the taxation district in which Harahvatiš was included (the Herodotean District No. 14) extended south-westward as far as the north-east shore of the Persian Gulf, to include the *Asagartiyā* (Sagartioi) in Kirmān, the *Yautiyā* (Outioi) in North-Eastern Lāristān, the *Mačiyā* (Mykoi) in South-western Lāristān, along the seaboard,[2] and the Median deportees ('the *déracinés*') on the inshore islands.[3]

On the evidence, which we have already noticed,[4] of variations in the order of the names on the official lists, we can conclude that *Zrăka* must have been transferred from the Viceroyalty of Parthava to the Viceroyalty of Harahvatiš between the dates of composition of 'DPe' and 'DZd', and we can discern two considerations, either or both of which may have moved Darius to make this change in the political map. On the one hand it would have the effect of diminishing the territory and population of a viceroyalty whose leading people had demonstrated its hostility to the Ariaramnan branch of the House of Achaemenes in 522–521 B.C., when the Parthians, as well as the Hyrcanians, had risen against their viceroy, Darius's father Hystaspes. In the second place, this transfer would widen the corridor between the loyal Viceroyalty of Harahvatiš and those dissident Persian tribes—the South-Eastern Asagartiyā in Kirmān and the South-Eastern Yautiyā and Mačiyā in Lāristān—whom Darius had attached to Harahvatiš for fiscal purposes after having degraded them to the ranks of his tax-paying subjects from their previously privileged status as constituent clans of the imperial people.

The *South-Eastern Asagartiyā* (Sagartioi) are described in the Herodotean field-state of Xerxes' expeditionary force[5] as being a still culturally conservative Nomad people[6] who fought only as cavalry and whose master weapon was the lasso. Their language was Persian, and in 480 B.C. they were attached to the Persian infantry in Xerxes' army, but their equipment was betwixt and between the Persian and the Pactyan; and this last piece of Herodotean information suggests that these Sagartians' country must have been Kirmān (O.P. Karmāna; *Latinè* Carmania), which lay immediately to the north-east of Lāristān and Fars,[7] while it faced Zrăka and Harahvatiš across the south-eastern end of the Central Desert of Iran. In the twentieth century of the Christian Era a people who made their livelihood by stock-breeding could not have

1 See p. 589, with n. 3, above.

2 See p. 622, above. In the field-state of Xerxes' expeditionary force the Outioi and Mykoi are paraded in Paktyan equipment, but the Outian and Mykan contingents are brigaded with one another under a separate command (see Herodotus, Book VII, chap. 68).

3 See pp. 602 and 623, above.

4 On p. 589, above.

5 In Book VII, chap. 85.

6 They still had a prejudice against metal weapons, except for poignards ('enkheiridia').

7 According to Strabo: *Geographica*, Book XV, chap. ii, § 8 (C 723), Carmania marched with the south-eastern paraitaka of Media: i.e. Carmania included the latter-day canton of Yazd, as is expressly stated by Ptolemy: *Geographia*, Book VI, chap. vi, § 2. 'Karmāna is mentioned in DSf, § 35, as a source of gold for Darius's palace at Susa.'—Professor Roland G. Kent.

won a living off a landscape that had come to be a desert punctuated at rare intervals with oases intensively cultivated by irrigation. This desert, however, was at least partly man-made. As recently as the ʿAbbasid Age the forests with which the mountains of Kirmān had originally been clothed had not yet all been cut down,[1] and in an earlier age, when the forests were still intact, Kirmān seems likely to have had sufficient rainfall to keep large tracts of the country fit to serve as pasture-land, and its pastoral Sagartian occupants will have been proportionately numerous, prosperous, and powerful.

Though these south-eastern, unlike the north-western, Asagartiyā are not mentioned by name in Darius's inscription on the cliff at Behistan as having taken part in the disorders of 522–521 B.C., the fact that their name is mentioned in only one of the six official lists of *dahyāva*[2] suggests that they too were in disgrace. We may infer that they had been one of the Persian clans that had taken up arms against Darius under Vahyazdāta's leadership; and, since the force which Vahyazdāta detached to invade Gādāra could hardly have covered the immense distances that it did cover unless it had been mounted, we may guess that the Sagartian horse were the backbone of it.

As for the *Yautiyā*, who were Vahyazdāta's own clan, the measure of their disgrace might be gauged from the fact that their name was passed over in all the official lists; and the reason for this official ostracism was revealed in the creditably frank account of Vahyazdāta's movement which Darius had made public in his Behistan record.[3] The truth—and Darius does not attempt here to conceal it—was that Vahyazdāta's challenge to Darius's pretensions was by far the most dangerous of all the crises with which this Ariaramnan pretender to a Cyran imperial crown found himself confronted in that terrible year; for, while the Armenians may have been Darius's most resolute, and the Medes his most powerful, adversaries on a strictly military reckoning, Vahyazdāta was politically by far the most formidable of all Darius's competitors. The Elamites, Margians, Thatagu[? d or v]iyā and Sakā were fighting simply for the recovery of their local independence, while the Babylonians (without their former subjects' goodwill) and the Medes (with their former subjects' active support) were fighting for the re-establishment of their pre-Cyran empires; but none of these non-Persian opponents of Darius's aspired, as Darius himself aspired, to reign without a peer over the whole *Oikoumenê* as the acknowledged legitimate successor of the universal monarch Cyrus II. Vahyazdāta alone challenged Darius in terms of Darius's own pretensions.

Vahyazdāta of Tāravā, like Darius, was a Persian; and so, for that matter, had been Martiya of Kuganakā; but Martiya had aimed at nothing more ambitious than to put himself at the head of a nationalist movement in Elam, and he had accordingly proclaimed himself to be a scion of the Elamite royal family.[4] In sharp contrast to the modesty of

[1] See, for example, Le Strange, op. cit., pp. 315 and 316.
[2] In 'DPe'.
[3] See 'DB', §§ 40–48.
[4] See 'DP', §§ 22–23. Martiya's bid for the crown of Elam suggests that he may have been a Persian whose native city, Kuganakā, lay, not in Pārsa (Fars), but in Parsuwaš (Lūristān).

Martiya's pretensions, Vahyazdāta had the audacity to impersonate Cyrus II's son Smerdis himself, whose claim to the imperial throne, were he really still alive, was incontestably paramount over the claim of a usurper descended from the Ariaramnan branch of the Achaemenidae. Vahyazdāta's *pronunciamiento* won the support, not only of his own Yautiyā clansmen, but of a strong enough faction in Pārsa at large, including at least some of the garrison of the imperial palace there, to enable him to establish himself in Pārsa as king; and this *fait accompli* was a dire blow to Darius's cause, considering that Pārsa had been the appanage, not of Cyrus the great-grandfather of the Smerdis whom Vahyazdāta was impersonating, but of Darius's great-grandfather Ariaramnes.

Moreover, Vahyazdāta did not make the mistake of resting on his oars. Like Darius, he promptly sought to vindicate his pretension to legitimacy by vigorously taking the offensive against all who ventured to contest it; and, in his military operations for taking possession of Cyrus II's patrimony, he gave proof of high strategic ability. He made it his first objective to occupy the basin of the Kābul River in Gādāra—a node of strategic routes[1] where, once entrenched, he would have been able at once to cut the communications between Darius's two principal supporters the viceroys of Harahvatiš and Bākhtriš, to establish contact between his own forces and the insurgents in the Panjab (Thataguš),[2] and perhaps to rekindle the flames of revolt in the Viceroy of Bactria's disaffected canton Marguš, which marched with the disaffected cantons Parthava and Varkāna in Darius's father Hystaspes' viceroyalty of Parthia. The stakes for which Vahyazdāta was playing when he detached a force to occupy the Kābul Basin were nothing less than the establishment of his rule over the whole South-East and whole North-East of the Achaemenian Empire; and, if once this had been achieved, the provinces in the Indus Valley would inevitably also have fallen into his lap. If Vahyazdāta's eastern plan of campaign had succeeded, Darius's cause would have been lost, and Vahyazdāta could have afforded to wait for the news of Darius's death before attempting to settle accounts with the would-be restorer of the Median Empire, Fravartiš.

Vahyazdāta did come within an ace of success, for the Viceroy of Harahvatiš, Vivāna, did not succeed in making contact with Vahyazdāta's expeditionary force until this had reached the pair of twin cities[3]

[1] See p. 635, n. 1, above.

[2] Thataguš was in revolt, on the testimony of 'DB', § 21.

[3] Kāpišakāniš (written as a single word, like Budapest, without the use of the sign for dividing words that was possessed by the Old Persian script) is the name given to this pair of cities in 'DB', § 45. This is manifestly identical with the Kapisa-Alexandria of the post-Alexandrine Hellenic geographers (see Tarn, *The Greeks in Bactria and India*, pp. 96–98, 139–40, and 460–2, together with map 3 at the end of the book). Darius has here given us the pre-Hellenic name of the west-bank twin of the east-bank city of Kāpiša. Kāniš will have occupied the site which, in latter-day Pakhtu parlance, was called 'begram', 'the city', *par excellence* (see ibid., p. 462). This pair of cities attained the zenith of its importance in the Kushan Age. Kujula, the founder of the Kushan Empire (see ibid., p. 338), will have taken his surname Kadphises to commemorate his acquisition of a Kāpiša which had lost none of its strategic importance during the five and a half centuries that had passed since Vahyazdāta's cause had been lost, and Darius's won, in a battle at this key point in 522–521 B.C. Kujula Kadphises' second successor

astride the confluence of the Panjshir and Ghorband tributaries of the Kābul River, where the road running north-eastward from the *dahyāuš* of Harahvatiš in the Hilmand Basin via Ghaznah and Kābul (*Graecè* Kôphên, *Sinicè* Ki-pin) divided into three branches[1] threading their way through the Hindu Kush by as many different passes—one road making north-eastwards for the upper valley of the Oxus,[2] while the other two roads both led by diverse routes to Balkh, the capital of the Viceroyalty of Bactria. Even after Vahyazdāta's expeditionary force had been headed back by Vivāna's pursuing column out of Gādāra into Harahvatiš, the invaders turned and fought a second battle, this time on Arachosian soil, at Gandutava; and, after that, they marched on the capital of the Arachosian viceroyalty, Aršādā,[3] itself, and had arrived there before Vivāna was able to catch up with them again and to take them prisoners.

If any man other than Darius himself could claim to have won Cyrus II's imperial crown for the Ariaramnan branch of the Achaemenidae, that man was Vivāna; and Darius showed his recognition of the loyalty of the Eastern Paktyes and their viceroy in the year of his ordeal by extending this viceroyalty's area to include not only Zrāka but also the three disaffected Persian cantons in Kirmān and Lāristān—Asagarta, the Yautiyā, and Maka—and even the Median deportees who had been marooned on the islands in the Persian Gulf off the Maka coast.[4] Yet it could have been said of the Paktyes who had fought so effectively for Darius in 522–521 B.C., as aptly as it actually was said of the Croats who fought for Francis Joseph in A.D. 1848–9, that the loyalists received from the Emperor as their reward what the rebels received as their punishment;[5] for the enlargement of the viceroyalty of Harahvatiš was accompanied by an assessment of the corresponding taxation district—No. 14 in the Herodotean gazetteer—at the figure of 600 talents. The exorbitancy of this assessment on a district consisting of little else than steppes, mountains, and deserts is indicated by a comparison with the figure of 700 talents which was Darius's assessment on Egypt. As far as the three disgraced Persian clans and the deported Median offenders were concerned, this assessment was, no doubt, intended to be penal; but, in giving us the aggregate figure, Herodotus leaves us in the dark as to the quota which the loyal Harahvatiš and Zrāka had the honour to be invited to contribute.

As for the *Mačiyā* (Mykoi), their name cannot have been associated

Kanishka's name will have commemorated the future emperor's birth or upbringing in a Kāniš which will have reverted by his day to its pre-Hellenic appellation. Pliny's statement, in his *Historia Naturalis*, Book VI, chap. xxiii (xxv), § 92, that Kāpiša (*Latinè* Capisa) had been destroyed by Cyrus I indicates that it was he who had annexed the Kābul Basin (Gādāra) to the Achaemenian Empire.

[1] See the passage of Strabo's *Geographica* cited on p. 635, n. 1, above.

[2] An account of Captain John Wood's passage of this Pass of Khawak, from the Oxus Basin into the Panjshir Valley, in April 1838, will be found in his *A Journey to the Sources of the Oxus*, new ed. (London 1872, John Murray), pp. 272–5.

[3] The Elamite text of 'DB', § 47, informs us that Aršādā was the seat of Vivāna's administration. Tarn, in *The Greeks in Bactria and India*, pp. 94 and 470, locates it in the neighbourhood of the latter-day Qal'at-i-Ghilzai on the River Tarnak, north-east of Qandahar.

[4] See Herodotus, Book III, chap. 93, and the present Annex, pp. 602 and 623, above.

[5] See V. v. 293, n. 2, and p. 114, with n. 6, above.

in Ariaramnan Achaemenid minds with such unpleasant memories as the names of the Yautiyā and the Asagartiyā, considering that either they themselves or their country, Maka, are mentioned in every one of the six official lists. At the same time, the Mačiyā cannot have emerged from the ordeal of 522–521 B.C. with an altogether clean bill of political health, or they would not have been sentenced to share with the Yautiyā and Asagartiyā the punishment of being degraded to the status of tax-paying subjects.

The two cantons Yautiyā (Outioi) and Maka (Mykoi) can both be located approximately. Vahyazdāta's native city Tāravā[1] had bequeathed its name to a latter-day Tārum on the eastern edge of Lāristān. The mountain (*kaufa*) called Parga, where he made his last stand,[2] must be one or other of the twin cities Burk, standing on a hillock like a camel's hump, and Furg, with its castle on a hill, which were still in existence in the ʿAbbasid Age.[3] Maka (Mykoi) was commemorated in the ʿAbbasid Age in the place-name Māhān on the road running north-westward from the port of Huzū, on the Lārī coast opposite Qays Island, to Laghir *en route* for Shīrāz.[4] In the twentieth century of the Christian Era the name still survived on the Lārī coast itself at Mughan, near the mouth of the Darghaband River, and at Maghu or Mughu farther east, near the Lārī coast's southernmost point.

The islands on which the Median deportees were marooned were presumably those strung along the same coast, of which Kishm was the largest and Hormuz the only one that was eventually to become a famous name. In settling these disaffected Medes here, Darius was, no doubt, consciously achieving two purposes simultaneously. He was interning dangerous ex-rebels in a chain of prisons, provided for him by Nature, where they would be impotent to do any more mischief to his régime; and, in the act, he was confirming the hold of his empire upon one of its frontages on the Indian Ocean by planting penal settlements on islands that were too uninviting to attract voluntary colonists.[5] The choice of these islands as the places of internment for irreconcilable rebels was all of a piece with the opening up of a continuous water-route from the Indus-port Kaspapyros to the head of the Red Sea, and with the reopening of the canal from the head of the Red Sea to the Mediterranean via the Nile. These three measures must have been so many parts of a comprehensive plan for securing the command of the Indian Ocean and thereby obtaining a water-route round Arabia to supplement

1 'DP', § 40.

2 'DP', § 42.

3 See Le Strange, op. cit., p. 292. 'The *Fārs Nāmah* writes the name Purk or Purg' [compare the Greek word 'pyrgos'—A.J.T.] 'and says that its castle was impregnable, being built of stone and very large.'

4 See ibid., p. 257, n. 1.

5 Darius's Median deportees were not the only *déracinés* to be marooned on these islands. For example, Megabyzus, the Persian general who had reconquered Egypt for the Achaemenian Empire after the insurrection led by Inarôs, was exiled by Artaxerxes I to the Persian Gulf, where he was interned in a place called Cyrtae (see Ctesias: *Persica*, Books XIV–XVII, § 71 (40) in J. Gilmore's edition (London 1888, Macmillan), p. 154). In this context, Ctesias uses the same word as Herodotus: '*déraciné*' (*Graecè* 'anáspastos'). The survivors of the sack of Miletus in 494 B.C. were deported, not to the islands, but to the mouth of the River Tigris on the gulf coast of Babylonia (Herodotus, Book VI, chap. 20).

the long and devious land-route between the eastern and western extremities of Darius's empire.[1]

The two peoples—*Southern Parikanioi* and *Asiatic Ethiopians*—who, in the Herodotean gazetteer, together constitute Taxation District No. 17, do not either of them figure in any of the official lists, and they are not associated with one another in the Herodotean field-state. The Parikanioi are paraded here in Pactyan equipment under a separate command of their own;[2] the Asiatic Ethiopians are brigaded with the Indoi.[3] The survival of the name 'pairikās' ('heathen')[4] in the place-name Fārghān 60 kilometres to the east of Tārum and 120 kilometres to the north of Bandar ʿAbbās, under the shadow of a Mount Furghun, was evidence, as we have already noticed,[5] that these Southern Parikanioi were the Outians' (Yautiyā's) immediate neighbours towards the east. Their country will have been the south-eastern extremity of Kirmān and the western part of Makrān; and the eastern part of Makrān, between the Southern Parikanioi and Sind, will have been the country of 'the Asiatic Ethiopians'. We may presume that this district was annexed by Darius at or after the date of his annexation of Sind, as part of his policy of giving his empire a frontage on the Indian Ocean. While he made it a separate administrative unit for fiscal purposes, he will have attached it for political purposes either to the Viceroyalty of Harahvatiš or to Hīduš. In A.D. 1952 the first of these two possibilities seemed the more likely on considerations of geographical convenience, which was all that a historian then had to go upon, in the absence of documentary evidence on the point.

In the South-Eastern Quarter of the Achaemenian Empire the predominant culture was the Pactyan, to judge from the adoption of the Pactyans' equipment by their neighbours and administrative associates the Kaspioi, Outioi, Mykoi, and Parikanioi. On the same test we shall conclude that the Bactrian culture was predominant in the North-East, and that this culture was an offshoot of the Median; for the Bactrians are paraded in a sub-Median equipment,[6] and this Bactrian equipment

[1] In this enterprising and far-sighted combination of measures, Darius showed a more lively sense of the importance of sea-power in the Indian Ocean for an empire strung out athwart the Middle Eastern land-bridge than was shown in the sixteenth century of the Christian Era by the 'Osmanlis when they gave way in the Indian Ocean to the Portuguese. The counterpart, in the Mediterranean, of the voyage of exploration into the Indian Ocean on which Scylax of Caryanda was sent by Darius was the commission given by him to Dêmocêdês of Crôtôn to conduct a squadron on a corresponding voyage of exploration into Dêmocêdês' own native waters. This Mediterranean expedition of Darius's was abortive (see Herodotus, Book III, chaps. 135–8), but it is further evidence of Darius's sea-mindedness; and the story of Sataspes' attempt to circumnavigate Africa from the Mediterranean coast of Egypt via the Straits of Gibraltar (see Herodotus, Book IV, chap. 43) shows—though this enterprise, too, ended in failure—that Darius had bequeathed his sea-sense to his son and successor Xerxes.

[2] Herodotus, Book VII, chap. 68.

[3] Ibid., chap. 70.

[4] See p. 595, above.

[5] On p. 617, above.

[6] See Herodotus, Book VII, chap. 64. According to Herodotus, Book VII, chap. 61, the three distinctive features of the Median equipment were a soft felt cap, trousers, a dagger suspended from a belt and worn on the right thigh, and 'the great bow'. This description exactly corresponds to an equipment portrayed on the Achaemenian bas-reliefs as being worn by one of the two imperial peoples, and from this it follows that the other imperial people's equipment, as portrayed on the bas-reliefs—namely a taka (*Gallicè* toque) instead of a soft tiara ('Phrygian cap'), and an ample robe instead of a riding coat and trousers—must be the national dress of the Persians. Herodotus tells us

is worn by the Parthians, Chorasmians, Sogdians, Gandarians, and Dadicae, while the Areioi are equipped partly Bactrian fashion and partly Median fashion.[1]

When we go on to compare the grouping of the north-eastern peoples in viceroyalties and taxation districts with their grouping in military commands, we find that in the North-East, as in the South-East, the military and civilian organizations do not coincide. For example, the inhabitants of Hyrcania (Varkāna), who in the Achaemenian Age were, for civil administrative purposes, so subordinate an element in the Viceroyalty and Taxation District of Parthia (Parthava) that their name is not mentioned either in the official lists or in the Herodotean gazetteer, though it figures in Darius's narrative of the events of 522–521 B.C., are paraded in the field-state under a separate command and in Median equipment,[2] in contrast to the Bactrian equipment of the Parthians; and the Sogdians likewise appear here under a separate command, though in every one of the six official lists they are associated with the Bactrians. Conversely the Sakā Haumavargā of Farghānah are brigaded with the Bactrians in the field-state, though Farghānah and Bactria were not contiguous (Sogdiana lay in between), and though the Sakā Haumavargā, who were allies of the Achaemenian Empire, differed in status from the Bactrians, who were tax-paying subjects. The Chorasmians (Hvārazmiyā), again, are brigaded with the Parthians, though Khwārizm and Parthia were insulated from one another territorially by the Qāra Qum Desert and by the Dahā in Transcaspia.

The civil, as well as the military, administrative geography of the North-East Quarter is fairly clear. The Viceroyalty of *Parthava* (Parthia) —with which the Herodotean Taxation District No. 16 will have been coextensive—touched the south-east corner of the Caspian Sea in *Varkāna* (Hyrcania). To the north it included *Hvārazmiš* (alias *Hvārazmīy; Latinè* Chorasmia, *Arabicè* Khwārizm), along the lower course of the River Oxus (Amu Darya); and the Viceroyalty of Parthava must therefore also have included the *Dahā*, whose name—though it is mentioned in the Achaemenian official lists only in 'XPh' was still extant in the 'Abbasid Age in Dihistan[3] at the western end of Transcaspia. Parthava (Parthia) Proper was approximately conterminous with the latter-day provinces of Western Khurāsān and Kuhistan; and the viceroyalty extended, east of that, to include Haraiva (*Graecè* the Areioi, who had bequeathed their name to the city of Herat), but not

in Book VII, chaps. 61–62, that, on active service at any rate, the Persians wore the more practical Median dress, and that the Kissioi (? i.e. the Persian troops from Parsuwaš) did likewise, except for retaining their native headgear the mitre (perhaps this was a taka with a low crown). The Bactrians were not armed with the Median 'great bow', but they did wear the Median cap (see ibid., chap. 64). This cap was also worn by all the Eurasian Nomad peoples, from the Sakā Haumavargā in Farghānah to the Scyths on the Great Western Bay of the Eurasian Steppe, except for the 'Pointed-Hood' Massagetae; and we may guess that, whatever may have been the origin of the cap, the wearing of trousers had been taken over by the Medes from the Nomads when they were learning from them the art of riding a war-horse instead of driving him in a chariot.

1 See Herodotus, Book VII, chap. 66. The Areioi are armed with the Median 'great bow', not with the Bactrian 'reed bow', but are equipped like the Bactrians in other respects.

2 Herodotus, Book VII, chap. 62.

3 See Le Strange, op. cit., pp. 379–81.

Mārguš (Merv), which belonged to the viceroyalty of Bactria,[1] and *a fortiori* not Suguda (Sogdiana), whatever Herodotus may say.[2] Finally, on the south-east, the Viceroyalty of Parthava had, as we have seen,[3] included Zrāka, on the north-east shore of the Hamun-i-Hilmand, before the transfer of Zrāka to the Viceroyalty of Harahvatiš.

The Viceroyalty of *Bākhtriš* (Bactria)—with which the Herodotean Taxation District No. 12 will have been coextensive—included Bākhtriš Proper and *Suguda* (*alias* Sugda; the Sogdoi). Bākhtriš Proper, which had bequeathed its name to the city of Balkh, lay between the south bank of the River Oxus (Amu Darya) in the middle section of its course and the northern flank of the Hindu Kush. Suguda (Sogdiana) stretched north-eastwards from the north bank of the Oxus, opposite Bactria, to the south bank of the southern elbow of the River Jaxartes (Sir Darya), where Suguda marched with the Hauma-(?)drinking Sakā's country in Farghānah.[4] The heart of Sogdiana was the valley of 'the golden river' whose Old Persian name—translated into Greek as 'polytîmêtos', 'the precious', by the post-Alexandrine Hellenic geographers—had survived, down to the time of writing, as the Zarafshan on whose banks stood the latter-day cities of Samarqand and Bukhārā.

The *Sakā Haumavargā* (Sakai Amyrgioi)[5] adjoining Suguda in Farghānah[6] were under the Viceroy of Bactria's supervision, to judge by the fact that they are brigaded with the Bactrians both in Herodotus's field-state of Xerxes' expeditionary force and in Arrian's field-state of the army assembled by Darius Codomannus at Gaugamela in 331 B.C.;[7] but they were the Achaemenian Empire's allies, not its subjects,[8] and

[1] See 'DB', § 38. [2] See pp. 595–6, above.

[3] On pp. 589 and 637, above.

[4] These boundaries are given, on the authority of Eratosthenes, by Strabo in his *Geographica*, Book XI, chap. viii, § 8 (C 514).

[5] This 'Amyrgioi', to which the Iranian compound epithet 'Hauma-varga' has been contracted in its rendering into Greek, may be compared with 'Aspourgianoi'—a people located by Strabo (*Geographica*, Book XI, chap. ii, § 11 (C 495), and Book XII, chap. iii, § 29 (C 556)) on the north-east coast of the Black Sea, at the mouth of the River Kuban, whose name, as it appears in Greek, presumably represents an Iranian 'Aspavargā'. If the Old Persian root varga- means 'pressing out' or 'drinking' (see the note by Professor R. G. Kent on p. 587, above), 'Aspavargā' would be a label for a Eurasian Nomad people who milked mares or who drank qumīz. On either of these two conjectural interpretations, 'Aspavargā' and 'Haumavargā' would be complementary terms by which the Sakā would be classified according to the difference of the source from which they extracted their indispensable intoxicant. While the Sakā Aspavargā would be continuing to extract it from mare's milk, the Sakā Haumavargā would have learnt to extract it from a plant growing in the Central Asian highlands into which they had been driven by the pressure of more powerful hordes on the steppes.

See further Rostovtzeff, M.: *Iranians and Greeks in South Russia* (Oxford 1922, Clarendon Press) for the Aspourgianoi (pp. 152 and 160) and for Aspourgos, son of Asandrokhos, who became king of the Kingdom of the Cimmerian Bosporus towards the end of the last century B.C. (pp. 152–3, 156, 166).

[6] Sogdiana was bounded on the east by the farther bank of the Jaxartes (i.e. the north-western bank above the southern elbow) as far as the river's sources, according to Ptolemy: *Geographia*, Book VI, chap. xii, § 1.

[7] See Arrian: *Expeditio Alexandri*, Book III, chap. viii, § 3.

[8] Bêssus, the viceroy of Bactria, was in command of 'the Indoi who were next-door neighbours of the Bactrians', besides commanding the Bactrians themselves and the Sogdians. 'Brigaded with Bêssus's command were the Sakai—one of the Asiatic Scythian peoples—but, unlike the other three peoples, these Sakai were not subjects of Bessus's, but were serving because they were Darius's Allies' (Arrian, ibid.). According to Ctesias, Books X–XI, § 38 (7) in J. Gilmore's edition (London 1888, Macmillan), pp. 135–6, this alliance had been contracted with the Sakā Haumavargā (Sakai Amyrgioi) by Cyrus II.

this status is perhaps described in the name 'Aiglai' by which Herodotus refers to them without recognizing who these 'Aiglai' were; for Herodotus's word 'Aiglai' recurs in Ptolemy's 'Augaloi'[1] and perhaps also in the 'Augasioi' whose name was found by Stephanus in his text of Strabo's *Geographica*, Book XI, chap. viii, § 8 (C 513), where the reading had subsequently come to be 'Attasioi' in the text that had reached the hands of Modern Western scholars. It had been conjectured by Tomaschek that these were three independent attempts to reproduce in Greek an Iranian word 'aogazdáo', which would have been a derivative of the Avestan word 'aogañh', meaning 'strength',[2] and which might therefore have been coined to designate 'reinforcements', 'auxiliaries', 'allies'. The location of Ptolemy's 'Augaloi', as well as their name, would fit the Achaemenian Empire's Hauma-(?)drinking Sakā allies in Farghānah; for Ptolemy places them 'below' (i.e. south of) the Iatioi (i.e. the Jāts, *alias* Massagetae, *alias* 'Pointed-Hood Sakā') and the Takhoroi (i.e. Tokharoi); and he places these Iatioi and Takhoroi on the northern section of the Jaxartes (i.e. around and down stream from Tashkend).[3]

As for the *Sakā Tigrakhaudā* (the Pointed-Hood Sakā), whom Herodotus knows by their national name as Massagetae, they were presumably neighbours of the Sakā Haumavargā, since in the official lists 'DB' and 'DPe' the Sakā are mentioned simply as such, without any attempt to draw the distinction between two different kinds of Sakā that is drawn in all four later lists. According to Herodotus[4] the Massagetae marched with the Achaemenian Empire along the Oxus at the time when Cyrus II made his disastrously unsuccessful attempt to conquer them. Herodotus's description[5] of the marshes and lagoons in which all branches of 'the Araxes' lose themselves, except for one solitary branch that finds its way to the Caspian Sea, shows that 'Araxes' must mean 'Oxus' in this context; and his description of the denizens of these marshes[6] corresponds to the label by which, in 'DZd', 'the Sakā of the Marshes' are distinguished from 'the Sakā of the Plains'. There is, however, no evidence that either Herodotus's 'marshmen' or Darius's 'Sakā of the Marshes' are to be identified with the 'Water Sakā'—'Apa Sakā', *Graecè* 'Apasiakai'—whom Polybius[7] describes as a mounted Nomad people, living between the rivers Oxus and Don, who have to cross the Oxus in order to raid Hyrcania.

[1] Ptolemy: *Geographia*, Book VI, chap. xii, § 4.

[2] Professor R. G. Kent comments: 'It is very hazardous to see in Greek Aiglai, Augasioi, Augaloi a Grecizing of Avestan aogaz-da—(so properly transcribed), meaning 'strength-giving or -making' (roots dō- and dhē- are phonetically merged into one, dā-, in Iranian). The compound does not actually occur in the *Avesta*, but its form would be certain. If you cite the Avestan word for strength, it should be aogah- (from auges-), which is more perspicuous. The use of ñh for Avestan s > h between vowels is no longer current, as it develops only in certain intervocalic positions, while -h- is its phonetic antecedent even there. In the Greek words the Ai- and the Au- are difficult to equate, even as corrupt borrowings: unless there is some popular etymology to a more familiar word, or to something that seems to make meaning.'

[3] These locations for the Sakā Haumavargā, the Sakā Tigrakhaudā, and the Tokharoi are evidently those which they had occupied at the moment when the Tokharoi (*alias* Yuechi) had just been pushed westward out of the country of the Issedones (Wusun).

[4] See Herodotus, Book I, chap. 201. [5] See ibid., chap. 202.

[6] In loc. cit. Cp. Strabo: *Geographica*, Book XI, chap. viii, § 7 (C 513).

[7] See Polybius, Book X, chap. 48.

These Apasiakai are located in what would appear to be the same position—along the Oxus west of Bactria—by Eratosthenes, according to Strabo, if we accept Tarn's emendation of the passage;[1] and here the Apasiakai are associated with the Massagetae. Ptolemy brings the Massagetae south of the Oxus, into Marginanê (Marguš).[2] Darius tells us[3] that, in the campaign in which he re-subjected the insurgent Sakā whose prince was Skunkha, he had to cross the sea. We know, from the evidence of the head-dress worn by Skunkha on the Behistan bas-relief, that Skunkha's Sakā were 'the Pointed-Hoods' and not 'the Hauma-(?) drinkers'; and, since Herodotus's and Eratosthenes' location of the Massagetae somewhere along the right bank of the Oxus suggests that the sea which Darius had to cross in order to get at them must have been an arm of the Sea of Aral, we can perhaps locate the south-eastern borders of 'the Pointed-Hood Sakā', *alias* Massagetae, as adjoining the Oxus from a point below the western frontiers of Bactria and Sogdiana to some point as far north-west as the south-eastern extremity of Chorasmia, and their western borders as adjoining the Sea of Aral; but we do not know how far this great confederacy of Nomad peoples extended northwards into the heart of the Eurasian Steppe, or at what point on the course of the Jaxartes, to the north and north-west of the river's southern elbow, they marched with the Sakā Haumavargā. We can, though, be sure that, in addition to the Apa Sakā on the Middle Oxus and the marshmen in the Oxus Delta, there were other Massagetan peoples who, like the Sakā Haumavargā, were 'Sakā of the Plains' in fact, whether or not this latter label is used in 'DZd' to designate the Sakā Haumavargā exclusively.[4]

A link between the North-East Quarter of the Achaemenian Empire and its dominions in the Indus Basin was constituted by the *dahyāuš* which is called *Gādāra* in the Old Persian version, and *Pa-ar-ú-pa-ra-e-*

[1] See Strabo: *Geographica*, Book XI, chap. viii, § 8 (C 513), as amended by Tarn in *The Greeks in Bactria and India*, p. 91, n. 3, to read: 'And Eratosthenes says that the Apasiakai (*sic*, instead of 'the Arachôtoi') adjoin the Bactrians on the west along the Oxus.'

[2] See *Geographia*, Book VI, chap. x, § 2.

[3] In 'DB', in the tantalizingly mutilated § 74.

[4] If the Achaemenian imperial authorities found some difficulty in hitting upon labels or nicknames to distinguish 'the Hauma-(?)drinking Sakā' who were their allies from 'the Pointed-Hood Sakā' who were at least nominally their subjects, it is not surprising to find the Hellenic geographers confounding the two kinds of Sakā with one another. After accurately distinguishing 'the Heathen' ('Parikanioi') from 'the Pointed-Hoods' ('Orthokorybantioi') in his gazetteer without realizing that these two outlandish names that he is cramming into one of his four Median taxation districts have anything to do with the Sakā (see pp. 594–5, above), Herodotus falls, in his field-state (Book VII, chap. 64), into the blunder of identifying the Sakā who wear stiff pointed hoods with the Sakā whom the Persians call 'Amyrgioi' (i.e. 'Haumavargā'). On the other hand, Strabo is not conclusively convicted of being guilty of the same blunder when he states that Spitamenes, when Alexander had made Bactria and Sogdiana too hot to hold him, 'sought asylum with the Augasioi (*sic*, following Stephanus, instead of "Attasioi") and the Khorasmioi, who were two of the peoples belonging to the nation of the Massagetai and the Sakai' (*Geographica*, Book XI, chap. viii, § 8 (C 513)). Spitamenes may have taken refuge with the Augasioi (*alias* Sakā Haumavargā of Farghānah) first, and then moved on to the country of the more distant Khorasmioi; and this second asylum would have been safer politically, besides being more remote geographically, than the first, if at this date the Khorasmioi had become 'one of the peoples of the Massagetai' in the sense that they had transferred their allegiance from a declining Achaemenian Power to the formidable Nomad confederacy against which a now decrepit Achaemenian Imperial Government had ceased to be able to protect them.

sa-an-na in the Babylonian version, of the official lists, and *Gandarioi* in Herodotus's catalogue of the peoples in his Taxation District No. 7. The Babylonian synonym for an Old Persian 'Gădāra', which reappears in the post-Alexandrine Hellenic name 'Paropanisus', had been interpreted by Modern Western scholars, in terms of the language of the *Avesta*, as meaning [the country which is] 'beyond' ('para') [the mountain range that is] 'higher than the eagle' ['upāirisaēna'], i.e. the country that is 'trans Hindu Kush'. Since this poetic geographical expression must have been coined by speakers of the Avestan language in which it is couched, it must have designated people who lived on the opposite side of the Hindu Kush from the Oxus Basin, and this locates these 'Para-upāirisaēna' in the basin of the Kābul River. This was the location of Gădāra likewise; and the prima-facie inference from the official equation Gădāra = Para-upāirisaēna in the Achaemenian official lists is that, in the Achaemenian Age—whatever permutations and combinations in the administrative geography of this region may have been inaugurated by the Macedonian conquest[1]—the two names were synonyms for an identical administrative area in the Kābul River Basin.[2] Besides the Gandarioi, however, Herodotus, in his description of his Taxation District No. 7, mentions three other peoples whose homes we still have to locate.

Two of these other three peoples in the Herodotean District No. 7 could be identified through the survival of their names down to the time of writing. Herodotus's *Dadikai* were still on the map as the Tajiks who were to be found in the Kābul River Basin in the Kuh-i-Dāmān, between the Upper Kābul River and the Panjshir River, and in the Kuhistan, between that and the Hindu Kush,[3] as well as in the Upper Oxus Valley above Bactria and Sogdiana—on the left bank in Badakhshān and on the right bank in the territory that had been labelled Tajikistan in the administrative geography of the Soviet Union.[4] Herodotus's *Aparytai* ('highlanders')[5] were still on the map as the Afridis who were to be found at the eastern end of the Safid Kuh, on the watershed between the Kābul River and the Kurram River, just to the south of the Khyber Pass.[6]

1 See, for instance, Tarn, op. cit., p. 100.

2 These 'Paropanisadai', *alias* 'Gandarioi', must be the people described in Arrian's field-state of Darius III Codomannus's army at Gaugamela (III. viii. 3) as 'the Indoi who were next-door neighbours of the Bactrians' and who were brigaded with the Bactrians under Bêssus's command (see p. 644, n. 8, above).

3 See Elphinstone, M.: *An Account of the Kingdom of Caubul*, new ed. (London 1839, Bentley, 2 vols.), vol. i, pp. 408–11; Burnes, A.: *Cabool: A Personal Narrative of a Journey to, and Residence in, that City in the Years 1836, 7 and 8*, 2nd ed. (London 1843, John Murray), pp. 149–51.

4 We have no information about the boundary between the Dadikai—in the administrative, as distinct from the ethnic, sense—and Bactria in the administrative geography of the Achaemenian Empire. Ptolemy's statement (in *Geographia*, Book VI, chap. xii, § 1) that Sogdiana was bounded 'by Bactria and the Caucasian Mountains Proper' not only on the south along the Oxus River and on the west (i.e. by the Bactrian province Margiana), but also on the east, may signify that the Upper Oxus Valley on the north bank, and consequently also on the south bank, was included in Bactria, not in Dadikê.

5 According to Herzfeld, op. cit., p. 99, 'parvatā' was one of the Iranian words for 'mountain'. Professor Kent notes that the word 'parvatā', with epenthesis to 'paurvatā—,' is extant in Avestan.

6 These 'Aparytai' must be the people described in Arrian's field-state (III. viii. 4) as 'the Indians called the highland Indians' who in 331 B.C. were brigaded, not with

Neither of these peoples is named in any of the official lists; but the fourth people included in the Seventh Taxation District according to the Herodotean gazetteer are the *Sattagydai* who appear in the official lists as the *Thatagu*[? *d* or *v*]*iyā*; and *Thataguš*, the *dahyāuš* from which this people derive their name, is not so easy to locate. Considering that Para-upāirisaēna = Gādāra Proper had immediate next-door neighbours on the north in Bactria, on the west in Areia, and on the south in Arachosia, we are led to look for the Thataguš canton of the Herodotean Taxation District No. 7 in the country immediately to the east of Gādāra Proper—i.e. in the Panjab, which adjoined Gādāra across the Indus.[1] Herzfeld points out[2] that in the Achaemenian bas-reliefs the Thatagu [? d or v]iyā are portrayed in loin-cloths, which indicates that their country lay somewhere on the plains of the Indus Basin, and not up in the highlands of Eastern Iran; and the difficulty of finding a location for Thataguš anywhere within the limits of Gādāra to the west of the Indus certainly suggests that the Thatagu[? d or v]iyā must have lived to the east of the Indus—that is to say, on the plains, extending south-eastwards from the east bank of the Indus opposite the mouth of the Kābul River, which were watered by seven streams, from the Indus to the Sutlej's lost south-eastern neighbour inclusive.[3]

the Gandarians, but with the Arachosians under the satrap of Arachosia's command. In Ptolemy's *Geographia*, Book VI, chap. xviii, Herodotus's 'Aparytai' appear as the 'Parouêtai' (*sic*, instead of the reading 'Parsuêtai' in the latter-day text) who are the southernmost community of the Paropanisadae (§ 3) and who are presumably the inhabitants of the Parouêtan Mountains (the latter-day Safid Kuh) that constitute the boundary between the Paropanisadae and Arachosia, since they also figure (ibid., Book VI, chap. xx, § 3) as the northernmost community in Arachosia. This location on the border would account for their transfer to Arachosia from Gādāra at some date before 331 B.C. Ptolemy's 'Parautoi' (Book VI, chap. xvii, § 3), who are located in Areia next door to the Paropanisadai, are evidently likewise 'highlanders' Hellenized in a slightly different transliteration of the same underlying Iranian word, but their location suggests that their highland home lay in the country of the latter-day Hazaras, on the watershed of the rivers Kābul, Hilmand, and Hari Rud, and not in the Safid Kuh, where the name 'Aparytai-Parouêtai-Parautoi' was still borne by the latter-day Afridis.

1 The only substantial objection to locating Thataguš in the Panjab is a financial one. The Panjab must always have been a rich country in virtue of its agricultural and pastoral products, and therefore, if the Herodotean Taxation District No. 7 did include even only a part of the Panjab, it is surprising that it should have been assessed at a lower figure than any other district. Moreover, Thataguš, whether a rich country or a poor one, had been in rebellion in 522–521 B.C., and Darius was not the man to let off re-subjugated rebels lightly in their tax-assessments, as he showed by the enormous figure at which he assessed the poverty stricken South-Eastern Asagartiyā, Yautiyā, and Mačiyā. The lowness of the assessment on the Herodotean District No. 7 could perhaps be reconciled with a location of one of its constituent cantons in the wealthy Panjab on the supposition that, if Thataguš did lie in the Panjab, it included no more than a fraction of it—e.g. the north-western corner, to the north-west of the Salt Range.

2 In op. cit., p. 99.

3 i.e. the Indus, Jhelum, Chenāb, Rāvi, Beas, and Sutlej, together with a former river, south-east of the Sutlej, adjoining the Indian Desert, that had subsequently dried up. This lost river was remembered under divers names: 'Hakrā' and 'Wahindah' (see Smith, V. E.: *The Early History of India*, 3rd ed. (Oxford 1914, Clarendon Press), p. 92) and 'Sarasvati' (see Rapson, E. J., in *The Cambridge History of India*, vol. i, p. 45). The Panjab is designated accordingly as the land, not of five, but of seven, rivers in the Avestan gazetteer of the Zoroastrian World (*Vendidad*, i. 18), as well as in the *Vedas* (e.g. in *Rigveda*, viii. 24 and 27). The 'Haptā Hindu' of the *Avesta* and the 'Saptā Sindhava' of the *Vedas* are philological equivalents of one another; and Herzfeld, in loc. cit., taking this figure 'seven' as his cue, suggests that the name reproduced in Old Persian as 'Thataguš' may represent a compound, in some Iranian or Sanskrit dialect, of the Indo-European word for 'seven' with some word meaning 'stream'. The identification of the Haptā Hindu of *Vendīdād*, i. 18, with the Panjab is corroborated by the

This conclusion will be supported by our finding that, if we do not locate Thataguš here, we shall be left with a vacuum in a piece of territory that can hardly have lain outside the frontiers of an Achaemenian Empire which, before the end of Darius I's reign, had come to include not only the basin of the Kābul River down to the west bank of the Upper Indus but also the Lower Indus Valley as far north as a point where *Hĭduš* (Indoi)—the Herodotean Taxation District No. 20—marched with Harahvatiš ('the Pactyan country'). In one of the appendixes to his gazetteer, Herodotus[1] tells us, as we have already noticed,[2] that the northernmost of all the Indoi were next-door neighbours of the city of Kaspatyros and the Pactyan (not the Gandarian) country on the one hand and next-door neighbours of the Indian Desert on the other; and this means that, at the farthest, Hĭduš (Indoi) cannot have extended farther north than the southern extremity of the Panjab, i.e. than the neighbourhood of the latter-day city of Multān. Darius must have annexed the Lower Indus Valley from this point downwards to the sea as part of his comprehensive plan for opening up through communications by water, via the Indus, the Indian Ocean, the Red Sea, his Red Sea-Nile canal, and the Eastern Mediterranean, between the eastern and western extremities of his empire.[3]

The name Hĭduš (Indoi) means the country of the people known as the Sindhu or Sauvīra-Sindhu in Sanskrit literature. These had 'entered India shortly before the Persian period and worked southwards',[4] and both the date of their arrival and the contemporary occurrence of another people bearing the name Sindoi on the banks of the River Kuban, in the throat of the Great Western Bay of the Eurasian Steppe, suggests that the Indoi in Sind will have been the left wing of a Eurasian Nomad horde whose right wing will have diverged to the north of the Caspian Sea in the course of the Völkerwanderung of the eighth and seventh centuries B.C.[5] In giving their name to the province of Sind and to the

description of it, in this passage of the *Avesta*, as being a region of 'abnormal heat' (see Jackson, A. V. W., in *The Cambridge History of India*, vol. i, p. 324); but, even if the identification of the Achaemenian 'Thataguš', too, with the Panjab were also to carry conviction, the countries called Hapta Hindu and Thataguš might be geographically identical without there being any common element in the etymologies of their names. A different interpretation of 'Thataguš' from Herzfeld's is given by Kent in his *Old Persian: Grammar, Texts, Lexicon*, p. 187:

> 'Θatagu- sb. "Sattagydia", a province of the Persian Empire: Elam. *sa-ad-da-ku-iš*, Akk. *sa-at-ta-gu-ú*, Gk. *Σατταγυδιᾱ* . . . From *Θατα*—"hundred", Av. *sata-*, Skt. *śatám*, Gk. *ἑ-κατόν*, Lt. *centum*, N. Eng. *hundred*, pIE *kmto-m*,+*gav-* "cattle": "having hundreds of cattle" (hardly "[Land of] Seven Streams", with Hz. AMI 1.99n., 3.100–2, 8.73, König Ru 1D 63).'

The name 'having hundreds of cattle' fits the Panjab as aptly as the name 'Land of Seven Streams', and thus there seems to be no etymological obstacle to the equation Thataguš = Panjab, which is commended by the negative geographical consideration that there is nowhere else where we can locate Thataguš, and by the positive indication that is to be found in the tropical dress in which the Thatagu[? d or v]iyā are portrayed.

Professor G. G. Cameron comments: 'I find it very difficult to reconcile Thataguš with the Panjab. Must it not rather be on the slopes of the Hindu Kush?' But, if that had been its location, would it not have had to be labelled 'having hundreds of sheep and goats'? And would not its denizens have had to be portrayed, not half-naked, but muffled up in *sisyrnai*?

1 In Book III, chap. 102.

2 On p. 633, above.

3 See p. 634, with n. 6, above.

4 Tarn, op. cit., p. 171 based on H. Lüders.

5 See p. 608, n. 4, above.

great river by whose united waters this province was traversed, the left wing of the Sindoi will have started a process which was to end in their name being applied to the whole sub-continent embraced within the Sulaymān and Himalaya mountain ranges;[1] and we can already see the beginnings of this progressive extension of the name 'Indian' in Herodotus's usage.

While, in Herodotus's mind, the word 'Indoi' means in the first instance the nation inhabiting Darius's Twentieth Taxation District and living on the banks of '*the* river' [Indus],[2] and while he believes that Sind is the eastern edge of the *Oikoumenê*,[3] with nothing to the east of its inhabitants except the Indian Desert that set for them their eastern boundary, he also knows of Indians, living south of the Achaemenian province Hĩduš, who were independent of Darius;[4] he is aware that the Indians consist of many peoples not all speaking the same language;[5] and, when, both in the gazetteer[6] and in another context,[7] he calls the Indians 'by far the largest nation in the World', he is manifestly using the word 'Indians' to cover not merely the Indoi in Sind but all the inhabitants of Sind's vast south-eastern hinterland, where, between the Indian Desert and the Arabian Sea, it passes over into Gujerat and Malwa and Mahārāshtra and the Deccan. On the other hand, Herodotus's location of 'the northernmost of the Indoi' no farther north than the latitudes of 'the Pactyan country' (i.e. Arachosia) and the Indian Desert, and his statement in this context that these were the Indoi who were sent to get from the Desert the gold[8] in which the Indian taxation district paid its enormous annual contribution to the Achaemenian Imperial Treasury,[9] show that, unlike the source from which Arrian ultimately obtained his field-state of the army assembled by Darius III Codomannus at Gaugamela a hundred years or so after the date at which Herodotus was writing, Herodotus did not reckon among the Indoi any of the peoples then in occupation of the Indus Basin to the north of Hĩduš's northern boundary in the neighbourhood of Multān.[10]

In thus excluding from the limits of India Proper the Panjab as well as Gãdāra, Herodotus was in agreement with the Sanskrit Scriptures; and there is a piece of evidence which suggests that, without knowing

1 'Sanskrit "Sindhu-s" and Old Persian "hi(n)duš" agree absolutely in etymology, as original initial s before a vowel became h in Iranian, and the aspirated voiced stops became voiced non-aspirates in Iranian. This explains the variation between Hind and Sind; "India" is from the Iranian with loss of the initial h.'—Professor R. G. Kent.

2 See Herodotus, Book III, chap. 98.

3 See ibid.

4 See Book III, chap. 101.

5 See Book III, chap. 98.

6 See Book III, chap. 94.

7 In Book V, chap. 3.

8 See Book III, chap. 102.

9 See Book III, chaps. 94–95.

10 How was it that, at some date between the reigns of the first Darius and the last Darius, the name 'Indoi' came to be applied to the peoples in the basin of the Kābul River whom Herodotus calls 'Aparytai' and 'Gandarioi'? The explanation might be that Hĩduš, after its annexation to the Achaemenian Empire by Darius, was attached for political purposes to the *dahyāuš* Gãdāra to constitute a single viceroyalty, though for fiscal purposes it was erected into a separate taxation district (Herodotus's District No. 20, which appears in his gazetteer as a separate unit from his District No. 7). If Gãdāra was united with Hĩduš for political purposes, this would account for the extension of the name 'Indoi' to the peoples in the Kābul River Basin, and for their retention of the name even after the rest of the Indus Basin, including the home of the authentic 'Indoi' in Sind, had recovered its independence—as it had before Alexander's descent upon it.

it, he may have been following Vedic authority through a chain of intermediate informants.

In describing the gold-getting Indoi who were the northernmost of all the peoples bearing the name, Herodotus states[1] that these were 'the most warlike of the Indians' and that their culture (*Graecè* 'díaita') was 'approximately the same as that of the Bactrians'. This must be an echo of the usage of the term 'Bāhlīka' (i.e. 'Bākhtriš', 'Baktroi') in the Sanskrit Scriptures as a disapprobatory generic name—a counterpart of the Avestan term 'pairikās'—to cover the swarm of Eurasian Nomad peoples and the once sedentary victims of their invasion—including not only the Bactrians Proper (Bhallas), but also the Çibi (*Graecè* Sibai), Malavas (*Graecè* Malloi), Kshudrakas (*Graecè* Oxydrakai),[2] Madda, Maddava, Madra, Madraka, Bhadra, and what not—who, in the Völkerwanderung of the eighth and seventh centuries B.C., had poured out of the Eurasian Steppe into the Panjab and beyond, without troubling to legitimize themselves in Brahman eyes by conforming to the ritual demands of Vedic orthodoxy.[3] The national names of these intruders are not mentioned either by Herodotus or in any of the Achaemenian official lists. They have been preserved in Sanskrit and in post-Alexandrine Hellenic literature. But it seems reasonable to surmise that, in the administrative geography of the Achaemenian Empire, they figure anonymously as the Thatagu[? d or v]iyā (Sattagydai) together with those northernmost peoples of the Viceroyalty of Hīduš who were more Bactrian than they were Indian in their way of life.[4]

The name of one of these heathen Bāhlīka peoples that looms large in Sanskrit literature, and that had been located in the Kābul River Basin by students of Indic history,[5] is conspicuous by its absence from both the Achaemenian official lists and the Herodotean gazetteer. Where are the Kambojas? In Sanskrit literature they are described as living in a cold country and manufacturing warm clothes from wool and fur, and they are associated with the Yonas (Hellenes) by Açoka Maurya.[6] These indications point to a location in the Paropanisus; and this is in fact Ptolemy's location[7] of a people whom he calls 'Tambyzoi' and places on the southern frontier of Bactria, about half-way along. If we may conjecture that 'Tambyzoi' is a corruption of an original 'Kambyzoi', we learn from this passage of Ptolemy's *Geographia* that the national name which appears in Sanskrit as 'Kamboja' was transliterated into Greek on the same system as the personal name which appears in Old

[1] In Book III, chap. 102.

[2] A rearguard of these Oxydrakai who had made their way to the south-eastern edge of the Panjab is located by Ptolemy (*Geographia*, Book VI, chap. xii, § 4) in the mountains of Sogdiana under the name Oxydrankai.

[3] See de la Vallée Poussin, L.: *L'Inde aux Temps des Mauryas* (Paris 1930, Boccard), pp. 12–16; Tarn: *The Greeks in Bactria and India*, pp. 169–71.

[4] The portrayal of the Thatagu[? d or v]iyā in loin-cloths does not disqualify them from being reckoned among the Bāhlīkas, since, as is evident from Elphinstone's account quoted on p. 636, above, of the dress of the nineteenth-century Afghan occupants of the Darajāt, an immigrant Central Asian people on the plains of the Indus Valley might revert to its ancestral dress in the winter even if it had taken to wearing a tropical undress in the summer.

[5] e.g. by de la Vallée Poussin in op. cit., p. 15.

[6] See ibid.

[7] In *Geographia*, Book VI, chap. xi, § 6.

Persian as 'Ka[m]būjiya', in Elamite as 'Kan-bu-ṣi-ị̇a', in Akkadian as 'Kam-bu-zi-ia', and in Greek as 'Kambŷsês'.[1]

The question remains: Why did Kambūjiya I's father Kūruš I of Parsuwaš and Anšan name his son 'the Kamboja'? And this question raises an antecedent one: Why did Kūruš I's father Čišpiš (*Graecè* Teispes) name his son 'the Kuru'?[2] It is evident that the personal names that thenceforth alternated in the Cyran, in contrast to the Ariaramnan, branch of the Achaemenidae are taken from the national names of two non-Persian peoples; but it seems improbable that Cambyses I of Parsuwaš-Anšan (*regnabat circa* 600–559 B.C.) can have been named after the Kambojas whom we find subsequently established on the southern flank of the Hindu Kush, and *a fortiori* improbable that Cyrus I of Parsuwaš-Anšan (*regnabat circa* 640–600 B.C.) can have been named after the Kurus whose 'plain', the 'Kuru-kshetra', is located in Sanskrit literature near the north-eastern edge of the Indian Desert, on the divide between the basins of the Indus and the Ganges.[3]

A clue to the solution of this problem may perhaps be found in the appearance of the same two words 'Kamboja' and 'Kuru' as place-names in Transcaucasia as well as on the Hindu Kush and in the Indian sub-continent. Sanskrit literature had preserved a memory of Uttara-Kurus living beyond the Himalaya;[4] and at the time of writing the principal left-bank affluent of the River Aras was still called the Kur, while this River Cyrus, as it was likewise called by Hellenic geographers, had a left-bank affluent called by them the Cambyses, which gave the name 'Cambŷsênê'[5] to a north-western tongue of the steppe country, called by them Kaspianê,[6] in the Lower Kur-Aras Basin. Thus in Transcaucasia the two names Cyrus (Kuru) and Cambyses (Kamboja) were not only both on the map, as they were in India and on its north-west frontier, but were found in immediate juxtaposition, which suggests that in

1 A Modern Western scholar, Sylvain Lévi, cited by Tarn in op. cit., pp. 138 and 170, had tentatively equated the national name 'Kamboja' with the Paropanisadan place-name Kāpiša, one of the two constituents of the double city Kāpišakāniš (see p. 639, n. 3, above); but Professor R. G. Kent had pointed out to the present writer that in the Elamite usage of the cuneiform script—which, unlike the Old Persian usage, shows nasals before consonants, Old Persian 'Kāpišakāniš' is transcribed 'Qa-ap-pi-iš-ša-qa-nu-iš', in contrast to the Elamite rendering 'Kan-bu-ṣi-ị̇a' for Old Persian 'Kabūjiya'. This Elamite testimony showed that there was no nasal in the initial syllable of the name Kāpiša', and this discrepancy told against Lévi's equation Kāpiša = Kamboja.

2 See Weissbach, F. H., s.v. 'Kyros', in Pauly–Wissowa, *Realencyclopädie der Classischen Altertumswissenschaft*, Neue Bearbeitung, Supplementband IV, col. 1128.

3 There was another 'Kuru Plain' (*Graecè* Kyrou *alias* Kourou *alias* Korou Pedion) in Western Anatolia, round the confluence between the River Hermus and its right-bank tributary the Phrygius, just to the north of the city of Magnesia-under-Sipylus (for the location see Strabo: *Geographica*, Book XIII, chap. iv, § 5 (C 626) and § 13 (C 629); Beloch, K. J.: *Griechische Geschichte*, 2nd ed., vol. iv, Part II (Berlin and Leipzig 1927, de Gruyter), pp. 458–61). In Anatolia, as in Hindustan, 'the Kuru Plain' was a battle-field on which the political fate of a sub-continent was repeatedly decided. Kyroupedion was the scene of the overthrow of Lysimachus by Seleucus Nicator in 281 B.C. and of Antiochus III by the Romans in 190 B.C. Kurukshetra, between the River Jumna and the lost River Sarasvatī, was the historic battlefield of Pānīpat, besides being the scene of the legendary war between the Kurus and the Pandus which is the theme of the *Mahābhārata*.

4 See Keith, A. Berriedale, in *The Cambridge History of India*, vol. i, p. 118.

5 See Strabo: *Geographica*, Book XI, chap. iv, § 1 (C 501) and § 5 (C 502); chap. xiv, § 4 (C 528).

6 See pp. 627–8, above.

Transcaucasia the two peoples who thus stamped their national names on the local landscape must have been closely associated.

It is perhaps almost as unlikely that the Cyran Achaemenidae will have derived their personal names from a pair of peoples in Transcaucasia as it is that they will have derived them from two peoples in and near India. But the occurrence of the two names in Transcaucasia as well as in and near India—and in Transcaucasia at close quarters—indicates that we have here two more names of Eurasian Nomad peoples who took part, and this in one another's company, in the Völkerwanderung of the eighth and seventh centuries B.C.; and, if, like so many of their fellows, these Kurus and Kambojas split into two wings whose paths diverged so widely, it does not seem unwarrantable to guess that a central detachment of this pair of migrating peoples may have found its way to Lūristān and there have been taken into partnership by Kūruš I's father Čišpiš.

Čišpiš seems to have come, *circa* 670 B.C.,[1] under the suzerainty of a war-lord whom the Assyrian records knew as Kashtaritu (*Persicè* Khšathrita)[2] and located, at his first appearance, in the Kassite country[3] just to the north-east of Parsuwaš. This Khšathrita was the leader of an anti-Assyrian coalition in which Medes and Mannaeans were associated with migrant Eurasian Nomads—Cimmerians and Saparda[4]—and the accommodation of a Kuru-Kamboja detachment of this horde in Parsuwaš may have been part of the arrangement on which Khšathrita and Čišpiš of Parsuwaš came to terms. The settlement of Eurasian Nomad immigrants in Lūristān is attested by the 'animal style' of the local school of bronze-work;[5] and some such reinforcement of the Achaemenian Power would also account for the sudden vast extension of its domain, at some date during Čišpiš' (*Graecè* Teispes') reign (*regnabat circa* 675–640 B.C.), from Parsuwaš in Lūristān and Anšan in the Pusht-i-Kuh south-eastwards over Pārsa (Fars). Teispes himself, for that matter, was the namesake of the Cimmerian war-lord Teušpu who crossed swords with Teispes' Assyrian contemporary Esarhaddon (*regnabat* 681–668 B.C.),[6] even if he was not Teušpu himself; and the folk-tale in which the mother of Cyrus I was called 'the bitch'—'Spakô'—according to Herodotus[7] may reflect the memory of a dynastic marriage between the House of Achaemenes and the House of the Scythian war-lord Išpakai who was riding hard at the Cimmerians' heels.[8]

Whatever may be the correct historical interpretation of these Nomad names in the personal nomenclature of the Achaemenidae from Čišpiš

1 See Cameron, op. cit., p. 180.

2 Esarhaddon's Khšathrita was identified by Modern Western scholars with Herodotus's Phraortes (i.e. Fravartiš) on the strength of Darius's statement, in 'DB', § 24, that another Fravartiš, the pretender to the Median throne in 522 B.C., gave himself out to be 'Khsathrita of the House of Uvakhštra (Cyaxares)'. See Cameron, op. cit., p. 177, and König, F. W.: *Älteste Geschichte der Meder und Perser* (Leipzig 1934, Hinrichs), p. 30.

3 See Cameron, op. cit., p. 177.

4 See Cameron, op. cit., p. 178; König, op. cit., p. 27.

5 This point is made by Cameron, op. cit., pp. 183–4, and by König, op. cit., p. 32.

6 See Luckenbill, op. cit., vol. ii, pp. 516, 530, 546.

7 In Book I, chap. 110.

8 See König, op. cit., pp. 27–31; Luckenbill, op. cit., vol. ii, pp. 517 and 533.

(Teispes) onwards in the Cyran branch of the house, they must mean that the Cimmerians, the Kurus, the Kambojas, and the Scyths had played some part in Achaemenian history that had been auspicious as well as important.

Having now completed our review of the *dahyāva* to the east of Western Iran, the heartland of the Achaemenian Empire, we have next to survey the *dahyāva* to the west of the heartland. If we take ship at Kaspapyros, sail down the Indus out into the Indian Ocean, and then follow in the wake of Alexander's admiral Nearchus up the Persian Gulf, instead of following in the wake of Darius's admiral Scylax round Arabia, we shall come to port in the *dahyāuš* which is called *Bābiruš* in all the Achaemenian official lists, and *Babylonia* by every Hellenic geographer with the one exception of Herodotus, who, for some private reason of his own, systematically calls Babylonia 'Assyria'[1] (the ninth taxation district in his gazetteer).

In the South-West Quarter of the Achaemenian Empire, on which we have now set foot, the next *dahyāuš* to Bābiruš (Babylonia) is the *Asshur* of the Babylonian and *Athurā* of the Old Persian text of the official lists; and both the name and the area covered by it appear in Greek as the *Syroi*—defined as 'the whole of Phoenicia and the so-called Philistine Syria, together with Cyprus'—who constitute Herodotus's Taxation District No. 5.

The name 'Asshur', as applied to this *dahyāuš*, is manifestly the official term which, before the incorporation of the Neo-Babylonian Empire into the Achaemenian Empire, had been used in the Neo-

[1] It is certain that Herodotus does mean Babylonia by 'Assyria'. In the gazetteer, for instance, he writes 'Babylon and the rest of Assyria' in between 'Susa and the rest of the Cissians' country' and 'Ecbatana and the rest of Media' (Book III, chaps. 91–92). 'Assyria' must mean Babylonia here, and so it must likewise in the field-state, where he states that the Assyrian contingent included the Chaldaeans, who were, of course, in occupation of South-Western Babylonia at this date (Book VII, chap. 63). In another place he calls Nabonidus 'king of Assyria' (Book I, chap. 188), and in another he uses 'the Babylonian country' and 'the Assyrian country' as synonyms in consecutive sentences, and explains that he is talking about an official administrative area: a 'satrapy' in the sense of a viceroyalty (Book I, chap. 192). Thus Herodotus's 'Assyria' certainly includes the whole of Babylonia—Book III, chap. 155, is another example of this usage—and there is no evidence that it includes anything besides; for, in a passage describing the down-stream coracle traffic on the River Euphrates, his words 'the Armenians who live above (i.e. up-stream in relation to) the Assyrians' (Book I, chap. 194) can hardly be compelled to yield the meaning that his 'Assyria' was conterminous with his Armenia and therefore included Mesopotamia as well as Babylonia. The *dahyāuš* officially styled 'Asshur' in Akkadian and 'Athurā' in Old Persian did include Mesopotamia, as we shall see, but this official Assyria, unlike Herodotus's private 'Assyria', did not include Babylonia. It is the *dahyāuš* that Herodotus calls 'the Syroi' (Book III, chap. 91). Herodotus is aware that this, and not Babylonia, is the district that is called Assyria by 'the Barbarians' (i.e. the Orientals). 'The Barbarians', he writes in Book VII, chap. 63, 'used the name "Assyrioi" to mean the people whom the Hellenes called "Syrioi" '—and these 'Syrioi' are the people whom Herodotus includes in his Fifth Taxation District ('the whole of Phoenicia and the so-called Philistine Syria, together with Cyprus'), not the people of an 'Assyria' which contains Babylon and which is the ninth district in his list.

Why did Herodotus deliberately adopt this private and peculiar usage of the word 'Assyria' to mean Babylonia? His words in Book I, chap. 178, suggest that his intention was to convey the historical truth that, in his day, Babylonia was the sole extant representative of a civilization, common to a still surviving Babylonia and a now extinct Assyria, which Herodotus labels 'Assyriac' (e.g. in Book I, chap. 199), not 'Babylonic', because he is aware that Assyria, before her downfall and annihilation, had been the paramount Power in this society.

Babylonian Empire's administrative geography to designate that part of the defunct Assyrian Empire that had fallen to Babylon's share in the partition of—or scramble for—Assyria's spoils between Babylon, Media,[1] Egypt, and Cilicia; but the exact limits of this Neo-Babylonian dominion labelled 'Assyria' which the Achaemenian Empire had inherited are not easy to ascertain.

We may be sure that the Neo-Babylonian Empire's 'Assyria' did not include the border cantons of Babylonia on the east and north-east—e.g. Gambalu, Dêr, and Kar-Asshur—which Assyria had detached from Babylonia and annexed to herself in and after the reign of Tiglath-Pileser III (*regnabat* 746–727 B.C.).[2] These authentically Babylonian cantons must simply have been 'disannexed', and it is also possible that the Babylonians may have now taken their revenge by annexing to Babylonia cantons higher up the Tigris, in the direction of the City of Asshur, which were as authentically Assyrian as Kar-Asshur and Dêr were Babylonian. But how far up the Tigris had the Neo-Babylonian Empire's writ run? We know from Herodotus's itinerary of the Achaemenian Empire's Great North-West Road[3] that neither the section of this highway east of the Tigris, running from Susa to the neighbourhood of Nineveh, nor the section west of the Tigris, running from the neighbourhood of Nineveh to the southern boundary of Armina, somewhere just north-west of Mardīn, traversed either Bābiruš or Athurā (*alias* Asshur, *alias* Syria) at any point; and this means that the Median share of the Assyrian Empire must have included, in addition to the metropolitan territory of Assyria east of the Tigris, at least the portion of the Department of Nineveh that lay on the west bank, together with three departments—Tille, Nasibina (i.e. Nisibin), and Izalā—which, on the post-Alexandrine Hellenic map, were embraced in the province labelled with the imported Macedonian name 'Mygdonia'.

This, however, was not the south-western limit of the ex-Assyrian territory west of the Tigris that the Medes had occupied. Though, in 609 B.C., during the Allies' final campaign against the remnant of the Assyrian Army in the neighbourhood of Harrān, Nabopolassar had penetrated (if we are to accept his claim) as far as Izalā and even Urartu, not only these countries but Harrān itself had fallen into Median hands in the event; Harrān had remained in Median hands from *circa* 607–606 B.C. onwards; and it had not been acquired by the Neo-Babylonian Empire *de facto*, whatever the position may have been *de jure* during the intervening half century, till 555 B.C.[4]—that is to say, till Astyages of Media was already so gravely preoccupied with the insubordinateness of Cyrus II of Anšan that Nabonidus of Babylon could venture to eject the Median garrison from Harrān with impunity. Since in the Achaemenian Age the country round Harrān (i.e. the upper basin of the River Balikh) was certainly not included either in Armenia or in Cilicia or in the fragment of a partitioned Media which Herodotus labels 'Matiênê',

1 See Herodotus, Book I, chap. 106.

2 See Forrer, op. cit., pp. 95–102, with the map of 'the development of Assyria, 745–606.'

3 Herodotus, Book V, chaps, 49–54.

4 According to Olmstead, op. cit., pp. 36–37. According to Adontz, op. cit., pp. 283–5 and 296–9, the date of Nabonidus's occupation of Harrān was 553 B.C.

this eleventh-hour acquisition of the Neo-Babylonian Empire's must have been left within the bounds of the Neo-Babylonian province of Asshur by Cyrus II when, after his conquest of the Neo-Babylonian Empire in 539 B.C., he kept it territorially intact as a single viceroyalty within his own universal state.

Wherever the northern boundary of the Achaemenian *dahyāuš* and Darian taxation district called Athurā-Asshur-Syria may have run, we know that—like the Syria of A.D. 1952—it comprised territory to the east as well as territory to the west of the River Euphrates; for the country through which, in 401 B.C., Xenophon and his comrades found themselves marching after they had crossed from the right to the left bank of the Euphrates was still Syria;[1] and, in Arrian's copy of both the field-state and the order of battle of Darius III Codomannus's army at Gaugamela in 331 B.C., the Syrians from Syria 'Between the Rivers' were brigaded with the Syrians from 'the Hollow Syria' under the single command of Mazaeus.[2] The portion of the province and taxation district labelled Syria-Asshur-Athurā which lay west of the Euphrates was called 'Hollow' by the Hellenes because it was traversed by the northernmost section of the Great Rift Valley which—after breaking southward out of the Taurus at Marʿash and running up the Orontes Valley, through the Biqāʿ, down the Jordan Valley, and through the Wādi ʿArabah, the Gulf of Suez, the Red Sea, and the Danākil Trough—continues up the Valley of the River Hawash in Abyssinia into Kenya Colony along a track punctuated, at this southern, as at the northern, end by lakes. The Babylonian name for the portion of Syria known on this account as 'Hollow Syria' in Greek was 'Beyond the River' (*Babyloniacè* Ebir-nari, *Aramaïcè* ʿAbar-Nahara)[3]—i.e. beyond the River Euphrates, as distinguished from the portion of Syria 'Between the Rivers' Euphrates and Tigris. The capital of this Achaemenian *dahyāuš* 'Athurā', the province comprising the Neo-Babylonian Empire's eventual share of the Assyrian Empire's spoils, was situated in the portion 'Beyond the River', 15 parasangs (i.e. just over 89 kilometres) to the north-west of the crossing of the Euphrates at Thapsacus.[4]

For the capital of a province astride the western elbow of the Euphrates, this position was well chosen, since it was within easy reach of the more extensive but less populous and less wealthy eastern portion of the *dahyāuš* that lay 'Between the Rivers', while it stood just within the portion, lying 'Beyond the River', which contained the industrially, commercially, and navally important Phoenician city-states with their miniature *imperia in imperio*.[5] Indeed, the 'Beyond the River' portion of Athurā-Asshur-Syria overshadowed the 'Between the Rivers' portion

[1] See Xenophon: *Expeditio Cyri*, Book I, chap. iv, § 19.

[2] See Arrian: *Expeditio Alexandri*, Book III, chap. viii, § 6, and chap. xi, § 4.

[3] In a letter to the present writer, Professor G. G. Cameron points out that, in the Akkadian text of 'DSf', § 3g, ll. 30–35, 'Ebir-nari' is employed as the translation for 'Kāra hya Athuriya' ('the Assyrian people') of the Old Persian text. Since the passage states that 'the cedar timber, this—a mountain by name of Lebanon—from there was brought; the Assyrian people, it brought it to Babylon' (Professor R. G. Kent's translation in *Old Persian*, p. 144), it is certain that Syria between the west bank of the Euphrates and the eastern shore of the Mediterranean was comprised within the Achaemenian *dahyāuš* labelled 'Athurā'.

[4] See Xenophon, op. cit., Book I, chap. iv, §§ 10–11.

[5] See p. 582, above.

to such a degree that in popular, as distinct from official, usage the term 'Beyond the River' was employed as a name for the whole province. This popular usage is followed in private business documents drawn up in Babylonia in the reigns of Cyrus, Cambyses, and Darius I[1] and in the Book of Ezra, and eventually even in the Aramaic inscriptions on provincial coins struck *circa* 340 B.C. by the governor of Athurā, Mazaeus,[2] though we know from the field-state and the order of battle preserved by Arrian that 'Between the Rivers', as well as 'Beyond the River', was included in Mazaeus's province.

In all the Achaemenian official lists Athurā-Asshur is mentioned as a different *dahyāuš* from Bābiruš, but this does not mean that Athurā was from first to last a separate viceroyalty, any more than the mention of Suguda, side by side with Bākhtriš, means that Suguda was not under the Viceroy of Bākhtriš's administration. Athurā is, in fact, placed in immediate juxtaposition to Bābiruš in the three latest of the official lists ('DSe', 'DNa', 'XPh'), as well as in the earliest ('DB'); and this is an indication that Athurā and Bābiruš, like Suguda and Bākhtriš, still constituted a single viceroyalty down to the year in which 'XPh' was inscribed. The Babylonian private documents that mention Athurā under the popular name 'Ebir-nari' inform us in so many words that this *dahyāuš* was under the administration of the Viceroy of Babylon until at least the sixth year of Darius I's reign.[3] On the other hand the governor of '‘Abar-Nahara' (i.e. Athurā), Tatnai, and the Emperor Darius I corresponded with one another direct, and not via the Viceroy of Bābiruš, according to the Aramaic document embedded in the Book of Ezra (chapter v. 6–chapter vi. 12), whatever the value of this document may or may not be as historical evidence.[4] Perhaps we may infer that Darius I left the original Viceroyalty of Babylon, which included Athurā as well as Babylonia, still intact on the political map, but dissected it, on his new fiscal map, into two separate taxation districts. Athurā had, however, certainly been separated from Bābiruš for political as well as for fiscal purposes by the time when Xenophon and his comrades traversed Athurā *en route* for Bābiruš in 401 B.C. Indeed, in that year the two provinces were not even conterminous; for, after crossing the River Khabur ('Araxes') just above its confluence with the Euphrates, Cyrus the Younger's expeditionary force, on the next stage of its advance down the left bank of the Euphrates, found itself marching through Arabia (*Persicè* Arabāya) for a distance of 125 parasangs (i.e. about 742½ kilometres) before entering Babylonia[5] at a point not more

[1] See Leuze, O.: *Die Satrapieneinteilung in Syrien und im Zweistromlande von 520–320* (Halle (Saale) 1935, Niemeyer), pp. 25, 36–37, and 70.

[2] See Leuze, op. cit., p. 110.

[3] See Leuze, op. cit., pp. 36–37 and 70. On the occurrence of the formula *Pahat Babili u Ebir-nari* in Babylonian texts, Professor G. G. Cameron comments in a letter to the present writer: 'When a Babylonian says "Babylon and Ebir-nari", he can only mean that there was a single administrative unit comprising Babylon and Assyria [i.e. the *dahyāuš* known in Old Persian as Athurā] in official terms.'

[4] 'It is difficult to regard this . . . as historical, or at any rate as belonging to the period in question. It looks as though it had originally referred to some other episode at some later time' (Oesterley, W. O. E.: *A History of Israel*, vol. ii (Oxford 1932, Clarendon Press), p. 85).

[5] See Xenophon, op. cit., Book I, chap. v, §§ 1 and 5, and chap. vii, §§ 1 and 14–16.

than about $13\frac{1}{2}$ parasangs (i.e. just over 80 kilometres) to the north-west of 'the Median Wall'.

The *dahyāuš* called *Arabia* in Greek and *Arabāya* in Old Persian, which in 401 B.C. thus extended across the middle course of the Euphrates into the desert and steppe country of South-Eastern Mesopotamia according to Xenophon, also extended, according to Herodotus,[1] to the shore of the Mediterranean at the south-east corner of that sea, along a short stretch of coast between a point south-west of Gaza and a place called Iênysos. Since the next stretch of the coast, extending from Iênysos south-westwards, for the distance of a three days' journey, to the north-east corner of Egypt, was, according to Herodotus in the same context, part of Athurā (Syria), it looks as if a corridor of territory had been cut out of Athurā and granted to Arabāya by the Achaemenian Imperial Government expressly in order to give Arabāya an outlet on the Mediterranean; and we can read between Herodotus's lines[2] that this cession of territory had been a reward for services rendered by the Arabs to Cambyses in assisting his passage across the desert from Syria when he was invading Egypt.

In thus placing their Arab allies in charge of the desert sections of two such vital lines of Imperial communication as the route from Babylonia to Syria up the Euphrates and the route from Syria to Egypt along the Mediterranean coast, the Achaemenian Imperial Government were no doubt moved by the same considerations that had led them to place their Hauma-(?)drinking Sakan allies in charge of their borderland over against the Great Eurasian Steppe. They had realized that, in a steppe and desert country, the only effective police force that a sedentary Power could find to perform the task of keeping the local Nomad occupants in order was the local Nomad nation-in-arms itself, and that, if these high-spirited and self-confident Nomads were to be induced to police themselves on the Achaemenian Empire's behalf, they must be given the honourable status of free allies. The Achaemenidae were assuredly wise thus to adopt Nabonidus's fruitful policy of conciliating the Arabs instead of reverting to the Assyrians' sterile policy[3] of trying to crush them on a *terrain* on which the Arabs were bound in the long run to have the advantage over the troops of any sedentary Power. The Arabs had to be brought to a halt by diplomacy if not by military operations, since they had been erupting out of Arabia into 'the Fertile Crescent' simultaneously with the Iranian Nomads' eruption out of Central into South-Western Asia in the eighth and seventh centuries B.C.[4] Indeed, the Arabian frontier that Darius had inherited was perhaps little less formidable than the Central Asian one.

We have no information about the boundaries of the Achaemenian *dahyāuš* Arabāya at other points. We know that the temple-state of Jerusalem lay, not in Arabāya, but in Athurā, though Judah had never

1 See Herodotus, Book III, chap. 5.

2 In Book III, chaps, 4–7 and 88.

3 See Abbott, N.: 'Pre-Islamic Arab Queens', pp. 4–5, in *The American Journal of Semitic Languages and Literatures*, vol. lviii, No. 1, January 1941 (Chicago 1941, University of Chicago Press), pp. 1–22, for Arab-Assyrian relations from the reign of Tiglath-Pileser III to that of Asshurbanipal inclusive.

4 See III, iii. 423.

been included in the Assyrian Empire, but had been annexed to the Assyrian province of the Neo-Babylonian Empire by Nebuchadnezzar. Presumably Nabonidus had intended to annex Edom likewise to Asshur when he had conquered Edom in 553 B.C.,[1] but here the Arabs were the *tertii gaudentes*, for, when the remnant of Edom reappears on a post-Alexandrine Hellenic map, this 'Idumaea' lies as far north as the Negeb, in the former territory of the Hebrew tribe of Simeon, while the former territory of Edom in the Wādi ʿArabah, round Petra, has become the domain of 'the Agricultural Arabs' ('the Nabataeans'). We may guess that, in addition to Petra, the oasis of Taymā, in the North-Western Hijāz, which Nabonidus had reached and had liked so well that he had preferred it to Babylon as a residence, had subsequently become part of the Achaemenian Empire's Arabian sphere of influence.

It will be seen that the Achaemenian *dahyāuš* Arabāya embraced at least as much of the North-West Arabian and South-East Mesopotamian Steppe as the Arab phylarchy of the Banu Ghassān, which was in charge of the Roman Empire's Arabian marches on the eve of the Primitive Muslim Arab conquerors' eruption out of the interior of the Arabian Peninsula. The status of the Achaemenian *dahyāuš* Arabāya must also have been much the same as that of this Ghassanid phylarchy and its Lakhmid counterpart which performed the equivalent service for the Roman Empire's rival and the Achaemenian Empire's successor the Sasanian Empire.[2] In all three cases, Arab Nomad peoples whose pastures adjoined the borders of a sedentary Power were recognized by that Power as its autonomous allies in consideration of their undertaking the wardenship of the desert marches. We do not know, however, whether 'the King of the Arabs'[3] with whom Cambyses negotiated for his expeditionary force a free passage overland from Syria to Egypt was the ruler merely of a local Arab principality that had supplanted the Edomites at Petra, or whether the same Arab prince's authority also extended south-eastward to Taymā in the Hijāz and perhaps north-eastward, as well, to Hatra in Mesopotamia.

Mudrāya was Egypt; the *Putāyā* appear to have been the Libyans[4] to the west of Egypt as far as the hinterland of the cluster of Greek city-states on the bulge of Cyrenaica; *Kūša* was the Napatan Kingdom which occupied the south of the Egyptiac World.[5] Herodotus includes the two Hellenic communities *Kyrênê* and *Barkê*, as well as *the Libyans adjoining Egypt*, in the same taxation district—his Number Six—as Egypt itself, and we may assume that, on the political map, they were likewise brigaded with Egypt in the same viceroyalty. On the other hand Herodotus reckons the Ethiopians who were Egypt's next-door neighbours as gift-bringing allies and not as tax-paying subjects;[6] and the maintenance of a permanent garrison of professional troops at

1 See Olmstead, op. cit., p. 37.
2 See p. 131, n. 3, above, and VIII. viii. 50–51.
3 See Herodotus, Book III, chaps, 5 and 7.
4 See Cameron, G. G., in the *Journal of Near Eastern Studies*, vol. ii (Chicago 1943, University of Chicago Press), p. 309.
5 See II. ii. 116–17.
6 See Book III, chap. 97.

Elephantinê by the Achaemenian Imperial Government[1] is evidence that its control over the Kingdom of Napata was only nominal.

The North-Western Quarter of the Achaemenian Empire—which was probably the quarter that was of least account in Persian eyes before the shocking disaster of 480–479 B.C.—begins with the *dahyāuš* named *Armina* (*alias* Arminiya; *Graecè* Armenia), which figures in Herodotus's description of his Taxation District No. 13 as one of its three constituent parts. We have already given reasons[2] for believing that, in the Darian division of a re-established Achaemenian Empire into taxation districts, the Armenian sub-empire was dissected into three districts: Armenia Proper; the strip of country between the northern boundary of Armenia Proper and the south shore of the Black Sea; and a western district consisting of Cappadocia-cum-Dascylîtide. And we have suggested that Herodotus has inadvertently preserved the description of a Viceroyalty of Armenia in which all these three taxation districts were comprised thanks to his having mistaken this description of a political unit for a description of one of its three fiscal subdivisions. The taxation district in question was, on this view, confined in reality to Armenia Proper; and this was 'a small country'[3] consisting of the Upper Tigris Basin together with the north-west corner of the Upper Euphrates Basin. The boundary between the taxation district consisting of this Armenia Proper and its western neighbour, the taxation district Cappadocia-cum-Dascylîtide, will have run to the east of the road from the latter-day city of Sivas (*Graecè* Sebasteia) on the Upper Halys to the latter-day city of Malatīyah (*Graecè* Melitênê, *Assyriacè* Meliddu). The boundary between Armenia Proper and its northern neighbours the coastal peoples will have followed approximately the watershed between the Upper Euphrates Basin and the Black Sea.

What was the boundary between an Achaemenian Armenia and its eastern neighbour Urartu which, on the political map of the Achaemenian Empire, was included in the Viceroyalty of Media[4] and which, on the Darian fiscal map, was associated, as is recorded in the Herodotean gazetteer,[5] with the Hyspirîtis and with a Matiênê or Matianê which embraced the Median share of Assyria as well as the basin of Lake Urmīyah? Under the Achaemenian régime at as early a date as 401 B.C. the western frontier of Urartu over against Armina already ran rather farther to the east than Urartu's Assyrian adversaries Tiglath-Pileser III and his successors had ever succeeded in pushing this frontier back; for when, in 401 B.C., Xenophon and his comrades, marching northwards, crossed the watershed between the Upper Tigris Basin and the basin of the Eastern Euphrates (Murād Su), and debouched into the valley of the Eastern Euphrates' left-bank affluent the Teleboas (the stream draining the plain of Mush), they found themselves passing out of Armenia, not into Urartu, but into another Armenia called 'the Armenia to the West'.[6] This valley of the Teleboas and the

[1] See p. 119, with n. 7, above.
[2] See pp. 604–11, above.
[3] Strabo: *Geographica*, Book XI, chap. xiv, § 5 (C 528).
[4] See pp. 603–4, above.
[5] See pp. 628–32, above.
[6] See Xenophon, op. cit., Book IV, chap. iv, § 4.

section of the Eastern Euphrates Valley into which it opened[1] thus lay on the Armenian side of the boundary between Armenia and Urartu in the Achaemenian Age; but in the Assyrian Age they had lain inside the Urartian Kingdom's frontiers. The conquest of this piece of territory by King Menuas of Urartu (*regnabat circa* 828–785 B.C.)[2] is recorded in an inscription on a stele found near Mush in the village of Trmd.[3] We may perhaps infer that during the bout of anarchy in South-West Asia at the turn of the seventh and sixth centuries B.C., between the collapse of the Assyrian and the establishment of the Median Power, Gurdi's Mushkian war-band which was then overrunning the former Assyrian territory of Naïri in the Tigris Basin overran the former Urartian territory in the Teleboas Valley as well, and that, when the Medes eventually imposed their rule on the autochthonous Urartians and on the intrusive Mushkians alike, they respected this accomplished fact in settling the boundary between an Urartu which they were incorporating into Media itself and an Armenia which they were making into a sub-empire within a Median Commonwealth.

If the valley of the Teleboas had in fact thus been transferred from Urartu to Armenia at some date between the end of the Assyrian and the beginning of the Median Age, this might prove to be the explanation of two puzzling pieces of nomenclature. In the first place it might explain how the Mushkian (i.e. Phrygian) followers of Gurdi,[4] who, in their own language, called themselves Haik,[5] came to be known in the Achaemenian official terminology neither as Haik nor as Mushki nor as Gordians, but as 'Arminiyā'. This Old Persian ethnikon of a place-name 'Arminiya' may represent the Urartian word Urmeniuhi-ni which occurs in Menuas' inscription found in the neighbourhood of Mush as the name of one of the conquered local cities which he had rased to the ground; and, in confirming the cession of this Urartian canton called Urmeniuhi-ni to the Mushki intruders who called themselves Haik, the Medes, and the Persians after them, may have labelled these new owners of this transferred piece of Urartian territory with the Urartian local place-name. If this conjecture carried conviction, it might also explain why the *dahyāuš* that is labelled 'Arminiya' or 'Armina' in the Old Persian text of the Achaemenian official lists is labelled 'Ú-ra-aš-ṭu (i.e. 'Urartu') in the Babylonian texts. Now that Urartu, save for the one district of Urmeniuhi-ni, had been swallowed up in the *dahyāuš* labelled 'Māda', the Babylonian archivists might have applied the label 'Urartu' to a *dahyāuš* which contained the only piece of ex-Urartian territory that had not lost its identity and that had been labelled with its historic Urartian local name in the Old Persian official nomenclature.[6]

1 The two districts together constituted the Tarônîtis of Strabo: *Geographica*, Book XI, chap. xiv, § 5 (C 528).

2 According to Adontz, op. cit., pp. 185 and 193.

3 See Adontz, op. cit., pp. 153–4 and 221, and Prášek, J. V.: *Geschichte der Meder und Perser* (Gotha 1906, Perthes, 2 vols.), vol. i, p. 148.

4 See pp. 604–5, above.

5 Presumably taking this name from their jumping-off ground in a Hayasa, to the north-west of the north-western elbow of the Western Euphrates (*Turcicè* Frat Su, *alias* Qāra Su), which eventually acquired the name 'Lesser Armenia' (see p. 610, n. 2, above).

6 This tentative explanation of the origin of the name 'Arminiya' or 'Armina' is, of

'The Armenia to the West', which Xenophon and his comrades entered in entering the valley of the Teleboas, must in 401 B.C. have been a separate province of the Achaemenian Empire from the 'Armenia' which they had entered when they had left the country of the Kardoukhoi behind them in crossing from the south to the north bank of the Centrîtês (Bohtān); for these two Armenias were under the administration of different viceroys: 'Armenia' under Orontes and Artuchas;[1] 'the Armenia to the West' under Tiribazus.[2] The portion of 'Armenia' through which they marched from the north bank of the Centrîtês to the headwaters of the Eastern Tigris was the province which the Assyrians had called Ulluba[3] and which the post-Alexandrine Hellenic geographers were to call Arzanênê; and the village, containing a residence for the viceroy, through which they passed *en route*,[4] will have been the seat of administration for Orontes' and Artuchas' viceroyalty. As for Tiribazus's viceroyalty 'the Armenia to the West', its name indicates that it must have included the westernmost parts of Armenia Proper, and this means that it must have extended westwards from the Tarônîtis down the valley of the Eastern Euphrates (*Turcicè* Murād Su) through Acilisênê[5] into the extreme north-west corner of the Upper Euphrates Basin, beyond the right bank of the Western Euphrates (*Turcicè* Frat Su, *alias* Qāra Su), which the Hittites had called Hayasa and which, in the Roman Age of Hellenic history, eventually came to be labelled 'Armenia Minor' to indicate that it was the only piece of Armenian territory left outside the 'Armenia Major' which King Artaxias and his successors had united under the sovereignty of their house since 190 B.C.[6] We may also presume that 'the Armenia to the West', which Tiribazus was administering in 401 B.C., included Sophênê, the

course, highly speculative. One alternative possible derivation for 'Armina' is 'Erimena', the name of the father of the last known king of Urartu, Rusas III (*regnabat* 610–585 B.C. according to Adontz, op. cit., p. 193). Another possible derivation is 'Arumu-ni', meaning the country of the Aramaeans who had flooded out of the North Arabian Steppe into Naïri at the turn of the second and the last millennium B.C. (see p. 604, above) and whose name had eventually come to the ears of Hellenic explorers of the southern shore of the Black Sea as the 'Arimoi' of the *Iliad*, Book II, line 783. This last of our three alternative etymologies for the name 'Armina' is commended by the Upper Tigris Basin's latter-day name 'Diyār Bakr', which signifies in Arabic the lands occupied by an Arab Nomad tribe called the Bakr which had pushed its way in from Mesopotamia some time before the Muslim Arab conquest of the Upper Tigris Basin (see Le Strange, G.: *The Lands of the Eastern Caliphate* (Cambridge 1905, University Press), p. 86. On this analogy it might be conjectured that the Upper Tigris Basin had derived its Old Persian name 'Armina', representing an Urartian 'Arumu-ni', from a previous wave of Semitic-speaking Nomad immigrants from the South.

1 See Xenophon, op. cit., Book IV, chap. iii, §§ 3–4.

2 See ibid, chap. iv, § 4.

3 See Forrer, op. cit., pp. 85–87.

4 See Xenophon, op. cit., Book IV, chap. iv, § 2.

5 Strabo makes Acilisênê march with Sophênê along the Antitaurus (i.e. along the watershed between the Upper Tigris Basin and the Upper Euphrates Basin) and also lie between the Taurus and the Euphrates valley bottom ('potamia') above the point where this bends southward (*Geographica*, Book XI, chap. xiv, § 2 (C 527)). The two indications in this passage can be reconciled if 'the Taurus' here means the Dersim Mountains in the quadrilateral between the two arms of the Euphrates, and if 'the Euphrates' here means the Eastern Euphrates (*Turcicè* Murād Su). Acilisênê would then be approximately coextensive with the latter-day Turkish vilayet of Kharpūt. Another passage (*Geographica*, Book XII, chap. iii, § 28 (C 555)), in which Strabo says that Acilisênê is demarcated by the Euphrates from Armenia Minor, would be reconcilable with the previous passage if, in this second passage, 'the Euphrates' means the Western Euphrates (*Turcicè* Frat Su, *alias* Qāra Su).

6 See pp. 626–7, above, and 664–6, below.

Armenian canton in the Upper Tigris Basin[1] which lay immediately to the west of Arzanênê.

If these were approximately the bounds of 'the Armenia to the West' which was one of the political divisions of the Achaemenian Empire in 401 B.C., Tiribazus's viceroyalty was perhaps the matrix of an Armenian successor-state of the Achaemenian Empire, with its capital at Arsamosata in the lower valley of the Eastern Euphrates, in the neighbourhood of Kharpūt, whose King Xerxes[2] was brought to heel by the Seleucid King Antiochus III *circa* 212 B.C.[3] Since Xerxes was subsequently liquidated by his Seleucid conqueror,[4] it looks as if Xerxes' *ci-devant* kingdom, and Tiribazus's *ci-devant* viceroyalty, survived in an Armenian province of the Seleucid Monarchy—consisting of Acilisênê, Sophênê, Odomantis,[5] 'and other territories'—whose military governor, Zariadris,[6] declared his independence after his former Seleucid master Antiochus III's catastrophic defeat by the Romans in 190 B.C.[7]

Zariadris' Armenian successor-state of the Seleucid Empire did not include 'Armenia Minor', to the north-west of the north-western elbow of the Western Euphrates, since we know[8] that, soon after the year 183 B.C., Armenia Minor was under the rule of a 'satrap' of its own, named Mithradates, whose acts show that, notwithstanding his title, he was an independent prince *de facto*. We do not know whether this *de facto* independence had been acquired by Armenia Minor at the time of the fall of the Achaemenian Empire or at the time of the liquidation of Xerxes of Arsamosata or at the time of Zariadris of Sophênê's secession from the Seleucid Empire in 190 B.C. We do know, however, that Zariadris had a brother military governor of a sister Armenian province of the Seleucid Empire who seceded simultaneously, and that the Armenian province which this colleague of Zariadris' named Artaxias was administering at the time lay on the middle course of the River Aras, in the district where, at some date between 190 and 183 B.C.,[9] he laid out a new capital which he called Artaxata after his own name.

1 Strabo, in his *Geographica*, Book XI, chap. xiv, § 2 (C 527), states that Sophênê lay between Mount Masius (i.e. the watershed between the Upper Tigris Basin and the Khabūr Basin) and the Antitaurus (i.e. the watershed between the Upper Tigris Basin and the Upper Euphrates Basin).

2 The name of this King Xerxes of Arsamosata was perhaps commemorated in the name of the province called Xerxênê or Derxênê (the latter-day Dersim) astride the Western Euphrates above Acilisênê and Armenia Minor and below the Caranîtis.

3 See Polybius, Book VIII, chap. 23 (25), as interpreted by Edwyn Bevan in *The House of Seleucus* (London 1902, Edward Arnold, 2 vols.), vol. ii, pp. 15–16.

4 See Bevan, ibid.

5 Odomantis is likely, to judge by its Macedonian name, to have lain on the Mesopotamian side of Mount Masius, between an Anthemusias and a Mygdonia which had likewise been named after cantons of the Seleucids' Macedonian homeland.

6 'The name "Zariadris" obviously contains as its first element Avestan "zaⁱri-", Sanskrit "hari-", meaning "yellow, gold-coloured, yellow-green". In trying to identify its second element, the -dr- in "Zariadris" makes me think of Avestan "vazra-", Sanskrit "vajra-" (the first element in Old Persian "vazraka", meaning "great"), with Median z = Old Persian d from Indo-European ĝ(h), meaning the club of Indra in Sanskrit, which was the thunderbolt or lightning. So "Zariadris" = "zaⁱri-vadri-š" or "zaⁱri-vazri-š", meaning "having (or wielding) the yellow club (the lightning)".'—Note by Professor R. G. Kent.

7 See Strabo, Book XI, chap. xiv, § 5 (C 528) and § 15 (C 531–2).

8 See Bevan, op. cit., vol. ii, p. 123.

9 This must be the *terminus ante quem*, if Strabo (*Geographica*, Book XI, chap. xiv, § 6 (C 528)) is correct in reporting that Artaxias employed Hannibal's services in this piece of town-planning.

If, in Achaemenian parlance, the name 'Armina' or 'Arminiya' had signified, as we have argued that it did, not the former Chaldian Kingdom of Urartu, but its western neighbours Hayasa (*Latinè* Armenia Minor) and Naïri (*Latinè* Acilisênê, Sophênê, and Arzanênê), which, at the moment of the collapse of the Assyrian Empire, had been overrun by Gurdi's war-band of Phrygian-speaking Mushki barbarians, the Haik, it is surprising to find the name Armenia adhering, in 190 B.C., to a district on the course of the Middle Aras which not only lay, as the Teleboas Valley likewise lay, within the former frontiers of the Kingdom of Urartu, but was actually situated in the extreme north-eastern corner of the Kingdom of Urartu's former domain, at the farthest possible remove from the region, adjoining the western and south-western frontiers of Urartu, which had been overrun by Gurdi's war-band at the turn of the seventh and sixth centuries B.C. At what date, and in what circumstances, had the name 'Armenia' come, by the year 190 B.C., to extend as far afield as the middle course of the Aras Valley, where at that date Artaxias was administering an Armenian province on the Seleucid Monarchy's behalf, and where, after declaring his independence, he founded the city of Artaxata?

Recollecting that, in the Achaemenian official lists, the Old Persian name 'Armina' is rendered as 'Urartu' in the Babylonian versions of the texts, we might be inclined, on first thoughts, to jump to the conclusion that, when Gurdi's war-band had crossed the north-western elbow of the Western Euphrates (Frat Su, *alias* Qāra Su) towards the close of the seventh century B.C., they had overrun, not only the Assyrian dominions in Naïri and the Teleboas Valley, but the whole of the adjoining Kingdom of Urartu as well, and that, in consequence, Urartu had been brigaded by Median and Persian empire-builders with Naïri and Hayasa to constitute the Achaemenian *dahyāuš* called 'Armina' within a sub-empire that also included both Cappadocia and the strip of country between Armina and the Black Sea, instead of being brigaded with the Urmīyah Basin (Matianê) and Adiabênê to constitute Herodotus's Taxation District No. 18 within a Greater Media. Might not this association be just another of Herodotus's blunders? And would not the identification of Xenophon's 'Armenia' with Urartu, and of Xenophon's 'Armenia to the West' with Naïri plus Hayasa, make sense of Xenophon's data as well as Strabo's? This explanation of the adhesion of the name 'Armina' to the middle course of the River Aras in 190 B.C. would be an attractively simple one, but, on further consideration, we shall see that, after all, it will not fit the facts.

In the first place, Xenophon's 'Armenia', which lay in the Upper Tigris Basin between the north bank of the River Centrîtês (Bohtān) and the Tigris-Euphrates watershed, can hardly have formed part of the same Achaemenian viceroyalty as Urartu if the Teleboas Valley belonged to a different viceroyalty called 'the Armenia to the West', since the head of the Teleboas Valley is traversed by the only practicable route between the Upper Tigris Basin and the Basin of Lake Van, which had been the former Kingdom of Urartu's nucleus and heart, so that an 'Armenia to the West' that comprised the Teleboas Valley would virtually have insulated 'Armenia' and Urartu from one another. In the second place the passage (whatever its provenance may be) in which Strabo informs us that, in 190 B.C., the middle valley of the River Aras was already Armenian territory, contains further information which indicates that this was the only part of the former domain of the Kingdom of Urartu that, at this date, was, as yet, Armenian. Strabo not only states explicitly[1] that Armenia had been 'a small country' down to the time of Zariadris' and Artaxias' simultaneous declarations of independence in 190 B.C.; he goes on, in this passage and in a subsequent one,[2] to give a catalogue of the successive territorial acquisitions by which Artaxias and his successors progressively built up a Kingdom of Armenia Major which, in Strabo's own day, extended from the east bank of the Western Euphrates to the western shore of the Caspian Sea round the debouchure of the rivers Aras and Kur, and from the watershed between the Khabūr and the Tigris along Mount Masius to the south bank of the River Kur and to the farther side of its head-waters.

This progressive aggrandisement of Artaxias' Armenian kingdom was crowned by his descendant Tigranes' annexation of the sister Armenian kingdom of the House of Zariadris;[3] but this eventual preponderance of the Artaxiads over the Zariadrids was the cumulative result of a previous progressive expansion of the Artaxiad dominions in other quarters at the expense of divers non-Armenian peoples and states; and, in this context, Strabo gives us three pieces of information which throw light on our present problem. In the first place the Armenian language—i.e. the historic Armenian language, of Indo-European origin, which had been carried from Hayasa to the east side of the Euphrates by Gurdi's Phrygian-speaking Mushki followers whose own name for themselves was 'Haik'—had become the common language of the heterogeneous population of Armenia Major only as a consequence of the political unification of all these peoples under the Artaxiad Crown. In the second place, one of the countries at whose expense the Artaxiads had enlarged their dominions had been Media. In the third place the Median territories which the Artaxiads had annexed to their expanding Kingdom of Armenia Major had been Kaspianê, Phaunîtis, and Basoropeda.[4]

Of these three territories which, according to Strabo, had previously belonged to Media, one, namely Basoropeda (*Armeniacè* Vaspuragan), lay on the east side of the Van Basin in the heart of Urartu and therefore within the limits of the canton which Herodotus calls 'Alarodioi' and which he associates, not with Armenia, but with the Saspeires and the Matiênoi who, together with these Alarodioi, constitute, as we have seen,[5] his Taxation District No. 18. Another of the three ex-Median districts annexed by the Artaxiads, namely Kaspianê, lay in the Lower Aras-Kur Basin and is assigned by Herodotus, as we have likewise seen,[6] to his Taxation District No. 15, labelled 'Sakai and Kaspioi'. We must infer that in 190 B.C. both the Lower Aras-Kur Basin and the

[1] In *Geographica*, Book XI, chap. xiv, § 5 (C 528).
[2] Ibid., § 15 (C 531–2).
[3] Ibid., § 15 (C 532).
[4] Ibid., § 5 (C 528).
[5] On pp. 628–32, above.
[6] On pp. 626–8, above.

Van Basin were still Median, and not yet Armenian, in the political sense, and *a fortiori* that they were then still non-Armenian-speaking countries, considering that, according to Strabo, the Armenian language made its way there only in the wake of the Artaxiad House's conquests.

The Media to which these two districts thus still belonged in 190 B.C. will have been the Media Atropatênê (the latter-day Azerbaijan) that was one of the Iranian successor-states of the Achaemenian Empire; and we may infer that, in the scramble for possession of the former Achaemenian dominions after the overthrow of the last Darius by Alexander, the territories on which Atropates, the founder of the successor-state that came to be called after him, had succeeded in laying hands had been the Herodotean Taxation District No. 18, save for Adiabênê, together with the Herodotean Taxation District No. 15. Media Atropatênê will have continued to hold the portions of these ex-Achaemenian territories comprised in Kaspianê, Basoropeda (Vaspuragan), and the Phaunîtis until it lost them to a rising Artaxiad Power at some date subsequent to the year 190 B.C. But, like the Basin of Lake Van, which still belonged to Media Atropatênê at that date, the middle valley of the River Aras, which was the nucleus of the Artaxiad Kingdom and which was already Armenian in 190 B.C., had been part of the former Kingdom of Urartu and must therefore likewise have been included in the Herodotean Taxation District No. 18 originally. At what date, then, had this section of the Aras Valley become Armenian instead of Median?

In the absence of any other information on this point, we can only say that there is no evidence to indicate that the transfer had taken place until after the fall of the Achaemenian Empire, while there is one piece of evidence which suggests that the district in the middle valley of the Aras, of which Artaxias was military governor, on behalf of the Seleucid King Antiochus III, in 190 B.C., may have been taken from Media Atropatênê and annexed to Armenia by Antiochus III himself after his liquidation of the Armenian King Xerxes of Arsamosata at some date after his subjugation of Xerxes in 212 B.C. The conqueror, whoever he may have been, who annexed the middle valley of the Aras to Armenia must have arrived there by forcing his way into the Aras Basin up the valley of the Western Euphrates and over the Frat Su (Qāra Su)-Aras watershed; and, if there is any substance in our conjecture[1] that the name of the province called Derxênê (Xerxênê), astride the Western Euphrates immediately above Acilisênê, commemorates Xerxes of Arsamosata's conquest and annexation of this district, we may further infer that Derxênê also marks the limit of Xerxes' conquests in this direction. If so, the middle course of the Aras must have been annexed to Armenia by some successor of Xerxes; and his only successor, down to the year 190 B.C., had been Antiochus III.

On this showing, we may abide by our previous finding that, in the Achaemenian Age, no portion of the former Kingdom of Urartu except the Teleboas Valley (the Tarônîtis) was included in the *dahyāuš* whose Old Persian name was 'Armina', notwithstanding the fact that the

[1] On p. 663, n. 2, above.

official Babylonian rendering of 'Armina' is 'Urartu'; and we may confirm our identification of the Achaemenian 'Armina' with a territory confined to the Upper Tigris Basin and the north-west corner of the Upper Euphrates Basin, corresponding to the Assyrian 'Naïri' together with the Hittite 'Hayasa'.[1]

The peoples lying between Armenia Proper and the Black Sea whose country was embraced, on the political map, in the Viceroyalty of Armenia, while it constituted, on the fiscal map, the Herodotean Taxation District No. 19, were, as enumerated by Herodotus in his gazetteer and rearranged in their apparent geographical sequence from east to west, the refugee *Mâres* who had inherited their name from the Hurrian or perhaps Eurasian Nomad 'mariannu'[2] and were to bequeath it to the latter-day Georgian canton Imerethia in the upper basin of the River Rhion (Phasis); the refugee *Moskhoi* who were to bequeath their name to the latter-day Georgian canton Meskhethi round the head-waters of the River Kur; the *Makrônes* on the northward descent from the watershed on which, in 400 B.C., Xenophon and his comrades were to catch their first glimpse of the Black Sea;[3] the *Mossynoikoi* along the seaboard to the west of Trebizond;[4] and the *Tibarênoi* along the seaboard to the west of the Mossynoikoi.[5]

The Herodotean Taxation District No. 19, which these peoples occupied between them, must have been bounded on the west, like Armina, by the Viceroyalty of Katpatuka, and on the east by 'the Kolkhoi and adjoining peoples as far as the Caucasis Range' who, according to Herodotus,[6] were 'gift-bringers' and not tax-payers. In 400 B.C. there were Colchians astride the road leading from the country of the Makrônes to Trebizond;[7] and, if, in the Achaemenian Age, the Colchians occupied the seaboard without a break from this point eastwards to the Caucasus, they must have insulated the Mâres and Moskhoi from the Makrônes, Mossynoikoi, and Tibarênoi—unless the Mâres and Moskhoi were at this time located somewhere farther to the west than the Georgian cantons that were eventually to be called after them.[8] However that may

[1] In this connexion it is noteworthy that, in the field-state of Xerxes expeditionary force (Herodotus, Book VII, chap. 73), the Armenians are associated, not with the Urartians ('Alarodioi'), but with the Phrygians and other peoples of Central Anatolia. They are equipped like, and are brigaded with, the Phrygians (of whom they are stated, in this passage, to be an offshoot); and the Armeno-Phrygian equipment is described as being a sub-variety of the Paphlagonian. We may guess that the culture represented by this equipment was really Hittite rather than Paphlagonian in origin.

[2] See the Note on Chronology in x. 200–2.

[3] See Xenophon, op. cit., Book IV, chap. vii, § 27, and chap. viii, § 1.

[4] See ibid., Book V, chap. iv.

[5] See ibid., Book V, chap. v, §§ 1–3.

[6] In Book III, chap. 97.

[7] See Xenophon, op. cit., Book IV, chap. viii, §§ 8–9.

[8] In Anatolia, as in Iran, the brigading of the national contingents, as described in the field-state of Xerxes' expeditionary force, partly cuts across their grouping for civil administrative purposes, as described in the gazetteer of Darius's taxation districts. The two peoples at the two extremities of District No. 19—the Moskhoi and the Tibarênoi—are brigaded under one command; the Makrônes and Mossynoikoi under another; and the Mâres with the Colchians, who were a non-tax-paying people not included within the bounds of the Nineteenth District. To judge by Herodotus's description of their equipment, the Colchians, as well as all the peoples of the Nineteenth District, belonged to the same cultural group as the Saspeires and the Alarodioi. The Tibarênoi, Makrônes, and Mossynoikoi are paraded in Moschian equipment, the Kolkhoi, Alarodioi, and

be, Herodotus's 'Kolkhoi and adjoining peoples as far as the Caucasis Range' seem more likely than the peoples in his Taxation District No. 19 to represent the *Ākaufačiyā* ('the People of the Mountains') whose name appears in 'XPh' alone among the official lists.

The Kingdom called *Cilicia* in Greek and *Khilakku* in Assyrian is left unmentioned in the official lists of *dahyāva* in deference to its juridical status of sovereign independence, though its *de facto* relation to the Achaemenian Empire may be more accurately conveyed by Herodotus in his erroneous inclusion of it among Darius's original twenty taxation districts as his District No. 4.[1]

At the turn of the eighth and seventh centuries B.C. Khilakku had been merely one of nine or ten petty principalities in South-Eastern Anatolia, between the Upper Euphrates and the Upper Halys, over which the Assyrians had asserted a suzerainty that had been short-lived and at no time very firmly established; but, in the subsequent scramble at the turn of the seventh and sixth centuries B.C. for Assyria's derelict dominions, Khilakku had distinguished herself from her neighbours by her Autolycan deftness as 'a snapper-up of unconsidered trifles'[2] and by the tact—almost equal to the Vicar of Bray's—with which she had succeeded in keeping on good terms with surrounding Great Powers who were on bad terms with one another. The measure of her achievement was that, after having enlarged her original patrimony four- or five-fold, she had succeeded, without having to forfeit any of her territorial gains, in securing a place for herself within the framework of the Achaemenian universal state on the juridical footing of a sovereign independent ally of the Imperial Power.

Three indications of the *tracée* of the Kingdom of Cilicia's expanded frontiers within the Achaemenian imperial framework are to be found in Herodotus's history. This Achaemenian Cilicia marched with the Viceroyalty of Armenia along a navigable section of the River Euphrates where the Great North-West Road crossed the river out of Armenia into Cilicia.[3] On the Mediterranean shore—and the once land-locked statelet of Cilicia now had a long and valuable coastline on the Mediterranean—the boundary between Cilicia and the Viceroyalty of Syria was Cape Posidêïum (*Arabicè* Ras-al-Basit), that is to say, a point on the coast to the south of the mouth of the River Orontes.[4] On the Anatolian Plateau, in the region containing the city of Mazaka—where, on a post-Alexandrine Hellenic map, the name 'Cilicia' still attached to one of the provinces of a latter-day Kingdom of Inland Cappadocia—the Kingdom of Cilicia in the Achaemenian Age bestrode the River Halys from a point below the river's exit from the Armenian highlands where it had its source to a point beyond its southward bend where Cilicia gave way on the right bank to the country of the Western Matiênoi and on the left bank to Phrygia.[5]

Saspeires in sub-Moschian equipment. We may guess that the culture represented by this equipment was really Urartian rather than Mushkian in its origin.

[1] See pp. 592–3, above.

[2] Shakspeare: *The Winter's Tale*, Act IV, scene ii.

[3] Herodotus, Book V, chap. 52.

[4] Book III, chap. 91.

[5] Book I, chap. 72.

In terms of the political geography of the Assyrian Age, these indications tell us that, to the south, Khilakku had annexed at least six once independent principalities: Tukhāna (*Graecè* Tyana) and Atuna or Tuna (*Graecè* Tynna) between the original Khilakku and the Taurus Range; Tabal (Bit Burutash) in the Antitaurus; Qu'e[1] (*Graecè* Akhaioi);[2] Sam'al[3] in the North Amanus; and Unqi, astride the lower reaches of the River Orontes, where first Antigonus Monophthalmus and then Seleucus Nîcâtôr was to choose the site for the capital city of a South-West Asian empire.[4] To the east, Khilakku must have annexed at least two principalities, for, as we have seen,[5] the Cilician territory on the west bank of the Euphrates into which the Great North-West Road ran after crossing the river out of Armenia must have been the region round Malatīyah (*Graecè* Melitênê, *Assyriacè* Meliddu), and Khilakku could not have annexed Meliddu without having also annexed at least the intervening south-western part of the principality of Kammanu.[6]

We may also guess that Khilakku had acquired Kummukhu (*Graecè* Commagênê) along the Euphrates immediately to the south of Meliddu and immediately to the north of the river's western elbow, and Gurgum (whose capital Marqasi was to bequeath its name to Mar'ash) between Kummukhu and Sam'al. On the other hand the Babylonians must have managed to lay hands on Carchemish, Arpaddu, and Til Turi between the elbow of the Euphrates and the eastern frontiers of Sam'al and Unqi; for they undoubtedly had access overland, through territory of their own, from the elbow of the Euphrates to their dominions in Ebir-nari. Again, Herodotus's itinerary of the Great North-West Road informs us that Til-Garimmu—a province of Kammanu in the upper basin of the Tokhma Su right-bank tributary of the Euphrates, immediately adjoining Meliddu to the north-west—must also have lain outside the bounds of the Kingdom of Cilicia and must have been included within the Achaemenian *dahyāuš* Katpatuka.

We can be sure of this because Herodotus tells us[7] that, from the point where the Great North-West Road entered Cilicia after crossing the Euphrates out of Armenia, this road ran through Cilician territory for the distance of only $15\frac{1}{2}$ parasangs (just over 89 kilometres); and, on the assumption that the point of entry into Cilicia was the river-crossing on the road from Kharpūt to Malatīyah, Herodotus's figure yields us

1 Qu'e, with its well-placed ports and with the largest area of prime agricultural land to be found anywhere in Anatolia west of Lydia and the Dascylîtis, was Khilakku's greatest prize.

2 Hyp-Akhaioi according to Herodotus, Book VII, chap. 91.

3 The name survived as late as A.H. 163, in the reign (A.D. 775–85) of the 'Abbasid Caliph Mahdī (see Ahmad al-Balādhurī: *Kitab Futūh al-Buldān*, vol. i, translated by P. K. Hitti (New York 1916, Columbia University Press), pp. 263–4).

4 See p. 201, above.

5 On p. 629, n. 4, *ad finem*, above.

6 While this principality of Kammanu that was Khilakku's eastern neighbour perhaps derived its name from the city of Comana, the latter-day province of the Kingdom of Inland Cappadocia called Chammanênê, in the bend of the Halys where Herodotus locates the Western Matiênoi, was possibly called after Prince Kamanā or Kamamas (? *Hebraicè* Haman, *Graecè* Haimôn) of Carchemish, whose father King Aias campaigned in South-East Anatolia in the first half of the eighth century B.C. (see Cavaignac, E.: *Le Problème Hittite* (Paris 1936, Leroux), p. 165; Delaporte, L.: *Les Hittites* (Paris 1936, La Renaissance du Livre), pp. 335–6).

7 In Book V, chap. 52.

two pieces of information: from the Euphrates crossing the road must have run north-westwards over the Uzun Yaila to Sivas in the upper valley of the Qyzyl Irmāq (Halys), and it must have run out of Cilicia into Cappadocia only a short distance to the north-west of Malatīyah town, that is to say, at the boundary between the former principality of Meliddu and Til-Garimmu.[1] Herodotus's figure of 15½ parasangs allows of no other location for this sector of the frontier between Cilicia and Cappadocia, and *a fortiori* it allows of no other alinement for the Great North-West Road in this stretch; for either of the two alternative routes running westward from Malatīyah via Mazaca (the latter-day Qaysari), in contrast to either of those running north-westward from Malatīyah via Sivas, would carry the road through what must indubitably have been Cilician territory for many times the distance—only 15½ parasangs—that Herodotus gives for this Cilician section. An alinement via Sivas also has two other points in its favour: it would allow for the at first sight surprisingly long distance of 104 parasangs which Herodotus gives for the Cappadocian section of the road from the Cilician-Cappadocian frontier to the crossing of the Halys out of Cappadocia (in the narrower sense) into Phrygia; and it would allow for an alinement through Hattusas (Boghazqalʿeh), the site of the former capital of the Hittite Empire, which must once have been the centre from which all roads in Eastern Anatolia radiated.

What were the affinities of the people, called Khilakku in Assyrian and Kilikes in Greek, who had built this miniature empire *circa* 600 B.C.? When the principality of Khilakku makes its first appearance in history at the turn of the eighth and seventh centuries B.C. it has Mita's Mushki

1 Herodotus tells us that, where the road crossed the Cilico-Cappadocian frontier, it ran through a pair of gates and passed by a pair of guard-houses. This description in the Herodotean itinerary of the Great North-West Road is to be interpreted in the light of an eyewitness's account of the security arrangements on the Cilico-Syrian frontier in 401 B.C. At this point in their anabasis, Xenophon and his comrades passed through a pair of gates in a pair of walls extending from the Mediterranean shoreline to the cliffs overhanging it. The north wall was manned by a Cilician garrison, the south wall (in normal times) by an imperial garrison, and there was a no-man's-land, three hundred yards wide, in between (Xenophon, op. cit., Book I, chap. iv, §§ 4–5). Evidently this was the layout at road-crossings between autonomous and imperial territory where there was no frontier river to provide a natural insulator such as the Euphrates provided between Cilicia and Armenia, and the Lower Khabūr between Arabāya and Syria. There were gates, for example, between Arabāya and Bābiruš (see ibid., chap. v, § 5); and Xenophon's mention of a pair of guard-houses, as well as a pair of gates, on the frontier between Cilicia and Syria suggests that, on the Great North-West Road, the pair of gates mentioned by Herodotus may have been located at the point, a few miles to the north-west of Melitênê on the more easterly of the two Melitênê–Sebasteia roads, which is labelled 'praetorium' in the Roman itineraries (see J. G. C. Anderson's map *Asia Minor* (London 1903, John Murray)).

It may be noted, in passing, that Xenophon's account of his itinerary shows that the territory of the 'sovereign independent' Kingdom of Cilicia had been drastically reduced, since the date of Herodotus's official sources, by the Imperial Power which was in theory Cilicia's ally. In 401 B.C. Dana (i.e. Tyana) was already part of an Imperial Viceroyalty of Cappadocia (Xenophon, op. cit., Book I, chap. ii, § 20); and this means that the Imperial Government must have detached from Cilicia by this time not only Tyana but the Cilicia astride the River Halys which had been the historical nucleus of the Cilician Kingdom. Moreover, the pair of gates and guard-houses which in 401 B.C. marked the frontier between Cilicia and an Imperial Viceroyalty of Syria stood between the shore of the Mediterranean and the cliffs of the Amanus on the east coast of the Gulf of Alexandretta (ibid., chap. iv, §§ 1–5); and this means that by this time the former principality of Unqi had been transferred from Cilicia to Syria. Thus by 401 B.C. Cilicia had already been reduced to its latter-day limits between the Taurus and the Amanus.

for its neighbours on the south-west in Lycaonia and the ubiquitous Gurdi's Mushki for its neighbours first on the south, in Tyana, in the reign of Tiglath-Pileser III of Assyria (*regnabat* 746–727 B.C.),[1] and then on the north-east in Til-Garimmu, astride the road running south-east via Naïri to Assyria, in 695 B.C.[2] Our line of least resistence would be to guess that the Khilakku were Phrygians like their neighbours; and this guess would not conflict with the Hellenic evidence; for, in the earliest appearance of the Kilikes in Hellenic literature, they are located in the south-west corner of Hellespontine Phrygia, at the head of the Gulf of Edremid (Adramyttium), in Thêbê under Mount Plakos. Hector's wife Andromachê was one of them, and her father had been king of this north-western Cilicia till Achilles had killed him and sacked Thêbê.[3] It looks as if the Kilikes had been the advance-guard of the Phrygian barbarians who had broken out of South-East Europe into the Hittite World at the turn of the thirteenth and twelfth centuries B.C. The Kilikes who had settled at Thêbê would be a detachment that had wheeled to the right after their passage from the European to the Asiatic shore of the Dardanelles; the Khilakku of Mazaka would be a detachment that had wheeled to the left, marched eastwards along the plain between Dascylium and the Mysian Olympus, and climbed on to the Anatolian Plateau at In Önü, like their Hittite predecessors and like their Galatian successors some fifteen hundred years later.

Herodotus's Taxation District No. 3, which included the *dahyāuš* called *Katpatuka* (Cappadocia), had two peculiarities. The first of these was its size. From the upper basin of the Tokhma Su tributary of the Euphrates and from the upper reaches of the Halys it extended right across Anatolia to the Asiatic shore of the Dardanelles, and it was broad as well as long, for there is no indication that it embraced less than the whole of Inland Phrygia, and that country extended south-westwards into the upper basin of the River Maeander. The second peculiarity of this taxation district was that it straddled a former international frontier —uniting, as it did, ex-Median territory to the east of the Middle and Lower Halys with ex-Lydian territory to the west of it.

This feature of Herodotus's District No. 3 was peculiar without being unique, considering that his District No. 14 similarly united Harahvatiš with the three south-eastern cantons of Pārsa; and, even if there had not been this parallel case, there could not have been any doubt about the facts. The administrative union of ex-Lydian territory to the west of the Halys with the ex-Median *dahyāuš* Katpatuka was attested by the consensus of several different pieces of evidence, positive as well as negative. In the first place it was on record that a territory administered from Dascylium, on or near the south shore of the Sea of Marmara, had been detached from Lydia since Cyrus II's day.[4] In the second place this ex-Lydian territory did not appear under any separate and distinctive

[1] See König, op. cit., p. 15.
[2] See Forrer, op. cit., p. 80.
[3] *Iliad*, Book VI, ll. 395–7 and 414–28.
[4] We know from Herodotus, Book III, chaps. 120, 126, and 127, that Orœtes, who had been appointed Viceroy of Sardis (Sparda) by Cyrus II, had a colleague and rival named Mitrabates who was governor of 'the province of Dascylium', i.e. the northern and north-eastern parts of the former Lydian Empire (see p. 611, n. 1, above).

name of its own in any of the official lists of *dahyāva*;[1] and, among all the *dahyāva* named in any of the lists, there is no *dahyāuš* except Katpatuka to which this ex-Lydian territory could have been attached—as it must have been attached to one or other recognized *dahyāuš* if it was not recognized as a separate one in its own right. The only *dahyāva* on the mainland of Anatolia that are named in any of the lists are Sparda (Sardis), which was the viceroyalty from which the Dascylîtis had been detached; 'the Ionians on the mainland', who were insulated from Dascylium by the Viceroyalty of Sardis; Karkā (Caria), which was insulated from Dascylium *a fortiori*; and Katpatuka. The process of exhaustion seems to force upon us the conclusion that, at the dates at which all our six official lists were drawn up, the ex-Lydian territory whose seat of administration was at Dascylium was attached to the ex-Median *dahyāuš* Katpatuka.

This conclusion, which is thus presented to the investigator by the negative evidence of the official lists taken in conjunction with Herodotus's mention of a separate governorship of Dascylium in the days of Orœtes' administration at Sardis, is positively corroborated by Herodotus's description of the third taxation district in his gazetteer; for he describes this district as including, in addition to the Cappadocians (*alias* Syrioi), who lived to the east of the River Halys, five peoples who lived to the west of the Halys: namely the *Paphlagones* immediately to the west of the Lower Halys; the *Mariandynoi* to the west of the Paphlagones, in the hinterland of the Hellenic city Heraclea Pontica; the *Asiatic Thracians*, between the debouchure of the River Sangarius into the Black Sea and the Asiatic shore of the Bosphorus; the *Phrygians*, whose domain extended from the southern shore of the Sea of Marmara southwards to the headwaters of the River Maeander and south-eastwards, through Lycaonia, to the north-western face of the Taurus Range; and the *Asiatic Hellespontine Hellenes* along the Anatolian shore of the Bosphorus, the Sea of Marmara, and the Dardanelles. The names of two other peoples in this district—the *Western Matiênoi* within the southward bend of the River Halys and the enigmatic *Ligyes*—are added in the field-state of Xerxes' expeditionary force.[2]

[1] Arguments against the conjecture that this continental territory may be the *dahyāuš* designated by the label 'those in the Sea' are set out on p. 679, n. 1, below.

[2] See Herodotus, Book VII, chap. 72, and, for the Western Matiênoi, also Book I, chap. 72. The evidence about the location of the Western Matiênoi is examined in the Note on Chronology in x. 201. As for the Ligyes, it is not inconceivable that they might have been the left wing of the Latin-speaking people whose right wing comes into the light of history in the second century B.C. along the French and Italian Rivieras and in the North-Western Appennines. The Hittites themselves were an Indo-European-speaking people of the centum group whose language—extant in some of the documents in the Hittite Imperial Archives retrieved at Boghazqal'eh—was considered by Modern Western philologists to have a closer affinity with Latin than with any other Indo-European language. In this connexion it might be noted that the Illyrians—another Indo-European-speaking people of the centum group who on the European side of the Black Sea Straits were at this time wedged in between the Italici and the Thracians—had also made their way into Anatolia, to judge by the name of the Mount Ellurya (i.e. Illyria) which figures in the political geography of the Hittite World in the second millennium B.C. as the scene of a battle between the Hittites and the Gasga in the sixteenth year of Mursil II's reign (see Delaporte, L.: *Les Hittites* (Paris 1936, La Renaissance du Livre), p. 122). An immigration of Illyrian peoples into Anatolia is also attested by the name of the Veneti, occupying a strip of the Anatolian coast to the east of the Mariandynoi, whom the field-state of the Trojans' allies in the Second Book of the *Iliad* (ll. 851–5) appears to equate

Another piece of information which confirms the official lists' testimony *ex silentio* that the Dascylîtis was at this time united with Katpatuka is Ctesias' statement[1] that, as a prelude to Darius's campaign beyond the Bosphorus against the Scythian horde on the Great Western Bay of the Eurasian Steppe, the Viceroy of Cappadocia was sent on a naval reconnaissance; for the viceroyalty whose viceroy was selected for this mission is likely to have been the north-westernmost viceroyalty in the Achaemenian Empire within the imperial frontiers as these stood before Darius inaugurated the forward movement into Europe.

In the light of the divers pieces of evidence reviewed above, we may perhaps now take it as proven that the Achaemenian viceroyalty designated 'Cappadocia' by Ctesias in this passage embraced the whole of Herodotus's Taxation District No. 3, including the ex-Lydian territory, to the west of the River Halys, that was administered from Dascylium.[2] But in the light of Herodotus's description of his Taxation District No. 13—if we have been right in interpreting this as the description of a viceroyalty which has been mistakenly applied by Herodotus to one of this viceroyalty's fiscal subdivisions[3]—we have now to ask ourselves whether the viceroyalty designated 'Cappadocia' by Ctesias may not have included other taxation districts besides Herodotus's District No. 3. If the formula 'Paktyïkê and Armenioi and the adjoining peoples as far as the Black Sea' does in reality designate, not just a taxation district, but a viceroyalty embracing the three taxation districts numbered 13, 3, and 19 in Herodotus's gazetteer, then the viceroyalty in which Herodotus's Taxation District No. 3 was embraced will have united an ex-Lydian Dascylîtis not merely with an ex-Median Cappadocia, but with an ex-Median Armenia as well, and this viceroyalty will have extended eastwards from the eastern shores of the Straits not merely as far as the upper reaches of the Halys but as far as the eastern boundaries of an Achaemenian Armenia over against an Achaemenian Urartu and Adiabênê that were included in Herodotus's Taxation District No. 18 and in the Viceroyalty of Media.[4] It will, in fact, have included all the country on the Asiatic side of the Straits that had been overrun by Phrygian invaders from Europe between the end of the thirteenth and the beginning of the sixth century B.C.

This conclusion that Armenia and Cappadocia-cum-Dascylîtide together constituted a single viceroyalty in Darius's day is not impugned by the appearance of both the names 'Arminiya' and 'Katpatuka' side by side in all our six official lists. We have already noticed[5] that at least nine of the other *dahyāva* named in the lists never constituted either separate viceroyalties or even separate taxation districts so far as we know; and, if Modern Western scholars were right in taking the repeated

with the Paphlagonians, and by the name of the city of Dardanus, which was to cling to the straits on whose Asiatic shore this Dardanian settlement had once stood.

1 See Ctesias: *Persica*, Books XII–XIII, § 47 (16), in J. Gilmore's edition (London 1888, Macmillan), pp. 150–1.

2 Professor G. G. Cameron comments: 'Almost—but not quite—I am fully persuaded now that the Greek Dascylium is Katpatuka.'

3 See pp. 604–11, above.

4 The *tracée* of these boundaries is discussed on pp. 660–7, above.

5 On p. 589, above.

juxtaposition of names of *dahyāva* in the lists—e.g. the juxtaposition of Suguda and Bākhtriš in all six—as evidence that *dahyāva* thus bracketed together were included in one and the same viceroyalty,[1] this would apply to Arminiya and Katpatuka, which are placed next to one another, in that order, in four out of Darius's five lists (namely in 'DB', 'DPe', 'DSe', 'DNa'), while in the fifth Darian list, 'DZd', they appear to have been separated only by the single name 'Yauna'. This is presumptive evidence that, at any rate down to the end of Darius's reign, Arminiya and Katpatuka, like Bākhtriš and Suguda, were combined to constitute a single viceroyalty.[2]

A viceroyalty of this size proved, however, too unwieldy to be retained intact. In the field-state of Xerxes' expeditionary force the constituent peoples of the Herodotean Taxation District No. 3 alone are already distributed among no less than four separate brigades—one consisting of the Paphlagones and Western Matiênoi and a second of the Mariandynoi, Ligyes, and Cappadocians, while the Asiatic Thracian contingent constitutes an independent command and the Phrygians are brigaded with the Armenians of Herodotus's Taxation District No. 13. At least as early as 408 B.C., when Cyrus the Younger was appointed by his father King Darius II to an extensive civil jurisdiction and military command in Anatolia, the original Viceroyalty of Armenia-cum-Cappadociâ was broken up; for Cyrus the Younger was made Viceroy of Cappadocia and of 'Great Phrygia' (i.e. Southern Phrygia), but Northern (*alias* 'Hellespontine') Phrygia was not—though Lydia was—included in his sub-empire,[3] and we may gather *ex silentio* that Armenia was not included in it either. By 401 B.C. the Viceroyalty of Cappadocia had been compensated for its loss of Armenia and the two Phrygias by having been enlarged, at the expense of the Kingdom of Cilicia, by the addition of the Tyanîtis[4] and therefore also, by implication, of Cilicia-

1 See p. 589, above.

2 Since it is hardly conceivable that the whole of a viceroyalty embracing Armenia can have been administered from Dascylium, at the far western extremity of its domain, we must suppose that Orœtes of Sardis' contemporary Mitrabates of Dascylium was, not a viceroy in his own right, but the lieutenant-governor of a viceroy whose seat of administration was more centrally situated. 'Lieutenant-governor' is the literal meaning of the Greek word ὕπαρχος, by which Herodotus designates Mitrabates in Book III, chap. 126; and, considering the vagueness of the Hellenic usage of such terms, this interpretation is not invalidated by the use of the same designation in chap. 120 for Orœtes, who was certainly a viceroy and not a viceroy's subordinate. Considering that the Dascylîtis must have been detached by Cyrus II from Lydia as a precautionary measure to guard against the possibility of a repetition of Paktyas' revolt (see pp. 588–9, above), we should have expected *a priori* to find the Dascylîtis not merely detached from a dissident viceroyalty but attached, in order to make assurance doubly sure, to some other viceroyalty on whose loyalty Cyrus II could rely—as we may presume that he could rely on the loyalty of Armenia, in virtue of his being Astyages' heir. Even as it was, Orœtes found himself able to liquidate Mitrabates and re-annex the Dascylîtis to the Viceroyalty of Sardis (Sparda) during the anarchic year 522–521 B.C. If the Dascylîtis had been erected into a separate viceroyalty on its own account, and had not been attached to Armenia besides being detached from Lydia, it would have remained still more helplessly exposed to the risk of aggression by an ambitious viceroy of Sardis.

3 See Xenophon, op. cit. Book I, chap. ix, § 7, cited on p. 183, n. 7, above, and in IX. viii. 548, n. 1. Considering that Pharnabazus, the governor of the Dascylîtis, was not subordinated to Cyrus the Younger in 408 B.C., we may perhaps infer that Pharnabazus had already, before that, been a viceroy in his own right, and that his father Pharnacês, who had been governor of the Dascylîtis as early as the summer of 430 B.C. (see Thucydides, Book II, chap. 67), had previously enjoyed the same status.

4 See Xenophon, op. cit., Book I, chap. ii, § 20.

on-Halys as well. By the same date, Armenia had not merely been detached from Cappadocia but had been partitioned into two separate viceroyalties, as we have seen.[1]

The *dahyāuš* called *Sparda* in the official lists is Herodotus's Taxation District No. 2, whose constituent peoples are the *Mysoi*, *Lydoi*, *Lasonioi*, *Kabalioi*, and *Hygennees*.

The Spardiyā—whose name was adopted as the official label for this *dahyāuš* because it had already attached itself to Sardeis, the city that was the seat of the local administration in virtue of having once been the capital of a Lydian Empire—were the western vanguard of the host of Eurasian Nomad peoples who had broken out of the Steppe into South-Western Asia between the Caspian Sea and the Pamirs before the end of the eighth century B.C.[2]

At their first emergence above our historical horizon, we see the Saparda (as the Assyrians called them), already poised on the western rim of the Iranian Plateau, astride the road leading down via Behistan towards Babylonia.[3] In the third decade of the seventh century B.C. we find Esarhaddon battling with a coalition of Medes, Saparda, and Cimmerians under the leadership of the barbarian war-lord Kashtaritu (Khšathrita);[4] and, though Assyria's victory in this round of the struggle was registered in the establishment of three new departments labelled Madai, Bit Kari, and Saparda, these territorial gains had all been lost again before 667 B.C.[5] The next 150 years or so in the history of the Saparda are a blank; but, after leaving a trace of their westward passage in the course of those years in the Sevordi-k who long afterwards, in the eighth century of the Christian Era, were to assert themselves in Uti, in the angle above the confluence of the rivers Kur and Aras,[6] the Spardiyā (as they are called in Old Persian) reappear in the Achaemenian official lists of *dahyāva* as the eponyms of a *dahyāuš* named Sparda at the western extremity of Anatolia in the country known in Greek as Lydia.[7]

1 On p. 662, above.

2 See pp. 608–10, above.

3 These Saparda will have been the right wing of the horde, if the same national name is to be detected in the 'Sabadioi' who are located by Ptolemy, *Geographia*, Book VI, chap. xi, § 6, in the south-east corner of Bactria.

4 See p. 653, with n. 2, above.

5 See Forrer, op. cit., p. 93; König, op. cit., pp. 27 and 37.

6 See p. 610, n. 2, above.

7 Professor G. G. Cameron comments: 'It is surely only by straining that one can connect the name of the *dahyāuš* Sparda with the Saparda in Media.' Certainly at first sight a mere accidental coincidence might seem to be the most likely explanation of the appearance of the same name in locations as far apart as Western Iran and Western Anatolia at dates separated by as long a Time-interval as 150 years. The writer offers the following reasons for thinking that a more probable explanation is to be found in the migration of a Nomad horde which had carried its name with it. (i) We know that at least one other horde, the Cimmerians, did in fact migrate, within those same 150 years, from Western Iran to Anatolia, carrying its name with it (see p. 610, n. 1, above). (ii) We know that the Saljūq Turks likewise travelled from Western Iran to Anatolia in the eleventh century of the Christian Era, and the Mongols of Hūlāgū's horde in the thirteenth century. (iii) We know that in the Aras Basin, which both the Saljūqs and the Mongols traversed *en route*, the name that had made its appearance in the seventh century B.C. in Media as Saparda, and in the sixth century B.C. in Lydia as Sapardiyā, was borne in the eighth century of the Christian Era by a then still extant people called Sevordi-k. The writer would submit that facts (i) and (ii) show that his explanation is credible, and that fact (iii) indicates that it is probable.

Sargon claims to have conquered Harhar and to have added Saparda to it in his sixth year (Luckenbill, op. cit., vol. ii, pp. 11 and 14). In a list of receipts of tribute

We must conclude that the Spardiyā had invaded Anatolia in company with their previous associates the Cimmerians, and that they had subsequently entered the service of Alyattes King of Lydia (*regnabat circa* 614–557 B.C.) to fight for him against their former comrades. This conjecture would explain not only how their name had come to attach itself first to the capital city of Lydia and eventually to Lydia as a whole, but also how Alyattes had managed to turn the tide in Lydia's favour in her struggle with her Cimmerian assailants and also to make a beginning of the conquest of the Hellenic city-states along the west coast.[1] Alyattes' Spardiyan *foederati* will have supplied Lydia with the redoubtable cavalry who, by 585 B.C., had won for her the dominion of all Anatolia west of the River Halys and of the Kingdom of Cilicia, except for a Lycia that was shielded by mountains[2] and for a Miletus that could feed itself from overseas. The Achaemenian official use of the name 'Sparda' to designate Lydia must have lived on in popular usage long enough for the Jews to label the diasporà in the Roman province of Asia 'Sephardim' (i.e. 'Saparda') to distinguish them from the 'Ashkenazim' in the Scythian[3] wilderness into which some of the more adventurous spirits among the diasporà had been drawn by the commercial openings along the Roman Empire's Continental European frontiers.

The Eurasian Nomad origin of the Saparda, *alias* Spardiyā, gives us a clue to the provenance of one of the peoples located in the Achaemenian *dahyāuš* 'Sparda' by Herodotus. These 'Hygennees' of the gazetteer—who must also be the people whose name has dropped out of the text of the field-state between the Asiatic Thracians and the Kabêlees[4]—are manifestly the left wing of the Sigynnai whom Herodotus locates[5] somewhere beyond the Danube, in the hinterland of the Veneti at the head of the Adriatic. In this remote north-western settlement the Sigynnai were still advertising their Eurasian Nomad origin by continuing to wear 'Median' (i.e. Sakan) dress. The missing link between these Sigynnai in the Austrian Alps and the Hygennees in South-Western Anatolia is supplied by Strabo's description[6] of the Siginnoi whom, in company with the Derbikes and the Kaspioi, he locates somewhere in the east–west chain of mountains constituted by the Elburz and the Caucasus.[7]

during his eighth campaign (714 B.C.), Sargon records, as received from Saparda, 'prancing horses, swift mules, camels native to their land, cattle and sheep' (Luckenbill, op. cit., vol. ii, p. 147). This is just the tribute that is to be expected from a Eurasian Nomad horde that has only recently erupted out of the Steppe. On the other hand, Professor Cameron's scepticism would be vindicated if Sargon's Saparda should prove to have been identical with the land of Shepardi which, together with Azalzi, was annexed to Assyria by Tukulti-Ninurta I in the thirteenth century B.C. (Luckenbill, op. cit., vol. i, p. 152).

[1] See Herodotus, Book I, chaps. 15–16.

[2] See ibid., chap. 28.

[3] According to Prášek, op. cit., vol. i, p. 115, n. 5, the 'Ashkenaz' in the latter-day text of Gen. x. 3 is a corruption of 'Ashkuz', which is the form in which the *nomen Scythicum* appears in the Assyrian records.

[4] See Herodotus, Book VII, chap. 76.

[5] In Book V, chap. 9.

[6] Strabo: *Geographica*, Book XI, chap. xi, § 8 (C 520).

[7] While Strabo's account of these Siginnoi agrees with Herodotus's account of his Sigynnai in the description of their peculiar breed of horses (see p. 688, below), the independence of Strabo's source is attested, not merely by the difference in geographical location, but also by the difference in the Hellenization of the name; by the labelling of the people's cultural affinity, not as 'Median', but as 'Persian'; and by the mention of

As for the other peoples mentioned in Herodotus's description of his Taxation District No. 2, the Mysoi, in the highlands between Lydia and Hellespontine Phrygia, are convicted, by the survival of their name in the Lower Danube Basin in the form 'Moesi', of having been one of the Phrygian-speaking barbarian peoples who had broken out of South-Eastern Europe into the north-west corner of the Hittite World in the second millennium B.C.

The Kabêlees, whose name reappears on the post-Alexandrine Hellenic map of Anatolia in the names Cabalia and Cibyra, to the north-west of the Lycian Milyas, and who figure on the Hittite map of Anatolia as the principality of Hapalla, must have occupied the country between the south-east border of Lydia and the north-west border of Pisidia. Herodotus associates the Kabêlees (Kabalioi) with the Lydians in calling both of them 'Mëïones',[1] and Strabo supports this association by his statement[2] that Lydian was one of four languages that were current in the Cibyrâtis. At the same time the Kabêlees also had cultural associations with their eastern neighbours, to judge by Herodotus's parade of both the Kabêlees and the Lasonioi in a Cilician equipment and by the presence of a detachment of Kabêlees at the eastern end of the Pamphylian coast, where there was another city named Cibyra.[3]

Herodotus's Lasonioi are as enigmatic as his Asiatic Ligyes. If they are not identical with the Kabalioi,[4] the only space still vacant for them on the map is Pisidia, and the only name of which their name is reminiscent is 'Rasena', which is said to have been the Etruscans' own name for themselves. This conjectural location and conjectural affinity are at any rate not incompatible with one another; for the only section of the coastline of Anatolia from which the Anatolian progenitors of the Etruscans could have taken to the sea was the section between the eastern end of the Greek settlements along the coast of Pamphylia and the northern end of the Phoenician settlements along the coast of Syria.[5]

The *dahyāuš* called *the Yaunā who are on the Mainland* ('Yaunā tyaiy uškahyā') in Official List 'DPe', and, with less precision, *the Yaunā sans phrase* in 'DSe' and 'XPh' and *Yauna* (i.e. the name of the country, not the people) in 'DB' and 'DNa', is coextensive with Herodotus's Taxation District No. 1, constituted by the *Iônes*, *Asiatic Magnêtes*, *Aiolees*,

points that are not mentioned by Herodotus—e.g. that their chariots are four-horse chariots, that the charioteers are women, that the best female charioteer is rewarded by being given licence to practise sexual promiscuity, and that they indulge in cranial deformation. Strabo's testimony to the existence of 'Siginnoi' who were Persian in their culture and who lived somewhere within or immediately adjoining what had once been the domain of the Achaemenian Empire is corroborated by the name of Themistocles' confidential slave Sikinnos (see Herodotus, Book VIII, chaps. 75 and 110), who is described in Plutarch's *Life of Themistocles*, chap. 12, as being 'a Persian by birth', and whom Themistocles employs as his go-between in his secret negotiations with Xerxes in 480 B.C. On the analogy of the latter-day Attic slave-names that were Latinized as 'Davus' and 'Geta', the name 'Sicinnus' would inform us that Themistocles' confidential agent was by birth a member of an ex-Eurasian Nomad people akin to the Getae and the Dahae.

1 Herodotus, Book VII, chaps. 74 and 77.

2 See Strabo: *Geographica*, Book XIII, chap. iv, § 17 (C 631).

3 See ibid., Book XIV, chap. iv, § 2 (C 667).

4 Herodotus seems to identify them with the Kabêlees in the field-state (Book VII, chap. 77), though he gives no indication of their being identical when he mentions the Kabalioi and the Lasonioi side by side in the gazetteer (Book III, chap. 90).

5 See I. i. 114, n. 3.

Kâres, *Lykioi*, *Milyai*, and *Pamphyloi* (the *Asiatic Dorians* are added in the field-state).[1] All these peoples, including the non-Greek-speaking Carians, Lycians, and Milyans, were Hellenes or sub-Hellenes in culture, and all of them except the Milyai were on the seaboard. The Milyai, who on the post-Alexandrine Hellenic map of Anatolia survive in the immediate hinterland of the Lycian coast and in Western Pisidia,[2] will have been a refugee remnant of the eponymous people of a country called Mirā which, on the Hittite map of Anatolia, had perhaps extended as far north as the upper course of the Phrygian Cayster in the neighbourhood of Afyun Qāra Hisār.[3]

In the three latest of the official lists—'DSe', 'DNa', and 'XPh'—the name *Karkā*, as well as the name Yauna or 'the Yaunā' (*sans phrase*), makes it appearance; and, if the identification of Karkā with Caria is correct, the introduction of the name signifies that the original *dahyāuš* Yauna had been partitioned and that the detached portion, now labelled 'Karkā', was made up of the last four peoples named in Herodotus's description of his First Taxation District. The reduced Yauna and the new Karkā, between them, like the original Yauna, will have extended round the Aegean coast of Anatolia and the western half of its Mediterranean coast continuously, all the way from the southern border of the Asiatic Hellespontine Hellenes in the taxation district Dascylîtis-cum-Cappadociâ to the western frontier of the seaboard of the Kingdom of Cilicia. The *dahyāuš* known as Sparda will thus have been completely landlocked; but there is no evidence that any of the cantons of Yauna and Karkā, except Caria Proper and Lycia, were ever under the administration of any other authority than the Viceroy of Sparda. In practice, Sparda, the whole of a reduced Yauna, and at least the Pamphylian canton of Karkā seem usually to have constituted a single viceroyalty; and this association is indicated in the official lists by the immediate juxtaposition to one another of Sparda and Yauna in 'DB', 'DPe', 'DSe', and 'DNa', and their separation only by a single intervening name in 'DZd', and 'XPh'.

Though, even in combination, these three *dahyāva* covered a very small area by comparison with the size of the taxation district Cappadocia-cum-Dascylîtide, and *a fortiori* with the size of the Viceroyalty Arminiya-plus-Katpatuka, the ratio between the two Anatolian viceroyalties, as measured in human terms of population and wealth, is indicated by Herodotus's figures. The combined annual assessment of his Taxation Districts Nos. 1 and 2 is 900 Euboic talents—200 more than the assessment on Egypt and only 100 less than the assessment on Babylonia[4]—while the combined annual assessment of Herodotus's

[1] See Herodotus, Book VII, chap. 93.

[2] See Strabo: *Geographica*, Book XIII, chap. iv, § 17 (C 631), and Book XIV, chap. iii, § 9 (C 666).

[3] See 'A note on Hittite Sites and Locations on Maps 15–16', in vol. xi.

[4] The mercantile and industrial seaboard of the Achaemenian Empire from the Black Sea Straits to the Philistine coast inclusive, together with the Empire's two great cereal-producing viceroyalties, Egypt and Babylonia, would appear to have been on a markedly higher level of wealth than the peoples of the interior on the Iranian, Armenian, and Anatolian plateaux, if the equipment paraded in the field-state of Xerxes' expeditionary force may be taken as an approximate indication of comparative standards of living, and

three Taxation Districts Nos. 3, 13, and 19 amounts, notwithstanding the enormously greater extent of their aggregate area, to only 1,060 talents in all—that is, to only 160 talents more than the combined figure for Districts Nos. 1 and 2.

The *dahyāuš* called *Those in the Sea* ('tyaiy drayahyā') in 'DB', 'DPe', and 'DSe', and *Those who live in the Sea* ('tya[iy] drayahiyā dārayatiy') in 'XPh', must be identical with *the Isles* (Nêsoi) in the Aegean Archipelago[1] which are mentioned by Herodotus, in an appendix to his

if body armour and metal helmets may be taken as the two criteria of affluence. On this test the western seaboard, Egypt, and Babylonia stand out against the foil of their vast poverty-stricken north-eastern hinterland. It is also noticeable that, among the non-Hellenic peoples of the western seaboard, the specifically Hellenic type of elaborate and costly equipment is gaining ground. It is worn by the Philistines and Phoenicians (Herodotus, VII. 89), as well as by the non-Greek-speaking Cilicians (VII. 91), Lycians (VII. 92), and Carians (VII. 93), and by the Greek-speaking but imperfectly Hellenic Cypriots (VII. 90).

1 The locative case of the Old Persian word 'draya', 'sea', must mean '*in* the Sea' in the sense in which an island is in the sea. It could not mean 'on sea' in the sense in which Boulogne was 'on sea' in virtue, not of being surrounded by the water like an island or floating on the water like a ship, but of standing on the continent, though on the coast of it. When the draftsman wants to describe the continental Yaunā as being situated on the coast, he does this by using the locative, not of the word 'sea', but of the word 'mainland'. He calls them 'Yaunā tyaiy uškahyā' (in 'DPe': see p. 677, above). To convey this meaning through the use of the word 'sea' he would have had to introduce a preposition meaning 'alongside of' or 'near' to govern the substantive. Moreover, the label 'those alongside of the sea', if the draftsman had used it (and as a matter of fact he did not use it), would have been useless as a distinguishing mark; for, whereas the Aegean Archipelago was the only *dahyāuš* in the Achaemenian Empire that lay *in* the sea, there were at least eighteen *dahyāva*, even before the separation of Hellespontine Phrygia from Cappadocia, that were *on* sea in the sense in which Boulogne was on sea. Besides Cappadocia, the viceroyalties or taxation districts or autonomous territories of Sparda together with 'the Yaunā on the Mainland', Karkā, Cilicia, Syria, Arabāya, Egypt, the Coastal Peoples north of Armenia, Colchis, Kaspianê, Parthia-cum-Hyrcaniâ, the Pointed-Hood Sakā, Babylonia, Hūja, Pārsa, Harahvatiš-cum-Maka, the Asiatic Ethiopians, and Hīduš all had seaboards on some sea or other: the Sea of Aral, the Caspian Sea, the Black Sea, the Sea of Marmara, the Aegean Sea, the Mediterranean, the Red Sea, the Persian Gulf, the Indian Ocean. If it had occurred to Darius to label any of these continental *dahyāva* with a sea-front 'the viceroyalty on the seaside' *par excellence*, the *dahyāuš* on which he would have conferred this title would certainly not have been the Dascylîtis-cum-Cappadociâ. It would have been Hīduš, the viceroyalty which he himself had added to the Empire for the sake of its seaboard on the Ocean—a seaboard that was invaluable for Darius because the acquisition of it had enabled him to open an oceanic line of communications between the eastern and western extremities of his dominions.

Professor G. G. Cameron comments: 'Your note is by no means convincing. We are scarcely in a position to put ourselves in a draftsman's shoes.' And a chronological point telling against the identification of the *dahyāuš* called 'those in the Sea' with the islands of the Aegean Archipelago has been brought to the writer's attention in the following comments by Professor R. G. Kent:

'Regarding your equation "tyaiy drayahyā = those in the Sea", I note that, while the term occurs in the "DB" list, at the very beginning of Darius's reign, Herodotus says specifically, in Book III, chap. 96, that "as time went on, however, other revenue came in also from islands and from the peoples living in Europe as far as Thessaly". This seems to me to indicate that the twenty districts did not, at the time of Darius's accession, include any significant island element, certainly not enough to have a place in the "DB" list. Therefore I cannot yet abandon the interpretation that George Cameron gave me, possibly starting from our late friend A. T. Olmstead, that "tyaiy drayahyā" means "those *by* the Sea", namely a section with their capital at Dascylium. As Dascylium seems to be associated with certain lakes (see any classical dictionary s.v. Dascylium or Daskylion), the term "those by the Sea" might not be very inexact after all. Further, the islanders were no very important element in the Persian Empire, as they contributed only 17 triremes to the Persian fleet (Hdt. VII. 95), whereas even the Pamphylians and the Asiatic Dorians each contributed 30, and no other national or territorial unit sent less than 50.'

In answer to this objection of Professor Kent's, the present writer would venture to

gazetteer,[1] as one of the new districts subsequently added to Darius's original twenty. In the field-state, in which the Islanders (Nesiôtai) duly appear among the naval contingents,[2] they are explicitly described as being Ionians of the same Athenian origin as the Ionians of the Anatolian mainland, and as wearing the Hellenic equipment.

When the five Old Persian texts in the official lists are checked off against one another, it becomes clear[3] that, besides Herodotus's literal translation 'the Islanders', 'those in the Sea' have a second synonym in 'the toque-wearing Yaunā' ('Yaunā Takabarā') who figure in 'DNa'—the only one of these five lists in which 'those in the Sea' do not appear. The headgear of the Achaemenids' far western subjects, the Hellenic

recall that, while Herodotus does speak of the tribute from the Aegean islands as being supplementary and subsequent to the tribute assessed by Darius on his original twenty taxation districts, Herodotus also goes on to indicate that Darius embarked on his forward policy in Hellenic waters almost immediately after he had completed the effective reassertion of his authority throughout the Achaemenian Empire. The sequence of events, as Herodotus gives it, is (i) the liquidation of Orœtes the satrap of Sparda, who had been Cyrus's appointee and who had played for his own hand during the interregnum between Cambyses' death and Darius's triumph (III. 126–8); (ii) the deportation of Dêmocêdês from Sardis to Susa (III. 129); (iii) the dispatch of a naval reconnoitring expedition from Sidon, with Dêmocêdês on board, which made a systematic survey of the coasts of the Hellenic World and penetrated as far to the west as Dêmocêdês' homeland Crôtôn on 'the ball' of 'the toe' of Italy before its activities were brought to an end by Dêmocêdês' machinations (III. 136–8); (iv) 'after this, Darius made the first of his annexations of foreign territory, Hellenic or non-Hellenic, by occupying Samos' (III. 139). From this sequence of events in Herodotus's narrative two points seem to emerge: (i) the annexation to the Achaemenian Empire of one important Aegean island, Samos, occurred rather soon after Darius's effective assertion of his sovereignty over Sparda and 'the Yaunā on the mainland' (who must also have been under Orœtes' jurisdiction before his liquidation); (ii) the annexation of Samos was the second move in a deliberate and ambitious plan for a forward policy of maritime expansion in the Hellenic World (see further IX. viii. 433–4), in which the first move had been the dispatch of a naval reconnoitring expedition to Magna Graecia. It seems not improbable that the list of *dahyāva* in 'DB', in which 'those in the Sea' already figure, was not inscribed until after the annexation of Samos. The mighty work at Behistan, where the cliff-face had to be chiselled smooth before the long record was inscribed on it, must, after all, have taken a considerable time to carry out; and, if, by then, Samos was already in Darius's hands, that might have sufficed, in his eyes, to justify the mention, in 'DB', of a new *dahyāuš* of which Samos was, in Darius's ambitious intentions, only a first instalment.

As regards Professor Cameron's identification of 'those in the Sea' with the inhabitants of the territory whose capital was Dascylium, the test of its convincingness is, surely, the applicability of this descriptive appellation, not just to Dascylium itself (whether the south shore of the Sea of Marmara or the north-east shore of Lake Manyas was the site of this local administrative centre), but to the whole of the area that the Governor at Dascylium administered. If we are right in thinking that the Dascylîtis was part of a viceroyalty embracing Cappadocia and Armenia (see pp. 671–7 above), this will have been one of the most conspicuously 'continental' and 'non-maritime' viceroyalties of the Achaemenian Empire; and, even if the Dascylîtis at this date had already constituted a separate viceroyalty confined to Hellespontine Phrygia, the metropolitan area—which was the great plain stretching east and west from the foot of the Mysian Olympus to the east bank of the River Granicus—would have been most unlikely to suggest the descriptive label 'in the Sea', since, although the plain does run parallel to the south shore of the Sea of Marmara, it gives the visual impression of being landlocked because it is secluded from the Marmara by a coastal range of hills. The sea is out of the picture, as the present writer could testify from a first-hand acquaintance with the country. He knew the eastern end of the great plain well, and he had also had two glimpses of the western end—the first between 3.0 and 4.0 p.m. on the 22nd April, 1923, *en route* by train from Izmir (Smyrna) to Banderma (Panormos), and the second on the evening of the 28th October, 1948, when there was still just light enough for him to catch a bird's-eye view of the landscape *en route by* air from Athens to Istanbul.

[1] See Book III, chap. 96. [2] See Book VII, chap. 95.

[3] For visual evidence, see the masterly Table II in Kent, R. G.: 'Old Persian Texts IV: the Lists of Provinces', in the *Journal of New Eastern Studies*, vol. ii, January–October 1943 (Chicago 1943, University of Chicago Press), pp. 302–7.

islanders, like the headgear of their far north-eastern subjects the Massagetan Sakā Nomads ('Sakā Tigrakhaudā', 'the Pointed-Hoods'), must have struck the Imperial Authorities as being so quaintly distinctive as to warrant the use of an allusive nickname as an official label. The word 'toque', which was the current French name for the headgear that, in A.D. 1952, was still being worn by members of the legal profession in France and by shepherds and brigands in Baluchistan, informs us that the authentic 'taka' was the fluted outward curving tall hat—a top-hat without a brim—in which the Persians are portrayed on Achaemenian bas-reliefs; but there is evidence that the Aegean Islanders' peculiar headgear, notwithstanding the official designation of it as a 'taka', was not, in fact, this Persian 'stove-pipe' hat, but was the low-crowned or crownless broad-brimmed hat that was known in Greek by the alternative names 'kausia' ('scorcher') and 'petasus' ('wide-awake'). In the Akkadian version of 'DNa' the Old Persian words 'Yaunā Takabarā' are paraphrased in the words 'the Second Ionians who wear shields on their heads'.[1] To post-Alexandrine Athenian eyes the crownless variety of the same headgear, as worn by an impostor dressed up as an Asiatic Macedonian from Seleucia, looked like a mushroom.[2]

This mushroom-like or shield-like Aegean insular headgear was to have a romantic history in a post-Achaemenian age. From the Archipelago the fashion spread westward to Attica—as is attested by its appearance here and there, on the Elgin Marbles, upon the heads of riders in the Panathenaic procession—and northward to Macedonia, where it became so characteristic a feature of the national dress that—'gorgeously transfigured'[3]—it established itself as one element in the royal insignia.

> 'As worn by the kings, it was dyed crimson with the precious juice won by immense labour from the sea, and the diadem was in some way tied round it or under it, its ends hanging loose about the neck. The diadem itself was inwrought with golden thread.'[4]

The sudden replacement of the Achaemenian Empire by a bevy of Macedonian successor-states, founded by officers who had served under King Alexander, ennobled a headgear that had once been the quaint monomark of one of the most outlandish of all the Achaemenian Empire's subject peoples into the sovereign emblem of royalty throughout an *Oikoumenê* extending from the Nile to the Ganges;[5] and in

[1] '[matuIa]-ma-nu ša-un-tú ša ma-ǵi-na-ta ina qaqqādī-šu-nu na-šú-u.'

[2] See Plautus: *Trinummus*, Act III, scene iii, ll. 43–44, and Act IV, scene ii, ll. 3 and 9–10. When the sycophant makes his appearance in his Asiatic Macedonian outfit, Charmides exclaims:

> Pol, hicquidem fungino generest: capite se totum tegit.
> Hilurica facies videtur hominis, eo ornatu advenit.

This crownless variety of the 'petasus' is portrayed on coins of King Antimachus, the brother, and King Demetrius II, the son, of King Demetrius the Euthydemid Bactrian Greek conqueror of the Mauryan Empire (see the plate of coin-portraits following p. 539 in Tarn, W. W.: *The Greeks in Bactria and India* (Cambridge 1938, University Press)).

[3] Bevan, E. R.: *The House of Seleucus*, vol. ii, p. 274.

[4] Ibid. Cp. Bouché-Leclercq, A.: *Histoire des Seleucides* (Paris 1913, Leroux, 2 vols.), vol. i, p. 475.

[5] This romantic change in the significance of the petasus came to be reflected in a

A.D. 1952, nearly two thousand years after the fall of the last of the post-Alexandrine Macedonian *peritura regna*, the petasus—duly dyed purple and duly girt with a diadem whose ends hung loose in a symmetrical pair of pendant tassels—could still be seen, on state occasions, adorning the heads of the ecclesiastical princes of a Roman Christian Church under the latter-day name of 'the cardinal's hat'.

In 'DPe' 'the Yaunā who are on the Mainland' and 'those in the Sea' (described in 'DNa' as 'the shield-shaped-toque-wearing Yaunā) are distinguished both from one another and from another *dahyāuš* called '*the Lands that are beyond the Sea* (dahyāva tyā para draya)' with complete clarity in the sequence 'the Yaunā who are on the Mainland *and* those in the Sea *and* the Lands that are beyond the Sea'. This third formula recurs in 'DSe' as 'those who are beyond the Sea (tyaiy para draya),' and in 'XPh' as 'those who live beyond the Sea (tyaiy para draya dārayatiy)', while 'DNa', which designates 'those in the Sea' as 'the shield-shaped-toque-wearing Yaunā', designates 'those beyond the Sea' as 'the Sakā beyond the Sea (Sakā tyaiy para draya)'. The Nomads to whom the word 'Sakā' in this phrase refers cannot be identified for certain. We cannot tell whether they are the Scyths on the Great Western Bay of the Eurasian Steppe to the north of the Black Sea or the Getae in the Lower Danube Basin (an advanced guard of the Massa-getae on the Oxus) or the Odrysae in the valley of the River Maritsa (*Graecè* Hebros). Whatever the reference here may be, it is clear that, just as the undifferentiated 'Sakā' of 'DB' and 'DPe' are sorted out in 'DSe', 'DNa', and 'XPh' into 'Hauma-(?)drinking Sakā' and 'Pointed-Hood Sakā', so, in the same three later lists, the undifferentiated 'Lands that are beyond the Sea' of 'DPe'—which is rendered by Herodotus as '*the peoples living in Europe as far as Thessaly*'[1]—are sorted out into an easterly overseas *dahyāuš*, to which 'DNa' applies the name 'Sakā', and a westerly one which is called 'Skudra' in 'DSe', 'DNa', and 'XPh' alike.

The location of this last-mentioned Achaemenian *dahyāuš* is established by the reappearance of its label in Ptolemy's geography and in Stephanus of Byzantium's gazetteer as the name of a Macedonian townlet that is just not too obscure to be ignored. Ptolemy[2] locates this townlet called Skydra in Emathia, and mentions it between Tyrissa and Myeza. The Achaemenian Empire's loss of all Darius's Continental European acquisitions except Doriscus[3] as a consequence of the disaster of 480–

corresponding change in the connotation of the term by which it had been designated in 'DNa'. The Old Persian compound word 'taka-barā', used in this context to describe a subject people wearing a peculiar national head-dress, was taken over into the Armenian language in the form 't'agawor' to denote the wearer of the 'taka' in the different sense of a king's crown. 'In Armenian the word "t'agawor" is the usual word for "king" . . . The takfūr of Sīs is, of course, the Armenian "t'agawor", Old Iranian [actually, not Old Iranian, but Middle Iranian or Pahlawī, as Professor Kent points out—A.J.T.] "taga-bara", "crown bearer" ' (Frye, R. N., in the *Harvard Journal of Asiatic Studies*, vol. x, No. 2, September 1947, pp. 237 and 236). In Ottoman Turkish the same compound word was taken over in the form 'tekfūr', and was used in the Armenian, as distinct from the Achaemenian, sense as a technical term to denote the East Roman Emperor. For example, in Turkish the ruin of the East Roman Imperial Palace Blachernae was called 'Tekfūr Serayī', and Mount Ganos, on the European shore of the Sea of Marmara, 'Tekfūr Daghī'.

[1] Herodotus, Book III, chap. 96. [2] *Geographia*, Book III, chap. xiii, § 39.

[3] See Herodotus, Book VII, chaps. 105–7, cited on p. 120, above.

479 B.C. was to cost Skydra the fulfilment of a manifest destiny. In the choice of Skydra for the seat of administration of a province that was intended soon to include the whole of Continental European Greece, the lieutenants of Darius who were organizing his new Continental European dominions for him showed the same eye for the structure of the military and political geography of the Balkan Peninsula as Ghāzi Evrenòs, the lieutenant of the Ottoman Sultan Murād I (*imperabat* A.D. 1360–89), was to show when he established a powerful Ottoman military colony on the same Emathian plain at Yenijé Vardar,[1] in the neighbourhood of the site of Pella. Emathia, as King Philip Amyntou of Macedon was to demonstrate, afforded a base of operations from which a land power could dominate Continental European Greece in one direction and the Morava Basin in another. If Xerxes had been as successful as either Philip or Murād I in his empire-building enterprise in South-Eastern Europe, an Achaemenian Skydra might have lived to play as great a part in history as a Macedonian Philippi or Philippopolis or as a Roman Lugdunum or Colonia Agrippina.

If we now cast our minds back over this survey of the administrative geography of the Achaemenian Empire, we can perhaps make out the lineaments of the viceroyalties, as well as the taxation districts, into which it was divided during the period of forty-two years between the disaster of 522–521 B.C. and the disaster of 480–479 B.C. The vice-royalties in this period were large in size and consequently few in number. They were:

I. Greater Media, including Adiabênê, Urartu, the Hyspîrîtis, and the Lower Aras-Kur Basin, as well as Media Proper, and embracing Herodotus's Taxation Districts Nos. 10, 11, 15, and 18.

II. Greater Elam, including Anšan and Parsuwaš, and coextensive with Herodotus's Taxation District No. 8.

III. Harahvatiš, including Zrāka, South-Eastern Pārsa, and Makran as well, and embracing Herodotus's Taxation Districts Nos. 14 and 17.

IV. Parthava, including Gurgān, Dihistān, Khwārizm, and Herat as well, and coextensive with Herodotus's Taxation District No. 16.

V. Bākhtriš, including Suguda and Marguš as well, and coextensive with Herodotus's Taxation District No. 12.

VI. The Indus Basin, consisting of Gādāra and Hīduš, and embracing Herodotus's Taxation Districts Nos. 7 and 20.

VII. Pahat Babili u Ebir-nari, consisting of Bābiruš together with Athurā, and embracing Herodotus's Taxation Districts Nos. 9 and 5.

VIII. Egypt together with Libya, coextensive with Herodotus's Taxation District No. 6.

1 *Graecè* Yanitzá (see Khalkokondhýlis, 'Laónikos' (i.e. Nikólaos): *De Origine et Rebus Gestis Turcarum*, Book IV, *ad finem*, on p. 218 of I. Bekker's ed. (Bonn. 1843, Weber); Hammer, J. von: *Histoire de l'Empire Ottoman*, vol. i (Paris 1835, Bellizard, Barthès, Dufour et Lowell), pp. 224–5; Gibbons, H. A.: *The Foundation of the Ottoman Empire* (Oxford 1916, Clarendon Press), pp. 146–7; Mordtmann, J. H., s.v. 'Evrenos', in *The Encyclopaedia of Islam*, vol. ii (London 1927, Luzac), pp. 34–35).

IX. 'Paktyïkê and Armenioi and the adjoining peoples as far as the Black Sea', embracing Herodotus's Taxation Districts Nos. 13, 19, and 3.

X. Sardis, together with 'the Yaunā who are on the mainland' and Karkā, embracing Herodotus's Taxation Districts Nos. 1 and 2.

As for 'Those in the Sea' and 'The Lands that are Beyond the Sea', these two titles would seem, like the names of the two Roman provinces Germania Superior and Germania Inferior, to commemorate ambitious programmes of conquest which were frustrated at an early stage, and the title Sakā Tigrakhaudā may be placed in the same category, considering how unlikely it is that Darius I's punitive expedition against Skunkha will have had any lasting results.

The Achaemenian Empire's Historical Background

Our survey of the administrative geography of the Achaemenian Empire has also brought to light some of the reasons why Cyrus II was able to extend his rule so rapidly and easily over so vast an area and why thereafter Darius and Xerxes, when they set out to add new dominions to Cyrus's bequest, ran up against unforeseen limits which they found themselves unable to pass. The area which Cyrus had conquered and which Darius had resubjugated after a sharp recrudescence of anarchy in 522–521 B.C. was an area in which the hearts of the population had been prepared by previous sufferings for the acceptance of an oecumenical peace at almost any price. From the Indus Basin to 'the Yaunā on the Mainland', and from Egypt to the countries lying under the lee of the Caucasus, the peoples' spirit had been broken by one or other or both of two scourges: the third bout of Assyrian militarism that had been launched by Tiglath-Pileser III in 745 B.C., and the third eruption of aggressive Nomad peoples from the Eurasian Steppe, which had broken upon the eastern frontiers of Assyria and Urartu *circa* 715–714 B.C. The peoples who had come within the range of either the *furor Assyriacus* or the *terror Scythicus* had been schooled to become the Achaemenian Empire's victims or beneficiaries, in whichever of the two alternative lights they might look upon a fate that was mild by comparison with Assyrian cruelty or Cimmerian savagery, however poorly it might compare with idealized memories of a parochial sovereign independence that had long ago ceased to be practical politics. But the expectations of docility which the Achaemenian empire-builders had come to take for granted as a result of their facile successes in a psychologically devastated area were rudely disappointed as soon as they attempted to impose the same oecumenical peace outside the limits within which the Assyrians and the Sakas had ploughed up the ground for them.

Cyrus II himself, for example, paid with his life for his failure to foresee that, when he attacked the Eurasian Nomads on their own *terrain*, he was going to encounter a much more vehement resistance than had been offered to him by neighbouring sedentary peoples for whom their submission to his dominion had brought with it some security against Nomad raids in compensation for the loss of an illusory national independence. Darius I was lucky to escape with his life when—emboldened, perhaps, by his success in momentarily subduing 'the Pointed-Hood Sakā' on the River Oxus and the Aral Sea, who had been Cyrus's bane—he went on to attack the more distant 'Sakā beyond the Sea' on the Great Western Bay of the Eurasian Steppe. Finally, Xerxes brought upon himself a disaster from which the Achaemenian Empire did not ever completely recover when he tried to deal with the Continental European Hellenes, who had never felt the touch of either the Assyrian or the Scythian lash, as Cyrus had found himself able to deal with 'the Yaunā on the Mainland', who had previously been broken in by the Cimmerians and the Spardiyā.[1] In their encounters with unbroken peoples, whether sedentary or Nomad, the Achaemenidae were only successful in so far as they showed a politic generosity. Their Arab neighbours, for instance, to whom they accorded the status of autonomous allies, do not seem to have given them the trouble that these Arabs' forebears had given to high-handed Assyrian militarists; and 'the Hauma-(?)drinking Sakā' of Farghānah, to whom the same status had been accorded by Cyrus II, proved their faithfulness to the alliance by fighting magnificently for the last Darius at Gaugamela in 331 B.C.

The historical importance of the Eurasian Nomad Völkerwanderung of the eighth and seventh centuries B.C. is one of the features in the background of the Achaemenian Empire that our survey has thrown into relief.[2] When Darius boasted that 'a Persian fighting-man's spear has pressed forward far',[3] a Massagetan Skunkha might have commented—if his ruthless Achaemenian conqueror had left him life in his body and a tongue in his head—that the Saka fighting-man's battle-axe had pressed forward farther. The Persians might have caught up and conquered the Sindoi on the shore of an ocean which was to be labelled with the Sindians' name when Darius's admiral Scylax sailed on over it to the Red Sea coast of Egypt; but they had never come within striking distance of the Sindians' right wing on the banks of the Kuban. 'The peoples to the north of the Caucasus snap their fingers at the Persians down to this day', as Herodotus wrote at some date during the reign of Xerxes' successor Artaxerxes I.[4] Again, the Persians might have caught up and conquered the Thatagu[? d or v]iyā on the cow-pastures of the Panjab, but they had never subjugated the Kuru on their plain between the Sutlej and the Jumna. They might have caught up and conquered the advance-guards of the Scyths, Cimmerians, Paktyes, and Spardiyā in Anatolia, but they had been foiled by the Scyths' right wing on the steppe to the north of the Black Sea. They might have momentarily imposed their rule on the Odrysai in the Maritsa Basin

1 The psychological limit to Achaemenian annexations that was set by the physical limits of previous Assyrian and Eurasian Nomad ravages is noticed again in IX. viii. 430–1.

2 Professor G. G. Cameron comments: 'The Völkerwanderung of the eighth and seventh centuries is, I see, to you, as it is to me, a terrific development hitherto insufficiently emphasized.'

3 'DNa', §4, quoted on pp. 589–90, above.

4 Herodotus, Book III, chap. 97.

and even on the advance-guard of the Getai in the Lower Danube Basin,[1] but the solitary[2] lost tribe of the Odrysai on the Hungarian Alföld had remained immune, and 'the Great Horde' of the Getai—the Massagetai whom the Persians called 'the Pointed-Hoods'—quickly shook off an ineffective Persian yoke. The Achaemenian tax-collectors had never come near the Agathyrsoi, and we may guess that they were not able to pester the 'Pointed-Hoods' for more than a few years.

It will be seen that Skunkha could have made a telling retort to Darius, and he could have crowned it by reminding him that, where the Eurasian Nomad invaders *in partibus agricolarum* had eventually been brought to heel by sedentary Powers, this had been achieved through the prowess of renegade Nomads who had enlisted in these sedentary Powers' service. If the Lydian Monarchy had broken the force of the Cimmerian horde in Anatolia and had imposed its own rule as far eastward as the River Halys, the Lydians had owed their success to the valour of their mercenary Spardiyā Nomad cavalry;[3] and, as for the conquest of the World by the elder branch of the House of Achaemenes, did not the alternating names Kūruš and Kambūjiya, borne by their princes from Cyrus I onwards, testify that their fortune had been made for them by the valour of Kuru and Kamboja Nomad reinforcements?[4]

In order to take the full measure of the impetus of this Eurasian Nomad Völkerwanderung that carried the Achaemenidae into power in South-West Asia, we have to remind ourselves that this was not the only front on which it had erupted. In the opposite hinterland of the Steppe, in the Upper Basin of the Yellow River, it had broken eastwards upon the Chóu Power in 771 B.C.,[5] more than half a century before it had broken westwards upon Assyria and Urartu. This eruption in the eighth century B.C. was comparable in violence to the eruption in the eighteenth or seventeenth century B.C. which had carried the 'mariannu' into Anatolia and Syria and the Mitanni into Anatolia and Mesopotamia, if not into Midian.[6] On the other hand, in contrast to both these eruptions, the intervening eruption, which had carried the ancestors of the Medes and Persians out of the Eurasian Steppe on to the Iranian Plateau, must have been relatively mild; for their advent left no mark on the Assyrian records; as we have seen,[7] the Assyrians do not mention them earlier than the third quarter of the ninth century B.C., and then only because the Assyrians themselves have pushed their way up on to the plateau, and not because the Medes and Persians have descended upon the plains. The only trace of Medo-Persian penetration to the west of the Zagros Range before the eve of the overthrow of Assyria

[1] See Herodotus, Book IV, chaps. 92–96.

[2] Supposing that 'ag-' in the name rendered 'Agathyrsoi' in Ionic Greek may be equated with the Sanskrit 'éka-' meaning 'one'. For the relation between the Agathyrsoi and their namesakes the Odrysai (in the rendering of whose name the d is the Macedonian Greek equivalent of an Ionic Greek th), see III. iii. 425, n. 2.

[3] See p. 676, above.

[4] See pp. 652–4, above.

[5] See Hirth, F.: *The Ancient History of China* (New York 1908, Columbia University Press), p. 176.

[6] See the Note on Chronology in x. 201, n. 3.

[7] On p. 608, n. 3, above.

in the seventh century B.C. is the appearance, in the annals of Tiglath-Pileser III (*regnabat* 746–727 B.C.), of the two personal names Kundašpi and Kuštašpi in Kummukhu (Commagênê), between the western elbow of the River Euphrates and the south-east face of the Taurus Range.[1]

Can we account for this striking difference in degree of force between the first and third eruptions on the one hand and the second eruption on the other? The explanation may be that, in the Medo-Persian Völkerwanderung, the invading Nomads were not equipped, as they were in the other two Völkerwanderungen, with a potent new weapon. In the eighteenth or seventeenth century B.C. it was their chariotry, and in the eighth century B.C. their cavalry, that enabled the Nomad invaders to carry all before them;[2] but we know of no comparable Nomad military invention in the intervening bout.

To break in the wild horses of the Steppe, and to invent a spoked wheel light enough to be drawn at a gallop yet strong enough not to break, were two *chefs-d'œuvre* of human skill.

> The mane that shaketh
> For his slave he taketh.[3]

The breaking-in of chariot-horses was, however, only the first of two great achievements in the Eurasian Nomad's handling of the horse. His second achievement was to breed a horse with a strong enough backbone to carry a rider in battle instead of merely conveying him to the battle-field on wheels.

'When we first meet it in Egypt, very soon after its introduction [by Maryanni Eurasian Nomads], the horse was a small and very lightly built animal which was rarely mounted except by stable boys who rode it bareback to water or who exercised it around the paddock. . . . The early horse was not built for carrying a rider any distance, being little more than a pony. The wooden figure of a mare which is in New York is somewhat sway-backed, with a rather large head ending in a big muzzle, and probably with a very short mane, which in that example has been clipped off. . . . A pair of these little steeds could draw no more than two men at the most, and in mountainous Syria even a single man often had to get out and walk, carrying the chariot on his shoulder. . . . The animal itself and the vehicle which it drew played highly important parts in the unparalleled success of the invasion of Egypt by the Hyksos. The latter were probably of Nomadic origin, of whatever race and language stock they may have been. Their animals were probably small and, being weak-backed, were always driven from a chariot; for it is only the Syrian goddess 'Anat who is shown mounted as a rule.'[4]

This passage in a book written by a twentieth-century Western

1 See König, op. cit., p. 15.

2 Professor G. G. Cameron comments: 'I agree with your observation that the rapidity and effectiveness of the Völkerwanderung of the eighth and seventh centuries B.C. were due to the riding horse. The Assyrian liver omens (which tell the truth, in contrast to the annals) make it clear that the search for the better riding horse was Esarhaddon's motive for sending parties of men up on to the Iranian plateau as far as Pateiskhoreis [see p. 616, above]. The whole subject is highlighted by the oft repeated Persian claim that the empire "possesses good horses and (i.e. as well as) good men".'

3 Sophocles: *Antigonê*, ll. 350–1, Gilbert Murray's translation.

4 Winlock, H. E.: *The Rise and Fall of the Middle Kingdom of Thebes* (New York 1947, Macmillan), pp. 153–5.

scholar, which is actually a description of an Egyptiac work of art made on the morrow of the Eurasian Nomad Völkerwanderung of the eighteenth or seventeenth century B.C., might have been a paraphrase of either Herodotus's description, written in the fifth century B.C., of a horse still in use among the Sigynnai in the Austrian Alps, or Strabo's description, written or copied round about the beginning of the Christian Era, of a horse still in use among the Siginnoi in the Elburz or the Caucasus; and the correspondence is the more impressive considering that there is no indication in Winlock's book of his being acquainted with either of these two passages of Hellenic literature.

'Their horses', writes Herodotus in his account of the Sigynnai, 'are said to be shaggy all over, with a coat five fingers thick. They are small, with snub muzzles, and cannot carry a rider, but they fly like the wind when yoked to a chariot, and consequently the people of that country are charioteers.'[1]

'The Siginnoi', writes Strabo in his account of these, 'have small shaggy ponies (*hipparia*) which cannot carry the weight of a rider, so they yoke them in four-in-hands.'[2]

Strabo's Siginnoi and Herodotus's Sigynnai were evidently the descendants of participants in the Eurasian Nomad Völkerwanderung of the eighteenth or seventeenth century B.C. who had strayed into the fastnesses of the Elburz or Caucasus and the Alps and had survived there as 'living museums' of the chariot-driving conquerors whose wheel-borne fleets had swept across South-West Asia into Egypt some twelve or thirteen hundred years before Herodotus's day and some sixteen or seventeen hundred years before Strabo's.[3] It was left for the Spardiyā, Paktyes, Cimmerians, Scyths, Kaspioi, and other hordes of the swarming 'Umman Manda' to surpass the feat of their forerunners the Maryanni and Mitanni by breeding horses that a fighting-man could ride; and, after this Sakan light cavalry had gone the way of the Hyksos chariotry, it was left for the Sarmatians to surpass the feat of their forerunners the Cimmerians and the Scyths by breeding 'the great horse' whose backbone could bear the weight, not only of a man, but of a man clad in mail cap-à-pie, in addition to the horse's own hardly less complete suit of armour[4]—a horse which was to carry to victory the Goths at Adrianople in A.D. 378 and the Normans at Hastings in A.D. 1066, besides playing his part, beyond the opposite shore of the Great Eurasian Steppe, in bringing a Sinic Civilization to the ground and rearing a Far Eastern Civilization to replace it. In the Achaemenian Age the cataphract is already in the arena. At Plataea in 479 B.C. he is represented by Masistius,[5] and at Gaugamela in 331 B.C. by the Sakā

1 Herodotus, Book V, chap. 9.

2 Strabo: *Geographica*, Book XI, chap. xi, § 8 (C. 520).

3 Another surviving remnant of the chariot-driving Eurasian Nomad host that had erupted out of the Steppe in the eighteenth or seventeenth century B.C. is perhaps to be detected in the Heniochoi ('Chariot-drivers') who, in the post-Alexandrine Age of Hellenic history, were to be found in the fastness between the north-east shore of the Black Sea and the north-west end of the Caucasus Range (see Strabo: *Geographica*, Book II, chap. iii, § 31 (C. 129); Book XI, chap. ii, § 1 (C. 492) and §§ 12–14 (C. 495–6); Book XI, chap. v, § 6 (C 506); Book XVII, chap. iii, § 24 (C 839)).

4 See IV. iv. 439, n. 4.

5 See Herodotus, Book IX, chap. 22.

Haumavargā in the heavy brigade that contested the field with the Macedonian horse so stubbornly.[1] In 331 B.C., however, the cataphract's great days were still to come. The cavalry of the age were the Umman Manda light horse who had opened the way for the establishment of the Achaemenian Empire by their wild ride from the heart of the Steppe to the Jumna and the Indus Delta and the Aegean and the Carpathians and beyond the Carpathians into the Hungarian Alföld.

[1] See the account, in Arrian: *Expeditio Alexandri*, Book III, chap. xiii, §§ 2–4, of the opening engagement between Darius's Bactrian and Sakan cavalry and Alexander's mercenary cavalry and Paeonians. In this engagement 'Alexander's troops suffered heavy casualties, not only because they were overborne by the Orientals' superiority in numbers, but because the Sakas and their horses had the advantage of being more efficiently protected by defensive armour'.

VI. C (ii) (*c*) 4, ANNEX

MOSCOW'S CHANGES OF FORTUNE AND THEIR HISTORICAL CAUSES

BOTH the eclipse of Moscow in the early eighteenth century and her recovery of her pristine status of being the capital of All the Russias in the early twentieth century can be explained, at least in part, in terms of the relaxation and reapplication of an external pressure.

Though Moscow had begun her career as an outpost of Russian Orthodox Christendom against the primitive pagan tenants of the north-eastern forests,[1] she had made her political fortune from the fourteenth century onwards as the main bulwark of a remnant of Russian Orthodox Christendom against an aggressive Western Christendom which had advanced eastward, overrunning the White Russian and Ukrainian marches of Russia, till, by the middle of the fifteenth century, the eastern frontier of Poland-Lithuania had come to lie within a short march of Moscow's western gate. The situation thus established had persisted for more than a century and a half. It was not till after the Polish occupation of Moscow itself in A.D. 1610–12[2] that the tide turned and Muscovy began to liberate Russian Orthodox Christian territory that had been conquered by Poland-Lithuania at earlier dates. By the beginning of the eighteenth century, however, Poland-Lithuania had become so feeble that the pressure on Russia from that quarter had diminished to vanishing-point, and in consequence Moscow had lost the significance—previously attaching to her as the defender of Russia's march against the Western World—which had been one of the causes of Moscow's both gaining and keeping a position of primacy inside the Russian World itself. During the ninety-two years that elapsed between the removal of the capital of the Russian Empire from Moscow to Saint Petersburg and the completion of the eighteenth-century partition of Poland, the balance of power on Russia's western march tipped more and more heavily in Russia's favour until in A.D. 1795 Russia recovered the last of the Russian Orthodox Christian territories that had been conquered by Western Christian Powers since the fourteenth century, with the sole exception of Eastern Galicia. In this rather exceptional chapter in the history of Russia's politico-military relations with the West along this land-frontier, Moscow's role of serving as guardian of the gate was naturally at a discount,[3] and it was probably no accident that this was also the age in which Moscow was at her nadir and Saint Petersburg at her zenith in the domestic history of the Russian body social.

However that may be, there can be no doubt that Moscow's recovery of prestige, which was the necessary prelude to her reattainment of her lost prerogative of serving as the political capital of All the Russias,

[1] See II. ii. 154. [2] See II. ii. 157. [3] See II. ii. 158, n. 1.

began from the moment when the pressure of the Western World on Russia once again became formidable. When the Polish Western invaders' feat of occupying Moscow in A.D. 1610–12 was repeated by French Western invaders in A.D. 1812, Moscow once again played the *beau rôle* while Saint Petersburg was enjoying an inglorious security;[1] and thereafter the successive German invasions of Russia in A.D. 1915 and A.D. 1941 indicated to Russian minds that the renewal of Western aggression under Napoleon's leadership had been, not a meaningless curiosity of history, but an earnest of a danger against which any government of Russia would have, in future, to be perpetually on its guard. The Polish and French invaders who in turn had momentarily occupied Moscow, and the German invaders who had only just failed to repeat the exploit, had all made their way into Great Russia along 'the duck walk' of comparatively dry ground between the parallel upper courses of the Dniepr and the Baltic Dvina, and the attractiveness of this narrow passage for Western invaders re-established the strategic importance of Moscow, in view of her situation covering 'the duck walk's' eastern exit.

It will be seen that, at the time when the Bolsheviks retransferred the seat of government from Saint Petersburg to Moscow, the original capital of the Russian Empire offered the same double advantage that had drawn the capital of the Roman Empire away from Rome to the neighbourhood of the Bosphorus in the time of Diocletian and Constantine the Great. In the 'geopolitical' circumstances of the day, Moscow was not only more conveniently situated than Leningrad for serving as the administrative capital of the Soviet Union as a whole; it was at the same time a more convenient point of vantage for simultaneously keeping an eye on that frontier from beyond which the most formidable threat to the Soviet Union's security was now to be apprehended.

A reader who is interested in this 'geopolitical' question may perhaps think it worth while to compare this Annex with II. D (v), vol. ii, pp. 157–8, in which the same vicissitudes in the fortune of Moscow and Saint Petersburg have been rather differently interpreted. When writing that passage in A.D. 1931, the writer did not realize that Moscow had now again become a bulwark of Russia on a once more dangerous western land-frontier, besides continuing to possess the attraction, which she had never ceased to possess, of being the most convenient centre of administration for the interior. What had become obvious to the present writer in A.D. 1952 after a German invader had all but encircled Moscow in the war of A.D. 1939–45 had no doubt been manifest to Lenin and his companions twenty-five years earlier.

[1] See II. ii. 400.

VII. A (i) AND (ii), ANNEX

CHURCHES AS GHOSTS

A 'DIE-HARD' upholder of the thesis that the histories of churches are incidental to the histories of civilizations might still be unwilling to confess defeat, even if he found himself unable to refute our argument that the churches are neither cancers preying upon civilizations nor chrysalises serving them for the reproduction of their kind. He might still fall back on a third hypothesis. If the churches are neither chrysalises nor cancers, may they not be ghosts? In the main stream of this Study we have not checked our course in order to discuss a third possible alternative presentation of churches in terms of civilizations which is even less convincing than the other two; but this explanation of churches as being the ghosts of civilizations perhaps deserves brief consideration in an annex.

The most plausible piece of evidence that can be cited in support of this diagnosis is the last phase in the history of the Egyptiac Civilization. When, in the eleventh century B.C., 'the New Empire' petered out, the Pharaonic Crown was assumed by the Chief Priest of Amon-Re of Thebes;[1] and thereafter, when, in the tenth century, this ecclesiastical continuation of 'the New Empire' collapsed in its turn and the greater part of the Egyptiac World was 'peacefully penetrated' by Libyan barbarians, an uncontaminated remnant of the Egyptiac social heritage was still preserved in four temple-states under the rule of the priests of the local divinities: Amon-Re of Thebes, Ptah of Memphis, Re of Heliopolis, and Horus of Letopolis. These four ecclesiastical principalities were left inviolate by the barbarian squatters who occupied the rest of the Egyptiac Civilization's domain.[2] What was the source of the prestige that enabled Hrihor to make himself master of the Imperial Throne, and the four local corporations of priests, in the next chapter of the story, to take over the government of their respective cities? If these local ecclesiastical principalities were respected by the incoming barbarians, was that not because they were recognized as being legatees of the Egyptiac culture? And was not Hrihor's political standing due, more specifically, to his ecclesiastical status as Chief Priest of a once local god who had become the High God of an Egyptiac Pantheon because his city had become the capital of an Egyptiac universal state which had been both founded and refounded by local Theban princes?[3] Would Hrihor have found himself in a position to step into Pharaoh's shoes[4] if his ecclesiastical office had not carried with it, *ex officio*, the presidency of a Pan-Egyptiac 'established church' which had been organized by the Emperor Thothmes III some four hundred years before Hrihor's day?[5]

[1] See II. ii. 116, n. 1; IV. iv. 421 and 515–17; and p. 190, above.

[2] See IV. iv. 422; V. v. 269–70 and 352–3.

[3] See pp. 213–15, above.

[4] The possibility that Hrihor may have usurped the Chief Priest's throne as a step towards usurping Pharaoh's has been noticed on p. 190, n. 1, above.

[5] See I. i. 145, n. 5; IV. iv. 421; and V. v. 530.

We may go on to observe that the local temple-states, in which the Egyptiac culture was preserved, like a fly in amber, from the tenth century B.C. onwards for some fourteen hundred years,[1] had had their counterparts in the derelict domains of other broken-down civilizations. For example, the Hittite Civilization, which suffered a violent death soon after the turn of the thirteenth and twelfth centuries B.C., was still living an ecclesiastical life-in-death in Strabo's day,[2] some twelve hundred years later, in the twin temple-states which had crystallized round the shrines of the Goddess Ma in the Pontic Cappadocian city of Comana and in its South Cappadocian namesake.[3] In the same sense the temple-state at Jerusalem, which was licensed by Cyrus the founder of the Achaemenian Empire and was extinguished by the Edomite usurper Herod the Great, was an ecclesiastical 'ghost' of a secular Syriac parochial state Judah that had been done to death by Nebuchadnezzar.

After the temple-state at Jerusalem, in its turn, had gone the way of the original Kingdom of Judah, Jewry still contrived to preserve its communal identity in diasporà thanks to a corporate religious life that survived the loss of its historic ecclesiastical citadel; and this Jewish achievement will remind us that a temple-state is only one variety of a social phenomenon which, in this Study, we have learnt to think of as a 'fossil'. If we now call to mind other examples of the general phenomenon that is exemplified in a post-Exilic Jewry, we shall observe that a majority of our 'fossils' had been preserved in an ecclesiastical sheath. The Tantric Mahayanian Buddhist fossil of an extinct Indic Civilization was, in fact, still embodied, at the time of writing, in a number of living temple-states: the ecclesiastical principality of the Dalai Lama in Tibet and its satellite temple-states in Mongolia.[4] The fossil of an extinct Babylonic Civilization that survived in the Mesopotamian city of Harrān down to the time of the 'Abbasid Caliphate preserved its identity by remaining faithful, in a Christian and Muslim environment, to an ancestral pagan religion and astral philosophy.[5] The Monophysite, Nestorian, and Zoroastrian fossils of an extinct Syriac Civilization managed, like Jewry, to retain their identity in diasporà by maintaining their corporate religious organization.

The existence of temple-states in particular, and 'fossils' in general, does suggest that there are such things as ecclesiastical 'ghosts' of defunct secular societies; and this impression will be reinforced if we

[1] The temple-state of Amon-Re at Thebes did not have so long a life as its three sisters in the Delta. It perished in the struggle for possession of the Egyptiac World between Napatan, Assyrian, and Saïte competitors in the eighth and seventh centuries B.C. (see IV. iv. 422, n. 3).

[2] See Strabo: *Geographica*, Book XII, chap. ii, § 3 (C 535), for the South Cappadocian Comana; Book XII, chap. iii, §§ 32–36 (C 557–9), for the Pontic Comana; Book XII, chap. iii, § 31, for the shrine of Men Pharnacis at Cabeira.

[3] These two Hittite ecclesiastical principalities were the most remarkable representatives of a group which also included, among others, those ruled by the priests of Cybele at Pessinus and by the priests of Mên at Pontic Cabeira and in the piece of Central Anatolian territory that was eventually converted into the domain of the Seleucid Greek city-state of Antioch-towards-Pisidia (see IV. iv. 312, n. 1).

[4] The writer did not know whether, in the year A.D. 1952, these temple-states still survived in Outer Mongolia under a Communist régime.

[5] See IV. iv. 101, n. 1; V. v. 125, n. 1; and IX. viii. 408, n. 5.

turn over the page of an historical atlas of Christendom; for this will show us at a glance that, while ecclesiastical geography is apt to reflect political geography, the political map that an ecclesiastical map reproduces is usually not the map of the political world of the day but a map which, on the political plane, has long since been obsolete. In another context[1] we have already observed that in the ecclesiastical map of a Medieval France the archbishoprics are 'ghosts' of the provinces of the Diocletianic Roman Empire, while the bishoprics are 'ghosts' of the Roman municipalities of Gallia Togata and the independent cantons of Gallia Comata as they had stood on the eve of Julius Caesar's conquests. In the ecclesiastical map of a Medieval Italy the archbishoprics commemorate the competition of Milan and Ravenna with Rome, between the third and the eighth century of the Christian Era, for the distinction of serving as a regional centre of Roman imperial administration, while the bishoprics are ghosts of the municipalities of the Italy of the Emperor Augustus. In the ecclesiastical map of a Medieval East Roman Empire the archbishoprics correspond, not to the army-corps districts (*themata*) which were the units of contemporary provincial organization,[2] but to the provinces of the Roman Empire in the Age of Justinian.

In this medieval ecclesiastical map of Eastern Orthodox Christendom, what is true of the boundaries of the archbishoprics is not true of the boundaries of the patriarchates; for, as we have noticed elsewhere,[3] the lines of demarcation between these major units of medieval ecclesiastical organization do not correspond, as they might be expected to correspond, to those between the major units of political organization in the Roman Empire of either Constantine's or Justinian's day. In contrast to the politically anachronistic boundaries between the bishoprics, the boundaries between the patriarchates turn out to be politically up to date; and, when we look into the historical reason for this anomaly, we find that it was the result of action deliberately taken by the Medieval East Roman Government, which had enlarged the area of its own metropolitan Patriarchate of Constantinople, at the expense of the two neighbouring patriarchates of Antioch and Rome, to make the Patriarchate of Constantinople coincide in area with the Medieval East Roman Empire itself. This modification of traditional ecclesiastical frontiers by political fiat was a characteristic East Roman act of state; for we have seen in another context[4] that the assertion of the supremacy of the State over the Church was a constant aim of East Roman imperial policy; and, when the East Roman Imperial Government found itself unable to control the Patriarchs of Antioch and Rome because their sees were situated in territories where the East Roman Government's writ did not run, it made the best of what was a bad job from its standpoint by high-handedly annexing to its own tame Patriarchate of Constantinople, whose incumbent was under the Emperor's thumb, those outlying fringes of the ecclesiastical dominions of the Patriarch of Antioch and the Pope of Rome—Western Cilicia

[1] On p. 192, above.
[2] See II. ii. 79–81 and 153–4; and IV. iv. 332.
[3] On p. 191, above.
[4] In IV. iv. 320–408 and 592–623.

in the one case and Greece, Sicily, and the 'toe' and 'heel' of Italy in the other case—which happened to lie within the East Roman Empire's political frontiers.

This alteration of the boundaries of the patriarchates to serve the East Roman Government's purposes can be seen, on a longer historical perspective, to have been a passing incident in a rivalry between these ecclesiastical Great Powers which was an old story by the time when the East Roman Empire was conjured up in the eighth century of the Christian Era by the genius of Leo Syrus, and which did not cease when the East Roman Empire perished, at the turn of the twelfth and thirteenth centuries, at the hands of Western Christian 'crusaders'. In this light we can see that the patriarchates too, like the archbishoprics and the bishoprics, of Christendom are ecclesiastical 'ghosts' of defunct bodies politic. Whereas the bishoprics are ghosts of city-states and cantons, and the archbishoprics are ghosts of Diocletianic Roman provinces, the patriarchates are ghosts of political Great Powers that had contended with one another in the international arena of the Hellenic World in the third and second centuries B.C. before the balance of power had been overthrown by the triumph of the Roman Commonwealth over all its competitors. On this view, the Papacy is the ghost of the Roman state; the Patriarchate of Alexandria is the ghost of a Ptolemaic successor-state of the Achaemenian Empire; the Patriarchate of Antioch is the ghost of a Seleucid successor-state of the same *ci-devant* oecumenical power; the Patriarchate of Constantinople is the ghost of the ephemeral appanage of the Macedonian war-lord Lysimachus, whose realm had once momentarily straddled the Straits and extended from Rhodope to Taurus before it was extinguished in 281 B.C. in the final round of the conflict for the division of the spoils of Darius between the successors of Alexander the Great.

This latter-day re-emergence, in an ecclesiastical guise, of an abortive political successor-state of the Achaemenian Empire which had been snuffed out more than six hundred years before the foundation of Constantinople is a striking exemplification of the thesis that churches are ghosts of defunct secular polities and societies. On the morrow of the Battle of Corupedium a victorious Seleucus Nicator and Ptolemy Lagus would have been astonished to learn that their defeated and slain rival Lysimachus was one day to take the field against them again in a ghostly warfare between the Patriarchates of Antioch, Alexandria, and Constantinople.[1] The Roman soldiers and statesmen who imposed

[1] Constantinople's success in forcing an entry into the ring of patriarchal sees was a remarkable feat. The patriarchal status of Rome, Alexandria, and Antioch had been established *de facto* already before the parvenue New Rome on the Bosphorus was founded, and all three sees were expressly confirmed in their customary rights, *iure canonico*, by Canon 6 of the Oecumenical Council of Nicaea (*sedebat* A.D. 325). The Oecumenical Council of Constantinople (*sedebat* A.D. 381) declared (Canon 2) that there were five patriarchates in the East. This was the logical 'layout' for an ecclesiastical map of the Roman Empire that was to follow the pattern of the political map (see pp. 191–2, above); for the patriarchal sees of Alexandria and Antioch corresponded respectively to the civil 'diœceses' of Egypt and the Orient, and this gave each of the three other eastern 'diœceses'—Pontus, Asiana, and Thrace—a presumptive title to be the locus of a separate patriarchal see. As it turned out, Constantinople contrived to bring the areas of all these three civil 'diœceses' under her own patriarchal jurisdiction.

Rome's yoke upon the necks of the Seleucids and the Ptolemies would have been no less surprised to see these subjugated Macedonian monarchies come back to life to challenge Rome's supremacy in an ecclesiastical arena. Yet the Eastern Orthodox patriarchates' rejection of the Roman See's claim to supremacy was, *sub specie historiae*, the reopening of an issue that had been closed on the political plane by Scipio's victory at Magnesia and Octavian's victory at Actium.

Does the evidence so far presented suffice to obtain judgement in favour of the advocates of 'the ghost theory' of the relation between churches and civilizations? The Roman instance is the classic example, and it would seem reasonable to take this as our test case. Is not Hildebrand's attempt to build a *Respublica Christiana* on the foundation of the Roman See a true parallel to Hrihor's attempt to sustain a tottering 'New Empire' of Egypt by placing the Pharaonic Crown on the head of the Chief Priest of Amon-Re of Thebes? And is not the subsequent temporal power of the Popes, and of the other prince-bishops in Western Christendom, in their local ecclesiastical principalities, a true parallel to the temporal power of the temple-states of Thebes, Memphis, Heliopolis, and Letopolis after the failure of Hrihor's more ambitious enterprise?[1]

This theory is applied to the Papacy by Thomas Hobbes of Malmesbury in a celebrated passage:

> 'If a man consider the originall of this great Ecclesiasticall Dominion, he will easily perceive that the *Papacy* is no other than the *Ghost* of the deceased *Romane Empire*, sitting crowned upon the grave thereof; for so did the Papacy start up on a Sudden out of the Ruines of that Heathen Power.'[2]

The voices of 'the barefooted fryars . . . singing Vespers in the Temple of Jupiter'[3] must indeed have sounded like the ghostly echo of a pagan Roman liturgy when they floated into Gibbon's ears on the evening of the 15th October, 1764,[4] though, when he harvested the inspiration that had germinated in his mind on that memorable occasion, Gibbon came to adopt, not 'the ghost theory', but 'the cancer theory', of the relation between the Roman Church and the Roman Empire.[5] 'The ghost-theory', however, was implicit in a phrase of Bossuet's (*vivebat* A.D. 1627–1704) which Gibbon appears to have been consciously echoing[6] when he summed up *The History of the Decline and Fall of the Roman Empire* by saying that he had 'described the triumph of Barbarism and Religion'.[7] Bossuet had said: 'Rome, devenue la proie des barbares, a conservé par la religion son ancienne majesté';[8] and

[1] This parallel has been suggested already in IV. iv. 471, n. 2.

[2] Hobbes, Th.: *Leviathan*, Part IV, chap. 47.

[3] *The Autobiographies of Edward Gibbon*, edited by Murray, J. (London 1896, Murray), p. 302, quoted in IV. iv. 59–60.

[4] See the passage quoted from Pickman on pp. 533, above.

[5] See XIII. x. 105–107.

[6] The echo of Bossuet's phrase in Gibbon's has been pointed out by Meissner, P., in *Grundformen der Englischen Geistesgeschichte* (Stuttgart and Berlin 1941, Kohlhammer), p. 8.

[7] Gibbon, E.: *The History of the Decline and Fall of the Roman Empire*, chap. lxxi, already quoted in I. i. 42 and IV. iv. 58.

[8] Bossuet, J.-B.: *Discours sur l'Histoire Universelle*, Book III, chap. 1.

Gibbon, in another passage of his work,[1] explicitly made Bossuet's point in his own observation that, 'after the loss of her legions and provinces, the genius and fortune of the popes again restored the supremacy of Rome'. It will be seen that Bossuet's dictum agrees with Hobbes' as a statement of Christian Rome's relation to her pagan predecessor, though these two seventeenth-century Western philosophers are poles apart in the inference that they draw from an identical hypothesis.[2] What to Hobbes' mind is a damning exposure is to Bossuet's mind a crowning glory; and, in taking this auspicious interpretation for granted, the seventeenth-century bishop is taking his cue from a fifth-century Pope. Preaching in Rome on the festival of the Apostles Peter and Paul, Pope Leo the Great (*pontificali munere fungebatur* A.D. 440–61) called his heroes 'the true founders of the city'.

'It is they who have raised thee to thy present pinnacle of glory, in order that—as a holy family, a chosen people, a priestly as well as a royal city that has become the capital of the World in virtue of being Blessed Peter's Holy See—thou mightest reign over a wider realm in the strength of our divine religion than in the exercise of an earthly dominion. Successive victories have added to thy territories till thou hast extended thy sovereignty far and wide over land and sea; yet the empire that has been made subject to thee by thy prowess in war is not so far flung as the domain that has been brought into thy fold by a Christian Peace.'[3]

[1] In chap. xlix.

[2] Mr. Martin Wight notes: 'The ghost theory had a special appeal for English common lawyers, who after the Reformation were apt to regard Canon Law as a malignant form of haunting. The point is made by Charles II's lord chief justice Sir Matthew Hale (*vivebat* A.D. 1609–76), in *The History of the Common Law of England*, chap. v (2nd ed. (London 1739, Walthoe), pp. 71–72):

> "Rome, as well Ancient as Modern, pretended a kind of universal Power and Interest; the former by their Victories, which were large, and extended even to *Britain* itself; and the later upon the Pretence of being Universal Bishop or Vicar-General in all Matters Ecclesiastical; so that, upon Pretence of the former, the Civil Law, and, upon Pretence of the later, the Canon Law was introduc'd, or pretended to some kind of Right, in the Territories of some absolute Princes, and among others here in *England*."

'Bryce makes the same point, with more detachment, in *Studies in History and Jurisprudence* (Oxford 1901, Clarendon Press, 2 vols.), vol. ii, pp. 245–6. Cp. Heine, Heinrich: *Zur Geschichte der Religion und Philosophie in Deutschland*: "Rom wollte herrschen; 'als seine Legionen gefallen, schickte es Dogmen in die Provinzen' " (*Religion and Philosophy in Germany*, translated by John Snodgrass (London 1882, Trübner), p. 22: "Rome always desired to rule; when her legions fell she sent dogmas into the provinces").'

[3] 'Isti sunt qui te ad hanc gloriam provexerunt, ut—gens sancta, populus electus, civitas sacerdotalis et regia—per sacram Beati Petri sedem caput Orbis effecta, latius praesideres religione divinâ quam dominatione terrenâ. Quamvis enim multis aucta victoriis ius imperii terrâ marique protuleris, minus tamen est quod tibi bellicus labor subdidit quam quod pax Christiana subiecit.'—Pope Leo the Great: *Sermo* lxxxii, *In Natali Apostolorum Petri et Pauli* (Migne, P.-J.: *Patrologia Latina*, vol. liv (Paris 1846, Migne), cols. 422–3 (quoted in Vogt, J.: *Orbis Romanus* (Tübingen 1929, Mohr), pp. 31–32). In the present Study, on p. 72, above, we have already quoted another passage of the same sermon in which Pope Leo points out the services rendered, not by Christianity to Rome, but by the Roman Empire to the Christian Church. This pair of complementary ideas is anticipated in a passage of a memorial, addressed to the Emperor Marcus Aurelius (*imperabat* A.D. 161–80) by his Christian contemporary and subject, Bishop Melito of Sardis, which is quoted by Eusebius (*Historia Ecclesiastica*, Book IV, chap. xxvi, §§ 7–11). Melito points out that the Church and the Empire are coeval (the propagation of Christianity through the Empire having started in the reign of the founder of the Empire, Augustus); he also suggests that the Empire, even during the first two centuries of its, and the Church's, history, has gained more from the spiritual support of the Church than the Church has gained from the mundane convenience of the *Pax Romana* (see p. 72, n. 1, above).

In this vision of Rome's destiny as it appears to Leo's eagle eye, the Christian 'ghost' of Rome is more robust than its pagan 'originall'. Which of these two appearances is the wraith, and which is the creature of flesh and blood? Is Hobbes right in maintaining that Romulus and Remus have made the fortunes of Peter and Paul? Or is Leo right in maintaining that Peter and Paul have saved the situation for Romulus and Remus? This issue was debated in public between a successor of Leo and a servitor of Leviathan during an episode in a conflict between the Papacy and the Kingdom of Italy which had been formally settled by the signature of three agreements at the Papal Palace of the Lateran on the 11th February, 1929,[1] but which smouldered on, and kept on flaring up, because it was an incident in a still undecided battle, on a wider front, between the worship of God and the worship of Man's corporate self.

In a speech delivered in the Chamber of Deputies at Rome on the 14th May, 1939,[2] Benito Mussolini reopened the issue by suggesting that Christianity would never have become a universal religion if the grandeur—and decadence—of Imperial Rome had not given her her opportunity.

'Italy has the singular privilege, of which we ought to be proud, of being the one European nation that is the seat of a universal religion. That religion was born in Palestine, but Rome was the place where it became Catholic. Had it stayed in Palestine, most probably it would have been one of those innumerable sects that flourished in that derelict environment—sects like the Essenes and the Therapeutae, for instance—and most probably, too, it would have flickered out without leaving a trace of its influence. . . .

'It was in Rome that Christianity found its favourable environment. It found it, in the first place, in the lassitude of the governing classes and the consular families, who, in the time of Augustus, had become effete, run to fat and gone sterile; it found it, above all, in the swarming ant-heap of Levantine humanity which was the plague of Rome's social sub-soil—a public for whom a speech like the Sermon on the Mount opened up horizons of revolt and revenge.'[3]

This offensively patronizing and provocatively controversial parenthesis in a militant political pronouncement drew fire from Pope Pius XI in an address which he gave next day to a deputation from the

[1] For this settlement and its aftermath, see Toynbee, A. J., and Boulter, V. M.: *Survey of International Affairs, 1929* (London 1930, Milford), pp. 422–78.

[2] The text will be found in Mussolini, B.: *Scritti e Discorsi*, vol. vii (Milan 1934, Hoepli), pp. 34–35.

[3] 'L'Italia ha il privilegio singolare, di cui dobbiamo andare orgogliosi, di essere l'unica nazione europea che è sede di una religione universale. Questa religione è nata nella Palestina, ma è diventata cattolica a Roma. Se fosse rimasta nella Palestina, molto probabilmente sarebbe stata una delle tante sette che fiorivano in quell' ambiente arroventate, come ad esempio quelle degli Esseni e dei Terapeuti, e molto probabilmente si sarebbe spenta, senza lasciare traccia di sé. . . .

'Il Cristianesimo trova il suo ambiente favorevole in Roma. Lo trova, prima di tutto, nella lassitudine delle classi dirigenti e delle famiglie consolari, che ai tempi di Augusto erano diventate stracche, grasse e sterili, e lo trova, sopra tutto, nel brulicante formicaio dell' umanità levantina che afliggeva il sottosuolo sociale di Roma, e per la quale un discorso come quello della Montagna apriva gli orizzonti della rivolta e della rivendicazione.'

Jesuit College of Mondragone; and, when Mussolini—taken aback by the reception of his ill-considered excursion into the interpretation of history—sought, in the Senate on the 25th May, to improve the defences of an exposed position without overtly surrendering any ground, his elaboration of his thesis led him floundering deeper into the mire and gave his formidable adversary an opening for striking a winning blow. In a letter of the 30th May, 1929, addressed to Cardinal Gasparri, the Pope had the last word.

'Least of all did We expect to be treated to heretical pronouncements on the very essence of Christianity and Catholicism. There has been an attempt to emend them, but this attempt has not been altogether successful, to Our mind. . . . The divine mission to all the nations preceded the calling of Saint Paul; and this was also preceded by the mission of Saint Peter to the Gentiles. Thus the universality of the Church—both by right and in fact—is already there at the very outset of the Church's history and of the Apostles' preaching. Through the work of the Apostles and of their apostolic fellow-labourers, this universality very soon surpassed the limits of the Roman Empire—which, as everybody knows, was very far indeed from being coextensive with the whole World [as] known [to the Ancients]. If all that was intended was a reference to the facility for the diffusion and organisation of the Church that was providentially provided in the organisation of the Roman Empire, all that was necessary was a reference to Dante and Leo the Great—two great Italians who, in a few magnificent words, have stated, in lapidary form, the substance of what has become a commonplace in second-hand restatements by innumerable other voices.'[1]

In this encounter, Pope Pius discomfited Mussolini as signally as Pope Leo had discomfited Attila; and the invocation of the Apostles on Christian Rome's behalf was indeed an argument to which there was no retort. Thomas Hobbes himself, shrewd in argument though he was, had simple-mindedly let the cat out of the bag in a sentence immediately preceding the passage of his *Leviathan* that we have quoted. In defining the period in which the Papists' 'whole Hierarchy or Kingdome of Darknesse may be compared not unfitly to the *Kingdome of Fairies*' by dating it 'from the time that the Bishop of Rome had gotten to be acknowledged for Bishop Universall by pretence of Succession to Saint Peter',[2] Hobbes has made, in advance, the admission that the Papacy is what it is in virtue of being the heir of the Apostolic Christian Church, and not in virtue of being the ghost of the pagan Roman Empire.

These findings may confirm us in the conclusion, reached in an

[1] 'Men che tutto Ci aspettavamo espressioni ereticali sulla essenza stessa del Cristianesimo e del Cattolicismo. Si è cercato di rimediare: non Ci sembra con pieno successo. . . . Il mandato divino alle genti universe è anteriore alla chiamata di San Paolo; anteriore a questa il mandato di San Pietro ai gentili; l'universalità si riscontra già di diritto e di fatto agli inizi primi della Chiesa e della predicazione apostolica; questa per opera degli apostoli e degli uomini apostolici ben presto più vasta dell' Impero Romano, che, come è noto, non era di gran lunga tutto il mondo conosciuto; se si voleva soltanto ricordare l'utilità providenzialmente preparata alla diffusione e organizzazione della Chiesa nella organizzazione dell' impero romano, bastava ricordare Dante e Leone Magno, due grandi Italiani, che in poche e magnifiche parole dissero e scolpirono la sostanza di quanto poi innumeri altri ridissero.'

[2] Hobbes, op. cit., loc. cit.

earlier context,[1] that 'the analogy between Hildebrand's Roman hierocracy and Hrihor's Theban hierocracy breaks down'; and, if our Roman case in point is a fair test case, as we have taken it to be, we may infer that the higher religions cannot be accounted for as being the ghosts of civilizations any better than they can be explained as being their cancers or their chrysalises.

[1] In IV. iv. 517.

VII. A (iii) (*a*), ANNEX I

SPIRITUAL ACHIEVEMENT AND MATERIAL ACHIEVEMENT: ARE THEY ANTITHETICAL OR INTERDEPENDENT?

In previous passages[1] we have suggested that the circumstances favourable to spiritual and to secular progress are not only different but are antithetical. This is one of the themes of the Parable of the Sower: 'Some fell among thorns, and the thorns grew up and choked it, and it yielded no fruit';[2] but we arrived at our conclusion, not intuitively, but empirically, as a result of tracing backwards in time a process of progressive spiritual enlightenment of which Christianity was the latest stage and, in Christian belief, the highest so far reached. We found that each of those preceding stages of spiritual advance had taken place in social circumstances which, like those which saw the birth of Christianity, were marked by a failure of mundane endeavours and by the suffering which such failure entails. When we turn from Christianity to consider the other three living higher religions, we find their histories likewise conforming to our apparent 'law' that spiritual achievement and material achievement are antithetical.

Christianity was born of a disintegrating Hellenic Civilization's experience of suffering at the climax of its Time of Troubles, and it came of age in the social interregnum following the Hellenic Civilization's final dissolution at the break-up of the Roman Empire. The histories of the Mahāyāna, Hinduism, and Islam reveal the same pattern of relation between spiritual and secular life. The Mahāyāna and Hinduism[3] both emerged during a period, running from the second century B.C. to the fourth century of the Christian Era, when the Indic World was suffering under an intrusion of the Hellenic Civilization in the form of military invasions by Bactrian Greek war-lords and their Kushan successors. Thereafter, the Mahāyāna captivated Far Eastern hearts during a social interregnum that followed the dissolution of the Sinic Civilization upon the break-up of the Empire of the Posterior Han at the turn of the second and third centuries of the Christian Era. As for Islam, it achieved its amazing metamorphosis from being the heresy of a barbarian prophet into being a higher religion in its own right under the Arab Caliphate, which was the second and last phase of a Syriac universal state; and it rose to the occasion in an age when the break-up of the Caliphate was announcing the dissolution of the Syriac Civilization. In the history of Islam at this stage the rise of Christian monasticism and Christian mysticism had its parallel in the dervish movement and in Islamic

[1] On pp. 425 and 551, above. See also pp. 759–68, below.

[2] Mark iv. 7. Cp. Matt. xiii. 7 and Luke viii. 7.

[3] Hinduism, that is, in the sense—to which the use of the term is confined in this Study—of the devotional religion which grew up, beneath the crust of the ritual religion of the Vedas, contemporaneously with the growth of devotional Mahayanian Buddhism beneath the crust of an ascetic Hinayanian Buddhism.

mysticism; and in this case, as in that, an outburst of spiritual life at a moment of mundane catastrophe was the secret of the triumphant religion's success in converting both the human sheep left shepherdless by the disappearance of a secular universal state and the wolf-like invading barbarians.

The same 'law' seems to be exemplified in the history of Zoroastrianism. In another context[1] we have observed that this higher religion forfeited its prospect of becoming a universal church when it was conscripted to serve as the ecclesiastical instrument of a Sasanian State dedicated to the political mission of expelling an intrusive Hellenism from the Syriac World. In the light of this spiritual penalty which Zoroastrianism incurred as the price of obtaining the political patronage of an Imperial Power in the third century of the Christian Era, it is significant that her previous loss of the patronage of an Imperial Power, through the overthrow of the Achaemenian Empire by Alexander the Great in the fourth century B.C., had been followed by a marked increase of intensity in the radiation of her spiritual influence.

'The end of the Persian period by no means saw the end of Parsee [i.e. Zoroastrian] influence on Jewish eschatology. Indeed, on the contrary, from this time onwards the influence becomes much stronger and more forceful and apparently more conscious, in contrast to the previous chapter of history, in which the adoption of Parsee ideas [by Judaism] was generally a more unconscious process. It is a peculiar phenomenon, of which there are many examples, that states and peoples do not exert their cultural and spiritual influence effectively until after their own political collapse. The culture of Ancient Greece was not transmitted to the Ancient World (it would be substantially true to say) until after the independence of the Greek city-states had been decisively abolished by Philip of Macedon; and the culture of Rome was not acquired, in the true sense, by the Germans before Rome's world empire had collapsed under the blows of the Teutons. There seems to be something like a law of Nature that peoples cannot sow, from a full hand, the golden seed of their spiritual treasures until they have renounced, or been compelled to renounce, earthly goods. This is certainly true of the religious ideas of Parseeism, and indeed of Iranian religion in general. These ideas radiate, with an unprecedented penetrative power, all over the domain of an expiring Ancient World when, but only when, the Persian Monarchy has collapsed.'[2]

It will be noticed that the student of religious history who is the author of the passage just quoted draws attention to our apparent 'law' of antithesis governing the conditions that make respectively for spiritual and for material achievement, but that, in the examples of its working which he cites, he does not confine himself to the field of Religion, but compares the case of Zoroastrianism with secular cultural phenomena which may be classified likewise as being 'spiritual' though they do not fall within the religious sphere of spiritual life. This raises the question whether our 'law', if it is a law for Religion, is likewise a law for spiritual life in a wider sense, in which the term 'spiritual' would cover aesthetic

1 In V. v. 659–61.
2 Gall, A. von: *Βασιλεία τοῦ Θεοῦ* (Heidelberg 1926, Winter), pp. 263–4.

and other non-religious cultural experiences and activities. Our 'law' has in fact been propounded, with this wider application, by an exiled Russian Orthodox Christian philosopher-prophet, Nicolas Berdyaev, in pursuance of an idea originally suggested by the German philosopher Oswald Spengler's sharply drawn antithesis between the connotations of the two German words *Kultur* and *Zivilisation*.

'Culture has always proved Life's greatest failure. An antithesis would seem to divide culture from the "life" that Civilisation attempts to realise. When a mighty German state is finally established, Capitalism and Socialism accompany it; and its main efforts are directed to assert its will to world power and organisation. But Goethe, the great idealists and romantics, great philosophy and art, will be missing from this mighty Imperialist and Socialist Germany. They will have been supplanted by technique, which has its repercussions even upon philosophical thought (in the gnosiological currents). Conquest is the method now applied in all spheres at the expense of the integral-intuitive apprehension of Being. The mighty civilisation of the British Empire holds no place for either Shakspeare or Byron, just as Dante and Michelangelo are inconceivable in [the] Modern Italy which erected the ponderous monument to Victor Emmanuel and established Fascism. And herein lies the tragedy of both Culture and Civilisation.'[1]

Does a 'law' which has thus suggested itself independently to the minds of divers students of history fit the facts of non-religious spiritual life as unequivocally as it appears to fit the facts of religious experience? In the field of Religion we have noticed a number of signal testimonies to this law's validity without so far having stumbled upon any conflicting evidence. Is this equally true in the field of secular culture? If we extend our empirical survey into this other province of spiritual life, we shall find here that the examples of the working of the law are also striking, but that they are contradicted, in this province, by some no less signal breaches of it.

One of the classic examples of the working of our 'law' in the secular cultural field is cited by Berdyaev in the passage just quoted. In the history of the Modern Western secular culture in Germany it is notorious that the great age of German music, literature, and art falls within the period of political and economic adversity that began for Germany with the Thirty Years War (*gerebatur* A.D. 1618–48) and that ended for her with the foundation of the Second Reich in A.D. 1871. And this classic German instance is not a solitary one. 'The golden day' in which a wave of artistic creativity, set in motion by a Medieval Italian Renaissance, touched New England, in her turn,[2] after having fructified Germany, was extinguished by the political triumph of winning the Civil War and by the economic triumph of winning the West.

'The law of inverse operation' is likewise illustrated by the history of Persian literature. Just as the religious tendril of the Iranian genius flowered after the fall of the Iranian Empire of the Achaemenidae and withered after the rise of the Iranian Empire of the Sasanidae, so its aesthetic potentiality in the medium of Poetry did not reveal itself until

[1] Berdyaev, N.: *The Meaning of History*, English translation (London 1936, Bles), p. 212.

[2] See III. iii. 137.

after the fall of the Sasanian Empire had opened an Islamic chapter of Iranian history; and, even then, it had to wait until after the Persian genius had been decisively expelled from the arena of political life. The Islamic Persian literature did not come to flower during an age when the Persians, after their momentary military and political overthrow at the hands of the Primitive Muslim Arab conquerors, had come back into political power in the Syriac World, first as henchmen and ministers of the ʿAbbasid Caliphs[1] and then as founders and rulers of successor-states of a crumbling ʿAbbasid Empire. The Islamic Persian literature—in which the Persian language served as the vehicle for poetry such as had never before been begotten by the Persian artistic genius—came to flower at a moment when the Persian successors of the ʿAbbasids were being supplanted by barbarian Turkish war-lords; the patron of Firdawsī was the Turk Mahmūd of Ghaznah; and, under Turkish and Mongol barbarian patronage, Persian literature continued to flourish so long as the Persians remained fast bound in the misery and iron[2] of political adversity. But, when, nine hundred years after the fall of the Sasanian Empire and five hundred years after the fall of the Samanid march-state in Transoxania,[3] a Turkish-speaking dynasty paradoxically re-established a powerful and militant Persian national state, the golden chain of Persian poets broke off short as abruptly as the chain of German composers of music when, two hundred years after Germany's political and economic catastrophe in the Thirty Years War, a materially puissant Prussia-Germany was conjured into existence by Bismarck.[4]

The law of inverse operation can also be seen at work in the aesthetic field in the province of Visual Art, as well as in the provinces of Music and Literature. In another context[5] we have noticed that, in a latter-day museum at Sparta, the specimens of an original, distinctive, and promising 'pre-Lycurgean' Lacedaemonian art are sundered from the specimens of a commonplace 'post-Lycurgean' art by a gap corresponding chronologically to the period during which Lacedaemon was a formidable political and military power in the Hellenic World in virtue of her devotion to a 'Lycurgean' *agôgê* which deliberately and cold-bloodedly concentrated on producing military efficiency and prowess at the cost of sacrificing every other aim in life. We have also noticed, in the same connexion, that the fifth, fourth, and third centuries B.C., during which the 'Lycurgean' régime held Sparta in its grip and inhibited her from indulging her previously manifest artistic genius, were the very centuries in which, in other Hellenic city-states, the visual arts were at their apogee.

This contrast between the artistic promise of 'pre-Lycurgean' Sparta and the conspicuousness of Art by its absence in the Sparta of the 'Lycurgean' Age has an historical parallel in the contrast between the masterly perceptiveness with which an Upper Palaeolithic Man depicted on the walls of his cave-dwellings the animals that were his game, and

[1] See pp. 148–51, above. [2] Ps. cvii. 10. [3] See II. ii. 142.

[4] The apparent inability of the Persian genius to express itself simultaneously in poetry and in politics has been noticed already in I. i. 360, n. 1, and II. ii. 77, n. 1. Compare I. i. 363, n. 3, and the passage quoted ibid., pp. 393–4, from Mirzā Muhammad Khan of Qazwīn.

[5] In III. iii. 66–67.

the unimaginativeness of the perfunctory decorations scratched or painted on the pottery of this magnificent primitive artist's Neolithic successor, who not only forged ahead of his aesthetically superior predecessor in the technique of fashioning stones into tools, but also demonstrated his own all-round superiority in economic capability by capping his invention of earthenware with the discovery of agriculture—a revolution in the material conditions of human life which, at the time of writing, still remained unsurpassed by any of the material achievements of any of the civilizations. If the dumb archaeological record that, midway through the twentieth century of the Christian Era, was the only extant evidence for the transition from the Upper Palaeolithic to the Neolithic way of life were ever to be illuminated by the dawning glimmer of an historical twilight that had revealed something of the inner history of the transition from a 'pre-Lycurgean' to a 'Lycurgean' Sparta, would it become apparent in the earlier, as in the later, tragedy that the artist's genius had been stifled by a will to power?

These parallels, in the spiritual provinces of Visual Art, Music, and Literature, to our examples of the working of 'the law of inverse operation' in the field of Religion are impressive as far as they go; but an unprejudiced survey reveals that, in the non-religious field of spiritual life, such evidences of the validity of our 'law' are counterbalanced by instances of breaches of it.

The case of Sparta, for example, is offset by the case of Athens; for the Periclean Athens who made herself 'the education of Hellas'[1] in the fifth century B.C. did not have to purchase her artistic and intellectual pre-eminence in the Hellenic World of that age at the price of renouncing the material power which an artistically barren contemporary Sparta was cultivating at the cost of everything else. On the contrary, at the very time when the Athenians were creating their exquisite works of art and literature, they were also building up their material power—and this on a basis far broader than any that the Spartans had ever dreamed of—to a pitch at which Athens, single-handed, proved almost strong enough to impose her dominion upon all the other city-states of Hellas. On this practical, power-building side of their multifarious activity in 'the Classical Age' the Athenians had begun by carrying through the economic revolution of abandoning subsistence-farming in favour of cultivating specialized crops, and manufacturing specialized industrial wares, for export in exchange for imports of foodstuffs for their own consumption at home;[2] in order to expedite this profitable new foreign commerce they had built up a merchant marine; and, on the twofold foundation of their newly acquired wealth and maritime experience, they had founded a navy which, as a weapon of war, outclassed the Spartan phalanx in subtlety as notably as in range. The potency of the Athenian Navy in the fifth century B.C. is expounded as follows by an anonymous Athenian student of public affairs whose observation of the Athenian democracy of his day was as keen as his dislike of it:

'[The] accidents [of geography] have played into the hands of Athenian

[1] A phrase attributed to Pericles himself by Thucydides, Book II, chap. 41.
[2] See I. i. 24–25; II. ii. 36–42; and III. iii. 122.

sea-power. The subjects of a land-power can club together a number of small communities and then go into action [against the paramount power] with concentrated forces; the subjects of a sea-power, in so far as they are islanders, are not in a position to bring their communities together in a physical union; they are insulated from one another by salt water; the paramount power rules the waves; and, even if the islanders could manage to slip through the blockade and concentrate their forces on a single island, they would [simply] die of hunger. As for Athens' subject communities on the mainland, the big ones are kept in subjection by intimidation and the small ones really by a [latent] economic sanction, since there is no community [in the world] that can do without imports and exports, and these will be denied to any community that does not show itself amenable to the rulers of the sea. And then the rulers of the sea can [count on being able to] do something that the rulers of land empires can do [only] occasionally: they can devastate the territory of their superiors in military strength. They can coast along an enemy shore-line where the enemy is either not on the spot at all, or anyway not in strength, and then, on the approach of [substantial] enemy forces, they can retire on board ship and stand out into the offing—tactics which condemn the enemy's relieving land-force (ὁ πεζῇ παραβοηθῶν) to have the worst of it. Then the rulers of the sea can make a naval expedition to any distance you like from their home base, while a land-power's range of action from its home base is limited to a few days' journey (marching overland being a slow business, and the ration-carrying capacity of a land-force being limited to not more than a few days' supply). Moreover, a land-force must either have friendly country to traverse or must fight its way through, whereas a naval force [is master of the initiative]: where it finds itself in superior strength it can disembark a landing-party; in the contrary event it is under no compulsion to try a landing at that particular point; it can [just] go coasting along till it reaches either friendly country or an enemy in inferior strength.'[1]

The versatility of the Athenians of the Periclean Age in simultaneously cultivating diverse capacities of human nature is eulogized, as a distinctive quality which is the secret of their greatness, in the Thucydidean version of a famous Periclean speech:

'We cultivate the Arts without extravagance and the Intellect without effeminacy. . . . Our politicians do not neglect their private affairs, and the rest of us devote ourselves to business without losing touch with politics. We are unique in regarding men who take no part in politics as being not merely unambitious but unprofitable; and we are all sound judges, if not creative statesmen, in public affairs. . . . In short, I maintain that the Commonwealth of Athens is the School of Hellas and that the individual Athenian will never meet his equal for gallantry, self-reliance, adaptability, versatility, and distinction, in whatever situation he may find himself. The proof that this is no empty boast, but is sober reality, is afforded by the power of our country, which is the fruit of our national character.'[2]

This simultaneous pre-eminence in artistic and material prowess, which is characteristic of Periclean Athens—though not of Sparta or

[1] Auctor Atheniensis Anonymus: *Institutions of Athens* (edited by Kalinka, E.: Berlin and Leipzig 1913, Teubner), chap. ii, §§ 2–5.

[2] Thucydides, Book II, chap. xl, §§ 1–2, and chap. xli, §§ 1–2.

Persia or Germany in any age—had had parallels in a Modern Western World in both seventeenth-century Holland and seventeenth-century France. The apogee of Dutch painting and Dutch scholarship had been contemporaneous with the apogee of Dutch commerce and Dutch naval, military, and political power; and in the twentieth century of the Christian Era France looked back to the reign of Louis Quatorze as 'le Grand Siècle' because in that age she had performed the twin feats of only just failing to impose her dominion upon all the other countries of the West and completely succeeding in making herself 'the education of Europe' thanks to the simultaneous brilliance of her achievements in the Arts. Thereafter, when Great Britain was harvesting the lion's share of the political and economic fruits of Holland's pyrrhic victory over Louis XIV's France, the consequent expansion of British commercial and naval power was accompanied in the realm of Literature by the achievement of a minor 'Augustan Age'; and the classic prototype of all 'Augustan ages', in which a Latin literature had come to its finest flower, had been contemporary with a reprieve which had been won by a Roman political genius for a disintegrating Hellenic Civilization through the establishment of an Augustan Peace.

If, with these conspicuous breaches of our 'law' in mind, we now re-examine the passage, quoted above, in which Berdyaev propounds this 'law' as one that governs the ebb and flow of secular culture, we shall find flaws in the particular pieces of evidence that he cites in support of his thesis.

If, in his citation of English history, Berdyaev had argued his case in terms of Music, he could have pointed out that, in the musical province of secular cultural life, A.D. 1688 was as inauspicious a date in England's history as A.D. 1871 in Germany's, and he could have inferred that a Modern Western bourgeoisie was apt to bury its musical talent as soon as it began to make money in business. Even in this province, however, the English example only partially bears out a 'law of inverse operation' to which the German example conforms with exactitude; for, while it is true of English, as of German, history that music 'slumped' when business began to boom, it is not true, in the English case, that music did not begin to blossom until the country's economic and political life had been overtaken by adversity. The *floruit* of German classical music, whose *terminus ante quem* is A.D. 1871, has also a *terminus post quem* in A.D. 1648; for, as we have noticed, this *floruit* is exactly coincident in duration with the 'trough' in the curve of Germany's political and economic fortunes between the Thirty Years War and the foundation of the Second Reich. On the other hand the musical talent of the English bourgeoisie, which ceased to be cultivated when 'the Glorious Revolution' of A.D. 1688 was followed by a steep and steady rise in British commercial prosperity and naval power, was already being cultivated with ardour in the Elizabethan Age—in which the English were enjoying an intoxicating spell of naval and commercial power—without having to wait for the doldrums of the seventeenth century in order to come into its own.[1]

[1] Mr. Martin Wight notes: 'French music partially bears out the law of inverse

Thus, in English history, even Music only partially bears out our 'law', while Poetry—which is the secular art that Berdyaev singles out for citing in his English illustration of his thesis—yields perhaps more evidence against his argument than in favour of it. Berdyaev's contention that 'the mighty civilisation of the British Empire holds no place for either Shakspeare or Byron' is, no doubt, borne out, as far as Byron is concerned, by the portentous spectacle of the eclipse that overtook the muse of Byron's older contemporary Wordsworth after the post-Napoleonic triumph of a British Industrial Revolution. If Byron (*vivebat* A.D. 1788–1824)—or, for that matter, Shelley (*vivebat* A.D. 1792–1822) or Keats (*vivebat* A.D. 1795–1821)—had lived to the same ripe old age as Wordsworth (*vivebat* A.D. 1770–1850), Wordsworth's history suggests that these younger contemporaries of his likewise might have found the spiritual climate of a Victorian England adverse to their poetic genius. On the other hand, Shakspeare's life-span was, of course, coeval with the Elizabethan Age, and this chronological correspondence is no mere coincidence, for the poet was neither hostile nor indifferent to the political and economic triumphs of his countrymen in his lifetime; the excitement of sighting opportunity, and the exultation of rising to the occasion, which was the stimulus of the Elizabethan English pirate and merchant adventurer, was likewise the inspiration of the Elizabethan English playwright and man of letters. The same fire coursed through all Elizabethan English veins; and this feature of an Elizabethan Age of English history reappears in a Victorian Age. Tennyson and Browning were children of the Victorian Age in the same significant sense in which Shakspeare was a child of the Elizabethan; and the last decade of the nineteenth century of the Christian Era, in which the resurgence of Germany's material power was celebrated by the death of the last of the German classical composers of music,[1] saw the recession of Victorian England's material power portended by the deaths[2] of the two most characteristic of the Victorian English poets.[3]

operation: it reached its greatest heights (as did French painting) during the first fifty years of the régime of the Third Republic [i.e. during a half-century in which, on the military and political plane, France was under the shadow of the catastrophe of A.D. 1870–1]. Martin Cooper's recent book on *French Music* (London 1951, Oxford University Press) bears the sub-title "From the Death of Berlioz to the Death of Fauré" (A.D. 1869–1924), which is the richest and most varied period in the history of French music. It may be noticed that this is an example of Music's flourishing in a period which, on the plane of practical affairs, was one of *political* decline but of *economic* prosperity. In France, at any rate, the bourgeoisie proved to be as good a patron of the Arts as the Crown had once been.'

Mr. John Lodge comments on Mr. Martin Wight's note: 'I think that this is a matter of opinion. Bizet (*vivebat* A.D. 1838–1875) died young but was a composer of genius as well as charm, and Berlioz (*vivebat* A.D. 1803–1869) is to French music what Hugo and Delacroix are to French poetry and French [visual] art. He is their greatest romantic. If you prefer the French Impressionists and Post-Impressionists in painting, you will probably prefer their contemporaries in music.'

1 Brahms died in A.D. 1897.

2 Tennyson died in A.D. 1892, Browning in A.D. 1889.

3 Mr. Martin Wight comments: 'In this application of the law of inverse operation to the history of English poetry, the argument is open to two criticisms: (i) It assumes the comparability and literary-historical equivalence of all the poets that you mention, and (ii) those that you mention are arbitrarily selected. The main massifs in the poetic range do roughly coincide with periods of political power: Spenser, Shakspeare, Donne, with the Elizabethan-Jacobean expansion; Milton with the Cromwellian epoch (if one regards him, like Clarendon, as a personal example of Withdrawal-and-Return, writing his masterpiece in a retirement from politics during the Restoration doldrums); Dryden

Nor, in the provinces of Poetry and the Visual Arts, is our 'law' borne out by Italian history any more convincingly than it is by English history. It is true, as Berdyaev points out, that a Cavourian Italy, like a Bismarckian Germany, blindly buried what survived of her artistic talent in her obsession with the pursuit of material power; but the two arts of which Dante and Michelangelo were respectively masters neither survived in Italy to wilt at the advent of the Risorgimento nor waited in Italy to blossom until the Italians had tasted the political and economic adversity that began to overtake them at the turn of the fifteenth and sixteenth centuries of the Christian Era. The *floruit* of the Italian school of Western Poetry, Painting, Sculpture, and Architecture was coeval with the age in which the city-states of Northern and Central Italy were successful in maintaining their political independence and in making their country the workshop and emporium of the World;[1] and in a Late Medieval Italy, as in an Elizabethan and in a Victorian England, the contemporaneity of the blossoming of these arts with the achievement of material power was not just a chronological coincidence. Here, too, there was an inner psychological connexion between these two diverse manifestations of *virtù*. To find an Italian illustration of the working of our 'law' in the secular field, Berdyaev would have had to surrender Poetry and the Visual Arts and take his stand on Music; for here the Italian pattern is in truth the same as the German. A golden chain which begins with Palestrina (*vivebat* A.D. 1526–94) and ends with Verdi (*vivebat* A.D. 1813–1901) does exactly span the political and economic 'trough' in Italian history which extends from Charles VIII's crossing of the Alps in A.D. 1494[2] to Victor Emmanuel's entry into Rome in A.D. 1870. The zenith of the Italian Opera coincides in date with the nadir of Italian wealth and power, and this synchronism is too suggestively reminiscent of its German counterpart for us to be able to dismiss it as a freak of Chance.

What is the upshot of the foregoing survey? It has already made two things clear. In the first place, our 'law' that spiritual achievement and material achievement are antithetical proves not to have equal validity in all cultural provinces. Its manifest operation in the field of Religion was the clue which originally led us to formulate it; and we can now see that we might also have arrived at it by another road if our starting-

and Pope with the age of William and Marlborough (but in the later Augustan Age we lack a poetic peak to correspond to Chatham: Gray scarcely fills the bill, though Johnson, whose genius was not poetic, would exactly fill it); and the Romantics, from their conventional beginning with the publication of *Lyrical Ballads* in 1798 down to their dim 'Georgian' swan-song with Rupert Brooke dying at Scyros in 1915, with the post-Napoleonic *Pax Britannica*. But most critics would judge that the general level of poetical genius in this series *descends*, running transversely to the ascending line of political power: they would see the Elizabethans as a Golden Age and Tennyson in terms of a Silver Age. And by common consent the two highest poetical peaks, Shakspeare and Milton, come at the beginning of the range. So perhaps one gets the law of inverse operation working within the limits of a broad coincidence of poetical and political achievement.

'It is worth noting that there is a fairly considerable massif, whose chief peaks are Yeats and Eliot, rising out of the waste land of Britain's loss of Great Power status in the twentieth century—fairly considerable, but not big enough in relation to the whole range to show a poetical efflorescence succeeding or coinciding with a collapse of political power.'

[1] See III. iii. 342.

[2] See ibid.

point had been, not Religion, but Music. If, however, our starting-point had been Poetry, the Persian and German exemplifications of the working of the 'law' would have been offset by the Attic, Italian, French, and English breaches of it; while, if we had started with a survey of the social conditions in which the Visual Arts have blossomed and wilted, we might have been led, by the evidence in this field, to formulate the precisely contrary 'law' that spiritual achievement and material achievement are, not antithetical, but interdependent; for the consensus of the Attic, Italian, and Dutch evidence in this sense would probably have weighed more heavily in our estimation than the contrary evidence from Sparta and from the Stone Age. Can we bring any order out of the apparent confusion into which our well-tried empirical method of inquiry might appear to have led us in this instance?

One conclusion that is suggested by the facts now before us is that there is an intrinsic incompatibility between the quest of the Beatific Vision, which is the goal of Religion, and the pursuit of material power in any of its forms. Another conclusion is that the secular vein of spiritual activity is a middle term between Religion on the one hand and the pursuit of material power on the other. When we dissect this secular spiritual activity into its diverse expressions in Music, Poetry, and Visual Art, we find that Music is apt to obey the same 'law' of ebb and flow as Religion, and Visual Art the same 'law' as the pursuit of power, while Poetry behaves equivocally—reacting in German and Persian history like Music and Religion, and in Attic, Italian, French, and English history like Visual Art and the pursuit of power. These tentative conclusions seem warrantable; for the truth is that Human Life on Earth is lived in two societies simultaneously—the Ergastulum of Leviathan and the Commonwealth of God[1]—and each of these ways of life has its own spiritual dynamic: the inspiration of the Grace of God and the stimulus of the Pride of Life.[2] The evidence suggests that Visual Art is apt to respond to the Pride of Life more readily than to a Grace of which the price is material adversity; that those adverse conditions of material life that are propitious for Religion are also propitious for Music; and that Poetry, in contrast to both her sister arts, is a turncoat chamaeleon, who can take colour from the stimulus of Pride as readily as from the inspiration of Grace.

The classic case in which Poetry had followed the course of Religion in first blossoming at the breath of mundane adversity and then wilting at the breath of mundane prosperity was presented by the Islamic chapter of Persian history; and in this case it was manifest that Poetry had drawn its inspiration from a religious source. 'The close connexion between Poetry and Belles Lettres on the one hand and Sufi-ism and Mysticism on the other, at any rate in Persia, is obvious, so that the extinction of the one necessarily involves the extinction of the other.'[3]

[1] See V. vi. 149–68 and 365–9; and pp. 558–61, above.

[2] 'Fecerunt itaque civitates duas amores duo, terrenam scilicet amor sui usque ad contemptum Dei, caelestem vero amor Dei usque ad contemptum sui' (St. Augustine: *De Civitate Dei*, Book XIV, chap. 28).

[3] Letter, dated the 24th May, 1911, from Mirzā Muhammad Khan of Qazwīn to Professor E. G. Browne, quoted in I. i. 394 (cp. loc. cit., p. 363, n. 3).

After the forcible conversion of Persia from the Sunnah to the Shīʿah by the Safawīs, the triumphant Shīʿī divines waged a relentless war against the dervish monasteries, and Poetry as well as Mysticism was eradicated in the destruction of a religious institution in which Mysticism and Poetry alike had found a spiritual home.

We may also cite one conspicuous case in which the course of Religion had been followed by Visual Art. A classical Hellenic art which had gone into decline at the onset of the second bout of an Hellenic Time of Troubles at the turn of the third and second centuries B.C.[1] had been eventually discarded—by an latter-day generation of Hellenes whose experience of suffering had sickened them of the Pride of Life—in favour of a revolutionary Byzantine art whose aim was not to portray the body but to minister to Religion by expressing the Soul.[2]

Note by MARTIN WIGHT *on VII. A (iii) (a), Annex I*

SPIRITUAL AND MATERIAL ACHIEVEMENT: THE LAW OF INVERSE OPERATION IN ITALIAN VISUAL ART

I think your generalization about the *floruit* of Italian art is so broad as to be inaccurate: it requires closer analysis.

The four great poets come squarely at the beginning and at the end of the political independence of the city-states: Dante and Petrarch in the fourteenth century, when Italy finally emancipated itself from the remains of Imperial and Papal political control; Ariosto (*vivebat* A.D. 1474–1533) and Tasso (*vivebat* A.D. 1544–95) in the sixteenth century, when Italy fell under Spanish control. The fifteenth century, which was the political heyday of the city-states, produced no great poet. Here there is something of inverse operation.

It is also visible in Painting, Sculpture, and Architecture. These ascended steadily up to the High Renaissance in the two generations after the collapse of the city-state cosmos in A.D. 1494, and the supreme artists lived through or were stimulated by the 'invasion of the barbarians'. Botticelli was deeply influenced by Savonarola and experienced the destruction of Florence as a Great Power. Raphael, whose life has fewest political *rapports*, was summoned to Rome by Julius II, the last pope under whom the Papal States played the role of a Great Power. Leonardo was in the service of Lodovico Sforza, under whom Milan lost its Great Power status, and he ended his life in the service of the French conqueror. Michelangelo's life was interwoven with the collapse of the Papacy as a temporal Great Power, and he was practically the last engineer of the fortifications of republican Florence before the city was finally reduced to being a satellite of Spain through the Medici restoration of A.D. 1530. Venetian art ascended from the Bellini through Giorgione (*vivebat* A.D. 1475?–1510) to its peak in Titian (*vivebat circa* 1485–1576) and Tintoretto (*vivebat* 1518–94), while Venice lost her Great Power status in the twin battles on land and sea of Agnadello and Diù

1 See V. vi. 287–91.

2 See IV. iv. 54–55.

in 1508; and Berenson sees the political catastrophe as a challenge by responding to which the Venetian artistic tradition was etherialized and carried to its greatest heights.

'But even while such pictures [as the early works of Titian] were being painted, the spirit of the Italian Renaissance was proving inadequate to Life. . . . Life began to show a sterner and more sober face than for a brief moment it had seemed to wear. Men became conscious that the passions for knowledge, for glory, and for personal advancement were not at the bottom of all the problems that Life presented. Florence and Rome discovered this suddenly, and with a shock. In the presence of Michelangelo's sculptures in San Lorenzo, or of his "Last Judgement", we still hear the cry of anguish that went up as the inexorable truth dawned upon them. But Venice, although humiliated by the League of Cambrai, impoverished by the Turk, and by the change in the routes of commerce, was not crushed, as was the rest of Italy, under the heels of Spanish infantry, nor so drained of resource as not to have some wealth still flowing into her coffers [an example of the golden mean of the stimulus of blows?]. Life grew soberer and sterner, but it was still amply worth the living, although the relish of a little stoicism and of earnest thought no longer seemed out of place. The spirit of the Renaissance had found its way to Venice slowly; it was even more slow to depart.

'We therefore find that towards the middle of the sixteenth century, when elsewhere in Italy painting was trying to adapt itself to the hypocrisy of a Church whose chief reason for surviving as an institution was that it helped Spain to subject the World to tyranny, and when portraits were already exhibiting the fascinating youths of an earlier generation turned into obsequious and elegant courtiers—in Venice painting kept true to the ripened and more reflective spirit which succeeded to the most glowing decades of the Renaissance. . . .

'It is scarcely to be wondered at that the Venetian artist, in whom we first find the expression of the new feelings, should have been one who by wide travel had been brought into contact with the miseries of Italy in a way not possible for those who remained sheltered in Venice. Lorenzo Lotto, when he is most himself, does not paint the triumph of Man over his environment, but in his altar-pieces, and even more in his portraits, he shows us people in want of the consolations of religion, of sober thought, of friendship and affection. They look out from his canvases as if begging for sympathy.

'But real expression for the new order of things was not to be found by one like Lotto, sensitive of feeling and born in the heyday of the Renaissance, to whom the new must have come as a disappointment. It had to come from one who had not been brought in personal contact with the woes of the rest of Italy, from one less conscious of his environment, one like Titian who was readier to receive the patronage of the new master than to feel an oppression which did not touch him personally; or it had to come from one like Tintoretto, born to the new order of things and not having to outlive a disappointment before adapting himself to it.'[1]

Thus, while superficially there seems to be a broad contemporaneity between the blossoming of Italian art and the achievement of material power by the city-states, if it is examined more closely a different relationship is seen. There is a time-lag between the political zenith and

1 Berenson, Bernhard: *The Italian Painters of the Renaissance*, revised ed. (London 1932, Oxford University Press), pp. 31–33.

the artistic zenith. The supreme artistic achievements of the High Renaissance are an after-glow of the political Golden Age of the city-states whose passing Guicciardini laments at the beginning of his history, or like the shower of stars emitted by a rocket when it reaches the highest point of its trajectory, Michelangelo and Titian being the two brightest and most long-lasting—just as El Greco was a still more delayed coruscation of the East Roman Empire (cp. IV. iv. 360–1).

There are two other striking examples of such inverse operation in the history of European Visual Art. One is provided by Spanish painting: Velasquez is to the decline of the Spanish Monarchy as Titian is to the decline of Venice, or as Michelangelo to the decline of Florence and Papal Rome. The other is a more important example. The only movement in European painting which can be compared with the Italian Renaissance, in the richness of its variety within a coherent tradition and in its profusion of great artists, is the French painting of the nineteenth century; and this appears as a 'compensation' for the post-Napoleonic political decline of France. 'Impressionism' was first used as the name of a school in A.D. 1863, and the *floruit* of the great Impressionists and Post-Impressionists was in the generation and a half between 1871 and 1914.

Against these three examples of inverse operation can be put the Dutch school, which, as you say above (p. 707), had its apogee in Rembrandt contemporaneously with the apogee of Dutch power, and the British school, which, if we roughly identify it with Reynolds, Gainsborough, Constable, and Turner, runs from A.D. 1723 when Reynolds was born to 1851 when Turner died,[1] and coincides closely enough with British political supremacy.

Perhaps the Flemish Renaissance could be pressed into service on the side of the examples of inverse operation, and seen as having the same relation to the independent Burgundian Power as the Italian Renaissance has to the Italian city-states, with Bruegel in the role of Michelangelo or Titian. 'The whole school provided, in fact, a kind of Gothic swan-song with Pieter Brueghel [*sic*] as its final climax.'[2] The German Renaissance is more difficult to fit into the pattern; and Rubens escapes through the net altogether. But perhaps enough has been said to suggest that there is at least as much inverse operation as interdependence in the case of the Visual Arts, and that the Visual Arts are therefore not less ambiguous than Poetry in this respect.

However, three last points need to be made. (i) This is only a cursory survey of European painting. To discover a 'law' of the Visual Arts that could claim any validity one would have to examine the art of at least the Byzantine World, Persia, India, and China as well. And probably the findings would be equally ambiguous. For example, 'it is noticeable that, throughout Indian history, architecture and sculpture have followed the moving centres of political power'.[3] Similarly the Mughal

[1] Mr. John Lodge comments: 'I would add Hogarth (*vivebat* A.D. 1697–1764), and so cover the period more completely.'

[2] Newton, Eric: *European Painting and Sculpture* (London 1941, Pelican Books), p. 92.

[3] John Irwin in *Indian Art*, essays . . . edited by Sir Richard Winstedt (London 1947, Faber), p. 92.

Empire at its zenith produced a great school of painting; on the other hand, Rajput painting seems to have been stimulated by the decentralization of art patronage that accompanied the decline of the Mughal Rāj, and flowered in the eighteenth and nineteenth centuries.

(ii) The danger of seeking to define the relationship between artistic and material achievement is that the political environment, which is only a conditioning factor, becomes subtly exaggerated into the determinant. For example, were the French Impressionists a response to a challenge of the political decline of France, or a development of the inspiration of Constable and Turner? An art historian would prefer the latter explanation. El Greco was born in Crete, worked in Venice perhaps as Titian's pupil, and settled in Spain when Philip II was at the height of his power. Is he to be treated as a late coruscation of the East Roman Empire, as an apprentice of the Venetian school at its zenith, or as the artistic epiphenomenon of the Spanish political apogee? Or was he an inspired vagrant who cross-fertilized schools like a wandering bee? Most art historians would regard him as an isolated figure who cross-fertilized only his own genius and whose influence was not fully felt until the French Post-Impressionists. With Rubens, again, was not the inspiration that he gained from the Italian masters when he was in Mantua more important than the political régime of the archduke Albert and archduchess Isabella in Flanders which enabled him to develop the inspiration, so that he must properly be described in terms of an international baroque movement? It seems that individual genius in art is more closely conditioned by artistic tradition than artistic tradition itself is conditioned by the political and social environment. The ultimate truth about artistic activity, as about all spiritual activity, is in terms of the wind blowing where it listeth and 'light caught from a leaping flame'.

(iii) The concept of 'inverse operation' needs to be analysed with much more precision before it can be really useful. At least three different kinds of inverse operation are seen from your discussion. (*a*) There is the time-lag or 'after-glow', when an artistic tradition has been established during a period of political prosperity, but produces its supreme achievements after political prosperity has ended. The Italian Renaissance is the classic example. (*b*) There is what might be called, by contrast, the 'radiant morning', when an outburst of artistic genius accompanies the beginnings of political power, but the artistic level sinks as material power expands. I have suggested that English poetry illustrates this.[1] (*c*) There is simple compensation, when an artistic efflorescence comes after the loss of material power, and the artistic tradition has not in any notable way been established earlier. The classic examples are German or Italian music.

Can we say that (*a*) tends to be illustrated by the Visual Arts, (*b*) by Poetry, and (*c*) by Music? It looks as if a tradition in the Visual Arts ascends slowly to its highest point and then falls sheer away, while a tradition in Poetry scales its highest point in about a generation and then descends gradually away. But this would be a generalization from far too few examples, and every example changes its shape, like Proteus,

[1] See p. 708, n. 3, above.

when you try to pin it down and classify it. For instance, the great German poetical efflorescence coincides with the musical efflorescence and seems therefore to illustrate (*c*) rather than (*b*). But on second thoughts they can both be made to illustrate (*b*). For it is inaccurate to regard the period from 1648 to 1871 as a continuous undifferentiated nadir of material adversity for Germany. From 1740 onwards the prostrate giant was stirring and preparing himself for 1871, and we could if we chose regard Lessing, Goethe, Schiller, and Hölderlin as the expression of the political renaissance of Germany, just as we regard the Elizabethan poets as the expression of the English *Befreiungskrieg* against Spain. The same is true of Music, for did not Bach, the first of the supreme masters, regard it as the climax of his career when in 1747 he was summoned to visit Frederick the Great at Potsdam?

It is this protean quality of our paradigms, rather than their insufficient quantity,[1] which makes an inquiry of the kind pursued in this Annex so unsatisfactory to the social scientist, who requires scientific precision and seeks firm laws in dealing with human history. But it seems to me that spiritual and artistic activity is intrinsically not susceptible to treatment by the scientific method, and that the 'laws' which you discuss do not aim to be demonstrable and universally valid, but are of a quite different character. Their aim is to refine the appreciation of a relationship between spiritual facts and their material contexts, not to demonstrate a causal connexion; their method is qualitative, not quantitative; and they are apprehended, not by the scientific mind, but by something much more like the aesthetic sensitivity of the critic—of which the quotation from Berenson above is an example.

[1] Mr. John Lodge comments: 'There is so much that has had to be passed over. How about Camoens in relation to Portuguese voyaging and its consequences, and Cervantes, Lope de Vega and Calderón in the Spanish picture? How about Pushkin and Tchaikovsky (not to mention Tolstoy, Dostoyevsky and others) in the story of Russia?'

VII. A (iii) (*a*), ANNEX II

HIGHER RELIGIONS AND PSYCHOLOGICAL TYPES

IN the main stream of this Study[1] we have struck upon the probability that each of the higher religions might satisfy some widely experienced human need, and the possibility that each of them might correspond and minister to one of the psychological types into which Human Nature appears to be differentiated. These vistas of which we have caught a glimpse in passing are perhaps worth exploring further.

We may begin with a point on which we touched in an earlier passage of the same chapter.[2] Each of the higher religions had been apt to lay stress on some particular aspect of God's relation to Man, or of the individual soul's relation to the religious community, or of the religious community's relation to the political; and, even when it had not repudiated the complementary antithetical aspects in theory, it had been apt to ignore them in practice owing to the difficulty of bringing opposite poles together into a single harmonious *Weltanschauung* and way of life. When this insistence on one aspect, to the depreciation of others, had been carried far, it had been apt to evoke a counter-insistence on opposing aspects which could not be suppressed with impunity because they, too, had a truth and value which Human Nature could not afford to sacrifice. The counter-movement might take the form either of a new current within the old religion or of a new religion altogether; and, when it declared itself, it was apt to 'compensate' for the previous depreciation of the aspect which it was championing by unduly emphasizing this aspect in its turn—thereby laying itself open to a reaction against itself in the original direction against which it had set its own face.

The difficulty of reconciling the two poles of an antithesis cannot in fact be solved by holding to the one and despising the other;[3] and a man is constrained to serve two masters as best he may, when he cannot dispense with either. On the plane of Religion the feminine epiphany of the Godhead as the Great Mother is difficult to reconcile with Its masculine epiphany as the Father of gods and men. The forbidding aspect of God as a jealous aloof judge is difficult to reconcile with the consoling aspect of God as a loving intimate saviour. The aspect of worship as a social act performed by a congregation, under the leadership of a priest who is a necessary mediator between the laity and God because he has a monopoly of the power to celebrate the liturgy, is difficult to reconcile with the aspect of worship as a direct communion between the individual soul and God, in a 'flight of the alone to the Alone'[4] without witnesses or intermediaries. The primitive undifferentiated identity of the religious with the secular community is difficult

[1] On pp. 442–3, above. [2] On pp. 426–9, above.

[3] Luke xvi. 13; cp. Matt. vi. 24.

[4] Φυγὴ μόνου πρὸς μόνον.—Plotinus: *Enneades*, VI. ix. 11 (the closing words of the whole Corpus Plotinianum as arranged by Porphyry).

to reconcile with the separation of Church from State which was a specific characteristic of the higher religions.[1] These psychological difficulties had left their mark on the history of the higher religions' relation with one another.

The victory of Christianity in its competition with Isis-worship and Cybele-worship for the allegiance of the internal proletariat of a disintegrating Hellenic Society had not availed permanently to suppress altogether an Isiaco-Cybelene vision of a triune godhead in which the first of the three persons had worn a feminine aspect.[2] In the victorious Christian presentation of the Trinity the genius of Motherhood had not only been deposed from the first place; it had been ejected from the Godhead altogether in the doctrine of an Incarnation in which the Second Person of the Trinity was held to have been born of a human mother at the cost of deliberately divesting Himself of His divine power and glory.[3] But a Trinity in which even the Third Person, as well as the First and the Second, had been reduced to masculine form had left the Psyche baulked of all means of satisfaction for its persistent and imperious impulse to pay worship to a principle of Motherhood which was both the primal and the dominant experience of every child born into the World; and the Great Mother had no sooner been thrust down from Heaven to Earth than She was raised again from Earth to Heaven in the transfiguration of Mary the human mother of Jesus of Nazareth into a Great Mother of God (*Theotókos*) capable of filling the intolerable vacuum that had been created by the previous deposition of Isis and Cybele. Yet this had not been the end of the story; for an antimatriarchal feeling that had once asserted itself in the replacement of an Isiac or Cybelene by a Christian presentation of the Trinity had eventually reasserted itself in an Islamic, Iconoclast, and Protestant series of revolts against 'Mariolatry'; and the Protestant attack on what looked, to Protestant eyes, like an avatar of Isis-worship and Cybele-worship within the bosom of a Western Christian Church had evoked in its turn, in Catholic Western Christian hearts, a more fervent devotion to the threatened person of Our Lady which had found expression in the successive promulgations of the dogmas of the Immaculate Conception and the Assumption.

The forbidding aspect of God, as Power, which had been presented in the Mosaic matrix of Judaism, had not been ousted completely or permanently by the consoling aspect of God as Love which had been presented in the Christian revelation. Islam had broken with Christianity in order to reinstate Yahweh under the name of Allah; and, in the Christian scheme itself, the lineaments of Yahweh were recognizable not only in the First Person of the Trinity, who had become Man's Father without having ceased to be his Lord, but also in the Second Person, who had become Man's judge as well as Man's saviour. This aspect of Christ as the Almighty Judge (*pantokrátor*) had been emphasized by the Eastern Orthodox Church, and the stern and melancholy bearded figure which was the latter-day conventional representation of

[1] See pp. 433–5, above.

[2] See pp. 437, 457–8, and 467 above.

[3] Ἑαυτὸν ἐκένωσε — Phil. ii. 7.

Christ in this role in Orthodox iconography bore no recognizable resemblance to the mild and gracious likeness of Orpheus in which the Primitive Church had depicted her conception of the Good Shepherd on the walls of the Catacombs. In a Western Christian Church the same Judaizing reversion from emphasis on God's loving intimacy with Man to emphasis on God's formidable transcendence had asserted itself, at a later stage, in the Protestant Reformation; and, when the enforcement of the political regulation *Cuius Regio Eius Religio*[1] had deprived Western Christians of the opportunity of making a personal choice between Catholicism and Protestantism, and had made Religion in Western Christendom depend again upon the accident of the subject's birthplace, the craving for a return to a more Judaic view of God, which had been debarred from expressing itself any longer through the channel of Protestantism in a France in which Catholicism had succeeded in re-establishing itself as the religion of the state, had found satisfaction on French soil in Jansenism, which was the nearest approach to Calvinism that could be contrived within a Catholic framework.[2]

Thus, where the intimate aspect of God's relation to Man had been to the fore, the transcendent aspect had persistently reasserted its claim to due consideration; but, in obedience to the same 'law' of psychological compensation, the converse tendency had likewise been persistently at work where the transcendent aspect had been dominant. The Christian revelation of God incarnate in Jesus Christ had not been the first intimation to Jewish souls of the truth that God is Love. The Mosaic presentation of Yahweh as a Jealous God, readily moved to anger, had been supplemented by the Prophetic presentation of Him as abounding in mercy and loving-kindness seven hundred years before the Christian Gospel was first preached; and this pre-Christian Judaism had even relaxed the rigidity of its monotheism so far as to associate with its One and Indivisible God a Word[3] and a Wisdom which—when personified on the excuse that the one was merely an utterance and the other merely an attribute—had come near to anticipating the Second and Third Persons of the Christian Trinity in Unity. It is noteworthy that the same craving to give expression to the intimate aspect of God's relation with Man should have asserted itself in Islam, which had originally stood for an uncompromising reversion to a Jewish monotheism from a Christian 'polytheism'.

The orthodox Islamic Sunnah had no sooner established itself than it was challenged by a Shīʿah which had found new suffering saviours incarnate in the persons of ʿAlī, Hasan, and Husayn and which was carried by enthusiasts to the extreme of identifying ʿAlī with God. The

[1] See V. v. 646–712.

[2] 'Can it be wholly by chance that, whereas Cassian advocated free will, frequent communion and holy dissimulation, the Jesuits of the seventeenth century did likewise; and that, whereas Augustine and Prosper of Aquitaine disapproved of free will and of holy dissimulation, the Jansenists did likewise? And may not this coincidence betray two natural dispositions of mind rather than mere attachment to two traditional schools of thought?' (Pickman, E. M.: *The Mind of Latin Christendom* (London 1937, Oxford University Press), p. 481, n. 78). For the significance of Jansenism, see further XI. ix. 304.

[3] See the passages in Eduard Meyer's *Ursprung und Anfänge des Christentums* cited in V. v. 539, n. 4, and in V. vi. 270, n. 3.

strength and ubiquity of the demand for a divine saviour in human form in an Islamic World that was officially dedicated to the dogmas of unitarianism and transcendence is indicated by the persistent revival of Shiʿism after persistent attempts to repress it in almost every province of Dār-al-Islām; and, when, in the early years of the sixteenth century of the Christian Era, the political regulation *Cuius Regio Eius Religio* was imposed in the Iranic Muslim World, a generation before its imposition in Western Christendom, in consequence of a personal clash between Ismāʿīl Shah Safawī and Sultan Selīm I ʿOsmanlī,[1] the same thing happened in sixteenth-century Turkey as in seventeenth-century France. When Muslims were deprived of the opportunity of making a personal choice between the Sunnah and the Shīʿah owing to the official establishment of Sunnism as the religion of the Ottoman Empire and Shiʿism as the religion of the Safawī Empire, the craving for a God Incarnate found satisfaction on Ottoman soil in the Bektashi Order of Dervishes and in the Qyzyl Bāsh village communities that were affiliated to it.[2] Bektashism was a crypto-Shiʿism which discreetly refrained from advertising its religious beliefs and from translating them into political action in favour of the Safawī cause; and the Ottoman Government found it politic tacitly to tolerate this politically innocuous version of Shiʿism, because it realized that this was the smallest ration of an indispensable spiritual vitamin, lacking in the Sunnah, to which the spiritually starved subjects of a Sunnī Government could safely be reduced without danger of a political explosion. It was notorious that Bektashism was the regimental religion of the Janissaries, and it has been estimated that, under the Later Ottoman Empire, more than half of the Turkish-speaking Muslim population was addicted to crypto-Shiʿism in some form.[3]

The pre-emergence in Judaism, and re-emergence in Islam, of the intimate aspect of God's relation to Man which is prominent in Christianity is not, however, so remarkable as the assertion of this intimate aspect in Buddhism, where the apparently ubiquitous and perpetual human craving for an expression of it actually availed to bring about the *tour de force* of conjuring the Mahāyāna—a consoling popular religion offering salvation by faith in a bodhisattva[4]—out of the forbidding Primitive Buddhist philosophy of the Hīnayāna.[5]

If we pass now from the question of God's relation to Man to the tension between congregational and individual worship, we shall encounter, in this different field, the same spectacle of a tug-of-war between two antithetical but equally importunate spiritual needs. The 'priestcraft' and 'ritualism' which Primitive Christianity had rejected in reaction to a priest-ridden and law-bound Judaism had conspicuously

1 See I. i. 382–400.
2 See Birge, J. K.: *The Bektashi Order of Dervishes* (London 1937, Luzac).
3 See IV. iv. 68–69 and V. v. 111 and 295, in the present Study; and Birge, op. cit., pp. 13–15.
4 See V. v. 133–6, 552; and V. vi. 20.
5 See V. v. 133–4; V. vi. 18 and 142–3. In these contexts it has been pointed out that we have no warrant for assuming that the tenets of the Hinayanian philosophy reproduce the personal beliefs of the Buddha, Siddhārtha Gautama, himself, about the Soul and God.

reasserted itself in both the Eastern Orthodox and the Western Catholic Christian Church; and in the Protestant Western Christian Church—which, on this issue, had originally been a reversion, not to Judaism, but to Primitive Christianity—it had again reasserted itself in Episcopalianism in general and in Anglo-Catholicism in particular. A priesthood and ritual reminiscent of those of the Orthodox and Catholic Christian churches had likewise been conjured by the Mahāyāna out of the simple fellowship of the Primitive Buddhist monastic community. Yet the institutional form of worship had never been exempt from challenge by the personal form that was its antithesis. Both Islam and Protestantism stood, in general, like Primitive Christianity, for a reversion from 'priestcraft' to a direct personal communion between the individual soul and God; and this perennial need, which had asserted itself as Protestantism in a Western Christendom, had similarly asserted itself in a Russian Orthodox Christendom in divers dissenting sects.[1]

Finally, if we glance at the vicissitudes in the relation between Church and State, we shall observe that, on this issue, Islam had stood for a reversion from Christianity to a 'totalitarian' paganism of the Hellenic type; and we shall also observe that, by contrast with a Western Christendom, an Eastern Orthodox Christendom, in its re-subjection of the Church to the State,[2] as in its re-minting of the image of Christ in the likeness of the First Person of the Trinity, had moved in the same direction as Islam, though without having had quite that courage of its convictions which had been one of Islam's virtues. The same tendency had eventually overtaken the Western Church in its turn since the failure of the Medieval Papacy to achieve the Hildebrandine ideal of a *Respublica Christiana* in which a commonwealth of parochial secular states was to find its unity under the auspices of the Apostle at Rome;[3] and it was significant that, in a Modern Western Christendom, this re-subjection of the Church to the State had not been confined to Protestant countries in which the supreme ecclesiastical power had been transferred, since the Reformation, from the Pope to the secular sovereign of a parochial principality. Catholic sovereigns had been as Orthodox-minded as their Protestant cousins in the keenness of their appetite to arrogate to themselves as many of the Pope's ecclesiastical prerogatives as they might find themselves able to filch without putting themselves outside the pale of the Catholic Communion.[4]

Thus the tension produced by the separation of the Church from the State at the birth of the higher religions had persistently sought relief in a remerging of the Church into an undifferentiated 'totalitarian' social order of the primitive kind. Yet the tendency to separation had no less persistently reasserted itself. In Islam it had been reasserted in the Shīʿah; and in a Safawī and post-Safawī Persian Empire, in which the Shīʿah had been converted into the established religion of a state by a *tour de force*, the secular authorities had never succeeded in taming the *mujtahids*—not even those who were resident at Qum, under the Persian

[1] For these Russian Orthodox Christian Non-conformists, see II. ii. 222.
[2] See IV. iv. 320–408 and 592–623.
[3] See IV. iv. 512–84.
[4] See IV. iv. 578.

Government's nose,[1] not to speak of their still more authoritative brethren who laid down the law for the Persian Government's subjects from fastnesses in the Shīʿī holy cities of ʿIrāq which had been beyond the range of the Persian Government's arm since A.D. 1546, when Suleymān the Magnificent had carried the Ottoman frontier right down to the head of the Persian Gulf.[2] This latent power, exercised on critical occasions, of not only defying but coercing the otherwise omnipotent secular authorities was characteristic, not only of the *mujtahids* in and on the margin of a Shīʿī Persian Empire, but of the anchorites in Orthodox Christian states.[3] Even in the realm of the Sunnah, the Commander of the Faithful, omnipotent though he had been in secular affairs, had had to defer, in matters of religion, to a consensus (*ijmāʿ*) of the doctors of the religious law (*Sharīʿah*);[4] and, in Protestant countries in which the secular sovereign had succeeded in acquiring the ecclesiastical prerogatives of an East Roman Emperor in Orthodox Christendom, the inevitable Shīʿah had presented itself in the shape of nonconformist 'free churches'.

This ebb and flow in which, in the history of the higher religions, antithetical features of religious life had asserted and reasserted themselves against one another in divers fields, without any of them ever either succeeding in permanently suppressing their opposites or succumbing to being permanently suppressed for their own part, might throw some light on the relations between the elemental practices and beliefs of the higher religions and the permanent needs of the Human Psyche.

The historical phenomena suggested that the distinctive spiritual stance of each of the higher religions must have been so oriented as to give some of the more important of these permanent psychic needs their due satisfaction, but that, just because each single religion had been thus effectively oriented towards satisfying certain particular needs, any single religion would inevitably prove not to be sufficiently catholic to be able to meet all the Psyche's permanent needs without making a tacit confession of its own congenital limitations by the impressively humble act of borrowing from one or more of the other historic higher religions some of the elements that inevitably would be lacking in the debtor religion's own spiritual gamut. In thus receiving from abroad elements overlooked in, because antithetical to, its own distinctively limited standpoint, a religion would be found guilty of inconsistency and self-stultification only in the verdict of a judge who took seriously the claim—officially filed by each of the Judaistic higher religions—that it alone was a uniquely complete and all-sufficient revelation of the Truth and vehicle of Salvation for all human souls on Earth, and that any other so-called 'religions' that might have had the hardihood to file

[1] In Persia in A.D. 1924 the *mujtahids* of Qum had prevented the dictator Rizā Khān Pahlawi from following his Ottoman Turkish contemporary Mustafā Kemāl's example by proclaiming a republic (see *Survey of International Affairs, 1925*, vol. i (Oxford 1927, University Press), p. 537).

[2] See I. i. 390.

[3] See pp. 388–90, above.

[4] A crucial case in which the Grand Muftī Sheykh Jemālī is reported to have prevailed over the formidable Ottoman Pādishāh Selīm the Grim, has been noticed in V. v. 706, n. 1, and in V. vi. 204, n. 1.

an identical claim were debased coins, which a rash soul would accept at their face value at its mortal peril since in these other currencies the best part of Religion's essential gold content had been replaced by an alloy.[1] It would be more just, as well as more merciful, to judge the attitude of each religion towards its fellows, not by its official professions, but by its practical conduct, and, on this practical criterion, a receptivity that was inconsistent with a pretension to self-sufficiency was to be taken as a sign of grace because it would be a sign of a practical humility underlying a verbal parade of hybris.

It might further be inferred from this historic receptivity of each of the higher religions to the diversely distinctive genius of each of the other representatives of its species that a claim to catholicity, which, when filed by any single higher religion, was tacitly refuted by the record of its own syncretistic practice, might be valid if it were to be filed on behalf, not of any single higher religion exclusively, but of all the higher religions collectively. A salutary impulse, in the hearts of some, at least, of the adherents of each higher religion, to win access to this catholic revelation of the Truth and catholic means of Salvation, that were to be found in all the higher religions taken together, would then account for those constant psychological tensions in the bosom of the body social and in the secret places of the individual soul which, in the institutional history of Religion, had been reflected in the constant antithetical tendencies that have been coming to our notice in this Annex.

If these tensions and conflicts are thus to be diagnosed as symptoms of a struggle to achieve a catholicity in Religion which was not to be found in the distinctive standpoint of any single one of the historic higher religions, the question then arises whether the limitations displayed by each of the higher religions were merely unfortunate historical accidents, or whether the historic orientation of each religion, from which each religion's distinctive limitations had manifestly arisen, was the inevitable adaptation of a human institution to some intrinsic and fundamental feature in the pattern of Human Nature. Some light on the answer to this question might perhaps be obtained by a confrontation of the phenomena which we have just been considering in the history of Religion with certain apparently analogous phenomena in the structure of the Psyche that had been brought to light in one of the leading schools of a post-Modern Western science of Psychology. If, in the light of these religious phenomena, we look at the chart of psychological types which had been plotted out by the pioneer explorer C. G. Jung,[2] can we tentatively discern any correspondences between these permanent types of psychic orientation and the historic orientations of the living higher religions, and (to push our analysis a stage further) between the sub-varieties of the psychological types and the orientations of the sects into which each of the higher religions had come to be divided?

[1] A Catholic friend of the writer's comments: 'A Catholic believes that there is a lot of good in other religions, but he does also believe that there are elements in the Catholic Faith which are necessary for all men: Redemption and the Sacraments.'

[2] See Jung, C. G.: *Psychological Types*, English translation, new impression (London n.d., Kegan Paul), *passim*, but especially pp. 412–517; Wickes, F. G.: *The Inner World of Man* (New York 1938, Holt), pp. 56–64.

Jung distinguishes two antithetical attitudes and four diverse faculties[1] of the Psyche which occur in a variety of combinations—though not all the mathematically conceivable combinations are possible in real life. The two attitudes are an 'introversion' towards the inner world of the Psyche (the microcosm) and an 'extraversion' towards the outer world of Objective Reality (the macrocosm). The four faculties are thinking, feeling, sensation,[2] and intuition.[3] Both the attitudes and all the four faculties are to be found in the psychological 'make-up' of every human being; the psychological differences between individuals which stamp them as representatives of different psychological types arise, not from the presence or absence of this or that psychological element (all the six elements being present in every psyche), but from differences in these omnipresent elements' relative strength and degree of development. Thus the 'introvert' and 'extravert' types are those in which respectively 'introversion' and 'extraversion' is the dominant attitude but not the exclusive one, since the subordinate attitude is not eliminated but is merely repressed into the Subconscious; and similarly, in a classification by faculties instead of by attitudes, the thinking, feeling, sensory,[4] and intuitive types are those in which the faculty from which the type is named is the predominant one in the sense of being the faculty of which the Consciousness is the most clearly aware and over which the Will has the greatest power of control. The faculties that are subordinated in each type are not eliminated in that type; if they cannot be taken into the service of the predominant faculty as its auxiliaries, they are repressed into the Subconscious, where they lead an outlaw's life of their own beyond the range of the Consciousness and the Will—hovering as qāzāqs on the fringe of the Great Khān's realm[5] and awaiting their opportunity to take their revenge (if the repression is unduly severe) by breaking out into disconcerting revolts against the ascendancy of a consciously organized and deliberately directed upper level of the Psyche.

The four faculties range themselves in two pairs:

'Thinking and feeling are rational—controlled by judgement and proceeding in accordance with logical steps. . . . Intuition and sensation, on the other hand, are essentially irrational [even] in their differentiated [i.e. in their conscious] form. They do not proceed by logical steps, but their conclusions seem to come of themselves without the intervention of the intermediary processes. Intuition suddenly finds itself at the end of the road, but has no idea of how it got there; whereas sensation finds itself sitting firmly upon an established fact, without any concern as to the implications of that fact or its relation to past and future—it simply *is* a fact.'[6]

1 The word 'faculty' is used here in place of Jung's own word 'function'.

2 In this Jungian terminology, 'sensation' means an uncritical and unorganized apprehension of brute facts in isolation from one another.

3 A Catholic friend of the writer's comments: 'If we remember the story of Martha and Mary, we have there in simple form the two different kinds of soul: extravert and introvert. If we examine the first disciples, we find the various types.'

4 'Sensory' is used here as the adjective corresponding to the substantive 'sensation' in Jung's meaning of this latter word.

5 See V. v. 282–4.

6 Wickes, op. cit., pp. 57–58.

This grouping of the faculties is the limiting factor in the articulation of the main psychological types into sub-types. For while the predominant faculty always has one auxiliary which is likewise on the level of Consciousness, so that the main types defined by predominant faculties fall into sub-types defined by their auxiliaries, it is not practically possible for the dominant faculty to associate with itself, as its auxiliary, every one of the three other faculties. It cannot enter into this relation with the sister faculty belonging to the same pair as itself (the discriminating rational or the perceptive irrational pair, as the case may be). This sister faculty is condemned, *ex officio affinitatis*, to be repressed into the Subconscious, because the Consciousness cannot serve two masters simultaneously, even when one of them is under the other's command, if they have an identical *modus operandi* but make use of it for incompatible purposes;[1] and for this reason the predominant faculty's choice of auxiliary faculties is confined to one between the two faculties of the opposite pair—either of which is a possible junior partner for the predominant faculty, because it operates in a different psychic style, so that there is no possibility of a clash between the two associates. This means that each main type is articulated in practice into only two sub-types and not into the mathematically conceivable three.

In the light of this summary exposition of the Jungian classification of psychological types we may perhaps tentatively draw the equations, set out on the accompanying table,[2] between types and religions.

In the classification by attitudes the four living higher religions seemed to range themselves clearly into an 'introvert' and an 'extravert' pair on the criterion of their respective readings of the nature of Ultimate Reality. In the eyes of the two religions of Indic origin, Hinduism and Buddhism, Ultimate Reality—the *Brahman* of the Hindu theology and the *Nirvāna* of the Buddhist—was impersonal and the approach to It was to be found by the conscious personality in turning inwards to remerge itself in the Subconscious. By contrast, in the eyes of the two religions of Judaic origin, Christianity and Islam, the Ultimate Reality was a Personal God, and the approach to Him was to be found by the human soul in turning outwards to enter into a communion with God which would prove to be, not a relinquishment of personality, but the human personality's *raison d'être* and consummation.

When we come to the classification by faculties we find that, unlike the classification by attitudes, it cuts across the grouping of the religions according to their historical origins, Indic and Judaic; for the rationally discriminating pair of faculties was represented by Hinduism and Christianity, and the irrationally perceptive pair by Islam and Buddhism. The predominant faculty in Hinduism was thinking; for its mainspring was a thought (inherited by Hinduism from the Indic school of philosophy) which was perhaps the most difficult that was conceivable for the Rational Human Intellect. This key-thought of Hinduism was the comprehension, by the Consciousness, of its psychic antithesis the Subconscious, and the realization that this subconscious underworld of the consciously individual soul was, not merely impersonal, but supra-

[1] This point is explained by Jung in op. cit., p. 515. [2] Table VII, facing p. 772.

personal.[1] By contrast, the predominance in Christianity of the faculty of feeling was proclaimed in the three words 'God is Love',[2] which were the heart of the Christian revelation. The predominance in Islam of the faculty of 'sensation', in the Jungian meaning of an uncritical apprehension of matters of fact, was no less clearly displayed in the Islamic confession of faith—'There is no god but *the* God, and Muhammad is The Apostle of *the* God'—and in the Islamic commandments to observe the five hours of prayer and to make the pilgrimage to the Holy Cities of the Hijāz. The predominance in Buddhism of the faculty of intuition was intimated in the sudden flash of enlightenment in the soul of the Founder in which his way of salvation had first revealed itself and which the followers of the Zen school of the Mahāyāna strove to recapture. In that supreme moment of his vigil under the Bōdhi Tree, there had burst upon the Buddha's soul a perception that Desire is the fuel of Pain, and that the extinction of Desire is the means of self-release from the Sorrowful Wheel of Existence into a peace that passeth all understanding: the haven of *Nirvāna*.

To follow out our interpretation of the higher religions in terms of psychological types, we have also to consider the sub-types and to take note of the faculties that, in each type and sub-type, are not even taken into partnership with the predominant faculty as auxiliaries, but are repressed into the Subconscious.

In Hinduism one of the predominant thinking faculty's two auxiliaries was the faculty of sensation, which here found expression in ritual; and, since the stimulation of thought by sensation in the service of an 'introvert' religion was an elsewhere unfamiliar phenomenon,[3] this combination of these two faculties with the 'introvert' attitude in Hinduism accounted for the impression—made on non-Hindu observers—of an incongruity between the etherially sophisticated conceptions of the Hindu theology and the crassly primitive rites that were practised by the esoterically instructed adepts as well as by the ignorant masses. The truth, no doubt, was that, for the Hindu adept, an external rite had an inner meaning that eluded the mental eye of the non-Hindu critic.

The other auxiliary faculty in Hinduism was intuition; and the partnership between intuition and thought in an 'introvert' religion had borne fruit in the psychological exercise and experience of Hindu mysticism (*yoga*). Mysticism and ritualism might appear to stand at opposite poles; yet, if this had been the gamut of Hinduism's spiritual capacity, it would still have been so inadequate a response to Man's

[1] In the language of the Indic school of philosophy this truth was conveyed in the proposition that the *Ātman* (Soul) was identical with *Brahman* (Ultimate Reality). If this proposition was to be taken, *au pied de la lettre*, as signifying a complete equation of 'God' with the 'Collective' Subconscious underlying the 'Personal' Subconscious that underlies the Conscious Personality (in terms of Jung's psychology), the Indic philosophers and their disciples the Hindu theologians had assuredly gone beyond the evidence, and, in the belief of the writer of this Study, their guess had also missed the mark on an issue which was the supreme question in the quest for religious truth. On this point see pp. 468–9 and 497–8, above.

[2] 1 John iv. 8 and 16.

[3] The stimulation of thought by sensation in the service of an 'extrovert' and secular intellectual pursuit had, of course, been the driving force behind a Modern Western scientific activity.

spiritual needs that it never could have won and retained the allegiance of a quarter of the Human Race.

One crying need of Human Nature—which had been amply satisfied in Christianity, Islam, and the Mahayanian sub-type of Buddhism—is Man's craving for a personal God with whom he, as another personality, can establish a relation; and in Hinduism this universal and importunate human demand had been met by the worship of Vishnu in his innumerable avatars in human form.[1] In this 'extraverted' worship of the Ultimate Reality in personal epiphanies, Hinduism might be said to be making a concession to Human Nature at the price of doing some violence to its own genius, if its mainspring was correctly described as an 'introverted' intellectual comprehension of the impersonal underworld underlying a Human Consciousness. There were, however, other aspects of the worships of Vishnu and of Shiva in which they showed themselves true to Hindu type; for an unsophisticated Hindu could find 'sensational' satisfaction in the liturgies of the Shaiva and Vaishnava churches, while an esoterically instructed Hindu would understand that even the personalities of the Gods were 'in the last analysis' ephemeral and illusory phenomena, and that their significance lay in symbolizing in myriad guises an intuitively perceived rotation of the Wheel of Existence, in which *Maya* was ever arising out of *Brahman*, and ever sinking back into It again—like the misty exhalations which the Sun's lust is ever drawing up out of the Ocean in order ever to be letting them drop down again to Earth in the falling rain, to run back to the Ocean in the flowing rivers.[2]

Thus Hinduism, which was dedicated to 'introverted' thought, had widened the range of its psychological appeal by making the most of the partnership of Hindu thought with both sensation and intuition. The faculty for which Hinduism had found no recognized place was thought's incompatible sister, feeling. It was true that, inasmuch as no fundamental faculty of the Psyche can ever be completely and permanently banished, the faculty of feeling had forced its way up again from the subconscious on to the conscious level of Hindu religious life. In the worships of Shiva and Vishnu there was an emotional element in the personal relation between the worshipper and his God which, on the worshipper's side, took the form of personal devotion (*bhakti*)[3] and on the God's side was expressed in his sexual passion for his female consort (*sakti*). This emotional element was manifestly akin to the feeling which was the leading note in Christianity and also in the Shīʿī form of Islam and in the Mahayanian form of Buddhism,[4] though,

[1] The two gods Vishnu and Shiva had been the product of a syncretism of a host of more or less like-natured local divinities, and the two syntheses in which the Hindu conception of *Brahman* in a personal epiphany had thus been polarized were readily reducible to unity on Hindu lines of thought, since creation and destruction are the two alternating beats of a single rhythm of phenomenal life. If the worshippers of Shiva and Vishnu had nevertheless been content to see their respective deities live and let live, they had been practising the tolerance which was characteristic of the Hindu religious êthos (see V. vi. 47–49, and the anecdote quoted from Radhakrishnan by Wight on p. 746, below).

[2] Compare Charon's simile in the passage of Lucian quoted in V. vi. 133.

[3] See V. v. 135–8.

[4] Read, for example, the *Tiruvāçagam* ('Sacred Utterance') of the Tamil poet, saint,

by comparison with these other expressions of it, some of its expressions in Hinduism looked crudely archaic to non-Hindu eyes and felt repulsively sensual to non-Hindu susceptibilities.

An apparent absence of love and absence of zeal for righteousness were the negative aspects of Hinduism that were apt to strike non-Hindu observers the most painfully.[1] They would recall the opening colloquy between Arjuna and Krishna in the *Bhagavadgītā*, in which, on a battlefield before battle is joined, the human hero confides to the god his heart-rending doubt whether Man can be justified, even in 'a good cause', in doing such evil as to fight and slay his fellow human beings; and they would be shocked by the coldness of Krishna's metaphysical solution for Arjuna's moral problem.

'Your words are wise, Arjuna, but your sorrow is for nothing. . . . That Reality which pervades the Universe is indestructible. No one has power to change the Changeless. Bodies are said to die, but That which possesses the body is eternal. It cannot be limited or destroyed. Therefore you must fight.

'Some say this Ātman
Is slain, and others
Call It the slayer:
They know nothing.
How can It slay
Or who shall slay It?'[2]

To non-Hindu observers, whose approach to Religion was not an essentially intellectual one, Krishna's academic exposition of the Subconscious as being the Ultimate Reality would seem so irrelevant to Arjuna's pressing practical problem of conduct that it might be suspect of being deliberately evasive,[3] were it not notorious that Hindu minds

and sage Mānikka-Vāçagar, which has been translated into English by G. U. Pope (Oxford 1900, University Press). An appreciation of the *Tiruvāçagam* will be found in Eliot, Sir Ch.: *Hinduism and Buddhism* (London 1921, Arnold, 3 vols.), vol. ii, pp. 215–19. 'It is not, like the Baghavad-Gītā, an exposition *by* the Deity, but an outpouring of the Soul *to* the Deity. . . . The remarkable feature . . . is the personal tie which connects the Soul with God. . . . Not only its outline but its details strikingly resemble the records of devout Christian lives in Europe.'

[1] See V. vi. 145–6 and 151–2.

[2] *Bhagavadgītā*, ii, English translation by Swami Prabhavananda and Christopher Isherwood (London 1947, Phoenix Press), pp. 40–41. The first sentence here quoted immediately precedes the last sentence quoted, from Barnett's English translation, in V. vi. 146.

[3] A Hindu philosopher who was familiar with the Christian Gospels might perhaps aptly reply that Krishna's exposition was, not deliberately evasive, but deliberately shocking; that, in this point of psychological construction, it resembled the parables of the Importunate Widow, the Talents, the Unjust Steward, the Labourers in the Vineyard, and the Prodigal Son; and that the motive for presenting a lesson in this vein was the same in the Hindu genre of edifying religious literature as in the Christian genre: namely, the mystification of philistines on whom the lesson would be lost in any case in any presentation of it. Manifestly the parables above mentioned would be above the head of a catechumen who could see no more in the first and in the second than a comparison of God Almighty with an unjust human judge and with a hard employer; no more in the third than a recommendation to the faithful to enter into a conspiracy with their employers' debtors for defrauding their employers of their due; and no more in the fourth and the fifth than a penalization of industry and virtue in the interests of sloth and vice. These shocking features in these parables are so many traps to catch the philistine, because, while it is true that they are shocking, it is at the same time true that they are irrelevant to the point which it is the purpose of the parable to make. On

were utterly sincere in their belief that Man's spiritual nourishment was to be found in an intellectual stone and not in moral bread[1] (to give their Christian names to Hindu values). The non-Hindu reader of the *Bhagavadgītā* would suffer the same moral shock when he turned from the classic Hindu religious poem to gaze upon a visual presentation of Shiva dancing the rhythmic ebb and flow of the phenomenal aspect of the Cosmos. In one of these masterpieces of the Tamil bronze-caster's art the naïve non-Hindu spectator would marvel at the virtuosity with which the snake-like swarm of writhing arms and legs was weaving a pattern for which the whirling Wheel of Existence had provided a frame, till he would be horrified by noticing the contrast between the misery of the trampled human figure on whose back one gracefully dancing divine foot was poised,[2] and the unconcerned serenity of the divine countenance. If that bronze could speak, its utterance could be nothing but

'I am indifferent to all born things; there is none whom I hate, none whom I love.'[3]

When we pass from Hinduism to Christianity, we find that the here predominant feeling faculty's pair of auxiliaries is the same as the thinking faculty's pair in the Hindu *Weltanschauung*, and that, here again, the auxiliary faculty of sensation finds expression in ritual. In the congregational rite of the Eucharist the Christian worshipper achieved an experience of entering into communion with a God who was Love. This association, in Christianity, of the two faculties of feeling and sensation in the service of an 'extravert' religion accounted for the impression—made on non-Christian observers—of an incongruity between the etherially sublime feelings that united with his worshippers a God who had become man and had suffered death on the Cross, and the strangely primitive rite in which this communion was consummated. What had Christ to do with Tammuz, or Christ's body and blood with the corn and wine that were deified because they were the material food of *Homo Agricola*?[4] The answer was that, in Christian hearts for whom God was Love, the ritual of a primitive food-god had become a vehicle for Christian feeling.

In Christianity, as in Hinduism, the other auxiliary faculty was

the same lines a Hindu exegete of the *Bhagavadgītā* might submit that the undeniable shockingness of Krishna's solution for Arjuna's moral problem is irrelevant to the metaphysical truth which it is the purpose of the poem to expound.

1 Matt. vii. 9; Luke xi. 11.

2 '"This theme . . . shows Siva, usually surrounded by a halo of flames, performing his dance of regeneration at Tillai, the mythical centre of the Universe. The demon he crushes beneath his feet symbolises Evil" (John Irwin in *Indian Art*, essays by H. G. Rawlinson, K. de B. Codrington, J. V. S. Wilkinson, and John Irwin, edited by Sir Richard Winstedt (London 1947, Faber), p. 102). I do not know whether this is the accepted interpretation or whether it is an etherializing gloss by an abashed Hindu theologian. If it *is* the right interpretation, then the figure of Siva Nataraja illustrates, not the predominant thinking faculty in Hinduism, but the faculty of feeling pushing its way up (see p. 726, above). I suppose the faculty of feeling is represented by the desire—which I do not think you mention in this Annex—for atonement, for redemption from sin, which is one of the basic religious impulses, if not the basic one.'—Martin Wight.

3 *Bhagavadgītā*, ix. 29, Barnett's translation, quoted in V. vi. 146.

4 A partial answer to this vexed question has been attempted on pp. 457 and 494, above.

intuition; and, in Christianity likewise, the partnership of intuition with the predominant faculty had borne fruit in mysticism—though in an 'extravert' religion for whose followers the Ultimate Reality was a Personal God the mystic's goal had been a Beatific Vision in which the human party to the encounter would retain the personality without which he would be unable to glory in God—in contrast to the Hindu mystic's goal of a Beatific Union in which the personality would be merged in an impersonal reality transcending it.[1] Yet neither the 'extravert' mystical nor the 'extravert' sacramental way of communion adequately met the spiritual needs of 'introverted' Christian souls; and, in psychological terms, this explained why the Protestant movement in a Western Christian Church had parted company with the Western Catholics as well as with their Eastern Orthodox co-religionists on the issue of the method and mode of communion between God and Man.

In the Jungian terminology, Protestantism was an attempt to provide, within a Christian framework, for the psychological needs of 'feeling introverts' by doing some violence to the genius of a religion which, in its classic form, appealed specifically to 'feeling extraverts'. In the Protestant's experience the real presence of Christ was to be found neither in the Beatific Vision nor in the rite of the Eucharist, but in the overwhelming spiritual event of a sudden ineffable change in the Christian's heart which certified its own authenticity by carrying with it a conviction that the sinner was saved. Yet even this *tour de force* of leading a Protestant canal out of the river of Catholic and Orthodox Christian tradition had not availed to bring the living waters of Christianity within the reach of every soul that was athirst. Introversion could never be complete in a religion for which the Ultimate Reality was a personal God; and the Protestantism that had succeeded in giving a limited expression to the 'introvert' attitude was as much at a loss as every other form of Christianity in its dealings with the faculty of thought. A Hindu observer of Christianity could hardly fail to be struck by the repression here of a thinking faculty which in Hinduism was dominant; and the Hindu critic would not be much impressed when, in reply, the Christian apologist pointed to an historic chain of mighty Christian thinkers extending from the author of the Fourth Gospel to Saint Thomas Aquinas.

'It is true', our Hindu would retort, 'that, when you drive Nature out with a pitch-fork she will insist on coming back sooner or later.[2] You have already suggested to me that the feeling faculty, which is repressed in Hinduism, has reasserted itself in the archaic form in which it presents itself in *bhakti*; and I readily concede that in Christianity the repressed faculty of thinking has re-asserted itself likewise. Considering that the earliest Christian mission-field happened to be the domain of an Hellenic Society which was almost as intellectual as its Indic contemporary, and further considering how prone you Hellenistic Westerners

[1] This distinction between the respective goals of mysticism in the 'extravert' and the 'introvert' philosophies and religions has been touched upon by anticipation in V. vi. 143, n. 3, and on p. 429, above.

[2] 'Naturam expelles furcâ, tamen usque recurret.' (Horace: *Epistulae*, Book I, Ep. x. l. 24).

and Byzantines have been to fall under the spell of an ancestral Hellenic mode of thought, what else could Christian Evangelists and Christian Fathers do but make an attempt at translating the Christian mythology into the language of the Hellenic school of philosophy? I am not surprised at the attempt, but I am also not impressed by the achievement. In the great Gothic cathedral, of which your Christian *Weltanschauung* reminds me, a re-intruding Intellect has advertised its presence in the ingeniously intricate tracery of the windows and in the gorgeously coloured glass; but the tracery does not fulfil any architectural function; if the whole of it were removed, the roof and the tower would still rest securely, as now, on the massive masonry of irrational walls and columns; and, as for the stained glass, if you were to remove that too, why, you would be letting in the sunshine in all its glory to put to shame the 'dim religious light'[1] now cast by the few discreetly selected rays which the glass admits—and tones down in their transit.

'To drop parables and use plain language', our Hindu exegete might proceed, 'I feel little respect for the Christian application of thought to Christianity because your Christian thinkers do not dare to have the courage of their convictions. The characteristic virtue of thought is to follow the argument whithersoever it may lead; if thought flinches from fulfilling this first commandment of intellectual honesty, it commits a stultifying sin against its own nature; and this is the moral infirmity by which your Christian thinking is invalidated. Your imposing *Summa Theologiae* is confined within the prison-walls of a mythology which your hearts have dictated to your heads; and in matters of religion Christianity allows the Intellect to operate only under a perpetual edict serving notice "Thus far and no farther". What is the World to think of a Christian intelligence that consents to work under conditions that make nonsense of the Intellect's essential function? Your Christian moral sensibilities are excruciated, you say, in the *Bhagavadgītā*, by Sri Krishna's intellectual liquidation of Arjuna's moral scruples. But is not the ruthless trenchancy of the poem's reasoning, which to you is repugnant, the best evidence of its intellectual integrity? If you are morally shocked by Krishna, I am intellectually unconvinced by Aquinas; and I am proud—however high your Christian judgement may rate the moral price—that my Hinduism does not sacrifice honest thinking to prejudiced sentiment.'

This mutual misunderstanding between two higher religions in which the thinking faculty and the feeling faculty were respectively predominant was perhaps inevitable on the showing of the Jungian psychology. These two 'rational' faculties were at odds with one another because they were using the same discriminatory *modus operandi* at cross-purposes. To conclude our inquiry we have still to review the two other higher religions, in which the 'irrational' perceptive faculties, sensation and intuition, were predominant, and in which thinking and feeling were auxiliary.

In Islam, in which the predominant faculty was an apprehension of matters of fact which Jung had labelled 'sensation', the thinking faculty

[1] Milton: *Il Penseroso*.

had played a more responsible part than in Christianity—not in the sense that Islamic theologians could be held to have surpassed their Christian confrères in intellectual prowess, but because in Islam the Intellect had enjoyed the advantage of doing its work as a junior partner of the predominant faculty and not as an unauthorized intruder. In building the Founder's modest legacy of isolated and unorganized tenets and commandments into the vast and solid structure of the *Sharīʿah*, the Sunnī theologians had, it is true, laboured under the same restrictive building regulations as their Christian brother masons. They had been constrained to make use of the materials handed out to them, and to take these materials as they had found them, however inappropriate these might have been for use in an intellectual structure. But they had profited by the paucity of the *disjecta membra* that they had inherited from the Prophet—like the architects of the Kaʿbah, who had had a free hand to build all the rest of their fane in whatever material and whatever style might suit them best, so long as they duly embedded in it, undesecrated by the chisel, one single uncouth but sacrosanct Black Stone, whereas the Christian theologians, under instructions to elicit a law of logic out of the law of Love, might be likened on our analogy to builders who had found themselves furnished with the fruit of the Tree of Life in quantities sufficient for building a Tower of Babel if only fruit-pulp were a practicable building material.

While the Sunnī *Sharīʿah* was a monument of the thinking faculty's service as an auxiliary to the matter-of-fact sensory faculty in Islam, the feeling faculty, which here had been the other auxiliary, had expressed itself in the Shīʿah—'the sect' *par excellence*, which had broken away from the Sunnah in order to minister to an elemental human need that the Sunnah could not satisfy.

Though orthodox Islam shared with Christianity the 'extravert' vision of Ultimate Reality as a personal God, the significant aspect of the divine personality was not the same in the sight of the two religions. If a Sunnī Muslim were called upon to describe God in three words, he would be constrained to write, not 'God is Love', but 'God is Power'. But this hard fact of God's power is no satisfying substitute for the warm feeling of God's love; and, if the eruption of Islam in reaction to Christianity was evidence that God's aspect as Power could not be depreciated with impunity, the break-away of the Shīʿah from the Sunnah within the bosom of Islam was an illustration of the nemesis incurred by depreciating God's aspect as Love. The portrait of the One True God that had been painted by Muhammad belied the conventional epithets that had followed His name into the Qur'ān like echoes from the New Testament and from the Prophets of Judah and Israel. The God to whose love Muhammad had paid lip-service by calling him 'the Merciful, the Compassionate' (*ar-Rahmān*, *ar-Rahīm*) had been depicted by Him as aloof and arbitrary and vindictive; and accordingly Muslim hearts that had been athirst for Love had found in an intimately human ʿAlī what they had been unable to find in an inhumanly transcendant Allah.

For Shīʿīs, ʿAlī had the pathos of the incarnate saviour who 'came unto his own, and his own received him not';[1] and the Passion of 'Alī's martyred son Husayn was annually commemorated in the Shī'ī World with an emotion that reminded a Christian spectator of the traditional Christian feeling about the Passion of Christ. Indeed, as we have seen,[2] there were Shī'ī extremists who, in their unavowed esoteric doctrine, identified 'Alī with God and ascribed the same divinity to his physical descendants the Imāms;[3] and these outright 'Alī-worshippers would have no consciousness of blasphemy in applying to their God Incarnate the context of the verse from the Gospel according to Saint John that we have quoted above as expressing the feelings of the more moderate followers of the Shī'ah. The extremists would assert of 'Alī that 'the World was made by Him',[4] and they would arrogate to themselves the daring claim that, 'as many as received Him, to them gave He power to become the sons of God, even to them that believe on His name'.[5]

Yet, while the Shī'ah offered the Muslim an intimate instead of a forbidding epiphany of a personal God, both sects of Islam would have repressed the faculty of intuition and the attitude of 'introversion' if these two ubiquitous elements in 'the make-up' of the Human Psyche had not risen in revolt and forced their way back into the conscious life of Islam, in defiance of a system in which there was no acknowledged room for them. 'Islamic mysticism', like 'Christian philosophy', was virtually a *contradictio in adjecto*. Yet, just as the Religion of Love had managed to find a place for a magnificent intellectual construction that had no organic function in the Christian scheme of things, so the Religion of Matter of Fact had contrived to harbour a school of mysticism which could bear comparison with its Christian counterpart—though no doubt, in both Hindu and Mahayanian eyes, this Christian and Islamic *yoga* would seem to be all but stultified by an apparently wilful refusal to see through a Judaic hallucination (as the Beatific Vision would seem to be in Indic eyes) of a personal God masquerading as the Ultimate Reality.

In Buddhism the same two sister discriminatory faculties that served as alternative auxiliaries in Islam had lent their services to a predominant perceptive faculty which in this case was not sensation but intuition. The thinking faculty co-operated with intuition in the Hīnayāna, and the feeling faculty in the Mahāyāna. The Hīnayāna was a school of practical philosophy, in which the Buddha's intuition that conscious life is pain, and that therefore pain cannot be cured except by extinguishing conscious life, had been followed up by thinking out an uncompromisingly ascetic course of self-mortification for bringing the adept to his goal of *Nirvāna*. In the Mahāyāna the alternative auxiliary faculty of feeling had entered into a paradoxical partnership with the Buddha's master-intuition that Desire is the root of all evil and that the last enemy that shall be destroyed is, not Death, but Life.[6]

[1] John i. 11.

[2] On p. 718, above.

[3] This combination of the two concepts of Incarnation and Metempsychosis seemed as alien from the Judaistic *Weltanschauung* of Islam as it was native to the Indistic *Weltanschauung* of Hinduism and Buddhism. It was reminiscent of the avatars of Vishnu and of the Buddha in his Mahayanian metamorphosis.

[4] John i. 10.

[5] John i. 12.

[6] 1 Cor. xv. 26.

The Mahayanian Buddhist had substituted for the arhat, whom his Hinayanian co-religionist revered and followed as his guide towards his goal of *Nirvāna*, a bodhisattva who deserved and received the Mahayanian Buddhist's love because the bodhisattva had 'so loved the World'[1] that, though he had already won his own way to the goal of human endeavours and was free to enter into his rest,[2] he had deliberately made the sacrifice of postponing his self-extinction for an indefinite time to come, in order that whosoever believeth in him[3] should learn from him how to follow in his footsteps. On these lines the alchemy of Love had transmuted a negative fellowship, in which the arhat followed the Buddha's lead towards the goal of *Nirvāna*, into a positive fellowship in which the faithful—including the mundane masses as well as a cloistered *élite*—could look forward to being with their bodhisattva in Paradise.[4] In theory, Amitabha's Paradise was a transient experience, like Christ's Millennium in the Christian eschatology; and, considering that *Nirvāna* was still the official goal of the bodhisattva and his followers alike, and this on the strength of the Buddha's key-intuition that life is pain, it was difficult for an outsider to understand how this paradise could be a paradise at all, and not rather a purgatory. The outsider could only register the fact that, for Mahayanian Buddhist hearts, the Mahayanian Paradise was a virtual equivalent of the Christian Heaven.

An 'introverted' intuitive religion might thus paradoxically accommodate Love, but it could give no official scope for 'extraversion' and no official value to matter of fact. Yet in Buddhism, as in the other living higher religions, Human Nature had rebelliously asserted its need to find some vent for all its divers faculties and attitudes. 'Extraversion' requires a manifestation of Ultimate Reality in a personal form; the sensory faculty requires a tangible object to apprehend (the Black Stone, the wood of the True Cross, the blood of Saint Januarius); and the Primitive Buddhist Community lost no time in providing for both these requirements. The breath was hardly out of the Buddha's body before his disciples were disputing over the possession of his mortal remains with a view to treasuring as sacred relics these material débris of a soul that had successfully remerged itself in *Nirvāna*; and the thus beatified human founder of the Buddhist Community had been transfigured by Hinayanian piety into a superhuman being long before the historical personality of Siddhārtha Gautama, the Sakya prince of the sub-Himalayan city-state of Kapilavastu, had been eclipsed, in the Mahayanian imagination, by other avatars, past and future, of an ever-recurrent Buddha, which better satisfied the human need for an epiphany of a personal God because they were untrammelled by intractable historical associations.

In the Mahayanian apotheosis of the Bodhisattva Amitabha, as in the Shī'ite apotheosis of the Caliph 'Alī, an *anima naturaliter Christiana in partibus peregrinis* was offered an equivalent of the Second Person of the Christian Trinity, while a metamorphosis of the Bodhisattva Avalokita into the Goddess of Mercy, Kwanyin, had provided the Far

[1] John iii. 16.
[2] Ps. xcv. 11.
[3] John iii. 16.
[4] Luke xxiii. 43.

Eastern moiety of Mankind with the spiritual consolation which, in the other half of the Old World, had been offered by the Great Mother in her divers avatars. Moreover, these very gods that had been discovered by, or revealed to, the Mahayanian Church were worshipped by her in liturgies that resembled those of Orthodox and Catholic Christianity with a verisimilitude that startled the Early Modern Western Christian missionaries.[1]

Our psychological interpretation of the four living higher religions, cursory and superficial though it has been, perhaps warrants us in drawing conclusions that may be summarized as follows. In the Human Psyche there are divers faculties and attitudes that are, all alike, importunate in seeking vent. These are all to be found in every individual human being, but this in different combinations and different relative strengths which display themselves in a variety of psychological types. There is not, and cannot be, any psychological type in which all the psychological elements can have full play at the conscious level; in every type there are, and are bound to be, some elements that are repressed into the Subconscious, and in every type the repressed elements seize, and are bound to seize, every opportunity of flooding back, unbidden, into Consciousness. These psychic phenomena prove to have been reflected in Religion. Each of the living higher religions, and each of their principal sects, had been attuned to some particular psychological type or sub-type;[2] and each religion was ever seeking, like the psychological type which it served, to achieve the impossible feat of ministering to the whole gamut of the Psyche's elemental needs for expression. The feat was impossible because there was not, and could not be, any spiritual organ capable of playing a psychic diapason; and therefore any existing higher religion that aspired to become *the* Universal Religion was doomed to disappointment, while any that claimed already to be *the* Universal Religion must be unaware of its own intrinsic limitations. The heavenly music that would satisfy every need of the Soul was not inaudible on Earth, but it was never audible in a solo; it could be heard only in a symphony. The divers higher religions must resign themselves to playing limited parts, and must school themselves to playing these parts in harmony, in order, between them, to fulfil their common purpose of enabling every human being of every psychological type to enter into communion with God the Ultimate Reality.

[1] See p. 460, n. 1, above, for the two alternative traditional Christian explanations of this likeness.

[2] A Catholic friend of the writer's comments: 'Should the Christian Faith really penetrate into the East, I am confident that aspects of it which are almost dormant in the West will flourish exceedingly. Let us suppose that the other three higher religions had not arisen, and that the Christian message had reached the East: I presume that the human beings there, being, as they are, of a different stamp to the extraverted Westerners, would have received the message *secundum modum recipientis*. They would have stressed some elements which remain almost unstressed in the West. This is even evident in the two approaches to Christian doctrine followed respectively by the Catholic and by the Orthodox Church, the one tending more to devotion through the humanity of Christ, the other more to devotion through the wisdom of God. I think it is a matter of more and less, not of [an exclusive choice between] either the one thing or the other.'

This conclusion that none of the living higher religions was superfluous left open the question of their relative value. 'One star differeth from another star in glory.'[1] An orchestra would not be capable of playing a symphony at all if there were not a conductor and a first violin. In the orchestra of Religion, does one psychic faculty count for more than another? Our answer to this question will be determined by our view of the nature and destiny of Man. If the true end of Man is to glorify God and fully to enjoy Him for ever, Man's master-faculty must be the one through which God is accessible to him, and this inestimably precious conductive faculty is not the Intellect, which is the distinctive organ of *Homo Sapiens*. Man enters into communion with God through the faculty of feeling which *Homo Peccator sed Capax Dei* shares with other living creatures. On this showing, the most valuable instruments in the orchestra of Religion would be those that played the music of Love; and, on an order of merit determined by that criterion, Christianity would head the list because, in Christianity, feeling was the predominant faculty, while the Shīʿah and the Mahāyāna would be next to Christianity in glory because, in each of them, feeling was the predominant faculty's auxiliary.

On this finding, Hinduism would stand at the bottom of our list; and the non-Hindu critic might even go so far as to suggest that the Intellect, which is at a discount when it is 'introverted' for service as the predominant faculty in a higher religion, is more profitably employed when it is 'extraverted' for secular purposes. Let the Intellect occupy itself in begetting Science, which is generated by a union of 'extraverted' thought with the faculty that apprehends matters of fact, and in begetting Philosophy, which is generated by a union of 'extraverted' thought with intuition. Yet it would be open to Hinduism to retort that, when she was weighed in the balance and found wanting[2] by a unanimous verdict of Christianity, the Shīʿah and the Mahāyāna, the judgement must be held to be invalidated by the patent intellectual incompetence and emotional prejudice of this self-constituted jury. What, for instance, would the Sunnah and the Hīnayāna have to say? And does the last word lie with a living God or with a brooding Brahman?

Meanwhile, at the time of writing, midway through the twentieth century of the Christian Era, Hinduism was to be found, not at the rear of the procession of living higher religions, but in its van, in virtue of a characteristically Hindu spirit of spontaneous charity towards all revelations—past, present, and to come—which was the first spiritual requirement in an age in which the whole of Mankind had been united in a single Great Society through 'the annihilation of distance' by a Western technology.

'In a restless and disordered world which is unbelieving to an extent which we have all too little realised, where sinister superstitions are setting forth their rival claims to the allegiance of men, we cannot afford to waver in our determination that the whole of Humanity shall remain a united people, where Muslim and Christian, Buddhist and Hindu shall stand together bound by a common devotion not to something

[1] 1 Cor. xv. 41. [2] Dan. v. 27.

behind but to something ahead, not to a racial past or a geographical unit, but to a great dream of a world society with a universal religion of which the historical faiths are but branches. We must recognise humbly the partial and defective character of our isolated traditions, and seek their source in the generic tradition from which they all have sprung. . . . In their wide environment, religions are assisting each other to find their own souls and grow to their full stature. . . . We are slowly realising that believers with different opinions and convictions are necessary to each other to work out the larger synthesis which alone can give the spiritual basis to a world brought together into intimate oneness by Man's mechanical ingenuity.'[1]

[1] Radhakrishnan, S.: *Eastern Religions and Western Thought*, 2nd edition (Oxford 1940, University Press), pp. 347–8.

VII. A (iii) (*a*), ANNEX III

THE CRUX FOR AN HISTORIAN BROUGHT UP IN THE CHRISTIAN TRADITION

By MARTIN WIGHT

THE Christian critic will read the whole of this Part with sympathy and admiration, above all for the comprehensive charity with which you endeavour to see all the Higher Religions *sub specie aeternitatis.*[1] But he may well have misgivings about your main arguments, and believe that you do not maintain the full tension inherent in the Christian problem of comparative religion. It is convenient to sum up some criticisms at this point.

1. Your description of Christianity is philosophical rather than historico-theological, 'Hellenic' rather than 'Hebraic'. You define Christianity in terms of the assertion that 'God is Love',[2] or as 'unique in revealing God to Man as Man's father and brother'.[3] But this is only true as far as it goes, and it does not go far enough. The central declaration of Christianity is not that God *is* something, but that God *has done* something; it is Hebraic first and Hellenic second; its uniqueness is primarily historico-theological, and only consequentially theologico-philosophical. God *has done* something in history; He has acted *in history* to show the meaning of history. If the Gospels say anything, they say this; and, since it is the common theme of the Synoptics and of St. John, perhaps the greatest modern Anglican commentary on St. John's Gospel may be quoted on the point:

'Modern study of the Fourth Gospel has pressed upon the Church the problem of historicity; the author of the Fourth Gospel, however, with greater theological insight, presses upon his readers the far more important, far more disturbing, problem of History itself and of its meaning. Confronted by the flesh of Jesus, the son of man, he demands that men should remember what He had said (xiv. 26), nay more, that they should eat His flesh and drink His blood (vi. 52–6). Jesus—Son of Man—words—flesh—blood! It is difficult to imagine language that fixes attention more steadily upon the importance of History. But, with equal conviction, the Evangelist refuses to permit his readers to rest even upon this important and particular history. *It is the spirit that quickeneth, the flesh profiteth nothing.* Only in relation to Spirit and Truth are the words of Jesus significant (vi. 63); only in relation to His Word is this speech able to be understood (viii. 43). It therefore follows necessarily that His words, His actual words, require for their understanding the interpretation that the Spirit of Truth alone is able to provide (xiv. 26). In Himself, as a product of the evolution of history, the Son of Man is merely—a son of man (viii. 54); and His words and actions, if they be thought of merely

1 On p. 428, above.

2 e.g. on pp. 439 and 443, and in VII. A (iii) (*a*), Annex II, 'Higher Religions and Psychological Types', p. 725, above.

3 On p. 427, above.

as historical episodes, are trivial and meaningless (vii. 16–18). This is the witness of the author of the Fourth Gospel: a witness thrust like a dagger straight into the heart of the "World" in so far as the World is regarded as existing of itself and in its own right; plunged like a dagger into the heart of History, if History contains within itself its own evident, analysable, and describable meaning. . . .

'The modern reader must by an effort of historical imagination first endeavour to place himself in the position of those for whom the gospel was originally written. Only he must not rest until this position is found to be charged with universal significance, until he stands here naturally because it is his inevitable position as a man. He must not rest until he stands where the Jews once stood and did not apprehend, and where Abraham and Isaiah once stood and did apprehend; until he stands confronted, not by the evolution of History, not even by the development of the Church, but by the Last Hour; until, that is to say, he stands confronted by the Truth, until the present time is confronted by eternity, and until the present place is met by the meaning of History—in fact, until he stands before God.'[1]

The Christian reader misses, in your account of Christianity, this insistence upon its springing from a unique and particular historical event which is charged with eschatological significance, and upon its therefore providing, alone among the Higher Religions except Islam, and far more fully than Islam, an answer to the question of the meaning of History.

2. It follows upon this that the Christian critic may think that you misrepresent the relationship between Christianity and Judaism, and consequently misrepresent Judaism itself. (*a*) Christianity did not 'break decisively with Judaism by recognizing and proclaiming that God is Love',[2] but by declaring that the promise of that Love, already contained in Judaism, was now fulfilled. 'L'abîme qu'il y a entre l'Ancien et le Nouveau Testament, c'est l'abîme qu'il y a entre l'annonce de quelque chose et la réalité de cette chose.'[3] It is curious to see you, side by side with your sympathetic treatment of Abraham, Moses, and the Prophets as the Judaic *praeparatio evangelica*, consistently identifying Judaism with Yahweh-religion, and emphasizing the Judaic God's jealousy[4] and 'Power.'[5] As regards the primitive religion of Yahweh, moreover, surely its important feature is not its inferiority in relation to Judaism and Christianity, but its superiority to the debased Canaanitish religions by which it was surrounded; not that it was only a partial revelation of the True God, but that it was indeed His revelation of Himself to the unpromising and backsliding people that he had chosen for His purposes. (*b*) Similarly, while Christianity did not 'break decisively' with Judaism in apprehending that God is Love, neither did it 'break decisively' in abandoning the apprehension that God is jealous—which simply means that His love makes exclusive

[1] Hoskyns, Edwyn Clement: *The Fourth Gospel*, edited by F. N. Davey, 2nd ed. (London 1947, Faber), pp. 58 and 49.

[2] p. 439, the first draft.

[3] Daniélou, Jean: *Le Mystère de l'Avent* (Paris 1948, Éditions du Seuil), p. 13.

[4] p. 439.

[5] VII. A (iii) (*a*), Annex II, 'Higher Religions and Psychological Types', p. 717, above.

claims. As there is more love in the Jewish conception of God than you allow, so is there more jealousy in the Christian conception. When you speak of the 'readmittance of the incongruous Israelitish concept' of a jealous God into Christianity,[1] and even of 'a fourteen-hundred-years-long' perversion of Christianity by the same concept,[2] though this again appears to be contradicted or corrected,[3] you are misrepresenting the Christian doctrine of God. For God's love is not a mere benevolence: it is a love that is identical with Holiness and Justice. This of course involves the human mind in paradox and great intellectual tension. It is only necessary here to point out that Jesus spoke of a God Whose response to obdurate evil is not only long-suffering but is also very terrible, and that the concept of the Wrath of God runs right through the New Testament.[4] Indeed the Love of God as it is shown throughout the Bible, for here there is no disagreement between the Old Testament and the New, is not an undemanding benignity, but something perhaps more like the condition of 'being in love'—a love that makes exclusive claims upon its object. 'O Jerusalem, Jerusalem, thou that killest the prophets, and stonest them which are sent unto thee, how often would I have gathered thy children together, even as a hen gathereth her chickens under her wings, and ye would not.'[5] 'No man cometh unto the Father, but by me.'[6] 'Neither is there salvation in any other; for there is none other name under heaven given among men, whereby we must be saved.'[7] The description of Christianity is falsified if this intrinsic exclusiveness and 'jealousy' in it is slurred over. (*c*) Where Christianity does seem to 'break decisively' with Judaism is not in its proclamation of Love, nor in its exclusiveness, but in its universality. It was not simply, as you say,[8] 'an intervention of God Himself to redeem the Jews of Jesus' day'. In the Synoptic tradition no less than in John there is a clear refusal to limit the sphere of the call of God.[9] The Old Israel which was limited to the seed of Abraham is superseded by the New Israel which embraces all who will repent and believe: the nature of the Christian Revelation is such that its promise and its claims are universal. But here again the discontinuity with Judaism is only superficial, for Judaism, inasmuch as it was an abortive Higher Religion, was also potentially universalist, and the Prophets had foretold the bringing of God's salvation to the Gentiles.[10]

3. The apparent under-estimation of the exclusiveness and universality of Christianity (the Christian critic might continue) throws your comparison of Christianity with the other Higher Religions out of focus. The inquiry necessarily begins from the assumption of the comparability of the Higher Religions, but the assumption is not sufficiently re-examined in the course of the discussion. It is only in the last two paragraphs of the Annex 'Higher Religions and Psychological

[1] p. 439. [2] p. 440. [3] On p. 563, above.

[4] e.g. Matt. iii. 7–8. Cp. Luke iii. 7–8, Rom. i. 18, Eph. v. 6, Col. iii. 6, 1 Thess. i. 10, Rev. xiv. 19.

[5] Matt. xxiii. 37. Cp. Luke xiii. 34. [6] John xiv. 6.

[7] Acts iv. 12. [8] On p. 552, above, in the first draft.

[9] e.g. Matt. viii. 11. Cp. Luke xiii. 29, Matt. xiii. 37–38, John x. 16.

[10] e.g. Isa. xlii. 6, xlix. 6, lii. 15, lvi. 8; Mic. iv. 2.

Types' that there are signs that you might want to discard it. Thus you seem to exaggerate the similarity of the Higher Religions' aims and contents: to exaggerate the unity of the species at the expense of the differences between its representatives. At the outset you attribute to all of them the same kind of exclusive claims,[1] though later you admit that the two Indic religions are not exclusive, or are 'exclusive' in a quite different way;[2] nor do you distinguish with any consistency between the prophetic or Judaic religions on the one hand and the non-prophetic or Indic on the other,[3] though the distinction is implicitly made in VII. A (iii) (*b*), on p. 453, n. 2. The reader may well feel that the comparative study of the Higher Religions never gets under way. Is there not a fundamental difference between the two Higher Religions of the Indic tradition, which are pantheistic, immanentist, non-historical, world-denying, and the two Higher Religions of the Judaic tradition, which are prophetic, transcendentalist, historical, and world-affirming?

But there is a methodological criticism that perhaps goes deeper. Your limitation of the discussion to the four Higher Religions that at present partition the World between them is really as arbitrary as it would be to limit your comparison of civilizations to the contemporary representatives of the species. It hinders your attempt to see the existing Higher Religions *sub specie aeternitatis*, because it commits you to assuming a finality about them which, in view of the many potential or abortive Higher Religions which have come into being in the past and either died or survived only as fossils, is manifestly illusory. There is no reason *a priori* to suppose that the 'fully-fledged Higher Religions . . . derived from the secondary civilizations'[4] are the collective final term in the history of Religion. Nor is any evidence or argument produced for your assertion that it is their 'destiny . . . that they should all become world-wide without conflicting with one another'[5] except for the theory that they correspond to Jung's psychological types; and this (fascinating, illuminating, and important as it is) cannot be more than a 'rationalization' of a particular historical constellation.

The 'illusion of finality' is most apparent when you argue[6] that 'if these religions did not genuinely satisfy some widely experienced human need' it is hardly conceivable that they should each have secured so wide an allegiance. This assumes, first, that the apprehension of human spiritual needs remains constant, and secondly, that the means of satisfying them are all equivalent, whereas the history of Religion shows that the apprehension of spiritual needs undergoes progressive development, and adherence to any one of the Higher Religions implicitly denies the adequacy of the means of satisfying those needs which are offered by the Primitive Religions. Your argument that prevalence indicates value could have been used in the Roman Empire to show the superiority of Paganism to Christianity, as you yourself suggest when you say in another connexion that the contemporary observer is 'most unlikely to be able to foresee the spiritual shape of things to come'.[7] Was Jung's

[1] p. 430, above.
[2] pp. 438 and 440, above.
[3] e.g. on p. 473, above, and in 'Holy Writ', on p. 750, below.
[4] On. p. 421, above.
[5] p. 443, the first draft.
[6] p. 443, above.
[7] p. 418, above.

typology applicable within the Roman Empire under the Antonines? If not, then his types do not have permanent validity. If yes, then the contemporary division of the World between the four existing Higher Religions does not have permanent validity. Indeed, it is surely plain that the present constellation of Higher Religions is due not to psychological typology but to that much wider thing (in which psychological typology may play its part) which we can only call cultural history. The psychological theory could only be upheld if it could be shown that there is a numerical predominance of each psychological type in the region of the World where its 'corresponding' Higher Religion has the ascendancy, and for this there is no evidence whatever. It is just as likely that the Higher Religions mould psychology as that 'each of them may correspond and minister to one of the psychological types into which Human Nature appears to be differentiated',[1] or, in a word, as that psychology determines the Higher Religions.

4. You admit the concept of a *praeparatio evangelica* throughout in your interpretation of Judaism, and in your account of Paganism,[2] though you only use the phrase itself twice, I think, *en passant*.[3] But from the Christian point of view it is the fundamental principle for explaining the relationship between Christianity and other religions, and for reconciling their truths and insight with the exclusive claims of the Christian Revelation, and the Christian critic may wish that you had developed it more thoroughly. It is expressed in the quotation from Temple,[4] and it could be expressed in the very fine metaphor of the veils which you use in a different connexion.[5] (It is magnificently stated in the passage from Bevan's *Jerusalem under the High Priests* which you quote in V. vi. 132: a passage which not only states the purpose and scope of the *praeparatio*, but also emphasizes the uniqueness and transcendence of That which was prepared for). The *praeparatio evangelica* was recognized from the earliest days of the Church, especially by St. Paul, when he preached at Athens,[6] and in his acknowledgement of the validity of Natural Law among the Gentiles.[7] In the second century A.D. the conception was elaborated, first of all, of course, to explain the relations between Christianity and Judaism, by St. Irenaeus in answer to Marcion, but also, more tentatively, to explain the relations between Christianity and Paganism, by St. Justin and Clement of Alexandria. 'Nous trouvons chez ces deux hommes l'idée que, dans les philosophies païennes, il y a une certaine présence du Verbe, du *Logos*, une certaine lumière divine qui éclaire les hommes et leur communique la part de vérité qu'il y a en eux.'[8] Perhaps this French writer whom I have quoted, a Jesuit who besides being a Patristic scholar is profoundly concerned with the theology of missionary activity, may be quoted

[1] VII. A (iii) (*a*), Annex II, 'Higher Religions and Psychological Types', p. 716, above.
[2] On pp. 458–60, above.
[3] On p. 532, above, and in VII. C (ii) (*a*), Annex, 'The Prehistoric Background', p. 766, n. 3, below.
[4] On p. 429, above.
[5] On pp. 461–3, above.
[6] Acts xvii. 22–31.
[7] Rom. ii. 14–15.
[8] Daniélou, Jean: *Le Mystère de l'Avent* (Paris 1948, Éditions du Seuil), p. 10.

further for a modern liberal Catholic statement of the conception of the *praeparatio evangelica* as the Christian doctrine of comparative religion:

'Il est très frappant de voir que les premiers chrétiens se sont trouvés, vis-à-vis du monde dans lequel ils étaient, exactement dans la situation dans laquelle se trouvent nos missionnaires en pays païens: une petite minorité d'hommes apportant un message étranger dans un monde qui leur était totalement fermé et hostile. Par exemple quand saint Paul pour la première fois est allé à Athènes et a commencé à prêcher l'Évangile sur l'Aréopage, il se trouvait dans la même situation que les premiers missionnaires qui sont allés en Chine ou au Japon et qui ont parlé aux sages de là-bas. . . .

'L'angoisse qui oppresse certaines âmes aujourd'hui, consiste à se demander si le christianisme n'est pas dépassé, s'il n'est pas vieilli. Ceci ne concerne que certaines structures tout extérieures du christianisme, mais non son essence: le christianisme est, et restera toujours, jeunesse du monde, parce qu'il est précisément chronologiquement au terme du développement de l'Histoire. Et la vraie relation du christianisme avec toutes les autres religions, c'est justement que ces religions à son égard sont antérieures, sont périmées. Je ne dis pas qu'elles sont fausses en tous points: le judaïsme n'est pas faux, le bouddhisme n'est pas faux, les civilisations fétichistes ne sont pas fausses; elles sont vieilles, c'est-à-dire que, par rapport au christianisme, elles sont dans un état d'antériorité chronologique et, en quelque sorte, des survivances; le christianisme, qui les achève, est apparu et désormais tout ce qu'il y a de bon en elles est accompli dans le christianisme. Entre le christianisme et elles, nous avons la juxtaposition dans l'espace de choses qui sont historiquement successives et c'est un fait curieux que ce rapport de simultanéité entre des réalités entre lesquelles le rapport essentiel est un rapport de succession.'[1]

I think the Christian critic might point to two places where your emphasis is different, and implies the spiritual equivalence of the four Higher Religions rather than the *praeparatio evangelica*. You describe Matteo Ricci as having sought 'a reconciliation, on Christian initiative, between hitherto exclusive-minded religions'.[2] But the above passage from Daniélou is the authentic position of Matteo Ricci, who 'approached these alien faiths with sympathy, understanding and reverence', not because he thought that they were as good as Christianity, but because he saw them in the way in which St. Paul saw the Law, as 'our schoolmaster to bring us unto Christ'.[3] Christian charity will always enjoin respect for the genuine agnosticism of a Symmachus,[4] but belief in the Christian Revelation is not compatible with an acceptance of Symmachus's position, and, although you infer the contrary, there would surely be no difference between St. Ambrose and Father Ricci on that point. Again, the resemblance between the sacraments and rituals of Christianity and Paganism cannot be adequately described for the Christian by 'the simple truth that it is a family likeness',[5] which once more implies spiritual equivalence.

'Ce que nous rencontrons là, c'est cette espèce de sacramentalisme universel qui est à la fois une sorte d'intuition profonde du sens sacral des

[1] Daniélou, op. cit., pp. 10 and 21–22. [2] p. 441, above.
[3] Gal. iii. 24. [4] p. 442, above. [5] p. 459, above.

choses et en même temps qui ne donne pas la grâce, qui la signifie seulement. C'est une sorte de pierre d'attente, d'appel. . . . Que fera le christianisme? Créera-t-il des rites distincts de ceux des autres religions? Pas du tout. Le christianisme prendra tous ces gestes sacrés de toutes les religions, mais il les chargera de la grâce du Christ. Alors cette eau du Gange, dans la mesure où elle devient le baptême, devient le moyen de la régénération surnaturelle des hommes. C'est bien le même repas, mais ce pain qui aura été brisé n'est pas seulement un symbole, effectivement il nous fait communier à la réalité même de Jésus-Christ. Alors nous voyons très bien ce qui se ressemble et ce qui est différent. C'est presque pareil et c'est totalement différent. C'est pareil quant au geste mais c'est différent parce qu'il y a toute la différence entre la figure et la réalité, entre le geste qui est un geste d'attente et le don. Et c'est là l'essentiel du christianisme: le don par Dieu de la grâce divine et de la vie divine.'[1]

5. But there has always been a tension in the relationship of Christianity with other religions: a tension between apprehending them as a *praeparatio evangelica* and apprehending them as obstacles to the spreading of the Gospel. This tension reflects the inherent ambiguity of other religions, which are at the same time both 'precursors' and 'adversaries'; and it springs from the essential nature of a revelation which is at once exclusive and universal, which proclaims itself as Truth among partial truths and falsehoods, which makes absolute claims and knows (in a sense) that they will be rejected, which is a light shining in a darkness that has not comprehended it.

'Some speak grudgingly or fault-findingly about the heights of the non-Christian religions and are inclined to lay all stress on their horrible depths. Others assiduously emphasise the heights of these religions but remain largely silent about the dark sides. Both, therefore, have a distorted view of these religions, not so much because they unduly vituperate or unduly praise them (although they certainly do so), but because they have a distorted view of Man, whose nature is angelic and satanic. We must honestly recognise the angel as well as the demon in Man, wherever we find him, in Christendom, in Hinduism, in China or anywhere else.'[2]

You describe the 'diabolical' theory of Paganism as an 'ingenious hypothesis' of 'Early Modern Western Christian missionaries'.[3] But it goes back at least to St. Paul, who saw Paganism as bondage to *τὰ στοιχεῖα τοῦ κόσμου*.[4] You imply that it is a perverse 'hypothesis'. Perverse and uncharitable, of course, its application can be and often has been, but it originates in spiritual insight into the intrinsically demonic potentialities of Paganism. What St. Paul describes in Rom. i. 20–25 is part of the experience of every missionary: that other religions are not only foreshadowings of Christianity, but also genuine autonomous idolatries, manifestations of the forces of spiritual evil that Christ came to vanquish.[5] Consequently Christian missionary thought has always moved

1 Daniélou, op. cit., pp. 75–76.

2 Kraemer, Hendrik: *The Christian Message in a Non-Christian World* (London 1938, published for the International Missionary Council by the Edinburgh House Press), p. 286.

3 VII. A (iii) (*a*), Annex II, 'Higher Religions and Psychological Types', in the first draft; cp. p. 459, above.

4 Gal. iv. 3 and 9; Col. ii. 8.

5 Matt. xii. 29, Luke x. 18, John xii. 31, xvi. 11. Cp. Col. i. 13, ii. 15, 1 John iii. 8.

between two poles, an emphasis on the similarities in Paganism to Christianity, and an emphasis on the radical otherness of Christianity. The first view is perhaps represented most clearly today by Roman Catholics like Daniélou, who are in the tradition of Matteo Ricci, while the 'radical' view has its classic modern expression in the book already quoted of Kraemer's, a Calvinist scholar who has had long missionary experience in the Far East. The two views are complementary: there is not contradiction between them, but a necessary tension. Therefore

'le rapport du christianisme aux autres religions . . . est d'une part historique, c'est-à-dire qu'il y a entre le christianisme et les autres religions une relation "chronologique", dans la mesure où il représente ce à quoi tout le reste aboutit; mais c'est en même temps une relation "dramatique", c'est-à-dire que, s'il est vrai que le christianisme achève, il faut dire aussi qu'il détruit et que, par conséquent, les religions païennes d'une part s'épanouissent en lui, et d'autre part meurent pour lui faire place.'[1]

The 'dramatic' relationship becomes most apparent at the point where another religion rejects its vocation of being a precursor of Christianity and passes over into the attitude of an adversary, as the Jews themselves did when confronted with Jesus Christ. This is how Daniélou sees the ultimate opposition between the Syriac tradition and the Indic tradition:

'Bouddha a été l'un des grands précurseurs du Christ et sera son dernier adversaire. Bouddha, représentant éminent de la religion cosmique, prébiblique, est à la fois celui qui dans les profondeurs du passé a préparé mystérieusement l'Inde à recevoir Jésus-Christ, en faisant l'éducation de son âme, et c'est encore lui qui dans le drame spirituel suprême du monde, quand Israël lui-même "sera intégré",[2] disputera l'âme de l'Inde au Christ, en opposant à l'universalisme chrétien l'universalisme de la religion cosmique, qui est ce qui lui ressemble le plus, la caricature de la catholicité, le syncrétisme.'[3]

Perhaps the most that can be said about the history of this tension in the Christian attitude to other religions is that, as Christianity has become less concerned with primitive religions of the kind that it superseded in the Roman Empire and has become more concerned with the other Higher Religions, so its emphasis has shifted from apprehension of the demonic character of other religions to recognition of their *praeparatio evangelica*. But this, once again, has taken place within the abiding framework of tension, of a 'dramatic' relationship, because these spring from the very nature of spiritual life and of Christianity itself. Now, as always, Christianity comes not only to fulfil, but also to purge.

'When the word "approach" is taken in the sense of Christianity as a total religious system approaching the non-Christian religions as total religious systems, there is only difference and antithesis, and this must be so because they are radically different. To minimise this results in a weakening and blurring of the true character of Christianity. Wilamowitz in his . . . book on *The Faith of the Greeks* mentions as one of the principal reasons of the victory of Christianity in the Ancient World the fact that it rejected all other gods and proclaimed the absolute monarchy of the

[1] Daniélou, op. cit., p. 9. [2] Rom. xi. 51. [3] Daniélou, op. cit., pp. 67–68.

One Living God; in other words, that it remained true to its essential nature. To remain true to its essential character is also to-day the unbreakable law of Christianity.'[1]

Let it be added that for a Christian to speak of the demonic potentialities of other religions does not preclude recognition of the possibility of demonic perversion of Christianity itself: it implies it. The Christian will be grateful for your insistence that 'the intransigence of the Christian martyrs degenerated into the intolerance of Christian persecutors',[2] and will confess the spiritual truth in your criticisms of Christianity,[3] even when he disagrees with the way in which they are formulated. *Corruptio optimi pessima.* For the Christian, the discussion of the relations between Christianity and the other Higher Religions has to start from its recognition that Christians, more than anyone else, are under judgement.

'The only valid and indestructible foundation of missions is the apostolic consciousness of joyful obedience to God's Will as manifested in the revelation in Christ, and our gratitude for this divine gift. All questions of superiority in the field of cultural experience or psychological religious experience are irrelevant in this context. No pretensions whatever, derived from presumably superior ethical or religious or cultural elements, have anything to do with the apostolic claim and obligation of Christianity. Its only foundation is the objective and plain reality of God's revelation in Christ, and therefore, speaking fundamentally, it is quite immaterial whether the World asks for it or not. The only way to become wholly purged from all kinds of superiority-feeling is, not the direct pursuit of a sympathetic or generous spirit towards other cultural experiences, however praiseworthy and valuable this may be, but the radically apostolic attitude; for this presupposes the not less radical humility that issues from the fact that all men of all civilisations (the "Christian" included) are, in the light of God's revelation, forlorn sinners and rebellious children of God.'[4]

6. For these reasons the Christian critic will, I think, be dissatisfied with your handling of 'the crux for an historian brought up in the Christian tradition', and will hold that your solution of the problem of the relationship between Christianity and the other Higher Religions fails to be in Christian terms. He will be able to accept neither your premiss of the spiritual equivalence of the Higher Religions derived from the secondary civilizations nor the conclusion, to which it inevitably leads, that they have a common destiny.[5] He will note that in due course you qualify your assumption by tentatively suggesting a spiritual deficiency in the Indic religions which has led to an apparently inconsistent assimilation to Christianity;[6] but it will seem to him that in the end, with your argument of the 'harmony' or 'symphony' of the Higher Religions,[7] you yourself capitulate to a Hindu mode of thought.

[1] Kraemer, op. cit., pp. 300–1.
[2] On p. 439, above.
[3] On pp. 440–1 and 452, above.
[4] Kraemer, op. cit., p. 300.
[5] pp. 442–3, above.
[6] VII. A (iii) (*d*) 3, Annex, 'Immortality and Karma', p. 758, below; VII. A (iii) (*a*), Annex II, 'Higher Religions and Psychological Types', pp. 719, 725, n. 1, and 735, above; cp. V. vi. 45–47.
[7] p. 428, above, and VII. A (iii) (*a*), Annex II, 'Higher Religions and Psychological Types', p. 735.

'Hinduism is wholly free from the strange obsession of the Semitic faiths that the acceptance of a particular religious metaphysic is necessary for salvation. . . . The main note of Hinduism is one of respect and good will for other creeds. When a worshipper of Viṣṇu had a feeling in his heart against a worshipper of Śiva and he bowed before the image of Viṣṇu, the face of the image divided itself in half and Śiva appeared on one side and Viṣṇu on the other, and the two smiling as one face on the bigoted worshipper told him that Viṣṇu and Śiva were one. . . .

'To obliterate every other religion than one's own is a sort of bolshevism in religion which we must try to prevent. We can do so only if we accept something like the Hindu solution, which seeks the unity of religion not in a common creed but in a common quest. Let us believe in a unity of spirit and not of organisation, a unity which secures ample liberty not only for every individual but for every type of organised life which has proved itself effective. For almost all historical forms of life and thought can claim the sanction of experience and so the authority of God. The World would be a much poorer thing if one creed absorbed the rest. God wills a rich harmony and not a colourless uniformity. The comprehensive and synthetic spirit of Hinduism has made it a mighty forest with a thousand waving arms each fulfilling its function and all directed by the spirit of God. Each thing in its place and all associated in the divine concert making with their various voices and even dissonances, as Heraclitus would say, the most exquisite harmony should be our ideal.'[1]

This is the same position that you finally arrive at, in words very similar to your own.[2] Nor will the Christian critic be touched by the argument which governs your discussion throughout, and is at once its starting-point and its conclusion, that 'each religion is ever seeking, like the psychological type which it serves, to achieve the impossible feat of ministering to the whole gamut of the Psyche's elemental needs for expression. The feat is impossible because there is not, and cannot be, any spiritual organ capable of playing a psychic diapason; and therefore any existing higher religion that aspires to become *the* Universal Religion is doomed to disappointment'.[3] He will reject this psychological relativism, first, because of the methodological doubts which I have suggested above; secondly, because it attributes an established scientific validity to a typological theory which is only one (and not the most widely accepted) among many, and which is at best no more than the intuitive schematizing of a great psychological artist; and, thirdly, because the evidence which you abundantly provide suggests that each Higher Religion in fact attains considerable success, by its internal development and articulation, in 'ministering to the whole gamut of the Psyche's [hypothetical] elemental needs for expression'. But he will reject it also for the *a priori* reason that the Christian Revelation is nonsense if there is only an 'arbitrarily favoured fraction of Mankind that happens to be psychologically equipped'[4] for the acceptance of the Gospel.

'We Catholics do not quarrel with the methods of the religious historian,

[1] Radhakrishnan, S.: *The Hindu View of Life* (London 1927, Allen & Unwin), pp. 37 and 58–59.

[2] Cp. Clement Webb's criticism of Hinduism, quoted ibid., p. 48.

[3] VII. A (iii) (*a*), Annex II, 'Higher Religions and Psychological Types', p. 734, above, transposed from the past tense into the present.

[4] p. 443, above.

so long as he keeps within his proper limits, within the limits of historical data and proved historical fact, and so long as he does not claim in his classification of religious types to pass decisive judgment upon the essential nature of the religious structure which he has under examination. We Catholics acknowledge readily, without any shame, nay with pride, that Catholicism cannot be identified simply and wholly with primitive Christianity, nor even with the Gospel of Christ, in the same way that the great oak cannot be identified with the tiny acorn. There is no mechanical identity, but an organic identity. And we go further and say that thousands of years hence Catholicism will probably be even richer, more luxuriant, more manifold in dogma, morals, law and worship than the Catholicism of the present day. A religious historian of the fifth millennium A.D. will without difficulty discover in Catholicism conceptions and forms and practices which derive from India, China and Japan, and he will have to recognise a far more obvious "complex of opposites". It is quite true, Catholicism *is* a union of contraries. But contraries are not contradictories. Wherever there is life, there you must have conflict and contrariety. . . . All peoples, each with their special aptitudes, are her [the Catholic Church's] children, and all bring their gifts into the sanctuary. The elasticity, freshness of mind and sense of form of the Roman combine with the penetration, profundity and inwardness of the German, and with the sobriety, discretion and good sense of the Anglo-Saxon. The piety and modesty of the Chinaman unite with the subtlety and depth of the Indian, and with the practicality and initiative of the American. It is unity in fullness, fullness in unity. The individual life of men and peoples—the most precious thing in the World and unique in character—flows with its rich and sparkling waters in all the innumerable courses and channels dug by missionaries in far lands; and those countless tributaries flow into the Church, and, purified in the Holy Spirit by its infallible teaching, merge into a single mighty stream, into one great flood which flows through all Humanity, fertilizing and purifying as it goes. That is the true conception of the Catholic Church.'[1]

The difference between this passage and the quotation from Radhakrishnan above, which is so close to your own view, is the difference between Catholicism and syncretism. Karl Adam is a Roman Catholic; Protestants see the development of the Church in federal rather than unitary terms as the propagation of autonomous and self-propagating indigenous churches.[2] Indeed, the reason why Protestants of the Reformed tradition would hesitate to accept the quotation from Karl Adam with the substitution of 'Christianity' for 'Catholicism' is because of the belief that the Roman Catholic theory of the development of doctrine compromises the purity of the original κήρυγμα and that Roman Catholicism already goes too far in the direction of syncretism.[3] But this issue between the Roman Catholic Church, the members of the World Council of Churches, and the Moscow Patriarchate, which together compose the Christian World today (which is also an issue *within* each church, as it was between Matteo Ricci and Clement XI, who finally condemned his methods) is nothing compared with their common distance from your

[1] Adam, Karl: *The Spirit of Catholicism*, translated by Dom Justin McCann, O.S.B., (London 1929, Sheed & Ward), pp. 2 and 146.

[2] Cp. the writings of K. S. Latourette and Kraemer, op. cit., pp. 405–27.

[3] Cp. Kraemer, op. cit., pp. 403–4.

own conclusion. For it is a debate within the common ground of conviction that the Church (however defined, and whatever its proper methods) is in the World to redeem it and that its *raison d'être* is to convert all nations. Paul's doctrine of the gathering of the Gentiles[1] is only a development of Christ's own declaration of the oecumenical character of His mission, and is foreshadowed, in simpler terms, by the Prophets' vision of an ultimate day in which all the World will acknowledge the God of Israel.

'And it shall come to pass in the last days, that the mountain of the Lord's house shall be established in the top of the mountains, and shall be exalted above the hills; and all nations shall flow unto it. And many people shall go and say, Come ye, and let us go up to the mountain of the Lord, to the house of the God of Jacob; and He will teach us of His ways, and we will walk in His paths: for out of Zion shall go forth the law, and the word of the Lord from Jerusalem. . . . In that day shall there be an altar to the Lord in the midst of the land of Egypt, and a pillar at the border thereof to the Lord. And it shall be for a sign and for a witness unto the Lord of hosts in the land of Egypt: for they shall cry unto the Lord because of the oppressors, and He shall send them a saviour, and a great one, and He shall deliver them. And the Lord shall be known to Egypt, and the Egyptians shall know the Lord in that day, and shall do sacrifice and oblation; yea, they shall vow a vow unto the Lord, and perform it. And the Lord shall smite Egypt: He shall smite and heal it: and they shall return even to the Lord, and He shall be intreated of them, and shall heal them. In that day, shall there be a highway out of Egypt to Assyria, and the Assyrian shall come into Egypt, and the Egyptian into Assyria, and the Egyptians shall serve with the Assyrians. In that day shall Israel be the third with Egypt and with Assyria, even a blessing in the midst of the land: Whom the Lord of hosts shall bless, saying, Blessed be Egypt my people, and Assyria, the work of my hands, and Israel mine inheritance.'[2]

But, while he will disagree with so much that you say, the Christian critic will be deeply grateful to you for this Part, because it will appear to him that, just as you have abandoned your original judgement that all civilizations are philosophically equivalent and have found that 'civilizations . . . have ceased to constitute intelligible fields of study for us and have forfeited their historical significance except in so far as they minister to the progress of Religion',[3] so the suppressed logic of your argument (rather than the weight of your evidence) drives on towards discarding your assumption that all higher religions are spiritually equivalent, and to the conclusion that the higher religions in their turn cease to be intelligible fields of study and forfeit their historical significance except in so far as they are related to Christianity.

1 e.g. Gal. iii. 28, Eph. i. 10, ii. 11–14, Col. iii. 11.
2 Isa. ii. 2–3 (cp. Mic. iv. 1–2), xix. 19–25.
3 p. 449, above.

VII. A (iii) (*c*), ANNEX

HOLY WRIT

THE recentness of the epiphany of the higher religions was advertised by the importance of the role that Holy Writ played in their life; for writing and reading were highly sophisticated media of mental intercourse, inasmuch as they were devices which reduced to a minimum the element of physical action entailed.

When Faust[1] substitutes 'Deed' for 'Word' in the opening verse of the Gospel according to Saint John in which the Evangelist declares what 'was in the beginning', the audacious reviser is showing himself a good historian; for a lively form of action is the natural means by which Man communicates his wishes, feelings, and thoughts to his fellows; and, in the progressive development of the semantic art, we may guess that a choric mime preceded a choric drama in which physical action was accompanied by intelligible words, as we know that words chanted by a choir as an accompaniment to dramatic action preceded words sung or recited by an individual prophet or bard to a listening audience. This living word disengaged from corporate physical action must have seemed a poor substitute at first, before the gradual exploration of its latent potentialities; and, if the sounding word that lives on the speaker's lips and in the hearer's ear would seem a bloodless medium of intercourse to the ecstatic participant in a Bacchic chorus, he would feel, *a fortiori*, that the silent word engraved, inscribed, or printed on stone, potsherd, parchment, or paper was too jejune to be taken seriously. The art of writing had, however, been coeval with the species of Society that we have called 'civilizations', at any rate in the Old World; and the possession of 'household books', sacred or profane, had been characteristic of Old World civilizations of all generations later than the first—though the inanimate means of preserving these literary treasures, which had always been available since they had first been brought into existence, had been spurned, through long ages, in favour of a living transmission of 'Homer' from rhapsode to rhapsode, and of the Qur'ān from *hāfiz* to *hāfiz*, 'not in tables of stone but in fleshy tables of the heart'.[2]

These 'household books' had been of two kinds. There had been epics inspired by the experience of barbarians belonging to the external proletariat of an antecedent civilization,[3] and there had been sacred books inspired by the different experience of an antecedent civilization's internal proletariat. The Bible and the Qur'ān were classic examples of the Sacred Book, and 'Homer', the Mahabharata, and the Icelandic Saga of the Epic. Usually the Epic had been in the ascendant in a civilization that had been affiliated to a predecessor through a barbarian heroic age, and the Sacred Book in a civilization that had been affiliated to a predecessor through a church. Broadly speaking, 'Homer' had held in Hellenic life the place that the Bible had held in the lives of Western

[1] Goethe: *Faust*, Part I, ll. 1224–37.

[2] 2 Cor. iii. 3.

[3] See V. v. 194–337, *passim*.

and Orthodox Christendom. Like the Bible, the Homeric Epic had been taken for granted, had been treasured as a κτῆμα ἐς αἰεί,[1] had been consulted as an oracle, had been quoted for emotional and aesthetic effect, and had been constantly reinterpreted, to suit the needs of different ages, till meanings had been read into it that would have been unintelligible to its makers. But this distinction between two classes of Civilization differentiated by different types of 'household book' was not clear-cut. In Western Christendom, for example, there had been an abortive Teutonic Epic which might conceivably have lived to play the part of 'Homer' if the Bible had not eclipsed it at the dawn of Western history,[2] while in the Indic World the epic poetry of the barbarian Aryas had not indeed been eclipsed, but been decidedly outshone, by a sacred book, in the shape of the Vedas, of which the nucleus, at any rate, had been bequeathed to the Indic Society by the same barbarians.

Barbarian sacred books, however, were as rare as religious epics; and this was no accident; for the normal association of sacred books with higher religions derived from a characteristic of higher religions that was one of their distinguishing features. The higher religions had been founded and developed by personalities that had become historic through impressing themselves on the imagination of Posterity; and the medium through which they had made this personal impression on disciples who had never seen them in the flesh had been a message enshrined in a sacred book preserved 'in the tables of the heart' if not on paper.[3]

[1] Thucydides, Book I, chap. 22.

[2] See I. i. 449, n. 2, and II. ii. 320–1.

[3] As the writer of this Study saw it, the Mahāyāna had been conjured out of the philosophy of the Buddha by the lives and works of Aśvaghosha, Nagarjuna, and Vasubandhu (see Eliot, Sir Ch.: *Hinduism and Buddhism* (London 1921, Edward Arnold, 3 vols.), vol. ii, pp. 82–89), while the post-Buddhaic and anti-Buddhaic Hinduism which was one of the four principal living higher religions in the writer's day had been inspired from the same source in the life and works of Šankara (see Eliot, op. cit., vol. ii, pp. 206–11). The conformity in this respect between the Buddhaistic and the Judaistic higher religions, which had struck the writer's eye, was queried by Mr. Martin Wight in the following comment:

'Surely neither Hinduism nor the Mahāyāna was founded by an historic personality, and neither has a sacred book which enshrines such a personality's message. Is there not a radical difference between the two higher religions of the Judaic tradition, which are prophetic religions, with historical founders and sacred books *sensu stricto*, and on the other hand the two higher religions of the Indic tradition, which are non-historical and non-prophetic (except in the indirect degree in which the Mahāyāna derives from the Hīnayāna), and whose sacred literature is heterogeneous?

'The following distinctions seem to me, if they are not very wide of the mark, to belong to your exposition:

'(i) Hinduism: sacred literature of the barbarian epic kind, as you say;

'(ii) Hīnayāna: The Pali Canon, at least in *The Discourses of the Buddha* and perhaps *The Book of the Great Decease*, is analogous to the Gospels in being the record of an historic personality; but, since you classify Gautama as a philosopher, not a prophet, perhaps one should say analogous to the Platonic and Xenophontic record of Socrates and to the Confucian *Analects*;

'(iii) Mahāyāna: the Sanskrit Canon, in so far as I can grasp its nature, consists in a tiny kernel of historic and prophetic record (such kernel as can be found in the lives of the Buddha), if one is to think of the Buddha as having been posthumously transmogrified from a philosopher into a prophet in the development from the Hīnayāna into the Mahāyāna, surrounded by a vast pulpy fruit of devotional and theologico-philosophical writings in the *Sutras* and related documents. Would it be a fair comparison to say that the Mahayanian sacred literature resembles the Christian Patristic writings divorced from the Old and New Testaments?'

The writer would agree that in the two Buddhaistic higher religions, as compared with the two Judaistic, the part played by historical personalities and by scriptures purporting to enshrine their personal teaching was not of the same overwhelming

Such sacred books had not established their authority without a struggle, however great might have been the prestige of the prophets whose messages they had embodied; for they had never found the domain of Religion untenanted. A traditional corporate liturgy, operated by a priesthood, had always been before them in the field, and, in so far as they had succeeded in winning their way against such time-honoured rites and securely vested interests, they had triumphed through managing to meet some importunate unsatisfied social need.

One emergency that had made the fortune of sacred books had been the social calamity of deracination. 'Displaced persons', whether they be refugees or deportees, are physically prevented by their geographical removal from continuing to worship at their ancestral shrines; and, since the due celebration of a rite at the proper place may be as essential to the religious efficacy of the proceedings as the performance of the proper gestures and the utterance of the proper words, the members of an exiled community may find themselves debarred from perpetuating the liturgy that has been their traditional means of communion with their god and with one another. In exile, this communion will have become more than ever precious, since it will be the sole remaining sustenance of a communal life which has lost its roots in a soil that the exiles can no longer call their own; and there will be a proportionately strong incentive to find some new medium of religious communion to replace the liturgy that has been abandoned perforce. In this desperate emergency a sacred book recorded in the tables of the heart—or even in the less durable, but hardly less portable medium of ink and paper—may save the situation by taking the lost liturgy's place.

The classic example of this enforced replacement of a liturgy by a book is, of course, the ritual revolution which was Jewry's response to the ordeal of being dispersed abroad among the Gentiles. In the Jewish communities of the Diasporà the priest offering sacrifices at the altar in the Temple at Jerusalem had to be supplanted by a reader reciting from the books of the Law and the Prophets on a reading-stand in the synagogue; and after the destruction of the Temple and the Roman Government's ban on the residence of Jews in Aelia Capitolina—the Hellenic city founded by Hadrian on the site where Jerusalem had stood—the Diasporà's form of worship was the sole form surviving. This triumph of the Torah in the Jewish Diasporà is manifestly an example of the same stimulating effect of new ground that we have observed already in another context,[1] where we have noticed how the Hellenic and Teutonic Epic and the Scandinavian Saga all flowered overseas—in Ionia, in Britain, and in Iceland—after a migration on board ship which had given the diction of poetry an opportunity to shake itself free from the trammels of an earth-bound ritual in order to become a

importance as it was in Christianity and Islam. On the other hand, he would maintain that the resemblance in this respect between the two pairs of living higher religions became not merely apparent but significant when they were viewed against the foil of antecedent primitive religions in which the alpha and the omega of piety consisted in the corporate performance of traditional rites, and in which neither scriptures nor historical personalities played any part at all.

[1] In II.ii. 92–96.

vehicle for expressing experiences that were, not corporate and repetitive, but personal and unique.

Another emergency that had made the fortune of a sacred book had been a revolutionary change in the direction of mimesis—a revolution precipitated, not by external forces driving a community into physical exile, but by a voluntary and deliberate transfer of allegiance from an ancestral tradition preserved by a priesthood to a revelation proclaimed by a prophet. If the formidable authority conferred on the priests by their custody of tradition is to be challenged, the challenge can be delivered only by the word of God Himself as revealed in His prophet's message; for, if that message is once recognized to be authentic, it must override the rulings of priests who are not God's spokesmen but merely His ministers; and, though the winged words of God's living human spokesman will be likely to have both a greater virtue[1] and a greater effect than any written testament, dumb scripture has one decisive posthumous advantage over the living voice. Scripture can attain a longevity which, at second hand, will multiply a hundredfold the brief life-span of the prophet whose message this frozen echo perpetuates. Holy Writ that purports to enshrine prophetic revelation is thus a *malleus presbyterorum* that is a literal godsend to rebels against sacerdotal authority. The followers of the Prophets of Israel and Judah and of Zarathustra made effective use of this weapon against the priests of their day; the Scribes and Pharisees used it against the Sadducees; the Protestant Reformers used it against the Papal Church.

This revolutionary attack in the name of Holy Writ had been met by the priests with varying degrees of success in different cases. The Jewish priesthood was eventually worsted by a combination of adverse circumstances: the Babylonish Captivity; the permanent preponderance of the Diasporà over a reconstituted temple-state at Jerusalem; the destruction of Jerusalem by the Romans and consequent cessation of the Hierosolymitan liturgy of sacrifice; and, above all, the gradual change of outlook and êthos in Jewry from a communal towards an individual relation to God. On the other hand the Magi signally defeated Zarathustra by playing upon his too simple-minded followers the confidence-trick which the English King Richard II sought to play upon a rebel peasantry when he cried 'I will be your leader!'; and, by an equally skilful use of similar tactics, the Brahmans had managed to survive the epiphanies of a long series of sacred books, from the Vedas onwards. The error of short-sighted priests who had clumsily ensured the prophets' triumph by ill-advisedly putting them to death had been retrieved by those priests' far-sighted children, who had contrived to sterilize the martyrs' spiritual legacies by building their sepulchres;[2] and the efficacy of this stratagem had been so great that it had proved able to weather even a

[1] 'The main force in promoting higher spirituality or morality among men has been the apparition of prophetic souls whose teaching cannot be accounted for by what went before them, and who appear by their commanding influence to drive men by a new impulse in a new direction. The new impulse is, perhaps, never afterwards wholly exhausted or lost. But it becomes merged in the general channel with other currents, and, though it adds something to the whole, it tends to become less and less distinctive' (Gore, Charles: *The Philosophy of the Good Life* (Everyman edition), p. 58).

[2] Matt. xxiii. 29–31; Luke xi. 47–48.

scathing exposure. They 'say: If we had been in the days of our fathers, we would not have been partakers with them in the blood of the prophets.'[1] The priest had drawn the sting of the prophet's message when, under the cloak of a feigned repentance, he had constituted himself the official interpreter of the prophetic books.

The tale of sacred books whose fortunes had been made either by the accident of physical exile or by the act of spiritual revolt had subsequently been increased by the working of the motive of emulation; for an established sacred book is an impressive instrument of power which confers on its possessors an enviable prestige in the estimation of parvenus who have no Scriptures of their own to pit against it; and the obvious remedy for a new religion is to put itself on equal terms with its seniors by producing a distinctive sacred book of its own. The Primitive Christian Church created the Bible by adding the New Testament to an Old Testament that was its scriptural heritage from Jewry. The children of the Arabs of 'the Days of Ignorance' could hold up their heads in face of the Jewish and Christian 'People of the Book' when they had received the Qur'ān from the divinely inspired lips of their own prophet Muhammad. The Sikhs challenged the Qur'ān by compiling the Granth; Joseph Smith challenged the Bible by producing the Book of Mormon, and Mary Baker Eddy by publishing *Science and Health*.[2]

Thus emulation, revolt, and exile had all played their part in providing opportunities for Holy Writ to assert its authority at the expense of 'priestcraft'. This conflict between priest and book was one expression of a more fundamental antagonism between the incubus of a traditional collectivism and the aspiration of an individual soul to enter into personal communion with God, and on this showing the future might appear to lie with Holy Writ—though this tentative judgement might be discounted as a Jewish, Protestant, Muslim, and Sikh aberration by Catholic Christian champions of sacerdotalism. In any event, experience indicated that priestcraft was not likely to be driven off the field either quickly or easily, considering the ability that it had already shown in quoting scripture to its purpose.

'The established religion [always] appeals to [the sacred books]. It declares their contents to be everlasting and sacrosanct; but in reality it is the Establishment, and not the Scriptures, that determines, at its own discretion, the content of its doctrine. What is in agreement with the Establishment's position is deduced from the text of the sacred book; everything else is twisted round and very often interpreted into the very opposite of its original meaning, or else is simply ignored; and woe to him who should venture to appeal to this [original meaning] or to declare

[1] Matt. xxiii. 30.

[2] Mr. Martin Wight notes: 'And the same process appears to have occurred, not deliberately but subconsciously, in Marxian Communism as it has developed into a religion, so that the writings of Marx and Engels have come to occupy the place of the Old Testament in Christian holy writ, the writings of Lenin (in whose life the Marxian meaning of History became incarnate, as the Christian meaning of History became incarnate in the Life and Passion of Christ) have become the counterpart of the Gospels, and the writings of Stalin have come to resemble the Pauline Epistles—the principal authorised interpretation of the historical revelation, which shallow and mistaken critics regard, in either case, as having been a perversion, but which was, in either case, a formulation and fulfilment.'

it to be binding. The last word lies, not with the sacred book, but with the tradition that the Church has created and now embodies. The Vedic hymns (to take one example) contain not a word about Brahma, not a word about Shiva, and very little about Vishnu; the Bible contains not a word about the fundamental doctrines of the Catholic Church: about the commanding position of the priesthood and the Papacy, about the cult of the Saints, the worship of the Host, the sacraments, Purgatory, confession, and so on.[1] Conversely the Holy Scriptures include books that have nothing in the world to do with Religion: historical works, sagas and romances; collections of erotic poetry like the Song of Songs; and sceptical philosophical works like *Qoheleth*, which are transformed into revelations of religious mysteries by master-strokes of ecclesiastical interpretation. Paradoxical though this may sound, it can positively be maintained that, for any fully developed religion, the contents of its sacred books are virtually a matter of complete indifference: any book in the world may become a sacred book through some freak of Chance.'[2]

This cynically written passage would appear, on consideration, to be neither so paradoxical nor so shocking as it might seem at first sight; for, while it was true that the original meaning of Holy Writ always might be, and sometimes had been, misinterpreted to suit the institutional interests of a church that was hypocritically professing a scrupulous respect for the divine revelation of which it claimed to be the divinely appointed trustee, it was also true that the reading of new

[1] Hindu and Christian apologists would, no doubt, retort to this sweeping assertion by copious citations of Holy Writ as a warrant for their practices and beliefs.—A.J.T.

[2] Meyer, E.: *Geschichte des Altertums*, vol. i, Part II, 4th ed. (Stuttgart and Berlin 1921, Cotta), p. 60.

Mr. Martin Wight comments: 'This is a fascinating quotation, but, if you end on this Voltairean note and implicitly commit yourself to an acceptance of Chance as the determining factor, you will seem once again to swing the balance too far and to speak inconsistently with what you say elsewhere. The reader may legitimately feel that you cannot be *both* as sceptical and anti-providential in your historical conclusion about the Christian Scriptures *and* as Christian as, in general, you are throughout this Part.' To this the writer would reply that a feeling which might be legitimate for his reader might at the same time be, for the writer, an illegitimate temptation to evade an ordeal which he had been challenged to encounter and to endure. *Sentio et excrucior*; but the painfulness of a tension between unreconciled dictates of Heart and Head gives Dipsychus no warrant for evading the pain by opting exclusively for one or other of these two conflicting masters, so long as the price of thus cutting the knot is the deliberate sacrifice of sincere convictions. So far from that, the natural human impulse to find and apply an anaesthetic, without counting the cost, might be a temptation that ought to be strenuously resisted. The boddhisattva who refrains from fading out into *Nirvāna* when this is at last within his reach may be doing better than the arhat who recognizes and pursues no other goal than that of entering into his rest, if the boddhisattva's motive for thus deliberately tarrying in the painful realm of mental strife is a sincere desire to continue to play one creature's tiny part in a common search for 'the glorious liberty' in quest of which 'the whole creation groaneth and travaileth in pain together until now' (Rom. viii. 21–22). The war between Heart and Head by which the writer's generation in a Westernizing World was being ravaged seemed to him to be a tribulation which that generation must expect to continue to endure all the days of its brief life on Earth. Its vocation seemed to him to be, not to seek release from this ordeal, but to play a manful part in serving God by humbly helping Him to turn His creatures' tribulation to account for His own creative purposes. The tribulation of being vouchsafed no more than a Pisgah sight of the Promised Land was visited by the Lord upon Moses and was accepted by Moses at the Lord's hand without repining; and this last trial was the consummation of a lifetime of toil and frustration. Yet this servant of the Lord who thus died without ever crossing the Jordan had not lived in vain on that account; for he had lived to play his part, through forty years of wandering in the Wilderness, in finding a way for Israel to reach the borders of a Promised Land from the providentially opened doors of a House of Bondage.

meanings into old words was one of the Human Spirit's well-tried and well-justified methods of gaining fresh spiritual insight; and thus a Holy Writ which had originated as an imperfect vehicle for commemorating the inspired message of a dead prophet, and had survived to be perverted into an effective instrument for promoting the mundane interests of a living church, might come to serve, in a third chapter of the story, as an organ for expressing new inspirations in the souls of the prophet's followers in latter days when prophet and church in turn had passed away.

VII. A (iii) (*d*) 3, ANNEX

IMMORTALITY AND KARMA

If, as has been suggested in a previous passage,[1] History wins meaning and value for Man in so far as Man co-operates in History with God, this meaning and value of History must be found in some mode of being which transcends that of Human Life on Earth; for, while God is master of History, as of all things, God's life, in which Man shares by co-operating with Him, is not confined to the dimensions of Time and Space. God's infinity is not just ubiquity, nor His eternity just everlastingness; and, on these analogies, the immortality attained by Man in virtue of a relation with God cannot be just Human Life disengaged from Space and prolonged in Time *in saecula saeculorum.* Time and Space had been shown by a Modern Western Science to be each unthinkable apart from the other; for they had been proved to be no more than abstractions from a Reality which included both these theoretical components in so far as it could be said to include either. The bearing of this recent Western philosophic insight upon human destiny had been anticipated by an Epicurean school of Hellenic philosophy through an empirical observation of the trajectories of human lives in their passage through This World.

> Praeterea gigni pariter cum corpore et unâ
> crescere sentimus pariterque senescere mentem.
> nam velut infirmo pueri teneroque vagantur
> corpore, sic animi sequitur sententia tenvis.
> inde, ubi robustis adolevit viribus aetas,
> consilium quoque maius et auctior est animi vis.
> post, ubi iam validis quassatum est viribus aevi
> corpus, et obtusis ceciderunt viribus artus,
> claudicat ingenium, delirat lingua, labat mens,
> omnia deficiunt et uno tempore desunt.[2]

Whether the life-curve is thus carried to its natural term of a death ushered in by a gradual decay of physical and psychic faculties, or whether it is broken off short by a premature death through accident, it is inconceivable that this curve can be prolonged after death in the Time-dimension in which it has been either completed or interrupted in the course of life.

Nor can Man's immortality be retrieved in the Time-dimension by equating it with the lasting difference which is made to the whole social future of Mankind on Earth by even the shortest life of the most insignificant personality. No doubt every human life-trajectory does have this enduring effect, just as the motion of a single atom or electron affects the equilibrium of the whole physical universe. But this so-called 'impersonal immortality' is no redemption of Man's role in terrestrial history; it is the heart of the nightmare of Human Life on Earth without the

[1] On pp. 512–13, above.

[2] Lucretius: *De Rerum Natura*, Book III, ll. 445–54.

fellowship of God; and the nightmare would not be dispelled even if we were warranted in inverting the poet's melancholy reflexion that

> The evil that men do lives after them;
> the good is oft interrèd with their bones.[1]

If our acts in This Life are the stuff of which our immortality is made, this is in virtue of their influence, not on human affairs on Earth, but on the relation between the human actor and God, and we must believe that in God's sight the spiritual balance-sheet of a human life on Earth is, for good or evil, of equal moment whether that life has been socially significant or insignificant and whether it has been long or short.

> For such my faith or fondness—which you will—
> This strange conviction would possess me still:
> That by heroic act or generous deed,
> Agony, abnegation, loving heed,
> Our mortal nature could from Time be freed,
> And suddenly outsoar, while still on Earth,
> Its long, low drag of days between the grave and birth,
> And touch a plane of life transcending Time's,
> As a dull-ticking clock suddenly chimes.
>
> . . . .
>
> Free of Time's trammel, clear of Earth and Skies,
> In that immortal instant will they rise,
> And with a loftiness of being live
> Beyond the summits happiness can give:
> Fulfilled, though stricken; absolute, though bound;
> Effaced on Earth, and yet, beyond it, found;
> Traceless, and yet with more than fame renowned.[2]

The sum of the spiritual values, positive and negative, that arise from the acts of a human being in his passage through Life on Earth had been designated *Karma* ('the product of action') by philosophers of the Indic school, and they had perceived that the spiritual plane on which *Karma* waxes and wanes must be in a different dimension altogether from the dimensions of Space and Time. It would follow that *Karma*, once generated, would have an existence of its own that would not be affected by the death on Earth of the personality from whose earthly acts it had sprung; and this Indic vision might give Judaic souls an insight into the nature of an immortality which is not in Time but is both 'now' and 'always', if the two parties did not disagree in their judgement of the implications.

In the sight of Judaically oriented souls, immortality was bound to seem an inestimable boon, even though the Soul's hope of Heaven might be haunted by a fear of Hell; for the hope of Heaven was a hope of communion with God in the Beatific Vision. In the sight of Indically oriented souls, immortality would be an intolerable burden, even if they did not believe, as they did believe, that a debit balance of *Karma* would condemn the vehicle of it to return to the sorrowful treadmill of birth-

[1] Shakspeare: *Julius Caesar*, Act III, scene ii, ll. 38–39.
[2] Skinner, Martyn: *Letters to Malaya*, v (London 1947, Putnam), pp. 74 and 76.

death-birth. A liberating purgatory had been desired by compassionate Buddhist hearts as wistfully as by their Christian counterparts; but the immortality from which Buddhist arhats sought liberation was not just an immortality in Hell; it was immortality itself—against which the arhat would consistently repine even if it were the immortality of Heaven. Can Man release himself from immortality, as the Buddha believed and taught, by dissolving *Karma* into *Nirvāna*? *Nirvāna* resembles its opposite, the quintessence of personality, in being indifferent to Space and Time, but this not through rising above them into communion with the personality of God, but through sinking below them into the abyss of Subconsciousness. Supposing that *Nirvāna* were attainable by the Buddha's prescription, would the attainment of it be the highest good for Man or the worst catastrophe?

The answer to this last question would depend on whether it were felt that a retention of Consciousness was worth its price of pain, or were felt that a release from pain was worth its price of oblivion. Was the Wheel of Existence merely an infernal machine for tormenting Ixion by revolutions that were vain repetitions? Or was it the wheel of a chariot of fire on which a human being might ascend to Heaven if he could bear the ordeal? The choice between alternative answers would turn on whether the Ultimate Reality was, or was not, believed to be a personal Living God. One answer had been given by Judaism, the other by an Indic school of philosophy; and so sharp a contradiction on a point of such supreme importance might have cleft an unbridgeable schism between the Judaic and the Indic pair of higher religions, if Hinduism and the Mahāyāna had not crossed the gulf, on their own initiative, to the Muslim-Christian side in defiance of their own philosophical first principles.

VII. C (ii) (*a*), ANNEX

THE PREHISTORIC BACKGROUND TO THE HISTORY OF THE HIGHER RELIGIONS

In the present Part of this Study we have been investigating the historical role of the higher religions, and we have seen that their epiphany had been a very recent event on the Time-scale of History that had been revealed by the discoveries of Modern Western geologists and astronomers.[1] This stage of Mankind's religious experience was the latest chapter of what must have been a very long story. Were any of the previous chapters accessible to latter-day Western students of History?

The Hebrew tradition that had been inherited by the higher religions of Judaic origin gave an account of Man's religious history that purported to carry the story right back to the origins of the Human Race. According to this account 'the Call of Abraham', with which the history of the Judaistic higher religions opened, had not created a relation between God and Man that had never existed before; it had re-created a relation that had once existed between God and Abraham's forefather, the first man Adam, but had been broken by Adam's fall. On this view the genesis of the higher religions presented itself as a 'palingenesia': a rebirth of something old which might also be the birth of something new.[2] In the Pauline Christian version of the Jewish plot of the drama of Man's spiritual history 'it is written: The first man Adam was made a living soul; the last Adam was made a quickening spirit.'[3]

When a Modern Western Rationalism had asserted its independence of the Christian tradition, one of its first acts had been to reject, as a figment of imagination, this picture of an original communion between Primitive Man and a One True God. The existence of the God of Abraham, Moses, and Jesus was held to be an illusion, and the belief that this illusion had already captivated Primitive Man was held to be an anachronism. The adherents of the higher religions, it was suggested, had sought to lend authority to a theological invention of their own by naïvely presenting it as being the revival of a primordial revelation; but, in the higher critic's eye, this hypothesis of a primitive monotheism was as unsubstantial as it was facile; for, while the Modern Western scholar would not doubt that Primitive Man's theological ideas, if he had any, were illusory, he would consider it impossible to ascertain which of the innumerable illusions lying in wait for Primitive Man was the one into which he had happened to fall in the first flight of his infantile fancy. This archaic Modern Western scepticism had been shaken by the subsequent progress of anthropological research. By the time of writing, some light had been thrown on Primitive Man's religion by a study of the religion of the least sophisticated human societies still surviving. This evidence had to be used with great caution, since neither the facts nor the inferences

[1] See pp. 452–4, above.

[2] See V. v. 27, n. 2, and V. vi. 172–3.

[3] I Cor. xv. 45.

to be drawn from them were by any means beyond dispute. Yet, as far as the evidence went, it did not conflict with the Hebrew legend and seemed, indeed, to bear it out.

The evidence up to date indicated two things: that there was a remarkable measure of uniformity in the practices and beliefs of the least sophisticated surviving societies, and that this distinctive common element in their religion was spiritually higher (in terms of the spiritual standards of the higher religions) than the religion of other uncivilized societies that were the superiors of these unsophisticated peoples in technology and in social organization.

The measure of uniformity was remarkable because, at the time when the evidence was collected by Modern Western anthropologists, the unsophisticated peoples were scattered, far apart from one another, over the face of the Earth, in holes and corners that had been left to them by materially more efficient competitors who had been driving them from pillar to post. If ever there had been a time when these societies had been in geographical contact with one another, that contact must have been broken several thousand, and perhaps several hundred thousand, years ago. Therefore the points of likeness between their respective religions could not have been the result of any direct borrowings by one of these societies from another. They could only have been the result either of some wave of cultural influence, radiating from one or more of the civilizations, which had reached and affected all these unsophisticated societies alike[1] at dates subsequent to their dispersion, or else of some primitive cultural heritage, once common to all Mankind, which each of the unsophisticated societies had sluggishly or simple-mindedly retained for itself after its more enterprising neighbours had discarded it.[2]

As between these two possible explanations, the hypothesis of a relatively recent cultural radiation from an identic external source had been favoured by Mrs. N. K. Chadwick in an attempt to account for a common theme in modern oral literature whose 'distribution . . . follows a great arc on the periphery of the Eastern Hemisphere, stretching from the Chathams in South Polynesia, round Siberia to Russia, and including the mountain masses and backward districts of Central Asia'.[3] The alternative hypothesis of isolated local survivals of an original common human heritage had been favoured by Father W. Schmidt as the explanation of a similar common theme in the religion of societies of a still less sophisticated and even more widely scattered stratum: the Pygmies and Pygmoids in the mountains and forests of the extreme South and South-East of Asia and the adjacent islands; the Blackfellows in the extreme South-East of Australia and their neighbours the Tasmanians; the Negrillos in the impenetrable primeval forest of Tropical Africa and the Bushmen in the Kalahari Desert; the Samoyeds, Kamchadals, Koryaks,

[1] See II. i. 187 and V. v. 197.

[2] 'These tribes have, apparently, never departed from the original state in which Man is contained by Nature as an animal is contained by the law of its species . . . and . . . their attitude towards the so-called boons of Civilisation is usually that of polite but adamant refusal' (Baynes, H. G.: *Mythology of the Soul* (London 1940, Baillière, Tindall, & Cox; 1949, Methuen), pp. 250–2).

[3] Chadwick, N. K.: *Poetry and Prophecy* (Cambridge 1942, University Press), p. 94; cp. pp. xiv–xvi.

and Ainu in Northern Asia; the Algonkins in the extreme North-East of North America and on the prairies; the Californian Indians in the narrow corner of the west coast of North America between the Rocky Mountains and the Sea; and the denizens of Tierra del Fuego, the bleak antarctic tip of South America.[1]

'No later culture can boast of a distribution which encircles the whole Earth so completely. But, if it is clear that, wherever remnants of the primitive peoples are still discoverable over this huge area, they show belief in a Supreme Being, then it is likewise manifest that such a belief is an essential property of this, the most ancient of human cultures, which must have been deeply and strongly rooted in it at the very dawn of Time, before the individual groups had separated from one another.'[2]

It will be seen that the difference between Father Schmidt's and Mrs. Chadwick's explanation of the presence of a common theme in the cultures of unsophisticated peoples whose latter-day habitats were widely scattered was not an irreconcilable one; for, though Mrs. Chadwick warns us 'to abandon the assumption that the culture of the most backward communities of the present day bears any relationship to that of truly "primitive" or Early Man',[3] she agrees with Father Schmidt in finding that 'the farther back we can carry our researches, the higher the culture becomes and the more the immediate sources of these cultures tend to converge';[4] and it is evident that, while this might be because the spiritually higher features in the cultures of the unsophisticated peoples had a common origin in influences recently radiated by the civilizations, these common features might have an alternative origin in a common heritage which the unsophisticated societies had retained from the dawn of human history. Whatever the source of this unsophisticated culture might be, our two Modern Western authorities concur in esteeming it to be a spiritual treasure of great price.

'In Asia, in Polynesia, even in Africa,' Mrs. Chadwick testifies, 'Man's chief intellectual pre-occupations and speculations are with spiritual adventure. . . . These spiritual adventures are the journeys which we take in our minds into the past, the hidden or distant present, and the future. The lonely pioneering of the Soul in these spheres and the defeat or success of its quest forms the principal theme in the oral literature of the Old World. . . .

'The more immediate objects of these journeys are many and various. . . But undoubtedly everywhere the principal *motifs* are the rescue of souls from hostile spirits and the securing of the water of life and the herb of healing. Directly or indirectly the quest for immortality is the most outstanding *motif* both in Asia and in Polynesia. . . .

'This quest of immortality, the effort of men and women to master matter by spirit, is the chief intellectual pre-occupation of the men and women outside the sphere of Civilisation to-day.'[5]

1 Schmidt, Father W.: *The Origin and Growth of Religion*, English translation by Rose, H. J. (London 1921, Methuen), pp. 252–3.

2 Schmidt, op. cit., pp. 260–1. Cp. Baynes, op. cit., pp. 250–2 and 457–8.

3 Chadwick, op. cit., p. xv. The same point has been made in the present Study, II. i. 185–7 and V. v. 197.

4 Chadwick, op. cit., loc. cit.

5 Chadwick, op. cit., pp. 91–94.

From this spectacle of contemporary Man's still unfaded intimations of immortality in the least unchildlike of the living human societies, Father Schmidt draws an inference—in which Mrs. Chadwick would perhaps hesitate to follow him—regarding the spiritual activities of Primeval Mankind.

'Primaeval Man was far from being [a] sluggish dreamer . . . standing in stupid astonishment and fright at the world that was so new to him. The pre-historic tools and weapons and those of the ethnologically oldest peoples of to-day are alone enough to show that he was a vigorous and daring man of action. . . . He grasped the conception of cause and effect, and then adapted that to the relationship of means to end. His means, to effect the ends he desired, were his tools, which he invented and used. Now all this sufficed to lead him to a real religion, to the recognition of a supreme Personal Being; for he was able to apply these same mental powers to the contemplation of the Universe as a whole.'[1]

Father Schmidt's inference reinstates, in terms of a Modern Western science, the picture of the spiritual condition of Primeval Man that is presented in mythological terms in the Book of Genesis. Supposing that we entertain Father Schmidt's thesis provisionally for the sake of the argument, shall we find the rest of the spiritual drama working out 'in modern dress' on the lines of the Biblical plot? Are there explanations, in our sophisticated terms, of Primeval Man's fall from a state of innocence and of Fallen Man's access to redemption through the grace of God? Perhaps the most promising approach to these questions will be to apply to the history of Primitive Man an empirically attested 'law' of the working of Human Nature which has already served us as a key to an understanding of the history of Man in process of Civilization.

In the history of Western Man we have seen that a rise in spiritual standards thanks to the influence of a higher religion can incidentally produce a consequent rise in material well-being, and that this incidental mundane effect of spiritual progress exposes Man to a temptation to which he readily succumbs. The material harvest of spiritual travail is apt to divert Man's energies from spiritual into material channels; and thus a spiritual regression may be the result of a material advance which a previous spiritual advance has brought in its train.[2] Conversely, in the histories of civilizations which had broken down and disintegrated through transferring their treasure from the Commonwealth of God to the Commonwealth of Swine, we have seen that Man's disillusioning experience of losing his life through setting his heart upon saving it had opened Man's eyes to the vanity of This World and reopened his ears to God's word, which had been uttered to him at this stage through higher religions.[3] Both the need and the opportunity for the epiphany of the higher religions had sprung from the failures of Fallen Man's mundane civilizations of the first and second generations, and Man's subsequent abandonment of his allegiance to a saving higher religion in order to go a whoring after a mundane civilization of the third generation wore the

[1] Schmidt, op. cit., pp. 135–6.
[2] See pp. 546–8, above.
[3] See pp. 425, 551–2, and 701–2, above.

aspect of a second Fall. Did this fall of a Sophisticated Man throw light on a Primeval Man's fall and its sequel?

The history of Primitive Man could be tentatively reconstructed on the analogy of the history of Man in Australia since the advent there of the pioneers of a Western way of life. Primeval Man's state on the morrow of his becoming human could be inferred from the state in which the first White settlers in Australia had found their Black predecessors.

'These Black People were intimately related to the land over which they roamed. In its sacred places were the spirits of their ancestors and the ancient heroes of their myths. Their own spirits lived in it before they were born. Even the animals and birds and fruits of the Earth had their spirits also, and a close affinity was maintained with this spirit world by long-established sacred rites and ceremonies. Spirits, land, and people were one close-knit community, and each needed the other for life to be possible and complete.'[1]

These unsophisticated souls had hardly been tempted to throw over their unselfconscious communion with God in order to worship their own achievements; for, when their Modern Western destroyers broke in upon them at the turn of the eighteenth and nineteenth centuries of the Christian Era, the Australian Blackfellows, in their hitherto secluded corner of the World, were still living in the Palaeolithic Age. Their domicile at this date testifies, however, that, in thus still remaining in a relative state of innocent inefficiency, they had been exceptions to the general run of Mankind. Long before the Westerners' violation of the Blackfellows' ultimate sanctuary, other societies had already outstripped the Blackfellows in material achievement sufficiently far to have driven them, by stages, into the precarious asylum where a globe-encompassing Western Civilization eventually hunted them down and finished them off.

'The Black Man . . . was controlled by Nature. He functioned as a part of it. He dared not disturb it. It lived in him. The Civilised Man, on the other hand, set out to exploit Nature. . . . The Australian version of the Garden of Eden in which the Black Man lived naked and unashamed had no appeal to the White. The White Man had eaten of the Tree of Knowledge and had changed completely his attitude to the World of Nature and of Man. As he clothed and adorned his body with the garments of Civilisation, he unclothed his mind and will of all customary restraints and sacred sanctions. At length the will to power in Man stood forth naked and unashamed. . . . More and more he freed himself from all guidance from Nature until, in an illusion of freedom, he stood over against Nature, using it for his purposes and subduing it to his will. This led to the point where Civilised Man no longer meets God at all on the ground of Nature. God is ignored: Civilised Man is confident that "he has no need of that hypothesis." This, in effect, makes Man his own God.'[2]

This regress-in-progress of a Modern Western Man is a repetition of the story of this Western Man's forerunners, the majority of Mankind, who,

[1] Burgmann, Bishop E. H.: *The Church's Encounter with Civilisation* (London 1948, Longmans), p. 8.

[2] Burgmann, op. cit., pp. 16 and 15.

for good or evil, had left the Blackfellows behind in embarking on the course of material achievement that was to culminate in the rises—and falls—of civilizations. Modern Western archaeological research had rediscovered an early sign of the times in the replacement of a Palaeolithic Man, cultivating a gift for expressing himself in Visual Art without being ambitious to improve upon his rudimentary tools, by an aesthetically insensitive Neolithic Man[1] producing a crop of revolutionary technical inventions which had not only been epoch-making in their day but had not been surpassed in importance by any subsequent material achievements of Neolithic Man's successors up to date.[2] In view of the affinity between the aesthetic and the religious faculty of the Human Psyche,[3] we might expect this impoverishment of Man's aesthetic life, which was the price of the Neolithic technological revolution, to be found associated with a religious regression; and this expectation is borne out—if we accept Father Schmidt's divination of the former religion of Primeval Man from the present religion of the least sophisticated and efficient of the extant human societies—by the contrast between the relatively aetherial spiritual activities, beliefs, and aspirations of these 'backward' peoples, as described by Father Schmidt and Mrs. Chadwick, and the crass paganism of societies that had forged far ahead of them in the race for wealth and power.

In another context[4] we have noticed Man's proneness to abandon the worship of God for the worship of some work of God which Man has newly discovered or newly mastered. In the work from which we have been quoting, Father Schmidt has laid bare, with a master's hand, the inner relation between divers forms of material achievement and the forms of idolatry that in his day were to be found in association with each of them in living societies which, by mundane standards, had raised themselves high above the level of the 'backward' worshippers of a Supreme Being. In this place it would be superfluous to recapitulate Father Schmidt's survey, but we may notice, in passing, the principal directions that these religious aberrations proved to have taken. In the rank jungle-growth of idolatry we can distinguish two main types. When Man begins to gain control over his non-human environment, he takes to worshipping fellow creatures that he has harnessed for his own immediate service, especially for supplying himself with food. The hunter's worship of his game breeds totemism; the husbandman's worship of his crop breeds the religion of the ἐνιαυτὸς δαίμων.[5] As Man gains in knowledge, he begins to worship more remote, pervasive, and abstract forces of Nature which appear to him to exercise an ultimate control over the creatures that can be directly harnessed to Man's service; and these path-finding hypotheses—correct or erroneous—of the burgeoning Scientific Mind breed worships of a Weather, a Nile, and a Sun that manifestly decide the fortunes of the pastures and the fields, and a worship of stars whose courses apparently determine the course of terrestrial events. These idolatrous cults of cosmic forces are intellectually sophis-

1 See III. iii. 160, and pp. 704–5, above.
2 See III. iii. 158–9.
3 See VII. A (iii) (*a*), Annex I, pp. 701–11, above.
4 On pp. 460–4, above.
5 See III. iii. 256–9.

ticated versions of a primitive idolatrous worship of particular non-human creatures; but, as Man gains in power, he transfers his devotion to a different, and a more sinister, idol when he begins to worship the collective organization of human activities through which he mobilizes his Science and Technology for the subjugation of the Material Universe. The original style of Man's corporate self-worship is parochial: he begins by worshipping a personification of his tribe (Athênê Poliûchus or Fortuna Praenestina) and the genii of his household (the Hebrew Teraphim and the Latin Lares et Penates). The ultimate style is oecumenical: he ends by worshipping a mundane human saviour with the sword[1] who is the god incarnate of a universal state.

These two types of idolatry that are spiritual by-products of Man's mundane success both have the same inauspicious effect of putting Man out of communion with the One True God by diverting Man's devotion from the Creator to the creature and screening the Beatific Vision behind an idolized creation;[2] and the short history of Man's mundane progress up to date had already shown, a number of times over, that the demoralizing spiritual effect of this idolatry was Man's Achilles' Heel. If Man's progress in technology, science, and social organization accounted for the geneses and growths of civilizations, his concomitant spiritual infirmity accounted for their breakdowns and disintegrations; and, if this had been the end of the story, human life on Earth would indeed have been 'nasty, brutish and short'.[3] Happily for Man, God's providence had offered him grace to find a cure for his spiritual sickness in the very direness of its consequences and to re-enter, as a spiritual adult, schooled by the creative experience of suffering, into a communion with his Maker which he had once enjoyed as a spiritual child in the primeval chapter of the history of the Human Race. In the higher religions that had sprung from the civilizations' catastrophes, Man had been re-endowed with the spiritual treasure that he had possessed (if Father Schmidt's thesis was the truth) in the days of his primeval inefficiency and had then jettisoned in his self-centred scramble up the treacherous ladder of material progress.

If this interpretation of the historical background of the higher religions commended itself, it suggested two reflections: the Devil had lost one throw in his perennial wager with God,[4] but the Devil had not so lost heart as to have given up the game.

The Devil's defeat in a round which had opened with the fall of Pri-

[1] See V. vi. 178–213.

[2] Mr. Martin Wight notes: 'These types of idolatry have a correspondence with the three covenants of the Judaic-Christian tradition. (i) Nature-worship corresponds with the covenant with Noah, which survived in its pure and pristine form to greet Abraham in the person of Melchisedek the priest-king offering bread and wine (Gen. xiv. 18), but whose corruption and perversion was seen in the Canaanitish idolatry which the Prophets of Israel combatted and in the paganism which St. Paul denounced in Rom. i. 21–25. (ii) Parochial corporate self-worship corresponds with the betrayal and denial of the covenant with Abraham, which had conferred a particular destiny and responsibility on the archetype of all chosen peoples. (iii) Oecumenical corporate self-worship corresponds with the betrayal and denial of the final covenant with the Human Race, revealed by Christ and sealed by His body and blood. This third type of idolatry corresponds, then, theologically to the New Testament doctrine of Antichrist.'

[3] Hobbes, Thomas: *Leviathan*, Part I, chap. 13.

[4] See II. i. 271–99.

meval Man and had ended in the epiphany of the higher religions was attested by the difference in spiritual stature between the Innocent and the Saint. The saintly soul that was the spiritual flower of the higher religions was not, perhaps, in closer communion with God than the innocent soul that, on Father Schmidt's hypothesis, had been the spiritual flower of the primeval dispensation; but, if Christianity was right in holding that a spiritually creative suffering was a human experience in which God Himself had participated in virtue of His incarnation,[1] then the Saint's communion with God, though no closer than the Innocent's, was nevertheless a communion on less unequal terms; and, if in this sense sainthood was the higher form of spiritual attainment, the Devil's defeat in this round was registered in the reflection that the mortified idolator could never have been transfigured into a saint who was a more enlightened and effective servant of God than the Innocent if that primeval worshipper of the One True God had not lost his innocence through lapsing into idolatry.

'All spiritual knowledge "goes in circles", that is to say that it has to do with re-birth, which is itself a return to the beginning on a different psychic level.'[2]

The measure of the Devil's defeat in this particular encounter with God was given by the fact that the higher religions had not only brought it within Man's reach to re-enter into communion with God on a higher spiritual level than any that had been accessible to Man in his days of innocence; the higher religions had even spoiled the Egyptians by gleaning a harvest from the jungle-growth of Man's idolatrous days of ignorance.[3] Yet we have also to recognize and take to heart the no less manifest fact that the severity of these reverses had not driven the Devil to withdraw from the field. At the time of writing, the living higher religions were being challenged by insurrections of civilizations of a third generation which had armed themselves for revolt by evoking potent ideas and institutions from the graves of their dead pagan predecessors.[4] A fresh advance, of unprecedented swiftness and perhaps unprecedented vigour, in Man's mastery of the Material Universe had launched idolatry on the war-path again; and, in this formidable recrudescence of a once transcended error, Man's corporate self-worship, which was the more pernicious of the two main lines of religious aberration, now had the whole field to itself.

The other type of idolatry, in which Nature had been substituted for

[1] A Christian theologian might object to this attempt at a statement of the Christian belief on this point on the ground that God does not have experiences because God is Being, whereas experience signifies a process of becoming. Yet the same theologian must hold that the Christ 'who suffered' was 'perfect God and perfect man . . . who, although He be God and man, yet He is not two, but one Christ'; and, on these premisses, it is hard for a layman to see how a theologian could assert, without taking, in the act, either a Nestorian or a Eutychian departure from the line of Catholic Christian orthodoxy, that God had not participated in the human experience of suffering when, in the exercise of His almighty power, He had chosen to become incarnate.

[2] Layard, J.: *The Lady of the Hare: A Study of the Healing Power of Dreams* (London 1944, Faber), p. 185.

[3] For the pagan *praeparatio evangelica*, see pp. 457–60, above.

[4] See pp. 539–41, above, and X. ix, *passim*.

God, had borne a fearful crop of wickedness and benightedness in its time; but its reign had been transitory; for Man's progress in the mastery of his environment, which had first brought this type of idolatry into existence, had subsequently swept it out of existence again. A natural phenomenon that Man has deified on an impulse of wonder and gratitude, when he has first succeeded in coaxing it into performing some highly valued service, cannot retain its divinity in his clearer-seeing eyes after it has been thoroughly broken in and domesticated by successive advances in Technology; and the vaster and more elusive forces of Nature that even a latter-day Western Man could hardly aspire to manipulate by his technological 'know-how' had likewise forfeited their illusory divinity as they had become intelligible to Man's scientific understanding. In the darkness before the dawn of the higher religions, Paganism had culminated in the worship, not of the corn-god or the sun-god, but of the man-god Caesar—the incarnate symbol of Man's terrible collective power—and the transformation of Nature from an object of worship into an object of exploitation and investigation had left Man facing the single question: 'Which is God? God or Man?'

The message of the higher religions had been that Man, like Nature, is not God but is God's creature; and this message had won Man's ear at the moment when the collapse of a man-made mundane civilization had been demonstrating to Man the limitations of his power through the first-hand evidence of a painful and humbling experience. But this lesson was readily forgotten when the mundane welfare that was a by-product of spiritual regeneration tempted the Heirs of the Promise to reinvest their treasure in This World. In the second Fall of Man there had been no recurrence of Nature-worship, but, for this very reason, a recurrent Man-worship, unchecked and unbalanced, this time, by the claims of any competing idols, was now raging in men's souls with an unprecedented virulence.[1] The Neo-Pagan man-worshipper believed Man to be, not Nature's co-divinity, but Nature's lord the One True God, and, being in this degree more impious than his pristine pagan forerunner, he was in the same degree more lonely—in a loneliness which aggravated itself by driving him into an ever more frantic pursuit of the idolatry that was the cause of it.

'Wandering, as they are, in the wilderness of distracted minds, . . . people everywhere feel insecure. They are no longer rooted anywhere. There is intense and widespread loneliness, . . . [and] they seek comradeship anywhere at any price. The day of the tribe returns. . . . Man is seeking for some strong tribal body, with its tribal leader, to relieve him of the responsibility of making personal decisions . . . and the modern tribe is larger than in the days of old. Now it can be a nation, or the people of a continent, or of continents. In the Western World it represents the retreat of a people who have lost the guidance and support of a higher faith. This emotional regression is a very serious matter in a highly rationalised and artificial environment.'[2]

[1] The resurgence of Caesar-worship in the Orthodox Christian and Western worlds has been touched upon on pp. 439–40 and 537–9, above.

[2] Burgmann, op. cit., pp. 14–15.

In this Neo-Pagan worship of a collective Humanity, the higher religions were being confronted with a repetition of the challenge to which they had responded victoriously in the first chapter of their history; and the struggle upon which they were entering in a twentieth-century Westernizing World threatened to be a sharper ordeal than any to which they had ever before been subjected.

TABLE I. *Universal States*

Civilization	*'Time of Troubles'*	*Universal State*	*Pax Oecumenica*	*Provenance of Empire-builders*
Sumeric	*c.* 2522–2143 or 2458–2079 B.C.	The Empire of Sumer and Akkad ('The Realm of the Four Quarters')	*c.* 2143–1750 or 2079–1686 B.C.	Founders metropolitans (from Ur); restorers marchmen (Amorites)
Babylonic	–610 B.C.	The Neo-Babylonian Empire	610–539 B.C.	Founders metropolitans [?][1] (Chaldaeans); successors barbarians (Achaemenidae) and aliens (Seleucidae)
Indic	–322 B.C.	The Mauryan Empire	322–185 B.C.	Founders metropolitans [?][2] (from Magadha)
		The Guptan Empire	A.D. 390–*c.* 475	Founders metropolitans (from Magadha)
Sinic	634–221 B.C.	The Ts'in and Han Empire	221 B.C.–*c.* A.D. 172	Founders marchmen (from Ts'in); successors metropolitans (Prior and Posterior Han)
Hellenic	431–31 B.C.	The Roman Empire	31 B.C.–A.D. 378	Founders marchmen (Romans); restorers marchmen (Illyrians)
Egyptiac	*c.* 2425–2050 B.C.	The Middle Empire	*c.* 2050–1675 B.C.	Marchmen (from Thebes)
		The New Empire	*c.* 1580–1175 B.C.	Marchmen (from Thebes)
Orthodox Christian (in Russia)	*c.* A.D. 1075–1478	The Muscovite Empire	A.D. 1478–1881	Marchmen (from Moscow)
Far Eastern (in Japan)	A.D. 1185–1597	Hideyoshi's dictatorship and the Tokugawa Shogunate	A.D. 1597–1868	Marchmen (from the Kwanto)
Western (medieval cosmos of city-states)	*c* A.D. 1378–1797	The Napoleonic Empire	A.D. 1797–1814	Marchmen (from France)
Western (carapace against assaults of 'Osmanlis)	*c.* A.D. 1128[3]–1526	The Danubian Hapsburg Monarchy	A.D. 1526–1918	Marchmen (from Austria)
Andean	–*c.* A.D. 1430	The Incaic Empire ('The Realm of the Four Quarters')	*c.* A.D. 1430–1533	Founders marchmen (from Cuzco); successors aliens (Spaniards)
Syriac	*c.* 937–525 B.C.	The Achaemenian Empire	*c.* 525–332 B.C.	Barbaro-marchmen (from Iran)
		The Arab Caliphate	*c.* A.D. 640–969	Barbarians (from Arabia)
Far Eastern (main body)	A.D. 878–1280	The Mongol Empire	A.D. 1280–1351	Barbaro-aliens (Mongols)
		The Manchu Empire	A.D. 1644–1853[4]	Barbaro-marchmen (Manchus)
Central American	–A.D. 1521	The Spanish Viceroyalty of New Spain	A.D. 1521–1821	Forerunners barbaro-marchmen (Aztecs); founders aliens (Spaniards)
Orthodox Christian (main body)	A.D. 977–1372	The Ottoman Empire	A.D. 1372–1768	Aliens ('Osmanlis)
Hindu	*c.* A.D. 1175–1572	The Mughal Rāj	*c.* A.D. 1572–1707	Aliens (Mughals)
		The British Rāj	*c.* A.D. 1818–1947	Aliens (British)
Minoan	–*c.* 1750 B.C.	'The Thalassocracy of Minos'	*c.* 1750–1400 B.C.	No evidence

[1] The Chaldaeans in Babylonia might be classified either as metropolitans or as marchmen.

[2] Magadha might be regarded either as part of the interior of the Indic World of the Pre-Mauryan and the Mauryan Age or else as the eastern march of the Indic World in those ages.

[3] The date of the outbreak of the first of the wars between Hungary and the 'Osmanlis' East Roman forerunners the Comneni (see IV. iv. 403, n. 3).

[4] The date of the capture of Nanking by the T'aip'ing insurgents.

Table II. *Philosophies*

Civilization	*Philosophy*
Egyptiac	Atonism (abortive)
Andean	Viracochaism (abortive)
Sinic	Confucianism
	Moism
	Taoism
Syriac	Zervanism (abortive)
Indic	Hinayanian Buddhism
	Jainism
Western	Cartesianism
	Hegelianism[1]
Hellenic	Platonism
	Stoicism
	Epicureanism
	Pyrrhonism
Babylonic	Astrology

[1] Hegelianism confined to the field of social affairs = Marxism; Marxism transplanted from the Western World to Russia = Leninism.

Table III. *Higher Religions*

Civilization	*Higher Religion*	*Source of Inspiration*
Sumeric	Tammuz-worship	indigenous
Egyptiac	Osiris-worship	alien [?] (Sumeric [?])
Sinic	The Mahāyāna	alien (Indo-Helleno-Syriac)
	Neotaoism	indigenous but imitative (of the Mahāyāna)
Indic	Hinduism	indigenous
Syriac	Islam	indigenous
Hellenic	Christianity	alien (Syriac)
	Mithraism	alien (Syriac)
	Manichaeism	alien (Syriac)
	The Mahāyāna	alien (Indic)
	Isis-worship	alien (Egyptiac)
	Cybele-worship	alien (Hittite)
	Neoplatonism	indigenous (*ci-devant* philosophy)
Babylonic	Judaism	alien (Syriac)
	Zoroastrianism	alien (Syriac)
Western	Bahaism	alien (Iranic)
	The Ahmadīyah	alien (Iranic)
Orthodox Christian (main body)	Imāmī Shi'ism	alien (Iranic)
	Bedreddinism	semi-alien (Iranic tincture)
Orthodox Christian (in Russia)	Sectarianism	indigenous
	Revivalist Protestantism	alien (Western)
Far Eastern (main body)	Catholicism	alien (Western)
	T'aip'ing	semi-alien (Western tincture)
Far Eastern (in Japan)	Jōdo	semi-alien (from Far Eastern, main body)
	Jōdo Shinshū	indigenous (from Jōdo)
	Nichirenism	indigenous
	Zen	semi-alien (from Far Eastern, main body)
Hindu	Kabirism and Sikhism	semi-alien (Islamic tincture)
	Brahmō Samāj	semi-alien (Western tincture)

TABLE VIII. *A Diagram to illustrate the Relation between Higher Religions and Psychological Types*

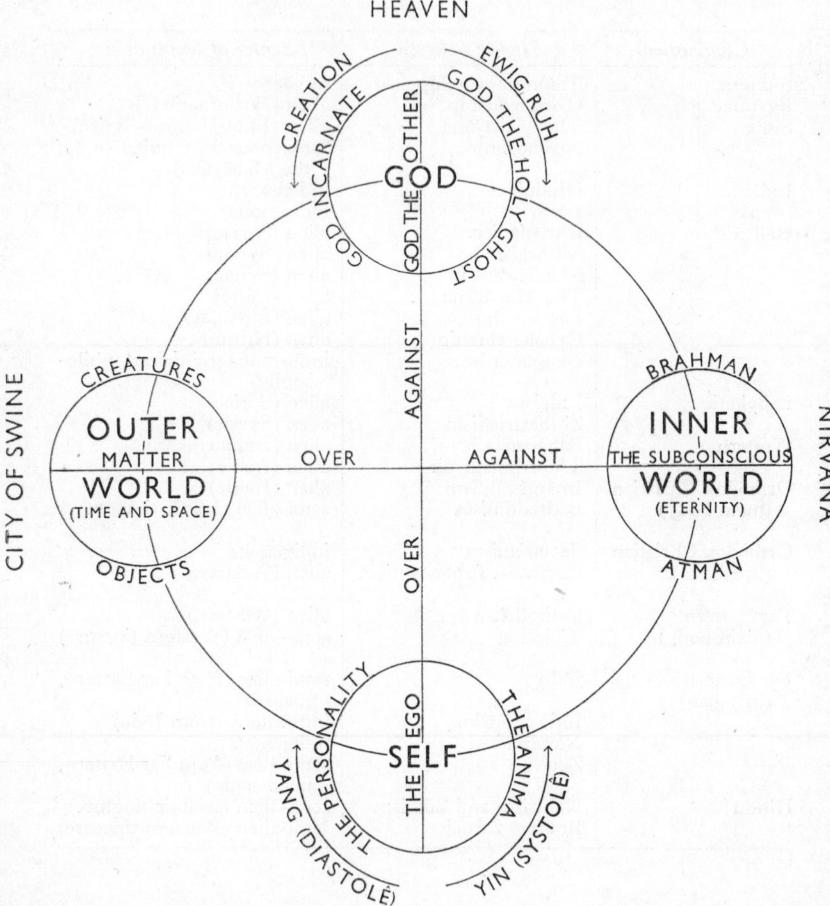

The Objectives of Divers Historic Weltanschauungen

Heaven is the objective of a Zoroastrian-Jewish-Muslim-Christian *Weltanschauung*.
Nirvāna is the objective of an Indic and an Hellenic *Weltanschauung*.
The City of Swine is the objective of a Materialist *Weltanschauung*.
Hell is the objective of a Satanist *Weltanschauung*.

TABLE IV. *Primitive Societies, Civilizations, Higher Religions*

(in serial order)

1. PRIMITIVE SOCIETIES

2. PRIMARY CIVILIZATIONS

(all derived direct from primitive societies)

Egyptiac Andean Mayan Sumeric Indus Culture Minoan Shang Culture

RUDIMENTARY HIGHER RELIGIONS

(created, adapted, or adopted by internal proletariats of primary civilizations)

- *The Worship of Osiris and Isis* (? adopted by the internal proletariat of the Egyptiac Civilization from the internal proletariat of the Sumeric)
- *The Worship of Tammuz and Ishtar* (? created by the internal proletariat of the Sumeric Civilization)

3. SECONDARY CIVILIZATIONS

(derived from the primary civilizations)

(*a*) through their dominant minorities

- Yucatec (from Mayan)
- Babylonic (from Sumeric)

(*b*) through their external proletariats

- Mexic (from Mayan)
- Abortive First Syriac, Hittite (from Sumeric)
- Indic (from Indus Culture)
- Syriac, Hellenic (from Minoan)
- Sinic (from Shang Culture)

4. HIGHER RELIGIONS

(created, adapted, or adopted by internal proletariats of secondary civilizations)

- *Judaism*, *Zoroastrianism* (created by the internal proletariat of the Babylonic Civilization)
- *Hinduism* (created by the internal proletariat of the Indic Civilization)
- *Islam* (created by the internal proletariat of the Syriac Civilization)
- *Isis-Worship*, *Cybele-Worship*, *Mithraism*, *Christianity*, *Manichaeism* (created by the internal proletariat of the Hellenic Civilization)
- *Neoplatonism* (adapted by the Hellenic internal proletariat from one of the philosophies of the Hellenic dominant minority)
- *The Mahāyāna* (adapted by the Hellenic internal proletariat from one of the philosophies of the Indic dominant minority, and adopted by the Sinic internal proletariat)
- *Neotaoism* (adapted by the Sinic internal proletariat from one of the philosophies of the Sinic dominant minority)

5. TERTIARY CIVILIZATIONS

(derived from secondary civilizations through chrysalis churches constructed by their internal proletariats)

- Hindu (derived from Indic through *Hinduism*)
- Iranic, Arabic (derived from Syriac through *Islam*)
- Abortive Far Eastern Christian (derived from Hellenic and Syriac through *Christianity*)
- Western Christian, Orthodox Christian, Orthodox Christian in Russia (derived from Hellenic through *Christianity*)
- Abortive Far Western Christian (derived from Hellenic through its external proletariat and through *Christianity*)
- Abortive Scandinavian (derived from Hellenic through its external proletariat)
- Far Eastern, Far Eastern in Korea and Japan (derived from Sinic through the *Mahāyāna*)

6. SECONDARY HIGHER RELIGIONS

- *Kabirism*, *Sikhism*, *Brahmō Samaj* (created by the internal proletariat of the Hindu Civilization)
- *Baha'ism*, *The Ahmadīyah* (created by the Iranic wing of the internal proletariat of the Western Civilization)
- *Bedreddinism* (created by the internal proletariat of the main body of the Orthodox Christian Civilization)
- *Russian Orthodox Christian Sects* (created by the internal proletariat of the Orthodox Christian Civilization in Russia)
- *The T'aip'ing* (created by the internal proletariat of the Far Eastern Civilization in China)
- *Jōdo*, *Zen* (adapted by the internal proletariat of the Far Eastern Civilization in Japan from the *Mahāyāna*)
- *Jōdo Shinshū*, *Hokke* (alias *Nichirenism*) (created by the internal proletariat of the Far Eastern Civilization in Japan)

Table VI. *A Tentative Reconstruction of Darius's Original Dissection of the Achaemenian Empire into Twenty Taxation Districts*

(following the geographical order adopted in the Concordance, Table V, above)

Location of District	*Number in New Order*	*Number of Herodotus's Gazetteer*	*Names of Peoples and/or Countries in Herodotus's Presentation*	*Names of Countries or Peoples in the Official Lists*
Southern Media: latter-day Hamadān, Kirmānshāh, Ispahān	1	10	'Agbatana and the rest of Media'	Māda
Central Media: Tabrīz, Khamsah, Ardalān (?), Qazwīn, Caspian Gates	2	11	Kaspioi, Pausikai, Pantimathoi, Dareitai	
North-Eastern Media: lower basin of rivers Aras and Kur	3	15	Sakai, Kaspioi	
North-Western Media: portion of 'Irāq to the north-east of the Jabal Hamrīn; basins of lakes Urmīyah and Van; upper valleys of rivers Aras, Choroq, Frat (*alias* Qāra) Su, Murād Su; middle valley of Kur (?)	4	18	Matiênoi, Saspeires, Alarodioi	
Khūzistān, Baktīyārī-land, Lūristān	5	8	'Sousa and the rest of the country of the Kissioi'	Hūja
Southern Afghanistan, the Darajāt, Kirmān, Lāristān	6	14+13	Thamanaioi (14), *alias* 'the Pactyan country' (13), Sagartioi, Outioi, Mykoi, *déracinés* planted in islands in Persian Gulf	Harahvatiš, Asagarta, Maka
Persian and Pākistānī Baluchistān	7	17	Parikanioi and Asiatic Aithiopes	
Khurāsān, Herāt, Seistan, Gūrgān (Astarābād), Western Transcaspia, Khwārizm (Khiva)	8	16+14	Parthoi, Areioi, Sarangai (14), Khorasmioi	Parthava, Haraiva, Zrāka, Varkāna, Dahā, Hvārazmiš
Upper basin of River Oxus (Amu Darya) and basin of River Zarafshān, as far to the north-east as the southward elbow of River Jaxartes (Syr Darya), together with Merv oasis	9	12+16	'the Baktrianoi as far as the Aiglai' [implicitly including the Sogdoi (16)]	Bākhtriš, Suguda, Marguš
Oxus Delta and steppes to the north-east of Lower Oxus and astride Middle Oxus	10	10	Orthokorybantioi	Sakā Tigrakhaudā
Kābul River basin and Northern Panjab	11	7	Gandarioi, Dadikai, Aparytai, Sattagydai	Gādāra, Thataguš
Southern Panjab, Multān, Bahawalpur, Sind	12	20	Indoi	Hiduš
'Iraq as far to the north-east as the Jabal Hamrīn	13	9	'Babylon and the rest of Assyria'	Bābiruš
Mesopotamia (the Jazīrah), Syria, Jordan, Lebanon, Israel, Cyprus	14	5	'The Whole of Phoinîkê and the so-called Philistine Syria and Cyprus'	Athurā
Egypt and Cyrenaïca	15	6	Egypt, Libyes, Kyrênê, Barkê	Mudrāya, Putāyā
Upper Tigris basin and north-west corner of Euphrates basin	16	13	Armenioi	Arminiya
Eastern section of Black Sea seaboard of Anatolia	17	19+13	Moskhoi, Tibarênoi, Makrônes, Mossynoikoi, Mâres, *alias* 'the adjoining peoples as far as the Black Sea' (13)	
Northern and Central Anatolia, extending as far to the north-west as the Anatolian shores of the Bosphorus, Sea of Marmara, and Dardanelles, as far to the south-west as the headwaters of the River Maeander, and as far to the south-east as Lycaonia	18	3+13	Syrioi, *alias* 'the Pactyan country' (13) [i.e. Kappadokiê], Paphlagones, Mariandynoi, Asiatic Thrâkes, Phryges, Hellespontine Hellenes	Katpatuka
South-Western Anatolia, excluding the seaboard	19	2	Mysoi, Lydoi, Lasonioi, Kabalioi, *alias* Kabêlees, Hygenees	Sparda
The western and south-western seaboard of Anatolia	20	1	Iônes, Asiatic Magnêtes, Aiolees, Kâres, Asiatic Dôriees, Lykioi, Milyai, Pamphyloi	'The Yaunā on the Mainland', Karkā
Districts Subsequently Added				
The Aegean Archipelago (intended to expand over maritime transmarine Hellas, as far to the west as Magna Graecia and Sicily)	21	..	Isles	'Those in the Sea', *alias* 'the hatted Yaunā'
Thrace, the Maritsa basin and the Lower Danube basin	22	..	'The inhabitants of Europe as far as Thessaly'	'Those beyond the Sea', *alias* 'the Sakā beyond the Sea'
Macedonia (intended to expand over Continental European Greece)	23			Skudra
Countries Externally Associated with the Achaemenian Empire				
Farghānah	..	10	Sakai Amyrgioi	Sakā Haumavargā
North-western Arabia, touching the south-east corner of the Mediterranean Sea and bestriding the Euphrates between Syria and 'Irāq	..	..	Arabioi	Arabāya
Nubia and the Eastern Sūdān	..	..	Aithiopes marching with Egypt	Kūša
Western Transcaucasia	..	..	'The Kolkhoi, and the adjoining peoples as far as Mount Kaukasis'	The Ākaufačiyā
South-eastern Anatolia, from the country astride the River Qyzyl Irmāq, just above its southward elbow, as far to the east as the right bank of the Euphrates and as far to the south as Cape Basit on the coast of Syria to the south of the mouth of the Orontes	..	4	Kilikes	——

Table VII. *Correspondences between Higher Religions and Psychological Types*

Religion	*Predominant Attitude*	*Predominant Faculty*	*Auxiliary Faculties*	*Religious Expression of Unrepressed Psychic Elements*	*Repressed Attitude*	*Repressed Faculty*	*Religious Expression of Repressed Psychic Elements*
Hinduism	Introversion	Thinking	Sensation Intuition	Hindu Ritual Hindu Mysticism	Extraversion	Feeling	Extraversion has found a limited expression in the worship of personal epiphanies of an impersonal Ultimate Reality (the avatars of Vishnu); feeling has found expression in the worshipper's devotion to the god of his choice (*bhakti*).
Christianity	Extraversion	Feeling	Sensation Intuition	The Eucharist Christian Mysticism	Introversion	Thinking	Introversion has found an incomplete expression in the Protestant's psychological experience of 'being saved'; thinking has found a limited expression in Christian theology.
Islam	Extraversion	Sensation	Thinking Feeling	The Sunnah The Shīʿah	Introversion	Intuition	Introversion has found a limited expression, but intuition has found a full expression, in Islamic Mysticism.
Buddhism	Introversion	Intuition	Thinking Feeling	The Hīnayāna The Mahāyāna	Extraversion	Sensation	Extraversion has found expression in the Mahayanian metamorphosis of bodhisattvas into personal gods; sensation, in the fetish worship of relics.